ORACLE® *Oracle Press*™

Oracle Certified Professional™ Application Developer Exam Guide

Jason S. Couchman
Christopher Allen

Osborne/**McGraw-Hill**

Berkeley New York St. Louis San Francisco
Auckland Bogotá Hamburg London Madrid
Mexico City Milan Montreal New Delhi Panama City
Paris São Paulo Singapore Sydney
Tokyo Toronto

Osborne/**McGraw-Hill**
2600 Tenth Street
Berkeley, California 94710
U.S.A.

For information on translations or book distributors outside the U.S.A., or to arrange bulk purchase discounts for sales promotions, premiums, or fund-raisers, please contact Osborne/**McGraw-Hill** at the above address.

Oracle Certified Professional Application Developer Exam Guide

Information has been obtained by Publisher from sources believed to be reliable. However, because of the possibility of human or mechanical error by our sources, Publisher, or others, Publisher does not guarantee to the accuracy, adequacy, or completeness of any information included in this work and is not responsible for any errors or omissions or the results obtained from the use of such information.

1234567890 DOC DOC 90198765432109

ISBN 0-07-211975-6

Publisher
  Brandon A. Nordin

**Associate Publisher and
Editor in Chief**
  Scott Rogers

Development Editor
  Jeremy Judson

Project Editor
  Ron Hull

Editorial Assistant
  Monika Faltiss

Technical Editor
  Christian Bauwens

Copy Editor
  Dennis Weaver

Proofreader
  Carol Burbo

Indexer
  Irv Hershman

Computer Designers
  Jani Beckwith
  Ann Sellers

Illustrators
  Beth Young
  Bob Hansen

Series Design
  Jani Beckwith

Cover Design
  Lisa Schultz

For Stacy

Jason Couchman

For Grace

Christopher Allen

ORACLE®
Certified Professional

About the Oracle Certification Exams

The expertise of application developers is integral to the success of any company that needs to create sophisticated, effective applications. The best Oracle application developers strive to be more productive and deliver more effective business application solutions. The Oracle Certified Application Developer Track provides developers with tangible evidence of their skills with Oracle development tools.

The Oracle Certified Professional (OCP) Program was developed by Oracle to recognize technical professionals who can demonstrate the depth of knowledge and hands-on skills required to maximize Oracle's core products according to a rigorous standard established by Oracle. By earning professional certification, you can translate the impressive knowledge and skill you have worked so hard to accumulate into a tangible credential that can lead to greater job security or more challenging, better-paying opportunities.

Oracle Certified Professionals are eligible to receive use of the Oracle Certified Professional logo and a certificate for framing.

Requirements for Certification

To become an Oracle Certified Application Developer you must pass the following five separate, scenario-based tests:

- Exam 1: Introduction to Oracle: SQL and PL/SQL

- Exam 2: Develop PL/SQL Program Units

- Exam 3: Developer Forms I

- Exam 4: Developer Forms II

- Exam 5: Oracle Developer Reports

Recertification

Oracle announces the requirements for upgrading your certification based on the release of new products and upgrades. Oracle will give six-month's notice announcing when an exam version is expiring.

Exam Format

The computer-based exams are multiple-choice tests, consisting of 60-90 questions that must be completed in 90 minutes.

Special 10% Exam Discount Offer

You can qualify for a special 10% discount when you register for the OCP exam by contacting the number listed below. You must specifically request the discount and mention extension 47. Offer valid through September 30, 1999. To register for an Oracle test and be eligible for the 10% discount, call Sylvan Prometric at:

1-800-891-EXAM, ext. 47 (1-800-891-3296, ext. 47).
Outside the U.S. call +1.612.820.5000.

Contact your local Oracle Education Representative for exam preparation courses and materials. Or download the *Candidate Guide* at **http://education.oracle.com/certification** for specific exam objectives and preparation methods.

Contents

UNIT I
Preparing for OCP DBA Exam 1: SQL and PL/SQL

UNIT III

Preparing for OCP Exam 3: Building Forms I

UNIT IV
Preparing for OCP Exam 4: Building Forms II

Preface

e have made it our goal to make the Oracle Certified
Professional (OCP) Exam Guides from Oracle Press the most
comprehensive and well-supported OCP preparation method
available. This book is divided into five units, one covering
each exam in the Developer track of the Oracle Certified
Professional program, as follows:

- Unit I: Preparing for OCP DBA Exam 1—SQL and PL/SQL

- Unit II: Preparing for OCP Exam 2—Developing PL/SQL
  Program Units

- Unit III: Preparing for OCP Exam 3—Building Forms I

- Unit IV: Preparing for OCP Exam 4—Building Forms II

- Unit V: Preparing for OCP Exam 5—Building Reports

Each unit consists of several chapters covering the material you need to
know to pass the exam. All of the chapters follow the format described in
this preface.

At the end of the book, an appendix explains the materials you should review for the Release 2 upgrade exam. You only need to take this exam if you are certified on Developer Release 1 and want to upgrade certification to Release 2.

How Chapters Are Organized

Each chapter in the book follows the same format, as described here.

Discussion Sections

Within each chapter, there are several discussion sections. These sections correspond directly to subject areas tested in the OCP exams.

Chapter Summaries

After presenting the main content, each chapter offers a summary of the material presented. This digest information is designed for quick review after reading the chapter and doing the exercises. In the days prior to your OCP exam, you can reread the chapter review to familiarize yourself with the information covered.

Two-Minute Drills

Each chapter also contains a series of bullet points designed to be a fact drill for final preparation on the OCP exams. These bullets are designed to be your crib notes for the final night of preparation before you take the exams. The key points of information are presented as nuggets designed to jog your memory of the main concepts covered in the chapter.

Chapter Questions and Answers

Each chapter also contains multiple choice questions patterned after the actual exam. These questions will familiarize you with the style of OCP questions. They will also test your knowledge of the Oracle material presented in the chapter. You should attempt to answer these questions after reviewing the chapter material. Finally, to help you understand the test material, each chapter contains the answers to the chapter questions, along with an explanation of each answer.

Conventions Used in This Book

Commands and keywords that the user enters are presented in boldface, while new terms and emphasized facts are presented in italics. Interspersed with the discussion are figures, tables, and code blocks. An example code block is shown here:

```
This is a sample code block.
```

Especially important information is set apart from the body text in a special format called *tips*. A sample tip appears here:

TIP
Read the important tips for additional test preparation. They contain special information and facts to remember, often with memorization tricks that will help you retain the facts you need to pass the test.

Using the Accelerated Reading Method

In order to get the most from reading this book, you should first ask yourself the following question: What is my level of Oracle experience? The reason you need to ask yourself this question is that there are two ways to read the chapters of this book. If you are a professional with a beginner/intermediate level of Oracle experience, you should use the standard method for studying the material in this book. Start at the beginning of each chapter, read it from start to finish, and *do the exercises*. Then, review the material by reading the chapter summary and two-minute drill, followed by taking the chapter questions and reviewing the answers. The standard method should give you the facts you need to understand in order to pass the OCP exams, presented in several different ways to help you retain that information. If you have reviewed the material thoroughly, answering the exercise questions and studying the chapter summary and the drill for all chapters in the unit, you should do well on the OCP exam.

However, advanced users of Oracle seeking to prepare for OCP exams quickly can also use the book's *accelerated reading method*. Skip directly to the chapter summary and read it to understand the content of the chapter.

Then, review the two-minute drill, and try the chapter questions. If you find yourself getting 80 percent or more of the questions right, you may be ready to take the test. Even if you are missing questions, you will probably have a better idea of the areas you need review. You can then flip back to the specific area in the chapter content to help refresh your memory.

A Note to Developer 1.0 OCP Test-Takers

This book is meant to assist candidates for OCP taking both the Developer 1.0 and 2.0 certification exams. To aid in the process, a few important notes are in order. The first concerns overlap between the two versions of the Developer track. First, Exam 1 (Introduction to SQL and PL/SQL and Exam 2 (Developing PL/SQL Program Units) are the same for both versions of the Developer track. So, if you've taken these two exams but not the Forms and Reports exams, you can easily choose between versions 1 and 2 without having to retake a single exam. Units I and II of this book will help you prepare for the first two exams in the OCP Developer track.

Third, the content of Units III through V of this book covers OCP Exams 3 through 5. They were primarily developed from use of Developer 2.0 and 2.1. If you are taking the Developer 1.0 track, you can use this guide to supplement your preparation; however, you should understand that the content was developed primarily for version 2. If you haven't taken the Forms I, Forms II, and Reports exams in the Developer track, we strongly advise you to upgrade your skill set to version 2.0 by using this guide and taking the version 2.0 exams. The book assumes that, if you are going to use it for Developer 1.0 exam preparation, you know enough Developer 1.0 to distinguish mention of versions. For example, the version of Oracle Forms included with Developer 1.0 is Forms 4.5, while for Developer 2.0 it is Forms 5.0. You may need to remember these items when taking your OCP Developer exams.

Also, there are some features of Developer 2.0 that are not included in Developer 1.0. You may want to review the appendix for assistance in identifying differences between versions. The appendix identifies content in the book that can be used for preparing for the Developer 1.0 to 2.0 Upgrade Exam to determine which features of Developer 2.0 are not included in 1.0, in addition to the intended use of preparing for the upgrade exam.

Additional Information and Support

Finally, if you have comments or questions about the book, visit ExamPilot.Com on the Web. ExamPilot.Com is an OCP test preparation company that has designed a competitively priced preparation service that is tightly integrated with OCP Exam Guides from Oracle Press. It features thousands of online practice questions, answers to all section questions, and advanced exam-taker tips. The service is available exclusively on the Web, and you can find out more about it at **http://www.exampilot.com**.

Acknowledgments

O ver a year has passed since I began writing the OCP Exam Guide series from Oracle Press. I have learned more about Oracle than ever before, and I am eager to pass this knowledge along to you. Several folks have been tremendously helpful along the way. I want to thank Rob Pedigo, Julia Johnson, Sundar Nagarathnam, and Jennifer Mastropolo, and Christian Bauwens of Oracle for helping tremendously with this project. Let's not forget the usual suspects at Osborne for their help, Scott Rogers, Jeremy Judson, Monika Faltiss, Ron Hull, Marc Miller, Dennis Weaver, and the rest of the OMH team. It was nice meeting all of you at that killer party at OpenWorld last November. Thanks to Greg Zipes, who once again provided great insight and the ability to ask the right questions. Of course, my undying loyalty to Stacy, Spanky, and Athena for putting up with *another* book, and much love to my mother and father for understanding the last-minute trip cancellations that invariably seem part of making these things happen. Finally, I owe a debt of gratitude to Christopher Allen, who stepped out of the ether and pulled the project together at its darkest hour. Thanks to all for a job well done.

Jason Couchman

Jason has done a good job of covering the people who contributed to this work. In addition, I would like to offer special kudos to Jeremy Judson and Ron Hull, for managing this project so smoothly; to Christian Bauwens, for perceptive technical editing; to Dennis Weaver, for "A1" copy editing (he'll probably want to change that to "A-1" or some such); and to Monika Faltiss, for getting everything where it needed to be, before it needed to be there. Each of these people showed unwavering dedication to making this book the best it can be. I also salute Jason Couchman for his driving spirit, and for being very easy to work with. Finally, I thank my sweet wife Grace, who held down the fort with a smile and a cup of hot tea while my head was buried in computers.

Christopher Allen

Introduction

he Oracle Certified Professional (OCP) Developer Certification Exam series is the second track in Oracle's certification program. The Developer certification track represents the culmination of many people's request for objective standards in one of the hottest markets in the software field—Oracle development tools. The presence of OCP on the market indicates an important reality about Oracle as a career path. Oracle is mature, robust, and stable for enterprise-wide information management. However, corporations facing a severe shortage of qualified Oracle professionals need a measure for Oracle expertise.

The OCP certification track for developers consists of five exams in several areas of the Oracle Developer product. As of this printing, each test consists of 50-60 multiple-choice questions pertaining to the recommended usage of the Oracle Developer product. You have 90 minutes to take each exam. Two versions of the OCP Developer certification track exist, and there is some overlap between those versions. Obtaining certification for the Oracle Developer product is contingent on taking and passing *all five* examinations. The following list identifies the exams in the Developer track, and the overlaps between the two tracks:

- Introduction to SQL and PL/SQL (same for both releases)

- Developing PL/SQL Program Units (same for both releases)

- Using Oracle Forms I (Forms 4.5 for Release 1, Forms 5.0 for Release 2)

- Using Oracle Forms II (Forms 4.5 for Release 1, Forms 5.0 for Release 2)

- Using Oracle Reports (Reports 2.5 for Release 1, Reports 3.0 for Release 2)

Why Get Certified?

If you are already an Oracle developer, you may wonder—why certify? Perhaps you've had a successful career thus far, enjoying the instant prestige your résumé gets with the magic word on it. With market forces currently in your favor, you're right to wonder. But, while no one is saying you don't know Developer when you put the magic word on your resume, can you prove how well you know Oracle *without* undergoing a technical interview? You might be surprised to find out that, even after years of using Oracle, there are areas you *don't* know. A good way to find out is by taking the time and putting forth the effort to get certified.

If you're looking for another reason to become certified in Oracle Developer, consider the situation many computer professionals with Novell NetWare experience were in during the late 1980s and early 1990s. It seemed that anyone with even a little experience in Novell could count on a fantastic job offer. Then Novell introduced its CNE/CNA programs. At first, employers were fine, hiring professionals with or without the certificate. As time went on, however, the want ad demographics changed. Employers no longer asked for computer professionals with Novell NetWare experience—they asked for CNEs and CNAs. A similar phenomenon can be witnessed in the arena of Microsoft Windows NT, where the MCSE has already become the standard by which those professionals are measuring their skills. If you want to be competitive in the field of Oracle development, your real question shouldn't be *if* you should become certified, but *when*.

If you are not in the field of Oracle development, or if you want to advance your Oracle career, there has never been a better time to do so.

OCP is already altering the playing field for DBAs by changing the focus of the Oracle skill set from "how many years have you used Oracle" to "are you certified?" Developer certification will likely do the same. That shift benefits organizations using Oracle as much as it benefits the professionals who use Oracle, because the emphasis is on performance, not attrition.

Managers who are faced with the task of hiring Oracle professionals should breathe a sigh of relief with the debut of OCP. By seeking professionals who are certified, managers can spend less time in an interview figuring out if the candidate knows Oracle well enough to develop their enterprise applications, and more time determining the candidate's work habits and compatibility with the team. What is interesting, however, is that many organizations are loath to jump on the Oracle certification bandwagon. There are many reasons for management's hesitation, but the biggest is retention. Ironically, the ability to leverage a significant salary gain in a job switch is a reason many professionals cite *for* getting certified. Hopefully, computer professionals and management won't always be at cross purposes. As the computer professional in this situation, your best bet is to focus on getting certified.

How Should You Prepare for OCP?

If you spend your free time studying things like the name of the PL/SQL exception in Oracle Reports that terminates the report execution when raised explicitly by the programmer, you are probably ready to take the OCP Developer exams now. For the rest of us, there are many training options available to learn Oracle, such as instructor-led training from Oracle Education. Those classes can be useful—their content forms the basis of the OCP exams, after all. But, not everyone has an employer willing to pay for instructor-led training. Now, you have another option—this book! By selecting this book, you demonstrate two excellent characteristics—that you are committed to a superior career in the field of Oracle development, and that you care about preparing for OCP correctly and thoroughly. And by the way, the name of the exception that terminates report execution when raised in a PL/SQL block is **program_abort**, and it is stored in the SRW package. This fact, along with many others, is on the OCP Developer exam—and covered in this book.

What is more, the OCP Exam Guides from Oracle Press are the best-supported exam preparation guides on the market today.

ExamPilot.Com is a Web-based OCP preparation program that is tightly integrated with the OCP Exam Guides from Oracle Press. ExamPilot.Com is recognized as the leader in OCP preparation by organizations like Oracle Education Seminars and IOUG. When you subscribe to ExamPilot.Com, you gain access to the answers to all the exercise questions in this book, lesson plans to help you organize your study time, thousands of practice exam questions, tips to improve your exam performance, and much more. Best of all, this support is no further away than your desktop. Check out ExamPilot.Com on the Web at **http://www.exampilot.com**.

Oracle Certification, Past and Present

Oracle certification started in the mid-1990s with the involvement of the Chauncey Group International, a division of Educational Testing Service. Chauncey's certification exam covered several different topic areas in one test. Oracle Corporation took certification several giant leaps ahead with the advent of OCP, and is now extending its reach across other Oracle products, such as Oracle Financials, Oracle Designer, and Oracle Developer (the topic of the book you are holding). Oracle has also committed to including scenario-based questions on the OCP examinations, and preparation material for these new questions is included in this book as well. Scenario-based questions require you not only to know the facts about Oracle, but also to understand how to apply those facts in real-life situations.

Oracle's final contribution to the area of Oracle certification is a commitment to reviewing and updating the material presented in the certification exams. Oracle certified developers will be required to maintain their certification by retaking certification exams periodically—meaning that those who maintain their certification will stay on the cutting edge of Oracle products better than those who do not.

There is one final bonus to beginning your certification process right now. If you have taken the Introduction to SQL and PL/SQL and the Developing PL/SQL Program Units exams toward Developer certification, you can leverage the knowledge you already have of Developer 1.0 to get certified on Developer 2.0 to obtain a demonstrated credential of expertise on the new version. This guide is written primarily for OCP Developer 2.0 exam preparation. However, you can use it for Developer 1.0 certification as well as for the version 1 to version 2 upgrade exam, if you have some knowledge of the Developer product and if you use ExamPilot.Com to help you prepare.

The Oracle Assessment Test

You begin your preparation for the OCP Developer certification exams by taking the Oracle Assessment Test. You can load the Oracle Assessment Test from the CD-ROM included with this book. You should load it onto your Windows-based computer and take the exams to determine which areas you need to study. Figure 1 shows the Assessment Test graphical user interface. The features of the interface are indicated in the figure. Several of the main features of the assessment test interface are explained here. The Assessment Test interface is very similar to the actual Sylvan Prometric OCP Developer Exam test driver, with a few exceptions as noted. At the top of the interface is a box that tells you how much time has elapsed and the number of questions you have answered.

On the actual OCP exam only, there is also a check box in the upper left-hand corner of the interface. You can use this check box to mark questions you would like to review later. In the main window of the interface is the actual production question, along with the choices. The interface generally allows the user to select only one answer, unless the question directs you to select more answers. In this case, the interface will allow you to select only as many answers as the question requests. After answering a question, or marking the question for later review, the candidate can move onto the next question by clicking the appropriate button in the lower left-hand corner. The next button over on the bottom allows you either to print the Assessment Test or to return to the previous question on the OCP exam. Next, in the Assessment Test only, you can score your questions at any time by pressing the Grade Test button on the bottom right-hand side. The final point feature to cover is the Exhibit button. In some cases, you may require the use of an exhibit to answer a question. If the question does not require use of an exhibit, the button will be grayed out.

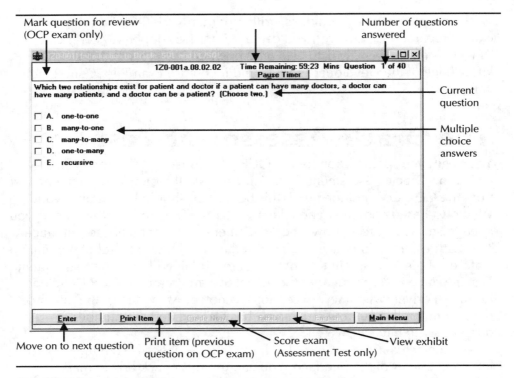

FIGURE 1. *The Oracle Assessment Test user interface*

The Assessment Test indicates your performance by means of a grade window like the one that appears in Figure 2. It details the number of questions you answered correctly, along with your percentage score based on 100 percent. Finally, a bar graph indicates where your performance falls in comparison to the maximum score possible on the exam. The OCP exam reports your score immediately after you exit the exam, so you will know right then whether you pass or not, in a similar fashion as the Assessment Test. Both interfaces offer you the ability to print a report of your score.

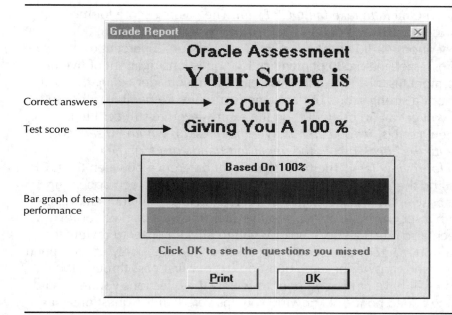

Correct answers ——————→ 2 Out Of 2

Test score ——————→ Giving You A 100 %

Bar graph of test performance ——→

FIGURE 2. *Grading your test performance*

Taking the OCP Exams

The score range for each OCP Exam is between 200 and 800. There is a 600-point range for potential scores, and typically there are 50-60 questions on each test in the track. The OCP Developer certification exam is administered at Sylvan Prometric test centers. To schedule OCP exams in the United States, call Sylvan Prometric at 800-891-EXAM (800-891-3926). For contact information outside the USA, refer to the Assessment Test software, or to the OCP Candidate Certification guide, available on the Web at **http://education.oracle.com/certification**.

Some preliminary items are now identified for you with regard to taking the OCP exams. The first tip is, *don't wait until you're the world's foremost authority on Oracle to take the OCP Exam*. The passing score for most exams is usually 650 out of 800—remember, you start out with 200 points—or about 48-50 questions right. That's about 75 percent of the exam. To be safe, target getting 80 percent, or four questions right out of five on the assessment test or in the chapters before you consider taking the OCP exam. That's a strong score, but not a perfect score. Remember, it doesn't matter if you get a 650 or an 800 on the exams—you're still certified.

The next item is, *if you can't answer the question within 30 seconds, mark it with the check box in the upper left-hand corner of the OCP interface for review later*. The most significant difference between the OCP interface and the Assessment Test interface is a special screen appearing after you answer all the questions. This screen displays all your answers, along with a special indicator next to the questions you marked for review. This screen also offers a check box for you to click in order to review the questions you marked. You should use this feature extensively. If you spend only 30 seconds answering each question in your first pass through the exam, you will have at least an hour to review the questions you're unsure of, with the added bonus of knowing you answered all the questions that were easiest to you first.

Third, *there is no penalty for guessing*. If you answer the question correctly, your score goes up, if not, your score does not change. If you can eliminate any choices on a question, you should take the chance in the interest of improving your score. In some questions, the OCP exam requires you to specify two or even three choices—this can work in your favor, meaning you need to eliminate fewer choices to get the question right.

Finally, unless your level of expertise with Oracle is high in a particular area, *it is recommended that you take the exams in the sequential order listed*. This is especially recommended for readers whose background in Oracle is more on the beginner/intermediate level, and even more important if you are using this book to prepare for the exam. This is because each subsequent chapter of the book builds on information presented in the previous chapters. As such, you should read the book from beginning to end, and take the test accordingly. Taking the exams in this manner will help you get the most out of this book.

Good luck with certification and best wishes with your Oracle career!

UNIT
I

Preparing for OCP DBA Exam 1: SQL and PL/SQL

CHAPTER
1

Selecting Data from Oracle

n this chapter, you will understand and demonstrate knowledge in the following areas:

- Selecting rows
- Limiting and refining selected output
- Using single-row functions

The first exam in the OCP series covers basic areas of database usage and design. Every Oracle user, developer, and DBA should have complete mastery in these areas before moving on into other test areas. This unit assumes little or no prior knowledge of Oracle in order to help you go from never using Oracle to having enough expertise in the Oracle server product to maintain and enhance existing applications and develop small new ones. The five chapters in this unit will function as the basis for understanding the rest of the book. This chapter will cover several aspects of data retrieval from the Oracle database, including selecting rows, limiting the selection, and using single-row functions. This chapter covers material comprising 17 percent of test content of OCP Exam 1.

Selecting Rows

In this section, you will cover the following areas related to selecting rows:

- Writing **select** statements
- Performing arithmetic equations
- Handling NULL values
- Creating column headings with column aliases
- Putting columns together with concatenation
- Editing SQL queries within SQL*Plus

Experience with Oracle for many developers, designers, DBAs, and power users begins with usage of an existing Oracle application in an organization. The first tool many people see for selecting data directly from

the Oracle relational database management system is SQL*Plus. When users
first start SQL*Plus, in most cases they must enter their Oracle username and
password in order to begin a session with the Oracle database. There are
some exceptions to this rule that utilize the password authentication provided
with the operating system. The following examples show how you might
begin a session with Oracle from a command line operating system such as
UNIX. From Windows, you can instead click on Start | Programs | Oracle for
Windows | SQL*Plus or double-click on the SQL*Plus icon on your desktop if
one appears there.

```
$> sqlplus jason/athena
```

or

```
$> sqlplus /
```

A *session* is an interactive runtime environment where you enter
commands to retrieve data and Oracle performs a series of activities to
obtain the data you ask for. Think of it as a conversation, which in turn
implies language. You communicate with Oracle using Structured Query
Language, or SQL for short. (SQL can be pronounced either as three
individual letters or as "sequel.") SQL is a "functional" language. A
functional language is one that allows you to specify the types of things you
want to see happen in terms of the results you want. Contrast this approach
to other languages you may have heard about or programmed in, such as
C++ or COBOL, which are often referred to as "procedural" programming
languages because the code written in these languages implies an end result
by explicitly defining the means, or the procedure, by which to get there. In
contrast, SQL explicitly defines the end result, leaving it up to Oracle to
determine the method by which to obtain the data. Data selection can be
accomplished using the following code listing:

```
SELECT *
FROM emp
WHERE empid = 39334;
```

This SQL statement asks Oracle to provide all data from the EMP table
where the value in a certain column called EMPID equals 39334. The
following block of code from an imaginary procedural programming

language similar to C illustrates how the same function may be handled by explicitly defining the means to the end:

```
Include <stdio.h>
Include <string.h>
Include <rdbms.h>

Int *empid;
Char *statement;

Type emp_rec is record (
Int            empid;
Char[10]       emp_name;
Int            salary; )

Void main()

  Access_table(emp);
  Open(statement.memaddr);
  Strcpy("SELECT * FROM EMP WHERE EMPID = 39334",statement.text);
  parse(statement);
  execute(statement);
  for (I=1,I=statement.results,I+1)
    fetch(statement.result[I],emp_rec);
    printf(emp_rec);

  close(statement.memaddr);
```

Of course, that C-like block of code would not compile anywhere but in your imagination, but the point of the example is clear—other languages define a process, while SQL defines the result.

Writing SELECT Statements

The most common type of SQL statement executed in most database environments is the *query*, or **select** statement. **Select** statements pull requested data from tables in a database. A table in Oracle is similar in concept to Table 1-1. For more information about tables, see Chapter 3. You can issue a simple **select** statement that is designed to pull all data from the table shown in Table 1-1. The following code block demonstrates SQL*Plus in action. You will see a **select** statement used to obtain data from a table called EMP, owned by a user called HRAPP. Sometimes Oracle developers and DBAs

Empid	Lastname	Fname	*Salary*
39334	Smith	Gina	*75,000*
49539	Qian	Lee	*90,000*
60403	Harper	Rod	*45,000*
02039	Walla	Rajendra	*60,000*
49392	Spanky	Stacy	*100,000*

TABLE 1-1.   *EMP*

refer to database objects being part of something called a "schema." A schema is a logical grouping of database objects, like tables, according to the owner. Thus, the EMP table you will see is part of the HRAPP schema.

```
SQL*Plus: Release 8.1.0.0.0 - Production on Tue Feb 03 18:53:11 199
Copyright (c) Oracle Corporation 1979, 1998.  All rights reserved.
Connected to: Oracle8 Release 8.1.0.0.0
With the distributed and replication options
PL/SQL Release 8.1.0.0.0 Production

SQL> SELECT * FROM HRAPP.EMP;

EMPID    LASTNAME    FIRSTNAME    SALARY
-----    --------    ---------    ------
39334    SMITH       GINA          75000
49539    QIAN        LEE           90000
60403    HARPER      ROD           45000
02039    WALLA       RAJENDRA      60000
49392    SPANKY      STACY        100000
```

The first part containing the copyright information in this code block is a "welcome" message from SQL*Plus. If you wanted, you could suppress this information in your call to SQL*Plus from the operating system command line (such as UNIX) by entering "**sqlplus –s**" and pressing ENTER, where the **–s** extension indicates SQL*Plus should run in silent mode. The line in bold in this excerpt illustrates the entry of a simple SQL statement. The query requests Oracle to give all data from all columns in the EMP table. Oracle replies with the contents of the EMP table as diagrammed in Table 1-1. Note that you did not tell Oracle how to retrieve the data, you simply expressed the data you wanted using SQL syntax and Oracle returned it. For now, make sure you understand how to specify a schema owner, the table name, and the column name in a **select** statement in SQL*Plus. The following code block demonstrates proper usage:

```
SELECT table_name.column_name, table_name.column_name
FROM schema.table_name;
```

TIP
*Always use a semicolon (;) to end SQL statements when entering them directly into SQL*Plus.*

The main components of a **select** statement are the **select** clause and the **from** clause. A **select** clause contains the list of columns or expressions containing data you want to see. The first statement used a *wildcard* (*****) character, which indicates to Oracle that you want to view data from every column in the table. The **from** clause tells Oracle what database table to pull the information from. Often, the database user will need to specify the schema, or owner, to which the table belongs, in addition to naming the table from which the data should come, as we did in this next example with a *schema.tablename* notation as well:

```
SELECT empid, lastname, salary
FROM HRAPP.EMP;


EMPID      LASTNAME     SALARY
-----      --------     ------
39334      SMITH         75000
49539      QIAN          90000
60403      HARPER        45000
02039      WALLA         60000
49392      SPANKY       100000
```

For review, the statement issued in the code block gets its information from the table called HRAPP.EMP. This means that Oracle should pull data from the EMP table in the HRAPP schema. When a user is granted the ability to create database objects, the objects he or she creates belong to you. Ownership creates a logical grouping of the database objects by owner, and the grouping is called a *schema*.

TIP
*A schema is a logical grouping of database
objects based on the user that owns the object.*

Exercises

1. What is a **select** statement? Name the two required components of a **select** statement.

2. How should you end a **select** statement in SQL*Plus?

3. What is a schema?

Performing Arithmetic Equations

In addition to simple selection of data from a table, Oracle allows you to perform different types of activities using the data. All basic arithmetic operations are available in Oracle. The operators used to denote arithmetic in Oracle SQL are the same as in daily use.

Assume, for example, that you are performing a simple annual review that involves giving each user a cost-of-living increase in the amount of 8 percent of their salary. The process would involve multiplying each person's salary by 1.08. Oracle makes this sort of thing easy with the use of arithmetic expressions, as shown below:

```
SELECT empid, lastname, salary, salary*1.08
FROM HRAPP.EMP;


EMPID    LASTNAME    SALARY    SALARY*1.08
-----    --------    ------    -----------
39334    SMITH       75000          81000
49539    QIAN        90000          97200
60403    HARPER      45000          48600
02039    WALLA       60000          64800
49392    SPANKY     100000         108000
```

Performing Arithmetic on Numeric Expressions

Select statements in Oracle require you specify columns or expressions following the **select** keyword and a table name after the **from** keyword. However, you may not always want to perform arithmetic calculations on data from a table. For example, say you simply want to add two fixed values together. Every **select** statement must have a **from** clause, but since you are specifying fixed values, you don't want Oracle to pull data from a real table. So why not pull data from a fake one? A special table called DUAL can be used in this query to fulfill the **from** clause requirement. Execute a **select * from** DUAL and see for yourself there is no data stored here. Now issue the following statement, and see results from the DUAL table:

```
SELECT 64+36
FROM DUAL;

64+36
-----
  100
```

There is no meaningful data actually in DUAL; it simply exists as a SQL construct to support the requirement of a table specification in the **from** clause. The DUAL table contains only one column called DUMMY and one row with a value, "X."

TIP
*DUAL is used to satisfy the SQL syntax construct stating that all SQL statements must contain a **from** clause that names the table from which the data will be selected. When a user does not want to pull data from any table, but rather wants simply to use an arithmetic operation on a constant value, she can include the values, operations, and the **from DUAL** clause.*

Exercises

1. How can you perform arithmetic on selected columns in Oracle?

2. What is the DUAL table? Why is it used?

3. How do you specify arithmetic operations on numbers not **select**ed from any table?

Handling NULL Values

Sometimes, a query for some information will produce a nothing result. In database terms, nothing is called *NULL*. In set theory, the mathematical foundation for relational databases, NULL represents the value of an empty dataset, or a dataset containing no values. Unless specified otherwise, a column in a table is designed to accommodate the placement of nothing into the column. An example of retrieving NULL is listed in the SPOUSE column of the following code block:

```
SELECT empid, lastname, firstname, spouse
FROM HRAPP.EMP;

EMPID     LASTNAME    FIRSTNAME    SPOUSE
-----     --------    ---------    ------
39334     SMITH       GINA         FRED
49539     QIAN        LEE
60403     HARPER      ROD          SUSAN
02039     WALLA       RAJENDRA     HARPREET
49392     SPANKY      STACY
```

However, there arise times when you will not want to see nothing. You may want to substitute a value in place of nothing. Oracle provides this functionality with a special function called **nvl( )**. Assume that you do not want to see blank spaces for spouse information. Instead, you want the output of the query to contain the word "unmarried." The query in the next code block illustrates how you can obtain the desired result.

```
SELECT empid, lastname, firstname,
NVL(spouse, 'unmarried')
FROM HRAPP.EMP;

EMPID     LASTNAME    FIRSTNAME    NVL(spous
-----     --------    ---------    ---------
39334     SMITH       GINA         FRED
49539     QIAN        LEE          unmarried
60403     HARPER      ROD          SUSAN
02039     WALLA       RAJENDRA     HARPREET
49392     SPANKY      STACY        unmarried
```

If the column specified in **nvl( )** is not NULL, the value in the column is returned, while when the column is NULL, the special string is returned. The **nvl( )** function can be used on columns of all datatypes, but remember that the "value if NULL" argument must be the same datatype as the column specified. Basic syntax for **nvl( )** is as follows:

```
NVL(column_name, value_if_null)
```

Exercises

1. What does NULL mean in the context of Oracle SQL?

2. What is the **nvl( )** function? How is it used?

Changing Column Headings with Column Aliases

When Oracle returns data to you, Oracle creates headings for each column so that you know what the data is. Oracle bases the headings it creates on the name of the column passed to Oracle in the **select** statement:

```
SELECT empid, lastname, firstname, NVL(spouse,'unmarried')
FROM HRAPP.EMP;
```

EMPID	LASTNAME	FIRSTNAME	NVL(spous
39334	SMITH	GINA	FRED
49539	QIAN	LEE	unmarried
60403	HARPER	ROD	SUSAN
02039	WALLA	RAJENDRA	HARPREET
49392	SPANKY	STACY	unmarried

By default, Oracle reprints the column name exactly as it was included in the **select** statement, including functions if there are any. Unfortunately, this method usually leaves you with a bad description of the column data, compounded by the fact that Oracle truncates the expression to fit a certain column length corresponding to the datatype of the column returned. Fortunately, Oracle provides a solution to this situation with the use of column aliases in the **select** statement. Any column can be given another name by you when the **select** statement is issued. This feature gives you the ability to fit more descriptive names into the space allotted by the column datatype definition.

```
SELECT empid, lastname, firstname,
NVL(spouse,'unmarried') spouse
FROM HRAPP.EMP;

EMPID    LASTNAME    FIRSTNAME    SPOUSE
-----    --------    ---------    ---------
39334    SMITH       GINA         FRED
49539    QIAN        LEE          unmarried
60403    HARPER      ROD          SUSAN
02039    WALLA       RAJENDRA     HARPREET
49392    SPANKY      STACY        unmarried
```

As indicated in bold, the SPOUSE column is again named SPOUSE, even with the **nvl( )** operation performed on it. In order to specify an alias, simply name the alias after identifying the column to be selected, with or without an operation performed on it, separated by white space. Alternately, you can issue the **as** keyword to denote the alias. The SPOUSE column with the **nvl( )** operation is an example of using the **as** keyword to denote the alias in the following code block:

```
SELECT empid, lastname, firstname,
NVL(spouse,'unmarried') AS spouse
FROM HRAPP.EMP;

EMPID    LASTNAME    FIRSTNAME    SPOUSE
-----    --------    ---------    ---------
39334    SMITH       GINA         FRED
49539    QIAN        LEE          unmarried
60403    HARPER      ROD          SUSAN
02039    WALLA       RAJENDRA     HARPREET
49392    SPANKY      STACY        unmarried
```

Column aliases are useful for adding meaningful headings to output from SQL queries. As shown, aliases can be specified in two ways: either by naming the alias after the column specification separated by white space, or with the use of the **as** keyword to mark the alias more clearly. Here's the general rule:

```
SELECT column_with_or_without_operation  alias, ...;
```

or

```
SELECT column_with_or_without_operation  AS alias, ...;
```

Exercises

1. What is a column alias? For what situations might column aliases be useful?

2. What are two ways to define aliases for columns?

Putting Columns Together with Concatenation

Changing a column heading in a **select** statement and using the **nvl( )** operation are not the only things that can be done to change the output of a query. Entire columns can be glued together to produce more interesting or readable output. The method used to merge the output of two columns into one is called *concatenation*. The concatenation operator is two pipe characters put together, or | |. You can also use the **concat( )** operation, passing it the two column names. In the following example, you change the name output to the format *lastname, firstname*:

```
SELECT empid, lastname||', '||firstname full_name,
NVL(spouse,'unmarried') spouse
FROM HRAPP.EMP;

EMPID    FULL_NAME           SPOUSE
-----    ---------------     ---------
39334    SMITH, GINA         FRED
49539    QIAN, LEE           unmarried
60403    HARPER, ROD         SUSAN
02039    WALLA, RAJENDRA     HARPREET
49392    SPANKY, STACY       unmarried

SELECT empid, concat(lastname,firstname) full_name,
NVL(spouse,'unmarried') spouse
FROM HRAPP.EMP;

EMPID    FULL_NAME           SPOUSE
-----    ---------------     ---------
39334    SMITH, GINA         FRED
49539    QIAN, LEE           unmarried
60403    HARPER, ROD         SUSAN
02039    WALLA, RAJENDRA     HARPREET
49392    SPANKY, STACY       unmarried
```

By using the concatenation operator in conjunction with a text string enclosed in single quotes, the output of two or more columns became one column to express new meaning. For good measure, the use of column aliases is recommended in order to make the name of the concatenated columns more meaningful.

Exercises

1. What is column concatenation?

2. What special character sequence is used to concatenate columns?

Editing SQL Queries Within SQL*Plus

The SQL*Plus work environment is very much a fair-weather coworker. It works well when you don't make mistakes, but it is unforgiving to the fat-fingered once you have pressed ENTER to move to the next input line. So far, this limitation of the SQL command line hasn't presented much difficulty. However, as the queries you can write get more and more complicated, you will grow frustrated. SQL*Plus does allow some correction of statement entry with the use of a special command called **change**, abbreviated as **c**. Consider the following example to illustrate the point:

```
SELECT empid, lastname||', '||firstname full_name,
NVL(sppuse,'unmarried') spouse
FROM HRAPP.EMP;

NVL(sppuse,'unmarried') spouse
       *
ERROR at line 2:
ORA-00904: invalid column name

SQL> 2

2> NVL(sppuse,'unmarried') spouse, FROM HRAPP.EMP;

SQL> c/sppuse/spouse

2> NVL(spouse,'unmarried') spouse, FROM HRAPP.EMP;

SQL> /
```

```
EMPID    FULL_NAME           SPOUSE
-----    ----------------    ---------
39334    SMITH, GINA         FRED
49539    QIAN, LEE           unmarried
60403    HARPER, ROD         SUSAN
02039    WALLA, RAJENDRA     HARPREET
49392    SPANKY, STACY       unmarried
```

In this example, you issued a **select** statement containing a typographical error, **sppuse**. Oracle notices the error and alerts you to it with **ORA-00904**. To change it, you first reference the line number containing the mistake, in this case with the number 2. Oracle indicates the current version of that line of the SQL statement. Then you issue the **change** command, abbreviated as **c**. The old text appears after the first slash, and the new text follows the second slash. Oracle makes the change and then displays the new version of the line. You can then execute the SQL statement, using the slash (/) command. Other errors that may be produced include:

ORA-00923: FROM Keyword Not Found Where Expected

This error indicates that the **from** keyword was not included or was misspelled. Here is another:

ORA-00942: Table or View Does Not Exist

This error indicates that the table or view typed in does not exist. Usually, the reason for **ORA-00942** is a typo in the name of the table or view, or because the schema owner was not specified in front of the table name. This error is fixed either by correcting the typing problem or by adding the schema owner onto the front of the table name. An alternative solution exists for the latter cause in creating synonyms for tables that are accessible to other users. This solution will be discussed later.

In any case, the method used to correct the typing problem is to first type the line number containing the error and then use the **change** command using the following syntax:

c/old_value/new_value

After making the change to the *first* appearance of *old_value* in the current line, Oracle redisplays the current line with the change made. Note that the change will be made to the first appearance of *old_value* only. If the change must be made to a specific place in the line, more characters can be added to the *old_value* parameter as appropriate. Finally, the corrected text can be reexecuted by entering a slash (/) at the prompt as indicated.

Oracle makes provisions for you to utilize your favorite text editor to edit the statement created in **afiedt.buf**, the file into which SQL*Plus stores the most recently executed SQL statement. You simply type **edit** (abbreviated **ed**). This action causes Oracle to bring up the SQL statement in **afiedt.buf** into the operating system's default text editor. On UNIX systems, that text editor is usually VI or EMACS, while Windows environments use Notepad. To change the text editor used, issue the **define _editor='*youreditor*'** statement from the SQL*Plus prompt.

Using a text editor rather than the line editor native to SQL*Plus offers many benefits. First and foremost is the benefit of using a text editor you know well, creating a familiarity with the application that is useful in adapting to SQL*Plus quickly. Second, it is helpful with large queries to have the entire block of code in front of you and immediately accessible.

TIP
When running SQL statements from scripts, do not put a semicolon (;) at the end of the SQL statement. Instead, put a slash (/) character on the line following the script. Do this if you encounter problems where Oracle says it encountered an invalid character (the semicolon) in your script.

It is possible to write your entire query in a text editor first and then load it into SQL*Plus. If you do this, be sure you save the script with a **.sql** extension so that SQL*Plus can read it easily. Later, when you load the file into SQL*Plus, three commands are available for this use. The first is **get**. The **get** command opens the text file specified and places it in **afiedt.buf**.

Once loaded, you can execute the command using the slash (/) command. Or, you can simply load SQL statements from the file into **afiedt.buf** and execute in one step using the @ command.

```
SQL*Plus: Release 8.1.0.0.0 - Production on Tue Feb 03 18:53:11
1999
Copyright (c) Oracle Corporation 1979, 1998.  All rights reserved.
Connected to Oracle8 Release 8.1.0.0.0
With the distributed and replication options
PL/SQL Release 8.1.0.0.0 - Production

SQL> GET select_emp
SELECT * FROM emp
SQL> /

EMPID    LASTNAME    FIRSTNAME    SALARY
-----    --------    ---------    ------
39334    SMITH       GINA          75000
49539    QIAN        LEE           90000
60403    HARPER      ROD           45000
02039    WALLA       RAJENDRA      60000
49392    SPANKY      STACY        100000

5 rows selected;

SQL> @select_emp

SELECT * FROM emp
/

EMPID    LASTNAME    FIRSTNAME    SALARY
-----    --------    ---------    ------
39334    SMITH       GINA          75000
49539    QIAN        LEE           90000
60403    HARPER      ROD           45000
02039    WALLA       RAJENDRA      60000
49392    SPANKY      STACY        100000

5 rows selected;
```

Notice that the **.sql** extension was left off the end of the filename in the line with the **get** command. SQL*Plus assumes that all scripts containing

SQL statements will have the **.sql** extension, so it can be omitted. Notice also that after the file is brought in using **get**, it can then be executed using the slash (/) command. In the second case, illustrated by the example, the same file is read into **afiedt.buf** and executed in one step, eliminating the need for the slash (/) command by using the @ command. Again, the **.sql** extension is omitted. When using the **get** or @ commands, if a full pathname is not specified as the filename, then Oracle SQL*Plus assumes the file is in the local directory.

Exercises

1. What two mechanisms are available to enter and modify SQL statements within SQL*Plus?

2. What is the edit command in the SQL*Plus command line? How can SQL scripts be loaded from files into SQL*Plus? How are they run?

3. What command is used to define a text editor for SQL*Plus to use?

Limiting and Refining Selected Output

In this section, you will cover the following areas related to limiting and refining selected output:

■ The **order by** clause

■ The **where** clause

Obtaining all output from a table is great, but usually you must be more selective in choosing output. Most database applications contain a lot of data. How much data can a database contain? Some applications contain tables with a million rows or more, and the most recent release of Oracle8 will store up to 512 petabytes of data. Needless to say, manipulating vast amounts of data like that requires you to be careful. Always ask for *exactly* what you want, and no more.

The ORDER BY Clause

Data within a table need not have any order. Another quick look at the output from the EMP table will demonstrate:

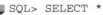

```
SQL> /

EMPID    LASTNAME    FIRSTNAME    SALARY
-----    --------    ---------    ------
39334    SMITH       GINA          75000
49539    QIAN        LEE           90000
60403    HARPER      ROD           45000
02039    WALLA       RAJENDRA      60000
49392    SPANKY      STACY        100000
```

   Notice that the data returned is in no particular order on any column, either numeric or alphabetical. That's fine for the database, but not always fine for people. Oracle allows you to place order on output from **select** statements using the **order by** clause, included in **select** statements at the end of the statement. The general syntax for the **order by** clause is to include both the clause and the column(s) or column alias(es) on which Oracle will define order, optionally followed by a special clause defining the direction of the order. Possible directions are **asc** for ascending and **desc** for descending. The default value is **asc**, and the output for **desc** as shown here:

```
SQL> SELECT *
  2> FROM emp
  3> ORDER BY empid DESC;

EMPID    LASTNAME    FIRSTNAME    SALARY
-----    --------    ---------    ------
60403    HARPER      ROD           45000
49539    QIAN        LEE           90000
49392    SPANKY      STACY        100000
39334    SMITH       GINA          75000
02039    WALLA       RAJENDRA      60000
```

   Order by can impose sort order on one or many columns in ascending *or* descending order in each of the columns specified. The **order by** clause can be useful in simple reporting. It can be applied to columns that are of NUMBER, text (VARCHAR2 and CHAR), and DATE datatypes. You can even use numbers to indicate the column on which Oracle should order the output from a statement. The use of numbers depends on the positioning of each column. For example, if you issue a statement similar to the one in the following code block, the order for the output will be as shown. The number 2 indicates that the second column should be used to define order in the output. But, since the second column is something different in each statement, the order of the output will be different as well.

```
SELECT empid, lastname FROM emp ORDER BY 2 DESC;

EMPID    LASTNAME
-----    --------
02039    WALLA
39334    SMITH
49392    SPANKY
49539    QIAN
60403    HARPER

SELECT lastname, empid FROM emp ORDER BY 2 DESC;

LASTNAME EMPID
-------- -----
HARPER   60403
SMITH    39334
SPANKY   49392
QIAN     49539
WALLA    02039
```

Exercises

1. How can a user put row data returned from a **select** statement in order? What are the various sort orders that can be used with this option?

2. What are the two ways to specify the column on which sort order should be defined?

The WHERE Clause

The **where** clause in Oracle **select** statements is where the really interesting things begin. This important clause in **select** statements allows you to single out a few rows from hundreds, thousands, or even millions like it. The **where** clause operates on a basic principle of comparison:

```
SELECT * FROM emp WHERE empid = 49392;

EMPID     LASTNAME    FIRSTNAME    SALARY
-----     --------    ---------    ------
49392     SPANKY      STACY        100000
```

Assuming the EMPID column contains all unique values, instead of pulling all rows from EMP, Oracle pulls just one row for display. To determine what row to display, the **where** clause performs a comparison operation as specified by the query—in this case, the comparison is an equality operation, **where** *empid* = 49392. However, equality is not the only means by which Oracle can obtain data. Some other examples of comparison are demonstrated in the following list:

$x = y$	Comparison to see if x is equal to y.
$x > y$	Comparison to see if x is greater than y.
$x >= y$	Comparison to see if x is greater than or equal to y.
$x < y$	Comparison to see if x is less than y.
$x <= y$	Comparison to see if x is less than or equal to y.
$x <> y$ $x\ != y$ $x\ ^= y$	Comparison to see if x is not equal to y.
like	A special comparison used in conjunction with the character wildcards (**%** **or** _) to find substrings in text variables.
soundex	A special function used to introduce "fuzzy logic" into text string comparisons by allowing equality based on similarly spelled words.
between	A range comparison operation that allows for operations on dates, numbers, and characters that are similar to the following numeric comparison: Y "is between" X and Z.
in	A special comparison that allows you to specify multiple equality statements by defining a set of values, any of which the value can be equal to. An example of its usage may be x **in** (1,2,3,4,5).

Every comparison between two values in Oracle boils down to one or more of these operations. Multiple comparisons can be placed together using the following list of operations. The operator is listed along with the result that is required to fulfill the criteria based on the presence of this operator.

x **and** *y*	Both comparisons in *x* and *y* must be true.
x **or** *y*	One comparison in *x* or *y* must be true.
not *x*	The logical opposite of *x*.

Exercises

1. What is a **where** clause? On what principle does this clause operate to determine which data is selected?

2. What are some operations available to assist in the purpose of comparison? What are some operations that allow you to specify more than one comparison in the **where** clause?

Using Single-Row Functions

In this section, you will cover the following areas related to using single-row functions:

■ Various single-row functions explained

■ Using functions in **select** statements

■ Date functions

There are dozens of functions available in Oracle that can be used for many purposes. Some functions in Oracle are designed to alter the data returned by a query, such as the **nvl( )** function already presented. The functions in this category are designed to work on columns of any datatype to return information in a different way. One commonly used example of this type of function is **decode( )**. The **decode( )** function works on the same principle as an **if-then-else** statement works in many common programming languages, including PL/SQL.

```
SELECT DECODE(column, val1, return1, val2, return2, ...
,return_default)
...
```

The **decode( )** function allows for powerful transformation of data from one value to another. Some examples of **decode( )** in action will appear later in the chapter.

Various Single-Row Functions Explained

From this point on, all functions described have limitations on the datatype on which they can perform their operations. Several functions exist in Oracle that manipulate text strings. These functions are similar in concept to **nvl( )** and **decode( )** in that they can perform a change on a piece of data, but the functions in this family can perform data change on only one type of data—text. Some are as follows.

lpad($x,y[,z]$) **rpad**($x,y[,z]$)	Returns the column "padded" on the left or right side of the data in the column passed as x to a width passed as y. The optional passed value z indicates the character(s) that **lpad( )** or **rpad( )** will insert into the column.
lower(x) **upper**(x) **initcap**(x)	Returns the column value passed as x into all lowercase or uppercase, or changes the initial letter in the string to a capital letter.
length(x)	Returns a number indicating the number of characters in the column value passed as x.
substr($x,y[,z]$)	Returns a substring of string x, starting at the character in position number y to the end, which is optionally defined by the character appearing in position z of the string.

Others are designed to perform specialized mathematical functions such as those used in scientific applications like sine and logarithm. These operations are commonly referred to as math or number operations. The functions falling into this category are listed next. These functions are not all that are available in Oracle, but rather are the most commonly used ones that will likely be used on OCP Exam 1.

abs(*x*)   Obtains the absolute value for a number. For example, the absolute value of (-1) is 1, while the absolute value of 6 is 6.

ceil(*x*)   Similar to executing **round** on an integer (i.e., **round(x,0)**, except **ceil** always rounds up. For example, **ceil(1.6)** = 2. Note that rounding "up" on negative numbers produces a value closer to zero (e.g., **ceil(-1.6)** = -1, not -2).

floor(*x*)   Similar to **ceil**, except **floor** always rounds down. For example, **floor(1.6)** = 1. Note that rounding "down" on negative numbers produces a value further away from zero (e.g., **floor(-1.6)** = -2, not -1).

mod(*x*,*y*)   The modulus of *x*, defined in long division as the integer remainder left over when *x* is divided by *y* until no further whole number can be produced. An example is **mod(10,3)** = 1, or **mod(10,2)** = 0.

round(*x*,*y*)   Round *x* to the decimal precision of *y*. If *y* is negative, round to the precision of *y* places to the left of the decimal point. For example, **round(134.345,1)** = 134.3, **round(134.345,0)** = 134, **round(134.345,-1)** = 130.

sign(*x*)   Displays **integer** value corresponding to the sign of *x*, 1 if *x* is positive, -1 if *x* is negative.

sqrt(*x*)   The square root of *x*.

trunc(*x*,*y*)   Truncate value of *x* to decimal precision *y*. If *y* is negative, then truncate to *y* number of places to the left of the decimal point.

vsize(*x*)   The storage size in bytes for value *x*.

The final category of number functions discussed here is the set of list functions. These functions are actually used for many different datatypes, including text, numeric, and date.

greatest(*x*,*y*,...)   Returns the highest value from list of text strings, numbers, or dates (*x*,*y*...).

least(*x*,*y*,...)   Returns the lowest value from list of text strings, numbers, or dates (*x*,*y*...).

Another class of data functions available in Oracle correspond to the DATE datatype. The functions that perform operations on dates are known as date functions. There is a special keyword that can be specified to give Oracle users the current date. This keyword is called **sysdate**. In the same way that you calculated simple arithmetic in an earlier part of the chapter using the DUAL table, so too can you execute a **select** statement using **sysdate** to produce today's date:

```
SELECT sysdate FROM DUAL;

SYSDATE
---------
15-MAY-99
```

The functions that can be used on DATE columns are listed in the following definitions:

add_months(x,y)	Returns a date corresponding to date x plus y months.
last_day(x)	Returns the date of the last day of the month that contains date x.
months_between(x,y)	Returns a number of months between y and x as produced by y-x. Can return a decimal value.
new_time(x,y,z)	Returns the current date and time for date x in time zone y as it would be in time zone z.

The functions available in Oracle are highly useful for executing well-defined operations on data in a table or constant values and often save time and energy. Make sure you understand these functions for OCP.

Exercises

1. Identify some of the character, number, and date functions available in SQL. What are two functions that allow you to transform column values regardless of the datatype?

2. What are other types of functions that perform operations on columns of specific datatypes?

Using Functions in SELECT Statements

The previous section introduced the many functions available in Oracle. The definitions in that section should suffice for reference; however, there is no substitute for actual usage. This section will show the functions listed in action. The first example details use of the **decode( )** function. Assume that you select data from the EMP table. The data in the SEX column of EMP is populated with M for male and F for female. Instead of displaying a letter, the following code block lets you write out the full word for each sex:

```
SELECT empid, lastname, firstname,
DECODE(sex,'M','MALE','F','FEMALE') sex FROM emp
ORDER BY empid DESC;

EMPID    LASTNAME    FIRSTNAME    SEX
-----    --------    ---------    ------
60403    HARPER      ROD          MALE
49539    QIAN        LEE          FEMALE
49392    SPANKY      STACY        FEMALE
39334    SMITH       GINA         FEMALE
02039    WALLA       RAJENDRA     MALE
```

The **decode( )** command has five variables, the first of which is the name of the column. This must always be present. The second variable corresponds to the value that could be found in the SEX column, followed by the value that **decode( )** should return if SEX in this row is equal to 'M'. The next set of variables answers the question of what **decode( )** should return if the value in the column is 'F'. This matching of column values with appropriate return values can continue until you have identified all cases you would like **decode( )** to handle. The last variable according to the definition of **decode( )** is used for the default return value, which is optional.

Now look at some text or character function examples. The first of these examples is for **rpad( )** and **lpad( )**. As shown in the following code, these two functions can be used to place additional filler characters on the right or left side of data in a column out to a specified column width:

```
SELECT empid, lastname, firstname,
RPAD(DECODE(sex,'M','MALE','F','FEMALE'),10,'-') sex FROM emp
ORDER BY empid DESC;
```

```
EMPID    LASTNAME    FIRSTNAME    SEX
-----    --------    ---------    ----------
60403    HARPER      ROD          MALE------
49539    QIAN        LEE          FEMALE----
49392    SPANKY      STACY        FEMALE----
39334    SMITH       GINA         FEMALE----
02039    WALLA       RAJENDRA     MALE------
```

The output from one SQL function can be used as input for another, as demonstrated here. The **rpad( )** operation will pad the decoded SEX column out to ten characters with dashes. If the **lpad( )** operation had been used instead, the result would have been as follows:

```
SELECT empid, lastname, firstname,
LPAD(DECODE(sex,'M','MALE','F','FEMALE'),10,'-') sex FROM emp
ORDER BY empid DESC;
```

```
EMPID    LASTNAME    FIRSTNAME    SEX
-----    --------    ---------    ----------
60403    HARPER      ROD          ------MALE
49539    QIAN        LEE          ----FEMALE
49392    SPANKY      STACY        ----FEMALE
39334    SMITH       GINA         ----FEMALE
02039    WALLA       RAJENDRA     ------MALE
```

Some of the simpler character functions are next. Two straightforward examples of SQL queries are sometimes referred to as "case translators," because they perform a simple translation of case based on the text string passed:

```
SELECT LOWER(title) TITLE_NOQUOTE,
UPPER(artist) ARTIST1, INITCAP(artist) ARTIST2 FROM SONGS;
```

```
TITLE_NOQUOTE              ARTIST1      ARTIST2
-------------------        ---------    ---------
"happy birthday"           ANONYMOUS    Anonymous
"diamonds and rust"        ANONYMOUS    Anonymous
"amazing grace"            ANONYMOUS    Anonymous
```

Another straightforward and useful character function is the **length( )** function, which returns the length of a text string:

```
SELECT title, LENGTH(title) LENGTH
FROM SONGS;
```

```
TITLE                   LENGTH
------------------      ------
"HAPPY BIRTHDAY"            16
"DIAMONDS AND RUST"        19
"AMAZING GRACE"            15
```

Note one interesting thing happening in this query—spaces and double quotes are all counted as part of the length! Another extraordinarily useful function related to character strings is the **substr( )** function. This function is commonly used to extract data from a longer text string. The **substr( )** function takes as its first variable the full text string to be searched. The second variable contains an integer that designates the character number at which the substring should begin. The third parameter is optional and specifies how many characters to the right of the start of the substring will be included in the substring. Observe the following output to understand the effects of omitting the third parameter:

```
SELECT title, SUBSTR(title,5,5) CHARS
FROM SONGS;

TITLE                   CHARS
------------------      -----
"HAPPY BIRTHDAY"        Y BIR
"DIAMONDS AND RUST"     ONDS
"AMAZING GRACE"         ING G

SELECT title, SUBSTR(title,5) CHARACTERS
FROM SONGS;

TITLE                   CHARACTERS
------------------      ---------------
"HAPPY BIRTHDAY"        Y BIRTHDAY"
"DIAMONDS AND RUST"     ONDS AND RUST"
"AMAZING GRACE"         ING GRACE"
```

The number or math functions are frequently used in scientific applications. The first function detailed here is the **abs( )** or absolute value function that calculates how far away from zero the parameter passed lies on the number line:

```
SELECT ABS(25), ABS(-12) FROM DUAL;

ABS(25)    ABS(-12)
-------    --------
     25          12
```

The next single-value function that will be covered in this section is the **ceil( )** function, which automatically rounds the number passed as its parameter up to the next higher integer:

```
SELECT CEIL(123.323), CEIL(45), CEIL(-392), CEIL(-1.12) FROM DUAL;

CEIL(123.323)    CEIL(45)    CEIL(-392)    CEIL(-1.12)
-------------    --------    ----------    -----------
          124          45          -392             -1
```

The next single-value function is the **floor( )** function. The **floor( )** is the opposite of **ceil( )**, rounding the value passed down to the next highest integer:

```
SELECT FLOOR(123.323), FLOOR(45), FLOOR(-392), FLOOR(-1.12) FROM
DUAL;

FLOOR(123.323)    FLOOR(45)    FLOOR(-392)    FLOOR(-1.12)
--------------    ---------    -----------    -----------
           123           45           -392             -2
```

The next function covered in this section is related to long division. The function is called **mod( )**, and it returns the remainder or modulus for a number and its divisor:

```
SELECT MOD(12,3), MOD(55,4) FROM DUAL;

MOD(12,3)    MOD(55,4)
---------    ---------
        0            3
```

After that, you should look at **round( )**. This important function allows you to round a number off to a specified precision:

```
SELECT ROUND(123.323,2), ROUND(45,1), ROUND(-392,-1), ROUND
(-1.12,0) FROM DUAL;

ROUND(123.323,2)    ROUND(45,1)    ROUND(-392,-1)    ROUND(-1.12,0)
----------------    -----------    --------------    --------------
          123.32             45              -390                -1
```

The next function is called **sign( )**. It assists in identifying a number to be positive or negative. If the number passed is positive, **sign( )** returns 1, and if the number is negative, **sign( )** returns –1. If the number is zero, **sign( )** returns zero:

```
SELECT SIGN(-1933), SIGN(55), SIGN(0) FROM DUAL;

SIGN(-1933)   SIGN(55)     SIGN(0)
----------    -----------  -------
        -1            1          0
```

The next example is the **sqrt( )** function. It is used to derive the square root for a number:

```
SELECT SQRT(34), SQRT(9) FROM DUAL;

SQRT(34)    SQRT(9)
---------   ----------
5.8309519          3
```

The next single-value number function is called **trunc( )**. Similar to **round( )**, **trunc( )** truncates a value passed into it according to the precision that is passed in as well:

```
SELECT TRUNC(123.232,2), TRUNC(-45,1), TRUNC(392,-1), TRUNC(5,0)
FROM DUAL;

TRUNC(123.232,2) TRUNC(-45,1) TRUNC(392,-1) TRUNC(5,0)
---------------- ------------ ------------- ----------
         123.23          -45           390          5
```

The final single-row operation that will be covered in this section is the **vsize( )** function. This function is not strictly for numeric datatypes, either. The **vsize( )** function gives the size in bytes of any value for text, number, date, ROWID, and other columns.

```
SELECT VSIZE(384838), VSIZE('ORANGE_TABBY'), VSIZE(sysdate) FROM
DUAL;

VSIZE(384838)     VSIZE('ORANGE_TABBY')     VSIZE(SYSDATE)
-------------     ---------------------     --------------
            4                        12                  8
```

Exercises

1. What is the purpose of the **nvl( )** function? What datatypes does it accept? What is the purpose of a **decode( )** statement? What datatypes does it accept?

2. Name some character functions? Can two functions be combined? Why or why not?

3. Name some single-value number functions. What types of applications are these functions typically used in?

4. What function is used to determine the size in bytes of a given value or column?

Date Functions

There are several date functions in the Oracle database. The syntax of these functions has already been presented. This section will discuss each function in more detail and present examples of their usage. The Oracle database stores dates as integers, representing the number of days since the beginning of the Julian calendar. This method allows for easy format changes and inherent millennium compliance.

The first function is the **add_months( )** function. This function takes as input a date and a number of months to be added. Oracle then returns the new date, which is the old date plus the number of months:

```
SELECT ADD_MONTHS('15-MAR-99',26)
FROM DUAL;

ADD_MONTHS('15
--------------
     15-MAY-01
```

The next date function, **last_day( )**, helps to determine the date for the last date in the month for the date given:

```
SELECT LAST_DAY('15-MAR-00') FROM DUAL;

LAST_DAY('15-M
--------------
     31-MAR-00
```

The next date function determines the number of months between two different dates given. The name of the function is **months_between( )**. The syntax of this command is tricky, so it will be presented here. The syntax of this command is **months_between(y,x)**, and the return value for this function is *y-x*:

```
SELECT MONTHS_BETWEEN('15-MAR-99','26-JUN-98') FROM DUAL;

MONTHS_BETWEEN
--------------
     8.6451613
```

The last example of a date function is **new_time( )**. It accepts three parameters, the first being a date and time, the second being the time zone the first parameter belongs in, and the last parameter being the time zone you would like to convert to. Each time zone is abbreviated in the following way: *X*ST or *X*DT, where *S* or *D* stands for standard or daylight saving time, and where *X* stands for the first letter of the time zone (such as *A*tlantic, *B*ering, *C*entral, *E*astern, *H*awaii, *M*ountain, *N*ewfoundland, *P*acific, or *Y*ukon). There are two exceptions: Greenwich mean time is indicated by GMT, while Newfoundland standard time does not use daylight saving. So far, none of the queries used to demonstrate the date functions have required that much precision, but the following example will. In order to demonstrate the full capability of Oracle in the **new_time( )** function, the NLS date format can be changed to display the full date and time for the query. The following example demonstrates both the use of **nls_date_format** to change the date format and the **new_time( )** function to convert a timestamp to a new time zone:

```
ALTER SESSION
SET NLS_DATE_FORMAT = 'DD-MON-YYYY HH24:MI:SS';

SELECT NEW_TIME('15-MAR-1999 14:35:00','AST','GMT')
FROM DUAL;

NEW_TIME('15-MAR-199
--------------------
15-MAR-1999 18:35:00
```

Exercises

1. What is **nls_date_format**? How is it set? How is it used?

2. Which date functions described in this section return information in the DATE datatype? Which one returns information in a datatype other than DATE?

3. How are dates stored in Oracle?

Conversion Functions

Still other functions are designed to convert columns of one datatype to another type. These functions do not actually modify the data itself; they just return the converted value. Several different conversion functions are available in the Oracle database, as listed below:

to_char(x)	Converts noncharacter value x to character
to_number(x)	Converts nonnumeric value x to number
to_date(x[,y])	Converts nondate value x to date, using format specified by y
to_multi_byte(x)	Converts single-byte character string x to multibyte characters according to national language standards
to_single_byte(x)	Converts multibyte character string x to single-byte characters according to national language standards
chartorowid(x)	Converts string of characters x into an Oracle ROWID
rowidtochar(x)	Converts a string of characters x into an Oracle ROWID
hextoraw(x)	Converts hexadecimal (base-16) value x into raw (binary) format
rawtohex(x)	Converts raw (binary) value x into hexadecimal (base-16) format
convert(x[,y[,z]])	Executes a conversion of alphanumeric string x from the current character set optionally specified as z to the one specified by y
translate(x,y,z)	Executes a simple value conversion for character or numeric string x into something else based on the conversion factors y and z

The following text illustrates the most commonly used procedures for converting data in action. These are the **to_char( )**, **to_number( )**, and

to_date( ) functions. The first one demonstrated is the **to_char( )** function. In the example of **new_time( )**, the date function described earlier, the **alter session set nls_date_format** statement was used to demonstrate the full capabilities both of Oracle in storing date information and Oracle in converting dates and times from one time zone to another. That exercise could have been accomplished with the use of the **to_char( )** conversion function as well, however. Using **to_char( )** in this manner saves you from converting **nls_date_format**, which, once executed, is in effect for the rest of your session, or until you execute another **alter session set nls_date_format** statement. Rather than using this method, you may want to opt for a less permanent option offered by the **to_char( )** function, as shown below:

```
SELECT TO_CHAR(NEW_TIME(TO_DATE('15-MAR-1999 14:35:00',
'DD-MON-YYYY HH24:MI:SS'),'AST','GMT'))
FROM DUAL;

NEXT_DAY('15-MAR-9
------------------
15-MAR-99 18:35:00
```

Note that this example also uses the **to_date( )** function, another conversion function in the list to be discussed. The **to_date( )** function is very useful for converting numbers, and especially character strings, into properly formatted DATE fields. The next function to consider is **to_number( )**, which converts text or date information into a number:

```
SELECT TO_NUMBER('49583') FROM DUAL;

TO_NUMBER('49583')
------------------
            49583
```

Although there does not appear to be much difference between the output of this query and the string that was passed, the main difference is the underlying datatype. Even so, Oracle is actually intelligent enough to convert a character string consisting of all numbers before performing an arithmetic operation using two values of two different datatypes, as shown in the following listing:

```
SELECT '49583' + 34 FROM DUAL;

'49583'+34
----------
     49617
```

Exercises

1. Identify some conversion functions. Which conversion functions are commonly used?

2. What is **nls_date_format**? How is it used?

Chapter Summary

This chapter provides an introduction to using Oracle by demonstrating basic techniques for use of **select** statements. The areas discussed in this chapter are selecting row data from tables using the **select from** statement, limiting the rows selected with the **where** clause of the **select from** statement, and using the single-row functions available in Oracle to manipulate selected data into other values, formats, or meanings. This chapter is the cornerstone for all other usage in Oracle, as well as for passing the OCP Exam 1. Material covered in this chapter comprises 17 percent of test content on OCP Exam 1.

The first area covered in this chapter is information about selecting data from Oracle. The most common manipulation of data in the Oracle database is to **select** it, and the means by which to select data from Oracle is the **select** statement. The **select** statement has two basic parts, the **select** clause and the **from** clause. The **select** clause identifies the column(s) of the table that you would like to view contents of. The **from** clause identifies the table(s) in which the data **select**ed is stored. In this chapter, data from only one table at a time was considered. In the next chapter, the concept of pulling or "joining" data from multiple tables is considered.

Often, users will want to perform calculations involving the data selected from a table. Oracle allows for basic, intermediate, and complex manipulation of data **select**ed from a database table through the use of standard arithmetic notation. These operators can be used to perform math calculations on the data **select**ed from a table or as math operators on numbers in calculator-like fashion. In order to perform calculations on numbers that are not **select**ed from any table, you must utilize the DUAL table. DUAL is simply a table with one column that fulfills the syntactic requirements of SQL statements like **select**, which need a table name in the **from** clause in order to work.

When manipulating data from a table, you must remember to handle cases when column data for a particular row is nonexistent. Nonexistent column data in a table row is often referred to as being NULL. These NULL values can be viewed either as blank space, by default, or you can account for the appearance of NULL data by using a special function that will substitute NULL fields with a data value. The name of this special function is **nvl( )**. The **nvl( )** function takes two parameters: the first is the column or value to be investigated for being NULL, and the second is the default value **nvl( )** will substitute if the column or value is NULL. The **nvl( )** function operates on all sorts of datatypes, including CHAR, VARCHAR2, NUMBER, and DATE.

When performing special operations on columns in a **select** statement, Oracle often displays hard-to-read headings for the column name because Oracle draws the column name directly from the **select** clause of the **select** statement. You can avoid this problem by giving a column alias for Oracle to use instead. For example, the following **select** may produce a cryptic column heading: **select nvl(LASTNAME,'DOE') ...**, while a column alias would allow Oracle to provide a more meaningful heading: **select nvl(LASTNAME,'DOE') LASTNAME ...**. Column aliases are specified as character strings following the function and/or column name the alias will substitute. Be sure to include white space between the function and/or column name and the alias.

Concluding the introduction to SQL **select** statements, the use of concatenation and entering the actual statements was discussed. Columns can be concatenated together using two pipe (||) characters. This operation is useful for making two columns into one, or to use special characters, such as commas or others, to separate the output. The SQL statement itself is entered using the SQL*Plus tool. If a user makes an error while typing in the line of SQL, you can use the BACKSPACE key to erase characters until you reach the mistake; however, this approach only works if you are still on the same line in the SQL entry buffer. If you have already proceeded to another line, or if you tried to execute the command, then you can type in the number corresponding to the line to be corrected to **select** that line for editing. Then, you can type in the **change** command, abbreviated **c/**old**/**new, where old is the existing version of the string containing the mistake, and new is the correction. If this all sounds complicated, you can simply type **edit**, or **ed**, from the prompt in SQL*Plus, and Oracle will immediately bring up your favorite text editor. The text editor used here can be specified or changed with the **define _editor="**youreditor**"** command.

The number or order of selected rows from the database can be limited or refined with various options. The option for refining data discussed is **order by**. This is a clause that allows you to specify two things—the first is a column on which to list the data in order, and the second is whether Oracle should use ascending or descending order. Usage of the **order by** clause can make output from an Oracle **select** statement more readable, since there is no guarantee that the data in Oracle will be stored in any particular order.

The means of limiting selected output is the **where** clause. Proper use of this clause is key to successful usage of Oracle and SQL. In the **where** clause, you can specify one or more comparison criteria that must be met by the data in a table in order for Oracle to **select** the row. A comparison consists of two elements that are compared using a comparison operator, which may consist of a logic operator such as equality (=), inequality (<>,!=, or ^=), less than (<) or greater than (>), or a combination of less or greater than and equality. Alternatively, you can also utilize special comparison operators that enable pattern matches using **like %**, range scans using **between** x **and** y, or fuzzy logic with the **soundex**(x) = **soundex**(y) statement. In addition, one or more comparison operations may be specified in the **where** clause, joined together with **and** or the **or** operator, or preceded by **not**.

Data selected in Oracle can be modified with the use of several functions available in Oracle. These functions may work on many different types of data, as is the case with **nvl( )** functions called **decode( )**, **greatest( )**, or **least( )**. Alternatively, their use may be limited to a particular datatype. These functions may be divided into categories based on the types of data they can handle. Typically, the functions are categorized into text or character functions, math or number functions, and date functions.

Usage of Oracle built-in functions enables you to perform many different operations. In general, the use of a function comprises specifying the name of the function and the passing of variables to the function. For example, to change the characters in a text string requires identifying the function that performs this task, followed by passing the function a value. To perform the task in this example, the following function call could be made: **upper**(*lowercase*).

The chapter also detailed the usage of all the functions available in Oracle, and provided examples for most of them. For brevity sake, they will not reappear here; however, it should be noted that many of the functions

can be used together and in conjunction with the multitype functions like
decode( ). For example, the usage of **decode(sqrt(x), 4, 'HARVEY',5,'JILL',
'BRAD')** is permitted. In essence, this functionality allows you to incorporate
the output from one function as input for another. An entire set of
conversion functions is also available to change datatypes for values, or to
create ciphers, or even to change the character sets used in order to move
data onto different machines. Again, for the sake of brevity, the functions
themselves are not listed here; however, it should be stated that the
conversion functions can be used in conjunction with many of the other
functions already named.

Two-Minute Drill

- Data is retrieved from Oracle using **select** statements.

- Syntax for a **select** statement consists of **select ...from...;**.

- When entering a **select** statement from the prompt using SQL*Plus, a
  semicolon(**;**) must be used to end the statement.

- Arithmetic operations can be used to perform math operations on
  data selected from a table, or on numbers using the DUAL table.

- The DUAL table is a table with one column and one row used to
  fulfill the syntactic requirements of SQL **select** statements.

- Values in columns for particular rows may be empty, or NULL.

- If a column contains the NULL value, you can use the **nvl( )** function
  to return meaningful information instead of an empty field.

- Aliases can be used in place of the actual column name or to
  replace the appearance of the function name in the header.

- Output from two columns can be concatenated together using a
  double-pipe (||).

- SQL commands can be entered directly into SQL*Plus on the
  command line.

- If a mistake is made, the change (**c**/*old*/*new*) command is used.

- Alternatively, the **edit** (**ed**) command can be used to make changes in your favorite text editor.

- You can specify a favorite text editor by issuing the **define _editor** command at the prompt.

- The **order by** clause in a **select** statement is a useful clause to incorporate sort order into the output of the file.

- Sort orders that can be used are **ascending** or **descending**, abbreviated as **asc** and **desc**. Order is determined by the column identified by the **order by** clause.

- The **where** clause is used in SQL queries to limit the data returned by the query.

- The **where** clauses contain comparison operations that determine whether a row will be returned by a query.

- There are several logical comparison operations, including =, >, >=, <, <, <>, !=, ^=.

- In addition to the logical operations, there is a comparison operation for pattern matching called **like**. The % and _ characters are used to designate wildcards.

- There is also a range operation called **between**.

- There is also a fuzzy logic operation called **soundex**.

- Finally, the **where** clause can contain one or more comparison operations linked together by use of **and**, **or**, and preceded by **not**.

- Several SQL functions exist in Oracle.

- SQL functions are broken down into character functions, number functions, and date functions.

- A few functions are usable on many different types of data.

- There are also several conversion functions available for transforming data from text to numeric datatypes and back, numbers to dates and back, text to ROWID and back, etc.

Chapter Questions

1. **Which of the following statements contains an error?**

   A. select * from EMP **where** EMPID = 493945;

   B. select EMPID **from** EMP **where** EMPID = 493945;

   C. select EMPID **from** EMP;

   D. select EMPID **where** EMPID = 56949 **and** LASTNAME = 'SMITH';

2. **Which of the following correctly describes how to specify a column alias?**

   A. Place the alias at the beginning of the statement to describe the table.

   B. Place the alias after each column, separated by white space, to describe the column.

   C. Place the alias after each column, separated by a comma, to describe the column.

   D. Place the alias at the end of the statement to describe the table.

3. **The NVL( ) function**

   A. Assists in the distribution of output across multiple columns

   B. Allows you to specify alternate output for non-NULL column values

   C. Allows you to specify alternate output for NULL column values

   D. Nullifies the value of the column output.

4. **Output from a table called PLAYS with two columns, PLAY_NAME and AUTHOR, is shown next. Which of the following SQL statements produced it?**

```
PLAY_TABLE
---------------------------------------
"Midsummer Night's Dream", SHAKESPEARE
"Waiting For Godot", BECKETT
"The Glass Menagerie", WILLIAMS
```

    A. select PLAY_NAME|| AUTHOR **from** PLAYS;

    B. select PLAY_NAME, AUTHOR **from** PLAYS;

    C. select PLAY_NAME||', ' || AUTHOR **from** PLAYS;

    D. select PLAY_NAME||', ' || AUTHOR **play_table from** PLAYS;

5. **Issuing the DEFINE _EDITOR="emacs" will produce which outcome?**

    A. The emacs editor will become the SQL*Plus default text editor.

    B. The emacs editor will start running immediately.

    C. The emacs editor will no longer be used by SQL*Plus as the default text editor.

    D. The emacs editor will be deleted from the system.

6. **Which function can best be categorized as similar in function to an IF-THEN-ELSE statement?**

    A. sqrt( )

    B. decode( )

    C. new_time( )

    D. rowidtochar( )

7. **Which three of the following are number functions? (Choose three of the four)**

    A. sinh( )

    B. to_number( )

    C. sqrt( )

    D. round( )

8. You issue the following statement. What will be displayed if the EMPID selected is 60494?

SELECT DECODE(empid,38475, 'Terminated',60494, 'LOA', 'ACTIVE') FROM emp;

A. 60494

B. LOA

C. Terminated

D. ACTIVE

9. Which of the following is a valid SQL statement?

A. select to_char(nvl(sqrt(59483), '0')) from dual;

B. select to_char(nvl(sqrt(59483), 'INVALID')) from dual;

C. select (to_char(nvl(sqrt(59483), '0')) from dual;

D. select to_char(nvl(sqrt(59483), 'TRUE')) from dual;

10. The appropriate table to use when performing arithmetic calculations on values defined within the SELECT statement (not pulled from a table column) is

A. EMP

B. The table containing the column values

C. DUAL

D. An Oracle-defined table

11. Which of the following keywords are used in ORDER BY clauses? (Choose two)

A. ABS

B. ASC

C. DESC

D. DISC

12. **Which of the following statements are NOT TRUE about ORDER BY clauses?**

    A. Ascending or descending order can be defined with the **asc** or **desc** keywords.

    B. Only one column can be used to define the sort order in an **order by** clause.

    C. Multiple columns can be used to define sort order in an **order by** clause.

    D. Columns can be represented by numbers indicating their listed order in the **select** clause within **order by**.

13. **Which of the following lines in the SELECT statement here contain an error?**

    A. **select decode**(EMPID, 58385, 'INACTIVE', 'ACTIVE') **empid**

    B. **from** EMP

    C. **where substr**(LASTNAME,1,1) > **to_number**('S')

    D. **and** EMPID > 02000

    E. **order by** EMPID **desc**, lastname **asc**;

    F. There are no errors in this statement.

Answers to Chapter Questions

   1. D.   **select** EMPID **where** EMPID = 56949 **and** LASTNAME
   = 'SMITH';

Explanation   There is no **from** clause in this statement. Although a **select**
statement can be issued without a **where** clause, no **select** statement can be
executed without a **from** clause specified. For that reason, the DUAL table
exists to satisfy the **from** clause in situations where you define all data
needed within the statement.

   2. B.   Place the alias after each column, separated by white space, to
   describe the column.

Explanation   Aliases do not describe tables, they describe columns, which
eliminates choices A and D. Commas in the **select** statement separate each
column selected from one another. If a column alias appeared after a
column, then Oracle would either select the wrong column name based on
information provided in the alias or return an error.

   3. C.   Allows you to specify alternate output for NULL column values

Explanation   The **nvl( )** function is a simple **if-then** operation that tests
column value output to see if it is NULL. If it is, then **nvl( )** substitutes the
NULL value with the default value specified. Since this function only operates
on one column per call to **nvl( )**, choice A is incorrect. Choice B is incorrect
because it is the logical opposite of choice C. Choice D is incorrect because
nvl( ) is designed to substitute actual values for situations where NULL is
present, not nullify data.

   4. D.   **select** PLAY_NAME||', ' || AUTHOR **play_table from** PLAYS;

Explanation   This question illustrates the need to do careful reading. Since
the output specified for the question contained a column alias for the output
of the statement, choice D is the only one that is correct, even though
choice C also performed the correct calculation. Choice A is incorrect
because it specified an inaccurate concatenation method, and choice B is
wrong because it doesn't specify concatenation at all.

5. A.   The emacs editor will become the SQL*Plus default text editor.

Explanation   The **define_editor** statement is designed to define the default text editor in SQL*Plus. Changing the definition will not start or stop the editor specified from running, which eliminates B and D. Choice C is the logical opposite of choice A and therefore is incorrect.

6. B.   **decode( )**

Explanation   The **decode( )** function is a full-fledged **if-then-else** statement that can support manipulation of output values for several different cases plus a default. The **sqrt( )** statement simply calculates square roots, eliminating choice A. Choice C is incorrect because **new_time( )** is a date function that converts a time in one time zone to a time in another time zone. Choice D is incorrect because it is a simple conversion operation.

7. A, C, and D.   **sinh( )**, **sqrt( )**, and **round( )**

Explanation   The only function in this list is the **to_number( )** function, which is a conversion operation. Several questions of this type appear throughout the OCP exams, whereby the test taker will choose multiple answers. For more information about number functions, refer to the discussion or examples of their usage.

8. B.   LOA

Explanation   The **decode( )** statement has a provision in it that will return LOA if the EMPID in the row matches the EMPID specified for that case, which also eliminates choice D. Also, since a default value is specified by the **decode( )**, there will never be an EMPID returned by this query. Therefore, choice A is incorrect. Choice C is also eliminated because Terminated is only displayed when 38475 is the column value.

9. A.   **select to_char(nvl(sqrt(59483), '0')) from dual;**

Explanation   Functions such as these can be used in conjunction with one another. Though usually the datatype of the "value if NULL" and the column specified for **nvl( )** must match, Oracle performs many datatype conversions implicitly, such as this one.

10. C.   DUAL

Explanation   When all data to be processed by the query is present in the statement, and no data will be pulled from the database, users typically specify the DUAL table to fulfill the syntactic requirements of the **from** clause.

11. B and C.   ASC and DESC

Explanation   The **abs( )** function is the absolute value function, which eliminates choice A. The **disc( )** function is not an actual option either, eliminating choice D.

12. B.   Only one column can be used to define the sort order in an **order by** clause

Explanation   Notice first of all there is a logical difference between B and C, meaning you can eliminate one of them on principle. Multiple columns can be used to define order in **order by** statements, thereby eliminating choice C automatically. Choice A is incorrect because you can use **asc** or **desc** to specify ascending or descending order in your **order by** clause. Finally, choice D is incorrect because you can use numbers to represent the column you want to place order on, based on how the columns are listed in the **select** statement.

13. C.   **where substr**(LASTNAME,1,1) > **to_number**('S')

Explanation   Characters that are alphabetic like S cannot be converted into numbers. When this statement is run, it will produce an error on this line.

CHAPTER 2

Advanced Data Selection in Oracle

n this chapter, you will understand and demonstrate knowledge in the following areas:

- Displaying data from multiple tables
- Group functions and their uses
- Using subqueries
- Using runtime variables

This chapter covers the advanced topics of Oracle data selection. The first area of understanding discussed in this chapter is the table join. The chapter will cover how you can write **select** statements to access data from more than one table. The discussion will also cover how you can create joins that display data from different tables even when the information in the two tables does not correspond completely. Finally, the use of table self joins will be discussed. The chapter also introduces the **group by** clause used in **select** statements and group functions. Use of the subquery is another area covered in this chapter as well. Finally, specification and use of variables is presented. The material in this chapter will complete the user's knowledge of data selection and comprises 22 percent of OCP Exam 1.

Displaying Data from Multiple Tables

In this section, you will cover the following areas related to displaying data from multiple tables:

- **Select** statements to join data from more than one table
- Creating outer joins
- Joining a table to itself

The typical database contains many tables. Some smaller databases may have only a dozen or so tables, while other databases may have hundreds. The common factor, however, is that no database has just one table that contains all the data you need. Oracle recognizes you may want data that resides in multiple tables drawn together in some meaningful way. In order to show data from multiple tables in one query, Oracle allows you to perform *table joins*. A table join is when data from one table is associated with data from another table according to a common column in both tables.

TIP
*There must be at least one column shared between two tables in order to join the two tables in a **select** statement.*

If a column value appears in two tables, a relationship can be defined between them if one of the columns appears as part of a primary key in one of the tables. A *primary key* is used in a table to identify the uniqueness of each row in a table. The table in which the column appears as a primary key is referred to as the *parent table*, while the column that references the other table in the relationship is often called the *child table*. The column in the child table relates to the parent table as something called a *foreign key*. Figure 2-1 demonstrates how the relationship may work in a database.

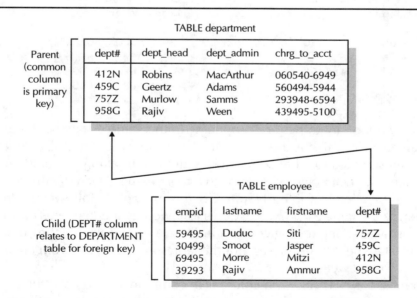

FIGURE 2-1.   *Primary- and foreign-key relationship between tables*

Select Statements That Join Data from More than One Table

When a primary- or foreign-key relationship exists between several tables, then it is possible to join their data. As described in the last chapter, a **select** statement can have three parts: the **select** clause, the **from** clause, and the **where** clause. The **select** clause is where you list the column names you want to view data from, along with any single-row functions and/or column aliases. The **from** clause gives the names of the tables where the data is stored. In a table join, two or more tables are named as sources for data. The final clause is the **where** clause, which contains comparison operations that will filter out the unwanted data from what you want to see. The comparison operations in a table join statement also have another purpose—to describe how the data between two tables should be joined together, as shown in the following code:

```
SELECT a.antique_name, a.antique_cost,
a.storage_box_number, b.box_name, b.box_location
FROM antique a, storage_box b
WHERE a.antique_name in ('VICTROLA','CAMERA','RADIO')
AND a.storage_box_number = b.storage_box_number;


A.ANTIQUE_N  A.ANTIQ  A.STOR  B.BOX_NAME  B.BOX_LOCATION
-----------  -------  ------  ----------  --------------
VICTROLA      150.00       3  ALPHA-3     ALPHA BLDG
CAMERA         75.00       4  ALPHA-4     ALPHA BLDG
RADIO         200.00       4  ALPHA-4     ALPHA BLDG
```

Many important things are happening in this sample statement, the most fundamental of which is the table join. The **from** clause in this statement is the clearest indication that a table join statement is taking place. In this statement, the **from** clause contains two table names, each of which is followed by a letter. Table ANTIQUE in this example is followed by the letter a, while table STORAGE_BOX is followed by the letter b. This display demonstrates an interesting concept in Oracle—not only can the columns in a **select** statement have aliases, but the tables named in the **from** clause can have aliases as well.

In most cases, tables with columns in common should have the same name for those columns, because then it becomes easier to identify that they contain the same data. However, this common name can lead to ambiguity when the Oracle SQL processing mechanism attempts (also known as the RDBMS) to parse the statement and resolve all database object names. If each column isn't linked to the particular tables identified in the **from** clause, Oracle will return an error. By specifying an alias for each table in the **from** clause, and then prefixing each column name in the **select** statement with the alias, you avoid ambiguity in the SQL statements while also avoiding the need to type out a table name each time a column is specified. The following code block illustrates the extra coding necessary when referencing columns if table aliases aren't used:

```
SELECT antique_name, antique_cost,
antique.storage_box_number, box_name, box_location
FROM antique, storage_box
WHERE antique_name in ('VICTROLA','CAMERA','RADIO')
AND antique.storage_box_number = storage_box.storage_box_number;

ANTIQUE_NAM  ANTIQUE  ANTIQU  BOX_NAME  BOX_LOCATION
-----------  -------  ------  --------  ------------
VICTROLA      150.00       3  ALPHA-3   ALPHA BLDG
CAMERA         75.00       4  ALPHA-4   ALPHA BLDG
RADIO         200.00       4  ALPHA-4   ALPHA BLDG
```

Notice something else. Neither the alias nor the full table name need be specified before a column that appears in only one table specified by the **from** clause. Ambiguity is only produced when the column appears in two or more of the tables specified in the **from** clause.

The next area to cover in creating queries that join data from one table to data from another table is the use of comparison operations in the **where** clause of the statement. The **where** clause must include one comparison that links the data of one table to the data in the other table. Without this link, all data from both tables is generated as output from the query in something referred to as a *Cartesian product*. A Cartesian product is the product of all data coming from one table multiplied by the product of the other.

There are two possibilities available in order to link the data from one table to another: equality comparisons or inequality comparisons. Tables joined on equality statements in the **where** clause are referred to as an "inner" join, or equijoin. An *equijoin* will return data where the value in one column in one table equals the value in the column of the other table. In the situation where the tables are being joined based on an inequality statement in the **where** clause, typically the data returned may have less meaning unless a range of data is specified and the actual link between the two tables is an equality statement.

```
SELECT antique_name, antique_cost,
antique.storage_box_number, box_name, box_location
FROM antique, storage_box
WHERE antique_name IN ('VICTROLA','CAMERA','RADIO')
AND antique.storage_box_number < storage_box.storage_box_number;
```

ANTIQUE_NAM	ANTIQUE	ANTIQU	BOX_NAME	BOX_LOCATION
VICTROLA	150.00	3	ALPHA-1	ALPHA BLDG
VICTROLA	150.00	3	ALPHA-2	ALPHA BLDG
VICTROLA	150.00	3	ALPHA-3	ALPHA BLDG
VICTROLA	150.00	3	ALPHA-4	ALPHA BLDG
CAMERA	75.00	4	ALPHA-1	ALPHA BLDG
CAMERA	75.00	4	ALPHA-2	ALPHA BLDG
CAMERA	75.00	4	ALPHA-3	ALPHA BLDG
CAMERA	75.00	4	ALPHA-4	ALPHA BLDG
RADIO	200.00	4	ALPHA-1	ALPHA BLDG
RADIO	200.00	4	ALPHA-2	ALPHA BLDG
RADIO	200.00	4	ALPHA-3	ALPHA BLDG
RADIO	200.00	4	ALPHA-4	ALPHA BLDG

This is junk data. It illustrates that when an inequality operation is specified as part of the **where** clause joining data from one table to another, there is no way to guarantee that the inequality operation will be satisfied for *all* values in the column for *both* tables. There is also a high possibility that the data returned by an inequality join will look suspiciously like a Cartesian product. A better alternative for drawing data from a table that satisfies an inequality operation but does not produce a Cartesian product is to specify the inequality operation outside the comparison that produces the join, as shown here:

```
SELECT antique_name, antique_cost,
antique.storage_box_number, box_name, box_location
FROM antique, storage_box
WHERE box_location in ('VICTROLA','CAMERA','RADIO')
AND antique.storage_box_number = storage_box.storage_box_number
AND antique.storage_box_number > 3;
```

ANTIQUE_NAM	ANTIQUE	ANTIQU	BOX_NAME	BOX_LOCATION
CAMERA	75.00	4	ALPHA-4	ALPHA BLDG
RADIO	200.00	4	ALPHA-4	ALPHA BLDG

This **select** statement will produce all results joined properly using the equality operation to link the rows of two tables in an inner join, while also satisfying the comparison needed to obtain data for only those storage boxes greater than box #3. In general, it is best to specify an equality operation for the two columns linking the tables for the join, followed by an inequality operation on the same column in *one* of the tables to filter the number of rows that will be linked in the join.

Generally speaking, the query used to produce a table join must contain the right number of equality operations to avoid a Cartesian product. If the number of tables to be joined equals *N*, the user should remember to include at least *N*-1 equality conditions in the **select** statement so that each column in each table that exists in another table is referenced *at least once*.

TIP
*For N joined tables, you need at least N-1 join conditions in the **select** statement in order to avoid a Cartesian product.*

Exercises

1. What is a table join? How is a table join produced?

2. Why is it important to use equality operations when creating a table join?

3. How many equality conditions are required to join three tables? Six tables? Twenty tables?

Creating Outer Joins

In some cases, however, you need some measure of inequality on the joined columns of a table join operation in order to produce the data required in the return set. Say, for example, that you want to see all Victrolas not in storage boxes as well as those that are boxed. One limitation of "inner" join or equijoin statements is that they will not return data from either table unless there is a common value in both columns for both tables on which to make the join.

```
SELECT antique_name, antique_cost,
antique.storage_box_number, box_name, box_location
FROM antique, storage_box
```

```
WHERE box_location = 'VICTROLA'
AND antique.storage_box_number = storage_box.storage_box_number;

ANTIQUE_NAM  ANTIQUE  ANTIQU  BOX_NAME  BOX_LOCATION
-----------  -------  ------  --------  ------------
VICTROLA      150.00       3  ALPHA-3   ALPHA BLDG
```

Notice only Victrolas that have corresponding storage box entries in the STORAGE_BOX table are included in the return set. In an attempt to obtain a list of Victrolas that are not boxed, the user then issues the following nonjoin query:

```
SELECT antique_name, antique_cost
FROM antique;

ANTIQUE_NAM ANTIQUE
----------- -------
VICTROLA     150.00
VICTROLA      90.00
VICTROLA      45.00
```

This query is a little closer to the mark, returning data on antique Victrolas regardless of whether or not they are boxed, but the user still needs to see storage box information for those Victrolas that are boxed. In order to force the join to return data from one table even if there is no corresponding record in the other table, the user can specify an *outer join* operation. The previous inner join statement can be modified in the following way to show records in the ANTIQUE table that have no corresponding record in the STORAGE_BOX table:

```
SELECT antique_name, antique_cost,
antique.storage_box_number, box_name, box_location
FROM antique, storage_box
WHERE box_location = 'VICTROLA'
AND antique.storage_box_number = storage_box.storage_box_number
(+);

ANTIQUE_NAM  ANTIQUE  ANTIQU  BOX_NAME  BOX_LOCATION
-----------  -------  ------  --------  ------------
VICTROLA      150.00       3  ALPHA-3   ALPHA BLDG
VICTROLA       90.00
VICTROLA       75.00
```

Outer join statements such as these produce result sets that are "outside" the join criteria as well as inside it. Notice the special (**+**) character string called the *outer join operator* at the end of the comparison that forms the join. This marker denotes which column can have NULL data corresponding to the non-NULL values in the other table. In the previous example, the outer join marker is on the side of the STORAGE_BOX table, meaning that data in the ANTIQUE table can correspond either to values in STORAGE_BOX or to NULL if there is no corresponding value in STORAGE_BOX.

TIP

*For "inner" joins, there must be shared values in the common column in order for the row in either table to be returned by the **select** statement.*

Exercises

1. How does an outer join remedy the situation where a lack of corresponding values in the shared column of two tables causes rows from neither table to be selected?

2. What is the special character used to denote outer joins?

Joining a Table to Itself

In special situations, it may be necessary for you to perform a join using only one table. Well, you really are using two copies of the tables — you join the table to itself. This task can be useful in certain cases where there is a possibility that some slight difference exists between two rows that would otherwise be duplicate records. If you want to perform a self join on a table, you should utilize the table alias method described earlier in the chapter to specify the same table for Oracle to understand that a self join is being performed.

The following example of a self join shows how to use this technique properly. For the example, assume that there is a table called TEST_RESULTS on which users at various locations administer a test for employees of a large corporation. The test is designed to determine if a given employee is ready for promotion. If an employee fails the test, he or she must wait a full year before taking the test again. It is discovered that there is a bug in the system that allowed some employees to circumvent the rule by taking the test at a different location. Now, management wants to find out which employees have taken the test more than once in the past year. The columns in the TEST_RESULTS table are listed as follows: EMPID, LOCATION, DATE, and SCORE. In order to determine if an employee has taken the test twice in the last year, you could issue the following SQL **select** that uses self join techniques:

```
SELECT a.empid, a.location, a.date, b.location, b.date
FROM test_results a, test_results b
WHERE a.empid = b.empid
AND a.location <> b.location
AND a.date > trunc(sysdate-365)
AND b.date > trunc(sysdate-365);
```

A.EMPID	A.LOCATION	A.DATE	B.LOCATION	B.DATE
94839	St. John	04-NOV-98	Wendt	03-JAN-98
04030	Stridberg	27-JUN-98	Wendt	03-AUG-97
59393	St. John	20-SEP-98	Wendt	04-OCT-97

The output from this self join shows that three employees took the test in different locations within the last 12 months. The clause used to determine DATE highlights the flexibility inherent in Oracle's internal method for storing DATE datatypes and **sysdate** as numbers representing the number of days since the beginning of the Julian calendar. The storage method Oracle uses allows you to perform simple mathematical operations on dates to obtain other dates without worrying about taking into account factors like the number of days in months between the old date and new, whether the year in question is a leap year, etc.

Those users who must perform self joins on tables should be extremely cautious about doing so in order to avoid performance issues or Cartesian products. Usually, the required number of equality operations is usually at least *two* in the situation of self joins, simply because only using one equality condition usually does not limit the output of a self join to the degree that the output must be limited in order to obtain meaningful information.

TIP
*The number of equality operations usually needed in the **where** clause of a self join should be greater than or equal to 2.*

It should be stated that a self join typically requires a long time to execute, because Oracle must necessarily read all data for each table twice sequentially. Ordinarily, Oracle will read data from two different tables to perform the join, but since the operation in this case is a self join, all data comes from one table. Without a proper comparison operation set up in the **where** clause, you may wind up with many copies of every row in the table returned, which will certainly run for a long time and produce a lot of unnecessary output.

Exercises

1. What is a self join? How might a self join be used?
2. How many equality operations should be used to create a self join?
3. What performance issues do self joins present?

Group Functions and Their Uses

In this section, you will cover the following areas related to group functions and their uses:

- Identifying available group functions
- Using group functions
- Using the **group by** clause
- Excluding group data with the **having** clause

A group function allows you to perform a data operation on several values in a column of data as though the column was one collective group of data. These functions are called group functions also, because they are often used in a special clause of **select** statements called a **group by** clause. A more complete discussion of the **group by** clause appears in the second discussion of this section.

Identifying Available Group Functions

An important difference group functions have with single-row functions is that group functions can operate on several rows at a time. This advantage allows functions to be used that calculate figures like averages and standard deviation. The list of available group functions appears here:

avg(x)	Average for all x column values returned by the **select** statement
count(x)	A total number of non-NULL values returned by the **select** statement for column x
max(x)	The maximum value in column x for all rows returned by the **select** statement
min(x)	The minimum value in column x for all rows returned by the **select** statement
stddev(x)	The standard deviation for all values in column x in all rows returned by **select** statements
sum(x)	The sum of all values in column x in all rows returned by the **select** statement
variance(x)	The variance for all values in column x in all rows returned by **select** statements

Exercises

1. What is a group function? How do they differ from single-row functions?

2. Name several group functions.

Using Group Functions

Examples of output from each of the following group functions appear over the next several pages. Since these functions require the use of several rows of data, the EMP table from the previous chapter will be used frequently. The EMP table appears in Table 2-1.

The **avg( )** function takes the values for a single column on all rows returned by the query and calculates the average value for that column. Based on the data from the previous table, the **avg( )** function on the SALARY column produces the following result:

```
SELECT AVG(salary)FROM EMP;

AVG(salary)
-----------
      74000
```

The second grouping function illustrated is **count( )**. This function is bound to become the cornerstone of any Oracle professional's repertoire. The **count( )** function returns a row count for the table given certain column names and/or **select** criteria. Note that the fastest way to execute **count( )** is to pass a value that resolves quickly in the SQL processing mechanism. Some values that resolve quickly are integers and the ROWID pseudocolumn.

```
SELECT COUNT(*),  -- Slow
       COUNT(1),  -- Fast
       COUNT(rowid) -- Fast
FROM EMP;

COUNT(*)  COUNT(1) COUNT(rowid)
--------  -------- ------------
       5         5            5
```

Empid	Lastname	Firstname	Salary
39334	Smith	Gina	75,000
49539	Qian	Lee	90,000
60403	Harper	Rod	45,000
02039	Walla	Rajendra	60,000
49392	Spanky	Stacy	100,000

TABLE 2-1.   *The EMP Table*

The asterisk (*) in the previous query is a wildcard variable that indicates all columns in the table. For better performance, this wildcard should not generally be used because the Oracle SQL processing mechanism must first resolve all column names in the table, a step that is unnecessary if one is simply trying to count rows. Notice that one of these examples uses the special pseudocolumn called ROWID. A ROWID is a special value that uniquely identifies each row. Each row in a table has one unique ROWID. The ROWID is not actually part of the table; rather, ROWID is a piece of information stored internally within Oracle. Thus, it is considered a "pseudocolumn." Note that index-only tables in Oracle8 do not have a ROWID.

TIP

*Do not use **count(*)** to determine the number of rows in a table. Use **count(1)** or **count(ROWID)** instead. These options are faster because they bypass some unnecessary operations in Oracle's SQL processing mechanism.*

The next pair of grouping functions to be covered are the **max( )** and **min( )** functions. The **max( )** function determines the largest value for the column passed, while **min( )** determines the smallest value for the column passed, as shown here:

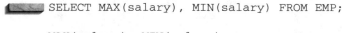

```
SELECT MAX(salary), MIN(salary) FROM EMP;

MAX(salary)  MIN(salary)
-----------  -----------
     100000        45000
```

Another group function details the **variance( )** of all values in a column. The variance of a set of numbers represents a measure of variability—the mean squared deviation from the expected value for the set, as shown below:

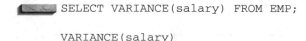

```
SELECT VARIANCE(salary) FROM EMP;

VARIANCE(salary)
----------------
       492500000
```

Related to **variance( )** is the next example in this section—the **stddev( )** function. It produces the standard deviation for values in the column specified. *Standard deviation* is the square root of the variance for the set— a measure of variability. The number produced represents the margin of variance or error for a set of numbers.

```
SELECT STDDEV(salary) FROM EMP;

STDDEV(salary)
--------------
    22192.341
```

The final group function is used commonly in simple accounting reports. The **sum( )** function gives the total of all values in a column.

```
SELECT SUM(salary) FROM EMP;

SUM(salary)
-----------
     370000
```

In general, the group functions will operate on columns of datatype NUMBER because many of the functions they represent in mathematics are numeric operations. For example, it makes little sense to take the standard deviation for a set of 12 words, unless the user wants to take the standard deviation of the length of those words by combining the use of the **length( )** function with the **stddev( )** function. There is one notable exception to this general rule, though—that exception is the **count( )** function. The **count( )** function will operate on a column of any datatype.

TIP
Group functions ignore NULL values by default. This is an essential piece of information you should know for OCP.

Exercises

1. How are group functions incorporated into **select** statements? How many rows of output can usually be expected from a query using a group function?

2. What is ROWID? Is ROWID stored in a table?

Using the GROUP BY Clause

Sometimes it gives more meaning to the output of a **select** statement to collect data into logical groupings. For example, to perform calculations on the populations of several cities in America, you may issue a query against all records in the CITIES table. The **select** statements, such as ones containing **order by**, may work well for specific queries against particular cities in this table, such as listing data in order based on an alphabetized list of cities and states, such as the SQL statement below:

```
SELECT state, city, population
FROM cities
ORDER BY state, city;

STATE              CITY             POPULATION
---------------    --------------   ----------
ALABAMA            AARDVARK             12,560
ALABAMA            BARNARD             176,000
...
```

Consider the following example, however. There arises a situation where you want to perform specific calculations on the cities in each state separately. For example, you want to find out the average city population for each of the states listed on the table. This **select** statement works fine for producing the raw data you need to calculate the average city population for each state; however, there is an easier way for you to determine this information based on usage of the **group by** clause in SQL statements.

```
SELECT state, AVG(population)
FROM CITIES
GROUP BY state;

STATE              AVG(POPULA
-----------------  ----------
ALABAMA                 49494
ALASKA                  14349
NEW YORK                85030
ARIZONA                 35003
CALIFORNIA              65040
...
```

The **group by** clause in this example saves you from performing a great deal of work by hand. Instead, Oracle shoulders most of the work and shows only the results you need. The **group by** clause works well in many situations where you want to report calculations on data according to groups or categories. There are two possible error messages with **group by** operations. They are shown here with examples:

```
SELECT job,avg(sal),deptno
FROM emp;

ORA-00937:  not a single-group group set function

SELECT job,avg(sal),deptno
FROM emp
GROUP BY deptno;

ORA-00979: not a GROUP  BY expression
```

To illustrate the usage of **group by** in another example, assume that you now want to calculate the average salary for all employees in a corporation by department. The EMP table contains the following columns: EMPID, LASTNAME, FIRSTNAME, SALARY, and DEPT. However, in addition to obtaining the average employee salary by department, you want the information in order from highest average salary to lowest.

```
SELECT dept, AVG(salary)
FROM emp
GROUP BY dept
ORDER BY avg(salary) DESC;

DEPT  AVG(SALARY)
----  -----------
201B       103020
594C        94030
493W        71039
201C        50403
```

In this example, the **order by** clause was combined with the **group by** clause to create a special order for the output. This order gives the data some additional meaning. You're not limited to grouping data by only one selected column, either. If you want, more than one column can be used in the **group by** statement—provided that the same nonaggregate columns specified in the select clause of the query match the columns specified in the group by clause. The following example illustrates proper usage of **group by** with more than one column specified. It assumes the addition of a column, COUNTRY, which names the country containing the city.

```
SELECT country, state, AVG(population)
FROM cities
GROUP BY country, state;
```

Exercises

1. How is the **group by** clause of a **select** statement used?

2. Identify some situations where statements containing the **group by** clause return errors.

Excluding GROUP Data with HAVING

One initial problem encountered when using the **group by** statement is that once the data is grouped, you must then analyze the data returned by the **group by** statement in order to determine which groups are relevant and which are not. It is sometimes useful to *weed out* unwanted data. For example, in the final query from the previous section, suppose you only wanted to see which departments paid an average salary of $80,000 or more per year. In effect, you are attempting to put a **where** clause on the **group by** clause.

This effect can be gained with the use of a special clause in Oracle called **having**. This clause acts as a modified **where** clause that only applies to the resultant rows generated by the **group by** expression. Consider the application of the previous modifications to the query of employee salary by department. If you want to view only those departments whose employees make an average of $80,000 or more, you may want to issue the following query. The **having** clause in this case is used to eliminate the departments whose average salary is under $80,000. Notice that this selectivity cannot easily be accomplished with an ordinary **where** clause, because the **where** clause is selective to the precision of individual rows while you require selectivity for eliminating groups of rows.

```
SELECT dept, AVG(salary)
FROM emp
GROUP BY dept
HAVING avg(salary)>80000
ORDER BY avg(salary) DESC;

DEPT   AVG(SALARY)
----   -----------
201B        103020
705B         94030
```

In this query, you successfully limit output on the **group by** rows by using the **having** clause. But the **having** clause need not be limited by some arbitrary number you key in manually. In addition to performing a comparison operation on a constant value, the **having** clause can perform a special operation to derive the required data with the use of a *subquery*. A subquery is another SQL query embedded within the overarching query being executed that derives some special value required by a part of the entire query. Subqueries are useful to incorporate into **select** statements when there is a need for valid value data that you don't know the value of, but know the manner in which to obtain it.

```
SELECT dept, AVG(salary)
FROM emp
GROUP BY dept
HAVING AVG(salary) >
   (SELECT salary
FROM emp
WHERE empid=49394)
ORDER BY avg(salary) DESC;

DEPT   AVG(SALARY)
----   -----------
201B        103020
569A         96120
```

Exercises

1. What is the **having** clause, and what function does it serve?

2. How can the user specify values to fulfill **having** criteria without actually knowing what the values themselves are?

Using Subqueries

In this section, you will cover the following topics related to using subqueries:

- Nested subqueries
- Subqueries in other situations
- Putting data in order with subqueries

There are several different ways to include subqueries in **where** statements. The most common method used is through the equality comparison operation, or with the **in** comparison, which is in itself similar to a **case** statement offered in many programming languages because the equality can be established with one element in the group. Another useful item for inclusion of a subquery in the **where** clause of a **select** statement is the **exists** clause. When you specify the **exists** operation in a **where** clause, you must include a subquery that satisfies the **exists** operation. If the subquery returns data, then the **exists** operation returns TRUE. If not, the **exists** operation returns FALSE. These and other uses for subqueries will be discussed shortly.

TIP

*A subquery is a "query within a query," a **select** statement nested within a **select** statement designed to limit the selected output of the parent query by producing an intermediate result set of some sort.*

Nested Subqueries

Subqueries can be used to obtain search criteria for **select** statements. The way subqueries work is as follows. The **where** clause in a **select** statement has one or more comparison operations. Each comparison operation can contain the name of a column on the left side and a given search method to obtain unknown data on the right side by means of a subquery.

```
SELECT empid, dept, salary
FROM emp
WHERE dept =
  (select dept
from emp
where empid = 78483);
```

The portion of the SQL statement that is highlighted is the subquery portion of the statement. On one side is the DEPT column, on which a comparison will be based to determine the result dataset. On the other side is the unknown search criteria, defined by the subquery. At the time this **select** statement is submitted, Oracle will process the subquery *first* in order to resolve all unknown search criteria, then feed that resolved criteria to the outer query. The outer query then can resolve the dataset it is supposed to return.

The subquery itself can contain subqueries. This process is known as nested subqueries. Consider the following example. You are trying to determine the salary of employees in the same department, as an employee who has submitted an expensive invoice for payment on the company's relocation expenditure system. The tables involved in this **select** statement are the EMP table, which has been described, and the INVOICE table, which consists of the following columns: INVOICE_NUMBER, EMPID, INVOICE_AMT, and PAY_DATE. The only information you have about the employee you are looking for is the invoice number the employee submitted for relocation expenses, which is 5640.

```
SELECT e.empid,
        e.salary
FROM emp e
WHERE e.dept =
  (SELECT dept
FROM emp
WHERE empid =
    (SELECT empid
FROM invoice
WHERE invoice_number = 5640));
```

In this statement, there are two subqueries: the subquery to the main **select** statement highlighted in bold, and the nested subquery in italics. Each subquery produces unknown criteria to fulfill the main search occurring in the **select** statement, the first producing the department information and the second producing the employee ID for the person submitting the invoice. These two details are crucial for completing the **select** statement, yet the data is unknown at the time the **select** statement is issued. Oracle must first resolve the innermost nested subquery in italics to resolve the next level. After that, Oracle will resolve the subquery level in bold to resolve the outermost level of the **select** statement issued.

Subqueries can be nested to a surprisingly deep level. The rule of thumb used to be that you could nest 16 or more subqueries into a **select** statement. In reality, the number of nested subqueries can be far higher. However, if you need to nest more than five subqueries, you may want to consider writing the query in PL/SQL or in a programming language like PRO*C or PRO*COBOL, or some other programming language that allows embedded SQL statements and cursors. At the very least, you may want to consider rewriting a query that makes heavy use of subqueries into a query that performs extensive join operations as well. Database performance degrades substantially after about that level when processing nested subqueries on all but the most powerful database servers and mainframes.

Exercises

1. What is a subquery? When might a user want to incorporate a subquery into a database **select** statement?

2. What are some situations where a **where** clause may be sufficient in place of a subquery?

3. What performance issues might revolve around the use of subqueries?

Subqueries in Other Situations

The previous discussion covered many areas of using subqueries in data manipulation statements. However, that discussion barely scratches the surface on the power of subqueries. A subquery can be used for complicated step-by-step joins of data that use data from one subquery to feed into the processing of its immediate parent. However, subqueries also allow you to "jump" subquery levels to perform incredibly complex, almost counterintuitive processing that necessarily must involve some discussion of a programming concept known as *variable scope*. If you are not familiar with the term, variable scope refers to the availability or "viewability" of data in certain variables at certain times.

Sometimes a variable has a local scope. That is to say that the variable can only be seen when the current block of code is being executed. Consider the columns in comparison operations named in subqueries to be variables whose "scope" is *local* to the query. Additionally, there is another type of scope, called global scope. In addition to a variable having local scope within the subquery where it appears, the variable also has *global* scope in all subqueries to that query. In the previous **select** statement example, all variables or columns named in comparison operations in the outermost **select** operation are local to that operation and global to all nested subqueries, given in **bold** and *italics*. Additionally, all columns in the subquery detailed in **bold** are local to that query and global to the subquery listed in *italics*. Columns named in the query in *italics* are local to that query only; since there are no subqueries to it, the columns in that query cannot be global. The nested query example from the previous discussion is featured in Figure 2-2.

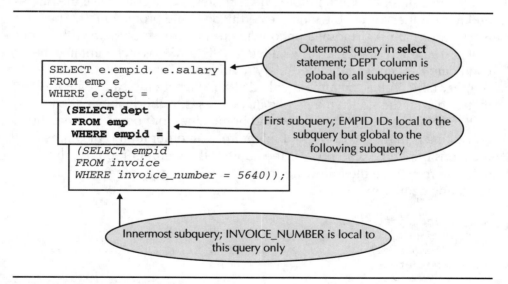

FIGURE 2-2. *Nested query example*

TIP
The scope of a variable defines which code blocks will have the variable and its defined value available to it. There are two different types of variable scope—local and global. If a variable has global scope, then it and its value are available everywhere in the code block. If a variable has local scope, then it and its value are available only in the current code block running in the memory stack.

In certain cases, it may be useful for a subquery to refer to a global column value rather than a local one to obtain result data. The subquery architecture of Oracle allows you to refer to global variables in subqueries as well as local ones to produce more powerful queries. An example of this type of global scope usage, sometimes also referred to as *correlated subqueries,* is as follows. Assume that there is a recruiter for a national consulting firm who wants to find people in Minneapolis who are proficient in Oracle SQL skills. Furthermore, the recruiter only wants to see the names and home cities for people who are certified Oracle professionals. The recruiter has at her disposal a nationwide resume search system with several tables. These tables include one called CANDIDATE, which contains the candidate ID, candidate name, salary requirement, and current employer. Another table in this example is called SKILLS, where the candidate ID is matched with the skill(s) the candidate possesses. A third table, called COMPANIES, contains the names and home cities for companies that the consulting firm tries to draw their talent from. In order to find the names and locations of people who possess the abilities the recruiter requires, the recruiter may issue the following **select** statement against the national recruiting database:

```
SELECT   candidate_id,
         name,
         employer
FROM candidate
```

```
WHERE candidate_id IN
  (SELECT candidate_id
   FROM skills
   WHERE skill_type = 'ORACLE SQL'
   AND certified = 'YES')
AND employer IN
  (SELECT employer
   FROM companies
   WHERE city = 'MINNEAPOLIS');


CANDIDATE_ID  NAME       EMPLOYER
------------  --------   ---------------
60549         DURNAM     TransCom
```

This query produces the result set the recruiter is looking for. Notice in the last subquery the use of the **in** keyword. Recall from Chapter 1 that the **in** operation allows you to identify a set of values, any of which the column named in the **in** clause can equal in order to be part of the result set. Thus, if the **where** clause of the **select** statement contains **and** NUMBER **in (1,2,3)**, that means only the rows whose value in the NUMBER column are equal to 1, 2, or 3 will be part of the result set.

Another complicated possibility offered by subqueries is the use of the **exists** operation. Mentioned earlier, **exists** allows the user to specify the results of a **select** statement according to a special subquery operation. This **exists** operation returns TRUE or FALSE based on whether or not the subquery obtains data when it runs. An example of the usage for the **exists** subquery is the relocation expenditure tracking system. The tables involved in this system are the EMP table, which has been described, and the INVOICE table, which consists of the following columns: INVOICE_NUMBER, EMPID, INVOICE_AMT, and PAY_DATE. Let's assume that you want to identify all the departments that have employees who have incurred relocation expenses in the past year.

```
SELECT distinct e.dept
FROM emp e
WHERE EXISTS
```

```
(SELECT i.empid
 FROM invoice i
 WHERE i.empid = e.empid
 AND i.pay_date > trunc(sysdate-365));
```

There are several new things that are worthy of note in this **select** statement. The first point to be made is that global scope variables are incorporated in the subquery to produce meaningful results from that code. The second point to make is more about the general nature of **exists** statements. Oracle will go through every record in the EMP table to see if the EMPID matches that of a row in the INVOICE table. If there is a matching invoice, then the **exists** criteria is met and the department ID is added to the list of departments that will be returned. If not, then the **exists** criteria is not met and the record is not added to the list of departments that will be returned. This can sometimes be a slow process, so be patient.

Notice that there is one other aspect of this query that has not been explained—the **distinct** keyword highlighted in bold in the **select** column clause of the outer portion of the query. This special keyword identifies a filter that Oracle will put on the data returned from the **exists** subquery. When **distinct** is used, Oracle will return only one row for a particular department, even if there are several employees in that department that have submitted relocation expenses within the past year. This **distinct** operation is useful for situations when you want a list of unique rows but anticipate that the query may return duplicate rows. The **distinct** operation removes duplicate rows from the result set before displaying that result to the user.

Exercises

1. Name a TRUE/FALSE operation that depends on the results of a subquery to determine its value.

2. What is variable scope? What is a local variable? What is a global variable?

3. What is the **distinct** keyword, and how is it used?

Putting Data in Order with Subqueries

As with other types of **select** statements, those statements that involve subqueries may also require some semblance of order in the data that is returned to the user. In the examples of subquery usage in the previous discussion, there may be a need to return the data in a particular order based on the columns selected by the outermost query. In this case, you may simply want to add in the usage of the **order by** clause. The previous example of selecting the departments containing relocated employees could be modified as follows to produce the required department data in a particular order required by the user:

```
SELECT distinct e.dept
FROM emp e
WHERE EXISTS
  (SELECT i.empid
   FROM invoice i
   WHERE i.empid = e.empid
   AND i.pay_date > trunc(sysdate-365))
ORDER BY dept;
```

By using the **order by** clause in the outermost statement, the data returned from the outermost statement can be sorted into ascending or descending order. You cannot, however, incorporate order into the data returned by the subquery.

```
SELECT distinct e.dept
FROM emp e
WHERE EXISTS
  (SELECT i.empid FROM invoice i
   WHERE i.empid = e.empid
   AND i.pay_date > trunc(sysdate-365)
   ORDER BY i.empid); -- WILL NOT WORK!
```

In another example, the points made before about global and local scope will be reinforced. A recruiter from the national consulting firm mentioned earlier tries to issue the following **select** statement, similar to the original one discussed with that example:

```
SELECT candidate_id,
       name,
       employer
FROM candidate
WHERE candidate_id IN
( SELECT candidate_id
  FROM skills
```

```
WHERE employer IN
  ( SELECT employer
    FROM companies
    WHERE city = 'MINNEAPOLIS'))
ORDER BY salary_req;
```

When the recruiter attempts to issue the preceding **select** statement, Oracle will execute the statement without error because the column specified by the **order by** clause need not be part of the column list in the **select** column list of the outermost **select** statement, though it must be part of the table in the **from** clause of the outermost query.

Exercises

1. Can you use the **order by** clause within **select** statements with subqueries? Why or why not?

2. What about within the subquery itself? Explain.

Using Runtime Variables

In this section, you will cover the following topics related to using runtime variables:

- Entering variables at run time
- Automatic definition of runtime variables
- The **accept** command

SQL is an interpreted language. That is, there is no "executable code" other than the statement you enter into the command line. At the time that statement is entered, Oracle's SQL processing mechanism works on obtaining the data and returning it to you. When Oracle is finished returning the data, it is ready for you to enter another statement. This interactive behavior is typical of interpreted programming languages.

```
SELECT name, salary, dept
FROM emp
WHERE empid = 40539;

NAME        SALARY   DEPT
--------    -------   ----
DURNAP       70560    450P
```

In the above statement, the highlighted comparison operation designates that the data returned from this statement must correspond to the EMPID value specified. If you run this statement again, the data returned would be exactly the same, provided that no portion of the record had been changed by the user issuing the query or anyone else on the database. However, Oracle's interpretive RDBMS mechanism need not have everything defined for it at the time you enter a SQL statement. In fact, there are features within the SQL processing mechanism of Oracle that allow you to identify a specific value to be used for the execution of the query as a runtime variable. This feature permits some flexibility and reusability of SQL statements.

Entering Variables at Run Time

Consider, for example, the situation where you pull up data for several different employees manually for the purpose of reviewing some aspect of their data. Rather than rekeying the entire statement in with the EMPID value hard-coded into each statement, you can substitute a variable specification that forces Oracle to prompt you to enter a data value in order to let Oracle complete the statement. The earlier statement that returned data from the EMP table based on a hard-coded EMPID value can now be rewritten as the following query that allows you to reuse the same code again and again with different values set for EMPID:

```
SELECT name, salary, dept
FROM emp
WHERE empid = &empid;

Enter value for empid: 40539
Old 3: WHERE empid = &empid;
New 3: WHERE empid = 40539;
```

```
NAME      SALARY   DEPT
------    -------  ----
DURNAP     70560   450P
```

After completing execution, you now have the flexibility to rerun that same query, except now you can specify a different EMPID without having to reenter the entire statement. Notice that a special *ampersand* (**&**) character precedes the name of the variable that will be specified at run time. This combination of ampersand and identifier creates a *substitution variable*. If you don't want to use the ampersand, the character can be changed with the **set define** command at the SQL prompt in SQL*Plus. You can reexecute the statement containing a runtime variable declaration by using the slash (**/**) command at the prompt in SQL*Plus.

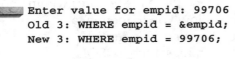

```
Enter value for empid: 99706
Old 3: WHERE empid = &empid;
New 3: WHERE empid = 99706;

NAME      SALARY   DEPT
-------   -------  ----
MCCALL    103560   795P
```

This time, you enter another value for the EMPID, and Oracle searches for data in the table based on the new value specified. This activity will go on as listed above until you enter a new SQL statement. Notice that Oracle provides additional information back to you after a value is entered for the runtime variable. The line as it appeared before is listed as the old value, while below the new value is presented as well. This presentation lets you know what data was changed by your input.

Exercises

1. What special character is used to specify a runtime variable?

2. How does Oracle prompt for runtime variable change?

3. What special character is used to reexecute a statement in SQL*Plus if the statement is stored in the current buffer? Can you recall the name of the file in which the SQL*Plus statement buffer is stored?

Automatic Definition of Runtime Variables

In some cases, however, it may not be useful to have you entering new values for a runtime variable every time the statement executes. For example, assume that there is some onerous reporting process that you must perform weekly on every person in a company. A great deal of value is added to the process by having a variable that can be specified at run time because you can then simply reexecute the same statement over and over again, with new EMPID values each time. However, even this improvement is not streamlining the process as much as you would like. Instead of running the statement over and over again with new values specified, you could create a script that contained the SQL statement, preceded by a special statement that defined the input value automatically and triggered the execution of the statement automatically as well. Some basic reporting conventions will be presented in this example, such as **spool**. This command is used to designate SQL*Plus that all output generated by the following SQL activity should be redirected to an output file named after the parameter following **spool**:

```
SPOOL emp_info.out;
DEFINE VAR_EMPID = 34030

SELECT name, salary, dept
FROM emp
WHERE empid = &var_empid;

UNDEFINE VAR_EMPID
DEFINE VAR_EMPID = 94059

SELECT name, salary, dept
FROM emp
WHERE empid = &var_empid;
```

When you execute the script, the time spent actually keying in values for the variables named in the SQL **select** statement is eliminated with the **define** statement. Notice, however, that in between each execution of the SQL statement there is a special statement using a command called **undefine**. In Oracle, the data that is defined with the **define** statement as corresponding to the variable will remain defined for the entire session unless the variable is undefined. By *undefining* a variable, the user allows another **define** statement to reuse the variable in another execution of the same or a different statement.

TIP
*You can also use the **define** command if you want to reuse substitution variables over different SQL statements, allowing you to pass a value from one statement to another.*

Exercises

1. How are variables defined within the SQL*Plus session to be used by **select** statements?

2. How can the user change a value set for a defined variable?

ACCEPT: Another Way to Define Variables

After executing a few example SQL statements that incorporate runtime variables, you may notice that Oracle's method for identifying input, though not exactly cryptic, is fairly nonexpressive.

```
SELECT name, salary, dept
FROM emp
WHERE empid = &empid
AND dept = '&dept';

Enter value for &empid: 30403
Old 3: WHERE empid = &empid
New 3: WHERE empid = 30403

Enter value for &dept: 983X
Old 4: WHERE dept = '&dept';
New 4: WHERE dept = '983X';

NAME        SALARY    DEPT
--------    --------  ----
TIBBINS      56700    983X
```

You need not stick with Oracle's default messaging to identify the need for input. Instead, you can incorporate into scripted SQL statements another method for the purpose of defining runtime variables. This other method allows the creator of the script to define a more expressive message that the user will see when Oracle prompts for input data. The name of the command that provides this functionality is the **accept** command. In order to use the **accept** command in a runtime SQL environment, you can create a script in the following way. Assume for the sake of example that you have created a script called **emp_sal_dept.sql**, into which the following SQL statements are placed:

```
ACCEPT var_empid PROMPT 'Enter the Employee ID Now:'
ACCEPT var_dept PROMPT 'Enter the Employee Department Now:'

SELECT name, salary, dept
FROM emp
WHERE empid = &var_empid
AND dept = '&var_dept';
```

At this point, the user can run the script at the prompt using the following command syntax:

```
SQL> @emp_sal_dept
```

or

```
SQL> start emp_sal_dept.sql
```

Oracle will then execute the contents of the script. When Oracle needs to obtain the runtime value for the variables that the user identified in the SQL statement and with the **accept** statement, Oracle will use the prompt the user defined with the **prompt** clause of the **accept** statement.

```
SQL> @emp_sal_dept
Enter the Employee ID Now: 30403

SELECT name, salary, dept
FROM emp
WHERE empid = &var_empid
AND dept = '&var_dept';

Old 3: WHERE empid = '&var_empid'
New 3: WHERE empid = 30403

Enter the Employee Department Now: 983X

SELECT name, salary, dept
```

```
FROM emp
WHERE empid = 30403
AND dept = '&var_dept';

Old 4: WHERE dept = '&var_dept'
New   4: WHERE dept = '983X'

NAME       SALARY   DEPT
--------   -------  ----
TIBBINS     56700   983X
```

Using the **accept** command can be preferable to Oracle's default output message in situations where you want to define a more accurate or specific prompt, or you want more output to display as the values are defined. In either case, the **accept** command can work well. Oracle offers a host of options for making powerful and complex SQL statements possible with runtime variables. These options covered can be used for both interactive SQL data selection and for SQL scripts.

TIP
*By default, the datatype for a variable defined with the **accept** command is CHAR. You can also explicitly specify the datatype in the **accept** command.*

Exercises

1. What is the **accept** command and how is it used?

2. What benefits does using the **accept** command offer?

3. What is the **start** command?

Chapter Summary

This chapter continues the discussion presented last chapter of using the **select** statement to obtain data from the Oracle database. The **select** statements have many powerful features that allow the user to accomplish many tasks. Those features include joining data from multiple tables, grouping data output together and performing data operations on the groups of data, creating **select** statements that can use subqueries to obtain criteria that is unknown (but the method for obtaining it is known), and using variables that accept values at run time. Together, these areas comprise the advanced usage of SQL **select** statements. The material in this chapter comprises 22 percent of information questioned on OCP Exam 1.

The first area discussed in this chapter is how data from multiple tables can be joined together to create new meaning. Data in a table can be linked if there is a common or shared column between the two tables. This shared column is often referred to as a foreign key. Foreign keys establish a relationship between two tables that is referred to as a parent/child relationship. The parent table is typically the table in which the common column is defined as a primary key, or the column by which uniqueness is identified for rows in the table. The child table is typically the table in which the column is not the primary key, but refers to the primary key in the parent table.

There are two types of joins. One of those types is the "inner" join, also known as an equijoin. An "equijoin" is a data join based on equality comparisons between common columns of two or more tables. An "outer" join is a nonequality join operation that allows you to obtain output from a table even if there is no corresponding data for that record in the other table.

Joins are generated by using **select** statements in the following way. First, the columns desired in the result set are defined in the **select** clause of the statement. Those columns may or may not be preceded with a table definition, depending on whether or not the column appears in more than one table. If the common column is named differently in each table, then there is no need to identify the table name along with the column name, as Oracle will be able to distinguish which table the column belongs to automatically. However, if the column name is duplicated in two or more tables, then you must specify which table you would like to obtain data from, since Oracle must be able to resolve any ambiguities clearly at the time the query is parsed. The tables from which data is selected are named in the **from** clause, and may optionally be followed by a table alias. A table alias is similar in principle to a column alias, which was discussed in the last chapter. The **where** clause of a join statement specifies how the join is performed. An inner join is created by specifying the two shared columns in each table in an equality comparison. An outer join is created in the same way, with an additional special marker placed by the column specification of the "outer" table, or the table in which there need not be data corresponding to rows in the other table for that data in the other table to be returned. That special marker is indicated by a (**+**). Finally, a table may be joined to itself with the use of table aliases. This activity is often done to determine if there are records in a table with slightly different information from rows that are otherwise duplicate rows.

Another advanced technique for data selection in Oracle databases is the use of grouping functions. Data can be grouped together in order to provide additional meaning to the data. Columns in a table can also be treated as a group in order to perform certain operations on them. These grouping functions often perform math operations such as averaging values or obtaining standard deviation on the dataset. Other group functions available on groups of data are **max( )**, **min( )**, **sum( )**, and **count( )**.

One common grouping operation performed on data for reporting purposes is a special clause in **select** statements called **group by**. This clause allows the user to segment output data and perform grouping operations on it. There is another special operation associated with grouping that acts as a **where** clause for which to limit the output produced by the selection. This limiting operation is designated by the **having** keyword. The criteria for including or excluding data using the **having** clause can be identified in one of two ways. Either criterion can be a hard-coded value or it can be based on the results of a **select** statement embedded into the overarching **select** statement. This embedded selection is called a subquery.

Another advanced function offered by **select** statements is the use of subqueries in the **where** clause of the **select** statement. There is no theoretical limit to the number of queries that can be nested in **select** statements, but it is not generally advisable to put more than half a dozen or so based on performance. Subqueries allow the user to specify unknown search criteria for the comparisons in the **where** clause as opposed to using strictly hard-coded values. Subqueries also illustrate the principle of data scope in SQL statements by virtue of the fact that the user can specify columns that appear in the parent query, even when those columns do not appear in the table used in the subquery.

Another use of subqueries can be found in association with a special operation that can be used in the **where** clause of a **select** statement. The name of this special operation is **exists**. This operation produces a TRUE or FALSE value based on whether or not the related subquery produces data. The **exists** clause is a popular option for users to incorporate subqueries into their **select** statements.

Output from the query can be placed into an order specified by the user with the assistance of the **order by** clause. One final advanced technique covered in this chapter is the specification of variables at run time. This technique is especially valuable in order to provide reusability in a data selection statement. In order to denote a runtime variable in SQL, the user should place a variable name in the comparison operation the user wants to specify a runtime value for. The name of that variable in the **select** statement should be preceded with a special character to denote it as a variable. By default, this character is an ampersand (**&**). However, the default variable specification character can be changed with the use of the **set define** command at the prompt.

Runtime variables can be specified for SQL statements in other ways as well. The **define** command can be used to identify a runtime variable for a **select** statement automatically. After being defined and specified in the **define** command, a variable is specified for the entire session or until it is altered with the **undefine** command. In this way, the user can avoid the entire process of having to input values for the runtime variables. The final technique covered in this chapter on **select** statements is the usage of **accept** to redefine the text displayed for the input prompt. More cosmetic than anything else, **accept** allows the user to display a more direct message than the Oracle default message for data entry.

Two-Minute Drill

- **Select** statements that obtain data from more than one table and merge the data together are called joins.

- In order to join data from two tables, there must be a common column.

- A common column between two tables can create a foreign key, or link, from one table to another. This condition is especially true if the data in one of the tables is part of the primary key, or the column that defines uniqueness for rows on a table.

- A foreign key can create a parent/child relationship between two tables.

- One type of join is the inner join, or equijoin. An equijoin operation is based on an equality operation linking the data in common columns of two tables.

- Another type of join is the outer join. An outer join returns data in one table even when there is no data in the other table.

- The "other" table in the outer join operation is called the outer table.

- The common column that appears in the outer table of the join must have a special marker next to it in the comparison operation of the **select** statement that creates the table.

- The outer join marker is as follows: (**+**).

- Common columns in tables used in join operations must be preceded either with a table alias that denotes the table in which the column appears, or the entire table name if the column name is the same in both tables.

- The data from a table can be joined to itself. This technique is useful in determining if there are rows in the table that have slightly different values but are otherwise duplicate rows.

- Table aliases must be used in self join **select** statements.

- Data output from table **select** statements can be grouped together according to criteria set by the query.

- A special clause exists to assist the user in grouping data together. That clause is called **group by**.

- There are several grouping functions that allow you to perform operations on data in a column as though the data were logically one variable.

- The grouping functions are **max( )**, **min( )**, **sum( )**, **avg( )**, **stddev( )**, **variance( )**, and **count( )**.

- These grouping functions can be applied to the column values for a table as a whole or for subsets of column data for rows returned in **group by** statements.

- Data in a **group by** statement can be excluded or included based on a special set of **where** criteria defined specifically for the group in a **having** clause.

■ The data used to determine the **having** clause can either be specified at run time by the query or by a special embedded query, called a subquery, which obtains unknown search criteria based on known search methods.

■ Subqueries can be used in other parts of the **select** statement to determine unknown search criteria as well. Including subqueries in this fashion typically appears in the **where** clause.

■ Subqueries can use columns in comparison operations that are either local to the table specified in the subquery or use columns that are specified in tables named in any parent query to the subquery. This usage is based on the principles of variable scope as presented in this chapter.

■ Variables can be set in a **select** statement at run time with use of runtime variables. A runtime variable is designated with the ampersand character (**&**) preceding the variable name.

■ The special character that designates a runtime variable can be changed using the **set define** command.

■ A command called **define** can identify a runtime variable value to be picked up by the **select** statement automatically.

■ Once defined, the variable remains defined for the rest of the session or until undefined by the user or process with the **undefine** command.

■ A user can also modify the message that prompts the user to input a variable value. This activity is performed with the **accept** command.

Chapter Questions

1. **Which of the following is not a group function?**

    A. avg( )

    B. sqrt( )

    C. sum( )

    D. max( )

2. **In order to perform an inner join, which criteria must be true?**

   A. The common columns in the join do not need to have shared values.

   B. The tables in the join need to have common columns.

   C. The common columns in the join may or may not have shared values.

   D. The common columns in the join must have shared values.

3. **Once defined, how long will a variable remain so in SQL*Plus?**

   A. Until the database is shut down

   B. Until the instance is shut down

   C. Until the statement completes

   D. Until the session completes

4. **To alter the prompt Oracle uses to obtain input from a user:**

   A. Change the prompt in the **config.ora** file.

   B. Alter the **prompt** clause of the **accept** command.

   C. Enter a new prompt in the **login.sql** file.

   D. There is no way to change a prompt in Oracle.

5. **Which of the following options is appropriate for use when search criteria is unknown for comparison operations in a SELECT statement? (Choose two)**

   A. select * from emp where empid = &empid;

   B. select * from emp where empid = 69494;

   C. select * from emp where empid = (select empid from invoice where invoice_no = 4399485);

   D. select * from emp;

6. **The default character for specifying substitution variables in SELECT statements is**

A. Ampersand

B. Ellipses

C. Quotation marks

D. Asterisk

7. **A user is setting up a join operation between tables EMP and DEPT. There are some employees in the EMP table that the user wants returned by the query, but the employees are not assigned to department heads yet. Which SELECT statement is most appropriate for this user?**

   A. **select** e.empid, d.head **from** emp e, dept d;

   B. **select** e.empid, d.head **from** emp e, dept d **where** e.dept# = d.dept#;

   C. **select** e.empid, d.head **from** emp e, dept d **where** e.dept# = d.dept# (+);

   D. **select** e.empid, d.head **from** emp e, dept d **where** e.dept# (+) = d.dept#;

8. **Which three of the following uses of the HAVING clause are appropriate? (Choose three)**

   A. To put returned data into sorted order

   B. To exclude certain data groups based on known criteria

   C. To include certain data groups based on unknown criteria

   D. To include certain data groups based on known criteria

9. **A Cartesian product is**

   A. A group function

   B. Produced as a result of a join **select** statement with no **where** clause

   C. The result of fuzzy logic

   D. A special feature of Oracle server

10. **The default character that identifies runtime variables is changed by**

    A. Modifying the **init.ora** file

    B. Modifying the **login.sql** file

    C. Issuing the **define** *variablename* command

    D. Issuing the **set define** command

11. **Which line in the following SELECT statement will produce an error?**

    A. **select** dept, **avg**(salary)

    B. **from** emp

    C. **group by** empid;

    D. There are no errors in this statement.

Answers to Chapter Questions

1. B. **sqrt( )**

Explanation Square root operations are performed on one column value. Review the discussion of available group functions.

2. B. The tables in the join need to have common columns.

Explanation It is possible that a join operation will produce no return data, just as it is possible for any **select** statement not to return any data. Choices A, C, and D represent the spectrum of possibility with regard to the shared values that may or may not be present in common columns. However, joins themselves are not possible without two tables having common columns. Refer to the discussion of table joins.

3. D. Until the session completes

Explanation A variable defined by the user during a session with SQL*Plus will remain defined until the session ends or until the user explicitly **undefine**s the variable. Refer to the discussion of defining variables from earlier in the chapter.

4. B. Alter the **prompt** clause of the **accept** command

Explanation Choice D should be eliminated immediately, leaving the user to select between A, B, and C. Choice A is incorrect because **config.ora** is a feature associated with Oracle's client/server network communications product. Choice C is incorrect. **login.sql** is a special file Oracle users can incorporate into their usage of Oracle that will automatically configure aspects of the SQL*Plus session, such as the default text editor, column and NLS data formats, and other items. This file does not configure input prompts, however. Only **accept** does that. Refer to the description of the use of the **accept** command.

5. A and C.

Explanation Choice A details usage of a runtime variable, which can be used to have the user input an appropriate search criteria after the statement has begun processing. Choice C details usage of a subquery, which allows the user to select unknown search criteria from the database using known methods for obtaining the data. Choice B is incorrect because the statement simply provides a known search criteria, while choice D is incorrect because it provides no search criteria at all. Review the discussion of defining runtime variables and subqueries.

6. A.   Ampersand

Explanation   The ampersand (**&**) character is used by default to define runtime variables in SQL*Plus. Review the discussion of the definition of runtime variables and the **set define** command.

7. C.   **select** e.empid, d.head **from** emp e, dept d **where** e.dept# = d.dept# (+);

Explanation   Choice C details the outer join operation most appropriate to this user's needs. The outer table in this join is the DEPT table, as identified by the (+) marker next to the DEPT# column in that table in the comparison operation that defines the join.

8. B, C, and D.

Explanation   All exclusion or inclusion of grouped rows is handled by the **having** clause of a **select** statement. Choice A is not an appropriate answer because sort order is given in a **select** statement by the **order by** clause.

9. B.   Produced as a result of a join **select** statement with no **where** clause.

Explanation   A Cartesian product is the result dataset from a **select** statement where all data from both tables is returned. Some potential causes of a Cartesian product include not specifying a **where** clause for the join **select** statement. Review the discussion of performing join **select** statements.

10. D.   Issuing the **set define** command

Explanation   Choice A is incorrect because a change to the **init.ora** file will alter the parameters Oracle uses to start the database instance. Use of this feature will be covered in the next unit. Choice B is incorrect because although the **login.sql** file can define many properties in a SQL*Plus session, the character that denotes runtime variables is not one of them. Choice C is incorrect because the **define** command is used to define variables used in a session, not an individual statement. Review the discussion of defining runtime variables in **select** statements.

11. C.   **group by** empid;

Explanation   Since the EMPID column does not appear in the original list of columns to be displayed by the query, it cannot be used in a **group by** statement. Review the discussion of using **group by** in **select** statements.

CHAPTER
3

Creating the Oracle Database

n this chapter, you will understand and demonstrate knowledge in the following areas:

- Overview of data modeling and database design
- Creating the tables of an Oracle database
- The Oracle data dictionary
- Manipulating Oracle data

The topics covered in this chapter include data modeling, creating tables, the data dictionary, and data manipulation. With mastery of these topics, the user of an Oracle system moves more into the world of application development. Typically, it is the application developer who creates database objects and determines how users will access those objects in production environments. The DBA is then the person who is responsible for migrating developed objects into production and then managing the needs of production systems. This chapter will lay the foundation for discussion of Oracle database object creation and other advanced topics, so it is important to review this material carefully. The OCP Exam 1 will consist of test questions in this subject area worth 15 percent of the final score. With these thoughts in mind, move on now to the topic at hand.

Overview of Data Modeling and Database Design

In this section, you will cover the following topics related to data modeling:

- The stages of system development
- The basic types of data relationships
- The relational database components
- Reading an entity-relationship diagram

Computer programs are the most animate of inanimate objects. Like the people who use, develop, and maintain them, software applications are dynamic creatures that are subject to the same constraints and realities as the very realities they try to model. Software applications are also subject to economic constraints, as any analyst who has spent months planning a project only to have the project's funds pulled at the last minute will attest. In so attempting to model reality, software applications become reality.

Stages of System Development

The first part of the software development life cycle is generally the one that most people pay attention to. This period of development is followed by a production phase, which may or may not involve the creation of enhancements. As time goes on, the users and developers of the project attempt to incorporate features into the production system. After quite a long time, usually, advances in the industry or the emergence of system requirements that the original technology cannot handle will cause the system's use to wane, until finally the data from the system will be archived or converted into a new system and the old system itself retired. The steps involved in the software development life cycle are as follows:

- Needs assessment
- Database design
- Application development
- Performance tuning
- Enhancements

Needs Assessment

A database system begins as an idea in someone's head. At this early stage in the game, a database application's possibilities can seem endless—however, this stage is as wrought with danger as other stages in the model. *Many questions should be answered by the end of this planning stage.* The first question that can be asked about an application is—will this application support large-volume data entry, or is the fundamental point of this application to make data viewable to users? In many cases, the answer is both. By the end of needs assessment, the designer of an application should have a clear idea about the following questions:

- Who will use the application?

- What use will the application fill in the organization?

- How do people plan on using the application?

Recent successes involving user-facilitated meetings show that the success of a project can often be improved with the early and frequent involvement of users on the project. Once the users' needs have been assessed, there is an activity that takes place allowing the developers to determine what data and tools are available for use. In this phase of software development, the developers of a software application must assess many things, such as process flow for data within the system and the method by which to present data to the user both on the screen and in reports. Generally, a software application involving a database involves three parts, all of which should be planned before creating them. The three components of a database application generally consist of user interface, the database, and reports.

Database Design

This activity in creating a database application lays the groundwork for success in supporting current and future needs of the application. To design a database requires two steps. The two steps of designing a database are

- Creating an entity-relationship diagram

- Translating an entity-relationship diagram into a logical data model

Creating an entity-relationship diagram and translating it into a logical data model is an involved process. The steps to execute this process, however, are important to ensure correct design of the tables that will support both the user interface and the reports. So, even though the users will interface with the database in a controlled manner via the application, it is still important for the success of the application to have a strong database design. More on this process will appear later in the discussion.

Application Development

Once the users' needs are assessed and the database design in place, the building of the application logic can begin. Some components of the application that may be placed within the database include integrity constraints and triggers, stored procedures and/or packages, and tuned SQL statements that take into account how Oracle optimizes its processing. Application development is often a task that involves stepwise refinement. As needs arise, or as hidden intricacies of a current process are uncovered, the application software that models business rules will undoubtedly grow complex. PL/SQL, the programming language of Oracle database packages, supports many constructs that allow for modularization and abstract datatypes, as well as other useful programming constructs that will simplify the logic used to represent complex business rules.

Performance Tuning

No application is harder to use than a slow one. The source of most performance issues in applications using Oracle databases is the application code itself. The application developers should, wherever possible, explore alternative methods for providing the same data to the user interface or reports in order to find the method that performs best. This step may involve development of alternative blocks of code that pull the same data from the database and executing benchmark tests to compare performance. This step may also involve the maintenance of two different databases, or at the very least, the ability to stop and restart a database with initialization parameters set to handle different periods of operation, such as daily production and weekend maintenance.

Database Security

The guarded usage of the database application created will ensure that its use is appropriate. Database security is an important factor in any database, allowing the developers and managers for the database system to handle large user populations, if necessary, and to limit database access to those users that require it. One key activity that should occur early on in the development of an application is the determining of levels of data access that will be afforded to each user or type of user in the system. At this early stage of the project, users should be divided into rough categories for the purpose of determining what data they need access to in order to perform their tasks. Furthermore, once general access and usage levels for various users are established, there are features within the Oracle database that allow the developer or the DBA to limit users to only their access level or to restrict their usage of the database to only what they need. Some key terms to know here are privileges and roles for managing user access, and resource profiles to manage system hardware usage.

Enhancements

Enhancements are often as important as the actual application in the minds of the users, because they represent an evolution of the business process that must be modeled by the application supporting that business process. However, in some ways developing enhancements is often riskier than developing the application itself. Some of the advantages of the initial application development, such as reduced production burden on the developers of the application, a structured project plan, funding, and management attention, are lost once the application sees its first few months of successful production life. When enhancements are requested, the developers often have to do double duty—they are both the enhancement developer who has to rework existing code *and* the analyst that has to handle the production issues of the application as they arise. However, these obstacles represent as much of an opportunity for success as they do for failure. Strong project management in these situations generally helps the enhancement development effort to succeed.

Exercises

1. What are the stages of the software development life cycle?

2. What important questions should be answered before the application is developed?

Basic Types of Data Relationships

The focus of this discussion is to present the areas of data modeling and database design. In order to model data, there must be relationships between the various components that make up a database design. These components are stored as data, while the relationships between data can be defined explicitly via the use of integrity constraints and/or database triggers that model business rules, or implicitly by the data manipulation statements that **select** data for viewing or populate the database with new data. The following list of data relationships will be discussed in this section:

- Primary keys
- Functional dependency
- Foreign keys

One type of data relationship starts in the tables that comprise the Oracle database. So far, we have seen many tables containing data. One common element in all the tables seen is that they contain multiple columns that "hang" off of one main column, called a primary key. This primary key is the column(s) that determines the uniqueness of every row in the database. In the primary key, there can be no duplicate value for any row in the entire table. Each column that is not part of the primary key is considered to be "functionally dependent" on the primary key. This term simply means that the dependent column stores data that relates directly to or modifies directly each individual column value for that row.

One other relationship to discuss in this section is the idea of a foreign key. This relationship is often referred to as a parent/child relationship because of where the data must appear in each table to create the foreign-key relationship. In the "child" table, the data can appear either as part of the primary key or as a functionally dependent column. However, in the "parent" table, the referenced column must appear in the primary key.

Exercises

1. What are three types of data relationships?
2. What is functional dependency?
3. What is required of two tables in order for the tables to be related?

Relational Database Components

A relational database consists of many components, some of which already have been covered. These components include objects to store data, objects to aid in accessing data quickly, and objects to manage user access to data.

Additionally, there are objects in the database that contain the code that is used to manipulate and change data, produce reports of data, and otherwise use data to produce the desired result. Some of the objects that are part of the relational database produced by Oracle that are used in the functions mentioned earlier are as follows:

- **Tables, views, and synonyms**   Used to store and access data
- **Indexes and the SQL processing mechanism**   Used to speed access to data
- **Triggers and integrity constraints**   Used to maintain the validity of data entered
- **Privileges, roles, and profiles**   Used to manage database access and usage
- **Packages, procedures, and functions**   Used to code the applications that will use the database

A relational database works on principles of relational data within tables. The relational data models real-world business situations through the use of datasets, called tables, that can contain different elements or columns. These columns then are able to relate to other columns in other tables, or simply to the primary key via functional dependency.

Exercises

1. What is a relational database model?

2. What are the components of a relational database? How are they used?

Reading an Entity-Relationship Diagram

Every database starts out as an entity-relationship diagram. In order to model a business process, the developers of an application must first map out the different components of a system. This map of a business process is often referred to as the entity-relationship diagram, or *ERD* for short. The ERD consists of two different components, which are listed here:

- **Entity** A person, place, thing, or idea involved in the business process flow

- **Relationship** The ties that bind entities together

In order to understand the process of creating an ERD, an example will be presented. This example is of a business process used by employees of an organization to obtain reimbursement for expenses that they may have incurred on behalf of their employer. See Figure 3-1. Already, a few entities have emerged in the description of the application to be created, namely *employee* (a person), *expenses* (things), and the *employer* (a person or group of people). A relationship has also been identified, *obtain reimbursement*, or "pay," which is an activity.

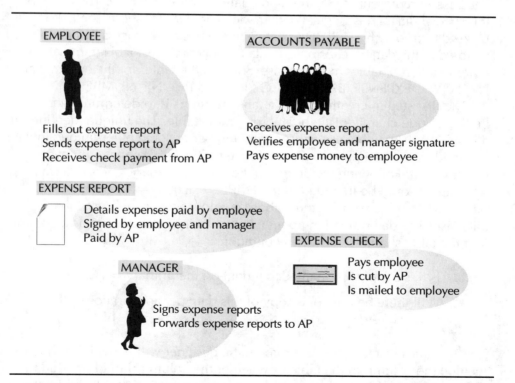

EMPLOYEE

Fills out expense report
Sends expense report to AP
Receives check payment from AP

ACCOUNTS PAYABLE

Receives expense report
Verifies employee and manager signature
Pays expense money to employee

EXPENSE REPORT

Details expenses paid by employee
Signed by employee and manager
Paid by AP

EXPENSE CHECK

Pays employee
Is cut by AP
Is mailed to employee

MANAGER

Signs expense reports
Forwards expense reports to AP

FIGURE 3-1. *An entity-relationship diagram of the employee expense system*

Often, a database application begins with looking at the process as it already exists. For this example, assume there is inefficiency in the current process. There may be several different points of entry of data, and there is the possibility that copies will get lost. Finally, there is the turnaround lag in paying employees. If there is a problem, the employee will not know about it for several weeks. On top of that, it may take several more weeks for the problem to be corrected. These reasons are enough to justify the need for a more automated process, and the ERD is the mechanism to model that process.

From ERD to LDM

An entity-relationship diagram is helpful to understand the process flow of data through the system. Once an entity-relationship diagram is created, the developer must then create a special diagram that models the data stored in a database to represent the entities and relationships in the ERD. The name of this special diagram is "logical data model," or LDM for short. The LDM will be used to display how all data relating to the business process being modeled is stored in the database. A logical data model consists of a diagrammatic representation of tables in a database. Some of the tables for the example are EMPLOYEE, EXPENSE, BANK_ACCOUNT, and PHONE_NUMBER.

The first step in creating a list of table columns is to determine what will be the unique characteristic of any row in the table. The unique identifier for all employees may be a social security number or some other unique integer assigned by the company to an employee for the term of that employee's employment. Following the determination of the primary key is determining what items could be included in the EMPLOYEE table—the developer will need to determine what features about employees must be stored in the database. The determination about whether to incorporate data as a column into the table should rest on two conditions:

- Is this data functionally dependent on the primary key?

- Will there be only one copy of this data per appearance of the primary key?

Once these factors are determined, the designer will know if he should include the column in the table or whether the column should be used to define another table. In this example of defining the EMPLOYEE table, the designer may want to include a few different elements, such as the person's name, hire date, age, spouse name, various telephone numbers, and supervisor's name.

In the case of bank accounts, employees may have several, each with a set of corresponding information such as bank name and ABA routing number. The additional storage overhead makes it difficult to store all bank account information in the EMPLOYEE table. Data components that have no functional dependency to the other data in a table record should be placed in separate tables. The designer may create a separate table containing bank account information, called BANK_ACCOUNT. The primary key of this table may be the bank account number and the associated employee who owns the account. In addition, there may be several columns that share a common functional dependency on the primary key. One final point is that since the bank account does eventually get associated back to an employee, it is required that there be some method to associate the two tables—a foreign key.

TIP
Data normalization is the act of breaking down column data to place in tables where each column in the table is functionally dependent on only one primary key. This process reduces data storage costs by eliminating redundancy and minimizes dependency of any column in the "normalized" database to only one primary key.

Role of Ordinality

Related to the discussion of foreign keys and table relationships is an aspect of data relationships relating to a special term called *ordinality*. This term represents two important features about a relationship between two tables. The ordinality of a table relationship is a message the designer uses to identify two facts about the relationship:

■   Is the relationship mandatory or optional for these objects?

■   Does one record in the table correspond to one or many records in the other table?

The ordinality of a table relationship contains two elements and is generally represented on the logical data model as an "ordered pair," usually (0,N) or (1,1), or (1,N), etc. In some cases, the relationship between two entities may not be required. Consider the following example of employees and expenses. This relationship works in two directions: from employees to expenses and from expenses to employees. In the direction of employees to expenses, the relationship is optional. That is to say, an employee need not have ever incurred expenses on behalf of the company. However, in the other direction, from expenses to employees, the relationship is mandatory because each and every expense submitted to the employee expense system will correspond to an employee. To answer the second question, in the direction of employees to expenses there is a one-to-many relationship, as each employee in the company may have submitted one or more expense reports in the course of their employment, or none at all. In contrast, on the other direction, each expense submitted will always have one and only one employee who submitted it, as shown in Figure 3-2.

Quality data models are more a product of experience than formula. Even though there are many theories on data normalization, the process of it is fairly arbitrary. In fact, most database designers break the so-called "rules" of normalization constantly in an attempt to improve performance. As the saying goes, "normalize until it hurts, denormalize until it works."

Exercises

1. What is an entity-relationship diagram and how is it read?

2. What is a logical data model? Identify some methods used to translate an entity-relationship diagram into a data model.

3. What is ordinality and how is it significant?

Creating the Tables of an Oracle Database

In this section, you will cover the following topics related to creating tables:

- Creating tables with integrity constraints
- Using table naming conventions

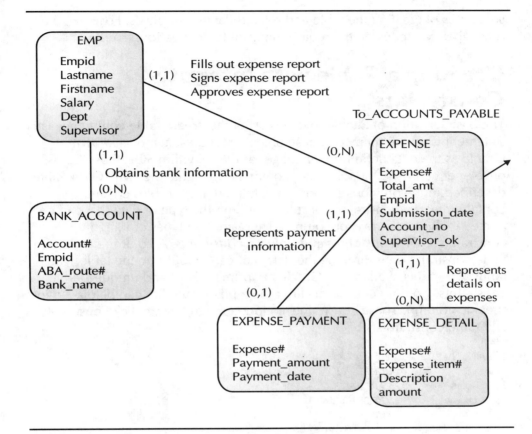

FIGURE 3-2. *The logical data model for the employee expense system*

- Indexes created by constraints

- Creating one table with data from another

The next step in creating a database application is defining the database objects that will comprise the logical data model. A major component in this process is creating the tables. This discussion will explain the basic syntax required of developers and DBAs in order to produce the logical database object in Oracle known as tables. At this point, the developer should understand that the only material presented here is the syntax and semantics of creating the table and related database objects. For now, the developer can focus on the requirements of table creation.

Creating a Table with Integrity Constraints

The basic creation of a table involves using the **create table** command. This statement is one of many database object creation statements known in Oracle as the data definition language, or *DDL*. Within SQL*Plus, the developer can issue the following command to create the EMPLOYEE table described in the previous section on data modeling. Tables created can contain integrity constraints, or rules that limit the type of data that can be placed in the table, row, or column. There are two types of integrity constraints: *table constraints* and *column constraints*. A column can have a table constraint on it, limiting the data that can be put into the table. The table constraints available in Oracle are primary keys and unique constraints. Column constraints limit the type of data that can be placed in a specific column. These constraints include foreign keys, check constraints, and table constraints.

```
CREATE TABLE employee
(empid          NUMBER(10),
lastname        VARCHAR2(25),
firstname       VARCHAR2(25),
salary          NUMBER(10,4),
CONSTRAINT      pk_employee_01
PRIMARY KEY     (empid));
```

What does this **create table** statement tell the developer about the table being created? First of all, there are several columns, each with a corresponding datatype, or a specification of the "type" of data that can be stored in this column. The types of data available in an Oracle database will be described shortly. There are four columns defined, which correspond to the four columns that the data modeling session from the previous discussion identified. Finally, the statement scratches the surface of data relationships by defining the EMPID column to be the primary key. This definition means that data in the EMPID column can be used to identify every row in the table as a unique row.

The definition of a column as the primary key in a table produces a few noticeable effects within the database itself. The term "primary key" itself refers to a special designation for a constraint that says to Oracle, "don't let any row insert a column value for EMPID that is NULL or that is the same as a column value that already exists for another row." There are some special methods Oracle will use to enforce this integrity constraint. Column values that are part of primary keys have the following conditions enforced on them. Any value in the column for any row must be unique. Secondly, no row can define the value in a column as NULL if that column is part of the primary key. No employee in the EMPLOYEE table can have a NULL value defined for EMPID.

TIP

Integrity constraints are rules that are defined on table columns that prevent anyone from placing inappropriate data in the column. There are five types of integrity constraints: primary key, foreign key, unique, NOT NULL, and check.

Take another moment to review the definition that was determined for the BANK_ACCOUNT table. Remember that the BANK_ACCOUNT table was supposed to have the BANK_ACCT_NO column be its primary key, because that column defines the data that is unique about each row in the table. However, remember also that there is a special relationship between the BANK_ACCOUNT table and the EMPLOYEE table.

```
CREATE TABLE bank_account
(bank_acct_no          VARCHAR2(40),
empid                  NUMBER(10),
BANK_ROUTE_NO          VARCHAR2(40),
BANK_NAME              VARCHAR2(50),
CONSTRAINT             pk_bank_acct_01
PRIMARY KEY            (bank_acct_no),
CONSTRAINT             fk_bank_acct_01
FOREIGN KEY (empid) REFERENCES employee (empid));
```

Notice that in addition to the definition of a primary-key constraint, this table also has a foreign-key constraint. The syntax for the definition allows the column to reference another table's column, of either the same or a different name. In order for a foreign-key constraint to be valid, the columns in both tables must have exactly the same datatypes. A fuller discussion of datatypes and their significance will appear later in the chapter. The designation "foreign key" tells Oracle that the developer would like to create referential integrity between the EMPID column in the BANK_ACCOUNT table and the EMPLOYEE table. This fact prevents a column in the child table (BANK_ACCOUNT) from containing a value that does not exist in the referenced column in the parent table (EMPLOYEE).

An option that can be specified along with the foreign key relates to the deletion of data from the parent. If someone attempts to **delete** a row from the parent table that contains a referenced value from the child table, Oracle will block the deletion unless the **on delete cascade** option is specified in the foreign-key definition of the **create table** statement. When the **on delete cascade** option is used, Oracle will not only allow the user to **delete** a referenced record from the parent table, but the deletion will cascade into the child table as well.

```
CREATE TABLE bank_acct
    (bank_acct_no          VARCHAR2(40),
    empid                  NUMBER(10),
    BANK_ROUTE_NO          VARCHAR2(40),
    BANK_NAME              VARCHAR2(50),
    CONSTRAINT             pk_bank_acct_01
    PRIMARY KEY            (bank_acct_no),
    CONSTRAINT             fk_bank_acct_01
    FOREIGN KEY (empid) REFERENCES employee (empid)
    ON DELETE CASCADE);
```

Other integrity constraints abound. There are five types of integrity constraints in all, including primary and foreign keys, unique constraints, NOT NULL constraints, and check constraints.

```
CREATE TABLE employee
    (empid         NUMBER(10),
    lastname       VARCHAR2(25),
    firstname      VARCHAR2(25),
    salary         NUMBER(10,4),
    home_phone     number(15),
    CONSTRAINT     pk_employee_01
    PRIMARY KEY    (empid),
    CONSTRAINT     uk_employee_01
    UNIQUE         (home_phone));
```

The definition of a unique constraint on HOME_PHONE prevents anyone from defining a row that contains a phone number that is identical to the phone number of anyone else already in the table. There are two weaknesses in this definition. The first is that having a unique constraint on a home phone number makes it difficult to store records for employees who are spouses with the same telephone number, or who are roommates. Another point to be made about unique constraints, and foreign-key constraints for that matter, is that there is no data integrity enforced on data in a row that has NULL defined for its value. This is a special case scenario that applies only to NULL data in columns with foreign-key, unique, and check constraints defined on them.

TIP
Foreign-key, check, and unique integrity constraints for a column are not enforced on a row if the column data value for the row is NULL.

The final two types of constraints are NOT NULL constraints and check constraints. The first type of constraint identified prevents the data value defined by any row for the column to be NULL if the column has the NOT NULL constraint defined on it. By default, primary keys are defined to be NOT NULL. All other constraints are NULLable unless the developer explicitly defines the column to be NOT NULL.

```
CREATE TABLE employee
 (empid              NUMBER(10),
 lastname            VARCHAR2(25)      NOT NULL,
 firstname           VARCHAR2(25)      NOT NULL,
 salary              NUMBER(10,4)      CHECK(salary<500000),
 home_phone          number(15),
 CONSTRAINT          pk_employee_01
 PRIMARY KEY         (empid),
 CONSTRAINT          uk_employee_01
 UNIQUE              (home_phone));
```

Notice that in this table definition, there are *three* columns defined to be NOT NULL, including the primary key. The two others are the LASTNAME column and the FIRSTNAME column. When defined, the NOT NULL table constraint will be applied to the columns, preventing anyone from creating a row for this table that does not contain a first and last name for the employee.

Notice also that an additional constraint has been created on this table. The final integrity constraint that will be identified by this section is the check constraint. Check constraints allow Oracle to verify the validity of data being entered on a table against a set of constants. These constants act as valid values. If, for example, someone tries to create an employee row for the table defined earlier with a salary of $1,000,000 per year, Oracle will return an error message saying that the record data defined for the SALARY column has violated the check constraint for that column. Check constraints have a number of limitations, all centering around the fact that the constraint can only refer to a specific set of constant values or operations on those values. A check constraint cannot refer to another column or row in any table, including the one the constraint is defined on, and it cannot refer to special keywords that can have values in them, such as **user**, **sysdate**, or **rowid** (see following *TIP*). Thus, the check constraint in the table definition earlier is valid, but the one in the following excerpt from a table definition is not:

```
CREATE TABLE address
(...,
city    VARCHAR2(80)  check(city in (SELECT city FROM cities))
...);
```

TIP
There are some special keywords that contain information about certain database conditions. These keywords are ***user****,* ***sysdate****, and* ***rowid****. The* ***user*** *keyword gives the username of the owner of the current session. The* ***sysdate*** *keyword gives the current date and time at the time the statement is issued. The* ***rowid*** *keyword gives the ROWID of the row specified. These keywords cannot be used in conjunction with a check constraint.*

Exercises

1. What command is used to create tables?

2. What is an integrity constraint? What are the five types of integrity constraints?

Using Table Naming Conventions

There are many philosophies around the naming of variables, tables, columns, and other items in software that come from the early days of computing. More often than not, available memory and disk space was small on those early machines. As such, the names of variables in these environments were small. This cryptic method was born out of necessity. In many systems today, however, developers are not faced with that restriction. As a result, the names of variables, columns, and tables need not be bound by the naming rules of yesteryear. However, some standard for naming tables and columns still has value, if only for the sake of readability.

Keep Names Short and Descriptive

A naming convention used in the Oracle database may be compact, but someone viewing variables in the database for the first time should also have some idea of what the variable is supposed to represent. For example, using the name EMP_LN_FN_SAL instead of EMPLOYEE for the table created previously would not be as easily understood as simply calling the table EMPLOYEE, or even EMP.

Relate Names for Child Tables to Their Parent

In certain situations, the developers of an application may find themselves creating multiple tables to define a logical object. The developer may have a logical entity that is represented by several tables, which have a one-to-many relationship among them. Consider the EXPENSE table, which was defined to hold the expense summaries that employees submit in order to generate a feed to the AP system. The developer could define a second table in conjunction with the EXPENSE table called EXPENSE_ITEM, which stores detail information about each expense incurred. Both are descriptive names, and it is obvious by those names that there is some relationship between them.

Foreign-Key Columns Should Have the Same Name in Both Tables

In the case of creating foreign-key relationships between columns in two different tables, it also helps if the referring and the referenced columns in both tables share the same name, making the potential existence of a foreign key a bit more obvious.

Names of Associated Objects Should Relate to the Table

Other naming conventions in the database related to tables include giving all integrity constraints, triggers, and indexes meaningful names that identify both the type of constraint created and the table to which the constraint belongs. Consider some of the names chosen in the previous examples. They include PK_EMPLOYEE_01, which is a primary key (PK) on the EMPLOYEE table; or FK_EMPLOYEE_01, which is a foreign key defined for the EMPLOYEE table. The name of the foreign key includes reference to the table to which the foreign-key constraint belongs.

Avoid Quotes, Keywords, and Nonalphanumeric Characters

You can't use quotes in the name of a database object. Nor can you use a nonalphanumeric character. This rule has three exceptions: the dollar sign ($), the underscore (_), and the hash mark (#). The dollar sign is most notable in the use for naming dynamic performance views. In general, you should steer clear of its use. The underscore is useful for separating two words or abbreviations, such as EXPENSE_ITEM, or BANK_ACCOUNT.

Exercises

1. Describe some table naming conventions.

2. What should be included in the name of a table that has a referential integrity constraint with another table, in which the table referring to the other table is the child table?

Datatypes and Column Definitions

The usage of datatypes to identify the "type" of data a column can hold has been mentioned a few times so far. At this point, it is necessary to discuss the available datatypes in the Oracle database. A few obvious ones should come to mind, as there have already been several tables defined and discussed in the preceding few chapters. Loosely speaking, the types of data a column will allow that have been used so far are alphanumeric datatypes that store text strings such as CHAR and VARCHAR2, the NUMBER datatype that stores numeric data only, and the DATE datatype.

Here's a list of datatypes and their descriptions:

VARCHAR2	Contains variable length text strings of up to 2,000 bytes (4,000 in Oracle8)
CHAR	Contains fixed text strings of up to 255 bytes (2,000 in Oracle8)
NUMBER	Contains numeric data
DATE	Contains date data
RAW	Contains binary data of up to 255 bytes (2,000 in Oracle8)
LONG	Contains text data of up to 2 gigabytes
LONG RAW	Contains binary data of up to 2 gigabytes
ROWID	Contains disk location for table rows
BLOB	Large binary object (Oracle8 only)
CLOB	Large character-based object (Oracle8 only)
NCLOB	Large single- or multibyte character-based object (Oracle8 only)
BFILE	Large external file (Oracle8 only)

Some other datatypes may not be so obvious. For example, the alphanumeric datatypes identified here are not one simple datatype, but two—a CHAR datatype and a VARCHAR2 datatype. Some people may ask, why does VARCHAR2 have the "2" on the end, and the reason is that there may be a VARCHAR datatype defined in future releases of Oracle; so, although VARCHAR and VARCHAR2 for now are synonymous, they may not be in the future. Both the CHAR and the VARCHAR2 variable datatypes can be defined to hold character strings, but there are some subtle differences. First, the CHAR datatype only supports character strings up to a length of 255 bytes in Oracle7 (2,000 for Oracle8), while the VARCHAR2 datatype supports character strings up to a length of 2,000 characters in Oracle7 (4,000 for Oracle8). Second, and perhaps most important, when Oracle stores data in a CHAR datatype, it will pad the value stored in the column up to the length of the column as declared by the table with blanks. In contrast, Oracle will not store padded blank spaces if the same value is stored in a column defined to be datatype VARCHAR2. To illustrate, if a column called LASTNAME was defined as CHAR(50) and the value someone attempted to store in it was "BRADY," the value Oracle would store would actually be "BRADY" with 45 blank spaces to the right of it. That same value stored in a column that was defined as datatype VARCHAR2 would be stored simply as "BRADY."

The NUMBER datatype that is used to store number data can be specified either to store integers or decimals with the addition of a parenthetical precision indicator. For example, if you had a column defined to be datatype NUMBER(15,2), the number 49309.593 would be stored as 49309.59, because the number specified after the comma in the parenthetical precision definition of the datatype represents the number of places to the right of the decimal point that will be stored. The number on the left of the comma shows the total width of allowed values stored in this column, including the two decimal places to the right of the decimal point. A column declared to be of type NUMBER(9) will not store any decimals at all. The number 49309.593 stored in a column defined in this way will appear as 49310, because Oracle automatically rounds up in cases where the value in the precision area that the declared datatype will not support is 5 or above.

Another type that has already been discussed is the DATE datatype, which stores date values in a special format internal to Oracle represented as the number of days since December 31, 4713 B.C.E., the beginning of the Julian date calendar. This datatype offers a great deal of flexibility to users who want to perform date manipulation operations, such as adding 30 days to a given date. In this case, all the user has to do is specify the column declared as a DATE datatype and add the number of days. Of course, there are also numerous functions that handle date operations more complex than simple arithmetic. Another nice feature of Oracle's method for date storage is that it is inherently millennium compliant.

Beyond these datatypes, there is an entire set of important options available to the developer and DBA with respect to type declaration. In Oracle7, these datatypes include LONG, RAW, LONG RAW, and MLSLABEL. RAW datatypes in Oracle store data in binary format up to 255 bytes long in version 7. It is useful to store graphics and sound files when used in conjunction with LONG to form the LONG RAW datatype, which can accommodate up to 2 gigabytes of data. The developer can declare columns to be of LONG datatype, which stores up to 2 gigabytes of alphanumeric text data. There can be only one column declared to be of type LONG in the database as of Oracle7. The entire operation of storing large blocks of data has been reworked significantly for Oracle8, where BLOB, CLOB, and NCLOB objects, which can be up to 4 gigabytes, and are used to store binary, single-byte, and multibyte character-based objects in the Oracle database through the use of pointers. This is in contrast to Oracle7, where the actual LONG or LONG RAW data is stored inline with the rest of the table information.

TIP
"Inline" means that the data in a LONG datatype column is stored literally "in line" with the rest of data in the row, as opposed to Oracle storing a pointer to LONG column data somewhere else inline with row data.

Finally, the ROWID datatype is considered. This datatype stores information related to the disk location of table rows. Generally, no column should be created to store data in type ROWID, but this datatype supports the **rowid** virtual column associated with every table.

Exercises

1. Name several different datatypes available in Oracle7. Which ones are introduced for Oracle8.

2. What are some of the differences between the CHAR and the VARCHAR2 datatype?

3. How is data stored in the DATE datatype? What is the ROWID datatype?

Indexes Created by Constraints

Indexes are created in support of integrity constraints that enforce uniqueness. The two types of integrity constraints that enforce uniqueness are primary keys and unique constraints. Essentially, unique constraints in Oracle are the same as primary-key constraints, except for the fact that they allow NULL values. When the primary-key or the unique constraint is declared, the index that supports the uniqueness enforcement is also created, and all values in all columns are placed into the index.

The name of the index depends on the name given to the constraint. For example, the following table definition statement creates one index on the primary-key column EMPID. EMPID cannot then contain any NULL values or any duplicates. The name of the index is the same as the name given to the primary key. Thus, the name given to the index created to support uniqueness on the primary key for this table is called PK_EMPLOYEE_01. There are performance benefits associated with indexes that will be discussed in the next chapter, but for now it is sufficient to say that the creation of an index in conjunction with the definition of a primary key is a handy feature of table declaration in Oracle.

```
CREATE TABLE employee
(empid           NUMBER(10),
lastname         VARCHAR2(25)       NOT NULL,
firstname        VARCHAR2(25)       NOT NULL,
salary           NUMBER(10,4)       CHECK(salary<500000),
home_phone       number(15),
CONSTRAINT       pk_employee_01
PRIMARY KEY      (empid),
CONSTRAINT       uk_employee_01
UNIQUE           (home_phone));
```

Another important case to consider is the unique constraint index. If the unique constraint is defined in the manner detailed in the previous code example, then the name of the corresponding index in the database created automatically by Oracle to support enforcement of the uniqueness of the column will be UK_EMPLOYEE_01. However, there is another method for declaring a unique constraint on a column such that the index created will remain somewhat anonymous, as shown below:

```
CREATE TABLE employee
(empid           NUMBER(10),
lastname         VARCHAR2(25)       NOT NULL,
firstname        VARCHAR2(25)       NOT NULL,
salary           NUMBER(10,4)       CHECK(salary<500000),
home_phone       number(15)         UNIQUE,
CONSTRAINT       pk_employee_01
PRIMARY KEY      (empid));
```

The unique constraint created in this situation will have the same properties as the unique constraint created in the previous code example. It will also enforce uniqueness on that column just as well as the constraint defined in the previous example. If you don't name your constraint, Oracle will name it for you. The name Oracle will generate in this situation is SYS_C*xxxxx*, where *xxxxx* is a six-digit number.

In summary, indexes are used to support the enforcement of unique integrity constraints, such as the primary-key and the unique constraints. The associated indexes can either be named with something corresponding to the name given to the constraint if the constraint is explicitly named, or the constraint can be given a relatively anonymous name automatically by Oracle when the unique index is created. It is important to bear in mind that with the creation of a table comes the creation of an associated primary-key index.

TIP
*When a table is created, an index corresponding to the primary key of the table is also created to enforce uniqueness and to speed performance on data selection that uses the primary key in the **where** clause of the **select** statement.*

Exercises

1. Identify two constraints that create indexes.

2. What determines the name given to an index created automatically?

3. What two purposes does the index serve in the enforcement of its associated constraint?

Creating One Table with Data from Another

The final area of discussion in this section on creating tables is one on how to create a table with prepopulated data. In most cases, when a developer creates a table in Oracle, the table is empty—it has no data in it. Once created, the users or developers are then free to populate the table as long as proper access has been granted. However, there are some cases in which the developer can create a table that already has data in it. The general statement used to create tables in this manner is the **create table as select** statement, as shown below:

```
CREATE TABLE employee
(empid,
lastname,
firstname,
salary,
home_phone,
CONSTRAINT      pk_employee_01
PRIMARY KEY     (empid))
AS SELECT * FROM hrglobal.empl;
```

The final **as select** clause instructs Oracle to **insert** data into the table it just created from the HRGLOBAL.EMPL table specified. In order to use **select ***, the columns in the table from which data will be selected must be identical to the column specification made in the table just created. Alternately, an exact copy of a table can be made without declaring any columns at all with the code block shown here:

```
CREATE TABLE employee
AS SELECT * FROM hrglobal.empl;
```

Finally, it is also possible for the developer to specify any option in the **select** statement that makes a copy of data that the developer could use in any other **select** statement in the database. This feature includes the specification of column concatenation, selecting only a limited number of columns, limiting the number of rows returned with the **where** clause, or even using arithmetic and other single-row operations to modify data in virtually any way available on other **select** statements.

Exercises

1. How can a table be created with data already populated in it?

2. What limits are there on the data that can be selected in creating a table from existing data?

The Oracle Data Dictionary

In this section, you will cover the following topics related to the Oracle data dictionary:

- Available dictionary views
- Querying the data dictionary

Few resources in the Oracle database are as useful as the Oracle data dictionary. Developers, DBAs, and users will find themselves referring to the data dictionary time and time again to resolve questions about object availability, roles and privileges, and performance. Whatever the information, Oracle has it all stored in the data dictionary. This discussion will introduce the major components of the data dictionary in the Oracle database, pointing out its features and the highlights in order to set groundwork for fuller discussions on the data dictionary in later chapters. It is worth having the major concepts related to the data dictionary down before moving on, as data dictionary views will be referred to in many other areas throughout the rest of the guide.

Available Dictionary Views

There are scores of dictionary tables available in the Oracle data dictionary, used to keep track of many of the database objects that have been discussed. The dictionary tells you just about anything you need to know about the database, including which objects can be seen by the user, which objects are available, the current performance status of the database, etc. There are a few basic facts about the data dictionary that you should know. First, the Oracle data dictionary consists of tables where information about the database is stored. The SYS user in Oracle is the only user allowed to **update** those dictionary tables. Oracle processes routinely do this as part of their processing, but a user such as the DBA should never do so except to periodically **update** and **delete** records from the SYS.AUD$ table, which stores audit trail records.

Rather than having users manipulate the dictionary tables directly, Oracle has available several *views* on the dictionary tables through which users get a distilled look at the dictionary contents. A view is a database object loosely akin to the idea of a "virtual table." The data in a view is pulled from a real table by way of a **select** statement and stored in memory. The Oracle data dictionary allow users to see the available database objects to various depths, depending on their needs as users.

The views of the data dictionary are divided into three general categories to correspond to the depth of the database to which one is permitted to view. The three general categories of views are listed as follows, along with a general description of the objects the view will allow the user to see. The text in all caps at the beginning of each bullet corresponds to text that is prefixed onto the name of the dictionary view categories in question.

- **USER_**   These views typically allow the user to see all database objects in the view that are owned by the user accessing the view.

- **ALL_**   These views typically allow the user to see all database objects in the view that are accessible to the user.

- **DBA_**   This powerful set of views allows those who may access them to see all database objects that correspond to the view in the entire database.

The USER_ views are generally those views with the least scope. They only display a limited amount of information about the database objects that the user created in his or her own schema. One way that tables can be referred to is by their schema owner. For example, assume there is a database with a user named SPANKY. SPANKY creates some tables in his user schema, one of which is called PRODUCTS, and then grants access to those tables to another user on the database called ATHENA. User ATHENA can then refer to SPANKY's tables as SPANKY.PRODUCTS, or SPANKY.*tablename* for a more general format. However, if user ATHENA attempts to look in the USER_TABLES view to gather more information about table PRODUCTS, she will find nothing in that view about it. Why? *Because the table belongs to user SPANKY.*

The next level of scope in dictionary views comes with the ALL_ views. The objects whose information is displayed in the ALL_ views correspond to any database object that the user can look at, change data in, or access in any way, shape, or form. In order for a user to be able to access a database object, one of three conditions must be true. Either the user herself must have created the object, or the user must have been granted access by the object owner to manipulate the object or data in the object, or the owner of the object must have granted access privileges on the object to the PUBLIC user. The PUBLIC user in the database is a special user who represents the access privileges every user has. Thus, when an object owner creates a table and grants access to the table to user PUBLIC, then every user in the database has access privileges to the table created.

The final category of data dictionary views available on the database is DBA_ views. These views are incredibly handy for DBAs to find out information about every database object corresponding to the information the view captures in the database. Thus, as mentioned earlier, the DBA_TABLES view displays information about every table in the database. At this point, the developer should note that this view allows the user to see objects in the database that the user may not even have permission to use. It can be a violation of security concerns to have certain users even aware of the existence of certain tables. Usually, the developer will not have access to DBA_ views.

The name of each view has two components, which are the scope or depth to which the user will be able to see information about the object in the database (USER_, ALL_, DBA_), followed by the name of the object type itself. For example, information about tables in the database can be found in the USER_TABLES, ALL_TABLES, or DBA_TABLES views. Some other views that correspond to areas that have been discussed or will be discussed, along with some information about the contents of the view, are listed here:

- **USER_, ALL_, DBA_OBJECTS**   Gives information about various database objects.

- **USER_, ALL_, DBA_TABLES**   Displays information about tables in the database.

- **USER_, ALL_, DBA_INDEXES**   Displays information about indexes in the database.

- **USER_, ALL_, DBA_VIEWS**   Displays information about views in the database.

- **USER_, ALL_, DBA_SEQUENCES**   Displays information about sequences in the database. A sequence is a database object that generates numbers in sequential order.

- **USER_, ALL_, DBA_USERS** Displays information about users in the database.

- **USER_, ALL_, DBA_CONSTRAINTS** Displays information about constraints in the database.

- **USER_, ALL_, DBA_CONS_COLUMNS** Displays information about table columns that have constraints in the database.

- **USER_, ALL_, DBA_IND_COLUMNS** Displays information about table columns that have indexes in the database.

- **USER_, ALL_, DBA_TAB_COLUMNS** Displays information about columns in tables in the database.

Exercises

1. What is the data dictionary?

2. What are the three categories of views that a user may access in the dictionary? How much information about the database is available in each view?

3. Who owns the data dictionary? Are users allowed to access the tables of the dictionary directly? Why or why not?

Querying the Data Dictionary

The introduction to the views available in the data dictionary now will be used to present ways for you to select data from the dictionary to understand better how useful the data dictionary is in Oracle. Consider first the need to get information about tables. For the purposes of this presentation, the ALL_ views will be used, except where noted. The first thing every user should learn how to do related to the data dictionary is to list the columns available in a table. A listing of the columns in a table can be obtained from the dictionary with the use of the **describe** command, often abbreviated as **desc**.

 DESC spanky.products

```
NAME                NULL?          TYPE
---------           -----          ------
PRODUCT             NOT NULL       NUMBER(10)
PRODUCT_NAME        NOT NULL       VARCHAR2(35)
QUANTITY                           NUMBER(10)
```

The user can find out any information about the database tables that is available for their usage with the ALL_TABLES view. In order to apply the description of any of these views to its sibling in the USER_ or DBA_ family, substitute the scope "available to the user" with "created by the user" or "all those created in the database" for USER_ or DBA_, respectively. ALL_TABLES displays information about who owns the table, where the table is stored in the database, and information about storage parameters that a table is using.

```
SELECT owner, table_name
FROM all_tables
WHERE owner = 'SPANKY';
```

Some of the other object views are similar to ALL_TABLES. For example, ALL_INDEXES contains information about the indexes on tables that are available to the user. Some of the information listed in this view corresponds to the features of the index, such as whether or not all values in the indexed column are unique. Other information in the view corresponds to the storage parameters of the index and where the index is stored.

```
SELECT owner, index_name, table_name, uniqueness
FROM all_indexes
WHERE owner = 'SPANKY';
```

The next data dictionary view represents a slight departure from the previous pattern. The ALL_VIEWS data dictionary view gives information about all the views in the database available to the user. It lists the schema owner, the view name, and the query that was used to create the view. The column containing the text that created the view is stored in LONG format. To obtain data from this column of the view, the user may need to issue the **set long** command to set the formatting that SQL*Plus will use to display to a LONG column to something large enough to display the entire query used to create the view. Typically, **set long 5000** will suffice. More information about creating views in Oracle will be covered in the next chapter.

```
SET LONG 5000

SELECT owner, view_name, text
FROM all_views
WHERE owner = 'SPANKY';
```

The next view is the USER_USERS view. This view is used to tell the current user of the database more information about his or her environment. Contained in this view are the default locations where objects created by the user will be stored, along with the user profile this user will abide by. There are several other pieces of information that will be more useful to DBAs than developers.

```
SELECT * FROM user_users;
```

The next few views discussed cover some more interesting material related to constraints. There are several views in this category that will be discussed, and the first one is the ALL_CONSTRAINTS view. This view is used to display information about the constraints that have been defined in the database. This view is particularly useful in determining the referenced column in cases where referential integrity constraints have been created on a table. This view gives the name of the constraint, the owner of the constraint, the name of the table the constraint is created on, and the name of the referenced table and column if the constraint created is a foreign key.

```
SELECT constraint_name, table_name, r_owner, r_constraint_name
FROM all_constraints
WHERE table_name = 'PRODUCTS' and owner = 'SPANKY';
```

The next view discussed also relates to constraints. The view is called ALL_CONS_COLUMNS, and it presents information about the columns that are incorporated into constraints on a table. For example, it is possible to create a primary key for a table that uses as its unique identifier two or more columns from the table. This definition of the primary key is sometimes referred to as a *composite primary key*. The ALL_CONS_COLUMNS view gives information about the columns that are in the primary key and which order they appear in the composite index.

```
SELECT constraint_name, table_name, column_name, column_position
FROM all_cons_columns
WHERE table_name = 'PRODUCTS' and owner = 'SPANKY';
```

The final dictionary view discussed in this section is related to the ALL_CONS_COLUMNS view, but extends the scope of that view by providing information about all the indexed columns on the database.

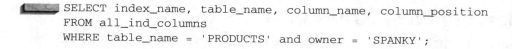

```
SELECT index_name, table_name, column_name, column_position
FROM all_ind_columns
WHERE table_name = 'PRODUCTS' and owner = 'SPANKY';
```

Exercises

1. Describe usage of object views. What purpose do the constraint views serve?

2. What is a composite index?

3. What purpose does the COLUMN_POSITION column serve in some of the dictionary views?

Manipulating Oracle Data

In this section, you will cover the following topics related to manipulating Oracle data:

■ Inserting new rows into a table

■ Making changes to existing row data

■ Deleting data from the Oracle database

■ The importance of transaction control

In this section, an introduction to all forms of data change manipulation will be covered. The three types of data change manipulation that exist in the Oracle database include updating, deleting, and inserting data. These statements are collectively known as the data manipulation language of Oracle, or *DML* for short. Furthermore, a treatment of *transaction processing* will also be included. Transaction processing is a mechanism that the Oracle database provides in order to facilitate the act of changing data. Without transaction-processing mechanisms, the database would not be able to guarantee that the users would not overwrite one another's changes midprocess, or select data that is in the process of being changed by another user.

Inserting New Rows into a Table

The first data change manipulation operation that will be discussed is the act of inserting new rows into a table. Once a table is created, there is no data in the table, with the one exception of creating a table populated by rows selected from another table. Even in this case, the data must come from somewhere. This somewhere is from users who enter data into the table via **insert** statements.

An **insert** statement has syntax different from a **select** statement. The general syntax for an **insert** statement is listed in the following code block, which defines several rows to be added to the PRODUCTS table owned by SPANKY. This table has three columns, titled PRODUCT#, PRODUCT_NAME, and QUANTITY. User SPANKY now wants to put some data in his table, so he executes the following statement designed to place one new row into the PRODUCTS table:

```
INSERT INTO products (product#,product_name, quantity)
VALUES (7848394, 'KITTY LITTER', 12);
```

Notice a few general rules of syntax in this statement. The **insert** statement has two parts, the first is one in which the table to receive the inserted row is defined, in conjunction with the columns of the table that will have the column values specified inserted into them. The second portion of the statement defines the actual data values that comprise the row to be added. This portion of the statement is denoted by use of the **values** keyword.

There are several variations Oracle is capable of handling in order to **insert** data on a table. For example, it is generally only required for the user to define explicit columns of the table in which to **insert** data when all columns of the table are not going to have data inserted into them. For example, if user SPANKY only wanted to define the product number and the name at the time the row was inserted, then SPANKY would be required to list the PRODUCT# and PRODUCT_NAME columns in the **into** clause of the **insert** statement. However, since he named column values for all columns in the table, the following statement would be just as acceptable for inserting the row into the PRODUCTS table:

```
INSERT INTO products
VALUES (7848394, 'KITTY LITTER', 12);
```

One important question to ask in this situation is "how does Oracle know which column to populate with what data?" Assume further about the table that the column datatypes are defined to be NUMBER for PRODUCT# and QUANTITY, and VARCHAR2 for PRODUCT_NAME. What prevents Oracle from placing the 12 in the PRODUCT# column? Again, as with the discussion of column positions in composite indexes as displayed by some of the views in the last section, position can matter in the Oracle database. The position of the data must correspond to the position of the column as it is created in the table. The user can determine the position of each column in a table by using the **describe** command or the output from the USER_, ALL_ or DBA_TAB_COLUMNS dictionary view using the column indicating position as part of the **order by** clause. The order in which the columns are listed from the **describe** command is the same order that values should be placed in if the user would like to **insert** data into the table without explicitly naming the columns of the table.

Another variation of the **insert** theme is the ability **insert** has to populate a table using the data obtained from other tables using a **select** statement. This method of populating table data is similar to the method used by the **create table as select** statement, which was discussed earlier in the chapter. In this case, the **values** clause can be omitted entirely. Also, the rules regarding column position of the inserted data apply in this situation as well, meaning that if the user can **select** data for all columns of the table having data inserted into it, then the user need not name the columns in the **insert into** clause.

```
INSERT INTO products
(SELECT product#, product_name, quantity
 FROM MASTER.PRODUCTS);
```

In order to put data into a table, a special privilege must be granted from the table owner to the user who needs to perform the **insert**. A more complete discussion of object privileges will appear in the next chapter.

Exercises

1. What statement is used to place new data into an Oracle table?

2. What are the three options available with the statement that allows new data to be placed into Oracle tables?

Making Changes to Existing Row Data

Often, the data rows in a table will need to be changed. In order to make those changes, the **update** statement can be used. Updates can be made to any row in a database, except in two cases. Data that a user does not have enough access privileges to **update** cannot be updated by that user. Data is updated by the user when an **update** statement is issued, as shown below:

```
UPDATE spanky.products
SET quantity = 54
WHERE product# = 4959495;
```

Notice that the typical **update** statement has three clauses. The first is the actual **update** clause, where the table that will be updated is named. The second clause is the **set** clause. In the **set** clause, all columns that will be changed by the **update** statement are named, along with their new values. The final clause of the **update** statement is the **where** clause. The **where** clause in an **update** statement is the same as the **where** clause in a **select** statement. There are one or more comparison operations that determine which rows Oracle will **update** as a result of this statement being issued.

The **update** and **set** clauses are mandatory in an **update** statement. However, the **where** clause is not. Omitting the **where** clause in an **update** statement has the effect of applying the data change to every row that presently exists in the table. Consider the following code block that issues a data change without a **where** clause specified. The change made by this statement will therefore apply to every column in the table.

```
UPDATE spanky.products
SET quantity = 0;
```

Every operation that was possible in the **where** clauses of a **select** statement are possible in the **where** clauses of an **update**. The **where** clause in an **update** statement can have any type of comparison or range operation in it, and can even handle the use of the **exists** operation or other uses for subqueries.

Exercise

What statement is used to change data in an Oracle table? What clauses in this statement are mandatory?

Deleting Data from the Oracle Database

The removal of data from a database is as much a fact of life as putting the data there in the first place. Removal of database rows from tables is accomplished with the use of the **delete** statement in SQL*Plus. The syntax for usage of the **delete** statement is detailed in the following code block. Note that in the next example there is no way to **delete** data from selected columns in a row in the table; this act is accomplished with the **update** statement where the columns that are to be "deleted" are set to NULL by the **update** statement.

```
DELETE FROM spanky.products
WHERE product# = 4959394; -- all column values removed
```

As in the case of database updates, **delete** statements use the **where** clause to help determine which rows are meant to be removed. In the same way as an **update** or **select** statement, the **where** clause in a **delete** statement can contain any type of comparison operation, range operation, subquery, or any other operation acceptable for a **where** clause. In the same way as an **update** statement, if the **where** clause is left off the **delete** statement, then the deletion will be applied to all rows in the table.

Data deletion is a careful matter to undertake. It can be costly to replace data that has been deleted from the database, which is why the privilege to **delete** information should only be given out to those users who really should be able to **delete** records from a table.

Exercises

1. What statement is used to remove data from an Oracle table? What clauses in this statement are mandatory?

2. When can a user not remove data in a table?

The Importance of Transaction Control

One of the first realities that a user of the Oracle database must understand is that a change to data made in the Oracle database is not saved immediately. Oracle allows users to execute a series of data change statements together as one logical unit of work, terminated by either saving the work in the database or discarding it. This period allotted to a user to make changes is called a transaction.

Transaction processing consists of a set of controls that allow a user issuing an **insert**, **update**, or **delete** statement to declare a beginning to the series of data change statements he or she will issue. When the user has completed making the changes to the database, the user can save the data to the database by explicitly ending the transaction. Alternatively, if a mistake is made at any point during the transaction, the user can have the database discard the changes made on the database in favor of the way the data existed before the transaction.

Transactions are created with the use of two different concepts in the Oracle database. The first concept is the set of commands that define the beginning, breakpoint, and end of a transaction. These commands are listed in the following set of bullets. The second concept is that of special locking mechanisms designed to prevent more than one user at a time from making a change to row information in a database. Locks will be discussed after the transaction control commands are defined.

- **SET TRANSACTION**   Initiates the beginning of a transaction and sets key features

- **COMMIT**   Ends current transaction by saving database changes and starts new transaction

- **ROLLBACK**   Ends current transaction by discarding database changes and starts new transaction

- **SAVEPOINT**   Defines breakpoints for the transaction to allow partial rollbacks

SET TRANSACTION

This command can be used to define the beginning of a transaction. If any change is made to the database after the **set transaction** command is issued but before the transaction is ended, all changes made will be considered part of that transaction. The **set transaction** statement is not required because a transaction begins as soon as you log onto Oracle via SQL*Plus, or immediately after issuing a **rollback** or **commit** statement to end a transaction. By default, a transaction is **read write** unless you override this default by issuing **set transaction read only**.

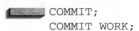

```
SET TRANSACTION READ ONLY;
SET TRANSACTION READ WRITE;
```

COMMIT

The **commit** statement in transaction processing represents the point in time where the user has made all the changes she wants to have logically grouped together, and since no mistakes have been made, the user is ready to save her work. The **work** keyword is an extraneous word in the **commit** syntax that is designed for readability. Issuing a **commit** statement also implicitly begins a new transaction on the database because it closes the current transaction and starts a new one. It is important also to understand the implicit **commit** that occurs on the database when a user exits SQL*Plus or issues a DDL such as a **create table** statement.

```
COMMIT;
COMMIT WORK;
```

ROLLBACK

If you have at any point issued a data change statement you don't want, you can discard the changes made to the database with the use of the **rollback** statement. After the **rollback** command is issued, a new transaction is started implicitly by the database session. In addition to rollbacks executed when the **rollback** statement is issued, there are implicit **rollback** statements conducted when a statement fails for any reason or if the user cancels a statement with the CTRL-C **cancel** command.

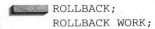

```
ROLLBACK;
ROLLBACK WORK;
```

SAVEPOINT

In some cases involving long transactions or transactions that involve many data changes, you may not want to scrap all the changes made simply because the last statement issued contains unwanted changes. Savepoints are special operations that allow you to divide the work of a transaction into different segments. You can execute rollbacks to the savepoint only, leaving prior changes intact. Savepoint usage is great for situations like this where part of the transaction needs to be recovered in an uncommitted transaction. At the point the **rollback to savepoint so_far_so_good** statement completes in the following code block, only changes made before the savepoint was defined are kept when the **commit** is issued:

```
UPDATE spanky.products
SET quantity = 55
WHERE product# = 59495;

SAVEPOINT so_far_so_good;

UPDATE spanky.products
SET quantity = 504;

ROLLBACK TO SAVEPOINT so_far_so_good;
COMMIT;
```

Locks

The final aspect of the Oracle database that allows the user to have transaction processing is a lock, the mechanism by which Oracle prevents data from being changed by more than one user at a time. There are several different types of locks, each with its own level of scope. Locks available on a database are categorized into table-level locks and row-level locks. A table-level lock makes it so that only the user holding the lock can change any piece of row data in the table, during which time no other users can make changes anywhere on the table. A row-level lock is one that allows the user the exclusive ability to change data in one or more rows of the table. However, any row in the table that is not held by the row-level lock can be changed by another user.

TIP

*An **update** statement acquires a special row-level lock called a "row-exclusive" lock, which means that for the period of time the **update** statement is executing, no other user in the database can view or change the data in the row. The same goes for **delete** or **insert** operations. Another **update** statement, the **select for update** statement, acquires a more lenient lock called the "share row" lock. This lock means that for the period of time the **update** statement is changing the data in the rows of the table, no other user may change that row, but users may look at the data in the row as it changes.*

Exercises

1. What is transaction processing?

2. Identify the mechanisms that support transactions.

Chapter Summary

This chapter covered the foundational material for understanding the mechanics of creating an Oracle database. The material in this chapter corresponds to 15 percent of the test material in OCP Exam 1 and represents the foundation on which other exams will build. This understanding is required in order to move the casual user who understands material related to selecting data from an Oracle database to a full-fledged expert on the Oracle database server product. Understanding this material is crucial to understanding several areas in the rest of this guide, including the management of tables, using transaction processing, locks and the contention issues they often produce, and proper management of the data dictionary.

The first portion of this chapter discussed the concepts of data modeling. In order to create a database in Oracle, it is important that all stages of system development be executed carefully. Some of the stages covered include needs assessment, requirements definition, database design, application development, performance tuning, security enforcement, and enhancements development. The enhancement stage in that life cycle is really a miniature version of the first several stages rolled into one. The needs assessment stage is a critical one. It is the period of time where the users of the system are identified, and the desired and required features of the system are documented. After needs assessment, a full list of requirements should be agreed upon and documented so as to avoid costly rework later. Once the requirements of the system are completely understood, the developers of the database portion of the application should model the business process required into an entity-relationship diagram, which consists of entities, or persons, places, things, or ideas involved in the process flow, and the relationships between each entity. This entity-relationship diagram will then be used to create a logical data model, or a pictorial diagram of the tables that will represent each entity and the referential integrity constraints that will represent each relationship. Ordinality is a key point here. Ordinality defines whether the relationship is mandatory for the entities partaking of the relationship, and the record-to-record correspondence of one record in a database. There are three types of record-to-record correspondence in the database—one-to-one, one-to-many, and many-to-many. A one-to-one correspondence means that one record of one table corresponds to one record in another. One-to-many correspondence means that one record from one table corresponds to many records of another table. Many-to-many correspondence means that several records from one table correspond to several records of another table.

Once the planning is complete, then developers can move forward with the process of actually creating the database. The syntax for creating a table with column definitions and constraints is covered in this chapter. A table can be created with several different columns. The allowed datatypes for these columns in Oracle7 are VARCHAR2, CHAR, NUMBER, DATE, RAW, LONG, LONG RAW, MLSLABEL and ROWID. More datatypes are available in Oracle8, such as BLOB, CLOB, NCLOB, and BFILE. One or more of these columns is used to define the primary key, or element in each row that distinguishes one row of data from another in the table. A primary key is one type of integrity constraint. Another type of integrity constraint is the foreign key, which defines referential integrity on the table, creating table relationships and often modeling the relationships between entities from the entity-relationship diagram. Referential integrity produces a parent/child relationship between two tables. Sometimes it is useful to name tables according to conventions that have the child objects take on the name of the parent object as part of their own name. The three other constraints available on the database are unique, check, and NOT NULL. Unique constraints prevent duplicate non-NULL values from appearing in a column for two or more rows. Check constraints verify data in a column against a set of constants defined to be valid values. NOT NULL constraints prevent the entry of NULL data for a column on which the NOT NULL constraint is defined. Two of the five constraints create indexes to help enforce the integrity they are designed to enforce. Those two constraints are the ones designed to enforce uniqueness: the unique constraint and the primary key. Finally, a table is created with no data in it, except in the case of the **create table as select**. This statement allows the user to create a table with row data prepopulated from another table. All options available for regular **select** statements are available in this statement as well.

The next portion of this chapter discussed the Oracle data dictionary. The data dictionary contains information about all objects created in the database. It also contains a listing of available columns in each object created in the database. Information about table columns can be obtained using the **describe** command, followed by the name of the table you want to view the columns on. Information is kept in data dictionary tables about the objects created in Oracle, where they are stored, and performance statistics. However, you will not usually access the tables of the data dictionary directly. Rather, you generally will look at that data using data dictionary views. Data can be selected from views in the same way it can be selected from tables. No user is able to **delete** data from the data dictionary, because doing so could permanently damage the Oracle database. All tables and views in the Oracle data dictionary are owned by SYS.

Several data dictionary views are available to find out information about the objects discussed in this unit. Those views are divided into three general categories that correspond to the scope of data availability in the view. The USER_ views show information on objects owned by the user, the ALL_ views show information on all the objects accessible by the user, and the DBA_ views show information on all objects in the database. Data dictionary views are available on every type of object in the database, including indexes, constraints, tables, views, synonyms, sequences, and triggers. Additionally, information is available to help the user understand which columns are available in indexes or primary-key constraints. Several views exist to show the position of columns in composite indexes, which are indexes that contain several columns.

The remainder of the chapter discussed the usage of SQL statements for the purpose of changing data in a database. There are three types of data change statements available in the Oracle database. They are **update**, **insert**, and **delete**. The **update** statement allows you to change row data that already exists in the database. The **insert** statement allows you to add new row data records to the tables of a database. The **delete** statement allows you to remove records from the database. The various data change operations are supported in Oracle with the use of transaction-processing control. There are several different aspects to transaction processing. These include the commands used to set the beginning, breakpoint, and end of transactions, and the locking mechanisms that allow one and only one user at a time to make changes to the data in the database.

Two-Minute Drill

- The stages of system development include needs assessment, requirements definition, database design, application development, performance tuning, database security enforcement, and enhancement development.

- The basic types of data relationships in Oracle include primary keys and functional dependency within a table, and foreign-key constraints from one table to another.

- A relational database is composed of objects to store data, objects to manage access to data, and objects to improve performance on accessing data.

- Within database planning, it is necessary to create an entity-relationship diagram that acts as a visual representation of the business process being modeled. The diagram consists of people, places, things, and ideas, called entities, which are related to one another using activities or a process flow called "relationships."

- Once an entity-relationship diagram has been created for an application, it must be translated into a logical data model. The logical data model is a collection of tables that represent entities and referential integrity constraints that represent relationships.

- A table can be created with five different types of integrity constraints: primary keys, foreign keys, unique constraints, NOT NULL constraints, and check constraints.

- Referential integrity often creates a parent/child relationship between two tables, the parent being the referenced table and the child being the referring table. Often, a naming convention that requires child objects to adopt and extend the name of the parent table is useful in identifying these relationships.

- The datatypes available in Oracle7 for creating columns in tables are CHAR, VARCHAR2, NUMBER, DATE, RAW, LONG, LONG RAW, ROWID, and MLSLABEL.

- Datatypes added by Oracle8 include BLOB, CLOB, NCLOB, and BFILE.

- Indexes are created automatically in conjunction with primary-key and unique constraints. These indexes are named after the constraint name given to the constraint in the definition of the table.

- Tables are created without any data in them, except for tables created with the **create table as select** statement. These tables are created and prepopulated with data from another table.

- There is information available in the Oracle database to help users, developers, and DBAs know what objects exist in the Oracle database. The information is in the Oracle data dictionary.

- To find the positional order of columns in a table, or what columns there are in a table at all, the user can issue a **describe** command on that table. The Oracle data dictionary will then list all columns in the table being described.

- Data dictionary views on database objects are divided into three categories based on scope of user visibility: USER_, for what is owned by the user; ALL_, for all that can be seen by the user; and

DBA_, for all that exists in the database, whether the user can see it or not.

■ New rows are put into a table with the **insert** statement. The user issuing the **insert** statement can **insert** one row at a time with one statement, or do a mass **insert** with **insert into** *table_name* (**select ...**).

■ Existing rows in a database table can be modified using the **update** statement. The **update** statement contains a **where** clause similar in function to the **where** clause of **select** statements.

■ Existing rows in a table can be deleted using the **delete** statement. The **delete** statement also contains a **where** clause similar in function to the **where** clause in **update** or **select** statements.

■ Transaction processing controls the change of data in an Oracle database.

■ Transaction controls include commands that identify the beginning, breakpoint, and end of a transaction, locking mechanisms that prevent more than one user at a time from making changes in the database.

Chapter Questions

1. **Which of the following integrity constraints automatically create an index when defined? (Choose two)**

   A. Foreign keys

   B. Unique constraints

   C. NOT NULL constraints

   D. Primary keys

2. **Which of the following dictionary views give information about the position of a column in a primary key?**

   A. ALL_PRIMARY_KEYS

   B. USER_CONSTRAINTS

    C. ALL_IND_COLUMNS

    D. ALL_TABLES

3. **Developer ANJU executes the following statement: CREATE TABLE animals AS SELECT * from MASTER.ANIMALS; What is the effect of this statement?**

    A. A table named ANIMALS will be created in the MASTER schema with the same data as the ANIMALS table owned by ANJU.

    B. A table named ANJU will be created in the ANIMALS schema with the same data as the ANIMALS table owned by MASTER.

    C. A table named ANIMALS will be created in the ANJU schema with the same data as the ANIMALS table owned by MASTER.

    D. A table named MASTER will be created in the ANIMALS schema with the same data as the ANJU table owned by ANIMALS.

4. **User JANKO would like to insert a row into the EMPLOYEE table, which has three columns: EMPID, LASTNAME, and SALARY. The user would like to enter data for EMPID 59694, LASTNAME Harris, but no salary. Which statement would work best?**

    A. insert into EMPLOYEE values (59694,'HARRIS', NULL);

    B. insert into EMPLOYEE values (59694,'HARRIS');

    C. insert into EMPLOYEE (EMPID, LASTNAME, SALARY) values (59694,'HARRIS');

    D. insert into EMPLOYEE (select 59694 from 'HARRIS');

5. **Which components are parts of an entity relationship diagram? (Choose two)**

    A. Referential integrity constraints

    B. Entities

    C. Relationships

    D. Triggers

6. **Which of the following choices is the strongest indicator of a parent/child relationship?**

   A. Two tables in the database are named VOUCHER and VOUCHER_ITEM, respectively.

   B. Two tables in the database are named EMPLOYEE and PRODUCTS, respectively.

   C. Two tables in the database were created on the same day.

   D. Two tables in the database contain none of the same columns.

7. **Which of the following are valid database datatypes in Oracle? (Choose three)**

   A. CHAR

   B. VARCHAR2

   C. BOOLEAN

   D. NUMBER

8. **Omitting the WHERE clause from a DELETE statement has which of the following effects?**

   A. The **delete** statement will fail because there are no records to delete.

   B. The **delete** statement will prompt the user to enter criteria for the deletion.

   C. The **delete** statement will fail because of syntax error.

   D. The **delete** statement will remove all records from the table.

9. **Which line of the following statement will produce an error?**

   A. **create table** GOODS

   B. (GOODNO **number,**

C. GOOD_NAME **varchar2 check**(GOOD_NAME in (**select** NAME FROM AVAIL_GOODS)),

D. constraint PK_GOODS_01

E. primary key (GOODNO));

F. There are no errors in this statement.

10. **The transaction control that prevents more than one user from updating data in a table is called**

A. Locks

B. Commits

C. Rollbacks

D. Savepoints

Answers to Chapter Questions

1. B and D.   Unique constraints and primary keys

Explanation   Every constraint that enforces uniqueness creates an index to assist in the process. The two integrity constraints that enforce uniqueness are unique constraints and primary keys. Refer to the discussion of creating a table with integrity constraints.

2. C.   ALL_IND_COLUMNS

Explanation   This view is the only one listed that provides column positions in an index. Since primary keys create an index, the index created by the primary key will be listed with all the other indexed data. Choice A is incorrect because no view exists in Oracle called PRIMARY_KEYS. Choice B is incorrect because although ALL_CONSTRAINTS lists information about the constraints in a database, it does not contain information about the index created by the primary key. Choice D is incorrect because ALL_TABLES contains no information related to the position of a column in an index.

3. C.   A table named ANIMALS will be created in the ANJU schema with the same data as the ANIMALS table owned by MASTER.

Explanation   This question requires you to look carefully at the **create table** statement in the question, and to know some things about table creation. First, a table is always created in the schema of the user who created it. Second, since the **create table as select** clause was used, choices B and D are both incorrect because they identify the table being created as something other than ANIMALS, among other things. Choice A identifies the schema into which the ANIMALS table will be created as MASTER, which is incorrect for the reasons just stated. Refer to the discussion of creating tables for more information.

4. A.   **insert into** EMPLOYEE **values** (59694,'HARRIS', NULL);

Explanation   This choice is acceptable because the positional criteria for not specifying column order is met by the data in the **values** clause. When you would like to specify that no data be inserted into a particular column, one method of doing so is to **insert** a NULL. Choice B is incorrect because not all columns in the table have values identified. When using positional references to populate column data, there must be values present for every column in the table. Otherwise, the columns that will be populated should be named explicitly. Choice C is incorrect because when a column is named for data **insert** in the **insert into** clause, then a value must definitely be specified in the **values** clause. Choice D is incorrect because using the multiple row **insert** option with a **select** statement is not appropriate in this situation. Refer to the discussion of **insert** statements for more information.

5. B and C.   Entities and Relationships

Explanation   There are only two components to an entity-relationship diagram: entities and relationships. Choices A and D are incorrect because referential integrity constraints and triggers are part of database implementation of a logical data model. Refer to the discussion of an entity-relationship diagram.

6. A.   Two tables in the database are named VOUCHER and VOUCHER_ITEM, respectively.

Explanation   This choice implies the use of a naming convention similar to the one discussed. Although there is no guarantee that these two tables are related, the possibility is strongest with this option. Choice B implies the same naming convention, and since the two tables' names are dissimilar, there is little likelihood that the two tables are related in any way. Choice C is incorrect because the date a table is created has absolutely no bearing on what function the table serves in the database. Choice D is incorrect because two tables can *not* be related if there are no common columns between them. Refer to the discussion of creating tables with integrity constraints, naming conventions, and data modeling.

7. A, B, and D.   CHAR, VARCHAR2, and NUMBER

Explanation   BOOLEAN is the only invalid datatype in this listing. Although BOOLEAN is a valid datatype in PL/SQL, it is not a datatype available on the Oracle database, meaning that you cannot create a column in a table that uses the BOOLEAN datatype. Review the discussion of allowed datatypes in column definition.

8. D.   The **delete** statement will remove all records from the table.

Explanation   There is only one effect produced by leaving off the **where** clause from any statement that allows one—the requested operation is performed on all records in the table.

9. C.   GOOD_NAME **varchar2 check**(GOOD_NAME in (**select** NAME **from** AVAIL_GOODS)),

Explanation   A check constraint cannot contain a reference to another table, nor can it reference a virtual column such as ROWID or SYSDATE.

10. A.   Locks

Explanation   Locks are the mechanisms that prevent more than one user at a time from making changes to the database. All other options refer to the commands that are issued to mark the beginning, middle, and end of a transaction. Review the discussion of transaction controls.

CHAPTER
4

Creating Other Database Objects in Oracle

n this chapter, you will understand and demonstrate knowledge in the following areas:

- Altering tables and constraints
- Creating sequences
- Creating views
- Creating indexes
- Controlling user access

At this point, you should know how to **select** data from a database, model a business process, design a set of database tables from that process, and populate those tables with data. These functions represent the cornerstone of functionality that Oracle can provide in an organization. However, the design of a database does not stop there. There are several features in the Oracle architecture that allows the user to give richer, deeper meaning to the databases created in Oracle. These features can make data "transparent" to some users but not to others, speed access to data, or generate primary keys for database tables automatically. These features are collectively known as the advanced database features of the Oracle database. This chapter covers material in several different areas tested in the OCP Exam 1. The material in this chapter comprises 17 percent of the material covered on the exam.

Table and Constraint Modifications

In this section, you will cover the following topics related to altering tables and constraints:

- Adding and modifying columns
- Modifying integrity constraints
- Enabling or disabling constraints
- Dropping tables
- Truncating tables

- Changing names of objects

- Dictionary comments on objects

Once a table is created, any of several things can happen to make the needs of the database change such that the table must be changed. The database developer will need to understand how to implement changes on the database in an effective and *nondisruptive* manner. Consider the implications of this statement. For example, there are two ways to cure an ingrown toenail. One is to go to a podiatrist and have the toenail removed. The other is to chop off the toe. Although both approaches work, the second one produces side effects that most people can safely do without. The same concept applies to database changes. The developer can do one of two things when a request to add some columns to a table comes in. One is to add the columns, and the other is to re-create the entire table from scratch. Obviously, there is a great deal of value in knowing the right way to perform the first approach.

Adding and Modifying Columns

Columns can be added and modified in the Oracle database with ease using the **alter table** statement and its many options for changing the number of columns in the database. When adding columns, a column added with a NOT NULL constraint must have data populated for that column in all rows before the NOT NULL constraint is enabled, and only one column of the LONG datatype can appear in a table in Oracle. The following code block is an example of using the **alter table** statement:

```
ALTER TABLE products
ADD (color VARCHAR2(10));
```

If the developer or the DBA needs to add a column that will have a NOT NULL constraint on it, then several things need to happen. The column should first be created without the constraint, then the column should have a value for all rows populated. After all column values are NOT NULL, the NOT NULL constraint can be applied to it. If the user tries to add a column with a NOT NULL constraint on it, the developer will encounter an error stating that the table must be empty.

Only one column in the table may be of type LONG within a table. That restriction includes the LONG RAW datatype. However, many columns of datatype BLOB, CLOB, NCLOB, and BFILE can appear in one table as of Oracle8. It is sometimes useful to emulate Oracle8 in Oracle7 databases by having a special table that contains the LONG column and a foreign key to the table that would have contained the column in order to reduce the amount of data migration and row chaining on the database.

TIP
Row chaining and row migration is when the Oracle RDBMS has to move row data around or break it up and save it in pieces inside the files on disk that comprise an Oracle database. This activity is a concern to DBAs because it hurts database performance.

Another important facet about table columns is the configuration of the datatype that is permitted for storage in the column. On a table called PRODUCTS, there is a column called SERIAL# of type VARCHAR2(10). The retailer has just begun to carry a new line of products whose serial number is substantially longer than the serial numbers of other products the store carries. A developer is called in to determine if the longer serial number will present a problem to the database. As it turns out, the average serial number for this new line of products is 23 characters long. In order to resolve the issue, you can issue a statement that will make the column length longer.

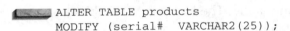

```
ALTER TABLE products
MODIFY (serial#  VARCHAR2(25));
```

Several conditions apply to modifying the datatypes of existing columns or to adding columns to a table in the database. The general rule of thumb is that increases are generally OK, while decreases are usually a little trickier. Some examples of increases that are generally acceptable are listed as follows:

- Increases to the size of a VARCHAR2 or CHAR column

- Increases in size of a NUMBER column

- Increasing the number of columns in the table

Decreasing the size of various aspects of the table, including some of the column datatypes or the actual number of columns in the table, requires special steps to accomplish. Usually, the effort involves making sure that the relevant column (or columns) has all NULL values in it before executing the change. In order to execute these types of operations on columns or tables that contain data, the developer must find or create some sort of temporary storage place for the data in the column. One acceptable method is creating a table using the **create table as select** statement where the **select** statement used draws data from the primary key and the column(s) in question that will be altered. Another method is spooling the data in a table to a flat file and reloading later using SQL*Loader, a utility provided with Oracle for loading data into tables from flat files. The following list details the allowable operations that decrease various aspects of the database:

- Reducing the size of a NUMBER column (empty column for all rows only)

- Reducing the length of a VARCHAR2 or CHAR column (empty column for all rows only)

- Changing the datatype of a column (empty column for all rows only)

Exercises

1. What statement is used to change the definition of a table?

2. What process is used to change a NULLable column to one with a NOT NULL constraint?

3. What are some of the rules and guidelines for changing column definitions?

Modifying Integrity Constraints

There are several changes that can be made to constraints. These changes include altering the constraint and disabling, enabling, or removing the constraint from the column or table of the database. These processes allow the developer to create, modify, or remove the business rules that constrain data. The first activity that a developer may need to do related to supporting constraints on a database is to add constraints to a database. This process can be easy or difficult, depending on the circumstances. If a constraint cannot be created with the database, it can be added to the database before data is populated into the database with the most ease of any scenario in which a constraint must be added to the database.

```
ALTER TABLE products
MODIFY (color  NOT NULL);

ALTER TABLE products
ADD (CONSTRAINT pk_products _01 PRIMARY KEY (product#));

ALTER TABLE products
ADD (CONSTRAINT fk_products _02 FOREIGN KEY (color)
REFERENCES (AVAIL_COLORS.color));

ALTER TABLE products
ADD (UNIQUE (serial#));

ALTER TABLE products
ADD(size CHECK (size in 'P','S','M','L','XL','XXL','XXXL'));
```

Notice that in the first statement in the list of examples the **modify** clause is used to add a NOT NULL constraint to the column, while the **add** clause is used to add all other types of integrity constraints. The column must already exist in the database table. No constraint can be created for a column that does not exist in the table. Some of the restrictions on creating constraints are listed here:

- **Primary keys** Columns cannot be NULL and must have all unique values.

- **Foreign keys** Referenced columns in other tables must contain values corresponding to all values in the referring columns or the referring columns values must be NULL.

- **Unique constraints** Columns must contain all unique values or NULL.

■ **Check constraints** The new constraint will only be applied to data added or modified after the constraint is created.

■ **NOT NULL** Columns cannot be NULL.

If any of the conditions for the constraints just listed are not met for the respective constraint to which the rule applies, then creation of the constraint *will fail.*

Exercises

1. What are some of the ways integrity constraints can be changed on a table?

2. What are some rules that must be adhered to for modification of each type of constraint?

Enabling or Disabling Constraints

What happens to a constraint if the creation of the constraint fails? This question is answered by examining the concept of enabling or disabling a constraint. Think of a constraint as a switch. When the switch is enabled, the constraint will do its job in enforcing business rules on the data entering the table. If the switch is disabled, the rules defined for the constraint are not enforced, rendering the constraint as ineffective as if it had been removed. Examine the process of enabling a disabled constraint. This process may be executed after you have taken steps to correct the reason the integrity constraint failed during creation in the first place. When the problem has been corrected or when the load completes, you may want to take steps to put the constraints back in order again.

```
ALTER TABLE products
ENABLE CONSTRAINT pk_products_01;

ALTER TABLE products
ENABLE CONSTRAINT uk_products_03;
```

Note that in this situation, only constraints that have been defined and are currently disabled can be enabled by this code. A constraint that has not been created cannot be enabled. As just discussed, a constraint that fails on creation will automatically be disabled. There are situations where you may want to disable a constraint for some general purpose. *Be careful when using this approach, however!* If data is loaded into a table that violates the integrity constraint while the constraint was disabled, your attempt to enable the constraint later with the **alter table** *TABLE_NAME* **enable constraint exceptions into** EXCEPTIONS statement will fail. The following error messages may be seen when this situation arises:

```
/* Values in the column do not satisfy the constraint*/
ORA-02296: cannot enable constraint table_name.constraint_name - found non-complying values

/* Constraint enabling failed because there are orphan records in a foreign key */
ORA-02298: cannot enable constraint table_name.constraint_name - parent keys not found

/* Constraint enabling failed because values in the column are not unique. */
ORA-02299: cannot enable constraint table_name.constraint_name - duplicate keys found
```

Precautions should be taken to ensure that data loaded into a table that has disabled constraints on it does not violate the constraint rules so that the enabling of the constraint later will be a smooth process. The following code block demonstrates some sample statements for your understanding:

```
ALTER TABLE products
DISABLE PRIMARY KEY;

ALTER TABLE products
DISABLE UNIQUE (serial#);
```

Furthermore, you may have a problem when you attempt to disable a primary key when foreign keys exist that depend on that primary key. The following error will ensue in this situation:

```
ORA-02297: Cannot disable constraint table_name.constraint_name - dependencies exist
```

If you try to drop a primary key when there are dependent foreign keys depending on it, the **cascade** option is required as part of the **alter table disable** *constraint*, as shown in the following code block:

```
ALTER TABLE products
DISABLE PRIMARY KEY CASCADE;
```

TIP
Disabling a constraint leaves the table vulnerable to inappropriate data being entered into the table. Care should be taken to ensure that the data loaded during the period the constraint is disabled will not interfere with your ability to enable the constraint later.

Usually, there is little about a constraint that will interfere with your ability to remove it, so long as the person attempting to do so is either the owner of the table or granted the appropriate privilege to do so. When a constraint is dropped, any associated index with that constraint (if there is one) is also dropped.

```
ALTER TABLE products
DROP CONSTRAINT uk_products_01;

ALTER TABLE products
DROP PRIMARY KEY CASCADE;
```

TIP
*Several anomalies can be found when adding, enabling, disabling, or dropping NOT NULL constraints. Generally, the **alter table modify** clause must be used in all situations where the NOT NULL constraints on a table must be altered.*

Exercises

I. How do you enable a disabled constraint?

2. What are some restrictions on enabling constraints?

Dropping Tables

Sometimes, the "cut off your toe" approach to database alteration is required to make sweeping changes to a table in the database. All requirements to executing that approach have been discussed so far except one—eliminating the offending table. In order to delete a table from the database, the **drop table** command must be executed.

```
DROP TABLE products;
```

However, dropping tables may not always be that easy. Recall from the earlier lesson that when you disable constraints like primary keys that have foreign-key constraints in other tables depending on their existence, you may have some errors. The same thing happens when you try to drop the table that has a primary key referenced by enabled foreign keys in another table. If you try to drop a table that has other tables' foreign keys referring to it, the following error will ensue:

```
ORA-02266: unique/primary keys in table referenced by enabled foreign keys
```

When there are foreign-key constraints on other tables that reference the table to be dropped, then you can use **cascade constraints**. The constraints in other tables that refer to the table being dropped are also dropped with **cascade constraints**. There are usually some associated objects that exist in a database along with the table. These objects may include the index that is created by the primary key or the unique constraint that is associated with columns in the table. If the table is dropped, Oracle automatically drops any index associated with the table as well.

```
DROP TABLE products
CASCADE CONSTRAINTS;
```

Alternately, you can disable or drop the foreign key in the other table first using syntax explained in the previous lesson, and then issue the **drop table** statement without the **cascade constraints** option. However, with this method you run the risk that many other tables having foreign keys that relate back to the primary key in the table you want to drop will each error out, one at a time, until you disable or drop every foreign-key constraint referring to the table. If there are several, your **drop table** activity may get extremely frustrating.

Exercises

1. How is a table dropped?

2. What special clause must be used when dropping a table when other tables have foreign-key constraints against it?

3. What happens to associated objects like indexes when a table is dropped?

Truncating Tables

There is a special option available in Oracle that allows certain users to delete information from a table quickly. Remember, in the last chapter the **delete** statement was discussed. One limitation of the **delete** statement is the fact that it uses the transaction-processing controls that were also covered in the last chapter. Sometimes, in large tables or when the DBA or privileged developer is sure he or she wants to remove the data in a large table, the **delete** option is an inefficient one for accomplishing the job.

As an alternative, the DBA or developer may use the **truncate** statement. The **truncate** statement is a part of the data definition language of Oracle, like the **create table** statement, unlike the **delete** statement, which is part of the DML. Truncating a table removes all row data from a table quickly while leaving the definition of the table intact, including the definition of constraints and indexes on the table. The **truncate** statement is a high-speed data deletion that bypasses the transaction controls available in Oracle for recoverability in data changes. Truncating a table is almost always faster than executing the **delete** statement without a **where** clause, but once complete, the data cannot be recovered without having a backed up copy of the data.

 `TRUNCATE TABLE products;`

TIP
Truncating tables affects a characteristic about them that Oracle calls the highwatermark. This characteristic is a value Oracle uses to keep track of the largest size the table has ever grown to. In the event you truncate the table, Oracle resets the highwatermark to zero.

Exercises

1. What are two options for deleting data from a table?

2. Is truncating a table part of DML or DDL? Explain.

3. What is a highwatermark, and how does it work?

Changing Names of Objects

Changing object names in Oracle is accomplished using the **rename** command. This command allows you to change the name of one table to another by taking data from one table and automatically moving it to another that is called something else. The following code block demonstrates use of this command:

```
RENAME products TO objects;
```

The effect of renaming a table can be duplicated through the use of synonyms. A synonym gives users an alternate name with which they can refer to the existing table. Synonyms in Oracle are used to offer an alternate name to the table without altering the details of the table's definition. Synonyms can be public or private. If the synonym is private, it will only be accessed by the user who owns it. If a synonym is public, it will be accessible by any user in the database. The following code block demonstrates the statements used to create private and public synonyms, respectively:

```
CREATE SYNONYM objects FOR products;
CREATE PUBLIC SYNONYM objects FOR products;
```

Exercises

1. How is a database object name changed? What are some of the effects of renaming a table?

2. What is another way to duplicate the effect of renaming a table?

Viewing Dictionary Comments on Objects

The Oracle data dictionary carries many different items about the table, including the description of the columns in the table. This is provided by the data dictionary with use of the **describe** command. More object information that can be found in the data dictionary is the use of object commenting. Comments are useful for recording data modeling information or any other information about the database objects directly within the data dictionary. To add a comment to a table or column, use the **comment on** statement, as demonstrated in the following code block. To view these comments, query the ALL_TAB_COMMENTS for tables, or ALL_COL_COMMENTS for columns on tables.

```
COMMENT ON TABLE product IS 'your_comment';
COMMENT ON COLUMN product.serial# IS 'your_comment';
```

Exercises

1. How can table remarks be entered and where are they stored?

2. How can you reference comments on a database object?

Sequences

In this section, you will cover the following topics related to creating sequences:

- Role of sequences
- Creating sequences
- Using sequences
- Modifying the sequence definition
- Removing sequences

In database development, sometimes it becomes necessary to populate a column with a series of integers on an ongoing basis. These integers may be used as numbers to identify the records being entered as unique. For example, a doctor's office may have a client tracking system that assigns each new patient a unique integer ID to identify their records. There are several ways to produce this integer ID through programmatic means, but the most effective means to do it in Oracle is through sequences.

Role of Sequences

A sequence is a special database object that generates integers according to specified rules at the time the sequence was created. Sequences have many purposes in database systems, the most common of which is to generate primary keys automatically. This task is common in situations where the primary key is not important to use for accessing data to store in a table. The common use of sequences to create primary keys has some drawbacks, though. With the use of sequences for this purpose, the primary key itself and the index it creates are rendered somewhat meaningless. But, if you don't care that you're creating a nonsense key, it is perfectly alright to do so.

Sequences operate on the following principle. Users **select** data from them using two special keywords to denote virtual columns or *pseudocolumns* in the database. The first pseudocolumn is CURRVAL. This column can be used to see what the current value generated by the sequence is. The second pseudocolumn is NEXTVAL. This column is the next value that the sequence will generate according to the rules developed for it. Selecting NEXTVAL on the sequence effectively eliminates whatever value is stored in CURRVAL. Data may only be drawn from a sequence, never placed into it. These pseudocolumns are available for **select** access, but users can incorporate a call on the sequence's CURRVAL or NEXTVAL to use the value in either of the two columns for **insert** or **update** on a row of another table.

Some restrictions are placed on the types of statements that can draw on CURRVAL and NEXTVAL of sequences as well. Any **update** or **insert** statement can make use of the data in a sequence. However, it generally is not advisable to set up an **insert** or **update** statement to do so in a trigger, as this has a tendency to cause the SQL*Plus session that fires the trigger to end abnormally with the **ORA-03113** error, possibly arising from self-referencing integrity constraint violations. In addition, subqueries of **select** statements (including those with **having**), views, **select** statements using set operations such as **union** or **minus**, or any **select** statement that requires a sort to be performed are not able to contain reference to a sequence.

Exercises

1. What is a sequence? What are some ways a sequence can be used?
2. What are CURRVAL and NEXTVAL? What happens to CURRVAL when NEXTVAL is selected?

Creating Sequences

Many rules are available on sequences that allow the developer to specify how the sequence generates integers. These rules are useful for the definition of sequences that produce integers in special order, or with increments in a certain way. There is even a feature related to sequences that allows the developer to improve performance on a sequence. The explanation of each clause in the statement, along with some options for configuring that clause, appear in the following list:

- **start with *n*** Allows the creator of the sequence the ability to identify the first value generated by the sequence. Once created, the sequence will generate the value specified by **start with** the first time the sequence's NEXTVAL virtual column is referenced.

- **increment by *n*** Defines the number by which to increment the sequence every time the NEXTVAL virtual column is referenced. Default for this clause is 1 if not explicitly specified.

- **minvalue *n*** Defines the minimum value that can be produced by the sequence. If no minimum value is desired or not explicitly specified, the default **nominvalue** keyword can or will be used.

- **maxvalue *n*** Defines the maximum value that can be produced by the sequence. If no maximum value is desired or not explicitly specified, the **nomaxvalue** keyword can or will be used.

- **cycle** Allows the sequence to recycle values produced when the **maxvalue** or **minvalue** is reached. If recycling is not desired or not explicitly specified, the **nocycle** keyword can or will be used.

■ **cache *n*** Allows the sequence to cache a specified number of values to improve performance. If caching is not desired or not explicitly specified, the **nocache** keyword can or will be used.

■ **order** Allows the sequence to assign values in the same order requests are received by the sequence. If **order** is not desired or not explicitly specified, the **noorder** keyword can or will be used.

Consider now some various examples for defining sequences. The integers that can be specified for sequences as they are created can be negative as well as positive. Consider the following example of a sequence that generates decreasing numbers into the negatives. The **start with** integer in this example is positive, but the **increment by** integer is negative, which effectively tells the sequence to decrement instead of incrementing. When zero is reached, the sequence will start again from the top. This sequence can be useful in countdowns for programs that require a countdown before an event will occur.

```
CREATE SEQUENCE countdown_20
START WITH 20
INCREMENT BY 1
NOMAXVALUE
CYCLE
ORDER;
```

The next code block illustrates a sequence that generates numbers between zero and 1,000 without repeating a sequence value during the life of the sequence:

```
CREATE SEQUENCE some_num
MINVALUE 0
MAXVALUE 1000
NOCYCLE;
```

Exercises

1. What statement is used for creating a sequence?

2. What are the options used for sequence creation?

Using Sequences

Once the sequence is created, it is referenced using the CURRVAL and NEXTVAL pseudocolumns. This reference may occur in a few different ways. Sometimes the users of the database may want to view the current value of the sequence by means of a **select** statement. The next value generated by the sequence can be generated with a **select** statement as well. Notice the reappearance of the DUAL table. Since sequences themselves are not tables—only objects that generate integers via the use of virtual columns—the DUAL table acts as the "virtual" table to pull virtual column data from. As stated earlier, values cannot be placed into the sequence, only selected from the sequence. Once the NEXTVAL column is referenced, the value in CURRVAL becomes the value in NEXTVAL, and the prior value in CURRVAL is lost.

TIP

CURRVAL has no meaning or is undefined until NEXTVAL is referenced for the first time after sequence creation.

```
SELECT some_num.currval CURRENT,
some_num.nextval NEXT,
some_num.currval CURRENT
FROM dual;

CURRENT  NEXT   CURRENT
-------  ----   -------
      1     2         2
```

Generally, however, users do not use **select** statements to draw data from sequences. Instead, that functionality can be incorporated directly into data changes made by **insert** or **update** statements. The statements here illustrate usage of sequences directly in changes made to tables:

```
INSERT INTO expense(expense_no, empid, amt, submit_date)
VALUES(some_nums.nextval, 59495, 456.34, '21-NOV-99');

UPDATE product
SET product_num = some_num.currval
WHERE serial_num = 34938583945;
```

This direct usage of sequences in **insert** and **update** statements is the most common use for sequences in a database. In the situation where the sequence generates a primary key for all new rows entering the database table, the sequence would likely be referenced directly from the **insert** statement. Note, however, that this approach sometimes fails when the sequence is referenced by triggers. Therefore, the best method to use when referencing sequences is within the user interface or within stored procedures.

Exercises

1. Identify a way to refer to a sequence with the **select** statement. Why is use of the DUAL table important in this method?

2. Identify a way to refer to a sequence with the **update** and **insert** statements.

Modifying a Sequence Definition

Like tables, there may come a time when the sequence of a database will need its rules altered in some way. For example, in the employee expense application, you may want to start the box numbering at some different number in order to start a new fiscal year. For another example, a sequence may have generated several primary keys for the rows in a database. When the sequence is re-created, you may need to set the first value produced by the sequence in order to avoid primary-key constraint violations. Any parameter of a sequence can be modified by issuing the **alter sequence** statement.

```
ALTER SEQUENCE countdown_20
INCREMENT BY 4;
```

The effect is immediate—the statement will change the COUNTDOWN_20 to decrement each NEXTVAL by 4. Any parameter of a sequence that is not specified by the **alter sequence** statement will remain unchanged. The COUNTDOWN_20 sequence will now be changed to run through one countdown from 20 to zero only. After the sequence hits zero, no further references to COUNTDOWN_ 20.NEXTVAL will be allowed.

```
ALTER SEQUENCE countdown_20
NOCYCLE;
```

The final example of usage for the **alter sequence** statement involves the SOME_NUM sequence created earlier. The next code block is designed to change the range of values that can be generated by the sequence from 1,000 to 10,000:

```
ALTER SEQUENCE some_nums
MAXVALUE 10000;
```

Modification of sequences is a relatively simple process. However, the main concern related to changing sequences is monitoring the effect on tables or other processes that use the values generated by the sequence. For example, resetting the value returned by the sequence from 1,150 back to zero is not a problem to execute. Once performed, there could be repercussions if the sequence was used to generate primary keys for a table, of which several values between zero and 1,150 were already generated. When the sequence begins generating values for **insert** statements that depend on the sequence for primary keys, there will be primary-key constraint violations on the table inserts. Although these problems don't show up when the sequence is altered, the only way to solve the problem (other than deleting the records already existing in the table) is to alter the sequence again.

Exercises

1. What statement is used to modify a sequence definition?

2. When do changes to a sequence take effect?

Removing Sequences

Removing a sequence may be required when the sequence is no longer needed. In this case, the DBA or owner of the sequence can issue the **drop sequence** statement. Dropping the sequence renders its virtual columns CURRVAL and NEXTVAL unusable. However, if the sequence was being used to generate primary-key values, the values generated by the sequence will continue to exist in the database. There is no cascading effect on the values generated by a sequence when the sequence is removed.

```
DROP SEQUENCE some_num;
```

Exercises

1. How are sequences dropped?

2. What are the effects of dropping a sequence?

Views

In this section, you will cover the following topics related to creating views:

■ Data dictionary views

■ Creating simple and complex views

■ Creating views that enforce constraints

■ Modifying views

■ Removing views

It has been said that eyes are the windows to the soul. That statement may or may not be true. What is definitely true is that eyes can be used to view the data in a table. In order to make sure the right eyes see the right things, however, some special "windows" on the data in a table can be created. These special windows are called *views*. A view can be thought of as a virtual table. In reality, a view is nothing more than the results of a **select** statement stored in a memory structure that resembles a table. To the user utilizing the view, manipulating the data from the view seems identical to manipulating the data from a table. In some cases, it is even possible for the user to **insert** data into a view as though the view *was* a table. The relationship between tables and views is illustrated in Figure 4-1.

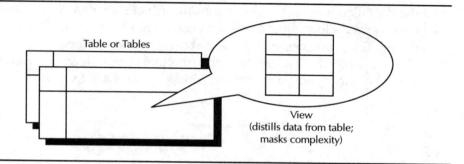

FIGURE 4-1. *Tables and views*

Data Dictionary Views

The use of views in the data dictionary prevents you from referring to the tables of the data dictionary directly. This additional safeguard is important for two reasons. First, it underscores the sensitivity of the tables that store dictionary data. If something happens to the tables that store dictionary data that should cause either the data to be lost or the table to be removed, the effects could seriously damage the Oracle database, possibly rendering it completely unusable. Second, the dictionary views distill the information in the data dictionary into something highly understandable and useful. Those views divide information about the database into neat categories based on viewing scope and objects referred to.

Dictionary views are useful to draw data from the data dictionary. Some of the following examples illustrate selection of data from the data dictionary views that have already been identified in the previous chapter as ones containing information about the objects covered in this chapter. Review the following code blocks:

```
SELECT * FROM all_sequences;
SELECT * FROM dba_objects;
SELECT * FROM user_tables;
```

Other dictionary views provide information about the views themselves. Recall that a view is simply the resultant dataset from a **select** statement, and that the data dictionary actually contains the **select** statement that creates the view. As shown below, view definitions can be quite complex. There are several functions specified in the **select** statement that produce ALL_TABLES. Don't worry if you don't understand the structure of this view, you won't need to know what the meanings of these columns are for OCP Exam 1.

```
SET LONG 9999;
SELECT text FROM all_views WHERE view_name = 'ALL_TABLES';

TEXT
----------------------------------------
select u.name, o.name, ts.name, co.name,
t.pctfree$, t.pctused$,
t.initrans, t.maxtrans,
s.iniexts * ts.blocksize, s.extsize * ts.blocksize,
s.minexts, s.maxexts, s.extpct,
decode(s.lists, 0, 1, s.lists), decode(s.groups, 0, 1, s.groups),
decode(bitand(t.modified,1), 0, 'Y', 1, 'N', '?'),
t.rowcnt, t.blkcnt, t.empcnt, t.avgspc, t.chncnt, t.avgrln,
lpad(decode(t.spare1, 0, '1', 1, 'DEFAULT', to_char(t.spare1)), 10),
lpad(decode(mod(t.spare2, 65536), 0, '1', 1, 'DEFAULT',
to_char(mod(t.spare2, 65536))), 10),
lpad(decode(floor(t.spare2 / 65536), 0, 'N', 1, 'Y', '?'), 5),
decode(bitand(t.modified, 6), 0, 'ENABLED', 'DISABLED')
from sys.user$ u, sys.ts$ ts, sys.seg$ s, sys.obj$ co, sys.tab$ t, sys.obj$ o
where o.owner# = u.user#
and o.obj# = t.obj#
and t.clu# = co.obj# (+)
and t.ts# = ts.ts#
and t.file# = s.file# (+)
and t.block# = s.block# (+)
and (o.owner# = userenv('SCHEMAID')
or o.obj# in
(select oa.obj#
from sys.objauth$ oa
where grantee# in ( select kzsrorol from x$kzsro))
or /* user has system privileges */
exists (select null from v$enabledprivs
where priv_number in (-45 /* LOCK ANY TABLE */,
-47 /* SELECT ANY TABLE */,
-48 /* INSERT ANY TABLE */,
-49 /* UPDATE ANY TABLE */,
-50 /* DELETE ANY TABLE */)))
```

Exercises

1. Why are views used by Oracle in the data dictionary?

2. What are two reasons for using views, both in the data dictionary and elsewhere?

Creating Simple and Complex Views

One example statement for creating a view has already been identified—the one for creating the ALL_VIEWS dictionary view in the Oracle database. Again, though, don't worry about understanding the minutiae of creating every Oracle data dictionary view. The most important things to remember about views can be summarized by the following bullets:

- Views add extra security to data, such as the definition of a view on the EMP_SALARY table that only shows salary information for the user performing the **select** against the view.

- Views hide data complexity, as in the situation of complex views (covered shortly).

- Views can hide real column names that may be hard to understand behind easier names.

To delve further into the requirements for creating views, the following discussion is offered. Creating a view is accomplished by using the **create view** statement. Once created, views are owned by the user who created them. They cannot be reassigned by the owner unless the owner has the **create any view** system privilege. More about privileges will be covered in a later section of this chapter.

Creating Simple Views

There are different types of views that can be created in Oracle. The first type of view is a *simple view*. This type of view is created from the data in one table. Within the simple view, all single-row operations are permitted. In addition, data can be placed in specific order by the **order by** clause of the **select** statement. Options not allowed for a simple view include reference to more than one table via a table join, no grouping or set operations, no **group by** clauses, no hierarchical queries (those queries containing a **connect by** clause), and no queries with the **distinct** keyword. The following code block demonstrates creation of a simple view:

```
CREATE VIEW employee_view
AS (SELECT empid, lastname, firstname, salary
FROM employee
WHERE empid = 59495);
```

Users of a simple view can **insert** data in the underlying table of the view if the creator of the view allows them to do so. A few restrictions apply. First, the data that the user attempts to **insert** into an underlying table via the view must be data that the user would be able to **select** via the view if the data existed in the table already. However, updating or inserting data on rows or columns on a table that the view itself would not allow the user to see is only permitted if the **with check option** is not used. The following statement demonstrates data change via a view:

```
UPDATE employee_view
SET salary = 99000
WHERE empid = 59495;
```

The restrictions on inserting or updating data to an underlying table through a simple view are listed here:

- The user may not **insert**, **delete**, or **update** data on the table underlying the simple view if the view itself is not able to **select** that data for the user if the **with check option** is used.

- The user may not **insert**, **delete**, or **update** data on the table underlying the simple view if the **select** statement creating the view contains **group by** or **order by,** or a single-row operation.

- No data may be inserted to simple views that contain references to any virtual column such as ROWID, CURRVAL, NEXTVAL, and ROWNUM.

- No data may be inserted into simple views that are created with the **read only** option.

Users will have problems inserting data into views if the underlying table has NOT NULL constraints on it. This can be eliminated with use of a default value for the NOT NULL column in the table definition.

Creating Complex Views

Complex views have some major differences from simple views. Complex views draw data from more than one table in addition to possibly containing single-row operations and/or references to virtual columns. Complex views can contain **group by** clauses. However, no data may be **insert**ed, **update**d, or **delete**d from underlying tables for complex views under most circumstances. Complex views are excellent for hiding complicated data models and/or conversion operations behind a simple name for the user to reference the view. The complex view allows data to be joined from multiple tables in addition to all the features of simple views, such as using **order by** in the **select** statement that creates the view.

```
CREATE VIEW employee_view
AS (SELECT e.empid empid, e.lastname lastname, e.firstname firstname,
e.salary salary, a.address, a.city, a.state, a.zipcode
FROM employee e, employee_address a
WHERE e.empid = a.empid);
```

Complex views cannot allow data to be changed on the underlying table because of the join that is performed in order to obtain the result set displayed in the view. As such, it is not necessary for the creator of the view to specify the **read only** option on the view, as the view already is assumed to be read only.

Exercises

1. What is a simple view? How does it differ from a complex view?

2. Which view allows the user to **insert** data into the view's underlying table? Explain.

Creating Views that Enforce Constraints

Tables that underlie views often have constraints that limit the data that can be added to a table. Views have the same limitations placed on data that may enter the table. In addition, the view can define special constraints for data entry. The option used to configure view constraints is the **with check option**. These special constraints force the view to review the data changes made to see if the data being changed is data the view can **select**. If the data being changed will not be selected by the view, then the view will not let the user make the data change. The following view will now guarantee that any user who tries to **insert** data into EMPLOYEE_VIEW for an employee other than EMPID# 59495 will not be able to do so:

```
CREATE VIEW employee_view
AS (SELECT empid, lastname, firstname, salary
FROM employee
WHERE empid = 59495)
WITH CHECK OPTION;
```

Exercises

1. How can constraints be created and enforced on views?

2. On what principle does a view constraint operate?

Modifying Views

There may be situations where the creator of a view may need to change the view. However, views don't follow the syntax conventions of other database objects. While there is an **alter view** statement in the Oracle SQL language, used to recompile or revalidate all references in the view *as it exists already*, the statement used to alter the definition of a view is the **create or replace view** statement. When a **create or replace view** statement is issued, Oracle will disregard the error that arises when it encounters the view that already exists with that name, overwriting the definition for the old view with the definition for the new. The following code block illustrates the use of the **create or replace view** statement:

```
CREATE OR REPLACE VIEW employee_view
AS (SELECT empid, lastname, firstname, salary
FROM employee
WHERE empid = user)
WITH CHECK OPTION;
```

TIP
*A view becomes invalid due to the redefinition
or deletion of a table that underlies the view.
To fix this, the creator of the view must either
re-create the underlying table and issue the
alter view command, or modify the view with
the **create or replace view** statement.*

The invalidation of a view as a result of the removal of the underlying
table illustrates an example of object dependency in the Oracle database.
That is to say, certain objects in Oracle depend on others in order to work.
Some examples of object dependency that have been presented so far are
indexes depending on the existence of the corresponding tables and views
depending on the existence of underlying tables.

Exercises

1. What statement is used to recompile or revalidate an existing view
definition?

2. What statement is used to alter the definition of a view?

3. What is object dependency?

Removing Views

Like other database objects, there may come a time when the view creator
needs to remove the view. The command for executing this function is the
drop view statement. There are no cascading scenarios that the person
dropping a view must be aware of. The following code block illustrates
the use of **drop view** for deleting views from the database:

```
DROP VIEW employee_view;
```

Exercise

How are views dropped?

Indexes

In this section, you will cover the following topics related to creating indexes:

- Manual and automatic indexes
- Uses for indexes
- Index structure and operation
- Creating indexes
- Removing indexes
- Guidelines for creating indexes

Indexes are synonymous with performance on the Oracle database. Especially on large tables, indexes are the difference between an application that drags its heels and an application that runs with efficiency. However, there are many performance considerations that must be weighed before making the decision to create an index. This discussion focuses on introducing the usage of indexes on the database. Some usage of indexes has already been presented with the discussion of constraints. However, the indexes that are created along with constraints are only the beginning. In Oracle7, indexes can be created on any column in a table except for columns of the LONG datatype. However, performance is not improved simply by throwing a few indexes on the table and forgetting about it. The following section will discuss the usage of indexes.

Manual and Automatic Indexes

So far, the indexes that have been presented have been ones that are created automatically via the primary-key or unique constraints on tables. Those indexes are identified in the data dictionary in the DBA_INDEXES view. Their name corresponds to the name of the primary-key or unique constraint that can be given if the creator of the table chooses to name indexes. Alternatively, if the creator of the table chooses to use unnamed constraints, then the name given to the constraint and the index will be something akin to SYS_C*XXXXX*, where *XXXXX* is an integer. However, there are many more indexes that can exist on a database. These indexes are the manual indexes that are created when the table owner or the developer issues the **create index** command to bring indexes into existence. Once created, there is little to distinguish an

index that was created automatically by Oracle from an index that was
created manually.

The most commonly used way to distinguish automatic from manual
indexes is through naming conventions. Take, for example, the table
EMPLOYEE. The primary-key constraint on this table might be named
EMPLOYEE_PKEY_01, while an index created on some other column in the
table might be called EMPLOYEE_INDX_01. In this fashion, it is easier for
the DBA or creator of the database objects to distinguish which objects are
which when selecting dictionary data.

Another way for the developer to distinguish manually created indexes
from automatically created ones is by looking at the actual columns in the
index. The information about the columns in an index can be found in the
ALL_CONS_COLUMNS data dictionary view. The columns in an index can
give some indication as to whether the index was created automatically to
someone who is familiar with the design of the database tables. Finding
indexes automatically created for columns that have unique constraints can
be trickier. It may require an in-depth knowledge of the application or an
additional call to the ALL_CONSTRAINTS table to verify the name of the
constraint generated automatically by Oracle, if not named explicitly by
the creator of the table.

Exercises

1. What are some differences between manual and automatic indexes?

2. How can you distinguish between indexes created manually and
   those created automatically?

Uses for Indexes

Indexes have multiple uses on the Oracle database. Indexes can be used
to ensure uniqueness on a database. Indexes also boost performance on
searching for records in a table. This improvement in performance is gained
when the search criteria for data in a table includes a reference to the indexed
column or columns. So far, all uses for indexes discussed involved unique
indexes, where all the values in the column indexed are unique. However,
data in this form is not required for creating an index of the table. Although
the best performance improvement can be seen when a column containing

all unique values has an index created on it, similar performance improvements can be made on columns containing some duplicate values or NULLS. However, there are some guidelines to ensure that the traditional index produces the performance improvements desired. The guidelines for evaluating performance improvements given by traditional indexes and whether it is worth the storage trade-off to create the index will be presented later in this discussion. Up to 16 columns in a table can be included in a single index on that table.

Exercises

1. Identify two reasons for using indexes.

2. Must all the data in an index be unique? Explain.

Index Structure and Operation

When data in a column is indexed, a special structure is created that allows Oracle to search for values in that column quickly. This discussion will highlight the features of the index structure, explaining why it works and what works best with it. This discussion covers traditional indexes and bitmap options that are available in Oracle. The traditional index in the Oracle database is based on the principle governing a highly advanced algorithm for sorting data called a *B-tree*. A B-tree contains data placed in layered, branching order, from top to bottom, resembling an upside-down tree. Consider the following, slightly simplified explanation of how a traditional index works in Oracle, based on an object known in computing as a binary search tree. The midpoint of the entire list is placed at the top of the "tree" and called the "root node." The midpoints of each half of the remaining two lists are placed at the next level, and so on, as illustrated in Figure 4-2.

It has been proven by computer scientists that this mechanism for searching data can produce a match for any given value from searching a list containing one million values in a *maximum* of 20 tries. By using a "divide and conquer" method for structuring and searching for data, the values of a column are only a few hops on the tree away, rather than several thousand sequential reads through the list away. However, traditional indexes work best

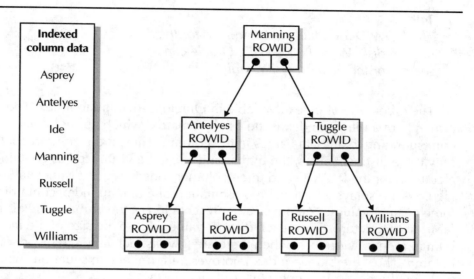

FIGURE 4-2.   *A B-tree index, displayed pictorially*

when there are many distinct values in the column, or when the column is unique. The binary search tree sees success in the same way. Its algorithm works as follows:

- Compare the given value to the value in the halfway point of the list. If the value at hand is greater, discard the lower half the list. If the value at hand is less, then discard the upper half.

- Repeat the process on the half remaining until a value is found or the list exhausted.

Along with the data values of a column, the individual nodes of an index also store a piece of information about the column value's row location on disk. This crucial piece of lookup data is called a "ROWID." The *ROWID* for the column value points Oracle directly to the location on disk in the table of the row corresponding to the column value. A ROWID consists of three components to identify the location on disk of a row—down to the row in the data block in the datafile on disk. With this information, Oracle can then find all the data associated with the row in the table.

TIP
The ROWID for a table is an address for the row on disk. With the ROWID, Oracle can search for the data on disk rapidly.

The other type of index available in Oracle is the bitmap index. The principle of a bitmap index is the use of a matrix, which has columns corresponding to all data values in the column. Thus, if the column contains only three distinct values, the bitmap index can be visualized as containing a column for the ROWID and three columns, one for each distinct value. Figure 4-3 displays a pictorial representation of a bitmap index containing three distinct values. The physical representation of the bitmap index is not far from the picture. Since each distinct value adds to the size of the index, bitmap indexes work best when there are few distinct values allowed for a column. Thus, the bitmap index improves performance in situations where traditional indexes are not useful, and vice-versa.

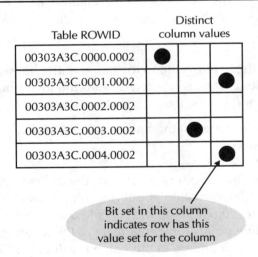

FIGURE 4-3. *A bitmap index, displayed pictorially*

Exercises

1. What is a B-tree index? How does it work? In what situations does it improve performance?

2. What is a bitmap index? How does it work? In what situations does it improve performance?

Creating Indexes

You can create a unique index on a column manually using the **create index** statement. This process is the manual equivalent of creating a unique constraint or primary key on a table. Remember, unique indexes are created automatically in support of that task. The index created is a B-tree index. The **create index** statement used to create a unique index must contain the **unique** keyword. You can index a column that contains NULL values as well, simply by eliminating the **unique** keyword. Creating a composite index with more columns named is possible as well. Finally, you can create a bitmap index by substituting the **unique** keyword with the **bitmap** keyword.

```
-- unique indexes
CREATE UNIQUE INDEX employee_lastname_indx_01
ON employee (lastname);

-- nonunique indexes
CREATE INDEX employee_lastname_indx_01
ON employee (lastname);

-- composite indexes
CREATE UNIQUE INDEX employee_last_first_indx_01
ON employee (lastname, firstname);

-- bitmap indexes
CREATE BITMAP INDEX employee_status_indx_01
ON employee (empl_status);
```

Once created, there can be little altered about an index other than some storage parameters. In order to replace the definition of the index, the entire index must be dropped and re-created. Once the index is created, there are several different ways to find information about it. The ALL_INDEXES dictionary view displays storage information about the index, along with the name of the table to which the index is associated. The ALL_OBJECTS dictionary view displays object information about the index, including the index status. The ALL_IND_COLUMNS view displays information about the columns that are indexed on the database. This last view is especially useful for determining the order of columns in a composite index.

Exercises

1. What method is used to create a unique index? A nonunique index?

2. How do you create a bitmap index?

3. In unique indexes containing more than one column, how do you think uniqueness is identified? Explain.

Removing Indexes

When an index is no longer needed in the database, the developer can remove it with the use of the **drop index** command. Once an index is dropped, it will no longer improve performance on searches using the column or columns contained in the index. No mention of that index will appear in the data dictionary any more, either. Additionally, if the index is used in relation to a primary-key or unique constraint, then the index will no longer continue to enforce that uniqueness constraint. The syntax for the **drop index** statement is the same, regardless of the type of index being dropped. If you wish to rework the index in any way, you must first drop the old index and then create the new one.

```
DROP INDEX employee_last_first_indx_01;
```

Exercises

1. How is a bitmap index dropped? How is a unique index dropped?

2. What are the effects of dropping an index?

Guidelines for Creating Indexes

The usage of indexes for searching tables for information can provide incredible performance gains over searching tables using columns that are not indexed. However, care must be taken to choose the right index. Although a completely unique column is preferable for indexing using the B-tree structured index, a nonunique column will work almost as well if only about 10 percent of its rows have the same value. "Switch" or "flag" columns, such as ones for storing the sex of a person, are a bad idea for B-tree indexes. So are columns used to store a few "valid values," or columns that store a token value representing valid or invalid, active or inactive, yes or no, or any types of values such as these. Bitmap indexes are more appropriate for these types of columns.

TIP
The uniqueness of the values of a column is referred to as "cardinality." Unique columns or columns that contain many distinct values have "high cardinality," while columns with few distinct values have "low cardinality." Use B-tree indexes for columns with high cardinality and bitmap indexes for columns with low cardinality.

Exercises

1. What is cardinality?

2. When might the DBA use a B-tree index to improve performance? When might the DBA use a bitmap index to improve performance?

User Access Control

In this section, you will cover the following topics related to controlling user access:

■ Oracle database security model

- System privileges
- Using roles to manage database access
- Object privileges
- Changing passwords
- Granting and revoking object privileges
- Using synonyms for database transparency

The most secure database is one with no users, but take away the users of a database and the whole point of creating a database is lost. In order to address the issues of security within Oracle, a careful balance of limiting access to the database and controlling what a user can see once a connection is established is required. Oracle provides a means of doing so with its security model. The Oracle database security model consists of several options for limiting connect access to the database and controlling what a user can and cannot see once connection is established. This section will focus on the presentation of security on the Oracle database, from user creation to password administration to administering security on individual objects in the database.

Oracle Database Security Model

Oracle security consists of two parts. The first part of the Oracle database security model consists of password authentication for all users of the Oracle database. Password authentication is available either directly from the Oracle server or from the operating system supporting the Oracle database. When Oracle's own authentication system is used, password information is stored in Oracle in an encrypted format. The second part of the Oracle security model consists of controlling what database objects a user may access, the level of access a user may have to the object, and the authority to place new objects into the Oracle database. At a high level, these controls are referred to as privileges.

The key to giving database access is creating users. Users are created in Oracle with the **create user** command. Along with a password, several storage and database usage options are set up with the creation of a user. The following statement can be issued by a user with the **create user** privilege in Oracle to create new users:

```
CREATE USER athena IDENTIFIED BY greek#goddess
```

Security in the database is a serious matter. In most organizations, it is a set of functions handled either by the DBA or, more appropriately, by a *security administrator*. This person is the one with the final say over creating new users and determining the accessibility of objects in the database. As a general rule, the larger the organization is and the more sensitive the information, the more likely it is that security will be handled by a special security administrator. However, it is important that developers, DBAs, and users all understand the options available in the Oracle security model for the version of Oracle the organization uses.

Exercises

1. What are the two parts of database security?

2. Who should manage database security such as user and password administration?

Granting System Privileges

System privileges grant the user the ability to create, modify, and eliminate the database objects in Oracle that store data for the application. In fact, in order to do anything in the Oracle database, the user must have a system privilege called **create session**. Within the scope of system privileges, there are two categories. The first is the set of system privileges that relate to object management. These objects include tables, indexes, triggers, sequences and views, packages, stored procedures, and functions. The three actions on objects managed by system privileges are defining or creating the object, altering definition, and dropping the object.

The other category of system privileges refers to the ability of a user to manage special system-wide activities. These activities include functions such as auditing database activity, generating statistics to support the cost-based optimizer, and setting up Oracle to allow access to the database only to users with a special system privilege called **restricted session**. These privileges should generally be granted only to the user or users on the database who will be performing high-level database administration tasks.

All granting of system privileges is managed with the **grant** command. In order to grant a system privilege, the grantor must either have the privilege granted to herself **with admin option**, or she must have **grant any privilege** granted to them. Granting a privilege **with admin option** signifies that the grantee may further grant or revoke the system privilege to any user on the database, with or without the **with admin option**. Users can create objects in their own schema with a system privilege such as **create table**. However, the user can create objects in any schema if the **any** keyword is added to the system privilege when it is granted, as in **create any table**.

```
GRANT CREATE PROCEDURE, CREATE FUNCTION, CREATE PACKAGE TO spanky;
GRANT CREATE TABLE, CREATE VIEW, CREATE TRIGGER, CREATE SEQUENCE TO athena;
GRANT CREATE TABLE TO athena WITH ADMIN OPTION;
```

Revoking system privileges is handled with the **revoke** command. In general, there are no cascading concerns related to revoking system privileges. For example, user ATHENA created 17 tables with the **create table** privilege while she had it, and granted the **create table** privilege with and without the **with admin option** to several users as well. Another user revokes the privilege from her, along with the **with admin option**. The revocation of **create table** from user ATHENA would have no effect either on the tables she created or the users to which she granted the **create table** privilege.

Exercises

1. What is a system privilege? What abilities do system privileges manage?

2. How are privileges granted and revoked?

3. What does **with admin option** mean, and how is it used?

Using Roles to Manage Database Access

When databases get large, privileges can become unwieldy and hard to manage. You can simplify the management of privileges with the use of a database object called a *role*. Roles act in two capacities in the database. First, the role can act as a focal point for grouping the privileges to execute certain tasks. The second capacity is to act as a "virtual user" of a database, to which all the object privileges required to execute a certain job function can be granted, such as data entry, manager review, batch processing, and others.

The amount of access to the objects of the database can be categorized using database roles to administrate the privileges that must be granted for database usage. In order to use roles, two activities must occur. The first is that you must logically group certain privileges together, such as creating tables, indexes, triggers, and procedures. Using the privileges that are granted to a role can be protected with a password when a special clause, called **identified by**, is used in role creation.

```
CREATE ROLE create_procs IDENTIFIED BY creator;
GRANT create any procedure TO create_procs WITH ADMIN OPTION;
```

The second aspect of work you must complete is logically grouping the users of a database application together according to similar needs. The most effective way to manage users is to identify the various types of users that will be using the database. You determine the activities each type of user will carry out, and list the privileges that each activity will require. These types or categories will determine the access privileges that will then be granted to roles on the database. The next step is to create roles that correspond to each activity, and to grant the privileges to the roles. Once this architecture of using roles as a "middle layer" for granting privileges is established, the administration of user privileges becomes very simply granting the appropriate role or roles to the users that need them.

```
CREATE ROLE ofc_developer;

GRANT CREATE TABLE TO ofc_developer;
GRANT SELECT ANY TABLE TO ofc_developer;
GRANT DROP USER TO ofc_developer;

GRANT ofc_developer TO athena;
GRANT ofc_developer TO spanky;
```

Roles can be altered to support the requirement of a password using the **alter role identified by** statement. Deleting a role is performed with the **drop role** statement. These two options may only be executed by those users with the **create any role**, **alter any role**, or **drop any role** privileges, or by the owner of the role. Privileges can be revoked from a role in the same way as they can be revoked from a user. When a role is dropped, the associated privileges are revoked from the user granted the role. Figure 4-4 shows how privileges can be managed with roles.

In order to use the privileges granted to a user via a role, the role must be enabled for that user. In order for the role to be enabled, it must be the default role for the user, or one of the default roles. The status of a role is usually enabled, unless for some reason the role has been disabled. To

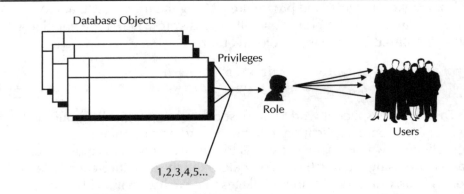

Database Objects

Privileges

Role

Users

1,2,3,4,5...

FIGURE 4-4. *Using roles to manage privileges*

change the status of a role for the user, the **alter user default role** statement can be issued. Some of the keywords that can be used in conjunction with defining roles are **all**, **all except**, and **none**; these keywords limit the roles defined for the **alter user** statement.

```
ALTER USER spanky DEFAULT ROLE ALL;
ALTER USER spanky DEFAULT ROLE ALL EXCEPT sysdba;
ALTER USER spanky DEFAULT ROLE app_dev, sys_aly, unit_mgr;
ALTER USER spanky DEFAULT ROLE NONE;
```

Exercises

1. What is a role? How are privileges granted to a role?

2. What is a default role? Can a user exercise privileges granted through a role if the role is disabled? Explain.

Granting Object Privileges

Once an object in the Oracle database has been created, it can be administered by either the creator of the table or by a user who has the **grant**

any privilege system privilege available to them. Administration of a database object consists of granting privileges that will allow users to manipulate the object by adding, changing, removing, or viewing data in the database object. Sometimes, object privileges are referred to by developers as *SUDI* (Select, Update, Delete, Insert) privileges. Other object privileges refer to the ability to refer to database objects, or to use them in some way that will not drop or change them in any way. These object privileges are **references** and **execute**. The **references** privilege allows the grantee of the privilege to create foreign-key constraints on the referenced column of a table. The **execute** privilege allows the user to run a compiled stored procedure, package, or function. Other object privileges manage the alteration and creation of certain database objects. These include the **alter table**, **alter sequence**, and **index table** privileges.

The object privileges for any database object belong to that user and to users with appropriate **any** system privileges granted to them. Object privileges can be granted to other users for the purpose of allowing them to access and manipulate the object, or to administer the privileges to other users. The latter option is accomplished via a special parameter on the privilege called **with grant option**.

Exercises

1. What are object privileges? Name some of the object privileges?

2. What option is used to grant an object privilege with the ability to grant the privilege further to others?

Changing Passwords

Once the user ID is created, the users can change their own passwords by issuing the following statement:

```
ALTER USER athena IDENTIFIED BY blackcat;
```

Exercise

How is the user password changed?

Granting and Revoking Object Privileges

All granting of object privileges is managed with the **grant** command. In order to **grant** an object privilege, the grantor must either have the privilege granted to herself with the **grant option**, or she must have **grant any privilege** granted to her, or she must own the object. Granting an object privilege must be managed in the following way. First, the grantor of the privilege must determine the level of access a user requires on the table. Then, the privilege is granted. Granting object privileges can allow the grantee of the privilege the ability to administer a privilege as well when **with grant option** is used. Administrative ability over an object privilege includes the ability to **grant** the privilege or revoke it from anyone, as well as the ability to **grant** the object privilege to another user with administrative ability over the privilege.

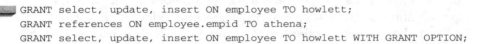

```
GRANT select, update, insert ON employee TO howlett;
GRANT references ON employee.empid TO athena;
GRANT select, update, insert ON employee TO howlett WITH GRANT OPTION;
```

Revoking object privileges is handled with the **revoke** command. In general, there are no cascading concerns related to revoking object privileges other than the removal of a user's ability to use the privilege. For example, user HOWLETT creates the EMPLOYEE table and inserts several rows in it. She then grants the **select** privilege along with the **with grant option** on the EMPLOYEE table to user ATHENA. User ATHENA then revokes the privilege from user HOWLETT, along with the **with grant option**. The revocation of these privileges from user HOWLETT would have no effect either on the data she created or on user ATHENA's continued ability to use the privileges granted by user HOWLETT. User HOWLETT, however, will no longer be able to access data as she once could before the object privilege was revoked.

Using Synonyms for Database Transparency

Database objects are owned by the users who create them. The objects are available only in the user's schema unless the user grants access to the objects explicitly to other users or to roles granted to other users. However, even when granted permission to use the object, the user must be aware of the boundaries created by schema ownership in order to access the data objects in Oracle. For example, assume the EMPLOYEE table exists in user SPANKY's schema, and user ATHENA attempts to access the table. Instead of returning the data associated with EMPID 96945, however, Oracle tells the user that the object does not exist. The reason this user could not see the table in the SPANKY schema is because user ATHENA did not refer to the table as being in the schema owned by SPANKY.

```
SELECT * FROM employee
WHERE empid = 96945;

SELECT * FROM employee
              *
ORA-00942: table or view does not exist.

SELECT * FROM spanky.employee
WHERE empid = 96945;
```

If that extra piece of information seems to be unnecessary to remember, synonyms may be used on the database. A synonym allows the users of the database to refer to the objects of a database without prefixing the name of the owner of the object. A public synonym can be created by a privileged user to allow other users in the database to access a particular table without having to prefix the schema name to the table reference. For example, a synonym can be created on the EMPLOYEE table. After creating a synonym, user ATHENA can access the table by use of it.

```
- Executed by SPANKY
CREATE PUBLIC SYNONYM employee FOR spanky.employee;

- Executed by ATHENA
SELECT * FROM employee
WHERE empid = 96945;
```

EMPID	LASTNAME	FIRSTNAME	SALARY
96945	AHL	BARBARA	45000

Another type of synonym is the "private synonym." This is a synonym you can create for yourself that allows only you to refer to a table in another schema by the table name only. No other user can access the table via your private synonym, they must create their own. The following code block illustrates ATHENA's use of private synonyms to achieve the same result as before:

```
- Executed by ATHENA
CREATE SYNONYM employee FOR spanky.employee;

- Executed by ATHENA
SELECT * FROM employee
WHERE empid = 96945;

EMPID       LASTNAME        FIRSTNAME       SALARY
-----       --------        ---------       ------
96945       AHL             BARBARA         45000
```

TIP
Synonyms do not handle the actual access to data in a table. Only privileges can do that. Synonyms only allow you to refer to a table without prefixing the schema name to the table reference.

Exercises

1. What is schema transparency?

2. How are synonyms used to facilitate schema transparency? What is a public synonym? What is a private synonym? How do they differ, and how are they the same?

Chapter Summary

This chapter covered several sections of required information for OCP Exam 1 related to the advanced creation of database objects. Some of the areas this chapter covered were altering tables and constraints, creating sequences, creating views, creating indexes, and controlling user access. The material in this chapter comprises about 17 percent of OCP Exam 1.

The first area of discussion for this chapter is the altering of tables and constraints. There are several activities a developer or DBA can do in order to alter tables and constraints. Some of these activities include adding columns or constraints, modifying the datatypes of columns, or removing constraints. Adding and modifying columns is accomplished with the **alter table** command, as are adding or modifying constraints on the table. There are several restricting factors on adding constraints, centering around the fact that adding a constraint to a column means that the data already in the column must conform to the constraint being placed upon it.

With respect to adding columns or changing the datatype of a column, there are some general rules to remember. It is easier to increase the size of a datatype for a column, and to add columns to the table. More difficult is changing the datatype of a column from one thing to another. Generally, the column whose datatype is being altered must have NULL values for that column specified for all rows in the table. A table can be dropped with the **drop table** statement. Once dropped, all associated database objects like triggers and constraints, and indexes automatically created to support the constraints, are dropped as well. Indexes that were manually generated by the DBA to improve performance on the table will also be dropped.

The chapter also covered several other tricks to table alteration. If you want to **delete** all data from a table but leave the definition of the table intact, you can use the **truncate** command. Alternately, the **delete from** *table_name* command can be used, but on large tables you may see a noticeable difference in performance between these two commands. Also, you cannot issue the **rollback** statement after a **truncate** and get all your data back the way you can after a **delete** statement. A database object can be renamed with use of the **rename** command. Alternatively, you can create a synonym, which allows users to reference the database object using a different name. One final option offered to you is to make notes in the database about objects by adding comments. Comments are added with the **comment on** statement.

Creation of sequences is another important area of advanced Oracle object creation. A sequence is an object that produces integers on demand according to rules that are defined for the sequence at sequence creation time. One use for a sequence include using a sequence to generate primary keys for a table. Creating a sequence is accomplished with the **create sequence** command in Oracle. To use a sequence, you must reference two pseudocolumns in the sequence, known as CURRVAL and NEXTVAL. The CURRVAL column stores the current value generated by the sequence, while referencing NEXTVAL causes the sequence to generate a new number and replace the value in CURRVAL with that new number. Several rules can be used to govern how sequences generate their numbers. These rules include the first number the sequence should generate, how the sequence should increment, maximum and minimum values, whether values can be recycled, and others. Modifying the rules that govern sequence integer generation is accomplished with the **alter sequence** statement, while removal of the sequence is accomplished with the **drop sequence** statement.

Creating views is another area of database object creation covered in this chapter. Views are used to distill data from a table that may be inappropriate for use by some users. Other uses for views include the creation of views that mask the complexity of certain data (such as joins from multiple tables), data that has single-row operations performed on it, and other things. One common example of view usage is the data dictionary, which stores all data about the Oracle database in tables but disallows direct access to the tables in favor of providing views through which the user can **select** data. There are two categories of views: simple and complex. A simple view is one that draws data from only one table. A complex view is one that draws data from two or more tables. Simple views sometimes allow the user to **insert**, **update**, or **delete** data from the underlying table, while complex views never allow this to occur. There are some other differences between simple and complex views covered in the chapter, and you should be sure you understand those differences before taking OCP Exam 1. A view can also have the option of enforcing a check on the data being inserted. This means that if you try to make a change, insertion, or deletion to the underlying table, the view will not allow it unless the view can then **select** the row being changed. Modifying the definition of a view requires dropping the old view and re-creating it or, alternatively, creating the view again with the **or replace** option. The **alter view** statement is used for recompiling an existing view due to a problem with the object dependencies of the database. Removing a view from the database is done with the **drop view** statement.

Creating an index is another area covered in this chapter. There are several indexes created automatically to support enforcement of uniqueness constraints such as the primary-key or the unique constraint. However, the DBA can also create nonunique indexes to support performance improvements on the database application. The traditional index consists of a B-tree structure. The search algorithm supported by this structure is similar to a binary search tree, the operation of which was covered in the chapter. In order for a column to be indexed and used effectively using the B-tree index, the cardinality, or number of distinct values in the column, should be high. To change the number of columns in an index, the index must be dropped and rebuilt. To drop an index, use the **drop index** statement. Another index available in Oracle is the bitmap index, and you should understand its usage before taking OCP Exam 1. Bitmap indexes work well for improving performance on columns with few distinct values.

Controlling user access on the database is the final area covered by this chapter. The Oracle database security model contains three major areas—user authentication, system privileges to control the creation of database objects, and object privileges to control usage of database objects. To change a password, the user can issue the **alter user identified by** statement, specifying the person's username and the desired password. System privileges govern the creation of new database objects, such as tables, sequences, triggers, and views, as well as the execution of certain commands for analyzing and auditing database objects. Three general object maintenance activities are governed by system privileges, and they are the creation, change, and dropping of database objects. Object privileges govern access to an object once it is created, such as **select**, **update**, **insert**, and **delete** statements on tables, execution of packages or procedures, and reference of columns on tables for foreign-key constraints.

In situations where there are many users and many privileges governing database usage, the management of privilege granting to users can be improved using roles. Roles act as "virtual users" of the database system. You first define the privileges a user may need, group them logically by function or job description, then create an appropriate role. Privileges to support the function or the job description are then granted to the role, and the role is granted to the user. Roles help to alleviate the necessity of granting several privileges each time a user is added to an application.

Finally, the use of synonyms for data transparency is discussed. Database objects are owned by users and accessible to their schema only, unless permission is explicitly granted by the owner to another user to view the data in the table. Even then, the schema owning the object must be referenced in the statement the user issues to reference the object. Public synonyms can eliminate that requirement, making the schema ownership of the database object transparent. A public synonym is created with the **create public synonym** statement.

Two-Minute Drill

- Adding or modifying a table column is done with the **alter table** statement.

- Columns can be added with little difficulty, if they will be NULLable, using the **alter table add** *column_name* statement. If a NOT NULL constraint is desired, add the column, populate the column with data, and then add the NOT NULL constraint separately.

- Column datatype size can be increased with no difficulty using the **alter table (modify** *column_name datatype***)** statement. Column size can be decreased or the datatype can be changed only if the column contains NULL for all rows.

- Constraints can be added to a column only if the column already contains values that will not violate the added constraint.

- Adding a constraint is accomplished with the **alter table add** *constraint_name* statement.

- Dropping a constraint is accomplished with the **alter table drop** *constraint_name* statement.

- If a constraint that created an index automatically (primary keys and unique constraints) is dropped, then the corresponding index is also dropped.

- If the table is dropped, all constraints, triggers, and indexes created for the table are also dropped.

- Removing all data from a table is best accomplished with the **truncate** command rather than the **delete from** *table_name* statement because **truncate** will reset the table's highwatermark and deallocate all the table's storage quickly, improving performance on **select count( )** statements issued after the truncation.

- An object name can be changed with the **rename** statement or with the use of synonyms.

- A comment can be added to the data dictionary for a database object with the **comment on** command. The comment can subsequently be viewed in DBA_TAB_COMMENTS or DBA_ COL_COMMENTS.

- A sequence generates integers based on rules that are defined by sequence creation.

- Options that can be defined for sequences are the first number generated, how the sequence increments, the maximum value, the minimum value, whether the sequence can recycle numbers, and whether numbers will be cached for improved performance.

- Sequences are used by selecting from the CURRVAL and NEXTVAL virtual columns.

- The CURRVAL column contains the current value of the sequence.

- Selecting from NEXTVAL increments the sequence and changes the value of CURRVAL to whatever is produced by NEXTVAL.

- Modifying the rules that a sequence uses to generate values is accomplished using the **alter sequence** statement.

- Deleting the sequence is accomplished with the **drop sequence** statement.

- A view is a virtual table defined by a **select** statement.

- A view is similar to a table in that it contains rows and columns, but different because the view actually stores no data.

- Views can distill data from tables that may be inappropriate for some users, or hide complexity of data from several tables or on which many operations have been performed.

- There are two types of views: simple and complex.

- Simple views are those that have only one underlying table.

- Complex views are those with two or more underlying tables that have been joined together.

- Data cannot be inserted into complex views, but may be inserted into simple views in some cases.

- The **with check option** clause on administering any object privilege allows the simple view to limit the data that can be inserted or otherwise changed on the underlying table by requiring that the data change be selectable by the view.

- Modifying the data selected by a view requires re-creating the view with the **create or replace view** statement, or dropping the view first and issuing the **create view** statement.

- An existing view can be recompiled if for some reason it becomes invalid due to object dependency by executing the **alter view** statement.

- A view is dropped with the **drop view** statement.

- Some indexes in a database are created automatically, such as those supporting the primary-key and the unique constraints on a table.

- Other indexes are created manually to support database performance improvements.

- Indexes created manually are often on nonunique columns.

- B-tree indexes work best on columns that have high cardinality, or a large number of distinct values and few duplicates in the column.

- B-tree indexes improve performance by storing data in a binary search tree, then searching for values in the tree using a "divide and conquer" methodology outlined in the chapter.

- Bitmap indexes improve performance on columns with low cardinality, or few distinct values and many duplicates on the column.

- Columns stored in the index can be changed only by dropping and re-creating the index.

- Deleting an index is accomplished by issuing the **drop index** statement.

- The Oracle database security model consists of two parts: limiting user access with password authentication and controlling object usage with privileges.

- Available privileges in Oracle include system privileges for maintaining database objects and object privileges for accessing and manipulating data in database objects.

- Changing a password can be performed by a user with the **alter user identified by** statement.

- Granting system and object privileges is accomplished with the **grant** command.

- Taking away system and object privileges is accomplished with the **revoke** command.

- Creating a synonym to make schema transparency is accomplished with the **create public synonym** command.

Chapter Questions

1. **Dropping a table has which of the following effects on a nonunique index created for the table?**

   A. No effect.

   B. The index will be dropped.

   C. The index will be rendered invalid.

   D. The index will contain NULL values.

2. **Which of the following statements about indexes is true?**

   A. Columns with low cardinality are handled well by B-tree indexes.

   B. Columns with low cardinality are handled poorly by bitmap indexes.

   C. Columns with high cardinality are handled well by B-tree indexes.

3. **To increase the number of NULLable columns for a table:**

   A. Use the **alter table** statement

   B. Ensure that all column values are NULL for all rows

   C. First increase the size of adjacent column datatypes, then add the column

   D. Add the column, populate the column, then add the NOT NULL constraint

4. **To add the number of columns selected by a view:**

   A. Add more columns to the underlying table

   B. Issue the **alter view** statement

C. Use a correlated subquery in conjunction with the view

D. Drop and re-create the view with references to select more columns

5. **A user issues the statement SELECT COUNT(*) FROM EMPLOYEE. The query takes an inordinately long amount of time and returns a count of zero. The most cost-effective solution is**

A. Upgrade hardware

B. Truncate the table

C. Upgrade version of Oracle

D. Delete the highwatermark

6. **Which of the following choices are valid parameters for sequence creation?**

A. identified by

B. using temporary tablespace

C. maxvalue

D. on delete cascade

7. **The following statement is issued against the Oracle database. Which line will produce an error?**

A. create view EMP_VIEW_01

B. as select E.EMPID, E.LASTNAME, E.FIRSTNAME, A.ADDRESS

C. from EMPLOYEE E, EMPL_ADDRESS A

D. where E.EMPID = A.EMPID

E. with check option;

F. This statement contains no errors.

8. **The following statement is issued on the database: COMMENT ON TABLE empl IS 'Do not use this table.' How can this data be viewed?**

A. Using the **describe** command

B. Issuing a **select * from empl** statement

    C. Selecting from ALL_COMMENTS

    D. Selecting from ALL_TAB_COMMENTS

9. **Which system privilege allows the user to connect to a database in restricted session mode?**

    A. create table

    B. create user

    C. restricted session

    D. create session

10. **Which of the following statements is true about roles? (Choose three)**

    A. Roles can be granted to other roles.

    B. Privileges can be granted to roles.

    C. Roles can be granted to users.

    D. Roles can be granted to synonyms.

11. **User MANN has granted the CREATE ANY VIEW WITH ADMIN OPTION privilege to user SNOW. User SNOW granted the same privilege WITH ADMIN OPTION to user REED. User MANN revokes the privilege from user SNOW. Which statement is true about privileges granted to users REED, MANN, and SNOW?**

    A. REED and MANN have the privilege, but SNOW does not.

    B. REED and SNOW have the privilege, but MANN does not.

    C. MANN and SNOW have the privilege, but REED does not.

    D. MANN has the privilege, but SNOW and REED do not.

12. **After referencing NEXTVAL, the value in CURRVAL**

    A. Is incremented by one

    B. Is now in PREVVAL

    C. Is equal to NEXTVAL

    D. Is unchanged

Answers to Chapter Questions

I. B. The index will be dropped.

Explanation Like automatically generated indexes associated with a table's primary key, the indexes created manually on a table to improve performance will be dropped if the table is dropped. Choices A, C, and D are therefore invalid. Refer to the discussion of dropping indexes in the chapter summary.

2. C. Columns with high cardinality are handled well by B-tree indexes.

Explanation Columns with low cardinality are the bane of B-tree indexes, eliminating choice A. Furthermore, bitmap indexes are primarily used for performance gains on columns with low cardinality, eliminating choice B. The correct answer is C. Review the discussion of how B-tree indexes work if you do not understand.

3. A. Use the **alter table** statement.

Explanation The **alter table** statement is the only choice offered that allows the developer to increase the number of columns per table. Choice B is incorrect because setting a column to all NULL values for all rows does simply that. Choice C is incorrect because increasing the adjacent column sizes simply increases the sizes of the columns, and choice D is incorrect because the steps listed outline how to add a column with a NOT NULL constraint, something not specified by the question.

4. D. Drop and re-create the view with references to select more columns

Explanation Choice A is incorrect because adding columns to the underlying table will not add columns to the view, but will likely invalidate the view. Choice B is incorrect because the **alter view** statement simply recompiles an existing view definition, while the real solution here is to change the existing view definition by dropping and re-creating the view. Choice C is incorrect because a correlated subquery will likely worsen performance and underscores the real problem—a column must be added to the view. Review the discussion of altering the definition of a view.

5. B.   Truncate the table

Explanation   Choices A and C may work, but an upgrade of hardware and software will cost far more than truncating the table. Choice D is partly correct, as there will be some change required to the highwatermark, but the change is to reset, not eliminate entirely, and the method used is to truncate the table.

6. C.   **maxvalue**

Explanation   The **maxvalue** option is a valid option for sequence creation. Choices A and B are both part of the **create user** statement, while choice D is a part of a constraint declaration in an **alter table** or **create table** statement. Review the discussion on creating sequences.

7. F.   This statement contains no errors.

Explanation   Even though the reference to **with check option** is inappropriate, considering that inserts into complex views are not possible, the statement will not actually produce an error when compiled. Therefore, there are no errors in the view. This is not something that can be learned. It requires hands-on experience with Oracle.

8. D.   Selecting from ALL_TAB_COMMENTS

Explanation   Choice A is incorrect because comments will not appear in the description of the table from the data dictionary. Instead, the user must select comments from the ALL_, USER, or DBA_TAB_COLUMNS views. Choice C is incorrect because ALL_COMMENTS is not a view in the Oracle data dictionary, while choice B is incorrect because selection of data from the table commented yields only the data in that table, not the comments. Refer to the discussion of adding comments to tables.

9. C.   RESTRICTED SESSION

Explanation   Choice A is incorrect because the **create table** privilege allows the user to create a table, while choice B is incorrect for a similar reason—**create user** allows the user to create new users. Choice D is required for establishing connection to an open database, while choice C is the only privilege listed that allows the user to connect to a database in **restricted session** mode. Refer to the discussion and review of roles and privileges.

10. A, B, and C.

Explanation Choice D is the only option not available to managing roles. Roles cannot be granted to synonyms. Refer to the discussion of roles and privileges in this chapter.

11. A. REED and MANN have the privilege, but SNOW does not.

Explanation The only result of revoking a system or object privilege in Oracle is that the user the privilege is revoked from is the only user who loses it. If the user has granted the privilege to someone else, that other user will still have the privilege. Review the discussion of cascading effects of granting privileges.

12. C. Is equal to NEXTVAL

Explanation Once NEXTVAL is referenced, the sequence increments the integer and changes the value of CURRVAL to be equal to NEXTVAL. Refer to the discussion of sequences for more information.

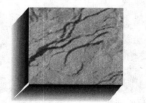

CHAPTER
5

Introducing PL/SQL

n this chapter, you will understand and demonstrate knowledge in the following areas:

- Overview of PL/SQL
- Developing a PL/SQL block
- Interacting with the Oracle database
- Controlling PL/SQL process flow
- Explicit cursor handling
- Error handling

In Oracle, there is a special language available for developers to code stored procedures that seamlessly integrate with database object access via the language of database objects, SQL. However, this language offers far more execution potential than simple **update**, **select**, **insert**, and **delete**. This language offers a procedural extension that allows for modularity, variable declaration, loops and other logic constructs, and advanced error handling. This language is known as PL/SQL. This chapter will present an overview of PL/SQL syntax, constructs, and usage. This information is tested on OCP Exam 1, and comprises 22 percent of the test material. Since PL/SQL comprises a massive portion of Oracle development, it is crucial you understand this language.

Overview of PL/SQL

In this section, you will cover the following topics related to overview of PL/SQL:

- Using PL/SQL to access Oracle
- Variable value assignment

PL/SQL offers many advantages over other programming languages for handling the logic and business rule enforcement of database applications. It is a straightforward language with all the common logic constructs associated with a programming language, plus many things other languages don't have, such as robust error handling and modularization of code blocks. The PL/SQL code used to interface with the database is also stored directly on the Oracle database, and is the only programming language that interfaces with the Oracle database natively and within the database environment. This overview will cover the details of benefits associated with using PL/SQL in the Oracle database and the basic constructs of the PL/SQL language.

Using PL/SQL to Access Oracle

Many applications that use client/server architecture have one thing in common—a difficulty maintaining the business rules for an application. When business rules are decentralized throughout the application, the developers must make changes throughout the application and implement system testing that will determine whether the changes are sufficient. However, in tight scheduling situations, the first deployment item to get left off is almost invariably testing. One logical design change that should be implemented in this scenario is the centralization of logic in the application to allow for easier management of change. In systems that use the Oracle database, a "middle layer" of application logic can be designed with PL/SQL. The benefits are as follows:

- PL/SQL is managed centrally within the Oracle database. You manage source code and execution privileges with the same syntax used to manage other database objects.

- PL/SQL communicates natively with other Oracle database objects.

- PL/SQL is easy to read and has many features for code modularity and error handling.

The features of PL/SQL that manage centralized code management make PL/SQL the logical choice for a database-centric client/server application that uses stored procedures for business logic and allows the client application developer to focus mainly on the user interface. Storing application logic centrally means only having to compile a change once, and then it is immediately accessible to all users of the application. With business logic stored in the client application, the effort of distributing code includes the recompilation of the client application (potentially on several different platforms). There is an additional distribution cost to getting the new executable version of the client on every user's desktop, as well as overhead for communication and support to make sure all users of the application are on the right version. Decentralized computing has increased the capacity of organizations to provide easy-to-use and fast applications to their customers. But some centralization improves the job even further by allowing the application development shop the ability to eliminate distribution channels for business logic changes and focus the client-side developers' efforts on the client application. Figure 5-1 shows an example of the difference between centralized and decentralized business logic code management.

Exercises

1. What are some advantages of using PL/SQL to access the database?

2. Where is PL/SQL compiled and stored?

PL/SQL Program Constructs

There are many different programming constructs to PL/SQL, from the various types of modules available, to the components of a PL/SQL block, to

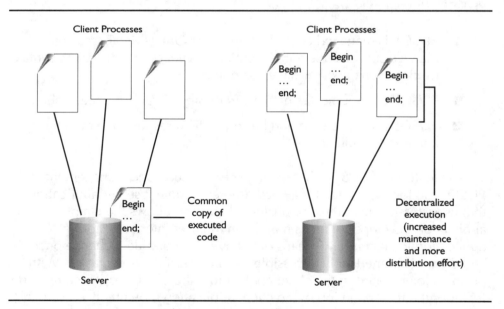

FIGURE 5-1.   *Centralized vs. decentralized business logic code management*

the logic constructs that manage process flow. This section will identify each component of the PL/SQL language and give some highlights about each area of the language.

Modularity

PL/SQL allows the developer to create program modules to improve software reusability and to hide the complexity of the execution of a specific operation behind a name. For example, there may be a complex process involved to add an employee record to a corporate database, which requires records to be added to several different tables for several different applications. Stored procedures may handle the addition of records to each of the systems, making it look to the user that the only step required is entering data on one screen. In reality, that screen's worth of data entry may call dozens of separate procedures, each designed to handle one small component of the overall process of adding the employee. These components may even be reused data entry code blocks from the various pension, health care, day-care, payroll, and other HR applications, which have simply been repackaged around this new data entry screen. Figure 5-2 shows how modularity can be implemented in PL/SQL blocks.

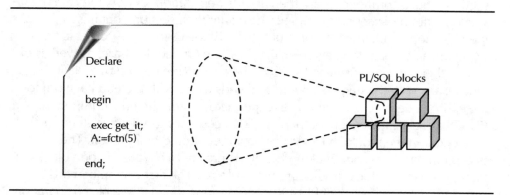

FIGURE 5-2. *Modularity and PL/SQL blocks*

Procedures, Functions, Triggers, and Packages

The modules of PL/SQL code are divided into four categories. Those categories are stored procedures, functions, packages, and triggers. To summarize, the four types of PL/SQL code blocks are as follows.

- *Procedure*—A series of statements accepting and/or returning zero or more variables.

- *Function*—A series of statements accepting zero or more variables that returns one value.

- *Package*—A collection of procedures and functions that has two parts: a specification listing available procedures and functions and their parameters, and a body that contains the actual code for the procedures and functions.

- *Trigger*—A series of PL/SQL statements attached to a database table that execute whenever a triggering event (**update**, **insert**, **delete**) occurs.

Components of a PL/SQL Block

There are three components of any PL/SQL block named in the previous section. Those components are the *variable declaration section*, the *executable section*, and the *exception handler*. The declaration section contains identification of all variable constructs that will be used in the code block. A variable can be of any datatype available in the Oracle database, as well as of some other types exclusive to PL/SQL. The executable section of a PL/SQL block starts with the **begin** keyword and ends either with the **end** keyword for the entire code block or with the **exception** keyword. The final component of a PL/SQL block is the exception handler. This code portion defines all errors that may occur in the block and specifies how they should be handled. The exception handler is optional in PL/SQL. There are two types of code blocks in PL/SQL—named blocks and anonymous blocks. The first example in this section is a named block of PL/SQL code—a function. It contains a declaration block, an executable block, and an exception handler.

```
FUNCTION convert_money
    (amount          IN NUMBER,
    from_currency    IN VARCHAR2,
    to_currency      IN VARCHAR2
```

```
)   IS    /* denotes the beginning of the declaration section. */
    my_new_amt number(10) := 0;
    bad_data exception;
BEGIN    /* begins the executable section of a code block. */
    IF my_new_amt > 3 THEN
       . . .
    ELSE
       . . .
    END IF;
EXCEPTION  /*Begins the Exception Handler */
    WHEN bad_data THEN
       DBMS_OUTPUT.PUT_LINE('Error condition');
END;
```

The other class of PL/SQL blocks is known as an unnamed or *anonymous* block. It is easier to identify the declaration section of an anonymous PL/SQL block because the declaration section is preceded by the **declare** keyword. It too contains a declaration section, an executable section, and an exception handler.

```
DECLARE  /* begins the declaration section in an anonymous block */
    my_convert_amt          NUMBER(10);
    my_convert_currency     VARCHAR2(5);
    my_old_currency         VARCHAR2(5);
    bad_data                EXCEPTION;
BEGIN /* begins the executable section of a code block. */
    IF my_convert_amt=6 THEN
       . . .
    ELSE
       . . .
    END IF;
EXCEPTION  /*Begins the Exception Handler */
    WHEN bad_data THEN
       DBMS_OUTPUT.PUT_LINE('Error condition');
END;
```

TIP
*The call to DBMS_OUTPUT.**put_line( )** in one of the code blocks is used to write a line of output to the SQL*Plus interface. In order to view the line of output produced, use the **set serveroutput on** command.*

Process Flow and Logic Constructs

PL/SQL offers the programmer logic constructs such as **for** loops, **while** loops, **if-then-else** statements, assignments, and expressions. Other logic constructs include PL/SQL tables and records. These "procedural" constructs are the items in PL/SQL that allow it to be both a programming language for supporting business rules and a functional language for providing data.

Cursors

One of the real strengths of PL/SQL, however, is its ability to handle cursors. A cursor is a handle to an address in memory that stores the results of an executed SQL statement. They are extremely useful for performing operations on each row returned from a **select** statement. Therefore, the PL/SQL programmer often finds herself using the looping procedural constructs of PL/SQL in conjunction with cursor manipulation operations.

Error Handling

Errors are called *exceptions* in PL/SQL, and they are checked implicitly anywhere in the code block. If at any time an error occurs in the code block, the exception corresponding to that error can be raised. At that point, execution in the executable code block stops and control is transferred to the exception handler. There are many different types of exceptions in Oracle, some of which are user defined. Others are defined by Oracle.

Exercises

1. What is PL/SQL? Name some benefits to accessing the Oracle database with PL/SQL.

2. What are the three parts of a PL/SQL code block? Name four different types of code blocks in Oracle. What are some program constructs available in PL/SQL?

3. What is the difference between a named and an anonymous code block?

Developing a PL/SQL Block

In this section, you will cover the following topics related to developing a simple PL/SQL block:

- Declaring and using variables
- Variable value assignment

A couple of sample PL/SQL blocks have already been offered. This section will cover in more detail some of the technical aspects of creating PL/SQL blocks. The topics that will be covered in this section include advanced usage and declaration of variables and constants in the declarative section of the PL/SQL block, and a refresher on assigning values to variables in the executable section.

Declaring and Using Variables

PL/SQL offers a great deal of flexibility in variable declaration. So far, two examples of variable declaration in different code blocks have been presented. Both of these examples used simple declaration of datatypes. The ones used were datatypes that have been presented as valid datatypes on the Oracle database.

Database Datatypes

There are several datatypes that can be used in PL/SQL that correspond to the datatypes used on the database. These types are as follows:

- **NUMBER(***size*[*,precision*]**)**   Used to store any number.
- **CHAR(***size***), VARCHAR2(***size***)**   Used to store alphanumeric text strings. The CHAR datatype pads the value stored to the full length of the variable with blanks.
- **DATE**   Used to store dates.
- **LONG**   Stores large blocks of text, up to 2 gigabytes in length.

- **LONG RAW**   Stores large blocks of data stored in binary format.

- **RAW**   Stores smaller blocks of data stored in binary format.

- **MLSLABEL**   Used in Trusted Oracle.

- **ROWID**   Used to store the special format of ROWIDs on the database.

- **BLOB, CLOB, NCLOB, BFILE**   Large object datatypes from Oracle8.

Nondatabase Datatypes

There are also several other PL/SQL datatypes that are not designed for use in storing data to a table:

- **DEC, DECIMAL, REAL, DOUBLE_PRECISION**   These numeric datatypes are a subset of the NUMBER datatype that is used for variable declaration in PL/SQL.

- **INTEGER, INT, SMALLINT, NATURAL, POSITIVE, NUMERIC**   These numeric datatypes are a subset of the NUMBER datatype that is used for variable declaration in PL/SQL.

- **BINARY_INTEGER, PLS_INTEGER**   These datatypes store integers. A variable in either format cannot be stored in the database without conversion first.

- **CHARACTER**   Another name for the CHAR datatype.

- **VARCHAR**   Another name for the VARCHAR2 datatype.

- **BOOLEAN**   Stores a TRUE/FALSE value.

- **TABLE/RECORD**   Tables can be used to store the equivalent of an array, while records store variables with composite datatypes.

%TYPE

In general, the variables that deal with table columns should have the same datatype and length as the column itself. Rather than look it up, you can use PL/SQL's special syntactic feature that allows you simply to identify the table column to which this variable's datatype should correspond. This syntax uses a special keyword known as **%type**. When using the **%type** keyword, all you need to know is the name of the column and the table to which the variable will correspond. Additionally, a variable can be declared with an initialization value by setting it equal to the value in the declaration section. Notice the characters used to set the variable to a value:

```
DECLARE
    my_employee_id       employee.empid%TYPE;
BEGIN …

DECLARE
    my_salary        employee.salary%TYPE  := 0;
    my_lastname      employee.lastname%TYPE:= 'SMITH';
BEGIN …
```

%ROWTYPE

There is another variable declaration method that uses the same reference principle described in the previous text. It is called **%rowtype**, and it permits the developer to create a composite datatype in which all the columns of a row in the table referenced are lumped together into a record. For example, if the EMPLOYEE table contains four columns—EMPID, LASTNAME, FIRSTNAME, and SALARY—and you want to manipulate the values in each column of a row using only one referenced variable, the variable can be declared with the **%rowtype** keyword. Compare the use of **%rowtype** to manual record declaration:

```
DECLARE
    my_employee        employee%ROWTYPE;
BEGIN …
```

or manually:

```
DECLARE
    TYPE t_employee IS RECORD (
      my_empid       employee.empid%TYPE,
      my_lastname    employee.lastname%TYPE,
      my_firstname   employee.firstname%TYPE,
      my_salary      employee.salary%TYPE);

    my_employee    t_employee;
BEGIN…
```

TIP
Blocks of PL/SQL code can be nested, that is to say that a procedure can have subprocedures. In this case, the same principles of variable scope discussed in Chapter 2 also apply to nested PL/SQL blocks.

Constant Declaration

It may be useful for you to declare constants in the declaration section of the PL/SQL blocks developed as well. Constants make a good substitute for the use of hard-coded values, or "magic numbers." A magic value in programming is a value that is required to perform an operation or calculation but does not have any sort of meaning in the code block to help others identify why the value is there. Take, for example, a function that calculates the area of a circle, which is the number pi times radius squared. The number pi is well known to most people, but imagine if it was not, how difficult it would be to understand the reason for having the number 3.14159265358 in the middle of the function. Assume also that in the Oracle database there is a table called CIRCLE with a column called RADIUS, whose datatype you want to refer to in the function, as **circle.radius%TYPE**, shown here:

```
CREATE FUNCTION find_circle_area (
    p_radius    IN    circle.radius%TYPE
) RETURN NUMBER IS
    my_area    number(10)  := 0;
    pi         constant number(15,14)   := 3.14159265358;
BEGIN
    my_area := (p_radius*p_radius)* pi;
    Return (my_area);
END;
```

Exercises

1. Identify some of the database and nondatabase datatypes that can be used in PL/SQL.

2. How can you declare PL/SQL variables without explicitly identifying the datatype?

3. How do you declare a variable with an initialized value?

4. How do you declare a constant? Why might you use a constant?

Variable Value Assignment

As noted, it is possible to assign an initial value to a variable in the declaration section of the code block, and it is also possible to assign a value to a variable at any point during execution by using the assignment character: the colon followed by an equals sign. Note that the use of the equality (=) operation is for comparison only. Note also that variable assignment can be accomplished in a variety of ways in the executable section, including the use of the return value from a function call to populate a variable, or the use of the current value in a variable in an arithmetic equation to produce a new value.

```
DECLARE
    my_area      circle.area%TYPE := 0;
BEGIN
    my_area := find_circle_area(493);
    my_area := my_area + 45;
END;
```

Exercises

1. Where can a variable be assigned a value?

2. What is the assignment operator? How does it differ from the equality operator?

Interacting with the Oracle Database

In this section, you will cover the following topics related to interacting with Oracle:

■ Using **select**, **insert**, **update**, and **delete** in PL/SQL code

■ Using implicit cursor attributes

■ Transaction processing in PL/SQL

No usage of PL/SQL is complete without presenting the ease of use involved in interacting with the Oracle database. Any data manipulation or change operation can be accomplished within PL/SQL without the additional overhead typically required in other programming environments. There is no ODBC interface, and no embedding is required for database manipulation with PL/SQL.

Using SQL Statements in PL/SQL

Using a **select** statement in the sample PL/SQL code block shown shortly illustrates how seamless the integration of PL/SQL and the Oracle database is. Note that there are no special characters that must precede the PL/SQL variables in SQL statements. The one concession PL/SQL must make is the **into** clause, which places the return values from the **select** statement into the **%rowtype** record created in the declaration section. You are not forced to use **%rowtype**; a manual record declaration or even three stand-alone variables declared as the same datatypes for each of the columns you use in your **select** statement will suffice. Even so, the utility for declaring a complex record with **%rowtype** has already been proven to be more efficient than manual record declaration. The same ease of use can be seen in **update** statements. The use of the *record.element* notation to refer to the components of a record variable is illustrated as well. Using **insert** statements in PL/SQL is as straightforward as the other statements available in PL/SQL. The same is true for the **insert** statement. And, as one might expect, the usage of **delete** is as straightforward as the usage of other SQL statements in PL/SQL.

```
DECLARE
    my_employee         employee%ROWTYPE;
    my_lastname         VARCHAR2(30)    := 'SAMSON';
    my_firstname        VARCHAR2(30)    := 'DELILAH';
    my_salary           NUMBER(10)      := 49500;
BEGIN
    SELECT *
    INTO my_employee
    FROM employee
    WHERE empid = 49594;

    UPDATE employee
    SET salary = my_employee.salary + 10000
    WHERE empid = my_employee.empid;
```

```
    INSERT INTO employee (empid, lastname, firstname, salary)
    VALUES (emp_sequence.nextval, my_lastname, my_firstname,
my_salary);

    my_employee.empid := 59495;

    DELETE FROM employee
    WHERE empid = my_empid;
END;
```

Exercises

1. What special characters are required for using data manipulation statements in PL/SQL?

2. Explain how Oracle assigns values to elements in a record.

Using Implicit Cursor Attributes

After the SQL statement executes, several things can happen that a developer may care about. For example, assume that a block of code is designed to **select** data from a table. If there is no data selected, then a special message should appear to let the user of the PL/SQL block know that no data was found. There are two ways to handle this situation. The first option is straightforward enough. Check the variable into which data from the **select** statement will be placed. If the variable is NULL, no data was found. However, this programmer's trick is fooled when the table you **select** from contains NULL values for an existing row. The second option, using cursor attributes, is more powerful, elegant, and harder to fool. Cursor attributes are a set of built-in "checks" that you can use to identify when certain situations occur during SQL statement processing in PL/SQL blocks. The cursor attributes that will be discussed in this chapter are listed in the following series of bullets:

- **%notfound**   Identifies whether the **fetch** executed on the cursor returned any row data. If no data returned, this attribute evaluates to TRUE; otherwise, it evaluates to FALSE.

- **%rowcount**   Identifies the number of rows that were processed by this cursor. Returns a numeric value.

- **%found** Identifies whether the **fetch** executed on the cursor returned any row data. If no data returned, this attribute evaluates to TRUE; otherwise, it evaluates to FALSE.

- **%isopen** Identifies whether the cursor referred to is opened and ready for use. Returns a TRUE if cursor is open, and FALSE if cursor is not.

In order to understand fully the use of cursor attributes, a discussion of cursor processing is required. For now, it is sufficient to know that cursors are generally named something, and that the syntax for using the cursor attributes just identified is to name the cursor, followed by the attribute. This syntax is similar to that used for the **%type** and **%rowtype** variable declaration attributes. For example, the open or close status of cursor EMPLOYEES can be referred to by its cursor attribute, with the user entering EMPLOYEES**%isopen**, which will return TRUE if the cursor is open or FALSE if the cursor is closed. More details about using cursor attributes and general cursor processing are discussed later in the chapter.

Exercises

1. What value can implicit cursor attributes serve in PL/SQL code?
2. What are some of the implicit cursor attributes a developer can use in PL/SQL?

Transaction Processing in PL/SQL

The same options for transaction processing that are available in SQL statement processing are available in PL/SQL processing. Those options include specifications that name the beginning, logical breakpoint, and end of a transaction. The database options that provide lock mechanisms to ensure that only one user at a time has the ability to change a record in the database are still available within the database, regardless of whether SQL or PL/SQL is used to reference the database objects.

The three transaction specifications available in PL/SQL are **commit**, **savepoint**, and **rollback**. An important distinction to make between executing SQL statements in PL/SQL blocks and the iterative entering of SQL statements with SQL*Plus is that the beginning and end of a PL/SQL block does not generally denote the beginning or end of a transaction. The

beginning of a transaction in the PL/SQL block is the execution of the first
SQL data change statement. In general, in order to guarantee that statements
executed that make changes in the database have those changes saved, the
PL/SQL code block should explicitly contain a **commit** statement. Likewise,
to discard changes made or to specify a breakpoint in a transaction, the
developer should code in **rollback** and **savepoint** operations appropriately.
Also, since the **set transaction** statement is not available in PL/SQL to
denote the beginning of the transaction or to set the transaction's database
access to **read only**, Oracle provides the DBMS_TRANSACTION package.
Within this package, there are several different functions that allow the user
to start, end, and moderate the transaction processing within PL/SQL blocks.

Exercises

1. What transaction-processing features are available in PL/SQL?

2. What is DBMS_TRANSACTION?

Controlling PL/SQL Process Flow

In this section, you will cover the following topics related to controlling
PL/SQL process flow:

- Conditional statements and process flow
- Using loops

No programming language is complete without the use of semantic
devices to control the processing flow of its code. Some mention has already
been made of the two categories of PL/SQL process flow statements, which
are conditional expressions and loops. This section will cover the details of
using both conditions and loops to moderate the processing of a PL/SQL
block. As these concepts are fairly standard among procedural programming
languages such as COBOL or C, most developers with programming
experience should have no problem with the concepts. The more specific
area of the chapter, and the one that will be tested in OCP Exam 1, is the
area of syntax and appropriate usage. You should focus on these areas to
gain the best background in preparation for the test.

Conditional Statements and Process Flow

A condition in a program equates directly with the idea of making a decision. The fundamental idea behind conditional processing is that of Boolean logic. Boolean logic, named for Charles Boole, a mathematician from the 19th century, is TRUE or FALSE logic. Some of the questions at the end of this chapter illustrate the idea behind TRUE or FALSE logic. The values TRUE and FALSE are conditions that can be applied to certain types of statements, called *comparison operations*. Some comparisons are as follows:

- $3 + 5 = 8$
- Menorahs hold ten candles
- $4 = 10$
- Today is Tuesday

Note that these comparison operations can all be evaluated for their validity, or whether they are TRUE or FALSE. In the first case, the statement is TRUE because 3 plus 5 equals 8. In the second, a menorah (used to commemorate the Jewish Feast of Lights around the same time as Christmas) usually contains eight or nine candles, but never ten. Therefore, the statement is FALSE. In the third example, 4 definitely does not equal 10, so the statement is FALSE. The final example illustrates an interesting principle about comparison operations; sometimes today is Tuesday, but sometimes it is not. The validity of the statement, then, depends on when the comparison is made.

Conditional statement-processing mechanisms allow you to structure code such that certain statements may or may not execute based on the validity of a comparison operation. The general syntax for conditional statements is "**if** the comparison is TRUE, **then** do the following." PL/SQL also offers an optional add-on, called **else**, which says essentially, "otherwise, do whatever the **else** clause says."

```
BEGIN
    IF TO_CHAR(sysdate,'DAY') = to_char(to_date('26-JAN-99'),'DAY') THEN
        find_hypotenuse(56,45,my_hypotenuse);
    ELSE
        My_hypotenuse := derive_hypotenuse(56,45);
    END IF;
END;
```

Note that single-row operations are allowed in comparison statements, so long as they resolve to a datatype that can be compared properly. If, for example, one side of the comparison operation resolves to a number and the other side is a text string, then that will be a problem. Additionally, note that the **else** statement can contain another **if** statement, allowing for nested **if** statements that amount to a **case** operation.

```
BEGIN
    IF TO_CHAR(sysdate,'DAY') = to_char(to_date('26-JAN-99'), 'DAY') THEN
        find_hypotenuse(56,45,my_hypotenuse);
    ELSIF TO_CHAR(sysdate,'DAY') = to_char_(to_date('28-JAN-99'), 'DAY') THEN
        my_hypotenuse := derive_hypotenuse(56,45);
    ELSE
        my_hypotenuse := 0;
    END IF;
END;
```

Once again, if the first condition is TRUE, the first block of PL/SQL will execute. If the second condition is TRUE, then the second block of PL/SQL code will execute. If neither of the preceding code blocks is TRUE, then the third PL/SQL block will execute. To end an **if** statement, there must be the **end if** keywords. Otherwise, the code after the conditional expression will be treated as part of the **else** clause, which will cause the PL/SQL compiler to error out.

Exercises

1. What statement allows you to handle conditional statement processing?

2. What is a comparison operation? What is Boolean logic?

Using Loops

Another situation that arises in programming is the need to execute a set of statements repeatedly. The repetitions can be controlled in two ways: the first is to repeat the code for a specified number of times, and the second is to repeat the code until some condition is met, thus rendering a comparison operation to TRUE. The types of loops that are available in PL/SQL are as follows:

- **Loop-exit** statements, also called basic loops
- **While-loop** statements
- **For-loop** statements

LOOP-EXIT Statements

The **loop-exit** statement is the simplest type of loop that can be written in PL/SQL. The **loop** keyword denotes the beginning of the code block that will be repeated, and the **end loop** keywords denote the end of the code block that will be repeated. The **exit** keyword specified by itself denotes that process should break out of the loop, while the **exit when** keywords denote a comparison operation that will test whether the statement is finished executing.

```
DECLARE
    my_leg                NUMBER(10) := 0;
    my_hypotenuse         NUMBER(10) := 0;
BEGIN
    LOOP
       my_leg := my_leg + 1;
       find_hypotenuse(my_leg,my_leg,my_hypotenuse);
       IF my_leg = 25 THEN
          EXIT;
       END IF;
    END LOOP;
END;
```

The **if-then** statement is designed to determine if the conditions within the loop are such that the loop should terminate. The **exit** statement instructs the PL/SQL execution mechanism to leave the loop. An alternative to setting up an **if-then** statement to determine if the loop should end is to add a **when** condition to the **exit** statement. The **when** condition contains the comparison operation that the **if-then** statement would have handled. An example of a simple **loop** statement that uses an **exit when** statement is listed in the following code block. Note that the code is essentially a revision of the simple **loop** block.

```
DECLARE
    my_leg               NUMBER(10) := 0;
    my_hypotenuse        NUMBER(10) := 0;
BEGIN
    LOOP
      my_leg := my_leg + 1;
      find_hypotenuse(my_leg,my_leg,my_hypotenuse);
      EXIT WHEN my_leg = 25;
    END LOOP;
END;
```

The **when** clause is very useful for the developer because it offers an elegant solution to defining when the loop will end, as opposed to hiding an **exit** statement inside an **if-then** statement. However, there are other possibilities for developing loops to handle repetition in coding.

WHILE-LOOP Statements

The next type of loop that approximates the usage of a **loop-exit when** statement is the **while loop** statement. The code in the previous block can be rewritten to include the **while loop**. The only difference between the **while loop** statement and the **loop-exit when** statement is where PL/SQL evaluates the **exit** condition. In a **while loop** statement, the exiting condition is evaluated at the beginning of the statement, while in the **loop-exit when** statement, the **exit** condition is evaluated wherever the **exit when** statement is placed. In one sense, the **loop-exit when** statement offers more flexibility than the **while loop** statement does because **loop-exit when** allows the developer to specify the **exit** condition wherever he wants. However, the flexibility that the **while-loop** statement may lack is made up for by its comparative elegance, in that there is no need for an **exit** statement.

```
DECLARE
    my_leg               NUMBER(10) := 0;
    my_hypotenuse        NUMBER(10) := 0;
BEGIN
    WHILE my_leg =< 25 LOOP
      my_leg := my_leg + 1;
      find_hypotenuse(my_leg,my_leg,my_hypotenuse);
    END LOOP;
END;
```

FOR-LOOP Statements

The final example of looping constructs to be presented is the **for loop** statement. This type of loop allows the developer to specify exactly the number of times the code will execute before PL/SQL will break out of it. To accomplish this process, the **for loop** statement specifies a loop counter and a range through which the counter will circulate. Optionally, you can circulate through the loop counter in reverse order, or in numeric descending order. The loop counter is then available for use by the statements in the **for loop** statement.

TIP
For loop statements have a built-in counter, which automatically increments itself by 1. Other options for incrementing the counter are also available.

```
DECLARE
    My_leg           NUMBER(10)  := 0;
    My_hypotenuse    NUMBER(10)  := 0;
BEGIN
    FOR my_leg IN 1..25 LOOP
        find_hypotenuse(my_leg,my_leg,my_hypotenuse);
    END LOOP;
END;
```

Notice that the use of a **for loop** statement made this code block even more elegant. No longer necessary is the statement that increments the *my_leg* variable, since the **for loop** statement handles the incrementation activity automatically. There is another type of **for loop** statement related to cursor handling that offers the same elegance and utility as the **for loop** statement detailed in the previous code block. Its usage, as well as the more general usage of cursors, will be covered in the next section of this chapter. The following code block shows the previous anonymous PL/SQL block again, this time with the **for loop** statement executing in reverse order. Notice that you don't need to change the beginning and end digit value any differently, Oracle handles everything properly with the **reverse** keyword.

```
DECLARE
    My_leg           NUMBER(10)  := 0;
    My_hypotenuse    NUMBER(10)  := 0;
BEGIN
```

```
      FOR my_leg IN REVERSE 1..25 LOOP
        find_hypotenuse(my_leg,my_leg,my_hypotenuse);
      END LOOP;
END;
```

PL/SQL does not allow you to increment or decrement your counter in the **for loop** statement by anything other than 1 natively. You can build this functionality with the use of a **mod( )** function in your **for loop** statement, as shown in this following code block:

```
DECLARE
     My_leg            NUMBER(10) := 0;
     My_hypotenuse     NUMBER(10) := 0;
BEGIN
     FOR my_leg IN 1..25 LOOP
       IF mod(my_leg,2) = 0 THEN
           find_hypotenuse(my_leg,my_leg,my_hypotenuse);
       END IF;
     END LOOP;
END;
```

Exercises

1. How is nested conditional statement processing handled?

2. What are three different types of loops? What is an **exit when** statement? What is a loop counter, and for which type of loop is it most commonly used? Which type of loop doesn't require an explicit **exit** statement?

Explicit Cursor Handling

In this section, you will cover the following topics related to using cursors in PL/SQL:

■ Implicit vs. explicit cursors

■ Declaring and using explicit cursors

■ Parameters and explicit cursors

■ Writing **cursor for** loops

The definition of a cursor has already been presented. To recap, a cursor is an address in memory where a SQL statement is processed. Cursors are frequently used in PL/SQL to handle loop processing for a set of values returned by a **select** statement, and they have other uses as well. This discussion will present the uses for cursors, along with the different types of cursors available in Oracle. Creation of all types of cursors will be presented, along with a more detailed discussion of creating the **cursor for** loop for cursor data handling.

Implicit vs. Explicit Cursors

Every time a user executes SQL statements of any sort, there is activity on the database that involves cursors. There are two types of cursors in PL/SQL: implicit and explicit cursors. The implicit cursor is an unnamed address where the SQL statement is processed by Oracle and/or the PL/SQL execution mechanism. Every SQL statement executes in an implicit cursor, including **update**, **insert**, and **delete** statements, and **select** statements that do not execute in explicit cursors.

TIP
Every SQL statement executed on the Oracle database is an implicit cursor, and any implicit cursor attribute can be used in conjunction with them.

An explicit cursor is one that is named by the developer. The cursor is little more than a **select** statement that has a name. Any sort of **select** statement can be used in an explicit cursor using the **cursor** *cursor_name* **is** syntax. When a **select** statement is placed in an explicit cursor, the developer has more complete control over the statement's execution.

```
DECLARE
    CURSOR employee_cursor IS
        SELECT * FROM employee;
    END;
BEGIN ...
```

There is really no such thing as determining "the best time" to use an implicit cursor, but the developer can determine the best time to use an explicit one. Every time a SQL operation is requested, an implicit cursor is used. When the developer wants to perform some manipulation on each record returned by a **select** operation, she will use an explicit cursor. Most serious processing of data records is done with explicit cursors; however, there are some operations that work with implicit cursors as well. For example, many of the cursor attributes identified in an earlier section of this chapter can be applied to implicit cursors with useful results. To refresh the discussion, the list of cursor attributes available are **%notfound**, **%found**, **%rowcount**, and **%isopen**. **%notfound** identifies whether the **fetch** executed on the cursor did not return a row. The return value is the opposite of that which is returned by **%found**, which identifies whether the **fetch** executed on the cursor returned a row. These two attributes return a TRUE or FALSE value. **%rowcount** identifies the number of rows that were processed by this cursor and returns a numeric value. **%isopen** identifies whether the cursor referred to is opened and ready for use, and returns a TRUE or FALSE value.

Using an implicit cursor in conjunction with cursor attributes may consist of executing some statement and then finding out if the results were successful. In the following example, a user attempts to update an employee salary record. If there are no employees in the EMPLOYEE table that correspond with the EMPID he would like to modify, then he wants the process to add an employee record.

```
DECLARE
    my_empid      employee.empid%TYPE := 59694;
    my_salary     employee.salary%TYPE := 99000;
    my_lastname   employee.lastname%TYPE := 'RIDDINGS';
BEGIN
    UPDATE employee
    SET salary = my_salary
    WHERE empid = my_empid;

    IF SQL%NOTFOUND THEN
        INSERT INTO EMPLOYEE (empid, lastname, salary)
        VALUES(my_empid, my_lastname, my_salary);
    END IF;
END;
```

There are two implicit cursors in this example. The first is the **update** statement, and the second is the **insert** statement. If the **update** statement produces a change on no rows, the **if sql%notfound then** statement will trap the error and force some operation to happen as a result of the condition. Note that in the situation of an implicit cursor, 'SQL' is the name you use to refer to the most recent implicit cursor. In this situation, the developer should specify **sql%notfound**, or **sql%found**, or use 'SQL' followed by the cursor attribute. That 'SQL' represents the most recently executed SQL statement producing an implicit cursor.

Exercises

1. What is an implicit cursor and what is the syntax for creating one?

2. What is an explicit cursor? Why might a developer use an explicit cursor rather than an implicit one?

3. What is the syntax for creating an explicit cursor?

Declaring and Using Explicit Cursors

Most of the time, developers spend their efforts working with explicitly defined cursors. These programming devices allow the developer to control processing outcome based on manipulation of individual records returned by a **select** statement. As stated, a cursor is defined with the syntax **cursor** *cursor_name* **is**, which is then followed by a **select** statement. Once defined, the cursor allows the developer to step through the results of the query in a number of different ways.

```
DECLARE
    /* extract from a salary review program */
    high_pctinc    constant    number(10,5)    := 1.20;
    med_pctinc     constant    number(10,5)    := 1.10;
    low_pctinc     constant    number(10,5)    := 1.05;
    my_salary      employee.salary%TYPE;
    my_empid       employee.empid%TYPE;
    CURSOR employee_crsr IS
        SELECT empid, salary
        FROM employee;
BEGIN …
```

Consider the definition of EMPLOYEE_CRSR. The two keywords used are **cursor** and **is**. Note that the syntactic requirements of the **select** statement are fairly standard. The declaration of a cursor does not actually produce the cursor, however. At this point, the cursor definition simply stands ready for action. The cursor will not actually exist in memory until it is opened and parsed by the SQL execution mechanism in Oracle. Data will not populate the cursor until the cursor is executed.

Attention should turn now to the process of invoking the cursor in memory. In this example, the employees of the company will be selected into the cursor for the purpose of salary review. Once selected, the review will be conducted as follows. Every employee of the company will obtain a midlevel raise as defined by the percentage increase listed for *mid_pctinc*. There are four exceptions: two employees will get a large raise as defined by the percentage increase listed for *high_pctinc*, while two other employees will get low performance increases as defined by *low_pctinc*. The process flow will be governed by a conditional statement, along with a loop.

```
DECLARE
    /* extract from a salary review program */
    high_pctinc   constant    number(10,5)      := 1.20;
    med_pctinc    constant    number(10,5)      := 1.10;
    low_pctinc    constant    number(10,5)      := 1.05;
    my_salary     employee.salary%TYPE;
    my_empid      employee.empid%TYPE;
     CURSOR employee_crsr IS
        SELECT empid, salary
        FROM employee;
BEGIN
    /* The following statement creates and */
    /* executes the cursor in memory */
    OPEN employee_crsr;

    LOOP  /* sets a loop that allows program to step through */
          /* records of cursor */
       FETCH employee_crsr INTO my_empid, my_salary;
       EXIT WHEN employee_crsr%NOTFOUND;  /* stop looping when no */
                                          /* records found */
       IF my_empid = 59697 OR my_empid = 76095 THEN
          UPDATE employee SET salary = my_salary*high_pctinc
          WHERE empid = my_empid;
       ELSIF my_empid = 39294 OR my_empid = 94329 THEN
          UPDATE employee SET salary = my_salary*low_pctinc
          WHERE empid = my_empid;
       ELSE
          UPDATE employee SET salary = my_salary*mid_pctinc
          WHERE empid = my_empid;
       END IF;
    END LOOP;
END;
```

The main cursor manipulation operations are the **open**, **loop-exit when**, **fetch**, and *cursor*%**notfound** statements. The cursor is first opened with the **open** command, which implicitly parses and executes the statement as well. The loop is defined such that it should run until all records from the cursor are processed. The **exit** condition uses the **%notfound** attribute, preceded by the name of the explicit cursor. Pay particular attention to the **fetch** statement. This operation can only be performed on explicit cursors that are **select** statements. When a call to **fetch** is made, PL/SQL will obtain the next record from the cursor and populate the variables specified with values obtained from the cursor. If the **fetch** produces no results, then the **%notfound** attribute is set to TRUE. The cursor **fetch** statement can handle variables of two sorts. The **fetch** command in the preceding code block illustrates use of stand-alone variables for each column value stored in the cursor. The **fetch** statement depends on positional specification to populate the variables if this option is used. Alternately, the use of a record that contains the same attributes as those columns defined by the cursor is also handled by **fetch**. Positional specification is used here as well, so it is required for the order of the variables in the declared record to match the order of columns specified in the cursor declaration.

```
DECLARE
    /* extract from a salary review program */
    high_pctinc   constant   number(10,5)   := 1.20;
    med_pctinc    constant   number(10,5)   := 1.10;
    low_pctinc    constant   number(10,5)   := 1.05;
    TYPE t_emp IS RECORD (
        t_salary   employee.salary%TYPE,
        t_empid    employee.empid%TYPE);
    my_emprec   t_emp;
    CURSOR employee_crsr IS
        SELECT empid, salary
        FROM employee;
BEGIN
    /* The following statement creates and executes the cursor in
memory */
    OPEN employee_crsr;
    LOOP  /* sets a loop that allows program to step */
         /* through records of cursor */
        FETCH employee_crsr INTO my_emprec;
        EXIT WHEN employee_crsr%NOTFOUND;  /* stop looping when no */
                                            /* records found */
```

```
        IF my_emprec.t_empid = 59697 OR my_emprec.t_empid = 76095
THEN
        UPDATE employee SET salary =
my_emprec.t_salary*high_pctinc
        WHERE empid = my_emprec.t_empid;
    ELSIF my_emprec.t_empid = 39294 OR my_emprec.t_empid = 94329
THEN
        UPDATE employee SET salary = my_emprec.t_salary*low_pctinc
        WHERE empid = my_emprec.t_empid;
    ELSE
        UPDATE employee SET salary = my_emprec.t_salary*mid_pctinc
        WHERE empid = my_emprec.t_empid;
    END IF;
  END LOOP;
END;
```

The additional code required to support records in this case may well be worth it if there are many variables in the PL/SQL block. Records give the developer a more object-oriented method for handling the variables required for cursor manipulation.

Exercises

1. What must be done in order to make a cursor exist in memory?

2. What step must be accomplished to put data in a cursor?

3. How is data retrieved from a cursor?

Parameters and Explicit Cursors

At times, there may be opportunities for the reuse of a cursor definition. However, the cursors demonstrated thus far either **select** every record in the database or, alternately, may be designed to **select** from a table according to hard-coded "magic" values. There is a way to configure cursors such that the values from which data will be selected can be specified at the time the cursor is opened. The method used to create this cursor setup is the use of parameters. For example, assume the developer wanted to set up so that the cursor would select a subset of values from the database to run the salary review program on, based on the first letter of the last name. This process could be accomplished with the use of cursor parameters. The developer could allow the cursor to accept a low and high limit, and then **select** data from the table for the cursor using that range.

```
DECLARE
/* extract from a salary review program */
   high_pctinc   constant   number(10,5)   := 1.20;
   med_pctinc    constant   number(10,5)   := 1.10;
   low_pctinc    constant   number(10,5)   := 1.05;
   TYPE t_emp IS RECORD (
       t_salary    employee.salary%TYPE,
       t_empid     employee.empid%TYPE);
       my_emprec   t_emp;
   CURSOR employee_crsr(low_end in VARCHAR2, high_end in VARCHAR2)
IS
       SELECT empid, salary
       FROM employee
       WHERE substr(lastname,1,1) BETWEEN UPPER(low_end) AND
UPPER(high_end);
BEGIN …
```

With the parameter passing defined, the developer can set up the cursor with more control over the data that is ultimately processed. For example, if the developer wants only to process salary increases for employees whose last names start with A through M, she can develop the following code block:

```
DECLARE
/* extract from a salary review program */
   high_pctinc   constant   number(10,5)   := 1.20;
   med_pctinc    constant   number(10,5)   := 1.10;
   low_pctinc    constant   number(10,5)   := 1.05;
   TYPE t_emp IS RECORD (
       t_salary    employee.salary%TYPE,
       t_empid     employee.empid%TYPE);
       my_emprec   t_emp;
   CURSOR employee_crsr(low_end in VARCHAR2, high_end in VARCHAR2)
IS
       SELECT empid, salary
       FROM employee
           WHERE UPPER(substr(lastname,1,1)) BETWEEN UPPER(low_end)
AND UPPER(high_end);
BEGIN
/* The following statement creates and executes the cursor in
memory */
```

```
      OPEN employee_crsr('A','M');
      LOOP  /* sets a loop that allows program to step */
           /* through records of cursor */
         FETCH employee_crsr INTO my_emprec;
         EXIT WHEN employee_crsr%NOTFOUND;  /* stop looping when no */
                                           /* records found */
         IF my_emprec.t_empid = 59697 OR my_emprec.t_empid = 76095
THEN
            UPDATE employee SET salary =
my_emprec.t_salary*high_pctinc
            WHERE empid = my_emprec.t_empid;
         ELSIF my_emprec.t_empid = 39294 OR my_emprec.t_empid = 94329
THEN
            UPDATE employee SET salary =
my_emprec.t_salary*low_pctinc
            WHERE empid = my_emprec.t_empid;
         ELSE
            UPDATE employee SET salary =
my_emprec.t_salary*mid_pctinc
            WHERE empid = my_emprec.t_empid;
         END IF;
      END LOOP;
END;
```

Notice that this code block—the **open** statement that opens, parses, and executes the cursor—now contains two values passed into the cursor creation as parameters. This parameter passing is required for the cursor to resolve into a set of data rows.

Exercises

1. What value does passing parameters to a cursor provide?

2. How can a cursor be defined to accept parameters?

Writing CURSOR FOR Loops

As given evidence in the previous examples, quite a bit of usage surrounding cursors involves selecting data and performing operations on each row returned by the cursor. The code examples presented thus far illustrate how to perform this activity. However, each one of the examples illustrates also that there is some overhead for handling the looping process correctly. Depending on the type of loop used, the overhead required can be substantial. Take, for example, the use of a simple **loop-exit** statement. Not only must the code that will execute repeatedly be enclosed in the **loop** syntax construct, but the test for the **exit** condition must be defined explicitly. Other looping statement examples do simplify the process somewhat.

There is one other loop that is ideal for the situation where a developer wants to pull together some rows of data and perform a specified set of operations on them. This loop statement is called the **cursor for** loop. The **cursor for** loops handle several activities implicitly related to loop creation. The items handled implicitly by a **cursor for** loop are the opening, parsing, executing, and fetching of row data from the cursor, and the check to determine if there is more data (and thus if the loop should exit). Moreover, the declaration of a record variable to handle the data fetched from the cursor by the **cursor for** loop is also handled implicitly. The sample PL/SQL block is reprinted below with the addition of a **cursor for** loop statement to handle all cursor processing:

```
DECLARE
/* extract from a salary review program */
   high_pctinc   constant   number(10,5)   := 1.20;
   med_pctinc    constant   number(10,5)   := 1.10;
   low_pctinc    constant   number(10,5)   := 1.05;
   CURSOR employee_crsr(low_end in VARCHAR2, high_end in VARCHAR2)
IS
      SELECT empid, salary
      FROM employee
      WHERE UPPER(substr(lastname,1,1)) BETWEEN UPPER(low_end) AND
UPPER(high_end);
BEGIN
/* The following statement creates and executes the cursor in
memory */
/* sets a loop that allows program to step through records of
cursor */
   FOR my_emprec in employee_crsr('A','M') LOOP
     IF my_emprec.empid = 59697 OR my_emprec.empid = 76095 THEN
        UPDATE employee SET salary = my_emprec.salary*high_pctinc
        WHERE empid = my_emprec.empid;
     ELSIF my_emprec.empid = 39294 OR my_emprec.empid = 94329 THEN
        UPDATE employee SET salary = my_emprec.salary*low_pctinc
        WHERE empid = my_emprec.empid;
     ELSE
        UPDATE employee SET salary = my_emprec.salary*mid_pctinc;
```

```
      WHERE empid = my_emprec.empid;
    END IF;
  END LOOP;
END;
```

Take an extra moment to review the code block detailing a **cursor for** loop and confirm the following features the loop handles implicitly. Note that the benefit of using a **cursor for** loop is that there are fewer requirements to set up the loop, resulting in fewer lines of code, fewer mistakes, and easier-to-read programs. The features that **cursor for** loops handle implicitly are listed here:

■ The **cursor for** loop handles opening, parsing, and executing the cursor automatically.

■ The **cursor for** loop fetches row data implicitly for each iteration of the loop.

■ The **cursor for** loop handles the *cursor_name*%**notfound** condition implicitly and appropriately terminates the loop when the attribute is TRUE.

■ The **cursor for** loop handles the definition of a record to store the row values returned by the cursor **fetch** automatically, resulting in a smaller declaration section.

Exercises

1. What steps in cursor loop handling does a **cursor for** loop handle implicitly?

2. How is the **exit** condition defined for a **cursor for** loop?

Error Handling

In this section, you will cover the following areas related to error handling:

■ The three basic types of exceptions

■ Identifying common exceptions

■ Coding the exception handler

The handling of errors in PL/SQL is arguably the best contribution PL/SQL makes to commercial programming. Errors in PL/SQL need not be trapped and handled with **if** statements directly within the program, as they are in other procedural languages like C. Instead, PL/SQL allows the developer to *raise exceptions* when an error condition is identified and switch control to a special program area in the PL/SQL block, called the *exception handler*. The code to handle an error does not clutter the executable program logic in PL/SQL, nor is the programmer required to terminate programs with **return** or **exit** statements. The exception handler is a cleaner way to handle errors.

Three Basic Types of Exceptions

The three types of exceptions in Oracle PL/SQL are *predefined* exceptions, *user-defined* exceptions, and *internal* exceptions. Exception handling in PL/SQL offers several advantages. These advantages are simplicity and flexibility. Predefined exceptions offer the developer several built-in problems that can be checked. User-defined and internal exceptions allow for additional flexibility to build in a level of support for errors defined by the user into PL/SQL. The following discussions will illustrate the use of predefined, user-defined, and internal exceptions.

Predefined Exceptions

In order to facilitate error handling in PL/SQL, Oracle has designed several "built-in" or predefined exceptions. These exceptions are used to handle common situations that may occur on the database. For example, there is a built-in exception that can be used to detect when a statement returns no data, or when a statement expecting one piece of data receives more than one piece of data. There is no invoking a predefined exception—they are tested and raised automatically by Oracle. However, in order to have something done when the predefined error occurs, there must be something in the exception handler both to identify the error and to define what happens when the error occurs. Later, in the section "Identifying Common Exceptions," several of the most common exceptions will be presented.

TIP
In order to trap a predefined exception, there must be an exception handler coded for it in the exceptions section of the PL/SQL block.

User-Defined Exceptions

In addition to predefined exceptions, there can be created a whole host of user-defined exceptions that handle situations that may arise in the code. A user-defined exception may not produce an Oracle error; instead, user-defined exceptions may enforce business rules in situations where an Oracle error would not necessarily occur. Unlike predefined exceptions, which are implicitly raised when the associated error condition arises, a user-defined exception must have explicit code in the PL/SQL block designed to raise it. There is code required for all three sections of a PL/SQL block if the developer plans on using user-defined exceptions. The required code is detailed in the bullets that follow:

- **Exception declaration** In the declaration section of the PL/SQL block, the exception name must be declared. This name will be used to invoke, or *raise*, the exception in the execution section if the conditions of the exception occur.

- **Exception testing** In the execution section of the PL/SQL block, there must be code that explicitly tests for the user-defined error condition, which raises the exception if the conditions are met.

- **Exception handling** In the exception handler section of the PL/SQL block, there must be a specified **when** clause that names the exception and the code that should be executed if that exception is raised. Alternately, there should be a **when others** exception handler that acts as a catchall.

The following code block provides an example for coding a user-defined exception. In the example, assume that there is some problem with an employee's salary record being NULL. The following code will select a record from the database. If the record selected has a NULL salary, the user-defined exception will identify the problem with an output message.

```
DECLARE
    my_empid            employee.empid%TYPE := 59694;
    my_emp_record       employee%ROWTYPE;
    my_salary_null      EXCEPTION;
BEGIN
    SELECT * FROM employee
    INTO my_emp_record
    WHERE empid = my_empid;
```

```
    IF my_emp_record.salary IS NULL THEN
RAISE my_salary_null;
END IF;
EXCEPTION
    WHEN NO_DATA_FOUND THEN
        DBMS_OUTPUT.PUT_LINE('No Data Found');
    WHEN my_salary_null THEN
DBMS_OUTPUT.PUT_LINE('Salary column was null for employee');
END;
```

Note that code must appear for user-defined exceptions in all three areas of the PL/SQL block. Without one of these components, the exception will not operate properly and the code will produce errors.

Internal Exceptions

The list of predefined exceptions is limited, and overall they really do nothing other than associate a named exception with an Oracle error. You can extend the list of exceptions associated with Oracle errors within your PL/SQL code with the use of **pragma exception_init** keywords. This statement is a compiler directive that allows the developer to declare the Oracle-numbered error to be associated with a named exception in the block. This usage allows the code to handle errors that it might not have handled previously, without requiring the developer to program an explicit **raise** statement for the exception. For example, assume that the developer is inserting data on the EMPLOYEE table, and this table defined a NOT NULL constraint on SALARY. Instead of allowing the PL/SQL block to terminate abnormally if an **insert** occurs that does not name a value for the SALARY column with an **ORA-01400** error, the declaration of an exception allows the PL/SQL block to handle the error programmatically.

```
DECLARE
    my_emp_record        employee%ROWTYPE;
    my_salary_null exception;
    PRAGMA EXCEPTION_INIT(my_salary_null, -1400);
BEGIN
    my_emp_record.empid := 59485;
    my_emp_record.lastname := 'RICHARD';
    my_emp_record.firstname := 'JEAN-MARIE';
    my_emp_record.salary := 65000;
```

```
        INSERT INTO employee(empid,lastname,firstname,salary)
        VALUES(my_emp_record.empid, my_emp_record.lastname,
               my_emp_record.firstname, my_emp_record.salary);
EXCEPTION
        WHEN NO_DATA_FOUND THEN
            DBMS_OUTPUT.PUT_LINE('No Data Found');
        WHEN my_salary_null THEN
DBMS_OUTPUT.PUT_LINE('Salary column was null for employee');
END;
```

An advantage to using the **exception_init** pragma when the user-defined error produces some Oracle error is that there is no need for an explicit condition test that raises the exception if the condition is met. Exceptions defined with the **exception_init** pragma enjoy the same implicit exception handling as predefined exceptions do.

Exercises

   1. What is a predefined error? How are they invoked?

   2. What is a user-defined error? Where must code be defined in order to create a user-defined exception?

   3. What can be used to associate an Oracle error with a user-defined error?

Identifying Common Exceptions

There are many common exceptions that Oracle PL/SQL allows developers to define and handle in their programs. Some of the predefined cursors are listed here:

- **invalid_cursor**   Occurs when an attempt is made to close a nonopen cursor.

- **cursor_already_open**   Occurs when an attempt is made to open a nonclosed cursor.

- **dup_val_on_index**   Unique or primary-key constraint violation.

- **no_data_found**   No rows were selected or changed by the SQL operation.

- **too_many_rows** More than one row was obtained by a single-row subquery, or in another SQL statement operation where Oracle was expecting one row.

- **zero_divide** An attempt was made to divide by zero.

- **rowtype_mismatch** The datatypes of the record to which data from the cursor is assigned are incompatible.

- **invalid_number** An alphanumeric string was referenced as a number.

Of these operations, the developer may expect to use the **no_data_found** or **too_many_rows** exceptions most frequently. In fact, the user can incorporate checks for these areas using cursor attributes. As mentioned, in order to use an exception, the developer must *raise* it. Raising an exception requires usage of the **raise** statement. However, one of the best features about the predefined exceptions is that there is no need to raise them. They must simply be included in the exception handler for the PL/SQL block, and if a situation arises where the error occurs, then the predefined exception is raised automatically. The following code block illustrates the use of an exception handler, along with a predefined exception:

```
DECLARE
    my_empid    number(10);
    my_emprec employee%rowtype;
BEGIN
    my_empid := 59694;
    SELECT * FROM employee INTO my_emprec
    WHERE empid = my_empid;
EXCEPTION
    WHEN NO_DATA_FOUND THEN
        DBMS_OUTPUT.PUT_LINE('No Data Found');
END;
```

Notice that there is no code that explicitly tells PL/SQL to write the output message if no data is found in the particular **select** statement in the executable portion of the block. Instead, the exception is implicitly raised when a predefined exception condition occurs. This layer of abstraction is useful because the additional **if** statement required for checking this condition manually is unnecessary.

Exercises

I. What predefined exception is used to identify the situation where no data is returned by a **select** statement?

2. What predefined exception is used to identify when the datatype of the information returned is not the same datatype as the declared variable?

Coding the Exception Handler

Special attention should be paid now to the actual code of the exception handler. So far, the exceptions handled in previous code blocks have had simple routines that display an error message. There are more advanced options than those presented, of course. This discussion will focus on a few of the options provided.

A named or user-defined exception in the declaration and executable section of the PL/SQL block should have an associated exception handler written for it. The way to handle an exception is to name it specifically using the **when** clause in the exceptions block of the PL/SQL program. Following the **when** clause, there can be one or several statements that define the events that will happen if this exception is raised. If there is no code explicitly defined for the exception raised, then PL/SQL will execute whatever code is defined for a special catchall exception called **others**. If there is no explicit code defined for a particular exception and no code defined for the **others** exception, then control passes to the exception handler of the procedure that called the PL/SQL code block. The exception handler is perhaps the greatest achievement gained by using PL/SQL to write stored procedures in Oracle. Its flexibility and ease of use make it simple to code robust programs.

```
EXCEPTION
    WHEN NO_DATA_FOUND THEN …
        /* does some work when the NO_DATA_FOUND predefined
exception is
        raised implicitly. */
    WHEN OTHERS THEN …
        /* this code will execute when any other exception is
raised,
        explicitly or implicitly. */
END;
```

TIP
*Once an exception is raised, PL/SQL flow
control passes to the exception handler. Once
the exception is handled, the PL/SQL block will
be exited. In other words, once the exception is
raised, the execution portion of the PL/SQL
block is over.*

Exercises

1. What are the components of an exception handler?

2. What is the **others** exception, and how is it used?

Chapter Summary

PL/SQL programming is the topic of this chapter. The subject areas discussed
include overview of PL/SQL, modular coding practices, developing PL/SQL
blocks, interacting with Oracle, controlling process flow with conditional
statements and loops, cursors, and error handling. The PL/SQL areas of OCP
Exam 1 comprise about 22 percent of the overall test. PL/SQL is the best method
available for writing and managing stored procedures that work with Oracle
data. PL/SQL code consists of three subblocks: the declaration section, the
executable section, and the exception handler. In addition, PL/SQL can be used
in four different programming constructs. The types are procedures and
functions, packages, and triggers. Procedures and functions are similar in that
they both contain a series of instructions that PL/SQL will execute. However, the
main difference is that a function will always return one and only one value.
Procedures can return more than that number as output parameters. Packages
are collected libraries of PL/SQL procedures and functions that have an interface
to tell others what procedures and functions are available as well as their
parameters, and the body contains the actual code executed by those
procedures and functions. Triggers are special PL/SQL blocks that execute when
a triggering event occurs. Events that fire triggers include any SQL statement.

The declaration section allows for the declaration of variables and
constants. A variable can have either a simple or "scalar" datatype, such as
NUMBER or VARCHAR2. Alternatively, a variable can have a referential
datatype that uses reference to a table column to derive its datatype.

Constants can be declared in the declaration section in the same way as variables, but with the addition of a **constant** keyword and with a value assigned. If a value is not assigned to a constant in the declaration section, an error will occur. In the executable section, a variable can have a value assigned to it at any point using the assignment expression (**:=**).

Using PL/SQL allows the developer to produce code that integrates seamlessly with access to the Oracle database. Examples appeared in the chapter of using all SQL statements, including data selection, data change, and transaction-processing statements. There are no special characters or keywords required for "embedding" SQL statements into PL/SQL, because SQL is an extension of PL/SQL. As such, there really is no embedding at all. Every SQL statement executes in a cursor. When a cursor is not named, it is called an implicit cursor. PL/SQL allows the developer to investigate certain return status features in conjunction with the implicit cursors that run. These implicit cursor attributes include **%notfound** and **%found** to identify if records were found or not found by the SQL statement; **%rowcount**, which tells the developer how many rows were processed by the statement; and **%isopen**, which determines if the cursor is open and active in the database.

Conditional process control is made possible in PL/SQL with the use of **if-then-else** statements. The **if** statement uses a Boolean logic comparison to evaluate whether to execute the series of statements after the **then** clause. If the comparison evaluates to TRUE, the **then** clause is executed. If it evaluates to FALSE, then the code in the **else** statement is executed. Nested **if** statements can be placed in the **else** clause of an **if** statement, allowing for the development of code blocks that handle a number of different cases or situations.

Process flow can be controlled in PL/SQL with the use of loops as well. There are several different types of loops, from simple **loop-exit** statements to **loop-exit when** statements, **while loop** statements, and **for loop** statements. A simple **loop-exit** statement consists of the **loop** and **end loop** keywords enclosing the statements that will be executed repeatedly, with a special **if-then** statement designed to identify if an **exit** condition has been reached. The **if-then** statement can be eliminated by using an **exit when** statement to identify the **exit** condition. The entire process of identifying the **exit** condition as part of the steps executed in the loop can be eliminated with the use of a **while loop** statement. The **exit** condition is identified in the **while** clause of the statement. Finally, the **for loop** statement can be used in cases where the developer wants the code executing repeatedly for a specified number of times.

Cursor manipulation is useful for situations where a certain operation must be performed on each row returned from a query. A cursor is simply an address in memory where a SQL statement executes. A cursor can be explicitly named with the use of the **cursor** *cursor_name* **is** statement, followed by the SQL statement that will comprise the cursor. The **cursor** *cursor_name* **is** statement is used to define the cursor in the declaration section only. Once declared, the cursor must be opened, parsed, and executed before its data can be manipulated. This process is executed with the **open** statement. Once the cursor is declared and opened, rows from the resultant dataset can be obtained if the SQL statement defining the cursor was a **select** using the **fetch** statement. Both individual variables for each column's value or a PL/SQL record may be used to store fetched values from a cursor for manipulation in the statement.

Executing each of the operations associated with cursor manipulation can be simplified in situations where the user will be looping through the cursor results using the **cursor for** loop statement. The **cursor for** loops handle many aspects of cursor manipulation explicitly. These steps include opening, parsing, and executing the cursor statement, fetching the value from the statement, exiting the loop when no data is found, and even implicitly declaring the appropriate record type for a variable identified by the loop in which to store the fetched values from the query.

The exception handler is arguably the finest feature PL/SQL offers. In it, the developer can handle certain types of predefined exceptions without explicitly coding error-handling routines. The developer can also associate user-defined exceptions with standard Oracle errors, thereby eliminating the coding of an error check in the executable section. This step requires defining the exception using the **exception_init** pragma and coding a routine that handles the error when it occurs in the exception handler. For completely user-defined errors that do not raise Oracle errors, the user can declare an exception and code a programmatic check in the execution section of the PL/SQL block, followed by some routine to execute when the error occurs in the exception handler. A special predefined exception called **others** can be coded into the exception handler as well to function as a catchall for any exception that occurs that has no exception-handling process defined. Once an exception is raised, control passes from the execution section of the block to the exception handler. Once the exception handler has completed, control is passed to the process that called the PL/SQL block.

Two-Minute Drill

- PL/SQL is a programming environment that is native to the Oracle database. It features seamless integration with other database objects in Oracle and with SQL.

- There are three parts to a PL/SQL program: the declaration area, the execution area, and the exception handler.

- There are two categories of PL/SQL blocks: named and anonymous blocks. Named blocks include procedures, functions, packages, and triggers.

- Procedures allow the developer to specify more than one output parameter, while functions only allow one return value. Other than that, the two PL/SQL blocks are similar in function and usage.

- Variables are defined in the declaration section.

- Variables can have a scalar datatype like NUMBER or VARCHAR2, or a referential datatype defined by use of a table and/or column reference followed by **%type** or **%rowtype**.

- Constants are declared the same way as variables, except for the fact that the **constant** keyword is used to denote a constant and the constant must have a value assigned in the declaration section.

- Variables can have values assigned anywhere in the PL/SQL block using the assignment operator, which looks like (**:=**).

- Any SQL statement is valid for use in PL/SQL. This includes all SQL statements such as **select** and **delete**, and transaction control statements such as **commit** or **rollback**.

- Conditional processing is handled in PL/SQL with **if-then-else** statements.

- **If-then-else** statements rely on Boolean logic to determine which set of statements will execute. If the condition is TRUE, the statements in the **then** clause will execute. If the condition is FALSE, the statements in the **else** clause will execute.

- The **if** statements can be nested into one another's **else** clause.

- Several loops also control the repetition of blocks of PL/SQL statements.

- The **loop-exit** statement is a simple definition for a loop that marks the beginning and end of the loop code. An **if-then** statement tests to see if conditions are such that the loop should exit. An **exit** statement must be specified explicitly.

- The **if-then** statement can be replaced with an **exit when** statement, which defines the **exit** condition for the loop.

- The **while** statement eliminates the need for an **exit** statement by defining the **exit** condition in the **while loop** statement.

- If the programmer wants her code to execute a specified number of times, the **for loop** can be used.

- Every SQL statement executes in an implicit cursor. An explicit cursor is a named cursor corresponding to a defined SQL statement.

- An explicit cursor can be defined with the **cursor** *cursor_name* **is** statement. Cursors can be defined to accept input parameters that will be used in the **where** clause to limit the data manipulated by the cursor.

- Once declared, a cursor must be opened, parsed, and executed in order to have its data used. This task is accomplished with the **open** statement.

- In order to obtain data from a cursor, the programmer must **fetch** the data into a variable. This task is accomplished with the **fetch** statement.

- The variable used in the **fetch** can either consist of several loose variables for storing single-column values or a record datatype that stores all column values in a record.

- A special loop exists to simplify use of cursors: the **cursor for** loop.

- The **cursor for** loop handles the steps normally done in the **open** statement, and implicitly fetches data from the cursor until the **%notfound** condition occurs. This statement also handles the declaration of the variable and associated record type, if any is required.

- The exception handler in PL/SQL handles all error handling.

- There are user-defined exceptions, predefined exceptions, and pragma exceptions in PL/SQL.

- Only user-defined exceptions require explicit checks in the execution portion of PL/SQL code to test to see if the error condition has occurred.

- A named exception can have a **when** clause defined in the exception handler that executes whenever that exception occurs.

- The **others** exception is a catchall exception designed to operate if an exception occurs that is not associated with any other defined exception handler.

Chapter Questions

1. **Developer JANET receives an error due to the following statement in the DECLARATION section:**

   PI CONSTANT NUMBER;

   The problem is because:

   A. There is not enough memory in the program for the constant.

   B. There is no value associated with the constant.

   C. There is no datatype associated with the constant.

   D. PI is a reserved word.

2. **Which statement most accurately describes the result of not creating an exception handler for a raised exception?**

   A. The program will continue without raising the exception.

   B. There will be a memory leak.

   C. Control will pass to the PL/SQL block caller's exception handler.

   D. The program will return a **%notfound** error.

3. **Which of the following statements is true about implicit cursors?**

   A. Implicit cursors are used for SQL statements that are not named.

   B. Developers should use implicit cursors with great care.

   C. Implicit cursors are used in **cursor for** loops to handle data processing.

   D. Implicit cursors are no longer a feature in Oracle.

4. **Which of the following is not a feature of a CURSOR FOR loop?**

   A. Record type declaration

   B. Opening and parsing of SQL statements

   C. Fetches records from cursor

   D. Requires **exit** condition to be defined

5. **A developer would like to use referential datatype declaration on a variable. The variable name is *EMPLOYEE_LASTNAME*, and the corresponding table and column is EMPLOYEE, and LASTNAME, respectively. How would the developer define this variable using referential datatypes?**

   A. Use employee.lname%**type**.

   B. Use employee.lname%**rowtype**.

   C. Look up datatype for EMPLOYEE column on LASTNAME table and use that.

   D. Declare it to be type LONG.

6. **After executing an UPDATE statement, the developer codes a PL/SQL block to perform an operation based on SQL%ROWCOUNT. What data is returned by the SQL%ROWCOUNT operation?**

   A. A Boolean value representing the success or failure of the **update**

   B. A numeric value representing the number of rows updated

    C. A VARCHAR2 value identifying the name of the table updated

    D. A LONG value containing all data from the table

7. Which three of the following are implicit cursor attributes?

    A. %found

    B. %too_many_rows

    C. %notfound

    D. %rowcount

    E. %rowtype

8. If left out, which of the following would cause an infinite loop to occur in a simple loop?

    A. loop

    B. end loop

    C. if-then

    D. exit

9. The OTHERS exception handler is used to handle the OTHERS raised exception.

    A. TRUE

    B. FALSE

10. Which line in the following statement will produce an error?

    A. **cursor** action_cursor **is**

    B. **select** name, rate, action

    C. **into** action_record

    D. **from** action_table;

    E. There are no errors in this statement.

11. **The command used to open a CURSOR FOR loop is**

    A. open

    B. fetch

    C. parse

    D. None, **cursor for** loops handle cursor opening implicitly.

12. Which of the following statements are true about WHILE loops?

    A. Explicit **exit** statements are required in **while** loops.

    B. Counter variables are required in **while** loops.

    C. An **if-then** statement is needed to signal when a **while** loop should end.

    D. All **exit** conditions for **while** loops are handled in the **exit when** clause.

Answers to Chapter Questions

1. B.   There is no value associated with the constant.

Explanation   A value must be associated with a constant in the declaration section. If no value is given for the constant, an error will result.

2. C.   Control will pass to the PL/SQL block caller's exception handler.

Explanation   If the exception raised is not handled locally, then PL/SQL will attempt to handle it at the level of the process that called the PL/SQL block. If the exception is not handled there, then PL/SQL will attempt to keep finding an exception handler that will resolve the exception. If none is found, then an error will result.

3. A.   Implicit cursors are used for SQL statements that are not named.

Explanation   Implicit cursors are used for all SQL statements except for those statements that are named. They are never incorporated into **cursor for** loops, nor is much care given to using them more or less, which eliminates choices B and C. They are definitely a feature of Oracle, eliminating choice D.

4. D.   Requires **exit** condition to be defined

Explanation   A **cursor for** loop handles just about every feature of cursor processing automatically, including **exit** conditions.

5. A.   Use employee.lname%**type**

Explanation   The only option in this question that allows the developer to use referential type declaration for columns is choice A. Choice B uses the **%rowtype** referential datatype, which defines a record variable, which is not what the developer is after.

6. B.   A numeric value representing the number of rows updated

Explanation   **%rowtype** returns the numeric value representing the number of rows that were manipulated by the SQL statement.

7. A, C, D.   **%found, %notfound, %rowcount**

Explanation   These three are the only choices that are valid cursor attributes.

8. D.   exit

Explanation   Without an **exit** statement, a simple loop will not stop.

9. B.   FALSE

Explanation   There is no **others** exception. The **others** exception handler handles all exceptions that may be raised in a PL/SQL block that do not have exception handlers explicitly defined for them.

10. C.   **into** action_record

Explanation   The **into** clause is not permitted in cursors.

11. D.   None, **cursor for** loops handle cursor opening implicitly.

Explanation   The **cursor for** loops handle, among other things, the opening, parsing, and executing of named cursors.

12. D.   All **exit** conditions for **while** loops are handled in the **exit when** clause

Explanation   There is no need for an **exit** statement in a **while** loop, since the exiting condition is defined in the **while** statement, eliminating choice A. Choice B is also wrong also because you don't specifically need to use a counter in a **while** loop the way you do in a **for** loop. Finally, Choice C is incorrect because even though the **exit** condition for a **while** loop evaluates to a Boolean value (i.e., **exit when** (*this_condition_is_true*), the mechanism to handle the exit does not require an explicit **if-then** statement.

UNIT
II

Preparing for OCP
Exam 2: Developing
PL/SQL Program
Units

CHAPTER
6

Procedures and Functions in PL/SQL Development

n this chapter, you will cover the following areas of PL/SQL development:

- Developing stored procedures and functions

- Using SQL*Plus to develop procedures and functions

- Using Procedure Builder to develop procedures and functions

- Handling exceptions in PL/SQL

At the end of the last section, you covered several key introductory areas of developing PL/SQL. Items like **cursor for** loops and block structure are the building blocks for understanding how to code using Oracle's procedural extension to SQL. However, these items are like I-beams—strong enough to hold together a building, but by themselves they are just a ton of metal. This chapter will introduce you to the creation of blueprints that hold PL/SQL building blocks together in the same way that an architectural blueprint holds a building together. These blueprints are called *stored procedures and functions.*

Stored procedures and functions are similar to anonymous PL/SQL blocks in that they have declaration sections, execution sections, and exception handlers. However, stored procedures and functions have at least two significant differences from anonymous PL/SQL blocks. The first difference is that a stored procedure or function has a name, while an anonymous PL/SQL block has no name, thus being anonymous. You simply submit the anonymous PL/SQL block and Oracle runs it, while a stored procedure or function is stored in the database and can be called upon to do its thing without having to be resubmitted by the user. The second key difference is that stored procedures and functions allow you to pass in parameters, while anonymous PL/SQL blocks allow no parameter passing. This feature makes stored procedures and functions flexible and usable again and again without the need to recompile the code.

There are also some differences between stored procedures and functions themselves. A stored procedure can accept one or many parameters, or none at all, and return one or many values, or none at all. In contrast, a function can accept one or many parameters, or none at all, but a function must always return one and only one value, without exception. In this chapter, you will learn more about developing stored procedures and functions using different Oracle products. The use of SQL*Plus for developing stored procedures and functions is covered. Additionally, the use of Procedure Builder to develop both client-side and server-side PL/SQL procedures and functions will be covered. Since this exam is the same for both 1.x and 2.0 OCP Application Developer certification tracks, you will focus your attention on Procedure Builder 2.0 in these chapters. Overall, the contents of this chapter comprise about 24 percent of OCP Exam 2 test content.

Developing Stored Procedures and Functions

In this section, you will cover the following points on developing stored procedures and functions:

- Permissions and PL/SQL programs

- Creating PL/SQL procedures

- Parameter passing

- Creating PL/SQL functions

This section will cover several important areas of client-side and server-side PL/SQL development. There are many ways to create PL/SQL code, and several ways to invoke it as well. This section will discuss the server-side creation of procedures and functions with Oracle's workhorse interface, SQL*Plus. In recognition of the ungainliness of a command line interface for everything, however, Oracle offers the PL/SQL developer a tool for writing and working with client-side PL/SQL code. This tool is called Procedure Builder, and it is part of the overall Oracle development package covered by the OCP Application Developer track. Procedure Builder has many features that other tools for PL/SQL development have, plus a few that others don't. In addition to introducing you to Procedure Builder, this section will discuss the invocation of procedures and functions from both the SQL command line in SQL*Plus, within Procedure Builder, and within other PL/SQL programs. Finally, a discussion on handling exceptions will be offered.

Permissions and PL/SQL Programs

Procedures and functions are the plan through which the power of PL/SQL constructs is delivered. Many books offer a discussion of the importance of using procedures and functions to encapsulate complex programming logic beneath a simple procedure or function call. For certification purposes, you will need to know what modularization is and how procedures and functions offer it. However, more important for passing OCP is that you know how to apply the appropriate methods to create procedures and functions. First, we explore the methods for creating procedures and functions in SQL*Plus.

A system privilege called **create procedure** governs the user's ability to compile stored procedures and functions and store them on the Oracle server. Without this privilege, the user may develop PL/SQL code in anonymous blocks, compile those blocks and run them, but will not be able to compile and load functions and procedures into Oracle for later use. Usually, this privilege is granted by the DBA for the system. The statement the DBA will use for granting **create procedure** looks similar to the following code block:

```
GRANT create procedure TO athena;
```

Once developed, anyone can invoke a stored procedure or function provided they have security permissions set to do so. The issuance of security privileges and/or roles is usually owned by either a security administrator or the DBA in most IS organizations. However, during periods of intense development, it is beneficial to allow developers to manage their own security. From an administration perspective, the ability to run a stored procedure or function is an object privilege called **execute**. To allow a user the ability to execute a procedure or function, either the procedure owner or privileged user (such as the DBA) should issue the following command from SQL*Plus. In this block, the ability to execute the **delete_employee( )** function is granted to lucky user ATHENA.

```
SQL> GRANT execute ON delete_employee TO athena;
```

Important to note is that, if user SPANKY owns the **delete_employee( )** procedure for which **execute** privileges were just granted to user ATHENA, then user ATHENA executes **delete_employee( )** with all the same object access privileges granted to user SPANKY. This is a general rule in PL/SQL, with one exception. If user SYS grants user ATHENA access to develop dynamic

SQL with the use of the DBMS_SQL package, this does not mean ATHENA can execute any possible SQL statement on the access authority of SYS. But other than that situation, the user executing the PL/SQL block does so with the object access privileges of the owner of the procedure, not their own.

Exercises

1. What is the name of the privilege required to create a procedure or function in Oracle?

2. What permission is required to run a function or procedure in Oracle?

Creating PL/SQL Procedures

Recall in Chapter 5 the discussion of anonymous PL/SQL blocks. When a user submits an anonymous block to Oracle for processing, the RDBMS parses the code into something it can process and then processes it. When Oracle is done processing the code, the parsed PL/SQL block eventually goes away—either if the user doesn't execute the anonymous block again or when the user ends their session. Unless the user kept the PL/SQL in a file stored external to the Oracle database, the user loses all that programming time and effort. Consider the following block of code:

```
DECLARE
    my_raise_empid      VARCHAR2(20) := '40593';
    my_delete_empid     VARCHAR2(20) := '59384';
    my_employee_rec     employee%ROWTYPE;
BEGIN
    SELECT *
    INTO my_employee_rec
    FROM employee
    WHERE empid = my_raise_empid;

    INSERT INTO process_emp_raise
    (empid, lastname, firstname, salary)
    VALUES (my_raise_empid, my_employee_rec.lastname,
            my_employee_rec.firstname,
my_employee_rec.salary+10000);

    DELETE FROM employee
    WHERE empid = my_delete_empid;
END;
```

This anonymous PL/SQL block will be forgotten by Oracle unless the user creates a way for the code to be remembered. Procedures and functions are the way for Oracle to remember. The keywords **create procedure** allow the user to define the preceding anonymous PL/SQL block in such a way that Oracle will *not* execute the block when the user submits it. Rather, Oracle will compile it and store it so that the user can execute the code later or whenever he or she wants. The result is a stored procedure in the Oracle database. The following code block demonstrates the creation of a procedure using the PL/SQL from the anonymous block, with modifications necessary for this purpose:

```
CREATE PROCEDURE raiseanddelete(
    p_raise_empid              IN VARCHAR2,
    p_delete_empid             IN OUT VARCHAR2
) AS
my_employee_rec    employee%ROWTYPE;
BEGIN
    SELECT *
    INTO my_employee_rec
    FROM employee
    WHERE empid = p_raise_empid;

    INSERT INTO process_emp_raise (empid, lastname, firstname,
salary)
    VALUES (p_raise_empid, my_employee_rec.lastname,
            my_employee_rec.firstname,
my_employee_rec.salary+10000);

    DELETE FROM employee
    WHERE empid = p_delete_empid;

    p_delete_empid := '00000';
END;
```

When the user submits this statement, Oracle will parse and compile this program into an executable form, and store the executable form in the database as a named procedure. Oracle will not execute the **select**, **insert**, or **delete** statements, but only store them as SQL statements that will execute when the user calls the procedure. The procedure is then available for usage.

Notice a few differences in the named procedure and the anonymous block. First, there is no keyword **declare**. Does that mean there is no declaration section? No, instead the declaration section is signified by the keyword **as**, highlighted in the fourth line of the preceding code block. This keyword must be used when the developer wants to declare variables other than those being passed in as parameters to the procedure. If the developer has no additional variables to declare, the developer can substitute the keyword **is** for **as**.

TIP

*It is sometimes difficult to distinguish the **is** keyword from **as**, and often they are interchangeable. You may want to try using one and if there are problems with compilation, you may switch later.*

To alter an existing program unit, the **or replace** syntax is a useful addition to the more basic **create procedure**, **create function**, **create package**, or **create package body** commands. The following code block shows how to use **or replace** in the definition of a procedure that already exists in Oracle:

```
CREATE OR REPLACE PROCEDURE raiseanddelete(
   p_raise_empid            IN VARCHAR2,
   p_delete_empid           IN VARCHAR2,
) AS
my_employee_rec     employee%ROWTYPE;
BEGIN
   SELECT *
   INTO my_employee_rec
   FROM employee
   WHERE empid = p_raise_empid;

   INSERT INTO process_emp_raise (empid, lastname, firstname,
salary)
   VALUES (p_raise_empid, my_employee_rec.lastname,
         my_employee_rec.firstname,
my_employee_rec.salary+10000);

   DELETE FROM employee
   WHERE empid = p_delete_empid;
END;
```

Exercises

1. What syntax is used to create procedures in PL/SQL?

2. In what area of a named procedure is variable declaration handled?

3. What is the difference between **is** and **as**?

Parameter Passing

Notice also the keyword **in**, highlighted in the second and third lines of the preceding block. This keyword indicates that the procedure will accept a value passed in for that parameter, but will not return a value. Other keywords that can be substituted for **in** are **out** and **in out**. Their meanings are as follows:

- **in**   Value passed in for this parameter, but not returned

- **out**   Value passed out for this parameter, but none passed in

- **in out**   Values are passed in and returned for this parameter

The keywords used in the declaration of variables that will have values passed in as parameters to the procedure call are highly important. An **in** parameter will specify that the variable named will be assigned that value passed into the procedure in the appropriate place specified. The **out** keyword specifies that the caller of the procedure will put a variable in the procedure call. When the procedure is done processing, whatever value is in that variable will be returned to the caller of the procedure. The **in out** keyword combination states that the procedure should expect to receive a value into the variable defined to handle that parameter, and whatever value is in that variable within the stored procedure when the procedure is done executing will be passed back to the caller. The following block illustrates the principles behind parameter passing and the **in**, **out**, and **in out** keywords referring to the **raiseanddelete( )** procedure that has already been defined. Since the second parameter variable is defined as an **in out** variable, a value may not be passed in as a parameter, but rather a variable must be defined at the procedure caller level that contains a value passed in and can hold a value passed out.

```
raiseanddelete('50398','54984'); /* No, 2nd parm won't accept
return value */
raiseanddelete('59483',delete_variable); /* OK! */
```

TIP
*You are not required to use **in** keywords in your procedures or functions. However, you will receive an error if you try to assign a value in your procedure or function to a parameter not defined either as **in out** or **out**.*

Shortly, you will cover the three ways or *modes* parameter values can be passed to a block, which are: positional, named association, and a combination of the two.

Exercises

1. What are the three ways PL/SQL will move parameters back and forth between program units?

2. Explain how each parameter passing method works in PL/SQL.

Creating PL/SQL Functions

The next type of named PL/SQL block we will discuss is the function. Like a procedure, you can create a function to execute a series of PL/SQL statements. Once the function is compiled and stored in the system, those granted **execute** privileges on that function can then use it. The main clause for changing an anonymous PL/SQL block to a stored function is **create function**. It is used in the same way as **create procedure**. The following code block demonstrates the code of a sample function:

```
CREATE FUNCTION find_mouse(
p_mouse_name        IN VARCHAR2,
p_house_name        IN OUT VARCHAR2 /* In/out parm in functions not
advised*/
) RETURN VARCHAR2 IS
my_room   mouse_house.room%TYPE;
BEGIN
    SELECT room  /* get the data */
```

```
    INTO my_room
    FROM mouse_house
    WHERE mouse_name = p_mouse_name
    AND house_name = p_house_name;
    RETURN (my_room); /* return the result */
END;
```

The function above has one purpose—it accepts two values and returns a value. There are two variables defined after the **create function** keywords to store the values users will pass into the function as parameters. The second to last line in the block contains a new keyword—**return**. This keyword highlights an important point you should remember about function process structure. A function accepts one or many values as parameters, or none at all. But, a function always returns exactly *one* result. You must remember to code a function call to handle a result when you call it. More information will be provided on procedure and function calls later. For now, simply recall that a function always returns a value.

TIP

A procedure accepts one or more values as parameters (or none at all), and can return one or more values (or none at all). A function accepts one or more values as parameters (or none at all), but always returns a result.

Although it will compile and run, there is an error in the **find_mouse( )** function! Can you find out where? The error relates back to the original definition of a function. A function accepts zero or more parameters, and returns one. Notice that the second variable defined for accepting values in as parameters is defined as an **in out** variable. Although this definition is permitted by the PL/SQL engine, it is not generally advised to define functions with **in out** parameters. A function should return only the value defined for the variable specified in the **return** statement in the last line of the function in order to conform to a higher purity level for optimization and prevention of ill side effects. The correct listing for this stored function is listed in the following code block:

```
CREATE FUNCTION find_mouse(
p_mouse_name        IN VARCHAR2,
```

```
p_house_name       IN VARCHAR2
) RETURN VARCHAR2 IS
my_room   mouse_house.room%TYPE;
BEGIN
    SELECT room   /* get the data */
    INTO my_room
    FROM mouse_house
    WHERE mouse_name = p_mouse_name
    AND house_name = p_house_name;
    RETURN (my_room); /* return the result */
END;
```

TIP

*The use of **in** parameters in a function
exclusively helps you to conform to the
required purity level in order to use the
function in SQL statements. In addition, all
parameter and variable datatypes must be
Oracle internal datatypes like NUMBER and
VARCHAR2, not datatype extensions like
PLS_INTEGER. Also, the function must only
work on row data, not group data.*

Finally, notice that the **return** command is the last statement in the
function. This design choice is done for a reason. First, once the **return**
command is issued the function will return control to the caller. Also, this
command defines what value will be returned to the caller. Say, for
example, the developer wants the function to do a series of tests. Execution
of a subsequent test depends on whether the previous test failed, and will
return different values based on the result of a test. The function may
contain a series of tests, each with its own return value. The following code
block contains an example to illustrate:

```
CREATE FUNCTION test_mouse_type (
p_fur_color  IN VARCHAR2,
p_tail_length IN VARCHAR2
) RETURN VARCHAR2 IS
BEGIN
    IF p_fur_color = 'ORANGE' AND p_tail_length = 'SHORT' THEN
      RETURN 'SHORT-TAILED ORANGEY ONE';
```

```
    ELSIF p_fur_color = 'RED' AND p_tail_length = 'LONG' THEN
      RETURN 'LONG-TAILED FIREY ONE';
    END IF;
END;
```

Exercises

1. What syntax is used to create functions in PL/SQL?

2. What parameter passing type is not allowed in functions that is allowed in procedures?

3. What is a functions "purity level" and what are the conditions for meeting that purity level? If that level is met, can you call the function from a SQL statement? Why or why not?

Using SQL*Plus to Create Procedures and Functions

In this section, you will cover the following points about using SQL*Plus to create procedures and functions:

- Entering PL/SQL code in SQL*Plus

- Invoking procedures and functions in SQL*Plus

- Code compilation in Oracle using SQL*Plus

Once your PL/SQL code has been developed, it must be placed somewhere to be effective. This place may be on the Oracle server or within a client application. You must have some mechanism to get PL/SQL from the typed word to executable code. This section covers one method for doing it. The tool you will use in this section is SQL*Plus, Oracle's workhorse application for interfacing with the database. This application will allow you to enter PL/SQL code for compilation and execution on the Oracle database server, making it a solution for server-side PL/SQL development. You will cover the creation of PL/SQL in SQL*Plus as well as compiling code with it, along with how to run the named code you compile with SQL*Plus.

Entering PL/SQL Code in SQL*Plus

With an idea of the keywords required in mind, shift your attention now to the process of entering the procedure or function into Oracle. For that purpose, the developer may choose to use SQL*Plus. The entry of PL/SQL at the SQL prompt is the same as entry of SQL statements, presented in Chapter 1. However, entry of PL/SQL in this way falls victim to the same difficulties as entry of SQL statements. Once you press ENTER on the line of code you keyed in, you can no longer edit that line without going through a lengthy process of referencing the line number and using the **change** command. The challenge of entering PL/SQL code directly from the SQL prompt in SQL*Plus is shown in Figure 6-1.

There are alternatives. The first is to edit the PL/SQL code with the **edit** command from the SQL*Plus prompt. This command invokes a text editor and places the code currently being written into that editor. This allows the developer to write code in a more user-friendly environment. This process is described in Chapter 1 and demonstrated in Figure 6-2. The other alternative is to write the entire PL/SQL block using a text editor and save the file with a **.sql** extension. Then, in SQL*Plus, the code can be loaded using the **get** command. Assuming there is a file containing a PL/SQL block called **delete_employee.sql**, the following example shows how the user can

```
Oracle SQL*Plus                                              _ □ ×
File  Edit  Search  Options  Help
Wrote file afiedt.buf

  1  create or replace function test_mouse_type (
  2  p_fur_color in varchar2,
  3  p_tail_length in varchar2
  4  ) return varchar2 is
  5  begin
  6   if p_fur_color = 'ORANGE' and p_tail_length = 'SHORT' then
  7      return 'SHORT-TAILED ORANGEY ONE';
  8   elsif p_fur_color = 'RED' and p_tail_length = 'LONG' then
  9      return 'LONG-TAILED FIREY ONE';
 10   end if;
 11* end;
SQL> /

Function created.

SQL>
```

FIGURE 6-1. *Entering function code directly into SQL*Plus*

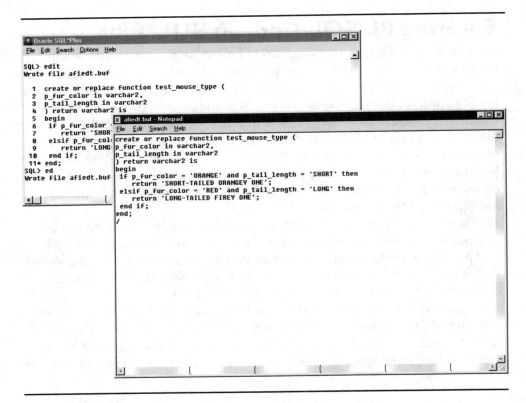

FIGURE 6-2. *Invoking a text editor from SQL*Plus*

load that script into SQL*Plus for modification or execution. The **get** command loads the contents of the script into the SQL*Plus buffer, while the @ command actually loads the contents of the script into SQL*Plus and then submits the code to Oracle for compilation. Once compiled, the PL/SQL code is stored as part of the Oracle database.

```
SQL> get test_mouse_type.sql
  1>CREATE FUNCTION test_mouse_type (
  2>p_fur_color  IN VARCHAR2,
  3>p_tail_length IN VARCHAR2
  4>) RETURN VARCHAR2 IS
  5>BEGIN
```

```
 6>    IF p_fur_color = 'ORANGE' AND p_tail_length = 'SHORT' THEN
 7>       RETURN 'SHORT-TAILED ORANGEY ONE';
 8>    ELSIF p_fur_color = 'RED' AND p_tail_length = 'LONG' THEN
 9>       RETURN 'LONG-TAILED FIREY ONE';
10>    END IF;
11>END;
SQL> /
Function created.
```

Or,

```
SQL> @test_mouse_type
Function created.
```

Exercises

1. What command is used to load a SQL script into SQL*Plus?

2. What command is used to load and execute the script at the same time in SQL*Plus?

3. What does the Oracle database do when you load and execute a PL/SQL script containing an anonymous PL/SQL block in SQL*Plus? What does Oracle do when you load and execute a script containing a named PL/SQL block?

Invoking Procedures and Functions in SQL*Plus

Recall at the end of the lesson on parameter passing that some mention of the modes for parameter passing was made. In this lesson, you will expand your understanding of the three modes for parameter passing. Once **execute** privileges are established, the procedure or function can be invoked in several ways. These methods include invocation from SQL*Plus or from other PL/SQL procedures and functions. You will explore invoking stored procedures and functions from SQL*Plus first. Executing stored procedures in SQL*Plus is handled with the **execute** command. The syntax is **execute** *procedurename(val1,...)* followed by a semicolon. The *val1* item refers to values that are passed into the procedure. If there are no values passed in, there needn't be any parentheses. From the SQL prompt, the commands issued may look something like the following code block:

```
SQL> EXECUTE delete_employee('49384');
PL/SQL procedure successfully completed.
SQL> EXEC raise_salary_for_employee('49849','10','PERCENT');
PL/SQL procedure successfully completed.
SQL> EXECUTE compare_apple_to_orange('APPLE59385','ORANGE59438893');
PL/SQL procedure successfully completed.
```

Note that in this example, the procedures all use positional parameter passing mode. In other words, the values passed into the procedure will be assigned to parameters according to the position of the value and the position of the parameter. The first value gets assigned to the first parameter, the second to the second, and so on. Alternately, for procedures that accept multiple parameters, you can use the parameter name and a reference pointer to identify passed values that are not in the order specified by the procedure. The following code block demonstrates this:

```
SQL> EXECUTE
compare_apple_to_orange(p_orange=>'ORANGE59438893',p_apple=>
'APPLE59385');
```

Notice in the previous block that the user can abbreviate the **execute** command with **exec**. However, Oracle gives no indication of how the procedure performed, or even if it did what it was supposed to do. In a later section, "Managing Procedures and Functions," you will explore how to make Oracle identify its progress and other pertinent information about the performance of the procedures and functions you execute. Notice also that in the code block an actual value must be passed. Finally, an interesting error will occur if you attempt to refer to a procedure from the SQL prompt without the **execute** command—Oracle treats the procedure name as though it is a reference to a variable, and reports that the variable has not been declared.

TIP
*The **run** command, used for executing SQL statements stored in the **afiedt.buf** statement buffer of SQL*Plus, is not an acceptable substitute for the **execute** command. You should test this functionality on your Oracle database.*

If the developer wants to use variables and call the PL/SQL procedure or function repeatedly, there will need to be some additional development. This leads the developer to considering how to call PL/SQL procedures and functions from within PL/SQL. Functions are called most effectively from other PL/SQL blocks. At the very least, the developer must code an anonymous PL/SQL block to declare a variable to hold the return value that the function must produce. The developer does not call a function directly and independently as she does with a procedure; rather, the call is made usually in reference to a variable, or as a function in a **select** statement, as with any other SQL function. Consider the following function call. A variable is defined in the anonymous block's declaration section, and populated with a result from a function, which accepts two numeric values and returns one.

```
DECLARE
    my_return_var       NUMBER;
BEGIN
    my_return_var := return_hypotenuse(3,4);
END;
```

Or,

```
SELECT return_hypotenuse(3,4)
FROM dual;
```

Or even,

```
DECLARE
    my_return_var NUMBER;
BEGIN
    SELECT return_hypotenuse(3,4)
    INTO my_return_var
    FROM DUAL;
END;
```

Procedures can be called from anonymous or named PL/SQL blocks as well. The syntax is actually quite simple for calling a PL/SQL procedure from another procedure. Simply name the procedure and pass in either the variables or appropriate values the procedure expects. There is not even a need to use the **execute** command—the name of the procedure being called will suffice.

```
BEGIN
    process_junk(x,y);
END;
```

Exercises

1. What command is used to run a stored procedure from the SQL prompt in SQL*Plus? What error occurs when the procedure name is entered without this command?

2. How are functions called using SQL*Plus? How do you pass parameters out of order from how the function or procedure defines them?

3. How is the **run** command used? How is it not used?

Code Compilation in Oracle Using SQL*Plus

Compiling PL/SQL code using SQL*Plus and PL/SQL stored in text files on your operating system can be a challenge. After running your **create procedure** statements as demonstrated, if there are problems, Oracle will return with a message saying **"Warning: Procedure created with compilation errors."** Your problems arise when you attempt to find out where the problem resides exactly. There is a view in the Oracle data dictionary called USER_ERRORS or ALL_ERRORS that lists the errors encountered in this compilation. The following code block shows you trying to obtain your errors from the USER_ERRORS view.

```
SQL> select * from user_errors;
```

One of the biggest problems you will encounter in trying to find and correct your errors is when you **select** your errors from USER_ERRORS or ALL_ERRORS. The line number Oracle places in this errors table relates directly to the line in the buffer just executed containing your PL/SQL code. The problem is that SQL*Plus saves only the most recent statement in the memory buffer, which at this point is your **select** statement. You are essentially left to your own devices to figure out where the problem in your PL/SQL code resides, modify your code, and recompile it several times before the thing works. More discussion on compiling and debugging your code with SQL*Plus and Procedure Builder will come shortly.

SHOW ERRORS: An Alternative

One popular method for getting your compilation errors out of SQL*Plus is to use the **show errors** command. This command gives you the errors the PL/SQL compilation engine encountered when compiling your program unit—with the added bonus of not losing your buffer, making it easier to locate and correct your errors from SQL*Plus. The following code block illustrates this:

```
SQL> create procedure flibber as
  2> begin
  3> select * where my_thing = 6;
  4> end;
  5> /

Warning: Procedure created with compilation errors.

SQL> show errors
Errors for PROCEDURE FLIBBER

LINE/COL ERROR
--------
------------------------------------------------------------------
3/10     PLS-00103: Encountered the symbol "WHERE" when expecting
one of
         the following:
         from into
```

Shortly, you will also see how Procedure Builder allows you to compile your code more easily than in SQL*Plus, even when you use the **show errors** command, because of Procedure Builder's GUI that shows you the errors on the same screen where you manipulate the code.

Exercise

Describe a problematic situation you encounter when compiling code in SQL*Plus. What are some ways to resolve it within SQL*Plus?

Creating Procedures and Functions with Procedure Builder

In this section, you will cover the following points about creating procedures and functions with Procedure Builder:

- Using Procedure Builder command line to develop PL/SQL
- Parts of the Procedure Builder GUI
- Using Procedure Builder GUI to develop client-side PL/SQL
- Using Procedure Builder GUI to develop server-side PL/SQL
- Running PL/SQL programs in Procedure Builder

You may be a little surprised that, at the onset, it looks like OCP covers a fair amount of Procedure Builder usage. It doesn't. Instead, you should focus your attention on learning core concepts about developing PL/SQL programs first, then learning Procedure Builder second. That said, it is still not a waste of your time to learn Procedure Builder as it is covered in this text. Procedure Builder is a good tool, because as shown, entering procedures and functions with SQL*Plus is possible, if a little ungainly. Instead, you can use components of the Developer/2000 program development suite. In particular, Oracle's Procedure Builder product allows the user to develop stored procedures and functions in Oracle. Many developers have found the SQL*Plus and favorite text editor approach cumbersome. Oracle addresses issues of ease of program development, debugging, and version control with various Procedure Builder features. This discussion will describe the use of Procedure Builder to develop procedures and functions in PL/SQL on both the client side and the server as well.

NOTE
The text identifying features of Procedure Builder were developed using Developer/2000 Version 2.0—however, there is little difference between Procedure Builder on Version 1.6 and 2.0. What's more, most of the functionality of Procedure Builder isn't even tested in OCP Exam 2, so spend less time getting hung up on Procedure Builder minutiae and use it more to develop your core knowledge of PL/SQL.

Using Procedure Builder Command Line to Develop PL/SQL

There are two ways for developing code in Procedure Builder: line mode and with the GUI. Procedure Builder line mode is similar to SQL*Plus in that you must enter all your code and operations via the command line interface. This method is used mainly for development of PL/SQL client-side procedures and functions. There are several commands for Procedure Builder on the command line that are different both from SQL and SQL*Plus. In general, you can use the **help** command to find out what the commands in PL/SQL are and the **help** *command_name* syntax for information about a specific command. Figure 6-3 demonstrates Procedure Builder's command line interface.

TIP

Before getting too far into learning Procedure Builder GUI, remember that you don't need to know too much about it to pass OCP other than Procedure Builder packages, covered in Chapter 7. However, use of Procedure Builder will aid in your learning of core PL/SQL concepts that are tested.

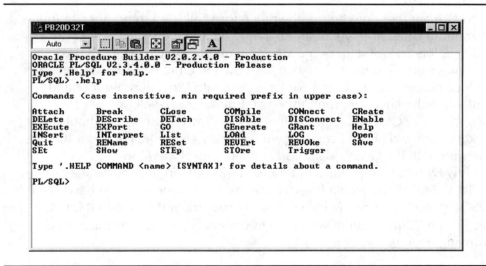

FIGURE 6-3. *Procedure Builder command line mode*

Creating a procedure at the command line in Procedure Builder is a simple process. When you initiate Procedure Builder in line mode, you actually put yourself into an interactive PL/SQL coding environment where any PL/SQL statement is valid. It is virtually identical to writing PL/SQL code in SQL*Plus, without some of the additional overhead. For example, if the user wanted to write the classic "Hello, World." program in PL/SQL using SQL*Plus, she may write the following:

```
SQL> set serveroutput on;
SQL> execute dbms_output.put_line('Hello, World.');
Hello, World.

PL/SQL program successfully completed.
SQL>
```

You execute a valid PL/SQL statement, but the problem is clear—you need to write a minimum of two lines in order to obtain only one result. Thus, although SQL*Plus is capable of Procedure Builder functionality, you can use Procedure Builder to execute the same process more easily. Consider the same program done in Procedure Builder:

```
PL/SQL> text_io.put_line('Hello, World.');
Hello, World.
PL/SQL>
```

Notice another difference—the procedure call used to produce output is different. In Chapter 5, you learned a little bit about the DBMS_OUTPUT package. It is a PL/SQL package available on the Oracle server that contains procedures and functions designed to allow the Oracle database server to produce output. TEXT_IO is a package built into Procedure Builder and available only when you run Procedure Builder for development of client-side PL/SQL code. Later in this unit, you will learn more about what packages are and how to create them, and also about the packages that are built into both the Oracle database and into Developer/2000.

However, the capabilities of Procedure Builder in line mode are very similar to SQL*Plus, with a few differences. For example, if you have some PL/SQL stored in a text file called **find_mouse.sql**, you can load it into the SQL*Plus execution buffer with the **get** command, as demonstrated in the following code block:

```
SQL> get find_mouse.sql
```

There are actually two different types of PL/SQL code in Procedure Builder, and they are files and libraries. A file can be thought of as the equivalent of a stand-alone procedure or function in a file in SQL*Plus, while a PL/SQL library is more like a package in that it can contain several different procedures and functions for use. The equivalent command in Procedure Builder to the **get** command in SQL*Plus would be **load file**. If, however, you want to use a library of PL/SQL procedures and functions, you would attach the library for use. Both methods are demonstrated in the following block:

```
PL/SQL> .load file find_mouse.sql
PL/SQL> .attach library mouse_lib_01a.pll
```

Notice both in the code block and in Figure 6-3 that a period (**.**) precedes the command for loading files in Procedure Builder. This period is important to remember, because otherwise Procedure Builder will return an error stating it was expecting you to treat the word "load" as if it were the name of a variable.

TIP

A period (.) must precede commands in Procedure Builder. Otherwise, Procedure Builder will not recognize it as a command.

A new type of file introduced here is the PL/SQL library file, suffixed by **.pll** as noted in the code block above. One final point to remember about Procedure Builder in line mode is that you don't necessarily need to be logged in to an Oracle database in order for your PL/SQL to work. This is because Procedure Builder line mode has a PL/SQL Interpreter built into it. This feature works well if you want to write PL/SQL and execute it interactively with Oracle, but if you want to write stored procedures and functions, you must be connected to the Oracle database so that Procedure Builder has somewhere to store them. This fact is true of SQL*Plus as well, but since the user views database login as an implicit part of SQL*Plus, it's easy to forget that the stored procedures are actually kept in the Oracle database and not available to you when not logged in.

Exercises

1. What special character precedes commands in Procedure Builder line mode? Once loaded or attached, how can you run procedures in Procedure Builder?

2. Do you need to be logged in to a database in order to use Procedure Builder? Why or why not?

3. Are regular PL/SQL statements valid for entry at the Procedure Builder PL/SQL prompt? Why or why not?

Parts of the Procedure Builder GUI

The second way to use Procedure Builder is with the graphical user interface. The Procedure Builder GUI consists of five different modules to help you develop code. Figure 6-4 features the Procedure Builder GUI with two modules displayed, the Object Navigator and the PL/SQL Interpreter.

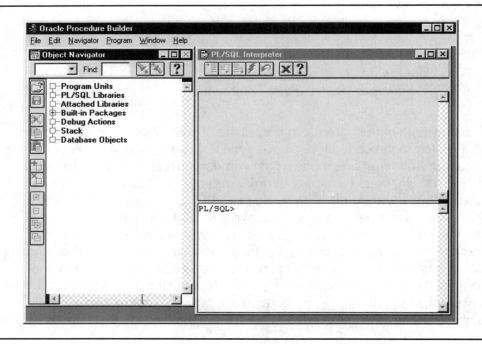

FIGURE 6-4. *Procedure Builder GUI mode*

The use of Procedure Builder in GUI mode requires understanding the different modules available. Here, we will cover a tour of viewing and using each of the modules, along with some key facts on their usage.

Object Navigator

The Object Navigator is a module that allows the developer to look at all PL/SQL program units, attached and built-in libraries, debug options, stacks, and database objects available for use. This interface treats all PL/SQL program objects like directories in a file system, and allows you to drill down into different code types to see exactly what's out there for your use.

Program Unit Editor

The Program Unit Editor is a module that allows the developer to rapidly develop client-side PL/SQL procedures, functions, package specifications, and package bodies. If you write a lot of PL/SQL, this tool will become your favorite quickly, because it builds the basics for different types of PL/SQL blocks automatically, and allows you to compile your code and see errors interactively so that you can cut the time you spend debugging. More on the challenges of debugging PL/SQL using SQL*Plus and the Oracle database and how Procedure Builder simplifies that process later.

PL/SQL Interpreter

The Interpreter is a module that allows the developer to run and debug client- and server-side PL/SQL commands interactively with a stand-alone PL/SQL Interpreter engine. Having already used the Procedure Builder in line mode, you should already find this component of the GUI to be familiar—or at least recognizable. This component is essentially the same as Procedure Builder line mode, with its ability to read PL/SQL statements interactively and the need to place a period before each special command like **load**. Notice, however, some key differences in the GUI approach with the availability of buttons at the top of the window. These buttons are used for debugging, which we will cover shortly.

Database Trigger Editor

The Database Trigger Editor is a module that allows the developer to develop, compile, and run server-side database triggers. Triggers are objects in the database that work in conjunction with tables. They execute or "fire" automatically when a specified activity takes place. For example, a **delete** trigger will fire every time a user attempts to **delete** data from the table the trigger is attached to. If you are not connected to the database, this option will be grayed out.

TIP
As of Oracle 7.3, database triggers are stored within the database in compiled format.

Stored Program Unit Editor

The Stored Program Unit Editor is a module that allows the developer to code and modify server-side PL/SQL code of the Oracle database. To use it, you must be connected to a database and able to browse through the database stored procedures, functions, and packages. The main difference between this editor and the Program Unit Editor is that this editor is for procedures and functions stored on the database and the Program Unit Editor is for works in progress or for PL/SQL code that exists outside the Oracle database. If you are not connected to the database, this option will be grayed out.

Exercises

1. Name and describe the program modules of Procedure Builder running in GUI mode.

2. Which Procedure Builder GUI module is similar to Procedure Builder running in line mode?

Using Procedure Builder GUI to Develop Client-Side PL/SQL

Probably the easiest way to develop a named PL/SQL block in Procedure Builder is to use the Program Unit Editor. If this module is not running already, you can open it by clicking on Program | Program Unit Editor on the Procedure Builder menu bar. Review Figure 6-4 to find the location of the Program pull-down menu. Alternately, you may go into the Object

Navigator module, highlight the Program Units node and click on the Create button in the vertical toolbar on the left-hand side of the screen.

Once in the Program Unit Editor, you can click on the New button at the top and center of the module, and you will be automatically prompted to type in a name for your new PL/SQL block, and to select a block type using the radio buttons. There are four options. The first two options are procedure and function, the use for both of which you should understand by now. The other two options may be a bit less familiar. They are the package specification and the package body. You will cover package development and use later in the unit, but for now you should understand that a package is basically a control structure for other PL/SQL code like stored procedures and functions. Other PL/SQL blocks can be bundled together into a package for portability and encapsulation of global variables that may be shared by several procedures and functions, and for other reasons. There are two parts to every package, a package specification and a package body. The specification contains a list of procedures and functions along with the required parameters for each, and optionally some comments about the functionality and use of each package component. The package body contains the source code for each procedure and function in the package.

TIP
A package specification lists all variables, exceptions, procedures, and functions available for use in a package, along with their parameters. A package body contains the source code for procedures and functions named in the corresponding package specification.

Once you have named your PL/SQL block and defined the block type, click OK. Procedure Builder then builds the basic components of the PL/SQL block you selected. If you want to build a function called **find_mouse( )** using the Program Unit Editor, Figure 6-5 displays what you put into the new program unit interface and Figure 6-6 displays the result Procedure Builder provides for you. Although you need to code the rest of the function yourself, Procedure Builder saves you the time it takes to debug trivial problems that may arise from incorrect **create function** statements.

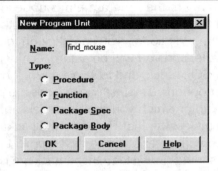

FIGURE 6-5. *Creating a new program unit with Program Unit Editor*

Once you have developed your PL/SQL code, it should be compiled. In the same area at the top of the Program Unit Editor as the New button is another button titled Compile. Pressing this button causes Procedure Builder

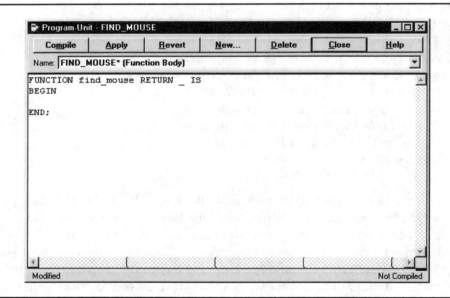

FIGURE 6-6. *Basic code constructs provided by Program Unit Editor*

to compile your PL/SQL block. If there are any errors, Procedure Builder notifies you and you can correct them. Otherwise, if the PL/SQL compilation works, then you can close the PL/SQL program unit with the Close button at the top of the Program Unit Editor display and the program unit will be stored as a program unit in the Object Navigator module, as shown in Figure 6-7. After developing the program unit, you can place that unit into a library by simply dragging and dropping the created program unit from under program units and placing it under PL/SQL libraries in the Object Navigator module.

Finally, a note about files containing client-side PL/SQL code in Procedure Builder. When you save a program unit, Procedure Builder stores your code in a binary file with the extension **.pll** attached to it. If you want to dump your PL/SQL code to flat file, you can do so by choosing the File | Export command from the menu. This way, you have a copy of the PL/SQL you just developed if you want to load the code into Oracle via SQL*Plus later.

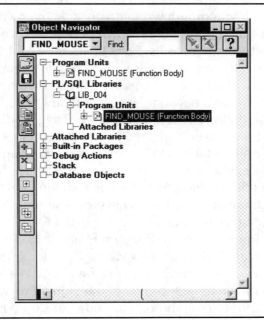

FIGURE 6-7. *Storage of program units in Object Navigator*

Exercise

What module is used for rapid PL/SQL program unit development in Procedure Builder GUI mode, and how is it used?

Using Procedure Builder GUI to Develop Server-Side PL/SQL

Using Procedure Builder to develop server-side stored procedures and functions is slightly different. First of all, you must be connected to the database in order to work with server-side PL/SQL. This is done by clicking on menu options File | Connect or CTRL-J, and you provide an Oracle login ID and password, along with a SQL*Net connection string so Procedure Builder knows where to look for its network connection information.

Once logged in, you will see a plus (+) sign in the box next to the Database Objects node in the Object Navigator. If you click on the box, you will see a list of database objects available to Procedure Builder categorized by schema owner. If you drill down into your schema owner, Procedure Builder will show you a further breakdown of objects owned by this schema by database objects, program units, PL/SQL libraries, tables, and views. Further drill-down into program units will list out all stored procedures in the database already. Rather than working with an existing procedure or function, you will create a new one. If you pull down the Program menu, notice that now all options including Database Trigger Editor and Stored Program Unit Editor are now darkened in and ready for use. The appearance of the Procedure Builder GUI at this point is shown in Figure 6-8.

Now you will develop a server-side stored procedure. You can either click on Program | Stored Program Unit Editor menu item to bring up the Stored Program Unit Editor module to develop a stored procedure, or double-click on the Database Objects node in the Object Navigator module, then again on the Stored Program Units node. This may take a moment as Procedure Builder obtains source code for your existing PL/SQL code. To modify an existing program, click on the DOWN ARROW next to the Name pull-down menu at the top-right of the Stored Program Unit Editor window. You may then scroll through to find your stored program unit. To create a new stored procedure, click on the New button above the Owner pull-down menu at the topmost-left of the Stored Program Unit Editor window. As with developing client-side program units, you are prompted to enter a name for your new PL/SQL block along with its type. When finished,

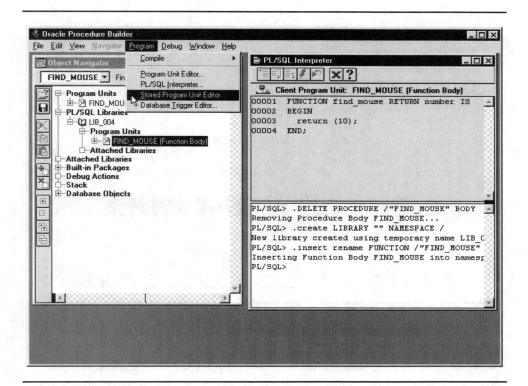

FIGURE 6-8. *Developing server-side PL/SQL with Procedure Builder*

click OK, and you will then be brought to the Stored Program Unit Editor module window, where you can modify the code provided until your procedure is developed.

Compiling your stored PL/SQL code in the Stored Program Unit Editor is almost as simple as compiling client-side program units, yet there is no Compile button in the Stored Program Unit Editor module. So, instead you must click the Save button, and Procedure Builder attempts to save your code in the Oracle database. However, if there is an error, Procedure Builder will still notify you in a new bottom window of the Stored Program Unit Editor, allowing you to change it. In Figure 6-9, you see how Procedure Builder responds to your entry of procedure **elaborate_calc( )**, which refers to the TEXT_IO package. However, recall that TEXT_IO is a client-side

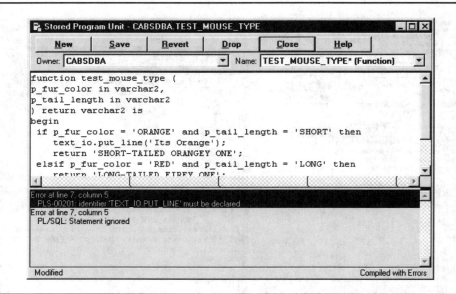

FIGURE 6-9. *Developing and saving PL/SQL with Stored Program Unit Editor*

package only, and its equivalent is DBMS_OUTPUT on the database side. So, the Stored Program Unit Editor reports an error. If you then modify the code and try saving it again with the Save button, the error and entire bottom window goes away. The code is now written, saved in the database, and you can click the Close button to send the Stored Program Unit Editor module away.

TIP
*If there are problems with your code but you do not see errors when you press the Save button, try entering **alter {procedure | function | package | package body}** proc_name **compile** from the PL/SQL Interpreter module PL/SQL prompt.*

Exercises

1. What event must occur before you can use the Stored Program Unit Editor?

2. Describe the process of developing server-side PL/SQL code. How is code compiled in the Stored Program Unit Editor? What command can be used to compile PL/SQL blocks that seem to be having problems?

3. How are compile errors usually reported in the Stored Program Unit Editor?

Running PL/SQL Programs in Procedure Builder

PL/SQL can be invoked in Procedure Builder with slightly less effort than in SQL*Plus. Recall that unnamed or anonymous PL/SQL code can run against the PL/SQL Interpreter without being compiled. Individual PL/SQL statements run interactively as well at the PL/SQL Interpreter prompt. Named PL/SQL blocks on the client side can be invoked in a different way. Once the program unit is compiled and stored, you can invoke it simply by typing in the name of the procedure at the interactive PL/SQL prompt within the Procedure Builder GUI. The code that would appear in the PL/SQL Interpreter window for a procedure called **list_available_mice( )** that prints all mice available at a pet store after a certain date is in the following block:

```
PL/SQL> LIST_AVAILABLE_MICE('09-NOV-2000');
MOUSE       AVAILABILITY
-----       ------------
BILLY       20-NOV-2000
MILLY       21-NOV-2000
JILLY       05-DEC-2000
EEEKY       26-DEC-2000
GRUB        04-JAN-2001
```

Invoking a PL/SQL block with Procedure Builder in line mode is accomplished in the same way. However, when working in Procedure Builder from the command line you usually must first attach the library containing the PL/SQL block or Procedure Builder won't know what to

execute. Assume for this example that you have a library called
MICE_LIB_01a, containing procedure **list_available_mice( )**. To invoke this
procedure from the command line in Procedure Builder, you must first
attach the library to Procedure Builder and then you may execute the
PL/SQL block. The following code listing demonstrates this:

```
PL/SQL> .attach library MICE_LIB_01a
Attaching library in file MICE_LIB_01a.pll, BEFORE other attached
libs...
PL/SQL> LIST_AVAILABLE_MICE('09-NOV-2000');
MOUSE     AVAILABILITY
-----     ------------
BILLY     20-NOV-2000
MILLY     21-NOV-2000
JILLY     05-DEC-2000
EEEKY     26-DEC-2000
GRUB      04-JAN-2001
```

You can also open or attach libraries in the Object Navigator module of the
Procedure Builder GUI. Do this by clicking either on the PL/SQL Libraries node
for opening libraries or on the Attached Libraries node for attaching libraries,
respectively, and then clicking on the Open button on the vertical toolbar of the
module. Remember an important difference in working with PL/SQL libraries in
Procedure Builder: If your library is open—that is to say it is located as a
drill-down item under the PL/SQL libraries item in the Object Navigator—that
means it is open and the PL/SQL code bodies are available for modification.
Those PL/SQL blocks are not necessarily ready to be run, however. An example
is when you have opened your PL/SQL library with the **.open library**
library_name command. When your PL/SQL library is attached, however, the
code is available for execution in the PL/SQL Interpreter module. You use the
.attach library *library_name* command to do this.

TIP
*If you compile a PL/SQL block and seem to
have problems executing it from the PL/SQL
Interpreter module, try clicking the Save button
on the left margin of the Object Navigator
module to save the library containing the
PL/SQL block. If there are still problems, try
closing the library entirely and typing **.attach
library** your_library_name from the command
PL/SQL Interpreter module prompt.*

Server-side PL/SQL is executed in the same way from the PL/SQL Interpreter module, by referring to the PL/SQL block by name, followed by a semicolon. However, to execute server-side PL/SQL properly, you must be connected to the database.

Exercises

1. How do you invoke anonymous PL/SQL within Procedure Builder? What about named PL/SQL?

2. How does invoking named PL/SQL within the PL/SQL Interpreter module differ from invoking named PL/SQL from Procedure Builder line mode?

Handling Exceptions in PL/SQL

In this section, you will cover the following points about handling PL/SQL exceptions:

- Handling Oracle-defined exceptions
- Handling user-defined exceptions
- Using **raise_application_error( )**

Error handling in PL/SQL is performed using the exception handler. In the last chapter, you covered the basic coding constructs of an exception handler. There are three different types of exceptions: Oracle-defined, user-defined, and internal exceptions. Several exceptions are already built into PL/SQL, such as **no_data_found** and others. The best part about Oracle-defined exceptions is that they are raised automatically. In addition, it was shown that you create your own exceptions by declaring and raising them appropriately yourself in the PL/SQL block. Finally, internal exceptions allow you to associate an exception name with an Oracle error condition. In this section, you will learn more about how to handle Oracle-defined and your own exceptions. You will also learn how to use an important procedure in PL/SQL—the **raise_application_error( )** procedure—for reporting PL/SQL errors.

Handling Oracle-Defined Exceptions

Recall from Chapter 5 the presence of Oracle-defined exceptions within the Oracle database. These exceptions are raised automatically whenever they occur in your PL/SQL code. There is a tip in Chapter 5 stating that, if you do not code an exception handler (either the specific exception name or the **when others then** clause) for predefined exceptions, you will not trap them in your code. This is true, and what's more, your users will receive the error message if you don't attempt to trap all possible exceptions that may occur. So, make sure you code your PL/SQL exception handlers to detect and resolve Oracle-defined exceptions. Remember, *Oracle **always** raises its own exceptions when they occur.*

To review, some of the exceptions that can occur are when your **select into** statement returns no data or too much data, or when data selected into a variable does not match the variable's type declaration. Also, Oracle will raise an exception if an attempt to divide by zero is made, a primary key or unique constraint violation is made, or if a cursor manipulation is made on a closed cursor. There are some others, but these several should be enough to refresh your memory. Refer back to Chapter 5 if you're still confused, or if you want the exact names of the Oracle-defined exceptions.

Assume your PL/SQL block contains a **select into** statement, similar to **select_emp( )** in the following code block. If no data is returned from the EMPLOYEE table related to the EMPID passed into the procedure, Oracle will raise its own exception.

```
CREATE PROCEDURE select_emp(
   p_empid            IN VARCHAR2
) AS
   my_employee_rec    employee%ROWTYPE;
BEGIN
   SELECT *
   INTO my_employee_rec
   FROM employee
   WHERE empid = p_raise_empid;
END;
```

What's more, since there is no coded exception handler for Oracle's own exception, you will receive an error when you execute it. The following code block illustrates what will happen if you compile and

execute the **select_emp( )** procedure from the **select_emp.sql** file within
SQL*Plus as it is written above:

```
SQL> @select_emp
Procedure created.
SQL> execute select_emp('593485');
*
ERROR at line 1:
ORA-01403: no data found
ORA-06512: at SPANKY.SELECT_EMP, line 5
ORA-06512: at line 1
SQL>
```

Not exactly the type of thing you want to pass to your users, is it? So, you
must add an exception handler. This procedure block requires only a simple
one. You can do it in one of two ways. First, you can identify the
Oracle-defined exception(s) by name in your exception handler and define
how it should be handled. Alternately, you can identify the special catchall
exception, **others**, and define something special to happen in that way.
Consider the first option, shown in the following code block:

```
CREATE PROCEDURE select_emp(
   p_empid               IN VARCHAR2
) AS
   my_employee_rec    employee%ROWTYPE;
BEGIN
    SELECT *
    INTO my_employee_rec
    FROM employee
    WHERE empid = p_raise_empid;
EXCEPTION
WHEN NO_DATA_FOUND THEN
DBMS_OUTPUT.PUT_LINE('select_emp(): Found no data in EMPLOYEE.');
END;
```

Alternately, the catchall exception can be used, with appropriate change to
the output. Remember, **others** will be the exception handler for any one of the
variety of things that can go wrong. Observe in the following code block:

```
CREATE PROCEDURE select_emp(
   p_empid               IN VARCHAR2
) AS
   my_employee_rec    employee%ROWTYPE;
BEGIN
```

```
SELECT *
INTO my_employee_rec
FROM employee
WHERE empid = p_raise_empid;
EXCEPTION
WHEN OTHERS THEN
DBMS_OUTPUT.PUT_LINE('select_emp(): An error occurred.');
END;
```

Of course, you can code any number of exceptions to be handled in a multitude of different ways. Just remember that an unhandled exception is passed to the caller of the PL/SQL block. Adding a **when others** clause to your exception handler to trap your Oracle-defined exceptions is usually a small preventive measure that yields a more robust application. Better still, code exception handlers for all Oracle-defined exceptions to identify exactly what has occurred, although in some cases you may find this to be overkill. Finally, you should code a special catch-all exception handler called **when others then** as the last handler to take care of all situations not explicitly coded for in other exception handlers.

TIP
*Remember that process control returns to the caller if an unhandled exception is raised. You may want to use it to your advantage in some situations by only coding an exception handler that uses **others** at the procedure caller's level to detect more serious problems with the application.*

Exercises

1. Identify some Oracle-defined exceptions. When are Oracle-defined exceptions raised?

2. Where is PL/SQL execution control passed if an unhandled exception is raised?

3. What is the **others** exceptions handler, and how is it used?

Handling User-Defined Exceptions

In addition to Oracle-defined exceptions, PL/SQL allows you to define your own exceptions to be raised by the application. Recall from Chapter 5 that user-defined exceptions must have code in all parts of the PL/SQL block, including declarations, execution, and exception sections. This is different from Oracle-defined exceptions, which need only have code in the exception section of the block in order to be handled properly. Observe the following version of **select_emp( )**. This version has a check in the code to see if this employee is active. If the STATUS column contains an "R" or "L," that means the employee is retired or on leave, respectively.

```
CREATE PROCEDURE select_emp(
   p_empid            IN VARCHAR2
) AS
   my_employee_rec    employee%ROWTYPE;
   bad_status         exception;
BEGIN
   SELECT *
   INTO my_employee_rec
   FROM employee
   WHERE empid = p_raise_empid;
   IF my_employee_rec.status = 'R' OR my_employee_rec.status = 'L'
THEN
RAISE bad_status;
   END IF;
EXCEPTION
   WHEN NO_DATA_FOUND THEN
       DBMS_OUTPUT.PUT_LINE('select_emp(): Found no data in
EMPLOYEE.');
WHEN BAD_STATUS THEN
DBMS_OUTPUT.PUT_LINE('select_emp(): Employee on leave or
retired.');
END;
```

Note that all components of the PL/SQL block have something in them addressing the user-defined exception. If the exception is not defined, raising it will itself produce an error at compile time. If the exception is not raised, then Oracle will never behave appropriately in the presence of that exception. If there is no exception handler for the user-defined exception, control will pass to the exception handler of the calling block in search of code that will handle the exception, in the same way as happens with an Oracle-defined exception.

One final note on handling user-defined exceptions—the **others** exception handler will handle a user-defined exception as well as it will handle Oracle-defined exceptions. The same conditions about unhandled exceptions passing control to their callers applies in this situation as well. In general, user-defined exceptions are useful in that you employ Oracle's overall process of exception handling for situations where Oracle errors might not occur to signal an application-defined problem. However, they do require some coding overhead, such as a condition check and an explicit **raise** statement.

Exercises

1. In what parts of a PL/SQL block must code appear supporting a user-defined exception? How is a user-defined exception raised?

2. Does the **others** exception handler support user-defined exceptions? Explain.

Using RAISE_APPLICATION_ERROR( )

Sometimes in PL/SQL programming, you may want error handling that is more robust than simple one-line output. In situations where you have dozens or even hundreds of PL/SQL programs working together as one application, it helps if the error-handling methods being used allow you to detect which procedure or function experienced the error and why in order to speed resolution time on specific issues. You can create unique ID numbers for the errors themselves as well. In PL/SQL, there is a special built-in procedure available that helps you build a more robust application whose errors meld well into Oracle's own methods for notifying you that an error condition exists.

The **raise_application_error( )** procedure allows for that more seamless integration. This procedure allows you to define more descriptive error messages in conjunction with a given error situation. In addition, this procedure accepts a user-defined error number that Oracle will report when an error arises that calls **raise_application_error( )** in such a way that the error message and error number will look like it's coming directly from Oracle. To summarize, the following items are passed to this procedure:

- *Error_Num* An integer value between –20,000 and –20,999 that should be used to identify uniquely each procedure and/or error in the application, allowing up to 1,000 procedures, functions, or errors in the application, package, or library to be so uniquely identified.

- *Error_Msg* A text string of no more than 512 characters that describes the error that occurred.

- *Keep_Recs* (Optional, default FALSE) A TRUE or FALSE value stating whether Oracle should keep previous exceptions that may have been raised in conjunction with this one.

TIP
*The **raise_application_error( )** procedure works well when you run server-side procedures from Procedure Builder and want to see errors.*

By incorporating **raise_application_error( )** into your exception handler, you can design a higher level of application error handling, which offers more information about the error and the exact procedure that raised it. The following code block shows incorporation of the **raise_application_error( )** procedure to allow you to see exactly what the problem was in the procedure:

```
CREATE PROCEDURE select_emp(
    p_empid              IN VARCHAR2
) AS
    my_employee_rec      employee%ROWTYPE;
    bad_status           exception;
BEGIN
    SELECT *
    INTO my_employee_rec
    FROM employee
    WHERE empid = p_raise_empid;
    IF my_employee_rec.status = 'R' OR my_employee_rec.status = 'L'
THEN
RAISE bad_status;
END IF;
EXCEPTION
    WHEN NO_DATA_FOUND THEN
```

```
      raise_application_error(-20100,'Found no data in EMPLOYEE for
' || to_char(p_empid) || '.');
WHEN BAD_STATUS THEN
raise_application_error(-20100,'Employee ' || to_char(p_empid) || '
is on leave or retired.');
END;
```

In this example, the error number identifies this procedure uniquely. Another option is for you to identify uniquely a specific user-defined exception like BAD_STATUS. In that case, the numbers passed to **raise_application_error( )** in each portion of the exception handler should be different. Consider how Oracle now replies to an error situation where employee with EMPID 40394 is on maternity leave, with its new calls to **raise_application_error( )**.

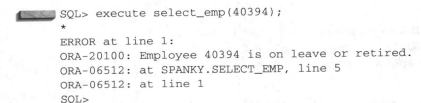

```
SQL> execute select_emp(40394);
*
ERROR at line 1:
ORA-20100: Employee 40394 is on leave or retired.
ORA-06512: at SPANKY.SELECT_EMP, line 5
ORA-06512: at line 1
SQL>
```

TIP
It usually works better to use **raise_application_error( )** *to identify each procedure and/or function in the application uniquely than to identify particular user-defined errors uniquely, because to extrapolate the uniqueness of each procedure from the unique exception number requires that you name and handle each exception uniquely.*

Exercises

1. What parameters are passed to the **raise_application_error( )** procedure?

2. Describe two things that can be identified uniquely by using **raise_application_error( )**.

3. Describe how exceptions are reported when the **raise_application_error( )** procedure is used.

Chapter Summary

In this chapter, you have covered a substantial amount of information on how to develop PL/SQL programs. Several topics are covered, including the required keywords and components in procedures and functions, the development of server-side procedures and functions with SQL*Plus and your favorite text editor, and the development of server- and client-side procedures and functions with Procedure Builder. In addition, the execution of PL/SQL code was covered in various ways, along with the development and requirements of exception handlers in your PL/SQL code. All in all, this chapter comprises about 24 percent of material tested on OCP Exam 2.

The first area you covered was the development of PL/SQL code. The permissions involved in PL/SQL programming were identified to be the **create procedure** system permission for server-side PL/SQL coding, and none for client-side PL/SQL coding. Execution of a server-side PL/SQL block created by a user in the database is granted both to the owner of the code and to anyone who has been granted the **execute** object permission. Issuing both of these permissions is handled with the **grant** command.

The creation of procedures and functions is handled with either the **create procedure** or **create function** statement. Packages have their own creation statement, to be covered in Chapter 9. There are special syntactic conditions to be met in creation of procedures. The first is an overall syntax flow, similar to **create procedure** proc_name (var direction datatype) **is begin … end**. The next is the syntax requirements for PL/SQL statements within the procedure. Once the user has created the procedure, she can submit the procedure to the Oracle database for compilation. Once compiled, if there are no errors, Oracle will store the procedure in the database, ready for execution. One main difference between anonymous PL/SQL blocks and named blocks is in the declaration of variables. Anonymous blocks use a **declare** keyword explicitly, while an implicit area for variable declaration exists between the **is** or **as** keyword and **begin**.

Parameter passing is an important area to understand in PL/SQL that is most directly attributed to use in procedures. Parameters can be passed in three directions. They can be passed into a procedure only, out of a procedure only, or into and out of a procedure. These directions are represented in the parameter variable definition area after the **create procedure** keywords with the use of the **in**, **out**, or **in out** keywords, respectively.

Functions are created with slightly different syntax from procedures. First, the keywords **create function** are used to define the function. Next, recall that a function *always* returns a value. As such, a return datatype must be defined for the function. The general syntax for function creation is **create function** *name* (*var* **in** *datatype*) **return** *datatype* **is begin ...return** *something* **... end**. Note that you should define your variable parameters as **in** variables. Although it is technically possible for PL/SQL functions to return values in **out** or **in out** variables, good coding practice stipulates that the only **out** variable is the one returned by the function. At some point in the function, the **return** command must be used to define the value the function will return to the caller.

After establishing the basic premises of PL/SQL development, some of which was review, your attention turned to the use of various tools like SQL*Plus and Procedure Builder to develop PL/SQL code for the client and server. SQL*Plus can be used to enter stored or server-side procedures in the same way as it is used to enter server SQL statements. You can code in anonymous blocks or named blocks directly at the SQL prompt and submit them for compilation. Or, you can write the PL/SQL code in a flat file using your favorite text editor, load the file into SQL*Plus with the **get** command and compile it into your Oracle database by typing a slash (/). Alternately, after writing the PL/SQL code in a flat file using your favorite text editor, you can load and compile it into Oracle with the @ character affixed to the front of the filename that contains the PL/SQL code, sans the suffix of the file (usually **.sql**).

Once created and compiled successfully, the procedure is considered a part of the Oracle database; thus, the term "stored procedure" applies. You can then execute the stored procedure from SQL*Plus using the **execute** *procedure_name*; statement. Alternately, this command can be abbreviated **exec**. In the case of executing a stored function from SQL*Plus, a small consideration must be made. Since a value will be returned from the function execution, a variable assignment statement must accompany (encompass, really) a stored function call. Thus, you wouldn't say **execute** *function_name* from the SQL prompt, you would write an anonymous block (or named procedure) that declared a variable to store the return value from the stored function. The actual line within that PL/SQL block may look like *variable_name* := *function_name(var1, var2)*;. The following code block illustrates:

```
DECLARE
   my_var NUMBER(10);
BEGIN
   my_var := sqrt(3);
END;
```

Compiling your server-side stored procedures is a bit ungainly in SQL*Plus when you encounter an error. This is because Oracle stores your compilation errors in either the USER_ERRORS or ALL_ERRORS dictionary views. Oracle also stores the line number where the error was found in these views; however, this line information is based on the location of the error in the SQL*Plus statement buffer (known as the file **afiedt.buf**), and that buffer only stores the most recent SQL or PL/SQL statement. Thus, as soon as you type **select * from user_errors**, you lose your buffer containing the location of your PL/SQL block. One solution is to have two sessions open at once, one for code compilation and the other for selecting errors. The other solution is to use **show errors**. However, SQL*Plus is not a particularly effective tool for server-side PL/SQL development.

Oracle combats the situation with Developer/2000. In particular, this development toolset includes a program called Procedure Builder. Procedure Builder runs in two modes, line and GUI. When at the Procedure Builder line mode, you can enter any valid PL/SQL statement, procedure, or function name, and Procedure Builder will run it. Contrast this to SQL*Plus, which requires the use of the **execute** command. This is because Procedure Builder contains its own PL/SQL execution engine, separate from the one in the Oracle database.

There are two types of client- and server-side code in Procedure Builder, and those types are files and libraries. Files usually contain stand-alone procedures and functions, while libraries contain multiple procedures, functions, and sometimes even packages. Recall that the concept of packages was introduced. A package is a structure in PL/SQL that allows the developer to bundle several procedures or functions together, offering the code definitions and required variables as a specification and hiding the procedure or function source code in a package body. A new file type was introduced as well that stores PL/SQL libraries. These files carry the **.pll** suffix. However, these files are stored as binaries. If you want to load a PL/SQL block you develop in Procedure Builder into Oracle server via SQL*Plus, you must export the program unit to a flat file with extension **.pls** using the File | Export command as described in the text. The same PL/SQL code developed in a flat file that can be loaded into SQL*Plus can also be loaded into Procedure Builder using the **load file** command. Alternately, if PL/SQL procedures are stored in client-side libraries, the library itself must be attached using the **attach library** command. However, you must remember to precede special commands like **load** and **attach** with a period (**.**) in Procedure Builder.

Although it can be run in line mode, more frequently you will find yourself working with the Procedure Builder GUI. The application itself consists of five elements called modules. They are the Object Navigator, the PL/SQL Interpreter, the Program Unit Editor, the Stored Program Unit Editor, and the Database Trigger Editor. The latter two modules are for server-side PL/SQL development of PL/SQL blocks and table triggers, respectively. The Program Unit Editor is used to develop client-side PL/SQL code—either stand-alone or in a library. The PL/SQL Interpreter is used for interactive execution of PL/SQL code on both the client and server. Finally, the Object Navigator provides a visual representation of an overall development environment for both client- and server-side PL/SQL code.

One major advantage Procedure Builder offers you is to cut the effort to develop code. The easiest way to develop a client-side PL/SQL block is to use the Program Unit Editor module. The module's graphical interface makes it easy to name the code and define its PL/SQL block type. Once named and its type defined, the Program Unit Editor will open a window containing the basic keywords and constructs of the PL/SQL block you want. All that remains is for you to fill in the loops, variables, **if-then** statements, and other PL/SQL constructs required for your program. What's more, the Program Unit Editor window simplifies compilation by offering you a Compile button. Once your code is written, you can compile it. If there are errors, the Program Unit Editor will notify you immediately what the problem was, and point the way clearly to the offending code. Note one important point about client-side PL/SQL programming—you needn't be connected to the database in order to write it, because Procedure Builder has its own built-in PL/SQL execution engine.

For development of server-side PL/SQL code, you must be connected to the database. Creation of stored procedures and functions is done with the Stored Program Unit Editor. The process for creating new stored PL/SQL is similar to that of creating client-side PL/SQL units, but with the exception that the stored program unit module has no Compile button. Instead, you must click on the Save button and Oracle will reply if it was able to compile and store your procedure on the database or not. Other specifics on development of client- and server-side PL/SQL are covered in the text, along with figures that show the status of Procedure Builder at the various stages of development.

Once compiled on either the client or server, your programs can be run in the following way. You can type the name of the procedure into the PL/SQL Interpreter module or Procedure Builder command line mode, so long as your client library or file is attached or loaded. If you are trying to run server-side PL/SQL, you must be connected and able to see the compiled and stored PL/SQL in the database. Recall also that an anonymous block can be entered at the PL/SQL Interpreter prompt, along with any valid PL/SQL statement, so you can run things that way, too.

The final area covered in this chapter is proper use of the exception handler, and handling exceptions in general in PL/SQL. Several different types of exceptions were covered, including Oracle-defined and user-defined exceptions. Important to remember is that Oracle always raises its own exceptions automatically. Thus, if you, for example, are to divide by zero in a function, Oracle will raise an exception automatically. If you haven't coded an appropriate exception handler for the situation, control returns to the caller of the procedure or function. If you are not careful about trapping all possible exceptions and handling them in your code, you may encounter situations where users receive errors they shouldn't have to deal with, causing your application to seem less robust. Chapter 5 lists the Oracle-defined exceptions; to handle them in your exception handler requires only that you include a **when** *Ora_defnd_exception* **then** clause, where *Ora_defnd_exception* is either the name of the Oracle-defined exception or a special catchall exception called **others**.

The user-defined exceptions are handled slightly differently. Remember, a user-defined exception must be declared, raised, and handled explicitly by the PL/SQL block. You get none of the freebies associated with Oracle-defined exceptions here. However, the importance of handling a raised user-defined exception is no less important than handling an Oracle-defined exception. Recall that in all cases where a raised exception is not handled by the current PL/SQL block, control passes to the exception handler of the calling block.

Last, the use of a special procedure called **raise_application_error( )** was covered in this chapter. This procedure allows you to create specially numbered custom error messages that are reported by Oracle whenever a server-side stored procedure or function hits a handled exception. This procedure accepts three variables as parameters, including *error_num* between –20,000 and –20,999, *error_msg* of 512 characters or less, and *keep_recs*, a TRUE or FALSE value that tells Oracle to keep or not keep other errors that have come before this one when reporting problems. By incorporating a call to **raise_application_error( )** in your exception handler, you allow more unique identification of either the stored PL/SQL block or of the error that occurred.

Two-Minute Drill

- To create PL/SQL code, keep in mind two permissions required: **create procedure** to write the code and **execute** to run it. These permissions are given with the **grant** command.

- Syntax for procedure creation is **create procedure** (*var direction datatype*) **is begin ... end**. Variables are declared between the **is** and **begin** keywords. This contrasts to anonymous PL/SQL blocks, where variables are declared after the **declare** keyword.

- Direction must be stated for parameter passing in procedures. Possibilities for direction include **in**, **out**, and **in out**.

- When submitting **create procedure** statements to the Oracle database for processing, you are compiling and storing the program unit, not running it.

- Syntax for function creation is **create function** (*var direction datatype*) **return** *datatype* **is begin ... return** *something* **... end**.

- Functions always have a return value. Thus, the datatype of that return value must be declared, and the **return** *something* statement must be included in the function code body.

- Functions accept as input zero or more variables, and return one.

- To meet Oracle's purity level for calling functions from SQL statements, good coding practice necessitates you define no parameter variable for a function call as an **out** or **in out** parameter, and you must use all Oracle internal datatypes like NUMBER and VARCHAR2 to declare variables and parameters, not PL/SQL datatype extensions like TEXT, PLS_INTEGER, and the like.

■ Note that the **create procedure** permission also allows you to create functions.

■ SQL*Plus can be used to create and submit for compilation server-side PL/SQL programs. The entry of lines of PL/SQL code must follow PL/SQL language constructs, and can happen at the SQL prompt.

■ Changing lines of code involves invoking the line number and using the **change** command to alter character strings in the current line. Alternately, you can invoke your favorite text editor and modify the current statement buffer using the **edit** command. See Chapter 1 for more information.

■ You can load PL/SQL source code stored in flat files into the SQL*Plus command prompt for code compilation with the **get** command, followed by slash (/) to compile and store in the Oracle database. Or, you can use the @*filename.sql* command to perform these activities in one fell swoop.

■ When running a PL/SQL block, you pass parameters either positionally corresponding to the way the block declares the parameters, or with reference pointers in the form *parm_name=> 'value'*.

■ To run a function in SQL*Plus, you need to create an anonymous or named procedure block that references the function as part of variable assignment. Remember, functions always return data of some sort.

■ Compiling PL/SQL in SQL*Plus is a challenge because the errors reported in ALL_ERRORS or USER_ERRORS correspond to a line number of the error as stored in the current SQL*Plus statement buffer. That buffer no longer stores the PL/SQL block after you **select** the errors from the dictionary view, though. One solution is to have two sessions open to Oracle when compiling: one to **select** the errors, and the other to execute the compile.

■ Procedure Builder allows you to create server- and client-side PL/SQL code using an application designed to code programs.

- Procedure Builder runs in both line mode and as a GUI. The GUI is actually a superset of line mode, because the PL/SQL Interpreter is identical to PL/SQL line mode.

- Information about available commands in Procedure Builder can be found with the **help** command. Commands in Procedure Builder line mode must be preceded with a period (**.**).

- Procedure Builder's GUI has five modules. Their names and uses are listed here:

  - **Object Navigator**   Navigate client and server PL/SQL program modules

  - **PL/SQL Interpreter**   Interactive prompt for running PL/SQL code

  - **Program Unit Editor**   Create, edit, and compile client PL/SQL

  - **Stored Program Unit Editor**   Create, edit, and compile server PL/SQL

  - **Database Trigger Editor**   Create, edit, and compile database triggers

- You can develop stand-alone PL/SQL code for the client side in flat files suffixed by **.sql** and load them into Procedure Builder using **.load file** *filename.sql* command from the PL/SQL prompt in line mode or the PL/SQL Interpreter in GUI mode.

- Procedure Builder introduces the concept of code libraries, which are files with the suffix **.pll**. A library contains client-side PL/SQL procedures and functions available for use.

- You can use PL/SQL code that is part of a client-side library after attaching it. To attach a client-side PL/SQL library, use the **.attach library** *libname* in the PL/SQL Interpreter module or in Procedure Builder line mode. You can also use the File | Attach menu item to attach a library.

- You do not need to be connected to the database to create client PL/SQL in Procedure Builder. You must be connected to the database to create server stored procedures and functions or database triggers in Procedure Builder.

■ PL/SQL code is executed by calling it in the PL/SQL Interpreter. No **execute** command is required. Also, you can run any valid PL/SQL statement from the PL/SQL Interpreter.

■ Errors in PL/SQL code are managed by the exception handler.

■ There are two types of exceptions to recall: Oracle-defined exceptions and user-defined exceptions. A third type of exception, an internal exception, is explained in Chapter 5.

■ Oracle-defined exceptions do not need to be declared in your code. Oracle automatically raises its own exceptions, though, so you must remember to code an exception handler to trap Oracle's own exceptions.

■ User-defined exceptions must be declared, raised, and handled explicitly in your PL/SQL code.

■ A special exception handler exists in PL/SQL called **others**, which allows you to create **when** clauses in your exception handler that catch all exceptions that are not specifically handled by other exception handlers.

■ A special procedure called **raise_application_error( )** allows you to integrate stronger error messaging into Oracle's native error reporting methods.

■ The **raise_application_error( )** procedure accepts three parameters: *error_num, error_msg,* and optionally *keep_recs.*

■ Acceptable values for error numbers are between –20,000 and –20,999.

■ Generally, it works best to use error numbers to identify uniquely all stored procedures or functions in the Oracle database. Alternately, use error numbers to identify uniquely the different user-defined errors in your stored procedures.

Chapter Questions

1. The developer attempts to execute client-side procedure REMOVE_EMP( ) in library EMP_ACTIONS, which results in Oracle saying the REMOVE_EMP variable must be declared. The appropriate way to correct this error is to

   A. Reestablish connection to the Oracle database.

   B. Open the procedure using the Stored Program Unit Editor module.

   C. Execute **.attach library EMP_ACTIONS** from the PL/SQL Interpreter module.

   D. Execute **.open file REMOVE_EMP** from the PL/SQL Interpreter module.

2. When developing a PL/SQL library, the developer defines variable NUM2 as IN OUT in the ADD_NUMS( ) function. Which of the following statements may happen as a result of this?

   A. The **add_nums( )** function will not compile.

   B. Code running after **add_nums( )** that uses the NUM2 variable may behave unpredictably because NUM2's value was changed in **add_nums( )**.

   C. The **add_nums( )** function will return errors to the user when run.

   D. The **add_nums( )** function will cause a memory leak.

3. A procedure declares a user-defined exception but does not raise it explicitly. Which of the following statements is true about this function?

   A. The user-defined exception will never be raised.

   B. The user-defined exception will be handled by a **when others** exception handler.

   C. The procedure will fail on compile.

   D. The user-defined exception is defined incorrectly.

4. The RAISE_APPLICATION_ERROR( ) procedure defines errors returned in which of the following numeric ranges?

  A. −00000 and −99999

  B. −01200 and −01299

  C. −00030 and −00039

  D. −20000 and −20999

5. The @ command in SQL*Plus will do which of the following with a named PL/SQL block stored in a flat file?

  A. Load the PL/SQL code into its processing buffer only.

  B. Load PL/SQL code into its processing buffer and compile the code against the database only.

  C. Load PL/SQL code into its processing buffer and compile the code on the client side only.

  D. Load, compile, and run PL/SQL code against the Oracle database.

6. Which statement can be used in Procedure Builder to modify procedures in a client-side PL/SQL library?

  A. **.open library** *lib_name.*

  B. **Alter procedure** *proc_name* **compile;**

  C. **.attach library** *lib_name.*

  D. **.open file** *lib_name.*

7. An Oracle-defined exception is raised

  A. By the PL/SQL **raise** statement.

  B. In the PL/SQL exception handler.

  C. Automatically by Oracle.

  D. By the user.

8. Which of the following lines in the PL/SQL source code will return an error?

  A. **create procedure** estatus (

  B. eid NUMBER, statchar CHAR) is begin

   C. select status **into** statchar **from** EMP **where** EMPID = eid; **end**;

   D. There are no errors in this code block

9. **Which two of the following Procedure Builder modules are not usable unless you are connected to the Oracle database? (Choose two)**

   A. Stored Program Unit Editor

   B. Database Trigger Editor

   C. Program Unit Editor

   D. Object Navigator

10. **In which areas of the PL/SQL block must code be placed in order to handle Oracle-defined exceptions?**

   A. Declaration section only

   B. Declaration and executable sections only

   C. Exception handler only

   D. Declaration, executable, and exception handler sections

11. **Which two commands are available in SQL*Plus for editing PL/SQL blocks?**

   A. Attach

   B. Change

   C. Edit

   D. Load

12. **In which areas of a PL/SQL block must the developer place code for user-defined exceptions? (Choose three)**

   A. Command line PL/SQL block call

   B. Variable declaration section

   C. Executable section

   D. Exception handler

Answers to Chapter Questions

1. C. Execute **.attach library EMP_ACTIONS** from the PL/SQL Interpreter module

Explanation   When you attempt to execute a procedure in a library that is not currently attached to the Object Navigator, Procedure Builder returns an error stating that it expected the name of the procedure to be declared in some way. Choices A and B are incorrect because they both imply you are working with stored procedures, which is not the case according to information given in the question. Choice D is also incorrect because the **open** command will make the library source code available for modification, not execution.

2. B. Code running after **add_nums( )** that uses the NUM2 variable may behave unpredictably because NUM2's value was changed in **add_nums( )**.

Explanation   When executed, the **add_nums( )** procedure returns a modified NUM2 variable. The caller must be aware this is happening or else other procedures and functions using NUM2 will contain that modified value, not the value NUM2 had before **add_nums( )** was called. Choices A and C are incorrect; Oracle technically will allow functions to have **in out** parameters for compilation, and will allow you to run the function successfully as well. Choice D is patently incorrect.

3. A. The user-defined exception will never be raised.

Explanation   User-defined exceptions must be raised explicitly by the PL/SQL block. Oracle will never raise a user-defined exception unless it is a pragma exception, covered in Chapter 5. Choices C and D are incorrect because there is nothing syntactically wrong with not raising a declared exception, and it will cause no errors at run time. If it is raised and no exception is defined to handle it explicitly, however, the **when others** exception handler will pick it up if there is one.

4. D. −20000 and −20999

Explanation   The range of accepted values for use in **raise_application_error( )** should be between −20000 and −20999. You should take the short amount of time necessary to memorize this fact.

5. B.   Load PL/SQL code into its processing buffer and compile the code against the database only.

Explanation   The first thing to remember with this question is SQL*Plus is used for server-side PL/SQL. This fact alone eliminates choice C. Next, remember that a flat file can contain either anonymous or named PL/SQL code. If the block is anonymous, the @ command will load, compile, and execute it. But, the question said the block was named. Thus, SQL*Plus will simply load and compile, but not execute, the named PL/SQL block in the flat file given.

6. A.   **.open library** *lib_name*

Explanation   To connect a library to Procedure Builder in order to edit source code, the **.open library** command should be used. Choice C is incorrect because attaching a library allows you to execute its PL/SQL program units, not modify them. Choice D is incorrect because the PL/SQL block in the question is not stand-alone; thus, the keyword **file** is inappropriate. Finally, since this question is talking about client-side PL/SQL, use of Oracle database DDL statements that apply to server-side code is also inappropriate.

7. C.   Automatically by Oracle

Explanation   Remember, Oracle always raises its own exceptions. They do not need to be raised explicitly by the code, eliminating choice A. Exceptions are never raised in the exception handler; that is where they are resolved, eliminating choice B as well. Users generally don't raise exceptions, either—PL/SQL blocks raise exceptions either implicitly or explicitly behind the scenes.

8. C.   **select** status **into** statchar **from** EMP **where** EMPID = eid; **end**;

Explanation   You cannot assign a value to a parameter variable if that variable has not explicitly been set as an **in out** or **out** variable. If there is no direction defined for the parameter, PL/SQL assumes it is an **in** variable. This error occurs on compilation of your code.

9. A. and B.   Stored Program Unit Editor and Database Trigger Editor

Explanation   Since these two modules modify server-side objects like stored procedures and triggers, you must be connected to the Oracle database to use them.

10. C.   Exception handler only.

Explanation   Oracle defines and raises its own exceptions so the user doesn't have to. The only code required on the part of the developer is an exception handler to prevent situations where Oracle raises its own exceptions and causes errors to be returned unexpectedly to the caller.

11. B and C.   **Change** and **Edit**

Explanation   Choices A and D are incorrect because those commands are used in Procedure Builder's PL/SQL Interpreter. The **change** command is sometimes abbreviated **c**, and its syntax is **c**/*old*/*new*. This may look familiar, as it was covered in Chapter 1 also. The **edit** command was also covered in Chapter 1, and is sometimes abbreviated **ed**.

12. B, C, and D.

Explanation   For user-defined exceptions, code must be placed in the variable declaration, executable, and exceptions sections of your PL/SQL block. You should never have to code anything to handle an exception from the command line; it all should happen within the block.

CHAPTER
7

Debugging PL/SQL
Procedures and
Functions

n this chapter, you will cover the following areas of PL/SQL debugging:

- Methods of debugging server-side PL/SQL
- Debugging PL/SQL with Procedure Builder
- Using Oracle-supplied packages for debugging

Development of code often requires debugging. Problems can occur in compilation due to syntax errors. In addition, problems may occur later with the programming logic. Without careful debugging and testing, code gets released to users that doesn't satisfy their needs. Without good debugging tools, your task in compiling and ensuring stable PL/SQL code products is difficult. This chapter will cover several topics about PL/SQL debugging. The tools available will be covered, including those on the Oracle database and within Procedure Builder. The special role of Oracle-supplied packages in the debugging process will also be covered. Knowing how to perform this activity is important; however, OCP doesn't test this area extensively. The contents of this chapter comprise 5 percent of OCP test subjects.

Methods of Debugging Server-Side PL/SQL

In this section, you will cover the following points about debugging PL/SQL:

- Introducing the DBMS_OUTPUT package
- A tour of the DBMS_OUTPUT package
- DBMS_OUTPUT procedures in action

Though mentioned already, the DBMS_OUTPUT package is the topic of this section. It is an important package with many uses. Oracle incorporated this package after Oracle6 in order to help PL/SQL developers receive better output from their code. Prior to its introduction, debugging involved populating temporary tables. Fortunately, PL/SQL development has come a long way since those days. Its use is effective in the debugging of server-side PL/SQL code.

Introducing the DBMS_OUTPUT Package

For server-side PL/SQL developers, DBMS_OUTPUT was a godsend. No longer did you have to write all variable information in your server-side PL/SQL to a temporary table for debugging. Instead, Oracle allowed you to generate some text output to the session to tell you what was happening inside your code. Consider the following situation. You're working with a function that has many variables to hold different values in a complex transaction. The transaction doesn't do what you wanted it to, but you don't know where it is falling apart. To revise code on the function such that it will **insert** rows of data into a temporary table takes a great deal of code and server activity overhead. You add the burden of an **insert** statement every time you anticipate the function will change a variable and/or step through a particular area. You must also include the name of the variable, and information about the location within the function, or a time/date stamp. Add to this the fact that you will need to create the table to hold debugging data from the transaction in progress, and a report generation script, and suddenly debugging your PL/SQL code looks like a real pain. DBMS_OUTPUT changes all that in much the same way that the **printf( )** procedure helps a C programmer debug his code.

Exercises

1. What is the DBMS_OUTPUT package? What functionality does it provide? What types of PL/SQL code does it help to debug?

2. What alternatives are there for debugging PL/SQL?

A Tour of the DBMS_OUTPUT Package

There are seven procedures in this package, along with type definitions to support them. These procedures and functions are used to help you with code debugging. The contents of this package are listed and described here.

ENABLE( ) and DISABLE( )

These two procedures are for use in other PL/SQL program units so that the units can actually write output. The **enable( )** procedure enables or allows the block to access a buffer for writing output at the prompt within the

SQL*Plus session. This procedure accepts one number, used to determine the size of the buffer allocated. The call to the **disable( )** procedure disallows your PL/SQL block to use the output buffer, and it accepts no parameters. The calls to both **disable( )** and **enable( )** are demonstrated in the following code listing from a procedure called **elaborate_calc( )**:

```
CREATE PROCEDURE elaborate_calc (
  p_var1         IN NUMBER,
  p_var2         IN NUMBER,
  p_var3         IN VARCHAR2
) IS
  my_var4        NUMBER(10);
  my_var5        VARCHAR2(30);
BEGIN
  DBMS_OUTPUT.ENABLE(800000);
  ...
  DBMS_OUTPUT.DISABLE;
END;
```

TIP
*All output data over the size allocated by the number passed in the call to **enable( )** is discarded by Oracle and lost. Make sure you size the output buffer allocated by the call to **enable( )** large enough to capture the information you want. But beware—only a buffer size maximum of 1,000,000 bytes can be obtained!*

PUT( ) and PUT_LINE( )

The **put( )** procedure is used by the developer's PL/SQL to put information into the output buffer. This procedure points out an interesting concept in PL/SQL that will come more into play when you cover packages. The concept is called *overloading*, and its meaning is as follows. Several procedures or functions are called the same thing, and even perform the same functionality. The difference is that each version of the procedure accepts and handles parameters of a different datatype. One version of **put( )**, for example, accepts a variable of type NUMBER, while another accepts a variable of type DATE. The other procedure, **put_line( )**, allows the developer to put VARCHAR2 data as well as numbers and dates into the output buffer, and it represents overloading as well. The following code block illustrates some calls to both procedures:

```
BEGIN
    ...
    dbms_output.put('06-JAN-2000');
    dbms_output.put(56948954);
    dbms_output.put_line('The cat ate a hat and sat on a mat.');
END;
```

TIP
Overloading is an important concept in PL/SQL where the developer has several functions or procedures in a package, all called the same thing and essentially handling the same functionality, but accepting parameters of different datatypes.

GET_LINE( )

The **get_line( )** procedure fetches data from the output buffer and returns it in the variable passed as a parameter. The **get_line( )** procedure is not overloaded, it only accepts variables of VARCHAR2 datatype. Thus, the **get_line( )** procedure converts NUMBER and DATE data into VARCHAR2 upon retrieval. The **get_line( )** procedure accepts two **out** parameters: the line to be taken out of the output buffer and the other a status, which identifies if **get_line( )** was successful—and if so, are there no more lines. Use of these procedures requires variable declaration, so be sure to pass a variable for each. An example for syntax is illustrated in the following anonymous PL/SQL block:

```
DECLARE
    my_line      VARCHAR2(255);
    my_status    NUMBER(10);
BEGIN
    ...
    dbms_output.get_line(my_line, my_status);
END;
```

TIP
*Lines from the output buffer are generally 255
characters long, but that doesn't mean you
need to declare your line variable for the call to
get_line( ) as such.*

GET_LINES( )

A call to procedure **get_lines( )** obtains more than one line from the output
buffer. There are two variables passed as parameters. Their types are
CHARARR and NUMBER. The CHARARR type is a special datatype
defined in the DBMS_OUTPUT package, a table of VARCHAR2 datatypes.
To use the **get_lines( )** procedure, you must declare a variable using this
CHARARR type. The second variable is a NUMBER that defines how many
lines of data will be retrieved in the call to **get_lines( )**. The overall use of
this procedure is illustrated in the following PL/SQL block:

```
DECLARE
    my_lines    DBMS_OUTPUT.CHARARR;
    my_num      NUMBER;
BEGIN
    ...
    dbms_output.get_lines(my_lines,my_num);
END;
```

NEW_LINE( )

The **new_line( )** procedure puts a "carriage return line feed" character into
the output buffer. In C, this character is represented as **\n**, while in SQL
statements you can simulate newline character behavior with **chr(10)**, as in
select ...| | chr(10) from *table_name*. There are no variables or data to pass
as parameters. The following PL/SQL block illustrates this:

```
BEGIN
    ...
    dbms_output.new_line;
END;
```

Exercises

1. Which procedure in DBMS_OUTPUT is most similar to a regular C **printf( )** procedure?

2. Imagine you had a PL/SQL application that wrote several thousand lines of output whenever it ran. What might happen if your call to DBMS_OUTPUT.**enable( )** allocated only a 4,000 byte buffer?

DBMS_OUTPUT Procedures in Action

So much for the facts on DBMS_OUTPUT—now for how to use them on your elaborate PL/SQL debugging needs. There are two ways to do it. The first is to have the PL/SQL block show output depending on how far processing gets in it. This process involves putting **put_line( )** calls into the block at appropriate intervals. The second method is to have calls to **put_line( )** that display the values in important variables at different times. The following code block shows use of both techniques. Notice, however, that the calls to procedures in the DBMS_OUTPUT package are not too fancy. You can use those procedures in ways more elaborate than shown here, but this procedure shows "bread and butter" usage that should suffice in most cases.

```
CREATE PROCEDURE elaborate_calc (
 p_var1          IN NUMBER,
 p_var2          IN NUMBER,
 p_var3          IN VARCHAR2
) IS
 my_var4          NUMBER(10);
 my_var5          VARCHAR2(30);
BEGIN
 DBMS_OUTPUT.ENABLE(800000);
 DBMS_OUTPUT.PUT_LINE('Beginning procedure elaborate_calc.');
 DBMS_OUTPUT.PUT_LINE('Transform_var: p_var1 = ' ||
to_char(p_var1));
 DBMS_OUTPUT.PUT_LINE('Transform_var: p_var2 = ' ||
to_char(p_var2));
 DBMS_OUTPUT.PUT_LINE('Calling procedure transform_var');
 my_var4 := transform_var(p_var1,p_var2);
 DBMS_OUTPUT.PUT_LINE('Back from function transform_var');
 DBMS_OUTPUT.PUT_LINE('my_var4 = ' || to_char(my_var4));
 DBMS_OUTPUT.PUT_LINE('Compare my_var4 to 5000, if bigger change');
```

```
     IF my_var4 > 5000 THEN
       DBMS_OUTPUT.PUT_LINE('Now adding p_var1 and p_var2 and placing
in my_var4');
       my_var4 := p_var1 + p_var2;
     END IF;
  DBMS_OUTPUT.PUT_LINE('my_var4 = ' || to_char(my_var4));
  DBMS_OUTPUT.PUT_LINE('Begin changing text strings');
  my_var5 := 'Chagall is a french artist.';
  DBMS_OUTPUT.PUT_LINE(p_var3 = ' || p_var3);
  DBMS_OUTPUT.PUT_LINE(my_var5 = ' || my_var5);
  DBMS_OUTPUT.PUT_LINE('Concatenating text strings now');
  my_var5 := CONCAT(p_var3, my_var5);
  DBMS_OUTPUT.PUT_LINE('Done, my_var5 now: ' || my_var5);
  DBMS_OUTPUT.PUT_LINE('End of procedure elaborate_calc.');
  DBMS_OUTPUT.DISABLE;
END;
```

As you can see, even a simple procedure like this one will need many lines of code added to support debugging with DBMS_OUTPUT. However, it still is a lot simpler than inserting records into temporary tables for debugging. Consider the output from this procedure, shown using SQL*Plus. In the following block, you will see the **set serveroutput on** statement, which allows you to see the information coming back from Oracle using the DBMS_OUTPUT package. Also, assume the source code for the procedure above is stored in a file called **elaborate_calc.sql**, and invoked from SQL*Plus as was covered in the last chapter.

```
SQL> set serveroutput on;
SQL> @elaborate_calc
procedure successfully created.
SQL> execute elaborate_calc(123,456,'I like french art.');
Beginning procedure elaborate_calc.
Transform_var: p_var1 = 123
Transform_var: p_var2 = 456
Calling procedure transform_var
Back from function transform_var
my_var4 = 549584
Compare my_var4 to 5000, if bigger change
Now adding p_var1 and p_var2 and placing in my_var4
my_var4 = 579;
Begin changing text strings
p_var3 = I like french art.
my_var5 = Chagall is a french artist.
Concatenating text strings now
Done, my_va5 now: I like french art. Chagall is a french artist.
```

```
End of procedure elaborate_calc.

PL/SQL procedure completed successfully.
SQL>
```

The output from the calls to **put_line( )** give you enough information to find out how the procedure runs and what values are stored in variables at different times. Had the procedure failed during execution, you would know the line it failed on by what output was produced and what output was not produced. The nice thing about coding PL/SQL with calls to procedures in the DBMS_OUTPUT package is that you can turn off output simply by specifying **set serveroutput off** or by not specifying DBMS_OUTPUT.ENABLE(x) to be on. This allows you to have the debugging feature available in your code, but not actually used at all times.

TIP

*When debugging PL/SQL with DBMS_OUTPUT and SQL*Plus, be sure to issue the **set serveroutput on** statement or else Oracle will not show you information from the output buffer on the SQL*Plus command prompt.*

Another package is available on the Oracle server for debugging the runtime variable stack. This package, called DBMS_DEBUG, contains several different type declarations, constants, procedures, and functions to support runtime debugging. However, the challenge in debugging code in run time is having an interface that helps you understand all that is happening in Oracle while your PL/SQL runs. The next section will explain how Procedure Builder can help you with this task.

Exercises

1. Identify the functionality of the **put_line( )** procedure in DBMS_OUTPUT. Identify and describe the special datatype provided in DBMS_OUTPUT for use with the **get_lines( )** procedure. How long are lines of information in the output buffer?

2. What **set** statement is required to display output from the Oracle server when using the DBMS_OUTPUT package for debugging?

Debugging PL/SQL with Procedure Builder

In this section, you will cover the following points about debugging PL/SQL with Procedure Builder:

- Finding errors in code compilation
- Using breakpoints to debug PL/SQL
- Using debug triggers for debugging code execution

Although the process of debugging server-side PL/SQL is simplified greatly with the use of the DBMS_OUTPUT package, the previous section glosses over a point made earlier about compiling your PL/SQL using the database and SQL*Plus. Procedure Builder provides functionality that supports debugging in a much stronger way than DBMS_OUTPUT, and provides much better support for debugging compilation errors. To illustrate, you will revisit the PL/SQL code for the procedure **elaborate_calc( )**. There are several features in Procedure Builder that help you work with procedures to discover problems at compile and execution time.

Finding Errors in Code Compilation

Writing code in Procedure Builder's Program Unit Editor module allows you to compile against a PL/SQL engine right in the application. This functionality gives you PL/SQL to use on the client side, which is useful for developing forms and reports in Developer/2000. When you compile the code and there are errors, Procedure Builder allows you to view your code using the Program Unit Editor module and press the Compile button to compile the code. If Oracle doesn't like what you wrote, it points out the errors it encountered in a separate area below the original source code, making it easy for you to find the errors in your code and correct them. This functionality is available for when you write code on the server side as well. Procedure Builder obtains the compilation errors from the ALL_ERRORS table and ports them directly to the Stored Program Unit Editor so that you can find the problems and resolve them easily.

Debugging Client-Side Code Compilation

Figure 7-1 demonstrates use of the Program Unit Editor module to correct compilation problems. Once Procedure Builder identifies your problem, you can correct it with relative ease. As soon as you correct your code, you can recompile the code by pressing the Compile button. Once your code compiles properly, the lower window—opened to show compilation errors as demonstrated in Figure 7-1—goes away. When this occurs, you may save your code by pressing the Close button at the top of the interface. You now have debugged your client-side code.

Debugging Server-Side Code Compilation

Finding errors in your server-side code is slightly different. Recall that to develop server-side PL/SQL code, you must use the Stored Program Unit Editor module in Procedure Builder. First, connect to the Oracle database by

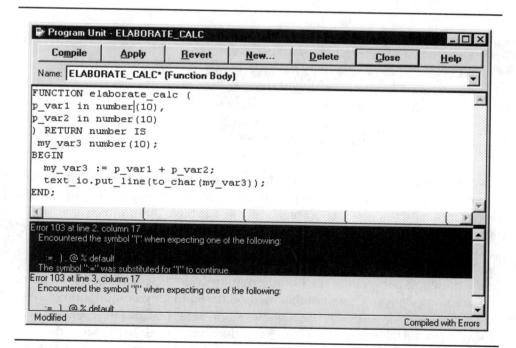

FIGURE 7-1.   *Debugging compile errors in Procedure Builder*

double-clicking on the Database Objects node in the Object Navigator or choosing the File | Connect menu option, and then enter the user, password, and connect string information. Once connected, you open the Stored Program Unit Editor by clicking on Program | Stored Program Unit Editor menu selection, or simply go to the expanded node in the Object Navigator module and double-click on the icon in front of the name of the program unit. You can then open the stored procedure you wish to edit by pulling down the list of available stored procedures on the right-hand top of the Stored Program Unit Editor module, scrolling down until you find your procedure, and then clicking on the procedure you wish to edit. These operations should be familiar to you from the last chapter. Alternately, you can create a new stored procedure or function by clicking on the New button in the module. You should be familiar with the process for creating new PL/SQL blocks using this interface as well. If not, take a moment to review appropriate discussions of creating stored procedures with Procedure Builder in Chapter 6.

TIP
If you want to modify a server-side stored procedure, but do not have the appropriate permissions to do so, click and drag the server-side procedure over to the client side, make the change, and then compile the procedure as a client-side procedure.

Once your procedure is complete, you compile it. However, again recall from Chapter 6 that there is no Compile button in Procedure Builder's Stored Program Unit Editor module. Thus, you use the Save button instead. This step causes the stored program unit to attempt creation of your new PL/SQL block. If there is an error from the database with the source code, PL/SQL will display the error in a new bottom window in the module. Thus, it is as easy to debug compilation of stored program code as it is to debug the client code's compilation. Compare this method to debugging compilation errors using one or even two SQL*Plus sessions and **select * from user_errors** or **show_errors** statements. Procedure Builder shows its ease of use in this area over SQL*Plus. Figure 7-2 illustrates the similarity between the two modules in debugging compile-time errors.

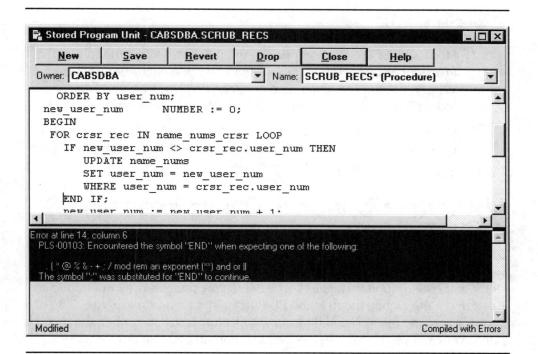

```
Stored Program Unit - CABSDBA.SCRUB_RECS                    _ □ ✕

   New      Save      Revert      Drop      Close      Help

Owner: CABSDBA              ▼   Name: SCRUB_RECS* (Procedure)    ▼

    ORDER BY user_num;                                           ▲
 new_user_num        NUMBER := 0;
 BEGIN
  FOR crsr_rec IN name_nums_crsr LOOP
    IF new_user_num <> crsr_rec.user_num THEN
        UPDATE name_nums
        SET user_num = new_user_num
        WHERE user_num = crsr_rec.user_num
    END IF;                                                      ▼
    new user num := new user num + 1·
◄                                                              ►

Error at line 14, column 6
  PLS-00103: Encountered the symbol "END" when expecting one of the following:

   . ( * @ % & - + ; / mod rem an exponent (**) and or ||
  The symbol ";" was substituted for "END" to continue.

Modified                                          Compiled with Errors
```

FIGURE 7-2. *Using Stored Program Unit Editor to compile PL/SQL*

TIP

*In some situations related to object dependencies, you may need to recompile stored procedures and functions. To compile stored procedures and functions from SQL*Plus, issue the **alter procedure** proc_name **compile** or **alter function** func_name **compile** statement. For more information, review Chapter 8.*

Exercises

1. How is PL/SQL code compiled in the database? What module of the Procedure Builder interface is used to compile client-side SQL code? What is the primary difference between the Program Unit Editor and Stored Program Unit Editor modules with respect to code compilation?

2. How does Procedure Builder display compile-time errors that occur in client-side programs? What method is used in the Stored Program Unit Editor to compile PL/SQL code?

Using Breakpoints to Debug Errors in Code Execution

Once your code is compiled, there are plenty of other ways to find problems with code execution. These methods include setting up breakpoints in the code, steps, and other important features. The debugging methods described here are listed under the Debug menu in the PL/SQL Interpreter module. Figure 7-3 shows where the menu is and illustrates the features available when the menu is pulled down. If you do not see the Debug menu on your window, make sure the PL/SQL Interpreter module is in the foreground of the application.

The debugging process in Procedure Builder consists of several methods. For your purposes, you will debug a client-side program unit that calls procedures stored in a PL/SQL library called LIB_020, and it contains the procedures **elaborate_calc( )** and **foomanchoo( )**. The following code block shows the definition for both procedures in library LIB_020:

```
PROCEDURE elaborate_calc (
p_var1 in number,
p_var2 in varchar2
)IS
 p_var3 number(10);
BEGIN
  p_var3 := p_var1 + p_var2;
  text_io.put_line(to_char(p_var3));
END;

PROCEDURE foomanchoo IS
BEGIN
  text_io.put_line('I am foo, who are you?');
END;
```

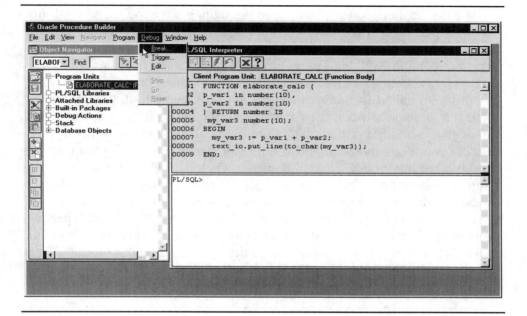

FIGURE 7-3. *Debug menu in the Procedure Builder's PL/SQL Interpreter*

TIP
The actual library name Procedure Builder generates for you is completely arbitrary, so don't get too bothered if yours is a little different.

After attaching your LIB_020 library, you create a new stand-alone program unit that calls your procedures and functions in that library. This procedure is called **call_procs( )**. After creating it, you bring up your new PL/SQL block in the upper window of the PL/SQL Interpreter module. The following code block indicates its definition as it would appear in the Program Unit Editor module:

```
PROCEDURE call_procs IS
BEGIN
  foomanchoo;
  elaborate_calc(123,'add');
END;
```

The first tool at your disposal when debugging code in Procedure Builder is a breakpoint. To create one is a simple task, just double-click on the line number you wish the breakpoint to occur in the source code display window of the PL/SQL Interpreter module. Notice what happens after you do so—in the bottom of the Object Navigator module, there is a node you can drill into called Debug Actions. If you drill down into it, you see that there is a Breakpoint node corresponding to the breakpoint you just created. Below that is another node you can drill into called Stack. When you execute your code by calling procedure **call_procs( )**, the PL/SQL Interpreter runs through the procedure until it encounters the breakpoint you created. There are several new items below the Stack node corresponding to the procedure running, and there is a new prompt in the interactive lower window of the PL/SQL Interpreter. Figure 7-4 demonstrates the **call_procs( )** procedure, shown in the PL/SQL Interpreter, with your breakpoints defined. Those breakpoints are also displayed in the Object Navigator module in that figure as well. The processing already handled in the PL/SQL Interpreter module is shown in the lower window of that module as well in the figure.

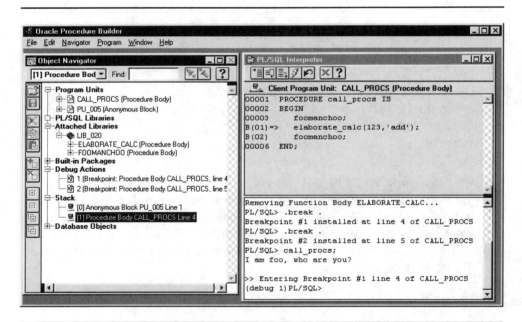

FIGURE 7-4. *Debugging PL/SQL blocks with breakpoints in Procedure Builder*

Observe the new prompt in the PL/SQL Interpreter—control is now passed back to it, allowing you to run the program you just developed interactively. In addition, you can observe values in the variables on the procedure stack using the appropriate drill-down menu. Now, notice back in the source code for the **elaborate_calc( )** procedure a type mismatch in the variables passed as arguments *p_var1* and *p_var2* and the declared variable used to hold the result, *p_var3*. In the procedure **call_procs( )**, you are currently stopped at a breakpoint after procedure **foomanchoo( )**, which simply writes the line "I am foo, who are you." To continue execution of this procedure, you must press the Go button, the one with the yellow lightning bolt in the PL/SQL Interpreter window. This act will cause the PL/SQL Interpreter to execute your code either until the end, the next breakpoint, or until it encounters an error. In this case, you will encounter an error due to the type mismatch and the values each argument variable contains. Figure 7-5 demonstrates this.

The point of this lesson is to illustrate a simple use of breakpoints. Once a breakpoint is created, it is available in the Object Navigator until you

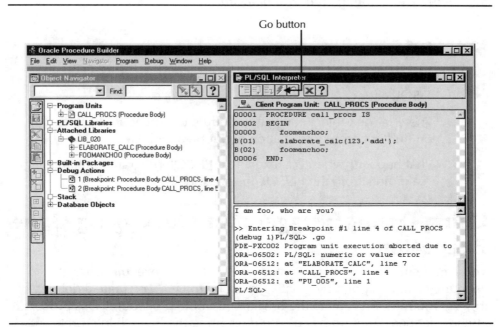

FIGURE 7-5. *Showing errors using breakpoints in Procedure Builder*

close or remove the program unit, PL/SQL library, or attached library. Another method for debugging PL/SQL processes is to create a debug trigger, which will execute every time the interpreter encounters a breakpoint. Several Procedure Builder built-in packages are available from Oracle to assist you with debugging your PL/SQL code. These packages are available for use in client-side PL/SQL debugging, and will be covered later in this section.

TIP
If your attempt to create a breakpoint is met with an error such as "invalid program unit," you may be trying to create breakpoints in a PL/SQL program that is not compiled. With the PL/SQL Interpreter module in the foreground of Procedure Builder, click on the Debug | Edit menu option to bring the PL/SQL procedure body up in the appropriate window, and click the Compile button to compile your procedure. Then, try creating the breakpoint again.

Exercises

1. What is a breakpoint? How do you place breakpoints into your PL/SQL code?

2. Where in the Object Navigator module of Procedure Builder can you find out more information about breakpoints?

3. What happens when you execute a PL/SQL program containing breakpoints from the PL/SQL Interpreter?

Using Debug Triggers for Debugging Code Execution

You can define a set of steps Procedure Builder will execute when it encounters a breakpoint by creating a debug trigger. To create a debug trigger, you must first create the breakpoint in the procedure. This process is already defined. After doing so, you must bring the PL/SQL Interpreter module to the front of the Procedure Builder screen, making it the active module. This changes the menu bar of the application to include your

Debug menu. Click on Debug | Trigger on the menu bar to bring up the PL/SQL trigger interface for creating debug triggers. Note that these triggers are slightly different from database triggers, to be covered later on in Chapter 10.

Debug triggers can be executed at three different times. Those times are at a specific line of PL/SQL code, at every breakpoint, or at every statement in the procedure or function. Triggers are fired before the PL/SQL Interpreter executes the line of code. A debug trigger can be used in many ways, particularly for creation of conditional breakpoints, where the breakpoint only happens when a certain condition exists in the PL/SQL code.

Debug Triggers for Client-Side PL/SQL Blocks

For this discussion, we will use the following PL/SQL code body to a slightly modified version of the procedure **elaborate_calc( )**, as shown in the following code block. Also shown in the block is a function, **transform_var( )**, which simply adds together two variables you pass it. Assume that you are having some problems with the execution of this code, and you want to inspect the values of variables in the procedure as it executes.

```
PROCEDURE elaborate_calc(
  p_var1          IN NUMBER,
  p_var2          IN NUMBER,
  p_var3          IN VARCHAR2
) IS
  my_var4          NUMBER(10);
  my_var5          VARCHAR2(30);
BEGIN
  my_var4 := transform_var(p_var1,p_var2);
  IF my_var4 > 5000 THEN
   my_var4 := p_var1 + p_var2;
  END IF;
  my_var5 := 'Chagall is a french artist.';
  my_var5 := CONCAT(p_var3, my_var5);
END;

FUNCTION transform_var (
p_var1 in number,
p_var2 in number
) RETURN number IS
BEGIN
  return (4999);
END;
```

Now examine the PL/SQL trigger interface, shown in Figure 7-6. First, the line at the top that reads **trigger: new** indicates you are creating a new debug trigger. Had you been modifying an existing trigger, this line would identify the number of that existing trigger. A check box is off to the right, telling you whether the trigger is enabled or disabled for use. The next important point about this interface is the Location pull-down menu. There are three potential source locations for debug triggers: the Program Unit, Debug Entry, or Every Statement. If Debug Entry is selected, then the trigger will be fired every time a breakpoint is encountered. If Every Statement is selected, then the trigger will fire before Procedure Builder executes every statement in the program. For every location except Program Unit, the program unit name and line boxes are grayed out. The last important area is the Trigger Body entry box, where the trigger code is placed. Don't worry about coding an explicit **begin** or **end;** these details are handled automatically.

Consider now the actual process of developing a trigger. Let's say you want to create a debug trigger that will fire before the program enters the **if then** statement in **elaborate_calc( )**. To do this, you create your breakpoint in the PL/SQL Interpreter window on line 10, then click on Debug | Trigger, pulling up the debug trigger interface. You will create a program unit trigger, to occur on line 10. If you review Figure 7-6, you will see that the definition

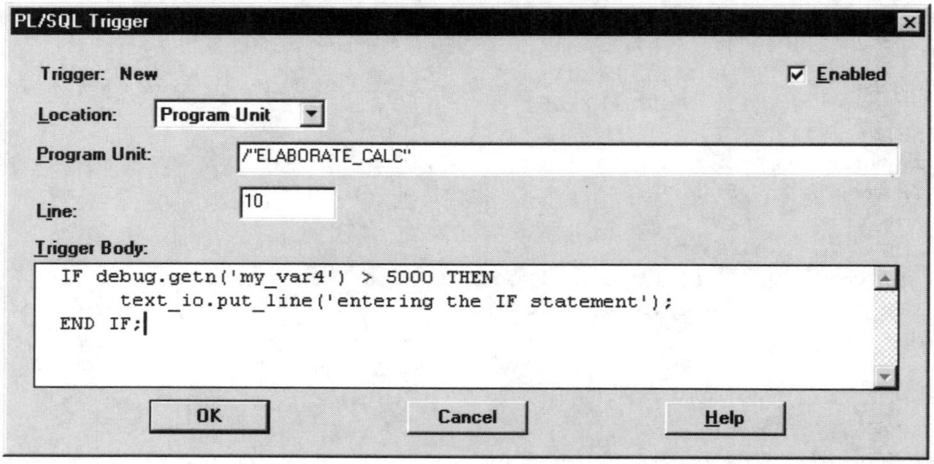

PL/SQL Trigger	☒

Trigger: New   ☑ **Enabled**

Location: `Program Unit ▼`

Program Unit: `/"ELABORATE_CALC"`

Line: `10`

Trigger Body:

```
IF debug.getn('my_var4') > 5000 THEN
     text_io.put_line('entering the IF statement');
END IF;
```

    OK   **Cancel**   **Help**

FIGURE 7-6. *Debug trigger creation interface*

of the trigger is present in the trigger creation interface window as it is described here.

Creation of debug triggers touches on Oracle-supplied packages for debugging, covered more extensively in Chapter 8. For now, you will use some functions in the DEBUG package to assist with creation of your debug trigger. There are two important classes of debugging functions in the DEBUG package used to obtain or change the value for a local variable in the program, called **get**x and **set**x, respectively. The character x refers to a character that represents the datatype of the variable you try to obtain: **n** for NUMBER, **c** for VARCHAR, **d** for DATE, or **i** for INTEGER. After entering the code for your trigger, you compile the trigger by clicking the OK button. For your example, the trigger body defined in Figure 7-6 is shown in the following code block:

```
BEGIN
    IF debug.getn('my_var4') > 5000 THEN
        text_io.put_line('Entering the IF statement');
    END IF;
END;
```

Notice a few items about this block. First, the **begin** and **end;** are added for readability, they are not actually required in the trigger body box in the trigger creation interface. Another important item to remember is in the call to **getn( )**, you must enclose the variable that **getn( )** will obtain in single quotes or else the trigger will return an error on compile. If you do receive an error on trigger compilation, you can see what the error was by looking in the interactive PL/SQL runtime area on the PL/SQL Interpreter module. Usually, if you didn't include single-quotes around your variable name in the call to DEBUG.**get**x( ), the error you receive will be that your variable must be declared. Once you successfully compile your debug trigger, notice a new item included under the Debug Actions node in the Object Navigator module corresponding to the trigger.

Debug Triggers for Server-Side PL/SQL Code

Creating debug triggers for server-side PL/SQL code is similar to creating debug triggers for client-side PL/SQL. After connecting to the database, you bring up your stored procedure by finding it with the Object Navigator module and then clicking on it to view the source with the PL/SQL Interpreter module. The breakpoint for server-side PL/SQL is created in the same way, by simply clicking on the line where you wish to create the breakpoint. However, there is a lot more happening behind the scenes. The following code block shows the contents of the PL/SQL Interpreter interactive window when you click on the line of a stored procedure to create a breakpoint on it:

```
PL/SQL> .break USER JASON PROGRAMUNIT CP_ACCUM_ALL_RESPS LINE 1011
Breakpoint #1 installed at line 1011 of CP_ACCUM_ALL_RESPS
```

Compare that to the contents of the PL/SQL Interpreter interactive window after you open your library to debug a client-side stored procedure. When you click on the line of a client-side procedure to create a breakpoint on it, a great deal less information is generated by Procedure Builder.

```
PL/SQL> .open LIBRARY D:\ORANT\BIN\LIB_020.pll FILESYSTEM
Opening library in file D:\ORANT\BIN\LIB_020.pll...
PL/SQL> .break .
Breakpoint #2 installed at line 10 of ELABORATE_CALC
```

Creating a trigger at this point is accomplished on a stored procedure in the same way as on a client-side procedure. You can use all the Oracle-supplied packages such as DEBUG and TEXT_IO to do so, as was shown before. Remember, however, that debug triggers are not the same as database triggers. A debug trigger is stored within Procedure Builder, not on the Oracle database. To view the debug actions available on the database, you can drill into that item on the Object Navigator module.

Exercises

1. Identify the purpose and uses of a debug trigger? How is a debug trigger created?

2. What locations are available for debug trigger definitions? When will a trigger be fired based on its location?

3. Identify the package and functions used to obtain and change variable values in debug triggers. How do you identify different datatypes for variables to be obtained to the function?

Using Oracle-Supplied Packages for Debugging

In this section, you will cover the following points on Oracle-supplied packages for debugging:

- Overview of Oracle-supplied packages in Procedure Builder

- Packages for application component communication

- Packages for tuning, portability, and compatibility

- Packages for debugging PL/SQL

- Case study of using Oracle-supplied packages for debugging

So far, a few Oracle-supplied packages have been identified and used in different aspects of client- and server-side debugging. These packages include DBMS_OUTPUT for server-side PL/SQL debugging, TEXT_IO for text output on the client side using Procedure Builder, and DEBUG for debug triggers. The use of other Oracle-supplied packages available within Procedure Builder for debugging will be covered in this section as well.

Overview of Oracle-Supplied Packages in Procedure Builder

Several packages exist in Procedure Builder, supplied by Oracle. Their functionality is varied, from text output packages to packages that help with debugging, and so on. To find the packages and their contents in the Procedure Builder application, you must use the Object Navigator module. The node you can examine is called "Built-in Packages." This node is always available in Procedure Builder, even if you are not connected to the database. Figure 7-7 shows the items that reside under this drill-down option.

These packages fall into many different categories. Some of these categories include debugging, communication between application components, tuning portability, and backward compatibility. A final

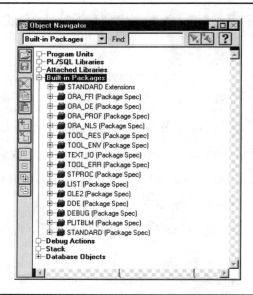

FIGURE 7-7.   *Oracle built-in packages in Procedure Builder*

package category is packages for internal use, which will be presented as well. The following discussions will identify each package category, along with the packages that fall into that category. A brief discussion of the use of each package in the category will follow.

Debugging PL/SQL Program Units

One of the value-added aspects of Procedure Builder is that the tool provides you with an ability to develop PL/SQL more rapidly than is available using conventional means like SQL*Plus and the Oracle database PL/SQL engine. To do so, Oracle provides some packages to help in the debugging process. The first package Oracle provides was introduced a short time ago, called DEBUG. This package helps you obtain and set values in different variables in your PL/SQL program. Another package offered by Oracle for the purpose of debugging is the TOOL_ERR package. This package contains several procedures and functions that help you manipulate the Procedure Builder error stack.

TIP
Recall that the DEBUG package is available through Procedure Builder only. A similar package called DBMS_DEBUG is available on the Oracle server for debugging server-side PL/SQL code using Procedure Builder breakpoints and debug triggers.

A final package offered for your benefit in this area has also been introduced, and is called TEXT_IO. This package allows you to manipulate text between the screen or a file and the application. Some usage of the TEXT_IO package suggests similarity to the **printf( )** command in C. In reality, this package has a great deal of flexibility for use, but since its closest counterparts on the Oracle database server side (DBMS_OUTPUT and UTL_FILE) are frequently used for debugging, you may want to treat TEXT_IO for that purpose among others as well.

Communicating Between Application Components

In a full-featured application, there may be many different components involved. These components may be part of the Developer/2000 product line, such as Forms or Reports, or they may be executable applications written in C. The first package that falls into this group is the DDE package. This package allows you to communicate between different components of the Developer/2000 application. Another package is the ORA_FFI package, which allows you to communicate between PL/SQL code and C programs. A final package that falls under this category is the OLE2 package, which allows you to use object linking and embedding in your PL/SQL application.

Furthermore, you may want to identify certain environment variables from your PL/SQL programs as well. There are Oracle-supplied packages that allow you to do this. The first is called TOOL_ENV. It allows you to interact with Oracle environment variables such as **oracle_sid** and **oracle_home**. The other package in this line is ORA_NLS. This package allows you to interact with national language settings.

Tuning, Portability, and Backward Compatibility

Another important use for Oracle built-in packages is for application timing. The ORA_PROF package contains many procedures and functions that can be used to tune the application by first timing the execution of parts of the application using this package. In situations where the application must be ported to a different language, there is another package that can be useful. This package is called TOOL_RES. For backward compatibility with PL/SQL release 1, the LIST package allows you a way to create arrays.

Internal Usage

The final area of usage for Oracle built-in packages is internal. Two packages fall into this category, the ORA_DE and STPROC packages. The ORA_DE package is used by Developer/2000 for internal purposes related to PL/SQL. The STPROC package is used by Developer/2000 to call stored procedures on the Oracle database. These calls are generated automatically by the Developer/2000 applications. Generally, you needn't worry about the contents of these packages, and therefore they will not be covered for the remainder of the section.

Exercises

1. Identify the major categories of PL/SQL packages available in Procedure Builder. What are the contents of each?

2. In what program module can information about each Oracle built-in package in Procedure Builder be found? Where within that program module can a listing of each package's contents be found?

Packages for Application Component Communication

Now that the package categories have been identified, the different packages that are available in Procedure Builder will be discussed in detail. In each subsection, the package contents will be identified, along with some guidelines for usage, tips, and examples. In this section, more in-depth use of certain packages for communication between application components will be covered. Turn attention now to the individual packages that comprise Procedure Builder.

The ORA_FFI Package

The ORA_FFI package offers the ability to integrate PL/SQL programs with foreign functions written in C, as in **.dll** files. The general process for integrating PL/SQL programs with foreign functions is to register the external functions, then generate PL/SQL code for them. There are several types, exceptions, and functions defined in this package, listed and used as follows. The **ora_ffi_error** exception is for use when errors occur while using the ORA_FFI package. Several type declarations exist in this package, including **funchandletype**, **libhandletype**, and **pointertype**. These type declarations are used to declare variables used to store handles to external procedures and functions.

Three functions are used for registration of external program components: **register_function( )** to register the function, **register_return( )** to register the return values for the functions, and **register_parameter( )** to register parameters passed to the functions. To locate registered components and return their handles to variables declared as the datatypes identified by the ORA_FFI package, the **find_function( )** and **find_library( )** functions are used. Note that you cannot use these until external programs are registered. A function can be used to determine if a variable contains a NULL value, called **is_null_ptr( )**. Once the external procedure or function is registered and loaded, the function **generate_foreign( )** can be used to create PL/SQL code for use by the PL/SQL program components. Once done, you can deallocate the foreign procedures and functions with the **unload_library( )** function.

The ORA_NLS Package

Every language has its own names for general concepts, such as the days of the week, months of the year, local time format, and other character constants. Furthermore, there often are numeric constants to a particular language as well, such as the placement and character used to define currency format. The first set of functions belies the American origin of Oracle products. One is **american( )**, which returns a TRUE or FALSE value based on whether the current NLS character set is American English. The second is **american_date( )**, which returns TRUE or FALSE for whether the current date format corresponds to American custom.

The next set of functions demonstrates how to obtain information about the current language corresponding to character or numeric constant. These functions include **get_lang_scalar( )** for numerics, and **get_lang_str( )** for strings. Several of these functions return Boolean values in response to implied questions about the current language, such as **modified_date_fmt( )** or whether the date format has been altered, and **right_to_left( )** or whether the current language is read from right to left. Also, **linguistic_collate( )** is used to decide if standard sorting methods will yield a proper sort order according to the rules of the language, **linguistic_specials( )** is used to determine if special cases exist and are in place for this language, and the **simple_cs( )** function determines if the current language is simple—meaning it is a single-byte language with no special characters or sort order required. The **single_byte( )** function determines if the current character set is single or multibyte. Finally, several exceptions are part of the package, including **bad_attribute**, **no_item**, and **not_found**.

The TOOL_ENV Package

This package is very simple—only one procedure is part of it, called **getvar( )**. To use it, you pass the name of the environment variable you want and a variable to hold the environment value.

The OLE2 Package

This is a fairly large package used to support the creation and usage of OLE2 objects such as spreadsheets, documents, and presentations produced by third-party vendors. As with the other built-in packages, there are type declarations and exceptions to support the work, along with procedures and functions that actually do the work. In this case, the types available are **list_type** and **obj_type**, which allow you to declare variables that hold argument list and OLE2 object handles. The exceptions include **OLE_error** (that's OH-EL-EE, not 'ole!), which is raised if an error occurs in another procedure or function on the OLE2 package, and the **OLE_not_supported** exception, raised when object linking and embedding is not supported by the platform. A function that works in conjunction with the **OLE_error** exception is called **last_exception( )**, and it returns the message of the last error raised in the OLE2 package. Another function working in conjunction with the **OLE_not_supported** exception is the **issupported( )** function, which returns TRUE if object linking and embedding is supported by the platform, FALSE if it is not.

The rest of this package contains procedures and functions related to the invoking, linking, and embedding of program objects into PL/SQL program units. To create a handle for PL/SQL to refer to the OLE2 object, the **create_obj( )** function is used. Each object can be passed argument lists, which are created with the **create_arglist( )** function. To add arguments to created lists, the **add_arg( )** procedure can be used. Alternately, to add object arguments to lists, the **add_arg_obj( )** procedure can be used. Several procedures are available for obtaining OLE2 object properties. They are **get_char_property( )**, **get_num_property( )**, **get_obj_property( )**, while the procedure to set the value for a property is **set_property( )**. Several procedures are available for obtaining numeric, character, or object type values from the OLE2 object. They are **invoke_num( )**, **invoke_char( )**, and **invoke_obj( )**. The object itself is invoked using the **invoke( )** procedure. When OLE2 work is complete, you can get rid of argument lists and objects with the **destroy_arglist( )** and **release_obj( )** procedures, respectively.

The DDE Package

This package in Developer/2000 is used to handle data interchange between the Developer/2000 application and other Windows clients. The components of the package, though not extensive, belie the complexity of use. There are quite a number of Windows-defined formats for data passed between these two applications, as well as Oracle-defined exceptions for this package's use.

Exercises

1. What is the package used to handle data interchange between Developer/2000 and other Windows clients? What package handles interchange with external code written in C?

2. If you wanted to embed a spreadsheet into your Procedure Builder PL/SQL code, what Oracle-supplied package might you use?

Packages for Tuning, Portability, and Compatibility

In this section, more in-depth use of certain packages for tuning, portability, and compatibility will be covered. An introduction to this area of functionality was covered in the overview. To recap, these packages include ORA_PROF, TOOL_RES, and LIST. Turn attention now to the individual packages that comprise Procedure Builder for the functionality of tuning, portability, and compatibility.

The ORA_PROF Package

This package aids in the performance tuning of PL/SQL programs in general by giving you the ability to track the time it takes a piece of code to run. This task is accomplished with timers, and ORA_PROF allows you to manage timers with relative ease. Timers are identified with names of type VARCHAR2. The first task in working with timers should be obvious—you create them. This happens with **create_timer( )**. You can start, stop, and reset timers with the **start_timer( )**, **stop_timer( )**, and **reset_timer( )** procedures. To eliminate a timer, you can use the **destroy_timer( )** procedure. To figure out the amount of time that has elapsed since the last call to **reset_timer( )** for that timer, you use the **elapsed_time( )** function. Finally, if any procedure or function is passed an invalid timer name, a special exception called **bad_timer** will be raised.

The TOOL_RES Package

Porting applications from one language to another can prove difficult. To do so, Procedure Builder allows you to put all text information into a resource file and read from that resource file. There are several functions in this package. The functions include **rfhandle( )** to allocate a handle to a resource file, **rfopen( )** and **rfclose( )** to open and close resource files, and **rfread( )** to read the text data from resource files. Several exceptions exist in the package as well. These are **bad_file_handle**, **buffer_overflow**, **file_not_found**, and **no_resource**.

The LIST Package

Backward compatibility is often a concern in an application. Toward this end, Oracle provides the LIST package in Developer/2000 as a holdover from PL/SQL version 1 for the creation and maintenance of lists of character strings to create arrays. There is one type definition and one exception created as part of this package. The type is called **listofchar**, and it defines a datatype to store a handle to a list you will create and manipulate. The exception is called **fail**; appropriately enough, it is raised if any other list operation fails.

TIP
OCP Developer track tests PL/SQL up to version 2.3.

The rest of the package contains definitions and code bodies for procedures and functions. The first two functions covered are **make( )** and **destroy( )**, used to make new lists and destroy them when needed, respectively. To find out how many items are in the list, you can use the **nitems( )** function. To obtain data from a list at a certain point, use the **getitem( )** function. The next set of procedures is used to write data to a list. They are **appenditem( )** to append items to the end of a list, **prependitem( )** to prepend items to the beginning of a list, **insertitem( )** to place an item in a list at any other point than the beginning or end, and **deleteitem( )** to remove an item from any point in the list.

Exercises

1. If you are a developer of a German application, and you want to bring your product to market in the United States, what Procedure Builder package might you consider using to port output to English?

2. What package is available for determining how long a particular PL/SQL program takes to run? What package handles backward compatibility with PL/SQL version 1? What version of PL/SQL is tested by OCP?

Packages for Debugging PL/SQL

In this section, more in-depth use of certain packages for debugging will be covered. There are three, as was described in the overview. To recap, those packages are DEBUG, TOOL_ERR, and TEXT_IO. Turn attention now to the individual packages that comprise Procedure Builder's debugging features.

The DEBUG Package

The DEBUG package is one you will likely find yourself using most heavily. This package contains utilities and exceptions designed to help you to identify and resolve bugs in your PL/SQL code. Start with the exceptions. There is only one, called **break**. It is raised inside debug triggers explicitly in order to activate a breakpoint. A suggested use for this exception is for conditional breakpoints, though you may think of other uses as well. Note, however, that you do not need to raise this exception explicitly in your PL/SQL program if you wish to create a breakpoint in that program. Procedure Builder handles breakpoints for you at that level.

There are four basic procedures in DEBUG, two of which have already been covered. The first two are **get**x( ) and **set**x( ), and they are used to obtain and define values in variables in PL/SQL blocks from debug triggers, respectively. Recall from earlier discussion that the x is replaced by a character to signify the datatype of the variable whose value will be obtained or set by the procedure. The allowed replacements for x in the procedure name are **n** for NUMBER, **c** for VARCHAR, **d** for DATE, and **i** for INTEGER.

TIP

*Note that the datatypes supported by **get**x( ) and **set**x( ) procedures are all available on the Oracle database, except INTEGER, which is available only in PL/SQL.*

The other two procedures available in Procedure Builder are designed to emulate the processes both of interactive PL/SQL interpretation and of returning control to the PL/SQL Interpreter in temporary suspension of your PL/SQL code. The first procedure is called **interpret( )**. It executes whatever string of text you pass in with it as if it was PL/SQL. If you have functions you would like to call from your debug trigger, you can do so easily with this procedure. The other procedure is called **suspend( )**. It accepts no variables, merely holds execution of the current PL/SQL program, and temporarily returns control to the Interpreter for debugging.

> **TIP**
> *Although several procedures exist in the DEBUG package for getting and setting variable values, this is not a good example of overloading. Why? Because the names of the procedures are different, though their functionality is the same.*

The TOOL_ERR Package

The TOOL_ERR package works in conjunction with the DEBUG package to help you retrieve more advanced error messaging from the Procedure Builder error stack. This package contains several procedures and functions, as well as a constant and an exception. The constant, **toperror**, refers to the newest or topmost error on the error stack for easy reference. The exception, **tool_error**, can be raised whenever one or more errors have been pushed onto the error stack.

The rest of the procedures and functions will now be explained. The entire error stack can be discarded with the **clear( )** procedure. To find the number of errors currently on the error stack, use the **nerrors( )** function. To retrieve an error code for a specific error on the stack, you use the **code( )** function, passing it the number of the error you wish to see. To view the message that corresponds to the code of the error you just obtained with the **code( )** function, use the **message( )** function. If you want to discard the topmost error on the error stack, use the **pop( )** procedure.

The TEXT_IO Package

Although its counterpart on the Oracle server, DBMS_OUTPUT, is used most commonly to supplement the functionality provided by print statements like **printf( )** in C, the TEXT_IO package in Procedure Builder in reality offers far more. Several procedures and functions are available in TEXT_IO to handle writing information to and reading information from files and standard output. Some of these functions will look familiar to you, as they are similar to functions and procedures in DBMS_OUTPUT.

The first set of procedures in TEXT_IO to be covered include the procedures to open and close files and a function to test if a file is open. These procedures are **fopen( )** and **fclose( )**, and the function is **is_open( )**, respectively. Related to these procedures and function is a special type for file handle declaration, called **file_type**. The next procedure is designed to read a line of text from the open file and is called **get_line( )**. This procedure accepts two parameters: a variable declared as type **file_type**, and a variable to hold the line of data retrieved from the file. The last set of procedures and functions are designed to place data into an open file, and those procedures include the **put( )** procedure for placing information of various datatypes, **new_line( )** for placing a specified number of carriage returns, **putf( )** for placing a line of formatted output to the file, and **put_line( )** for putting a line of text to the file.

TIP
TEXT_IO is a useful and robust package in Procedure Builder. It takes two packages on the Oracle server side to approximate its operation. DBMS_OUTPUT is the first; the second is UTL_FILE, a server-side package that handles file opening, closing, reading and writing.

Exercises

1. What server-side Oracle packager is TEXT_IO most comparable to? How does the functionality provided by TEXT_IO extend past that of its closest counterpart on the Oracle database?

2. What set of procedures in the DEBUG package handles obtaining variable values in debug triggers? What set of procedures changes those values?

Case Study of Debugging with Oracle-Supplied Packages

In the previous discussion, you learned more about the contents of the TOOL_ERR, DEBUG, and TEXT_IO packages for the purpose of debugging your PL/SQL procedures and functions. This discussion will demonstrate usage of some of these processes in an actual debugging situation. For the example, assume there is a table called NAME_NUMS that has two columns: USER_NAME and USER_NUM. This table lists the name of each user on the system and a sequential number corresponding to that user, starting with zero. The contents of the table are shown in the following code block:

```
SQL> select * from name_nums order by user_num;
USER_NAME      USER_NUM
---------- ----------
manfran                 0
flibber                 1
ellison                 2
howlett                 3
barbara                 5
anthony                 6
deborah                 7
spanky                  8
athena                  9
```

Now, let's say that the numbers are generated by the application, and for one reason or another those numbers are generated out of sequence. A stored procedure out on the database called **scrub_recs( )** can be run to put those numbers into the right order. The code for this procedure is listed in the following code block:

```
PROCEDURE scrub_recs IS
    CURSOR    name_nums_crsr IS
    SELECT    user_name,
              user_num
    FROM      name_nums
    ORDER BY user_num;
  new_user_num      NUMBER := 1;
  BEGIN
```

```
    FOR crsr_rec IN name_nums_crsr LOOP
      IF new_user_num <> crsr_rec.user_num THEN
         UPDATE name_nums
         SET user_num = new_user_num
         WHERE user_num = crsr_rec.user_num;
      END IF;
      new_user_num := new_user_num + 1;
    END LOOP;
    COMMIT;
  EXCEPTION
    WHEN DUP_VAL_ON_INDEX THEN
       rollback;
       raise_application_error(-20001,'primary key violation on
NAME_NUMS');
    WHEN OTHERS THEN
       rollback;
       raise_application_error(-20002,'General fault on
scrub_recs');
END;
```

Once the stored procedure is compiled on Oracle, the first step in debugging this process is to open the stored procedure up for debugging in the PL/SQL Interpreter window. This is accomplished by double-clicking on the name of the procedure in the Object Navigator module. After doing this, you will see the source code for this procedure in the top window of the PL/SQL, while the interactive PL/SQL Interpreter prompt appears in the second window. Since this code contains a **for** loop, it is fair game to want to see the contents of variables as the PL/SQL Interpreter steps through the loop for each record in the cursor. The process for creating a breakpoint is simple enough, and you have enough exposure to them now to know what a breakpoint looks like in the PL/SQL Interpreter window and what inserting a breakpoint does in the Object Navigator. What you see in your Procedure Builder session should match the contents of Figure 7-8.

Once your breakpoint is set inside the loop, you will want to define your debug trigger. Recall that this is done using the debug trigger editor made available by choosing the Debug I Trigger menu option and entering PL/SQL code you want to use as part of your trigger body. The following code block demonstrates the contents of the trigger body window for a simple trigger,

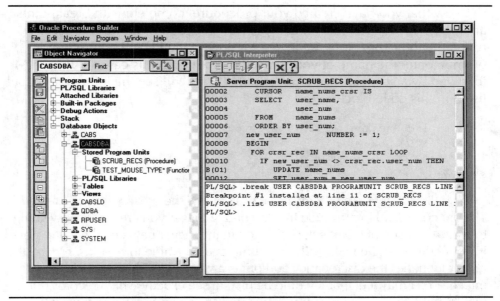

FIGURE 7-8. *Debugging procedures in Procedure Builder*

which obtains the values both for the USER_NUM column in the cursor and the NEW_USER_NUM that it should be:

```
if debug.getn('crsr_rec.user_num') <> debug.getn('new_user_num')
then
   text_io.put_line('These records do not match!');
end if;
```

TIP

*Remember, debug trigger bodies shouldn't contain the **begin** and **end** keywords because Procedure Builder adds them later. Also, if your trigger doesn't compile, you can check the PL/SQL Interpreter lower window to see what errors were produced on compilation.*

Now that you have created your procedure, complete with breakpoints and triggers, you are ready to analyze how Procedure Builder supports runtime debugging. From the lower window in the PL/SQL Interpreter prompt, enter the name of your procedure to run, in this case **scrub_recs( )**, followed by a semicolon, and press ENTER. You will see the following output listed in this code block:

```
>> Entering Breakpoint #1 line 10 of SCRUB_RECS
(debug 1)PL/SQL> .go
These records do not match!
PL/SQL>
```

The PL/SQL Interpreter indicates it has entered the breakpoint you created. The **.go** command informs you that the debug trigger you created is now going to fire. As a result of the check performed in the trigger between the value stored in your cursor for the USER_NUM column and the value in *new_user_num*, the trigger identifies the discrepancy and prints a warning: "These records do not match!" You may feel that it would be nice to see exactly which records don't match, but before changing your debug trigger, remember that you have the runtime stack at your disposal, too. Looking in the stack for the procedure name will show you what the values for each variable are. The stack and debug actions you should see in the Object Navigator module and the contents of the PL/SQL Interpreter module are in Figure 7-9.

Finally, to understand how to continue debugging the execution, you need to click on the Go button in the top-center of the PL/SQL Interpreter module. The Go button is the one with the yellow lightning bolt on it. This indicates to Procedure Builder that you're ready to continue debugging the execution of this procedure. Again, you will enter your breakpoint, and the debug trigger fires again to show you that once again the values in the USER_NUM column of the cursor and the *new_user_num* variable do not match, resulting in your text output. If you look in your runtime stack in the Object Navigator module, you notice that your values for both have incremented by only one digit. By now, you probably realize that your debug trigger is going to fire for every iteration because the numbers in the USER_NUM column of the table and cursor started with 0 while the initialized value for *new_user_num* started with 1. Recall that the initial usage for **scrub_recs( )** was to eliminate sequential gaps in USER_NUM, but not to change the initial value of the list to 1. At this point, you want to reset the execution of the procedure by pressing the Reset button next to the Go button, and modify the initialization value for *new_user_num* at line 10 in

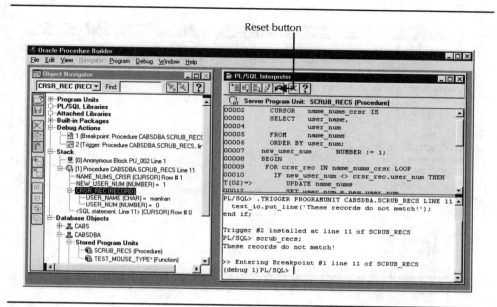

FIGURE 7-9. *Procedure Builder runtime stack*

the procedure to be 0, not 1. The Reset button is the one with the arched black arrow on it. Figure 7-10 shows the source code with the change.

After altering the code and recompiling it, you must step through the program again to ensure it executes properly. Your debug trigger and breakpoints may have disappeared; if so, simply re-create them. Then, run **scrub_recs( )**. Your program execution will stop at the breakpoint indicated, but notice this time that your trigger doesn't fire. The output in the PL/SQL Interpreter window is listed in the following code block:

```
PL/SQL> scrub_recs;

>> Entering Breakpoint #1 line 10 of SCRUB_RECS
(debug 1)PL/SQL>
```

The values for both USER_NUM in the cursor and the *new_user_num* match this time according to the runtime stack as well. You keep stepping through the loop by pressing the Go button until the debug trigger fires on user BARBARA, whose number is 5, not 4. Each step through **scrub_recs( )** will set this and all subsequent values as they are supposed to be according to variable *new_user_num*.

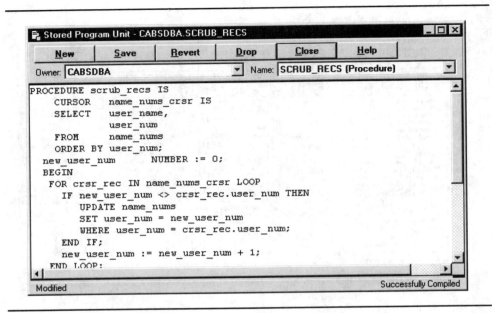

FIGURE 7-10. *Modified procedure in Stored Program Unit Editor*

TIP
The three buttons next to the Go button are Step Into, Step Past, and Step Out. They approximate the function of the Go button while in debug mode as the result of a breakpoint.

Exercises

1. What button is used to continue execution of a procedure past a breakpoint? How are values obtained from a procedure for use in a debug trigger?

2. Start Procedure Builder on your PC and step through this example again. Experiment with different execution buttons in the PL/SQL Interpreter module and with different types of debug triggers.

Chapter Summary

This chapter focuses on debugging PL/SQL programs. There are several areas covered, including methods of debugging server-side PL/SQL using server-side packages such as DBMS_OUTPUT. Another area covered in this chapter is debugging PL/SQL with Procedure Builder. The special role of Oracle-supplied packages for debugging within the Procedure Builder software is offered as well. All told, this chapter covers 5 percent of OCP exam content.

The first area covered describes methods of debugging server-side PL/SQL using methods like logging on to the database with SQL*Plus. The DBMS_OUTPUT package is a set of stored procedures and functions provided by Oracle to use for debugging your own procedures, functions, and packages. It is a package provided by Oracle that is stored on the database. It was introduced by Oracle to eliminate the use of temporary tables for debugging. Instead, the developer makes use of items in the package that allow for functionality similar to the **printf( )** procedure in C. There are seven procedures in this package. They include **enable( )** and **disable( )**, which handle the enabling and disabling of a special output buffer for storing output messages in Oracle, respectively. Some of the other functions include **put( )** and **put_line( )**, which put information into the output buffer. The last three procedures in DBMS_OUTPUT are **get_line( )**, **get_lines( )** and **new_line( )**, which pull a line or lines of text from the output buffer and add carriage returns to the current line in the buffer, respectively.

The most frequently used procedures in the DBMS_OUTPUT package include the **enable( )** and **disable( )** procedures, and the **put_line( )** procedure. When enabled, the DBMS_OUTPUT.**put_line( )** procedure behaves like a **printf( )** procedure as in C. An example was provided in the chapter that illustrated the benefits of using **put_line( )**, but also pointed out that frequently a great deal of code will need to be added to your stored procedures to support debugging with this method. One nice benefit for using DBMS_OUTPUT for debugging is the ability to turn it on and off, however, with the **disable( )** procedure, or from the SQL*Plus prompt with the **set serveroutput off** statement. Recall that in order to obtain output from your calls to procedures in DBMS_OUTPUT, you must issue the **set serveroutput on** statement.

Debugging PL/SQL in Procedure Builder offers the same features as the DBMS_OUTPUT package, plus a whole lot more. There are many different features in Procedure Builder for debugging that were covered in the chapter, including debugging your code compilation with Procedure Builder and using breakpoints and debug triggers for runtime code debugging. There are some subtle differences in debugging with Procedure Builder depending on your use of client-side or server-side PL/SQL code. For client-side PL/SQL, compiling is handled with the Program Unit Editor module. Within that module, the mechanism used for code compilation is the Compile button, while for coding stored procedures and functions, you would use the Stored Program Unit Editor module of Procedure Builder. In this case, use the Save button instead to handle your compilation and storage of the PL/SQL program in one motion. Either way, Oracle will indicate any errors immediately from within the program development module, allowing you to identify and correct the problem quickly. The equivalent method, using the **alter procedure** *proc_name* **compile** statement and viewing errors in the USER_ERRORS or ALL_ERRORS dictionary views is time-consuming and difficult. You need to use two sessions for debugging in order to avoid losing your statement buffer in SQL*Plus, thus rendering meaningless the line numbers provided by the error views.

Perhaps the greatest contribution to debugging Procedure Builder makes is the ability to debug your PL/SQL during run time. Procedure Builder allows you to do this with its breakpoint and debug trigger features. A breakpoint is inserted to a procedure once it has been compiled, stored either locally or on the server, and brought up in the PL/SQL Interpreter module for execution by double-clicking on the line you want procedure execution to suspend temporarily. Recall from the chapter that the breakpoint causes PL/SQL operation to cease *just prior* to the line on which the breakpoint has been created. Evidence of the breakpoint creation can be found in the PL/SQL Interpreter and in the Object Navigator module under the Debug Actions node.

Debug triggers work in conjunction with breakpoints. There are three potential ways for you to configure your debug trigger to fire: **program unit** for every time a breakpoint is entered in this program unit, **debug entry** for every time any breakpoint is entered, and **every statement** for every statement Procedure Builder executes. Using the Procedure Builder debug trigger interface is covered, including the trigger body window. Important to remember with the trigger body window is that you don't need to write an explicit **begin** or **end**, and the interface handles development of these components automatically. To create a debug trigger, select the Debug |

Trigger menu item. You must have the PL/SQL Interpreter in the foreground to use the Debug menu.

Within your debug triggers, you will find yourself using some or many of the Oracle-supplied packages. Probably the most important Oracle-supplied package is called DEBUG. Again, probably the most important function in this package allows you to obtain the value of a variable in your PL/SQL program. The function is called **get**x( ), where x is replaceable with **n, c, d,** or **i,** for NUMBER, VARCHAR2, DATE, or INTEGER, corresponding to the datatype of the variable you want to obtain. Another important package used in debugging is the TEXT_IO package. This package offers the same functionality as DBMS_OUTPUT, but TEXT_IO goes much further in its ability to read and write from files.

Other Oracle-supplied packages fall into a few defined categories, including application component communication; tuning, portability, and compatibility; internal functions; and debugging. You should review the section on Oracle-supplied packages to identify the various package names and their component functions, procedures, exceptions, and user-defined datatypes. For purposes of better understanding the overall process of debugging, you should focus your attention on the DEBUG, TEXT_IO, and TOOL_ERR packages. The text covered these areas of debugging through a case study. You should review it to understand the process of debugging in Procedure Builder.

Two-Minute Drill

- To obtain output from the Oracle database in the same manner as a **printf( )** command in C, you can use the DBMS_OUTPUT package, a PL/SQL package supplied as part of the Oracle database.

- DBMS_OUTPUT works in conjunction with a special output buffer that stores data for later retrieval.

- The DBMS_OUTPUT package consists of the following program units:

  - **enable( )** and **disable( )**: Enables and disables use of the output buffer with DBMS_OUTPUT.

  - **put( )** and **put_line( )**: Places information into the output buffer for retrieval later.

- **get_line( )** and **get_lines( )**: Retrieve information from the output buffer that was placed in the output buffer.

- **new_line( )**: Places a carriage return line separator into the text buffer—used often in conjunction with the **put( )** procedure.

■ Lines of output in the output buffer on the Oracle database are usually 255 characters.

■ Most commonly used in the DBMS_OUTPUT package for server-side PL/SQL debugging is the **put_line( )** procedure.

■ Use of DBMS_OUTPUT procedure calls can be activated within the SQL*Plus session or deactivated with the **set serveroutput on** and **set serveroutput off** statement.

■ Procedure Builder is used for debugging both server- and client-side PL/SQL programs.

■ One of Procedure Builder's most useful features is its ability to identify errors in client- and server-side code compilation.

■ A difference exists between the Program Unit Editor (client-side) and Stored Program Unit Editor (server-side) for compiling PL/SQL. In the Stored Program Unit Editor, you use the Save button, while in Program Unit Editor the button is actually Compile.

■ Procedure Builder allows you to debug runtime errors as well with the stack drill-down in the Object Navigator module.

■ The two features most used for debugging programs in runtime in Procedure Builder are breakpoints and debug triggers. Both these items are created in conjunction with the Debug menu on the PL/SQL Interpreter module.

■ A breakpoint allows you to stop PL/SQL midexecution and examine the contents of your runtime variable stack, and other aspects of code execution.

■ A debug trigger is a block of PL/SQL code that executes according to specific criteria that helps you debug your PL/SQL code execution.

■ The three options for debug trigger firing are

- **stored program**: In breakpoints on a particular program unit.

- **debug entry**: In all breakpoints across all program units.

- **every statement:** Before every PL/SQL statement issued.

- The options for debug trigger firing are defined in the create debug trigger interface.

- Debug trigger bodies are not defined with **begin** or **end** statements; Procedure Builder supplies those automatically.

- Any errors in debug trigger compilation can be found in the interactive PL/SQL window of the PL/SQL Interpreter module.

- The DEBUG package is used often in debug triggers to pull variable values from PL/SQL and highlight them for debugging purposes.

- The **get**x**( )** and **set**x**( )** functions are used often in debug triggers, and they allow you to obtain and define values for variables in your PL/SQL program, respectively.

- Four versions of each are provided, where x is replaced by a letter corresponding to the datatype of the variable being manipulated. Options are

  - **n** NUMBER
  - **i** INTEGER
  - **c** VARCHAR2 or CHAR
  - **d** DATE

- You need to encapsulate the variable whose value is being manipulated in single quotes on your call to **get**x**( )** and **set**x**( )**, respectively (i.e., **getc(**'*my_varchar2*'**)**).

- Debug triggers are not stored on the Oracle database, even if they correspond to stored procedures or functions.

- There are many different PL/SQL packages supplied by Oracle within the Procedure Builder software.

■ One category of Oracle-supplied packages includes those packages used for debugging. The packages in this category, along with their contents, are listed here. If you don't remember what the functions and procedures do, review the text and write their functions in the margins:

- ■ DEBUG—Debugging—**get**x**( )**, **set**x**( )**, **break( )**, **interpret( )**

- ■ TEXT_IO—Writing text output—**fopen( )**, **fclose( )**, **is_open( )**, **get_line( )**, **put_line( )**, **put( )**, **putf( )**, **new_line( )**. Types include **file_type**.

- ■ TOOL_ERR—Handling error stacks—**clear( )**, **nerrors( )**, **code( )**, **message( )**, **pop( )**. Exception and constant are **tool_error** and **toperror**, respectively.

■ Another category of Oracle-supplied packages includes those packages used for application component communication. The packages in this category, along with their contents, are listed here. If you don't remember what the functions and procedures do, review the text and write their functions in the margins:

- ■ ORA_FFI—Integrating C programs with PL/SQL—**register_function( )**, **register_parameter( )**, **register_return( )**, **find_function( )**, **find_library( )**, **is_null_ptr( )**, **generate_foreign( )**, and **unload_library( )**. Exception and type declarations include **ora_ffi_error**, **funchandletype**, **libhandletype**, and **pointertype**, respectively.

- ■ ORA_NLS—Obtaining language conventions and formats—**american( )**, **american_date( )**, **get_lang_scalar( )**, **get_lang_str( )**, **modified_date_fmt( )**, **right_to_left( )**, **linguistic_collate( )**, **linguistic_specials( )**, **simple_cs( )**, **single_byte( )**. Exceptions include **bad_attribute**, **no_item**, and **not_found**.

- ■ OLE2—Object linking and embedding—**create_obj( )**, **create_arglist( )**, **add_arg( )**, **add_arg_obj( )**, **get_char_property( )**, **get_num_property( )**, **get_obj_property( )**, **get_bool_property( )**, **set_property( )**, **invoke_num( )**, **invoke_char( )**, **invoke_obj( )**, **invoke( )**, **destroy_arglist( )**, **release_obj( )**.

- DDE—Interchange between Developer/2000 clients and other Windows clients.

- Another category of Oracle-supplied packages includes those packages used for tuning, portability, and compatibility. The packages in this category, along with their contents, are listed here. If you don't remember what the functions and procedures do, review the text and write their functions in the margins:

  - ORA_PROF—Performance tuning—**create_timer( )**, **start_timer( )**, **stop_timer( )**, **reset_timer( )**, **destroy_timer( )**, **elapsed_time( )**. Exception is **bad_timer**.

  - TOOL_RES—Porting applications across languages—**rfhandle( )**, **rfopen( )**, **rfclose( )**, **rfread( )**. Exceptions are **bad_file_handle**, **buffer_overflow**, **file_not_found**, and **no_resource**.

  - LIST—Handling text strings as lists in PL/SQL 1.*x*—**make( )**, **destroy( )**, **nitems( )**, **getitem( )**, **appenditem( )**, **prependitem( )**, **insertitem( )**, and **deleteitem( )**. Type and exception are **listofchar** and **fail** respectively.

Chapter Questions

1. **The developer needs to design an application that uses external procedures written in C. The Oracle-supplied package most appropriate for use in this situation is**

   A. TOOL_ERR

   B. TEXT_IO

   C. ORA_FFI

   D. OLE2

2. **The developer is debugging server-side PL/SQL from SQL*Plus. Text output has been embedded into the procedure, but output still is not appearing. The most appropriate fix is to**

   A. Execute **set serveroutput on**

   B. Recompile the procedure

    C. Use debug triggers

    D. Shut down and restart the computer

3. **A debug trigger has been coded to fire on every breakpoint within a certain PL/SQL program. The breakpoint will be entered when in relation to the code line on which the breakpoint appears?**

    A. After

    B. Before

    C. During

    D. Never, debug triggers fire only when disabled

4. **Type declarations for variables referenced in debug triggers are generally found in**

    A. The runtime procedure call

    B. PL/SQL programs

    C. Debug triggers

    D. Database triggers

5. **On compiling a debug trigger, the developer receives an error saying "identifier must be declared." Which three of the following are potential causes for this error?**

    A. Datatype mismatch between intended variable and function used

    B. Variable to be obtained not enclosed properly

    C. Function called without reference to package name

    D. Variable whose value to be obtained not present in the package

6. **When stepping through PL/SQL execution, which button terminates the run time and returns the interpreter to its prerun state?**

    A. Compile

    B. Go

    C. Step Through

    D. Reset

7. **The developer wants to modify the value of a PL/SQL variable from within a debug trigger. Which procedure or function is most appropriate?**

   A. DEBUG.interpret( )

   B. DEBUG.setc( )

   C. ORA_PROF.create_timer( )

   D. TEXT_IO.put_line( )

8. **The runtime error stack is found in which PL/SQL program module?**

   A. Stored Program Unit Editor

   B. Database Trigger Editor

   C. PL/SQL Interpreter

   D. Object Navigator

9. **Which Oracle-supplied package's procedures are called internally from Oracle?**

   A. TOOL_RES

   B. OLE2

   C. STPROC

   D. DEBUG

10. **The developer is using SQL*Plus for debugging. What data dictionary view contains information about compile-time errors on PL/SQL programs?**

    A. USER_ERRORS

    B. USER_SOURCE

    C. SOURCE#

    D. SYS

11. **With which two Oracle-supplied procedures can you emulate the functionality of the PL/SQL Interpreter module?**

    A. TOOL_RES.**rfread( )**

    B. DEBUG.**interpret( )**

    C. TOOL_RES.**rf_handle( )**

    D. DEBUG.**break( )**

12. **The GET( ) and SET( ) functions are part of which package?**

    A. TOOL_ENV

    B. ORA_FFI

    C. DEBUG

    D. LIST

Answers to Chapter Questions

I. C.   ORA_FFI

Explanation   The ORA_FFI package contains procedures and functions that assist with interfacing between PL/SQL programs and those written in C. The TOOL_ERR package handles obtaining and manipulating errors on the error stack, eliminating choice A. The TEXT_IO package handles reading and writing text messages to screen or to file, eliminating choice B, while the OLE2 package handles object linking and embedding in PL/SQL code, eliminating choice D.

2. A.   Execute **set serveroutput on**

Explanation   If calls to DBMS_OUTPUT are present, the developer can turn the output producing functionality on and off by using the **set serveroutput on** statement from the SQL prompt in SQL*Plus. The procedure being compiled is really not a factor, unless for some reason the code is invalidated. Restarting the computer is not a factor, either. Debug triggers are used when debugging from Procedure Builder, not SQL*Plus.

3. B.   Before

Explanation   Breakpoints are entered just before the statement on which the breakpoint appears in the PL/SQL Interpreter is executed, not after or during. Statement D is paradoxical, since a debug trigger would never fire if it had been disabled.

4. B.   PL/SQL programs

Explanation   A variable used in PL/SQL programs is declared in that PL/SQL program, with the exception of when global variables are used in packages. Neither the debug or database trigger is an appropriate place to declare variables for PL/SQL code. Occasionally, type definitions will be found in Oracle-supplied packages, but never the declaration of a variable to be that user-defined type.

5. B, C, and D.

Explanation   The "identifier must be declared" error will be encountered in each of the situations listed, from the variable not being declared, to the package reference not being present in a function call, to the single-quotes not being around the variable name on a **get( )** call. The only situation where you don't receive any errors on compilation is when the datatype expected in the **get( )** call doesn't match the datatype for the variable whose value is being obtained.

6. D.   Reset

Explanation   The Reset button is used to reset the PL/SQL Interpreter to the state just prior to PL/SQL code execution. Both Go and Step Through are used to move code execution forward after encountering a breakpoint. The use of Compile should be self-explanatory. Recall that the Reset button has a black loopback or return arrow on it in the PL/SQL Interpreter module.

7. B.   DEBUG.**setc( )**

Explanation   The **setc( )** function of the DEBUG package is used to modify values in variables from within a debug trigger. The **interpret( )** procedure in the same package is used to emulate interpretation of PL/SQL statements, while the **create_timer( )** program in ORA_PROF creates a device used for performance tuning called a timer. Finally, the **put_line( )** procedure in TEXT_IO is used to produce a line of output to the screen or add it to an output buffer.

8. D.   Object Navigator

Explanation   The Object Navigator contains drill-downs to help you locate any attached or open client- or server-side PL/SQL program unit available to Procedure Builder. Further, it provides drill-downs for the database objects, Oracle-supplied packages, debug actions and, of course, the error stack. The Stored Program Unit Editor is used to develop server-side PL/SQL, while the PL/SQL Interpreter is used to run PL/SQL programs. The Database Trigger Editor allows you to edit database triggers.

9. C.   STPROC

Explanation   Only the STPROC package contains procedures and functions called exclusively within Procedure Builder or Oracle. All others can be called explicitly by you.

10. A.   USER_ERRORS

Explanation   The USER_ERRORS view contains errors produced by the user in the most recent PL/SQL code compilation effort. USER_SOURCE contains source code for stored procedures owned by that user, while the SOURCE# is an underlying table owned by the SYS user that contains data made accessible via data dictionary views like USER_SOURCE.

11. B. and D.

Explanation   The **interpret( )** and **break( )** PL/SQL programs allow you to emulate both the interactive PL/SQL interpretation function provided by the PL/SQL Interpreter program module of Procedure Builder and the functionality of breakpoints. The **rfread( )** and **rfhandle( )** programs are both used in porting applications from one language to another, as in German to English and so on.

12. C.   DEBUG

Explanation   As two functions commonly employed for debug triggers, it should be obvious that these functions are part of the DEBUG package. If not, remember that the TOOL_ENV package consists of only one function used to obtain environment variable values. The ORA_FFI package handles interaction between PL/SQL programs and external processes written in C, while LIST handles text string manipulation.

CHAPTER
8

Managing Procedures, Functions, and Procedural Dependency

n this chapter, you will cover the following areas of PL/SQL program development:

- Managing procedures and functions
- Managing procedural dependency

Once developed, procedures and functions require some maintenance management for continued efficiency and performance. You need to understand some key points about the management of procedures and functions, and the dependencies Oracle enforces on procedures and functions stored in the Oracle database that use database objects like tables, views, indexes, and the like. This area, though perhaps less obvious to developers than how to construct **for** loops and **if – then** statements, is critical to maintenance programmers who must support PL/SQL running on production systems while simultaneously designing enhancements or new functionality into the production application. This subject area comprises 23 percent of OCP Exam 2 test content.

Managing Procedures and Functions

In this section, you will cover the following points on managing procedures and functions:

- Finding information about stored procedures in the data dictionary
- Security for owners and users on stored PL/SQL

Managing stored procedures and functions has many of the same challenges inherent in managing code for other environments. There are problems of where and how to find information about the code, and application security issues. Beyond the scope of Oracle certification, but certainly no less important, is source code version control. These issues form the core of what you need to know about source code management in Developer/2000. In this section, you will cover discussions in these areas.

Dictionary Views on Stored Procedures

There are many views in the data dictionary in Oracle that hold information about stored procedures and functions. Those views store everything from information about who owns the procedures to who can execute them, and even the source code of a stored procedure, function, trigger, or package. As stated in Chapter 3, there are three categories of data dictionary views, corresponding to the scope each view has over the total data in the Oracle database: USER_, ALL_ and DBA_. Sometimes the management of stored procedures and functions ultimately may fall on the DBA, like management of most database objects does. In some cases, there may be a production developer or maintenance and enhancement team that handles this functionality. The DBA_ views will be considered in this discussion, because they provide the most comprehensive view on the database, though you should bear in mind that the USER_ and ALL_ views will be of some limited use in source code management as well.

DBA_OBJECTS

The DBA_OBJECTS view stores a wide variety of information about objects in the database, including PL/SQL blocks. The columns in this view include OWNER, OBJECT_NAME, OBJECT_ID, OBJECT_TYPE, CREATED, LAST_DDL_TIME, TIMESTAMP, and STATUS. Pay attention to rows in this view where OBJECT_TYPE is 'PACKAGE', 'PACKAGE BODY', or 'PROCEDURE'. This view offers information about the PL/SQL block such as when it was created or last changed, and whether it's valid or not. Questions about the validity of a PL/SQL block touch on the topic of procedural dependency, covered later in the chapter. The formatting in this output is not standard—it has been modified for readability.

```
SQL> select owner, object_name, o_id, object_type, created, last_ddl, timestamp, status
  2> from dba_objects where object_type in
  3> ('PROCEDURE','PACKAGE','PACKAGE BODY') and owner = 'STACY';

OWNER    OBJECT_NAME   O_ID   OBJECT_TYPE   CREATED     LAST_DDL_   TIMESTAMP
-----    -----------   ----   -----------   ---------   ---------   -------------------
STATUS
------
STACY    FLURB         1079   PROCEDURE     07-SEP-99   07-SEP-99   1999-09-07:17:02:54
VALID

STACY    FOO           1078   PROCEDURE     06-SEP-99   06-SEP-99   1999-09-06:15:05:29
INVALID
```

DBA_SOURCE

Perhaps the most important of dictionary views related to PL/SQL blocks, DBA_SOURCE stores the source code for PL/SQL blocks. This source may either be in plaintext format or encoded using the PL/SQL wrapper. A *wrapper* is an encryption method that allows the developer of PL/SQL packages to distribute them in a portable format for use on other Oracle databases, yet in such a way as to prevent others from viewing the source code directly. This method allows an individual or company to protect complex logic, business rules, or other coding secrets while allowing others to use the functionality the procedures and functions provide. Many of Oracle's server packages such as DBMS_SQL are distributed using the PL/SQL wrapper.

The columns of the DBA_SOURCE dictionary view include OWNER, NAME, TYPE, LINE, and TEXT. The key to this dictionary view is that, when you want to view only the source code, you must remember to reference only the TEXT column in your **select** statements. Thus, **select * from DBA_SOURCE where NAME =** '*proc_name*'**;** is a bad idea that usually results in a buffer overflow error in SQL*Plus. Instead, you can switch the * to **TEXT**. This allows you to see only the source code corresponding to the PL/SQL block named by the query. The following block contains a statement that allows you to **select** data from this view for a procedure name that you can enter interactively. Note the use of the ampersand (**&**) character, which precedes any input variable, and the **upper( )** SQL built-in function, which converts characters to their uppercase form.

```
SQL> select text from dba_source where name = upper('&plsql_codename')
  2> order by line;
Enter value for plsql_codename: foo
old   1: select text from dba_source where name = upper('&plsql_codename')
new   1: select text from dba_source where name = upper('foo')

TEXT
-----------------------------------------------------------------------
procedure foo
begin
dbms_output.put_line('I am foo, who are you?');
end;
```

TIP
*Be sure always that you use the **order by** clause when obtaining source code from any of the SOURCE views.*

DBA_ERRORS

After covering debugging in Chapter 7, you know that the DBA_ERRORS, USER_ERRORS, or ALL_ERRORS dictionary views contain the errors produced during compilation of PL/SQL procedures, functions and packages. These errors only apply for the most recent compile. A new compile causes the old errors to be lost. As explained in Chapter 7, this view is a little difficult to use, because the line number it gives for error location corresponds to the line number of the PL/SQL code as it appears in the SQL statement buffer in SQL*Plus during the compilation. Thus, it is usually wise to view this information in a session separate from the session you use to perform the actual compile. The columns in the DBA_ERRORS view include OWNER, NAME, TYPE, SEQUENCE, LINE, POSITION, and TEXT, while USER_ERRORS subtracts the OWNER column that defines who owns the code producing these errors. The following code block shows a selection from DBA_ERRORS:

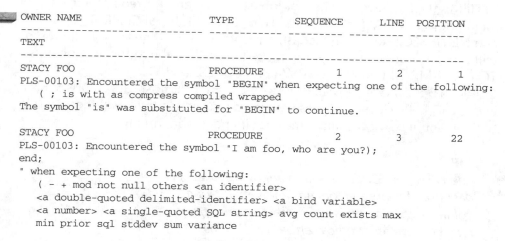

```
OWNER NAME                          TYPE           SEQUENCE    LINE  POSITION
----- ----------------------------  ------------   ---------   ----- ---------
TEXT
----------------------------------------------------------------------------
STACY FOO                           PROCEDURE           1         2       1
PLS-00103: Encountered the symbol "BEGIN" when expecting one of the following:
   ( ; is with as compress compiled wrapped
The symbol "is" was substituted for "BEGIN" to continue.

STACY FOO                           PROCEDURE           2         3      22
PLS-00103: Encountered the symbol "I am foo, who are you?);
end;
" when expecting one of the following:
   ( - + mod not null others <an identifier>
   <a double-quoted delimited-identifier> <a bind variable>
   <a number> <a single-quoted SQL string> avg count exists max
   min prior sql stddev sum variance
```

DBA_JOBS

The final dictionary view considered here is the DBA_JOBS view. This dictionary view on the Oracle database tracks information about the Oracle database job scheduler, which is used to run PL/SQL code for regularly scheduled batch operations without the use of job scheduling from the operating system or a third-party vendor. The benefit of using Oracle for job scheduling is that you don't need to develop support into the batch job to handle situations where the database is not available or a user's password has changed. Since these jobs are internal to Oracle, they will fire automatically as long as the database is running. If the database is not running, the job will not fail because the job will not be run. Also, Oracle automatically retries jobs for a period of time you specify, eliminating the need to retry a job manually when you learn it has not run.

Oracle-scheduled jobs can be used in conjunction with packages and features in the Oracle database like DBMS_OUTPUT and UTL_FILE to write text output to a file. This method of job scheduling is as effective as batch job scheduling with UNIX shell scripts, Pro*C programs, crontab, Windows services, or other operating system-driven methods.

The columns in the DBA_JOBS view give information about the jobs scheduled to run on the Oracle database. Several columns of data are provided, including JOB, a number used to identify uniquely each job entered in the database. Several columns track the different users that may be involved in job execution, including LOG_USER, PRIV_USER, and SCHEMA_USER. Several dates for job execution are tracked as well, including LAST_DATE, LAST_SEC, THIS_DATE, THIS_SEC, NEXT_DATE, and NEXT_SEC, indicating the last, current, and next time the job did run or will run. Several other things are tracked as well, in the following columns: TOTAL_TIME, BROKEN, INTERVAL, FAILURES, WHAT, CURRENT_SESSION_LABEL, CLEARANCE_HI, CLEARANCE_LO, NLS_ENV, and MISC_ENV. Several of these columns are used to track whether a job is broken, and if so, how many times has it ended abnormally.

TIP
The DBA_JOBS view is a little annoying to **select** *data from because it contains a few really long columns. When you issue a* **select** *against it, you may get a buffer overflow error in SQL*Plus. Issue* **set arraysize 5** *and* **set maxdata 32767** *from your SQL prompt and you should be fine.*

Exercises

1. What dictionary view would the developer use to determine if a package is invalid?

2. What dictionary view contains source code for most types of PL/SQL blocks? In what column is source code stored on that view?

3. Based on the things you have learned in this chapter, can you guess what dictionary view contains source code for triggers?

4. What **set** statement is used to ensure being able to see the trigger source in its entirety from SQL*Plus?

Security for Owner and User on Stored PL/SQL

Recall from Chapter 6 that, to create PL/SQL program components on the Oracle database, you require the **create procedure** system privilege granted by the DBA or some other privileged user on the database. This is required for server-side PL/SQL only; client-side PL/SQL can be created and used by anyone. To run server-side procedures, you must have the **execute** object privilege granted to you. If you're still wondering about system and object privileges related to PL/SQL code development, review Chapter 6.

There is an important factor to consider when running stored procedures and functions, related to what the function does and whether the user of the procedure or function is allowed to do it. Say, for example, that user ATHENA wants to run user SPANKY's procedure **find_mouse( )**. This procedure performs a **select** statement on the MOUSE_HOUSE table, for which ATHENA does not have **select** privileges but user SPANKY does.

You might think that ATHENA would not be able to run the **find_mouse( )** procedure, because even though she has **execute** privileges on that procedure, she doesn't have **select** privileges on MOUSE_HOUSE. This assumption is wrong, in fact. ATHENA can run the procedure successfully. Why? Because Oracle only cares that SPANKY, the owner of the procedure, has the **select** privilege required to execute the procedural components successfully. What's more, user SPANKY must have these privileges on the objects referenced in the program unit granted explicitly to him, not through a role, or else SPANKY's own compilation of his program unit will fail. Thus, the user of a procedure needn't have the underlying object privileges required to run the statements in a stored procedure or function; she need only have the **execute** privilege on the procedure. The owner of the procedure or function, however, must have *all* privileges required by the procedure for it to compile and run successfully. This fact touches on functional dependency, which is covered later this chapter as well.

TIP
The procedure owner must have all privileges required to run statements in a procedure. The user of that procedure needn't have the privileges required to execute every statement in the procedure, so long as the user has **execute** *privileges on the procedure.*

User ATHENA only needs to concern herself with obtaining **execute** privileges on that stored function. SPANKY, meanwhile, must have all privileges granted to him that are required to run the function successfully, even though the function will be run by other people. Thus, the developer of an application can not only modularize the application functionality by encapsulating logic into stored procedures and functions, she can modularize database access privileges via stored procedures as well.

TIP
The owner of any program unit must have all object privileges necessary to run the program unit granted directly to them. The privilege cannot be granted via roles.

By giving the *application schema owner* the actual object privilege to access table data, she can effectively moderate the actual access to the database any user may have. An application schema owner (SPANKY in this case, for example) owns the database access privileges and moderates them to user ATHENA by only allowing her to view as much data as the function **find_mouse( )** will provide her. So, the developer can then revoke **select** privileges to table MOUSE_HOUSE from ATHENA while still allowing her to do her job finding mice with the assistance of application code. Figure 8-1 illustrates the principle of maintaining security on the Oracle database by allowing users access to data programmatically.

Several advantages are offered with employment of this method throughout the database and application. The database is more secure

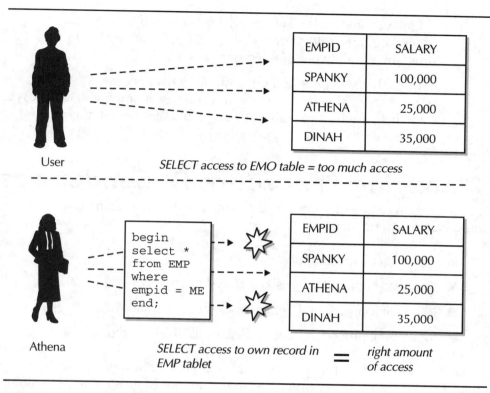

EMPID	SALARY
SPANKY	100,000
ATHENA	25,000
DINAH	35,000

User

SELECT access to EMO table = too much access

```
begin
select *
from EMP
where
empid = ME
end;
```

Athena

*SELECT access to own record in
EMP tablet*

EMPID	SALARY
SPANKY	100,000
ATHENA	25,000
DINAH	35,000

= *right amount
of access*

FIGURE 8-1. *Maintaining data security with programmatic access*

because no user other than the application schema owner has object privileges that would allow them to go out and run SQL statements that view or modify data that are not part of a stored procedure or function. This design limits the overall usage of the system to flow only through stored procedures and functions. Interestingly, it gives the user as much access as the procedure will allow, so even though ATHENA may not have **select** access on MOUSE_HOUSE, she can still see the data she needs to see in that table anyway. PL/SQL then extends the basic functionality provided by Oracle in the form of granting execution on program privileges to users that cannot otherwise access the data.

Exercises

1. Identify the privileges required to create and run PL/SQL programs.

2. Which user must have **select** privileges granted to them if a procedure must **select** from a table, the user running the PL/SQL program or the owner of the program?

3. Explain the principles behind controlling data access programmatically. What are the advantages of limiting data access to only that which can be given through PL/SQL? For what types of users might this approach *not* work?

Managing Procedure Dependencies

In this section, you will cover the following points about managing procedural dependencies:

- Tracking procedural dependencies
- Database object changes and stored procedures
- Managing procedural dependencies in one database
- Managing procedural dependencies in distributed databases

It has been said that no man is an island. That author, of course, neglected to realize that women, like men, are not islands, either. The point here is that people and things in a society are usually interconnected. The same holds true in Oracle, the software used to represent or model reality. Objects like tables, indexes, views, and program units are interconnected. As a result of this interconnectivity, there are dependencies placed on one object such that if the object were to fail or disappear, its absence would be noticed by its dependents. This section covers the management of dependency in PL/SQL applications. There are two different types of dependencies a PL/SQL block may have dependency on another PL/SQL block, called *procedural dependency*, and dependency on a database object, called *object dependency*. The tracking of procedural dependencies in the Oracle database will be covered in this section, along with analyzing the effects of database object changes on PL/SQL blocks. The special responsibilities involved in managing dependency on single and distributed databases are covered, too.

Tracking Procedural Dependencies

In the course of PL/SQL development, you will encounter many different types of applications, from financial applications and accounting software to HR and employee-related service applications, to telemarketing applications, to just about anything else you can think of. One common thread between all these applications, however, will be that there is a strong chance the application will be *big*. Take this to mean that you may be required to develop and maintain applications with several thousand or more lines of source code. Now, that's a complicated task, so you will need to understand the implications of maintaining such complexity.

Often, to simplify the complexity of a large application, you will want to use modularity in program design. This means you will take your overall program activity and break it down into logical units of work. Once this is complete, you will take your logical units of work and develop PL/SQL blocks to handle only the logical component. In particular, this method helps if there is a repeatable task that happens in the application, such as the selection of data for validation purposes. You simply develop your function or procedure to handle the logical mechanisms required, and define parameters to be passed in and out to handle the specifics of the work.

In this development scenario, you are creating procedural dependencies. Procedural dependency in this situation literally means "one procedure depends on another." When developing code in a modular fashion, beware the dependencies you create. For example, if a defect appears in a procedure that is called by 17 other procedures, then the defect will occur in at least that many places. Without a clear idea or knowledge of your overall application, you will become very frustrated very quickly unless you have methods available to track the dependencies one unit of code has on another.

DBA_DEPENDENCIES View

Fortunately, there are some items at your disposal for tracking procedural dependencies between database PL/SQL programs. There are a group of dictionary views that were held back from prior discussion that benefit your quest to find the procedural dependencies in your Oracle database. This group is the USER_DEPENDENCIES, ALL_DEPENDENCIES, and DBA_DEPENDENCIES views. As with most dictionary views, there are three possible limitations on scope, including the current user's dependencies, all dependencies in the database the current user can see, and all dependencies in the database, period. Due to the importance of tracking procedural dependencies in the Oracle database with respect to PL/SQL programs, the following is a list of columns in the DBA_DEPENDENCIES view, with an explanation of the contents of that column. Here we go:

- **OWNER** The user who owns the PL/SQL block, also known as an application schema owner.

- **NAME** The name of the PL/SQL block, in all-caps.

- **TYPE** The type of PL/SQL object, such as 'PROCEDURE', 'FUNCTION', 'PACKAGE' or 'PACKAGE BODY'.

- **REFERENCED_OWNER** The user who owns the referenced PL/SQL block.

- **REFERENCED_NAME** The name of the referenced PL/SQL block.

- **REFERENCED_TYPE** The type of the referenced object, like 'PROCEDURE', 'FUNCTION', 'PACKAGE', 'PACKAGE BODY', 'TABLE', and so on.

- **REFERENCED_LINK_NAME** The name of the database link used to access the referenced PL/SQL code block. This column contains a value only when the referenced object is on another Oracle database.

Let's examine now the usage of the DBA_DEPENDENCIES view. Assume we have a complicated set of procedures, functions, and packages on the Oracle database for an application that conducts international financial transactions. One of these functions, **convert_money( )**, is used to convert a monetary amount from one currency to another. The **convert_money( )** function accepts four variables, *from_crcy*, *to_crcy*, *from_amt* and *valid_date*, and returns data of type NUMBER. Notice this function violates the good programming practice of only using **in** parameters for functions, allowing it to return only one value. The code for this function appears in the following code block:

```
CREATE FUNCTION convert_money (
p_from_crcy          VARCHAR2,
p_to_crcy      IN OUT VARCHAR2,
```

```
p_from_amt              NUMBER,
p_valid_date            DATE
) RETURN NUMBER IS
  my_exch_rate NUMBER(15,4);
  my_ret_val   NUMBER(15,4);
BEGIN
  SELECT exch_rate INTO my_exch_rate FROM EXCH_RATE
  WHERE to_crcy = p_to_crcy AND from_crcy = p_from_crcy
  AND p_valid_date = TRUNC(sysdate);
  my_ret_val := p_from_amt*my_exch_rate;
  RETURN my_ret_val;
END;
```

As you can see, to perform its application logic, **convert_money( )** obtains an exchange rate from the EXCH_RATE table. The table consists of four columns, TO_CRCY, FROM_CRCY, EXCH_RATE, and VALID_DATE. The FROM_CRCY and TO_CRCY columns contains character strings that represent world currencies, like GBP for the British pound, USD for the U.S. dollar, or IR for Indian rupee, that represent the currency you convert from and to, respectively. The EXCH_RATE column contains a small number used as the conversion factor from the one currency to another. The last column, VALID_DATE, contains a date on which that value in EXCH_RATE is valid.

Several PL/SQL procedures in the applications call the **convert_money( )** function. Several of these procedures are experiencing difficulties in obtaining correct conversions for the day they pass into the application. You are the developer in this situation, and have been asked to take a look at the situation. To determine the different procedures that call the **convert_money( )** function, the SQL statement in the following code block can be used:

```
SQL> select name, referenced_name from dba_dependencies
  2> where referenced_name = 'CONVERT_MONEY';

NAME                    REFERENCED_NAME
------------------      ---------------------------
PROC_TODAY_TRAN         CONVERT_MONEY
PROC_YEST_TRANS         CONVERT_MONEY
PROC_MNTH_TRANS         CONVERT_MONEY
```

Based on the data coming from this view, you can now identify the three different procedures that depend on this function. Judging strictly by the names of the procedures that call **convert_money( )**, you can see that three types of transactions need to convert money: those that happen today, those that happened yesterday but are processed today, and those that happen monthly. Using this information, you should be able to determine the problem—simply run **proc_today_tran( )**, **proc_yest_trans( )** and **proc_mnth_trans( )** separately to determine which one converts money properly. Upon execution of each procedure, and further examination, you will notice that the error lies in the **convert_money( )** function, in that the **select** statement never actually uses *p_valid_day* at all—instead, **convert_money( )** uses the **sysdate** keyword in the overall selection criteria for obtaining the appropriate exchange rate—a semantic error that will only be obvious in processing yesterday's or monthly transactions!

TIP
DBA_DEPENDENCIES shows the procedural dependencies of a database, like the dependency of one code block on another. It also shows the object dependencies of the database, like the underlying tables used by procedures and functions.

So, the **proc_today_tran( )**, **proc_yest_trans( )**, and **proc_mnth_trans( )** procedures depend on the appearance and validity of the **convert_money( )** function. A procedure or function is valid only after successful compilation against the PL/SQL engine in the Oracle database. After you make the necessary change to this function and recompile, if for some reason the compilation failed, you not only cannot use **convert_money( )**, you cannot execute **proc_today_tran( )**, **proc_yest_trans( )**, or **proc_mnth_trans( )**, either.

DEPTREE and IDEPTREE

Another view for finding database dependencies can be used as well. This view is called DEPTREE. DEPTREE lists the dependency information stored in an underlying table called DEPTREE_TEMPTAB. Another view, called IDEPTREE, allows you to see dependency information such that dependent objects are shown below the objects they depend on, and indented. These views give both direct and indirect dependency information while DBA_DEPENDENCIES can give only direct procedure and object dependencies in the Oracle database. To make them available for your use, you must run the **utldtree.sql** script found in the **rdbms/admin** subdirectory under your Oracle software home directory to create the appropriate dependency objects and PL/SQL blocks that comprise this utility. Another object, the procedure called **deptree_fill( )**, actually populates the underlying table for your use. You should run it before trying to see the dependencies with DEPTREE or IDEPTREE, using the syntax provided in the following code block. NOTE: all three parameters are of type CHAR.

```
SQL> execute deptree_fill('obj_type','obj_owner','obj_name');
```

TIP
*You should experiment with use of the
Dependency Tree utility before taking OCP.*

The columns in the DEPTREE view include NESTED_LEVEL, OBJECT_TYPE, OWNER, OBJECT_NAME, and SEQ#. The column in IDEPTREE is DEPENDENCIES.

Exercises

1. Explain the concept of procedural dependency. In what state must a PL/SQL block be in order to allow other PL/SQL blocks to depend on it? What activity puts PL/SQL blocks in that state?

2. What dictionary views are used for identifying procedural dependency? Experiment with the one called DBA_DEPENDENCIES and determine what the REFERENCED_TYPE column in that view refers to.

3. Explain the use of the Dependency Tree utility. What are its components? What are the names of its views, and what are their columns? How is data populated into this utility?

Database Object Changes and Stored Procedures

Recall from Chapter 5 that SQL statements embed easily into PL/SQL. In fact, the main purpose of PL/SQL is to make it possible to design applications that reside partially or wholly within the Oracle database. Thus, you may find yourself developing PL/SQL programs that use SQL statements intensively. The sorts of statements that you might use include DML statements like **select**, **update**, **delete**, or **insert**. You may recall that PL/SQL does not permit the use of DDL statements directly like **create table** or **drop index**, but rather you must use dynamic SQL via a special package in Oracle called DBMS_SQL. More on the role of Oracle-supplied packages in the Oracle database in Chapter 9.

Every time you incorporate a SQL statement that calls a database object in your PL/SQL statement, you create a dependency on that object. Thus, if your PL/SQL block contains the statement **select * from** EMPLOYEE, your PL/SQL block then depends on the existence of the EMPLOYEE table in order to function properly. Tracking object dependency in your PL/SQL programs is highly important to ensure continued usage of your programs. Since an application may call dozens or even hundreds of tables in the course of its operation, the object dependencies a PL/SQL program will have on underlying tables are so pervasive it is difficult to tell the dependency exists between the PL/SQL program units until it is too late. The only real option to you as the developer or programmer is to understand each PL/SQL program unit in your application thoroughly.

Oracle has particular behavior in this situation. First, Oracle enforces dependency on database objects. Let's return to our **convert_money( )** function. In addition to the **proc_today_tran( )**, **proc_yest_trans( )**, and **proc_mnth_trans( )** procedures being dependent on the availability and validity of **convert_money( )**, so too must the EXCH_RATE table be valid and available or the **convert_money( )** function will not work properly. The trickle-down effect is in place as well, so execution of **proc_today_tran( )**, **proc_yest_trans( )**, and **proc_mnth_trans( )** will not work properly either. The cycle of direct procedural and object dependency and the indirect dependencies that ensue are all demonstrated in Figure 8-2.

Any statement that has the effect of changing a table referenced by a procedure or function will cause that procedure or function to become invalid. For example, a **drop table** statement that removes EXCH_RATE that the **convert_money( )** function selects will render the **convert_money( )** function invalid. The following code block demonstrates use of the DBA_OBJECTS table to determine PL/SQL code block validity before any activity on the Oracle database takes place. Remember that the DBA_OBJECTS view contains the all-important STATUS column, which describes the validity of any object for use in the Oracle database. Invalid

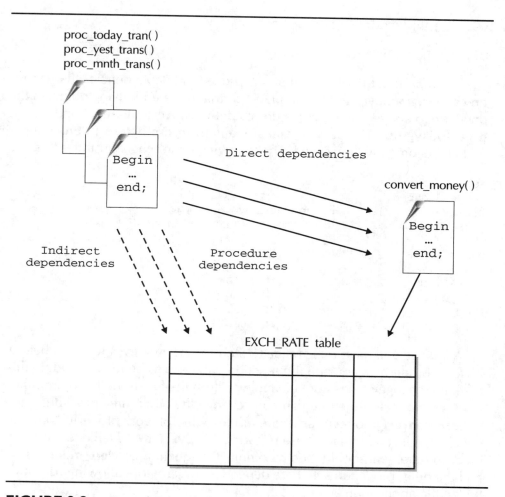

FIGURE 8-2. *Procedural and object dependencies in a sample application*

PL/SQL program units must be recompiled explicitly before you can use them again.

```
SQL> select object_name, object_type, status from dba_objects
  2> where object_name = 'CONVERT_MONEY';
```

```
OBJECT_NAME    OBJECT_TYPE STATUS
-------------  ----------- -------
CONVERT_MONEY  PROCEDURE    VALID
```

It is important to note also that any procedural dependencies that existed on **convert_money( )** are still in place, so that if the underlying object in the database to **convert_money( )** is dropped, the **convert_money( )** and the **proc_today_tran( )**, **proc_yest_trans( )**, and **proc_mnth_trans( )** procedures will all become invalid as well. The following code block illustrates this:

```
SQL> drop table exch_rate;
Table dropped.
SQL> select object_name, object_type, status from dba_objects
  2> where owner='SPANKY' and object_type = 'PROCEDURE';

OBJECT_NAME       OBJECT_TYPE STATUS
----------------  ----------- -------
CONVERT_MONEY     FUNCTION     INVALID
PROC_MNTH_TRANS   PROCEDURE    INVALID
PROC_TODAY_TRAN   PROCEDURE    INVALID
PROC_YEST_TRANS   PROCEDURE    INVALID
```

A change will have to be made to the **convert_money( )** function before it works properly again, and the function will need to be recompiled. In this case, the change is to restore the table or drop the function. If you drop the **convert_money( )** function, you must change the other three procedures to not call **convert_money( )** anymore or they will not work properly. Once the change is made, in this case restoring the EXCH_RATE table to its predrop state, you should then recompile the function **convert_money( )** and the other procedures that are dependent on it before allowing users to utilize the application again.

Recall from earlier discussion that the **alter procedure** *proc_name* **compile** or **alter function** *func_name* **compile** statement will recompile an existing procedure or function. If the underlying problem of a table missing has been corrected, there is no need to edit the source code for any of the procedures or functions involved. Bear in mind the order of procedural dependencies must be followed when recompiling these functions and procedures. The following code block illustrates this:

```
SQL> alter function CONVERT_MONEY compile;
Function altered.
```

```
SQL> alter procedure PROC_TODAY_TRAN compile;
Procedure altered.
SQL> alter procedure PROC_YEST_TRANS compile;
Procedure altered.
SQL> alter procedure PROC_MNTH_TRANS compile;
Procedure altered.
```

TIP
*Follow the order of procedural dependency
when recompiling invalid procedures or
functions. This means that the procedure or
function the others depend on should be
compiled first, followed by the procedures or
functions that depend on it.*

What about situations where the underlying object dependency is not
removed, merely changed? For example, say you do not create a table to
replace EXCH_RATE, instead creating a synonym EXCH_RATE from data for
another table. This act will allow you to recompile your procedures and
functions only if the function with the object dependency on EXCH_RATE
sees the same columns in the new underlying table as it did in EXCH_RATE.

Another situation to consider is when you issue an **alter table** statement
against EXCH_RATE that adds columns not related to the activities of
convert_money( ). Something interesting happens here that you should
remember. Even though the column added is not accessed by any of the
procedures and functions in your application, the mere act of redoing the
EXCH_RATE table is enough to invalidate the function and procedures. The
following code block illustrates this:

```
SQL> alter table exch_rate add (rate_comment varchar2(80));
Table altered.
SQL> select object_name, object_type, status from dba_objects
  2> where object_name = 'EXCH_RATE';

OBJECT_NAME       OBJECT_TYPE STATUS
--------------- ----------- ------
EXCH_RATE        TABLE        VALID

SQL> select object_name, object_type, status from dba_objects
  2> where owner='SPANKY' and object_type = 'PROCEDURE';
```

```
OBJECT_NAME        OBJECT_TYPE  STATUS
----------------   -----------  -------
CONVERT_MONEY      FUNCTION     INVALID
PROC_MNTH_TRANS    PROCEDURE    INVALID
PROC_TODAY_TRAN    PROCEDURE    INVALID
PROC_YEST_TRANS    PROCEDURE    INVALID
```

So, even though the underlying database object is valid, the PL/SQL code is not. This is a simple item to fix—simply recompile all functions and procedures affected by the database object change in the order of their procedural dependency. A more significant effort will be required if you eliminate the VALID_DATE column being used in the function **convert_money( )** that depends on the database object. If so, the **convert_money( )** programs that rely on this table must be altered in order to accommodate the table change. Refer to the discussion of creating PL/SQL functions and procedures in Chapter 6.

TIP
*Any **alter** or **drop** statement that affects a database object used in a PL/SQL program has the effect of invalidating that program. The USER_OBJECTS, ALL_OBJECTS, or DBA_OBJECTS dictionary view shows the current status of objects in the database. If the change impacts the function's behavior, the function must be changed or dropped before proceeding. PL/SQL code that has procedural dependency on code invalidated because of object dependency will be invalidated as well.*

One final thought—what happens if an object or procedural dependency other than **convert_money( )** or EXCH_RATE causes the **proc_today_tran( )** procedure to become invalid? What is the effect on **convert_money( )**? There is none, because **convert_money( )** doesn't share a procedural dependency with its caller—the caller is dependent on it, but the same in reverse does not hold true. So, if **proc_today_tran( )** performs a **select** against the TRANS_TABLE, and that table gets dropped, **proc_today_tran( )** will become invalid but **convert_money( )** will not.

Exercises

1. What happens to procedures and functions with object dependencies if that underlying object experiences the effects of a **drop** statement? An **alter** statement?

2. Does DBA_DEPENDENCIES show procedural dependencies, object dependencies, or both?

3. In what order should procedures and functions be recompiled after an object dependency issue causing code to become invalid is resolved?

Managing Procedural Dependencies in One Database

Obviously, there can be some challenges inherent in the management of dependency in an Oracle database. If the DBA alters the database objects in some way, it is likely that problems may ensue with the applications that perform DML operations against the database. Similarly, if there is a piece of PL/SQL code that many different code blocks depend on—such as those handling routine operations in the application, like **convert_money( )**— recompiling that PL/SQL block may cause invalidation of code for other PL/SQL blocks in the application.

TIP
*There are three types of SQL statements in Oracle. The first is DML, which are statements like **update**, **insert**, or **delete** that change data in the database. The next is DDL, which are changes to database objects produced by statements like **drop index** or **alter table**. The last are DCL, or statements that control the availability of the database, like **startup** or **shutdown**.*

In general, it makes sense that you understand what the procedural and object dependencies of the application are so as to understand procedure invalidation and its effects on that application. For example, you may have an application that consists of several different packages, one of which may contain utility procedures and functions used by several other procedures. You can't just make changes to this utility package or any procedure in the package without considering the effects on other parts of the application, because if you do, you will invalidate some or all of your application in the process.

To assist you with the task of managing procedural dependency in a single database, you need to understand how Oracle enforces procedural dependency. One of the methods Oracle uses for managing procedural dependency is called *timestamping*. Recall from earlier in the chapter the discussion on where to find information about PL/SQL in the Oracle database. One dictionary view used to identify dependency information was DBA_DEPENDENCIES. Another is DBA_OBJECTS.

Recall that DBA_OBJECTS contains information about the status of the procedure or function in the Oracle database. This information is stored in the STATUS column of the view. Another bit of information you will recall is the date and time the object's definition code was changed and/or compiled. Two columns are of use here: the LAST_DDL_TIME column and the TIMESTAMP column. Usually, the format of LAST_DDL_TIME will be Oracle's standard date output format, 'DD-MON-YY'. This is true even though the datatype for this information in the DBA_OBJECTS table is CHAR. The column format for LAST_DDL_TIME may be different depending on whether or not you have altered the format Oracle uses to show dates with the **alter session set nls_date_format =** '*format*' statement. The TIMESTAMP column, which is also stored as a character string, will always show both the date and time to seconds precision of the last occasion when you have changed the object definition or compiled the PL/SQL code. The format for timestamp is always the same, and that format is '*YYYY-MM-DD:HH24:MI:SS*'.

The use of DBA_OBJECTS and DBA_DEPENDENCIES will be combined now to give you a clearer idea of how Oracle enforces dependencies according to their timestamp. The following code block shows information about the procedures and functions that are part of the international financial application example. Both the query and the results are shown in order to demonstrate how you identify timestamping information. The reference to **chr(10)** allows you to put a carriage return into the output. The formatting has been cleaned up for readability, but you should get the general idea.

```
SQL> select d.name, d.type, o1.status, o1.timestamp, chr(10),
  2> d.referenced_name, d.referenced_type, o2.status, o2.timestamp, chr(10)
  3> from dba_dependencies d, dba_objects o1, dba_objects o2
  4> where o1.owner = 'SPANKY' and d.name = o1.object_name
  5> and d.owner = o1.owner and d.referenced_name = o2.object_name
  6> and d.referenced_owner = o2.owner;
```

D.NAME	D.TYPE	O1.STATUS	O1.TIMESTAMP

D.REFERENCED_NAME	D.REFERENCED_TYPE	O2.STATUS	O2.TIMESTAMP
CONVERT_MONEY	FUNCTION	VALID	1999-07-11:17:01:59
EXCH_RATE	TABLE	VALID	1998-09-30:09:15:34
PROC_MNTH_TRANS	PROCEDURE	VALID	1999-07-12:14:03:03
CONVERT_MONEY	FUNCTION	VALID	1999-07-11:17:01:59
PROC_TODAY_TRAN	PROCEDURE	VALID	1999-07-12:14:03:03
CONVERT_MONEY	FUNCTION	VALID	1999-07-11:17:01:59
PROC_YEST_TRANS	PROCEDURE	VALID	1999-07-12:14:03:03
CONVERT_MONEY	FUNCTION	VALID	1999-07-11:17:01:59

So, as you can see, all of the items in the output of this query are valid. Notice that the timestamps on every referenced item show an earlier point in time than the timestamps on the referring items. This is not by accident. If the times on the referenced items were later than the referring items, you would likely see that all the referring items would be invalid. So, you can see the evidence for the premise that referenced items must be compiled before referring items in order for everything to be valid in an application with procedural and object dependency.

Oracle works well with using the timestamp method for determining procedural dependency in local databases. Since time can be considered a constant across multiple database objects residing in the same database, it makes sense for Oracle to use this as the method of choice for handling procedural dependency. If a referenced program unit has been compiled later than a referring program unit, then the referring unit will be marked invalid by Oracle and must be recompiled before you can use it again.

Exercises

1. Where is object validity and status information found in the Oracle data dictionary?

2. What happens to a procedure that is dependent on another procedure when you recompile that other procedure?

3. How are timestamps used in conjunction with procedural dependency and PL/SQL code validity in Oracle?

Managing Procedural Dependencies in Distributed Databases

Consider the following problem. You have an application that takes care of travel expenditures and relocation costs for employees of a Fortune 500 corporation. This application works in online mode for situations when you are in the office and submitting your expenses. The application also works offline, so that as you travel and are out of the office, you can enter your expenses as you incur them. Some of the PL/SQL code components for the application are stored on the client machine, while others are stored on the Oracle server. The client PL/SQL program units are compiled and in use on January 02, 2001. However, the folks in IS determined a leftover bug from the millennium project and made the necessary changes, recompiling the server-side PL/SQL program units over the holiday weekend. The following Monday, however, some people traveling on business over the holidays return to the office to find that their application, which had worked fine offline and before they left, no longer works.

Based on the facts of this scenario, can you determine what the cause of the problem is? If you said timestamping, you're right! Another possible situation where this may occur is when the PL/SQL code on one database calls PL/SQL via a database link on another database, where the second PL/SQL block was recompiled. In order for the first block to use the second, the first must be recompiled, even though nothing changed about the first block. Unnecessary PL/SQL recompilation on the referring PL/SQL on the first database is annoying but not severe. A slightly more complicated situation is when the PL/SQL source code for the first block is not immediately available on the client machine, as is often the case in Forms applications where only the executable is available.

Consider another problem involving distributed systems. You are a developer in Utah coordinating compilation of a procedure with a developer in London. Your colleague in London has just compiled a procedure, call it **foo( )**, that you call in your procedure, called **foobar( )**.

When your procedure goes out to the Oracle database in London via database link to obtain a timestamp for **foo( )**, your compilation is not going to work, because the timestamp of **foo( )** is incorporated into the compilation of your procedure, **foobar( )**. Since **foo( )** was compiled at a "later" local time (remember, London is several time zones ahead of Utah) than **foobar( )**, timestamping renders the **foobar( )** procedure invalid.

A method used for solving this problem is present in Oracle PL/SQL version 2.3 and later. Rather than allowing Oracle to use timestamping to determine whether a PL/SQL block is valid or not, you can use the *signature* method. A signature is a piece of information that Oracle can store along with the procedure or function that helps determine when the PL/SQL block must be recompiled. A signature contains several bits of information about the procedure specification being compiled, including the datatype and position of parameters passed into the procedure or function.

Unlike a timestamp, which changes every time the DDL for a database object or PL/SQL block is altered, the signature changes only when the specification for the PL/SQL object changes. Thus, in the situation where logic in the procedure or procedures changes but the mechanism used to call the procedure (i.e., the specification) does not change, you have no need for recompiling the procedures that are dependent on this stored procedure or function.

Something needs to happen on the Oracle database in support of using the signature method for determining procedural dependency. There are basically three options for starting use of the signature method for determining procedural dependency. In the first, you change an initialization parameter in your **init.ora** file, used for starting the database. The initialization parameter in Oracle used to initiate the signature method for determining procedural dependency is REMOTE_DEPENDENCIES_ MODE. This parameter can be set to **signature** or **timestamp**. As you may assume, the **timestamp** value is the default for the Oracle database.

TIP
*The Oracle database can be set to run in specific ways according to specific parameters. DBAs use parameter files to specify these parameters and their values. Typically, Oracle documentation refers to this parameter file as the **init.ora** file, although it can have any name the DBA wants.*

You must remember that changing the value for an initialization parameter in the **init.ora** file doesn't guarantee the Oracle database will start using the new value for that parameter immediately. For any change in the **init.ora** file to take effect, you must shut down and restart the Oracle database. If you want the change from timestamp method to signature method for procedural dependency enforcement to take place immediately within the Oracle database, the statement in the following code block must be issued:

```
SQL> alter system set remote_dependencies_mode = SIGNATURE;
```

Only a user with the **alter system** privilege (usually SYS or comparable user) can issue this statement successfully. The effect will be immediate. In some cases, you may want to be more selective in which procedures and functions use the signature method and which use timestamping. Perhaps there are vast portions of applications on the Oracle database that are used locally and make no remote procedure calls. Rather than disrupting operations here, or even to ensure that those PL/SQL blocks must be recompiled if another block is changed, you can set the signature method of procedural dependency enforcement only to apply to procedures and functions compiled out of your current session. This is done with the statement in the following code block, which can be issued by any user with the **create session** privilege:

```
SQL> alter session set remote_dependencies_mode = SIGNATURE;
```

TIP
Oracle recommends that you use timestamping to enforce procedure dependency for server-side PL/SQL residing locally on one database, and the signature method of enforcing procedure dependency on PL/SQL residing on remote databases or client-side PL/SQL residing on the client machine.

After setup of the signature method for procedure dependency enforcement, you must recompile your PL/SQL code to create signatures for the PL/SQL blocks on the Oracle database. Use of the signature method for enforcing dependency is useful mainly for remote procedure calls on distributed databases. Several facts, behaviors, and conditions are worthy of note when using the signature method for enforcing procedural dependency in Oracle. They are as follows:

■ Signatures include the name of PL/SQL block, parameter datatype and direction (**in**, **out**, or **in out**), and return type (functions only).

■ Not included in signatures are parameter default values, parameter name, and implicit direction definition (i.e., omitting **in** from a parameter definition).

■ Certain changes to PL/SQL block specifications do not alter the signature. They include changing the name of a parameter or explicitly defining **in** for a parameter that was already an **in** parameter implicitly (i.e., direction had not been defined).

■ Only major datatype changes on parameters will alter the signature on a procedure or function. For example, changing a parameter from type VARCHAR2 to VARCHAR (or even ROWID) will *not* alter the signature, but a change from DATE to NUMBER (or DATE to ROWID) will.

■ Adding another procedure or function to the end of a package will not alter the other signatures in a package specification. Adding the procedure body somewhere in the middle or at the beginning will invalidate the signatures of procedures and functions in the package appearing after the new procedure or function.

■ Adding another procedure or function to an already overloaded procedure or function falls under the same rules as adding other procedures and functions to a package (i.e., its presence at the end will not cause the other signatures to become invalid). But, you will not be able to use the new procedure or function until the local procedure or function calling the new overloaded version is recompiled.

A point about major changes to parameter datatypes affecting signatures while minor changes not affecting the signature should be further clarified. A minor change in a datatype is one that alters the minutiae of a datatype but not the overall function. For example, changing the datatype of a parameter between INTEGER, NUMBER, REAL, FLOAT, DECIMAL,

DOUBLE_PRECISION, or SMALLINT does not alter the overall type of the parameter—that is to say the parameter will still be a number of some kind. The same can be said for altering a parameter between the VARCHAR2, VARCHAR, STRING, or ROWID datatypes. DATE datatypes are in their own category, so any type change from DATE to anything else, or from anything else to DATE, is by definition a major change. The same is true for MLS_LABEL. Changes between CHAR and CHARACTER are minor, as are changes between RAW and LONG RAW. A gray area in type changes resides in the change of certain numeric datatypes like INTEGER or NUMBER to other integer datatypes like PLS_INTEGER, POSITIVE, NATURAL, or BOOLEAN. These are actually major type changes and will affect signatures.

TIP
Although complex, it is vital that you understand the conditions that will and won't change a signature before proceeding to take OCP Exam 2.

Exercises

1. What is a signature? How is the signature method set up for use in Oracle?

2. What advantages does use of signatures afford when handling procedural dependency in distributed database environments? How may use of signatures in Oracle be a disadvantage (HINT: think overloading)?

3. In what compile-time situations will a signature be altered? When will a signature not be altered?

Chapter Summary

This chapter covers a number of important concepts related to management of procedures and functions. In addition, the topic of managing procedure dependency is covered. Finding information in the data dictionary and security options available for owners and users are also covered, along with the functions in Oracle that are available to track procedure and object dependency. Also, the special tasks involved in managing dependency both on individual databases and in a distributed database environment are covered. Together, these areas comprise about 23 percent of OCP Exam 2 test content. Although this chapter is slightly smaller than some of the others in the unit, it is highly important to understand these concepts in order to pass the test.

Managing procedures and functions involves the ability to find information about stored procedures in the data dictionary. Several views are available in the database dictionary for the purpose of finding information about stored procedures and functions. The first this chapter covered is the DBA_OBJECTS view. This one is important in its ability to provide status and timestamping information about a stored PL/SQL block (indeed, any database object). This timestamp is then used as a determinant in identifying procedure dependency, another topic of the chapter. To obtain information from DBA_OBJECTS related only to PL/SQL blocks, **select** against this view by where the value in the OBJECT_TYPE column is in the set ('PROCEDURE', 'FUNCTION', 'PACKAGE', 'PACKAGE BODY'). And make sure that your **select** statement has those PL/SQL types in uppercase, as they are shown here.

Other views used for PL/SQL source code management abound in the database. One is DBA_SOURCE, the view that offers the actual source code for the PL/SQL block. This is highly useful in the absence of effective source code control, because the view allows you complete access to the most current version of your application. Of course, if you want to revert to a previous version of the block, you have to store the source code yourself. Anyway, you should beware of selecting data from this view with the **select** * wildcard, because this causes several other items to be drawn from the table in addition to the source, which is stored in the TEXT column of this view. Instead, merely using the **select TEXT from DBA_SOURCE where NAME =** '*proc_name*' will work just fine for obtaining the source code for your procedures. Don't forget to issue the **spool** *filename*.**sql** statement before source code selection from the dictionary—most real-world procedures and functions are long, and it's a waste of time to type them over and over (although it does wonders for your abilities as a touch typist!).

It also makes sense to add the **order by LINE** clause to ensure that your source code is properly ordered in the output file, although experience tends to show the proper order is usually given by Oracle anyway. The

DBA_SOURCE view shows source code as of the most recent compile, so if you had a valid procedure in your database, recompiled it, and made it invalid, you now have the invalid version in DBA_SOURCE—not the valid one.

Another important view in the dictionary is DBA_ERRORS. It contains the most recent set of errors produced by code compilations for all users in the database. This view works best in conjunction with a tool to assist you with debugging, such as Procedure Builder. If you are not using a debugging tool to help with PL/SQL code compilation, you should have two sessions open during your compilation. The first session is used to perform the compile and the other to read the DBA_ERRORS table to ensure you are able to use the line number provided by DBA_ERRORS to find your error.

There is another important view in the data dictionary that you will use when you schedule PL/SQL process execution through the DBMS_JOB package (covered in Chapter 9). The view is called DBA_JOBS. This is important for batch scheduling and is used as an alternative to processing batch jobs via operating system scripts. Sometimes when using this view you get an error stating that there is a buffer overflow, which prevents you from obtaining the data in this view. To correct this, you can issue the **set arraysize 10** (or smaller) and **set maxdata 20000** (or greater, max. 32767) statements.

Oracle PL/SQL provides you with interesting opportunities to extend basic security functionality though the use of your application. To create a PL/SQL block, you need the **create procedure** system permission, and to run a named PL/SQL block, you must have **execute** permissions on that block. The chapter discussed that, if your procedure executes a database SQL statement, it is your obligation as owner of the procedure to ensure you have the required permission to execute the SQL statement, not the user executing your statement. All the user of your procedure needs is the privilege to **execute** the PL/SQL block.

On face value, it may seem that this is a security risk—after all, having people who don't have permission to perform certain SQL statements directly performing them under someone else's database access permissions sounds like you're sneaking around something, right? In reality, this feature actually allows you more flexibility in maintaining database security by allowing users only the access to the database they need via the application. Thus, for example you can give user ATHENA the ability to perform a certain **select** statement on the database by allowing her to execute **select_emp( )** instead of issuing a more broad **grant select on EMP to ATHENA** statement. Using PL/SQL applications to limit data access in this way gives the developer broad discretion in determining which users are allowed to see what data.

Procedure dependency is the other big topic this chapter covers. The chapter identifies two types of dependency in the Oracle database: procedure and object dependency. Procedure dependency is the reliance on usability a procedure has on the procedures or functions it calls. The example in the chapter was **proc_today_tran( )**, a procedure in a financial application that performs transactions in international currencies. It calls **convert_money( )** to perform the necessary conversions. This procedure, **proc_today_tran( )**, then has procedural dependency on **convert_money( )**, such that if **convert_money( )** gets dropped or invalidated for any reason, **proc_today_tran( )** will become invalid as well.

Object dependency is the reliance on underlying database objects like tables, views, sequences, and other things that a PL/SQL block may have in order to function properly. The example offered from the chapter was, again, the financial application. Within that application, you have the **convert_money( )** function, which uses exchange rates stored in the database as part of the EXCH_RATE table. If this table goes away, you lose the ability to use **convert_money( )** as well.

Oracle gives you the ability to track procedural dependencies with the data dictionary. A dictionary view called DBA_DEPENDENCIES stores the names of both PL/SQL blocks with procedure and object dependencies and the names of objects they depend on. This view allows you to find the dependencies your application has quickly and easily. Another set of views called DEPTREE and IDEPTREE offer information about the direct and indirect dependencies on a database.

If you need to make changes to one area of the application or database, such as dropping and re-creating a table, you will know where to look to find out what packages, procedures, or functions that act may have invalidated. These features help you prevent the situation on your database where you allow user access to Oracle after dropping and re-creating the table without recompiling the dependent PL/SQL blocks.

Several activities, then, will cause your PL/SQL program to become invalid. One is the invalidation of a program unit on which this program was dependent. The other is a change to the database objects it works with. Any change to the database applies, including a **drop** statement (as in **drop table** or **drop sequence**) or an **alter** statement. It does not matter if your **alter**

table statement is simply adding new columns that will never even be used by the application—the application component is still invalidated anyway.

If a PL/SQL block does become invalid, the process for making the application valid again must happen according to the procedure and object dependencies that exist on the database. Referenced objects must always be made valid first, followed by the referring object, in order to prevent the need for recompiling unnecessarily. Usually, the database objects like the underlying tables will need to be fixed first, followed by the PL/SQL blocks with only object dependencies on which other blocks have procedure dependencies. Finally, the referring PL/SQL blocks with those procedure dependencies can be compiled, after which all components of the Oracle database application should be valid and ready for use.

The mechanism and method used by Oracle for determining procedure and object dependency is called the timestamp method, or timestamping. The timestamp for a database object is stored in the data dictionary, and can be found in the DBA_OBJECTS table. This timestamp is stored and displayed in a specific date and time format, in the TIMESTAMP column. Though stored in the DBA_OBJECTS view as a CHAR(75) datatype, the format for timestamps corresponds to '*YYYY-MM-DD:HH24:MM:SS*' in DATE formatting terms. Using the timestamp method, PL/SQL database objects that depend on availability of other objects will be valid so long as the referring object's timestamp is younger than the timestamp of the referenced object. If the referenced object's timestamp is older, then the referring object will not be valid and will need to be recompiled.

Timestamping is an acceptable method for procedure dependency enforcement on the Oracle database when only one database is in use by the application. However, situations arise in use of distributed databases and the client/server application model that preclude use of timestamping to enforce procedure dependency in those cases. Though the timestamping method is always used in the case of database objects like tables, you can use alternatives to timestamping for enforcing procedure dependency in the Oracle database. Reasons not to use timestamping include situations where you have stored procedures on one database that reference stored procedures on another database via remote procedure calls through a database link. Another situation that your use of timestamping may not work well is when you have client-side PL/SQL programs that are stored on the client in executable form. If you recompile your server-side stored procedures, your client PL/SQL will be invalid the next time the user requires the procedure dependencies by way of the remote procedure calls. Since the source is not available to recompile, the user is stuck until they can get a new executable.

The signature method for procedural dependency enforcement can be an alternative. Using the signature method allows your PL/SQL on the client or on the local database to remain valid even when you execute certain types of recompilation on the remote PL/SQL block. A signature consists of several items correlating to the specification of the procedure or function. A specification is basically all the source code in a procedure or function that precedes the **is** or **as** keyword of the *main* execution section of the block. The name of the PL/SQL block is part of the signature, along with the parameters of the block, their types, and the direction of a parameter, like **in**, **out**, or **in out**, and the return datatype if the PL/SQL code block is a function. Items *not* part of the signature that *are* part of the specification include the name of the parameter and default value for the parameter. By definition, the body of any PL/SQL block is not considered part of the signature.

If signature methods are used on the database for enforcing procedure dependency, then only a PL/SQL compilation that alters the signature on the remote block will invalidate local PL/SQL blocks. Changing parameter default values, explicitly stating a parameter is an **in** parameter when it has already been defined that way implicitly (i.e., the **in** keyword was omitted), or "minor" changes to parameter datatype will not alter the signature. Changing the procedure body will never invalidate a signature unless the number of parameters the PL/SQL block accepts is also changed.

Items that will invalidate a signature include adding parameters, "major" changes to datatype in the specification, and changing the name of a code block. When using packages, if you add new procedures and functions to the package, you will not invalidate signatures on other code blocks in the package so long as you add your new block at the end of the package specification and body. If you add the code somewhere in the middle or at the beginning, every code block appearing after the new one will need its signature re-created.

Some tips about major and minor changes to datatypes. A major change to a parameter datatype includes any change that significantly alters the type of information the parameter will house. For example, a change from VARCHAR2 to ROWID or CHAR to CHARACTER is not significant, but a change from CHAR to DATE is. The final determinant for a minor or major datatype change rests with Oracle's grouping of like datatypes in PL/SQL. The chapter content indicates the major datatype groups, and the Two-Minute Drill lists each datatype in PL/SQL and what group it falls under.

To set up Oracle for use of the signature method for procedure dependency enforcement, you must do one of three things. Your DBA can change the REMOTE_DEPENDENCIES_MODE initialization parameter from **timestamp** to **signature** in the **init.ora** file for the Oracle database and shut down and restart the database. Alternately, your DBA can issue the **alter system set REMOTE_DEPENDENCIES_MODE = signature** as a user with **alter system** privileges. After one of these operations is complete and the signature method is being used, you then recompile all PL/SQL on the database that you want to have a signature attached to. You as an individual developer can use the **alter session set REMOTE_DEPENDENCIES_MODE = signature** to change your own session to use the signature method for enforcing constraints. You then recompile the PL/SQL blocks you own that you want Oracle to enforce procedure dependency on using the signature method.

Two-Minute Drill

- Dictionary views supporting stored PL/SQL in the Oracle database include:

  - DBA_OBJECTS: Shows validity and timestamp information about the block. Important columns to remember are TIMESTAMP, LAST_DDL_TIME, and STATUS.

  - DBA_SOURCE: Stores source code for the block. Important columns include TEXT to store line of source code and LINE to order by line number.

  - DBA_ERRORS: Shows compilation errors for the block. Important columns include NAME to show the name of the block that generated the error, TEXT to store the error message, and LINE to indicate the line on which the error appears.

  - DBA_JOBS: Displays information about job scheduling for the block. The output from this view may overload your output buffer. You may need to issue **set arraysize 10** (or less) and **set maxdata 32767**.

- The privilege to create PL/SQL blocks is **create procedure**. It must be granted to the would-be code owner. To run a procedure, the owner (or other privileged user) grants **execute** privilege to the user who wants to run it.

- The owner of a PL/SQL block must have all object permissions required to run any SQL statement present in the block. These permissions must be granted directly to the owner, not via a role. The only permission the user of that block needs is **execute** on the block.

- The fact presented in the previous point allows you to grant table access to a user via a PL/SQL program while revoking the more general **select** object privilege from the user.

- PL/SQL code can manage user access to the precision of a single SQL statement, giving you more security options than blanket **grant select on** *tblname* permission granting to your users.

- Two types of database dependencies available in Oracle are object and procedure dependency:

    - Object dependency is when a PL/SQL block relies on availability of a database object such as a table or sequence to do its job.

    - Procedure dependency is when a PL/SQL block relies on availability of another PL/SQL block to do its job.

- The DBA_DEPENDENCIES dictionary view in Oracle allows you to see the different procedure and object dependencies on the Oracle database.

- Important columns in the DBA_DEPENDENCIES view are NAME, which names the referring or calling program, REFERENCED_NAME, which names the referenced or called program, and REFERENCED_TYPE, which helps determine if this is an object or procedure dependency.

- Additionally, the REFERENCED_LINK_NAME column gives you a database link if the referring program depends on a remote procedure on another database.

- The DEPTREE and IDEPTREE views allow you to obtain indirect and direct dependency information for your application.

- DEPTREE shows information about direct and indirect dependencies in your database. The columns in the DEPTREE view include NESTED_LEVEL, OBJECT_TYPE, OWNER, OBJECT_NAME, and SEQ#.

- IDEPTREE shows similar information as DEPTREE, but in a simple graphical format where dependent objects are listed below and indented from the objects they depend on. The column in IDEPTREE is DEPENDENCIES.

- For PL/SQL blocks that perform SQL operations on a table, if the table is dropped or altered in any way, you will have to recompile any PL/SQL block that has an object dependency on that table.

- For PL/SQL blocks that call other blocks, the other block is called the referenced block. If the referenced block is recompiled or invalidated, the calling block will also be invalidated.

- To correct a situation where a procedure or object dependency invalidates several different items in an application, whatever corrections required must occur in the order of dependency, from referenced object to referring object, starting with object dependencies and ending with procedure dependencies.

- Object and procedure dependencies are enforced using timestamps in Oracle by default.

- An object's timestamp is a character string of the date and time the object was last modified or compiled.

- The timestamp format is YYYY-MM-DD:HH24:MI:SS.

- Timestamps have several drawbacks:

  - Time may not be synchronized across multiple machines in distributed systems. Machines may be in different time zones, making it difficult to revalidate programs with procedure dependencies if one is consistently compiled "later" than the other (remember the London-Utah example?).

  - In client/server applications, source code may not be available on the client machine to allow the server to recompile when required.

  - These difficulties stem from the use of a relative concept in an absolute way.

- Oracle provides the signature method for enforcing procedure dependency to allow you some flexibility in maintaining PL/SQL on distributed systems.

- Instead of using a timestamp to determine if the referring procedure is invalid, Oracle will check to see if the signature has changed. If so, the referring procedure is invalid.

- A signature is basically a conglomeration of different elements from a PL/SQL block specification. A PL/SQL block specification consists of the following:

  - PL/SQL block name

  - Number of parameters

  - Parameter datatype

  - Parameter direction, like **in**, **out**, or **in out**

  - Datatype returned (function only)

- A signature is invalidated when:

    - You change the number of parameters in the PL/SQL block specification.

    - You change the position of a parameter in the list of parameters for the block.

    - You make a "major" change to the datatype of a parameter.

    - You change the direction of a parameter (exception: implicit **in** to explicit **in**).

    - You change the return datatype of the function.

    - You add a procedure or function to a package before other procedures and functions that are already compiled parts of the package. If so, the procedures and functions after the one you added will have invalid signatures.

- A signature is *not* invalidated when:

    - You alter the body of a procedure only

    - You change the name of a parameter but not its position in the list, its datatype, or number of parameters in the block

    - You make a "minor" change to a parameter's datatype

    - You change the default value for a parameter

    - You change an implicit **in** parameter (i.e., one declared without a direction) to explicit **in**

- Minor datatype changes are changes from one type to another within one category. Major changes of datatypes are those changes that cause the parameter's datatype to switch to a new category. Categories are defined as follows:

    - **VARCHAR**   VARCHAR2, VARCHAR, STRING, LONG, ROWID

    - **CHAR**   CHAR, CHARACTER

    - **RAW**   RAW, LONG RAW

- **NUMERIC**   NUMBER, INTEGER, INT, SMALLINT, DECIMAL, DEC, REAL, FLOAT, NUMERIC, DOUBLE_PRECISION
- **INTEGER**   BINARY_INTEGER, PLS_INTEGER, BOOLEAN, NATURAL, POSITIVE, POSITIVEN, NATURALN
- **DATE**   DATE
- **TRUSTED**   MLS_LABEL

Chapter Questions

1. **UPDATE_PTABLE( ) performs some updates on an underlying table called PTABLE. According to the signature method of procedure dependency enforcement, if a column is added to PTABLE, what happens to UPDATE_PTABLE( )?**

   A. PTABLE is dropped

   B. Nothing, the specification of PTABLE did not change

   C. Procedure **update_ptable( )** is invalidated

   D. Nothing, the specification of **update_ptable( )** did not change

2. **The best source of timestamp information in the Oracle database is which of the following items?**

   A. USER_SOURCE dictionary view

   B. Source code for the PL/SQL program

   C. DBA_ERRORS dictionary view

   D. ALL_OBJECTS dictionary view

3. **What is the effect of revoking SELECT access on table EMPLOYEES from user JOYCE after granting her EXECUTE privilege on SELECT_EMP( ), a procedure containing SELECT * FROM EMPLOYEES?**

   A. Her execution of **select_emp( )** will work properly.

   B. Her execution of **select_emp( )** will work, but the **select** will encounter "permission denied" errors.

C. Her **execute** privilege on **select_emp( )** will be revoked.

D. Oracle will disconnect when **select_emp( )** is executed.

4. Function CALORIE_COUNT( ) is compiled on the Oracle database using the signature method of procedure dependency enforcement. In which three of the following situations will a signature be invalidated?

   A. When a parameter name is changed

   B. When a new parameter is added

   C. When **calorie_count( )** is part of a package and a new procedure is added to the package before it

   D. When an **in** parameter becomes **in out**

5. The developer wants to obtain a source code listing from Oracle. Which of the following statements is most appropriate for the task?

   A. select * **from** USER_SOURCE **where** NAME = '*proc_name*';

   B. select TEXT **from** USER_ERRORS **where** NAME = '*proc_name*'; **order by** LINE

   C. select LINE **from** USER_SOURCE **where** NAME = '*proc_name*';

   D. select TEXT **from** USER_SOURCE **where** NAME = '*proc_name*' **order by** LINE;

6. Procedure PROC1( ) calls function FUNC1( ), which in turn updates data on the TABLE1 table. The developer drops TABLE1 accidentally. What must be done to rectify the problem?

   A. Re-create TABLE1, then recompile **proc1( )**, then recompile **func1( )**

   B. Re-create TABLE1, then recompile **func1( )**, then recompile **proc1( )**

   C. Recompile **func1( )**, then recreate TABLE1, then recompile **proc1( )**

   D. Recompile **proc1( )**, then recompile **func1( )**, then recreate TABLE1

7. **Function FOO( ) references table FOOBAR via an invalid database link. If FOOBAR has not been modified, what should the status of FOO( ) be?**

A. Valid, because the underlying table hasn't been modified

B. Invalid, because the database link is invalid

C. Valid, because the signature method is being used to enforce procedure dependency

D. Invalid, because Oracle does not support object dependencies through database links

8. **Which two of the following methods specify PL/SQL signatures in effect for all sessions in the Oracle database?**

A. **alter system set** REMOTE_DEPENDENCIES_MODE=TRUE

B. **alter system set** REMOTE_DEPENDENCIES_MODE=**signature**

C. **alter session set** REMOTE_DEPENDENCIES_MODE=**timestamp**

D. Alter REMOTE_DEPENDENCIES_MODE in **init.ora** and set it to **signature**

9. **The developer wants to change a parameter's datatype from ROWID to something else, but doesn't want to invalidate the signature. Which of the following datatypes are acceptable alternatives?**

A. VARCHAR

B. DATE

C. CHARACTER

D. RAW

10. **Signatures are in use on the Oracle database. Function F1( ) is compiled containing an INSERT statement on table T1. A NOT NULL constraint is then added to T1. What is the status of function F1( )?**

A. Valid, because the signature on T1 did not change

B. Invalid, because timestamps are always used for enforcing object dependencies

C. Valid, because table T1 was not dropped

D. Invalid, because the constraint added altered the specification on function **F1( )**

11. **Which of the following cannot be altered about a function without invalidating its signature?**

A. Parameter names

B. Default values

C. Direction from implicit to explicitly defined **in**

D. Return datatype from CHAR to RAW

12. **The DBA_ERRORS dictionary view contains which of the following information?**

A. Compilation and runtime errors for all PL/SQL on the database

B. Compilation errors for user-owned PL/SQL code only

C. Compilation errors for all PL/SQL on the database

D. Runtime errors for user-owned PL/SQL code only

13. **Procedure P1( ) calls function F1( ), which contains a SELECT statement on table T1. All objects are stored on one database. Table T1 is dropped. What happens to procedure P1?**

A. Procedure **P1( )** is invalidated immediately

B. Procedure **P1( )** is invalidated the next time it is called

C. Procedure **P1( )** stays valid as long as function **F1( )** is never called

D. Procedure **P1( )** is dropped along with table T1

Answers to Chapter Questions

1. C.   Procedure **update_ptable( )** is invalidated

Explanation   The signature method of procedure dependency enforcement does not apply to database objects, which are marked only by their timestamp. If an object dependency is violated, then the referring object is invalidated. Choices A and B are not logically correct based on the data in the question. Choice D is irrelevant—you do not care about whether or not the specification for **update_ptable( )** changed, because again the problem lies with the object dependency. Beware of the mention of signature method in this question—it is potentially misleading.

2. D.   ALL_OBJECTS dictionary view

Explanation   Though in compilation a PL/SQL block will obtain the timestamp of all objects it depends on, neither the source code itself nor the view in which it is stored (USER_SOURCE) is a good place to find that information, knocking off choices A and B. DBA_ERRORS is also incorrect, eliminating choice C. Recall that DBA_OBJECTS and USER_OBJECTS both contain timestamp and status information for all database objects in the database and all objects owned by the current user, respectively.

3. A.   Her execution of **select_emp( )** will work properly.

Explanation   The only privilege user JOYCE needs in this situation is **execute** on **select_emp( )**. Once issued, any other privilege for viewing data on the tables accessible via the application can be revoked, limiting blanket access to data while supporting more narrow access programmatically. Only the owner needs **select** access on the underlying objects used by **select_emp( )**, eliminating choice B, the only other choice that can even pretend to be viable.

4. B., C., and D.

Explanation   Only choice A in this question offers an option that will leave a PL/SQL signature valid if executed. The name of a parameter can change so long as the direction and datatype for the parameter do not. In all other choices, the signature will become invalid. Careful review of signatures and the items that can and cannot invalidate them is the best way to ensure your understanding of this feature.

5. D.   **select** TEXT **from** USER_SOURCE **where** NAME = '*proc_name*' **order by** LINE

Explanation   The TEXT column of USER_SOURCE contains the actual source code for the PL/SQL block. Ordering by LINE will prevent any chance of source code being returned in incorrect order. Using the * wildcard to draw data out of the database is inappropriate in choice A because too much data will be selected, cluttering the source code file. Choice B is incorrect because compilation errors are stored in USER_ERRORS, not source code. Choice C will only give you the line numbers for the source code, and is incorrect.

6. B.   Re-create TABLE1, then recompile **func1( )**, then recompile **proc1( )**

Explanation   When dependencies have caused objects to become invalid, the right way to set things straight is to handle the underlying objects first, followed by those PL/SQL programs with object dependencies, followed by PL/SQL programs with procedure dependencies. Choice A is incorrect because the procedure dependencies are handled before the object dependencies in this situation. Choice C is wrong because the object dependencies are being handled before the object itself is corrected. Choice C is wrong because, again, the procedure dependencies are handled first.

7. B.   Invalid, because the database link is invalid

Explanation   Since the database link is an underlying database object, it must be corrected in order for **foo( )** to be recompiled. All options that state the function is valid are wrong outright, while the rationale given for invalidity in choice D is false.

8. B. and D.

Explanation   Setting REMOTE_DEPENDENCIES_MODE to **signature** can be done either in the **init.ora** file followed by restarting the database or by issuing the **alter system** statement to change the value set for this parameter. Choice C simply changes the dependency enforcement to **timestamp**, and furthermore only does so for the current session. Choice A is wrong because REMOTE_DEPENDENCIES_MODE is not a TRUE/FALSE parameter.

9. A.   VARCHAR

Explanation   According to the categories of datatypes in PL/SQL, the change from ROWID to VARCHAR is "minor," or within that category, while the others are "major," or from one category to another. Since signatures are not invalidated by minor datatype changes, choice A is correct.

10. B.   Invalid, because timestamps are always used for enforcing object dependencies

Explanation   This question is essentially the same as question 1. Review its explanation for rationale on why B is correct. Important to remember is that tables are marked for validity with timestamps, not signatures.

11. D.   Return datatype from CHAR to RAW

Explanation   As with parameter datatypes, the major change in return datatype for this function renders the signature invalid. All other changes will not impact the signature. Refer to the Two-Minute Drill for a treatment of the actions that invalidate signatures and those that leave signatures alone.

12. C.   Compilation errors for all PL/SQL on the database

Explanation   All compilation errors for all PL/SQL currently invalid in the database can be found in DBA_ERRORS. Choice B is almost right—except for the fact that the USER_ views contain information pertaining to the current user only, not DBA_ views. Choices A and D are both incorrect because runtime errors are not tracked in any of the ERRORS views on the data dictionary.

13. A.   Procedure **P1( )** is invalidated immediately

Explanation   Oracle wastes no time invalidating local PL/SQL code when dependencies are violated. Only in the case of remote PL/SQL on either the client or another Oracle database would Oracle wait to invalidate **P1( )** until it was called again. Choices C and D do not take into account many factors about the way Oracle enforces procedure and object dependency, and thus they are wrong.

CHAPTER

9

Developing and Using Packages

In this chapter, you will cover the following topics on developing and using packages:

- Developing PL/SQL packages
- Managing packages on the database
- Using Oracle server–supplied packages

Modularity should be the goal of every programmer. Modular code is more flexible and reusable because the procedures and functions only perform one or two tasks. Each module then becomes a building block that can be incorporated many different times in different places within the same or different programs. Originally, modularity and the use of procedures and functions was designed to phase out "spaghetti code" produced as a result of numerous **goto** statements in a large program block. However, large applications often have scores or hundreds of different procedures and functions. Each of them is modular, and perform only a few operations. But, hundreds of them available on one Oracle database creates a mess of its own, a needle in a haystack, if you will, in which you could really use that one program component—if you could only find it in the mass of named PL/SQL on the database. Packages are a way to change this scenario by grouping procedures and functions together logically, either by function, application, dependency, or any other category you can think of. This chapter will focus on packages, which have been mentioned in several different places so far. The development and use of packages will be considered, along with the special uses of a package you may have in an application. The usage and role of Oracle-supplied packages found inside the database server will be treated as well. Together, these topics comprise about 24 percent of test content on OCP Exam 2.

Developing PL/SQL Packages

In this section, you will cover the following points on developing PL/SQL packages:

- Overview of using PL/SQL packages
- Creating packages to bundle PL/SQL constructs

- Public and private objects in packages
- Debugging package compilation

Packages are perhaps one of the most significant achievements Oracle has made to commercial PL/SQL programming. Unlike stand-alone functions and procedures, packages allow you to take a full-scale approach to application development by combining the program units you have learned how to develop in the last several chapters into a cohesive and robust application. You already know of several packages in the Oracle database and in Procedure Builder, and now you will find out how packages work, and why. In addition, you will cover the mechanics of developing packages, along with methods for their debugging.

Overview of Using PL/SQL Packages

Oracle makes available special constructs called "packages" to help developers group blocks of loose PL/SQL code into logical units. You have already been introduced to several packages, both in the database like DBMS_OUTPUT, and in Procedure Builder like the DEBUG or TEXT_IO package. But, while you have been shown that there are packages, even shown how to call program units residing in packages, you may still wonder—what exactly is a package? A package is a PL/SQL development construct that allows you to combine several program units into one logical structure.

TIP
When you take OCP test 2, on your questions that involve looking at package source code, **make sure you read the question before you even look at the package code!** *Read the question first, then read the code later, and you'll waste little time getting correct answers on these questions.*

Rather than having dozens (or perhaps hundreds) of individual program units floating around in the Oracle database, it may be difficult for you as the developer to understand what each program unit does. If you're the lone developer, this may not be a problem for you since you wrote and now maintain all the code. But if you're like most developers, you work in a team, and without some cohesive development strategy, you may be less able to reuse a team member's code if you have little idea what those program units out there are doing.

Package Features and Benefits

Packages relieve some of the problems in this situation. They allow you to group several program units, types, exceptions, variables, and other PL/SQL language constructs together according to your needs or logical collection. For example, you may have 30 program units for an application that fall into roughly three areas: SQL statement processing, obtaining valid values, and manipulating temporary tables for complex accounting algorithms. Rather than simply allowing those 30 program units to sit out there loose, you instead may want to group those units together into three distinct packages according to business function.

Another option for grouping program units into packages relates to building an application. One unit in the package acts as the unit that calls all others, akin to a **main( )** procedure in C. The others act in a supporting capacity by performing the smaller, modular function. In this way, a package encapsulates all PL/SQL code for all program components of an application.

Still another benefit for using packages is the ability to hide program logic behind another layer of abstraction. A package allows procedures and functions within it to publish their specifications together, while the package body containing all program unit bodies relieves another programmer from having to think about whatever complexity lies "behind the curtain." You can use this feature in conjunction with the PL/SQL wrapper program as well, which allows you to encrypt the logic of each program unit to hide any trade secrets and prevent users from modifying your packages as well. Figure 9-1 illustrates the use of packages in the Oracle database, along with visual representation of some of the examples provided in this discussion.

Finally, you will see better performance on procedures and functions grouped as a package because calling one program unit in the package causes the whole package to be loaded into memory. This fact means that, when you call a different procedure in the package later, that different package will be loaded into memory as well, thus being more accessible for your use.

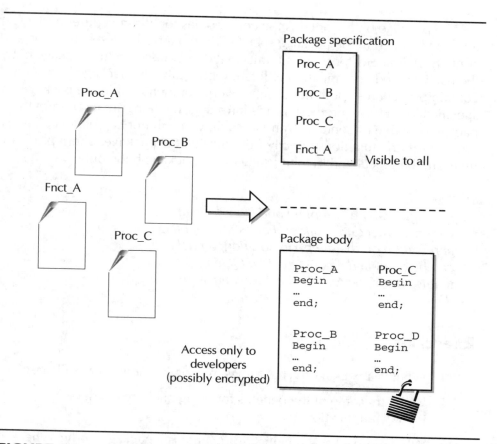

FIGURE 9-1. *Using packages for application development*

Package Specification and Package Body

A package consists of two structures: package specification and package body. These constructs come to PL/SQL from Ada, and the concept of specification and body stored as two separate modules is nothing new. A package specification is a unit of PL/SQL code that names the procedures, functions, exceptions, user-defined types, variables, and other PL/SQL constructs that are available as a part of this package. Consider a specification to be a package's "table of contents"—it lists what is available for use in the package body, without wallowing you in the mire of each unit's intricacies.

The package body contains the code bodies for all procedures and functions named in the package specification. If a package specification contains definitions for program units that don't appear in the package body, the package body compilation will fail. Optionally, the package body can contain procedures and functions that were not identified in the package specification. However, these procedures and functions are not part of the package's "table of contents," and as such, you will not be able to call those procedures and functions directly from outside the package. These program units are then localized in their usage to the package body only.

TIP
Packages can be compiled and stored locally within a Procedure Builder, Forms, or Reports application on the client. In addition, a package can be compiled against the PL/SQL engine that is part of the Oracle database and stored there as well.

Exercises

1. What is a package? What things may be included in a package?

2. What are some of the benefits for using packages to develop PL/SQL applications?

3. What is a package specification? What is a package body? Where can packages be stored?

Creating Packages to Bundle PL/SQL Constructs

Now that you understand the fundamental premise behind packages, turn your attention to creating them. Special syntactic and semantic constructs are required for creating a package, and both the creation of package specification and package body are covered in this discussion. An example to use for this discussion will now be described. You are enhancing functionality on the existing international financial application introduced in Chapter 8. Recall that the application consisted of **proc_today_tran( )**,

proc_yest_trans( ), and **proc_mnth_trans( )**, which are procedures that execute the actual transactions of the financial application. In addition, you have **convert_money( )**, called by all the other procedures to help with converting between different currencies as a part of the international financial transactions. The database includes the EXCH_RATE table, which stores your exchange rate information.

Assume there are hundreds of other procedures and functions on the database housing this application. Your enhancement goal is to convert the application from one that uses a lot of loose program units to one that encapsulates program units into packages according to functionality. Take a moment to look at these four program units. There are many different ways to categorize these according to functionality. One way is to categorize these program units according to those that process transactions and utilities that support transaction processing. Assuming you take this course of action, you may create two new packages called TRANS_PROCS and TRANS_UTILS.

Developing Package Specifications

First, you develop your package specifications. Let's look at the sample specifications for these packages. The sample is given in the following code block:

```
CREATE OR REPLACE PACKAGE trans_utils IS
    FUNCTION convert_money (
       p_from_crcy             VARCHAR2,
       p_to_crcy       IN OUT VARCHAR2, -- example only, do not try this at home
       p_from_amt              NUMBER,
       valid_date              DATE
    ) RETURN NUMBER;
END;

CREATE OR REPLACE PACKAGE trans_procs IS
    PROCEDURE proc_today_tran (
    p_today_date            DATE
    );
    PROCEDURE proc_yest_tran (
    p_yest_date             DATE
    );
    PROCEDURE proc_mnth_tran (
    p_mnth_name             VARCHAR2
    );
END;
```

Observe that the overall syntax for creating packages is **create package** *pkg_name* **as** ... **end**. Within the ellipses, you can place the program unit specifications for your functions and procedures, along with any record type declarations, exceptions, cursors, or anything else so long as it is not a PL/SQL code body. No code bodies are allowed. Each of the program unit specifications listed doesn't include the **create** keyword. This is because you are not creating the function, procedure, or any other component as an individual component, but rather you are creating a package comprised of those units.

TIP
You must compile a package specification before compiling its body.

The package specification is actually an excellent place to provide documentation on how to use the programs contained in the package. Commenting a line of code is done with a double dash (**--**). This method works for commenting one line of code only, while if you want to comment a substantial block of text, the standard C notation for comments (**/* */**) works nicely. The following block demonstrates use of comments in a package specification:

```
CREATE OR REPLACE PACKAGE trans_utils IS
-- This package contains utilities used by the transaction application
   FUNCTION convert_money (
-- This function converts money from one currency to another.
-- You pass in four parameters, the first two are the "from" currency and
-- the "to" currency. The function also returns the "to" currency you passed.
-- The next parameter is the amount you want to convert out of the "from"
-- currency. The last parameter tells Oracle what date to use for selection
-- of the appropriate exchange rate. The function returns a number,
-- corresponding to the monetary amount in "to" currency you passed in as
-- "from" currency.
      p_from_crcy          VARCHAR2,
      p_to_crcy    IN OUT VARCHAR2, -- example only, do not try this at home
      p_from_amt           NUMBER,
      valid_date           DATE
   ) RETURN NUMBER;
END;
```

Developing Package Bodies

After defining the package specification, you then must define and compile the package body. Because only the code for **convert_money( )** was given in Chapter 8, the discussion is simplified by only showing a package body for the TRANS_UTILS package. The package body is shown in the following code block:

```
CREATE OR REPLACE PACKAGE BODY trans_utils IS
    FUNCTION convert_money (
        p_from_crcy         VARCHAR2,
        p_to_crcy      IN OUT VARCHAR2, -- returning a value here, watch out!
        p_from_amt         NUMBER,
        valid_date          DATE
    ) RETURN NUMBER IS
        my_exch_rate NUMBER(15,4);
        my_ret_val   NUMBER(15,4); -- return value for the function
    BEGIN
        -- grab the exchange rate from the appropriate table
        -- and put it in MY_EXCH_RATE
        SELECT exch_rate INTO my_exch_rate FROM EXCH_RATE
        WHERE to_crcy = p_to_crcy AND from_crcy = p_from_crcy
        AND valid_date = sysdate;
        -- The big tricky calculation: convert the money to a new
        -- currency
        my_ret_val := p_from_amt * my_exch_rate;
        -- now, give it back to the caller
        RETURN my_ret_val;
    END;
END;
```

Observe the following points about developing package bodies. First, the general syntax for this operation is **create package body** *pkg_name* **is begin ...end**. Between the ellipses is where you place your PL/SQL code for the program units, as shown here for TRANS_UTILS.

Using Procedure Builder

The example presented is only a simple package specification and body to illustrate basic syntax and semantics of package creation. A real-world example would include different types of PL/SQL components, including PL/SQL program units, constants, variables, exceptions, types, and the rest.

Note that both flat files compiled against the server-side PL/SQL engine and use of Procedure Builder is acceptable for development of PL/SQL packages. For reasons of simplicity both in the development and ease of compilation, using Procedure Builder is recommended over SQL*Plus and text files containing your source code. You can create a new package stored program unit by first connecting to the database, and then drilling down to the Stored Program Units node in the Object Navigator for the user you connected as, and then clicking on the Create button in the left margin of the Object Navigator. Alternately, you can open the Stored Program Unit Editor using the Program | Stored Program Unit Editor menu option available when the PL/SQL Interpreter is in the foreground of Procedure Builder, then pressing the New button in that module. Either method brings you to the interactive window, displayed in Figure 9-2, where you define your package title, along with whether you will create a specification or a body. As with creation of other program units, Procedure Builder provides you with the fundamental syntax for package specification and body definition.

TIP
Remember, your package specification cannot name a program unit that is not also defined in the package body (public constructs). Your package body may contain program units not named in the specification, however (private constructs).

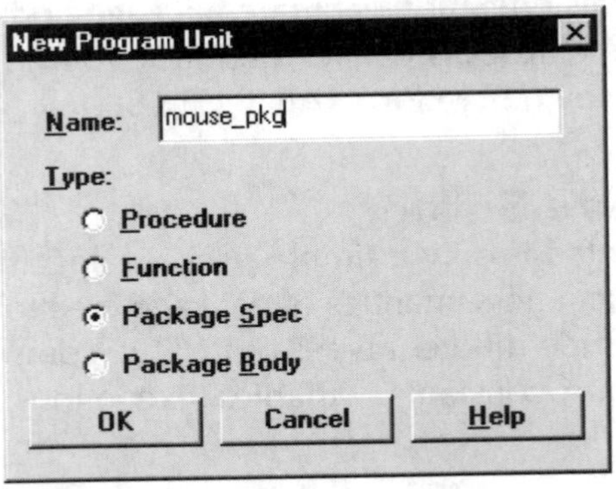

FIGURE 9-2. *Creating new packages in Procedure Builder*

It is important to remember that Procedure Builder allows you to specify less base unit code for package specification and package body creation. You merely need to say **package** *pkg_name* **is** in Procedure Builder instead of the full-blown **create or replace package** *pkg_name* **is** required for SQL. The extra keywords are filled automatically by Procedure Builder.

TIP

Beware the functions that do not restrict database references in Oracle!! You must specify your package and database state in Oracle for functions that change information on the database in the package specification. This is because your package body is hidden from the application at run time. Review the explanation of pragma **restrict_references** *appearing later in this chapter for more information.*

Exercises

1. What is the basic syntax for creating a package specification? Can you create program unit specifications for which there are no bodies in the package body? Why or why not?

2. What is the basic syntax for creating package bodies? How are comments indicated in packages? What parts of basic syntax does Procedure Builder handle that you must explicitly code in SQL*Plus?

Public and Private Objects in Packages

An important point made earlier about program units and packages will now be reiterated. If you define the specification for a program unit in the package specification, the package body must contain the source code for that code block or else the package body compilation will fail. *But what about the other way around?* Oracle is fine with your decision to include program units in the package body that are not declared in the specification. Say, for example, you want to write an application much like the typical C program, with a **main( )** procedure that calls several other procedures and functions. However, you don't want any other application other than this one to use the program units, because there is perhaps some sensitive trade secrets embedded into the source code. You may have 15 or more program units written into the package body to help the **main( )** procedure, but the package specification still looks like the code in the following block:

```
CREATE OR REPLACE PACKAGE trans_appl AS
    PROCEDURE MAIN;
END;
```

Now, the program units in the package body that were not defined in the package specification are considered *private* objects, while the **main( )** procedure that is defined as part of the package specification is considered a *public* object. The difference is self-evident—one is published to the world of Oracle database users. The **main( )** procedure can be called by users from the SQL*Plus sessions, from applications that interface with Oracle, from Procedure Builder, from Pro*C programs, and from other places.

The other procedures are private, which means that they can only be called and used by those procedures actually in the package body. For example, if the **foo( )**, **foobar( )**, and **barfoo( )** procedures and functions were defined as part of the package body, the **main( )** procedure can call them within package TRANS_APPL. You, on the other hand, cannot call **foo( )**, **foobar( )**, and **barfoo( )** from the Procedure Builder PL/SQL Interpreter, even if you were connected to the database.

Making program units within a package public and private, then, is a matter of including or excluding the program unit specification with or from the package specification. The same can be said for variables, constants, types, exceptions, and other PL/SQL constructs that are defined and used in the package body but not included in the specification. Remember, the package specification is like a table of contents—if you do not include information about your components in it, no one will know it is there, and even if they did, they couldn't use it.

An important benefit is provided with the use of packages that employ variables or cursors declared to be public, and are contained in the package specification. You can use these variables across all procedures and functions in your package, eliminating the need to populate the database with temporary information from one procedure only to **select** it back out for use somewhere else.

Exercises

1. Can package specifications contain procedure definitions that do not have bodies in the package body? Explain.

2. What is a public object? What is a private object? How is privacy in packages determined?

Compiling and Running Packages

Once you have developed your package specification and body code, you should compile it. Packages can be compiled either on the client side or the server, so long as there is a PL/SQL engine to use. Just as there are two ways to develop PL/SQL packages, so too are there two ways to compile them: with SQL*Plus and Procedure Builder.

The same issues with compiling procedures and functions with SQL*Plus against the Oracle PL/SQL server-side engine and the DBA_ERRORS view exist with compiling packages. In fact, given that most packages contain several PL/SQL blocks, the difficulties of locating errors in the code are often compounded. Because of this reason, you should strongly consider the advantages Procedure Builder offers for code compilation. Figure 9-3 shows you the use of the Stored Program Unit Editor module to develop and compile packages.

There is another important fact to remember about code compilation. The package specification must be compiled before the package body. Also, as mentioned, the package body must contain program unit code bodies for all program unit specifications or else the compilation of the package body will fail. One factor about package specifications and package bodies that does not impact compilation is program unit order. In other words, the program units defined in the package body needn't be listed in the same order as the specification.

Important to remember about packages is that you do not run the package itself—you run the components in it. But, you usually have to precede the program units in the package with the package name. After the code is compiled successfully, you can run code in the package by using the PKG_NAME.**proc_name( )** syntax. From SQL*Plus, you must precede references to code in packages with the **execute** command, while in Procedure Builder, you merely identify the procedure using the syntax

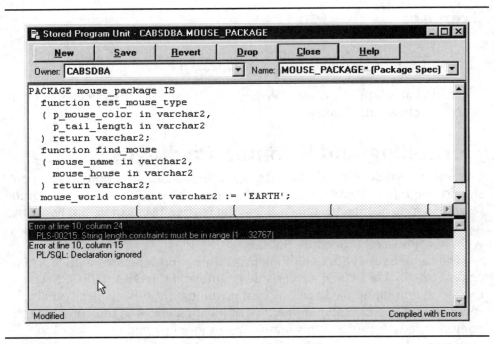

```
Stored Program Unit - CABSDBA.MOUSE_PACKAGE

  New        Save       Revert      Drop       Close       Help

Owner: CABSDBA                          ▼  Name: MOUSE_PACKAGE* (Package Spec) ▼

PACKAGE mouse_package IS
  function test_mouse_type
  ( p_mouse_color in varchar2,
    p_tail_length in varchar2
  ) return varchar2;
  function find_mouse
  ( mouse_name in varchar2,
    mouse_house in varchar2
  ) return varchar2;
  mouse_world constant varchar2 := 'EARTH';

Error at line 10, column 24
  PLS-00215: String length constraints must be in range (1 .. 32767)
Error at line 10, column 15
  PL/SQL: Declaration ignored

Modified                                            Compiled with Errors
```

FIGURE 9-3. *Developing and compiling packages*

mentioned previously. The following example presents a call to a procedure in a package from SQL*Plus, TRANS_APPL.**proc_today_trans( )**.

```
SQL> execute TRANS_APPL.proc_today_trans(sysdate);
```

Instead, in the PL/SQL Interpreter module of Procedure Builder, you still simply reference the package and procedure as follows.

```
PL/SQL> TRANS_APPL.proc_today_trans(sysdate);
```

TIP
On recompiling package bodies due to code changes, you only need to recompile the package specification when something about the parameters changes in a code body that makes the package body compilation fail.

Exercises

1. How do you compile packages in SQL*Plus? How about in Procedure Builder? How do you run code blocks in packages in SQL*Plus? What about Procedure Builder?

2. Say you make a change to a procedure in a package body. The parameters to the procedure do not change, only some program logic in the body. Do you need to recompile the package specification? Why or why not?

3. Can you think of a situation where you might need to recompile the package specification along with the body? Can you think of a situation where you might need to recompile the specification *without* recompiling the body?

Managing PL/SQL Packages on the Database

In this section, you will cover the following points on managing packages on the database:

- Managing package specification dependency
- Managing compilation dependency and packages
- Managing procedure dependency and packages
- Using pragma RESTRICT_REFERENCES
- Managing packages and security

You will recall the discussion of PL/SQL program unit management from the previous chapter. Several of the same issues of code management are present in packages as well. In this section, you will cover the issues associated with program unit dependency when the program units are part of packages. Various design methods are considered, along with their merits and shortcomings, with the ultimate offering of logically grouping program units into packages according to their dependencies. Finally, some security issues will be presented with respect to package code management.

Managing Package Specification Dependency

There is an important dependency related to packages that you may have identified already. That dependency is the one formed on the package specification by the package body. Say, for example, that you compile both the specification and body successfully. Both the specification and the body can be found in the DBA_OBJECTS dictionary view, complete with timestamp information and a status flag. The following code block identifies for example's sake the status of TRANS_APPL once you compile it:

```
SQL> select * from dba_objects where object_name = 'TRANS_APPL';

OWNER OBJECT_NAME O_ID OBJECT_TYPE  CREATED   LAST_DDL_ TIMESTAMP
----- ----------- ---- ------------ --------- --------- -------------------
STATUS
------
STACY TRANS_APPL  4060 PACKAGE      21-SEP-99 21-SEP-99 1999-09-21:17:02:54
VALID

STACY TRANS_APPL  4061 PACKAGE BODY 21-SEP-99 21-SEP-99 1999-09-21:18:05:29
VALID
```

Example 1: Package Body Compile Failures and Package Specification

Now, let's say a bug was located in the **proc_mnth_tran( )** procedure. You go into Procedure Builder and make the necessary modification to the package body without changing procedure specifications, and then you recompile the package body. Regardless of whether the body recompiles successfully, so long as you do not change the program unit specification the package specification should be fine. This is because your specification to the procedure did not change, although the logic did. This important *lack* of procedure dependency is what makes packages so great. Rather than having to recompile all PL/SQL programs that had procedure dependencies of the one you changed, you simply get to recompile the one you changed as part of a package body, and other parts of the application remain undisturbed. In fact, even if you attempt to change the program unit specification in your package body, the package specification is still valid even though the package body compilation fails. The following code block demonstrates package specification and body status if you recompile a package body and it fails due to syntax errors:

```
SQL> select * from dba_objects where object_name = 'TRANS_APPL';

OWNER OBJECT_NAME O_ID OBJECT_TYPE   CREATED   LAST_DDL_ TIMESTAMP
----- ----------- ---- ------------ --------- --------- -------------------
STATUS
------
STACY TRANS_APPL  4060 PACKAGE       21-SEP-99 21-SEP-99 1999-09-21:21:02:54
VALID

STACY TRANS_APPL  4061 PACKAGE BODY 21-SEP-99 21-SEP-99 1999-09-21:22:05:29
INVALID
```

Example 2: Package Specification Compile Failures and Package Body

However, if your package specification fails on compilation—say, because of a syntax error—the package body will fail on compilation as well. This is because a package body depends on the existence of its package specification in a valid state. If for some reason the package specification is invalidated, then the package body will invalidate as well. For example, a package specification will be invalidated if you recompile it and it contains errors. So, package bodies have a special package dependency on the package specification that must be satisfied for the body to compile successfully. The following code block demonstrates status on package specification and body if the specification is recompiled with syntax errors:

```
SQL> select * from dba_objects where object_name = 'TRANS_APPL';

OWNER OBJECT_NAME O_ID OBJECT_TYPE   CREATED   LAST_DDL_ TIMESTAMP
----- ----------- ---- ------------ --------- --------- -------------------
STATUS
------
STACY TRANS_APPL  4060 PACKAGE       21-SEP-99 21-SEP-99 1999-09-21:22:02:54
INVALID

STACY TRANS_APPL  4061 PACKAGE BODY 21-SEP-99 21-SEP-99 1999-09-21:22:05:29
INVALID
```

TIP
A package body has a dependency on the package specification, while the package specification does not have a dependency on its package body.

Exercises

1. Can compilation failure for a package body invalidate the package specification? Why or why not?

2. Can compilation failure for a package specification invalidate the package body? Why or why not?

Managing Compilation Dependency and Packages

Recall from the previous chapter that you will often create dependencies between program units and between those units and objects like tables in the Oracle database. Two types of dependency were introduced: procedure dependency and object dependency. Two procedures of functions experience procedure dependency when one of the procedures calls another as part of its regular function, like **proc_today_trans( )** did on **convert_money( )**. A procedure may also rely on the valid existence of a table in Oracle to perform its tasks as well, as **convert_money( )** did on EXCH_RATE.

Example 3: Referring Package Body Compile Dependency on Referenced Body

These procedure dependencies are still present when you recompile procedures and functions into packages. If you have programs that depend on other programs that also extend from one package to another, the referenced package body should be compiled before the referring package body. The specifications, however, can be compiled in any order. The following code block displays the package body status information from

DBA_OBJECTS for TRANS_UTILS and TRANS_APPL if you compile the
TRANS_APPL package body before compiling TRANS_UTILS. Note
that TRANS_UTILS is valid, but TRANS_APPL is not in this situation.

```
SQL> select * from dba_objects where object_type = 'PACKAGE BODY'
  2> and owner = 'STACY';

OWNER OBJECT_NAME O_ID OBJECT_TYPE   CREATED   LAST_DDL_ TIMESTAMP
----- ----------- ---- ------------ --------- --------- -------------------
STATUS
------
STACY TRANS_APPL  4061 PACKAGE BODY 21-SEP-99 21-SEP-99 1999-09-21:30:02:54
INVALID

STACY TRANS_UTILS 4040 PACKAGE BODY 21-SEP-99 21-SEP-99 1999-09-21:31:05:29
VALID
```

Example 4: Delayed Effect of Compile Errors in Referenced Package Body

In another example, say you go into TRANS_UTILS and make a change to
convert_money( ), but forgot to put a semicolon at the end of a line
somewhere. When you recompile the TRANS_UTILS procedure body, the
compilation fails. Note, however, that the status of TRANS_APPL, is still
valid until someone actually runs **proc_today_trans( )** and Oracle learns that
the referenced package body is invalid. The following code block shows the
status of both procedure bodies in the state after the error in compiling
TRANS_UTILS but before referencing the **proc_today_trans( )** procedure in
TRANS_APPL.

```
SQL> select * from dba_objects where object_type = 'PACKAGE BODY'
  2> and owner = 'STACY';

OWNER OBJECT_NAME O_ID OBJECT_TYPE   CREATED   LAST_DDL_ TIMESTAMP
----- ----------- ---- ------------ --------- --------- -------------------
STATUS
------
STACY TRANS_APPL  4061 PACKAGE BODY 21-SEP-99 21-SEP-99 1999-09-21:40:02:54
VALID

STACY TRANS_UTILS 4040 PACKAGE BODY 21-SEP-99 21-SEP-99 1999-09-21:41:05:29
INVALID
```

Example 5: Immediate Effects of Bad Referenced Package Specification Compile on Referring Package Body

Consider the same situation where you recompile the TRANS_UTILS package specification instead, and you forgot your semicolon somewhere. The TRANS_UTILS package specification compilation fails, which not only invalidates the TRANS_UTILS package body immediately, but also invalidates the TRANS_APPL package body. The TRANS_APPL specification remains valid, however.

```
SQL> select * from dba_objects where object_type in
  2>('PACKAGE','PACKAGE BODY') and owner = 'STACY'
  3> order by object_name, object_type;

OWNER OBJECT_NAME O_ID OBJECT_TYPE  CREATED    LAST_DDL_ TIMESTAMP
----- ----------- ---- ----------- --------- --------- -------------------
STATUS
------
STACY TRANS_APPL  4060 PACKAGE      21-SEP-99 21-SEP-99 1999-09-21:40:02:54
VALID

STACY TRANS_APPL  4061 PACKAGE BODY 21-SEP-99 21-SEP-99 1999-09-21:40:02:54
INVALID

STACY TRANS_UTILS 4039 PACKAGE      21-SEP-99 21-SEP-99 1999-09-21:41:05:29
INVALID

STACY TRANS_UTILS 4040 PACKAGE BODY 21-SEP-99 21-SEP-99 1999-09-21:41:05:29
INVALID
```

Exercises

1. How does recompiling a package body containing procedures referenced by other packages affect the status of those other package bodies? Their specifications?

2. How does recompiling a package specification containing procedures referenced by other packages affect the status of those other package bodies? Their specifications? Its own body?

Managing Procedure Dependency in Packages

Certain consideration should be given when planning packages to avoid dependencies that make packages impossible to compile. In addition, you should understand the conditions that may exist where it is advisable for you to put procedures together in one package. Code in packages should be logically grouped according to whether they are used for the same overall function in an application, or whether they are depended upon consistently by other applications.

Grouping Program Units Together that Work Together

The hallmark reason for putting procedures and functions together in a package is if they work together on the same functional area of the application. Say you have an application that has two functional uses: online transaction processing and reporting. Your functions and procedures that support OLTP work can be grouped into one package, while your reporting programs can be grouped together in another.

Procedures and functions may be grouped together according to their involvement in certain batch processes. Say, for example, that you have a database that has several different batch feeds happening at different times. You may package the PL/SQL programs that work on one batch feed together, while putting those that work on a different batch feed into another package.

Example 6: How Oracle Avoids Cyclical Dependency

Consider how Oracle performs in the following situation. Say you have three procedures—call them **a( )**, **b( )**, and **c( )**. Procedure **a( )** calls procedure **b( )**, which in turn calls procedure **c( )**. You want to create two packages: X and Y. Package X will contain procedures **a( )** and **c( )**, and Y will contain **b( )**. One might think that compiling X and Y is not possible, considering the cyclical nature of calls that would result from one package to another. However, there is no problem with this design. The reason for this fact lies with the package specifications. Although when Oracle attempts to compile the package body for X containing **a( )**, it will verify the existence of procedure **b( )** in package Y's specification and the validity of package specification Y, it does not actually check for the validity of Y's package body. The same is true when you compile the Y's package body. It checks X's package specification for the referenced procedure call and for validity, but does not check the package body. Thus, this design is possible.

Example 7: Forward Referencing

A special case of cyclical dependency exists called "forward referencing," which basically refers to situations where one program unit refers to another in a package before the other reference has been compiled. Say a package has two procedures, one called **award_bonus( )** and the other called **calc_rating( )**. If **award_bonus( )** refers to **calc_rating( )** before Oracle has seen any sort of reference to it—either in the package specification or package body—Oracle will compile the package with errors. The following code block illustrates an offender:

```
...
Procedure award_bonus(...) is
Begin
 Calc_rating(...);   --illegal reference
...
End;
Procedure calc_rating(...) is
Begin
...
End;
```

However, if you make forward reference to the PL/SQL block before using it either in the specification or the body, you can get away with calling the program unit from another unit before actually defining the program logic. The following block shows an acceptable block of code that uses forward referencing:

```
...
Procedure calc_rating(...);   --forward declaration
Procedure award_bonus(...) is
Begin
 Calc_rating(...);
...
End;
Procedure calc_rating(...) is
Begin
...
End;
```

Grouping Programs Referenced by Other Packages

Another method for designing packages is to place programs that are commonly relied upon by other programs. These referenced programs may be utilities commonly used by other programs. As such, they may belong in a utilities package that is referenced by all other programs. In this situation, you create a dependency architecture where one or several other packages have procedural dependencies into the utilities package. However, remember that the procedure dependency applies to the package bodies only. Thus, the package specifications can be compiled in any order you want. Compilation of the bodies of packages that reference the utilities package must happen after the utilities package specification is compiled. But, because other packages are procedurally dependent only on the utilities package specification, you can recompile the utilities package body as often as you need to so long as referring procedures aren't executed while the referenced package body is invalid.

Package Instantiation and Usage State

One final situation should be considered regarding procedure dependency. This situation is when a user has a session open where she is using a particular package. The user has her own private version of the package in memory for her session, which was valid as of the time she began use of the package. This version of the package in the user's session is called an *instantiation* of that package. However, let's say that as the developer, you invalidate both the package specification and the package body. This causes the instantiation of the user's package to be lost. The first time after the instantiation is lost, when the user calls program units in the package, she will receive the Oracle error **ORA-04068: existing state of packages has been discarded**. This error, though it appears threatening, is actually benign, and the next time she calls the programs in the package, it will reinstantiate for her without producing an error.

One-Time-Only Procedures

If you've seen a package body definition, you probably have noticed that it looks suspiciously similar to a procedure or function definition without an area for parameter definition. So similar, in fact, are package bodies to the procedures and functions they contain that the package body can also have some stand-alone PL/SQL defined within it, at the very end of the package body definition. This stand-alone PL/SQL is called a one-time-only procedure because it executes only once, when you submit the package body to Oracle for compilation. You may find one-time-only procedures useful in situations where you have some structures or variables you want to set up when you first compile the package. The following code block shows a greatly simplified example of a package body from Procedure Builder with a one-time-only procedure defined:

```
Package my_pkg is
    procedure my_proc ( … ) is
    begin
     …
    end;
    procedure my_proc_2 ( … ) is
    begin
    end;
begin -- one-time-only procedure
…
end;
```

Exercises

1. How does Oracle solve the problem of cyclical procedure dependency between packages?

2. If a package exists that contains code referenced by programs in other package bodies, what happens to the validity of those package bodies if the referenced body is compiled with errors?

3. What is package instantiation? Describe a situation that may arise when packages are recompiled while being used in sessions by users.

Using Pragma RESTRICT_REFERENCES

Packaging functions takes a small amount of extra effort to address the fact that the package body for the function is hidden when Oracle runs it. So, Oracle needs you to say explicitly what the function is doing with respect to writing to the database, reading from it, and other things. A *pragma* is a compilation directive you can set that defines items like whether the function will write information to the database among other things. You have already seen one pragma, the EXCEPTION_INIT pragma in Chapter 5, which is used to allow you to associate your own exception name with an Oracle error. RESTRICT_REFERENCES allows you to restrict how your function manipulates the Oracle database. There are several different ways to restrict how your function references the Oracle database. They are as follows:

- **WNDS**   Write No Database State tells Oracle to prevent the function from writing changes to the database.

- **WNPS**   Write No Package State tells Oracle to prevent the function from altering values for package global variables.

- **RNDS**   Read No Database State tells Oracle to prevent the function from issuing **select** statements against the database (highly restrictive).

- **RNPS**   Read No Package State tells Oracle to prevent the function from obtaining values in package global variables (highly restrictive).

Your use of this feature will take the following form in your specification: **pragma RESTRICT_REFERENCES(**func_name,**WNDS,** [optional_restrictions]**).** Optional restrictions in this case are WNPS, RNDS, and RNPS. Using pragma RESTRICT_REFERENCES requires you to add some lines to your package specification. In the following code block, you will reconsider your TRANS_UTILS package specification in light of using pragma RESTRICT_REFERENCES. Should you want to explicitly prevent your **convert_money( )** function from being able to write changes to the database, you will add a line telling Oracle to enforce this restriction on **convert_money( )**.

```
CREATE OR REPLACE PACKAGE trans_utils IS
   FUNCTION convert_money (
      p_from_crcy            VARCHAR2,
      p_to_crcy      IN OUT VARCHAR2,
      p_from_amt             NUMBER,
      valid_date             DATE
   ) RETURN NUMBER;
   pragma RESTRICT_REFERENCES(convert_money,WNDS);
END;
```

Now, if you compile this specification and your package body contains an **update** statement, the compilation of your package body will fail because it violates the RESTRICT_REFERENCES you have set for the function.

Exercises

1. What is a pragma? How does RESTRICT_REFERENCES influence Oracle's compilation of your functions in a package? Where is reference made to RESTRICT_REFERENCES, in the package specification or the body? Why is it needed for functions in packages but not stand-alone functions?

2. What is WNDS? WNPS? RNDS? RNPS? How do you formulate your **pragma RESTRICT_REFERENCES** statement?

3. If you set up a function to Read No Package State and then your function body contains a reference to a global package variable, what happens to the package body compilation?

Managing Packages and Security

The same security considerations given for procedures and functions apply to packages and package bodies. Only those users who may create a procedure or function may create a package. This ability is bestowed with the **create procedure** privilege. To run a program unit that is stored in a package, you must have the **execute** privilege on the package, not the procedure. So, on the one hand, packages allow you to make changes to source code for program unit bodies without disturbing the status of other programs with procedure dependencies on the unit. But, the execution of the procedure individually is impossible without granting **execute** privilege on all procedures and functions in the package. Thus, you may have to plan for this limitation in the way you allocate procedures and functions to various packages.

Another take on packages and security relates to the package body. Since your package body resides separately from the specification, you can hide information and application logic from your users while simultaneously allowing them to do their job by running the code. The PL/SQL wrapper allows you to store an encrypted version of your code body in the database for purposes of security as well.

TIP
Any information you need to find out about packages from the data dictionary can be found in the same views as those used for procedures, such as DBA_OBJECTS, DBA_SOURCE, and DBA_ERRORS.

Overloading Programs in Packages

One final area of package management is the ability you have to overload procedures and functions. You have already been exposed to overloading, so you know that an overloaded function may have three different functions out there with the same name, each handling different datatype arguments. An example is a function that returns the length of a variable in characters. Since you may want to find the length of noncharacter variables, you can overload this function in your package to save yourself extensive formatting on your variable from the function caller and extensive **if-then** statements in the function itself. The following code block shows the specification for the overloaded function:

```
CREATE OR REPLACE PACKAGE UTIL_FUNCS IS
   FUNCTION var_length (
    p_var CHAR
   ) RETURN NUMBER;
   FUNCTION var_length (
    p_var VARCHAR2
   ) RETURN NUMBER;

   FUNCTION var_length (
    p_var NUMBER
   ) RETURN NUMBER;

FUNCTION var_length (
   p_var DATE
   ) RETURN NUMBER;
END;
```

TIP
*Even though you have four functions in this package, Oracle will still work fine, even automatically detecting the datatype of the parameter you pass to **var_length( )** and directing it to the correct overloaded function.*

Exercises

1. What special considerations must be made concerning packages and security? What permissions are required to create packages? Are packages themselves executed? Why or why not?

2. Where can you go to find information about your packages?

3. What is overloading? What is a wrapper?

Using Oracle Server-Supplied Packages

In this section, you will cover the following points on using Oracle server-supplied packages:

- Overview of Oracle server-supplied packages
- Server packages for database and application administration
- Server packages for transaction processing
- Server packages for advanced application development
- Server packages for Oracle internal support

With all this talk about designing your own packages, you may have several ideas about designing packages to help you with several areas of basic functionality in the Oracle database. Oracle did, too, at one point, and from that they decided to create some basic packages to help you do your job. You need to know what the Oracle server-supplied packages are in order to pass OCP, and this knowledge will help you as you develop and maintain database applications. Several packages have already been covered, namely those packages that are part of Procedure Builder and can be used for debugging. This section covers the packages available as part of the Oracle database that can be used in many ways to improve the functionality of your applications.

Overview of Oracle Server-Supplied Packages

Several packages exist in the database to complement your development and administrative efforts. These packages are developed by Oracle and reside in the database. The Oracle server-supplied packages are owned by user SYS. In some cases, you must run scripts that come with the Oracle distribution software. For the most part, these scripts will be found in the **rdbms/admin** subdirectory of the Oracle home directory on the machine hosting the Oracle database. For more information about the scripts that must be run, consult *Oracle Certified Professional DBA Certification Exam Guide*. Oracle server-supplied packages fall into four different categories. These categories are transaction processing, application development, database and application administration, and internal support. The high-level category description and packages in each are described here, while the functionality highlights and program components for each package will be covered shortly. Be aware this is a survey of packages for exam preparation purposes. To find out more about use of an individual package, including parameters and other things, consult the comments in the package specification on your Oracle database.

Transaction Processing

Several different packages are available to support transaction processing. Transaction processing includes all activities related to locking database objects for data changes, along with **commit** and **rollback** operations, with some additional SQL statement functionality thrown in as well. The packages falling into this category include DBMS_ALERT, DBMS_LOCK, DBMS_SQL, and DBMS_TRANSACTION.

Application Development

The Oracle server makes several different packages available in the support of basic and advanced application development. This includes everything related to developing batch jobs, altering the session environment within the application, and intersession communication. The category also includes finding more information about program units available in the application, and file I/O. The packages falling into this category include DBMS_JOB, DBMS_SESSION, DBMS_PIPE, DBMS_DESCRIBE, DBMS_OUTPUT, DBMS_STANDARD, and UTL_FILE. Since the functionality of the DBMS_OUTPUT package is described in Chapter 7, it will not be described again here. Instead, you may want to refer to that discussion for information about the package.

Database and Application Administration

Many different packages help you with database and application administration. This includes everything related to recompiling packages or procedures, administration of the system, space management on the database, replication, and SGA. The packages falling into this category include DBMS_UTILITY, DBMS_DDL, DBMS_APPLICATION_INFO, DBMS_SYSTEM, DBMS_SPACE, and DBMS_SHARED_POOL.

Support for Data Replication

A few packages in Oracle also support data replication. They are DBMS_SNAPSHOT, DBMS_REFRESH, DBMS_DEFER, DBMS_DEFER_QUERY, DBMS_REPCAT, DBMS_REPCAT_AUTH, and DBMS_REPCAT_ADMIN. Since snapshots and data replication are not topics covered in OCP, they will not be covered here.

Oracle Internal Support

There are some packages available in the support of Oracle database internal activities as well. Oracle often uses a package wrapper to prevent you from viewing or modifying the code in these packages, as they support several fundamentals of the database. They also support other packages used more actively by you in other categories. The packages falling into this category include STANDARD, DBMS_IJOB, DBMS_DEFER_IMPORT_INTERNAL, DBMS_DEFER_SYS, DBMS_IREFRESH, DBMS_ISNAPSHOT, DBMS_SYS_ERROR, and DBMS_SYS_SQL. Note that

the STANDARD package is not the same as DBMS_STANDARD. The
STANDARD package defines all SQL built-in functions covered in Chapter
1, along with database datatypes and PL/SQL extensions to those types.
DBMS_STANDARD, on the other hand, defines items like
raise_application_error( ) and several important items that assist in PL/SQL
procedure and database trigger development. See Chapter 10 for more
information about the DBMS_STANDARD package.

Exercises

1. Where are Oracle server-supplied packages stored and who owns
them?

2. What are some categories for Oracle-supplied packages? Name
some packages in each.

Server Packages for Transaction Processing

Sometimes applications want more restrictive locks than the simple
row-exclusive lock granted for an **update** statement. Locks on database
objects can be obtained with the use of the DBMS_LOCK package. The
procedure **allocate_unique( )** is used to generate a numeric ID for a given
lock handle allocated by the application. An overloaded function called
request( ) allows the application to request the lock on the database object,
using either the integer or lock handle. Another function, called **convert( )**,
is used by an application to convert one type of database object lock into
another. This function is overloaded as well to handle either the lock ID or
the handle. The final procedure is called **sleep( )**, and it is used to suspend
session activity for a period of time.

The DBMS_TRANSACTION package supports transaction processing as
well. There are several program units in this package for performing
activities like **commit** and **rollback**, and also for defining savepoints and
other items throughout the application. The procedures for setting
transaction status, advising **commit** activity, and assigning **rollback**
statements include **read_only( )**, **read_write( )**, **advise_rollback( )**,
advise_commit( ), **advise_nothing( )**, and **use_rollback_segment( )**.
Procedures used to begin and end transactions and define savepoints are

begin_discrete_transaction( ), **commit_comment( )**, **commit_force( )**, **commit( )**, **rollback( )**, **savepoint( )**, **rollback_savepoint( )**, and **rollback_force( )**. You should note that some of these activities needn't be executed as procedures or functions. Statements like **commit** and **rollback** can be executed with that syntax instead of a full-blown procedure call.

The DBMS_SQL package allows you to construct SQL statements on the fly using text strings. Several procedures and functions are available. For manipulating SQL statements in memory, called cursors, the **open_cursor( )** function and **close_cursor( )** procedure are available. You turn a text string into a SQL statement with the **parse( )** procedure. Your SQL statement may contain a comparison operation in the **where** clause, so in order to incorporate the value in that statement, you use the **bind_variable( )** procedure. Two procedures must be used if your SQL is a **select** statement to set up the return values positionally. They are **define_column( )** and **define_column_long( )**. You then use the **execute( )** procedure to process the SQL statement. After processing, if you have run a **select** statement, you may then retrieve rows from the resultant cursor with **fetch_rows( )**, after which you can call **variable_value( )** to obtain specific values for columns from each row. Finally, you can use **column_value_long( )** to retrieve data from LONG columns a piece at a time.

TIP
The coverage here of the Oracle-supplied packages does not even pretend to explain these useful packages in any detail. You can find better coverage of use in a PL/SQL programming book. For now, concentrate on understanding usage concepts in order to pass OCP.

You may want to set up an activity that occurs based on a change in data on the database as the result of a transaction as well. The DBMS_ALERT package can help you accomplish this task. There are several procedures and functions available to you from DBMS_ALERT. Running the **register( )** procedure allows you to register your session as one that needs to pay attention to the alert named as a parameter. Running the **remove( )**

procedure specifies that you are no longer interested in being notified by the alert. When your application does something that others need to be alerted of, your application runs the **signal( )** procedure to signal the alert. Running the **waitany( )** procedure from your session causes your session to wait until any alert your session is registered to receive occurs. Instead, you may want to wait only for an individual alert you subscribe to, in which case you use the **waitone( )** procedure. Alerts are event-driven, meaning they occur as a result of an event such as a database change rather than as the result of a continuous polling loop (the **waitany( )** procedure is an exception). If you wish to use polling (such as for **waitany( )**), you may want to run **set_defaults( )** to set the frequency that Oracle will poll.

TIP

*When you use DBMS_ALERT.**waitany( )**, you essentially put your session on hold until one of your alerts occur—be careful to give up any database locks you have by ending all transactions before issuing the **waitany( )** call.*

Exercises

1. What package helps you to develop dynamic SQL? Which procedures do you use to generate, run, and release Oracle resources for a dynamic SQL statement?

2. What package helps you to work with alerts? Which procedures are called from the session wanting to be notified by the alert when it is signaled?

3. Which procedure is issued by the application to signal the alert? What happens when you execute **waitany( )** before your transaction is complete in an application?

4. Which package helps initiate, end, and define savepoints in transactions? Why wouldn't it be used too often for that purpose from PL/SQL programs? What package allows you to obtain table locks?

Server Packages for Advanced Application Development

The DBMS_JOB package helps you to develop batch processes that run within the Oracle database. The job run must be a PL/SQL stored procedure. To set up the job in the job queue, you run the **submit( )** procedure, while to get it out of the job queue, you can run **remove( )**. Jobs have a description, an interval or frequency of execution, and the next date defined for which they will run. These items can be changed individually with **what( )**, **interval( )**, and **next_date( )**, respectively. The more generalized **change( )** procedure can be used to change any of these things as well. Jobs that fail upon execution are marked "broken" by Oracle, and will not run again until they are fixed. Alternately, you can stop a job from being run by breaking it manually with **broken( )**. Once the job is fixed, you force job execution with **run( )**. If the job runs successfully, Oracle marks the job as not broken anymore.

The DBMS_SESSION package can be used to set the current role within anonymous PL/SQL blocks. It is not usable from stored procedures in order to avoid the security risks posed by allowing those blocks to modify their own security restrictions at run time. The procedures include **set_role( )** to set a role for the session. Another is **close_database_link( )**, use of which is self-explanatory. You can reinstantiate a package that has been compiled after you began using it in your session with **reset_package( )**. To set a NLS variable, use **set_nls( )**.

Communication between database sessions happens with the DBMS_PIPE package. Pipes in Oracle run through the SGA, and are lost after shutdown on the Oracle instance. Messages to be sent across pipes and received from pipes are stored in local buffers for the session. Trace the route a message will take from one session to another through a pipe. Optionally, a private pipe is created beforehand with **create_pipe( )** to handle message transfer between two sessions owned by the same user. The message is created and placed in the local buffer with **pack_message( )**, then sent on the pipe with **send_message( )**. If no pipe exists for **send_message( )** to use, it will create a public pipe for its own use. On the receiving end, the process runs **receive_message( )** to get it off the pipe and store it in the local buffer. From there, **unpack_message( )** is used to take the next message off the buffer. To create a variable to hold the message, you call

next_item_type( ) to obtain the datatype of the message. To eliminate the private pipe, call **remove_pipe( )**. To flush data out of a pipe, use **purge( )**. To flush data out of the local buffer, use **reset_buffer( )**.

TIP
*Public pipes can be read by any user so long as the user has **execute** privilege on DBMS_PIPE. Private pipes can only be read by the owner of the pipe or by privileged users like the DBA.*

The DBMS_DESCRIBE package can be used to find information about the stored procedures in an application that you may create. Items of importance in this package include two type declarations that define tables for storage of output from the one procedure DBMS_DESCRIBE houses, called **describe_procedure( )**. This procedure accepts as input the name of the object to be described and returns whether the procedure is overloaded, the parameters, their directions, datatypes, positions in the procedure call, and other items that help you determine the proper call to a procedure. Since there are many **out** parameters to **describe_procedure( )**, you must declare variables to hold the output using the VARCHAR2_TABLE and NUMBER_TABLE types provided in the DBMS_DESCRIBE package and pass them along with the call to the **describe_procedure( )** procedure.

The DBMS_STANDARD package houses many common PL/SQL constructs. The procedure for advanced error handling, **raise_application_error( )**, which has already been covered, is defined in the DBMS_STANDARD package. One nice thing about these items is that you don't need to refer to the DBMS_STANDARD package by name when using these items.

The UTL_FILE package handles file I/O from PL/SQL packages. This functionality allows you to develop code to handle almost any form of batch processing or batch feed to or from flat file, eliminating the need to use operating system scripts that call SQL*Plus. The procedures used to open and close procedures include **fopen( )**, **fclose( )**, and **fclose_all( )**, while the **is_open( )** function returns whether or not a file is already open. To obtain a line of data from the file, use **get_line( )**. To place a line of data into the file with an end-of-line marker, use **put_line( )**; otherwise, **put( )** is used to place data to the file without the end-of-line marker. The end-of-line marker can be added later with **new_line( )**. To place data into the file with specific formatting, use **putf( )**. Sometimes Oracle may write data to a file asynchronous to the actual calls listed above. To place all pending data into the file immediately, use **fflush( )**.

Exercises

1. What package is used for identifying parameters to be passed to a function? What is the name of the procedure in that package that performs this functionality?

2. What package contains the definition for **raise_application_error( )**? What package handles setup and execution of a batch process or job? What does it mean to say a job set up in this way is "broken?"

3. What package allows you to send messages between two sessions? What is the difference between a public and private pipe?

4. A package called TEXT_IO exists in Procedure Builder. What two packages on the Oracle server handle functionality similar to TEXT_IO?

Server Packages for DBAs and Application Administration

Several packages were presented that assist in administrating the Oracle database. Since only some of these packages are useful for application administration, only those packages will be covered in detail here. The packages that assist with *database* administration include DBMS_SYSTEM, DBMS_SPACE, and DBMS_SHARED_POOL for managing memory, disk, and other items. One important procedure in DBMS_SHARED_POOL is the **keep( )** procedure, which pins a package or program unit into memory for the life of the database instance. If you recompile a package that has already been instantiated, the new version will not be readily available because an outdated version of it is stuck permanently in memory. The **unkeep( )** procedure allows you to age this obsolete version of the package out of memory, but may not be supported in future releases of Oracle.

DBMS_UTILITY contains several procedures and functions used for database administrative tasks. One of interest to application developers is

compile_schema( ), which allows you to recompile all procedures, functions, and packages owned by you. DBMS_DDL offers similar functionality on specific PL/SQL program units with the **alter_compile( )** procedure.

Finally, DBMS_APPLICATION_INFO allows you to register your application with the Oracle database for tuning purposes. The procedure **set_module( )** allows you to establish a name for the application running, while **set_action( )** identifies the current action by name within the module. These functions identify your application for audit or timing purposes. The **set_client_info( )** procedure also sets information about the client running in that session. Procedures for reading information set about the client or application include **read_module( )** and **read_client_info( )**.

TIP
Again, it is unfortunate that the text glosses over the intricacies of each package. These areas are some of the most exciting in Oracle. However, there is still a lot of material left to cover for OCP certification, and the exams don't test your usage of individual packages in exhaustive detail.

Exercises

1. Identify two packages and two procedures that allow you to recompile other procedures or functions.

2. What are some packages that are for DBA use?

3. How might use of the DBMS_SHARED_POOL package interfere with instantiation of a package once it has been recompiled?

Chapter Summary

This chapter covers development and use of packages to manage PL/SQL program units more effectively. The subject areas covered are the overview of using PL/SQL packages, development of packages, managing packages on the database, and using Oracle server-supplied packages available on the database. This chapter covers 24 percent of OCP test 2 content.

Packages are constructs that consolidate stored procedures and functions on a database into two distinct objects: specifications and bodies. The specification contains procedure and function definitions along with the parameters passed, and the body contains program logic. Packages offer several benefits over individuated stored procedures and functions. The package groups related procedures and functions, making it easier to find those program units. Packages help reduce the burden of procedure dependency by divorcing the specification from the body. While other program units depend on the presence of the specification, you can recompile the body when needed. Package bodies can also hide program logic when used in conjunction with PL/SQL wrappers. Packages can offer improved performance when you use related procedures and functions because your use of one procedure in a package loads the entire package into memory. When you need another procedure from the package, that other procedure is in memory as well. You can also define multiple versions of the same procedure or function with a package, to handle operation of the same task on information of differing datatypes. This feature is called overloading.

Packages have two parts, a specification containing procedure and function specifications such as name, parameters, and return values, and a body containing program unit code logic. Packages can contain public and private program units. A public program unit is one whose program unit specification appears in the package specification. A private program unit is one defined exclusively in the package body. Public units can be called by other procedures outside the package, while private units are called only from within the package. However, a package body must always contain program unit logic if a package specification contains its specifications, or else the package body compilation fails.

Basic syntax for package specifications is **create or replace package** *pkgname* **is...end**. Within the ellipses of this basic syntax are the listings for all user-defined types, procedures, functions, constants, cursors, and exceptions. For procedures, functions, and types, the specification takes the form {**procedure**|**function**}*whatever* (*parm* **in datatype**...) [**return** *datatype*]; instead of the syntax for creating that individual unit, (i.e., **create or replace ...**).

Basic syntax for package bodies is **create or replace package body** *pkgname* **is...end**. Within the ellipses of this syntax are the listings and program logic for all procedures, cursors, and functions. Constants, types, and exceptions have already been defined in the specification and can be used in the body without further definition, however, you can declare more constants, types, and exceptions in the package body that will remain privately accessed by only procedures in the package body. Syntax for procedures and functions defined in a package is the same as that used for creating procedures and functions, minus the **create or replace** syntax. See Chapter 6 for more information about developing procedures and functions.

Several important points about package compilation were made in the text. A specification for a package must always be compiled before its body. If the body doesn't contain program logic for a unit defined in the specification, package body compilation fails. Package body compilation failure never invalidates the specification, but package specification compilation failure always invalidates its own body, along with the body of every package that has procedure dependency on program units in the failing specification.

Package specifications should contain comments that explain general program usage, while package bodies should contain comments explaining tricky program logic or hard-coded values, or other minutiae of the code. A package specification should always contain comments on using the program units defined, along with an explanation of every parameter passed **in** or **out**, and also return values, if appropriate. Package bodies may be easier to maintain if their program units have comments describing their design quirks. Single line comments are preceded by double dashes (--), while block comments are made with usual C notation, (/* */).

Coding and compiling your packages with Procedure Builder offers the same advantages it offered for program units. If you have a package already and you want to change the program unit logic, you need only recompile the specification when parameters into or out of the program unit change.

Several examples were provided to demonstrate packages and program dependency. To summarize, a package specification will almost never invalidate as the result of any dependency on the database. Package bodies that call procedures in other packages will not invalidate even when the package body containing the referenced procedure is recompiled or invalidated, so long as the specification remains valid and the program unit that references invalid code is not executed. As soon as you execute the procedure that calls invalid code, the referenced body will invalidate as well. If your recompilation of the package specification fails, the associated package body and all package bodies that reference code in the failed specification will invalidate.

Grouping program units together into packages according to dependency is usually a good idea. Grouping program units together according to application or functional area usually works as well. It is helpful to group utility program units that are called by several other program units into one utility package as well.

Package instantiation is another important area of package development. A package is instantiated by a session once a call is made to program units in that package. Once instantiated, a version of that package exists in session memory for that user. If the package should be recompiled after instantiation, the next reference to a program unit for that user will result in the **ORA-04068 – existing state of packages has been discarded.** This error is usually a red herring—simply calling the procedure again makes it go away.

The same privileges to create and run program units are used to allow creation of packages. One limitation on security enforcement on packages is that granting **execute** privileges on a package allows the user to execute all program units in the package. Ensure this fact is addressed when grouping program units together in a package. To find information about a package such as validity, timestamp, compilation errors, and source code, use the same dictionary views as those for procedures and functions, namely DBA_ERRORS, DBA_SOURCE, and DBA_OBJECTS.

Several packages are available on the Oracle database, and they are used for operation in many different areas. The general categories covered for server-supplied packages are transaction processing, application development, application/database administration, and Oracle internal support. Since this guide focuses on exam preparation, and given the fact that the use of each package is intricate, the text focused only on the basic usage of each program unit in the package, along with some facts about package usage likely to be tested on the OCP exam.

The first category is transaction processing. Packages in this category were DBMS_ALERT for asynchronous notification of changes made to the database and DBMS_LOCK for acquiring locks on the database that are higher than those given with **update** or **select for update** statements. Also included here were DBMS_SQL for dynamic generation of SQL DML and DDL statements and DBMS_TRANSACTION for execution of statements to begin and end transactions or set savepoints throughout a transaction.

The next category is application development. Packages in this category include DBMS_JOB for setting up batch operations of program units, DBMS_SESSION for changing aspects about the session running environment, and DBMS_PIPE for intersession communication between program units. Also included here are DBMS_DESCRIBE to identify key points about any procedure or function in the database, DBMS_OUTPUT and UTL_FILE to send text output to both the computer screen or a text file from your program unit, and the DBMS_STANDARD package, which contains definitions for **raise_application_error( )**.

Application and database administration is the next category. The Oracle-supplied packages in this category are DBMS_UTILITY, DBMS_DDL, DBMS_APPLICATION_INFO, DBMS_SYSTEM, DBMS_SPACE, and DBMS_SHARED_POOL. The two packages of importance to application development are DBMS_UTILITY and DBMS_DDL. These two packages contain procedures that recompile PL/SQL code, and as such may be useful in creating more robust applications. The rest of the packages in this category are more for database administration tasks, and so the application may not have much occasion to use them. One exception to this statement is DBMS_SHARED_POOL, which contains the **keep( )** procedure that allows the DBA to pin an object into Oracle's shared pool. If you recompile a package that is pinned in Oracle memory, no one will be able to use the new version because the old instantiation is never removed from memory.

Two other package areas are Oracle internals support and data replication, but since these are areas not covered for OCP, they will not be covered here.

Two-Minute Drill

- A package is a database construct that allows you to collect many program units into one database object.

- Packages consist of two components: a specification and a body. Benefits for using packages include the following:

  - Procedure dependency on referenced programs only extends to the package specification. The package body can be recompiled without regard to effect on other package bodies.

  - Performance improvements for related program units occur because all program units in a package are loaded into memory when any one program unit in the package is referenced.

  - Several program units of the same name can be created to handle data of many datatypes. This is called overloading.

  - Hiding application logic is possible with the structure of packages. A wrapper function can also be used to encrypt the package body, further protecting the source code.

- The specification contains program unit definitions, type definitions, exceptions, and constants only. No program unit logic can be included in a package specification.

- The body contains all program logic for all program units included in the package, plus any program logic for private program units as well.

- A private program unit is one that appears in a package body whose specification does not appear in the package specification. Private program units cannot be called from outside the package body.

- A public program unit is one whose specification appears in the package specification. The public program unit can be called from outside the package body.

■ Syntax for creating a package specification is **create or replace package** *pkgname*. Syntax for creating the package body is **create or replace package body** *pkgname*.

■ Compilation of a package specification must happen before compilation of its body. If there are several packages that will have procedure dependencies on one another, compilation of package specifications can happen in any order so long as they finish before any package body is compiled.

■ The procedure or function specification in the package body must conform to whatever the package specification has defined for that procedure or function. If there is any discrepancy, or if the package body does not contain program logic for a procedure defined in the specification, then the package body compilation will fail.

■ Functions in package bodies must conform to any restriction on references stated in the package specification via **pragma** RESTRICT_REFERENCES.

■ RESTRICT_REFERENCES allows you to restrict function references in four different ways:

  ■ **WNDS**   Write No Database State tells Oracle to prevent the function from writing changes to the database.

  ■ **WNPS**   Write No Package State tells Oracle to prevent the function from altering values for package global variables.

  ■ **RNDS**   Read No Database State tells Oracle to prevent the function from issuing **select** statements against the database (highly restrictive).

  ■ **RNPS**   Read No Package State tells Oracle to prevent the function from obtaining values in package global variables (highly restrictive).

■ Since function bodies are hidden within package bodies, Oracle must know how functions manipulate database and package data explicitly via your use of **pragma** RESTRICT_REFERENCES.

■ Package specifications will be invalid only if their compilation fails. In this case, the body for that package will also be marked invalid, along with any package bodies that reference program units in the invalid package specification.

■ If a package body containing program units referenced by a program in another package is rendered invalid, the referencing package will remain valid until the referencing program unit is called. Once the referencing package calls invalid code, it will also be rendered invalid.

■ When a user calls a program unit in a package, a version of that package is copied into memory for that user. This act is called instantiation of the package.

■ If someone recompiles the package, the next time a program unit from that package is called the user will receive error **ORA-04068: Existing state of package has been discarded**. Calling the procedure once more after this error is received will usually eliminate the problem.

■ Regarding security, the same permissions for program unit creation and execution apply to packages: **create procedure** and **execute**.

■ The same views are used to find information as for procedures and functions: DBA_OBJECTS, DBA_ERRORS, and DBA_SOURCE.

■ Oracle supplies several server-side packages for program development. Procedure Builder contains packages as well, which were covered in Chapter 7.

■ As an exercise, you should go back and review each of the Oracle server-supplied packages in both the book and in the package specifications given on your Oracle database. Use Procedure Builder to do so if it will help you gain some experience there as well.

- Some packages that handle aspects of transaction processing that will be on OCP Exam 2 include the following:

  - DBMS_ALERT
  - DBMS_LOCK
  - DBMS_SQL
  - DBMS_TRANSACTION

- Some packages that handle aspects of application development that will be on OCP Exam 2 include the following:

  - DBMS_JOB
  - DBMS_SESSION
  - DBMS_PIPE
  - DBMS_DESCRIBE
  - DBMS_OUTPUT
  - UTL_FILE
  - DBMS_STANDARD

- Some packages that handle aspects of application and database administration that will be on OCP Exam 2 include the following:

  - DBMS_UTILITY
  - DBMS_DDL
  - DBMS_APPLICATION_INFO
  - DBMS_SHARED_POOL

Chapter Questions

1. **Which of the following situations will cause a package specification to invalidate?**

    A. Syntax error in the specification

    B. Referenced procedure in another package invalidates

    C. Program unit specification in package body doesn't match

    D. Package body fails on compilation

2. **The developer finds a logic error in a program unit called by other programs in several different packages. The developer corrects the error and recompiles the package. Assuming no calls to the referenced program were made, what are the effects of her action?**

    A. The specification to the recompiled package body invalidates

    B. The bodies of other packages were invalidated

    C. The specification to other packages were invalidated

    D. Nothing, the referenced package specification did not invalidate

3. **Which of the following are good uses of comments in packages? (Choose two)**

    A. General descriptions of program usage in package body

    B. General description of program usage in package specification

    C. Detailed description of program logic in package specification

    D. Detailed description of program logic in package body

4. **Which of the following statements are true of a private program unit in a package?**

    A. The package specification will contain comments about a private program unit's general usage.

    B. Only the package body will contain references to the private program unit.

C. Any package can reference the private program unit.

D. Only the package specification will contain reference to the private program unit.

5. **After sending a message across a pipe, which of the following procedures would a developer use to retrieve the message from the pipe?**

A. pack_message( )

B. send_message( )

C. receive_message( )

D. unpack_message( )

6. **The user of a program unit has received the following error: "ORA-04068: existing package state has been discarded." The next step the developer should take is:**

A. Rerun the program unit just attempted

B. Recompile the package containing the program unit

C. Drop the package containing the program unit

D. Recompile the program unit individually

7. **The use of which of the following Oracle server-supplied program units may cause problems with instantiating a package after recompilation?**

A. DBMS_ALERT.**waitany( )**

B. DBMS_PIPE.**create_pipe( )**

C. DBMS_SESSION.**describe_procedure( )**

D. DBMS_SHARED_**POOL**.**keep( )**

8. **Which two Oracle server-supplied packages approximate the use of the TEXT_IO package supplied with Procedure Builder?**

A. DBMS_SESSION and DBMS_PIPE

B. DBMS_OUTPUT and UTL_FILE

C. DBMS_DDL and DBMS_UTILITY

D. STANDARD and DBMS_LOCK

9. **Which Oracle server-supplied program unit may cause locking issues if a COMMIT is not issued before its use?**

   A. DBMS_ALERT.**waitany( )**

   B. DBMS_PIPE.**create_pipe( )**

   C. DBMS_SESSION.**describe_procedure( )**

   D. DBMS_SHARED_POOL.**keep( )**

10. **The developer wants her PL/SQL program unit to issue DDL to create temporary tables to hold data. Which of the following methods should she use to do it?**

    A. Issue the create table statements directly from the program unit

    B. Use DBMS_SESSION to alter the environment such that the PL/SQL program unit can create tables

    C. Use the DBMS_OUTPUT and UTL_FILE packages to issue the **create table** statement from the operating system

    D. Use DBMS_SQL to generate the **create table** statement on the fly

11. **The datatype in a program unit specification in the package body does not match its counterpart in the specification. Which of the following events best describes what will happen?**

    A. The package body will fail on compile because the program unit specifications don't match.

    B. The specification will fail on compile because the program unit specifications don't match.

    C. Both the package body and package specification will compile fine.

    D. The package body will compile fine, but the package specification will fail.

12. **In which of the following scenarios when developing intersession communication in an application is the use of a private pipe appropriate?**

    A. When any user should be able to access information on the pipe

    B. When developers and users should be able to access information on the pipe

    C. When only the owner of the pipe should have access to information on that pipe

    D. When the pipe is being sent to a file

13. **The developer of an application wants the application to acquire table locks in order to execute its processing. Which of the following methods for acquiring that table lock are appropriate?**

    A. Issuing **update** statements with **where** clauses

    B. Issuing **select for update** statements where the **select** statement has a **where** clause

    C. Issuing calls to program units in DBMS_LOCK

    D. Issuing calls to program units in DBMS_TRANSACTION

14. **The term that best describes a situation where several procedures in a package all have the same name but accept parameters of different datatypes is:**

    A. Instantiating

    B. Overloading

    C. Datatyping

    D. Compilation error

Answers to Chapter Questions

1. A.   Syntax error in the specification

Explanation   Package specifications rarely invalidate because of another package specification or body changing on the database. This is because the package specification has no dependency on another database object. In choice B, the only time this situation occurs is when a package body referring to another invalid package body actually calls the other package body. In the case of choice C, Oracle favors the program unit specification in a package specification over that in a package body. Choice D is inappropriate because the failure of a package body to compile will never invalidate the specification.

2. D.   Nothing, the referenced package specification did not invalidate

Explanation   Since the referenced package specification did not become invalid, there is no reason for the referring package body to invalidate, thus eliminating choice B. Choices A and C are wrong because the recompilation of the referenced package body will never invalidate its specification, nor will it invalidate another package specification. Remember, there is little you can do to invalidate a package specification other than compile it with syntax errors.

3. B. and C.

Explanation   Good comment usage is demonstrated by Oracle server-supplied packages, where comments on general program unit usage, parameter passing options, and other general items on using the package appear in the package specification. This is because people who will actually use the package will look to the specification to understand what the contents of the package are. In the package body, comments explaining complex coding logic or answers to other program-related questions is useful because someone who has to maintain the application will want to understand the specifics of the application logic more than how the program should be used in general.

4. B.   Only the package body will contain references to the private
program unit.

Explanation   A private program unit is one that appears only in a package
body. No program unit exists in the package specification, so there is no
reason to explain general program usage. No one from outside the package
body can call the private program unit anyway. These last two statements
eliminate choices A and C. Choice D is incorrect because if the package
specification contains a program unit specification and the package body
doesn't contain application logic for that program unit, the compilation of
the package body will fail.

5. C.   **receive_message( )**

Explanation   To send a message across a pipe, you must first pack the
message into your local buffer and then copy the message from the buffer to
the pipe. The **pack_message( )** procedure handles packing the message
while **send_message( )** handles transmission of it. Reading the message off
the pipe into your local buffer is done with **receive_message( )** while
unpack_message( ) removes if from the local buffer, allowing you to
work with it.

6. A.   Rerun the program unit just attempted

Explanation   The program unit must be reinstantiated after recompilation in
order to be used. This error signals that this activity must take place. After
issuing it, Oracle instantiates the procedure and you can use it. Since the
package has already been recompiled, it doesn't need to be compiled again.
Dropping it will simply make it unavailable, and compiling the program unit
separately simply requires Oracle to instantiate it another time.

7. D.   DBMS_SHARED_POOL.**keep( )**

Explanation   The **keep( )** procedure in DBMS_SHARED_POOL forces
Oracle to pin the package into memory. Once there, no recompilation of
the package will be available until the instance is shut down and restarted,
or until the DBA issues the **unkeep( )** procedure to eliminate the
instantiation of the package from memory in favor of a new one. Thus,
keep( ) can interfere with the instantiation of recompiled packages.

8. B.   DBMS_OUTPUT and UTL_FILE

Explanation   The TEXT_IO package in Procedure Builder, covered in Chapter 7, allows you to write output from your procedure or function to both the screen and to a file. On the Oracle database, DBMS_OUTPUT allows you to write your output to the screen, while UTL_FILE allows you to write output to a file.

9. A.   DBMS_ALERT.**waitany( )**

Explanation   The **waitany( )** procedure in DBMS_ALERT forces the session to wait until it receives a signal from any of the alerts it is registered to receive. As you know from review for OCP test 1, as long as a transaction is in progress, the session holds all its locks until the transaction ends. Thus, **waitany( )** can force a session to hold locks unnecessarily if the transaction is not over.

10. D.   Use DBMS_SQL to generate the **create table** statement on the fly

Explanation   PL/SQL cannot execute DDL statements like **create table** directly, eliminating choice A. Instead, you must use DBMS_SQL to generate the **create table** statement and execute it. You cannot issue this sort of statement from the operating system, invalidating choice C. Finally, use of DBMS_SESSION is appropriate for changing environment parameters but not for creating tables, eliminating choice B.

11. A.   The package body will fail on compile because the program unit specifications don't match.

Explanation   The package body must conform to the package specification on matters of program unit specification. If any inconsistency appears, the package body, not the specification, fails to compile. This fact invalidates choices B, C, and D.

12. C.   When only the owner of the pipe should have access to information on that pipe

Explanation   A private pipe is readable by only the owner of the pipe and privileged users like the DBA. Public pipes, on the other hand, are readable by any user with **execute** privilege on the DBMS_PIPE package.

13. C.   Issuing calls to program units in DBMS_LOCK

Explanation   Table-level locks may only be acquired by an application when the DBMS_LOCK package is used. The two statements offered in choices A and B will acquire only row-level locks, and since a **where** clause is involved, it is fair to assume that only some (not all) of the rows in the table will have row-level locks on them. The DBMS_TRANSACTION package is used mainly for setting up and ending transactions, or defining savepoints in your transactions.

14. B.   Overloading

Explanation   The text of the question describes overloading. Instantiation is the storage of a version of a package in memory. Datatyping is a vague term that ultimately means nothing. No compilation error will ensue as a result of having several program units of the same name.

CHAPTER
10

Developing and Using Database Triggers

n this chapter, you will cover the following areas of developing and using database triggers:

- Developing database triggers
- Managing triggers

Sometimes you want something to happen when a certain type of database change happens. For example, a table may contain information pertaining to a sales order. Several different applications read the sales order and do something with it. Dependencies exist between the different applications, so the shipping application cannot process a record until the accounts payable application marks it paid, which cannot happen until the invoicing application makes and sends a bill for it, and so on. Each of these applications may update an order status flag stored in a column on the table. However, let's say someone wants to track the number of days it takes for the record to go from invoicing to delivery. You decide the best way to handle this situation is to populate a history table with the sales order, the new and old status, and the date the record changed. A database trigger will help you do the job. This chapter will explain how database triggers work and what other things they can do. How you develop and maintain database triggers using Procedure Builder and other means will also be covered. All told, the content of this chapter comprises 24 percent of OCP Exam 2 test content.

Developing Database Triggers

In this section, you will cover the following points regarding developing database triggers:

- Identifying different trigger types
- Creating statement triggers
- Creating row triggers
- Dictionary information about triggers

A trigger is a database object directly associated with a particular table that fires whenever a specific statement or type is issued against that table.

The types of statements that fire triggers are query and data manipulation statements like **update**, **delete** and **insert** statements. In this section, you will learn how to distinguish a database trigger from other types of triggers in Oracle, along with the syntax for defining triggers. The difference between a statement trigger and a row trigger in the Oracle database will be presented as well. For simplicity's sake, assume Procedure Builder is used to develop triggers, although you will be presented with the correct SQL statement syntax for building triggers—even though Procedure Builder builds it for you.

Identifying Different Trigger Types

One favorite question asked to distinguish Oracle server-side PL/SQL developers from Developer/2000 professionals is "What is the difference between a database trigger, a stored procedure, and a Forms trigger?" You haven't covered Oracle Forms yet, but now is as good a time as any to start distinguishing one trigger from another.

Part of the answer to the above question lies in where the trigger is stored. A database trigger is stored as a compiled object within the Oracle database. Its source code can be found in the Oracle data dictionary, and when running, its executable is loaded into Oracle's system global area, or SGA for short. The SGA is the memory area the Oracle database uses as it runs. The stored procedure is stored similarly, as compiled code in the database that gets loaded into SGA when necessary for use in an application. Another factor that makes a trigger similar to a stored procedure is that both are written at least partly with PL/SQL.

TIP

As of Oracle 7.3, database triggers are stored in the Oracle database in their compiled form, just like a stored procedure.

However, the substantial difference between a trigger and a stored procedure is when they run. A trigger runs automatically when statements of a certain type execute. For example, if you set up a trigger to fire whenever a user **update**s a record in the EXCH_RATE table, no action is necessary to get that trigger to fire other than updating a record in EXCH_RATE. In other words, you don't need to issue a call explicitly to the trigger. On the other hand, a stored procedure only runs when you call it explicitly from another procedure, or with the PL/SQL Interpreter in Procedure Builder, or with the **execute** command in SQL*Plus.

Finally, consider the Forms trigger. A Forms trigger consists of PL/SQL code that runs when a specific action takes place. So, in this respect a Forms trigger is similar to a database trigger. The difference is that a Forms trigger is stored in the Forms application, in turn stored on a client machine and not the database. The Forms trigger also fires when a specific event occurs on the application GUI, such as a button being pressed. In contrast, the database trigger fires when a database event happens, such as a new row of data being **insert**ed in the table.

Exercises

1. Define a database trigger. What programming language is a trigger developed with? Define a stored procedure. Where are database triggers and stored procedures stored?

2. How does a database trigger differ from a stored procedure?

3. What is a Forms trigger? What programming language is a Forms trigger written in? When does a Forms trigger fire? How is it similar to a database trigger? How is it different?

Creating Statement Triggers

The basic type of database trigger is a statement trigger. It will fire every time a triggering statement occurs on the table to which the trigger is attached. Let's assume you want to monitor the EXCH_RATE table **delete** activity to identify when exchange rates are removed from the table. You create a history table that logs the user that changes the EXCH_RATE table, along with the date/time information and a comment in VARCHAR2 format for tracking when data is removed. Then, you set up a trigger to populate the new EXCH_RATE_HIST table.

Trigger SQL code is sort of a hybrid between a database object creation statement (like **create table**) and straight PL/SQL code. Procedure Builder can be used to develop the trigger, as demonstrated in Figure 10-1. However, since Procedure Builder builds many of the basic SQL syntactic constructs required to compile a database trigger, the following code block demonstrates that basic SQL syntax. Compare the code block to Figure 10-1 in order to understand what work Procedure Builder does for you behind the scenes.

```
CREATE OR REPLACE TRIGGER rate_hist_trigger_01
BEFORE delete ON exch_rate
BEGIN
    INSERT INTO exch_rate_hist (chg_user, chg_date_time, comment)
    VALUES (user, to_char(sysdate,'YYYY-MM-DD HH:MIAM'),
            'Exchange rates removed from table on this date');
END;
```

Now, consider the syntax used to create this trigger. First, you consider the **create or replace trigger** *trig_name* portion. This code indicates the creation of a new trigger, but also states that if a trigger of the same name already exists, Oracle should go ahead and replace it. Reexamine Figure 10-1 now and notice that you don't need to specify this to Procedure Builder in order for it to create your trigger. The *trig_name* portion allows you to identify the trigger by a name of your making. Optionally, you can

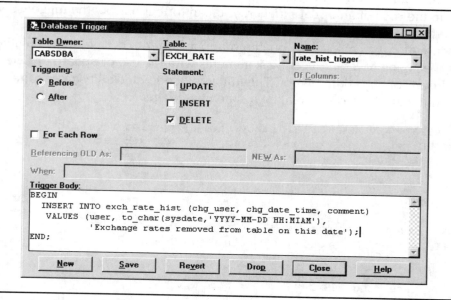

FIGURE 10-1. *Creating statement triggers in Procedure Builder*

identify the user who will own this trigger. Ideally, it will be the same schema owning the table you attach the trigger to. Notice also in Procedure Builder that if you do not want to write your own name for the trigger, the tool will generate one for you. This is not the case with writing a trigger in SQL*Plus—Procedure Builder generates this trigger name, not the Oracle database. So, if you are writing trigger code in a flat file and intend to load it using SQL*Plus, do not forget a trigger name or else your code will fail.

The next big line to consider is **before delete on** *tbl_name*. This line identifies three big components. First is when the trigger fires, either before the triggering statement is processed by Oracle or after it is processed by Oracle. Should you want to run the trigger after the **delete** statement takes place, change the **before** keyword to **after**. The second important point about this line of the trigger creation statement is the **delete** keyword. You can set up a trigger to run as the result of an **update** or **insert** statement in addition to **delete**. Procedure Builder allows you to set up this information with the use of the check boxes and text box in the middle portion of Figure 10-1, and their use should be fairly self-explanatory. If you are confused, you should try to create a trigger using the Database Trigger Editor module of Procedure Builder, but remember first to connect to the database.

In the case of an **update** trigger, you can further narrow the trigger scope to fire only when a particular column value is changed with the use of **update of** *col_name*. Also, you can set up a trigger to do multiple activities by specifying several triggering statements with the use of **update or delete or insert**, or a portion thereof. The following code block illustrates some of the different options for creating a statement trigger:

```
CREATE OR REPLACE TRIGGER stacy.rate_hist_trigger_01
BEFORE update on (exch_rate,valid_date) ON exch_rate
DECLARE
BEGIN
   ...
END;

CREATE OR REPLACE TRIGGER stacy.rate_hist_trigger_01
BEFORE insert OR update OR delete ON exch_rate
DECLARE
BEGIN
   IF inserting THEN...
   ELSIF updating THEN...
   ELSIF deleting THEN...
   END IF;
END;
```

The second example in the preceding block illustrates an interesting point about database triggers—you can set them up to fire for multiple triggering events. Within the trigger's PL/SQL, you can set up to distinguish different activities that correspond to the different events causing the trigger to fire. The keywords **inserting**, **updating**, and **deleting** are defined for you in the DBMS_STANDARD package, and can be used in a nested **if then** statement as the test criteria for branching your code for multiple triggering events. These items are called *conditional predicates*.

Use of **updating**, **inserting**, or **deleting** in your trigger segues into the final area of the trigger for you to consider—the PL/SQL block that executes as a result of the triggering event. Any valid PL/SQL statement is acceptable in the trigger body. Procedure Builder allows you to develop your trigger body within the Database Trigger Editor module, and again simplifies your work by putting together the **begin** and **end** keywords for you. Many SQL statements are permitted within a trigger body as well. Such statements include **select**, **update**, **delete**, or **insert**. The same restrictions on DDL statements (such as **create table** or **truncate table**) that are present in PL/SQL on stored procedures apply to triggers as well.

Exercises

1. Define the valid triggering events that can be defined for statement triggers. How can these events be combined into one trigger, and how then will Oracle be able to distinguish what should happen, and when?

2. What determines when a trigger will fire with respect to its triggering event (Hint: before or after)?

3. To what precision can you specify the statement trigger to restrict itself with respect to **update** triggering events?

Creating Row Triggers

Sometimes, with trigger development, you want to have more precision over work the trigger will accomplish than a statement trigger allows. For the sake of example, say you want to eliminate the VALID_DATE column from your EXCH_RATE table and simply have EXCH_RATE list the "from" and "to" currency along with an exchange rate, and you will simply assume the rate is valid. Your batch process will then come in and update the exchange rate every day—let's pretend it does so with only one **update** statement. You decide later that you want a history table that gives "from" currency, "to" currency, an old rate, a new rate, and the date the rate changed. However, these requirements may be beyond what a statement trigger provides. Remember, your statement trigger fires once for the **update** of the entire table, while you want a trigger that does something for every row.

A row trigger gives this functionality. A row trigger adds some syntax to the statement trigger to identify a method for accessing row data in the trigger's own table, both before the triggering statement executes and after. The following code block illustrates the syntactic changes that must occur in order for the statement trigger to become a row trigger. Pretend that for timestamp reasons you want to store your change data as a VARCHAR2 string in the EXCH_RATE_HIST table.

```
CREATE OR REPLACE TRIGGER stacy.rate_hist_trigger_01
AFTER update ON exch_rate
REFERENCING OLD AS old NEW AS new
FOR EACH ROW
BEGIN
    INSERT INTO exch_rate_hist (chg_user, chg_date_time, from_curcy,
                               to_curcy, old_rate, new_rate,
                               comment)
    VALUES (user, to_char(sysdate,'YYYY-MM-DD HH:MIAM'),
           :old.from_curcy,
           :old.to_curcy, :old.exch_rate, :new.exch_rate,
           'Exchange rates updated from table on this date');
END;
```

TIP
*Read trigger code as follows. The first line is the name of the trigger, and the second line is the triggering event. If you're working with statement triggers, the next line will be **declare** for variable declaration or **begin** to start the PL/SQL code body, if you're working with row triggers, the next line will define the reference names for your old and new data (optional), and the line after that will say **for each row**.*

Several neat things become possible with row triggers. First, your trigger gains the ability to access row data involved in the triggering statement, both as it existed before the triggering statement runs and after. This ability gives you tremendous flexibility. The two lines in the trigger creation statement to pay attention to for row triggers are **referencing old as** *old* **new as** *new* and **for each row**. For syntactic correctness, put these statements in this order in your trigger. When using Procedure Builder, you merely check the box next to "for each row" on the Database Trigger Editor module interface and the options for creating a row trigger are available to use.

Notice something peculiar about the code block also—the references to **:old.***col_name* or **:new.***col_name*. The **old** and **new** keywords can be used to identify both the old version and new version of column data in rows that are changing. These keywords must be preceded with a colon in your trigger PL/SQL. You can define different words to replace **old** and **new** in the column references line starting with the **referencing** keyword. You needn't include the line starting with **referencing** if you decide not to change your keywords **old** and **new**, and those keywords will still be available for you so long as you specify the trigger is a row trigger.

Finally, if you return your attention briefly back to Figure 10-1, you will see all the interface features Procedure Builder gives for building row triggers. You can change the name used for referencing old and new versions of row and column data with text boxes. Another text body is preceded with the phrase "When". This box corresponds with a feature in row triggers allowing you to restrict when the trigger fires based on a SQL condition that must be resolved in order for Oracle to fire the trigger. Should you want to use a **when** clause in Procedure Builder, simply add the restriction to the text box after the "When" phrase. If data for any row change causes the logic for the **when** clause to test FALSE, the trigger is not fired for the row. The **when** clause is checked for all rows, however. The code block produced by your inclusion of a **when** clause that causes the trigger only to fire when either the "from" currency or the "to" currency is the U.S. dollar (represented by USD in the table) is listed here:

```
CREATE OR REPLACE TRIGGER stacy.rate_hist_trigger_01
AFTER update ON exch_rate
REFERENCING OLD AS old NEW AS new
FOR EACH ROW
WHEN (new.from_curcy = 'USD' OR new.to_curcy = 'USD')
BEGIN
    INSERT INTO exch_rate_hist (chg_user, chg_date_time, from_curcy,
```

```
                           to_curcy, old_rate, new_rate,
                           comment)
       VALUES (user, to_char(sysdate,'YYYY-MM-DD HH:MIAM'),
   :old.from_curcy,
             :old.to_curcy, :old.exch_rate, :new.exch_rate,
             'Exchange rates updated from table on this date');
   END;
```

TIP
*Performance on a row trigger is usually better
when you set the trigger to be an **after** trigger
than a **before** trigger because only one read
from memory is required for both the trigger
and then for the triggering statement.*

Exercises

1. You have an **update** row trigger set to fire conditionally with a **when**
   clause. You issue an **update** statement that changes ten rows. On the
   third row, the **when** clause causes the trigger not to fire. Will the
   trigger fire for the fourth through tenth row? Why or why not?

2. What special character must precede a reference to old or new data
   involved in the row trigger execution?

3. With row triggers, is it more efficient to define the trigger to fire
   before or after the triggering event is complete? Why?

Dictionary Information about Triggers

Several dictionary views are available to show information about the triggers
on a database. They include DBA_TRIGGERS, USER_TRIGGERS, and
ALL_TRIGGERS. These different views all have alternate scope, including all
triggers on a database, all triggers on a database owned by the current user,
and all triggers on a database the current user can see. These views contain
basically the same columns, with the exception of the OWNER column
displaying trigger owner and the TABLE_OWNER column listing the owner
of the table the trigger is attached to. These two appear on only the
DBA_TRIGGERS and ALL_TRIGGERS views. Other columns in the

DBA_TRIGGERS view appear here. If the column datatype is unusual in any way, the datatype is listed:

- **TRIGGER_NAME**   The name of the trigger.

- **TRIGGER_TYPE**   Whether the trigger is a statement or row trigger.

- **TRIGGERING_EVENT**   The event that causes the trigger to fire, either **insert**, **update**, or **delete**.

- **TABLE_NAME**   The table to which the trigger is attached.

- **REFERENCING_NAMES**   The **old** or **new** referencing names you have chosen for the trigger. NULL for statement triggers.

- **WHEN_CLAUSE**   The **when** clause that determines if the trigger will fire for that row. NULL for statement triggers. Datatype VARCHAR2(2000).

- **STATUS**   Whether the trigger is enabled or disabled. When disabled, the trigger will not fire.

- **DESCRIPTION**   Contains basic information about the trigger, including everything after **create or replace** up to the PL/SQL section **begin**. Datatype VARCHAR2(2000).

- **TRIGGER_BODY**   Contains all PL/SQL code in the body of your trigger. Datatype LONG.

TIP
*Obtaining data from this view in SQL*Plus usually requires playing with several options. Using **set arraysize 5**, **set maxdata 32767**, and **set long 9999** should suffice to pull data back from this unusually sized view.*

DBA_TRIGGER_COLS, USER_TRIGGER_COLS, and ALL_TRIGGER_COLS are another set of views you can use to find out information about specific columns used in triggers. This view has several columns designed to show the use of columns within the trigger, such as those involved in the column-specific **update** that can be used to determine if a trigger will fire. This view is the same across the three levels of scope provided by USER_, ALL_, and DBA_, save that only the latter two have the

TRIGGER_OWNER and TABLE_OWNER columns. The rest of the columns of the view are shown in the following list, along with an explanation of their usage.

- **TRIGGER_NAME**   The name of the trigger.

- **TABLE_NAME**   The table to which the trigger is attached.

- **COLUMN_NAME**   The name of the column used by the trigger.

- **COLUMN_LIST**   A YES or NO value set if the column is used in a **for update of** clause on the trigger definition.

- **COLUMN_USAGE**   Displays the usage of the column both as a referenced value (i.e., **new** or **old**) and as a parameter to a stored procedure or function call (**in**, **out**, or **in out**).

TIP
*Whether you're talking the **when** clause, the trigger status, or PL/SQL code bodies in the trigger, it's all stored in DBA_TRIGGERS!*

Exercises

1. What are two dictionary views you can use to find information about triggers? In which will you find source code for the trigger body?

2. What **set** statements are useful for retrieving information from the trigger view containing trigger bodies?

Managing Triggers

In this section, you will cover the following points about managing triggers:

- Managing trigger development

- Security issues and trigger availability

- Trigger firing mechanisms

- Creating triggers that complement the Oracle database

With the initial design factors in place, you should now consider aspects of managing trigger development, maintenance, and usage. This section covers the facts you should know about the development of triggers, such as how many triggers can be out there on one table, considerations you need to make on triggers that fire other triggers, and other items. In addition, the security and permissions available to limit trigger development will be covered, along with how you limit trigger availability. Finally, you will consider how triggers fire, and how you can manage that aspect of trigger development as well.

Managing Trigger Development

Several factors govern the development of triggers. First of all, within the categories of triggers presented in the prior section, there are six possible subcategories. Three of these subcategories are **update**, **delete** and **insert**—the types of statements that induce trigger firing. These three categories then are matrixed across two subcategories determined by when the trigger fires with respect to the triggering event. Thus, you can have 12 triggers on a table for Oracle7 databases, 1 of each type. To explain further, the types are as follows:

- **before update** statement trigger
- **after update** statement trigger
- **before insert** statement trigger
- **after insert** statement trigger
- **before delete** statement trigger
- **after delete** statement trigger
- **before update** row trigger
- **after update** row trigger
- **before insert** row trigger
- **after insert** row trigger
- **before delete** row trigger
- **after delete** row trigger

This high number of database triggers you can attach to your tables should suffice for all but the most trigger-intensive applications. Given the number of options within Oracle to limit your trigger use, there won't be a need for more than maybe three or four triggers on each table in your database. However, if yours is the exception, you can design triggers for each category that fire for multiple triggering events, such **insert or update or delete**.

One situation to beware of is when the PL/SQL in your trigger causes other triggers to fire. Although the cascading effect of trigger firing isn't a problem by itself, necessarily, you must ensure the cascading trigger firing does not come back to haunt your table. For example, say trigger A on table A fires on **insert**. Trigger A inserts a row into table B, which in turn fires an **insert** trigger on table B, which inserts a row back into table A. As you may imagine, this will cause a problem, and is quite simply a poor design choice. Up to 32 cascading triggers can fire, subject to limitation by setting the MAX_OPEN_CURSORS initialization parameter on Oracle database startup.

Certain restrictions on using datatypes in triggers exist as well. For example, in Oracle7 the use of triggers to modify or populate columns declared to be datatype LONG or LONG RAW can get a little annoying. Triggers can **insert** data into a column declared as type LONG. Your variables in the trigger, however, cannot be declared as type LONG or LONG RAW. If you want to **select** data from a column declared as type LONG or LONG RAW, you have to convert your column to a constrained type such as VARCHAR2 as part of the **select**, and it cannot be longer than 32 kilobytes. Also, you cannot use **new** or **old** references on the column(s) of a table declared as type LONG or LONG RAW.

Use of procedures or functions in packages can cause problems when called from a trigger related to the cascading issue described earlier. Sometimes, when an **update** in a package program unit on the table whose firing trigger has called the package program unit, the two **updates** may conflict. This conflict can cause the **before** trigger's activity to roll back and refire several times before the conflict can be resolved. Obviously, this is a performance issue that can cause many problems that must be addressed in system design.

Row evaluation order may also be a factor when database triggers fire. Be aware that a trigger will not necessarily process row data in the order you want it to. Relational databases are not designed to enforce row order. Should you want to process data based on order, you may want to consider writing a stored procedure that uses a cursor with an **order by** statement after the fact.

Triggers also run into big problems when you don't handle exceptions and errors that may occur as part of their PL/SQL execution. Remember, triggers are just like other blocks of PL/SQL, so they can have exception handlers. And like other PL/SQL blocks, triggers are going to blow off if an unhandled exception occurs as the trigger executes, causing the activity happening in your trigger to roll back, and returning ugly errors to your users. But, on the bright side, your trigger's transaction processing rolls back, so you won't have data corruption issues.

The Problem of Mutating or Constraining Tables

Sometimes, triggers have errors in their execution due to mutating or constraining tables. A table mutates every time an **update**, **insert**, or **delete** statement is issued against it. A table constrains if SQL statements or referential integrity constraints must read data from it in order for a data change to happen to another table. Statement triggers never have problems due to mutating or constraining tables, but row triggers might in certain cases. A row trigger cannot read or modify data from the table it is attached to when firing except through referencing **old** and **new** values for that single row. In addition, the trigger cannot modify the table to which a changing column references via primary, foreign, or unique constraint. In other words, if you have an **insert** row trigger firing on an added record, and a column in that added record has a foreign key, the row trigger cannot go out to the referenced table and add a row to it to satisfy the foreign key constraint. The golden rule in this situation is that the trigger must be bound both by existing read consistencies and referential integrity. Figure 10-2 demonstrates the restrictions on row triggers related to mutating or constraining tables.

Exercises

1. How many triggers can be attached to a table? What are the different types of triggers you can attach? What datatype issues do you run into with triggers and the LONG datatypes?

2. What is a trigger called when it changes data in another table such that another trigger fires? How many times can this happen before Oracle gives an error?

3. What is a constraining table? A mutating table? What restrictions are there on row triggers regarding these two situations?

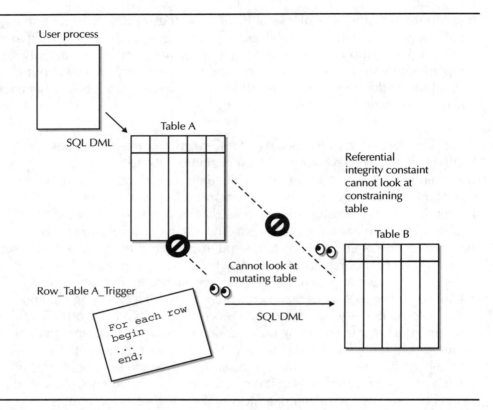

FIGURE 10-2. *Restrictions on row triggers and mutating or constraining tables*

Required Security and Trigger Availability

Security on trigger creation is managed with the **create trigger** privilege. Once created, you will own the trigger. If, on the other hand, you want to put the trigger in someone else's schema, you must have the **create any trigger** system privilege. However, trigger creation is one situation where the restrictions don't stop with mere privilege granting. In addition to possession of the **create trigger** privilege, you must have one of the following situations in your favor as well. They are as follows:

- Ownership of the table to which the trigger is attached

- Appropriate privileges to issue **alter table** statements against the table to which trigger is attached

■ The **alter any table** system privilege

Once created, the trigger will be enabled and ready for use. There are no specific privileges required to run a trigger, other than the privileges required to execute the triggering event, **update** if it is an **update** trigger, and so on. No special syntax to run the trigger, either—simply execute the triggering event and the trigger fires automatically.

Sometimes a situation will arise where you want to get rid of a trigger without actually getting rid of it. Say you want to execute a batch of **update** statements on a table with a trigger that maintains historical data for that table. You may want to turn the trigger off or disable it before running the event that would otherwise fire the trigger. To do this, you must issue an **alter trigger disable** statement. The following code block shows you how to disable our trigger on the EXCH_RATE table from SQL*Plus:

```
SQL> alter trigger RATE_HIST_TRIGGER_01 disable;
```

The nice thing about disabling triggers is that you can get them back in action easily by reenabling them. Disabling simply means the trigger won't fire; the compiled version of it still lives in the Oracle database. You may want to eliminate the trigger entirely, in which case you issue the **drop trigger** statement, such as the one listed in the following code block. The downside to dropping a trigger is that after the trigger is dropped, you must fully re-create it before it is available on the database again. The following code block demonstrates enabling and dropping triggers:

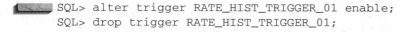

```
SQL> alter trigger RATE_HIST_TRIGGER_01 enable;
SQL> drop trigger RATE_HIST_TRIGGER_01;
```

TIP
*If you disable a trigger that handles some work when a certain type of statement occurs, and then perform that statement, the work the trigger would ordinarily handle **will not happen**. Furthermore, when you reenable the trigger later, the trigger will not go back and do that work for you. Reenabling triggers doesn't enforce things that happened while the trigger was disabled.*

Exercises

1. What security and permissions must be satisfied to create a trigger? How is a trigger fired? What security and permissions must be satisfied to run a trigger?

2. How is a trigger disabled? Once disabled, how do you get it back in action? How do you remove a trigger from the database?

Understanding Trigger Firing Mechanisms

Consider the following facts about statement and row triggers. A trigger fires as the result of a triggering event. You can specify the trigger to fire either before or after Oracle processes the triggering statement. You know this feature is set either by clicking on the radio button within Procedure Builder when creating the trigger or with the **before** or **after** keywords in the **create trigger** statement.

The **before** trigger fires in the following way. When a triggering statement occurs, Oracle processes the trigger first, along with its data changes, if any. Then, Oracle processes the triggering statement's data changes. As discussed, it is slightly less efficient to process the trigger before the triggering event for **update** row triggers, but in some cases it might work out better logically, such as in the case of **delete** triggers. However, there is no significant performance difference between execution of the trigger before or after the triggering event for statement triggers.

In contrast, the **after** trigger fires after Oracle completes processing for the triggering event. This method is slightly more efficient for **update** row triggers, as was discussed in the previous section. If you make the trigger wait and fire after the triggering event, then Oracle will already have the changed row stored in the buffer cache of the SGA, thus making it more available for the trigger processing.

One situation you must consider, however, is when triggers won't fire. Say, for example, you have a table with five million rows. To **delete** all data from this table with a **delete from** *tbl_name* statement will take a long time for Oracle to process. Instead, you may want to consider the **truncate table** *tbl_name*. Now, this statement will run a lot faster and is more efficient with disk space than the comparable **delete** statement. But, the **truncate table** statement is a DDL operation, not a DML statement like **delete**. DDL statements do not fire triggers. Thus, if you have some **delete** trigger out there and you truncate your table, figure on creating a stored procedure to run the operation before truncating the table.

Exercises

1. What are some performance considerations on row triggers that are set to fire before the triggering event's data gets processed?

2. On what data "change" operation won't a trigger fire?

Creating Triggers that Complement the Oracle Database

On some weaker databases in the market, triggers can be set up to perform several different types of activities that may be data-driven. For example, you may want to monitor or audit the **update** statements on a particular table to ensure that the users who change data are tracked. In addition, you may want to enforce a complex integrity constraint where the constraining data or table depends on the data being added to the database. Other examples include history tables and event logging. Unlike some of those weaker databases out there, Oracle allows you to perform many of these tasks with database features other than triggers. Features such as database auditing, declarative integrity constraints built into tables, and advanced replication with snapshots avoid some of the performance burdens associated with firing the substantial number of triggers inherent in a system that uses triggers to perform these tasks. Still, you should consider how triggers can be used to mimic functions on the Oracle database, and identify when triggers may handle functionality that other Oracle features do not.

The one type of activity where a trigger really shines is for creating data in one table based on a triggering event in another. Because this is one area where OCP will test you extensively, you should understand it thoroughly. Figure 10-3 shows pictorially the situation where you have an **insert** or other triggering statement that happens on the database, and you want to populate another table with some sort of information.

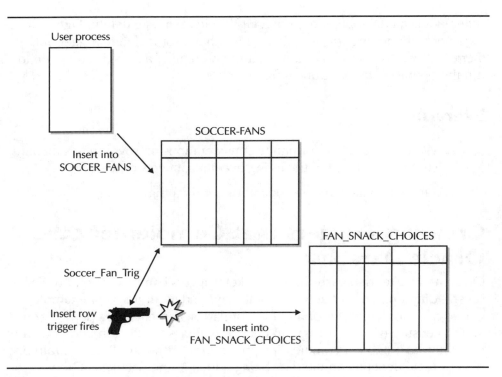

FIGURE 10-3. *Populating event or historical data with triggers*

Let's say you have a table called SOCCER_FANS that keeps track of all the soccer fans in the world. In each, you're converting to this format from a format where you had several soccer fans tables, one for each country in the world, like SOCCER_FANS_US, SOCCER_FANS_CAN, etc. To move the data into your SOCCER_FANS table, you might use a **insert into** SOCCER_FANS (**select * from** SOCCER_FANS_CAN) statement, substituting the name of each soccer fans table for each country in turn.

Let's assume you have a companion table for SOCCER_FANS in your new application that tracks each fan's snack choices to help the stadium concessions determine what to get for each soccer fan as they enter the stadium. However, this **update** will move many rows into the table at a time. If you use a statement trigger, the trigger fires only once per **update**, while the row trigger will fire for each row moved. Obviously, you want to use a row trigger. Assuming that your populated table is called FAN_SNACK_CHOICES with columns FAN_ID,

PREF_BVG1, PREF_BVG2, PREF_FOOD1 and PREF_FOOD2, your trigger might look something like the following code block:

```
CREATE OR REPLACE TRIGGER stacy.soccer_fan_snack_01
AFTER insert ON soccer_fans
FOR EACH ROW
 BEGIN
    INSERT INTO fan_snack_choices (fan_id, pref_bvg1, pref_bvg2,
                            pref_food1, pref_food2)
    VALUES (:new.fan_id,'BEER','SODA','HAMBURGER','ICE CREAM');
END;
```

Your ability to pass OCP will depend on your ability to read trigger code, understand what the trigger does, and figure out if that's what you want to do. For example, if you eliminate the **for each row** line, your trigger will not fire once per row; instead, it will fire once for the entire **insert** statement. You should also understand the whole mutating/constraining table issue as it relates to row triggers. First of all, mutating or constraining table issues don't relate to statement triggers, only row triggers. With this fact in mind, recall that within your row trigger you may not read or alter data on the table to which the trigger is attached, save for using the **old** and **new** keywords to reference the old version of the row data and the new. So, with your SOCCER_FAN_SNACK_01 triggery you cannot **select** data from SOCCER_FAN outright, but only reference new SOCCER_FAN row data using **:new.**fan_id.

Another important restriction relates to foreign keys. Say, for example, your FAN_SNACK_CHOICES table has a foreign key constraint on its FAN_ID column that references back to FAN_ID on SOCCER_FANS to ensure that snacks aren't added for which there are no corresponding soccer fans. When the row trigger fires, however, you receive an error saying something to the effect of "Your table is mutating, foreign key constraint may not see it." To correct this type of problem, drop the foreign key constraint, and SOCCER_FAN_SNACKS will not reference the SOCCER_FANS table on FAN_ID anymore.

TIP

In most cases, Oracle will not allow you to set up the trigger in this type of situation where the foreign key creates a constraining table situation.

Another situation where using triggers complements the Oracle database rather than mimicking existing other functionality is where you want to populate a history table. An application idea has already been given with the EXCH_RATE table change and related historical data population. Some issues to watch in that situation include the mutating/constraining table issue raised in the previous example, the selection of data from the table to which the row trigger is attached, and so on.

Exercises

1. Identify some uses for triggers that mimic other Oracle database features. Identify some trigger uses that don't mimic other Oracle features.

2. Describe a situation where a trigger will encounter a mutating table. How does Oracle respond in this situation? What can you do to correct problems that arise as the result of mutating tables?

Chapter Summary

Though this chapter is slightly more brief, it is highly important to understand it in order to pass OCP Exam 2. On the OCP exam, you will find about 24 percent of the test questions relate to usage of triggers. This chapter covers trigger usage, development of triggers, and management of both triggers and the issues that arise with their usage. The term "trigger" can be used to refer to many different objects around the Oracle database. For example, there are triggers within the Oracle database and triggers on Oracle Forms. There can be some blurring between triggers and other programs in Oracle that use PL/SQL code in them, too, like stored procedures, functions, and the like. To identify a database trigger, remember that the database trigger is stored within the database—unlike a Forms trigger, which is stored in the Forms application. And although stored procedures and functions also contain PL/SQL code, only the database trigger has a defined process set up for executing the PL/SQL code already defined.

The first key to passing OCP is your ability to identify the two main types of database triggers. There are statement triggers and row triggers. A statement trigger will fire when a triggering event occurs on the table, such as **update**, **insert**, or **delete**. It will fire once for that event and once only. A statement trigger is created with the basic **create or replace trigger** syntax in which the second line defines your triggering event, and after that you define the PL/SQL code that will comprise the body of your database trigger. Statement triggers do not allow you to access data being changed as part of the triggering event, but they may be used for simple purposes of counting the times a triggering statement occurs. Before taking OCP Exam 2, be sure you can identify a statement trigger based on looking at the trigger source code.

You name your triggers explicitly in Oracle, although each trigger needn't have a unique name. For example, if you have table FOO and you want to create a trigger called FOO, you can do that, although it may become confusing later when you have many triggers and many tables, and they all have the same names. Procedure Builder also generates unique names for your triggers automatically, but this is an application feature, not a database feature.

Row triggers are more flexible than statement triggers because row triggers can fire for every row processed by a triggering statement. In addition to the **create or replace trigger** statement and the line defining the triggering statement, the row trigger adds syntax to define how to access old and new column values for the individual row affected by the triggering statement. Also, the line **for each row** must be added to explicitly define this as a row trigger. Now, you need to make sure you can identify a row trigger when given a sample trigger source code statement. Specifically, you should make sure you understand that you cannot reference row data if the **for each row** line is not included to define the trigger as a row trigger.

A triggering statement is an **update**, **insert**, or **delete** statement on the database to which the trigger is attached that causes the trigger to fire. Oracle database triggers can fire either before the triggering event is processed or after, depending on how you code the trigger. The **before** keyword is used to specify the trigger process its thing before Oracle processes the triggering statement, as in **before insert on** DATADB. The **after** keyword is used to specify the trigger process after Oracle processes the triggering statement, as in **after delete on** DATADB.

Assuming you are using the standard **old** and **new** keywords for referencing old and new column values for rows as part of the row trigger, there is some special syntax for you to remember when writing code to reference that data. Think of **old** and **new** as being records defined to be the same type as the table on which the row trigger is defined. You then reference a particular column in the following way: either **:old.**col_name for old row values or **:new.**col_name for new ones. Do *not forget* the colon preceding **old** or **new** in your trigger code body or it will not compile. Use common sense when referencing old and new values—for example, there won't be an old value for an **insert** row trigger, nor will there be a new value for a **delete** trigger.

For all but the most obscure information about triggers, you should be able to find the information you need in the USER_TRIGGERS, ALL_TRIGGERS, or DBA_TRIGGERS dictionary views in the Oracle database. The columns in the DBA_TRIGGERS views include OWNER, TRIGGER_NAME, TRIGGER_TYPE, TRIGGERING_EVENT, TABLE_OWNER, TABLE_NAME, REFERENCING_ NAMES, WHEN_CLAUSE, STATUS, DESCRIPTION, and TRIGGER_BODY. Important to note is that you can find out the status of your trigger (i.e., enabled or disabled) in the STATUS column on DBA_TRIGGERS, not on the DBA_OBJECTS view like other database objects in Oracle. In addition, there is information in the DBA_TRIGGER_COLS column on the table columns in use within the trigger.

You are allowed to define up to 12 triggers on a table. Bear in mind, too, that you can specify multiple triggering events in the second line of your trigger creation code, as in **after insert or update on** DATADB. Within your trigger code body, you can specify certain code blocks to run for each triggering statement with the use of the special keywords **inserting**, **updating**, or **deleting**, which evaluate to TRUE or FALSE based on whether or not the triggering event is an **insert**, **update**, or **delete** statement, respectively. These conditional predicates are defined in the DBMS_STANDARD package.

Your 12 triggers on the table fall into the following categories. There can be six each of triggers that process before and after the triggering statement. Six triggers can be statement triggers and the other six can be row triggers. Within each of those categories, you can have three types of triggering events: **update**, **insert**, or **delete**. Given the fact that many activities you may have chosen to develop triggers for have specific Oracle features to address them, such as database auditing, replication, and other activities, you shouldn't usually exceed this limit, and very well may not even come close to it.

The following restrictions are present on database triggers. All variables and parameters passed to stored procedures in Oracle must have internal datatypes like DATE, NUMBER, RAW, LONG, LONG RAW, VARCHAR2, CHAR, or ROWID. No PL/SQL datatype extensions like PLS_INTEGER, POSITIVE, TEXT, or the like will be accepted. Related to this datatype limitation is another on columns of type LONG or LONG RAW. To **select** data from a column of type LONG within your trigger, you must convert it to a constrained datatype like VARCHAR2 and limit its size to 32K or less. In row triggers, you cannot reference columns of type LONG or LONG RAW using **old** or **new**. Another limit on triggers relates to other triggers that may fire when one trigger fires. This effect is called cascading. A trigger may cause up to 32 cascading triggers to fire, after which Oracle returns an error.

You should take care to handle all errors that may arise as the result of your trigger. You can code an exception handler into the PL/SQL block appearing as part of your trigger body that handles your errors. If you have an unhandled exception in your trigger body and Oracle raises it, both the work of your triggering statement and the trigger will be rolled back.

You must also factor in the effects of mutating or constraining tables as part of your trigger execution. Any DML statement such as an **update**, **insert**, or **delete** will cause a table to mutate. Similarly, any foreign key constraint or **select** lookup on another table containing valid values is a constraining table. If a row trigger performs a **select** statement on either the table it is attached to or another table that references the table the trigger is attached to via foreign key, the trigger may encounter mutating table errors. This problem is due to the fact that the trigger won't be able to see the change being made until the action is complete. In some cases, you simply cannot fix the problem other than not to **select** data from the table your trigger attaches to. If, instead, you are trying to **select** data from the table to which your trigger attaches, you should consider dropping the foreign key constraint if you want your trigger to work—or, alternately, you should enforce the foreign key constraint using a trigger rather than a declarative foreign key constraint.

To use a trigger, you must have appropriate permissions to run the triggering statement that causes the trigger to fire. There is no **execute** permission on triggers per se other than this permission. Creating a trigger requires the **create trigger** privilege along with one of the following: ownership of the table to which you associate the trigger, privileges to issue alter table statements against the table to which you associate the trigger, or the **alter any table** system privilege. A created trigger is enabled automatically. To disable it, issue **alter trigger** *trig_name* **disable**. Disabling a trigger causes it not to fire, but keeps its definition in the database. To eliminate the trigger entirely, issue the **drop trigger** statement.

Before taking OCP Exam 2, make sure you understand situations where triggers complement your use of the Oracle database. Most of the time, there is another feature in Oracle that substitutes for triggers very well; however, when it comes to populating other tables based on triggering statements on one table, triggers can't be beat. But wholesale replication is better accomplished with Oracle's replication features like snapshots.

Two-Minute Drill

- Two types of triggers that exist in Oracle are Forms triggers and database triggers.

- A Forms trigger is a prescribed set of PL/SQL actions that happen each time an event such as clicking a button occurs.

- A database trigger is a prescribed set of PL/SQL actions that happen each time a triggering statement such as an **update**, **insert**, or **delete** statement occurs on the database.

- Database triggers are similar to stored PL/SQL blocks both in that they are written primarily in PL/SQL and they are stored in the database. The two differ in that triggers also define how the PL/SQL code will execute.

- There are two types of database triggers: statement triggers and row triggers. A statement trigger will fire only once for a triggering statement. A row trigger fires once for every row affected by a triggering statement.

- Before taking OCP Exam 2, make sure you have looked at many different trigger code bodies and can identify the difference between a statement trigger and a row trigger.

- Row triggers have the following identifiable features:

  - A line in the source code saying **for each row**.

  - References to old and new column data for changed rows prefaced with special syntax such as **:old**.*col_name* or **:new**.*col_name*.

  - A line that defines alternatives for referencing old and new column data that reads **referencing old as** *old* **new as** *new*.

■ Any trigger definition that doesn't contain these distinguishing characteristics of row triggers is a statement trigger.

■ Triggers can be set to fire either before Oracle processes the triggering statement with the use of the **before** keyword in a trigger definition, as in **before delete on** EMPL, or after Oracle processes the triggering statement, as in **after insert on** EMPL.

■ Triggers that fire as a result of **update** statements can be set to fire only when a specific column is changed, with use of the **after update of** *col_name* **on** EMPL syntax. If an **update** statement occurs that doesn't change the column specified, the trigger does not fire.

■ You can define multiple triggering events for one trigger, and then distinguish the processing of the trigger with an **if-then-else** statement within the trigger body.

■ The keywords **inserting**, **updating**, or **deleting** can be used when multiple triggering events are defined to use in the **if-then-else** statement. These three keywords evaluate to TRUE or FALSE depending on what statement has fired the trigger.

■ Any valid PL/SQL statement is acceptable for use in a trigger.

■ Row triggers fire for every row that is affected by the triggering statement. You can, however, include a **when** clause into the definition of the trigger.

■ The **when** clause is a SQL statement that evaluates to TRUE or FALSE. If the **when** clause evaluates to TRUE, the trigger will fire for that row.

■ A **when** clause that evaluates to FALSE causes the trigger not to fire for that row. This does not prevent the row trigger from firing for another row.

■ Basically, all information set about a trigger, including status, **when** clause, trigger source code, table to which the trigger is attached, and other things, can be found in the DBA_TRIGGERS, ALL_TRIGGERS, and USER_TRIGGERS dictionary view in Oracle.

■ Up to 12 triggers can be associated with an Oracle table, or one trigger of any combination of the following features: **before** or **after**, **statement** or **row**, **update** or **insert** or **delete**.

- A trigger whose activities cause other triggers to fire is called a cascading trigger. Up to 32 cascades are permitted to fire as the result of one trigger; after that, Oracle returns an error and rolls back all changes.

- You are not permitted to reference LONG and LONG RAW columns using **old** and **new** syntax in your row trigger.

- You cannot **select** data from LONG or LONG RAW columns in your row trigger without converting the values to constrained datatypes like VARCHAR2. Even then, you're limited to seeing only 32K of the LONG or LONG RAW columns.

- Row triggers are limited by the effects of mutating or constraining tables. A mutating table is one that is affected by the triggering event. A constraining table is one containing valid values referenced by a column in the table affected by the trigger.

- You cannot perform a **select** statement on the table your row trigger is attached to from your row trigger.

- You cannot **update** or **insert** data into another table if one of the column values you add or modify has a foreign key constraint back to the table to which your trigger is attached.

- To create a trigger you must have the **create trigger** privilege. Additionally, you must:

  - Own the table associated to the trigger

  - Be able to issue **alter table** statements associated to the trigger

  - Have the **alter any table** privilege

- Once created, the trigger is enabled and ready to execute. Running the trigger requires no special privileges other than permission to use the triggering statement.

- You prevent the trigger from executing by disabling it. This is done with **alter trigger** *trig_name* **disable**. This allows you to stop trigger execution without eliminating the trigger definition from Oracle entirely.

- To eliminate the trigger from Oracle entirely, you issue the **drop trigger** *trig_name* statement.

■ A **truncate table** statement will not cause a trigger to fire. Importing data into Oracle with the IMPORT utility will cause triggers to fire.

■ Many uses for triggers, such as auditing use of **insert** or **delete** statements, duplicate the effects of other Oracle features. However, one use of triggers that complements the Oracle database is the population or change of data in one table based on a triggering statement executed on another. Such uses include the following:

  ■ Population of historical data tables or rows in child tables

  ■ Population of data for event tracking purposes

■ It's been said before, but you should hear it again—make sure you understand the effects of mutating and constraining tables on row triggers. They affect row trigger execution only, and prevent certain activities you may want the trigger to perform.

■ In general, if you're counting on data changes in the associated table made by the triggering statement to be there in order for the row trigger to work, your row trigger will fail because of mutating or constraining table errors.

Chapter Questions

1. The developer issues the following statement: CREATE OR REPLACE TRIGGER soccer_fans_snacks_02 BEFORE DELETE ON SOCCER_FANS FOR EACH ROW BEGIN DELETE FROM soccer_fans_snacks WHERE fan_id = :old.fan_id; END;. Which of the following statements best describes the trigger created?

   A. An **update** trigger that fires before Oracle processes the triggering statement

   B. An **insert** trigger that fires after Oracle processes the triggering statement

   C. An **insert** trigger that fires after Oracle processes the triggering statement

   D. A **delete** trigger that fires before Oracle processes the triggering statement

2. Which of the following trigger types will be impacted by constraining factors brought on by mutating tables?

   A. Row triggers only

   B. Statement triggers only

   C. Both row and statement triggers

   D. Neither row or statement triggers

3. The developer issues the following statement: CREATE OR REPLACE TRIGGER soccer_fans_snacks_02 BEFORE DELETE ON SOCCER_FANS BEGIN DELETE FROM soccer_fans_snacks WHERE fan_id = :old.fan_id; END;. Why will trigger creation fail?

   A. The row trigger does not properly reference the old value in FAN_ID.

   B. The statement trigger should have been defined as a row trigger.

   C. The statement trigger fires after the **delete** statement is processed.

   D. The row trigger does not properly define the associated table.

4. Table SOCCER_FAN_SEAT contains two columns: FAN and SEAT_NUM. A trigger is created in this table, whose triggering statement definition is AFTER UPDATE OF SEAT_NUM ON SOCCER_FAN_SEAT. You issue an UPDATE statement that changes column FAN only. Which of the following best describes what happens next?

   A. The trigger fires successfully.

   B. The trigger fires unsuccessfully.

   C. Nothing, the SEAT_NUM column was not updated.

   D. The trigger invalidates.

5. You define a trigger that contains the clause AFTER UPDATE OR DELETE ON SOCCER_FAN_SNACKS. Which two of the following keywords may be useful in your trigger source code to distinguish what should run, and when?

    A. inserting

    B. updating

    C. deleting

    D. truncating

6. **To find information about trigger status, which of the following views are appropriate?**

    A. ALL_TRIGGERS

    B. ALL_OBJECTS

    C. ALL_TRIGGER_COLS

    D. ALL_SOURCE

7. **The developer issues the following statement: CREATE OR REPLACE TRIGGER soccer_fans_snacks_02 BEFORE DELETE ON SOCCER_FANS FOR EACH ROW BEGIN DELETE FROM soccer_fans_snacks WHERE fan_id = :prechange.fan_id; END;. Why does the trigger fail on creation?**

    A. The statement trigger improperly references the changed row data.

    B. The row trigger does not define **prechange** as the referencing keyword for old column values.

    C. Row triggers cannot process before the triggering statement.

    D. Statement triggers cannot process before the triggering statement.

8. **The developer issues the following statement: CREATE OR REPLACE TRIGGER soccer_fans_snacks_02 BEFORE DELETE ON SOCCER_FANS FOR EACH ROW BEGIN DELETE FROM soccer_fans_snacks WHERE fan_id = :old.fan_id; END;. Which of the following permissions are required to run this trigger?**

    A. **execute** on SOCCER_FANS

    B. **execute** on SOCCER_FANS_SNACKS_02

c. delete on SOCCER_FANS_SNACKS_02

D. delete on SOCCER_FANS

9. The SOCCER_FANS table has a trigger associated with it that inserts data into SOCCER_FANS_SNACKS whenever rows are inserted into SOCCER_FANS. A foreign key constraint exists between FAN_ID on SOCCER_FANS and SOCCER_FANS_SNACKS. What happens when the trigger fires?

   A. The trigger processes normally.

   B. The trigger invalidates.

   C. The trigger execution fails because of a mutating or constraining table.

   D. The trigger execution succeeds because the trigger is a statement trigger.

10. To achieve better performance on row triggers, you should:

    A. Set the trigger to process after the triggering statement

    B. Set the trigger to process before the triggering statement

    C. Set the trigger to process in parallel with the triggering statement

    D. Set the trigger to **update** the triggering statement

Answers to Chapter Questions

1. D.   A **delete** trigger that fires before Oracle processes the triggering statement

Explanation   Key to understanding what sort of trigger you are dealing with is the ability to read the trigger creation statement. The key clause in this case is **before delete on** SOCCER_FANS. The trigger creation statement defines a trigger that fires only when **delete** statements are issued, and the trigger processing will happen before Oracle processes the triggering statement.

2. A.   Row triggers only

Explanation   Table mutation occurs when your triggering statement changes data in a table. Since statement triggers cannot see data in the table to which they are associated because they cannot issue **select** statements against that table, it stands to reason that mutating tables don't adversely impact statement triggers. However, since you can refer to old and new column values in rows affected by the triggering statement of your row trigger, mutating a table has the potential to adversely impact row trigger performance.

3. B.   The statement trigger should have been defined as a row trigger.

Explanation   Remember that key features of a row trigger include the mandatory **for each row** clause in the trigger definition. Since this trigger doesn't include that important clause, it cannot be a row trigger, eliminating choices A and D right away. A statement trigger cannot reference old and new column values in the affected rows; in fact, a statement trigger cannot reference rows affected by the triggering statement individually. Thus, the answer is B.

4. C. Nothing, the SEAT_NUM column was not updated.

Explanation   Since the trigger contains the clause **after update of** SEAT_NUM **on** SOCCER_FAN_SEAT, the trigger will not fire if an **update** statement affects the FAN column only. Thus, nothing happens when an

update statement comes along and only changes the value in the FAN column, because the SEAT_NUM column was not updated.

5. B. and C. **updating** and **deleting**

Explanation Since the trigger will fire for two triggering statements, **update** and **delete**, it stands to reason that you will want to place in your trigger an **if-then-else** statement that determines which block of code to run in the case of an **update** or **delete**, respectively. The **updating** and **deleting** keywords evaluate to TRUE if the triggering statement is **update** or **delete**, respectively, making them useful in your **if-then-else** statement.

6. A. ALL_TRIGGERS

Explanation The ALL_TRIGGERS view contains status information for triggers, along with source code, **when** clause (if any), and most every other component you define with the trigger. ALL_OBJECTS, though usually where you look for object status, is inappropriate in this situation. ALL_TRIGGER_COLS gives you the columns used by the trigger only, while ALL_SOURCE only contains source code for stored procedures, functions, and packages on the Oracle database.

7. B. The row trigger does not define **prechange** as the referencing keyword for old column values.

Explanation In order to use any keyword to reference old or new column values in rows affected by the triggering statement other than **old** or **new**, you must define the other keyword with the **referencing old as** *old* **new as** *new* clause. Otherwise, the trigger fails on creation.

8. D. **delete** on SOCCER_FANS

Explanation No other permission is required to execute a trigger than permission to run the triggering statement.

9. C. The trigger execution fails because of a mutating or constraining table.

Explanation   Because of the foreign key constraint between FAN_ID on one table and FAN_ID on the other table, the **insert** statement executed by the trigger must have read access to data being changed by the triggering statement. This is not possible in row triggers. In order to resolve the problem, you must drop the foreign key constraint.

   10. A.   Set the trigger to process after the triggering statement

Explanation   Processing the trigger execution after the triggering statement allows Oracle to perform the work necessary with fewer logical reads of data, thereby reducing overall processing time for the trigger and the triggering statement.

UNIT III

Preparing for OCP Exam 3: Building Forms I

CHAPTER
11

Introduction to Oracle
Developer/2000

I n this chapter, you will cover the following areas of Oracle Developer/2000:

- Overview of the Developer/2000 package
- Introduction to Developer/2000 tools
- Customizing your Developer/2000 session

This unit covers materials that are tested in OCP Exam 3, Building Forms I. The first section of this chapter gives a high-level overview of Developer/2000's features, along with the benefits of using it. The next section provides a first look at the components that make up the Developer/2000 package. The final section describes how you can tune the Developer/2000 application so it more closely matches the way you like to work.

Overview of the Developer/2000 Package

In this section, you will cover the following points about the Developer/2000 package:

- Features and benefits of using Developer/2000
- Component groups in Developer/2000

Developer/2000 is comprised of several powerful tools enabling developers to create robust, highly scalable client/server applications more quickly than would be possible using a programming language such as C, Visual Basic, or Java. With it, developers can use tools (known as *Builders* in Developer/2000) to create the different parts of an application, such as forms, reports, charts, queries, database objects, and procedures.

Features and Benefits of Using Developer/2000

Developer/2000 is a sophisticated, and some might say complicated, program. That is true of any application designed to do as many things as

Developer/2000. Learning it well takes time, but that investment will be rewarded with a broad array of powerful, time-saving features. Some of the benefits include enhanced productivity, the ability to design scalable applications, adherence to Oracle's standard of openness between applications, creation of reusable applications, dynamic visualization, and Web deployment of applications to take advantage of recent advances in Internet/Web technology.

Productivity

For individual developers, Oracle Developer/2000 speeds application design by employing object orientation, rapid application design (RAD) techniques, a unified client-server architecture, and online computer-based training modules. It allows components to be reused, and to be grouped into classes whose characteristics can be inherited by subclasses. You can use wizards—special interfaces that prompt you to specify values for certain components that then configure objects according to parameters you defined—to create application components quickly and easily. If you use Oracle's Designer/2000 CASE tool, you can have Developer/2000 base an application on a Designer/2000 model. In addition, Developer/2000 forms can interface with programs written in other languages (C, for instance) utilizing the Open API. The Open API can also be used to create or modify form modules.

For team development, Developer/2000's Project Builder can manage all of the Developer/2000 components, as well as components from third-party sources, such as documentation or multimedia files. When a project includes components created by programs other than Developer/2000, Project Builder is intelligent enough to use the correct third-party tools to edit and compile those components. Project Builder also provides facilities to interface with several other companies' version-control systems. When it is time to distribute an application, Developer/2000 can package the application's parts into a **.zip** or **.tar** file, and it can create customized installation scripts for the Oracle Installer program.

Scalability

Because Oracle Developer/2000 is designed to accommodate a multitiered client/server architecture, it has many features that help an application scale up to handle large quantities of data. At the server, it provides array data manipulation, such as array inserts and deletes. Available without writing a line of code, this feature can dramatically improve application performance, because the application sends inserts, updates, and deletes to the server in a batch. In addition, Developer/2000 can base forms on data returned from stored procedures run on the server, and when the user changes data a Developer/2000 application can recompute subtotals at the client, without having to run another server query. All of these features reduce network traffic, thereby increasing the number of users a given server can accommodate with reasonable performance. Developer/2000 provides a simple drag-and-drop interface to determine whether an object runs on the client or the server.

Openness

Developer/2000 provides a rich set of features for interacting with other applications. It accommodates OCX/ActiveX controls, Object Linking and Embedding (OLE), and Dynamic Data Exchange (DDE). In addition to its native Oracle database, Developer/2000 can work with data stored in SQL Server, Sybase, Informix, Rdb, and DB/2, as well as any database accessible via ODBC or the Oracle Gateway. It can even work with data from multiple databases simultaneously.

In addition, numerous third-party companies have created interfaces between their products and Developer/2000. Available from members of the Open Tools Initiative, these interfaces allow Developer/2000 to interact with CASE and modeling tools, configuration management (version control) tools, workflow engines, and transaction-processing (TP) monitors, among many others.

Usability

Developer/2000 provides a variety of features enabling you to create applications that are extremely easy to use. You can build intuitive drag-and-drop user interfaces; incorporate image and sound files that are stored either within the database or as individual files; call dynamic link library (**.dll**) files to take advantage of platform-specific features within your applications; and incorporate animations, tooltips, and pop-up menus.

Visualization

With a sophisticated feature called *Dynamic Visualization*, Developer/2000 enables you to create applications in which data and the graphics depicting the data can interact. This allows you to create features such as runtime chart editing, seamless Web reporting, graphical drill-down from overview to line-item detail, visual selection of data based on a graphic display, and conditional formatting of the display based on the content of the data within it.

Web Deployment

Developer/2000 Release 2 provides features enabling you to deploy your application on the Internet or an intranet with a minimum of effort. Data entry forms, graphics, and reports can all utilize a Web browser as the "client" portion of a client/server system. This feature utilizes Java, bringing with it the many benefits of platform independence. Using a Java-enabled browser, your application can run in any environment, including the Network Computing Architecture. This eliminates the need to install a runtime client, or to learn a new language to create applications for different environments.

Exercises

1. Name six important features of Developer/2000. Why are they important?

2. What new form of server data manipulation has been added to Developer/2000 2? What is the advantage of using it?

3. What is the benefit of using Java for database applications?

Component Groups in Developer/2000

Developer/2000 comes with a set of powerful tools for client/server development. It includes tools to manage the development project and develop the application's components. Developer/2000 includes capabilities to manage a development project from the top down. The

Project Builder component keeps track of the individual pieces of the project, so you have a single point from which to work on your project, compile it for use, and package it for delivery to users. Individual pieces of the project don't even need to be Oracle-related—they can be code files from other languages such as C, documentation files, and dynamic link library files, as well as others. For version control, there is a facility for integrating Developer/2000 with other source code management systems like ClearCase, PVCS, and Tuxedo. In situations where an application needs to be deployed in more than one language, the Translation Builder stores translated text between any number of languages supported by Oracle. It will then apply prior translation decisions to later versions of the application, thereby making subsequent translations very easy to do.

Components for Development

The major front-end development components of Developer/2000 are Forms, Reports, and Graphics. These components provide the front-end capabilities of an application: inserting and querying data, reporting on data, and displaying information in graphical formats. Client/server development is accomplished using other Developer/2000 components that allow manipulation of code and objects at the client and server level. The Reports Server and Reports Queue Manager components handle running reports on the application server, which can speed up their processing substantially. Developer/2000 Release 2 supports three-tier architecture: the database server, an application server, and the client computer. Queue Manager, in conjunction with Reports Server, typically resides on the middle tier.

Special features exist in Developer/2000 for back-end server development and for deployment of applications to the Web as well. For back-end development, Developer/2000 offers the Procedure Builder, Schema Builder, and Query Builder. These tools are designed to speed up the nuts-and-bolts work needed to put an application's essential infrastructure into place. Developer/2000 handles Web transactions and publishing through its Web components as well. In Release 2.0, the Developer/2000 Application Server allows applications to be accessed through any browser on the Web. Release 2.0's Graphics and Reports components also facilitate publishing data and reports on the Web.

Exercises

1. What are the limitations on the types of files that can be managed and compiled by the Project Builder?

2. What is the purpose of the Translation Builder?

Introduction to Developer/2000 Builder Tools

In this section, you will cover the following points about Developer/2000 Builder tools:

- Builder tools for project management
- Builder tools for front-end development
- Builder tools for back-end development

When you install Developer/2000, you have the option to install some or all the components. The following tools are the major components in the Developer/2000 package: Project Builder, Form Builder, Report Builder, Graphics Builder, Procedure Builder, Query Builder, Schema Builder, and Translation Builder. Project Builder, Query Builder, and Schema Builder are new components of Developer/2000 release 2.0. The Developer/2000 designers in versions before 2.0 have been renamed Form Builder, Report Builder, and Graphics Builder for release 2.0. The various Builders in Developer/2000 can be grouped into several categories. These include project management (Project Builder, Translation Builder), application front-end management (Form Builder, Report Builder, Graphics Builder), and application back-end management (Procedure Builder, Schema Builder, Query Builder). These components work together in a hierarchy that is depicted in Figure 11-1.

Builder Tools for Project Management

There are two tools for project management in Developer/2000, Project Builder and Translation Builder. The Project Builder gives you a single place

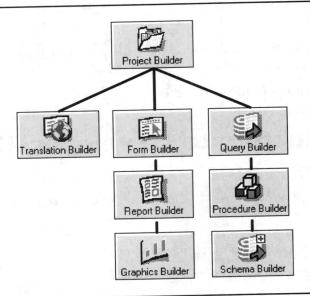

FIGURE 11-1. *Functional hierarchy of Developer/2000 components*

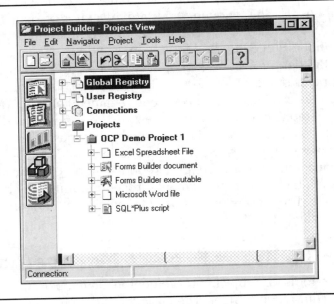

FIGURE 11-2. *Project Builder main screen*

to manage all the pieces of your Developer/2000 application. It starts by keeping track of the individual files that make up a project. Project Builder allows you to segregate the files into logical groups, such as Form Builder files, Report Builder files, word processing or spreadsheet files, and SQL scripts. It stores information about the project's files and database connections in one of two *Registries*: a *Global Registry* for information that is consistent for an entire development team, and one or more *User Registries* for information that is specific to an individual developer's files. A *Project Wizard* is available to walk you through the steps in defining a project. Figure 11-2 displays the Project Builder main screen.

The Translation Builder provides the means for developers to translate an application's text into other languages, and to store those translations in a repository to be used automatically when future versions of the application are translated. The Translation Editor performs the actual translation, and it also manages the translation strings so future translations can be accomplished more quickly. Figure 11-3 displays an example screen from Translation Builder to aid your understanding.

Exercises

1. What program keeps track of information about a project's files and database connections?

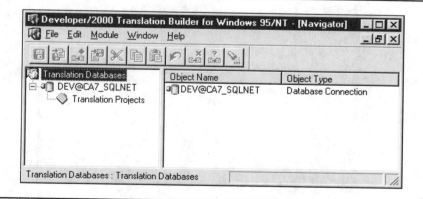

FIGURE 11-3. *Translation Builder example screen*

2. What is the difference between a Global Registry and a User Registry?

3. What are the benefits of using the Translation Builder?

Builder Tools for Front-End Development

Several other Builder components assist in building your GUI front end in Developer/2000. These tools include Form Builder, Report Builder, and Graphics Builder. The Form Builder simplifies the creation of data-entry screens, also known as *forms*. Forms are the applications that connect to a database, retrieve information requested by the user, present it in a layout specified by the form's designer, and allow the user to modify or add information. Form Builder allows you to build forms quickly and easily. Like the Project Builder, Form Builder works with a set of wizards to step you through various tasks. Figure 11-4 displays the Form Builder example screen to assist in your understanding.

FIGURE 11-4. *Form Builder example screen*

The Report Builder is the tool you use to create reports in a
Developer/2000 application. Reports display data from a database in a
layout specified by the report's designer, often including subtotals,
summaries, and graphics to help give the report's reader the "big picture."
Report Builder includes a wizard that walks you through creating a report
very quickly. Completed reports can be viewed in the Reports Live
Previewer, which allows you to change facets of a report and immediately
see the results. Reports can be created on remote servers using
Developer/2000's Reports Server application. When Reports Server is used
with a Reports Web Cartridge, reports can be run dynamically from a Web
browser. Figure 11-5 displays the main screen in Report Builder.

The Graphics Builder allows you to create interactive graphical displays
of the data in a database. These graphics can then be embedded in forms
and reports. Graphics Builder provides a complete set of drawing and
editing tools, along with a Chart Wizard to simplify the process of using the
tools. Graphics created with Graphics Builder can be designed to change
based on user interaction at run time. The program also allows you to

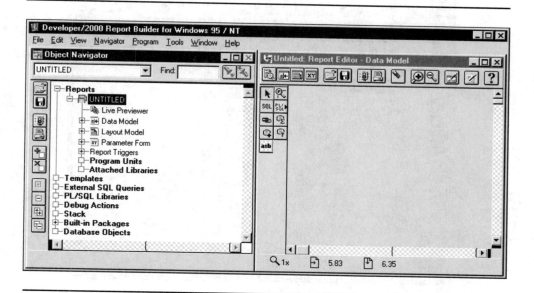

FIGURE 11-5.   *Report Builder main screen*

import and export a wide range of image formats. Figure 11-6 displays the Graphics Builder main screen.

Exercises

1. What is a database's "front end"?

2. What Builders would be used to create a data entry screen? A report showing the contents of a table? A pie chart?

Builder Tools for Back-End Development

Back-end server development is a task covered by Developer/2000 as well. Developing PL/SQL stored procedures, functions, and packages are not tasks that should be handled using flat files and SQL*Plus alone, as any seasoned

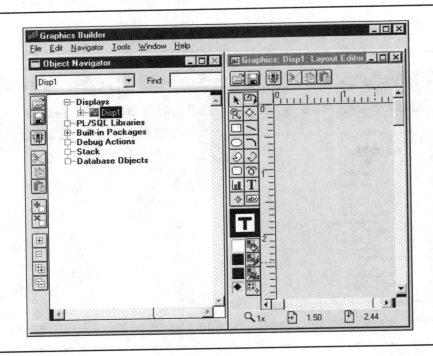

FIGURE 11-6. *Graphics Builder main screen*

developer who's struggled through it the hard way can attest. Instead, use Procedure Builder. In the last unit, you already saw how Procedure Builder allows manipulation of PL/SQL code for use by forms and reports. You can use this tool to work on code for either client-side or server-side execution. It incorporates a broad set of features to aid in creating, testing, and debugging PL/SQL code in program units, libraries, and triggers. Figure 11-7 displays an example screen from Procedure Builder.

Schema Builder is another useful tool that allows you to define the tables, views, snapshots, synonyms, constraints, and relationships that will make up your database. It lets you visualize a database design, including the tables, columns, data types, and relationships, and then execute that design. This tool is useful to both developers and DBAs, in that it manages all aspects of Oracle database object creation and then displays all those components with ease. Figure 11-8 displays an example screen from Schema Builder.

One final aspect of back-end server development in Developer/2000 is the creation of SQL statements. Building complex forms, reports, and graphics can require writing complicated SQL programming. Query Builder

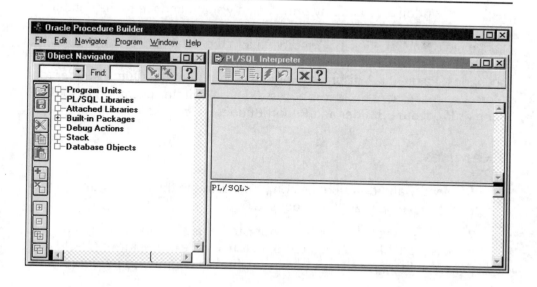

FIGURE 11-7. *Procedure Builder example screen*

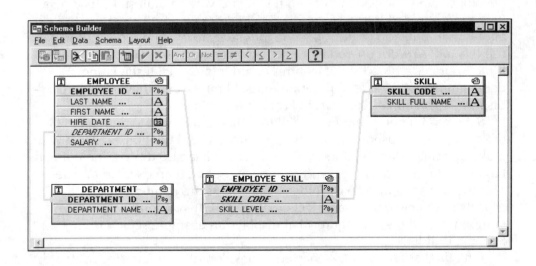

FIGURE 11-8. *Schema Builder example screen*

facilitates writing SQL code by providing a visual interface to the database objects being linked. Query Builder constructs SQL Data Manipulation Language (DML) queries that modify data in the database. Using this tool, an efficient query can be designed based on its performance in several scenarios. Figure 11-9 displays a sample screen from the Query Builder tool. Note also that Query Builder is accessible from within several other tools, such as Procedure Builder and Report Builder.

Exercises

1. Identify and describe the components in the three broad divisions of the Developer/2000 Builder set.

2. Which Developer/2000 Builder can be used to add rows to an existing table? Create a radio button to an existing form? Create a reusable trigger? Track common libraries and menus in forms?

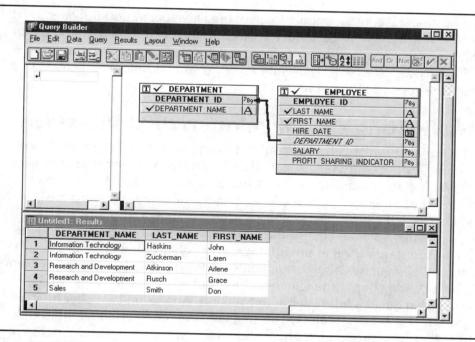

FIGURE 11-9.   *Query Builder example screen*

Customizing Your Developer/2000 Session

In this section, you will cover the following points on customizing your Developer/2000 session:

- Navigating the Developer/2000 interface
- Customizing Project Builder

Developer/2000 offers a variety of ways for you to customize how its programs look and operate. To learn about these features, you will first learn the rudiments of navigating the Project Builder interface. These basic navigational techniques apply to all of the Developer/2000 Builders. Next, you will learn how to customize Project Builder so it displays information and operates in a way that is tailored to your preferences. Your mastery of these two topics will be useful for your overall development efforts in the Developer/2000 package.

Navigating the Developer/2000 Interface

The Project Builder can serve as the starting point for the most-used tools within Developer/2000. Using the large buttons on the left side of Project Builder's screen—known as the *Launcher*—you can start the Builders for forms, reports, graphics, procedures, and queries. These buttons are indicated in the Project Builder toolbar that is shown in Figure 11-10.

Note that you can change the contents of the Launcher. You can add buttons to start any other program you wish; change the order of the buttons; change the label that appears when your mouse pointer hovers over a button; and change the icon a button displays. These features will be covered in detail a little later in this section. Above the Launcher toolbar, you will see another toolbar. This one contains shortcuts to often-used features of Project Builder. The features offered by these buttons include creating new Project Builder files, opening existing Project Builder files, and

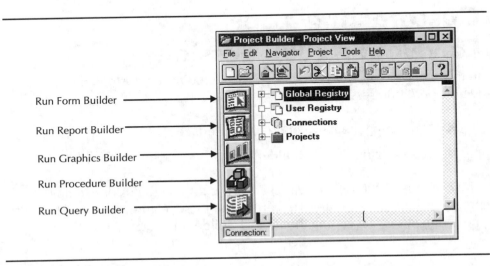

FIGURE 11-10. *Project Builder buttons for launching other tools*

starting the Project Wizard. Other buttons include Undo, Cut, Copy, and Paste. There are buttons for adding files to and removing files from projects, as well as a button for compiling selections and incremental compiles. Finally, if you need assistance, you can use the Project Builder Help button.

In the central portion of the screen you will see a tree containing groups that Project Builder calls *nodes*. The nodes are labeled: Global Registry, User Registry, Connections, and Projects. The Global Registry contains settings that affect all developers on your project. These settings can include:

- File extensions used to indicate a particular type of file

- Whether the file type is version controlled

- Whether the file type should be included in a delivered package

- What programs to use to open, edit, print, view, use version control, and deliver the file type

- What database connection to link to the file type

If you elect to override any of the global settings, your changes will be stored as a personal configuration in the User Registry node. The Connections node contains information about each database connection your project uses, including the database name, the username and password required to make the connection, and your own comments about the connection. Finally, the Projects node stores the actual project information. You will do most of your interaction with Project Builder within the Projects node. Each of these four nodes has a square to its left that is either empty or, if the node contains information, displays a plus or a minus. The plus indicates that there is information in that node's category, and that the information is not yet being shown. If you click on the plus once, that node's items will display, and the plus changes to a minus to denote that the node is showing its contents.

Exercises

1. Identify what features are built into Project Builder to make it function as the central point for your development efforts.

2. If you want to use a different text editor than the other developers in your group, where is the best place to have Project Builder store that information?

Customizing Project Builder

Project Builder allows many of its settings to be altered to suit your preferences. To see what settings can be changed, use the Tools | Preferences menu bar option. When you choose this option, you will see a dialog box like the one shown in Figure 11-11. The Preferences dialog box includes three tabbed pages: Display, Projects, and Launcher. The tab named Display contains a page that is divided into two groups: Environment and Project Navigator. Within the Environment group, the Show Launcher option enables you to turn the display of the Launcher toolbar on or off. The Show Toolbar option provides the same type of control over the standard toolbar located beneath the Project Builder menu bar. The *Show initial "Welcome" dialog* option turns on or off the display of the initial "Welcome" screen when you start Project Builder. This screen is shown in Figure 11-12.

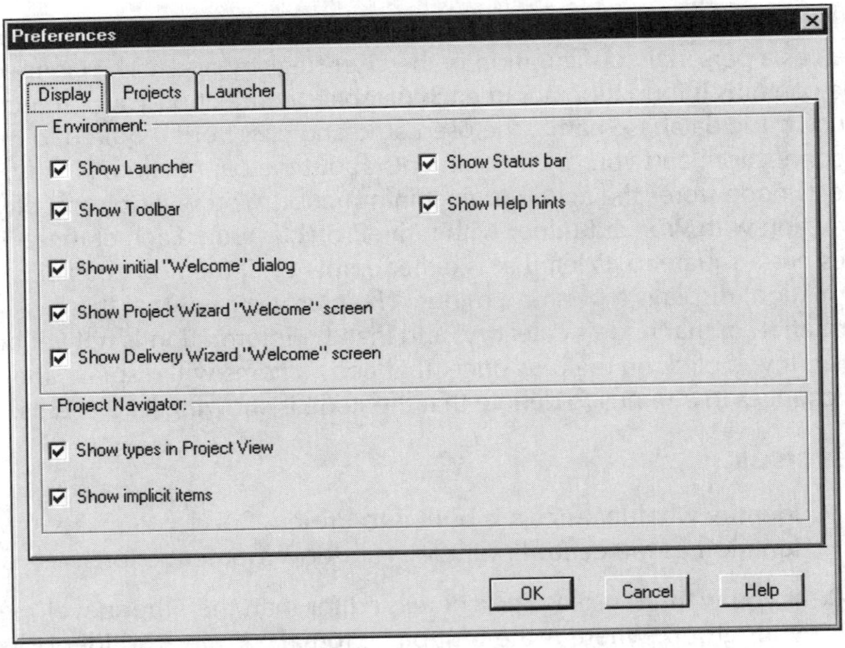

FIGURE 11-11. *Project Builder display preferences*

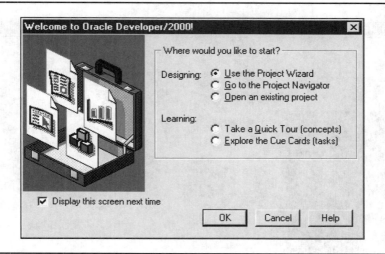

FIGURE 11-12.   *Project Builder initial welcome*

The Show Project Wizard "Welcome" screen option provides similar control over whether you see the screen shown in Figure 11-13 each time you start the Project Wizard. The Show Status bar option determines whether Project displays a line at the bottom of its screen identifying your current database connection and project name. The Show Help hints option enables a feature that uses the middle portion of the status bar (at the bottom of the Project Builder screen) to display helpful information about projects, file types, and menu and toolbar items.

In the Project Navigator group, some installations of Developer/2000 will have options called Show Global Registry and Show Local Registry. These turn on and off the display of the Global and User Registry nodes, respectively. All installations will display a Show types in Project View option, which causes Project Builder to group project files by file type when it displays them in "project view" mode (the default). This means that when you open a project, you will initially see a list of file types, instead of the individual filenames themselves. In order to see individual files, you have to click on the plus sign to the left of the desired file type. This may be unnecessary for projects with a small number of different file types, but it is very handy for projects with enough different types of files

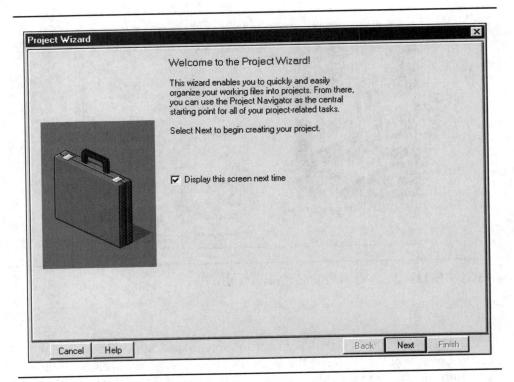

FIGURE 11-13. *Project Builder "Welcome" screen for the Project Wizard*

that having an additional layer of organization—by type—helps you find files more quickly.

The last option on this dialog box page, Show implicit items, instructs Project Builder to include implicit items in its display when you have changed its view to Dependency View with the Navigator | Dependency View menu command. An implicit item is a file that will exist, even if it does not yet. For instance, when you create a Form Builder document, Project Builder also adds an entry for a Form Builder executable file, even if one does not yet exist. It does this because it knows that an executable version must be created before the form can be used. Project Builder displays the names of real files in a bold font, and implicit files in a standard font.

The Preferences dialog tab named Projects contains fields allowing you to specify default values for a project's author, database connection, and

comments. This dialog is shown in Figure 11-14. The third and final
Preferences dialog tab, Launcher, divides its options into three frames:
Entries, Display, and Layout. It is shown in Figure 11-15.

The Entries frame is where you control the items in your Launcher
toolbar. This allows you to add buttons for other useful programs, like the
Oracle Schema Manager, SQL*Plus, or other tools. You can also change an
entry's parameters by clicking on it and then clicking the Edit button
beneath the list. (You can also right-click on it and select Edit Entry from the
context menu that appears.) In the dialog box that follows, you can specify
whether the button controls a single item or a group of items; whether it is
visible or hidden; what command it runs if the button invokes a single item;
what label should appear as a tooltip if you hover your mouse pointer over
the button; what helpful description should appear in the status bar for the
button; and what icon to display on the button.

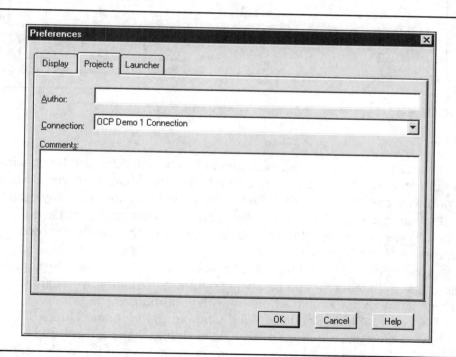

FIGURE 11-14. *Project Builder Projects preferences*

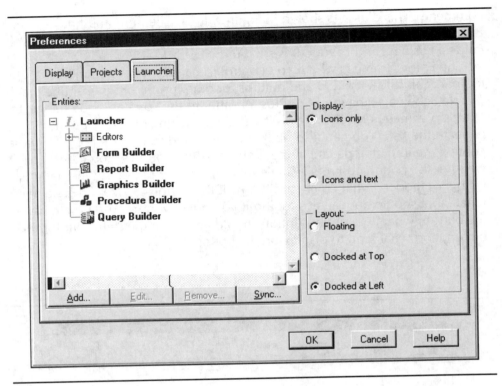

FIGURE 11-15. *Project Builder Launcher preferences*

You can change the order of the entries in the Launcher list by clicking on an entry and dragging it up or down to the new location. In the Display group, you can select whether the Launcher buttons should display both the button name and its icon, or only the icon. Beneath that, in the Layout group, you can specify whether you want the Launcher toolbar to be docked on the left side of your screen, docked at the top of the screen, or free-floating in a separate, movable toolbar. If you choose the latter option, the shape of the toolbar can be changed from horizontal to vertical by dragging any of the toolbar's borders with your mouse.

The Form Builder, Report Builder, Graphics Builder, and Query Builder all have preference functions offering very similar features for display customization, along with other options relevant to each Builder's respective functions. You can use the approach you learned in this chapter to customize the preferences of those programs, as well. The commands to invoke the Preferences dialog box are a bit different from Builder to Builder. In Form Builder and Report Builder, the menu bar command is Tools | Preferences. In the Graphics Builder, the command is Tools | Tool Options. In the Query Builder, it is Edit | Preferences.

Exercises

1. What three changes could you make to the Project Builder customization options to provide the largest amount of space for displaying information about items in your project?

2. How can you give yourself one-click access within Project Builder to programs other than those it provides?

Chapter Summary

This chapter provided an overview of the Developer/2000 Builder programs. It began by introducing the features and benefits you can enjoy by using Developer/2000. These features include productivity resulting from an object-oriented rapid application design (RAD) environment. Your productivity also benefits from reusable components, a unified client/server architecture, component classes whose characteristics can be inherited by subclasses, and wizards to quickly guide you through many common tasks. In addition, productivity is enhanced by having Project Builder as a single point from which you can manage all development projects, and by having direct links to Oracle's Designer/2000 CASE tool and third-party version-control systems.

The next feature is the scalability that comes from being able to easily specify whether objects execute on the client or the server, as well as bandwidth-saving features such array data manipulation for performing batch inserts, updates, and deletes without writing code. Scalability is also enhanced by the ability to base forms on server-run stored procedures, as well as the ability to recalculate aggregate values on the client without having to requery the server.

Another benefit of Developer/2000 is the openness resulting from support for OXC/ActiveX controls, Object Linking and Embedding (OLE), and Dynamic Data Exchange (DDE) to interact with other programs. Adding to Developer/2000's openness is its ability to work with data in many other databases, and its ability to interact with programs written by companies in the Open Tools Initiative, whose products provide CASE and modeling functions, configuration management (version control), and transaction-processing (TP) monitoring.

The next benefit is the high degree of usability you can build into your Developer/2000 applications. You can incorporate pop-up menus, tooltips, and animations to make your applications easier to use. You can build easy-to-understand drag-and-drop user interfaces, and you can have your apps include image and sound files, with the files being stored either within the database or as separate files. If your project prioritizes performance over portability, you can employ **.dll** files to access platform-specific features within your applications.

The next benefit is visualization, which enables you to create such handy features as runtime chart editing, graphical drill-down from overview to line-item detail, conditional formatting of a display based on its content, and visual selection of data based on a graphic display. Finally, Developer/2000 provides Web deployment features enabling you to create Web-browser–based applications with minimal effort. Without having to learn Java, your applications can run in any environment in which a browser is available, including the Network Computing Architecture.

Next, you learned about Developer/2000's two groups of components: management components and development components. The management components include the Project Builder and the Translation Builder. Project Builder's features for organizing your project's files give you the "big picture" when you need it, while still letting you get into individual files quickly just by double-clicking on them. Translation Builder keeps track of text strings within your application that you translate from one language to another, and when you have a future revision of that application to translate, Translation Builder automatically translates any strings that match those translated before. The development components include the Form Builder, Report Builder, Graphics Builder, Procedure Builder, Schema Builder, and Query Builder.

The next section covered Developer/2000's Builders in more detail. This section divided the development components of Developer/2000 into two subgroups: front-end development (items the user sees and interacts with) and back-end development (behind-the-scenes objects). Developer/2000 expedites front-end development with its Form Builder, Report Builder, and

Graphics Builder. For the back end, Developer/2000 helps you get work done quickly by offering the Procedure Builder, Schema Builder, and Query Builder.

The last section discussed two areas: how to navigate the Developer/2000 interface, and how to customize the appearance and operation of the programs. The Project Builder serves as the central point for your project navigation, because it allows you to launch other programs, store group and individual settings in the Global Registry and User Registry, and include project modules by adding them to nodes in the Project Builder project tree. You also learned how to set preferences within many of the Developer/2000 Builders. This feature lets you control the balance between convenient one-button access to all your tools and maximum screen real estate for your project tree. You also learned how to control the ways in which Developer/2000 tries to help you as you create and work with your projects; how to set default values that will be used as the starting point for new projects; and how to control the contents of the Launcher toolbar in the Project Builder.

Two-Minute Drill

- Developer/2000 is a package of several programs enabling developers to quickly produce database applications.

- In addition to increased productivity, Developer/2000 also offers developers a high degree of scalability, openness, usability, visualization, and ease of Web deployment.

- Developer/2000's productivity benefits come from its object orientation, unified client/server architecture, and use of rapid application design (RAD) techniques. It allows classing and subclassing of components; provides wizards to simplify common tasks; uses the Open API to interface with programs written in other languages; and can interface directly with Oracle's Designer/2000 CASE tool, as well as with version-control systems and other applications.

- Developer/2000's scalability features include the ability to identify whether an object runs on the client or the server simply by dragging and dropping it into the appropriate location within the Developer/2000 interface. It further promotes scalability with numerous features to reduce network traffic, such as array data manipulation, the ability to base forms on stored procedures running on the server, and the ability to recalculate aggregate values on the client without having to requery the server.

- Developer/2000 provides a high degree of openness by making it easy to interact with non-Oracle databases, as well as with other applications. Several major database platforms are supported, as well as any database accessible via ODBC or the Oracle Gateway. To interact with other applications, you can employ OCX/ActiveX controls, OLE, and DDE.

- To promote usability within your applications, Developer/2000 lets you include pop-up menus, tooltips, and animations in your interfaces; incorporate drag-and-drop functions; include image and sound files stored either as separate files or as objects within your database; and make calls to **.dll** files if you need to employ platform-specific features.

■ Developer/2000's Dynamic Visualization feature lets you include graphics in your applications and have the graphics interact with the data beneath them. This enables you to deploy features like graphical drill-down from overview to line-item detail; runtime chart editing; visual selection of data based on a graphic display; conditional formatting of a display based on its data; and seamless Web reporting.

■ Speaking of the Web, Developer/2000 enables you to produce forms and reports that run within any standard Web browser without having to learn another language or install a different runtime client for each client environment.

■ Developer/2000's programs can be divided into two main categories: management components and development components.

■ The management components provide overview and project-wide abilities through the Project Builder and Translation Builder.

■ Its development components include function-specific tools to create specific portions of your project. For front-end development, it offers the Form Builder, Report Builder, and Graphics Builder. For back-end development, it provides the Procedure Builder, Schema Builder, and Query Builder.

■ The Project Builder is designed to be the central focus point for your projects. Within the Project Builder, you can launch other programs, store group and individual settings, and manage project modules.

■ The Project Builder can accommodate any file type. It allows you to specify what program should be used to edit, print, and compile each type of file.

■ You can set preferences within most of the Developer/2000 Builders to tailor their appearance and operation to suite your work style.

Chapter Questions

1. **Which of the following are major features of Developer/2000? (Choose six)**

   A. Graphical depiction of business processes

   B. Ease of Web deployment

   C. Centralized control over user access levels

   D. Productivity

   E. Openness

   F. Wide acceptance by international standards committees

   G. Usability

   H. Radio buttons

   I. Scalability

   J. Visualization

2. **What new form of client data manipulation has been added to Developer/2000 2?**

   A. Bidirectional data links

   B. ODBC

   C. Array data manipulation

3. **What is the primary advantage of using the client data manipulation type referred to in question 2?**

   A. Minimal coding

   B. Reduced network traffic

   C. Web deployment

   D. Faster PL/SQL procedures

4. **What is the primary benefit of using Java in database applications?**

   A. More complete database functionality

   B. Can deploy on numerous platforms easily

   C. Cool addition to résumé

   D. Faster PL/SQL procedures

5. **What are the limitations on the types of files that can be managed and compiled by the Project Builder?**

   A. Files created by the Developer/2000 package

   B. Files created by any Oracle product

   C. Files from major software vendors whose file formats are well-known

   D. None

6. **What is this purpose of the Translation Builder?**

   A. Automatically translates your application into other languages

   B. Simplifies conversion of data from one database format to another

   C. Ensures that forms and reports are easy to understand

   D. Stores earlier translations performed manually and applies them to subsequent translations

7. **What Developer/2000 program keeps track of information about a project's files and database connections?**

   A. Schema Builder

   B. Enterprise Manager

   C. Translation Builder

   D. Project Builder

   E. Designer/2000

8. Which statement most accurately describes what Developer/2000 will do if it finds a parameter with different settings in the Global Registry and the User Registry?

   A. Prompts user to ask which setting to use

   B. Resets User Registry setting to match that in the Global Registry

   C. Uses the setting from the Global Registry

   D. Uses the setting from the User Registry

   E. Stops with an error message

9. Which of the following are among Developer/2000's management components? (Choose two)

   A. Form Builder

   B. Procedure Builder

   C. Project Builder

   D. Query Builder

   E. Report Builder

   F. Schema Builder

   G. Translation Builder

10. Which of the following are *not* among Developer/2000's front-end Development Components? (Choose three)

   A. Form Builder

   B. Graphics Builder

   C. Procedure Builder

   D. Project Builder

   E. Report Builder

   F. Schema Builder

11. Which of the following are among Developer/2000's back-end development components? (Choose three)

   A. Form Builder

   B. Graphics Builder

   C. Procedure Builder

   D. Project Builder

   E. Query Builder

   F. Report Builder

   G. Schema Builder

   H. Translation Builder

12. What Builders would be used to create a report containing a pie chart?

   A. Form Builder

   B. Graphics Builder

   C. Procedure Builder

   D. Project Builder

   E. Query Builder

   F. Report Builder

   G. Schema Builder

   H. Translation Builder

13. While working within Project Builder, you decide you would like to devote more of your screen to displaying project nodes and files. Which of the following menu commands would *not* accomplish this?

   A. Tools | Preferences | Display | Show Launcher (off)

   B. Tools | Preferences | Display | Show Toolbar (off)

   C. Tools | Preferences | Display | Show Status bar (off)

   D. Tools | Preferences | Display | Show Help hints (off)

Answers to Chapter Questions

1. B, D, E, G, I, J.   Ease of Web deployment, Productivity, Openness, Usability, Scalability, Visualization

Explanation   Graphical depiction of business processes is a feature of Oracle Designer/2000, not Developer/2000. Centralized control over user access levels comes from the Oracle server Security Manager. The level of acceptance by international standards committees is not relevant, since you distribute Developer/2000 applications in executable format, or design them to be used in Web browsers. And while radio buttons are certainly available as features within a Developer/2000 form, it cannot be considered a major feature.

2. C.   Array data manipulation

Explanation   Bidirectional data links would be essential to any form generator, so could not be a new feature in Developer/2000. ODBC capabilities were present in earlier version of Developer/2000.

3. B.   Reduced network traffic

Explanation   By allowing you to specify that inserts, updates, and deletes should occur in batches rather than one record at a time, array data manipulation reduces the number of transactions necessary to affect large numbers of records, thereby reducing network traffic, which generally improves an application's performance.

4. B.   Can deploy on numerous platforms easily

Explanation   Platform independence is Java's main claim to fame.

5. D.   None

Explanation   Project Builder can be configured to accommodate any type of file.

6. D.   Stores earlier translations performed manually and applies them to subsequent translations

Explanation   The Translation Builder does not automatically translate your application. It stores the translations you create manually when converting your application's front end from one language to another. It then remembers and reapplies those translations automatically during subsequent translations. It does not convert database data, or try to determine the ease of use of your forms or reports.

7. D.   Project Builder

Explanation   Project Builder's main purpose is managing a project's files. This includes storing information about the files' database connections.

8. D.   Uses the setting from the User Registry

Explanation   By definition, the Global Registry contains default settings that can be overridden by individual developers. When a setting is overridden, the overriding setting is stored in the individual's User Registry.

9. C, G.   Project Builder, Translation Builder

Explanation   The Project Builder and Translation Builder are the two Developer/2000 tools that have umbrella-like impact over modules created using the other Builders.

10. C, D, F.   Procedure Builder, Project Builder, Schema Builder

Explanation   The Developer/2000 tools designed to create front-end components—components the user interacts with directly—are the Form Builder, the Report Builder, and the Graphics Builder.

11. C, E, G.   Procedure Builder, Query Builder, and Schema Builder

Explanation   The Developer/2000 tools designed to create back-end components—components the user does not interact with directly—are the Procedure Builder, the Query Builder, and the Schema Builder.

12. B, F.   Graphics Builder, Report Builder

Explanation   Since the question identifies a report as the product, the Report Builder is clearly going to be involved. The Graphics Builder is included as well, because the report is going to contain a pie chart.

13. D.   Tools | Preferences | Display | Show Help hints (off)

Explanation   The Help hints display within existing screen space. They do not take up space that could be used by a project's nodes and files.

CHAPTER
12

Form Builder

n this chapter, you will learn about the following facets of Form Builder:

- Working in the Form Builder environment
- Creating basic form modules
- Running a Form Builder application

In this chapter, you will get a thorough introduction to Form Builder. You will start by learning about the Form Builder environment, the main Form Builder components, and the main objects in a form module. Next, you will step through the basics of creating form modules, and learn the four steps involved in creating and using a Developer/2000 form. You will create a new form module, generate data blocks to use within the module to access database data, and create a basic form layout for viewing the data. After modifying the data blocks and form layout a bit, you will learn how to compile form modules, and once your sample application is compiled, you will run it using the Forms Runtime program. Next, you will be introduced to Form Builder file formats and their characteristics. With that under your belt, you will go on to create a relationship between data blocks, and then modify your single-table form so it shows records from two tables synchronized in a master/detail relationship. In the final section, you will learn a variety of ways to run a Form Builder application, as well as how to filter the data retrieved into a Form Builder application. You will be shown time-saving techniques for inserting repetitive data, and you then will learn how to get detailed information about database errors in the Forms Runtime program. The OCP Exam 3 will include test questions in this subject area worth 12 percent of the final score.

Working in the Form Builder Environment

In this section, you will cover the following points about working in the Form Builder environment:

- Identifying the main Form Builder executables
- Identifying the main components of Form Builder
- Identifying the main objects in a Form module

It is time to move beyond theory and start learning about the nuts and bolts of building forms in Developer/2000's Form Builder. This section will begin by defining the main executable files that make up the Form Builder application. Next, you will learn about the main components that Form Builder makes available to you, and what each component does. Finally, you will take one of those components, the Form module, and get an understanding of the main objects within it.

Identifying the Main Form Builder Executables

As shown in Table 12-1, there are three executable programs that make up the Form Builder application in Developer/2000. All three are located in the **bin** directory beneath your Oracle software home directory. The executable programs for Windows environments are listed in the following table. To determine the name of the executable in UNIX environments, where 32-bit applications have been around long enough for it not to be so novel as to include mention of them in the executable filename, remove the **32.exe** from the end of the executable filename.

Program Name	Function	File Name	Reads File Type	Creates File Type
Form Builder	Development environment for creating Developer/2000 forms	**f50des32.exe**	N/A	**.fmb**
Form Compiler	Creates an executable **.fmx** file from an **.fmb** file	**f50gen32.exe**	**.fmb**	**.fmx**
Forms Runtime	Runs compiled Forms application **.fmx** files	**f50run32.exe**	**.fmx**	N/A

TABLE 12-1. *Form Builder Executables*

The Form Compiler program takes the **.fmb** file containing your Forms Builder application and compiles it so it can be run by the Forms Runtime program. This process compiles the PL/SQL code in your application's program units, producing an **.fmx** file as a result. The Forms Runtime program reads the **.fmx** file and runs your application. This entire process occurs automatically when you run your form from within Form Builder, as long as you leave the Build Before Running preference at its default setting of Yes. You can also compile your form at any time from within Form Builder by executing the Program | Compile menu command. (The File | Administration | Compile File menu command will do the same thing, but does not offer incremental compilation.)

Exercises

1. What are the Form Builder executables?

2. What does each Form Builder executable do?

Identifying the Main Components of Form Builder

A Form Builder application contains several different types of components, each providing a unique kind of functionality. The individual components are called *modules*. The modules can be grouped into the categories that follow:

- **Form modules**   Make up the bulk of most applications. It is within form modules that you define what data is presented to the user, how it is presented, and what they can do with it. This is also where you define relationships, PL/SQL triggers, limits on the number of records fetched, and similar parameters.

- **Menu modules**   Where you store information about custom menus you create for your application. In addition to storing the definitions and underlying code for menu and submenu items, a menu module keeps track of any libraries the menu uses, information about object grouping and classes/subclasses, help items associated with the menu, and visual attributes such as font name, size, weight, style, and spacing. Because a form's menus are stored in a Menu module, it is possible to customize or replace the default menus. This allows you to provide exactly the functionality your application requires.

■ **PL/SQL Library modules** Contain the client-side procedures, packages, and functions that you write. These modules are called by other modules within your application.

■ **Object Library modules** Enable you to store objects your application uses, and reuse them wherever you need them. This can speed development dramatically, as well as make it easier to enforce standards throughout your company.

Exercises

1. What are the four main components in Form Builder?

2. What default Form component can you modify or replace in order to tailor the functionality of a new application?

3. What are the benefits of using an object library?

Identifying the Main Objects in a Form Module

Most users see a data-entry form as a single object. As a developer, you need to think about a form's contents not only in more detail, but also in a hierarchical structure. In Developer/2000, a form module contains numerous "large" objects that, in turn, hold smaller objects. All of these form module objects come together into a single cohesive interface that lets the user interact with database data. What follows is a description of these objects, in order from largest to smallest. For your assistance in understanding, Figure 12-1 shows a sample form and the object types within it.

Window Objects

This is the outermost boundary for a form—an empty frame to hold objects. All of the visual objects in a Form Builder application are contained within windows. There are two types of windows: *document* and *dialog*.

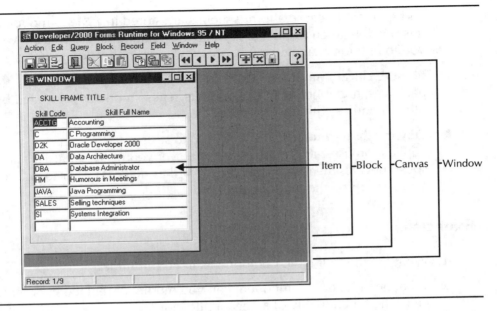

FIGURE 12-1. *Main objects in a form module*

DOCUMENT WINDOWS Document windows are used for standard data entry forms. If you are developing on a Windows platform, your application will automatically have a special type of document window called a multiple document interface (MDI) window that serves as a "parent" window containing all the other document windows. The MDI window usually holds the application's main menu and toolbar, as well. While the MDI window is not included in an application's list of windows, you can still maximize, minimize, and resize it via code. All other document windows—in other words, the ones you create—must fit within the confines of the MDI window. When a user is in a document window, they can generally enter and query data, move to other windows within the application, and interact with the application's menu and toolbars.

DIALOG WINDOWS Dialog windows are used for displaying messages to the user. When defining the properties of a dialog window, you can specify its size and position; whether or not it is *modal* (forcing users to respond to it before they can do anything else); whether the user can move, resize, maximize, minimize, or close it; and visual attributes such as colors, fill patterns, font name, size, weight, style, and spacing.

Canvas Objects

A window can contain one or more canvases, which are the visual backgrounds on which you place form objects. There are four types of canvases: content, stacked, tab, and toolbar.

CONTENT CANVASES   A content canvas is the essential background for any form window. Because of this, a content canvas is automatically placed in any new form layout you create. It is the default canvas type.

STACKED CANVASES   A stacked canvas resides on top of a content canvas, hiding a portion of the content canvas as it does so. The stacked canvas can look either similar to or different from the content canvas background, depending on the effect desired by the developer. You can use stacked canvases to make items seem to appear and disappear on the screen based on criteria you specify. You can also use a stacked canvas to create scrolling subwindows within a window, and to display a single form header above multiple forms without having to lay the header out in each form, among other things. A window can contain numerous stacked canvases.

TAB CANVASES   A tab canvas is a multiple-page object that is very familiar to users who have set the "options" for practically any Windows object. It allows the user to move between multiple pages of related information simply by clicking on intuitive *tabs* at the top of the pages. A tab canvas is most useful when you need to display a large quantity of related data while consuming relatively little screen space. A tab canvas resides on top of a content canvas, hiding a portion of the content canvas as it does so.

TOOLBAR CANVASES   Toolbar canvases are available in several flavors: horizontal, vertical, and MDI. A window can have one or more toolbars—even multiple horizontal or vertical toolbars—and you have programmatic control over which toolbars are visible at a given time, as well as over what items within each toolbar are visible. If you are developing within a Windows environment, you can also create toolbars for the MDI window.

Block Objects

In Forms Builder, a block is a logical container that holds form objects such as data items and control buttons. There are two types: *data* block and *control* block.

DATA BLOCKS   A data block creates a bridge between your form and the data in your database. It allows you to access data from a database table, a database view, a procedure, or a transactional trigger. Form Builder automatically puts a *frame* around a data block, and you can use the frame not only to move the block on the layout, but also to select the block for modification.

CONTROL BLOCKS   A control block holds items that do not interact directly with your data, but instead exert control over the application itself. For instance, when you add buttons to a form, you place them within a control block.

Item Objects

The *items* are the individual objects on your forms with which your users interact. The most common item is a *text item*, which contains fields enabling your users to view, enter, and modify database data. There are also items to display read-only data (*chart item, display item, image item*, and *OLE container*); to depict changeable data in a graphical representation (*check box, list item*, and *radio group*); to control the application (*button*); to manipulate audio objects (*sound item*); and to simplify the creation of user interfaces (*ActiveX control*).

Exercises

1. When you create a new form layout, what type of object is always automatically on it?

2. What is the relationship between a window and a canvas?

3. What are the types of canvases, and what are the differences between them?

4. What is the relationship between a block and an item?

5. What are the different kinds of blocks?

Creating Basic Form Modules

In this section, you will cover the following points about creating basic form modules:

- Creating a form module
- Using the Data Block Wizard to create and modify data blocks
- Creating and modifying layouts with the Layout Wizard
- Saving, compiling, and running a form module
- Form Builder file formats and their characteristics
- Creating data blocks with relationships
- Running a master/detail form module

When you want to create a new database form with Developer/2000, there are four steps to go through. First, you create a new form module in Form Builder. Next, you create a data block to supply the new form module with data. After that, you create a form layout depicting the data block's items on one or more canvases. Finally, you save, compile, and run the module. In this section, you will go through all of these steps. Starting with a sample requirement for a one-table form, you will create a new form module, give it a data block, lay the data block's items out on a form canvas, and compile and run it in the Forms Runtime environment. You will then learn about the different file types that Form Builder produces when you generate form modules. Next, you will learn how to create relationships between data blocks. The section will wrap up by stepping you through the process of creating a form utilizing a master/detail relationship.

Creating a Form Module

Creating a new form module is very simple. The first step is to start the Form Builder application. If you see the Welcome dialog box shown in Figure 12-2, deselect the **Display at startup** option. Then select the option labeled **Build a new form manually** and click on the OK button. You should see the Form Builder Object Navigator, with the Forms node open and a module showing, usually with the name MODULE1. If your Forms node does not have any modules, simply double-click on the node name **Forms** to create one.

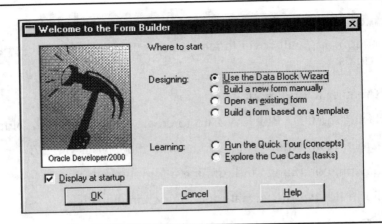

FIGURE 12-2. *Form Builder Welcome screen*

Take a moment to look at the form module that has been created on your screen. Examine the module nodes shown in the tree beneath the module name: Triggers, Alerts, Attached Libraries, etc. Notice that one of the nodes has a plus to the left of its name: Windows. Click on the plus sign to the left of Windows, and you will see that a default window has automatically been created for your form module. A form module must have at least one window, so Form Builder created one for you.

Exercise

When a new form module is created, what object does it automatically include?

Using Data Block Wizard to Create and Modify Data Blocks

In order to manipulate data, a form needs a data block to serve as a link between the form and the database—or more accurately, between the form and the data *source*, since a data block can be based not only on a table, but also on a view, a procedure, or a transactional trigger. Form Builder provides a Data Block Wizard to simplify the process of creating data blocks.

Before starting the Data Block Wizard, you will want to create the test tables used in this chapter. A listing of the SQL code to create and populate the test tables follows. For your reference, an entity-relationship diagram for the test tables is shown in Figure 12-3. If you would rather not type in the SQL code, you can find it in the file named **erdscript.sql** in the appropriate directory for this chapter on the book's CD-ROM.

```
CREATE TABLE DEPARTMENT
( DEPARTMENT_ID          NUMBER(8,0) NOT NULL,
  DEPARTMENT_NAME        VARCHAR2(25) NOT NULL );

CREATE UNIQUE INDEX DEPARTMENT_BRW_P1 ON DEPARTMENT
( DEPARTMENT_ID ASC );

ALTER TABLE DEPARTMENT
  ADD ( PRIMARY KEY (DEPARTMENT_ID) ) ;

CREATE TABLE EMPLOYEE
( EMPLOYEE_ID            NUMBER NOT NULL,
  LAST_NAME             VARCHAR2(20) NOT NULL,
  FIRST_NAME            VARCHAR2(15) NOT NULL,
  HIRE_DATE             DATE NOT NULL,
  DEPARTMENT_ID         NUMBER(8,0) NOT NULL,
  SALARY                NUMBER(8,2) NOT NULL
);

CREATE UNIQUE INDEX EMPLOYEE_BRW_P1 ON EMPLOYEE
( EMPLOYEE_ID ASC );

ALTER TABLE EMPLOYEE
  ADD ( PRIMARY KEY (EMPLOYEE_ID));

CREATE TABLE SKILL
( SKILL_CODE            VARCHAR2(8) NOT NULL,
  SKILL_FULL_NAME       VARCHAR2(30) NOT NULL);

CREATE UNIQUE INDEX XPKSKILL ON SKILL
( SKILL_CODE ASC );

ALTER TABLE SKILL
  ADD ( PRIMARY KEY (SKILL_CODE));

CREATE TABLE EMPLOYEE_SKILL
( EMPLOYEE_ID           NUMBER NOT NULL,
  SKILL_CODE            VARCHAR2(8) NOT NULL,
```

```
    SKILL_LEVEL              NUMBER(1,0) NOT NULL
                             CHECK (SKILL_LEVEL BETWEEN 1 AND 5 );

CREATE UNIQUE INDEX XPKEMPLOYEE_SKILL ON EMPLOYEE_SKILL
( EMPLOYEE_ID ASC, SKILL_CODE ASC );

ALTER TABLE EMPLOYEE_SKILL
  ADD (PRIMARY KEY (EMPLOYEE_ID, SKILL_CODE));

ALTER TABLE EMPLOYEE
  ADD (FOREIGN KEY (DEPARTMENT_ID) REFERENCES DEPARTMENT);

ALTER TABLE EMPLOYEE_SKILL
  ADD (FOREIGN KEY (SKILL_CODE) REFERENCES SKILL);

ALTER TABLE EMPLOYEE_SKILL
  ADD (FOREIGN KEY (EMPLOYEE_ID) REFERENCES EMPLOYEE);

CREATE INDEX XIF1EMPLOYEE ON EMPLOYEE
( DEPARTMENT_ID ASC );

CREATE INDEX XIF6EMPLOYEE_SKILL ON EMPLOYEE_SKILL
( EMPLOYEE_ID ASC );

CREATE INDEX XIF7EMPLOYEE_SKILL ON EMPLOYEE_SKILL
( SKILL_CODE ASC );

INSERT INTO DEPARTMENT VALUES (1, 'Sales');
INSERT INTO DEPARTMENT VALUES (2, 'Research and Development');
INSERT INTO DEPARTMENT VALUES (3, 'Information Technology');
INSERT INTO DEPARTMENT VALUES (4, 'Maintenance');

INSERT INTO EMPLOYEE VALUES
  (1001, 'Smith', 'Don', '30-JUN-72', 1, 45000);
INSERT INTO EMPLOYEE VALUES
  (1002, 'Atkinson', 'Arlene', '29-OCT-88', 2, 50000);
INSERT INTO EMPLOYEE VALUES
  (1003, 'Zuckerman', 'Laren', '30-JUN-97', 3, 41369);
INSERT INTO EMPLOYEE VALUES
  (1004, 'Rusch', 'Grace', '28-JUL-69', 2, 75000);
INSERT INTO EMPLOYEE VALUES
  (1005, 'Haskins', 'John', '29-OCT-98', 3, 95000);
INSERT INTO EMPLOYEE VALUES
  (1006, 'Smythe', 'Nancy', '15-SEP-88', 3, 105000);
INSERT INTO EMPLOYEE VALUES
  (1007, 'Campbell', 'Scott', '04-JAN-99', 4, 56000);
```

```
INSERT INTO EMPLOYEE VALUES
(1008, 'Miller', 'John', '06-DEC-99', 3, 87000);

INSERT INTO SKILL VALUES ('SALES', 'Selling techniques');
INSERT INTO SKILL VALUES ('ACCTG', 'Accounting');
INSERT INTO SKILL VALUES ('C', 'C Programming');
INSERT INTO SKILL VALUES ('DBA', 'Database Administrator');
INSERT INTO SKILL VALUES ('D2K', 'Oracle Developer 2000');
INSERT INTO SKILL VALUES ('DA', 'Data Architecture');
INSERT INTO SKILL VALUES ('SI', 'Systems Integration');
INSERT INTO SKILL VALUES ('JAVA', 'Java Programming');
INSERT INTO SKILL VALUES ('HM', 'Humorous in Meetings');

INSERT INTO EMPLOYEE_SKILL VALUES (1005, 'D2K', 5);
INSERT INTO EMPLOYEE_SKILL VALUES (1005, 'DBA', 4);
INSERT INTO EMPLOYEE_SKILL VALUES (1005, 'DA', 5);
INSERT INTO EMPLOYEE_SKILL VALUES (1004, 'D2K', 4);
INSERT INTO EMPLOYEE_SKILL VALUES (1004, 'DA', 2);
INSERT INTO EMPLOYEE_SKILL VALUES (1004, 'HM', 5);
INSERT INTO EMPLOYEE_SKILL VALUES (1002, 'SI', 5);
INSERT INTO EMPLOYEE_SKILL VALUES (1002, 'DA', 1);
INSERT INTO EMPLOYEE_SKILL VALUES (1001, 'SALES', 4);
INSERT INTO EMPLOYEE_SKILL VALUES (1006, 'DA', 4);
INSERT INTO EMPLOYEE_SKILL VALUES (1006, 'SI', 5);
INSERT INTO EMPLOYEE_SKILL VALUES (1006, 'ACCTG', 5);
INSERT INTO EMPLOYEE_SKILL VALUES (1006, 'JAVA', 4);
INSERT INTO EMPLOYEE_SKILL VALUES (1007, 'HM', 5);
INSERT INTO EMPLOYEE_SKILL VALUES (1008, 'DBA', 3);
INSERT INTO EMPLOYEE_SKILL VALUES (1008, 'C', 4);

COMMIT;
```

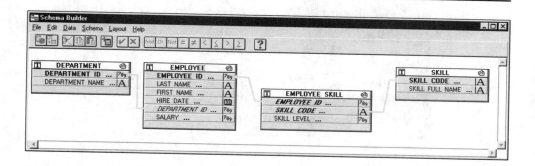

FIGURE 12-3.   *Entity-relationship diagram for test tables*

Creating a Data Block Using the Data Block Wizard

To start the Data Block Wizard, right-click on the Data Blocks node beneath your Form module, and select **Data Block Wizard** from the context menu that appears. You will be presented with the dialog box shown in Figure 12-4, asking whether to base the data block on a table, view, or stored procedure. Select the Table or View option and click on the Next button.

In the next page, the Data Block Wizard asks what table or view you wish to use as a base for your data block. For this first exercise, you will create a data block on the DEPARTMENT table. You can either type in the table's name and click the Refresh button to get a list of the table's columns, or you can click the Browse button, select Current user and Tables from the dialog box that results, click on the OK button, and then select the DEPARTMENT table. Whichever approach you prefer, you will end up with a dialog box filled in as shown in Figure 12-5. Press the button with the two right arrows on it to move all of the table's column names from the Available Columns area to the Database Items area of the dialog box. Then, click on the Next button. This will take you to the Finish page, which is

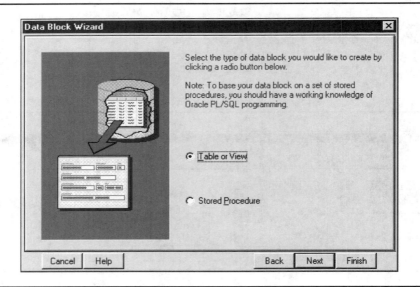

FIGURE 12-4. *Data Block Wizard Type page*

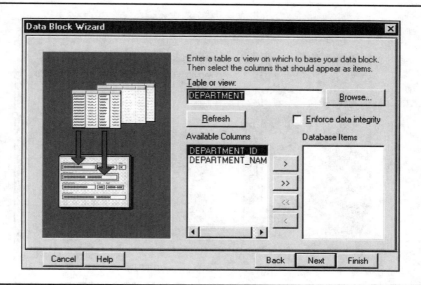

FIGURE 12-5.   *Data Block Wizard Table page*

depicted in Figure 12-6. Select the Just create the data block option and click on the Finish button.

Modifying a Data Block Using the Data Block Wizard

In addition to simplifying the creation of new data blocks, the Data Block Wizard can assist you in modifying existing data blocks. When used in this way, the Data Block Wizard offers the same options it did when you initially created the data block: control over the data source, selection of columns included, and ability to generate relationships between data blocks. To change other data block parameters, you must open the data block's property sheet, just like any other Form Builder object.

You can start the Data Block Wizard on an existing data block in either of two ways. You can either right-click on the data block and then choose Data Block Wizard from the context menu or you can click on the data block and then choose Tools I Data Block Wizard from the standard Form Builder menu. Once you have started the Data Block Wizard, you will see the familiar three tab pages to control the data block's type, table, and

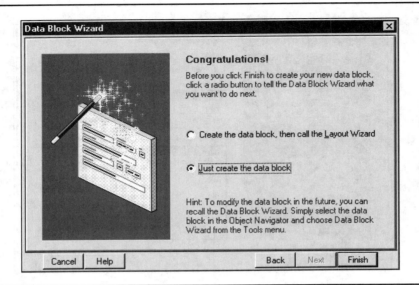

FIGURE 12-6. *Data Block Wizard Finish page*

master/detail relationships. For instance, in the tab page labeled Table, you can use the arrows between the Available Columns and the Database Items areas to change which columns are included in the data block, or to change their column order. Once your changes are complete, you click the Finish button to exit the Data Block Wizard.

Exercises

1. If you wanted to modify the way in which a data block was sorted, would you be able to do it with the Data Block Wizard? If so, on what Wizard page?

2. What are the two methods for starting the Data Block Wizard on an existing data block?

Creating and Modifying Layouts Using the Layout Wizard

The Layout Wizard is Form Builder's tool for creating and modifying forms quickly. It works by asking you a series of questions and then generating a basic form that fulfills the criteria you have specified. The Layout Wizard can later modify the form if you want to change its fundamental design or contents. You can also modify the layout manually, if you wish, to better suit your application's needs.

Creating a Layout Using the Layout Wizard

It is very simple to create a basic entry form using the Layout Wizard. First, open the Developer/2000 Form Builder application. Then, right-click the data block you would like to use as the basis for a form. If you do not yet have a data block with the desired data, create one using the steps in the previous section. For the purposes of this example, select the DEPARTMENT data block from the test data provided with this book.

Start the exercise by choosing Layout Wizard from the context menu that appeared when you right-clicked on your data block. You may or may not see the Layout Wizard Welcome screen, depending on how your system is configured. If you do see it, deselect the Display this page next time option and click the button labeled Next. You will see the dialog box shown in Figure 12-7.

The Canvas page starts by asking you what canvas you wish to use to display the form you are about to create. Remember, the canvas is the background that underlies all forms. If this is the first form you have created for this project, there will not be any existing canvases to select, so the proper choice for canvas is (New Canvas). For the canvas Type, leave the selection at the default choice of Content. Click the Next button.

You should now be on Layout Wizard's Data Block page, shown in Figure 12-8. On this page, you select the data block that the Wizard will use as the basis for this layout. By default, the data block you started with is displayed, although you can change that at this point. More likely, you will use this page to select which items (that is, data columns) from the data

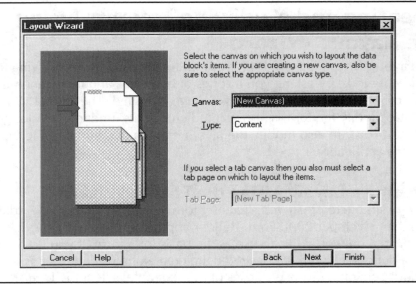

FIGURE 12-7. *Layout Wizard Canvas page*

block you wish to have displayed in the layout. Most developers are familiar with selection interfaces like the one used on the Data Block page. The left area, labeled Available Items, contains all the items in the data block you have selected. The right area, labeled Displayed Items, shows the items you have selected for inclusion in the layout. Move the DEPARTMENT_ID and DEPARTMENT_NAME items into the Displayed Items column. Then, click the Next button.

You should now be on the Layout Wizard Style page. Here you can change the onscreen prompt label that will be displayed next to each data item. If the label contains more than one word and there is a vertical bar (|) displayed between the two words, that means the Layout Wizard intends to split the prompt onto more than one line. Figure 12-9 demonstrates this in the prompt for the DEPARTMENT_NAME item. To the right of the Prompt column are two columns showing the field width and height that the Layout Wizard is planning to give each item. By default, these measurements are shown in points. There is no reason to change the measurements at this time, so you can just click the Next button.

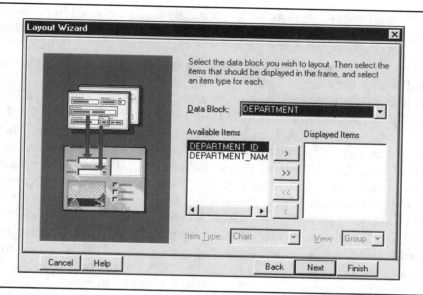

FIGURE 12-8. *Layout Wizard Data Block page*

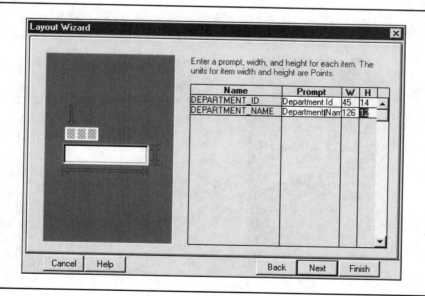

FIGURE 12-9. *Layout Wizard Items page*

You will next see the Layout Wizard's Style page, shown in Figure 12-10. Obviously, this is where you specify whether the data you selected should be depicted in a form layout, or in a table layout, which looks like a spreadsheet. For the purposes of this exercise, select the Tabular choice and click the Next button.

You should now be on the Layout Wizard Rows page. In this Layout Wizard page, shown in Figure 12-11, you start by entering a title for the frame the Layout Wizard is going to place around your data items. This frame serves as a container for all of the items. For the purposes of this exercise, enter **DEPARTMENT Frame Title** as the frame title. The next field, Records Displayed, allows you to specify how many records are shown at a time in this layout. Since you chose a tabular layout, it makes sense to design the layout so that more than one record shows at a time. Specify that five records should be shown at a time. The next field, Distance Between Records, specifies how much vertical space is placed between each row. This parameter only applies to layouts in which the Records Displayed option is set to more than one. Even then, it is generally better to leave the parameter at its default setting of zero. If for some reason the records prove

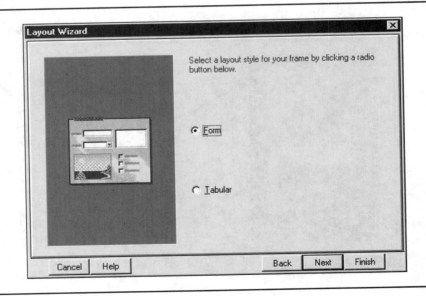

FIGURE 12-10. *Layout Wizard Style page*

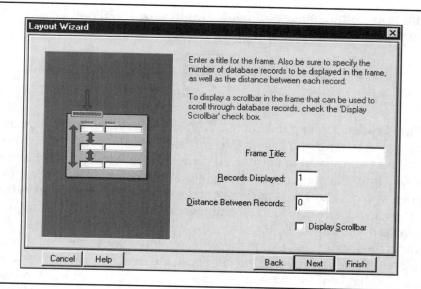

FIGURE 12-11.   *Layout Wizard Rows page*

to be too close together, you can easily increase the space between them in the Layout Editor, which provides versatile features for spreading items evenly and displays the results instantly so you can quickly determine the optimal amount of vertical space. The final field on this page specifies whether the frame will include a scrollbar to move through records. This can be a good idea if your layout will be displaying more than one record at a time. Since your DEPARTMENT layout will show more than one record at a time, click on the Display Scrollbar parameter so that it is enabled. Then click the Next button.

The Layout Wizard now displays its Finish page. Read the text on this page and then click the Finish button. Form Builder will generate your form and display it in the Layout Editor. Later sections of this book will go into great detail about the editing changes you can make to your form in the Layout Editor. For now, the discussion will be limited to modifications you can make using the Layout Wizard you just employed.

Modifying a Layout Using the Layout Wizard

By running the Layout Wizard again on an existing layout, you can make fundamental changes to the layout quickly. You can invoke the Layout

Wizard from within the Layout Editor by clicking the Layout Wizard toolbar button, which looks like this:

This is called running the Layout Wizard in *reentrant mode*. The most useful reason to rerun the Layout Wizard on an existing form is to add or remove data items from the displayed canvas. For instance, if you have an Employee form that includes sensitive information such as Social Security Number, you may be asked at some point to remove that information from a canvas so it is not displayed to all employees. It may seem natural to just open the canvas in the Layout Editor, select the item you no longer want to display, and press the Delete key. Doing this will certainly remove the item from your layout, but *it will also remove the item from the underlying data block*. If the form needs that item for some other purpose, but you do not want to display the item, that's the time to use the Layout Wizard. You can restart the Layout Wizard on that block in your layout, and move the appropriate items from the Displayed Items column back to the Available Items column. Once you have finished, your form will display only the items you want, while your data block continues to contain all the items it had originally.

You can also use the Layout Wizard to change the size of your data items. While you can do this in the Layout Editor just by clicking on an item's field and dragging its edges to make it shorter or longer, the Layout Wizard incorporates more intelligence about the block's physical layout on the canvas. If you use the Layout Wizard, rather than the Layout Editor, to increase the length of a field beyond what the data block's frame can contain, the Layout Wizard will automatically increase the size of the frame, and even rearrange the fields within the frame if necessary. Because of this ability, the Layout Wizard is your best tool for increasing a field's size when the increase is enough to make the field extend outside the data block's current frame. To finish this section, close the Layout Editor and return to the Object Navigator.

Exercises

1. What is the best way to remove an item from a form layout without removing it from the underlying data block?

2. What is the best way to increase the display width of a field when there is plenty of space around the field? What is the best way when there is no extra space around the field?

Saving, Compiling, and Running a Form Module

As you know, you can create form modules in Form Builder, but you cannot run them there. For that, you must invoke the Forms Runtime program. Before you do, however, you need to save the form and compile it.

Saving a Form in Form Builder

You will find this extremely easy. To save the form, perform either of these actions. Either execute the File | Save command from Form Builder's menu, or click the familiar Save button, whose icon is shown here:

TIP
You can configure Form Builder to automatically save your work each time you compile it. Go to Tools | Preferences, and under the General tab select the Save Before Building option. The rest of this chapter will assume that the Save Before Building option is enabled, so enable it on your system now.

Compiling a Form in Form Builder

The form modules you create in Form Builder cannot be run directly. There is an interim step in which the form module file is converted into a separate, executable file in a format that the Forms Runtime program can read. This process is called compiling. You can compile your form modules at any time by executing the File | Administration | Compile File menu command.

You can configure Form Builder to automatically compile your module before you run it. Go to Tools | Preferences, and under the General tab select the Build Before Running option. The rest of this chapter will assume that the Build Before Running option is enabled, so you should enable it on your system now. Note that this option does not cause the module to be saved, so you will need to either save the module manually, or enable the Save Before Building preference option discussed previously. In addition, the Build Before Running option does not cause library or menu modules attached to a form to be compiled when the form is compiled, so when you have an application that includes custom library or menu modules, you will need to compile them manually before running the form.

Running a Form Module

To run your form module, perform either of these actions. Either execute the Program | Run Form command, or click on the Run Form button, as shown in this illustration:

Form Builder will start the Forms Runtime program, which will load the executable version of your form. Figure 12-12 shows how the form will look.

The first thing you're likely to notice is that the form does not display any data. The Forms Runtime program is making an assumption that when you first open a form, you want to enter new data. If you want to see existing data, you must query the database. To do that, take either of these actions. Either run the Query | Execute menu command, or click on the Execute Query button shown here:

Later in this book, you will learn how to customize the form so it displays data as soon as it opens.

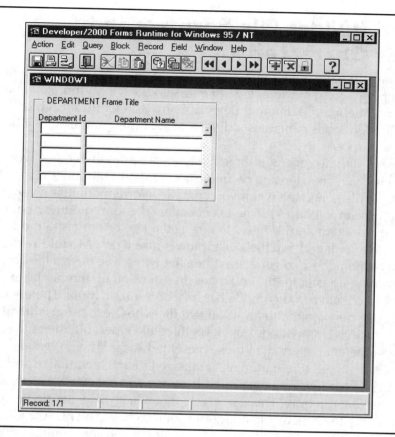

FIGURE 12-12. *Forms Runtime program*

Exercises

1. What is a compiled file?

2. What Developer/2000 program runs the form modules you create in Form Builder?

3. When you initially run a form, why doesn't it show any data?

Form Builder File Formats and Their Characteristics

Now that you have gone through a complete cycle of creating, compiling, and running a form module, it is time to step back for a moment and discuss a bit more theory: the different types of Form Builder files. Each of the main Form Builder nodes generates a different set of files, and each file has a different purpose.

The Form node generates three file types. The design file you work with directly is given an extension of **.fmb** (short for Form Module Binary). The executable file generated when you compile a form module is given an extension of **.fmx** (Form Module Executable). The form module's parameters can be exported to an ASCII text file using the File | Administration | Convert menu command, and that file's extension is **.fmt** (Form Module Text).

The Menu node also generates three file types. The design file you work with (coming up later in this book) has an extension of **.mmb**. The executable file generated when you compile has an extension of **.mmx**. The menu module can be exported to an ASCII text file whose extension is **.mmt**.

The PL/SQL Library node generates three file types, but their file extensions follow a different pattern than those presented so far. The design file is given an extension of **.pll** (Programming Language Library), and unlike any other node, the design version contains both source and executable code, and thus can be used at run time. The executable file, whose file extension is **.plx**, contains only the executable code—no source code. The PL/SQL Library can be exported to an ASCII text file, and that file's extension is **.pld**.

The Object Library node generates only two file types. The design file has the extension **.olb**. The Object Library can be exported to an ASCII text file, and that file's extension would be **.olt**.

Table 12-2 summarizes each of the Form Builder file types and characteristics.

Exercises

1. What is the difference between an **.fmb** file and an **.fmx** file?

2. What Form Builder file type contains compiled menu data?

3. What Form Builder file type contains both source code and executable code?

Module	Extension	Characteristic
Form	.fmb	Form design file
	.fmx	Form executable runfile
	.fmt	Form text export file
Menu	.mmb	Menu design file
	.mmx	Menu executable runfile
	.mmt	Menu text export file
PL/SQL Library	.pll	PL/SQL Library design file (can also be executed—contains both source and executable code)
	.plx	PL/SQL Library executable runfile (contains no source code)
	.pld	PL/SQL Library text export file
Object Library	.olb	Object Library design file
	.olt	Object Library text export file

TABLE 12-2. *Form Builder File Types*

Creating Data Blocks with Relationships

The sample tables used in this chapter include the DEPARTMENT and EMPLOYEE tables. The contents of these tables have inferred relationships; for instance, a department will have one or more employees. This particular type of relationship is often called a *master/detail* relationship. It is also called a *parent/child* relationship. In order for this type of relationship to exist, the master or parent table must have a primary key. A primary key consists of one or more columns that cannot be empty and that must contain unique values for every record. These unique primary-key values are what the detail, or child table stores and uses to refer to master table records. The detail table column(s) that store values from the master table's primary key are called the *foreign key* to the master table's primary key. So in a master/detail relationship, the master table's primary key is referred to by the detail table's foreign key.

It is very common for database applications to use a single form to display data that is in a master/detail relationship. Form Builder makes it very easy to define master/detail relationships between data blocks. Once this is done, any canvas containing both the master and the detail data block will also have automatic query synchronization between the two, so the detail data block will only show those records that are related to the selected record in the master data block.

Data Blocks and Relationships in Action

In order to experiment with this, you will modify the DEPARTMENT canvas so it displays two data frames: the current one for department data, and a new one that will show employees assigned to the selected department. To do this, you will create a new data block to get data from the EMPLOYEE table, and assign a master/detail relationship between the new Employee data block and the Department data block.

Follow the entire procedure described here. Within your Form Builder file, start the Data Block Wizard by either executing the Tools | Data Block Wizard command, or right-clicking on the Data Blocks item in the Forms node and selecting Data Block Wizard from the context menu that appears. On the Type page, specify that the data block will be based on a Table or View. On the Table page, specify that the data block should be based on the EMPLOYEE table. Move all six EMPLOYEE table columns from the Available Columns area to the Database Items area. Notice that the EMPLOYEE table includes a column called DEPARTMENT_ID. This will be the foreign key to the DEPARTMENT table's primary key. The next page you will see is new: the Master/Detail page. Click on the Create Relationship button. From the list of tables that appears, select DEPARTMENT and click OK. Your screen should now look like the one shown in Figure 12-13.

Note that the field labeled Detail Item currently shows EMPLOYEE_ID. This is the primary key for the EMPLOYEE table, but it is not the correct item to serve as the foreign key back to the DEPARTMENT table. Open the drop-down list for the Detail Item field, and you will see the DEPARTMENT_ID item in the list. Select the DEPARTMENT_ID item from the list. You will see that not only did the Detail Item change to the DEPARTMENT_ID item you selected, but the Data Block Wizard also

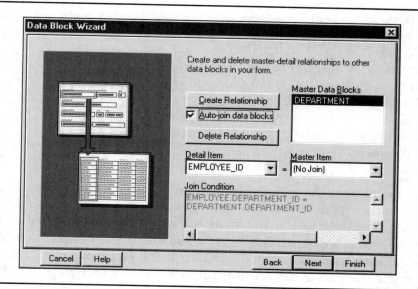

FIGURE 12-13. *Creating a master/detail relationship*

automatically placed DEPARTMENT_ID in the Master Item field. You can see the SQL join condition that this relationship creates in the following code:

```
EMPLOYEE.DEPARTMENT_ID = DEPARTMENT.DEPARTMENT_ID
```

Now, click on the Next button. This takes you to the Finish page. Select Create the data block, then call the Layout Wizard and click on the Finish button. When the Layout Wizard starts, ensure that the Canvas field shows the canvas that contains your Department data block, and not New Canvas. Click on the Next button. On the Data Block page, note that the Data Block field is grayed out—that is because you have already selected the data block indirectly by calling the Layout Wizard from the Data Block Wizard. In the Available Items column, select every item *except* DEPARTMENT_ID. Click the Next button.

> **TIP**
> *There is no need to display the DEPARTMENT_ID item in the Employee data frame, since the current department will be displayed elsewhere on the canvas. It was essential to have DEPARTMENT_ID in the Employee data block, however, because that item is the foreign key to the Department data block.*

You're close to the end. On the Items page, simply click on the Next button to accept all default values for item prompt, width, and height. On the Style page, select Tabular. On the Rows page, enter a frame title of **Employees in this department:** Increase the Records Displayed value to **5,** and enable the Display Scrollbar option. On the Finish page, click the Finish button to close the Layout Wizard. You will now see your form in the Layout Editor, with data frames for both Department and Employees. Close your form to return to the Object Navigator. Notice that the Object Navigator now shows two frames beneath the canvas you were working with: the first frame holds the Department data block, and the second frame holds the Employee data block.

Exercises

1. What must be true about a pair of tables in order to create a master/detail relationship between them?

2. What is a foreign key?

3. Does the detail frame of a master/detail form need to display the foreign key used to join the tables?

Running a Master/Detail Form Module

Running a master/detail form module is even easier than creating one. From within Form Builder, follow this process. First, select the Form module you want to run by clicking on the module name. If you have been following the exercises in this chapter, you will have only one form module available. Then, run the module using the Run button or the Program | Run Form menu command. When the form opens in the Forms Runtime program, populate it with data using the Execute Query button or the Query | Execute command. After that, select different Department records by clicking on either the records directly, or the Next Record and Previous Record buttons. Note that each time you select a different department record, the Employees frame changes to show only those employees in that department. Finally, use the Action | Exit menu command to close the Forms Runtime program and return to Form Builder.

Exercise

What steps do you have to take in a master/detail form to change the records included in the detail frame?

Running a Form Builder Application

In this section, you will cover the following points related to running a Form Builder application:

- Understanding the runtime environment
- Navigating a Form Builder application
- Understanding the two modes of Forms Runtime operation
- Retrieving data into a Form Builder application
- Inserting, updating, and deleting records
- Displaying database errors using the Help facility

You have now used Developer 2000's Forms Runtime program to run your first form. This is a good time to go into detail about the Forms Runtime program's purpose, requirements, and operational techniques. This section covers understanding the runtime environment and navigating the Form Builder application. You will also understand the two modes of Forms Runtime operation, and gain experience retrieving data into a Form Builder application. You will practice **insert**, **update**, and **delete** operations as well. Finally, you will learn how to display database errors using the Help facility.

Understanding the Runtime Environment

Each of the Builder programs provides an environment for creating application modules. However, they do not run those modules. For that, Developer/2000 supplies *runtime* programs. There are three runtime programs—one each for the Form, Report, and Graphics Builders. The runtime programs must be present on the client machine when the application is distributed, but the development programs do not need to be, and generally are not. This allows the development tool to be rich with convenience-enhancing features, while the runtime program can be lean and efficient. It also allows companies to distribute applications to many users while only having to purchase development-tool licenses for the actual developers.

To run an application built in Developer/2000, you call the appropriate runtime program. When you are developing an application and testing it, you will usually call the Forms Runtime program directly from within the Builder you are using. This is done by either clicking on the Run button—which was introduced earlier—or using the Program | Run Form command.

If you want to run the Forms Runtime program independently of any Builder, you can do so by opening the Start menu in Windows environments and navigating to Programs | Developer 2000 | Forms Runtime. When you do, you will see a screen similar to the one depicted in Figure 12-14.

Using this screen, you can enter all the information necessary to open and run a form module: the filename (remember that it will be looking for an **.fmx** file), the userid and password for logging into the database, and the alias for the database itself. There are also a number of other options, which are beyond the scope of discussion at this point.

To have the Forms Runtime program run the form you created in the previous section of this book, fill in the filename, userid, password, and database alias. When filled in, the Forms Runtime Options screen will look similar to the one shown in Figure 12-15. Once you have filled in the necessary information, click the OK button to run your form.

When you distribute an application, the client computers will need to have the runtime programs installed, as well as all the compiled files for your application. To enable you to start your application from a user-friendly icon and still specify runtime arguments, Developer/2000 provides a way for you to include the desired application's name and other parameters as command line arguments. For instance, this is an example of

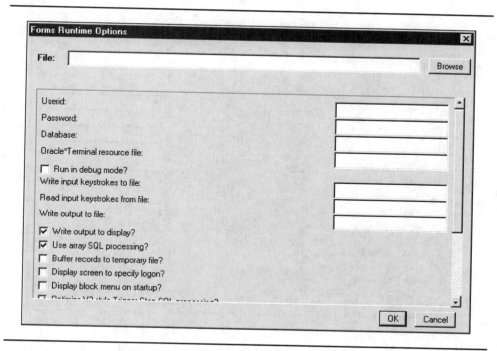

FIGURE 12-14. *Forms Runtime Options screen*

the command line used to call the Developer/2000 "Benefits and Features" demo program:

```
"C:\Program Files\Ora8Home\BIN\F50RUN32.EXE" start20.fmx
user@db_alias/password
```

Exercises

1. What is meant by the term "runtime environment" in Developer/2000?

2. What are the advantages of separating development and runtime tools?

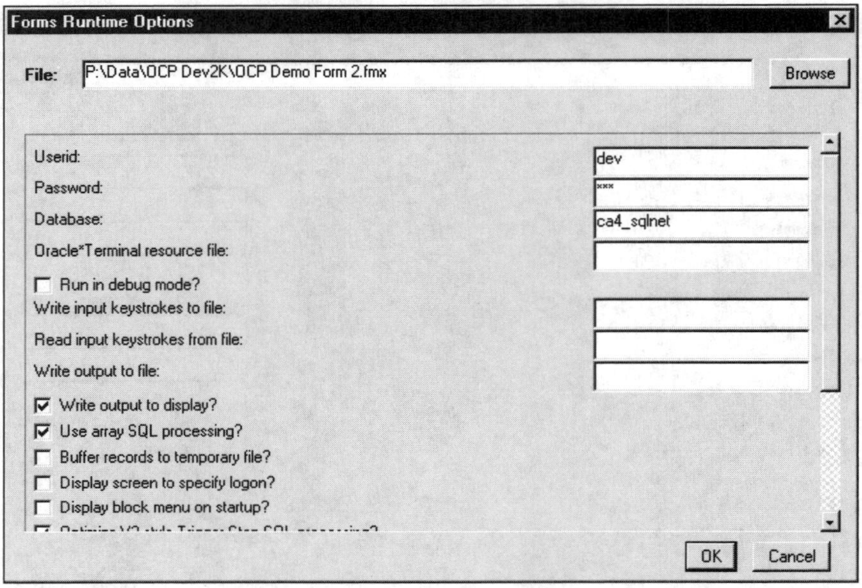

FIGURE 12-15. *Forms Runtime Options screen with essential data*

Navigating a Form Builder Application

Navigating a Form Builder application in the Forms Runtime program is relatively straightforward. This section will discuss the four parts of a standard Forms Runtime display: the *Menu, Toolbar, Form Area,* and *Console.*

Looking at the Menus

The default menu used in the Forms Runtime program is shown here:

Action   Edit   Query   Block   Record   Field   Window   Help

If you do not create a custom menu for your application, this is the menu that Forms Runtime provides. It is somewhat unusual in that its first menu category is not File. This is because a Runtime instance is specific to the **.fmx** file opened within it; close the **.fmx** file, and the Forms Runtime program will close as well. Thus there is no need for commands like File | Open.

The menus displayed are described as follows. The Action menu provides choices to commit data inserts, updates, and deletes; to clear all displayed records from the form (which does not remove them from the underlying tables—it simply blanks the form); to print the form; and to exit the Runtime program. The Edit menu provides the standard cut, copy, and paste commands, which operate at field-level granularity. Further down this menu, the Edit | Edit command opens a dialog box containing the contents of the currently selected field, with a convenient search-and-replace function for making repetitive changes within a large text field. The final choice on this menu, Edit | Display List, opens a List of Values (LOV) if the currently selected field has one.

Two other menus include the Query and Block menus. The Query menu provides functions to enter and utilize data-filtering criteria, including a very handy Counts Hits function to determine how many records will match your current criteria without having to actually retrieve the records. The Block menu provides navigational control, enabling the user to move between data blocks on a multiple-block canvas. The menu also includes a command to clear, or blank out, the records in the currently selected block. As with the Action | Clear All command, the Block | Clear command does not actually remove any data from the database; its function is purely cosmetic.

The Record menu provides standard navigation functions: previous and next record, along with scroll up and down (which act similar to a page down and page up within the data block's frame). It also provides commands to insert, lock, and remove records—and "remove" will actually delete the record from the underlying table when the action is committed, unlike the "clear" command farther down the menu. There is also a convenient duplicate function that, when invoked within a new blank row, copies the values from whichever existing record was more recently current. Many of these functions are also available from the Runtime toolbar, which will be addressed shortly.

Other menus abound. The Field menu provides a subset of the functions described on the Record menu: move to previous or next, clear, and duplicate. In this case, each function operates at the field level instead of the record level. For instance, when invoked from a new blank record, the Field | Duplicate command copies the contents of that field from the record just above the new one and places the contents into the new record. This can be useful when entering repetitive data. The Window menu offers standard windows-management commands for applications that employ more than one window. The Help menu provides a limited amount of help: details about the field you are currently in, a reminder of the keyboard shortcut keys available, and information about errors, if any have occurred.

Looking at the Toolbar

The next area for study is the toolbar. The default toolbar used in the Forms Runtime program looks like this:

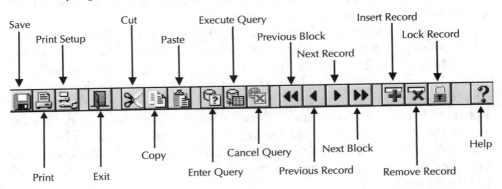

If you do not create a custom toolbar canvas for your application, this is the toolbar Forms Runtime provides. Several of its buttons will undoubtedly be familiar to you, while others are specific to the Developer/2000 environment. Remember that you cannot only create your own toolbar, you can create horizontal *and* vertical toolbars for your application, if you wish.

There are several remarks to be made about the items you will find in the Forms Runtime default toolbar. The Save button performs a SQL **commit** command, saving any inserts, updates, or deletions the user has performed. Its menu equivalent is Action | Save. The Print button prints the current form and its contents. Its menu equivalent is Action | Print. The Print Setup button provides standard options for page size, source, orientation, and margins. Its menu equivalent is Action | Print Setup. The Exit button closes the application and the Forms Runtime program. Its menu equivalent is Action | Exit. The Cut, Copy, and Paste buttons provide exactly the functions you would expect in any Windows program. Their menu equivalents are Edit | Cut, Edit | Copy, and Edit | Paste. Like their menu equivalents, the buttons operate at field-level granularity.

The Enter Query button places the user in a mode where they can enter query by example (QBE) data into the form. This function will be covered later in more detail. The button's menu equivalent is Query | Enter. The Execute Query button performs a **select** statement against the database, using whatever criteria are present from the Enter Query mode. If no criteria have been entered, all records are returned. The button's menu equivalent is Query | Execute. The Cancel Query button clears any criteria that were entered in Enter Query mode. It does not cause an additional **select** statement to be run, however, so the contents of the form will not change until the Execute Query function is performed again. The button's menu equivalent is Query | Cancel.

The Previous Block button moves the user's cursor to a prior data block on the current canvas. If the canvas has no prior data block but the form module contained additional canvases, the button causes the prior canvas to be displayed, with the cursor in the last data block on that canvas. The button's menu equivalent is Block | Previous. The Next Block button moves the user's cursor to the next data block on the current canvas. If the canvas has no succeeding data block but the form module contained additional canvases, the button causes the next canvas to display, with the cursor in the first data block on that canvas. The button's menu equivalent is Block | Next.

The Prior Record button causes the user's cursor to move up one record in the current data block. If the user is already on the block's first record, the button does nothing. Its menu equivalent is Record | Previous. The Next Record button causes the user's cursor to move down one record in the current data block. If the user is already on the block's last record, the button moves the cursor to a blank row and allows the user to enter a new record. Its menu equivalent is Record | Next. The Insert Record button creates a blank row below the user's current cursor location (or a blank form if the form is designed to show one record at a time) and allows the user to enter new data. The insertion will occur in the database when the user's next **commit** occurs. The button's menu equivalent is Record | Insert. The Remove Record button deletes the current record from the table. The deletion will occur in the database when the user's next **commit** occurs. The button's menu equivalent is Record | Remove. The Lock Record button attempts to lock the database row corresponding to the record at which the user's cursor is currently located. Its menu equivalent is Record | Lock.

Finally, The Help button shows detailed information about the field in which the user's cursor currently resides. This can be handy during development, but it is of little interest to most users, and so you may want to reprogram its function in a custom menu.

Looking at the Form Area

Beneath the default Forms Runtime toolbar is the form area. This is the area where your users will put most of their attention—as will you as a developer. Because this area simply displays the canvases you create, it will be covered in greater detail later in the book, in the portions dealing with customizing the canvas contents.

Looking at the Console

At the bottom of the Forms Runtime display is the console area. This area consists of two lines. The first line displays Oracle messages such as "FRM-40400: Transaction complete: 10 records applied and saved.", as well as informational items like "Enter a query; press F8 to execute, CTRL-Q to cancel." (By the way, that CTRL-Q command is case sensitive, so if you have the CAPS LOCK key on, it will not work.) The second line displays the record number the user's cursor is on, along with status information such as "Enter-Query" when the user is in Enter Query mode.

Exercises

1. What can you do if you decide that most of the buttons in the Forms Runtime toolbar are not of value to your users?

2. List all the ways you can cause a **commit** to occur from an application in the Forms Runtime program.

3. Explain the purpose of the console. Describe how it is laid out.

Understanding the Two Modes of Forms Runtime Operation

The phrase "Enter Query mode" has been used a few times already in this section, and it is time to explain this mode in more detail. A form running in the Forms Runtime program is always in either of two states: the normal insert/update/delete mode, or Enter Query mode. When the user invokes Enter Query mode, the form blanks its contents and waits for the user to enter data into the form that will serve as filtering criteria for a **where** clause when the user invokes the Execute Query command. The user can enter only one record's worth of criteria, although they can enter criteria into multiple fields on that record. This means that there is no record-to-record movement while in the Enter Query mode.

To test this operation, follow these steps. First, open your sample application in the Forms Runtime program. Then, invoke Enter Query mode by either clicking on the Enter Query button, performing the Query | Enter command, or pressing the F7 function key. Next, move to the Department Name field and type **Maintenance**. Finally, execute the query by either clicking on the Execute Query button, performing the Query | Execute menu command, or pressing function key F8. You will see that the Maintenance department record will appear, along with the employee record related to that department. You are now back in the normal mode—the only difference is that you are viewing a filtered subset of the available records. Since you are no longer in Enter Query mode, executing another query will produce a result set containing all records.

Exercises

1. Describe the difference between Enter Query mode and the Forms Runtime's normal mode for a form.

2. How is the user's movement among records restricted while in Enter Query mode?

Retrieving Data into a Form Builder Application

By doing the chapter exercises up to this point, you have already retrieved data into a Form Builder application by opening the application with the

Forms Runtime program and doing the Execute Query command. When you retrieve records without using selection criteria to limit the number of records returned, you are performing an *unrestricted query*. It's the same as using a **select** statement with no **where** clause. Unrestricted queries win points for simplicity, but they can hurt overall application performance by clogging the available network bandwidth with records the user does not really need.

The solution to this can be a *restricted query*, which utilizes selection criteria to limit the number of records returned. In the last section you used Enter Query mode to limit the department records retrieved to just those matching the name Maintenance. That was a restricted query. You can perform more sophisticated restricted queries as well, using Oracle wildcard characters and SQL statements.

Restricting Queries with Field-Level Criteria

There are a number of characters you can use as wildcards and comparison operators when entering field criteria for Enter Query mode. These characters are shown in Table 12-3.

Character	Function
_	Wildcard replacing any single character
%	Wildcard replacing any number of characters, including none
> and <	Greater than and less than (usable for numbers, strings, and dates)
<> or !=	Not equal to (usable for numbers and strings)
>= and <=	Less than or equal to, and greater than or equal to

TABLE 12-3. *Criteria Field Characters for Enter Query Mode*

Each of these would be valid criteria to enter into a field in Enter Query mode:

- Sm_th%
- Pine Ave%
- >50000
- <50000
- >G
- <01-JUL-2001
- <>Backup
- <>5
- !=5
- >=5
- <=5

If you enter search criteria into more than one field while entering a query, all of your search criteria will be combined with **and** clauses in the query's **where** clause.

TIP
While you are experimenting with different combinations of criteria, this is an excellent time to practice using the F7 function key to invoke Enter Query mode, and the F8 key to execute a query. Small timesavers like these can add up to a sizable overall time-savings.

Restricting Queries with SQL Statements

You can also employ full SQL statements to restrict the records returned in a query, and even to control their sort order. To try this, follow the process described here. First, open your sample application in the Forms Runtime program, if it is not open already. If necessary, execute a query to populate the Department frame with all four departments. Then, place your cursor on the department record Information Technology. Place your cursor on any record in the Employees data frame. Next, invoke Enter Query mode by either clicking on the Enter Query button, performing the Query | Enter menu command, or pressing function key F7. After that, move to the Last Name field and type **:LAST_NAME**. (The variable name does not have to be the same as the column name, but you might find it provides more clarity to make it so.) The colon at the beginning of the name indicates that the name is to be treated as a variable. Then, move to the Hire Date field and type **:HIRE_DATE**, and move to the Salary field and type **:SALARY**. Your screen should now look like Figure 12-16.

Continuing the process, execute the query by either clicking on the Execute Query button, performing the Query | Execute menu command, or pressing function key F8. You will see a dialog box titled Query/Where. Enter the following text as your query's **where** clause. After doing so, click OK. You will see that the number of Information Technology employees displayed has dropped from four to two, and that the two shown are the ones who fulfill the criteria you specified.

```
HIRE_DATE between '01-JAN-1998' and '31-DEC-1999'
    and SALARY < 100000
order by LAST_NAME asc
```

Exercises

1. Which of the following is *not* a valid criterion to place in a field while in Enter Query mode: **SEL_CT**, **WILDC*RD**, **>JKL** or **<6-DEC-1999**?

2. What must you place in front of a field name in Enter Query mode to cause the Forms Runtime program to treat the name as a variable?

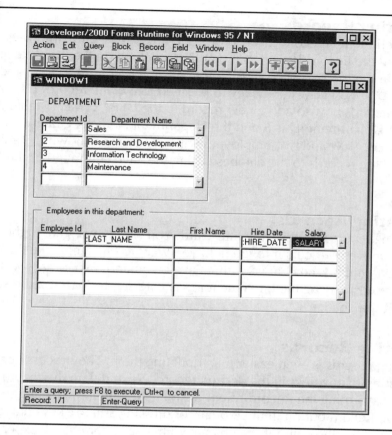

FIGURE 12-16. *Using variables in a Forms Runtime query*

Inserting, Updating, and Deleting Records

So far in this chapter, you have only queried existing records. Now it is time to add records of your own, change their contents, and delete them. Before you do, it is important to note that each of these Data Manipulation Language (DML) functions occurs with the records you are looking at locally; changes you make are not made in the underlying database until you **commit** the changes with a Save command. Each of the three topics that follows will assume that you have your sample application open in the Forms Runtime program.

Inserting Records

You can initiate a record-**insert** process in any of the following ways: choosing the Record | Insert menu option, clicking on the Insert Record button in the toolbar, or navigating to the last record in the table, and then use the DOWN ARROW cursor key to proceed to a blank record. Use one of these methods now to add a new record to the DEPARTMENT table. Specify that the Department ID is **5** and the Department Name is **Quality Assurance**. Now add two employees with information shown in Table 12-4. **Commit** the records to the database using the Save command or the Save button.

Updating Records

Updating records is very straightforward. You simply navigate to the desired record, move your cursor to the field you want to change, make the change, and then **commit** the change with a Save command. Experiment with this process by changing the hire date for Lois Paterson to **March 2**. Be sure to **commit** the change.

Deleting Records

Deleting records is even easier than updating them. The process begins with navigating to any field in the desired record. Next, **delete** the record by either performing the Record | Remove menu command, clicking on the Remove Record button in the toolbar, or pressing SHIFT-F6 keys on your keyboard. Finally, **commit** the change with a Save command. Experiment with this process by deleting the record for Bob Unca. Be sure to **commit** the deletion.

Employee ID	Last Name	First Name	Hire Date	Department ID	Salary
1009	Unca	Bob	25-NOV-1999	5	68000
1010	Paterson	Lois	01-MAR-2000	5	72000

TABLE 12-4. *Sample Employee Records to Add*

Exercise

You have just performed a Record | Remove command on the wrong record. What steps do you need to take to get the record back?

Displaying Database Errors Using the Help Facility

As a foundation for this topic, add the record shown in Table 12-5 to your sample application. If you have been following the exercises, this **insert** should fail when you try to **commit** it. As you probably noticed, the new record has the same Employee ID as a record that already exists. The Employee ID is the primary-key column for the EMPLOYEE table, so all records must have unique Employee ID values.

Look down at the console area of your Forms Runtime program, and you will see a message like the one shown in the following code block.

```
FRM-40508: ORACLE error: unable to INSERT record.
```

Unfortunately, the error message doesn't say *why* the **insert** failed. To get more information, you can use the Forms Runtime program's Help facility. Here is the process. First, choose the Help | Display Error menu option. You should see a dialog box similar to the one shown in Figure 12-17. The top half of the dialog box shows a segment of the code the application was attempting to execute. The bottom half has more useful information: the Oracle database error message. Here, you learn that the table has a unique constraint that your new record would violate. When you are finished reading the error information, click the OK button to close the Database Error dialog box and exit the Forms Runtime program without saving the new record.

Employee ID	Last Name	First Name	Hire Date	Department ID	Salary
1010	Trumble	Laren	10-JAN-2001	1	60000

TABLE 12-5. *Record with Duplicate Employee ID*

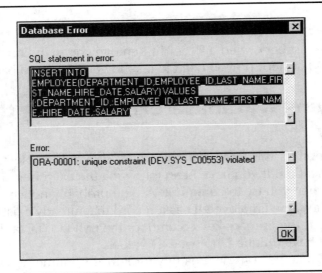

FIGURE 12-17. *Forms Runtime Database Error dialog box*

Exercise

What information is available from the Forms Runtime program's Help | Display Error command that is not available in the console area?

Chapter Summary

In this chapter, you have covered a substantial amount of information on Form Builder. You started by learning about the Form Builder environment: the main Form Builder executables (Form Builder, Form Compiler, and Forms Runtime), and the main Form Builder components (form modules, menu modules, PL/SQL libraries, and Object libraries). You then learned the main objects in a form module: window, canvas, block, and item.

In the next section, you covered the basics of creating form modules. You learned the four steps involved in creating and using a Developer/2000 form: creating a new form module in Form Builder, creating a data block to supply the new form module with data, creating a form layout depicting the data block's items on one or more canvases, and saving, compiling, and running the module using the Forms Runtime program. You then took the steps to actually create a new form module, and then utilized the Data Block Wizard to create data blocks to use within the module to access database data. Once you had access to data, you employed the Layout Wizard to create a basic form layout on a canvas, which you then viewed in the Layout Editor. Next, you modified the layout by rerunning the Layout Wizard in reentrant mode and changing specific parameters in the already-existing layout. You then learned about compiling form modules, and once your sample application was compiled, you ran it using the Forms Runtime program.

Next you learned to identify Form Builder file formats and their characteristics. The Form module file types are **.fmb** (Form Module Binary), **.fmx** (Form Module Executable), and **.fmt** (Form Module Text). The Menu module file types are **.mmb** (Menu Module Binary), **.mmx** (Menu Module eXecutable), and **.mmt** (Menu Module Text). The PL/SQL library file types are **.pll** (PL/SQL Library), **.plx** (PL/SQL eXecutable), and **.pld** (PL/SQL Documentation). The Object library file types are **.olb** (Object Library Binary) and **.olt** (Object Library Text). To finish up the section, you learned how to use the Data Block Wizard to create data blocks with relationships, generating a master/detail relationship between two data blocks. You then used the Layout Wizard to modify your single-table form layout so that it displayed both tables involved in the master/detail relationship. When you ran the resultant form in the Forms Runtime program, you saw how Developer/2000 automatically synchronizes the two tables so the contents of the details table changes each time a different master record is selected.

In the final section, you learned about running a Form Builder application. You started by getting an overview of the runtime environment, which included information about how to specify information about your compiled forms on the Forms Runtime command line. You then learned more about navigating a Form Builder application, learning details about the four sections of the runtime display: the menu, the toolbar, the form area, and the console. Next, you discovered the difference between the two modes of Forms Runtime operation: normal insert/update/delete mode and Enter Query mode. Then, you learned how to control what data a Form Builder application retrieves, either by employing field-level criteria utilizing the _, %, <, >, =, and != operators, or by implementing form variables allowing you to use statements similar to SQL **where** clauses. You learned the fine points of inserting, updating, and deleting records, including how to save time by using record-level and field-level duplicate commands to speed the entry of repetitive data. Finally, you learned how to display detailed database error information using the Help facility in the Forms Runtime program. All in all, the material in this chapter comprises about 12 percent of material tested on OCP Exam 3.

Two-Minute Drill

- The main Form Builder executables are Form Builder, Form Compiler, and Forms Runtime.

- The main Form Builder components are form modules, menu modules, PL/SQL libraries, and Object libraries.

- The four steps involved in creating and using a Developer/2000 form are (1) creating a new form module in Form Builder, (2) creating a data block to supply the new form module with data, (3) creating a form layout depicting the data block's items on one or more canvases, and (4) saving, compiling, and running the module using the Forms Runtime program.

- The main objects in a form module are, from largest to smallest: window, canvas, block, and item. When a data block is placed on a canvas, it is automatically surrounded by a frame that assists in selecting the data block for moving and editing.

- Form Builder provides a Data Block Wizard to simplify creating and modifying data blocks.

- Form Builder also provides a Layout Wizard to simplify creating and modifying form layouts.

- Form Builder generates different file types for each of its four main components. All of the components generate binary source files and text documentation files. All but the Object Library component create compiled executable files.

- The Form module file types are **.fmb** (Form Module Binary), **.fmx** (Form Module eXecutable), and **.fmt** (Form Module Text).

- The Menu module file types are **.mmb** (Menu Module Binary), **.mmx** (Menu Module eXecutable), and **.mmt** (Menu Module Text).

- The PL/SQL Library file types are **.pll** (PL/SQL Library), **.plx** (PL/SQL eXecutable), and **.pld** (PL/SQL Documentation).

- The Object Library file types are **.olb** (Object Library Binary) and **.olt** (Object Library Text).

- A master/detail relationship—also known as a parent/child relationship—is the most common relationship between two data blocks. In it, the master table's primary key is referenced by a foreign key in the detail table.

- Form Builder automatically synchronizes master/detail relationships so the detail table only shows records related to the currently selected record in the master table.

- Before a form can be run, it must be compiled. This can be done manually within Form Builder, or you can set Form Builder to do it automatically when you run a form.

- There are three ways to cause a form to run in the Forms Runtime program: (1) use the Run command in Form Builder, (2) start the Forms Runtime program and fill in the necessary filename/userid/password/database information when it presents its starting dialog box, or (3) invoke the Forms Runtime program from a command line or shortcut and append all the necessary data to the end of the command line.

- There are four sections in a standard Forms Runtime display: the menu, the toolbar, the form area, and the console.

- A form running in the Forms Runtime program is always in one of two states: normal insert/update/delete mode, or Enter Query mode.

- Enter Query mode allows you to control what data are retrieved into a Form Builder application.

- While in Enter Query mode, you can specify data filters using either field-level criteria with the _, %, <, >, =, and != operators, or form variables that enable you to use statements similar to SQL **where** clauses. Each form variable name must begin with a colon in the form, but not in the SQL clause.

- The Record | Duplicate menu command copies the values from the most recently selected record into a new record. The Field | Duplicate menu command does the same thing, but for only the field currently selected.

- When you encounter an error in the Forms Runtime program, you can often get more detailed information by invoking the Help | Display Error command.

Chapter Questions

1. **What are the main Form Builder executables?**

   A. Forms, menus, PL/SQL libraries, Object libraries

   B. Form module, data block, layout, runtime file

   C. .fmb, .fmx, .fmt

   D. Form Builder, Form Compiler, and Forms Runtime

2. **What are the main Form Builder components?**

   A. Form module, data block, layout, runtime file

   B. Form modules, Menu modules, PL/SQL libraries, Object libraries

   C. Form Builder, Form Compiler, and Forms Runtime

   D. .fmb, .fmx, .fmt

3. **You want to create a basic form module. What main steps will you take, and in what order? (Choose four)**

   A. Create a data block

   B. Create a master/detail relationship

   C. Create a form module

   D. Save, compile, and run the form module

   E. Create a layout

4. **You have created a Department data block and layout, both of which contain the items Department ID and Department Name. Now your requirements have changed: while you still need the Department ID in the data block for relational integrity reasons, you no longer want the layout to display it to the user. What is the best way to remove Department ID from the layout without removing it from the underlying data block?**

   A. It is not possible to remove a data item from a layout when it is still in the underlying data block. Thus, to remove it from the layout, you must remove it from the data block first.

   B. Open the Data Block Wizard and move the Department ID item from the Displayed Items column back to the Available Items column.

   C. Open the layout in the Layout Editor. Locate the Department ID item, select it, and press Delete.

   D. Open the canvas in the Layout Editor. Select the frame around the Department data block, and start the Layout Wizard. Move the Department ID item from the Displayed Items column back to the Available Items column.

5. **Which of the following file types is *not* ready to be run in the Forms Runtime program? (Choose one)**

   A. .fmx

   B. .pll

   C. .mmt

6. **When a new form module is created, what object does it automatically include?**

   A. Window

   B. Toolbar

   C. Tab canvas view

   D. Stacked canvas view

7. What are the main objects in a form module, and what is their size precedence, from largest to smallest? (Choose four)

   A. Frame

   B. Layout

   C. Block

   D. Window

   E. Item

   F. Canvas

8. You would like to create a master/detail relationship in Form Builder between two database tables. What must be true about the tables in order to accomplish this? (Choose three)

   A. The detail table must have a primary key.

   B. The master table must have a primary key.

   C. The form module must contain data blocks for at least one of the database tables.

   D. The form module must contain data blocks for both of the database tables.

   E. The master table must have a foreign-key column referencing the primary key of the detail table.

   F. The detail table must have a foreign-key column referencing the primary key of the master table.

9. Which of the following are *not* defining characteristics of Enter Query mode in the Forms Runtime program? (Choose as many as necessary)

   A. Allows entering SQL statements for record filtering

   B. Is the default mode

   C. Allows updating records

   D. Allows wildcard criteria such as the "*" character

   E. Allows movement from record to record

10. **You are creating a form for the DEPARTMENT table using the Data Block Wizard and the Layout Wizard. You know that the table's DEPARTMENT NAME column is wider than any of the actual department names, so you decide to change the width of that item on your display. Unfortunately, you underestimated the amount of screen space the department names would require, and as a result some of them are being cut off when displayed. On the canvas, the Department Name is tightly clustered with other data items, and there is no additional space within its data block's frame. What is the best way to increase the width of the Department Name item?**

   A. Open the canvas in the Layout Editor, click the Department Name item, and drag its right side to increase its display length.

   B. Open the Property Palette of the DEPARTMENT data block and change the Department Name's Maximum Length property to a larger number. The layout will update automatically to the new length the next time the module is compiled.

   C. Use the Data Block Wizard in reentrant mode to change the field's display size.

   D. Use the Layout Wizard in reentrant mode to change the field's display size.

   E. Both C and D.

11. **Which of the following are *not* ways to cause a form to run in the Forms Runtime program? (Choose as many as necessary)**

   A. Use the Run command in Form Builder

   B. Start the Forms Runtime program and fill in the necessary filename/userid/password/database information when it presents its starting dialog

   C. Include all the necessary data in the command line that calls the Forms Runtime program

   D. None of the above.

12. You create a form module that does not have a custom menu or toolbar defined. Which of the following items will be present when the form is run in the Forms Runtime program, and in what order, from the top of the display to the bottom? (choose as many as necessary)

   A. Toolbar

   B. Layout

   C. Form area

   D. Console

   E. Menu

13. You have created a new application and would like to customize it. Which of the following is a Form component that you can customize, or replace altogether?

   A. Message line

   B. Console

   C. Graph

   D. MDI window

   E. Default menu

Answers to Chapter Questions

1. D.   Form Builder, Form Compiler, and Forms Runtime

Explanation   The *executables* are the programs that make up this portion of the Developer/2000 package.

2. B.   Form modules, Menu modules, PL/SQL libraries, Object libraries

Explanation   The *components* are the nodes you see in the Form Builder object tree. They are the pieces that make up a Form Builder application.

3. C, A, E, D.   Create a form module, create a data block, create a layout, and save, compile, and run the form module

Explanation   A master/detail relationship is not an essential part of a basic form module. Of the remaining steps, you must create a form module first, because it contains the other components. The next essential step is creating a data block—without a data block, you have nothing to lay out. Once the data block is created and laid out, you have an application you can save, compile, and run in the Forms Runtime program.

4. D.   Open the canvas in the Layout Editor. Select the frame around the Department data block, and start the Layout Wizard. Move the Department ID item from the Displayed Items column back to the Available Items column.

Explanation   It is possible to keep an item in a data block while not displaying it in a layout. The Layout Wizard's Data Block page provides two areas for items: Available Items and Displayed Items. You select which items are displayed on a layout by moving them into or out of the Displayed Items area.

5. C.   **.mmt**

Explanation   **.pll** files contain both source code and executable code. The **.mmt** file, however, is a simple ASCII text file and, as such, cannot be executed.

6. A. Window

Explanation   Form Builder automatically creates a default window in each new form module it creates. No other items are created automatically.

7. D, F, C, E.   Window, Canvas, Block, Item

Explanation   A layout is the combination of all of these items; it is not an item itself. A window contains one or more canvases, each of which can contain one or more blocks. Each block is comprised of one or more items. A frame is not considered an item itself, but rather a boundary around a block. Review Figure 12-1 for a visual refresher.

8. B, D, F.   The master table must have a primary key, the form module must contain data blocks for both of the database tables, and the detail table must have a foreign-key column referencing the primary key of the master table.

Explanation   In order for database tables to be visible in a Form Builder application at all, there must be a Form Builder data block for each table. Once that is done, a master/detail relationship is possible as long as the master table has a unique primary key, which the detail table stores in one or more columns called a foreign key. Developer/2000 uses a detail record's foreign-key value to determine whether to display the record when a new master record is displayed.

9. B, C, D, E.   Is the default mode, Allows updating records, Allows wildcard criteria such as the "*" character, Allows movement from record to record

Explanation   The default mode for the Forms Runtime program is the normal insert/update/query mode. In Enter Query mode, any data you enter will be treated as selection criteria, thus it is not possible to **update** records while in it. And while the Enter Query mode does allow for wildcards, the multiple-character wildcard is "%", not "*". Finally, because Enter Query mode is inherently a one-record query-by-example form, it does not accommodate any movement from record to record.

10. D.   Use the Layout Wizard in reentrant mode to change the field's display size.

Explanation While you can increase the display size of an item by clicking and dragging its borders in the Layout Editor, the question stated that the data block in question has no additional space. The Layout Wizard's Items page contains parameters controlling display width, and the Layout Wizard will redo the layout of a data block if size changes to the items within the block cause them to no longer fit within the old data block layout. The Maximum Length property controls the length of data that can be displayed in an item, but does not affect the size of the field used to display that data. And the Data Block Wizard has nothing to do with display size.

11. D.   None of the above.

Explanation All of these are valid ways to cause a form to run in the Forms Runtime program.

12. E, A, C, D.   Menu, Toolbar, Form area, Console

Explanation Review the section titled "Navigating a Form Builder Application" for a refresher.

13. E.   Default menu

Explanation While you can place messages into the message line, you cannot replace it entirely. Since the message line is part of the console, the same holds true for the console. A graph is not inherently part of a form module, so you cannot "modify" it. The MDI window cannot be replaced. That leaves the default menu, which you can in fact modify or replace.

CHAPTER
13

Forms Design I

n this chapter, you will learn about the following facets of building forms:

- Working with data blocks and frames
- Working with text items
- Creating LOVs and editors

To create Form Builder applications in Developer/2000, you must understand the components that work together on a finished form. Most forms are based on data blocks, which provide the link between the form and the source of the data being displayed. In this chapter, you will learn quite a bit about data blocks, as well as the nondata version of form blocks: control blocks. You will also be introduced to the components of the Property Palette, where you specify how every object on a form will look and function. Once you are familiar with navigating the Property Palette, you will learn about specific groups of properties important for form development: properties that control the appearance and behavior of data blocks, the frames surrounding data blocks, and control blocks, among others. Next you will learn about text items—the objects on a form that enable the user to see and edit text, numbers, dates, or long data. You will learn about text item properties, including those you can use to enforce data-quality standards at the point of input. You will see how to create tooltips and hints for your users. Finally, you will practice creating Lists of Values (LOVs) and editors on your forms to enhance productivity.

Overall, the contents of this chapter comprise about 13 percent of OCP Exam 3 test content.

Working with Data Blocks and Frames

In this section, you will cover the following points related to working with data blocks and frames:

- Property Palette components
- Manipulating properties

- Controlling the behavior of data blocks
- Controlling frame properties
- Creating blocks that do not correspond to a database object
- Deleting data blocks and their components

In the previous chapter you used wizards to effect changes on a variety of objects and properties—the items included in data blocks, the relationships between blocks, the items displayed on a canvas, and so forth. While the wizards are very helpful for certain tasks, they give you access to only a small portion of the properties you can change. This section will introduce the Property Palette, which gives you much greater control over the objects you create. You will learn how the Property Palette works, how to use it to control the behavior of data blocks, and how to control frame properties with it. Building on this knowledge, you will learn about blocks that do not correspond directly to a database, and you will create a block of this type. Rounding out this section, you will learn how to delete data blocks and their components in two different ways, observing the characteristics of each approach as you experiment.

Property Palette Components

The Property Palette provides complete control over many facets of your objects. Using it efficiently requires understanding its components so you can select the best approach to setting the parameters you need.

To start learning about the Property Palette, start Form Builder and open the file containing your sample application from Chapter 12. Then open the Data Blocks node and double-click on the DEPARTMENT data block to open its Property Palette. You will see a window that looks similar to Figure 13-1.

Toolbar

The toolbar contains buttons giving convenient access to functions relevant to setting properties: property copy and paste, property add and delete, and property-class create and inherit. You will also see a button with a shape like an upside-down "U", which determines what properties are shown when you use a single Property Palette to show properties for multiple objects. When the "U" is upside down (the default setting), the Property

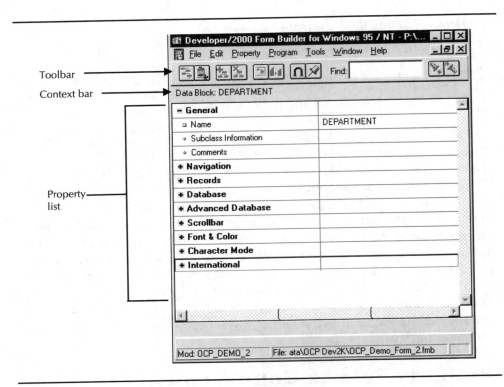

FIGURE 13-1. *Property Palette for DEPARTMENT data block*

Palette is in *Intersection mode* and shows *only the properties that are common* among all the objects you have selected. Clicking the button switches the Property Palette to *Union mode,* in which *every* property related to the selected items is displayed, *even if a property relates to only a single item.* In either mode, a shared property that has the same value for all selected objects will show that value, but if the value is not the same for every selected object, the property will display ***** instead of a value.

The next toolbar button, labeled Freeze/Unfreeze, helps work around a feature of the Property Palette that can be annoying in certain circumstances. Usually the Palette changes its contents each time you select a different object, so that the current object's properties are displayed. This is generally a convenience. However, when you have more than one Property Palette open, *all* of the Palettes will change their contents each time you select a new object. The Freeze/Unfreeze button solves this by forcing a Property Palette to continue showing properties for its current object, regardless of what objects you select from that point on. To see this in action, open your sample application. Open the Data Blocks node so you can see the DEPARTMENT and EMPLOYEE data blocks. Then open a Property Palette for the DEPARTMENT data block by double-clicking on its icon, or by right-clicking on it and selecting Property Palette from the Layout Wizard. Open a second Property Palette by holding down the SHIFT key and double-clicking on the icon for the EMPLOYEE data block. The second Property Palette will open in exactly the same position as the first one, so you will need to move or resize the second Property Palette in order to see both. Click once again on the DEPARTMENT data block. You will see that *both* Property Palettes shift their display to show properties for that data block. Click on the EMPLOYEE data block, or any other object, and you will see that both Property Palettes continue to follow your selection in lockstep. To solve this, click on the DEPARTMENT data block, and then in the first Property Palette you opened, click on the Freeze/Unfreeze button. This will force the Palette to keep its focus on the DEPARTMENT data block. Click on other objects in the Object Navigator, and you will see that the second Property Palette changes its contents to follow your selections, while the first Palette continues displaying properties for the DEPARTMENT data block. Click on the EMPLOYEE data block, and then in the second Property Palette you opened, click on the Freeze/Unfreeze button. This will force the second Property Palette to keep its focus on the EMPLOYEE data block. Click on other objects in the Object Navigator. You will see that no matter what item you select, both Property Palettes remain on their "frozen" objects.

To the right of the toolbar is a field labeled Find. This search field is very handy, because it makes the Property Palette quickly jump to specific properties. If the group containing the matching property is closed, the Find field will even open it up for you. For instance, if you want to change the sort order of the data returned by a data block, you can jump to that property by just typing the letter **O** in the data block's Property Palette's Find field. The focus will immediately move to the **order by** clause property.

Context Bar

Located beneath the toolbar, the context bar identifies which object is currently having its properties displayed by the Property Palette. The first text on the context bar line identifies the type of object: form module, trigger, data block, item, relation, etc. (When you test this on your own system, remember to unfreeze the Property Palette first.) The object type is followed by a colon and then the name of the selected object.

Property List

The main portion of the Property Palette, of course, is the property list. This two-column display shows the property names in the left column, and their current values in the right column. The properties are grouped by category, and a + in front of a category name indicates that the category is collapsed and not displaying its properties, while a – in front of a category name means that the category is expanded and that the properties within that category are all visible. You can toggle between these two states on a category-by-category basis by clicking on the + or – in front of each category name. Each object type in your application has different properties, and the Property Palette is smart enough to remember which property categories you like to have open and closed for each type of object.

Exercises

1. What is the difference between the Property Palette's Intersection and Union display modes?

2. How can you find a specific property quickly in the Property Palette?

3. What does freezing the Property Palette do?

Manipulating Properties

The Property Palette contains several different types of value fields. As you move from property to property, you will encounter the following field types in the Property Palette's value column:

- Alphanumeric fields for typing values

- Fields containing a button labeled More, which opens a dialog box for setting values

- Fields with a button showing an ellipsis (**...**), which opens a window for entering and editing lengthy text like comments or **where** clauses

- Drop-down lists of fixed, predefined values (such as Yes/No fields, or a data block's fixed Navigation Style options of Same Record, Change Record, and Change Data Block)

- Lists of Values (LOVs) containing lists whose contents can change (such as a canvas frame's *Layout Data Block* property, whose list will show whatever data blocks your application has)

You can change properties simply by clicking on the value field for the desired property and either typing in the correct value, selecting it from a list, or specifying it in a dialog box. For properties that have lists, you can iterate through the choices in the list by double-clicking on the property name. This can be particularly handy for Yes/No properties.

You can compare the properties of two or more objects by selecting all of the items you want to compare, and then perusing the Property Palette. As long as you are in the Property Palette's default Intersection display mode, the Palette will only show properties that are common among all of the selected objects. Properties having the same value in all selected objects will show the shared value, while properties that do not have the same value will display ***** for that property instead of a value. When you are showing the properties for multiple objects in a single Palette, any property you change will be changed in all of the selected objects, overwriting whatever prior settings the objects had for that property.

TIP
You can select multiple objects in the Object Navigator by employing the same techniques that work in Windows Explorer. After selecting an initial object, SHIFT-clicking on another object will select a contiguous range containing all the objects between the first selection and the second one. For noncontiguous sets of objects, use CTRL-clicking after the initial object is selected.

If you want to contrast the properties for more than one object, you can open multiple Palettes by SHIFT-double-clicking on the second and subsequent object icons.

The Property Palette's copy and paste functions operate just as you would expect for individual properties: you select the property that contains the value you want to copy, click on the Copy Properties button, move to the property to which you would like to copy the value, click on the Paste Properties button, and the value from the source property is written into the destination property. Now for the interesting information about copying and pasting:

■ You can select multiple properties to copy all at once, using the SHIFT and CTRL keys along with the mouse.

■ If any of the properties you selected are displaying *********—meaning your Property Palette is reflecting multiple objects, and some of those objects' shared properties do not have the same value—the Copy command will ignore those properties. The Copy command will only copy values from properties whose values are the same among all the source objects.

■ The destination object does not need to be the same type as the source object. For instance, you can copy the *Visual Attribute Group* properties from a data block to a canvas. The Paste command is flexible enough to only paste the properties that are appropriate for the destination object.

Exercises

1. What types of value fields will you find in a Property Palette?

2. What happens when you double-click on the name of a property that has a List of Values?

3. What problem could arise from pasting a group of properties into another object?

Controlling the Behavior of Data Blocks

The properties for a data block are divided into nine categories: General, Navigation, Records, Database, Advanced Database, Scrollbar, Font & Color, Character Mode, and International. From a developer's perspective, you can divide these categories into three main groups:

- **General properties**   This is where you can change the data block's name, subclass the data block beneath another object or property class, and enter comments about the data block. The General category offers similar properties for all Form Builder objects.

- **Behavior properties**   This includes the Navigation group, Records group, Database group, and Advanced Database group.

- **Appearance properties**   This includes the Scrollbar group, Font & Color group, Character Mode group, and International group.

The behavior properties are very important to developers. Several deserve special attention. The Query Array Size property controls how many records will be fetched from the database at a time. The Number of Records Buffered property specifies how many records the Forms Runtime program will keep in the client computer's memory when the form is run (records beyond this quantity are stored in a temporary disk file on the client). Increasing the number improves client performance but requires more RAM; decreasing it saves client RAM. The default value for Number of Records Displayed is + 3. The Query Allowed property determines whether the user (or application code) can execute a query in this data block. The **where** clause allows you to enter filtering criteria to limit the types of records returned. The **order by** clause lets you select how the returned data should be sorted. The Insert/Update/Delete Allowed property fills out the C.R.U.D. (Create/Read/Update/Delete) control of your block. (C.R.U.D. is not an Oracle term.) The Update Changed Columns Only property specifies that when the user changes an existing record, the **update** command sent to the server only includes the fields that were changed. While that may seem like a good idea in general, it forces Developer/2000 to reparse the **update** statement for every record being updated, which can degrade performance. It is useful when the record contains LONG values that are not likely to be updated, or if the user is likely to be updating the same one or two columns, or if you have column-specific triggers in your database that you do not want firing unnecessarily. The DML Array Size property controls the number of records that will be sent to the server in a batch. Increasing the number reduces network traffic and therefore improves system-wide performance, but requires more memory on the client computer. Since this command creates batch processing, it forces the Update Changed Columns Only property to No regardless of the property's set value. This property is ignored if the block includes a LONG RAW item.

Exercises

1. Which data block properties manipulate the balance between client computer memory and network traffic?

2. Which data block property gives you control over whether the block allows records to be inserted? Updated? Deleted? Which property determines whether the block will accept query criteria?

3. Which data block property would you consider changing if your records include LONG items that are not likely to be edited?

Controlling Frame Properties

There are a number of properties that will be of particular interest as you work with frames on your application's canvases. Frame Title Alignment lets you select the horizontal position of your frame title within the top border of the frame. The Number of Records Displayed property is a value that you initially specify while running the Layout Wizard. If you want to change it later, this is the property to use. You can also change this value by rerunning the Layout Wizard on a frame. The Distance Between Records property is also specified—and usually ignored—while running the Layout Wizard. If you decide you want a little more space between rows, you can make that modification using this property. You can also change this value by rerunning the Layout Wizard on a frame. The Bevel property lets you select from five different types of frame borders. The choices are Raised, Lowered, None, Inset (the default), and Outset. Figure 13-2 shows how each bevel type looks. The Frame Title Font & Color group property gives you control over the frame title's appearance—its font, size, spacing, and color, among other things. In order to standardize these frame appearance properties across your application, you may want to specify them as a Visual Attribute (one of the nodes under Forms in the Object Navigator) and then assign that visual attribute to the appropriate frames.

Exercises

1. What bevel types are available for your frames?

2. What is the purpose of a Visual Attributes object?

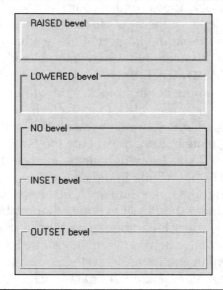

FIGURE 13-2. *Frame bevel types*

Creating Blocks That Do Not Correspond to a Database Object

So far, all the blocks you have created have been data blocks, which serve to provide a data link between a form and a database. There is another type of block—one that is not associated with a database object. This is called a *control block*. The items in a control block *are not related to database columns*. Instead, it contains either controls such as buttons, or a group of items with single values, such as calculated subtotals.

Unlike data blocks, control blocks have a two-part creation process: create the control block, and then manually create the items that go in the block. To get a taste of how this is done, open Form Builder. Within the Object Navigator form module where you wish to create the control block, click on the Data Blocks node. Start the process of creating a new block by clicking on the Create button, or executing the Navigator I Create command. From the New Data Block dialog box that appears, select the *Build a new data block manually* option, and then click on the OK button.

You will see a new block appear under your Data Blocks node. Double-click on the icon for the new block to open its Property Palette. Under the Database node in the Property Palette, change the property named Database Data Block to No. Change the block's name (under the General node) to **DEPARTMENT_EXIT**.

You now have an empty control block. You will place within it a single item: a button that the user may click to exit a form. In the Object Navigator, click on the Items subnode beneath the DEPARTMENT_EXIT block. Click on the Create button, or execute the Navigator | Create command. In the new item's Property Palette, change the item's Name property to **EXIT_BUTTON**. While in the General property node, change the Item Type to Push Button. Under the Functional node, change the Label value to Exit Form. Under the Physical node, change the Canvas property to the canvas containing your Department data block.

You now have a control item on your DEPARTMENT canvas. But the item doesn't do anything yet; it has no code beneath it. To add code, open the canvas containing your Department data block in the Layout Editor. Drag the control button from the top-left corner of the canvas to a position centered beneath the Department data block. Right-click on the button and select SmartTriggers from the context menu that appears. In the list of SmartTriggers, select WHEN-BUTTON-PRESSED. Form Builder will open the PL/SQL Editor. Enter this code to give the button its functionality:

```
BEGIN
    EXIT_FORM (ASK_COMMIT, NO_ROLLBACK);
END;
```

Run the form. When it opens in the Forms Runtime program, click on your new Exit Form button to see it perform.

Exercises

1. What is the definitive difference between a data block and a control block?

2. When a control block is created, what items does it contain?

Deleting Data Blocks and Their Components

There are two ways you can delete data blocks and data block components: from the Object Navigator, and from the Layout Editor. Each has as slightly different impact. The important thing to know is how closely linked Object Navigator objects are with those in the Layout Editor. It will probably not surprise you to find out that deleting an object in the Object Navigator will cause that object to be removed from any canvas in which it was used. Not so obvious, however, is that the reverse is also true: deleting an object from a canvas in the Layout Editor will remove that object from the Object Navigator as well.

To see this demonstrated, open the Form Builder and your sample project from this chapter, if it is not already open. If it is already open, save it now. This is important, because in this exercise you will be deleting items that cannot be undeleted. Then open the Data Blocks node so you can see the data blocks displayed. Open the Canvases node and double-click on the canvas that displays your DEPARTMENT data block. Arrange the Object Navigator window and Layout Editor window so you can see the contents of both simultaneously. In the Object Navigator, click on the DEPARTMENT data block and press the Delete key to delete it. Answer Yes to the confirmation prompt. Notice what happens on the canvas in the Layout Editor. The frame that contained your DEPARTMENT data block is now empty. The data block and its items are gone, while the frame and the frame title are still there.

TIP

Any text in a Developer/2000 application that you type is called boilerplate text. This is in contrast to text that is derived from the database, such as item names. The frame title is an example of boilerplate text, as is the label you placed on your Exit Form button earlier.

Open the Edit menu. Notice that the Undo command is not available. When you delete a data block or data block component from the Object Navigator, it cannot be undone with the Undo command. Now use the File | Revert command to revert your sample project to the state it was in before you deleted the data block. Your sample application is now exactly as it was before you deleted any objects.

Now it is time to see what happens when you delete data block items from the Layout Editor. Once again open the Data Blocks node. Then click on the + next to the DEPARTMENT data block so you can view its components, and click on the + next to the Items subnode so you can see the DEPARTMENT_ID and DEPARTMENT_NAME items. Open the Canvases node, then open the canvas containing your DEPARTMENT data block and position the windows again, if necessary, so you can see the contents of both the Object Navigator and the Layout Editor. In the Layout Editor, select the entire DEPARTMENT data block by clicking outside one of the block's corners and dragging the mouse to the opposite corner. You should see the entire block display selection marks, including the items, titles, and scroll bar within it. Notice that in the Object Navigator, several items are selected: the DEPARTMENT_ID and DEPARTMENT_NAME items in the data block, as well as the frame in your canvas that holds those items. Now delete the selected items in the Layout Editor by pressing the Delete key. Notice that this time there are differences in the result. In the Layout Editor, everything has been deleted except the scroll bar: the frame and its boilerplate text are gone, as well as the items the frame contained. In the Object Navigator, you can see that the items are also gone from the DEPARTMENT data block's Items subnode. The data block itself is still there as an empty data structure, buts its triggers and relations remain intact. Now open the Edit menu. Notice that the Undo command is available this time. When you delete a data block or data block component from the Layout Editor, you can get it back if you immediately issue an Edit | Undo command. Use the File | Revert command now to revert your sample project to the state it was in before you deleted the data block.

Exercises

1. Which approach to deleting data block items gives you the opportunity to undo the deletion?

2. Which approach to deleting a data block removes the data block's data structure but leaves its triggers and relations?

3. What is the only way to actually delete an entire data block, structure and all?

Working with Text Items

In this section, you will cover the following points about working with text items:

- Introduction to text items
- Modifying a text item's appearance
- Controlling the data in a text item
- Modifying the navigational behavior of a text item
- Enhancing the relationship between a text item and a database
- Modifying the functionality of a text item
- Including help messages in your applications

This section covers the most ubiquitous part of any form: text items. You will learn what text items are, and how they differ from display items. You will learn which properties are available to control the appearance of data within text items, and you will learn more about Visual Attribute Groups, which enable you to specify and store named sets of appearance properties that can be referred to by objects in your forms. This helps ensure that similar items look identical throughout your application, and it can save you an immense amount of time if you need to make application-wide changes to appearance later, because you simply change the appropriate Visual Attribute Groups. Next you will learn about the properties that give you control over what the users can, or must, enter. After that, you will be introduced to the properties that affect how users can move around your application, and then you will see which properties control how your Form Builder application interacts with a database. Next, you will learn about properties that affect the scope of queries, along with properties determining what items the user can insert or update. Following this, you will discover properties that control how text items get their value, whether they hide data entered by the user, and whether they are available for user interaction. Finally, you will learn about properties you can use to add user hints and tooltips to your application.

Introduction to Text Items

Form Builder uses the term *text item* to describe any control on your form that displays text, numbers, dates, or long data, and allows the data to be edited by the user. For instance, the fields that display your database items are text items. A text item differs from a *display item* in that the latter does not allow the user to change the data shown. A text item can be either single-line—the type used to display most database data—or multiple-line, which responds to the ENTER key by creating another line of text, instead of moving to the next item.

Exercises

1. What is the difference between a text item and a display item?

2. Describe how a multiple-line text item differs from a single-line text item.

Modifying a Text Item's Appearance

Since a text item is all about displaying data, it's important to understand how to control the appearance of the data it displays. You can access the appearance-oriented properties by opening your canvas in the Layout Editor, selecting the text item whose appearance you would like to change, and opening that item's Property Palette. Table 13-1 contains a number of the more relevant properties.

You undoubtedly noticed that Table 13-1 mentions the Visual Attribute Group twice. This handy feature allows you to create named groups of visual properties—font, colors, and fill, among other things—and then apply those properties to your forms. This feature is similar to the style sheets used in many word processors. If you change any of the default item appearance properties in your forms, it makes sense to use a Visual Attribute Group to do it. That way you can later modify the display properties in a single, centralized location, and have those modifications automatically propagate throughout your forms.

Exercises

1. Why would someone want to change the appearance of a text item?

2. What are the benefits of using a Visual Attribute Group to control the appearance of text items?

Property Node	Property Name	Function
Functional	Justification	Horizontal alignment of the item's contents in relation to the item's width
Data	Format Mask	Allows you to tailor how text, numbers, dates, and times are displayed
Records	Distance Between Records	Vertical distance between each row in a data block
Physical	Visible	Determines whether item is displayed to user
Font & Color	Visual Attribute Group	Allows you to reference an object in which you have already specified appearance properties
Prompt	Prompt	Text label to be displayed for the item
Prompt	Prompt Justification	Horizontal justification of the prompt text in relation to the item's width
Prompt Font & Color	Prompt Visual Attribute Group	Allows you to reference an object in which you have already specified appearance properties

TABLE 13-1. *Text Item Appearance Properties*

Controlling the Data In a Text Item

While controlling the appearance of a text item is important, the content of the data is even more important. Table 13-2 shows properties that give you control over what the users can, or must, enter.

To use the current date as a value in a text item property, set the Initial Value property to $$DATE$$. To use the current date and time, set it to $$DATETIME$$.

Property Node	Property Name	Function
Functional	Multi-Line	Determines whether the item allows for multiple lines of text data
Functional	Case Restriction	Converts value entered by user to uppercase or lowercase
Data	Data Type	Specifies what type of data the item accepts: number, date, etc.
Data	Maximum Length	Longest entry the item will accept
Data	Fixed Length	Only accepts entries containing exactly the number of characters specified by the Fixed Length property
Data	Initial Value	Default value for the item
Data	Required	When set to Yes, will not allow user to save the record unless the item contains a value
Data	Format Mask	Allows you to restrict the content of each character typed, and to control the length of each portion in a multiportion entry such as a date
Data	Lowest Allowed Value	Minimum valid value
Data	Highest Allowed Value	Maximum valid value
Calculation	Calculation Mode	Specifies that a formula or summary should populate the item

TABLE 13-2. *Text Item Data Control Properties*

Exercises

1. Which properties would you use to set valid range of values for a number field?

2. How can you ensure that a date is entered with a four-digit year?

3. Which property would enable you to specify that an item must contain three letters, a two-digit number, and another letter?

4. How could you configure a Date/Time field to have the current date and time automatically inserted each time a new record is created?

Modifying the Navigational Behavior of a Text Item

Once you have taken care of the quality of data the user enters, you can focus on the ease with which they can move around the application. Table 13-3 shows the properties you can employ that will help in this endeavor.

Property Node	Property Name	Function
Functional	Automatic Skip	Specifies that cursor will automatically jump to next item when the last character in the field has been added or changed
Navigation	Keyboard Navigable	When set to No, the item will never receive the input focus via "default navigation" (tabs, ARROW keys, ENTER key)—item can only receive input focus if the user clicks on it
Navigation	Previous Navigation Item	Identifies which item the default navigation should move to if the user moves backward
Navigation	Next Navigation Item	Identifies which item the default navigation should move to if the user moves forward
Physical	Show Vertical Scroll Bar	Specifies that the block should display a scroll bar

TABLE 13-3. *Text Item Navigational Behavior Properties*

Exercises

1. Which text item navigation property would help you minimize the number of keystrokes your users need to type?

2. If you wanted to change the default navigation in a table so users move down a column before they move across a row, which text item navigation properties would you change?

Enhancing the Relationship Between the Text Item and a Database

This section identifies properties that allow you to exert greater control over how your Form Builder application interacts with a database. There are properties that limit or expand the scope of queries users can perform, as well as properties to specify what items the user can **insert** or **update**, and under what conditions. Table 13-4 lists each of these properties in order and describes their purpose.

Exercises

1. Which text item database properties can restrict whether a user can **insert** new data?

2. Which text item data properties can expand the scope of a query beyond what the user explicitly entered?

3. What text item data property allows you to specify that an item cannot be changed once it is populated?

Modifying the Functionality of a Text Item

There are quite a few properties available that enable you to modify a text item's functionality. These properties control how a text item gets its value, whether it displays data as the user enters it, and whether the item is active in the first place. Table 13-5 lists these properties and describes each one.

Property Node	Property Name	Function
Database	Primary Key	Item corresponds to a database data block's primary-key column
Database	Query Only	Specifies that item can be queried but cannot be part of an **insert** or **update** command
Database	Query Allowed	Determines whether users or applications can perform a query using this block
Database	Query Length	Maximum length for a restricted query operation; a value of 0 means no limit
Database	Case Insensitive Query	When set to Yes, any text queries constructed by Form Builder will be case-insensitive; these rely on the queried column being indexed
Database	Insert Allowed	Determines whether user can manipulate the content of the item when inserting a new record
Database	Update Allowed	Determines whether user can change the contents of the item
Database	Update Only if NULL	Handy feature stating that the item can be changed only if it does not already have contents

TABLE 13-4. *Text Item Database Relationship Properties*

Exercises

1. What text item properties would you use to specify that a text item's value should be derived from the sum of an item in a different block?

Property Node	Property Name	Function
Functional	Enabled	Specifies whether the user can navigate to an item using the mouse or keyboard (Keyboard Navigable must also be Yes for keyboard access)
Functional	Conceal Data	Instructs Form Builder to hide characters typed into this item (often used for password fields)
Functional	Popup Menu	Allows you to attach a pop-up menu of your own design to an item
Data	Initial Value	Specifies a default value to populate the item each time a new record is created; value can be a hard-coded value, a form item, a global variable, a form parameter, or a sequence
Data	Copy Value from Item	Used primarily in master/detail relationships, specifies the item in the master block that should be used to filter records in the detail block, or should be automatically copied into this item in the detail block when a new detail record is created
Calculation	Calculation Mode	Allows you to specify that an item should derive its value from a formula or summary, rather than from a database column
Calculation	Formula	Stores a PL/SQL expression used to create the item's value if Calculation Mode property is set to Formula
Calculation	Summary Function	Works in conjunction with the Summarized Block and Summarized Item properties to define a calculation used to populate this item; choices are Average, Count, Max, Min, Standard Deviation, Sum, and Variance

TABLE 13-5. *Text Item Functionality Properties*

Property Node	Property Name	Function
Calculation	Summarized Block	Works in conjunction with the Summary Function and Summarized Item properties to define a calculation used to populate this item
Calculation	Summarized Item	Works in conjunction with the Summary Function and Summarized Block properties to define a calculation used to populate this item
List of Values (LOV)	List of Values	Defines the List of Values that should be attached to the text item
List of Values (LOV)	Validate from List	Used in a field that has an attached LOV, specifies whether data typed by the user should be validated against the LOV

TABLE 13-5. *Text Item Functionality Properties* (continued)

2. If you want a Date field in your form to automatically be populated with today's date for every new record, what text item property would you use to make that happen?

3. What text item property can increase a field's security?

Including Help Messages in Your Applications

Form Builder provides properties making it very easy to add helpful information for your users to see as they move from item to item. The helpful information can take two different forms: *hints* and *tooltips*. A hint displays in the message line (the first line of the two-line area called the console, at the bottom of the form display) when the user enters a particular text item. A tooltip displays adjacent to the mouse pointer when the pointer is hovering over a text item. Table 13-6 lists the properties that provide you with these capabilities.

Property Node	Property Name	Function
Help	Hint	Stores the hint text you would like to display to the users when they enter this text item
Help	Display Hint Automatically	Yes causes the hint to display in the message line instantly when the user enters the field; No keeps the hint from displaying until the user presses the HELP function key or executes the menu Help command
Help	Tooltip	Stores the tooltip text you would like to display to the user when the mouse pointer hovers over this text item
Help	Tooltip Visual Attribute Group	Allows you to specify a Visual Attribute Group for the tooltip text (the default <Null> setting results in the familiar black-on-yellow tooltip text)

TABLE 13-6. *Text Item Help Properties*

Exercises

What is the difference between a hint and a tooltip in Form Builder?

Creating LOVs and Editors

In this section, you will cover the following points about creating LOVs and editors:

- Introduction to LOVs and editors

- Creating LOVs

- Creating editors

This section covers two features that can make the forms you create much easier for users to work with: *Lists of Values* and *editors*. A List of Values (LOV) is a pop-up window that displays a series of choices from which the user selects. LOVs incorporate a feature called *autoreduction* that makes it possible for users to select the list item they want with an absolute minimum of keystrokes, which can save a substantial amount of time in high-volume production environments. In this section, you will create a new form and incorporate your own LOV into the form. After learning about LOVs, you will move on to editors. An editor is a dialog box that appears when the user is in a text item. You will see how to create custom editors that incorporate your own titles, visual attributes, and even a different editing program, if you wish.

Introduction to LOVs and Editors

A List of Values (LOV) is a specific type of pick list used in Developer/2000. It consists of a pop-up window that displays a series of choices relevant to the operation or text item from which it was called. The LOV window is modal, so the user has to either make a selection or dismiss the list. A sample LOV window is depicted in Figure 13-3, which shows the LOV of available triggers you would see if you created a new trigger from the Object Navigator.

One very useful feature in the LOV window is autoreduction, which filters the list's entries in real time as the user enters characters to identify the desired item. While many word processors offer a similar-sounding feature for operations like font selection, Developer/2000's is smarter: if the list includes items whose names have many identical characters, the user only needs to type the characters that differentiate one item from the next.

For example, consider a situation where you want to create a trigger for a KEY-DOWN event. (This book will cover triggers later, so just read along for now—don't try to follow this as an exercise.) To do this you would click on the Triggers node in your module and then invoke the Create procedure. You would immediately be presented with a list of the triggers available in Form Builder, as you saw in Figure 13-3. Since you want a KEY-DOWN trigger, you could type a **k** to reduce the list to only the items that start with "K." The result of this action is depicted in Figure 13-4. The only items

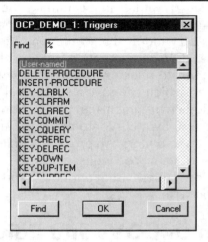

FIGURE 13-3. *List of Values window*

showing are those that start with the same letter: "K." In fact, they all start with the same word: "KEY," followed by a hyphen. All you need to do next is identify *which* key you want; you do not need to type the "EY-" that would be required in, for instance, a font list. So you could type a letter **d**, and the list would diminish to only those values whose second word started with "D." This is depicted in Figure 13-5. To select from that list, you would only need to type a letter **o**, and the list shortens to a single entry: the KEY-DOWN trigger, as shown in Figure 13-6. With only three keystrokes, you could select the desired trigger from a list of over one hundred potential triggers.

You can also search an LOV for strings that occur anywhere within the values, not just at their start. For instance, if you wanted to create a trigger that fires when an item is changed but cannot remember the exact name of the trigger, you can type the word **update** after the "%" in the Find field and click the Find button. The list of triggers will be filtered to show only the values that have "update" somewhere within their names, as shown in Figure 13-7. This same versatile functionality is available in LOVs you create for your users, enabling them to find people, products, or anything else quickly and easily.

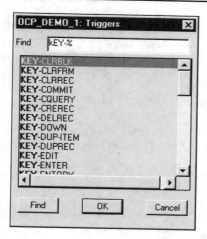

FIGURE 13-4. *List of Values filtered with one character*

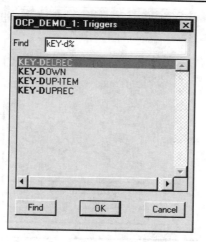

FIGURE 13-5. *List of Values filtered with two characters*

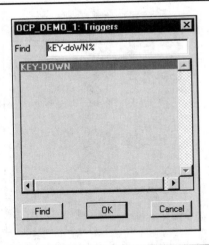

FIGURE 13-6. *List of Values filtered with three characters*

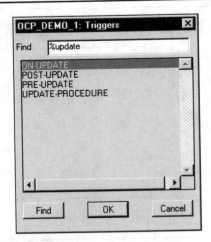

FIGURE 13-7. *List of Values filtered to show UPDATE triggers*

Exercises

1. What is a List of Values?

2. How many ways does an LOV give the user to find items in the list? What are the differences between them?

Creating LOVs

It is quite easy to create an LOV and use it in your forms. In this section, you will go through the steps of creating an LOV, configuring its properties, and assigning it to an item on a form. You will create an Employee form and design the Department ID field so it can be filled in from an LOV.

You will start by creating a new data block to get data from the EMPLOYEE table. (If you use the existing EMPLOYEE data block in a new canvas, it will be removed from the DEPARTMENT canvas where it already resides.) You will then create an LOV for DEPARTMENT data. Next, you will create a new canvas to display records from the EMPLOYEE data block. After testing your new canvas by running it in the Forms Runtime program, you will return to the Layout Editor and attach the DEPARTMENT LOV to the EMPLOYEE canvas. You will then run the Employee form again and see how it allows users to select a department by name and have the appropriate department number appear in the employee's record.

Using the Data Block Wizard, create a new data block. Base it on the EMPLOYEE table, and include all of that table's columns. Do not establish any relationships for the data block, and when the Data Block Wizard asks if you would like it to proceed to the Layout Wizard, tell it to just create the data block. Once the new data block has been created, change its name to **EMPLOYEE_2**. In the Object Navigator, select the LOVs node and then click on the Create button. In the New LOV dialog box, ensure that the choice New Record Group Based on the Query below... is selected. Then enter the following code as the source query for the LOV:

```
SELECT DEPARTMENT_ID, DEPARTMENT_NAME
FROM DEPARTMENT
ORDER BY DEPARTMENT_NAME
```

Click on the OK button to complete the procedure. Then open the Property Palette for the new LOV, and change its name to

DEPARTMENT_LOV. Navigate to the LOV's Functional properties group, and open the dialog box for Column Mapping properties. The dialog box should look like Figure 13-8. For the DEPARTMENT_ID column name, enter a Return Item property of **EMPLOYEE_2.DEPARTMENT_ID**. This specifies the *destination* into which the LOV will place the DEPARTMENT_ID value of whatever department record the user selects. Then enter a display width of **0**, which will cause DEPARTMENT_ID to become a *hidden* column. As a result, the LOV will display only department names. Click on the OK button to close the dialog box. In the Object Navigator, you will see that a record group has automatically been created under the Record Groups node to supply data to your new LOV. Change the record group's name to **DEPARTMENT_LOV**.

Now you have an LOV, but it isn't yet attached to a form. To do that, navigate to the Object Navigator's Canvases node and change the name of your existing canvas to **DEPARTMENT**. Then start the Layout Wizard to create a new canvas. Specify (New Canvas) for the canvas name, and move the Available Items into the Displayed Items area in the following order: LAST_NAME, FIRST_NAME, EMPLOYEE_ID, HIRE_DATE, SALARY, DEPARTMENT_ID. Specify a layout style of Form and a frame title of **Employee**. When the finished canvas is displayed in the Layout Editor, click

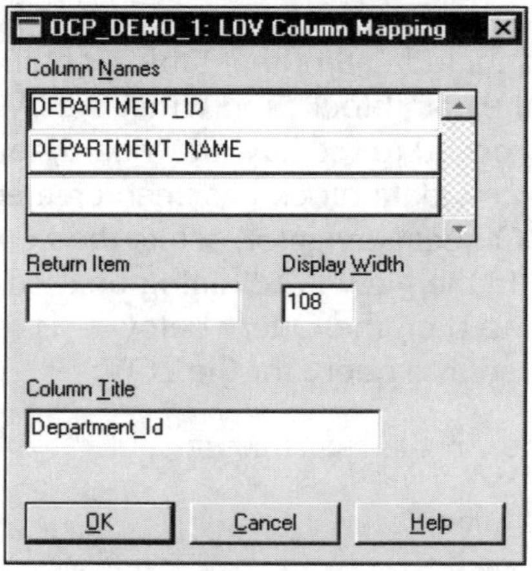

FIGURE 13-8. *Column Mapping properties dialog box for LOV*

on the background of the form to select the entire canvas, open the Property Palette (function key F4 is a shortcut to do this), and change the new canvas's name to **EMPLOYEE**.

Continue by selecting the DEPARTMENT_ID item. In the Property Palette, set the item's List of Values property to DEPARTMENT_LOV. Move farther down the Property Palette to the property named Validate from List, and set that property to Yes. Then run your form. Use the Next Block button on the toolbar to move from the DEPARTMENT form to the EMPLOYEE form. Enter the following values in a new record: Last Name **Carilla**, First Name **Bianca,** Employee ID **1011**, Hire Date **10–MAY-1999**, Salary **65000**.

When you move into the Department ID item, notice that the bottom line in the console displays the indicator "List of Values." This is your clue that you can enter data into this item using a list, as well as by typing directly. To see the LOV, press function key F9 or use the menu command Edit I Display List. You should see an LOV appear that looks like the one shown in Figure 13-9. Select the Quality Assurance department either by typing **Q** and clicking on the OK button, or by double-clicking on the Quality Assurance value in the list. When you do, you will see the Quality Assurance department's ID automatically appear in the item. Save the record by clicking on the Save button, and then exit out of the Forms Runtime program.

Once you have returned to Form Builder, close the Layout Editor and then open the Property Palette for the LOV named DEPARTMENT_LOV. Table 13-7 shows a number of properties you can use to tailor the look and feel of the LOV.

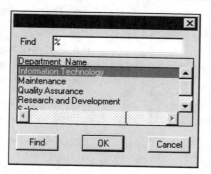

FIGURE 13-9. *DEPARTMENT LOV*

Property Node	Property Name	Function
Functional	Automatic Display	Causes the LOV to display automatically any time the user navigates into the relevant item
Functional	Automatic Refresh	A setting of Yes causes the LOV's underlying query to reexecute each time the LOV is displayed or the item's contents are validated, which takes additional time but ensures that the LOV contents are up-to-date; a setting of No means the query runs only the first time the LOV is used, a bandwidth-saving approach useful when the list's contents are not likely to change during the session
Functional	Automatic Select	When set to Yes, the LOV will automatically act on a list entry as soon as the user types enough characters to uniquely identify a single row in the list; eliminates need for user to click OK to return to the form
Functional	Automatic Skip	A setting of Yes causes focus to move immediately to next field on form after user makes an LOV selection
Functional	Automatic Position	Enables Developer/2000 to automatically position an LOV near the item that invoked it
Functional	Automatic Column Width	Lets Developer/2000 automatically set the widths of the LOV columns wide enough to accommodate their titles if the Display Width isn't wide enough to do so
Physical	X Position Y Position	Allows you to position an LOV precisely where you want it on the screen
Physical	Width Height	Enables you to tailor the size and shape of the LOV

TABLE 13-7. *LOV Functional Properties*

Exercises

1. What are the two purposes of a List of Values?

2. Which LOV properties give you control over the LOV's appearance?

3. What LOV property would you set to cause the LOV to appear automatically when the user enters a field?

4. What LOV property ensures that the values in the LOV are always up-to-date, as of the moment the LOV is opened?

Creating Editors

In Developer/2000, an *editor* is a dialog box that can appear when the user is in a text item. In addition to giving the user more space in which to type text, an editor provides Find and Replace functions that can be useful when modifying large blocks of text. You can open an editor any time your cursor is in a character, number, or date/time field by pressing CTRL-E (remember that in Developer/2000 the CTRL-key commands are case sensitive, so this command will work only if your CAPS LOCK key is off). This keystroke command will produce an editor window similar to the one shown in Figure 13-10. Clicking on the Search button takes you to the Search/Replace dialog box shown in Figure 13-11.

Since you can call up an editor any time already, why create your own? Customization. Designing your own editor allows you to specify what editing program is opened for the user, as well as customize the editor window's size, shape, title, and appearance.

Editor windows are most useful for character fields that will hold large amounts of text. The sample application you have created for this unit does not have any fields of this type, so to learn how to make a custom editor you will create one for the DEPARTMENT_NAME item. In Object Navigator, select the Editors node and then click on the Create button. Open the Property Palette for the new editor. Change the editor's Name property to **DEPARTMENT_NAME_EDITOR**. Change the Title property to **Department Name Editor**, and the Bottom Title property to **Sample Bottom Title**. Change the X Position property to **100**, the Y Position property to **25**, the Width to **400** and the Height to **300**. Change the Show Vertical Scroll Bar property to **Yes**. Then open your DEPARTMENT canvas and display the Property Palette for the DEPARTMENT_NAME item. Change the item's Editor property to

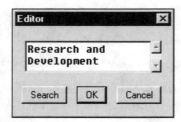

FIGURE 13-10. *Editor window*

DEPARTMENT_NAME_EDITOR. Then run your application. When the DEPARTMENT form opens in the Forms Runtime program, populate the form using the Execute Query button. Then move to a Department Name item, and press CTRL-E to invoke to editor. The editor window that appears should look very similar to Figure 13-12. When you are finished, close the editor window, exit from the Forms Runtime program, and return to Form Builder.

If you just want your user to have a more flexible editing window and do not care about custom titles or visual attributes, you can tell Developer/2000 to use the default system editor (Notepad in Windows systems) instead of Developer's internal editor. You can do this by opening the canvas in Layout Editor, selecting the relevant text item, and changing its Editor property to **SYSTEM_EDITOR**.

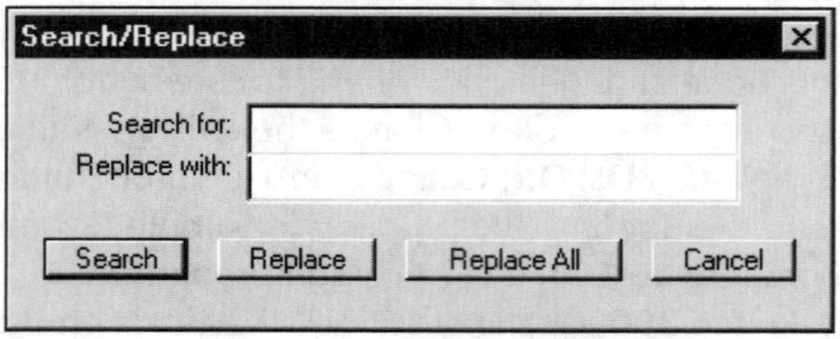

FIGURE 13-11. *Editor Find and Replace options*

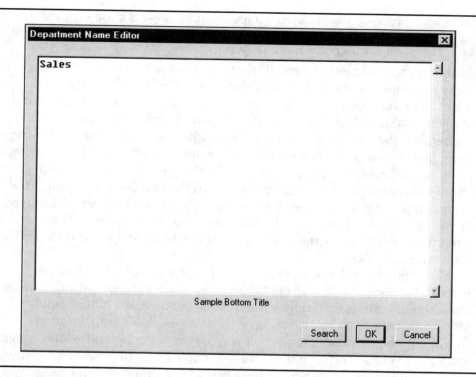

FIGURE 13-12.   *Custom editor window*

Exercises

  1. What benefits does the user enjoy from using an editor window while working with large text blocks?

  2. What are the advantages of creating a custom editor?

Chapter Summary

In this chapter, you have covered quite a bit of information about Forms design. You began by learning about the components of the Property Palette, which consist of the toolbar, context bar, and property list. The toolbar contains buttons giving convenient access to functions relevant to setting properties: property copy and paste, property add and delete, and property-class create and inherit. It also provides buttons that control whether a Property Palette invoked for multiple objects shows only the properties those objects have in common (intersection mode), or shows all of the properties for all objects (union mode). The next Property Palette toolbar button, labeled Freeze/Unfreeze, forces the Palette to continue showing properties for its current object, regardless of what objects you select from that point on. To the right of that button is a field labeled Find that lets you quickly jump to specific properties in the Property Palette.

Beneath the toolbar is the context bar, which identifies the object whose properties are currently being displayed by the Property Palette. Below that is the property list, the main portion of the Property Palette. The property list arranges properties into groups and provides the familiar + or − in front of each group name to open or close the group's properties. Each object type in your application has different properties, and the Property Palette remembers which property categories you like to have open and closed for each type of object.

Next you learned how to manipulate properties using the Property Palette. The Property Palette contains several different types of value fields: alphanumeric fields for typing values, fields containing a button labeled More... that opens a dialog box for setting values, fields with a button showing an ellipsis (...) that opens a window for entering and editing lengthy text such as comments or **where** clauses, pop-up lists of predefined values, and Lists of Values (LOVs) containing lists whose contents can change. You can compare the properties of two or more objects by selecting all of the items you want to compare: SHIFT-clicking allows you to quickly select contiguous groups of objects, and CTRL-clicking lets you select noncontiguous objects. When a Property Palette is displaying properties for multiple objects, it displays ***** for properties that do not have the same value for all the objects selected. You can change the properties for multiple objects simultaneously by selecting all the objects and then changing the desired property in the Property Palette. The Property Palette offers copy and paste functions for individual and multiple properties. When copying more than one property at a time, the Palette will paste only the properties for which an actual value is shown (as opposed to *****), and only the properties that are relevant in the object receiving the pasted properties.

You then learned about properties that control the behavior of data blocks. The General group of properties allows you to change the data block's name, subclass the data block beneath another object or property class, and enter comments about the data block. The data block behavior properties include the Navigation group, Records group, Database group, and Advanced Database group. The data block appearance properties include the Scrollbar group, Font & Color group, Character Mode group, and International group. Behavior properties that are especially useful to developers are Query Array Size, which controls how many records will be fetched from the database at a time; Number of Records Buffered, which specifies how many records the Forms Runtime program will keep in the client computer's memory when the form is run; and Query Allowed, which determines whether the user (or application code) can execute a query in a data block. The property named **where** clause enables you to enter filtering criteria to limit the types of records returned; **order by** clause allows you specify how the returned data should be sorted; Insert / Update / Delete Allowed lets you enable or disable the respective DML functions; Update Changed Columns Only specifies that when the user changes an existing record, the **update** command sent to the server only includes the fields that were changed; and DML Array Size controls the number of records that will be sent to the server in a batch. The properties relevant to the frame surrounding a data block include Frame Title Alignment, Number of Records Displayed, Distance Between Records, Bevel, and the Frame Title Font & Color group.

Next you learned how to create control blocks—blocks that do not directly correspond to a database. A control block contains either controls such as buttons, or a group of items with single values, such as calculated subtotals. Unlike data blocks, control blocks have a two-part creation process: create the control block, and then manually create the items that go into the block. When you delete data blocks and their components from the Object Navigator, the frame that contained the data block will remain on the canvas, as well as the frame's title, which is an example of boilerplate text. The frame will no longer contain the data block or data block items, and the deletion cannot be undone. In contrast, when you delete a data block's items and frame from the canvas in the Layout Editor, everything related to those items is deleted from the Layout Editor except the scroll bar: the frame and its boilerplate text are gone, as well as the items the frame contained. In the Object Navigator, the data block is still present but is an empty data structure. This action can be undone.

You then moved on to a new section discussing text items. A text item is any control on your form that displays text, numbers, dates, or long data, and allows the data to be edited by the user. This is in contrast to display items, which do not allow the user to change the data shown. You can modify a text item's appearance by manipulating properties such as Justification, Format Mask, Distance Between Records, Visible, Visual Attribute Group, Prompt, Prompt Justification, and Prompt Visual Attribute Group. For controlling the data within a text item, Developer/2000 offers properties such as Case Restriction, Data Type, Maximum Length, Initial Value, Required, Lowest and Highest Value, and Calculation Mode. You can change the navigational behavior of a text item with properties like Automatic Skip, Keyboard Navigable, Previous and Next Navigation Item, and Show Vertical Scroll Bar. To enhance the relationship between a text item and a database, you can utilize such properties as Primary Key, Query Only, Query / Insert / Update Allowed, Query Length, Case Insensitive Query, and Update Only if NULL. The properties designed to modify the functionality of a text item include Enabled, Conceal Data, Popup Menu, Initial Value, Copy Value from Item, Calculation Mode, Formula, Summary Function, Summarized Block, Summarized Item, List of Values, and Validate from List.

After digesting the capabilities of those properties, you proceeded to learn about others enabling you to provide item-level assistance for your user by creating hints and tooltips. These invaluable text item properties include Hint, Display Hint Automatically, Tooltip, and Tooltip Visual Attribute Group. Further enhancing individual text items are Lists of Values (LOVs) and editors. An LOV is a window that displays a series of choices users can use to populate a text item. The LOV window is modal, so the user has to either make a selection from the list or dismiss it. When presented with an LOV, the user can employ a feature called autoreduction to select the list item they want with a minimum of keystrokes. The user can also search an LOV for strings that occur anywhere within the list's values, not just at their start. An LOV can be customized using properties such as Automatic Display, Automatic Refresh, Automatic Select, Automatic Skip, Automatic Position, Automatic Column Width, X and Y Position, Width, and Height to tailor the look and feel of the LOV.

An editor is a dialog box that gives the user a larger space in which to type text. An editor provides Find and Replace functions, and you can customize its look and feel. You can also tell Developer/2000 to employ the operating system's default editor instead of Developer's internal editor by setting the Editor property to SYSTEM_EDITOR for the relevant text item.

All in all, this chapter comprises about 13 percent of material tested on OCP Exam 3.

Two-Minute Drill

- The components of the Property Palette are the toolbar, context bar, and property list.

- The toolbar on the Property Palette contains buttons giving convenient access to functions relevant to the setting properties: property copy and paste, property add and delete, and property-class create and inherit.

- The Intersection/Union button on the Property Palette toolbar controls whether a Property Palette invoked for multiple objects shows only the properties those objects have in common (Intersection mode), or all of the properties for all objects (Union mode).

- The Property Palette toolbar button labeled Freeze/Unfreeze forces the Palette to continue showing properties for its current object, regardless of what objects you select from that point on.

- The Property Palette toolbar field labeled Find causes the Property Palette to place its focus on the first property matching the characters you type.

- The Property Palette context bar identifies the object whose properties are currently being displayed by the Property Palette.

- The Property Palette can contain alphanumeric fields for typing values, fields containing a button labeled More... that opens a dialog box for setting values, fields with a button showing an ellipsis (...) that opens a window for manipulating lengthy text, pop-up lists of predefined values, and Lists of Values (LOVs) containing lists whose contents can change.

- You can compare the properties of two or more objects using just one Property Palette by selecting all of the items you want to compare. The Property Palette displays ***** for properties that do not have the same value for all the objects selected.

- You can change the properties for multiple objects simultaneously by selecting all the objects and then changing the desired property in the Property Palette. In doing so, you will overwrite whatever settings the selected objects had for those properties.

- The Property Palette can copy and paste individual or multiple properties. When copying multiple properties, the Palette will paste only the properties for which an actual value is shown, and only the properties that are relevant to the object receiving the pasted properties.

- The behavior of data blocks can be controlled using properties such as Query Array Size, Number of Records Buffered, Query Allowed, **where** clause, **order by** clause, Insert/Update/Delete Allowed, Update Changed Columns Only, and DML Array Size.

- The properties relevant to the frame surrounding a data block include Frame Title Alignment, Number of Records Displayed, Distance Between Records, Bevel, and the Frame Title Font & Color group.

- A control block does not directly correspond to a database, tables, or columns.

- Control blocks have a two-part creation process: create the control block, and then manually create the items that go in the block.

- When you delete data blocks and their components from the Object Navigator, the data blocks and components are irreversibly deleted, but the frame that contained them will remain on the canvas, along with the boilerplate text you entered for the frame's title.

- When you delete a data block's items from the canvas in the Layout Editor, everything related to that block is deleted from the Layout Editor except the scroll bar, and the data block remains in the Object Navigator but is an empty data structure. This action can be undone.

- A text item is any control on your form that allows the user to view and edit text, numbers, dates, or long data.

- A display item shows data but does not allow the user to change it.

- You can modify a text item's appearance by manipulating properties such as Justification, Format Mask, Distance Between Records, Visible, Visual Attribute Group, Prompt, Prompt Justification, and Prompt Visual Attribute Group.

- For controlling the data within a text item, Developer/2000 offers properties such as Case Restriction, Data Type, Maximum Length, Initial Value, Required, Lowest and Highest Value, and Calculation Mode.

- You can change the navigational behavior of a text item with properties like Automatic Skip, Keyboard Navigable, Previous and Next Navigation Item, and Show Vertical Scroll Bar.

- To enhance the relationship between a text item and a database, you can utilize such properties as Primary Key, Query Only, Query / Insert / Update Allowed, Query Length, Case Insensitive Query, and Update Only if NULL.

- The properties that can modify the functionality of a text item include Enabled, Conceal Data, Popup Menu, Initial Value, Copy Value from Item, Calculation Mode, Formula, Summary Function, Summarized Block, Summarized Item, List of Values, and Validate from List.

- The item properties enabling you to provide item-level assistance for your user are Hint, Display Hint Automatically, Tooltip, and Tooltip Visual Attribute Group.

- A Lists of Values (LOV) is a modal window that populates a text item based on a selection made by the user from the list.

- LOVs utilize autoreduction to filter the list in real time as the user types differentiating characters, making it possible to select the desired list item with an absolute minimum of keystrokes.

- The user can also search an LOV for strings that occur anywhere within the values, not just at their start. Only the first column in the LOV will be searched.

- An LOV can be customized using properties such as Automatic Display, Automatic Refresh, Automatic Select, Automatic Skip, Automatic Position, Automatic Column Width, X and Y Position, Width, and Height.

- An editor is a dialog box that can give the user a larger space in which to type text, as well as providing Find and Replace functions.

- You can customize the look and feel of the editor, and you can tell Developer/2000 to bring up the operating system's default editor instead of Developer's internal editor by setting the Editor property to SYSTEM_EDITOR for the relevant text item.

Chapter Questions

1. You open a single property sheet to display properties for your DEPARTMENT data block and DEPARTMENT canvas simultaneously. Which Property Palette display mode is likely to show more properties?

   A. Intersection

   B. Union

2. Which data block property would you consider changing if your records include LONG items that are not likely to be edited?

   A. Query Allowed

   B. Update Allowed

   C. Update Changed Columns Only

   D. DML Array Size

3. What would be the result of completely deleting a data block from the Object Navigator?

   A. The data blocks and components are deleted but can be retrieved using the Edit | Undo command.

   B. The data blocks and components are irreversibly deleted, and all components from the data block stay on the canvas and must be deleted manually.

   C. The data blocks and components are irreversibly deleted, and all components from the data block are removed from any canvas that contained them, including the data block's frame and boilerplate title text.

   D. The data blocks and components are irreversibly deleted, and all components from the data block are removed from any canvas that contained them, but the data block's frame and boilerplate title text will stay on the canvas.

4. You created an LOV for stock items and included a Quantity Currently In Stock column in the LOV. How can you ensure that the user sees accurate In Stock numbers each time the LOV is invoked?

A. Enable the LOV's Automatic Select property.

B. Programmatically requery all tables in the application when the user opens that canvas.

C. Enable the LOV's Automatic Refresh property.

D. There is no way to ensure this.

5. **You have created a SALES_TICKET form for a point-of-sale application. You now want to modify the Transaction_Date_Time item in the form so it is automatically populated with the current date and time each time a new record is created. How can you accomplish this?**

A. Set the Default Value property to $$DATETIME$$.

B. Set the Initial Value property to SYSDATE.

C. Set the Default Value property to SYSDATE.

D. Set the Initial Value property to $$DATETIME$$.

6. **What does freezing the Property Palette do?**

A. Enables you to change a property in multiple objects at one time

B. Forces the Palette to continue displaying properties for the currently selected object(s), regardless of what object(s) you select from that point on

C. Opens a second Palette for comparing multiple objects' properties

D. When multiple objects are selected, shows only those properties that all selected objects share in common

7. **What is the best way to ensure that an item cannot accept query criteria?**

A. Set the item's Query Allowed property to No

B. Set the item's Disable Query property to Yes

C. Set the item's Queryable property to No

D. Set the item's Query Length property to 0

8. **How many characters would you need to type in an LOV to select the WHEN-KEY-UP item from a list containing WHEN-BUTTON-PRESSED, WHEN-KEY-DOWN, and WHEN-KEY-UP, assuming they are the only items in the list and the LOV's properties are set to automatically display the LOV and automatically enter the value once a row is selected?**

   A. 1

   B. 2

   C. 3

   D. 10

9. **Which of the following data block properties affect the balance between client computer memory and network traffic? (choose all that apply)**

   A. DML Data Target Type

   B. DML Array Size

   C. DML Data Target Name

   D. Number of Records Buffered

   E. Number of Records Displayed

   F. Record Orientation

10. **You have created an LOV for a text item on your canvas, and you would like the LOV to appear automatically each time the user enters that text item. What is required to make that happen?**

    A. Set the Automatic Refresh property in the LOV Property Palette to Yes

    B. Set the Automatic Refresh property in the text item Property Palette to Yes

    C. Set the Automatic Display property in the LOV Property Palette to Yes

D. Set the Automatic Display property in the text item Property Palette to Yes

E. Set the Automatic Select property in the LOV Property Palette to Yes

F. Set the Automatic Select property in the text item Property Palette to Yes

G. You must code a trigger to make this happen

11. **When a control block is created, what items does it contain?**

A. Text items for all columns in the related database table.

B. None. You must manually create any items that will go into a control block.

C. None, because, you cannot put items in a control block.

12. **Which text item data properties can restrict whether a user can insert new data? (Choose all that apply)**

A. Primary Key

B. Query Only

C. Query Allowed

D. Insert Allowed

E. Lock Record

13. **What are the benefits of incorporating a List of Values in your application? (Choose as many as apply)**

A. Faster record retrieval

B. Enables user to make selections with minimum keystrokes

C. Efficient use of client computer memory

D. Can ensure that detail values are valid in master table

E. Makes application much cooler

Answers to Chapter Questions

1. B. Union

Explanation   The Intersection display mode shows only the properties that multiple selected objects have in common, while the Union display mode shows all properties for all selected objects, whether the objects share the properties in common or not.

2. C. Update Changed Columns Only

Explanation   If your records include LONG items that are not likely to be edited, this data block property can improve application performance by keeping the application from sending the voluminous LONG data back to the server during an **update** command.

3. D. The data blocks and components are irreversibly deleted, all components from the data block are removed from any canvas that contained them, but the data block's frame and boilerplate title text will stay on the canvas.

Explanation   Review the section titled "Deleting Data Blocks and Their Components" if you need a reminder on this topic.

4. C. Enable the LOV's Automatic Refresh property

Explanation   The Automatic Refresh property determines whether the LOV's underlying query executes every time the LOV is invoked, or only the first time it is invoked. Setting the property to Yes configures it to requery every time.

5. D. Set the Initial Value property to $$DATETIME$$.

Explanation   The is no Item property called Default Value, and while SYSDATE is a valid parameter in a SQL query, it will not work in the Initial Value property; you must use $$DATETIME$$.

6. B. Forces the Palette to continue displaying properties for the currently selected object(s), regardless of what object(s) you select from that point on

Explanation Review the section titled "Understanding the Components of the Property Palette" for a refresher on this topic.

7. A. Set the item's Query Allowed property to No

Explanation There are no properties named Disable Query or Queryable. Setting the Query Length property to 0 simply tells Developer/2000 to use the item's length as the maximum query length.

8. B. 2

Explanation Because all three choices begin with "WHEN-", the LOV only cares about the first differentiating character, which is the "K" that identifies the KEY group. The next character needed is the "D" to select DOWN, after which the row's key value will automatically be entered into the text item.

9. B, D. DML Array Size, Number of Records Buffered

Explanation Review the section titled "Controlling the Behavior of Data Blocks" if you need a reminder on this topic.

10. C. Set the Automatic Display property in the LOV Property Palette to Yes

Explanation No text item property would effect this change. Of the LOV properties listed, Automatic Refresh determines whether the LOV's contents are requeried each time it is opened, and Automatic Select specifies whether the selected LOV row is placed into the specified text item without the user having to double-click on the row or click on the OK button.

11. B. None. You must manually create any items that will go into a control block.

Explanation By definition, a control block is not related to a database table. And you can put items into a control block—that is what it's for. But you must do it manually after the block is created.

12. B, D. Query Only, Insert Allowed

Explanation When the Query Only property is set to Yes, records cannot be inserted. The same is true if the Insert Allowed property is set to No.

13. B, D. Enables user to make selections with minimum keystrokes, Can ensure that detail values are valid in master table

Explanation The autoreduction feature of LOVs allows them to select records with minimum keystrokes, and the fact that the LOV can be populated from a detail item's master table ensures that the selected values are valid as long as the item is set to validate entries against the LOV. Answer E was not intended as a serious answer, but don't mark your score down if you selected it.

CHAPTER
14

Forms Design II

n this chapter, you will cover the following aspects of building forms:

- Creating additional input items
- Creating noninput items
- Creating windows and content canvases
- Working with other canvases

This chapter covers a wealth of information you can use to make your applications much more sophisticated. You will learn about all the input item types available in Form Builder, and then practice creating check boxes, lists, and radio button groups. Next you will cover noninput item types, with practice at creating buttons, read-only fields, calculated fields, and items to display pictures and play sounds. Then, you will learn how to create applications with multiple windows, and you will create forms that incorporate toolbars, tabbed interfaces, and stacked canvases. The OCP Exam 3 will consist of test questions in this subject area worth 18 percent of the final score.

Creating Additional Input Items

In this section, you will cover the following points related to creating additional input items:

- Introduction to item types that allow input
- Creating a check box
- Creating a list item
- Creating a radio group

The most obvious task when creating forms is placing items on the form for the user to interact with. Several of the items you can place on a form are designed to let the reader enter or modify data. This section introduces those *input items* and takes you through exercises creating several different types of them.

Introduction to Item Types that Allow Input

Input items are form objects enabling the user to enter and change data. Table 14-1 shows the input items available in Form Builder, along with usage recommendations for each item type.

Item Type	Usage
Text Item	Allows user to enter and view data. Best for nonrepeating data that does not lend itself to being in a list of often-used choices.
Check Box	Used singly or in groups. Each check box represents a data item that can have only one of two values. They are used for yes/no status fields such as "transaction completed," "currently active," "include in report," and "flagged for review."
Radio Button	Used in groups of two or more. Represents data that has a fixed number of choices that are mutually exclusive. Examples include gender, ratings, and day of week.
Poplist	Familiar drop-down list that allows user to select one value. Autofills entry with matching list item as user types. Will not accept nonlist entries. Designed to be used with lists containing 15 or fewer choices.
T-List	Shows multiple rows of list options and highlights the one currently selected. Designed to be used when the user will select one row from a list containing 15 to 30 choices. The default display size shows at least five rows from the list, so it is best suited for a form that has plenty of screen space available.
Combo Box	Drop-down list that allows user to select one value. Does not autofill entry with matching list item as user types. Can accept nonlist entries if the developer has written a trapping trigger.
List of Values (LOV)	Can display an unlimited number of choices, and can display multiple columns of information for each choice.

TABLE 14-1. *Item Types That Allow Input*

Exercises

1. What item type would you use to allow users to select rows from a multicolumn list?

2. What is the main functional difference between a group of check boxes and a group of radio buttons?

Creating a Check Box

In order to add a check box to a form layout, the form's data block needs to include an item that can contain *only one of two possible values*. Currently, the sample application being used in this unit does not have a column that matches this criterion, so you will add one. Using SQL*Plus, add a profit-sharing column to the EMPLOYEE table by entering the following code:

```
ALTER TABLE EMPLOYEE
   ADD (PROFIT_SHARING_INDICATOR NUMBER(1,0) NULL
   CONSTRAINT BETWEEN_0_AND_1
   CHECK (PROFIT_SHARING_INDICATOR BETWEEN 0 AND 1));

COMMIT;
```

Now that the database can store a true/false value for profit sharing for each employee, you need to add the profit-sharing column to the data block underlying your Employee form. Open your sample application in Form Builder, open the Data Blocks node, right-click on the EMPLOYEE_2 data block, and select Data Block Wizard from the context menu that appears. In the wizard, click on the Table tab and then click on the Refresh button. After you see the PROFIT_SHARING_INDICATOR column appear in the Available Columns area, click once on the SALARY item in the Database Items area (to tell the wizard where it should add the new column), and then click on the > button to move PROFIT_SHARING_INDICATOR into the Database Items area. Complete the change by clicking on the Finish button.

Next, open your EMPLOYEE canvas in the Layout Editor. Right-click on the frame surrounding the Employee data block, and select Layout Wizard from the context menu that appears. In the Layout Wizard's Data Block page, click on DEPARTMENT_ID in the Displayed Items area and then click on the > button to move PROFIT_SHARING_INDICATOR from the

Available Items area to the bottom of the Displayed Items area. While
PROFIT_SHARING_INDICATOR is still selected, open the Item Type
drop-down list and choose Check Box from its choices. Then click on the
Finish button. Your form should look very similar to the one shown in
Figure 14-1.

Before you can run your modified form, you must set properties
identifying the check box's "on" and "off" values. Click on the check box to
select it, open the Property Palette, set the Value When Checked property to

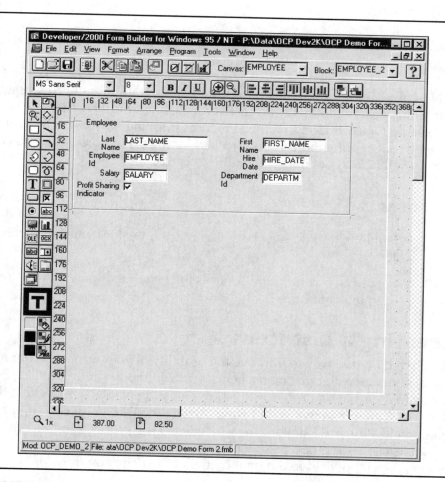

FIGURE 14-1. *Check box added to Employee layout*

1, and the Value When Unchecked property to **0**. In the property named Check Box Mapping of Other Values, change the property to Unchecked. Finally, change the Prompt property from Profit Sharing Indicator to simply Profit Sharing.

Your form is ready to run now, but none of the EMPLOYEE records currently have a "true" value for profit sharing, so it won't be immediately apparent if your check box is working. Using SQL*Plus, enter the following code to set the first record's profit sharing to "true":

```
UPDATE EMPLOYEE
   SET PROFIT_SHARING_INDICATOR = 1
   WHERE EMPLOYEE_ID = 1001;

COMMIT;
```

Now run your form. In the Forms Runtime program, use the Next Block button, if necessary, to make the EMPLOYEE canvas display. Then, click on the Execute Query button to retrieve records from the database. You will see that the Profit Sharing Indicator is checked for the first record—the one you set from SQL*Plus—but not for the other records.

Exercises

1. What limitation does a check box place on values within a database column?

2. What check box property controls the text that displays on the form next to the check box?

Creating a List Item

Lists are a common way to improve the usability of your form. In order to gain experience with creating list items, you will modify your EMPLOYEE canvas so it displays a drop-down list for Department. Start by opening the EMPLOYEE canvas in the Layout Editor. Select the **DEPARTMENT_ID** item and open its Property Palette. Change its Item Type property to List Item, and set its List Style property to Poplist. Locate the Elements In List property, click on the empty field to the right of it, and then click on the More button that appears. Amazingly, you must manually type the elements of the list the user will see, and Developer/2000 offers no way to automatically read the contents of a table to initially create the list elements. (You can write code to populate a list, but that is a subject more appropriate for a later chapter.) There is also no automatic sorting of the list, so the list elements you type must be in the order you want them displayed. Type the following values for the list elements and their corresponding list item values:

List Element	List Item Value
Information Technology	3
Maintenance	4
Quality Assurance	5
Research & Development	2
Sales	1

When you are done, click on the OK button to continue. Change the Prompt property to **Department**. In the Layout Editor, drag the right side of the DEPARTMENT_ID item so it is long enough to display "Research & Development" along with the Drop-Down List button (you will need to expand the data block's frame to the right to make the field large enough). Save your form and then run it. When the form compiles, the Form Compiler will display the following error message, which may be quickly covered up by the Forms Runtime program:

```
FRM-30188: No initial value given, and other values are not allowed

(item EMPLOYEE_2.DEPARTMENT_ID).

List DEPARTMENT_ID

Block: EMPLOYEE_2
```

Developer/2000 prefers that list boxes have a default value. Since that is not appropriate for a Department field, none was specified in the item's Property Palette. The form will run perfectly, however.

In the Forms Runtime program, navigate to the Employee form and then click on the Execute Query button to populate it. You will see that the Department field now displays department names, instead of their numbers. When you are done, exit the Forms Runtime program and dismiss the Compilation Errors dialog box presented by the Form Compiler. To keep the Compilation Errors dialog box from appearing dozens of times as you work with this form module, open the Property Palette for the DEPARTMENT_ID item in your EMPLOYEE_2 data block and change the item's Initial Value property to **1**.

Exercise

What are the differences between the various types of lists available in Form Builder?

Creating a Radio Group

Radio buttons are a popular way to depict data when an item has *two or more* defined possible values, and *only one of the values can be true at a given time*. Neither the DEPARTMENT nor EMPLOYEE tables contain columns that satisfy this criterion, but another table generated by **erdscript.sql** does: EMPLOYEE_SKILL. This table is designed to link the EMPLOYEE and SKILL tables, and it includes a column named SKILL_LEVEL that rates an employee's ability in a given skill, using the numbers 1, 2, 3, 4, or 5. This column is a good candidate for a group of radio buttons. To utilize the column, you must first create a data block for the EMPLOYEE_SKILL table and add that data block to the EMPLOYEE canvas. Then you will modify the EMPLOYEE_SKILL data block so the SKILL_LEVEL item displays as a radio group.

Start by right-clicking on the Data Blocks node in the Object Navigator. From the context menu that appears, select Data Block Wizard. Identify that the data block will be based on a Table or View, and specify the EMPLOYEE_SKILL table as the source. Move all available columns into the Database Items area, and enable the *Enforce data integrity* option. Proceed to the Master/Detail dialog page and click on the Create Relationship button, selecting EMPLOYEE_2 as the master data block. Ensure that both the Detail Item and the Master Item are set to EMPLOYEE_ID. Click on the Next button, select *Just create the data block*, and click on the Finish button.

In the Object Navigator, move to the new EMPLOYEE_SKILL data block and open the Items node beneath it. Select the SKILL_LEVEL item and open its Property Palette. Change the Item Type property to Radio Group. Back in the Object Navigator, click on the + to the left of the SKILL_LEVEL item to open the subnodes beneath it. Note that while there is an entry for Radio Buttons, there are no buttons beneath it. The Data Block Wizard does not generate radio buttons automatically—in order to do so, it would have to read the database and determine the unique values for the assigned column, and while this would be a handy feature, it doesn't exist. So, you will add radio buttons to the radio group manually.

There are two ways to add radio buttons to a radio group: in the Object Navigator, and in the Layout Editor. In order to give you experience with both approaches, the following exercise will have you create some radio buttons in the Object Navigator, and others in the Layout Editor. Normally, you would choose one location or the other to perform this task.

Start by opening the Property Palette for the SKILL_LEVEL item and changing its Initial Value property to 1 (this avoids an error message similar to the one seen for the poplist on the DEPARTMENT_ID field). Then click once on the Radio Buttons subnode beneath SKILL_LEVEL, then click on the Create button. A radio button will appear. Open its Property Palette and change its Name property to **SKILL_RADIO_1**. Change its Label property to 1 so the button has a "1" next to it when it is laid out, and change its Radio Button Value property to **1** so the button relates to a value of "1" in the SKILL_LEVEL data block column. Set the button's Width property to **36** so the button and its label have plenty of space. Then, return to the Object Navigator and click on the SKILL_RADIO_1 radio button object. Copy it by pressing CTRL-C and then paste four copies of it by pressing CTRL-V four times. Change the properties of each copy so that the Name, Label, and Radio Button Value for each button increment by one. When you are done, your Object Navigator should show radio buttons like those depicted in Figure 14-2.

TIP

You can also use the Label property to place text next to a radio button. The prompt text goes to the left of the button; the label text goes to the right of it. Remember both of these for the exam!

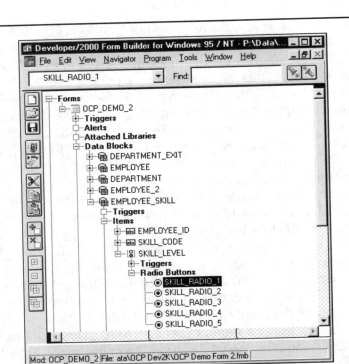

FIGURE 14-2. *Radio buttons in the Object Navigator*

You now have a data block for the EMPLOYEE_SKILL table, and a set of radio buttons to depict the values for the SKILL_LEVEL column in that table. The next step is to lay the data block out on the EMPLOYEE canvas. To do this, right-click on the EMPLOYEE_SKILL data block and select Layout Wizard from the context menu that appears. In the Layout Wizard, select the EMPLOYEE canvas as the destination for your new data block. On the next Wizard dialog page move SKILL_CODE and SKILL_LEVEL into the Displayed Items area. Continuing forward through the Wizard dialog pages, accept the default sizes for each item, and then specify that the layout style for the frame will be Tabular. In the next dialog page, enter a Frame Title of **Skills for this employee:** and specify that the frame will display **5** records at a time. Click on the Finish button to complete the process. Your EMPLOYEE canvas should now look similar to Figure 14-3.

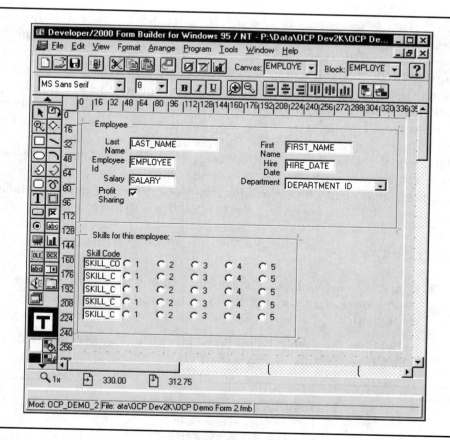

FIGURE 14-3. *EMPLOYEE canvas with radio button group*

Run your canvas. In the Forms Runtime program, navigate to the Employee form, and then click on the Execute Query button to populate the form. Move forward through the employee records using the Next Record button and you will see that the SKILL_LEVEL radio buttons change to reflect each employee shown. When you are done viewing records, exit the Forms Runtime program and return to Form Builder.

To see what happens when you add a radio button in the Layout Editor, view your layout for the EMPLOYEE canvas, click on the Radio Button button, shown here:

Then click anywhere within the EMPLOYEE_SKILL block. A modal window will appear asking whether you want to place the new radio button in an existing radio group—and if so which one—or if you would rather create a new radio group for this button. This window is shown in Figure 14-4. Click on the OK button to select the SKILL_LEVEL radio group. You will see that five closely positioned copies of the new radio button appear within the data block. There are five copies of the radio button because this data block's properties specify that it displays five records at a time. The spacing of the new radio button's instances does not match the record spacing already in place in the data block, however. If you were going to keep this radio button, you would alter its properties to make it fit with the existing data block. Since this new radio button is not going to be used, however, press the DELETE key to delete it now.

Exercises

1. You create a data block and specify that one of its items is to be represented as a radio group. How many radio buttons will be generated?

2. What does the Layout Editor do when you add a radio button to a block that contains a radio group?

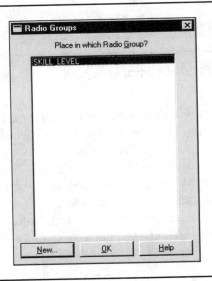

FIGURE 14-4. *Radio Groups selection window in Form Builder*

Creating Noninput Items

In this section, you will cover the following points about creating noninput items:

- Introduction to item types that do not allow input
- Creating a display item
- Creating an image item
- Creating a sound item
- Creating a button
- Creating a calculated field

In addition to items through which users can enter and change data, a form usually needs items that display read-only data or initiate actions. This section covers such *noninput* items. You will start by learning about the different types of noninput items. After that, you will experiment with creating noninput items of your own, including a display item, an image item, a sound item, a group of buttons, and a calculated field.

Introduction to Item Types that Do Not Allow Input

In contrast to input items, noninput items do not enable the user to enter or change data. Instead, they present nonchangeable data to the user and/or generate actions. Table 14-2 shows the noninput items available in Form Builder, along with a description for each item type.

Item Type	Description
Boilerplate Text	Any form text that was typed in manually rather than derived from the database by Form Builder.
Display Item	Form field that displays data but does not allow input. Useful for calculated data such as subtotals or totals, as well as read-only data such as ZIP code cities.

TABLE 14-2. *Item Types that Do Not Allow Input*

Item Type	Description
Image	Provides access to graphics files.
Sound	Provides access to audio files.
Push Button	Ubiquitous object for initiating actions; displays text or picture indicating what it does.
Icon	Button on a toolbar, best suited for frequently used operations. Displays text or picture indicating what it does.

TABLE 14-2. *Item Types that Do Not Allow Input* (continued)

Exercises

1. What is the difference between input items and noninput items?

2. Which noninput items present nonchangeable data to the user? Which provide informative text? Which generate actions?

Creating a Display Item

As its name suggests, a *display item* is a form object that shows data to the user but does not allow that data to be changed. The data can be calculated, or it can come directly from a database column.

Open your sample application, if it is not already open. If it is already open, save it now, because you will be performing some destructive actions during this exercise, and you'll want to be able to revert to the intact version on disk later. In the Object Navigator, open the EMPLOYEE_2 data block and delete its SALARY item. Then, open your EMPLOYEE canvas in the Layout Editor, and you will see that the Salary item is gone. To replace it, click on the Display Item button, shown here:

Then click on the location previously occupied by the Salary field. Change the resultant display item's Name property to **SALARY_DISPLAY**, and change its Column Name property—which identifies which data source column to read—to **SALARY**. Change its Height property to **14** so it matches the other fields, and change its background color to gray so the user doesn't expect it to be changeable. Now run the form. Once the form is open in the Forms Runtime program, populate it using the Execute Query button, and then move among the records using the Next Record and Previous Record buttons. The data in the display item changes with the current record, but it cannot be changed, or even selected.

When you are done, close the Forms Runtime program and return to Form Builder. Execute the File | Revert command to return the Employee form to its fully changeable state.

You can also create a read-only field by changing a text item's Insert Allowed, Update Allowed, and Keyboard Navigable properties to No, and changing its Background Color property to gray. However, even an unchangeable text item consumes more memory than a display item, so it is to your advantage to use display items whenever you want to display read-only data.

Exercises

1. What is the difference between a text item and a display item?

2. What are the benefits of using a display item instead of a text item for read-only data?

Creating an Image Item

Using Developer/2000 to load and store images is really quite easy. In order to experiment with this feature, you will need to create a table capable of holding image files. In SQL*Plus, enter the code that follows. (The table used in this example is based on the BLOB table in Developer/2000's demos. If after reading this section you would like a more in-depth treatment of image and sound files, you can dissect the **image.fmb** and **sound.fmb** files provided in the Developer/2000 demo directory.)

```
CREATE TABLE AV_DATA (
        BLOB_ID             NUMBER(10,0)  NOT NULL,
        BLOB_TYPE           VARCHAR2(10)  NOT NULL,
        DESCRIPTION         VARCHAR2(25)  NOT NULL,
        BLOB_DATA           LONG RAW NULL
);
```

```
ALTER TABLE AV_DATA ADD  (
      CONSTRAINT AV_PRIMARY_KEY PRIMARY KEY (BLOB_ID)
) ;

COMMIT;
```

Next, you need to create a new data block to forge a link between your new table and the sample application you have been working with. To do this, open the application, click on the Forms node, and then click on the Create button. Navigate to the new module that is created and change its name to **IMAGE_MODULE**. Click on the + to the left of the module's name in order to see the nodes it contains, and then click on its Data Blocks node, followed by the Create button. Elect to use the Data Block Wizard and specify that the block will be based on a Table or View. Select the AV_DATA table as the source, and move all columns into the Database Items area. Click on the Next button twice to proceed to the final Data Block Wizard page. Select the *Just create the data block* option and then click on the Finish button. When you see your new data block appear in the Object Navigator, change its name to **AV_DATA_IMAGE**. Open the Property Palette for the data block and change its **where** clause property to **blob_type = 'IMAGE'**. Because the AV_DATA table is going to store both image and sound files, this **where** clause property will ensure that the AV_DATA_IMAGE data block only retrieves image records from the table.

In order to ensure that all records entered through this data block are identified as image records, return to the Object Navigator and click on the Triggers subnode beneath the AV_DATA_IMAGE data block. Click on the Create button and select the PRE-INSERT trigger, which fires before a record is inserted. Type the following code into the PL/SQL Editor for the trigger:

```
:av_data_image.blob_type := 'IMAGE';
```

Click on the Compile button and look for the message "Successfully Compiled" in the bottom-right corner of the PL/SQL Editor. If you do not see that message, correct the syntax of the code and recompile it. When the trigger code is successfully compiled, click on the Close button to close the PL/SQL Editor. The code you just entered will cause the value of 'IMAGE' to be placed into the BLOB_TYPE item of any new record you create using this data block.

Now it is time to create a form for the data block. Right-click on the AV_DATA_IMAGE data block and select Layout Wizard from the context menu that appears. Specify that you want to lay the data out on a New Canvas. Move the BLOB_ID, DESCRIPTION, and BLOB_DATA items into the Displayed Items area. accept the default sizes for each item, and select Form as the layout style. Enter **Picture Test** as the Frame Title and then click on the Finish button. You should see a form that looks like Figure 14-5.

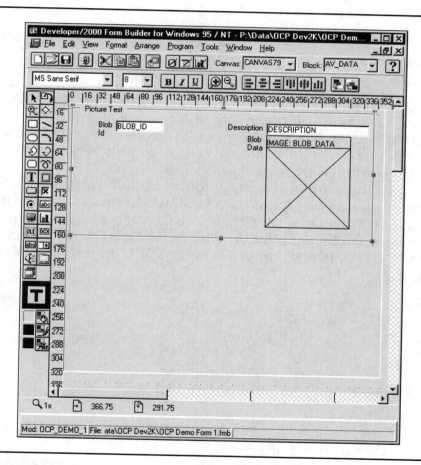

FIGURE 14-5. *Form Builder form with image item*

Click on the BLOB_DATA item and change its Sizing Style property to Adjust so that images will show in their entirety on your form, regardless of their size. (At least, that is the theory; in reality, large images are still cropped.) Then, close the Layout Editor and return to the Object Navigator. Change the name of your new canvas to **AV_DATA_IMAGE**.

In order to make this form useful, you need to give it the ability to read image files from disk and load them into your database. To do this, open the AV_DATA_IMAGE canvas once again in the Layout Editor. Locate the Button Tool button in the Tool Palette—shown next—and click on it.

Then click on an open area in your form, and a button will appear. Open the button's Property Palette and change its Name property to **LOAD_DISK_IMAGE**, its Label property to Load Disk Image, its Keyboard Navigable property to No, its Mouse Navigate property to No, and its Tooltip property to Load image stored on disk.

Now you need to add trigger code to the button. Return to the Object Navigator and beneath your AV_DATA_IMAGE data block locate the new item named LOAD_DISK_IMAGE. Click on the + to the left of the item, and then click on the Triggers subnode. Click on the Create button and select the WHEN-BUTTON-PRESSED trigger. In the PL/SQL Editor, enter the following code:

```
declare
    v_dirname    varchar2(255);
    v_filename   varchar2(255);
begin
    v_dirname := 'C:\';

    v_filename := get_file_name(v_dirname,NULL,
    'Bitmap files (*.bmp)|*.bmp|'          ||
    'JPEG files (*.jpg)|*.jpg|'            );

    if v_filename is not null then
        read_image_file(v_filename,'ANY','av_data_image.blob_data');
    end if;
end;
```

Click on the Compile button, and when the trigger code is successfully compiled, click on the Close button. You are done! Save your work, then run your form. When the Forms Runtime program opens, navigate to the AV_DATA_IMAGE canvas and click on your Load Disk Image button. Navigate to any disk directory you know will contain graphics files; your Windows directory is a safe bet, because it usually contains **.bmp** files used for wallpaper. Wherever you choose to search, select a graphics file and then click the OK button. Your image will appear inside the BLOB_DATA item, similar to the form shown in Figure 14-6. Enter values for the BLOB_ID and DESCRIPTION items, and then click on the Save button to store the image and description into your AV_DATA table. If you would like to store more image records, click on the Next Record button and repeat the process just described. When you are finished, exit the Forms Runtime program and return to Form Builder.

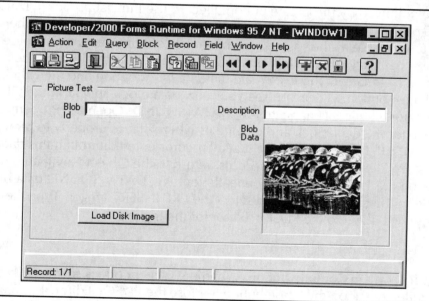

FIGURE 14-6. *Form Builder form with image item populated*

Exercises

1. What are the major steps necessary to create an image item and load images into it?

2. What database column type is used to store image data?

Creating a Sound Item

The process for adding a sound item is very similar to the process for adding an image item. Like images, sounds are stored in Oracle in a LONG RAW type column. You already have a database table suitable for storing sounds, so all you need to do is create a new data block to access that table, and then a form for reading sound files from disk and storing them in the table.

Starting in the Object Navigator, click on the Forms node, and then on the Create button. Navigate to the new module that is created, and change its name to **SOUND_MODULE**. Click on the + to the left of the module's name in order to see the nodes it contains, and then click on its Data Blocks node, followed by the Create button. Elect to use the Data Block Wizard, and specify that the block will be based on a Table or View. Select the AV_DATA table as the source, and move all columns into the Database Items area. Click on the Next button to proceed to the final Data Block Wizard page. Select the *Just create the data block* option and then click on the Finish button. When you see your new data block appear in the Object Navigator, change its name to **AV_DATA_SOUND**. Open the Property Palette for the data block and change its **where** clause property to **blob_type = 'SOUND'**. In order to ensure that all records entered through this data block are identified as sound records, return to the Object Navigator and click on the Triggers subnode beneath your AV_DATA_SOUND data block. Click on the Create button and select the PRE-INSERT trigger. Type the following code into the PL/SQL Editor for the trigger:

```
:av_data_sound.blob_type := 'SOUND';
```

Click on the Compile button. When the trigger code is successfully compiled, click on the Close button to close the PL/SQL Editor. To create the form, right-click on the AV_DATA_SOUND data block and select Layout Wizard from the context menu that appears. Specify that you want to lay the data out on a New Canvas. Move the BLOB_ID, DESCRIPTION, and

BLOB_DATA items into the Displayed Items area, and while in that Layout Wizard page change the Item Type for BLOB_DATA to Sound. Accept the default sizes for each item, and select Form as the layout style. Enter **Sound Test** as the Frame Title and then click on the Finish button. You should see a form that looks like Figure 14-7.

Click on the BLOB_DATA item and open its Property Palette. Change its Distance Between Records property to **0** and its Number Of Items Displayed property to **1**. Change its Width property to **140** and its Height property to **24**. Set Yes values for the properties Show Record Button, Show Rewind Button, and Show Fast Forward Button. If the changes to the BLOB_DATA item's size have caused it to extend outside the data block's frame, use your mouse to reposition the item to a more suitable location. Then, close the Layout Editor and return to the Object Navigator. Change the name of your new canvas to **AV_DATA_SOUND**.

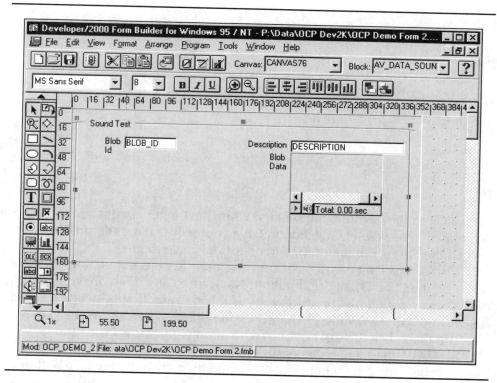

FIGURE 14-7.   *Form Builder form with sound item*

In order to give this form the ability to read sound files from disk and load them into your database, open the AV_DATA_SOUND canvas once again in the Layout Editor. Click on the Button Tool button in the Tool Palette and then click on an open area in your form. Open the newly-created button's Property Palette and change its Name property to **LOAD_DISK_SOUND**, its Label property to Load Disk Sound, its Keyboard Navigable property to No, its Mouse Navigate property to No, and its Tooltip property to Load sound stored on disk.

Now you need to add trigger code to the button. Return to the Object Navigator and locate the new item named LOAD_DISK_SOUND. Click on the + to the left of the item to see the subnodes beneath it, and then click on the Triggers subnode. Click on the Create button and select the WHEN-BUTTON-PRESSED trigger. In the PL/SQL Editor, enter the following code:

```
declare
   v_dirname    varchar2(255);
   v_filename   varchar2(255);
begin
   v_dirname := 'C:\';

   v_filename := get_file_name(v_dirname,NULL,
   'Wave files (*.wav)|*.wav|' );

   if v_filename is not null then
     read_sound_file(v_filename,'ANY','av_data_sound.blob_data');
   end if;
end;
```

Click on the Compile button, and when the trigger code is successfully compiled, close the PL/SQL Editor. Save your work, and then run your form. When the Forms Runtime program opens, navigate to the AV_DATA_SOUND canvas, click on the Insert Record button, and then click on the Load Disk Sound button. Navigate to any directory you know will contain sound files, such as your Windows **\media** subdirectory, which usually contains **.wav** files. Wherever you choose to search, select a sound file and then click the OK button. Your sound will appear inside the BLOB_DATA item. Enter values for the BLOB_ID and DESCRIPTION items, such as the ones shown in Figure 14-8, and then click on the Save button to

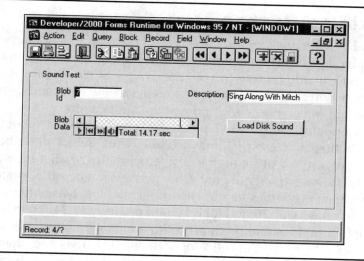

FIGURE 14-8.   *Form Builder form with sound item populated*

store the sound and description into your AV_DATA table. (Remember that your BLOB_ID cannot duplicate a BLOB_ID for an image file, since a single table is storing both types of data. In a production system, you would probably create an Oracle sequence to generate the BLOB_ID numbers, but that is not germane to this example.) If you would like to store more sounds, click on the Insert Record button and repeat the process just described. Since the sound item's Show Record Button property was set to Yes, you can also record new sounds from a microphone, your computer's CD-ROM drive (playing audio CDs), or any other audio input source your computer accommodates. When you are finished, exit the Forms Runtime program and return to Form Builder.

Exercise

What properties must you change on a sound item to enable it to record sound? To shuttle back and forth within a recording?

Creating a Button

Since you have already learned the basics of creating individual buttons in Form Builder, it is time to extend that knowledge by creating a group of buttons. You will add buttons to your AV_DATA_SOUND canvas to navigate between records, as well as to create a new record, delete an existing record, save your work, and exit the application.

Start by opening the AV_DATA_SOUND canvas in the Layout Editor. Create six buttons in close proximity to each other. Select all six buttons, and in the property sheet set their Iconic property to Yes. Set their Background Color property to gray. Change their Keyboard Navigable and Mouse Navigate properties to No. Next select the first two buttons and set their Width property to **26** and their Height property to **24**. Then select the remaining four buttons and set their Width and Height properties to **18**. To set button-specific properties, click on individual buttons and change their properties to match those shown in the table that follows. The names in the Icon Filename column of the table relate to **.ico** files that are provided in the **<oracle_home>\tools\devdem20\bin\icon** directory. Their location on your system can vary, so you may need to search your disk to find them. Note that you do not include the **.ico** file type when entering an icon file's name in the Property Palette.

Button Number	Name	Icon Filename	Tooltip
1	PREV_REC	W_prev	Move to previous record
2	NEXT_REC	W_next	Move to next record
3	SAVE	Save	Save work
4	NEW_REC	Addrow	Add new record
5	DEL_REC	Delrow	Delete current record
6	EXIT	Exit	Exit this application

After you have set the button-specific properties, select all of the buttons and use the Arrange | Align Objects menu command to line them up the way you wish. While they are all still selected, execute the Arrange | Group menu command to group the buttons. You will see that when this is done, the selection marks around the buttons change to indicate that a single group is selected, instead of six individual objects. In fact, it is impossible to select an individual object in the Layout Editor once that object has been made part of a group. To see this for yourself, click on any other object on the canvas, and then click on any of the six buttons you just created. You will see that clicking on a single button now results in the entire group of buttons being selected.

Close the Layout Editor now and return to the Object Navigator. Beneath the AV_DATA_SOUND data block, open the Items node and you will see items representing each of the six buttons you just created, in addition to the original items for database columns. Click on the + to the left of the PREV_REC item, and then click on the Triggers subnode beneath it. Click on the Create button and select the WHEN-BUTTON-PRESSED trigger. Once the PL/SQL Editor opens, type **previous_record;** as the trigger code. Compile the trigger and close it. Perform the same task with the other five buttons, using the following table as your guide.

Button Name	WHEN-BUTTON-PRESSED Trigger Code
PREV_REC	Previous_record;
NEXT_REC	Next_record;
SAVE	Commit work;
NEW_REC	Create_record;
DEL_REC	Delete_record;
EXIT	Exit_form(ask_commit, no_rollback);

Save your form, and then run it to test the buttons you have created. When you are done, close the Forms Runtime program and return to Form Builder.

Exercises

1. When you create a new button, what function is it automatically programmed to perform?

2. If you have combined numerous objects into a group, and you click on a single object within that group, what is selected?

Creating a Calculated Field

Calculated fields are an excellent way to keep the user updated on important status information without giving them the opportunity to change that information directly. Form Builder gives you functions to easily select a data block item and perform sum, average, count, min, max, variance, and standard deviation calculations on it. You can also specify your own formulas to fulfill more complicated mathematical requirements.

To see how to create a calculated field, open your AV_DATA_SOUND canvas in the Layout Editor. Click on the Display Item button in the Tool Palette. Then click on the canvas at the location where you would like to display the number of records in the underlying data table. Open the new display item's Property Palette and change its Name property to **TOTAL_RECORDS**. Change its Data Type property to Number, and its Calculation Mode property to Summary. Change its Summary Function property to Count, its Summarized Block property to **AV_DATA_SOUND**, and its Summarized Item property to **BLOB_ID**. Change its Width property to **25**. Then move back to the Tool Palette and click on the Text button, which is shown here:

Click on your canvas just to the right of the display item you just created. Type **Sound records in database** inside the text box, and line it up with the display item so they can be read as a single phrase. Close the Layout Editor and return to the Object Navigator. Under the Data Blocks node, click on the AV_DATA_SOUND data block and change its Precompute Summaries property to Yes so the calculated field will show the correct number as soon as you retrieve records. Then save the form, run it, retrieve records using the Forms Runtime program's Execute Query button, and watch your new TOTAL_RECORDS item display the calculated total as you add and delete sound records. When you are done, exit from the Forms Runtime program and return to Form Builder.

Exercises

1. What mathematical functions are automatically available for calculated fields in the Layout Editor?

2. What property must be changed in a canvas's underlying data block in order for a calculated field to work?

Creating Windows and Content Canvases

In this section, you will cover the following points about creating windows and content canvases:

- Introduction to windows and content canvases
- Window and content canvases properties
- Displaying a form module in multiple windows

Windows and content canvases are relatively simple objects, but not knowing how to work with them can cost you time, productivity, and quality in the final application. In this section, you will learn about key properties of windows and content canvases. You will then put your knowledge to use by creating a multiple-window application.

Introduction to Windows and Content Canvases

You may recall from Chapter 12 that whenever you create a new form module, Form Builder generates a multiple document interface (MDI) window for the module (assuming you are working in a Windows environment). The MDI window serves as a "parent" window containing all the other document windows, and it usually holds the application's main menu and toolbar. All other document windows—in other words, the ones you create—must fit within the confines of the MDI window. A window is the outermost boundary for a form—an empty frame to hold objects. All of the visual objects in a Form Builder application are contained within windows. There are two types of windows: *document* and *dialog*. A document window is used for standard data entry forms. When a user is in a document window, they can generally enter and query data, move to other windows within the application, and utilize the application's menu and toolbars. In contrast, a dialog window usually serves as a modal dialog box, requiring the user to acknowledge the dialog box in one way or another before proceeding to any other action.

Canvases are displayed within windows, and a single window can be used by one or more canvases. If a window contains more than one canvas, you can use the Next Block and Previous Block buttons to move from one canvas to another. There are four types of canvases: content, stacked, tab, and toolbar. All four types can coexist within a single window. The default canvas type—and the most common—is the content canvas. The content canvas completely occupies the content pane of its window, and *every window must have at least one content canvas*. All of the canvases you created in this unit so far have been content canvases.

Exercises

1. What are the four types of canvases?

2. Is it possible to have a window without a canvas? A canvas without a window?

3. Which is the "outermost" object, a window or a canvas?

Window and Content Canvases Properties

In order to thoroughly understand how to use windows and content canvases you must be well versed in their properties. This section presents the most important properties for you to know.

Window Properties

Table 14-3 shows key properties for use with windows.

Property Node	Property Name	Function
General	Name	Name of the window as it appears in the Object Navigator.
General	Subclass Information	Allows you to subclass this window's properties under another window's in order to simplify changing window properties globally.
Functional	Title	Allows you to specify text to display in the window's title bar at run time. If NULL, the window's name appears in the title bar by default.
Functional	Primary Canvas	Name of canvas that will be this window's primary content view.
Functional	Window Style	Selection between document and dialog window styles.
Functional	Hide on Exit	Applicable only to nonmodal windows, and specifies whether the window becomes hidden if the user navigates to another window.
Functional	Close Allowed	Specifies whether user can close the window.
Functional	Move Allowed	Specifies whether user can move the window.
Functional	Resize Allowed	Specifies whether user can resize the window.
Functional	Maximize Allowed	Specifies whether user can maximize the window.
Functional	Minimize Allowed	Specifies whether user can minimize the window.
Functional	Minimized Title	Specifies the title that appears with a window's icon if it is minimized.

TABLE 14-3. *Window Properties*

Property Node	Property Name	Function
Physical	X Position	Horizontal location of window's top-left corner.
Physical	Y Position	Vertical location of window's top-left corner.
Physical	Width	Width of window.
Physical	Height	Height of window.

TABLE 14-3. *Window Properties* (continued)

Content Canvas Properties

Table 14-4 shows key properties for use with content canvases.

Property Node	Property Name	Function
General	Name	Name of the canvas as it appears in the Object Navigator.
General	Canvas Type	Select between content, stacked, tab, or vertical or horizontal toolbar.
General	Subclass Information	Allows you to subclass this canvas under another in order to simplify changing global properties.
Functional	Raise on Entry	If the user navigates to an item that is covered by another canvas, should this canvas be raised to make the item visible?
Physical	Window	If the form module has more than one window, this property specifies which window should be used to display this canvas.
Physical	Width	Width of canvas.
Physical	Height	Height of canvas.

TABLE 14-4. *Content Canvas Properties*

Exercises

1. Which window property controls what title appears in the window's title Bar?

2. Which canvas property controls what title appears in the window's title bar?

3. What canvas property controls which window the canvas will display in?

Displaying a Form Module in Multiple Windows

To practice controlling the relationship between windows and content canvases, you will create a second window in your sample application. You will then assign the DEPARTMENT canvas to one window, and the EMPLOYEE canvas to the other.

Open your sample form module in Form Builder and navigate to the Windows node. Click on it and then on the Create button. Once the new window object appears, change its Name property to **DEPARTMENT_WINDOW**. Then, select your original window in the Object Navigator and change its Name property to **EMPLOYEE_WINDOW**. Move to the Canvases node in the Object Navigator, and select the DEPARTMENT canvas. Change its Window property to DEPARTMENT_WINDOW. Then, select the EMPLOYEE canvas and ensure that its Window property is set to EMPLOYEE_WINDOW. Run your application. Once it opens in the Forms Runtime program, click on the Next Block button until the second window opens. It may open directly on top of the first window if both windows have default settings for size and location. You can drag the windows to different locations on the screen, resize them, and position them so both windows are open at once. Thus, you can cause two or more canvases to appear in your application simultaneously simply by assigning each canvas to its own window. You can also use the window size and position properties to ensure that the windows do not overlap, if you wish.

Exercises

1. What must you do in Form Builder to enable two or more canvases to display simultaneously at run time?

2. What canvas property allows you to specify the window in which a canvas will be viewed?

Working with Other Canvases

In this section, you will cover the following points about working with other canvases:

- Introduction to canvas types
- Creating an overlay effect using stacked canvases
- Creating a toolbar
- Creating a tabbed interface

You have created numerous canvases in your sample application, but they have all been the same type: content. Now it is time to learn about the other canvas types Developer/2000 offers for forms.

Introduction to Canvas Types

In addition to the content canvas type, Form Builder enables you to create stacked, tab, and toolbar canvases. Each of these types is ideal for fulfilling certain requirements. In this section, you will practice creating all three types.

TIP
Earlier versions of Developer/2000 called a canvas a "canvas-view." This term is still used on some versions of the Certification Exams. If you see "canvas-view" on the exams, just think "canvas."

Stacked Canvas

As its name implies, a stacked canvas lays on top of—or "stacks" onto—a content canvas. In doing so, it hides whatever is beneath it; the user can see what is part of a stacked canvas, but not what it covers. Because of this, stacked canvases are useful for controlling the visibility of entire groups of objects. You can use a stacked canvas to display information that only needs to be viewed in certain situations, such as sensitive data, highly detailed data, or help text. A stacked canvas is also handy if you want to make a portion of the screen static, displaying a predictable group of data, while the user moves among other content canvases in the rest of the screen. Finally, because a stacked canvas can have its own set of scroll bars separate from those on the underlying content canvas, you can use a stacked canvas to show data in a tabular format that the user can scroll around in, while keeping important data like record IDs visible in a fixed location on the underlying content canvas.

Tab Canvas

Familiar to most computer users, the tab canvas is a very useful tool when you need to display a lot of information about a single subject but want to break the information into logical groups for reasons of simplicity or limited screen space. The tabs on a tab canvas essentially represent a group of stacked canvases, with each canvas page obscuring the rest when its tab is selected by the user.

Toolbar Canvas

Unlike the stacked or tab canvases, the toolbar canvas is not designed to display data from a data source. Instead, it contains the components that make toolbars for individual windows. You can make a toolbar either horizontal or vertical, and you can even have multiple toolbars in a single window.

Exercises

1. What type of canvas would most help you create an application that doesn't need a menu? (Assuming that the application already has a content canvas.)

2. How would you describe the difference between a tab canvas and a stacked canvas?

Creating an Overlay Effect Using Stacked Canvases

To see how stacked canvases work, you will modify your EMPLOYEE canvas so that it only shows the employee work skills when a button is activated. Start by opening your sample application. Click on the application's form module node—the one that displays the module's name—and open the Property Palette. Change the First Navigation Data Block property to **EMPLOYEE_2** so your EMPLOYEE canvas will show immediately each time the module is run. Next, move to the Object Navigator's Canvases node and double-click on the EMPLOYEE canvas to open it in the Layout Editor. Click on the Button Tool button, and then click on your canvas in the location shown in Figure 14-9 to create the button. This button will end up being

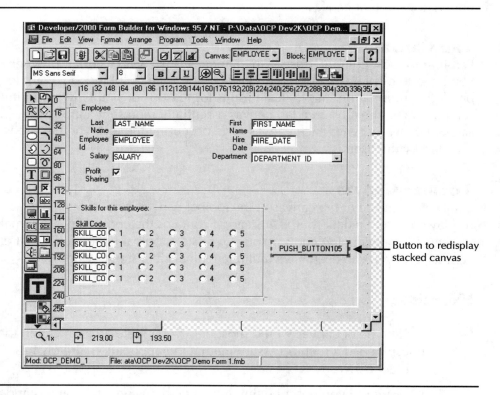

FIGURE 14-9. *Location of button to redisplay stacked canvas*

covered by the stacked canvas, and will therefore become visible to the user only when the stacked canvas is hidden. The button's job will be to make the stacked canvas visible again, thereby covering the button and the Employee Skills area at the same time. Open the button's Property Palette and change its Name property to **HIDE_SKILLS**. Change its Label property to **Hide Skills**. Set its Keyboard Navigable property to No and its Mouse Navigate property to No. Then, right-click on the button and select PL/SQL Editor from the context menu that appears. Select the WHEN-BUTTON-PRESSED trigger and enter the following code in the PL/SQL Editor:

```
go_block('EMPLOYEE_2');
show_view('EMPLOYEE_SKILL_COVER');
```

This command names a canvas that does not yet exist: EMPLOYEE_SKILL_COVER. You will create that canvas after setting the properties of this button, which will be hidden beneath it. To continue, compile your code and then close the PL/SQL Editor.

Now it is time to create the stacked canvas that will cover the employee skills area. Locate the Stacked Canvas button in the Tool Palette. The Stacked Canvas button looks like this:

Position your mouse over the top-left corner of the EMPLOYEE_SKILL frame in the bottom half of the canvas, hold down the mouse button, drag the mouse to the bottom-right corner of the EMPLOYEE_SKILL frame, and let the mouse button go. The EMPLOYEE frame will disappear from view, because it is covered by the stacked canvas. While the stacked canvas is still selected, open its Property Palette and change its Name property to **EMPLOYEE_SKILL_COVER**. Change the stacked canvas's Bevel property to None, and change its Background Color to gray.

All that is left to do now is give the user the ability to make the skill information visible, which requires hiding the stacked canvas. To do this, click on the Button Tool button, and then click on the stacked canvas in approximately the same location where you placed the first button. Change the second button's Name property to **SHOW_SKILLS**. Change its Label property to **Show Skills**. Set its Keyboard Navigable property to No and its Mouse Navigate property to No. Then, right-click on the new button and select PL/SQL Editor from the context menu that appears. Select the WHEN-BUTTON-PRESSED trigger and enter the following code in the PL/SQL Editor:

```
hide_view('EMPLOYEE_SKILL_COVER');
```

Compile the code and then close the PL/SQL Editor. Save your form module and then run it. Populate the Employee form in the Forms Runtime program by clicking on the Execute Query button. Then, click on your Show Skills button. The skills for each employee will appear, and they will stay visible until you click on the Hide Skills button. When you are finished experimenting with the form, close it and return to Form Builder.

Exercises

1. For what types of uses are stacked canvases best suited?

2. When you add a stacked canvas to a layout, what is the default visibility status of items beneath the stacked canvas?

Creating a Toolbar

You can create a toolbar containing exactly the functions your application's users need. To see how to do this, open your SOUND_MODULE form module, if it is not already open. In the Object Navigator, click on the module's Data Blocks node and then the Create button. Select Build a new data block manually from the dialog box that appears, and click on the OK button. Change the block's Name property to **TOOLBAR_ITEMS** and set its Database Data Block property to No.

Click on the Canvases node and then the Create button. Set the new canvas's Name property to **TOOLBAR_HORIZONTAL**, and set its Canvas Type property to Horizontal Toolbar. Double-click on the new canvas's icon to open it in the Layout Editor. Create four buttons, and set their properties to those shown in Table 14-5.

Property	Button 1	Button 2	Button 3	Button 4
Name	SAVE	DEPT	EMP	EXIT
Label		Department form	Employee form	
Iconic	Yes	No	No	Yes
Icon Filename	Save			Exit
Keyboard Navigable	No	No	No	No
X Position	0	24	160	236
Y Position	3	3	3	3
Width	18	70	70	18
Height	18	18	18	18
Tooltip	Save work	Open Department form	Open Employee form	Exit this application

TABLE 14-5. *Properties for Toolbar Buttons*

Click on the background canvas that all the buttons are located on. Change the canvas's Height property to **24**. Then, use the PL/SQL Editor to place the code shown in Table 14-6 into WHEN-BUTTON-PRESSED triggers behind each button.

Button	WHEN-BUTTON-PRESSED Trigger Code
SAVE	Commit work;
DEPT	Go_block('DEPARTMENT');
EMP	Go_block('EMPLOYEE_2');
EXIT	Exit_form(ask_commit, no_rollback);

TABLE 14-6. *Trigger Code for Toolbar Buttons*

Close the Layout Editor. In the Object Navigator, click on the module name and change its Form Horizontal Toolbar Canvas property to **TOOLBAR_HORIZONTAL**. Then, save your work and run the form to see the toolbar in action. When you are done, close the Forms Runtime program and return to Form Builder.

Exercise

What type of block stores the contents of a custom toolbar?

Creating a Tabbed Interface

A tabbed interface is an excellent way to squeeze large amounts of related information into a limited display space. It can also be useful for separating information into logical groups for purposes of clarity. To see how to produce one, create a new form module and name it **EMPLOYEE_TAB**. Using the Data Block Wizard, create new data blocks for the EMPLOYEE and EMPLOYEE_SKILL tables. Establish appropriate relationships between the two tables. Select the EMPLOYEE_SKILL data block and change its Number Of Records Displayed property to **5** so the user will be able to see up to five skills for each employee.

Form Builder doesn't like it when a single data block's items are split between a main canvas and a tab page residing on the same canvas; the program responds by hiding the main canvas items at run time. To avoid this, create a second data block for the EMPLOYEE table. In the Data Block Wizard page for relationships, deselect Auto-join data blocks and then click on the Create Relationship button. Select the EMPLOYEE data block and specify EMPLOYEE_ID for both the Detail Item and the Master Item. This will cause Form Builder to keep the two data blocks synchronized on any form that uses them both—such as the form you are about to create. Keep the new data block's default name of EMPLOYEE1.

Right-click on the EMPLOYEE data block and start the Layout Wizard. Create a new canvas containing the LAST_NAME and FIRST_NAME items from the EMPLOYEE data block. Select a form layout style, and enter a frame title of **Employee Data Sheet**. Once you are in the Layout Editor, click on the background to select the canvas, and change the canvas's Name property to **EMPLOYEE**. Then, click on the Tab Canvas button, shown next:

Move your mouse to a location just below the Employee Data Sheet's bottom-left corner, hold down the left mouse button, and drag the mouse down and to the right so it creates a rectangle approximately the same width as the Employee Data Sheet area and twice as deep. Your screen should look similar to Figure 14-10 at this point. Change the tab canvas's Name property to **EMPLOYEE_TAB**, and change its Background Color property to gray.

Return to the Object Navigator. Locate the EMPLOYEE_TAB canvas and click on the + to the left of its name in order to see its objects. Click on the + to the left of the Tab Pages node, and then select the first tab page beneath

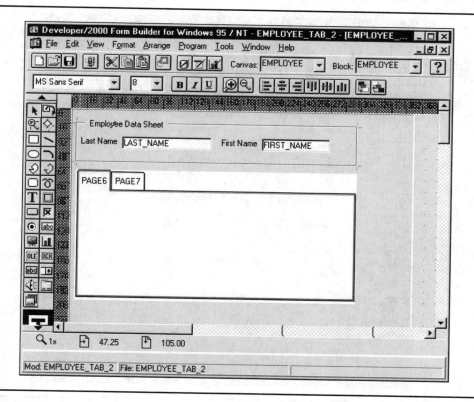

FIGURE 14-10. *Empty tab canvas*

it. Change the first tab page's Name property to **GENERAL_INFO**, and change its Label property to **General Info**. Change the second tab page's Name property to **SKILLS**, and change its Label property to **Skills**. Then, locate the EMPLOYEE1 data block in the Object Navigator—the "extra" employee data block—and select its EMPLOYEE_ID, HIRE_DATE, DEPARTMENT_ID, SALARY, and PROFIT_SHARING_INDICATOR items. Set the Canvas property for all five items to EMPLOYEE_TAB, and the Tab Page property to GENERAL_INFO. Next, move to the EMPLOYEE_SKILL data block and select its SKILL_CODE and SKILL_LEVEL items. Set the Canvas property for both items to EMPLOYEE_TAB, and set the Tab Page property to SKILLS. Return to the Layout Editor and arrange the items into an effective layout. One possible layout is shown in Figure 14-11. Now run

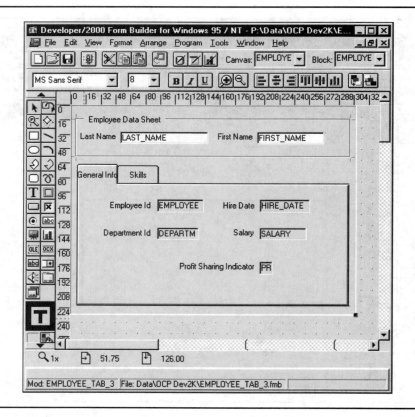

FIGURE 14-11. *Employee information on a tabbed canvas*

your form, populate it using the Execute Query button, and move between the two tab pages you created to see the results of your efforts.

Exercise

What uses are tabbed interfaces well suited for?

Chapter Summary

In this chapter, you have covered a substantial amount of information on forms design. Several topics were covered, including creating additional input items, as well as creating noninput items. You also learned to create windows and several kinds of canvases, including content canvases, toolbar canvases, stacked canvases, and tab canvases.

The first area you covered was creating additional input items. During the introduction you learned that an input item is a form object that enables the user to enter and change data. The input-item category includes text items, check boxes, drop-down lists, radio button groups, poplists, T-lists, combo boxes, and Lists Of Values (LOVs). A text item is most commonly used for entering and changing data, and it is best suited to data that is not repetitive and therefore does not belong in a list. A check box can be used singly or in groups, with each check box representing a data item that can have only one of two values. A radio button group is comprised of two or more radio buttons, and it represents data comprised of a limited number of mutually exclusive choices. A poplist provides a familiar drop-down list that allows user to select one value. It can autofill a user's entry by matching the user's typing with a list item as user types, and it will not accept nonlist entries. A T-List is designed for applications where the user will select one row from a list containing 15 to 30 choices. By default a T-list shows at least five rows from the list, so it is best suited for layouts that have plenty of screen space available. A combo box provides a drop-down list that allows the user to select one value. It does not autofill an entry as the user types, and it can accept nonlist entries as long as the developer has written a trapping trigger. A List of Values (LOV) can display an unlimited number of choices, and it can display multiple columns of information for each choice.

Next, you learned the steps necessary to create a check box. After adding a column to a database table to hold the yes/no data for which a check box is suited, you added the check box and set the properties necessary to make it work. You established the check box's "on" and "off" values by setting the Value When Checked property and the Value When Unchecked property. The property named Check Box Mapping Of Other Values tells the check box what to display if it encounters other values in the data source. Next, you learned to create a list item. You created a poplist, which required you to manually type the list elements in the exact order they should be displayed to the user. One benefit of attaching a poplist to a field containing codes or ID numbers is that it allows that field to display as user-friendly text instead of codes or numbers—as long as the codes or numbers are in the list. You then proceeded to create a group of radio buttons. This allowed the SKILL_LEVEL values stored in the EMPLOYEE_SKILL table to display in a more graphical fashion by having one radio button assigned to each possible value. You can produce a radio group from the Layout Wizard by specifying that a column in the Displayed Items area should be represented as a radio group; you can also create a radio group in the Object Navigator or the Layout Editor. Once a group is created, radio buttons can be added to it from the Object Navigator, as well as from the Layout Editor. Each radio button within a radio group must be assigned a unique number that it will represent for existing records and generate in new records. When you add a radio button to an existing radio group in the Layout Editor, a modal window appears asking whether you want to place the new radio button in an existing radio group—and if so which one—or if you would rather create a new radio group for this button.

You then moved on to a new section covering noninput items. This section provided an introduction explaining what noninput items are available in Developer/2000, and then gave detailed instructions for creating display items, image items, sound items, buttons, and calculated fields. Noninput items do not enable the user to enter or change data. Instead, they provide the user with information to view but not change, and they generate actions. The types of noninput items include boilerplate text, which is any form text that was typed in manually rather than derived from the database by Form Builder; display items, which are read-only form fields that are useful for calculated data such as subtotals or totals, as well as read-only data such as ZIP code cities; image items, which provide access to graphics files; sound items, which provide access to audio files; push buttons, which initiate actions; and icons, which are toolbar buttons best suited for frequently used operations. You then created a table capable of holding image files, followed by a canvas that could load and save them. Here, you got your first taste of a form PRE-INSERT trigger, which fires before a record is inserted; the trigger ensured that any record entered through the image canvas was given a blob type of "IMAGE". You added a variety of buttons to the canvas, and since new buttons contain no code by default, you utilized WHEN-BUTTON-PRESSED triggers to store the code each button would execute when activated. After the buttons were combined into a group, you learned that selecting any object in a group causes the entire group to be selected. Then, you applied your knowledge to creating a canvas for loading and storing sound files. Sound items allow you to customize how many controls are given to the user by setting properties such as Show Play Button, Show Record Button, Show Rewind Button, Show Fast Forward Button, Show Volume Control, Show Time indicator, and Show Slider.

The next subject you covered was creating calculated fields, which let you easily create display items showing sum, average, count, min, max, variance, and standard deviation values. In order for calculated fields to work automatically, the summarized data block's Precompute Summaries property must be enabled. Form Builder also lets you specify your own formulas to fulfill more complicated mathematical requirements.

Next you worked through a thorough discussion on creating windows and content canvases. Whenever you create a new form module, Form Builder generates a multiple document interface (MDI) window that serves as a "parent" window containing all the other document windows. There are two types of windows: document and dialog. A document window is used for standard data entry forms, allowing a user to enter and query data, move to other windows within the application, and interact with the application's menu and toolbars, while a dialog window usually presents a modal dialog box requiring the user to acknowledge the dialog box before proceeding to any other action. Both types of windows display canvases. The four types of canvases are content, stacked, tab, and toolbar. All four types can coexist within a single window, meaning that a single window can contain numerous canvases. Every window must have a content canvas, which will completely occupy the content pane of its window. You can create multiple-window applications simply by creating additional windows and assigning canvases to them by setting each canvas's Window property to the appropriate window.

The final area covered in this chapter is working with stacked, toolbar, and tab canvases. A stacked canvas lays on top of—or "stacks" onto—a content canvas, hiding anything beneath it. Stacked canvases are useful for controlling the visibility of entire groups of objects, and because they can have their own scroll bars separate from those on the underlying content canvas, they can provide a scrollable window separate from the main content canvas. A tab canvas is essentially multiple stacked canvases with handy "tabs" at the top to simplify moving from one canvas to another. Tab canvases are ideal for displaying a lot of information about a single subject in a small amount of screen space. Content, stacked, and tab canvases are all designed to display data. In contrast, a toolbar canvas contains buttons giving users quick access to whatever functions you choose. You can have multiple horizontal and vertical toolbars in a single window.

The content covered in this chapter represents about 18 percent of the material tested on OCP Exam 3.

Two-Minute Drill

- An input item is a form object that enables the user to enter and change data.

- Input items include text items, check boxes, drop-down lists, radio button groups, poplists, T-lists, combo boxes, and Lists of Values (LOVs).

- A text item is most commonly used for entering and changing data, and it is best suited to nonrepeating data that could not be in a list of often-used choices.

- A check box can be used individually or in groups, with each check box representing a data item that can have only one of two values.

- A radio button group is comprised of two or more radio buttons, and it represents data containing a limited number of mutually exclusive choices.

- A poplist provides a familiar drop-down list that allows user to select one value, and it can autofill a user's entry by matching the user's typing with matching list items as the user types. It will not accept nonlist entries.

- A T-list is designed for applications where the user will select one row from a list containing 15 to 30 choices. By default a T-list shows at least five items from the list, so it is best suited for layouts that have plenty of screen space available.

- A combo box provides a drop-down list that allows user to select one value. It does not autofill an entry as the user types. It can accept nonlist entries as long as the developer has written a trapping trigger.

- A List of Values (LOV) can display an unlimited number of choices, and it can display multiple columns of data for each choice.

- A check box item must have mutually exclusive "on" and "off" values defined by setting the Value When Checked property and the Value When Unchecked property.

- A poplist allows a text field to display as user-friendly text instead of codes or numbers.

- A radio button group allows values stored in a data source column to display in a more graphical fashion, by having one radio button assigned to each possible value.

- You can create a radio button group in the Object Navigator, Layout Wizard, or Layout Editor.

- Once a radio group is created, each radio button within it must be assigned a unique value that it represents for existing records or generates in new records.

- When you add a radio button to an existing radio group in the Layout Editor, a modal window appears asking whether you want to place the new radio button in an existing radio group—and if so, which one—or if you would rather create a new radio group for that button.

- Noninput items do not enable the user to enter or change data. Instead, they provide the user with information to view but not change, and they generate actions.

- The types of noninput items include boilerplate text, display items, image items, sound items, push buttons, and icons.

- Boilerplate text is any form text that was typed in manually rather than derived from the database by Form Builder.

- Display items are read-only form fields that are useful for calculated data such as subtotals or totals, as well as unchangeable data such as ZIP code cities.

- Image items provide access to graphics files, and sound items provide access to audio files.

- Push buttons initiate actions stored in their trigger code, as do icons, which do this from within toolbars.

- A form PRE-INSERT trigger fires before a record is inserted. It allows you to tailor the environment for the form by establishing the contents of memory variables or other parameters important to your application.

- A button's functionality is specified in its WHEN-BUTTON-PRESSED trigger.

- Once items are combined into a group, selecting any object in the group causes the entire group to be selected.

- Calculated fields display read-only information that is computed based on database or other data, rather than retrieved directly from the database.

- Form Builder gives you functions to easily perform sum, average, count, min, max, variance, and standard deviation calculations on any data block item. Form Builder also lets you specify your own formulas for more complicated mathematical requirements.

- Whenever you create a new form module, Form Builder generates a multiple document interface (MDI) window that serves as a "parent" window containing all the other document windows.

- The two types of windows are document and dialog. A document window is used for standard data entry forms, while a dialog window usually presents a modal dialog box that the user must acknowledge before proceeding to any other action.

- The four types of canvases are content, stacked, tab, and toolbar. All four types can coexist within a single window. A single window can display many canvases.

■ A content canvas is the basic background for all windows. Every window, regardless of type, must have at least one content canvas.

■ A stacked canvas lays on top of—or "stacks" onto—a content canvas, hiding anything it covers.

■ A tab canvas is essentially multiple stacked canvases with handy "tabs" at the top to simplify moving from one canvas to another. Tab canvases are ideal for displaying a lot of information about a single subject in a small amount of screen space.

■ A toolbar canvas contains buttons giving users quick access to whatever functions you choose.

■ You can have multiple horizontal and vertical toolbars in a single window.

■ You can create multiple-window applications by creating additional windows and assigning canvases to them by setting each canvas's Window property to the appropriate window.

Chapter Questions

1. **What mathematical functions are automatically available for calculated fields in the Layout Editor, without having to write any formulas? (Choose as many as apply)**

   A. average

   B. mean

   C. count

   D. max

   E. min

   F. standard deviation

   G. sum

   H. variance

2. **Users of your application have requested that they be able to see STOCK and CUSTOMER canvases on the screen simultaneously. You add a second window to the application. How can you make the CUSTOMER canvas use the second window?**

    A. Change the canvas's Visual Attributes group.

    B. Change the canvas's Window property.

    C. Change the window's Primary Canvas property.

    D. It is not possible to change a canvas's display window.

3. **Which check box property controls the text that displays next to the check box?**

    A. Text

    B. Name

    C. Label

    D. A check box's text is fixed and cannot be changed.

4. **Which type of canvas is best suited for displaying tutorial text on the same canvas as the form about which the user is being taught?**

    A. Toolbar

    B. Tab

    C. Viewport

    D. Stacked

    E. Content

5. **What visual controls can you add or remove from a sound item? (Choose all that apply)**

    A. Sound format

    B. Play button

    C. Compression

    D. Record button

    E. Mono/stereo

F. Rewind button

G. Fast Forward button

H. Sound quality

I. Volume control

J. Time indicator

K. Progress slider

6. **You are working with an existing radio group in the Layout Editor and try to add a radio button to the group. The Layout Editor responds by:**

   A. Offering to create a check box instead, since a radio button group already exists

   B. Displaying a warning message, and then returning you to the Layout Editor

   C. Presenting a dialog box giving you the chance to select a radio group for the new radio button, or create a new radio group for it

7. **Your Employee form includes a SALARY text item. You want to ensure that standard users cannot input or change a salary value, but you want the value to look exactly like a regular field. What is the best way to do this?**

   A. Set the item's Insert Allowed property to No, and its Update Allowed property to No.

   B. Set the item's Enabled property to No.

   C. Set the item's Enabled property to No, and its Update Allowed property to No.

   D. It is not possible for an unchangeable item to look like a changeable item.

8. **Which of the following are input items? (Choose all that apply)**

   A. Push button

   B. Check box

C. Radio button

D. Sound item

9. **What type of canvas can easily eliminate the need for a menu in your application?**

   A. Content

   B. Stacked

   C. Toolbar

   D. Tab

10. **The DEPARTMENT table in your database has been augmented with a BUDGET column. You want to add BUDGET as an item on your Department form, but the item should be a read-only text box so users cannot change it. The best way to do this is:**

    A. In the Layout Editor, create a display item and set its Insert Allowed property to No, its Update Allowed property to No, and its Database Item property to No.

    B. In the Data Block Wizard, move the BUDGET column into the Available Items area. Change the new data block item's Insert Allowed and Update Allowed properties to No. Proceed to the Layout Editor and add BUDGET as a text item.

    C. In the Layout Editor, create a display item and set its Column Name property to BUDGET.

    D. In the Data Block Wizard, move the BUDGET column into the Available Items area. Proceed to the Layout Editor and add BUDGET as a text item, and change the item's Insert Allowed and Update Allowed properties to No.

11. **You have created a form that contains two canvases, ten database items, and four buttons. The items have all been placed into a group, and the buttons have been placed into a separate group. What happens when you click on one of the buttons in the Layout Editor?**

    A. Nothing is selected

    B. The button is selected

C. The group of buttons is selected

D. All groups are selected

E. All items on the button's canvas are selected.

F. All items on all canvases are selected

12. **Which canvas type is most dissimilar to the others?**

   A. Content

   B. Stacked

   C. Toolbar

   D. Tab

13. **What is the primary difference between tab and stacked canvases?**

   A. A stacked canvas can contain push buttons.

   B. A tab canvas can contain multiple pages.

   C. A stacked canvas obscures what is beneath it.

   D. A tab canvas looks much cooler.

Answers to Chapter Questions

1. A, C, D, E, F, G, H.   average, count, max, min, standard deviation, sum, variance

Explanation   Review the section titled "Creating a Calculated Field" if you need a refresher on this topic.

2. B.   Change the canvas's Window property

Explanation   A canvas's Window property determines which window the canvas is visible in. The Visual Attributes Group has no window selection properties, and a window's Primary Canvas property specifies the primary canvas for a window that displays multiple canvases.

3. C.   Label

Explanation   Remember that both Prompt and Label can place text next to a radio button.

4. D.   Stacked

Explanation   The requirement that the tutorial text be visible on the same form limits the choices to either stacked or tab. A tab canvas might be useful for a multipage tutorial, but the requirements did not state the need for multiple pages, so a simple stacked canvas will fulfill the requirement.

5. B, D, F, G, I, J, K.   Play button, Record button, Rewind button, Fast Forward button, Volume control, Time indicator, Progress slider

Explanation   Review the section titled "Creating a Sound Item" if you need a refresher on this topic.

6. C.   Presenting a dialog box giving you the chance to select a radio group for the new radio button, or create a new radio group for it

Explanation   The Layout Editor is willing to add buttons to an existing radio group. It just needs to know which group will get the new button, or if a completely new group is what you desire.

7. A. Set the item's Insert Allowed property to No, and its Update Allowed property to No

Explanation Changing an item's Enabled property to No causes its contents to display with light gray characters instead of black. Therefore, the only valid choice is A.

8. B, C. Check box, Radio button

Explanation The definition of an input item is an item that allows the user to enter data. You cannot enter data through a push button; you can only run trigger code. A check box can enter data, as can a radio button. A sound item can only play back existing items; you must code a trigger to populate a sound item.

9. C. Toolbar

Explanation A toolbar canvas's sole purpose is holding buttons, which initiate actions. The buttons can replace every menu action your users would need to take.

10. C. In the Layout Editor, create a display item and set its Column Name property to BUDGET.

Explanation Setting an item's Database Item property to No keeps it from retrieving database data, so answer A cannot be correct. Answer B does work, but it creates a normal-looking text box that actually allows the user to type in data; it isn't until the user tries to save their work that the data block's Insert Allowed and Update Allowed properties halt the action. This is not optimal design. Answer D creates an application in which the field's data cannot be changed, but the user can still place focus on the field, which is also not optimal. Therefore, the best choice is answer C.

11. C. The group of buttons is selected.

Explanation The primary reason for groups is to ensure that when any item in the group is selected, all items are selected with it.

12. C.   Toolbar

Explanation   Content, stacked, and tab canvases are all intended to display database data. The toolbar canvas type is not; it is intended to display buttons that work in concert with the items on the other three canvas types.

13. B.   A tab canvas can contain multiple pages.

Explanation   The essence of a tab canvas is the fact that it consists of multiple pages of data, each page overlaying the others when it is selected by the user or developer. It is not possible to get this functionality from a single stacked canvas.

CHAPTER
15

Working with Triggers

In this chapter, you will understand and demonstrate knowledge in the following areas:

- Introduction to form triggers
- How to produce triggers
- Adding functionality to form items
- Using query triggers
- Debugging triggers

Triggers are the bread and butter of your work creating a Form Builder application. You have already worked briefly with triggers in prior chapters of this book. Now it is time for a more complete introduction. You will start by learning about trigger categories, types, scope, and properties. Next, you will learn how to attach triggers to a variety of different objects, utilizing trigger-specific components and subprograms. You will practice adding functionality to form items by attaching triggers to them, and see how to exert greater control over query results by employing query triggers. Then, you will learn how to use the form Debugger, which can provide major assistance when you need to track down misbehaving code. The content of this chapter represents about 22 percent of OCP Exam 3 test content.

Introduction to Form Triggers

In this section, you will cover the following points related to form triggers:

- Definition of a trigger
- Form trigger categories
- Form trigger types and scope
- Form trigger properties

You will learn about the numerous categories of triggers Form Builder offers; be introduced to the two form trigger types; learn how to control a trigger's scope; and see all of a form trigger's properties.

Definition of a Trigger

A trigger is a block of PL/SQL code that adds functionality to your application. Triggers are attached to objects in your application. When a trigger is activated, or *fired*, it executes the code it contains. Each trigger's name defines what event will fire it; for instance, a WHEN-BUTTON-PRESSED trigger executes its code each time the user clicks on the button to which the trigger is attached.

Form Trigger Categories

The triggers most commonly used in Form Builder fall into several functional categories. There are *block-processing* triggers such as ON-DELETE, *interface event* triggers like WHEN-BUTTON-PRESSED, *master/detail* triggers such as ON-POPULATE-DETAILS, *message-handling* triggers like ON-MESSAGE, *navigational* triggers such as WHEN-NEW-FORM-INSTANCE, *query-time* triggers like POST-QUERY, *transactional* triggers such as PRE-INSERT, and *validation* triggers like WHEN-VALIDATE-ITEM. Most of the triggers you deal with will fall into the category of interface event triggers. These fire as the user interacts with your application's GUI. Each time the user clicks on a button, chooses from a list, or changes a radio group or check box, a series of triggers is available to control the application's response.

Interface event triggers generally have names fitting the format WHEN-*object-action*. For instance, list triggers include WHEN-LIST-ACTIVATED and WHEN-LIST-CHANGED. For triggers that fire when a new instance of an object is created, the format WHEN-NEW-*object*-INSTANCE prevails. For instance, if you wanted to establish certain settings when a particular form opens, but did not want the application to bother reestablishing those settings just because the user navigated out of the form and then came back into it, the trigger WHEN-NEW-FORM-INSTANCE would do the trick. There are also quite a few triggers for mouse events, such as WHEN-MOUSE-CLICK, WHEN-MOUSE-DOUBLE-CLICK, WHEN-MOUSE-DOWN, WHEN-MOUSE-UP, WHEN-MOUSE-ENTER, and WHEN-MOUSE-LEAVE. In addition, there are over 40 triggers to respond to keystrokes; these use the naming format KEY-*keytype*. Examples include KEY-DOWN, KEY-UP, KEY-F1, KEY-ENTER, and a very useful addition, KEY-OTHERS. The KEY-OTHERS trigger fires whenever the user presses a key that can have a trigger *but does not*. It is an excellent way to disable unwanted function keys, or to perform one or more actions each time the user presses any key.

Exercises

1. What are the most common trigger categories in Form Builder?

2. If you see a trigger named WHEN-CHECKBOX-CHANGED, what category does the trigger fall into?

3. What trigger would fire each time a new record is created?

4. What is the purpose of the KEY-OTHERS trigger?

Form Trigger Types and Scope

Triggers can also be divided according to their *trigger type* and *trigger scope*. There are two types of triggers: *built-in* and *user-named*. Built-in triggers correspond to specific runtime events and are supplied with Form Builder. User-named triggers are not provided with Form Builder; they are written by developers like you, and their names can be whatever you, the developer, desire. User-named triggers are required only in special situations, and they can only be run using the EXECUTE_TRIGGER built-in procedure from within a user-named subprogram, built-in trigger, or menu item command.

A trigger's scope defines what event must occur in order for the trigger to fire as a result. The trigger scope is usually determined by the object to which it is attached: its scope encompasses the object itself, and any smaller objects contained therein. For instance, if you defined a WHEN-NEW-ITEM-INSTANCE trigger for a single item on a canvas, the trigger would fire whenever the user navigated to that item. If you moved the trigger to a block, it would fire each time the user navigated to any item in the block. Move the same trigger farther up to a form level, and it would fire when the user navigated to any item in any of the form's blocks.

Exercises

1. What is the difference between a built-in trigger and a user-named trigger?

2. What is meant by a trigger's "scope?" What determines a trigger's scope?

Form Trigger Properties

Triggers have relatively few properties. This makes sense for an object whose very name defines when it operates, and whose code content defines what it does. Table 15-1 shows the trigger properties and what they do.

Property Node	Property Name	Function
General	Name	Name of this trigger as it appears in the Object Navigator.
General	Subclass Information	Allows you to subclass this trigger under another in order to simplify changing global properties.
General	Comments	Developer comments about trigger.
Functional	Trigger Style	Allows you to select between a PL/SQL trigger and a V2-style trigger. The latter is available only for compatibility with previous versions, and it is not recommended.
Functional	Trigger Text	Contains a More... button that opens the PL/SQL Editor for entering and editing the trigger's code.
Functional	Fire in Enter-Query Mode	Specifies whether trigger should fire if the form is in Enter-Query mode. Only applicable for triggers related to actions that are valid in Enter-Query mode.
Functional	Execution Hierarchy	If a higher-level object contains a trigger with the same name, this property defines whether this trigger should override the higher-level one (the default), execute before it, or execute after it.

TABLE 15-1.   *Trigger Properties*

Property Node	Property Name	Function
Help	Display in 'Keyboard Help'	Useful only for KEY- triggers, specifies whether a description of the trigger will appear in the list produced by the Forms Runtime program's Help | Keys menu command.
Help	'Keyboard Help' Text	Text to display for a key trigger in the runtime Keys help screen.

TABLE 15-1. *Trigger Properties* (continued)

Exercises

1. Which property controls how a trigger interacts with other triggers?

2. Which property controls what actions a trigger will perform? (Hint: This is a trick question.)

How to Produce Triggers

In this section, you will cover the following points about producing triggers:

- Writing trigger code
- Understanding the use of built-in subprograms
- Introduction to the WHEN-WINDOW-CLOSED trigger

This section covers the basics of writing trigger code. It starts with an overview of the components you can use in a trigger code block. It then introduces the built-in subprograms that are supplied with Form Builder. It wraps up with an exercise in which you use a built-in subprogram within a form trigger.

Writing Trigger Code

Triggers consist of PL/SQL code blocks. The structure of these blocks will be familiar if you have completed the first two units of this book. (If you have not yet worked through those units, be sure to do so; the information they contain is essential to your success as a Developer/2000 developer.) Trigger code can contain a declaration section, a code section, and an error-trapping section. In addition, there are many new system variables enabling you to ascertain and control facets of the client/server environment provided by Form Builder; these are listed in Table 15-2. There are also many, many object properties that you can read and set using PL/SQL code. For instance, you could change the background color of an item in response to an event by placing code like this in the event's trigger:

```
DECLARE
   ITEM_ID item;
BEGIN
   ITEM_ID := find_item('NET_EARNINGS');
   set_item_property(ITEM_ID, visual_attribute, 'GREEN_TEXT_GROUP');
END;
```

In addition, there are many built-in packages containing PL/SQL constructs you can reference in your own code. Examples include CLEAR_ITEM, which clears a text item's current value, and GET_FILE_NAME, which causes a file-open dialog box to display and returns information about the file selected to the routine that called it. The next section covers built-ins in greater detail. As you work through this chapter and the chapters that follow, you will have many opportunities to expand your trigger-writing skills.

SYSTEM.BLOCK_STATUS	SYSTEM.MESSAGE_LEVEL
SYSTEM.COORDINATION_OPERATION	SYSTEM.MODE
SYSTEM.CURRENT_BLOCK	SYSTEM.MOUSE_BUTTON_PRESSED
SYSTEM.CURRENT_DATETIME	SYSTEM.MOUSE_BUTTON_SHIFT_STATE

TABLE 15-2. *Form Builder System Variables*

SYSTEM.CURRENT_FORM	SYSTEM.MOUSE_ITEM
SYSTEM.CURRENT_ITEM	SYSTEM.MOUSE_CANVAS
SYSTEM.CURRENT_VALUE	SYSTEM.MOUSE_X_POS
SYSTEM.CURSOR_BLOCK	SYSTEM.MOUSE_Y_POS
SYSTEM.CURSOR_ITEM	SYSTEM.MOUSE_RECORD
SYSTEM.CURSOR_RECORD	SYSTEM.MOUSE_RECORD_OFFSET
SYSTEM.CURSOR_VALUE	SYSTEM.RECORD_STATUS
SYSTEM.DATE_THRESHOLD	SYSTEM.SUPPRESS_WORKING
SYSTEM.EFFECTIVE_DATE	SYSTEM.TAB_NEW_PAGE
SYSTEM.EVENT_WINDOW	SYSTEM.TAB_PREVIOUS_PAGE
SYSTEM.FORM_STATUS	SYSTEM.TRIGGER_BLOCK
SYSTEM.LAST_QUERY	SYSTEM.TRIGGER_ITEM
SYSTEM.LAST_RECORD	SYSTEM.TRIGGER_RECORD
SYSTEM.MASTER_BLOCK	

TABLE 15-2.   *Form Builder System Variables* (continued)

Exercises

1. What features can you utilize as you write trigger code in Form Builder?

2. What are system variables?

Understanding the Use of Built-In Subprograms

In addition to system variables and object properties, there are many built-in subprograms, also known as *built-ins*, containing PL/SQL constructs you can use in your own trigger and subprogram code. Form Builder comes with hundreds of built-ins, and they are always available for use within your code. Examples include navigational functions such as NEXT_ITEM,

NEXT_RECORD, or NEXT_BLOCK, as well as programming conveniences like GET_FILE_NAME, which generates a file-open dialog box and returns information about the selected file to its calling routine. The built-ins provided with Form Builder are grouped by function into *packages*. You can view the built-in packages in the Object Navigator by opening the Built-In Packages node. Table 15-3 shows the packages and their functional areas.

Built-In Package Name	Functional Area
DDE	Dynamic Data Exchange support for Developer/2000 components
Debug	Procedures, functions, and exceptions for debugging PL/SQL program units
List	Procedures, functions, and exceptions for creating and maintaining lists of character strings
OLE2	PL/SQL API for creating and manipulating attributes of OLE2 automation objects
Ora_FFI	Public interface to call foreign (C) functions from PL/SQL
Ora_NLS	Extracts high-level information about your current language environment
Ora_Prof	Procedures, functions, and exceptions for tuning PL/SQL program units
PECS	Tools to utilize Form Builder's Performance Event Collection Services measuring resource usage
Standard Extensions	Core Form Builder built-ins such as CALL_FORM and CREATE_RECORD
Standard Package Spec	Comparison, number, text, date, record, and logical operators such as >=, BETWEEN, DECODE, LTRIM, ADD_MONTHS, CHARTOROWID, and XOR
Text_IO	Support for reading and writing information from and to files
Tool_Env	Tools to interact with Oracle environment variables

TABLE 15-3.   *Built-In Packages*

Built-In Package Name	Functional Area
Tool_Err	Allows you to manipulate error stack created by other built-in packages
Tool_Res	Extracts string resources from a resource file in order to make PL/SQL code more portable
VBX	Utilize VBX components in forms
Web	Utility for Web applications

TABLE 15-3. *Built-In Packages* (continued)

You have already used built-ins while doing this book's exercises. For instance, when you created a form to display images you included a button employing the GET_FILE_NAME built-in to let the user specify a graphics file to be loaded. For reminder's sake, the code used is shown here:

```
declare
  v_dirname    varchar2(255);
  v_filename   varchar2(255);
begin
  v_dirname := 'C:\';

  v_filename := get_file_name(v_dirname,NULL,
  'Bitmap files (*.bmp)|*.bmp|'           ||
  'JPEG files (*.jpg)|*.jpg|'             );

  if v_filename is not null then
    read_image_file(v_filename,'ANY','av_data_image.blob_data');
  end if;
end;
```

This code also used the READ_IMAGE_FILE built-in to load the selected image file into the application's current record memory. Both of these built-ins are part of the Standard Extensions package. When you use a built-in from a package other than the standard packages, you must precede its name with the name of the package; for instance, WEB.SHOW_DOCUMENT.

Restricted and Unrestricted Built-Ins

Because some of the built-ins provided in the Standard Extensions package are designed to cause navigation, a potential problem exists: what if a developer writes a trigger in response to a navigation event, and the trigger contains a built-in generating another navigation event causing the original trigger to fire again? This sort of circular-reference mistake would cause the application to hang, and it can happen with database transactions as well as navigation events. To keep this from happening, Form Builder prohibits navigation triggers from containing built-ins that move input focus or involve database transactions. These *restricted* built-ins cannot be called from PRE- and POST- triggers, because these triggers fire while the user navigates from one item to another. Examples of restricted built-ins include CLEAR_FORM, COMMIT_FORM, DELETE_RECORD, DOWN, ENTER, GO_ITEM, and NEXT_ITEM, among others.

TIP
Trigger names have hyphens between the words, and built-in subprogram names have underscores between the words. This is a handy thing to remember while taking the certification exam, because some questions ask about triggers and offer some answers containing underscores, or ask about built-in subprograms and offer some answers containing hyphens. Keeping their respective naming conventions straight will help you eliminate answers that are in the wrong category altogether.

Exercises

1. What is a built-in subprogram? A built-in package?

2. What naming convention must be observed when calling built-ins from packages other than the Standard packages?

3. Why are some built-ins classified as restricted? What is the restriction that is enforced?

Introduction to the When-Window-Closed Trigger

The WHEN-WINDOW-CLOSED trigger fires whenever the user employs the window-manager Close command to close a window. To create one, open your SOUND_MODULE application. In the Object Navigator, open the Windows node and change the name of the application's only window to **SOUND_WINDOW**. Then, go back up to the top of the Object Navigator and select the Triggers node directly beneath the module name. Click on the Create button, select the WHEN-WINDOW-CLOSED trigger, and click on the OK button. Enter the following code in the PL/SQL Editor for the trigger:

```
message('Executing the WHEN-WINDOW-CLOSED trigger. Preparing to
close form...', ACKNOWLEDGE);
exit_form;
```

Compile the code, close the PL/SQL Editor, and run your application. When the application opens in the Forms Runtime program, click on the Windows Close button in the top-right corner of your form window. (The trigger does not fire if you use the Close button in the outer MDI window, or the Action | Exit menu command.) You should see a dialog box appear that looks similar to the one shown in Figure 15-1. Click on the dialog box's OK button to return to Form Builder.

A key fact to remember about the WHEN-WINDOW-CLOSED trigger is that it is not attached to a window. Why? Look in the Object Navigator within the Windows node for your module. See any trigger subnodes? No—windows do not have triggers. So you have to go up a level, attaching

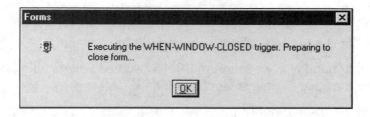

FIGURE 15-1. *Dialog box from WHEN-WINDOW-CLOSED trigger*

the WHEN-WINDOW-CLOSED trigger at the form level, where it will fire when *any* window in the module is closed. Because of this, it is common to have the WHEN-WINDOW-CLOSED trigger contain an **if** statement that selects the trigger's actions based on which window's closing fired the trigger. An example of this, from the **d2khelp.fmb** demo file provided with Developer/2000, follows:

```
if :system.event_window = 'WIN_REL_TOPICS'
then
    trt_hlp.hide_topics;
elseif :system.event_window = 'WIN_EXAMPLE'
then
    trt_hlp.hide_example;
else
    do_key('exit_form');
end if;
```

Exercises

1. When does the WHEN-WINDOW-CLOSED trigger fire?

2. At what level should a WHEN-WINDOW-CLOSED trigger be placed? Why?

Adding Functionality to Form Items

In this section, you will cover the following points about adding functionality to items on your forms:

- Supplementing the functionality of input items

- Supplementing the functionality of noninput items

The study of the triggers and built-in subprograms Form Builder offers for its input and noninput items is likely to be an ongoing process in your life as a developer. Here is an overview that will help you understand the forest as you learn about the trees.

Supplementing the Functionality of Input Items

All input items can have triggers attached to them. Because of the nature of their function—accepting data—input items commonly have triggers that fire when the user arrives on the item, leaves the item, or changes the item's data. Any input item can have a WHEN-NEW-ITEM-INSTANCE trigger that executes each time the user lands on the item, as well as a WHEN-VALIDATE-ITEM trigger containing code to determine whether the content entered by the user satisfies your integrity constraints. Input items that function by having the user change their state rather than enter a value—meaning all input items except text items—can have triggers that fire when their contents change; the format used in those triggers' names is WHEN-*itemtype*-CHANGED. Table 15-4 shows the common triggers for each type of input item.

Item Type	Common Triggers
Text Item	WHEN-VALIDATE-ITEM WHEN-NEW-ITEM-INSTANCE PRE-TEXT-ITEM POST-TEXT-ITEM
Check Box	WHEN-VALIDATE-ITEM WHEN-NEW-ITEM-INSTANCE WHEN-CHECKBOX-CHANGED
Radio Button	WHEN-VALIDATE-ITEM WHEN-NEW-ITEM-INSTANCE WHEN-RADIO-CHANGED
Poplist	WHEN-VALIDATE-ITEM WHEN-NEW-ITEM-INSTANCE WHEN-LIST-CHANGED
T-List	WHEN-VALIDATE-ITEM WHEN-NEW-ITEM-INSTANCE WHEN-LIST-CHANGED

TABLE 15-4. *Common Triggers for Input Items*

Item Type	Common Triggers
Combo Box	WHEN-VALIDATE-ITEM WHEN-NEW-ITEM-INSTANCE WHEN-LIST-CHANGED
List of Values (LOV)	WHEN-VALIDATE-ITEM WHEN-NEW-ITEM-INSTANCE WHEN-LIST-CHANGED

TABLE 15-4. *Common Triggers for Input Items* (continued)

Input item triggers can include built-ins to enhance their functionality. There are built-ins to manipulate data, such as CLEAR_ITEM, CLEAR_RECORD, ADD_LIST_ELEMENT, DELETE_LIST_ELEMENT, INSERT_RECORD, DELETE_RECORD, ENTER_QUERY, and EXECUTE_QUERY. There are also built-ins to move the input focus, such as GO_ITEM, GO_RECORD, GO_BLOCK; NEXT_ITEM, NEXT_RECORD, NEXT_BLOCK; and PREVIOUS_ITEM, PREVIOUS_RECORD, and PREVIOUS_BLOCK. In addition, there are built-ins to open specific items, such as SHOW_EDITOR and SHOW_LOV, as well as built-ins to control an item's availability, like DISABLE_ITEM and ENABLE_ITEM. These built-ins operate like a PL/SQL function, expecting specific input parameters when they are called.

Exercises

1. Describe the difference between a trigger and a built-in.

2. What trigger would you use to store code that should fire when a radio group's value is modified by the user?

3. Which built-in will cause an editor to display?

Supplementing the Functionality of Noninput Items

Like input items, noninput items can be augmented with triggers. Table 15-5 shows the common triggers for each type of noninput item.

Item Type	Common Triggers
Boilerplate text	Not applicable
Display Item	Not applicable
Image	WHEN-NEW-ITEM-INSTANCE WHEN-IMAGE-PRESSED WHEN-IMAGE-ACTIVATED
Sound	Available, but no triggers are specifically designed for sound items
Push Button	WHEN-NEW-ITEM-INSTANCE WHEN-BUTTON-PRESSED
Icon	WHEN-NEW-ITEM-INSTANCE WHEN-BUTTON-PRESSED

TABLE 15-5. *Common Triggers for Noninput Items*

Noninput item triggers can also employ built-ins to enhance their functionality. A noninput item trigger can employ any built-in used for an input item, as well as many other built-ins that control interface elements. Examples include CALL_FORM and CLOSE_FORM, ENTER_QUERY and EXECUTE_QUERY, OPEN_FORM and EXIT_FORM, and GET_TAB_PAGE_ PROPERTY and SET_TAB_PAGE_PROPERTY. You may also find usefulness in GET_BLOCK_PROPERTY, GET_CANVAS_PROPERTY, and GET_FORM_ PROPERTY; SET_BLOCK_PROPERTY, SET_CANVAS_ PROPERTY, and SET_FORM_PROPERTY; SHOW_PAGE, SHOW_VIEW, SHOW_WINDOW; HIDE_PAGE, HIDE_VIEW, and HIDE_WINDOW; and SHOW_MENU, HIDE_MENU, and EXIT_MENU.

Exercises

1. Which noninput items can you assign triggers to?

2. What built-in would you use to change a tab page's name?

Using Query Triggers

In this section, you will cover the following points about query triggers:

- Data block query process and triggers
- Writing triggers that screen query conditions
- Writing triggers to supplement query results

Believe it or not, a single query can fire over half a dozen triggers. There is a reason that Oracle Corporation expended the effort to offer this many points at which you can insert trigger code: *control*. Query triggers allow you to exert an enormous amount of control over the queries your application generates, both before they are created and after their data results have been returned. In this section you will learn how to utilize query triggers.

Data Block Query Process and Triggers

A query seems like a simple process: you identify what must be true about the records you want to see, and Oracle fetches them for you. When this is done via a Developer/2000 application, additional layers of actions are added relating to the presence of a user interface. The first group of actions falls under the category *entering the query*. When the user initiates a query in the Forms Runtime program, the program starts by checking whether the data block the user is in has its Query Allowed property set to Yes. If so, it checks to see if the block contains any items whose Query Allowed property is also Yes. If so, the Forms Runtime program allows the user to utilize Enter-Query mode to enter query conditions. The Forms Runtime program then takes the query conditions entered by the user in Enter-Query mode and adds whatever conditions were previously placed in the data block's **where** clause property (this property can be changed by a trigger at run time, as you will soon see). The Forms Runtime program also appends any ordering specifications you have placed in the data block's **order by** clause property (which can also be changed programmatically at run time).

The next stage is *executing the query*. Here, the Forms Runtime program once again checks whether the data block's Query Allowed property is set to Yes (it does this again because this point can be reached by other means). Once that succeeds, it navigates to the relevant data block, validates any records that aren't validated, and prompts the user to save any unsaved changes. Finally, it opens the query. If there are resulting records, it fetches the records, limiting their quantity to the number specified in the block's Query Array Size property if the property is set to a value other than zero.

In addition to performing the actions just described, Developer/2000 has the ability to fire a variety of triggers during the process of fulfilling a query. For instance, there are pre-query and post-query triggers that you can attach to blocks or forms. These usually are attached to a block, where they can exert such control as specifying additional **where** column conditions (via a pre-query trigger) and setting values in fetched records before showing the records to the user (via a post-query trigger). To give you a more complete picture of when query triggers fire, Table 15-6 shows the order in which query triggers and actions execute. *Whenever a trigger is on the same line as an action,* the Forms Runtime program checks for the presence of the trigger first, and if the trigger exists, it is fired and the corresponding action does not occur.

Stage	Triggers	Actions
Enter Query		Check whether query is allowed on data block
		Check whether data block contains any queryable items
		Accept user's query conditions via Enter-Query mode
Execute Query		Check whether query is allowed on data block
		Navigate to block
		Validate unvalidated records
		Prompt to **commit** unsaved changes
	Fire PRE-QUERY trigger	
		Check whether the block has a base table

TABLE 15-6. *Chronology of Query Actions and Triggers*

Stage	Triggers	Actions
		Build **select** statement
	Fire PRE-SELECT trigger	
	Fire ON-SELECT trigger	Execute **select** statement
	Fire POST-SELECT trigger	
	Fire WHEN-CLEAR-BLOCK trigger	
		Flush example query record from block
Fetch Records		Check whether buffer already contains fetched rows not yet placed in data block; if so, use those rows and skip to POST-CHANGE trigger
	Fire ON-FETCH trigger	Fetch one record, or quantity specified in Query Array Size property
		Place cursor at first record in buffer
	Fire POST-CHANGE trigger	
		Mark record and items as valid
	Fire POST-QUERY trigger once for each record	
		Loop to fetch next record

TABLE 15-6. *Chronology of Query Actions and Triggers* (continued)

Exercises

1. What are the three major steps in the process of querying a data block?

2. At what object level are PRE-QUERY and POST-QUERY triggers most often attached?

3. Does the PRE-QUERY trigger fire before or after the user enters criteria? Does the POST-QUERY trigger fire before or after records are shown to the user?

4. In what trigger would you place code to check whether the user specified criteria for an indexed item before running the query?

Writing Triggers That Screen Query Conditions

The PRE-QUERY trigger gives you the ability to check a query entered by the user before that query is executed, and modify or stop the query if you wish. For instance, you can use a PRE-QUERY trigger to ensure that the user's query includes at least one column that has an index, in order to maximize query turnaround speed and minimize server workload. You can also use a PRE-QUERY trigger to control how returned records are sorted, as well as to apply additional **where** clause criteria before the query is processed.

To practice this, you will modify your DEPARTMENT canvas so it lets users choose whether to sort departments by DEPARTMENT_ID or DEPARTMENT_NAME. Open your original sample application, click on the Data Blocks node, and click on the Create button. Select *Build a new data block manually* and click on the OK button. Change the new block's Name property to **DEPARTMENT_SORT_CONTROL** and change its Database Data Block property to No to make it a control block. In the Object Navigator, click on the block's Items node, followed by the Create button. Change the item's name to **SORT_SELECT**, its Item Type property to Radio Group, its Initial Value to **DEPARTMENT_ID**, and its Canvas property to DEPARTMENT. Back in the Object Navigator, click on the SORT_SELECT item's Triggers node, click on the Create button, select the WHEN-RADIO-CHANGED trigger, and enter the following code in the PL/SQL Editor:

```
go_block('DEPARTMENT');
execute_query;
```

Compile the trigger code and close the PL/SQL Editor. Now click on the SORT_SELECT item's Radio Buttons node, followed by two clicks on the Create button. Change the first radio button's Name and Label properties to **ID**, and its Radio Button Value property to **DEPARTMENT_ID**. Change the second radio button's Name and Label properties to **NAME**, and its Radio Button Value property to **DEPARTMENT_NAME**. Next, in the Object Navigator, right-click on the DEPARTMENT_SORT_CONTROL block's name and select *Layout Wizard* from the context menu that appears. Specify that you want to lay the control block out on the DEPARTMENT canvas, specify a form type of Form, enter a frame title of **Department Sort Order**, and then click on the Finish button. In the Layout Editor, move the control block so it is next to the DEPARTMENT block. Close the Layout Editor and return to the Object Navigator. Open the DEPARTMENT data block's node, click on the Triggers node, and click on the Create button. Select the Pre-Query trigger and enter the following code in the PL/SQL Editor:

```
set_block_property('DEPARTMENT', ORDER_BY,
  :department_sort_control.sort_select);
```

Compile the trigger code and close the PL/SQL Editor. Save your application and then run it. In the Forms Runtime program, navigate to the Department window, and then click on the NAME radio button. That should initiate a query whose results look very similar to those in Figure 15-2. When you are through, close the Forms Runtime program and return to Form Builder.

If you wanted to create a pre-query trigger to ensure that a user's query includes criteria on the indexed column DEPARTMENT_ID, you could do so with code similar to this:

```
if :DEPARTMENT.DEPARTMENT_ID is null then
   message('A Department ID is required. Please provide '||
        'a Department ID and re-run your query.');
   raise form_trigger_failure;
end if;
```

You can also specify additional **where** clause filtering by using code like the following (which assumes, for the sake of demonstration, that a check

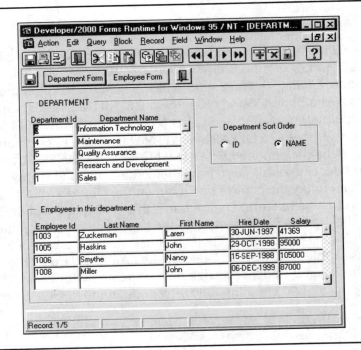

FIGURE 15-2. *Department form sorted by Pre-Query trigger*

box exists identifying whether the user wants their employee form to show only employees in the profit-sharing plan):

```
if checkbox_checked('EMPLOYEE_FILTER_CONTROL.PROFIT_SHARE_ONLY')
then
  set_block_property('EMPLOYEE', DEFAULT_WHERE,
'PROFIT_SHARING_INDICATOR = 1');
end if;
```

You can use all of these techniques together in a single Pre-Query trigger, giving you the assurance of index utilization while giving your users the ability to easily tailor the data returned without having to go through Enter-Query mode.

Exercises

1. What type of trigger gives you the ability to modify query criteria before records are selected?

2. What types of items can you add to your user interface to give the user a simple method of changing query criteria and rerunning a query?

Writing Triggers to Supplement Query Results

Because the Post-Query trigger fires after records are retrieved but before they displayed to the user, you can use it to augment a query's records in a number of ways. The Post-Query trigger can contain code to calculate running totals, generate statistics about the records retrieved, or populate control items, as well as items in other blocks.

The following example builds on the techniques you practiced in the section you just completed. The example code, designed to be run from an Employee form, uses the employee's DEPARTMENT_ID to retrieve that department's mission statement from the DEPARTMENT table and display it on the EMPLOYEE canvas. The example code assumes that the DEPARTMENT table has a column named MISSION to store mission statements, and that the Employee canvas has a display item named DEPT_MISSION_DISPLAY to show a mission statement.

```
DECLARE
   cursor MEM_DEPT_MISSION is
     select MISSION
     from    DEPARTMENT
     where   DEPARTMENT_ID=:EMPLOYEE.DEPARTMENT_ID;
BEGIN
   open MEM_DEPT_MISSION;
   fetch MEM_DEPT_MISSION into :EMPLOYEE.DEPT_MISSION_DISPLAY;
   close MEM_DEPT_MISSION;
END;
```

Exercises

1. When does the Post-Query trigger fire?

2. What are the potential benefits of using a Post-Query trigger?

Debugging Triggers

In this section, you will cover the following points about debugging triggers in your forms:

■ Running a form module in debug mode

■ Understanding the components of the Debugger

■ Debugging PL/SQL code

Nothing is more fun than debugging trigger code. Okay, that may not be true. But using decent debugging tools can make the process a lot more pleasant. This section covers the fundamentals of using the Forms Runtime program's Debugger. You will start with an overview of the debugging process used for Developer/2000 forms. Then, you will learn specifics about debugging options and initiating the debug process. Next, you will get a thorough explanation of the Debugger's screen components, followed by a walk-through on setting debug breakpoints, altering memory values while the application is paused, and seeing the impact of altered values when the application resumes.

Running a Form Module in Debug Mode

When you run your form module in debug mode, the Forms Runtime program starts, but instead of going immediately into your application, it first displays the Debugger. While in the Debugger you can create breakpoints and even write coded debug triggers that fire at specific times. After you have established breakpoints and debug triggers—or if you don't yet know where you will need them—you close the Debugger, and your application starts. From that point on, the evidence that you are in debug mode varies depending on how you configured your debug settings before running your form. You may see evidence that you are running in debug mode every time a trigger fires, or whenever the program's execution is interrupted with a **break** command in your code, or when you choose Help | Debug from the Forms Runtime menu.

You can start the Debugger from Form Builder by clicking on the Debug Mode button, shown here:

When this button is active, the Debugger will start each time you run your form from Form Builder. Behind the scenes, enabling this button causes Form Builder to include source code in the **.fmx** and **.mmx** files it generates before calling the Forms Runtime program. Since part of the Debugger's job is letting you view and modify source code at run time, it is necessary to have that source code in the executable file.

There is one other debug option you set from Form Builder: *Debug Messages.* To set this option, execute the Tools | Preferences | Runtime menu command. The resulting dialog box contains a check box labeled Debug Messages. When you run your form in debug mode with this option enabled, the Forms Runtime program displays an alert every time a trigger is about to fire. In addition, it displays in the form console the name of the trigger, along with the item that the trigger is attached to. This option can be valuable, because it lets you pinpoint precisely the spot in an application where a problem is occurring. On the other hand, simple actions can generate a lot of trigger events, and if you already have a good idea where a problem is occurring, your debugging may be slowed down substantially by enabling the Debug Messages option. For the sake of learning, enable it now and close the dialog box.

Before running your form, ensure that the Debug Mode button is enabled. Then click on the Run Form button to start the Forms Runtime program. Before your application starts, you will see the Debugger screen, which is discussed in detail in the next section.

Exercises

1. Assuming you already have a form module application, what are the steps for running it in debug mode?

2. What does Form Builder do differently to the **.fmx** and **.mmx** files it creates when it knows you will be running the application in debug mode?

Understanding the Components of the Debugger

In order to use the Debugger effectively you must be thoroughly acquainted with its components. Figure 15-3 shows the Debugger window and identifies its main components.

The Debugger toolbar provides quick access to functions commonly used while debugging. The toolbar is shown in detail in Figure 15-4. The

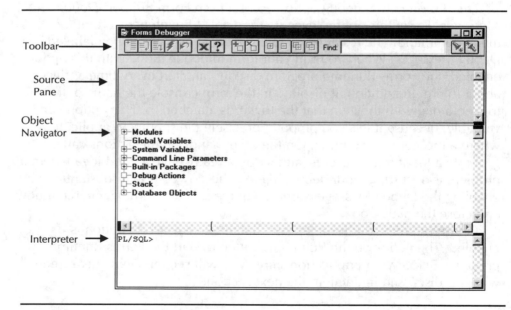

FIGURE 15-3. *Debugger components*

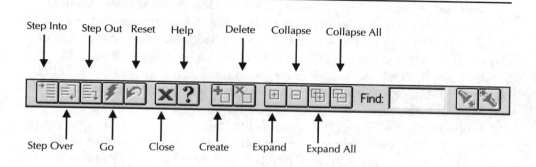

FIGURE 15-4. *Debugger toolbar*

Step Into button instructs the Debugger to step into subprogram calls. In contrast, the Step Over button disables stepping into called subprogram bodies. The Step Out button resumes execution, and stays in effect until the current subprogram has returned. The Go button also resumes program execution, remaining in effect until the thread currently executing terminates or is interrupted by a debug action. The Reset button stops program execution in the current debug level and returns program control to an outer level. The Close button closes the Debugger window so you can proceed to run your form. The Expand, Collapse, Expand All, and Collapse All buttons cause Object Navigator nodes to open and close, either individually or as a group.

Beneath the toolbar is the **Source Pane**, which displays the source code of whatever program unit you have selected in the Debugger's Object Navigator. The source code is read-only when viewed through the Source Pane; the pane is not designed for editing. The Source Pane also displays the program unit's line numbers along its left margin. In addition to line numbers, the left margin of the Source Pane sometimes shows other symbols. The pipe symbol (|) marks the current source location. The current scope location is marked with the symbol =>. If the current execution location is different than the current scope location, it will be marked with the symbol SYMBOL 224 \f "Wingdings" \s 12. Breakpoints are indicated with the letter *B* followed by a number representing the corresponding debug action ID. Debug triggers are marked with the letter *T* along with a number indicating the corresponding debug action ID.

Below the Source Pane is the Debugger's Object Navigator. This area lists all the modules that the Debugger is going to watch. You can see your module by clicking on the + to the left of the Modules node. When you do, you will see your sample application module. Open it, open its Blocks node, open the DEPARTMENT node, open the Triggers subnode, and click on the PRE-QUERY trigger. You will see the trigger's code appear in the Source Pane above.

Underneath the Object Navigator is the Interpreter. This is an interactive prompt at which you can enter commands that control the actions of the Debugger, such as creating breakpoints. Much of what you can do at the Interpreter prompt can also be done by selecting items in the Source Pane or the Debugger Object Navigator, or by executing commands from the new menu command groups that appear in your Forms Runtime menu when the Debugger is active: View, Navigator, Program, and Debug.

Exercise

Which Debugger menu buttons cause program execution to resume? What are the differences between them?

Debugging PL/SQL Code

When you run a form module in debug mode and the Debugger presents its screen, it is likely you will want to simply dismiss the Debugger and run your application until you observe the problem you are trying to solve. Dismiss the Debugger now by clicking on the Close button in its toolbar. Then navigate to your Department form. If you enabled the Debug Messages option in Form Builder, you will immediately be presented with an alert box stating simply "*Please acknowledge message.*" Down in the console, the message line will identify that a trigger is about to fire; it will name which trigger, and specify what object owns the trigger. Click on the alert box's OK button to proceed, and then populate the Department form by clicking on the NAME radio button in the Department Sort Order control block. This will cause several alert messages to display—one for each trigger that fires while the program fulfills your request. As you can see, the Debug Messages option gives you a very fine razor…and can get annoying after a while. To turn it off, exit from the Forms Runtime program, execute the Form Builder's Tools | Preferences | Runtime command, and uncheck the Debug Messages option. Then click on the OK button and rerun your form. This time, don't dismiss the Debugger right away. Within its Object Navigator, navigate to the PRE-QUERY trigger you created earlier for the DEPARTMENT table. When you find it, the trigger's code will be displayed in the Debugger's Source Pane. Double-click on the **set_block_property** line in the trigger code. You will see that its line number changes to 'B(01)'. You have just set a breakpoint, which will cause the Debugger to be invoked just before your application executes that line of trigger code. You can remove the breakpoint by double-clicking on the line again. You also could have established a breakpoint here when you created the trigger in Form Builder by including a line containing the following code:

```
break;
```

The **break** command can be especially handy as part of an **if** statement that checks for valid conditions and executes the **break** command if it finds a problem.

Ensure now that the **set_block_property** line in your trigger is marked as a breakpoint, and then click on the Close button to proceed to run your application. Navigate to the Department form and click on the NAME radio button. When the Forms Runtime program encounters the breakpoint in your PRE-QUERY trigger, it will stop and open the Debugger. At this point your screen should look similar to Figure 15-5. If you were tracking down a real problem, you would now use the Debugger's Object Navigator to investigate the values stored in your module, global variables, or system variables. For example, open the Object Navigator's Modules node and navigate down to your DEPARTMENT_SORT_CONTROL block. Open its Items node and you will see that the only item it has—SORT_SELECT—has a current value of DEPARTMENT_NAME. It has that value because the most recent action was initiated by the NAME radio button, and you assigned that radio button a value of DEPARTMENT_NAME when you created it. To see how you can use the Debugger to alter values during execution, click on the DEPARTMENT_NAME value to the right of the SORT_SELECT item, and replace the value with **DEPARTMENT_ID**. Press the ENTER key to make the new value "stick," and then click on the Go button to continue. You will see that the department data has been sorted by ID, and the radio group has its ID button marked, even though it was the NAME button that initiated the action. The results were different because you altered the value midstream using the breakpoint and the Debugger.

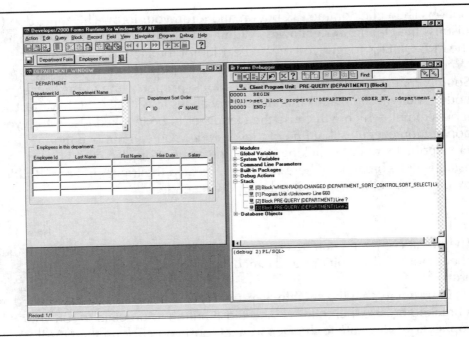

FIGURE 15-5.   *Debugger open in response to breakpoint*

Exercises

1. What is the difference between the Step Into, Step Over, and Step Out menu commands?

2. When you run a form in debug mode, how many different actions can cause the Debugger to appear?

Chapter Summary

In this chapter, you have covered a substantial amount of information on working with triggers. You started with an explanation of what triggers are and how they work. You then learned how to produce triggers, and you employed this knowledge while writing triggers that add functionality to items and queries. Next, you learned how to debug triggers using the Debugger.

The first area you covered was an introduction to form triggers. A trigger is a block of PL/SQL code that adds functionality to your application. Triggers are attached to objects in your application. When a trigger is fired, it executes the code it contains. Each trigger's name defines what event will fire it; for instance, a WHEN-BUTTON-PRESSED trigger executes its code each time the user clicks on the button to which the trigger is attached. The triggers most commonly used in Form Builder fall into several functional categories: Block Processing, Interface Event, Master/Detail, Message Handling, Navigational, Query, Transactional, and Validation. Most of the triggers you deal with will be interface event triggers, which fire as the user interacts with your application's GUI objects. Interface event triggers generally have names fitting the format of WHEN-*object-action*. Triggers that fire when a new instance of an object is created follow a naming format of WHEN-NEW-*object*-INSTANCE. Mouse event triggers use the naming format WHEN-MOUSE-*mouse action*, and triggers that respond to keystrokes use the format KEY-*keytype*. The KEY-OTHERS trigger fires whenever the user presses a key that can have a trigger but does not, and it is an excellent way to disable unwanted function keys. One trigger whose name does not represent the object it is attached to is WHEN-WINDOW-CLOSED. Because windows do not have triggers, the WHEN-WINDOW-CLOSED trigger is usually attached at the form level.

Triggers can also be grouped by their type and scope. The two types of triggers are "built-in" and "user-named." Built-in triggers are supplied with Form Builder, and they each correspond to a predefined runtime event. User-named triggers, on the other hand, are not provided with Form Builder; they are written by developers like you, and their names can be whatever the developer desires. A trigger's scope defines what event must occur in order for the trigger to fire, and is determined by the object to which the trigger is attached. Triggers have few properties, the most important of which are Execution Hierarchy, which determines how the Forms Runtime program handles triggers with identical names and overlapping scopes; and Display In Keyboard Help, which gives you the ability to add a description of a KEY- trigger to the key help in the Forms Runtime program.

After establishing the basic premises of trigger functions, categories, types, scopes, and properties, your attention turned to the techniques involved in producing triggers. Triggers consist of code blocks filled with PL/SQL instructions. Trigger code can also contain a variety of system variables, commands to read and set object properties, and built-in packages containing premade PL/SQL constructs for specific purposes. The built-ins provided with Form Builder are grouped by function into packages. When you use a built-in from a package other than the Standard packages, you must precede its name with the name of the package; for instance, WEB.SHOW_DOCUMENT. Built-ins that move input focus or involve database transactions cannot be used in navigation triggers, so as to avoid circular references that generate endless command loops. These built-ins are called restricted built-ins.

When addressing how to use triggers to add functionality to form items, you learned that all input items can have triggers attached to them. Input items commonly have triggers that fire when the user arrives on the item, leaves the item, or changes the item's data. Any input item can have a WHEN-NEW-ITEM-INSTANCE trigger that executes each time the user lands on the item, as well as a WHEN-VALIDATE-ITEM trigger to check the item's contents for integrity. Input items that function by having the user change their state rather than enter a value—meaning all input items except text items—can have triggers that fire when their contents change; the format used in those triggers' names is WHEN-*itemtype*-CHANGED. Input item triggers can make use of built-ins that manipulate data, move the input focus, open editors and LOVs, and control an item's availability. Like input items, noninput items can be augmented with triggers, generally including a WHEN-NEW-ITEM-INSTANCE trigger and a trigger that fires when the item is clicked with the mouse. Noninput item triggers can also employ built-ins to enhance their functionality. A noninput item trigger can make use of any built-in used for an input item, as well as many other built-ins that control interface elements.

You then proceeded to learn about query triggers. You started by learning the process involved in executing a data-block query, which consists of three steps: entering the query, executing the query, and fetching the records. A data query can have several triggers attached to it, the most useful of which are the PRE-QUERY trigger (which fires before the **select** statement is finalized) and the POST-QUERY trigger (which fires before selected records are presented to the user).

The final area covered in this chapter is debugging. The Debugger can be invoked by enabling the Debug Mode option in Form Builder and then running your form. When the Debug Mode button is active, the Debugger will start each time you run your form from Form Builder. Enabling this button causes Form Builder to include source code in the **.fmx** and **.mmx** files it generates before calling the Forms Runtime program. You can also choose to enable Debug Messages, which cause the Forms Runtime program to display an alert every time a trigger is about to fire, along with a message in the console identifying the trigger and object that owns it. The Form Debugger has four visual components: the toolbar, which contains buttons for often-used actions; the Source Pane, which shows the PL/SQL instructions in whatever code object you select; the Object Navigator, which displays Debugger objects in a hierarchical layout; and the Interpreter, which is an interactive prompt at which you can type Debugger commands. While in the Debugger, you can create temporary breakpoints and write coded debug triggers that fire in response to specific actions. You can also create breakpoints in Form Builder by adding the command **break** to your PL/SQL code. Whenever the Forms Runtime program encounters either type of breakpoint, it pauses execution of your application and starts the Debugger, which allows you to examine and change memory variables and program code.

All in all, this chapter comprises about 22 percent of material tested on OCP Exam 3.

Two-Minute Drill

- A trigger is a block of PL/SQL code that adds functionality to your application.

- Triggers are attached to objects in your application.

- When a trigger is fired, it executes the code it contains.

- Each trigger's name defines what event will fire it.

- The triggers most commonly used in Form Builder fall into several functional categories: Block Processing, Interface Event, Master/Detail, Message Handling, Navigational, Query, Transactional, and Validation.

- Most of the triggers you deal with will be interface event triggers, which fire as the user interacts with your application's GUI objects.

- Interface event triggers generally have names fitting the format of WHEN-*object-action*.

- Triggers that fire when a new instance of an object is created use a naming format of WHEN-NEW-*object*-INSTANCE.

- Mouse event triggers use the naming format WHEN-MOUSE-*mouse action*.

- Triggers that respond to keystrokes use the naming format KEY-*keytype*.

- The KEY-OTHERS trigger fires whenever the user presses a key that can have a trigger but does not.

- Because windows do not have triggers, the WHEN-WINDOW-CLOSED trigger is usually attached at the form level.

- The two types of triggers are *built-in* and *user-named*. Built-in triggers are supplied with Form Builder, while user-named triggers are written by developers.

- A trigger's scope defines what event must occur in order for the trigger to fire, and is determined by the object to which the trigger is attached.

- Triggers consist of code blocks filled with PL/SQL instructions.

- Trigger code can also contain a variety of system variables, commands to read and set object properties, and built-in packages containing premade PL/SQL constructs for specific purposes.

- The built-ins provided with Form Builder are grouped by function into *packages*.

- When you use a built-in from a package other than the Standard packages, you must precede its name with the name of the package; for instance, WEB.SHOW_DOCUMENT.

- Built-ins that move input focus or involve database transactions cannot be used in navigation triggers, so as to avoid circular references that generate endless command loops. These built-ins are called restricted built-ins.

■ Input items commonly have triggers that fire when the user arrives on the item, leaves the item, or changes the item's data.

■ Any input item will accept a WHEN-NEW-ITEM-INSTANCE trigger that executes each time the user moves focus to the item, as well as a WHEN-VALIDATE-ITEM trigger to identify how the item's contents should be checked for integrity.

■ All input items except text items can also have triggers that fire when their contents change; the format used in those triggers' names is WHEN-*itemtype*-CHANGED.

■ Noninput items can also be augmented with triggers, generally including a WHEN-NEW-ITEM-INSTANCE trigger and a trigger that fires when the item is clicked with the mouse.

■ A noninput item trigger can employ any built-in used for an input item, as well as many other built-ins that control interface elements.

■ The query process involves three steps: entering the query, executing the query, and fetching the records.

■ A data query can have several triggers attached to it, the most useful of which are the PRE-QUERY trigger (which fires before the **select** statement is finalized) and the POST-QUERY trigger (which fires before selected records are presented to the user).

■ The Debugger can be invoked by enabling the Debug Mode option in Form Builder and then running your form.

■ When the Debug Mode option is active, the Debugger will start each time you run your form from Form Builder.

■ Enabling this button causes Form Builder to include source code in the **.fmx** and **.mmx** files it generates before calling the Forms Runtime program.

■ If you enable Debug Messages, the Forms Runtime program will display an alert every time a trigger is about to fire, along with a message in the console identifying the item and trigger.

■ The Form Debugger has four visual components: toolbar, Source Pane, Object Navigator, Interpreter.

■ While in the Debugger, you can create temporary breakpoints and write coded debug triggers that fire in response to specific actions. You can also create breakpoints in Form Builder by adding the command **break** to your PL/SQL code.

■ Whenever the Forms Runtime program encounters a breakpoint, it pauses execution of your application and starts the Debugger, which allows you to examine and change memory variables.

Chapter Questions

1. **What trigger would you use to execute code each time a user modifies the value of a check box?**

   A. WHEN-CHECKBOX-CLICKED

   B. WHEN-CHECKBOX-CHECKED

   C. WHEN-CHECKBOX-UNCHECKED

   D. WHEN-CHECKBOX-CHANGED

   E. ON-NEW-CHECKBOX-INSTANCE

2. **You would like to create a trigger that fires each time a window is closed by the user. You will most likely place the trigger at the...**

   A. Item level

   B. Data block level

   C. Canvas level

   D. Window level

   E. Form level

3. **What trigger would fire each time a new record is created?**

   A. ON-NEW-RECORD

   B. WHEN-NEW-RECORD-INSTANCE

   C. WHEN-VALIDATE-RECORD

   D. WHEN-DATABASE-RECORD

4. **What do you need to do to within Form Builder to run a form module in debug mode?**

    A. Enable the Debug Mode button, run the form, and the Debugger will display automatically.

    B. Run the form, and in the Forms Runtime program execute the Help | Debug menu command.

    C. Enable Debug Messages and then run your form. The Debugger will appear automatically.

    D. Enable the Debug Mode button, run your form, and in the Forms Runtime program execute the Help | Debug menu command.

5. **When does the PRE-QUERY trigger fire?**

    A. Before the form enters Enter-Query mode

    B. After the form enters Enter-Query mode, but before the user enters query criteria

    C. After the user enters query criteria, but before the query executes

    D. After the query executes, but before records are shown to the user

6. **Which built-in will cause an editor to display for a text item?**

    A. SHOW-EDITOR

    B. WHEN-NEW-ITEM-INSTANCE

    C. SHOW_EDITOR

7. **You want to write a trigger that will screen a query condition. At what level will you place the trigger?**

    A. Item

    B. Record

    C. Block

    D. Form

8. **You wish to have certain values in a form initialized when the form is first opened. What trigger will you use?**

    A. WHEN-NEW-FORM

    B. WHEN-NEW-CANVAS

    C. WHEN-FORM-OPENED

    D. WHEN-NEW-FORM-INSTANCE

    E. WHEN-NEW-CANVAS-INSTANCE

9. **What part of a trigger specifies the trigger's actions?**

    A. Name

    B. Type

    C. Code

    D. Scope

10. **Which built-in will cause an LOV to display for a text item that has one defined?**

    A. WHEN-NEW-ITEM-INSTANCE

    B. WHEN-NEW-LOV

    C. GO_ITEM

    D. SHOW_LOV

11. **What trigger can you use to ensure that a query entered by the user includes at least one item that is indexed, and keep the query from occurring if not? (Choose all that apply)**

    A. PRE-QUERY

    B. ON-SELECT

    C. POST-SELECT

    D. WHEN-CLEAR-BLOCK

    E. ON-FETCH

    F. POST-CHANGE

    G. POST-QUERY

12. **What is the purpose of the KEY-OTHERS trigger?**

    A. Provides code to execute if a key's own trigger fails

    B. Provides code to execute if user presses wrong key

    C. Provides code to execute if user presses a key that has no trigger attached, but could

    D. Provides code that accesses another key's trigger and executes the code it contains

13. **Your data analysis application is slowing the network to a crawl. You analyze the queries users are performing and discover that the majority of their queries are too broad, returning many more records than necessary. You decide to require that any query have at least three fields containing criteria. What type of trigger can you use to enforce that requirement?**

    A. ON-NEW-QUERY-INSTANCE

    B. PRE-QUERY

    C. PRE-UPDATE

    D. POST-QUERY

    E. POST-UPDATE

Answers to Chapter Questions

I. D. WHEN-CHECKBOX-CHANGED

Explanation See the section titled "Supplementing the Functionality of Input Items" for a refresher on this topic.

2. E. Form level

Explanation Windows do not have triggers. Placing the WHEN-WINDOW-CLOSED trigger at the Form level allows it to fire when any window in the module is closed.

3. B. WHEN-NEW-RECORD-INSTANCE

Explanation Choice A is not a valid trigger name, and choices C and D fire at other times. Review the section titled "Supplementing the Functionality of Input Items" if you need a reminder on this topic.

4. A. Enable the Debug Mode button, run the form, and the Debugger will display automatically.

Explanation See the section titled "Running a Form Module in Debug Mode" for a refresher on this topic.

5. C. After the user enters query criteria, but before the query executes.

Explanation The PRE-QUERY trigger fires after Enter-Query mode but before a query's **select** statement has been finalized, and therefore before the query is executed.

6. C. SHOW_EDITOR

Explanation Choice A is formatted as a trigger, not a built-in, and doesn't exist. Choice B exists but is also a trigger, not a built-in.

7. D.   Form

Explanation   See the section titled "Writing Triggers that Screen Query Conditions" for a refresher on this topic.

8. D.   WHEN-NEW-FORM-INSTANCE

Explanation   None of the other choices are valid triggers.

9. C.   Code

Explanation   A trigger's actions are defined entirely by its code.

10. D.   SHOW_LOV

Explanation   The first two choices are triggers, not built-ins. GO_ITEM navigates to an item but does not open an LOV.

11. A.   PRE-QUERY

Explanation   While the other triggers listed are query triggers, only the PRE-QUERY trigger fires before the **select** statement is executed.

12. C.   Provides code to execute if user presses a key that has no trigger attached, but could.

Explanation   See the section titled "Form Trigger Categories" for a refresher on this topic.

13. B.   PRE-QUERY

Explanation   The PRE-QUERY trigger fires before a query's **select** statement has been finalized, and is therefore ideal for screening query criteria before the query is executed.

CHAPTER
16

Forms Processing

n this chapter, you will understand and demonstrate knowledge in the following areas:

- Forms Runtime messages and alerts
- Data validation
- Navigation
- Transaction processing

This chapter builds on the knowledge you gained in the preceding chapter about triggers and shows you how to apply it in several new areas. The chapter starts with an introduction to the messages produced by the Forms Runtime program. With that basis established, it goes on to show how you can create and present your own messages to the user. You will also learn about numerous triggers and techniques that can ensure the integrity of the data entered through your applications. Next, you will see how to move the focus from object to object in an application's GUI programmatically. The chapter wraps up by thoroughly covering the processes and triggers used in transaction processing, including information on how to use Oracle sequences and array DML in your applications. The OCP Exam 3 will consist of test questions in this subject area worth 23 percent of the final score.

Forms Runtime Messages and Alerts

In this section, you will cover the following points related to Forms Runtime messages and alerts:

- Introduction to the default messaging
- Handling errors using built-in subprograms
- Controlling system messages
- Creating and controlling alerts

At some point in your application's operation you will need to communicate with the user in a way they cannot ignore. The message may simply be informative; it may require them to make a decision; or it could be a warning about a problem. In this section, you will learn how to create these messages and redirect your code's execution path based on the user's response. You will also learn the basics of trapping error conditions. This is an essential part of creating robust, reliable, bulletproof applications.

Introduction to the Default Messaging

The Forms Runtime program has the ability to generate a wide variety of error messages in response to anomalous conditions. It displays these messages in either of two places: the message line within the console at the bottom of the Forms Runtime display, or in pop-up windows called *alerts*. Each message has an internally assigned severity level that defines how strongly it tries to be seen. The severity levels can be grouped into the following categories:

Message Severity Level	Message Severity Category
5	Describes a condition that is already apparent
10	Identifies a procedural mistake made by the user
15	User is trying to execute a function the form is not designed for
20	Outstanding condition or trigger problem that will keep user from continuing the action they intended
25	Condition that could cause the form to perform incorrectly
>25	Extreme severity; messages in this category cannot be suppressed by using the SYSTEM.MESSAGE_LEVEL system variable

As the last row in this table indicates, by setting a system variable named SYSTEM.MESSAGE_LEVEL in your code you can instruct the Forms Runtime program to suppress messages whose severity level is below a certain value. The technique to do this will be covered in detail later in this chapter.

Forms Runtime messages are divided into four types. The first type is the *Working* message, also known as a *Hint*. These Hints tell the user that the Forms Runtime program is processing data or instructions. They appear in the console message line. They are useful for messages that the user can ignore without interfering with processing. The second type of Forms Runtime message is the *Informative* message, which appears when the user needs to acknowledge the message but will not be required to make a choice in order to proceed. Informative messages consist of the message text, an OK button, and the Information icon. They are useful for messages such as "No records matching your criteria were found." The third type of Forms Runtime message is the *Warning* message, which appears when the user needs to make a choice before processing can continue. Warning messages consist of the message text, up to three buttons, and the Warning icon. They are useful when you want the user to answer a question or verify an action before processing proceeds. The last type of Forms Runtime message is the *Error* message, which appears when a condition has occurred that prevents the user from continuing whatever action they were taking. Error messages consist of the message text, the OK and Help buttons, and the Error icon.

Exercises

1. Which message type does not display a pop-up message window?

2. What is the function of the severity level assigned to each message?

Handling Errors Using Built-In Subprograms

Errors are bound to happen, and it is important that your application be ready to handle them gracefully. When a Forms application encounters an error, it *raises an exception*, halts execution of the PL/SQL code that was active when the error occurred, and looks in the current PL/SQL block for an EXCEPTION section to tell it what to do about the error. Developer/2000 divides errors into two types: *internal exceptions*, which include all the situations for which either Oracle Server or Oracle Forms already has preprogrammed error messages; and *user-specified exceptions*, which are defined by the developer. Form Builder provides a variety of built-ins for error handling. Table 16-1 shows the relevant built-ins along with explanations of each one.

All of the built-ins shown in Table 16-1 can be used in any PL/SQL code in your application. The ON-MESSAGE and ON-ERROR triggers can be defined at the form, block, or item level; form level is recommended, because it can be difficult for the Forms Runtime program to trap block- and item-level errors

Built-In Name	Data Returned
DBMS_ERROR_CODE	Error number of the most recent Oracle database error
DBMS_ERROR_TEXT	Message number and text of the most recent Oracle database error
ERROR_CODE	Error number of the most recent Forms Runtime error
ERROR_TEXT	Error-message text from the most recent Forms Runtime error
ERROR_TYPE	Three-character code indicating the message type of the most recent Forms Runtime error: FRM = Form Builder error, ORA = Oracle error
MESSAGE_CODE	Message number of the most recent Forms Runtime message
MESSAGE_TEXT	Message text from the most recent Forms Runtime message
MESSAGE_TYPE	Three-character code indicating the message type of the most recent Forms Runtime message: FRM = Form Builder message, ORA = Oracle message

TABLE 16-1. *Form Builder Error-Handling Built-Ins*

while it is performing internal navigation functions like committing records. The following code demonstrates a simple error-trapping routine that works when installed as an ON-ERROR trigger at the form level. This routine traps record-insertion problems and displays a message in the console's message line.

```
DECLARE
   DBERR_NUM number := dbms_error_code;
   ERR_NUM number := error_code;
   ERR_TXT varchar2(80) := error_text;
   ERR_TYP varchar2(3) := error_type;
BEGIN
   if ERR_NUM = 40508 then
     if DBERR_NUM = -1 then
```

```
        message('Primary key for new record duplicates key in
existing record.');
      else
        message('Cannot insert this record...reason undetermined.');
      end if;
    else
      message(ERR_TYP||'-'||to_char(ERR_NUM)||': '||ERR_TXT);
    end if;
end;
```

Exercises

1. At what level are error-trapping triggers best defined? Why?

2. Which built-ins are designed for handling error conditions? Which are designed to handle messages?

3. What is the difference between the DBMS_ERROR_CODE built-in and the ERROR_CODE built-in?

Controlling System Messages

There are two ways you can control system messages in Form Builder. The first approach is very similar to the technique you just learned for handling errors: You simply place the trapping code in an ON-MESSAGE trigger instead of an ON-ERROR trigger, and the trapping code contains MESSAGE_CODE, MESSAGE_TEXT, and MESSAGE_TYPE built-ins instead of ERROR_CODE, ERROR_TEXT, and ERROR_TYPE built-ins. An example of this type of code follows, utilizing the DISPLAY_ERROR built-in to show the error screen:

```
DECLARE
   MSG_NUM number := message_code;
   MSG_TXT varchar2(80) := message_text;
   MSG_TYP varchar2(3) := message_type;
BEGIN
   if MSG_NUM = 40301 then
     message('No records matching your criteria were found.');
     DISPLAY_ERROR;
   else
     message(MSG_TYP||'-'||to_char(MSG_NUM)||': '||MSG_TXT);
   end if;
end;
```

If your goal is to suppress low-priority messages entirely, you can do so using the SYSTEM.MESSAGE_LEVEL system variable. For instance, when the Forms Runtime program is at the first record of a table and the user clicks on the Previous Record button, the console's message line displays a rather terse "FRM-40100: At first record" in the console's message line. You could use the ON-MESSAGE trigger to change the message, using code similar to that shown in the previous listing. Or, you can set the SYSTEM.MESSAGE_LEVEL system variable so that the Forms Runtime program doesn't display the message at all. The severity level of the FRM-40100 message is 5, so the following instruction in a Form module's WHEN-NEW-FORM-INSTANCE trigger will keep the message from displaying:

```
:system.message_level := 5;
```

One other type of system message that is sometimes useful to suppress is the "Working…" message that appears in the console's message line while records are being retrieved. The message itself isn't the problem, but rather the fact that it usually causes the screen to update, which can generate unwanted delays. Because the message is generally useful, you may find it makes sense to suppress it only when you need to, rather than globally. Code like the following will do it:

```
:system.suppress_working := 'TRUE';
go_block('EMPLOYEE');
   execute_query;
go_block('EMPLOYEE_SKILL');
   execute_query;
go_block('EMPLOYEE');
:system.suppress_working := 'FALSE';
```

Exercises

1. What are the different types of control you can exercise over system messages?

2. What is the purpose of the SYSTEM.MESSAGE_LEVEL system variable?

Creating and Controlling Alerts

Form Builder offers a premade dialog box called an *alert* that shows the user a message of your choosing and provides one, two, or three buttons for their response. Your PL/SQL code then reads the user's response and selects subsequent actions based on it. There are three types of alerts: Note, Caution, and Stop. To experiment with alerts in your own application, take the following steps.

Open your AV_DATA_SOUND application. In the Object Navigator, click on the Alerts node, followed by the Create button. An alert object will appear in the Object Navigator (as opposed to all the other objects, which are probably snoozing). Open the alert's Property Palette, and change its Name property to **TEST_ALERT_NOTE**. Change its Title property to **Test Alert Note**, its Message property to **This is your sample message for the Test Alert Note**, its Alert Style property to **Note**, and its Button 1 Label property to **OK**. If the Button 2 Label or Button 3 Label properties have contents, delete those contents; this will cause your alert to only display one button. Your alert is now complete. To make it display, you must create a trigger or subprogram that calls for it. To do that, open the AV_DATA_SOUND canvas and create a new push button on it named **TEST_ALERT_NOTE**. Set the button's Label property to **Test Alert Note**. Right-click on the button and select SmartTriggers from the context menu that appears. Select the WHEN-BUTTON-PRESSED trigger, and enter the following code in the PL/SQL Editor:

```
DECLARE
   V_ALERT_USER_RESPONSE number;
BEGIN
   V_ALERT_USER_RESPONSE := show_alert('TEST_ALERT_NOTE');
END;
```

Compile your code and then close the PL/SQL Editor. Run your application, click on the Execute Query button to populate the form with records, and click on your Test Alert Note button. You should see a dialog box that looks like Figure 16-1. Click on the OK button to dismiss the alert and then exit the Forms Runtime program to return to Form Builder.

Informative alerts like this are useful, but there will be times when you want the alert to ask the user to make a choice. The SHOW_ALERT built-in returns specific numeric constant values depending on which of its three buttons the user selects. If the user clicks on the first button, the SHOW_ALERT built-in returns the value **alert_button1**, regardless of the label the button displays. If the user clicks on the second button, the SHOW_ALERT built-in returns the value **alert_button2**. Clicking on the third

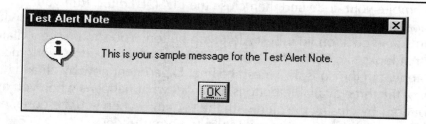

FIGURE 16-1.   *Note alert*

button, or exiting the alert without choosing a button, generates a return value of **alert_button3**. To see this in action, create another alert in the Object Navigator and name it **TEST_ALERT_STOP**. Change the alert's Title property to **Test Alert Stop**, and its Message property to **You are about to do something destructive. Continue?** Change its Alert Style property to **Stop**, and its three button labels to **Yes**, **Help**, and **No**. Then open your AV_DATA_SOUND canvas once again and add another push button. Set the button's Name property to **TEST_ALERT_STOP** and its Label property to **Test Alert Stop**. Right-click on the button and select SmartTriggers from the context menu that appears. Select the WHEN-BUTTON-PRESSED trigger, and enter the following code in the PL/SQL Editor:

```
DECLARE
  V_ALERT_USER_RESPONSE number;
BEGIN
  V_ALERT_USER_RESPONSE := show_alert('TEST_ALERT_STOP');
  if V_ALERT_USER_RESPONSE = alert_button1 then
    message('User selected button 1.');
  elsif V_ALERT_USER_RESPONSE = alert_button2 then
    message('User selected button 2.');
  else message('User selected button 3 or cancelled alert without
making a selection.');
  end if;
END;
```

Notice how this code compares the variable V_ALERT_USER_RESPONSE, which stores the user's response, with numeric constants named **alert_button1**, **alert_button2**, and **alert_button3**. This is how it determines which button the user clicked.

Compile your code and then close the PL/SQL Editor. Run your application, click on the Execute Query button to populate the form with records, and click on your Test Alert Stop button. You should see a dialog box that looks like Figure 16-2. Each time you select a button, your message will appear in the console's message line. Experiment now by clicking on each of the three available buttons. Find out what happens when you avoid the buttons by closing the alert with the ESC key. When you are done, exit the Forms Runtime program and return to Form Builder.

Exercises

1. What type of window does an alert produce?

2. When the SHOW_ALERT built-in is used, what value will it return for the first button in the alert? What value for the second button? The third button?

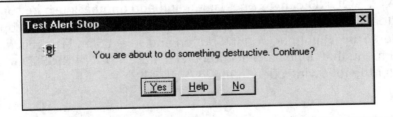

FIGURE 16-2. *Stop alert*

Data Validation

In this section, you will cover the following points about data validation:

- Effects of the validation unit on a form
- Introduction to Form Builder validation properties
- Controlling validation using triggers

As anyone who has studied popular psychology can tell you, validation is an important part of any interaction. In this section, you will learn everything you need to know to ensure that your data is properly validated. You will see how a validation unit affects a form, learn about the validation properties available in Form Builder, and practice controlling data validation by employing triggers.

Effects of the Validation Unit on a Form

The term *validation* refers to the process of ensuring that data satisfies whatever requirements you have specified. For instance, it makes sense to use validation to guarantee that a State field contains one of the 50 recognized two-character abbreviations; that a gender field contains only M or F; and that a salary figure is greater than zero. Validation can occur in the Oracle database, as well as in the client application.

On the client side, validation can occur each time the user enters an item, completes a record, leaves a data block, or leaves a form. This is known as the *validation unit:* the largest chunk of information a user can enter before the form starts the validation process. You specify this at the form module level, using a property named Validation Unit. *By default, the validation unit is at the Item level*, which causes the Forms Runtime program to perform validation when the user navigates out of an item, presses the ENTER key, or attempts to commit their changes to the database. If you change the validation unit to Record, data will not be evaluated until the user navigates out of the current record, or attempts to changes; when this occurs, all items within the current record will be validated. If the validation unit is set to Data Block or Form, the Forms Runtime program waits until the user tries to navigate out of the block or form, respectively, or until they attempt to commit changes to the database. At that time, *all* records in the block are validated.

Exercises

1. What does the phrase *validation unit* mean?
2. What are the different units, or levels, at which validation can occur?
3. What is the default Form Builder validation unit?
4. At what level do you normally specify the Validation Unit property?

Introduction to Form Builder Validation Properties

Client-side validation properties are usually defined at the item level. Text items have a number of properties that affect how they are validated. These properties are listed in Table 16-2. If the text item has an attached List of Values, setting the item's Validate From List property to Yes will cause the Forms Runtime program to check what the user has typed against the values

Property Node	Property Name	Function
Data	Data Type	Ensures that, for instance, a number field does not contain alphabetic characters
Data	Maximum Length	Defines the maximum number of characters the field will accept
Data	Fixed Length	If this property is set, requires input value to be exactly the maximum length
Data	Required	Value must be entered
Data	Lowest Allowed Value	Minimum value acceptable for the item
Data	Highest Allowed Value	Maximum value acceptable for the item
Data	Format Mask	Checks that user input matches the visual format defined by the developer
Database	Insert Allowed	Does field allow input at all?
Database	Update Allowed	Can the field's contents be changed?
Database	Update Only If NULL	When set to Yes, item can only be altered if it was NULL before
List of Values	Validate From List	Determines whether value entered by user should be validated against an attached List of Values

TABLE 16-2. *Form Builder Item-Validation Properties*

in the LOV's first column. If no LOV entry exactly matches what the user entered, the Forms Runtime program opens the LOV and autoreduces its contents so that only those rows that match what the user typed will be displayed. For instance, if the user enters just **A** in a State field with an attached LOV, when the field is validated the LOV will open and only those states that start with "A" will be shown.

Exercises

1. At what level are validation properties usually defined?

2. How does the behavior of a text item with an attached LOV change when you set the text item's Validate From List property to Yes?

Controlling Validation Using Triggers

You can augment the default validation of items or records by employing triggers. All you have to do is put PL/SQL code within the appropriate trigger to check the value you are concerned about. You can use the WHEN-VALIDATE-ITEM trigger to perform item-level validity checking. It is the last trigger to fire during item validation for new or changed items, and it can be assigned to the item, block, or form level. For record-level validity checking, the WHEN-VALIDATE-RECORD trigger comes into play. It is the last trigger to fire during record validation for new or changed records, and it can be assigned to the block or form level.

As an example, you could place the following PL/SQL code in a WHEN-VALIDATE-ITEM trigger connected to the EMPLOYEE_SKILL.SKILL_LEVEL item. Doing so would ensure that the skill values stay between 1 and 5. Combined with the fact that the SKILL_LEVEL item has a NUMBER(1,0) datatype that excludes decimal places, this trigger ensures that the user can only the values 1, 2, 3, 4, or 5.

```
if not(:EMPLOYEE_SKILL.SKILL_LEVEL BETWEEN 1 AND 5) then
   message('WHEN-VALIDATE-ITEM trigger failed on field
'||:system.trigger_field);
   raise form_trigger_failure;
end if;
```

Exercise

Which triggers can help you expand on the Forms Runtime program's default validation functions?

Navigation

In this section, you will cover the following points about navigation:

- Internal versus external navigation
- Using navigation triggers
- Introduction to built-ins that cause navigation

Controlling where the focus is in your application, and what happens at each point when movement occurs, is essential to creating a smooth, stable experience for the user. This section provides a thorough introduction to navigation in Form Builder applications. It starts by explaining the difference between internal and external navigation. You will learn how to employ navigation triggers to achieve an extremely high degree of control over movement-related actions, and you will be presented with step-by-step tables showing the order in which these triggers fire. After that, you will discover all the built-ins Form Builder provides for controlling movement and focus from within your PL/SQL code.

Internal vs. External Navigation

As a programmer, you undoubtedly already understand the difference between a movement the user makes from one object to another, and **goto**-like functions in code that occur behind the scenes. A similar dynamic exists in the realm of form navigation in Form Builder, and understanding it will help you determine where to place triggers to achieve the desired scope.

From the perspective of the Forms Runtime program, clicking on any input or noninput item that fires a trigger, or pressing a keyboard key to move from one object to another, creates an *external navigation* event. For instance, consider a user who is working with a form displaying two blocks. The user sees an object they wish to change, clicks on it, and the focus naturally moves to that object. That is external navigation. However, what the Forms Runtime program actually does to move from one object to another is substantially more involved. In the example just offered, the Forms Runtime program would respond to the user's click by going up the tree of object hierarchy: validating the item the user was on at the time, leaving the item, moving up to the next-larger object in the item's hierarchy (a record, in this case) and validating it, leaving the record, and leaving the block that contained the record. It would then go down the desired branch by entering the destination block, entering the destination record, entering the destination item, preparing the block for input, preparing the record for input, and preparing the item for input. This is *internal navigation*, and in this case it consisted of 11 discrete events, each of which could fire its own trigger.

Exercises

1. Describe the difference between internal and external navigation.

2. Which type of navigation does the user see?

3. Which type of navigation is more complicated? Why?

Using Navigation Triggers

Navigational triggers fire when internal navigation is occurring. There are triggers for each level in the object hierarchy: form, block, record, and item. Table 16-3 lists the navigation triggers, describes each one, and identifies the level(s) at which each can be used. To help you visualize the order of trigger firing and how it relates to actions perceivable by the user, Tables 16-4, 16-5, and 16-6 provide a chronology of user actions, triggers fired in response, and perceivable results when the user starts a Forms Runtime application, moves among records, and exits the Forms Runtime program.

Trigger Name	Description	Level
PRE-FORM	First trigger that fires when a form is run; fires before the form is visible. Useful for setting access to form items, initializing global variables, and assigning unique primary key from an Oracle sequence.	Form

TABLE 16-3. *Form Builder Navigation Triggers*

Trigger Name	Description	Level
PRE-BLOCK	Second trigger that fires when a form is run; fires before the form is visible. Useful for setting access to block items, and setting values of variables.	Block or form
POST-TEXT-ITEM	Fires when user leaves a text item. Useful for calculating or changing item values.	Item, block, or form
PRE-TEXT-ITEM	Fires when user navigates to a text item, before they are given the opportunity to change the item. Useful for storing the item's current value for later use.	Item, block, or form
WHEN-NEW-FORM-INSTANCE	Fires when form is entered.	Form
WHEN-NEW-BLOCK-INSTANCE	Fires when block is entered.	Block or form
WHEN-NEW-RECORD-INSTANCE	Fires when record is entered.	Block or form
WHEN-NEW-ITEM-INSTANCE	Fires when item is entered.	Item, block, or form
POST-BLOCK	Fires once when the user attempts to leave a block. Useful for validating the current record in the block.	Block or form
POST-FORM	Last trigger to fire before Forms Runtime program closes. Useful for erasing global variables and other cleanup tasks, as well as displaying an exit message to the user.	Form

TABLE 16-3. *Form Builder Navigation Triggers* (continued)

User Action	Trigger Fired	Visual Result on Form
Starting application in Forms Runtime program	PRE-FORM	
	PRE-BLOCK	
		Form appears without any data
	WHEN-NEW-FORM-INSTANCE	
	WHEN-NEW-BLOCK-INSTANCE	
	WHEN-NEW-RECORD-INSTANCE	
	WHEN-NEW-ITEM-INSTANCE	
		User is given access to form

TABLE 16-4. *Triggers That Fire When Starting Forms Runtime Application*

User Action	Trigger Fired	Visual Result on Form
TAB	WHEN-NEW-ITEM-INSTANCE	
		Focus moves to next field
NEXT RECORD	WHEN-NEW-RECORD-INSTANCE	
	WHEN-NEW-ITEM-INSTANCE	
		Next record appears

TABLE 16-5. *Triggers That Fire While Moving Among Records*

User Action	Trigger Fired	Visual Result on Form
Action	Exit	POST-BLOCK	
	POST-FORM	
		Forms Runtime program closes

TABLE 16-6. *Triggers That Fire When Exiting Forms Runtime Application*

Exercises

1. Which triggers can help you add auditing functions to your application?

2. If you set a data block's validation unit to Form, and then place a PRE-TEXT-ITEM trigger at the block level, will the trigger fire? Why or why not?

Introduction to Built-Ins That Cause Navigation

A key requirement of coding routines in a GUI environment is controlling the focus within the GUI. Form Builder provides several built-in subprograms you can use in your PL/SQL code to move the focus to different objects. These built-ins are shown in Table 16-7. These navigation built-ins are restricted, so they cannot be used in the PRE- or POST-navigational triggers. Instead, place them inside WHEN- triggers such as WHEN-BUTTON-PRESSED, WHEN-CHECKBOX-CHECKED, WHEN-NEW-FORM-INSTANCE, WHEN-NEW-BLOCK-INSTANCE, WHEN-NEW-RECORD-INSTANCE, and WHEN-NEW-ITEM-INSTANCE.

Built-In Name	Description	Sample Code
GO_ITEM	Moves focus to named item	`Go_item('EMPLOYEE.E MPLOYEE_ID');`
GO_RECORD	Moves focus to record matching number given	`Go_record( :control.last_recor d_number);`
GO_BLOCK	Moves focus to named block	`Go_block('EMPLOYEE_ 2');`
GO_FORM	Moves focus to named form	`Go_form('AV_DATA_SO UND');`
FIRST_RECORD	Moves focus to first record in current block	`First_record;`
LAST_RECORD	Moves focus to last record in current block	`Last_record;`
NEXT_RECORD	Moves focus to next record in current block, first navigable and enabled item	`Next_record;`
PREVIOUS_RECORD	Moves focus to prior record in current block, first navigable and enabled item	`Previous_record;`
UP	Moves focus to current item in previous record	`Up;`
DOWN	Moves focus to current item in next record	`Down;`

TABLE 16-7.   *Built-Ins That Cause Navigation*

Exercises

1. You place a GO_ITEM built-in in a PRE-BLOCK trigger, and an error message results. Why?

2. Which navigation built-in would move focus one record down, and keep it on the same item it was on when invoked?

Transaction Processing

In this section, you will cover the following points about transaction processing:

- Commit processing, transaction processing, and triggers
- Allocating automatic sequence numbers to records
- Implementing array DML

The information in this section will enable you to exert a high degree of control over the behind-the-scenes processing of your application's records. You will begin with a detailed account of the triggers available for your use during commit and transaction processing. Next, you will create an autonumbering sequence for one of your application's tables, and instruct the relevant data block in your application to use that sequence as its source for ID numbers. Finally, you will see how to cut transaction-processing time to a minimum using array DML.

Commit Processing, Transaction Processing, and Triggers

The phrase *commit processing* refers to posting data from a client application to the database, and then committing that data. Posting the data involves sending all of the client application's inserts, updates, and deletes to the database. Committing the data involves making the posted data permanent in the database, and therefore available to other users. A **commit** command causes both **post** and **commit** operations to take place, although you can use the **post** command to cause only the posting stage to occur; this is especially useful when you have entered new data in a master form and are going to open a detail form to augment it. Table 16-8 shows the most important commit and transaction triggers available in Form Builder applications.

The actual process of committing records and performing other transactions varies depending on the nature of the transaction. Table 16-9 shows the steps that occur when records are retrieved from a database into the client application. Tables 16-10 through 16-12 show the steps when records are added, changed, and deleted.

Trigger Name	Description	Level
ON-COMMIT	Replaces normal **commit** processing, and is therefore most useful for creating special conditions to accommodate committing to a non-Oracle database.	Form
ON-INSERT	Replaces normal **insert** processing.	Block or form
ON-UPDATE	Replaces normal **update** processing.	Block or form
POST-BLOCK	Fires once when the user attempts to leave a block. Useful for validating the current record in the block.	Block or Form
POST-CHANGE	Fires when an item contains changed data. *Included for backward compatibility with older Forms versions, and not recommended for current use.*	Item, block, or form
POST-DATABASE-COMMIT	Fires once following a database **commit**, just after the POST-FORMS-COMMIT trigger.	Form
POST-FORM	Fires once when a form is exited. Useful for clearing global variables, or for displaying a message to user when form is closed.	Form
POST-FORMS-COMMIT	Fires once between the time when changes are written to the database and the time when the Forms Runtime program issues the **commit** to finalize those changes. Useful for audit trails and other operations requiring an action each time a database **commit** is imminent.	Form
POST-INSERT	Fires once for each record inserted in a **commit** process. Useful for auditing transactions.	Block or form
POST-QUERY	Fires once for each record fetched into a block's list of records.	Block or form

TABLE 16-8. *Commit and Transactional Triggers*

Trigger Name	Description	Level
POST-RECORD	Fires once when focus moves out of a record.	Block or form
POST-SELECT	Fires once between a query's **select** phase and the actual retrieval of records. Useful for performing record counts or other actions reliant on the **select** phase.	Block or form
POST-TEXT-ITEM	Fires when user leaves a text item. Useful for calculating or changing item values.	Item, block, or form
POST-UPDATE	Fires once after each updated row is saved in a **post** or **commit** process.	Block or form
PRE-BLOCK	Fires once as user enters a block. Useful for controlling block access, or setting variable values.	Block or form
PRE-COMMIT	Useful for initiating an action before a database **commit** occurs. Fires before the Forms Runtime program processes records to change, and only fires if records have been inserted, updated, or deleted.	Form
PRE-DELETE	Fires once for each record marked for deletion. Fires before the **post** or **commit** processes occur. Useful for master/detail referential integrity checks.	Block or form
PRE-FORM	Fires once during form startup. Useful for controlling access to form, initializing global variables, and assigning a primary key from a sequence.	Form
PRE-INSERT	Fires once before each new record is inserted in a **post** or **commit** process. Useful for modifying item values or populating auditing fields such as User ID or Date.	Block or form

TABLE 16-8. *Commit and Transactional Triggers* (continued)

Trigger Name	Description	Level
PRE-QUERY	Fires once just before a query. Useful for modifying query criteria.	Block or form
PRE-RECORD	Fires when user navigates to a different record.	Block or form
PRE-SELECT	Fires during query operations, after the **select** statement is constructed but before the statement is issued. Useful for preparing a query string for use by a non-Oracle database.	Block or form
PRE-TEXT-ITEM	Fires when user navigates to a text item, before they are given the opportunity to change the item. Useful for storing the item's current value for later use.	Item, block, or form
PRE-UPDATE	Fires once before each updated record is saved in a **post** or **commit** process. Useful for modifying item values or populating auditing fields such as User ID or Date.	Block or form
WHEN-NEW-BLOCK-INSTANCE	Fires when focus changes from one block to another. Useful for executing restricted built-ins for navigation.	Block or form
WHEN-NEW-FORM-INSTANCE	Fires at form startup after focus has been moved to first navigable item. Useful for executing restricted built-ins for navigation.	Form
WHEN-NEW-RECORD-INSTANCE	Fires when focus moves to an item in a different record. Useful for executing restricted built-ins for navigation.	Block or form
WHEN-NEW-ITEM-INSTANCE	Fires when focus moves to an item. Useful for executing restricted built-ins for navigation.	Item, block, or form

TABLE 16-8. *Commit and Transactional Triggers* (continued)

User Action	Trigger Fired	Visual Result on Form
Open form in Forms Runtime module	PRE-FORM	Form not yet visible
	PRE-BLOCK	Form appears without any data
	WHEN-NEW-FORM-INSTANCE	
	WHEN-NEW-BLOCK-INSTANCE	
	WHEN-NEW-RECORD-INSTANCE	
	WHEN-NEW-ITEM-INSTANCE	Form is available to user
Click Execute Query button	PRE-QUERY	
	PRE-SELECT	
	POST-SELECT	
	POST-CHANGE	
	POST-CHANGE	
	POST-CHANGE	
	POST-QUERY	
	WHEN-NEW-RECORD-INSTANCE	
	WHEN-NEW-ITEM-INSTANCE	Data appears in form

TABLE 16-9. *Triggers That Fire When Retrieving Data*

User Action	Trigger Fired	Visual Result on Form
Insert record	WHEN-NEW-RECORD-INSTANCE	
	WHEN-NEW-ITEM-INSTANCE	Form data clears
Enter first field's data, then TAB to next field	WHEN-NEW-ITEM-INSTANCE	Focus moves to next field
...	... (loop through as many fields as necessary)	...
Save	POST-CHANGE	
	POST-CHANGE	
	WHEN-VALIDATE-RECORD	
	POST-BLOCK	
	PRE-COMMIT	
	PRE-INSERT	
	POST-INSERT	
	POST-FORMS-COMMIT	
		Console message line says "FRM-40400: Transaction complete: 1 records applied and saved."
	POST-DATABASE-COMMIT	
	PRE-BLOCK	
	WHEN-NEW-ITEM-INSTANCE	Control returns to user

TABLE 16-10. *Triggers That fire When Adding a Record*

User Action	Trigger Fired	Visual Result on Form
Change the data and click on Save button	POST-CHANGE	
	WHEN-VALIDATE-RECORD	
	POST-BLOCK	
	PRE-COMMIT	
	PRE-UPDATE	
	POST-UPDATE	
	POST-FORMS-COMMIT	
		Console message line says "FRM-40400: Transaction complete: 1 records applied and saved."
	POST-DATABASE-COMMIT	
	PRE-BLOCK	
	WHEN-NEW-ITEM-INSTANCE	Control returns to user

TABLE 16-11. *Triggers That Fire When Changing a Record*

User Action	Trigger Fired	Visual Result on Form
Remove record	WHEN-NEW-RECORD-INSTANCE	
	WHEN-NEW-ITEM-INSTANCE	Record counter decrements; control is returned to user
Save	POST-BLOCK	
	PRE-COMMIT	
	PRE-DELETE	

TABLE 16-12. *Triggers That Fire When Deleting a Record*

User Action	Trigger Fired	Visual Result on Form
	POST-DELETE	
	POST-FORMS-COMMIT	
		Console message line says "FRM-40400: Transaction complete: 1 records applied and saved."
	POST-DATABASE-COMMIT	
	PRE-BLOCK	
	WHEN-NEW-ITEM-INSTANCE	Control is returned to user

TABLE 16-12.   *Triggers That Fire When Deleting a Record* (continued)

When Oracle performs the **commit**, it processes record deletions before inserts or updates, because getting the deleted records out of the way could speed up subsequent **update** processes. Next it processes updates, again with the idea that waiting until after new records are inserted would only cause the **update** process to churn through additional records that presumably do not need updating. Finally, the new records are inserted. The whole process is depicted in Table 16-13, which shows the triggers that fire if you commit after adding one record, changing one record, and deleting one record. Looking at the chronology of events points out just how many triggers are available to you for controlling transactions.

User Action	Trigger Fired	Visual Result on Form
Change the data and click Save button	POST-CHANGE	
	WHEN-VALIDATE- RECORD	
	POST-CHANGE	

TABLE 16-13.   *Triggers That Fire During a Combined DML commit*

User Action	Trigger Fired	Visual Result on Form
	POST-CHANGE	
	WHEN-VALIDATE- RECORD	
	POST-BLOCK	
	PRE-COMMIT	
	PRE-DELETE	
	POST-DELETE	
	PRE-UPDATE	
	POST-UPDATE	
	PRE-INSERT	
	POST-INSERT	
	POST-FORMS-COMMIT	
		FRM-40400: Transaction complete: 3 records applied and saved.
	POST-DATABASE- COMMIT	
	PRE-BLOCK	
	WHEN-NEW-ITEM- INSTANCE	
		Control returned to user

TABLE 16-13. *Triggers That Fire During a Combined DML Commit* (continued)

Exercises

1. What is one common use for the WHEN-NEW-*object*-INSTANCE triggers?

2. What is the order in which **insert**, **update**, and **delete** functions are executed during a **commit** process?

Allocating Automatic Sequence Numbers to Records

A *sequence* is an Oracle construct that produces unique numbers, usually in sequential order. You can easily instruct your Form Builder applications to use sequences to get unique ID values for new records. To experiment with this, create a sequence using the following code:

```
create sequence SEQ_EMPLOYEE
  start with 1050
  nomaxvalue
  nocycle;

commit;
```

Now, open your sample application in Form Builder, open the EMPLOYEE_2 data block node, and then the Items node beneath it. Select the EMPLOYEE_ID item and set its Initial Value property to **:sequence.SEQ_ EMPLOYEE.nextval** to tell the item to retrieve ID values from the sequence you just created. Save the form and run it. When it opens in the Forms Runtime program, you will immediately see that the Employee ID field is already populated with a new number. Go ahead and fill out the new record with last name **Faltiss**, first name **Jeremy**, hire date **31-DEC-1998**, salary **102500**, department **Information Technology**, and profit sharing **True**. Save your record and exit the Forms Runtime program.

Exercises

1. When creating a sequence for an existing table, which sequence-creation parameter must take into account the table's existing contents?

2. Which property in Form Builder do you use to cause an item to utilize a sequence?

Implementing Array DML

You can control how many record inserts, updates, and deletes the Forms Runtime program can send in a single commit transaction. Increasing this number can improve overall application performance because each commit transaction has a certain amount of inherent overhead; combining multiple records into a single commit reduces that overhead as compared to issuing a commit for every individual record. The trade-off is that those uncommitted records have to be stored somewhere, and of course that somewhere is the client computer's memory. The larger the batch of records the client computer stores between each commit, the more memory it requires.

The need for this ability, known as *array data manipulation language (DML)*, varies depending on the content of each data block. Therefore, you can set the array DML quantity for each data block individually. The name of the property is DML Array Size. The Developer/2000 demo file **<oracle_home>\tools\devdem20\demo\forms\arraydml.fmx** contains a powerful example of the speed increases you can achieve by implementing array DML.

Exercises

1. What does the word *array* refer to in the phrase *array DML*?

2. At what object level do you establish array DML?

3. Which property do you use to establish array DML?

Chapter Summary

In this chapter, you have covered quite a bit of information on forms processing. The topics covered include Runtime messages and alerts, data validation, external and internal navigation, and transaction processing. All in all, this chapter comprises about 23 percent of material tested on OCP Exam 3.

The first area you covered was Runtime messages and alerts. Topics included an introduction to Form Builder's default messaging, how to handle errors with built-in subprograms, controlling system messages, and creating and controlling alerts. Messages can be presented in the console's message line or in pop-up alert windows. Every message has an internally assigned severity level that defines how strongly it tries to be seen. Forms Runtime messages are divided into four types. The first Forms Runtime message type is the *Working* message, also known as a *Hint*. These hints tell the user that the Forms Runtime program is processing data or instructions. They appear in the console message line. The second type of Forms Runtime message is the *Informative* message, which appears when the user needs to acknowledge the message but will not be required to make a choice before the message will go away. Informative messages consist of the message text, an OK button, and the Information icon. The third Forms Runtime message type is the *Warning* message, which appears when the user needs to make a choice before processing can continue. Warning messages consist of the message text, up to three buttons, and the Warning icon. The last type of Forms Runtime message is the *Error* message, which appears when a condition has occurred that prevents the user's action from continuing. Error messages consist of the message text, the OK and Help buttons, and the Error icon.

When a Forms application encounters an error, it raises an exception, halts PL/SQL code execution, and looks in the current PL/SQL block for an EXCEPTION section to tell it what to do about the error. Developer/2000 divides errors into two types: *internal exceptions*, which include all the situations for which Oracle Server or Oracle Forms already has preprogrammed error messages; and *user-specified exceptions*, which are defined by the developer. Form Builder provides a variety of built-ins for error handling, including DBMS_ERROR_CODE, DBMS_ERROR_TEXT, ERROR_CODE, ERROR_TEXT, ERROR_TYPE, MESSAGE_CODE, MESSAGE_TEXT, and MESSAGE_TYPE. All of these can be used in any PL/SQL code in your application. It is best to define the ON-MESSAGE and ON-ERROR triggers at the form level, because it can be difficult for the Forms Runtime program to trap block- and item-level errors while performing internal navigation functions like committing records. When you are trapping system messages with the ON-MESSAGE trigger, the useful built-ins are MESSAGE_CODE, MESSAGE_TEXT, and MESSAGE_TYPE, instead of ERROR_CODE, ERROR_TEXT, and ERROR_TYPE. You can use the SYSTEM.MESSAGE_LEVEL system variable to suppress low-level system messages entirely by placing a command like **system.message_level := 5;** in your form's WHEN-NEW-FORM-INSTANCE trigger. You can also control the display of the "Working…" message in the console's message line by including **system.suppress_working := 'TRUE';** and **system.suppress_working := 'FALSE';** commands at appropriate points in your code.

Next you learned about alerts. An alert is a modal dialog box containing message text, an icon indicating the severity of the alert, and from one to three buttons. Alerts are displayed via the PL/SQL command **show_alert**, which is usually placed in a trigger. The PL/SQL code can respond to the user's button selection by executing different code segments for each button.

There are three types of alerts: Note, Caution, and Stop. The only inherent difference between them is the icon they display with the text, although you will generally use them to convey the alert's importance to the user. The button the user selects is returned to the PL/SQL code in the form of numeric constants named **alert_button1**, **alert_button2**, and **alert_button3**.

The next subject you covered was data validation. Topics here included the effects of the validation unit on a form, an introduction to Form Builder's validation properties, and how to control validation using triggers. The term *validation* refers to the process of ensuring that data satisfies whatever requirements you have specified. Validation can occur in the Oracle database, as well as in the client application. On the client side, text items have several properties that assist with data validation, including Data Type, Maximum Length, Fixed Length, Required, Lowest Allowed Value, Highest Allowed Value, Format Mask, Insert Allowed, Update Allowed, Update Only If NULL, and Validate From List. If the text item has an attached List of Values, setting the item's Validate From List property to Yes causes the Forms Runtime program to check the user's entry against the LOV, and if no matching LOV value exists, the LOV is opened and autoreduced based on the user's entry. You can also utilize triggers to augment the default validation of items or records. The WHEN-VALIDATE-ITEM trigger performs item-level validity checking, while the WHEN-VALIDATE-RECORD trigger performs record-level validity checking. The form-level property Validation Unit determines the largest chunk of information a user can enter before the form fires validation triggers. The validation unit can be Item, Record, Block, or Form, with the default validation unit being the smallest one, Item.

Next, your attention turned to navigation. There are two types of navigation: external, which encompasses any change in focus on the GUI, and internal, which consists of the steps taken by the Forms Runtime program as it moves up and down object hierarchies to execute external navigation initiated by the user. Form Builder provides navigational triggers that fire at different stages of the navigation process. There are triggers for each level in the object hierarchy: form, block, record, and item. These triggers include PRE-FORM, PRE-BLOCK, PRE-TEXT-ITEM, POST-TEXT-ITEM, WHEN-NEW-FORM-INSTANCE, WHEN-NEW-BLOCK-INSTANCE, WHEN-NEW-RECORD-INSTANCE, WHEN-NEW-ITEM-INSTANCE, POST-BLOCK, and POST-FORM. Form Builder also provides a variety of built-ins to cause navigation, including GO_ITEM, GO_RECORD, GO_BLOCK, GO_FORM, FIRST_RECORD, LAST_RECORD, NEXT_RECORD, PREVIOUS_RECORD, UP, and DOWN. Because these navigation built-ins create movement, they are restricted and cannot be used in

PRE- or POST- navigational triggers, so as to avoid endless navigation loops. They can, however, be used in WHEN- triggers.

The final area you covered was transaction processing. Committing, or saving, data to the database actually includes two steps: posting the data to the database (available by itself via the **post** command) and then committing the data to make it permanent. Many triggers can fire during a **commit** transaction, including PRE-BLOCK, PRE-COMMIT, PRE-DELETE, PRE-FORM, PRE-INSERT, PRE-QUERY, PRE-RECORD, PRE-SELECT, PRE-TEXT-ITEM, and PRE-UPDATE; POST-BLOCK, POST-CHANGE, POST-DATABASE-COMMIT, POST-FORM, POST-FORMS-COMMIT, POST-INSERT, POST-QUERY, POST-RECORD, POST-SELECT, POST-TEXT-ITEM, and POST-UPDATE; and WHEN-NEW-BLOCK-INSTANCE, WHEN-NEW-FORM-INSTANCE, WHEN-NEW-RECORD-INSTANCE, and WHEN-NEW-ITEM-INSTANCE. When Oracle performs the **commit**, it processes record deletions first, then updates, and then inserts.

Implementing a sequence to provide unique numbers for a data block item is quite simple. After you create the database sequence with the **create sequence** command, you set the Initial Value property for the appropriate data block item to **:sequence.*sequence_name*.nextval**. Implementing array DML to gain the speed benefits of batch transactions is equally easy: You just set the relevant data block's DML Array Size property to the number of records that should be in each batch.

Two-Minute Drill

- The four types of messages are Working, Informative, Warning, and Error. Working messages display in the console's message line; the other three types display in modal pop-up windows.

- The three types of alerts are Note, Caution, and Stop.

- All messages have severity levels, which work together with the SYSTEM.MESSAGE_LEVEL system variable to let you suppress low-level messages from being displayed.

- Error-trapping triggers are best defined at the form level, because it can be difficult for the Forms Runtime program to trap block- and item-level errors while it is performing internal navigation functions like committing records.

■ Error messages can be trapped with the ON-ERROR trigger, and system messages can be trapped with the ON-MESSAGE trigger.

■ The built-ins designed to handle error conditions are DBMS_ERROR_CODE, DBMS_ERROR_TEXT, ERROR_CODE, ERROR_TEXT, and ERROR_TYPE. The DBMS_ built-ins handle Oracle database messages, and the ERROR_ built-ins handle Forms messages.

■ The built-ins designed to handle system messages are MESSAGE_CODE, MESSAGE_TEXT, and MESSAGE_TYPE.

■ When the SHOW_ALERT built-in is used, its buttons return the values **alert_button1**, **alert_button2**, and **alert_button3**, regardless of the labels displayed by the buttons.

■ The phrase *validation unit* defines the object size from which the user must navigate in order for validation triggers to fire. The choices are Item (the default), Record, Block, and Form.

■ Client-side validation properties are usually defined at the item level. These properties include Data Type, Maximum Length, Fixed Length, Required, Lowest Allowed Value, Highest Allowed Value, Format Mask, Insert Allowed, Update Allowed, Update Only If NULL, and Validate From List.

■ The item property Validate From List causes the Forms Runtime program to check the user's entry against the attached LOV, and if no matching LOV value exists, the LOV opens with an autoreduced list based on the user's entry.

■ The WHEN-VALIDATE-ITEM and WHEN-VALIDATE-RECORD triggers can help you expand on the Forms Runtime program's default validation functions.

■ External navigation consists of the GUI focus moving from one object to another. Internal navigation is the movement the Forms Runtime program goes through to move up the object hierarchy from the source object, and then down the object hierarchy to the destination object.

■ The Navigation built-ins UP and DOWN move to the prior or next records, respectively, placing the focus on the same item it was on when invoked.

■ You can work around the restriction prohibiting the use of navigational built-ins in navigational triggers by utilizing WHEN-NEW-*object*-INSTANCE triggers.

■ When records are committed to the database, **delete** operations are processed first, followed by **update** operations, and then **insert** operations.

■ You can make an item refer to a sequence to get default values for new records by setting the item's Initial Value property to **:sequence.*sequence_name*.nextval**.

■ You establish array DML at the data block level by setting the DML Array Size property.

Chapter Questions

1. **You have created an alert with three buttons. What value will be returned if the user selects the second button?**

   A. BUTTON2

   B. DIALOG_BUTTON2

   C. ALERT_BUTTON2

   D. It depends on the choice being offered by the button.

2. **What is the default level at which validation occurs in the Forms Runtime program?**

   A. Item

   B. Record

   C. Form

   D. Block

3. **How does the Forms Runtime program respond when a user enters text into a text item that has an LOV attached and the VALIDATE_FROM_LIST property set to Yes?**

   A. The Forms Runtime program ignores the LOV if the user types a value directly into the field.

   B. The Forms Runtime program populates the item automatically with the first value in the LOV that matches the user's entry.

   C. The Forms Runtime program will open the LOV and show only items that match what the user has typed so far.

   D. Validate From List is a Data Block property, not an Item property.

4. **How can you cause a block to use a database sequence to get unique IDs?**

   A. Set the Validate From List property to :sequence.*sequence-name*.nextval

   B. Set the DML Array Size property to :sequence.*sequence-name*.nextval

   C. Set the Initial Value property to :sequence.*sequence-name*.nextval

   D. This action is not possible.

5. **You have written a contact-tracking application that includes a field for the last date a client was contacted. You want to use a trigger to guarantee that whenever the date in that field is changed, the date entered is later than the date that was there before. What is the best trigger to use?**

   A. ON-UPDATE

   B. PRE-UPDATE

   C. PRE-COMMIT

   D. ON-COMMIT

   E. POST-UPDATE

   F. POST-COMMIT

6. Your form module's Validation Unit property is set to Form. The module includes a data block that has a PRE-TEXT-ITEM trigger. At what point will the trigger fire?

   A. Never

   B. When data is committed

   C. Before the form is validated

   D. After the form is validated

7. You want to add a delete-confirmation dialog to your application. You can do so by creating which type of object?

   A. Editor

   B. Message box

   C. Message

   D. Alert

8. You would like to keep the user from seeing the Forms Runtime program's "nn records applied and saved" messages. What would you put in the form's WHEN-NEW-FORM-INSTANCE trigger?

   A. :system.suppress_working := 'TRUE';

   B. :system.suppress_working := 'FALSE';

   C. :system.message_level := 0;

   D. :system.message_level := 5;

9. Which of the following are alert styles ? (Choose all that apply.)

   A. Working

   B. Note

   C. Informative

   D. Caution

   E. Warning

   F. Error

   G. Stop

10. **What is the last DML statement processed during a commit transaction?**

    A. INSERT

    B. UPDATE

    C. DELETE

    D. POST

11. **Which of these built-ins can you use in a PRE-UPDATE trigger? (Choose all that apply)**

    A. COMMIT_FORM

    B. DOWN

    C. GO_ITEM

    D. All of the above

    E. None of the above

12. **Which navigational built-in will move the focus to a subsequent record and place it on the same item it was on in the original record?**

    A. DOWN

    B. NEXT_ITEM

    C. NEXT_BLOCK

    D. The described action is not possible from a single built-in.

13. **You would like to modify your form so it uses array processing to send DML statements to the server in batches of 50. How would you do this?**

    A. Set the data block's DML Array Size property to 50.

    B. Set the canvas's DML Array Size property to 50.

    C. Set the window's DML Array Size property to 50.

    D. Array processing is limited to 25 records per batch.

Answers to Chapter Questions

1. C. ALERT_BUTTON2

Explanation   See the section titled "Create and Control Alerts" for a refresher on this topic.

2. A. Item

Explanation   By default, the Forms Runtime program validates an item immediately when the user tries to leave the item.

3. C. The Forms Runtime program will open the LOV and show only items that match what the user has typed so far.

Explanation   See the section titled "Introduction to Form Builder Validation Properties" for a refresher on this topic.

4. D. This action is not possible.

Explanation   Data blocks cannot read sequences, and in fact cannot store values at all. Items, on the other hand, can. Give yourself half a point if you answered C, which would have been the right answer if the question had referred to an item instead of a block, and remember to pay closer attention to the wording of questions. In some Oracle exam questions, a single word defines why one choice is right and another choice wrong.

5. C. PRE-COMMIT

Explanation   PRE-COMMIT is a form-level trigger that fires only once at the beginning of a transaction, so it cannot perform validation on a row-by-row basis. ON-UPDATE and ON-COMMIT only occur if you have replaced the default Forms Runtime transaction processing. POST-UPDATE occurs after the update has occurred, so it is too late for a validity check. POST-COMMIT does not exist. The remaining trigger, PRE-COMMIT, is perfect.

6. A. Never

Explanation   The trigger will not fire because the object level defined in the trigger name—item—is smaller than the module's validation unit.

7. D.   Alert

Explanation   See the section titled "Creating and Controlling Alerts" for a refresher on this topic.

8. D.   :system.message_level := 5;

Explanation   See the section titled "Controlling System Messages" for a refresher on this topic.

9. B, D, G.   Note, Caution, and Stop

Explanation   Working, Informative, Warning, and Error are message types.

10. A.   INSERT

Explanation   The **post** command does not perform a **commit**. Of the three remaining choices, their processing order is **delete**, **update**, and then **insert**.

11. E.   None of the above

Explanation   Each built-in listed is a navigational built-in, which cannot be used within the navigational trigger PRE-UPDATE.

12. A.   DOWN

Explanation   See the section titled "Introduction to Built-Ins that Cause Navigation" for a refresher on this topic.

13. A.   Set the data block's DML Array Size property to 50.

Explanation   See the section titled "Implementing Array DML" for a refresher on this topic.

CHAPTER
17

Forms Programming

n this chapter, you will cover the following areas of forms programming:

- Writing flexible code
- Sharing code and objects
- Managing multiple-form applications

As your applications become more complex, you need to start employing more sophisticated techniques to produce robust, powerful applications in a minimum of time. This chapter is here to help. It shows you how to leverage your effort by writing code that is flexible and reusable, employing techniques such as indirect object referencing, property classes, object groups, object libraries, and PL/SQL code libraries. The chapter wraps up by showing you how to create and manage applications incorporating multiple form modules. Overall, the contents of this chapter comprise about 12 percent of OCP Exam 3 test content.

Writing Flexible Code

In this section, you will cover the following points related to writing flexible code:

- Flexible code and system variables
- Advantages of using system variables
- Built-in subprograms that assist flexible coding
- Writing code to reference objects by internal ID
- Writing code to reference objects indirectly

The more flexible your code is, the more easily it can be reused, maintained, and expanded. This results in an overall reduction in the time you take to complete a project, which makes *you* more valuable to your employer or clients. There are an infinite number of ways to use the techniques shown in this section, so instead of showing every possible usage, one or two simple examples of each technique are provided. Once you understand how the techniques work, you can apply them in your own applications.

Flexible Code and System Variables

Flexible code is code that can be used by a variety of objects, in a variety of modules, without requiring changes to the code. While this type of code often takes longer to write initially, the investment of additional time pays major dividends later, with the benefits increasing each time the code is reused. Code flexibility comes from the way the code is written, as well as from its availability for use in applications other than the one for which it was originally written.

One technique that makes code substantially more flexible is giving it the ability to refer to objects and values with generic names that are evaluated at run time. Form Builder comes with dozens of *system variables* to provide this ability; they are listed in Table 17-1.

System Variable Name	Returns...
$$DATE$$	Current operating system date
$$DATETIME$$	Current operating system date and time
$$DBDATE$$	Current database date from an Oracle database
$$DBDATETIME$$	Current database date and time from an Oracle database
$$DBTIME$$	Current database time from an Oracle database
$$TIME$$	Current operating system time
SYSTEM.BLOCK_STATUS	NEW if all records in current block are new, CHANGED if one or more records in block have been changed, QUERY if all records are unchanged since being retrieved

TABLE 17-1. *System Variables*

System Variable Name	Returns...
SYSTEM.COORDINATION_OPERATION	Type of event that is causing coordination between related master and detail blocks
SYSTEM.CURRENT_BLOCK	NULL if current navigation unit is a form; name of current block if current navigation unit is block, record, or item
SYSTEM.CURRENT_DATETIME	Current operating system date and time in DD-MON-YYYY HH24:MI:SS format
SYSTEM.CURRENT_FORM	Name of current form
SYSTEM.CURRENT_ITEM	NULL if current navigation unit is record, block, or form; name of current item (without block name) if current navigation unit is item
SYSTEM.CURRENT_VALUE	Value of the current item
SYSTEM.CURSOR_BLOCK	NULL if current navigation unit is form; name of block where cursor is located if current navigation unit is block, record, or item
SYSTEM.CURSOR_ITEM	Name of item that has input focus, in format *block_name.item_name*
SYSTEM.CURSOR_RECORD	Number representing current record's physical order in a block's records
SYSTEM.CURSOR_VALUE	Value of item where cursor is located
SYSTEM.DATE_THRESHOLD	Changeable variable; used with $$DBDATE$$, $$DBTIME$$, and $$DBDATETIME$$, specifies how many minutes must have passed since the last database date/time retrieval to make the Forms Runtime program retrieve the information from the database again, instead of just adding the amount of elapsed local time to the last retrieved date/time value

TABLE 17-1. *System Variables* (continued)

System Variable Name	Returns...
SYSTEM.EFFECTIVE_DATE	Changeable variable; allows you to set the effective database date
SYSTEM.EVENT_WINDOW	Name of last window that fired a window event trigger
SYSTEM.FORM_STATUS	NEW if all records in current form are new, CHANGED if one or more records in block have been changed, QUERY if all records are unchanged since being retrieved
SYSTEM.LAST_QUERY	Most recent **select** statement used to populate a block
SYSTEM.LAST_RECORD	TRUE if current record is last record in block; FALSE if not
SYSTEM.MASTER_BLOCK	Name of master data block involved in a firing of an ON-CLEAR-DETAILS trigger
SYSTEM.MESSAGE_LEVEL	Changeable variable; message severity level at or beneath which messages will not be displayed
SYSTEM.MODE	NORMAL during normal processing, QUERY when query is being processed, ENTER-QUERY when form is in Enter-Query mode.
SYSTEM.MOUSE_BUTTON_PRESSED	1 if left mouse button was pressed, 2 if right button (on 2-button mouse) or middle button (on 3-button mouse) was pressed
SYSTEM.MOUSE_BUTTON_SHIFT_STATE	Shift+ if SHIFT key was held down when mouse button was clicked; Ctrl+ for CONTROL key; Alt+ for ALT key; Shift-Control+ for SHIFT-CONTROL keys
SYSTEM.MOUSE_CANVAS	NULL if mouse is not in a canvas; canvas name if it is
SYSTEM.MOUSE_FORM	Name of form mouse is in

TABLE 17-1. *System Variables* (continued)

System Variable Name	Returns...
SYSTEM.MOUSE_ITEM	NULL if mouse is not in an item; item name in *block_name.item_name* format if it is
SYSTEM.MOUSE_RECORD	0 if mouse is not in a record; number of record if it is
SYSTEM.MOUSE_RECORD_OFFSET	Used in multirecord blocks with more than one visible record, number representing offset from first visible record to record the mouse is in; 0 if mouse is not in a record
SYSTEM.MOUSE_X_POS	Horizontal position of mouse in relation to top-left corner of canvas, or top-left corner of item's bounding box if mouse is in an item
SYSTEM.MOUSE_Y_POS	Vertical position of mouse in relation to top-left corner of canvas, or top-left corner of item's bounding box if mouse is in an item
SYSTEM.RECORD_STATUS	NEW if current record is new, CHANGED if it has been changed since last validated, QUERY if its status is valid and it was retrieved from a database, or INSERT if it contains invalidated data and has not been saved to the database
SYSTEM.SUPPRESS_WORKING	Changeable variable; TRUE is "Working..." messages are suppressed, FALSE if not
SYSTEM.TAB_NEW_PAGE	Name of destination of tab-page navigation
SYSTEM.TAB_PREVIOUS_PAGE	Name of source of tab-page navigation
SYSTEM.TRIGGER_BLOCK	Name of block that was current when trigger fired

TABLE 17-1. *System Variables* (continued)

System Variable Name	Returns...
SYSTEM.TRIGGER_ITEM	Name of item that was current when trigger fired
SYSTEM.TRIGGER_RECORD	Number of record that was current when trigger fired

TABLE 17-1.   *System Variables* (continued)

Exercises

1. What is the difference between the $$DATE$$ and $$DBDATE$$ system variables?

2. What system variable will tell you the name of the current item? The number of the current record? The name of the current block?

Built-In Subprograms that Assist Flexible Coding

Form Builder provides quite a few built-ins that are useful when you want to make your code more flexible. The bulk of these either read or set specific properties for a wide variety of objects. These property-manipulation built-ins have names that make very clear what they do. The built-ins that read object properties include the following:

- GET_APPLICATION_PROPERTY
- GET_BLOCK_PROPERTY
- GET_CANVAS_PROPERTY
- GET_FORM_PROPERTY
- GET_ITEM_PROPERTY
- GET_LIST_ELEMENT_LABEL
- GET_LIST_ELEMENT_VALUE

- GET_LOV_PROPERTY
- GET_MENU_ITEM_PROPERTY
- GET_RADIO_BUTTON_PROPERTY
- GET_RECORD_PROPERTY
- GET_RELATION_PROPERTY
- GET_TAB_PAGE_PROPERTY
- GET_VIEW_PROPERTY
- GET_WINDOW_PROPERTY

The built-ins that set object properties are almost, but not quite, an exact mirror of the GET_ list; they include the following:

- SET_ALERT_BUTTON_PROPERTY
- SET_ALERT_PROPERTY
- SET_APPLICATION_PROPERTY
- SET_BLOCK_PROPERTY
- SET_CANVAS_PROPERTY
- SET_FORM_PROPERTY
- SET_ITEM_PROPERTY
- SET_LOV_COLUMN_PROPERTY
- SET_LOV_PROPERTY
- SET_MENU_ITEM_PROPERTY
- SET_RADIO_BUTTON_PROPERTY
- SET_RECORD_PROPERTY
- SET_RELATION_PROPERTY
- SET_TAB_PAGE_PROPERTY
- SET_VIEW_PROPERTY
- SET_WINDOW_PROPERTY

These built-ins require as parameters the name of the item you are interested in, the name of the property to read or set—use the property name from the Property Palette, with underscores to replace spaces between words—and the value to place into the property, if it is a SET_ built-in. For example, the following code would make your sample application's SALARY item unavailable for editing:

```
set_item_property('EMPLOYEE_2.SALARY', enabled, PROPERTY_FALSE);
```

Some of the more useful properties you can control when working with text items include ITEM_NAME, ITEM_TYPE, DATATYPE, ENABLED, LABEL, PROMPT TEXT, and VISIBLE. There are also properties you can GET_ and SET_ that do not show up in the Property Palette. For the GET_ITEM_PROPERTY built-in, for example, additional properties include BLOCK_NAME and ITEM_IS_VALID.

In addition to the GET_ and SET_ built-ins, Form Builder offers a handful of other built-ins that are useful when you are writing flexible code. Table 17-2 lists these and describes what they do. Of the built-ins in the list, the most unusual is SHOW_LOV, because it has the combined task of displaying an object (an LOV), and also returning a Boolean value to the calling program indicating whether or not the user selected a value from the LOV.

Exercises

1. What built-in will let you determine whether a specific field can be seen by the user?

2. What built-in has the ability to create a global variable?

3. What pair of built-ins could you use to control the labels on radio buttons programmatically? To set the labels for tab pages? To change canvas background colors?

Writing Code to Reference Objects by Internal ID

Each built-in example you have seen so far has used an object's name as a parameter. It is also possible to use an internal ID to reference objects in many built-ins. The internal object ID is created by Form Builder when the

Built-In Name	Description
ADD_GROUP_COLUMN	Adds a column to a record group
ADD_GROUP_ROW	Adds a row to a record group
ADD_LIST_ELEMENT	Adds an element to a list
ADD_PARAMETER	Adds a parameter to a parameter list
COPY	Copies a value from a literal, text item, or global variable into a text item or global variable; used to write values into items referenced via the NAME_IN built-in
DEFAULT_VALUE	Copies a value to a variable if the variable is currently NULL; creates the variable if it is an undefined global variable
DISPLAY_ITEM	Assigns a display attribute to an item
NAME_IN	Returns a value from a named variable or object
SHOW_LOV	Displays a list of values at specified coordinates, returns TRUE if user selects value from list and FALSE if user dismisses list with the Cancel button

TABLE 17-2. *Additional Built-Ins for Flexible Coding*

object is created, and it is not visible to the user. Referring to objects by their ID rather than by name benefits you in two ways. First, it speeds up program execution if an object is referred to more than once. Form Builder's native way of addressing objects is their object ID, and if you refer to an object by name, Form Builder has to go find that object's ID before processing can continue. Subsequent references to the object name will cause Form Builder to look up the object ID each time. Each of these lookups after the first one can be avoided by declaring a variable in your code to store the object's ID the first time it is looked up. After that, the ID is immediately available each time the object needs to be referenced: you just use the variable name in the referencing code statement. The second benefit is that it improves your code's flexibility and maintainability by storing the object name just once in a section of code, at the very beginning. If you wish to modify the object name in the code for maintenance reasons or so the routine can be used elsewhere, you need only change the object name once, because that is the only time the object is referred to by name.

You can obtain an object's ID by using the FIND_ built-in functions. Each object class has a matching FIND_ built-in; for instance, FIND_WINDOW, FIND_BLOCK, and FIND_LOV. Each of these built-ins returns its own unique VARCHAR2 value type; Table 17-3 shows each object type's FIND_ function and return data type. For example, the following code would return the object ID of the AV_DATA_SOUND form and then move focus to that form:

```
DECLARE
   v_form_id   formmodule;
BEGIN
   v_form_id := find_form('AV_DATA_SOUND');
   go_form(v_form_id);
END;
```

Once you have included code such as that just shown in a PL/SQL code block, you can refer to the object using the variable name (in the prior example, "v_form_id") instead of the object name. You can also use the FIND_ function directly as a parameter in another built-in, with a statement like **go_form(find_form('AV_DATA_SOUND'));**. However, because the form's ID does not get stored in a reusable variable, this approach provides no benefit over simply saying **go_form('AV_DATA_SOUND');**.

Exercises

1. What are the benefits of referencing objects by ID instead of by name?

2. How do you determine an object's ID?

Writing Code to Reference Objects Indirectly

There are probably going to be times when you need to write code that refers to variables and objects in a way that is even more abstract than using object IDs. One reason to do this is to make your code even more flexible; a routine that receives a value, processes it, and places it somewhere else can

Object Type	FIND_ Function	Return Data Type
Alert	FIND_ALERT	ALERT
Block	FIND_BLOCK	BLOCK
Canvas	FIND_CANVAS	CANVAS
Editor	FIND_EDITOR	EDITOR
Form	FIND_FORM	FORMMODULE
Item	FIND_ITEM	ITEM
List of Values	FIND_LOV	LOV
Menu Item	FIND_MENU_ITEM	MENUITEM
Parameter List	GET_PARAMETER_LIST	PARAMLIST
Record Group	FIND_GROUP	RECORDGROUP
Record Group Column	FIND_COLUMN	GROUPCOLUMN
Relation	FIND_RELATION	RELATION
Timer	FIND_TIMER	TIMER
View	FIND_VIEW	VIEWPORT

TABLE 17-3. *FIND_ Built-In Return Data Types*

achieve its maximum flexibility when it does not have the names of *any* source or destination objects hard-coded. Another reason is that you will soon be building applications that contain menu modules, library modules, and/or multiple form modules, and because each of these modules is compiled independently of the others, they cannot directly reference items or variables stored in a module other than their own. The solution in both of these situations is referencing objects indirectly.

The types of objects that cannot be referenced directly across modules are form items, system and global variables, and parameters. These are called *form bind variables*. There are two built-ins you can use to reference form bind variables: one to read values, and the other to write them. The built-in to read values is NAME_IN, and if you interpret its name somewhat loosely, it gets "the name that is in" a named object. The built-in to write values is COPY. The structure of each built-in follows:

```
name_in('block_name.item_name')
name_in('GLOBAL.variable_name')
name_in('SYSTEM.variable_name')
name_in('PARAMETER.parameter_name')
copy('value', 'block_name.item_name');
copy('value', 'GLOBAL.variable_name');
copy('value', 'SYSTEM.variable_name');
copy('value', 'PARAMETER.parameter_name');
```

You can nest NAME_IN inside the COPY built-in to give COPY the ability to place values into indirectly referenced locations. An example of this follows:

```
DECLARE
  GV_USER_TYPE varchar2(10);
BEGIN
  if :radio.choice = 1 then
    GV_USER_TYPE := 'STANDARD';
  else
    GV_USER_TYPE := 'ADMIN';
  end if;

  copy(name_in('logon_screen.userid'), 'GLOBAL.' || GV_USER_TYPE || '_ID' );
END;
```

The return value from a NAME_IN built-in is always a character string, even when it is retrieving data from a item with a data type of NUMBER or DATE. Use the TO_NUMBER and TO_DATE conversion functions to convert the character string to the appropriate type, as shown in the following code:

```
numeric_variable := to_number(name_in('block.numeric_item'));
date_variable := to_date(name_in('block.date_item'));
```

Exercises

1. What are the benefits of writing code that references objects indirectly?

2. What built-in allows you to derive the contents of a variable referenced indirectly?

3. What built-in allows you to place a value into a variable referenced indirectly?

Sharing Objects and Code

In this section, you will cover the following points about sharing code and objects:

- Inheriting properties from property classes
- Grouping related objects for reuse
- Reusing objects from an object library
- Reusing PL/SQL code

The allure of being able to reuse objects and code is powerful. It saves time and money. It reduces errors by eliminating re-creation of existing procedures and functions. It helps ensure uniform appearance and functionality with little effort. Form Builder offers sophisticated features to help you reuse objects and code: property classes, object groups, object libraries, and PL/SQL libraries.

Inheriting Properties from Property Classes

Every form module contains a node called Property Classes. A *property class* is an object that holds a collection of properties and property values that can be *inherited* by other objects. This allows you to create objects that automatically incorporate the properties you have taken the trouble to define previously, thereby cutting development time. It also assists in creating applications with a uniform look and behavior. An added benefit is that if you need to change a property later, you can change it in the property class and the change will automatically be propagated throughout your application, once again improving your productivity. A property class can hold any number of properties, including properties that apply to different object types. Once you have created a property class, you can use it as the basis for other objects, which will inherit the properties appropriate for their object types. In the objects based on the property class, you decide which properties are inherited by the object and which are overridden. A property class can also be subclassed into other modules.

Consider, for example, text items that display dollar values; the Salary field in your EMPLOYEE canvas is one example. By default the salary figures appear flush left in the field, without any commas or dollar signs, whereas numeric values are traditionally aligned to the right. You might also wish to have salary values of zero display with a red background to attract the user's attention. These design features would also be useful in *any* item showing dollar values. You can create a property class containing the properties that produce these features, and then have each dollar-oriented item refer to that property class, thereby producing the appearance and behavior you want in each item without having to set the properties manually every time.

To make this example more concrete, open your sample application in Form Builder. Open the EMPLOYEE canvas in the Layout Editor, and open the Property Palette for the HIRE_DATE item. Select the following properties (remember that you can hold down the CTRL key to select multiple properties):

- Item Type
- Justification
- Data Type
- Maximum Length
- Fixed Length
- Format Mask
- Width
- Height
- Hint

In the Property Palette toolbar, click on the Property Class button, shown here:

A dialog box will appear informing you that a property class was created; click on the OK button to dismiss it. Close the Layout Editor and open the Property Classes node in the Object Navigator. Click on the + to the left of your new property class to show its contents. Change the new property class's name to **DATE_PROPERTIES**. Change its Justification property to Right, and its Format Mask property to MM-DD-YYYY.

If you want to add additional properties to the property class, you can do so by clicking on the Add Property button in the Property Palette toolbar, shown here:

You can also delete unneeded properties by clicking on the Delete Property button in the Property Palette toolbar, shown next:

You now have a usable property class. To cause form items to inherit its properties, open your EMPLOYEE canvas once again in the Layout Editor and select the HIRE_DATE item. Open its Property Palette and select the Subclass Information property. Click on the More... button that appears in the property's value location, and you will see a dialog box similar to the one shown in Figure 17-1.

Click on the Property Class radio button, open the Property Class Name list, and select your DATE_PROPERTIES property class from the list. Then click on the OK button. When you do, you will see that some new symbols appear in the Property Palette to the left of the property names. The standard symbol is a small dot signifying that the property's value is unchanged from the default, as follows:

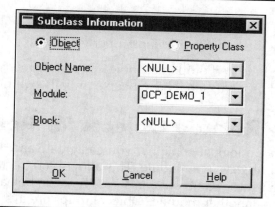

FIGURE 17-1.   *Subclass information dialog box*

Properties whose values have been changed manually are marked with a slightly larger square, which looks like this:

Properties displaying inherited values are marked with an arrow pointing to the right, as shown here:

Items whose values were inherited from a property class and then manually overridden are marked with an inheritance arrow whose point is replaced with a red "X", like the following:

Exercises

1. What are the benefits of using property classes?

2. How are inherited properties indicated in a Property Palette? Inherited properties that have been manually overridden?

Grouping Related Objects for Reuse

An *object group* is a logical container you can create and then place into it pointers to other objects in a module. This allows you to group related objects—even objects of different types—so they can be easily copied to, or subclassed within, another module. Object groups are available within form and menu modules. They are very easy to create: you simply click on the Object Groups node in the Object Navigator and then click on the Create button. To add pointers to the object group, just select the items you want to group together and drag them onto the object group's name. To remove an item from an object group, select the item within the object group (*not* the original item!) and click on the Delete button or press the DELETE key.

Exercise

What is the purpose of object groups?

Reusing Objects from an Object Library

While grouping objects into an object group is convenient, there are limitations inherent in this approach; for instance, subclassing the object group into another form module does not always work. A more powerful approach is to copy the original items into an *object library*, and subclass the object library items into each form module that needs them. Besides being a more robust approach to reusing objects, an object library lets you divide the objects visually onto tab pages of your own design so you can locate and select the ones you want more quickly.

To see this in action, you will create an object library to hold the objects necessary to save and load images to and from your AV_DATA table. Start by clicking on the Object Libraries node in Form Builder and then clicking on the Create button. Change the object library's name to **IMAGE_LIBRARY**. Beneath its entry in the Object Navigator you will see a subnode named

Library Tabs; double-click on the subnode to create your first tab, and then click on the Create button to create a second tab. Change the first tab's Name property to **BLOCKS** and its Label property to **Blocks**. Change the second tab's Name property to **CANVASES** and its Label property to **Canvases**. Now, double-click on the object library's icon in the Object Navigator to open it. You will see a window similar to Figure 17-2. To place items into your new object library, open the IMAGE_MODULE form in Form Builder. Drag its AV_DATA_IMAGE data block into the object library. Click on the object library's Canvases tab, and then drag the IMAGE_MODULE's AV_DATA_IMAGE canvas into the object library. Click on the object library's Save button to save the object library to disk under the name **image_library.olb**. Then, close the IMAGE_MODULE form module so that it is no longer present in the Object Navigator.

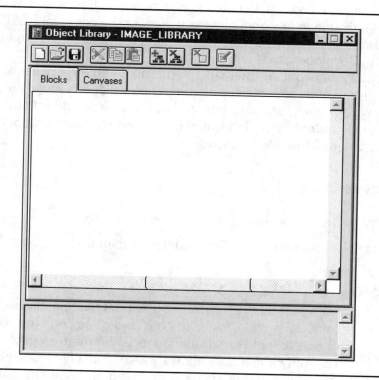

FIGURE 17-2.   *Object Library window*

Next, create a new form module in the Object Navigator. Then, return to the object library, click on the Blocks tab, and drag the AV_DATA_IMAGE data block from the object library onto the new form module's name. Form Builder will display a dialog box asking if you want to subclass the object library object or copy it. Select the Subclass option. Then, click on the object library's Canvases tab and drag the AV_DATA_IMAGE canvas from the object library onto the new form module. When asked, select the Subclass option for this object as well. Then click on the Object Navigator's Run button to run your new form. You will see that it runs exactly as the original IMAGE_MODULE form did. Bringing the functionality of the IMAGE_MODULE form into your new form module took only seconds—a good demonstration of the productivity benefits you can enjoy from using object libraries.

Object libraries are a powerful way to enforce standards across an organization's applications. One common approach is to have two object libraries used in a project: an enterprise-wide object library containing objects applicable to any application created for the company, and a second object library containing objects for a particular application or group, if necessary. Developer/2000 comes with an object library named STANDARDS that contains premade alerts, input and display items, canvas layouts, visual attribute groups, and components that can speed creation of a menu, wizard, pick list, navigator, and calendar. You will find this object library in the **stndrd20.olb** file located in the **<oracle_home>\tools\ devdem20\demo\forms** directory.

Exercises

1. What are the benefits of using an object library?

2. How is using an object library different than using an object group?

Reusing PL/SQL code

With all this talk about reusing objects, it is natural that the discussion turn to the subject of reusing code. You can copy and paste code just like any other object, of course, but Form Builder offers a far more elegant solution: *PL/SQL libraries*. A PL/SQL library allows you to store client-side program units and make them available to any form, menu, or library module. A

PL/SQL library stores subprograms, including functions, procedures, and packages. Once attached to a module, a PL/SQL library's program units can be called from your own routines, triggers, and menu item commands. You can attach multiple PL/SQL libraries to a single module, and many modules can attach to the same PL/SQL library. A library can even be attached to another library. A PL/SQL library is intelligent enough to only load its program units as an application needs them, thereby minimizing the demand for client-computer memory. This is called *dynamic loading*. PL/SQL libraries can also be handy for applications that need to be distributed in multiple languages: you can store different language versions of the display text in separate language-specific PL/SQL libraries, and then attach the appropriate library before the application is distributed to a specific region. PL/SQL libraries are created and modified under Form Builder's PL/SQL Libraries node. To use a PL/SQL library in a module, you attach it under the Attached Libraries node within the appropriate module; the attached library is read-only. Developer/2000 comes with several PL/SQL libraries to simplify common tasks; look in the directories **<oracle_home>\oca20\plsqllib**, **<oracle_home>\tools\devdem20demo\forms**, and **<oracle_home>\tools\open2k20\plsqllib**.

Exercises

1. What features do PL/SQL libraries offer to reduce the amount of memory needed on the client computer?

2. How do you work with server code in a PL/SQL library? (This is a trick question.)

Managing Multiple-Form Applications

In this section, you will cover the following points about multiple-form applications:

■ Defining multiple-form functionality

■ Calling one form from another

You have already seen how a single form module can contain different canvases. You can also integrate multiple form modules into a larger, coordinated application. Put on your seat belt!

Defining Multiple-Form Functionality

The Forms Runtime program can have more than one form module open simultaneously during a session. The application starts in the same familiar way—with a single form—but incorporates PL/SQL built-ins to invoke other forms. The additional forms can call other forms of their own, and so on. This can assist development of complicated applications by dividing functional groups into different forms. It also helps maximize the usability of client-computer memory because forms only consume memory when they are called, and their memory is released when they are closed. As an added bonus, using separate form modules lets you exercise a higher degree of control over what records are committed when the user performs a save procedure.

Form Builder gives you plenty of options related to running multiple forms. A newly opened form can run simultaneously with the one that called it, or the new form can replace the old one, causing the calling form to close. Multiple instances of the same form can be run. A form can be opened but kept in the background. And multiple forms can either share the same database connection or they can have multiple independent database connections, as if they were running on separate client computers. The next section provides all the dirty details.

Exercises

1. What are the benefits of creating multiple-form applications?

2. What kinds of multiple-form options are available to you as a developer? When might you use each?

Calling One Form from Another

Create a new form module in Form Builder, and name it **START_SCREEN**. Create a new data block within the module; change its name to **BUTTON_BLOCK**, and change its Database Data Block property to No. Create a new canvas manually by double-clicking on the Canvases node;

name the new canvas **BUTTON_CANVAS**. Open the canvas in the Layout Editor and add four push buttons to it. Set the properties of the buttons as follows:

Button Name	Button Label
RUN_SAMPLE_APP	Run Sample Application
RUN_SOUND_APP	Run Sound Application
RUN_IMAGE_APP	Run Image Application
EXIT_FORM	Exit

Your canvas should look similar to the one shown in Figure 17-3. Now create a WHEN-BUTTON-PRESSED trigger for the RUN_SAMPLE_APP button, and place inside it code similar to this:

```
open_form('sample_application_name');
```

Replace the *sample_application_name* with the name of your sample application as it appears on disk—not as it appears in the Object Navigator. You do not need to include a file extension of **.fmb** or **.fmx**. If you have been storing the sample application somewhere other than Form Builder's default path, you will need to specify that path in the OPEN_FORM built-in command (this is an excellent place to use a global variable in an application you are going to distribute). If your file specification includes spaces, you may need to use the old 8.3 filename format from DOS, which limits file and directory names to eight characters (excluding the three-character file extension) and no spaces. To convert a long file or directory name to this format, remove all spaces from the name, use the first six characters of what remains, and then add a tilde character (~) followed by a number indicating which number file or directory this is if more than one entry in this location could be matched by the first six characters you specified. It may take some experimenting with DIR and CD commands at a DOS prompt to find the right 8.3 format name. As an example, the modern filename of

```
P:\Data\OCP Dev2K\OCP Demo Form 1
```

converts into the following 8.3 format name:

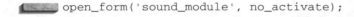

    P:\Data\OCPDev~1\OCPDem~1

Compile the button and close the PL/SQL Editor. Add similar triggers to the
sound and image buttons to open their respective form modules. For the Exit
button, create a trigger containing the command **exit_form;** to close the
START_SCREEN module. Then, save your form and run it. In the Forms Runtime
program, click on the first three buttons in your START_SCREEN application to
load and open the other form modules. Execute a query with each module, and
position them on your screen so their layout suits your taste. Your screen will
end up looking similar to Figure 17-4. When you are done experimenting with
your multiple forms, close them all and return to Form Builder.

If you wish to invoke a form module without immediately passing
control to it, you can do so by including the NO_ACTIVATE option in the
OPEN_FORM built-in command, like this:

```
open_form('sound_module', no_activate);
```

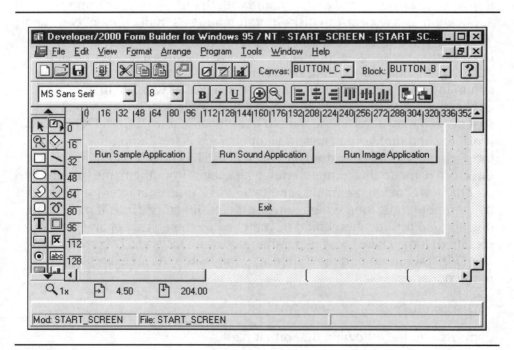

FIGURE 17-3. *Canvas with buttons to open other forms*

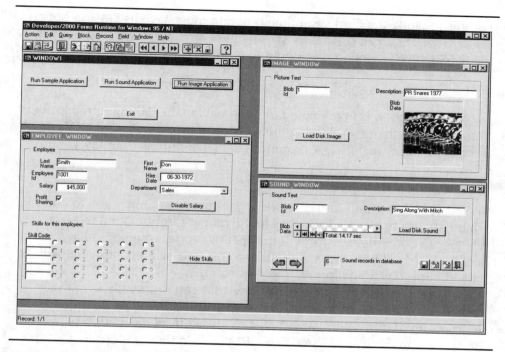

FIGURE 17-4. *Multiple forms running simultaneously*

You can also elect to have a new form opened with its own database connection, separate from whatever database connection is already running on that client computer. The benefit of doing this is that each form will have independent **commit** processing. When multiple forms are opened without this option—and therefore are using the same database connection—a **commit** in any form causes data in all forms to be saved. If the forms do not have a functional relationship—for instance, if one is a sales application and the other is a scheduler—you do not want records in one form to be saved just because records in another are. That is a situation where opening the forms with their database connections makes sense. To do this, include the SESSION option in the second form's OPEN_FORM built-in command, as shown:

```
open_form('sound_module', session);
```

For this to work, the Forms Runtime program must have its Session option set to TRUE. You can do that by starting the Forms Runtime program with the SESSION=YES option on its command line, like this:

```
f50run32 module=module_name userid=user/ID session=YES
```

Another option is invoking a form and having the calling form close automatically, thereby releasing the memory it consumed. The NEW_FORM built-in performs this task. An example of this built-in is as follows:

```
new_form('module_name');
```

The NEW_FORM built-in has optional parameters enabling you to control what happens to unsaved changes in the parent form before it closes, whether to open the new form in query-only mode, whether to have the new form share library data with other forms, and what parameters will be passed from the calling form to the new form.

To navigate between open forms, the user can simply click on the desired form, or use the Forms Runtime program's **Window** command to select a form if it is not in view. You can also control navigation between forms programmatically. The GO_FORM built-in moves focus to a form identified either by name or by internal ID, using the syntax **go_form('module_name');**. If you know the order in which forms were loaded, you can also employ the built-ins NEXT_FORM; and PREVIOUS_FORM; to move to the next or prior forms in the form stack.

Table 17-4 offers a reference table of form-related built-ins.

Exercises

1. Which built-in would you use to cause a form to run another form? Which would you use if you did not want to move focus to the new form immediately? Which would you use to run a form with its own database connection?

2. Why would you want to open a second form with its own database connection?

3. How can you cause your application to navigate between open forms?

Built-In Name	Purpose
CALL_FORM	Runs a form; with options to select whether the calling form maintains the focus, whether the two forms share library data, and whether the called form is to be run only in query mode
CLEAR_FORM	Flushes records from current form
CLOSE_FORM	Closes indicated form
COMMIT_FORM	Saves current form's records to database
EXIT_FORM	Closes current form
FIND_FORM	Returns internal ID of form module with a given name
GO_FORM	Moves focus to the indicated form
NEW_FORM	Enters the indicated form, exiting and closing the current form
NEXT_FORM	Moves focus to next form
OPEN_FORM	Opens indicated form, with options to select whether the called form gets focus, shares library data with other forms, and gets its own database connection if required
PREVIOUS_FORM	Moves focus to prior form

TABLE 17-4.   *Form Builder Built-Ins for Multiple-Form Applications*

Chapter Summary

This chapter covered a lot of ground in the area of form programming. You read explanations and did exercises focusing on writing flexible code, sharing objects and code, and creating multiple-form applications. The subjects covered in this chapter represent about 12 percent of the material tested on OCP Exam 3.

You started by learning about writing flexible code, which is code that can be used by a variety of objects, in a variety of modules, without modifying the code. Code flexibility comes both from the way code is written and from its availability for use by applications other than the one for which it was originally written. One technique that makes code substantially more flexible is giving it the ability to refer to objects and values with generic names that are evaluated at run time. Form Builder comes with many system variables to provide this ability, such as SYSTEM.CURRENT_FORM, SYSTEM.CURRENT_BLOCK, SYSTEM.CURSOR_RECORD, and SYSTEM.CURRENT_ITEM. In addition, there are dozens of built-ins to assist in writing flexible code by reading and writing object properties during run time; their names follow a pattern of GET_*objecttype*_PROPERTY and SET_*objecttype*_PROPERTY. Form Builder also offers a handful of other built-ins that are useful when you are writing flexible code, including ADD_GROUP_COLUMN, ADD_GROUP_ROW, ADD_LIST_ELEMENT, ADD_PARAMETER, COPY, DEFAULT_VALUE, DISPLAY_ITEM, NAME_IN, and SHOW_LOV. The most unusual of these is SHOW_LOV, because it both displays an object (an LOV) and returns a Boolean value indicating whether or not the user selected a value from the object.

Another technique that can increase the flexibility of your code is referencing objects by their internal ID rather than by name. Using internal IDs minimizes the number of places where you will have to change hard-coded names, and it allows you to run multiple instances of a single form simultaneously. As an added benefit, it speeds up your code because object names only need to be correlated with their internal IDs once. You can obtain an object's ID by employing one of several FIND_ built-in functions. Each object class has a matching FIND_ built-in; for instance, FIND_WINDOW, FIND_BLOCK, and FIND_LOV. If you want your form module to be able to access values in form items, parameters, and system and global variables in other form, menu, or library modules, you can use the NAME_IN and COPY built-ins to read and write values, respectively, in other modules. These items are called form bind variables, and the technique is known as *indirect referencing*.

The next subject you delved into was sharing objects and code. Reusing objects and code saves time and money, reduces rewriting errors, and ensures uniform appearance and functionality with minimal effort. The Form Builder features that support reusing objects and code include property classes, object groups, object libraries, and PL/SQL libraries. A property class is an object that holds a collection of properties, property values, and triggers that can be inherited by other objects, thereby ensuring that new objects can quickly take on the characteristics you have deemed important.

An added benefit is that if you need to change a property later, the change will automatically be propagated throughout your application. A property class can hold any number of properties, including properties that apply to different object types. Once you apply a property class to an object, you can still decide which property-class properties are inherited from the property class and which are overridden.

Performing a slightly different service are object groups. An object group is a logical container into which you place pointers to other objects in a module. This allows you to group related objects—even objects of different types—so they can be easily copied to, or subclassed within, another module. Providing a more powerful version of this functionality are object libraries, which are separate files you can create and then attach to a form as needed. An object library offers better subclassing features, and it lets you divide the objects visually into tab pages so you can locate the ones you want more quickly. Object libraries are a powerful way to make objects available to other applications, as well as to enforce standards across an organization's applications.

To facilitate reusing code in multiple modules, Form Builder offers PL/SQL libraries. These allow you to store client-side program units and make them available to any form, menu, or library module. A PL/SQL library stores subprograms, including functions, procedures, and packages. Once attached to a module, a PL/SQL library's program units can be called from your own routines, triggers, and menu item commands. You can attach multiple PL/SQL libraries to a single module, and many modules can attach to the same PL/SQL library. Because a PL/SQL library only loads its program units as an application needs them, it minimizes the demand for client-computer memory. PL/SQL libraries are created and modified under Form Builder's PL/SQL Libraries node. To use a PL/SQL library in a module, you attach it under the Attached Libraries node within the appropriate module; the attached library is read-only.

You then moved on to the subject of multiple-form applications. To create multiple-form applications, you write PL/SQL code incorporating built-ins that invoke other forms. The additional forms only consume client memory when they are called, so this is a good way to minimize your application's memory "footprint." Form Builder gives you plenty of options related to running multiple forms. A newly opened form can run simultaneously with the one that called it, or the new form can replace the old one, causing the calling form to close. Multiple instances of the same form can be run. A form can be opened but kept in the background. And multiple forms can either share the same database connection or they can have multiple independent database connections, as if they were running on separate client computers. The OPEN_FORM built-in opens a form and offers options to select whether the called form gets focus, shares library data with other forms, and gets its own database connection. The CALL_FORM built-in opens a form with options determining whether the calling form maintains the focus, whether the two forms share library data, and whether the called form is to be run only in query mode. The NEW_FORM built-in enters the called form and closes the calling form. The GO_FORM built-in moves focus to a specified form, and the EXIT_FORM built-in closes a form.

Two-Minute Drill

- You can get information about the current form, block, and item using the SYSTEM.CURRENT_FORM, SYSTEM.CURRENT_BLOCK, and SYSTEM.CURRENT_ITEM system variables, all of which return the name of the specified item. To determine the current record—remembering that records do not have names—you must use the SYSTEM.CURSOR_RECORD system variable, which returns the number of the record within its block.

- The difference between the $$DATE$$ and $$DBDATE$$ system variables is that the former gets its information from the client computer's operating system, while the latter gets it from the database.

- You can tell whether an item is visible using the GET_ITEM_PROPERTY(*item_name*, VISIBLE) system variable.

- The DEFAULT_VALUE built-in, whose primary job is to copy a value into variable if the variable is currently NULL, will create the destination variable if it is an undefined global variable.

- The SHOW_LOV built-in displays an LOV and returns a Boolean value to the calling program indicating whether or not the user selected a value from the LOV.

- The benefits of referencing objects by ID instead of by name are faster execution of code that references the object more than once, and improved code flexibility and maintainability.

- You can determine an object's ID by employing the FIND_*object _type* built-in.

- The benefits of writing code that references objects indirectly are flexibility (because you can write routines that have no item names hard-coded) and the ability to share data across separate form, menu, and library modules.

- You use the NAME_IN built-in to read a value from an indirectly referenced object, and the COPY built-in to place a value into an indirectly referenced object.

- The benefits of using property classes are (1) reduced development time due to being able to inherit customized settings for similar object types, (2) more uniform appearance and behavior, and (3) greater ease of propagating property changes throughout a system.

- In a Property Palette, a property whose value is unchanged from the default is marked with a small circle. Properties whose values have been changed manually are marked with a slightly larger square. Properties displaying inherited values are marked with an arrow pointing to the right. Properties whose inherited values have been manually overridden are marked with an inheritance arrow whose point is replaced with a red "X".

- Object groups enable you to group together pointers to related objects, and then copy or subclass the entire group of related items to other modules in one step.

- The benefits of using an object library include increased productivity due to reusing objects and standardization by having application objects subclassed under a central library.

- Object groups are designed to gather related objects of any type into one easy-to-copy group. An object library, on the other hand, is best at making objects available for subclassing into form and menu modules. The optimal blend of the two features is to group relevant items into an object group and then copy that object group to an object library to make it available to other modules.

- PL/SQL libraries work exclusively with client-side code.

- PL/SQL libraries offer dynamic loading so that program units are only placed in memory when the application needs them.

■ You can open form modules programmatically in the Forms Runtime program by using the OPEN_FORM built-in. If you do not want the new form to receive focus immediately, include the NO_ACTIVATE option. If you want the new form to have its own database connection, include the SESSION option.

■ When multiple forms are running simultaneously, a **commit** in one causes all forms to save their records to the database. This is undesirable if the forms are not functionally related. Using the OPEN_FORM built-in with the SESSION option allows a new form to open with its own database connection, and therefore its own **commit** timing.

■ You can cause your application to navigate between open forms by using the GO_FORM, NEXT_FORM, and PREVIOUS_FORM built-ins in your code.

Chapter Questions

1. **What built-in can you use to open a second form but keep the first form in control?**

    A. SYSTEM.CURRENT_FORM

    B. SYSTEM.MOUSE_FORM

    C. CALL_FORM

    D. FIND_FORM

    E. NEW_FORM

    F. OPEN_FORM

2. **Which system variable can tell you the record on which the user has placed focus?**

    A. CURRENT_ITEM

    B. CURRENT_RECORD

    C. CURSOR_ITEM

    D. CURSOR_RECORD

3. **Which of the following is not a benefit of referencing objects by internal ID? (Choose all that apply)**

   A. Faster program execution

   B. More secure code

   C. Greater ease of maintenance

   D. Smaller files

4. **You are modifying a Customer form so that it has the ability to place the contents of the customer's ZIP code into a separate form named Dealer. What built-in will you use?**

   A. WRITE_VALUE

   B. ADD_PARAMETER

   C. COPY

   D. SET_APPLICATION_PROPERTY

   E. NAME_IN

5. **You have added an LOV to a form and now want to add code to determine whether the user has made a choice from the LOV or dismissed it. What built-in will help you?**

   A. GET_LOV_PROPERTY

   B. WHEN-LIST-CHANGED

   C. SHOW_LOV

   D. KEY-LISTVAL

   E. POST-TEXT-ITEM

   F. WHEN-LIST-ACTIVATED

6. **Which of the following will allow you to collect objects and easily reuse them in other forms?**

   A. PL/SQL Library

   B. Object package

    C. Object group

    D. Trigger library

    E. Property class

7. You have created a client-lookup canvas, complete with code and all the necessary objects, that has proven popular enough that others want to use it in their applications. How can you make it available to the other applications from one central source point?

    A. Copy the canvas, code, and objects into a PL/SQL library

    B. Copy the canvas, code, and objects into an object library

    C. Copy the form module into a PL/SQL library

    D. Copy the form module into an object library

    E. Place the canvas, code, and objects into an object group that the other developers will reference

8. You have inherited an application from a developer who left to pursue a career in music. While looking through the SALARY item's Property Palette, you notice that to the left of its Data Type property is an arrow with an "X" at its point. What does this symbol indicate?

    A. The setting for this property is invalid

    B. The setting has been derived from a Visual Attributes group

    C. The setting has been derived from a property class

    D. The setting has been derived from a Visual Attributes group, but has been overridden

    E. The setting has been derived from a property class, but has been overridden

9. You want to read the value in an item on another form and use it in your current form. What built-in will you use?

    A. SET_ITEM_PROPERTY

    B. GET_ITEM_PROPERTY

    C. GET_ITEM_VALUE

    D. FIND_ITEM

    E. NAME_IN

    F. COPY

    G. SET_ITEM

10. **You create a module with two forms: Employee and Product. The application allows users to have the forms open simultaneously. The users notice that when they save an Employee record, any unsaved Product records are also committed; the reverse is also true. This is not the behavior they want. What can you do to change it?**

    A. Open the first form using the OPEN_FORM built-in with the SESSION option

    B. Open the second form using the OPEN_FORM built-in with the SESSION option

    C. Open the first form using the OPEN_FORM built-in with the ACTIVATE option

    D. Open the second form using the GO_FORM built-in with the ACTIVATE option

    E. Open the second form using the GO_FORM built-in with the NO_ACTIVATE option

11. **You need a built-in that will copy a value into a global variable, and create the variable if it is undefined. What built-in has this ability?**

    A. DEFAULT_VALUE

    B. COPY

    C. SET_VAR

    D. CREATE_VAR

12. **You are writing versatile code that checks whether your Employee form's Salary field is visible; if it is, the code hides it; if it isn't, the**

code shows it. What built-in can you use to determine which route the code will take?

A. GET_FORM_PROPERTY

B. GET_BLOCK_PROPERTY

C. GET_RECORD_PROPERTY

D. GET_ITEM_PROPERTY

E. GET_VIEW_PROPERTY

F. GET_WINDOW_PROPERTY

13. You want to use a single multipage tab canvas for different purposes. Which built-in will let you set the labels for the pages dynamically when the application is running?

A. SET_CANVAS_PROPERTY

B. SET_TAB_PROPERTY

C. SET_TAB_PAGE_PROPERTY

D. SET_PAGE_PROPERTY

Answers to Chapter Questions

1. F.   OPEN_FORM

Explanation   The OPEN_FORM built-in includes a NO_ACTIVATE option stipulating that the form being opened should not receive control.

2. D.   CURSOR_RECORD

Explanation   This is a record-level requirement, so the ITEM variables will not help you. There is no CURRENT_RECORD system variable.

3. B, D.   More secure code, Smaller files

Explanation   The type of object reference you use in your code does not affect security or guarantee smaller files. It does, however, improve the speed at which the code can run if the reference is used more than once, and it simplifies maintenance by allowing you to change an object's name only once within a code segment.

4. C.   COPY

Explanation   This question requires the use of form bind variables, which cannot be referenced directly across modules. The built-ins NAME_IN and COPY are used to read and write values across modules with form bind variables. In this case, COPY is the right choice, because you wish to place values in another field, rather than read them from the field.

5. C.   SHOW_LOV

Explanation   The SHOW_LOV built-in has the ability to display an object (an LOV), and also return a Boolean value to the calling program indicating whether or not the user selected a value from the LOV. If you selected one of the WHEN- or POST- choices, be sure to reread the chapter before the exam…those are triggers, not built-ins.

6. C.   Object group

Explanation   Review the section titled "Grouping Related Items for Reuse" if you need a refresher on this topic.

7. B.   Copy the canvas, code, and objects into an object library

Explanation   Review the section titled "Reusing Objects from an Object Library" if you need a refresher on this topic.

8. E.   The setting has been derived from a property class, but has been overridden

Explanation   A Data Type property can only be derived from a property class. The arrow indicates that this has been done. The "X" at its point indicates that the setting inherited from the property class has been manually overridden for this item.

9. E.   NAME_IN

Explanation   Some of the built-in names offered as choices don't exist. Of the ones that do, NAME_IN and COPY are used to read and write values from/to items in other form modules. In this case, NAME_IN is the right choice, because you wish to read a value in another field.

10. B.   Open the second form using the OPEN_FORM built-in with the SESSION option

Explanation   Review the section titled "Calling One Form from Another" if you need a refresher on this topic.

11. A.   DEFAULT_VALUE

Explanation   Review the section titled "Built-In Subprograms that Assist Flexible Coding" if you need a refresher on this topic.

12. D.   GET_ITEM_PROPERTY

Explanation   Visibility is an item-level property, so you would use the GET_ITEM_PROPERTY to determine the current status.

13. C.   SET_TAB_PAGE_PROPERTY

Explanation   Review the section titled "Built-In Subprograms that Assist Flexible Coding" if you need a refresher on this topic.

UNIT
IV

Preparing for OCP Exam 4: Building Forms II

CHAPTER
18

Project Builder

n this chapter, you will understand and demonstrate knowledge in the following area:

- Managing projects with Project Builder

This chapter covers everything you need to know to begin using Project Builder. Because the chapter contains only one main section—"Managing Projects with Project Builder"—you will find the introduction to the chapter's contents within that section's introduction. The contents of this chapter comprise about 8 percent of the OCP Exam 4 test content.

Managing Projects with Project Builder

In this section, you will cover the following points related to managing projects with Project Builder:

- Benefits of using Project Builder
- Creating projects and subprojects
- Adding files to a project
- Implicit and explicit dependencies
- Compile options
- Delivering a project
- Customizing a Project Builder environment

Project Builder is the central point from which you can keep track of all the files that make up one or more Developer/2000 application projects. In this section, you will learn the benefits that Project Builder has to offer, and learn the basic layout of the Project Builder display. Next, you will explore how to create projects and subprojects in Project Builder, how to add files to the projects and subprojects, and how to identify files that are dependent on each other. You will then learn how Project Builder makes it easy to compile part or all of your project in a single step, and how to create an installable group of files that comprise a deliverable application. Finally, you will discover the automated actions that Project Builder links to each file type, along with the dynamic variables you can insert into these actions to make them more versatile and flexible.

Benefits of Using Project Builder

Project Builder allows you to create and maintain a hierarchical list of the files that make up your application. From this central list, you can edit files, compile them, run their compiled versions, and combine them into a deliverable product complete with installation scripts for the Oracle Installer.

Project Builder offers a wealth of features to simplify the management of large, complicated, multiple-developer applications. It provides a *Global Registry* that stores settings identifying how each type of file should be handled. These settings include whether that file type should be delivered in the final application, whether it should be included under a version-control system, what database connection should be used with files of that type, what automated actions are available for that file type, and what variables are available to make those actions modify themselves dynamically. Project Builder also offers a *User Registry* that can contain user-specific settings that supersede Global Registry settings on a developer-by-developer basis. Project Builder also allows you to keep track of the database *connections* used in a project. And finally, Project Builder provides a familiar navigator-style *Projects* node, which can show your project's files grouped in a tree format in whatever subprojects you desire, and sorted either by file type or by dependencies between the files. When you add form, report, and graphics files to the Projects tree, Project Builder does not bring the physical files into your Project Builder file; instead, it creates *pointers* to the form, report, and graphics files, which themselves remain on disk. Project Builder doesn't stop at simply maintaining these pointers; it allows you to define how each file being pointed to should be edited and packaged into a deliverable Developer/2000 application.

The Project Builder has a basic set of onscreen components that are similar to those you learned about in Form Builder. Figure 18-1 shows these components. At the top of the display are a familiar menu and toolbar; the toolbar includes special buttons to start the Project Wizard and Delivery Wizard (which you will learn more about later), to add and remove files from a project, and to compile source files. On the left side of the display is the Launcher for starting other programs. Most of the screen space is devoted to the tree-oriented Project Navigator, which gives you convenient access to the files in your application.

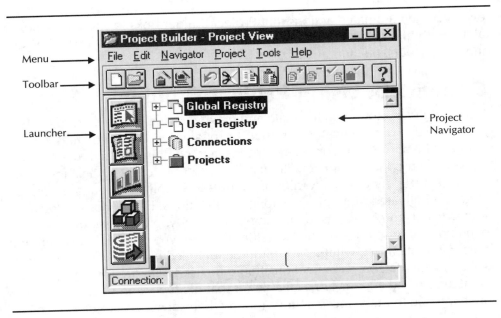

FIGURE 18-1. *Project Builder components*

Exercises

1. What are the main functions of Project Builder?

2. How does Project Builder make multiple-developer environments more consistent and efficient?

Creating Projects and Subprojects

To see how to add projects and subprojects in the Project Builder, start the program (if you haven't already) and double-click on the Projects node to start the Project Wizard. If you see a screen labeled *Welcome to the Project Wizard!*, deselect its *Display this screen next time* option and click on the Next button to proceed. The Project Wizard will start by asking you for the title, directory, and filename for your new project. Enter a title of **Oracle Press Samples**, identify the directory you would like to serve as the project's default directory, and enter a file name of **Oracle_Press_Samples** for the project's file name. Then click on the Next button to continue. The next Project Wizard screen allows you to enter an author name and select a database connection. These parameters will override the default settings established using Project

Builder's Tools | Preferences | Projects menu command. For now, just click on the Next button to continue. In the final Project Wizard screen, select the *Just create the project* radio button and click on the Finish button. Your screen should now look similar to Figure 18-2.

If, at a future time, you would like to create a project without using the Project Wizard, you would start by executing the File | New | Project menu command. Project Builder will immediately present a file-save dialog box; enter the name the project file should be saved under and click on the Save button. You can then change the name the project shows in the Project Navigator by opening the project's Property Palette.

You can also create subprojects beneath a project to provide further organization of the application's files. Right-click on your Oracle Press Samples project node and select New Sub-Project from the context menu that appears. Select the subproject's default directory—it can be the same as the main project's default directory—and click on the OK button. Change the subproject's name to **Standard**. Next, create a second subproject at the same level and name it **AV**. You now have a fine hierarchical structure to hold your project files. In the next section, you will add files to it.

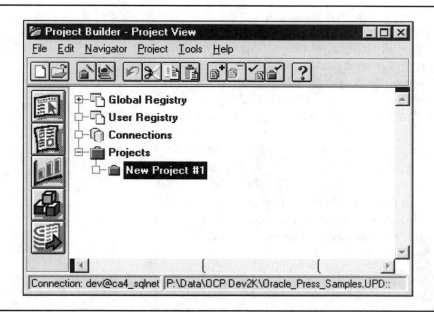

FIGURE 18-2. *Project Builder new project*

Exercises

1. What is the difference between a project's title and its filename?

2. What is the purpose of subprojects?

Adding Files to a Project

Double-click on your Standard subproject node to open the dialog box for adding files to the project. Navigate to the location where your form files from this book are stored and select the **.fmb** and **.fmx** files for your sample application. You can select multiple files by employing SHIFT-clicking for contiguous groups and CTRL-clicking for noncontiguous groups. When you are done selecting files, click on the Open button to continue. You should now see two new nodes beneath your Standard subproject: *Forms Builder document* and *Forms Builder executable*. Click on the + to the left of each node and you will see pointers to the files you selected. Your screen should now look similar to Figure 18-3 (which shows two **.fmb** files, while your project will probably only show one). Using the technique you just learned, add the Form Builder files for your **AV_DATA** forms to your project.

TIP
The number of files Project Builder can add to a project in one add-file command is limited. The program's documentation states that in a single command you can add up to 250 files that have Windows long filenames, and as many as 600 files that have names using the older 8.3 notation. In reality, the limit is far lower for files with long filenames. If you select too many files, Project Builder will either add some of them but not others, or will add none at all. If either of these events occurs, add the files in smaller quantities using multiple add-file commands.

Even though the items added to your project are pointers to your files, and not the files themselves, the pointers still have properties. Right-click now on the Project Builder pointer for your **image_module.fmb** file, and

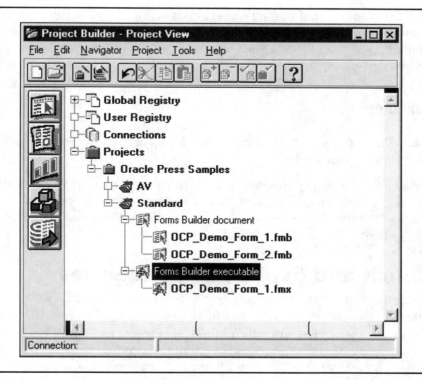

FIGURE 18-3. *Project Builder project with subproject and file pointers*

select Property Palette from the context menu that appears. The properties of particular interest include Project Directory, which identifies where the file being pointed to is stored; Version Control File, which—if you have implemented source control using a version-control product such as PVCS or ClearCase—determines whether multiple versions of the file are stored as the file is modified; Deliver File, identifying whether the file should be included in a delivered Developer/2000 application; a group of Actions properties, which determine what programs should be used to open, print, run, and perform other actions on a file; and the Macros group, in which you can specify command-line parameters for the applications defined in the Actions group.

When you are done looking at the project item's properties, close the Property Palette and return to Project Builder. Double-click on one of the source files represented in the Project Navigator and you will see that the file will be opened for editing in Form Builder. Double-click on one of the compiled files in the Project Navigator and the file will be run by the Forms Runtime program.

Exercises

1. Which portion of the Project Builder display shows the individual files in your project?

2. How can you change whether a specific file in a project is destined to be delivered in the distributed application? How can you determine where the physical file is stored? How can you change whether it is version controlled?

Implicit and Explicit Dependencies

In an application, certain files rely on the presence of other files. For instance, compiled forms with **.fmx** file types cannot exist without there first being a corresponding source form **.fmb** file. Project Builder offers a Navigator view type that arranges file pointers based on their dependency on other files, rather than by their file types. To see this *Dependency View* in action, execute the Navigator | Dependency View menu command. Your Project Navigator display will rearrange to show Project Builder's best understanding of which source files are the basis for other files. Unfortunately, Project Builder isn't that bright about connecting source and target files; if you add a *file_name*.fmb and a *file_name*.fmx file in the same add-files command, Project Builder will not understand that the **.fmx** file has a dependency on the **.fmb** file, even though they share the same name. You must state this dependency explicitly by adding the files in separate steps. First, you add the target file—in this case, the **.fmx** file—and after that file has been added to the Project Navigator, you select it and click on the Add Files to Project button in the Project Builder's toolbar, shown here:

In the add-files dialog box that appears, you then select the source file. This creates an *explicit dependency* that will be reflected when you have set the Project Builder to Dependency View.

While you are using Dependency View, you will notice that source files do not necessarily all display at the same hierarchy level: source files in explicit dependencies with target files display one level deeper than source files without such dependencies. This means that if you add the **image_module.fmx** file to your project, then add the **image_module.fmb** file beneath it in an explicit dependency, and next add the **sound_module.fmb** file to the project, the two **.fmb** files will not display at the same level. This can be visually confusing. To remedy this, Project Builder offers a display mode that creates "phantom" dependent items for source files that are not part of an explicit dependency. Displaying these phantom files is called showing *implicit dependencies*. To turn this feature on, execute the Tools | Preferences | Display command and enable the *Show implicit items* option. If your project includes any source files without explicitly defined target files, Project Builder will create phantom target files so all the source files display at the same level in the Project Navigator. Figure 18-4 shows a project with this option enabled. Notice how the AV subproject's pointers include two instances of **image_module.fmx** and **sound_module.fmx**. The instances in bold lettering are the ones you added manually, while the instances in regular lettering are implicit items and do not really exist. This brings up an important point: enabling the *Show implicit items* option does not cause Project Builder to automatically seek and add dependent items to your project when you add a source item; it merely causes the Project Navigator to display phantom dependent items so that source items are displayed at the same hierarchical level. It is a purely cosmetic change. It is also important to know that if you have a project displaying with implicit items and then manually add a file with exactly the same name as an implicit item, Project Builder will not replace the implicit item with the real one; it will display both.

Exercises

1. What is the difference between Project View and Dependency View?

2. If you have the *Show implicit items* option enabled and add an **.fmb** file to your project, will the corollary **.fmx** file be added automatically? If not, what must you do to ensure that the **.fmx** file is added?

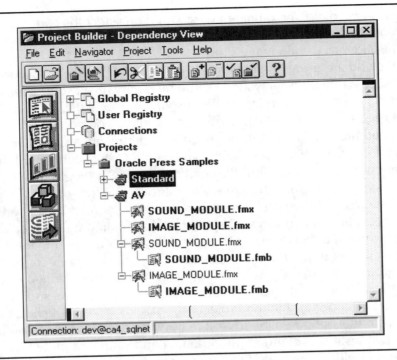

FIGURE 18-4. *Project Navigator with **Show implicit items option enabled***

Compile Options

You can create compiled versions of your source files from within Project
Builder. This can be a fast, convenient way to ensure that all the compiled
files you are about to package into a deliverable product are up-to-date. To
compile all the source files in a project or subproject, right-click on the
project name or subproject name in the Project Navigator. Then select
Compile All from the context menu that appears. You will see Project
Builder start the Forms Compiler program once for each **.fmb** file in your
project. (When you have applications containing other types of source files,
Project Builder can start the appropriate compiler for those file types as
well.) When the compile process is finished, it will display a dialog box
showing the compilation status as *Done* and offering a Close button. Click
on the button to return to Project Builder.

If you wish to compile only the source files that have changed since the
last time they were compiled—or that have never been compiled at

all—right-click on the appropriate project or subproject name and select Compile Incremental from the context menu that appears. To force a compile on one or more specific source files, select the file pointers in the Project Navigator and execute the Project | Compile Selection menu command.

Exercise

What is the difference between Compile All, Compile Incremental, and Compile Selection?

Delivering a Project

Considering how complex it can be to develop a sophisticated application, preparing it for delivery is remarkably simple. This is largely due to one of Project Builder's nicest features: the Delivery Wizard. The Delivery Wizard simplifies the process of preparing your finished application for distribution to users. It lets you select the files to include, and for patches, it is smart enough to only include the changed files. The Delivery Wizard copies the selected files to a "staging" area, which is simply a location in which copies of your application's files are placed, along with other files needed by the Oracle Installer. The staging area can be on a local or networked hard drive, or it can be a remote site accessed via File Transfer Protocol (FTP). Your final step for delivery will be copying files from the staging area to your distribution media, or making the staging area available for users on a network.

To see this in action, select your project's node in the Project Navigator and execute the Tools | Delivery Wizard menu command. If you are presented with a screen titled *Welcome to the Delivery Wizard!*, uncheck its *Display this screen next time* option and click on the Next button to continue to the first page of the Delivery Wizard, which is shown in Figure 18-5. Notice that the name of your project is already presented in the *What project would you like to deliver?* field. If you open that field, you will see that your subprojects are also available. For the time being, leave the field set to your main project. Enable the *Deliver all files* radio button, and then click on the Next button to continue. In the next wizard page, click on the *Deliver to a local staging area and create Oracle Installer scripts* radio button, and enter a name for the directory that you would like the Delivery Wizard to use as the staging area. It is recommended that you have a directory dedicated solely to this function. Also, note that each time you run the Delivery Wizard it replaces the contents of your staging directory, so if you are doing a "patch" release, you will want to place that release's files in a directory different from

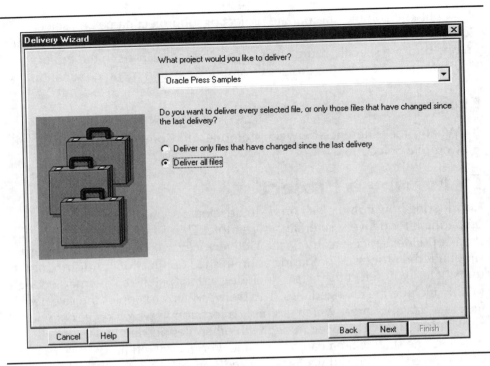

FIGURE 18-5. *Project Builder's Delivery Wizard first page*

the one containing the distribution files you are patching! After you have entered your staging directory name, click on the Next button to continue to the next wizard page. In the first field of this new page, labeled Script Name, enter up to eight alphanumeric characters that will serve as the filename portion of the Oracle Installer files the wizard generates for your application. The user does not need to see this name, so you can be cryptic if necessary. The next field on the page, Program Group Name, is the name the user will see in the Oracle Installer; it is also the name of the Windows Program Group that will be created for your application, and the name that the Installer will add to your Start menu to give the users access to the application's compiled files. Unlike the prior field, this one allows spaces, mixed-case words, and a friendly amount of space. The value you put in the third field, Version, will also show up in the Oracle Installer, appended to the Program Group Name. Below these fields is a radio group allowing you to specify whether you want the Developer/2000 Runtime environments

(Forms Runtime, Reports Runtime, and Graphics Runtime) included in the distributed product. Make your selection and then click on the Next button to proceed.

In the next wizard page you have the opportunity to select which of the compiled files you wish to include in your distributed application. Make any changes you wish, and click on the Next button to continue. The next Delivery Wizard page lets you enter the program labels that will appear in the user's Start menu after your application is installed. These labels can be mixed case and include spaces. Enter the labels you want your users to see, and then click on the Next button to move forward. The next wizard page allows you to specify environment variables that will be added to the user's Windows Registry when the application is installed. For the moment, just click on the Next button to proceed to the next page. There, you will see a summary of the actions the Delivery Wizard is about to take. Click on the Finish button and your application's compiled files will be copied to your staging directory, along with the files necessary to install them using the Oracle Installer.

Exercise

What is the purpose of the staging area?

Customizing a Project Builder Environment

One of the benefits of using the Project Builder is that it knows how to open, edit, print, and perform other operations based on a file's type. These operations rely on *actions* defined in the registries and Property Palettes. You can view and modify these actions yourself, and even create new ones of your own if you wish. Actions are hierarchical: the Global Registry defines actions for each file type, and those can be superseded by entries in a User Registry. Individual projects can have their own actions, as can subprojects and even individual files. This gives you a very high degree of control over how your files are handled while maintaining the benefits of having repetitive activities automated. Project Builder provides *predefined actions* that should be edited only by the project administrator—if at all—as well as *user-defined actions* that you can easily add yourself by right-clicking on a node and selecting Add Action from the context menu that appears. Don't do that quite yet, though, because you still need more information about how actions work.

Open your Global Registry node now in the Project Navigator and select the Form Builder document node. Open the Property Palette and, if necessary, open the Actions node. You will see property entries for all the actions currently defined in the Global Registry for this type of file. For instance, the Edit property will contain a value similar to this:

```
{ORACLE_HOME}\bin\f50des32 {ORACONNECT ? Userid={ORACONNECT}}
Module='"'{n}'"' {F50DESOPTS}
```

This is the command line that Project Builder will execute if you tell it you want to edit one of the Form Builder documents (**.fmb** files) in your project. The parts of the command line that are surrounded by braces ({ }) are variables called *macros*. When the command line is executed, the macros are replaced by text; for instance, the {ORACLE_HOME} macro is replaced by the path for your Oracle home directory. The values for macros are defined in the next node of the Property Palette, named Macros.

You may notice that some actions include macros that are not defined in the Macros section of the Property Palette. That is because certain macros cannot be changed; these are called *built-in macros*. They have one-character names and are shipped with Developer/2000. There are two other categories of macros: *predefined macros*, which appear in the Macros node of the Property Palette, are also provided with Developer/2000 but can be changed if you wish; and *user-defined macros*, which you create yourself to add dynamic variables to the command lines executed by actions. A complete treatise on actions and macros is beyond the scope of this book; the important thing to remember for the exams is that actions are file-type-specific commands that perform defined tasks, that you can create your own custom actions, that an action's command line can include macros to serve as dynamic variables in the action's command, and that you can create your own macros to add your own variables.

Exercises

1. What is an action, and why do they exist?

2. What are the two types of actions, and what is the difference between them?

3. What can you add to an action to alter the command string it creates dynamically?

4. What are the three types of macros, and what are the differences between them?

Chapter Summary

In this chapter, you got a thorough introduction to Project Builder. You started by exploring the benefits of using Project Builder, which include easy establishment of company-wide standards for file location, delivery, version control, database connections, and compilation, as well as an intuitive tree structure for displaying project, subprojects, and individual file names. From this central list, you can edit files, compile them, run their executable versions, and combine them into a deliverable product complete with installation scripts for the Oracle Installer. Project Builder's Global Registry stores settings identifying how each type of file should be handled. These settings can be superseded by individual developers, if necessary, using settings in the User Registry. Project Builder provides a tree-structured Project Navigator, which can show your application's files grouped into whatever subprojects you desire, and sorted either by file type or by dependencies between the files. When you add form, report, and graphics files to the Projects tree, Project Builder does not bring the physical files into your Project Builder file; instead, it creates pointers to them. Project Builder allows you to define how each file being pointed to should be edited and packaged into a deliverable Developer/2000 product.

Next, you learned how to create projects and subprojects. This can be done either using the Project Wizard or manually, using the File | New | Project menu command. You can then add files to a project either by double-clicking on the project's node, or by clicking on it once and then clicking on the Add Files to Project button. The pointers Project Builder creates to your files have properties allowing you to specify parameters on an individual-file basis. These parameters include file location, database connection, automated actions, macro variables, inclusion in the delivered application, and monitoring by a version-control system. When adding files, you can explicitly identify file dependencies by adding a dependent file first, selecting that file's pointer in the Project Navigator, and then adding the other files on which the first file depends. These dependencies can be displayed by executing the Navigator | Dependency View menu command. If your project contains source files without any corresponding executable files, you can cause the Project Navigator to display the source files at the same hierarchical level by executing the Tools | Preferences | Display command and enabling the *Show implicit items* option.

Project Builder also provides you with a fast, convenient way to compile your application's source files. In addition to being able to compile every source file in your application with a single command, it offers commands allowing you to compile only those that have changed since their last compilation, or only those you select manually. For packaging the compiled files into a deliverable application, Project Builder offers the Delivery Wizard. The Delivery Wizard lets you select the files to include, and for patches, it can automatically include only changed files. It copies the selected executable files to a staging area, along with other files necessary for the Oracle Installer to install the application. The staging area can be on a local or networked hard drive, or it can be a remote site accessed via File Transfer Protocol (FTP). Product-packaging operations such as these, as well as more common activities like opening and compiling files, are controlled by Project Builder properties called actions. Actions are file-type-specific commands that execute defined tasks. You can edit the actions to modify how they handle your files, and you can create actions of your own to add new functionality to Project Builder. Within an action's command string, you can incorporate dynamic variables called macros to insert values into the action command string at run time. There are three categories of macros: built-in macros, which are shipped with Developer/2000, have one-character names, and cannot be changed; predefined macros, which are also provided with Developer/2000, can be changed if you wish, and appear in the Macros node of the Property Palette; and user-defined macros, which you create yourself.

The contents of this chapter comprise about 8 percent of material tested on OCP Exam 4.

Two-Minute Drill

- The main functions of Project Builder are maintaining settings of how file types and individual files should be edited, compiled, delivered, and otherwise handled; displaying the names of a project's files in an easy-to-navigate hierarchical layout; and giving easy access to actions commonly performed on project files, such as editing, compiling, and delivering.

- Project Builder makes multiple-developer environments more consistent and efficient by offering a Global Registry to store file-specific settings that are used by all developers, and a User

Registry to store developer-specific settings when certain Global Registry settings need to be superseded.

■ A project's title is visible only within the Project Builder. It can contain spaces and mixed-case characters. A project's filename is the disk filename under which it is stored in your operating system, and Oracle products generally work with fewer problems if their disk filenames do not contain spaces.

■ The purpose of subprojects in the Project Builder is organization. Subprojects provide a means of segmenting very large projects into smaller groups of logically related files.

■ The portion of the Project Builder display that shows the individual files in your project is the Project Navigator.

■ You can change whether a specific file in a project is destined to be delivered in the distributed application by altering the Deliver File property in the file's Property Palette. The property identifying where the physical file is stored is Project Directory, and the property specifying whether it is version controlled is Version Control File.

■ In the Project Navigator, executing the Navigator | Project View menu command causes the Project Navigator to organize files within a project (or subproject) by file type. Executing the Navigator | Dependency View menu command causes the Project Navigator to organize files within a project (or subproject) by the target files' dependencies on source files.

■ Enabling the *Show implicit items* option causes the Project Navigator to display phantom dependent items for any source file that does not have a dependent file linked in an explicit dependency. It does *not* cause dependent files to automatically be added to a project when their source file is added.

■ The Compile All command forces all source files in the selected project or subproject to be compiled. The Compile Incremental command does this for only those files that either have changed since their last compile or have not been compiled at all. The Compile Selection command compiles one or more source files of your choosing.

- When you want to distribute an application, the staging area is the location where Project Builder's Delivery Wizard places copies of the compiled files you wish to distribute, along with the installation files necessary to install the application using the Oracle Installer.

- An action is a command line that is executed in order to accomplish a defined task. Actions are specific to each file type, and they can be defined at the global, user, project, subproject, and file levels.

- Project Builder comes with predefined actions for common tasks such as opening, printing, and compiling files. You can also create user-defined actions to add functionality of your own.

- An action's command line can be made more dynamic by incorporating macros. Surrounded in braces ({ }), macros are variables whose values are filled in when the action is executed.

- Project Builder comes with built-in macros, which have single-character names and cannot be changed; and predefined macros, which usually already contain values but can be altered. You can also create user-defined macros to add dynamic variables of your own to action commands.

Chapter Questions

1. **You inherit a project at work and discover that its several prior developers have been storing files in a variety of directories scattered throughout the network. You move all the files into a single directory. How can you adjust the Project Builder pointers to find the files in their new location without having to delete the pointers and re-create them and their dependencies?**

   A. Change the Project Directory property in the Global Registry.

   B. Change the Project Directory property in the User Registry.

   C. Change the Project Directory property for the project.

   D. Change the Project Directory property for each file pointer.

   E. You must delete the pointers in Project Builder and re-create them.

2. Which of the following are *not* among the benefits of Project Builder? (Choose all that apply)

A. Standardization of file locations

B. Localized file security

C. Standardization of compilation actions

D. Smaller installation files

3. What steps are necessary to establish an explicit dependency between two files?

A. Select the files and run the Dependency Wizard.

B. Select the files and execute the Project | Create Dependency menu command.

C. Add the files in the same Add Files command, and the dependency will be created automatically as long as the filenames are the same up to the file type extension.

D. Add the source file, select it in the Project Navigator, and add the dependent file.

E. Add the dependent file, select it in the Project Navigator, and add the source file.

F. It is not possible to create an explicit dependency between two files.

4. What allows you to see the relationship between source files and other files that are based on them?

A. Object View

B. Project View

C. Global Registry

D. Relationship View

E. Dependency View

F. Database Connection

5. **What steps are necessary to establish an implicit dependency between two files?**

    A. Select the files and run the Dependency Wizard.

    B. Select the files and execute the Project | Create Dependency menu command.

    C. Add the files in the same Add Files command, and the dependency will be created automatically as long as the filenames up to the extension are the same.

    D. Add the source file, select it in the Project Navigator, and add the dependent file.

    E. Add the dependent file, select it in the Project Navigator, and add the source file.

    F. It is not possible to create an implicit dependency between two files.

6. **You have created a group of custom actions to process all of your distribution files through an in-house encryption program before being packaged for distribution. The custom actions include command-line parameters for the encryption program, and the command-line parameters change often. What can you create so changes in encryption command-line parameters need only be made in one place, rather than in every custom action?**

    A. Macro

    B. Parameter

    C. Action

    D. Module

    E. Variable

7. **You have copied several .fmb source files from an existing application, and modified them to be used in a new application you are building. You now wish to add them to a Project Builder project. What must you do to ensure that any .fmx compiled files generated from these source files will be added to Project Builder as well?**

A. Execute the Tools | Compile Selection menu command after adding the **.fmb** files.

B. Enable the Tools | Preferences option to include implicit dependencies.

C. Select the **.fmx** files in an Add Files command.

D. You cannot add **.fmb** files from another application to a new Project Builder project.

8. **You inherit a project at work and need to know where the project is looking for files. Where can you acquire this information?**

   A. Global Registry

   B. User Registry

   C. Project Property Palette

   D. File Property Palette

   E. Project View

   F. Dependency View

9. **You have completed your predevelopment JAD sessions and written the resulting requirements in a series of word-processor documents. What component in Project Builder can you employ to gain access to these documents easily?**

   A. Subproject

   B. User Registry

   C. Global Registry

   D. Project Navigator

Answers to Chapter Questions

1. D.   Change the Project Directory property for each file pointer

Explanation   Neither the Global Registry nor the User Registry contain a Project Directory property. Projects do have a Project Directory property, but it will not help because the project's files are already subdivided into separate directories for each developer, so the project's Project Directory property is already being overridden. The only place to make this change is at the file level; each file pointer in Project Builder has a Project Directory property.

2. B, D.   Localized file security, Smaller installation files

Explanation   Project Builder does not address file security in any way, and while it makes it more convenient to create installation files, it does not offer any particular benefits in terms of file compression.

3. E.   Add the dependent file, select it in the Project Navigator, and add the source file.

Explanation   See the section titled "Implicit and Explicit Dependencies" for a refresher on this topic.

4. E.   Dependency View

Explanation   See the section titled "Implicit and Explicit Dependencies" for a refresher on this topic.

5. F.   It is not possible to create an implicit dependency between two files.

Explanation   By definition, an implicit dependency is displayed only when a source file exists in the Project Navigator without a corresponding dependent file.

6. A.   Macro

Explanation   See the section titled "Customizing a Project Builder Environment" for a refresher on this topic.

7. C.   Select the **.fmx** files in an Add Files command.

Explanation   The Tools | Compile Selection command creates **.fmx** files from **.fmb** files, but it does not add the **.fmx** files to your project. The Tools | Preferences command controls the display of dependencies between files already added to Project Builder; it does not cause compiled files to be added to Project Builder automatically when their source files are added. And Project Builder does not know or care whether **.fmb** or **.fmx** files have been used in another application. The only way to ensure that any file is added to a project is to select it explicitly during an Add Files command.

8. C.   Project Property Palette

Explanation   Since the question specified you need to know where the *project* is storing files, rather than where individual *files* may have their location set to, the answer is at the project level, and would be found in the project's Property Palette in the Project Directory property.

9. D.   Project Navigator

Explanation   Adding file types in either the User or Global Registry is of no use if the files have not been added to the Project Navigator. The same is true of subprojects, which can only help organize files that have already been added. So the answer is the Project Navigator, which provides easy access to the files by displaying pointers to them in a logical hierarchical tree.

CHAPTER
19

Working with Menu Modules

n this chapter, you will cover the following facets of working with menu modules:

- Creating menu modules

- Managing menu modules

Menus are a fact of life in modern application development. Form Builder has features that make it extremely easy to create custom menus for your applications. In this chapter, you will learn how to create custom menus and toolbars, including context-sensitive pop-up menus. In addition, you will learn to control menus programmatically, including determining which menu is active at a given time, and which items within the active menu are available to the user. The contents of this chapter constitute about 13 percent of the OCP Exam 4 test content.

Creating Menu Modules

In this section, you will explore the following points related to creating menu modules:

- Menu components

- Creating, saving, and attaching menu modules

- Setting menu properties using the Property Palette

- Creating menu toolbars

- Creating pop-up menus

This section lays the groundwork of knowledge you need to create your own menus and toolbars. You will start with an introduction to the components of a menu and the Menu Editor. With that as a basis, you will then learn how to create custom horizontal and vertical menus, how to easily generate horizontal and vertical toolbars containing buttons corresponding to items in your menus, and how to create context-sensitive pop-up menus that appear when the user right-clicks on an object.

Menu Components

Form Builder provides a Menu Editor enabling you to design menus graphically. Shown in Figure 19-1, the Menu Editor provides a layout that will be familiar by now: a toolbar of buttons at the top providing quick access to often-used functions, a drop-down list to change which object is being viewed, and a design area where you do your work graphically. In addition, starting the Menu Editor alters Form Builder's menus, replacing the View and Navigator menu categories with a single Menu category.

When you build a custom menu, the menu itself cannot do any work; it serves only to organize the objects contained within it. The *main menu* organizes *individual menus*. Each individual menu organizes *menu items*,

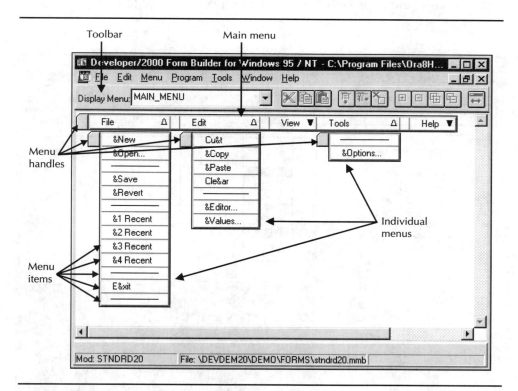

FIGURE 19-1. *Menu Editor sample screen*

which provide access to the actual functions you build into the menu system. While all of these different types of objects are stored in a single menu module (**.mmb**) file, they have a hierarchical relationship with each other. This is reflected within the Object Navigator by a traditional tree layout. Figure 19-2 depicts how selecting an item in the Menu Editor causes that item to be selected in the Object Navigator's object tree. The reverse is also true: select an item in the Object Navigator's object tree and it will be selected in the Menu Editor as well.

In the Menu Editor, individual menus can be expanded or collapsed by clicking on the arrow to the right of each menu name. For instance, in Figure 19-1 the File, Edit, and Tools menus are all open, and to the right of each of their names is a small, hollow upward-pointing arrow. Clicking on that arrow would cause the items in the individual menu to collapse

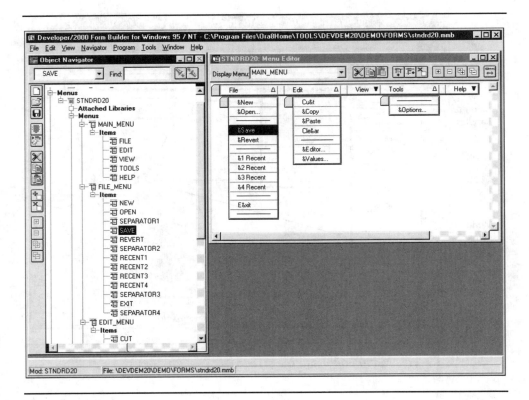

FIGURE 19-2. *Menu item selection coordination*

upward; the items would no longer be visible. Conversely, the View and Help menus are closed, reflected not only by the lack of menu items beneath them, but also by the small, solid, downward-pointing arrow to the right of their names. Clicking on that arrow would cause the menu to expand, exposing its items.

To the left of each menu's top-left corner is a small gray tab. This is the *menu handle*, which allows you to drag the entire menu from place to place.

Exercise

What actions can the main menu object perform?

Creating, Saving, and Attaching Menu Modules

To create a menu, you start by adding a new menu module to Form Builder. To do this, click on the Form Builder Menus node, followed by the Create button. Change the menu's name to **SOUND_MENU**. Then, double-click on your new menu module to open a Menu Editor for it. The editor will open with a single menu item whose name is MENU1 and whose label says <New_Item>. Change the label to **Action** and then click on the Create Right button to create an additional menu item to the right. Here is what the Create Right button looks like:

Label the new item **Edit**. Use the same technique to create three more menu items named **Record**, **Field**, and **Help**. Then return to the Object Navigator, and change the MENU1 menu's name to **MAIN_MENU**. You now have a main menu. To create individual menus beneath the File, Edit, and Help items, return to the Menu Editor and click on the Action menu item. Then, click on the Create Down button, shown here:

This will create a new individual menu whose name will show in the Object Navigator as ACTION_MENU. Change the label of the first item in this menu so that it reads **&Save** (the **&** in front of a character indicates that the character will give one-key access to that menu choice). Click on the Create Down button again, and label the new item **SEPARATOR1**. Add a third item, and label it **E&xit**. Continue this process until your menu structure looks like the one shown in Figure 19-3.

To make the menu items labeled SEPARATOR look like standard separator lines, select them all (using CTRL-clicking), open the Property Palette, and change their Menu Item Type property to Separator. If you want to change the order of items in the menus, you can either drag the items in the Menu Editor and let them go at their new position or perform the same type of drag-and-drop within the Object Navigator. Item order in the Menu Editor and the Object Navigator is inseparably linked.

Now that you have created the menu structure, you need to write the PL/SQL code that each menu item will execute. To do this, select your own menu's Action | Save item and open its Property Palette. Ensure that its Menu Item Type property is set to Plain, and that its Command Type

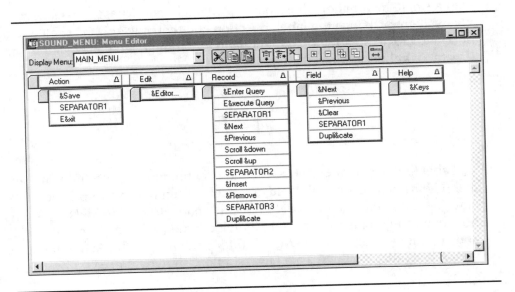

FIGURE 19-3. *Custom menu*

property is set to **PL/SQL**. Then click on the Menu Item Code property's value area, and a More... button will appear. Click on that button, and the PL/SQL Editor will open. Enter the following code:

```
do_key('commit_form');
```

You can stay in the PL/SQL Editor and enter code for every other menu item. Above the PL/SQL Editor's code-entry area, there is a field labeled Name that gives you access to the other menu items in the current menu. To change menus, utilize the field labeled Object. Use these now to enter the code shown in Table 19-1.

Menu Item	PL/SQL Code
Action	Save	`do_key('commit_form');`
Action	Exit	`do_key('exit_form');`
Edit	Editor	`do_key('edit');`
Record	Enter Query	`do_key('enter_query');`
Record	Execute Query	`do_key('execute_query');`
Record	Next	`do_key('down');`
Record	Previous	`do_key('up');`
Record	Scroll up	`do_key('scroll_up');`
Record	Scroll down	`do_key('scroll_down');`
Record	Insert	`do_key('create_record');`
Record	Remove	`do_key('delete_record');`
Record	Duplicate	`do_key('duplicate_record');`
Field	Next	`do_key('next_item');`
Field	Previous	`do_key('previous_item');`
Field	Clear	`do_key('clear_item');`
Field |Duplicate	`do_key('duplicate_item');`
Help	Keys	`Do_key('show_keys');`

TABLE 19-1. *PL/SQL Code for SOUND_MENU Menu*

You now have a complete, working menu. However, your SOUND_MODULE form module does not yet know about this menu. To attach this menu to the form module, save the menu module now. Then, select its SOUND_MENU menu module object in the Object Navigator and compile it by executing the File | Administration | Compile File command. This will create a sound_menu.mmx file on your disk; it is this file that you will attach to your form. To do this, select the SOUND_MODULE form module in the Object Navigator, open its Property Palette, and change its Menu Module property from DEFAULT&SMARTBAR to sound_menu. (If you stored the menu module somewhere other than Developer's default path, you will need to enter the entire file path, along with the filename.) Then, run your form. In the Forms Runtime program, execute your own menu's Record | Execute menu command to populate the form with data, and then experiment with your other menu items. When you are done, exit from the Forms Runtime program and return to Form Builder.

Now that you have seen how to create a menu, you will find it useful to look at the code underlying the default menu used by the Forms Runtime program. The source file for this menu is stored in the **<oracle_home>\ tools\devdem20\demo\forms** directory in a file named **menudef.mmb**. This **.mmb** file can be customized or can serve as a basis for a new menu module.

Exercises

1. Define the major steps necessary to create a menu module and attach it to a form.

2. What is the purpose of the Menu Editor?

3. Name two techniques for changing the order of items in a menu.

4. What is the most important difference in functionality between a menu and a menu item?

5. What file contains the default menu used by the Forms Runtime program?

Setting Menu Properties Using the Property Palette

There are numerous menu item properties that are valuable to know about. Table 19-2 shows these properties, their locations in the Property Palette, and what they do. Some of these properties will only be used when a menu item is created, while others are candidates for real-time manipulation using built-ins, which will be covered in a future section.

Property Node	Property Name	Function
Functional	Enabled	Controls whether item is available or grayed out
Functional	Menu Item Type	**Plain** Standard menu text item **Check** Boolean menu item the user checks on or off **Radio** Boolean item that is one choice within a larger radio menu group of mutually exclusive choices **Separator** Visual separating line **Magic** Item that implements predefined properties for Cut, Copy, Paste, Clear, Undo, Quit, Help, About, and Window. Predefined functionality includes item style, position, accelerator, and in the case of Cut, Copy, Paste, Clear, Quit, and Windows, functionality as well (other commands require developer to code PL/SQL commands)
Functional	Visible In Menu	Determines whether menu item appears at all at runtime
Functional	Visible In Horizontal Menu Bar	Allows you to customize which menu items appear based on whether the menu is display horizontally (the default)

TABLE 19-2.   *Menu Item Properties*

Property Node	Property Name	Function
Functional	Visible In Vertical Menu Bar	Allows you to customize which menu items appear based on whether the menu is displayed vertically
Menu Security	Item Roles	Allows you to implement menu security based on database roles; this will be covered in a future section
Menu Security	Display Without Privilege	Determines whether menu item appears for users who do not have the privileges necessary to access it

TABLE 19-2. *Menu Item Properties (continued)*

Exercises

1. Which menu item property could you manipulate at run time to gray out an item?

2. What type of menu item is best for implementing common functions such as Cut, Paste, and Quit?

Creating Menu Toolbars

The items you create in menus can also be represented in custom toolbars very easily. All you need to do is enable the Visible In Horizontal Menu Toolbar or Visible In Vertical Menu Toolbar property in the menu item's Property Palette, and specify an icon to depict the item's functionality in the toolbar. To see a quick example of this in action, open your SOUND_MENU menu in the Menu Editor, select your Action | Save menu item, and open its Property Palette. Change its Visible In Horizontal Menu Toolbar property to Yes, and its Icon Filename property to **rt_save**. Change the same properties for the Action | Exit menu item, using **rt_exit** as its Icon Filename property. Then, select the Record | Enter Query menu item and instruct it to become part of a *vertical* toolbar by setting its Visible In Vertical Menu Toolbar property to Yes, and its Icon Filename property to **rt_quer1**. Do the same for the Record | Execute Query menu item, using **rt_quer2** as its Icon Filename property. Then save your menu module, compile it, and run the SOUND_MODULE application. Your screen should look similar to Figure 19-4. The buttons appear in the toolbar in the same order their commands appear in the menu, so the only way to change the order of toolbar buttons is to change the order of the corresponding commands in the menu.

TIP
The icon files you just used are stored on disk in .ico files, just like those you used earlier in the book. The icons designed for runtime use start with rt_.

Exercises

1. What steps must you take to make a menu item in a custom menu appear in a toolbar?

2. How can you change the order of buttons in a menu toolbar?

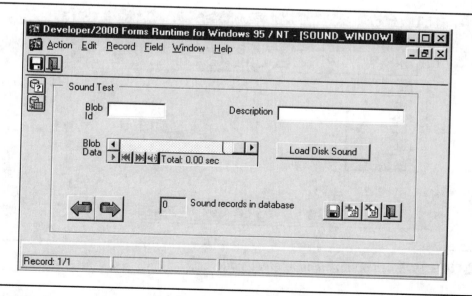

FIGURE 19-4. *Horizontal and vertical toolbars based on custom menu*

Creating Pop-Up Menus

Pop-up menus are context-sensitive "minimenus" that appear when you right-click on an object. They are intended to include only items relevant to the object they are attached to, so a robust application may have numerous pop-up menus, each of which is attached to many objects of the same type. Unlike the menu modules you just learned about, pop-up menus do not have module files of their own; they are owned by form modules. Look in the Object Navigator now, and you will see that one of the nodes beneath your form module is Popup Menus.

To experiment with making your own pop-up menus, open the SOUND_MODULE form module in the Object Navigator (if it is not already open) and double-click on its Popup Menus node to create a new pop-up menu. Change the new pop-up menu's name to **POPUP_TEXT**. Then, double-click on the pop-up menu item to open it in the Menu Editor. Use the techniques you learned in the previous section to create a menu like the one shown in Figure 19-5. Set the menu items' properties so they match the

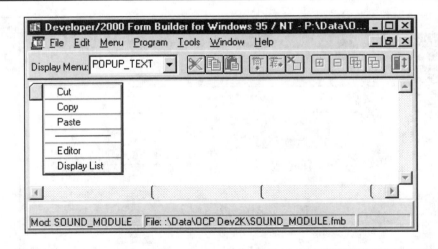

FIGURE 19-5. *Pop-up menu in Menu Editor*

properties shown in Table 19-3. Once that is done, you must attach the pop-up menu to the item(s) for which it will display. Pop-up menus can be attached to individual items in a data block, or to entire canvases; the latter option is useful if you want the user to be able to click on an application's background and get a pop-up menu. For this example, you will attach the pop-up menu to data block items. Open the AV_DATA_SOUND data block in the Object Navigator, select its DESCRIPTION item, and change its Popup Menu property to **POPUP_TEXT**. Then run your form, populate it, and right-click on the Description field. You should see your pop-up menu appear. Experiment with its functionality, and when you are done, exit from the Forms Runtime program and return to Form Builder.

Exercises

1. To what level in an application does a pop-up menu belong?

2. How many pop-up menus would you need to create to provide identical right-click functionality for 12 text items on four different canvases?

Menu Item	Menu Item Type	Magic Item	Menu Item Code
Cut	Magic	Cut	N/A
Copy	Magic	Copy	N/A
Paste	Magic	Paste	N/A
Editor	Plain	None	Edit_field;
Display List	Plain	None	Do_key('list_values');

TABLE 19-3. *Pop-Up Menu Item Properties*

Managing Menu Modules

In this section, you will cover the following points about managing menu modules:

- Controlling the menu programmatically
- Customizing menu modules with substitution parameters
- Implementing menu security

Once you have created a menu, you may find that you need to control its properties dynamically. You can use Form Builder features to modify menu properties when the menu loads, or dynamically while your application is running. You can also control access to specific menu items, ensuring that users are only able to execute commands appropriate for their work.

Controlling the Menu Programmatically

Form Builder offers a variety of built-ins you can use in your PL/SQL code to control menus programmatically. Table 19-4 lists these built-ins and provides a description of each one.

NOTE
Form Builder offers quite a few other menu built-ins that are included only for compatibility with older versions of the program. These include BACKGROUND_MENU, MAIN_MENU, MENU_CLEAR_FIELD, MENU_NEXT_FIELD, MENU_PARAMETER, MENU_PREVIOUS_FIELD, NEXT_MENU_ITEM, PREVIOUS_MENU, PREVIOUS_MENU_ITEM, SHOW_BACKGROUND_MENU, TERMINATE, and WHERE_DISPLAY. These built-ins will not be supported in the next major Form Builder release, so you should not use them. There are also built-ins that apply only to character-mode or block-mode environments: HIDE_MENU, MENU_REDISPLAY, SET_INPUT_FOCUS, and

Built-In Name	Description
APPLICATION_PARAMETER	Displays the current menu's parameters in the Enter Parameter Values dialog box
FIND_MENU_ITEM	Returns the internal ID of a specified menu item
GET_MENU_ITEM_PROPERTY	Identifies whether a specified menu item is checked, enabled, or visible; can also return the menu item's label
ITEM_ENABLED	Identifies whether a specified menu item is enabled; equivalent to GET_MENU_ITEM_PROPERTY (*menu_item*, ENABLED)
MENU_SHOW_KEYS	Displays runtime Keys screen for a menu module
QUERY_PARAMETER	Displays a Query Parameter dialog box containing current substitution parameters
REPLACE_MENU	Replaces current menu for all windows in an application with specified menu
SET_MENU_ITEM_PROPERTY	Modifies a menu item's checked, enabled, or visible properties; can also set the menu item's label

TABLE 19-4.   *Menu Built-Ins*

SHOW_MENU. If you are designing an application for a GUI environment, these built-ins will not be useful to you.

Exercises

1. Which menu built-in would let you gray out a menu item programmatically?

2. Which menu built-in could you use to determine if a menu item was checked by the user?

3. Which menu built-in allows you to keep specific menu items from showing at all?

Customizing Menu Modules with Substitution Parameters

Form Builder has a feature allowing you to specify code that it will run when a menu module is loaded at run time. It operates like an ON-NEW-MENU-INSTANCE trigger would, if such a trigger existed. This startup code is useful for initializing *substitution parameters*, which are variables that your menu items' command statements can reference. The menu startup code is also useful for initializing global variables, setting menu items' initial display states, and setting the initial status of check and radio menu items. This is a menu-level property, and can be entered by selecting the menu module in the Object Navigator and double-clicking on the Startup Code property. You can also create your own substitution parameters, if you wish. A full treatment of the use of substitution parameters in menu startup code is beyond the scope of this book, so this section will serve as an introduction you can follow up with on your own if you wish.

Form Builder comes with six built-in substitution parameters, which are shown in Table 19-5. All substitution parameter names are two characters long.

Substitution Parameter Name	Data Returned
AD	Directory storing current menu's runtime file
LN	Current language preference
PW	Password for current user
SO	Menu item currently selected (stands for Selected Option)
TT	Terminal type
UN	Name of current user

TABLE 19-5. *Form Builder Built-In Substitution Parameters*

Exercises

1. What is menu startup code? What are the advantages of using it?

2. What are substitution parameters?

3. What datatype and length are substitution parameter names?

Implementing Menu Security

Any form you build will automatically be limited by whatever security is in place on your Oracle server. In addition, you can also implement your own security in the client application so that certain menu items are grayed out or do not appear at all. This menu security is based on database roles—the group-rights feature built into Oracle server. Once you have roles active in your database, you can identify which roles may use which menu items.

NOTE
*If you are not familiar with database roles, refer to the Oracle documentation on the **create role** and **grant role** commands before continuing with this chapter.*

Menu security is implemented entirely within the menu module. There are three steps to implement menu security:

1. Enable the security function in the menu module as a whole.

2. Identify the database roles that have access to the entire menu module.

3. Identify which roles have access to each menu item.

For your convenience as a developer, there is a menu-module-wide property that determines whether menu security is implemented; this allows you to disable menu security temporarily for development purposes without having to alter your menu settings on an item-by-item basis. Turning this property on is the first step toward implementing menu security. To see this in action, open your SOUND_MENU menu module in Form Builder. Select the menu module in the Object Navigator and open its Property Palette. Locate the Use Security property under the Menu Security node and set the property to Yes. If you try to run your SOUND_MODULE form now, the form will load, but the menu attached to it will not.

Next, you need to tell the menu module which database roles will be candidates to access its items. To do this, double-click on the Module Roles property. You will be presented with a dialog box in which you will enter the names of the database roles that should be able to access the menu. Surprisingly, Form Builder does not have the ability to query the database and present you with a list of roles to choose from; you have to type the role names manually. Enter the **DBA** role now, as well as any other roles you want to add; for instance, clerk, manager, and administrator are common role types. Then click on the OK button to continue.

The last step is identifying which roles may access each menu item. You can do this in either the Object Navigator or the Menu Editor. Whichever method you choose, you can use traditional multiple-selection techniques to set the access roles for multiple menu items simultaneously. To do this from the Object Navigator, open the Menus node, followed by the MAIN_MENU node, and then the Items subnode beneath it. Select all five of the top-level menu items, and then in the Property Palette double-click on the Item Roles property. You will be presented with the list of role names you established earlier in the menu-level Module Roles property. Select one or more roles to access this menu item and then click on the OK button to continue. Repeat this process for the items within the individual menus, and be sure that at least one menu item is *not* set to give you access, so you have proof at run time that menu security as a whole is working. When you are done, save your menu module, compile it, and then run your SOUND_MODULE form. When you are done, exit from the Forms Runtime program and return to Form Builder.

Controlling Menu Security Programmatically

There are two built-ins that are especially useful for implementing menu security. The first is REPLACE_MENU, which changes what menu is displayed. The second is SET_MENU_ITEM_PROPERTY, which lets you control which menu items are enabled or visible in real time. For the SET_MENU_ITEM_PROPERTY built-in to work, you must set each item's Display Without Privilege property to Yes. While it may seem advantageous to have items not display when the user does not have the privileges to use them, if you do so you cannot control the items' properties programmatically, and therefore cannot make them visible again. Setting this property to Yes enables you to control an item's properties programmatically, including whether it is visible.

Exercises

1. What are the three steps to implementing menu security?

2. What property turns on the use of security throughout a menu, and at what level is the property set?

3. What built-in allows you to change what menu an application is displaying?

4. What built-in allows you to control what menu items are visible or enabled at run time?

Chapter Summary

In this chapter, you have covered a substantial amount of information about working with menu modules. The topics covered included creating menu modules, attaching them to form modules, and controlling the operation of menu modules when they run.

The first area you covered was identifying the components of menus and the Menu Editor. The menus you create start with a main menu, which contains one item for each of the individual menus. The individual menus consist of menu items, each of which performs a specific task such as Cut or Copy. The Menu Editor provides a graphical interface through which you can create and modify your menus. It displays a handle adjacent to the top-left corner of each menu; you can drag these handles to move menus from place to place. You can also move the menu items to different locations simply by dragging and dropping them. The menus and menu items are displayed both in the Menu Editor and in the Object Navigator; selecting an object in one selects it in the other at the same time. You can change the order of items from either place. You can add a separator to a menu by adding a menu item and setting its Item Type property to

Separator. You can also make individual menu items accessible with a letter of your choosing by preceding the letter with an ampersand character (**&**) in the menu item's Label property.

Once you have created the menu structure, you need to write the PL/SQL code that each menu item will execute. You do this through the menu item's Menu Item Code property, which opens a PL/SQL Editor. Finally, you compile the menu module and then attach it to a form module by setting the form module's Menu Module property to the name of the menu module.

You can see the source file for the default Forms Runtime menu by opening the **menudef.mmb** file in the **<oracle_home>\tools\devdem20\ demo\forms** directory.

There are numerous properties related to menu items that are valuable to know about. Some of these properties will only be used when a menu item is created, while others are candidates for real-time manipulation using built-ins. These properties include Enabled, which controls whether the menu item is available or grayed out; Menu Item Type, which specifies whether the menu item is a standard menu text item, check item, radio group, predefined magic function, or separator; Visible In Menu, which determines whether the menu item appears at all at run time; the property pair Visible In Horizontal Menu Bar and Visible In Vertical Menu Bar, which allow you to customize which menu items are visible depending on whether the menu is displayed horizontally (the default) or vertically; Item Roles, which allows you to implement menu security based on database roles; and Display Without Privilege, which determines whether a menu item is visible to users who do not have the privileges necessary to access it.

Next, you learned how to create toolbars whose buttons provide shortcuts to menu item functionality. These toolbars can be either horizontal or vertical. To create them, select the desired menu item and enable either the Visible In Horizontal Menu Toolbar or Visible In Vertical Menu Toolbar property in the Property Palette. (You can enable both, although there is rarely a reason to do so.) You must then specify an icon file to depict the item's functionality in the menu. Menu toolbars created in this way display buttons in the same order that the corresponding commands appear in the menu, so the only way to change the order of toolbar buttons is to change the order of commands in the menu. You can also create pop-up menus, which are context-sensitive "minimenus" that appear when you right-click on an object. You can also attach a single pop-up menu to many objects, on many canvases, within the form module that owns it.

After establishing the basic premises of creating menu modules, your attention turned to managing them. You can control menus programmatically using a variety of built-ins. These include APPLICATION_PARAMETER, which displays the current menu's parameters in the Enter Parameter Values dialog box; FIND_MENU_ITEM, which returns the internal ID of a specified menu item; GET_MENU_ITEM_PROPERTY, which identifies whether a specified menu item is checked, enabled, or visible, and can also return the menu item's label. Additional built-ins for controlling menus programmatically include ITEM_ENABLED, which identifies whether a specified menu item is enabled; MENU_SHOW_KEYS, which displays a runtime Keys screen for a menu module; QUERY_PARAMETER, which displays a Query Parameter dialog box containing current substitution parameters; REPLACE_MENU, which replaces the current menu for all windows in an application with a specified menu; and SET_MENU_ITEM_PROPERTY, which modifies a menu item's checked, enabled, or visible properties, and can also set the menu item's label.

The next topic you covered was customizing menu modules with substitution parameters. Form Builder's menu-level Startup Code property allows you to specify code that will be run when a menu module is loaded at run time. This startup code is useful for initializing substitution parameters, which are variables that your menu items' command statements can reference. The menu startup code is also useful for initializing global variables, setting menu items' initial display states, and setting the initial status of check and radio menu items. Form Builder comes with six built-in substitution parameters: AD, which returns the directory storing the current menu's runtime file; LN, which returns the current language preference; PW, which returns the password for the current user; SO, which returns the menu item currently selected; TT, which returns the terminal type; and UN, which returns the name of current user. You can also create your own substitution parameters.

The last topic covered was implementing menu security, which allows you to make specific menu items unavailable or keep them from displaying at all based on the database role assigned to the user. Menu security is implemented entirely within the menu module. There are three steps to implement menu security: enable the security function in the menu module as a whole, identify the database roles that have access to the menu module, and then identify which roles may access each menu item. You enable menu security using a menu module's Use Security property. Next, you identify which database roles will be candidates to access menu items by typing the role names into a list in the menu module's Module Roles property. Finally, you assign those roles to menu items using the item-level property Item Roles.

There are two built-ins enabling you to control menu security programmatically. REPLACE_MENU allows you to change which menu is displayed, as well as the role the menu is to use. SET_MENU_ITEM_PROPERTY lets you control which menu items are enabled or visible in real time. For SET_MENU_ITEM_PROPERTY to work, you must set each item's Display Without Privilege property to Yes; this enables you to control item properties programmatically.

All in all, this chapter comprises about 13 percent of the material tested on OCP Exam 4.

Two-Minute Drill

- A main menu object holds other menus, which themselves hold menu items that can perform actions. The menu items do the work; the menus are only organizers and cannot perform any actions on their own.

- The most important difference in functionality between a menu and a menu item is that a menu's only function is to organize items within it, while a menu item has the ability to initiate actions by executing PL/SQL code.

- The major steps necessary to create a menu module and attach it to a form (assuming you already have a form module) are creating the menu module, populating it with menu objects and menu items, placing PL/SQL code behind the menu items to define the tasks each item performs, saving and compiling the menu module, and setting the form module's Menu Module property to point to the compiled menu module **.mmx** file.

- The Menu Editor provides you with a graphical area in which to visualize, design, and create your menus.

- To change the order of the items in the menus, you can either drag the items in the Menu Editor and let them go at their new position or perform the same type of drag-and-drop within the Object Navigator. Item order is inseparably linked between the Menu Editor and the Object Navigator.

- The file containing the default menu used by the Forms Runtime program is named **menudef.mmb**. It is located in the directory **<oracle_home>\tools\devdem20\demo\forms**.

- The menu item property that controls whether a menu item is available or grayed out is Enabled.

- The Magic menu item type provides predefined properties for Cut, Copy, Paste, Clear, Undo, Quit, Help, About, and Window menu items. These predefined properties include Font Size, Font Style, and Keyboard Accelerator. Additionally, the actual functionality is predefined for the Cut, Copy, Paste, Clear, Quit, and Windows menu items.

- To make a menu item in a custom menu appear in a toolbar, set its Visible In Horizontal Menu Toolbar or Visible In Vertical Menu Toolbar property to Yes, and provide the name of the icon file to display on the toolbar button for that menu item.

- The only way to change the order of buttons in a menu toolbar is to change the order of the corresponding items in the underlying menu.

- Unlike menu modules, pop-up menus do not have module files of their own; they are owned by form modules. They reside in the Object Navigator in a form module's Popup Menus node.

- Pop-up menus can be attached to individual items or to canvases.

- A pop-up menu can be attached to an unlimited number of items in a form module. A single item can only have one pop-up menu.

- You can gray out menu items programmatically using the SET_MENU_ITEM_PROPERTY built-in with the ENABLED parameter.

- You can determine if a menu item was checked by the user by employing the GET_MENU_ITEM_PROPERTY built-in with the CHECKED parameter.

- You can keep specific menu items from showing at all using the SET_MENU_ITEM_PROPERTY built-in and its VISIBLE parameter.

- The SET_MENU_ITEM_PROPERTY built-in also allows you to control what menu items are visible or enabled at run time.

- Menu startup code is useful for initializing substitution parameters, global variables, menu item display states, and check and radio menu item selection status.

- Substitution parameters are variables that your menu item command statements can reference. The built-in substitution parameters provided with Form Builder return the user's name and password, current menu item, current menu file directory, terminal type, and language preference.

- Form Builder's built-in substitution parameters are AD, which returns the directory storing the current menu's runtime file; LN, which returns the current language preference; PW, which returns the password for current user; SO, which returns the currently selected menu item; TT, which returns the terminal type; and UN, which returns the name of current user.

- The three steps to implementing menu security are enabling the menu module's Use Security property, specifying in the menu module's Module Roles property the role names that may access the menu, and identifying what menu items each role can access by setting each menu item's Item Roles property.

- The Use Security property provides quick access to whether a menu is controlled by database roles, and is set at the menu module level.

- If your application has more than one menu, you can change which menu is displayed by employing the REPLACE_MENU built-in.

Chapter Questions

1. **What actions can a main menu object perform?**

   A. All File, Edit, and Help operations

   B. By default, only File | Exit

C. All File and Help operations

D. None of the above

2. **You have created a form module and a custom menu, and now would like to have the menu initialize certain parameters and variables when it starts. What feature will you use to accomplish this?**

   A. SET_MENU_PROPERTY

   B. SET_MENU_ITEM_PROPERTY

   C. WHEN-NEW-MENU-INSTANCE

   D. Menu startup code

3. **You are working in the Menu Editor and would like the order of items to be different from the order shown in the Object Navigator. How can you accomplish this?**

   A. Drag items in the Menu Editor to put them in your preferred order.

   B. Drag objects in the Object Navigator to put them in your preferred order.

   C. Using CTRL-clicking to select the object simultaneously in the Object Navigator and the Menu Editor, set the Property Palette to intersection display mode, and set the Item Order property for each one.

   D. It is not possible for the order of items in the Menu Editor to be different from the order shown in the Object Navigator.

4. **You have created a menu toolbar, but its buttons are not in the order you wish. How can you change the order of the menu toolbar buttons?**

   A. Rearrange the order of the items in the menu from which the toolbar is derived.

   B. Open the menu canvas in the Layout Editor and drag the buttons to your preferred positions.

   C. Using CTRL-clicking to select the toolbar objects simultaneously in the Object Navigator and the Menu Editor, set the Property Palette to intersection display mode, and set the Item Order property for each one.

D. It is not possible to change the order of buttons in a menu toolbar.

5. **You have created a main menu object in the Menu Editor. What do you need to do to add functionality to it that the user can utilize?**

   A. Open the PL/SQL Editor and add the appropriate code for the functionality you want to provide

   B. Create an Object Library containing the functionality you want to provide, and attach it to the menu module

   C. Create a PL/SQL Library containing the functionality you want to provide, and attach it to the menu module

   D. Add items to the menu, and use the PL/SQL Editor to add the appropriate code for the functionality you want to provide

6. **You have instituted menu security based on database roles. What is the best way to turn the menu security off temporarily during development without having to modify the security property of every menu item?**

   A. Set the form module's Use Roles property to False

   B. Set the menu module's Use Roles property to False

   C. Remove the values from the form's Module Roles property list

   D. Set the form module's Use Security property to False

   E. Set the menu module's Use Security property to False

   F. Remove the values from the menu's Module Roles property list

7. **Users have asked you to add pop-up menus to your HR application. Under which node in the Object Navigator will you create the pop-up menus?**

   A. Forms

   B. Menus

   C. PL/SQL Libraries

   D. Object Libraries

   E. Built-In Packages

F. Database Objects

8. **Which menu item property controls whether the user can execute an item they see in a menu?**

   A. AVAILABLE

   B. VISIBLE

   C. ENABLED

   D. CHECK

9. **How can you look at the structure of the Forms Runtime program's default runtime menu? (Choose as many as apply)**

   A. Open the **defmenu.mmb** file in Form Builder.

   B. Open the **def_menu.mmx** file in Form Builder.

   C. Decompile the **def_menu.mmx** file.

   D. Open the **menudef.mmb** file in Form Builder.

   E. Open the **menu_def.mmb** file in Form Builder.

   F. You cannot see the structure of the default menu.

10. **You want to add several items to a menu in the fastest way possible. One of the menu items will be an on/off choice; three others will be in a mutually exclusive group; and there are two others. None of the items will provide predefined functionality such as Cut or Copy. What menu item types will you use? (Choose all that apply)**

    A. Plain

    B. Check

    C. Radio

    D. Separator

    E. Magic

11. **What menu item type provides predefined functionality such as Cut and Paste?**

    A. Plain

    B. Check

    C. Substitution Parameter

    D. Enabled

    E. Separator

    F. Magic

12. Your SALES application is going out to two different groups of users: salespeople on the road with Windows laptops, and administrators in the central office on UNIX computers. The groups are assigned different database roles, and you have created a different menu for each group. What built-in is the best choice for displaying the correct menu for each group?

    A. MAIN_MENU

    B. WHERE_DISPLAY

    C. SHOW_MENU

    D. REPLACE_MENU

    E. SET_MENU_ITEM_PROPERTY

13. Which of the following is *not* a Form Builder built-in substitution parameter? (Choose as many as apply)

    A. AD

    B. Add

    C. LN

    D. MM

    E. PW

    F. SO

    G. TT

    H. UID

    I. UN

Answers to Chapter Questions

1. D. None of the above

Explanation A main menu object holds other menus, which themselves hold menu items that can perform actions. The main menu object is an organizer. It cannot perform any actions on its own.

2. D. Menu startup code

Explanation See the section titled "Customizing Menu Modules with Substitution Parameters" for a refresher on this topic.

3. D. It is not possible for the order of items in the Menu Editor to be different from the order shown in the Object Navigator.

Explanation See the section titled "Creating, Saving, and Attaching Menu Modules" for a refresher on this topic.

4. A. Rearrange the order of the items in the menu from which the toolbar is derived.

Explanation Menu toolbars always maintain the item order of the toolbar that generates them.

5. D. Add items to the menu, and use the PL/SQL Editor to add the appropriate code for the functionality you want to provide.

Explanation A menu has no means of providing functionality to the user directly, so you must add items to it before you can do anything else.

6. E. Set the menu module's Use Security property to False

Explanation The Use Security property is a menu-level property.

7. A. Forms

Explanation Pop-up menus are attached at the Forms level.

8. C. ENABLED

Explanation See the section titled "Setting Menu Properties Using the Property Palette" for a refresher on this topic.

9. D. Open the **menudef.mmb** file in Form Builder

Explanation See the section titled "Creating, Saving, and Attaching Menu Modules" for a refresher on this topic.

10. A, B, C. Plain, Check, Radio

Explanation The on/off menu item calls for a Check item type. The three menu items in a group will be Radio item types. The two remaining menu items will be Plain items, since they are not implementing predefined functionality—the realm of the Magic item type. Award yourself an extra half-point if you included Separator items for visual clarity—but don't expect any extra on the exam for it!

11. F. Magic

Explanation See the section titled "Setting Menu Properties Using the Property Palette" for a refresher on this topic.

12. D. REPLACE_MENU

Explanation MAIN_MENU and WHERE_DISPLAY are present in Form Builder only for compatibility with earlier versions, and will not be supported in future versions, so they should not be used. SHOW_MENU is for use only in character- or block-mode environments, so it is not appropriate for the graphical environments specified. SET_MENU_ITEM_PROPERTY allows you to control individual menu items, not entire menus. That leaves REPLACE_MENU, which fortunately fulfills the specified requirements.

13. B, D, H. Add, MM, UID

Explanation The built-in substitution parameters all have two-character names, which eliminates Add and UID. Of the remaining choices, "MM" is not a valid Form Builder built-in substitution parameter, but all the other acronyms offered are.

CHAPTER
20

Advanced Forms
Programming I

n this chapter, you will explore the following areas:

- Programming function keys
- Responding to mouse events
- Controlling windows and canvases programmatically
- Controlling data block relationships

This chapter, and the two that follow it, introduce you to the world of advanced Form Builder programming. This chapter begins by explaining how you can reprogram your application's response to function keys pressed by the user. It then explores mouse events, showing how you can create triggers to respond to any mouse action the user performs. Next, you will see how to control windows, and the canvases they display, programmatically. Finally, you will learn about the triggers, program units, and system variables that work together to control data block relationships. The OCP Exam 4 contains a large number of questions in these subject areas—32 percent of the final score—so you will want to pay special attention to this chapter, studying it thoroughly until you know the answers to every one of its exercises and chapter questions. Of course, you have studied every chapter before this just as thoroughly, right?

Programming Function Keys

In this section, you will cover the following points related to programming function keys:

- Redefining function keys
- Determining when KEY_ triggers should be used

Most applications currently being written are menu driven, but that doesn't mean the client computer's function keys should be ignored. The Forms Runtime program already has predefined functionality for many of the function keys; you can reprogram that functionality so the keys perform functions related to your application—or so they do nothing at all. A complete treatment of this topic is beyond the scope of this book, so this introduction provides the key concepts on what function-key triggers do and when to use them.

Redefining Function Keys

You can easily assign items in custom menus to function keys, as well as create entirely new functionality using KEY-Fn triggers. Form Builder provides 10 of these function-key triggers, numbered KEY-F0 through KEY-F9. It also provides a KEY-OTHERS trigger that automatically applies to every key that can have a key trigger associated with it but does not. The KEY-OTHERS trigger is useful for disabling function keys that are not germane to your application. When you use any of these techniques to assign functionality to function keys, the default functionality of the keys is overridden.

The default function key assignments are shown in Table 20-1. The triggers available for each of these assignments are shown in Table 20-2.

Exercises

1. What happens to a function key's default functionality when you assign a KEY-Fn trigger to it?

2. What happens to a function key's default functionality when you assign a KEY-OTHERS trigger to the form?

	F1	F2	F3	F4	F5	F6	F7	F8	F9	F10
Shift-	Display Error	Count Matching Records	Next Primary Key	Clear Record	Clear Block	Delete Record	Clear Form	Print		
Control-	Show Keys									
Normal	Help		Duplicate Field/Item	Duplicate Record	Block Menu	New Record	Enter Query	Execute Query	List of Values	Accept

TABLE 20-1. *Forms Runtime Default Function Key Assignments*

Function Key	Associated Key Trigger
[Accept]	Key-COMMIT
[Block Menu]	Key-MENU
[Clear Block]	Key-CLRBLK
[Clear Form]	Key-CLRFRM
[Clear Record]	Key-CLRREC
[Count Query Hits]	Key-CQUERY
[Delete Record]	Key-DELREC
[Down]	Key-DOWN
[Duplicate Item]	Key-DUP-ITEM
[Duplicate Record]	Key-DUPREC
[Edit]	Key-EDIT
[Enter Query]	Key-ENTQRY
[Execute Query]	Key-EXEQRY
[Exit]	Key-EXIT
[Help]	Key-HELP
[Insert Record]	Key-CREREC
[List of Values]	Key-LISTVAL
[Next Block]	Key-NXTBLK
[Next Item]	Key-NXT-ITEM
[Next Primary Key]	Key-NXTKEY
[Next Record]	Key-NXTREC
[Next Set of Records]	Key-NXTSET
[Previous Block]	Key-PRVBLK
[Previous Item]	Key-PRV-ITEM

TABLE 20-2. *Forms Runtime Function Keys and Corresponding Triggers*

Function Key	Associated Key Trigger
[Previous Record]	Key-PRVREC
[Print]	Key-PRINT
[Scroll Down]	Key-SCRDOWN
[Scroll Up]	Key-SCRUP
[Up]	Key-UP

TABLE 20-2.   *Forms Runtime Function Keys and Corresponding Triggers* (continued)

Determining When Key Triggers Should Be Used

There are certain tasks for which key triggers are especially useful, and also certain situations in which they cannot be used. Key triggers are a good choice when you need to enable and disable function keys dynamically, disable a function key's default behavior, or have a single keystroke perform multiple actions. Disabling default behavior and performing multiple actions are two of the more interesting capabilities, because they cannot be duplicated by a menu command like most function key actions can. Regarding their limitations, the KEY-Fn triggers are ignored in Edit mode, and the KEY-OTHERS trigger is ignored while the user is responding to a Forms Runtime prompt or viewing a list of values, the help or Keys screen, or an error screen. Also, certain function keys cannot be redefined, because they are often executed by the Forms Runtime program's user-interface management system or the Oracle terminal, rather than by Form Builder. Table 20-3 lists these *static function keys*.

Exercise

What are two features of KEY- triggers that cannot be attained using any existing menu command or toolbar button?

[Clear Item]	[First Line]	[Scroll Left]
[Copy]	[Insert Line]	[Scroll Right]
[Cut]	[Last Line]	[Search]
[Delete Character]	[Left]	[Select]
[Delete Line]	[Paste]	[Show Keys]
[Display Error]	[Refresh]	[Toggle Insert/Replace]
[End of Line]	[Right]	[Transmit]

TABLE 20-3.   *Static Function Keys*

Responding to Mouse Events

In this section, you will cover the following points about responding to mouse events:

- Introduction to mouse events
- Causing a form module to respond to mouse movement
- Causing a form module to respond to mouse button actions

Everything a user can do with a mouse in an application constitutes an event in Form Builder, and therefore can fire specific event triggers. In this section, you will be introduced to these triggers, learn what causes them to fire, and see how they can be used.

Introduction to Mouse Events

Form Builder comes with a variety of triggers that can fire in response to actions the user takes with the mouse. Table 20-4 lists the mouse triggers available and describes the action that causes each trigger to fire. To assist your programming efforts, Form Builder also provides a group of system variables appropriate for use in mouse triggers. These allow you to

Mouse Trigger	Is Fired When...
WHEN-MOUSE-DOWN	User presses down a mouse button within an item or canvas
WHEN-MOUSE-UP	User releases a mouse button within an item or canvas
WHEN-MOUSE-CLICK	User clicks mouse within an item or canvas
WHEN-MOUSE-DOUBLECLICK	User double-clicks mouse within an item or canvas
WHEN-MOUSE-ENTER	User moves mouse into an item or canvas
WHEN-MOUSE-LEAVE	User moves mouse out of an item or canvas
WHEN-MOUSE-MOVE	User moves mouse within an item or canvas

TABLE 20-4. *Mouse Event Triggers*

determine which mouse button the user pressed, and where the mouse pointer was when the button was pressed. Table 20-5 lists these mouse system variables and describes the data each one returns. When the Forms Runtime program executes the code in a mouse trigger, it initializes and populates any variables in the code just before running the code. Because of this, it is best to use mouse system variables only in mouse trigger code in order to ensure that the contents of the variables are up to date when a mouse trigger fires. You will see how to apply these triggers and system variables in the topics that follow.

Exercises

1. Which mouse event triggers fire when the user presses a mouse button and releases it?

2. Which mouse system variables are dedicated to identifying the mouse pointer's location?

3. Which mouse system variables tell you what mouse button the user pressed and whether the button was modified with SHIFT, CTRL, or ALT?

Mouse System Variable	Returns...
SYSTEM.MOUSE_BUTTON_PRESSED	Number representing the button the user pressed (1-2)
SYSTEM.MOUSE_BUTTON_MODIFIERS	Shift modifier held down while the mouse button was clicked
SYSTEM.MOUSE_CANVAS	Name of canvas mouse is currently in
SYSTEM.MOUSE_ITEM	Name of item mouse is currently in
SYSTEM.MOUSE_RECORD	Number of record mouse is currently in
SYSTEM.MOUSE_RECORD_OFFSET	Offset between first visible record and mouse record
SYSTEM.MOUSE_X_POS	Mouse's X-axis location on canvas or within item
SYSTEM.MOUSE_Y_POS	Mouse's Y-axis location on canvas or within item

TABLE 20-5. *Mouse System Variables*

Causing a Form Module to Respond to Mouse Movement

Three of the Form Builder mouse event triggers fire in response to mouse movement: WHEN-MOUSE-ENTER, WHEN-MOUSE-LEAVE, and WHEN-MOUSE-MOVE. All of these triggers can be defined at the form, block, or item level. When defined at the Form level, they are active in any canvas or item in the form. When defined at the block level, they are active in any item in the block. When defined at the item level, they are active only when the mouse enters, leaves, or moves within the item. These triggers fire only in response to mouse movement, so they will *not* fire if the user enters a canvas via menu commands. Similarly, pressing a mouse button will not fire any mouse-movement triggers, because pressing a mouse button does not constitute movement. There are other triggers to respond to mouse button presses, and they will be explored in the next topic.

Exercises

1. At what levels can mouse movement triggers be defined?

2. In what order are the mouse movement triggers likely to fire?

3. If a WHEN-MOUSE-ENTER trigger is defined at the Form level, will it fire when the user clicks on a field within a canvas? When they invoke a pop-up menu? When they open a normal menu?

Causing a Form Module to Respond to Mouse Button Actions

Four of the Form Builder mouse event triggers fire in response to mouse button presses: WHEN-MOUSE-DOWN, WHEN-MOUSE-UP, WHEN-MOUSE-CLICK, and WHEN-MOUSE-DOUBLECLICK. All of these triggers can be defined at the form, block, or item level. When used in conjunction with the SET_APPLICATION_PROPERTY built-in, the triggers enable you to change your application's cursor in real time. For instance, the following code in a WHEN-MOUSE-DOWN trigger would alter the mouse cursor depending on what mouse button the user has pressed:

```
DECLARE
  V_MOUSE_BUTTON_PRESSED varchar2(1);
BEGIN
  V_MOUSE_BUTTON_PRESSED := :system.mouse_button_pressed;
  if V_MOUSE_BUTTON_PRESSED = '1' then
    set_application_property(cursor_style, 'BUSY');
  else
    set_application_property(cursor_style, 'CROSSHAIR');
  end if;
END;
```

The action of the WHEN-MOUSE-DOWN trigger could be reversed by the following code in a WHEN-MOUSE-UP trigger:

```
set_application_property(cursor_style, 'DEFAULT');
```

Exercises

1. What triggers are available to respond to mouse button actions?

2. Which built-in allows you to change a cursor's display style?

Controlling Windows and Canvases Programmatically

In this section, you will cover the following points about controlling windows and canvases programmatically:

- Creating trigger code to interact with windows

- Controlling windows programmatically

- Controlling canvases

Almost by definition, a sophisticated application is likely to consist of multiple canvases and multiple windows. If your application has multiple canvases and multiple windows, you need to be able to control them programmatically. This section will get you started in the right direction, and will cover the topic to the degree necessary to answer the exam questions in this area.

Creating Trigger Code to Interact with Windows

Form Builder offers four different triggers that can fire in response to window-oriented events. The first window trigger, WHEN-WINDOW-ACTIVATED, fires when a window is opened, or when an open window receives focus. The second window trigger, WHEN-WINDOW-DEACTIVATED, fires when an open window loses focus. The third window trigger, WHEN-WINDOW-RESIZED, fires when a window's size is changed by the user or programmatically. The last window trigger, WHEN-WINDOW-CLOSED, fires when the user executes the window-close command intrinsic to their operating system.

Because windows themselves cannot have triggers, window-oriented triggers are defined at the next higher level in the object hierarchy: the Form level.

Exercises

1. What window-oriented triggers does Form Builder offer?

2. At what level in the object hierarchy do you establish window triggers?

3. What trigger can help you ensure that a window is always large enough to show its contents, even if the user changes its size?

Controlling Windows Programmatically

Form Builder provides quite a few built-ins enabling you to control your windows via PL/SQL code. These are shown in Table 20-6. Perhaps the most versatile of these is SET_WINDOW_PROPERTY, which allows you to set any of the properties you normally see in a window's Property Palette, such as window size, position, and title. There are also built-ins to manipulate a window's visual status: SHOW_WINDOW, HIDE_WINDOW, MOVE_WINDOW, and RESIZE_WINDOW.

Exercises

1. Which three window built-ins have the ability to set a window's position on the screen?

2. Which window built-in can you use to change a window's title dynamically at run time?

3. Which window built-in has the ability to speed up operation of the other window built-ins?

Controlling Canvases

Because Form Builder allows you to assign more than one content canvas to a window, you need some way to specify programmatically which content

Built-In Name	Description	Data Type Returned
FIND_WINDOW	Returns internal ID of named window	Window
GET_WINDOW_PROPERTY	Retrieves value of properties shown in window's Property Palette	VarChar2
HIDE_WINDOW	Hides named window	N/A
ID_NULL	Identifies whether an object created dynamically at run time (a window, in this case) exists	Boolean
MOVE_WINDOW	Moves named window to X/Y coordinates stated	N/A
RESIZE_WINDOW	Sets named window to width and height stated	N/A
SET_WINDOW_PROPERTY	Sets value of properties shown in window's Property Palette	N/A
SHOW_WINDOW	Displays named window; allows optional X/Y position specification	N/A

TABLE 20-6. *Window Built-Ins*

canvas a window should display. This task is accomplished using the REPLACE_CONTENT_VIEW built-in. Table 20-7 shows this and other built-ins useful for controlling canvases via PL/SQL code.

Exercises

1. What is the purpose of the REPLACE_CONTENT_VIEW built-in?

2. What built-in would you use to display a new canvas along with an existing canvas? To retrieve and set canvas properties?

Built-In Name	Description	Data Type Returned
REPLACE_CONTENT_VIEW	Display named content canvas, replacing prior canvas	N/A
SHOW_VIEW	Displays named canvas, does not replace prior canvas	N/A
GET_CANVAS_PROPERTY	Retrieves specified property for canvas named	VarChar2
SET_CANVAS_PROPERTY	Sets specified property for canvas named	N/A

TABLE 20-7. *Built-Ins for Controlling Canvases*

Controlling Data Block Relationships

In this section, you will cover the following points about controlling data block relationships:

- Definition of block coordination
- Creating and modifying relations
- Characteristics of relation-handling code
- Implementing a coordination-type toggle

This section introduces the Form Builder features related to coordinating master and detail data blocks in a master/detail relationship. You can use these techniques to work with non-Oracle databases, control when a detail block queries the database for records, and customize your application in other ways.

Definition of Block Coordination

As you probably know, creating a relationship between two blocks requires that the blocks share one or more columns in common. More specifically, the contents of the master block's primary-key column(s) must be referred to by one or more foreign-key columns in the detail block. When you define a master/detail relationship between such tables, Form Builder ensures that the detail block always displays records related to the current record in the master block, and that new detail records will automatically be assigned to the current master record. This is called *block coordination*, and it relies on triggers. Each time the user does something that causes the master record to change—moving up or down in the master data block, for example, or deleting the current master record—the Forms Runtime program considers it a *coordination-causing event*. Internally, it goes to the detail data block, flushes existing detail records, makes the next master record current, and then repopulates the detail block with a new query.

There are many facets of this process that you can control in order to customize your application's relation-handling capabilities, or to augment them with new features. These facets will be covered in upcoming topics.

Exercises

1. Describe block coordination.

2. What is a coordination-causing event?

Creating and Modifying Relations

A *relation* is a logical Form Builder object that defines how one master data block and one detail data block are related. The relation object is located under the master data block, in a node named Relations. You can create a relation in two ways: with the Data Block Wizard, or manually. Not surprisingly, using the Data Block Wizard is much less work. To see this approach, you will create a new form module and create a relation within it. Start now by creating a new form module and naming it **RELATIONSHIPS**. Then, use the Data Block Wizard to create a data block for the DEPARTMENT table. Include all the table's columns as database items. When given the option, elect to *Just create the data block*. Then, invoke the Data Block Wizard again to create a second data block, this time for the EMPLOYEE table. Include all the table's columns as database items. When presented with the Wizard's master/detail page, ensure that the *Auto-join data blocks* option is enabled and then click on the Create Relationship button. Identify the master data block for the relation by selecting the DEPARTMENT data block from the dialog box that appears, and then click the OK button. Open the Detail Item list and select DEPARTMENT_ID from the available items. Your Data Block Wizard screen should now look like Figure 20-1. Click on the Next button to continue. Elect to *Just create the data block* and click on the Finish button. Your screen should now look like Figure 20-2. Notice that in addition to the EMPLOYEE data block, Form Builder created a form-level ON-CLEAR-DETAILS trigger, two block-level ON- triggers under the master data block, a DEPARTMENT_EMPLOYEE relation under the master data block, and three form-level program units. These objects work together to perform block coordination.

To see the properties available for a relation, open the Property Palette for the DEPARTMENT_EMPLOYEE relation. Under the Functional node, you will see that the detail block is specified (there is no need to specify the master block, since this relation is owned by the master block), as well as

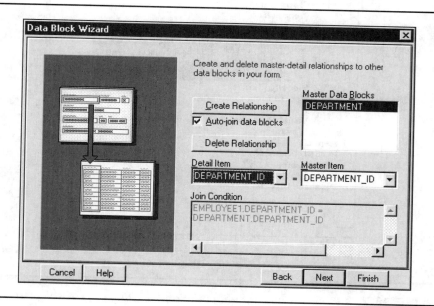

FIGURE 20-1. *Data Block Wizard master/detail page*

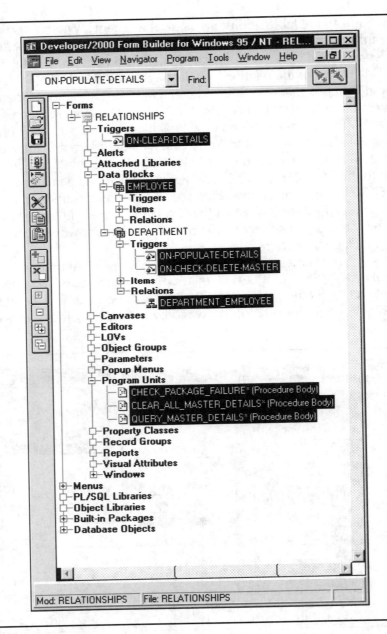

FIGURE 20-2. *Object Navigator with relation-handling objects selected*

the SQL join condition that synchronizes the blocks. Beneath that you will see the Delete Record Behavior property. This property controls how the Forms Runtime program responds when the user attempts to delete a master record that has related detail records. The first available setting for this property, Cascading, specifies that when a master record is deleted, any related detail records will also be deleted when the action is committed to the database. The second available setting, Isolated, allows master records to be deleted without deleting any related detail records—which could result in detail records with invalid values in their foreign-key columns pointing back to the master table. The third available setting, Non Isolated, causes the Forms Runtime program to refuse to delete a master record if it has related detail records. This is the default setting for this property. One fascinating facet of the Delete Record Behavior property is that changing it causes the master data block's triggers to be re-created. Setting the Delete Record Behavior property to Cascading causes Form Builder to generate PRE-DELETE and ON-POPULATE-DETAILS triggers immediately. Setting the property to Isolated causes the PRE-DELETE trigger to disappear, leaving only the ON-POPULATE-DETAILS trigger. Setting the property to Non Isolated causes the generation of an ON-CHECK-DELETE-MASTER trigger to accompany the ON-POPULATE-DETAILS trigger. The relationship between the settings for this property and the presence of data-block-level triggers is depicted in Table 20-8.

The next property, Prevent Masterless Operations, defines whether the user can insert detail records or query the detail data block when there is no current master record. The next two properties work together to specify when the detail block gets populated after a coordination-causing event. When the Deferred property is set to No, the detail block is repopulated immediately after any coordination-causing event in the master block. When

Property Setting	Triggers	
Cascading	ON-POPULATE-DETAILS	PRE-DELETE
Isolated	ON-POPULATE-DETAILS	
Non Isolated	ON-POPULATE-DETAILS	ON-CHECK-DELETE-MASTER

TABLE 20-8. *Triggers Generated by a Relation's Delete Record Behavior Property*

the Deferred property is set to Yes, the next property—Automatic Query—comes into play. When the Automatic Query property is set to Yes, the detail block will be repopulated as soon as the user navigates into the detail block. This allows the user to change master records often without being subject to potential delays from having the detail block repopulate each time. When the Automatic Query property is set to No, the user must navigate into the detail block *and* execute a query to populate the detail block.

Exercises

1. What are the three possible settings for a relation's Delete Record Behavior property, and what are the results of each setting?

2. What does a relation's Prevent Masterless Operations property do?

3. How many usable combinations of the Deferred and the Automatic Query properties can there be? What are the results of each combination? In what conditions would each be useful?

Characteristics of Relation-Handling Code

There may be times when you want to write your own block-coordination code: when you are using non-Oracle data sources, for instance, or when your application has especially long relation chains. There are three types of objects involved in relation handling: triggers, program units, and system variables.

Relation-Handling Triggers

Form Builder automatically generates up to three relation-handling triggers when you set a relation's Delete Record Behavior. There is always an ON-CLEAR-DETAILS trigger at the Form level, and an ON-POPULATE-DETAILS at the master block level. In addition, implementing cascading delete requires the use of a PRE-DELETE trigger; this trigger deletes related detail records; this must be accomplished *before* the master record is deleted, which is why a PRE-DELETE trigger is used. If the relation's Delete Record Behavior property is set to Non Isolated, an ON-CHECK-DELETE-MASTER trigger at the master block level is used to check whether detail records exist before a master record is deleted. Table 20-9 shows each of these triggers, what they do, where to use them, and what behavior they produce.

Trigger Name	Object Level	Purpose	Corresponding Setting of Relation's Delete Record Behavior Property
ON-CHECK-DELETE-MASTER	Master Block	Prohibits deletion of master record when detail records exist	Non Isolated
ON-CLEAR-DETAILS	Form	Clears records in a detail block	Cascading
			Isolated
			Non Isolated
ON-POPULATE-DETAILS	Master Block	Coordinates master and detail blocks	Cascading
			Isolated
			Non Isolated
PRE-DELETE	Master Block	Executes cascading deletes	Cascading

TABLE 20-9. *Relation-Handling Triggers*

Relation-Handling Program Units

The relation-handling triggers generated by Form Builder rely on the presence of three program units that are also created automatically when you define a relation. In your RELATIONSHIPS form module, you will find them in the form-level node named Program Units. The first program unit, CHECK_PACKAGE_FAILURE, is used by the other two program units to determine whether a PL/SQL statement completed successfully. The second program unit, CLEAR_ALL_MASTER_DETAILS, flushes detail records from the detail block when called by the ON-CLEAR-DETAILS trigger. The third, QUERY_MASTER_DETAILS, fetches a new batch of detail records into the detail block when called by the ON-POPULATE-DETAILS trigger. Table 20-10 lists these program units in an easy-to-reference format.

Program Unit Name	Purpose	Called by...
CHECK_PACKAGE_FAILURE	Determines whether prior PL/SQL statement executed successfully	ON-POPULATE-DETAILS trigger, CLEAR_ALL_MASTER_DETAILS and QUERY_MASTER_DETAILS program units
CLEAR_ALL_MASTER_DETAILS	Clears detail records	ON-CLEAR-DETAILS trigger
QUERY_MASTER_DETAILS	Fetches detail records	ON-POPULATE-DETAILS trigger

TABLE 20-10. *Relation-Handling Program Units*

Relation-Handling System Variables

Three of the system variables available in Form Builder are used in relation-handling code. All three are called by the CLEAR_ALL_MASTER_DETAILS program unit, which itself is called by the ON-CLEAR-DETAILS trigger. The first system variable is SYSTEM.BLOCK_STATUS, which determines whether any of the records in a block are new or changed. For instance, if you wanted to build a trigger that commits records in a block before the block is cleared, you could place the following code in a KEY-CLRBLK trigger:

```
if :system.block_status = 'NEW' then
    commit_form;
  elsif :system.block_status = 'CHANGED' then
    commit_form;
end if;
clear_block;
```

The second system variable is SYSTEM.COORDINATION_OPERATION, which returns one of 20 possible results identifying what type of coordination-causing event fired the ON-CLEAR-DETAILS trigger. It works together with the third system variable, SYSTEM.MASTER_BLOCK, which returns the name of the master block driving the relation. Table 20-11 lists each system variable and identifies where and why each is used.

To use these system variables, you create local variables in your code and store the values of the system variables into the local variables. An

System Variable Name	Purpose	Called By...
SYSTEM.BLOCK_STATUS	Reports whether a block's record status is NEW, CHANGED, or QUERY (unchanged since last query)	CLEAR_ALL_MASTER_DETAILS program unit
SYSTEM.COORDINATION_OPERATION	Identifies what type of coordination-causing event fired the trigger	CLEAR_ALL_MASTER_DETAILS program unit
SYSTEM.MASTER_BLOCK	Returns the name of the driving master block in a coordination event	CLEAR_ALL_MASTER_DETAILS program unit

TABLE 20-11. *Relation-Handling System Variables*

excellent example of this is found in the CLEAR_ALL_MASTER_DETAILS program unit (which is called by the ON-CLEAR-DETAILS trigger). This program unit's code follows, with boldface print used to identify the relevant system variables and the local variables used to store their values:

```
PROCEDURE Clear_All_Master_Details IS
   mastblk  VARCHAR2(30);   -- Initial Master Block Causing Coord
   coordop  VARCHAR2(30);   -- Operation Causing the Coord
   trigblk  VARCHAR2(30);   -- Cur Block On-Clear-Details Fires On
   startitm VARCHAR2(61);   -- Item in which cursor started
   frmstat  VARCHAR2(15);   -- Form Status
   curblk   VARCHAR2(30);   -- Current Block
   currel   VARCHAR2(30);   -- Current Relation
   curdtl   VARCHAR2(30);   -- Current Detail Block

   FUNCTION First_Changed_Block_Below(Master VARCHAR2)
   RETURN VARCHAR2 IS
     curblk VARCHAR2(30);   -- Current Block
     currel VARCHAR2(30);   -- Current Relation
     retblk VARCHAR2(30);   -- Return Block
```

```
BEGIN
   curblk := Master;
   currel := Get_Block_Property(curblk,  FIRST_MASTER_RELATION);
   WHILE currel IS NOT NULL LOOP
      curblk := Get_Relation_Property(currel, DETAIL_NAME);
      IF ( Get_Block_Property(curblk, STATUS) = 'CHANGED' ) THEN
        RETURN curblk;
      ELSE
        retblk := First_Changed_Block_Below(curblk);
        IF retblk IS NOT NULL THEN
           RETURN retblk;
        ELSE
           currel := Get_Relation_Property(currel, NEXT_MASTER_RELATION);
        END IF;
      END IF;
   END LOOP;

  RETURN NULL;
END First_Changed_Block_Below;

BEGIN
   mastblk  := :System.Master_Block;
   coordop  := :System.Coordination_Operation;
   trigblk  := :System.Trigger_Block;
   startitm := :System.Cursor_Item;
   frmstat  := :System.Form_Status;

   IF coordop NOT IN ('CLEAR_RECORD', 'SYNCHRONIZE_BLOCKS') THEN
     IF mastblk = trigblk THEN
       IF frmstat = 'CHANGED' THEN
         curblk := First_Changed_Block_Below(mastblk);
         IF curblk IS NOT NULL THEN
           Go_Block(curblk);
           Check_Package_Failure;
           Clear_Block(ASK_COMMIT);
           IF NOT ( :System.Form_Status = 'QUERY'
                    OR :System.Block_Status = 'NEW' ) THEN
             RAISE Form_Trigger_Failure;
           END IF;
         END IF;
       END IF;
     END IF;
   END IF;
```

```
  currel := Get_Block_Property(trigblk, FIRST_MASTER_RELATION);
  WHILE currel IS NOT NULL LOOP
    curdtl := Get_Relation_Property(currel, DETAIL_NAME);
    IF Get_Block_Property(curdtl, STATUS) <> 'NEW'  THEN
      Go_Block(curdtl);
      Check_Package_Failure;
      Clear_Block(NO_VALIDATE);
      IF :System.Block_Status <> 'NEW' THEN
        RAISE Form_Trigger_Failure;
      END IF;
    END IF;
    currel := Get_Relation_Property(currel, NEXT_MASTER_RELATION);
  END LOOP;

  IF :System.Cursor_Item <> startitm THEN
    Go_Item(startitm);
    Check_Package_Failure;
  END IF;

EXCEPTION
  WHEN Form_Trigger_Failure THEN
    IF :System.Cursor_Item <> startitm THEN
      Go_Item(startitm);
    END IF;
    RAISE;

END Clear_All_Master_Details;
```

Exercises

1. Which trigger is necessary to create a cascading delete? At what level is the trigger defined?

2. What are the three relation-handling program units created by Form Builder when you define a relation? Which ones are called when a detail block is populated? When it is cleared?

3. Which system variable will identify the type of coordination-causing event that fired a relation-handling trigger? Which system variable will return the name of the master block driving the relation?

Implementing a Coordination-Type Toggle

Earlier in this section you learned about the relation properties that control when a detail block is populated: Deferred and Automatic Query. Because these settings can effect your application's response time, as well as overall network and database demand, there may be times when you want to change the properties dynamically, or allow the users to do so. This can be accomplished using the SET_RELATION_PROPERTY built-in. To make a detail block repopulate immediately each time the user changes focus to a new master record, you can implement code like the following:

```
procedure make_coordination_immediate( RELATION_NAME varchar2 ) is
   RELATION_ID relation;
BEGIN
   RELATION_ID := find_relation(RELATION_NAME);
   set_relation_property(RELATION_ID, deferred, property_false);
   set_relation_property(RELATION_ID, autoquery, property_false);
END;
```

Similarly, you could use code like this to cause the detail block to repopulate only when the user navigates into it:

```
procedure make_coordination_immediate( RELATION_NAME varchar2 ) is
   RELATION_ID relation;
BEGIN
   RELATION_ID := find_relation(RELATION_NAME);
   set_relation_property(RELATION_ID, deferred, property_true);
   set_relation_property(RELATION_ID, autoquery, property_true);
END;
```

The corollary command built-in, GET_RELATION_PROPERTY, can return a variety of useful information, including whether coordination is automatic or deferred, the names of the master and detail blocks, and the names of master and detail relations.

Exercises

1. What built-in can you use to alter relation coordination behavior in real time?

2. What relation properties must be manipulated to effect this change?

Chapter Summary

In this chapter, you have covered a substantial amount of information on advanced forms programming. The topics covered include programming function keys, responding to mouse events, controlling windows and canvases programmatically, and controlling data block relationships. The material in this chapter comprises about 32 percent of material tested on OCP Exam 4.

The first area you covered was programming function keys. You can use KEY-Fn triggers to replace the default functionality of individual function keys, and the KEY-OTHERS trigger to disable any function key that can have a trigger assigned to it but does not. Key triggers are a good choice when you need to replace a function key's default behavior, enable and disable function keys dynamically, or have a single keystroke perform multiple actions.

The next area you covered was responding to mouse events. The triggers that respond to mouse movement are WHEN-MOUSE-ENTER, WHEN-MOUSE-LEAVE, and WHEN-MOUSE-MOVE. These triggers fire only in response to mouse movement; entering a canvas via menu commands will not fire the mouse-movement triggers. They can be defined at the form, block, or item level. When defined at the form level, they are active in any canvas or item in the form. Defined at the block level, they are active in any item in the block. Defined at the item level, they are active when the mouse enters, leaves, or moves within the item. There are also triggers that respond to presses of the mouse buttons: WHEN-MOUSE-DOWN, WHEN-MOUSE-UP, WHEN-MOUSE-CLICK, and WHEN-MOUSE-DOUBLECLICK. These can also be defined at the form, block, or item level. When used in conjunction with the SET_APPLICATION_PROPERTY built-in, the mouse-button triggers enable you to change your application's cursor in real time. Form Builder also provides a collection of mouse-oriented system variables enabling your code to determine which mouse button the user pressed, and where the mouse pointer was when the button was pressed. The system variables that return information about the mouse's location are SYSTEM.MOUSE_CANVAS, SYSTEM.MOUSE_ITEM, SYSTEM.MOUSE_RECORD, SYSTEM.MOUSE_RECORD_OFFSET, SYSTEM.MOUSE_X_POS, and SYSTEM.MOUSE_Y_POS. The system variables that return information about what mouse button was pressed are SYSTEM.MOUSE_BUTTON_PRESSED and SYSTEM.MOUSE_BUTTON_MODIFIERS.

You next explored controlling windows and canvases programmatically. Form Builder offers four triggers that can fire in response to window-oriented events: WHEN-WINDOW-ACTIVATED, which fires when a window is opened or receives focus; WHEN-WINDOW-DEACTIVATED, which fires when an open window loses focus; WHEN-WINDOW-RESIZED, which fires when a window's size is changed by the user or programmatically; and WHEN-WINDOW-CLOSED, which fires when the user executes the window-close command intrinsic to their operating system. Because windows themselves cannot have triggers, window-oriented triggers are defined at the next higher level in the object hierarchy: the Form level. Form Builder also provides quite a few built-ins enabling you to control your windows, including FIND_WINDOW, SHOW_WINDOW, HIDE_WINDOW, MOVE_WINDOW, RESIZE_WINDOW, GET_WINDOW_PROPERTY, and SET_WINDOW_PROPERTY. The SET_WINDOW_PROPERTY built-in allows you to set window properties such as window size, position, and title. For controlling canvases, Form Builder offers another group of built-ins: GET_CANVAS_PROPERTY, SET_CANVAS_PROPERTY, SHOW_VIEW, and REPLACE_CONTENT_VIEW. The REPLACE_CONTENT_VIEW and SHOW_VIEW built-ins allow you to select a window's current content canvas programmatically; the former built-in replaces the prior canvas, while the latter allows the prior canvas to remain.

The final area you covered was controlling data block relationships. This began with an explanation of block coordination, which is the process Form Builder uses to ensure that a detail block always displays records related to the current record in the master block, and that new detail records are automatically assigned to the current master record. Block coordination occurs when the user moves to a next or prior record in the master data block, or deletes a master record; these actions are called coordination-causing events.

A master data block is connected to its detail blocks with logical objects called *relations*. A relation defines how one master data block and one detail data block are related. The relation object is owned by the master data block. Once created, a relation's Delete Record Behavior property enables you to control how the Forms Runtime program responds when the user attempts to delete a master record that has related detail records. The options are Cascading, which causes any related detail records to be deleted before a master record is deleted; Isolated, which allows master records to be deleted without deleting any related detail records; and Non Isolated, which causes the Forms Runtime program to refuse to delete a master record if it has related detail records. Changing this property's setting causes Form Builder to re-create the master data block's triggers, because it is the triggers that enforce the settings when the application is run. The next relation property is Prevent Masterless Operations, which defines whether the user can insert detail records or query the detail data block when there is no current master record. The timing of block coordination is controlled by the next two properties: Deferred and Automatic Query. The Deferred property can be considered the more extensive of the two properties because it determines whether population of the detail block is deferred at all. If set to Yes, then the Automatic Query button specifies whether the detail block will be populated automatically when the user enters it, or only after the user enters it and executes a query within it. You can set these properties programmatically using the SET_RELATION_PROPERTY built-in.

If your application requires that you write your own relation-handling code, you will utilize specific triggers, program units, and system variables. In the area of triggers, there will always be an ON-CLEAR-DETAILS trigger at the Form level to clear detail-block records, along with an ON-POPULATE_ DETAILS trigger owned by the master data block. In addition, you can use an ON-CHECK-DELETE-MASTER trigger at the master block level to check whether detail records exist before a master record is deleted, or a PRE-DELETE trigger to implement a cascading delete from master records down to detail records. The relation-handling triggers created by Form Builder rely on the presence of three program units that are also generated automatically when you create a relation. The first, CHECK_PACKAGE_ FAILURE, is used by the other two program units to determine whether a PL/SQL statement completed successfully. The second, CLEAR_ALL_ MASTER_DETAILS, flushes detail records from the detail block when called by the ON-CLEAR-DETAILS trigger. The third, QUERY_MASTER_DETAILS, fetches a new batch of detail records into the detail block when called by the ON-POPULATE-DETAILS trigger. The CLEAR_ALL_MASTER_DETAILS program unit employs a number of relation-oriented system variables: SYSTEM.BLOCK_STATUS, which determines whether any of the records in a block are new or changed; SYSTEM.COORDINATION_OPERATION, which identifies what type of coordination-causing event fired the coordination trigger; and SYSTEM.MASTER_BLOCK, which returns the name of the master block driving the relation.

Two-Minute Drill

- A KEY-Fn trigger replaces the default functionality of whatever function key it is assigned to.

- A KEY-OTHERS trigger replaces the default functionality of any key that can have a key trigger associated with it but does not.

- The two functions KEY- triggers perform that cannot be attained using any existing menu command or toolbar button are replacing the default functionality of all undefined triggerable keys and executing multistep PL/SQL instructions.

- The mouse event triggers that fire when the user presses a mouse button and releases it are WHEN-MOUSE-DOWN, WHEN-MOUSE-UP, WHEN-MOUSE-CLICK, and WHEN-MOUSE-DOUBLE-CLICK.

- The mouse event triggers that fire when the user moves the mouse are WHEN-MOUSE-ENTER, WHEN-MOUSE-LEAVE, and WHEN-MOUSE-MOVE.

- Mouse triggers can be defined at the form, block, or item level.

- A WHEN-MOUSE-ENTER trigger can fire whenever the user clicks on an item on a canvas.

- The mouse system variables dedicated to identifying the mouse pointer's location are SYSTEM.MOUSE_CANVAS, SYSTEM.MOUSE_ITEM, SYSTEM.MOUSE_RECORD, SYSTEM.MOUSE_RECORD_OFFSET, SYSTEM.MOUSE_X_POS, and SYSTEM.MOUSE_Y_POS.

- The mouse system variable that tells you what mouse button the user pressed is SYSTEM.MOUSE_BUTTON_PRESSED. The mouse system variable that identifies whether the button was modified with SHIFT, CTRL, or ALT is SYSTEM.MOUSE_BUTTON_MODIFIERS.

- The SET_APPLICATION_PROPERTY built-in lets you change a cursor's display style to BUSY, CROSSHAIR, DEFAULT (the default, of course), HELP, or INSERTION.

- Form Builder's window triggers are WHEN-WINDOW-ACTIVATED, WHEN-WINDOW-DEACTIVATED, WHEN-WINDOW-RESIZED, and WHEN-WINDOW-CLOSED.

- Because windows cannot have triggers attached to them directly, you establish window triggers at the next higher level in object hierarchy: the Form level.

- The window built-ins that have the ability to set a window's position on the screen are MOVE_WINDOW, SET_WINDOW_PROPERTY, and SHOW_WINDOW.

- You can change use the SET_WINDOW_PROPERTY built-in to alter window properties such as size, position, and title dynamically at run time.

- The FIND_WINDOW built-in has the ability to speed up operation of the other window built-ins by providing the internal Oracle ID of a named window.

- The REPLACE_CONTENT_VIEW built-in causes the current window to display a different content canvas.

- The SHOW_VIEW built-in displays a specified canvas along with an existing canvas. GET_CANVAS_PROPERTY and SET_CANVAS_PROPERTY built-ins allow you to retrieve and set specific canvas properties.

- Block coordination is the process of ensuring that the detail block in a master/detail relationship always displays only the records related to the currently selected master record.

- A coordination-causing event is any action in the master record block that changes the current record. This can include adding, deleting, or moving among master block records.

- A relation's Delete Record Behavior property has three possible settings: Cascading, which specifies that when a master record is deleted, any related detail records will also be deleted; Isolated, which allows master records to be deleted without deleting any related detail records; and Non Isolated, which causes the Forms Runtime program to refuse to delete a master record if it has related detail records. This is the default setting for this property.

■ A relation's Prevent Masterless Operations property controls whether the user can insert records or query records in a detail data block when no master record is selected.

■ A relation's Deferred and Automatic Query properties work together to specify when the detail block gets populated. When the Deferred property is set to No, the detail block is repopulated immediately after any coordination-causing event in the master block. When the Deferred property is set to Yes and the Automatic Query property is set to Yes, the detail block will be repopulated when the user navigates into the detail block. When the Deferred property is set to Yes and the Automatic Query property is set to No, the user must navigate into the detail block *and* execute a query to populate the detail block.

■ Cascading deletes between master and detail blocks are executed by a PRE-DELETE trigger attached to the master block in the relation.

■ The three relation-handling program units created by Form Builder when you define a relation are CHECK_PACKAGE_FAILURE, CLEAR_ALL_MASTER_DETAILS, and QUERY_MASTER_DETAILS. Populating a detail block involves the QUERY_MASTER_DETAILS program unit, which also calls CHECK_PACKAGE_FAILURE. Clearing a detail block involves the CLEAR_ALL_MASTER_DETAILS program unit, which also calls CHECK_PACKAGE_FAILURE.

■ The SYSTEM.COORDINATION_OPERATION system variable identifies the type of coordination-causing event that fired a relation-handling trigger. The SYSTEM.MASTER_BLOCK system variable returns the name of the master block driving a relation.

■ You can alter a relation's coordination behavior dynamically using the SET_RELATION_PROPERTY built-in. The relation properties that control coordination behavior are Deferred and Automatic Query.

Chapter Questions

1. **Which of the following functions can be accomplished only with the use of key triggers? (Choose all that apply)**

    A. Navigating between blocks

    B. Disabling function keys

    C. Validating data

    D. Modifying data before it is committed

    E. Changing function keys' default functionality

    F. Controlling menu access

2. **Which built-in allows you to change window properties dynamically while the application is running?**

    A. SET_WINDOW_PROPERTY

    B. SET_CANVAS_PROPERTY

    C. SET_VIEW_PROPERTY

    D. GET_WINDOW_PROPERTY

    E. GET_CANVAS_PROPERTY

    F. GET_VIEW_PROPERTY

3. **At what object level do you place WHEN-WINDOW- triggers?**

    A. Form

    B. Canvas

    C. Window

    D. Block

4. **What happens to a function key's default functionality when you define a key trigger for the function key?**

    A. The default functionality is augmented by whatever code is contained in the key trigger.

B. The default functionality is replaced by whatever code is contained in the key trigger.

C. The default functionality overrides whatever code is contained in the key trigger.

D. Forms determines each time the function key is pressed whether it should execute the default functionality or the key trigger.

5. **Which of the following actions constitute mouse-movement events? (Choose all that apply)**

   A. Clicking on a form field

   B. Using the TAB key to leave a form field

   C. Entering a new canvas

   D. Clicking on a menu to open it

   E. Executing a pushbutton

6. **What program units does Form Builder create automatically when you define a relation? (Choose all that apply)**

   A. CHECK_ALL_MASTER_DETAILS

   B. CLEAR_ALL_MASTER_DETAILS

   C. QUERY_ALL_MASTER_DETAILS

   D. CHECK_MASTER_DETAILS

   E. CLEAR_MASTER_DETAILS

   F. QUERY_MASTER_DETAILS

   G. CHECK_PACKAGE_FAILURE

   H. CLEAR_PACKAGE_FAILURE

   I. QUERY_PACKAGE_FAILURE

7. **Which property and setting will prohibit the user from deleting a master record if related detail records exist?**

   A. Master block property Delete Record Behavior set to Cascading

   B. Master block property Delete Record Behavior set to Isolated

   C. Master block property Delete Record Behavior set to Non Isolated

   D. Relation property Delete Record Behavior set to Cascading

   E. Relation property Delete Record Behavior set to Isolated

   F. Relation property Delete Record Behavior set to Non Isolated

   G. Master block property Prevent Masterless Operations set to Yes

   H. Master block property Prevent Masterless Operations set to No

8. **What trigger can institute a default functionality, or no functionality, for every function key that does not have an explicit trigger?**

   A. KEY-FUNCTION

   B. KEY-NONE

   C. KEY-Fn

   D. KEY-OTHERS

   E. KEY-ELSE

9. **Which of the following properties can be set by the SET_WINDOW_PROPERTY built-in? (Choose all that apply)**

   A. Height

   B. Width

   C. Position

   D. Title

   E. Visible

   F. Canvas

10. **What built-in gives you the ability to change the cursor's appearance dynamically?**

   A. SET_APPLICATION_PROPERTY

   B. SET_CANVAS_PROPERTY

   C. SET_CONTEXT

   D. SET_FORM_PROPERTY

E. SET_ITEM_PROPERTY

F. SET_VIEW_PROPERTY

G. SET_WINDOW_PROPERTY

11. When you define a master/detail relation between two tables, Form Builder automatically creates ON-CLEAR-DETAILS and ON-POPULATE-DETAILS triggers. It also creates three program units, two of which are called by the ON-POPULATE-DETAILS trigger. Which two?

A. CHECK_PACKAGE_FAILURE

B. CLEAR_ALL_MASTER_DETAILS

C. QUERY_MASTER_DETAILS

12. What built-in allows you to dynamically control when a detail block is populated?

A. SET_BLOCK_PROPERTY

B. SET_ITEM_PROPERTY

C. SET_RELATION_PROPERTY

D. SET_WINDOW_PROPERTY

13. What trigger is necessary for implementing a cascading delete in a master-detail relation?

A. PRE-CASCADE

B. POST-CASCADE

C. PRE-DELETE

D. PRE-POST

E. PRE-UPDATE

Answers to Chapter Questions

1. B, E.   Disabling function keys, Changing function keys' default functionality

Explanation   The KEY-Fn and KEY-OTHERS triggers are the only ways to change what happens in your application when a function key is pressed.

2. A.   SET_WINDOW_PROPERTY

Explanation   See the section titled "Controlling Windows Programmatically" for a refresher on this topic.

3. A.   Form

Explanation   Windows do not have the ability to hold triggers, so you need to define a WHEN-WINDOWS- trigger one level higher in the object hierarchy: the Form level.

4. B.   The default functionality is replaced by whatever code is contained in the key trigger.

Explanation   See the section titled "Redefining Function Keys" for a refresher on this topic.

5. A.   Clicking on a form field

Explanation   The only mouse-movement triggers are WHEN-MOUSE-ENTER, WHEN-MOUSE-LEAVE, and WHEN-MOUSE-MOVE, and they only work in relation to an item or canvas. Clicking on a form field would fire the WHEN-MOUSE-ENTER trigger. Moving out of the field with the TAB key would not, since the change in focus was done with a key instead of the mouse. Entering a new canvas would qualify if it were done with a mouse, but that is not specified in the question. The same is true of executing a pushbutton. Clicking on a menu doesn't qualify because it is not a form item or canvas.

6. B, F, G.   CLEAR_ALL_MASTER_DETAILS, QUERY_MASTER_DETAILS, CHECK_PACKAGE_FAILURE

Explanation   See the section titled "Characteristics of Relation-Handling Code" for a refresher on this topic.

7. F.   Relation property Delete Record Behavior set to Non Isolated

Explanation   See the section titled "Creating and Modifying Relations" for a refresher on this topic.

8. D.   KEY-OTHERS

Explanation   The purpose of the KEY-OTHERS command is to replace the functionality of any key that can have a trigger assigned to it but does not.

9. A, B, C, D, E.   Height, Width, Position, Title, Visible

Explanation   See the section titled "Controlling Windows Programmatically" for a refresher on this topic.

10. A.   SET_APPLICATION_PROPERTY

Explanation   See the section titled "Causing a Form Module to Respond to Mouse Button Actions" for a refresher on this topic.

11. A, C.   CHECK_PACKAGE_FAILURE, QUERY_MASTER_DETAILS

Explanation   See the section titled "Characteristics of Relation-Handling Code" for a refresher on this topic.

12. C.   SET_RELATION_PROPERTY

Explanation   See the section titled "Implementing a Coordination-Type Toggle" for a refresher on this topic.

13. C.   PRE-DELETE

Explanation   The PRE-DELETE trigger is the only one that has the ability to intercept a master-record deletion, check to determine if related detail records exist, and delete those detail records before proceeding to delete the master record. There is no such thing as a PRE-CASCADE, POST-CASCADE, or PRE-POST trigger.

CHAPTER
21

Advanced Forms
Programming II

n this chapter, you will cover the following areas of advanced forms programming:

- Building multiple-form applications
- Defining data sources
- Working with record groups

This chapter introduces you to some exciting areas of the Form Builder design process. It starts by describing a variety of different ways to produce multiple-form applications, and explaining how to pass data between forms when they are opened. It then proceeds to a discussion of alternative data sources you can use to create a data block. The last section is on record groups—tabular data structures you can use not only to feed LOVs, but also to pass data to other forms, as well as to graphs and reports. Overall, the contents of this chapter comprise about 27 percent of OCP Exam 4 test content.

Building Multiple-Form Applications

In this section, you will cover the following points related to building multiple-form applications:

- Different ways to invoke forms
- Building robust multiple-form transactions
- Passing data between forms using parameter lists

In Chapter 17, you were introduced to the concept of multiple-form applications. The section you are about to read provides much more detailed information about the features and options you have available when you create multiple-form applications. You will explore different ways to invoke additional forms, learn how to move between forms with confidence, and see how to pass information from one form to another when a new form is opened.

Different Ways to Invoke Forms

Form Builder provides three separate built-ins capable of invoking forms: CALL_FORM, NEW_FORM, and OPEN_FORM. The standard built-in used for most multiple-form work is OPEN_FORM. Its syntax is shown here, with each available option included and set to its default value:

```
open_form ('form_name', activate, no_session,
            no_share_library_data, paramlist_id);
```

The first option, ACTIVATE, specifies that the newly opened form will immediately receive focus. The second option, NO_SESSION, specifies that the newly opened form will share the database connection used by the calling form, as opposed to opening its own database connection. The NO_SHARE_LIBRARY_DATA option specifies that any libraries attached to the newly opened form will not share data with matching libraries attached to other open forms. The last argument specifies the internal ID (or the name) of the parameter list you want to pass to the opened form.

If your application requires that you open a new form modally so that it is the only form that can receive focus until it is closed, use the built-in CALL_FORM. Its syntax is shown here, with each available option included and set to its default value:

```
call_form ('form_name', hide, no_replace, no_query_only,
            no_share_library_data, paramlist_id);
```

The first option, HIDE, causes the Forms Runtime program to make the calling form invisible to the user while the called form is active. The second option, NO_REPLACE, tells the Forms Runtime program to continue using the default menu module of the calling form, even if the called form has a default menu module of its own. The third option, NO_QUERY_ONLY, specifies that users should be able to insert, update, and delete records in the called form, as opposed to only being able to fetch them.

If you want to open a new form and close the one that was active, use the built-in NEW_FORM. Its syntax is shown here, with each available option included and set to its default value:

```
new_form ('form_name', to_savepoint, no_query_only,
            no_share_library_data);
```

The first option, TO_SAVEPOINT, specifies that changes that have not been committed will be rolled back to the calling form's last savepoint.

Table 21-1 compares the salient characteristics of each approach to opening forms.

When one form opens another and the calling form has pending transactions that have not been posted, the called form is opened in *post-only mode*. This means that the calling form cannot **commit** any transactions or perform a **rollback**; it can only **post** to the database whatever changes the user makes while in the called form. If the user makes changes in the called form and then exits, the Forms Runtime program displays an alert asking if they want to **post** their changes before returning to the calling form.

Built-In	CALL_FORM	NEW_FORM	OPEN_FORM
Purpose	Opens additional form as modal window	Closes calling form and opens new form	Standard built-in used for multiple-form applications
Parameters	HIDE / NO_HIDE, DO_REPLACE / NO_REPLACE, QUERY_ONLY / NO_QUERY_ONLY, SHARE_LIBRARY_DATA / NO_SHARE_LIBRARY_DATA	NO_ROLLBACK / FULL_ROLLBACK / TO_SAVEPOINT, QUERY_ONLY / NO_QUERY_ONLY, SHARE_LIBRARY_DATA / NO_SHARE_LIBRARY_DATA	ACTIVATE / NO_ACTIVATE, SESSION / NO_SESSION, SHARE_LIBRARY_DATA / NO_SHARE_LIBRARY_DATA
Calling Form Remains Open?	Y	N	Y
Calling Form Accessible While Called Form Is Open?	N	N/A	Y
Calling Form Remains Visible?	Y	N/A	Y
Allows Separate DB Session?	N	N/A	Y
Restricted Procedure?	N	Y	Y

TABLE 21-1. *Comparison of Built-Ins That Open Forms*

Exercises

1. Which built-in is the most commonly used for opening forms in a multiple-form application?

2. Which built-in allows you to open a form modally?

3. Which built-in opens a new form and closes the form that called it?

4. When does post-only mode occur, and what are its characteristics?

Building Robust Multiple-Form Transactions

When you create the ability to open multiple forms, you will soon be faced with a new array of needs: navigating between forms in controlled ways, determining within code what form is active and what form called it, and creating additional database connections without again asking the user for their logon information, for instance. This topic explores Form Builder features that satisfy those needs.

There are three built-ins enabling you to move between open forms: GO_FORM, NEXT_FORM, and PREVIOUS_FORM. The most versatile is GO_FORM, because it allows you to jump to any form, not just the next or previous one. Its syntax is shown here:

```
go_form('form_name');
```

To support applications in which multiple instances of the same form are opened, you can specify the destination form using its internal Oracle ID, instead of its (now nonunique) name.

To supply your PL/SQL code with information about the application's environment, you can use the GET_APPLICATION_PROPERTY built-in. To see an example of this, open a form module of your choosing, display a canvas in the Layout Editor, add a pushbutton to it, and enter the following code for its WHEN-BUTTON-PRESSED trigger:

```
DECLARE
  V_FORM_NAME varchar2(80);
BEGIN
  V_FORM_NAME := get_application_property(current_form_name);
  message ('Form: '||V_FORM_NAME);
END;
```

You can also use the GET_APPLICATION_PROPERTY built-in to provide a wealth of other system information. The most relevant of these items are listed in Table 21-2.

Exercises

1. What three built-ins give you the ability to change focus from one form to another?

2. What built-in allows you to determine the name and password of the current user? What parameters cause the built-in to return these data

Parameter Name	Data Returned
CALLING_FORM	If current form was invoked with CALL_FORM, returns name of calling form
CURRENT_FORM	Disk filename of currently active form
CURRENT_FORM_NAME	Name of currently active form
DATASOURCE	Type of current database: DB2, NCR/3600/NCR/3700, NONSTOP, NULL, ORACLE, SQLSERVER, or TERADATA
DISPLAY_HEIGHT	Height of display
DISPLAY_WIDTH	Width of display
OPERATING_SYSTEM	Name of current OS: HP-UX, MACINTOSH, MSWINDOWS, MSWINDOWS32, SunOS, UNIX, VMS, or WIN32COMMON
USER_INTERFACE	Type of current user interface: BLOCKMODE, CHARMODE, MACINTOSH, MOTIF, MSWINDOWS, MSWINDOWS32, PM, UNKNOWN, WEB, WIN32COMMON, or X
PASSWORD	Current operator's password
USERNAME	Current operator's username
USER_NLS_LANG	Current value of NLS_LANG environment variable

TABLE 21-2.   *GET_APPLICATION_PROPERTY Built-In Parameters*

items? What parameter would cause the built-in to return the current form name? The current form filename?

Passing Data Between Forms Using Parameter Lists

Using Form Builder, you can have one form module call another and pass parameters to the called form. There are two ways to do this: Create the parameters under the Parameters nodes in both form modules; or create the parameters in just the called form, and write PL/SQL code in the calling form that constructs the parameter list and then calls the second form. Either way, the called form must have the parameters defined already, so they must be established in the called form at design time.

To create parameters in either the calling form or the called form, click on its Parameters node and then click on the Create button. Give the new parameter a descriptive name; set its datatype and maximum length; and in the calling form, establish an initial value if the parameter is going to have a fixed value such as the name of the calling form. The parameter name, datatype, and length properties must be identical in both the calling form and the called form.

To create a parameter list dynamically in the calling form, use the CREATE_PARAMETER_LIST built-in. Invoking this built-in returns a numeric value that is the internal ID for the parameter list created; this internal ID can be used in further references to the parameter list. Once the empty parameter list is created, you add parameters to it using the ADD_PARAMETER built-in. Finally, you invoke the called form and include the parameter list's internal ID as the final command argument. Here is a sample bit of code showing how these built-ins work together:

```
DECLARE
   PARAM_LIST_ID paramlist;
BEGIN
   PARAM_LIST_ID := create_parameter_list('list_name');
   add_parameter(PARAM_LIST_ID, 'parameter_name', text_parameter,
                 'parameter value');
   open_form('form_name', PARAM_LIST_ID);
END;
```

Note that the ADD_PARAMETER built-in includes the argument **text_parameter**. This tells Form Builder that the value being passed is a VARCHAR2 text string; these have a maximum length of 255 characters. The alternative argument is **data_parameter**, which is a VARCHAR2 string containing the name of a record group in the calling form. This is useful for providing data when calling the Graphics Runtime or Reports Runtime programs, a subject that will be addressed later in the chapter.

If you choose to establish parameters in the calling program permanently by adding them under the Parameters node, those parameters will become part of a parameter list named DEFAULT that is kept internally by all form modules. To send this parameter list to a called form, include its name in the calling command, as shown here:

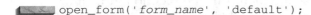

```
open_form('form_name', 'default');
```

Exercises

1. When can you define parameters to pass from a calling form?

2. When must you define parameters that will be received by the called form?

Defining Data Sources

In this section, you will cover the following points about defining data sources:

- Introduction to diverse data source types

- Selecting appropriate data sources for data blocks

This section provides a comparison of the features and shortcomings of each data source type, along with tips for selecting the appropriate data source for different application needs. These criteria will help you when the time comes to decide what data source type to explore further—after you have passed your certification exam.

Introduction to Diverse Data Source Types

So far in this book, every form data block you have created has been based on a database table. You can also create data blocks based on a database view, a **from** clause query, a stored procedure, or a transactional trigger. In the case of the stored procedure, there are two options for how the data is provided: Data is returned to the data block either in the form of a *ref cursor*, which is a pointer to a server-side cursor that is populated by a **select** statement; or as a *table of records*, which is an array-like structure sent to the client computer containing every record returned by the procedure.

The most common source for a data block is still a database table. However, there are definite advantages to other data source types: increased performance, reduced network traffic, increased control and security, and shifting of processing burden to the database server. Using an alternative data source is easy to do. For instance, if you have a stored procedure that you would like to use as the basis for a data block, you can simply select Stored Procedure in the Data Block Wizard's Type screen, identify the procedure in the following Procedure screen, and then select columns as you would from a database table. These steps are shown in Figures 21-1 and 21-2.

Selecting a **from** clause query as a data source type is almost as easy. You create a new data block manually, set its Query Data Source Type

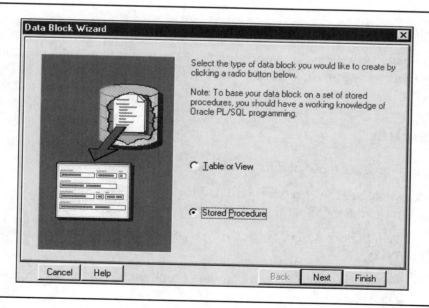

FIGURE 21-1. *Specifying a stored procedure as a data block source*

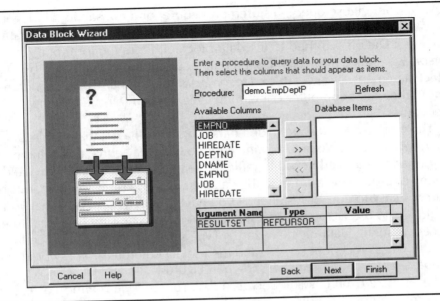

FIGURE 21-2. *Identifying the procedure name and selecting columns*

property to *FROM clause query*, and place the appropriate **select** statement in its Query Data Source Name property.

Exercises

1. Name six types of data block sources.

2. What are the two types of data block sources using stored procedures? What is the main difference between them?

3. What choices of data source types are offered by the Data Block Wizard?

4. Where do you specify that a data block should be based on a **from** clause query?

Selecting Appropriate Data Sources for Data Blocks

There are many factors to consider when deciding which data source type to use for a data block. Take a look at Table 21-3, which provides a

Data Source	DML?	Array Processing?	QBE?	Advantages	Shortcomings
Table	Yes	Yes	Yes	Simple to implement, standard technique, versatile.	Can be slow on large transactions.
View	Yes	Yes	Yes	Simple to implement.	View must be created beforehand.
FROM clause query	No	Yes	No	Can perform multiple-table joins, lookups, and calculations without having the DBA create a view on the server.	Query only; no DML.
Procedure | Ref Cursor	No	Yes	No	Can provide better performance than table data source.	Query only; no DML.
				Increased control and security.	If used to populate a detail block in a master/detail relationship, allows only the Isolated delete option.
				Can query and update multiple tables.	Disables any Count Query Hits calculation.
				Can perform complex computations.	Cannot receive a **where** or **order by** clause at run time.
				Can perform validation on the server.	Does not support Update Changed Columns Only property.
				Encapsulates logic within a subprogram.	

TABLE 21-3. *Data Source Type Comparison*

Data Source	DML?	Array Processing?	QBE?	Advantages	Shortcomings
Procedure | Table of Records	Yes	No	No	Creates very little network traffic. Requires only two network trips: one to execute the stored procedure, and the other to retrieve the entire set of returned records. Increased control and security. Can query and update multiple tables. Can perform complex computations. Can perform validation and DML on the server. Encapsulates logic within a subprogram.	Cannot use array processing. Disables any Count Query Hits calculation. Cannot receive a **where** or **order by** clause at runtime. Does not support Update Changed Columns Only property.
Transactional trigger	Yes	No	No	Useful when running an application with a non-Oracle database.	Cannot use array processing.

TABLE 21-3.   *Data Source Type Comparison* (continued)

comprehensive comparison of each data source type's advantages and shortcomings, and you will get an idea of the number of decisions that go into selecting the right data-block source type.

You can simplify the selection process and narrow your choices quickly by asking a few key questions about the reason you are considering other source types, and the data block's requirements. For instance, if you want to minimize the network traffic required to fetch large numbers of records, a stored procedure returning a table of records would be your first choice because it reduces network transactions to the bare minimum. If you need to get data from multiple data blocks and don't want to have the DBA (or yourself) create any new objects on the server, a **from** clause query is the way to go. If your users will need to update the records in the data block, your choices are limited to data source types of table, view, or stored procedure returning a table of records. If you are interacting with a non-Oracle database, a transactional trigger is likely to be your best choice. If the data block needs Query By Example capabilities, your choice of data source types is restricted to table or view. And if you want to implement array processing, you will limit your data source selection to table, view, **from** clause query, or a stored procedure returning a ref cursor.

Study Table 21-3 until you know it inside and out, and it will serve you well on your exam.

Exercises

  1. Which data source type allows you to join tables, perform lookups, and create calculations without having to create any new objects on the server?

  2. Which data source type has the greatest potential for reducing network traffic?

  3. Which data source types produce record sets that can be changed by the user?

Working with Record Groups

In this section, you will cover the following points about working with record groups:

  - Creating record groups at design time

  - Creating and modifying record groups programmatically

  - Building dynamic list items by using record groups

  - Applying record groups in other useful ways

  - Using a global record group to communicate between forms

A record group is a Form Builder object that makes tabular (column/row) data available to your application. By default, a record group is specific to the form module in which it is defined. You have worked with a record group already, when you created a DEPARTMENT_LOV list earlier in the book. Now it is time to learn more about record groups and what they can do for you. There are three types of record groups:

- *Query* record group, which is based on a SQL **select** statement. This provides a functionality similar to a database view, with two added benefits: The **select** statement that produces the record group can be dynamically created at run time, and you don't need to add a view to the database.

- *Nonquery* record group, which can also be created and populated dynamically at run time but has no underlying **select** statement.

- *Static* record group, whose structure and contents are defined at design time and cannot change as the application runs.

Creating Record Groups at Design Time

To create a query record group, click on the Record Groups node and then click on the Create button. You will see the New Record Group dialog box, as shown in Figure 21-3. Ensure that the Based on the Query below… option is selected, and then enter the following SQL **select** statement:

```
select d.department_name, e.last_name, e.first_name, e.salary
from department d, employee e
where d.department_id = e.department_id
order by d.department_name, e.salary;
```

Then click on the OK button to continue. You will see a new record group added beneath the Record Groups node. Change the record group's name to **DEPT_EMP_SALARY**. The record group is not currently populated; it can be populated at run time using the POPULATE_GROUP built-in, as shown here:

```
populate_group ('group_name');
```

To create a static record group, click on the Record Groups node and then click on the Create button. Select the Static Values option and then click on the OK button. You will be presented with a dialog box similar to

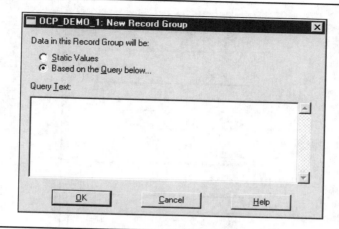

FIGURE 21-3. *New Record Group dialog box*

Figure 21-4, asking you to define the names, datatypes, lengths, and values for your static record group. For this example, create a sample STATE record group, as depicted in Figure 21-5. Then click on the OK button to complete the process. Change the name of the new record group to **STATE**.

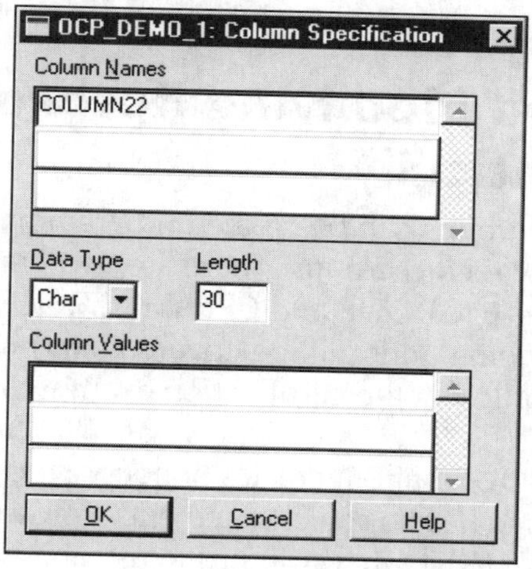

FIGURE 21-4. *Static Record Group Column Specifications dialog box*

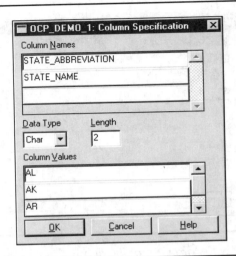

FIGURE 21-5. *Static Record Group example entries*

Exercise

What are the three types of record groups? What are the differences between them?

Creating and Modifying Record Groups Programmatically

Two types of record groups can be created programmatically: query record groups and nonquery record groups. There are two built-ins that create record groups: CREATE_GROUP and CREATE_GROUP_FROM_QUERY. The syntax of these commands will be covered later; what you need to know to pass this portion of the certification exam is which built-in to use for a specific task.

The CREATE_GROUP built-in creates nonquery record groups. Because a nonquery record group has no **select** statement to provide it with column information, you must tell it what columns to use and what to populate them with. There are two ways to do this. If your data is coming from a queryable data source, you can use the POPULATE_GROUP_WITH_QUERY built-in to specify a **select** statement that will define the record group's structure and contents. Populating the record group in this way essentially turns the nonquery record group into a query record group, a useful trick when you have a record group you thought wasn't going to change during the application's lifetime and—surprise!—it is going to change after all. If the values for the record group are going to be generated programmatically, the process of populating the record group is, of course, more involved. You first define the record group's columns using one ADD_GROUP_COLUMN built-in for each column. You then add and populate rows using one ADD_GROUP_ROW built-in for each row, along with one SET_GROUP_CHAR_CELL or SET_GROUP_NUMBER_CELL built-in for each item in the row you wish to populate.

The CREATE_GROUP_FROM_QUERY built-in creates query record groups. Once created, this type of group can be populated by simply executing the POPULATE_GROUP built-in. If you find you need to dynamically change the **select** statement that underlies an existing query record group, you can do so programmatically with the POPULATE_GROUP_WITH_QUERY built-in. This replaces the record group's **select** statement for the duration of that runtime session. This replacement works as long as the new **select** statement returns records with the same structure as the original **select** statement, and varies only in the *content* of the records returned.

Exercises

1. Which built-in will create a query record group? A nonquery record group?

2. What is the simplest way to populate a nonquery record group?

3. What built-in will let you change the **select** statement underlying a query record group?

Building Dynamic List Items by Using Record Groups

When you experimented with creating a List of Values earlier in this book, a record group was automatically created to feed data to the LOV. Every LOV needs a record group. However, you can create record groups without creating LOVs, and then later creating an LOV to view the records in an existing record group. The LOV can be considered a viewing portal into the record group's rows; each time the LOV is opened, the attached record group is populated automatically. You can also change the contents of the LOV dynamically, or even make the list show an entirely different record group.

To create an LOV based on an existing record group, click on the LOV's node in the form module, then click on the Create button. Select the Existing Record Group choice, then click on the Select button to choose the record group on which to base the LOV. Then click on the OK button to dismiss the Select dialog box and click on the next OK button to complete the process. Finally, rename the LOV so its name reflects its purpose.

To populate an LOV with values from a two-column record group created at runtime, use the POPULATE_LIST built-in. Its syntax follows:

```
populate_list('list_name', 'record_group_name');
```

If you want to modify an LOV so it shows values from a record group that wasn't necessarily created at run time, or that has more than two columns, use the SET_LOV_PROPERTY built-in. Its syntax is

```
set_lov_property('lov_name', GROUP_NAME, 'record_group_name');
```

Exercise

What are the two methods for changing the record group associated with an LOV? What are the differences between them?

Using a Global Record Group to Communicate Between Forms

Generally, record groups remain within the scope of the form module that owns them. You can, however, specify global scope for a record group, so that it is visible to all forms in an application. You can even make the contents of a record group available to other Developer/2000 products, such as Graphics Builder and Report Builder. This gives you the ability to alter the contents of a graphic or report at run time.

To make a record group available to all form modules, include the GLOBAL_SCOPE parameter in the built-in that creates the group. Thus, the syntax would be

```
create_group('record_group_name', GLOBAL_SCOPE, array_fetch_size);
```

or

```
create_group_from_query('record_group_name', 'query_text', GLOBAL_SCOPE,
                        array_fetch_size);
```

To pass a record group to a graph or report, use the RUN_PRODUCT built-in. To do this, the record group must have the same data structure as the query on which the graph or report is already based.

```
run_product(GRAPHICS, 'graph_module_name', SYNCHRONOUS, RUNTIME, FILESYSTEM,
            parameter_list_id, 'graph_block.graph_item');
```

An example of the code to realize this function follows. The example passes data from a record group called GRAPH_RECS to a graph named DPTGRAPH.

```
PROCEDURE Run_Department_Graph IS
  PARAM_LIST_ID ParamList;
BEGIN
  /* Check to see if the 'GRAPH_DATA' parameter list exists. */
  PARAM_LIST_ID := Get_Parameter_List('GRAPH_DATA');
  /* If parameter list exists, delete it to ensure it contains
  ** only the parameters we want. */
  IF NOT Id_Null(PARAM_LIST_ID) THEN
    Destroy_Parameter_List( PARAM_LIST_ID );
  END IF;
  /* Create the 'GRAPH_DATA' parameter list. */
  PARAM_LIST_ID := Create_Parameter_List('GRAPH_DATA');
  /* Populate the parameter list with a data parameter whose key is
  ** the name of the query currently driving the graph, and whose
  ** value is the name of the record group to pass from this form. */
  Add_Parameter(PARAM_LIST_ID,'GRAPH_QUERY',DATA_PARAMETER,'GRAPH_RECS');
  /* Run graph and pass it the parameter list */
  Run_Product(GRAPHICS, 'DPTGRAPH', SYNCHRONOUS,
              RUNTIME, FILEYSTEM, PARAM_LIST_ID, NULL);
END;
```

Exercises

1. How can you make a record group visible to all forms in your application?

2. What built-in can you use to pass a record group's data to other Developer/2000 applications?

Chapter Summary

In this chapter, you covered some fascinating information on advanced forms programming. The topics included building multiple-form applications, defining data sources, and working with record groups. The contents of this chapter represent about 27 percent of material tested on OCP Exam 4.

The first area you covered was building multiple-form applications. Form Builder provides three separate built-ins capable of invoking forms: CALL_FORM, NEW_FORM, and OPEN_FORM. The standard built-in used for most multiple-form work is OPEN_FORM. If you need to open a new form modally, use the built-in CALL_FORM. If you want to open a new form and close the one that was active, use the built-in NEW_FORM. When one form opens another and the calling form has pending transactions that have not been posted, the called form is opened in *post-only mode*, which means that the calling form cannot commit any transactions or perform a rollback; it can only post to the database whatever changes the user makes while in the called form. There are three built-ins enabling you to move between open forms: GO_FORM, NEXT_FORM, and PREVIOUS_FORM. The most versatile is GO_FORM because it allows you to jump to any form, not just the next or previous one.

To supply your PL/SQL code with information about the application's environment, you can use the GET_APPLICATION_PROPERTY built-in. This built-in can return the name of the current form, calling form, and current form filename; the type of data source, operating system, and user interface on the client computer; the display's height and width; the user's name and password; and the language in which the application is operating.

You can pass data between forms using parameter lists whenever one form module calls another. There are two ways to do this: Create the parameters under the Parameters nodes in both form modules, or create the parameters in just the called form, and write PL/SQL code in the calling form that constructs the parameter list and then calls the second form. Either way, the called form must have the parameters defined already, so they must be established in the called form at design time.

After establishing the basic premises of building multiple-form applications, your attention turned to defining data sources. You can create data blocks based on a database table, database view, **from** clause query, stored procedure, or transactional trigger. In the case of the stored procedure, there are two options for how the data is provided: Data is returned to the data block either in the form of a *ref cursor*, which is a pointer to a server-side cursor that is populated by a **select** statement; or as a *table of records*, which is an arraylike structure sent to the client computer containing every record returned by the procedure. Although a database table is still the most common source for a data block, the other data source types offer advantages in specific situations. If you want to minimize the network traffic required to fetch large numbers of records, a stored procedure returning a table of records would be your first choice. If you need to get data from multiple data blocks and don't want to create any new objects on the server, a **from** clause query is the way to go. If your users will need to update the records in the data block, you will look at data source types of table, view, or stored procedure returning a table of records. If you are interacting with a non-Oracle database, a transactional trigger is likely to be your best choice.

The final area covered in this chapter was working with record groups. A record group is a Form Builder object that makes tabular data available to your application. Record groups are the basis for all LOVs. There are three types of record groups: query, nonquery, and static. A query record group is based on a SQL **select** statement, and it provides a functionality similar to a database view, with two added benefits: The **select** statement that produces the record group can be dynamically created at run time, and you don't need to add a view to the database. A nonquery record group does not have an underlying **select** statement, and so must be populated explicitly each time it is used. A static record group's structure and contents are defined at design time and cannot change as the application runs. Query record groups and nonquery record groups can be created programmatically. To create a nonquery record group, you use the CREATE_GROUP built-in, and populate it either with the POPULATE_GROUP_WITH_QUERY built-in or with a series of ADD_GROUP_COLUMN, ADD_GROUP_ROW, SET_GROUP_ CHAR_CELL, and SET_GROUP_NUMBER_CELL built-ins. To create a query record group, you use the CREATE_GROUP_FROM_QUERY built-in, followed by a POPULATE_GROUP built-in to populate it. If you find you need to dynamically change the **select** statement that underlies an existing query record group, you can do so programmatically with the POPULATE_ GROUP_WITH_QUERY built-in, which replaces the record group's **select** statement for the duration of that runtime session.

An LOV acts as a viewing portal into the record group's rows; each time the LOV is opened, the attached record group is populated automatically. You can change the contents of the LOV dynamically, or make the list show an entirely different record group. To populate an LOV with values from a two-column record group created at run time, use the POPULATE_LIST built-in. If you want to modify an LOV so it shows values from a record group that wasn't necessarily created at run time, or that has more than two columns, use the SET_LOV_PROPERTY built-in.

If you want to make a record group visible to all forms in an application, include the GLOBAL_SCOPE parameter in the built-in that creates the group. If you wish to make the contents of a record group available to other Developer/2000 products, such as Graphics Builder and Report Builder, you can do so using the RUN_PRODUCT built-in.

Two-Minute Drill

- The most commonly used built-in for opening forms in a multiple-form application is OPEN_FORM.

- The built-in that allows you to open a form modally is CALL_FORM.

- The built-in that opens a new form and closes the calling form is NEW_FORM.

- Post-only mode occurs when a user opens a new form from a form that has uncommitted changes. While in post-only mode, the calling form cannot commit any transactions or perform a rollback; it can only post to the database whatever changes the user makes while in the called form. If the user makes changes in the called form and then exits, the Forms Runtime program displays an alert asking if they want to post their changes before returning to the calling form.

- The built-ins that give you the ability to change focus from one form to another are GO_FORM, NEXT_FORM, and PREVIOUS_FORM.

- The GET_APPLICATION_PROPERTY allows you to determine an application's current user and password, current form and form disk name, calling form, database type, display height and width, operating system and UI type, and language settings.

- You can pass values to a called form when it is opened by creating and using a parameter list.

- The calling form, which sends out the parameters, can define them either at design time by adding them to the Parameters node, or at run time by creating them with the CREATE_PARAMETER_LIST and ADD_PARAMETER built-ins.

- The called form, in contrast, can only accept passed values if the parameters were previously defined in the called form at design time.

- The six types of data block sources are table, view, **from** clause query, stored procedure returning a ref cursor, stored procedure returning a table of records, and transactional triggers.

- The main difference between the two types of data block sources using stored procedures is that one returns a ref cursor pointing to an array of returned records still on the server, whereas the other returns a table of records to the client computer containing all records returned by the procedure.

- The types of data sources made available by the Data Block Wizard are table, view, and stored procedure.

- You specify that a data block should be based on a **from** clause query by setting the data block's Query Data Source Type to *FROM clause query*.

- The data source type *FROM clause query* allows you to join tables, perform lookups, and create calculations without having to create any new objects on the server.

- The data source type *Stored Procedure Returning a Table of Records* has the greatest potential of reducing network traffic.

- The data source types that produce record sets that can be changed by the user are *Table, View, Stored Procedure Returning a Table of Records*, and *Transactional Triggers*.

- A record group is a two-dimensional table that provides data to a form module. There are three types of record groups: query, nonquery, and static.

- A query record group is based on a SQL **select** statement. It provides a functionality similar to a database view, with two added benefits: The **select** statement that produces the record group can be dynamically created at run time, and you don't need to add a view to the database.

- A nonquery record group can also be created and populated dynamically at run time but has no underlying **select** statement.

- A static record group is defined at design time, and its structure and content do not change when the application runs.

- Nonquery record groups are created with CREATE_GROUP. They are populated either with the POPULATE_GROUP_WITH_QUERY built-in, which essentially turns the nonquery record group into a query record group, or with a series of ADD_GROUP_COLUMN, ADD_GROUP_ROW, SET_GROUP_CHAR_CELL, and SET_GROUP_NUMBER_CELL built-ins.

- Query record groups are created with the CREATE_GROUP_FROM_QUERY built-in. They are populated with the POPULATE_GROUP built-in. As an alternative, you can populate a query record group with a different set of data using the POPULATE_GROUP_WITH_QUERY built-in, as long as the new **select** statement returns records with the same structure as the original **select** statement.

- The two methods for changing the record group associated with an LOV are POPULATE_LIST and SET_LOV_PROPERTY. POPULATE_LIST requires that the new record group be created at run time and contain exactly two columns. SET_LOV_PROPERTY works with any type of record group, with any number of columns.

- You make a record group visible to all forms in your application by including the GLOBAL_SCOPE parameter in the CREATE_GROUP or CREATE_GROUP_FROM_QUERY built-in that creates the record group.

- You can pass a record group's data to other Developer/2000 applications using the RUN_PRODUCT built-in.

Chapter Questions

1. **You need to add a display item to a form. The item will display a calculated total summarizing data from several different tables. You do not want to create any new objects in the database. What course of action is the best one to take?**

   A. Using the Data Block Wizard, create a block with a Stored Procedure as its data source type.

   B. Using the Data Block Wizard, create a block with a View as its data source type.

   C. After creating a data block manually, set its Query Data Source Type to *FROM clause query,* and write the appropriate **select** command in its Query Data Source Name property.

   D. After creating a data block manually, set its Query Data Source Columns property to the desired columns and write the appropriate **select** command in its Query Data Source Arguments property.

2. **What built-in allows you to replace the query associated with a record group?**

   A. ADD_GROUP_ROW

   B. CREATE_GROUP

   C. POPULATE_GROUP_WITH_QUERY

   D. SET_GROUP_QUERY

3. **What built-in can you use to open a second form modally?**

   A. CALL_FORM

   B. NEW_FORM

   C. OPEN_FORM

   D. RUN_PRODUCT

4. **What built-in can provide the name of the current form?**

   A. GET_APPLICATION_PROPERTY

   B. GET_BLOCK_PROPERTY

   C. GET_FORM_PROPERTY

   D. GET_WINDOW_PROPERTY

5. **What built-in can populate a dynamic list item on a form with values from a record group?**

   A. SET_LIST_VALUES

   B. POPULATE_LIST

   C. POPULATE_LIST_WITH_QUERY

   D. RETRIEVE_LIST

6. **What built-in allows you to change a nonquery record group into a query record group?**

   A. CREATE_GROUP_FROM_QUERY

   B. POPULATE_GROUP

   C. POPULATE_GROUP_WITH_QUERY

   D. POPULATE_LIST_WITH_QUERY

7. **How can you base a data block on a stored procedure that uses a ref cursor?**

   A. Using the Data Block Wizard, specify a data source type of Table.

   B. Using the Data Block Wizard, specify a data source type of Stored Procedure.

   C. After creating a data block manually, set the Query Data Source Name property to the appropriate stored procedure.

   D. After creating a data block manually, set the Query Data Source Columns property to the appropriate stored procedure.

8. **Name a benefit of using a FROM clause query as the basis for a data block.**

   A. Can utilize any PL/SQL code

   B. Can include user-defined parameters

   C. Can perform server joins, calculations, and lookups without needing specific access rights to tables

   D. Can perform server joins, calculations, and lookups without needing to create a view

9. **What built-in enables you to populate a record group with data that can be filtered dynamically at run time?**

   A. CREATE_GROUP_FROM_PARAMETER

   B. SET_GROUP_FILTER

   C. POPULATE_LIST

   D. POPULATE_GROUP

10. **You have created a sales application that uses one form for the sales ticket and a second form to list the items being purchased. When the second form is called, the sales ticket is still open and has pending changes. What mode will the second form be opened in?**

    A. Commit mode

    B. Enter-query mode

    C. Open-transaction mode

    D. Post-only mode

11. **What built-in allows you to change the contents of a static record group at run time?**

    A. POPULATE_GROUP_FROM_QUERY

    B. POPULATE_GROUP

    C. ADD_GROUP_ROW

    D. You cannot change the contents of a static record group at run time.

12. **What built-in allows you to pass data from a record group to a separate Oracle graph or report?**

    A. OPEN_REPORT_WITH_GROUP

    B. PASS_GROUP

    C. RUN_PRODUCT

    D. PASS_GROUP_DATA

13. **When you need to design a pair of forms in which one passes values to the other, when and where should you define the parameters that will accept the values?**

    A. In the calling form, at design time

    B. In the calling form, at run time

    C. In the called form, at design time

    D. In the called form, at run time

Answers to Chapter Questions

1. C. After creating a data block manually, set its Query Data Source Type to *FROM clause query*, and write the appropriate **select** command in its Query Data Source Name property.

Explanation You cannot use a Stored Procedure or a View because both of these require adding a new item to the database. The correct approach is using a **from** clause query.

2. C. POPULATE_GROUP_WITH_QUERY

Explanation See the section titled "Creating and Modifying Record Groups Programmatically" for a refresher on this topic.

3. A. CALL_FORM

Explanation CALL_FORM is the built-in that opens forms in a modal window.

4. A. GET_APPLICATION_PROPERTY

Explanation See the section titled "Building Robust Multiple-Form Transactions" for a reminder on this topic.

5. B. POPULATE_LIST

Explanation See the section titled "Building Dynamic List Items by Using Record Groups" for a reminder on this topic.

6. C. POPULATE_GROUP_WITH_QUERY

Explanation The purpose of the POPULATE_GROUP_WITH_QUERY built-in is to fill a record group with data based on a given query, even if the record group was originally a nonquery group.

7. B. Using the Data Block Wizard, specify a data source type of Stored Procedure.

Explanation The options detailing the creation of a data block manually specify using the name of the stored procedure in properties not designed to hold a procedure name. Using the Data Block Wizard, there is no reason to specify a data source type of Table when there is also an option for Stored Procedure.

8. D.   Can perform server joins, calculations, and lookups without needing to create a view

Explanation   The essence of the **from** clause query is its ability to nest SQL **select** statements in subqueries that perform lookups, table joins, and calculations without relying on a database view.

9. D.   POPULATE_GROUP

Explanation   See the section titled "Creating Record Groups at Design Time" for a refresher on this topic.

10. D.   Post-only mode

Explanation   See the section titled "Different Ways to Invoke Forms" for a refresher on this topic.

11. D.   You cannot change the contents of a static record group at run time.

Explanation   The definition of a "static group" is one whose contents cannot be changed at run time.

12. C.   RUN_PRODUCT

Explanation   The RUN_PRODUCT built-in is designed to open other forms, graphics, or reports in their respective runtime programs.

13. C.   In the called form, at design time

Explanation   A parameter that is to be received must be defined at design time, and of course it must be define in the called form. See the section titled "Passing Data Between Forms Using Parameter Lists" for a reminder on this topic.

CHAPTER
22

Advanced Forms Programming III

n this chapter, you will understand and demonstrate knowledge in the following areas:

- Including charts and reports in forms
- Applying timers to form objects
- Utilizing reusable components
- Using server features in Form Builder

You're in the home stretch now on the Forms exams! This chapter covers an assortment of interesting features related to advanced Form Builder programming. You will start by learning how to add graphic charts to your application's forms. Then, you will get a taste of the book's next section as you learn how to create a simple report and invoke it with a push button on a form. Next, you will create an experimental form showing how you can use multiple timers in your applications. After that comes an overview of the reusable components supplied with Form Builder, followed by tips on how to use server features more fully in your applications.

The OCP Exam 4 will consist of test questions in this subject area worth 20 percent of the final score.

Including Charts and Reports in Forms

In this section, you will cover the following points related to including charts and reports in forms:

- Using the Chart Wizard to embed charts in a form
- Using the Report Wizard to create and invoke reports in a form

In this section, you will get a taste of how to create visual output from your data. First, you will see how to create charts based on your application's data, and how to place those charts on your forms. Then, you will experiment with building a report and invoking that report from one of your forms.

Using the Chart Wizard to Embed Charts in a Form

It's very simple to create charts that display on your application's forms. Form Builder provides a Chart Wizard that steps you through the process. In order to see how this works, you will create a new form module and build within it a form that displays the total salaries allocated to each department. To provide data for the form and the chart, you will start by creating a database view that sums salaries by department. Using SQL*Plus or your favorite SQL editor, enter the following code:

```
create view DEPARTMENT_SALARIES as (
  select
    DEPARTMENT_NAME,
    sum(SALARY) TOTAL_SALARY
  from
    (select
      D.DEPARTMENT_NAME, E.SALARY
    from
      DEPARTMENT D, EMPLOYEE E
    where
      D.DEPARTMENT_ID = E.DEPARTMENT_ID
    )
  group by DEPARTMENT_NAME
);
```

Create a new form module and name it **GRAPH**. Then create a new data block based on the view you just built. (Note that this will require enabling the Views option in the Data Block Wizard's Tables dialog box so it will include the DEPARTMENT_SALARIES view in the list of available data sources.) When offered the choice, select the option Create the Data Block, then call the Layout Wizard.

Use the Layout Wizard to create a form that shows both view columns in a Tabular layout, displaying five records at a time. When the Layout Editor opens, click on the canvas's background to select the canvas, and change its Name property to **DEPARTMENT_SALARIES**.

To start the process of creating a chart item, click on the Chart Item button shown here:

Then, drag the mouse on the canvas to create a rectangular area that will hold the chart and its labels. This will cause a dialog box to appear asking whether or not to use the Chart Wizard to create the chart. Select the Use the Chart Wizard option and click on the dialog's OK button. In the Chart Wizard's Chart Title page, leave the Title field empty, select a chart type of Pie, a Chart Subtype of Plain, and then click on the Next button. The next page asks which of the form's data blocks should drive the pie chart. Since the form only has one data block, select DEPARTMENT_SALARIES and then click on the Next button to continue.

The next wizard page asks which item from the data block should produce the pie chart's labels. Ensure that the DEPARTMENT_NAME field is selected, click on the Right Arrow button to move it to the Category Axis area, and then click on the Next button to continue. The next wizard page wants to know which data block item will provide the values for the pie slices. Select the TOTAL_SALARY item, click on the Right Arrow button to move it into the Value Axis area, then click on the Next button. In the final wizard page, change the graph file's name to **dept_slr.ogd** and click on the Finish button to complete the process of creating your chart item.

What you see next will be somewhat of a mess—there will be one pie chart with four rectangular areas beneath it representing additional copies of the chart for each of the five records your data block displays on this form. To solve this, click on the pie chart to select it, open its Property Palette, change its Number Of Items Displayed property to **1**. While in the Property Palette, change the Background Color property to gray. Then run your form. Once it opens in the Forms Runtime program, populate the form by clicking on the Execute Query button. Your form should now look similar to Figure 22-1.

In the exercise you just completed, you created a graphics file named **dept_slr.ogd**. This file is separate from the form module, and is called by a chart item on a canvas within the form module. You can use this or any other preexisting graphics file in canvasses other than the ones in which they were created. To incorporate an existing graphics display into a form, you still start by using the Chart Item button in the Layout Editor. When the New Chart Object dialog box appears, select the Build a New Chart Manually option and click on the OK button. The **.ogd** file will be read by Form Builder, and its settings will be incorporated into the existing form. You then change several of the chart item's properties: Data Source Data Block, Data Source X Axis, and Data Source Y Axis. Expect to play with this for a while after you have taken your exam, because the Oracle documentation on this feature is somewhat sparse.

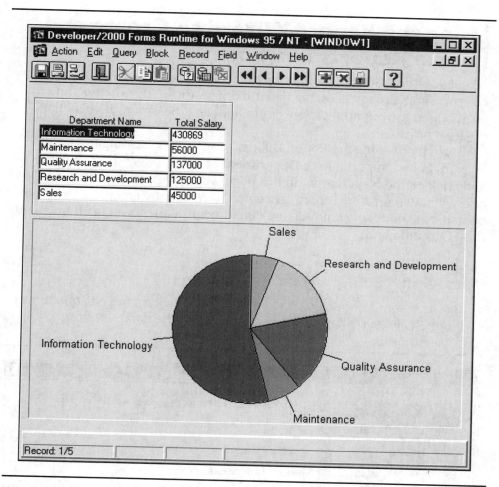

FIGURE 22-1. *Pie chart example*

Exercises

1. What property controls the relationship between the number of records displayed on your form and the number of chart repetitions displayed?

2. If you want to incorporate an existing graphic into a form, should you use the Chart Wizard or build the new chart manually?

Using the Report Wizard to Create and Invoke Reports in a Form

To get your first glimpse of report generation in Developer/2000, you will create a simple report showing department salaries. You will then add a push button to your application's form allowing the user to invoke that report at any time.

Begin by opening the Report Builder program and starting the Report Wizard. Enter a report title of **Department Salaries**, select the Tabular style, and click on the Next button. In this page, you are asked to enter the SQL query that will feed the report. Since you have already created a view that contains the code for summarizing department salaries, you need only enter this SQL command:

```
select * from department_salaries
order by department_name;
```

Your screen should now look like Figure 22-2. Click on the Next button to continue. Unless you have already connected to the database from within

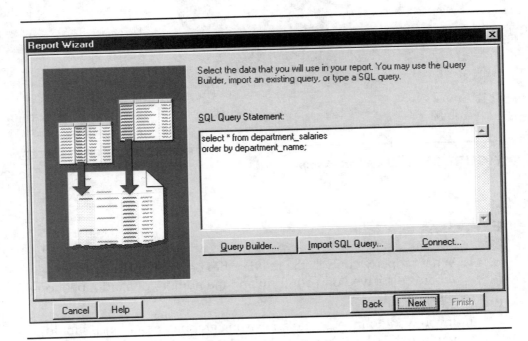

FIGURE 22-2. *Report Wizard query page*

Report Builder, you will be asked to log on to your database. Once that is accomplished, you will be asked which items from the data source should be included in the report. Move both items into the Displayed Fields area and click on the Next button. The next screen asks whether any of the fields should be totaled. Since that is not germane to the exam, simply click on the Next button to move on to the next page, where you can change the item labels or widths. Click on the Next button to move past this page as well. The Report Wizard then asks if you would like to apply a predefined template to the report's layout. Select the Corporate 1 template and click on the Finish button. You should now see a report preview that looks similar to Figure 22-3.

Close the report preview window. Save the report with the name **DEPARTMENT_SALARIES**. Close Report Builder and return to Form Builder. In your GRAPH form module, create a data block manually, name it **DEPARTMENT_CONTROL**, and set its Database Data Block property to No. Then open your DEPARTMENT_SALARIES canvas in the Layout Editor. Use the Block drop-down list in the toolbar to change the focus block to DEPARTMENT_CONTROL. Then, create a push button, change its Name property to **DEPARTMENT_REPORT_PUSHBUTTON**, and change its Label

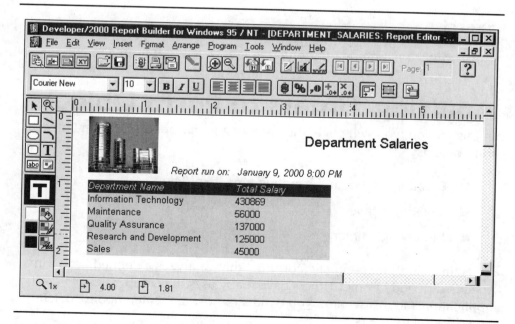

FIGURE 22-3. *Report preview screen*

property to **Run Report**. Create a WHEN-BUTTON-PRESSED trigger for the new push button, and enter the following code into it:

```
run_product(reports, 'DEPARTMENT_SALARIES', synchronous, runtime,
filesystem, '', null);
```

NOTE
If you stored your report file in a directory other than the default Form Builder directory, you need to include the file's path in the command before the DEPARTMENT_SALARIES filename. Use the 8.3 file-naming convention.

Run your form, and click on the new Run Report push button. While looking at your report in the on-screen previewer, you can print the report using the File | Print command. You can also use the File | Generate to File command to write the report out to files in a variety of formats: Adobe Portable Document Format (**.pdf**), Hypertext Markup Language (**.htm**), Rich Text Format (**.rtf**), and Postscript (**.eps**).

Exercise

What PL/SQL built-in allows you to invoke a report from a form?

Applying Timers to Form Objects

In this section, you will cover the following points about applying timers to form objects:

- Creating a timer and handling timer expiration

- Deleting a timer

- Modifying a timer

A timer is a programmatic construct that catalyzes a defined action in a specified period of time. Timers have many uses in certain types of applications. In this section, you will learn how to create, modify, delete, and respond to timers.

Creating a Timer

A timer's duration is set in milliseconds; one thousand milliseconds constitutes one second. With a valid range of 1 to 2,147,483,647 milliseconds, you can create a timer that waits almost 25 days before it expires. When you create a timer, you can specify whether or not it repeats after it expires.

The timer itself does not actually execute an action when it expires. That is the job of a WHEN-TIMER-EXPIRED trigger, which you define for a form module as a whole by placing it at the Form level. Since the trigger may be fired by more than one timer, you will see how to determine in the trigger what timer fired it.

To see how timers work, you will create a canvas that lets you run a few of them simultaneously. Start by creating a new form module named **TIMERS**. Create a new data block manually, change its name to **TIMER_CONTROL**, and change its Database Data Block property to No. Then, create a new canvas object, change its name to **TIMER_CANVAS**, and open it in the Layout Editor. Click on the Display Item button and draw a display item that is approximately 1" tall and 1 1/2" wide in the middle of your canvas. Name the display item **DISPLAY_1**, set its Initial Value property to **0**, its Database Item property to No, and its Font Size property to **48**. Now place a push button just above the display item, and change its name to **TIMER_1_PUSHBUTTON**. Change its Label property to **Start Timer 1**. Then, create a WHEN-BUTTON-PRESSED trigger for the push button, and enter the following code for the trigger:

```
DECLARE
  V_TIMER_1 timer;
BEGIN
  V_TIMER_1 := create_timer('ONE_SECOND_TIMER', 1000, repeat);
END;
```

Close the Layout Editor and return to the Object Navigator. Double-click on the TIMERS module's Triggers node to create a new trigger, and select the WHEN-TIMER-EXPIRED trigger. In the PL/SQL Editor, enter the following code:

```
:TIMER_CONTROL.DISPLAY_1 := :TIMER_CONTROL.DISPLAY_1 +1;
```

Run your form, and when it opens in the Forms Runtime program, click on your Start Timer 1 button. You will see your display item begin to increment in intervals of approximately one second. When you have been sufficiently entertained, close the Forms Runtime program and return to Form Builder.

TIP
There are a number of things in the Forms Runtime environment that take precedence over timer execution. Timer expiration will not necessarily occur at exactly the number of milliseconds you state.

Your application could have multiple timers operating simultaneously. Since there is only one WHEN-TIMER-EXPIRED trigger covering an entire form module, the trigger code needs a way to determine which timer fired. The GET_APPLICATION_PROPERTY built-in has the ability to identify the timer most recently fired. To see how it works, you will modify your TIMER form module so it has two timers running concurrently. Start by opening the TIMER_CANVAS canvas in the Layout Editor. Click on the Display Item button and draw a second display item next to the first one. Name the second display item **DISPLAY_2**, set its Initial Value property to **0**, its Database Item property to No, and its Font Size property to **48**. Click on the first push button to set its size as the current default, and then click on the Button toolbar button to create a second push button. Position the new push button above the new display item, and change its name to **TIMER_2_PUSHBUTTON**. Change its Label property to **Start Timer 2**. Then, create a WHEN-BUTTON-PRESSED trigger for the push button, and enter the following code for the trigger:

```
DECLARE
    V_TIMER_2 timer;
BEGIN
    V_TIMER_2 := create_timer('HALF_SECOND_TIMER', 500, repeat);
END;
```

Close the Layout Editor and return to the Object Navigator. Open the form-level WHEN-TIMER-EXPIRED trigger in the PL/SQL Editor, and modify its code to match the following:

```
DECLARE
    LAST_TIMER_EXPIRED char(20);
```

```
BEGIN
  LAST_TIMER_EXPIRED := get_application_property(timer_name);
  if LAST_TIMER_EXPIRED = 'ONE_SECOND_TIMER'
    then :TIMER_CONTROL.DISPLAY_1 := :TIMER_CONTROL.DISPLAY_1 +1;
  elsif LAST_TIMER_EXPIRED = 'HALF_SECOND_TIMER'
    then :TIMER_CONTROL.DISPLAY_2 := :TIMER_CONTROL.DISPLAY_2 +1;
  end if;
END;
```

Run your form, and when it opens in the Forms Runtime program, click on your Start Timer 1 and Start Timer 2 buttons. You will see both of your display items begin to increment at the time intervals you specified. After you have seen this, close the Forms Runtime program and return to Form Builder.

Exercises

1. What built-in would you use to make a timer that expires at one-minute intervals?

2. What object performs an action when a timer expires? At what level is this object usually defined?

3. What built-in can identify the timer that most recently expired? Why is this necessary in form modules with multiple timers?

Deleting a Timer

There may be times when you will want a timer to execute a certain number of times and then stop. This can be handled using the DELETE_TIMER built-in. To see how this works, modify the code of your form-level WHEN-TIMER-EXPIRED trigger to match the following:

```
DECLARE
  LAST_TIMER_EXPIRED char(20);
  LAST_TIMER_EXPIRED_ID timer;

BEGIN
  LAST_TIMER_EXPIRED := get_application_property(timer_name);
  LAST_TIMER_EXPIRED_ID := find_timer(LAST_TIMER_EXPIRED);

  if LAST_TIMER_EXPIRED = 'ONE_SECOND_TIMER'
```

```
    then
      if :TIMER_CONTROL.DISPLAY_1 < 10
        then :TIMER_CONTROL.DISPLAY_1 := :TIMER_CONTROL.DISPLAY_1 +1;
      else delete_timer(LAST_TIMER_EXPIRED_ID);
      end if;
  elsif LAST_TIMER_EXPIRED = 'HALF_SECOND_TIMER'
    then
      if :TIMER_CONTROL.DISPLAY_2 < 10
        then :TIMER_CONTROL.DISPLAY_2 := :TIMER_CONTROL.DISPLAY_2 +1;
      else delete_timer(LAST_TIMER_EXPIRED_ID);
      end if;
  end if;
END;
```

This code incorporates two new built-ins: FIND_TIMER and DELETE_TIMER. The FIND_TIMER built-in returns the internal ID number of whatever timer name is used as an argument. As you no doubt recall, using the ID number can speed up processing when the object will be referred to multiple times in a routine. The FIND_TIMER built-in can work together with the DELETE_TIMER built-in to identify which timer to delete. To see all of this in action, run your form, and when it opens in the Forms Runtime program, click on your Start Timer 1 and Start Timer 2 buttons. You will see both of your display items begin to increment at the time intervals you specified, and then they will each stop after reaching the value of 10, as shown in Figure 22-4. After you have seen this, close the Forms Runtime program and return to Form Builder.

Exercises

1. What is the purpose of the FIND_TIMER built-in?

2. Which built-in enables you to remove a timer?

Modifying a Timer

There are other ways you can modify a timer besides just deleting it. The SET_TIMER built-in allows you to change a timer's duration or iteration setting. The syntax of this built-in is as follows:

```
set_timer('timer_name', duration, iteration);
```

or

```
set_timer(timer_id, duration, iteration);
```

If you want to change a timer's duration but leave its iteration setting alone—or vice versa—you can specify NO_CHANGE for the value of the parameter you don't want to change. For example, the following code would set the HYPER_TIMER to expire every tenth of a second, without changing its iteration status:

```
set_timer('HYPER_TIMER', 100, no_change);
```

Exercises

1. What built-in allows you to modify an existing timer?

2. What parameters of an existing timer can you change? How do you avoid changing parameters you wish to leave alone?

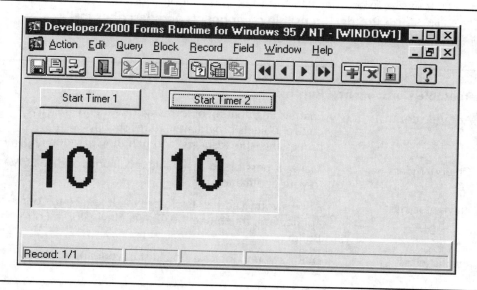

FIGURE 22-4.   *Multiple timers*

Utilizing Reusable Components

In this section, you will cover the following points about utilizing reusable components:

- Introduction to reusable components
- Using the Calendar class in an application

Reusability is the essence of object-oriented design. This section identifies the reusable components provided with Form Builder and gives an overview of how to utilize one common component, a calendar, in your own applications.

Introduction to the Reusable Components

Form Builder comes with an assortment of reusable components that can provide valuable functionality to your applications. In addition to giving you useful features requiring very little work to implement, reusing components makes it easier to standardize the look and feel of your application. Table 22-1 lists Form Builder's reusable components and describes the functionality each component offers.

Reusable Component	Purpose
ActiveX control	Enables augmenting of forms with predefined ActiveX control objects providing features such as word processing, spreadsheets, and handling of video clips.
Calendar class	Makes it possible to easily add a calendar or date LOV to your application.
Navigator class	Allows you to add an Explorer-type interface to your application, much like the Object Navigator in Form Builder.
Picklist class	Enables you to include a picklist in your applications.

TABLE 22-1. *Form Builder Reusable Components*

Reusable Component	Purpose
Standard Object Library	Contains a collection of predefined alerts, buttons, form input items, layouts, visual attribute groups, and the Calendar, Navigator, Picklist, and Wizard components. Can be extended or modified by the developer, and its objects can be set as standard or customized SmartClasses.
Wizard class	Allows you to create customized wizards for your applications.

TABLE 22-1.   *Form Builder Reusable Components* (continued)

Exercises

1. Which reusable component enables you to use third-party commercial objects to augment your application?

2. Which reusable component allows you to customize SmartClasses?

3. Which reusable component could you use to give your application's users access to other modules in an interface that looks like the Object Navigator?

4. Which reusable component can help you step users through complicated procedures?

Using the Calendar Class in an Application

The certification exam will not require that you attach the Calendar class to an application, but you will be expected to understand the process involved in doing so. There are four steps:

1. Create your form module, data block, and canvas.

2. Attach the Standard Object Library file **stndrd20.olb**. Copy or subclass the Calendar class from the resultant STANDARDS object library into your form module. This will add a variety of relevant objects to your application.

3. Attach the PL/SQL library file **calendar.pll** in order to gain access to the DATE_LOV package it contains.

4. To trigger the calendar from the appropriate date item in your form, create a KEY-LISTVAL trigger on the item. Place code in the trigger employing the DATE_LOV package to show the calendar.

The key to making these steps work is the triggering device: the KEY-LISTVAL trigger. Without that trigger, none of the functionality from the Standard Object Library or the Calendar PL/SQL Library will ever be used.

Exercises

1. What object library will you attach when adding a calendar object to your application? What PL/SQL library?

2. How can you allow the user to invoke a calendar from a date field that has an LOV attached?

Using Server Features in Form Builder

In this section, you will cover the following points about using server features in Form Builder:

- Introduction to Oracle Server features in Form Builder

- Partitioning PL/SQL program units

- Handling errors raised by the Oracle Server

- Performing DDL commands

As this chapter draws to a close, it is an excellent time to discuss incorporating the database server more completely within your applications. In this section, you will read about the abilities Developer/2000 offers to move a substantial amount of your application's processing to the server. More work done on the server means more potential for server errors, so you will also review how to handle database errors. The section, and the chapter, wrap up with examples showing how you can make your application generate and execute SQL Data Definition Language (DDL) commands dynamically at run time.

Introduction to Oracle Server Features in Form Builder

Form Builder provides features enabling you to easily create multitier applications. You can partition your application's program units, PL/SQL libraries, and triggers by simply dragging the objects into the Object Navigator's Database Objects node. Doing so can yield substantial rewards in system performance, data integrity, ease of maintaining standard objects, and simplicity. Performance can improve because record-oriented actions occur on the server, close to the data, thereby reducing network traffic and resultant delays. Data integrity benefits because anything you have defined to ensure data integrity is stored with the data tables, and will thus be available for action no matter what application is accessing the data. Standards benefit because often-used routines can reside on the server, where they are easy to locate and maintain.

When a program unit is placed on the server, it is called a *stored program unit*. Form Builder lets you create stored program units containing a procedure, function, package spec, or package body. These are stored in specific schema areas on the server. You can also attach a database trigger directly to a table, thereby ensuring the trigger will fire at the appropriate times regardless of the front-end application used to access the data.

This is not the same as storing the application itself on the server (a feature offered by Form Builder). This feature relates to where the application is stored for retrieval by users, and the options are the database server or a standard file system available to the user. The choice between these two options does not affect how the application partitions its operations once it is loaded into the client computer's memory.

Exercises

1. What object types can you store on the server to partition an application's functionality?

2. What are three benefits that can result from placing part of an application's functionality on the server?

Partitioning PL/SQL Program Units

To see how to create program units on the server, open the Database Objects node in the Object Navigator. Beneath that node, you will see each schema available via your current database connection. Open a schema, and you will see subnodes for Stored Program Units, PL/SQL Libraries, Tables, and Views. Double-click on the Stored Program Units node, and you will be given the opportunity to create a new procedure, function, package spec, or package body directly on the server. You can also copy program units from an existing client-side PL/SQL library into the Stored Program Units node of a schema simply by dragging the program units in the Object Navigator and dropping them on the appropriate Stored Program Units node.

When a procedure or function is created on the server, it can be called in exactly the same way as a procedure or function residing on the client computer. There are some limitations on what stored procedures can do, however. They cannot refer to bind variables: form items, global variables, or system variables. If you need to pass values to a stored procedure, you must do it using parameters. In addition, all form processing pauses when a stored procedure or function is called; the form waits until the procedure or function completes. So you will want to consider the performance of your server and network when deciding what parts of your application to store on the server.

Exercises

1. What is the hard-and-fast rule about partitioning applications for best performance? (Note: This is another trick question.)

2. What limitations exist for procedures and functions stored on the server?

Handling Errors Raised by the Oracle Server

As discussed in Chapter 16, you can trap errors returned by the Oracle server. This becomes especially important as you move more of your application's processing onto the server. Chapter 16 introduced one of the two ways to trap server error messages: the DBMS_ERROR_TEXT built-in, which returns the message text of the most recent Oracle database error. An example of its use follows:

```
DECLARE
   DBERR_NUM number := dbms_error_code;
   DBERR_TXT varchar2(80) := dbms_error_text;
   ERROR_TYPE varchar2(3) := error_type;
BEGIN
    if DBERR_NUM = -1 then
       message('Primary key for new record duplicates key in
existing record.');
    else
       message('Cannot insert this record...reason undetermined.');
    end if;
  else
    message(ERROR_TYPE || '-' || to_char(DBERR_NUM) || ': ' ||
DBERR_TXT);
  end if;
end;
```

Exercise

What built-in returns the text of the most recent DBMS error message?

Performing DDL Commands

You can write PL/SQL code in Form Builder that dynamically generates and executes DDL commands while the application is running. Based on the FORMS_DDL built-in, this very cool feature affords you a lot of flexible control over the database while your application is running. For instance, if you want to store posted records in a temporary database table until they are committed, you can have your application build the temporary table dynamically and then drop it when it is no longer needed. What follows is a very simple example of how to do this:

```
BEGIN
   forms_ddl('create table TEMP_RECS (COL_1 varchar2(20), COL_2
            number) ');
   if form_success then
     message ('Temporary table successfully created.');
   else
     message ('Temporary table could NOT be created.');
   end if;
END;
```

Note that in this example, the SQL DDL statement did *not* have its own terminating semicolon. For multiple-line SQL statements, you should include semicolons in the standard places, with the exception of the last, terminating semicolon. The contents of the SQL DDL command itself can be constructed dynamically at run time. One simple application of this is demonstrated in the following code, which is adapted from a clever example in the Oracle documentation:

```
PROCEDURE Create_N_Column_Number_Table (N number) is
   V_SQL_STRING varchar2(2000);
BEGIN
   V_SQL_STRING := 'create table tmp (COL1 number';
   for I in 2..N loop
     V_SQL_STRING := V_SQL_STRING || ',COL' || to_char(I) || '
number';
   end loop;
   V_SQL_STRING := V_SQL_STRING || ')';

   forms_ddl(V_SQL_STRING);
   if form_success then
     message ('Table successfully created.');
   else
     message ('Table could NOT be created.');
   end if;
end;
```

Exercise

What is the purpose of the FORMS_DDL built-in?

Chapter Summary

In this chapter, you have covered some powerful concepts regarding advanced forms programming. Several topics are covered, including embedding charts and reports into your forms, utilizing timers in your applications, incorporating reusable components, and using server features more fully in your applications.

The first area you covered was embedding charts and reports into your forms. To add a chart to a Form Builder form, all you need to do is make sure the form module has a data block that provides the data the chart needs, and then use the Chart Wizard to create the chart. The Chart Wizard generates a separate graphics file with a file type of **.ogd**, and then generates a chart item on your form to display the chart. That same graphics file can be used by other canvasses as well, by creating a chart item and setting its Data Source

Data Block, Data Source X Axis, and Data Source Y Axis properties. To create a report, you invoke the Report Builder program and start the Report Wizard. This, too, results in a separate file on disk, with a file type of **.rdf**. Once the report file is created, you can invoke it from a push button or any other code-containing object in your application, using the RUN_PRODUCT built-in. While the report is running, you can export its contents to files formatted into Adobe Portable Document Format (**.pdf**), Hypertext Markup Language (**.htm**), Rich Text Format (**.rtf**), and Postscript (**.eps**).

The next section you explored was timers. A timer is a programmatic construct that catalyzes a defined action in a specified period of time. A timer's duration is set in milliseconds, which are thousandths of a second. With a valid duration of 1 to 2,147,483,647 milliseconds, you can create a timer that waits almost 25 days before it expires. When you create a timer, you can specify whether or not it repeats after it expires. The timer itself does not execute code when it expires. That is the job of a WHEN-TIMER-EXPIRED trigger, which you define at the form level. Your application can have multiple timers operating simultaneously. Since all timers will cause the same WHEN-TIMER-EXPIRED trigger to fire, the trigger needs a way to determine what trigger within the timer fired it. The GET_APPLICATION_PROPERTY built-in allows you to determine the name of the timer most recently fired timer in an application, which you can use as the argument in an **if** statement within the trigger to determine what action to take based on which timer expired. You can delete a timer by using the DELETE_TIMER built-in. You can determine a timer's internal ID with the FIND_TIMER built-in. You can modify an existing timer using the SET_TIMER built-in, which allows you to change a timer's duration or iteration setting.

After working with timers, you were introduced to the reusable components supplied with Form Builder. These include the ActiveX control, Calendar class, Navigator class, Picklist class, Standard Object Library, and Wizard class. The ActiveX control enables augmenting your forms with predefined ActiveX control objects providing features such as word processing, spreadsheets, and handling of video clips. The Calendar class makes it possible to easily add a calendar or date LOV to your application. The Navigator class allows you to add an Explorer-type interface to your application, much like the Object Navigator in Form Builder. The Picklist class enables you to include a picklist in your applications. The Standard Object Library contains a collection of predefined alerts, buttons, form input items, layouts, visual attribute groups, and the Calendar, Navigator, Picklist, and Wizard components. It can be extended or modified by the developer, and its objects can be set as standard or customized SmartClasses. Finally, the Wizard class allows you to create customized wizards for your applications. You still have to do a little bit of work to use these classes; for instance, to use a Calendar class after all the pieces have been attached, you can create a KEY-LISTVAL trigger for your LOV field.

The last topic was the server features you can use in your Form Builder applications. Form Builder provides features enabling you to easily create multitier applications by partitioning your application's program units, PL/SQL libraries, and triggers between the client computer and the database server. You can move program units, PL/SQL libraries, and triggers to the server by dragging the objects into the Object Navigator's Database Objects node. When a program unit is placed on the server, it is called a stored program unit. You can also create new stored program units directly from within Form Builder. To catch and handle errors returned by the server when it executes stored program units, use the DBMS_ERROR_TEXT built-in, which returns the message text of the most recent Oracle database error. If you need to have your application dynamically generate and execute DDL commands at run time, you can do so using the FORMS_DDL built-in.

All in all, this chapter comprises about 20 percent of material tested on OCP Exam 4.

Two-Minute Drill

- When adding a chart to a canvas, use the Chart Wizard to create and add a new chart display. Create the chart item manually if you are incorporating an existing chart display.

- To invoke a report from a form, utilize the RUN_PRODUCT built-in.

- The built-in that generates timers is CREATE_TIMER.

- Timers do not perform actions. That is the province of the WHEN-TIMER-EXPIRED trigger. Usually defined at the form level, this trigger fires when any timer within the form module expires.

- The WHEN-TIMER-EXPIRED trigger can determine which timer expired by getting the timer's name with the GET_APPLICATION_PROPERTY(TIMER_NAME) built-in. It can also determine the ID of a timer using the FIND_TIMER built-in.

■ A timer can be removed using the DELETE_TIMER built-in.

■ A timer can be modified using the SET_TIMER built-in. You can change the timer's duration, its iteration status, or both. To leave one of the parameters as it is, use the constant NO_CHANGE for that parameter.

■ Form Builder comes with several reusable components: ActiveX control, Calendar class, Navigator class, Picklist class, Standard Object Library, and Wizard class.

■ The ActiveX control enables adding predefined ActiveX control objects to augment your forms with features such as word processing, spreadsheets, and video clips.

■ The Calendar class makes it possible to easily add a calendar or date LOV to your application.

■ The Navigator class allows you to add an Explorer-type interface to your application, much like the Object Navigator in Form Builder.

■ The Picklist class enables you to include a picklist in your applications.

■ The Standard Object Library contains a collection of predefined alerts, buttons, form input items, layouts, visual attribute groups, and the Calendar, Navigator, Picklist, and Wizard components. It can be extended or modified by the developer, and its objects can be set as standard or customized SmartClasses.

■ The Wizard class allows you to create customized wizards for your applications.

■ When adding a Calendar class object to your application, you attach the Standard Object Library to obtain an assortment of relevant objects, classes, and settings, and then attach the Calendar PL/SQL file to gain access to the DATE_LOV package. To invoke a calendar from a form, you can use a KEY-LISTVAL trigger.

■ When partitioning an application's functionality between the client computer and the server, you can store program units, PS/SQL libraries, and triggers on the server.

■ The benefits of partitioning an application between client and server computers include faster performance due to reduced network traffic and record-oriented procedures executing closer to the relevant data tables; improved data integrity from locating integrity-oriented triggers directly on the tables they protect; and easier maintenance and standardization by having commonly used objects located in one central location.

■ The decision about what parts of your application to place on your server depends on a variety of variables: the size of your organization, the amount of code that is used by more than one application, the speed of the server and client computers, and the speed of the network.

■ Stored procedures and functions have a number of limitations. They cannot refer to bind variables: form items, global variables, or system variables. If you need to pass values to a stored procedure, you must do it using parameters. In addition, all form processing pauses when a stored procedure or function is called.

■ When an error occurs, the DBMS_ERROR_TEXT built-in can provide you with the text of the most recent DBMS error message.

■ The FORMS_DDL built-in enables you to have your application generate and execute SQL DDL commands dynamically at run time.

Chapter Questions

I. **What reusable component allows you to step your users through complicated processes?**

A. ActiveX controls

B. Calendar class

C. Navigator class

D. Picklist class

E. Standard Object Library

F. Wizard class

2. **What reusable component allows you to create an Object Navigator-like interface for your own applications?**

   A. ActiveX controls

   B. Calendar class

   C. Navigator class

   D. Picklist class

   E. Standard Object Library

   F. Wizard class

3. **What Form Builder built-ins allow you to set the duration of a timer? (Choose all that apply.)**

   A. CREATE_TIMER

   B. FIND_TIMER

   C. SET_TIMER

   D. SET_TIMER_PROPERTY

   E. WHEN-TIMER-EXPIRED

4. **What built-in would allow you to find the internal ID of the EVERY_MINUTE timer?**

   A. CREATE_TIMER

   B. FIND_TIMER

   C. SET_TIMER

   D. SET_TIMER_PROPERTY

   E. WHEN-TIMER-EXPIRED

5. **What reusable component allows you to create a customized SmartClass?**

   A. ActiveX controls

   B. Calendar class

   C. Navigator class

    D. Picklist class

    E. Standard Object Library

    F. Wizard class

6. **What built-in would allow you to eliminate a timer?**

    A. DELETE_TIMER

    B. FIND_TIMER

    C. REMOVE_TIMER

    D. SET_TIMER

    E. SET_TIMER_PROPERTY

    F. WHEN-TIMER-EXPIRED

7. **You moved a number of your application's program units over to the server and started experiencing DBMS errors. What built-in can you use to capture these errors and the information they return?**

    A. DBMS_ERROR

    B. DBMS_ERROR_NUM

    C. DBMS_ERROR_STRING

    D. DBMS_ERROR_TEXT

8. **What trigger is used to respond to timers, and at what level is it most commonly defined?**

    A. ON-TIMER-BEGIN at the block level

    B. ON-TIMER-EXPIRE at the form level

    C. ON-TIMER at the window level

    D. WHEN-TIMER-BEGINS at the block level

    E. WHEN-TIMER-BEGINS at the form level

    F. WHEN-TIMER-BEGINS at the window level

    G. WHEN-TIMER-EXPIRED at the form level

    H. WHEN-TIMER-EXPIRED at the window level

9. **What trigger should you use to activate a calendar when the user presses the List Of Values function key while in a date field?**

   A. ON-LIST-OPEN

   B. KEY-LIST-OPEN

   C. ON-LISTVAL

   D. KEY-LISTVAL

   E. WHEN-LOV-OPEN

10. **What are the steps for embedding an existing chart on a form you have open in the Layout Editor?**

    A. Invoke the Chart Wizard, identify the chart file, and move the resulting chart to the correct position on the canvas.

    B. Execute the File | Import menu command, identify the chart file, and move the resulting chart to the correct position on the canvas.

    C. Create a chart item manually using the Chart Item button, identify the chart file in the item's Property Palette, and move the resulting chart to the correct position on the canvas.

11. **What built-in allows you to manipulate table structures at run time?**

    A. RUNTIME_DDL

    B. FORMS_RUNTIME

    C. FORMS_DDL

    D. DDL_FORMS

    E. DDL_RUNTIME

12. **What built-in gives you the ability to invoke reports from a form?**

    A. INVOKE_PRODUCT

    B. INVOKE_REPORT

    C. RUN_PRODUCT

    D. RUN_REPORT

    E. WHEN-BUTTON-PRESSED

13. **What built-in allows you to determine which timer fired a WHEN-TIMER-EXPIRED trigger?**

    A. SYSTEM.TIMER

    B. GET_TIMER_PROPERTY

    C. GET_APPLICATION_PROPERTY

    D. FIND_TIMER

Answers to Chapter Questions

1. F.   Wizard class

Explanation   The Wizard class enables you to create your own custom wizards, which can step users through complicated processes.

2. C.   Navigator class

Explanation   The Navigator class contains objects that make it easy to implement a Navigator interface in your own applications.

3. A, C.   CREATE_TIMER, SET_TIMER

Explanation   CREATE_TIMER generates a new timer with the duration specified. SET_TIMER alters the duration of an existing timer. If you included WHEN-TIMER-EXPIRED in your answer, take care to read the questions more carefully—this question asked for built-ins, and WHEN-TIMER-EXPIRED is a trigger.

4. B.   FIND_TIMER

Explanation   The FIND_TIMER built-in returns the internal ID of whatever timer's name is provided as an argument.

5. E.   Standard Object Library

Explanation   See the section titled "Introduction to the Reusable Components" for a refresher on this topic.

6. A.   DELETE_TIMER

Explanation   The DELETE_TIMER built-in's sole purpose is to deactivate and eliminate timers. There is no REMOVE_TIMER built-in.

7. D.   DBMS_ERROR_TEXT

Explanation   The DBMS_ERROR_TEXT built-in is designed specifically to return the text of error messages sent back by the database server.

8. G.   WHEN-TIMER-EXPIRED at the form level

Explanation   See the section titled "Creating a Timer" for a refresher on this topic.

9. D.   KEY-LISTVAL

Explanation   The KEY-LISTVAL trigger fires whenever the user presses the LOV function key.

10. C.   Create a chart item manually using the Chart Item button, identify the chart file in the item's Property Palette, and move the resulting chart to the correct position on the canvas.

Explanation   The Chart Wizard is only useful for creating new charts, so it is not a correct answer because the question specifies that you are dealing with an existing chart. There is no such command in Form Builder as File I Import. When dealing with an existing chart file, you bypass the Chart Wizard, create a new chart item manually, and alter the new item's properties to use the existing chart file.

11. C.   FORMS_DDL

Explanation   The FORMS_DDL built-in gives you the ability to execute SQL commands during run time. All other potential answers to this question were made up (FORMS_RUNTIME is a program, not a built-in).

12. C.   RUN_PRODUCT

Explanation   The RUN_PRODUCT built-in allows you to run separate report or graphics files from your form module.

13. C.   GET_APPLICATION_PROPERTY

Explanation   See the section titled "Creating a Timer" for a refresher on this topic.

UNIT V

Preparing for OCP Exam 5: Building Reports

CHAPTER
23

Introducing
Oracle Reports

In this chapter, you will cover the following areas of building reports in Oracle:

- Designing and running reports
- Report Builder concepts
- Using Report Wizard to create reports

OCP Exam 5 tests your knowledge of writing reports against the Oracle database server using Oracle Reports, a component of the Developer toolset. This chapter introduces you to using Oracle Reports to develop and execute reports against the Oracle server. Both the creation of reports and the use of Oracle Reports for this purpose are covered in the test, with emphasis on how to use the Reports toolset. This introduction covers designing and running reports, Report Builder concepts, and using the Report Wizard to create new reports quickly. The chapter content covers 15 percent of material found on OCP Exam 5.

As an aside, and before proceeding any further, make sure you understand the basics of usage for the other Builder components, and the other Developer/2000 tools that were covered in Chapter 11. In particular, make sure you understand Project Builder, Query Builder, and Chart Builder. Only about 3 percent of OCP Exam 5 content is directly focused in this area, but they are easy points to score! Plus, there are several questions in OCP Exam 5 that require an indirect knowledge of other Builder components, so the time studying this material is well spent.

Designing and Running Reports

In this section, you will cover the following points on designing and running reports:

- Style and structure of common business reports
- Using Runtime executable to run prebuilt reports
- Identifying various report destinations
- Viewing report output in the Report Previewer

Many applications and work environments require the use of reporting to make decisions. As the report developer, you need to understand a few basic items about the development of reports before proceeding into other areas of developing and managing reports with Oracle Reports. This section covers basic concepts on the style and structure of common business reports. In addition, you may find that, in some environments, there are reports already in production that require support. This section will acquaint you with the requirements for running prebuilt reports with the Reports Runtime executable. The section will cover the identification of reporting destinations such as file and printer. Finally, the section will show you how to view the output for a report using the Report Previewer.

Style and Structure of Common Business Reports

Business reports have a style and structure all their own. Several different types of reports may exist in a business, and each one may be used in a different way. Several different elements of commonality may exist between business reports, however. The most straightforward style of business report is a tabular report. This report shows data in a table format, similar in concept to the idea of an Oracle table. You may not have realized it, but you've already seen many examples of tabular reports in the form of output from SQL queries in SQL*Plus. Oracle, by default, returns output from your **select** statement in tabular format. Oracle Reports seeks mainly to beautify the output and add some features like showing totals on columns and other items that are helpful—particularly for financial reports. The following code block shows a simple tabular report:

```
EMPID    LASTNAME    FIRSTNAME    SALARY
-------  ----------  -----------  -------
059495   Flurb       David         25000
965383   King        Mustafa       56000
593834   Yojumbo     Bill          29380
```

Sometimes your simple tabular report will contain data where the columns on the right may contain unique data while the entries on the left are duplicates. For example, when your report displays a table join or **select** statement containing a **group by** clause, where there is a one-to-many relationship such as managers to employees, you may have a manager's name listed 20 times on the left, once for each unique employee. A group-left report can help to unclutter your output in this situation. Consider the following code block, which displays a simple group-left report:

```
MANAGER       EMPLOYEE
-----------   ------------
ROBERTS       MCBOOP
              DINNY
              LIVINGSTON
ELLISON       DAVIS
              FLUMPY
              GRUMPY
```

Another type of report common in business situation is a matrix report. This type of report adds another column to your basic tabular report containing a set of fixed items down the vertical axis. The matrix, then, shows the value at each intersection of fixed value along the horizontal axis at the top and the vertical axis on the left. Consider a simple example of a matrix report: a table showing a value by which you multiply your income to find how much you owe for income tax. Along the horizontal axis at the top you may see several categories corresponding to your filing status, such as married, single, and married filing separately. Along the left vertical axis, you will see various income brackets. The body of the report shows a multiplier that you use to determine your income. The following code block shows the simple example:

```
                | SINGLE | MARRIED | MFS
------------------------------------------
0-10000         | 0.18   | 0.15    | 0.17
10001-45000     | 0.21   | 0.19    | 0.20
45001-90000     | 0.25   | 0.21    | 0.23
90001-up        | 0.28   | 0.25    | 0.27
```

You may have combinations of report types as well, such as matrix with group. Other types of reports are reports containing multimedia objects like charts, graphics, sound clips, and the like. Another two types of reports include form letters and mailing labels. Oracle can store all these items in the database, so there's nothing preventing you from creating reports of these types and more. The examples shown here are only samples of the reports you may be required to do.

Exercises

1. Identify common types of business reports and describe some features of each.

2. Which type of report is commonly used for SQL*Plus output? What sort of report might be used to display a **select** statement containing a **group by** clause?

Using Runtime Executable to Run Prebuilt Reports

Many times, you will have a production environment where several reports already exist. An existing report that is compiled and ready to run using Reports Runtime will have the filename extension **.rep**. To process these reports, you must use Reports Runtime. This tool can be executed interactively in Windows-based environments or in batch from an operating system command line or shell script. This discussion will help you understand the use of Reports Runtime working in batch mode. To run a report from an operating system command line, you issue the appropriate command, passing in the appropriate parameters. The appropriate command depends on the version of Oracle Reports you are running: **r25run** for Developer/2000 1.*x* or **r30run32** for Developer/2000 2.0, respectively.

Reports Runtime behaves according to the runtime options you specify via command line parameters. Most of the parameters available for you to specify on the command line are included in Table 23-1. Those that aren't include parameters that handle runtime report tracing and some parameters usable only in character mode. To change any of these parameters from within the Reports Runtime interactive session, use the Edit | Runtime Options menu item to open the Runtime Options dialog box.

Once your parameters are defined either on the command line or in your command file, you are set to run your report from the operating system command prompt. Alternately, you may wish to define the execution of your report to happen from a script, allowing you to set up report execution as part of some time schedule. The following code block shows the

Parameter	Description
MODULE *filename* REPORT *filename*	The name of the file that is the report to be run, sometimes called a *runfile*. These files usually carry the **.rdf** or **.rep** suffix. REPORT and MODULE are synonymous, though REPORT is provided for backward compatibility.
BATCH **y/n**	Whether Reports Runtime is running in batch. If so, no terminal input will be accepted. If not, the interactive window opens.
USERID *user/pwd@db*	Valid user information for use when Reports Runtime accesses the database to create the report.
PARAMFORM **y/n**	Determines whether Reports Runtime shows the runtime parameter form in the Reports Runtime interactive window when you run the report. Not used if BATCH=**y**.
CMDFILE *filename*	The name of a file containing parameters and values for the execution of Reports Runtime.
TERM *termname*	The type of terminal used to run Reports Runtime. Valid only when the report is run in character mode, on environments such as UNIX.
ARRAYSIZE *num*	Size in K of the Oracle array Reports Runtime will use when executing the report. Usually a larger array helps reports process faster. Valid values for *num* range between 1 and 9999, default is 10.
DESTYPE *type*	Specifies the destination of the report. Valid values for *type* include **screen**, **file**, **printer**, **preview**, **sysout**, and **mail**.
DESNAME *name*	Name of a printer, filename, or Oracle Office username 1K in length that is the destination of the report.
DESFORMAT *fmt*	Allows you to specify a printer driver for use when you specify DESTYPE to be a file. Also specifies characteristics of your printer identified by DESNAME.
COPIES *num*	Specifies the number of copies Reports Runtime should produce. Only used if DESTYPE=**printer**. Valid values for *num* range between 1 and 9999, default is 1.
CURRENCY *char*	A character symbol Reports Runtime will use to specify currency on a number.

TABLE 23-1. *Reports Runtime command line parameters*

Parameter	Description
THOUSANDS *char*	A character symbol Reports Runtime uses to separate a number hundreds from thousands, hundred thousands from millions, etc. on a number (i.e., comma, as in 1,000,000 instead of 1000000).
DECIMAL *char*	The character symbol Reports Runtime uses to indicate the decimal place in a number.
READONLY **y/n**	Equivalent to **set transaction read only**, allows reports containing multiple **select** statements to have read consistency across them.
LOGFILE *filename*	Name of a log file to which all screen prints of reports in character mode will be saved. Default is **dfltrep.log**. If the file already exists, its contents are not overwritten. Instead, new screen prints are added at the end.
BUFFERS *num*	Amount of memory used to run your report. Default is 640K. Range is between 1 and 9999.
PROFILE *filename*	The name of a file that stores performance statistics on the report execution. Items included in the profile include total elapsed time, total time Reports Runtime spent running, time spent connecting to Oracle, parsing, and fetching data, SQL processing time, and CPU time.
RUNDEBUG **y/n**	Tells Reports Runtime to perform extra debugging to check for overwrite, layout, mode inconsistencies, or bind variable problems that don't produce runtime errors but will make the report look bad.
ONSUCCESS *action* ONFAILURE *action*	How Reports Runtime should end its transaction based on the success or failure of the report's execution. Valid values for *action* include **commit**, **rollback**, and **noaction**.
ERRFILE *filename*	File to which Reports Runtime writes all errors received this run.
LONGCHUNK	Size in K of chunks Reports Runtime retrieves from LONG type columns. Default 10K. Range is between 1 and 9999.
ORIENTATION *dir*	Orientation of report when printed. Valid values for *dir* include **portrait**, **landscape**, or **default**.

TABLE 23-1. *Reports Runtime command line parameters* (continued)

Parameter	Description
BACKGROUND **y/n**	Specifies whether the report will be run as a background process.
MODE *md*	Specifies whether report runs in bitmap or character mode. Valid values for *md* include **bitmap**, **character**, and **default**.
PRINTJOB	Defines whether the print job dialog interface will appear before the report is run to define printer options. Will not work for background report runs or when DESTYPE=**mail**.
AUTOCOMMIT **y/n**	Defines whether database changes should be committed automatically.
NONBLOCKSQL **y/n**	Allows or disallows other programs to execute while report is being created.
ROLE *name/pwd*	Specifies a role to be used when running this report.
PAGESIZE *num* x *num*	Identifies size of report page in inches, centimeters, picas, or characters.

TABLE 23-1. *Reports Runtime command line parameters* (continued)

command line you may use to run a report in batch from the operating system command prompt where you pass parameters:

```
c:\orant\bin> r30run32 module=jason.rep userid=jason/stacy background=y
```

Or, you can place all your parameters in the command file, as follows:

```
c:\orant\bin> r30run32 cmdfile=jasonrep.cmd
```

In this example, the contents of **jasonrep.cmd** appear in the following block:

```
MODULE=jason.rep
USERID=jason/stacy
BACKGROUND=y
```

Character Mode and Bitmap Mode

You can run a report executable in one of two modes: character and bitmap. Report running mode is determined by the MODE parameter, which can be set to character, bitmap, or default. Character mode is a holdover from older UNIX-based Oracle environments where the reports appeared on your UNIX character-based terminal. Bitmap mode is used for Windows-based environments and offers graphical output.

Some parameters for running reports using Reports Runtime are meant for character mode only while others are meant for bitmap only. For example, the TERM parameter is useful for reports running in character mode because Reports Runtime needs to know what type of terminal to format the distributed output for. TERM is not useful for bitmap reports, however, because the output for the bitmap report will be graphical, not character-based. Other parameters are interpreted differently based on whether the report is running in bitmap or character mode. For example, the PAGESIZE parameter measures size of page in inches, centimeters, or picas if you are running your report in bitmap mode, but measure in characters per page if you are running reports in character mode.

Exercises

1. Name two ways you can run an existing report.

2. Identify the purpose of the DESTYPE, RUNDEBUG, PROFILE, and ONFAILURE parameters. Which parameter can be used to identify a file containing parameters for the report run? Explore the Reports Runtime interactive session and determine how to change these parameters using the Runtime Options dialog box.

3. Identify some parameters used only for Reports Runtime when running in character mode. Identify some parameters used only for Reports Runtime when running in bitmap mode. Identify a parameter whose usage depends on which mode the report is running under.

4. Can parameters be used when starting execution of Report Builder? Why or why not?

Identifying Various Report Destinations

As you may have already surmised from your exposure to the DESTYPE Reports Runtime parameter, there are several different destinations to which a report can be sent. Some of these destinations include the printer, a file, email, the Report Previewer, the screen, or default system output (usually the screen). For the most part, production reports have one primary destination: the printer. Usually, the report goes to a business analyst that prefers hard copy to something on the computer screen. Another common destination is email. For some production purposes, this destination may be sufficient, although email is not 100 percent reliable. Still, a good many production reports find their way into email boxes in the office.

You can run your report interactively and send it to the printer or email as well. After starting the Reports Runtime executable, select the File | Print or File | Mail menu option, and Reports Runtime will prompt you to enter which report you want to run. After processing the report, the executable will send the report to the printer or email address you define.

Other destinations for reports are usually used for development of the report. For example, you may have written the SQL for a report but you are not sure if the data you queried is sufficient. Also, you may want to inspect other visual aspects of the report before allowing others to see it. Setting the destination to be the Report Previewer works best in this situation, or simply running the report using Reports Runtime interactive mode works well also. Bear in mind that if you send a report to the Report Previewer destination, you must run the report with BATCH=no.

A special output destination you may not find yourself using often but that has many uses nonetheless is sending the output to file. One interesting application for this destination in production is to send the output of the report execution to file, then simply print the file. This execution may be useful for those situations where your users frequently complain of lost reports, or want a copy of a report from several days ago. Rather than having to rerun the report to satisfy these requests, you can simply output your reports to file every day, print the file, and keep a soft copy around for a specified period of time.

The output to file destination option also allows you to store multiple copies of the report, corresponding to different file or printer types. For example, you may run the report and send the output to file once for PostScript printers, once for Portable Document Format files, and once for

HTML files for the Web. To send report output to file, you can either run the report from the operating system command prompt or set the runtime options in Reports Runtime using the Edit | Runtime Options menu option. In the following code block, you will see the appropriate parameters to set if you would like to run a report called **cats.rep** from the command line, sending the output to a file that can be put onto a Web site and made available for all:

```
/home/oracle/> r30run module=cats.rep userid=jason/stacy destype=file \
> desname=cats.html desformat=HTML
```

Exercises

1. Identify some different report destinations.

2. What uses are there for sending the report to the file destination?

Viewing Report Output in the Report Previewer

It is often useful in the development of reports to view the report output onscreen before printing a hard copy. The Report Previewer in Reports Runtime allows you to accomplish this task. To see report output online using Reports Runtime and the Report Previewer, execute the following steps. You can start the Windows-based Reports Runtime executable usually by clicking on whatever icon corresponds to Reports Runtime. From within the application, you click on the File | Run menu option to execute a specific report. Using the open file interface, choose the report you wish to run by clicking it once to highlight and then click the Open button. Your report must be in report executable format with the extension **.rep** in this situation. Reports Runtime will prompt you to provide user information to log on to the Oracle database on which the report runs. After connecting, Reports Runtime executes the report against the Oracle database and then shows the output for the report in a Report Previewer window. Figure 23-1 shows the Reports Runtime executable as it appears on your display.

Alternately, you can run the report from the command line with BATCH=no, and DESTYPE=previewer. Reports Runtime will simply come up in interactive mode, processing your report and then showing the

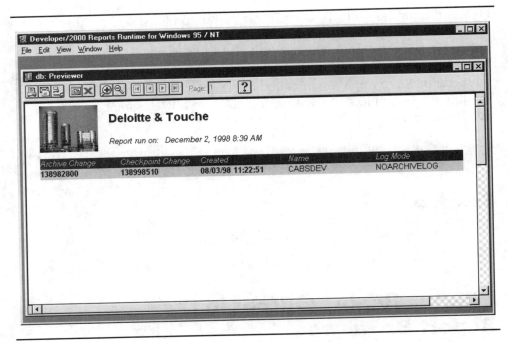

FIGURE 23-1. *Reports Runtime with report in Report Previewer*

result in the Report Previewer. You cannot bring up the report in the Report Previewer if BATCH=yes.

TIP
Make sure you understand the DESTYPE, DESNAME, and DESFORMAT parameters before proceeding!

Exercises

1. How do you bring a report up into the Report Previewer using Reports Runtime interactively? How can you accomplish the same task from the command line?

2. Can you view a report in the Report Previewer without being connected to the Oracle database? Why?

Report Builder Concepts

In this section, you will cover the following points on Report Builder concepts:

- Executable components of Oracle Reports

- Invoking Report Builder and its components

- Main objects in a report

With some of the business elements and facts about running existing reports covered, turn your attention now to understanding how to use Report Builder. This is the tool you use to create new reports in Oracle. It has several components that are designed to help you develop reports quickly, customize their appearance, and view how they will look in printed form online. This section will cover the executable components of a report, along with the components of Report Builder. Methods used to invoke Report Builder are covered as well. Finally, the section details the main objects in a report.

Executable Components of Oracle Reports

The discussion of Reports Runtime in the prior section functions as an introduction to the executable components of Oracle Reports within the Developer/2000 product. There are several other components within Developer/2000 that comprise the Reports toolset. The following discussions tell you what the components are and also give you a bit of information about their purpose for Oracle Reports in Developer/2000 2.0.

TIP

For Developer/2000 1.0 preparation, go back to Developer/2000 and make a mapping of executables in 2.0 that existed in 1.x, and study that listing. In most cases, the change in the name of the executable will be as simple as substituting "25" for "30".

Oracle Reports for Developer/2000 2.0

The following executable items are included in Oracle Reports for Developer/2000 2.0:

- **Report Builder** Tool for use when building new reports or modifying existing reports. Executable is **r30des**.

- **Reports Runtime** Tool for running reports in production from operating system command lines or within scripts. Executable is **r30run**. A similar executable allows you to run a report with the use of the Reports Server, and that executable is **r30cli**.

- **Reports Queue Manager** Tool for managing queued reports. Executables include **r30rqv** for UNIX, and **r30rqm32** for Windows.

- **Reports Server** Tool for use on multitier architectures for running reports. Allows for scheduling or report submission. Executables include **r30mts**.

- **Reports Web CGI** Tool allowing you to execute reports on the Reports Server from your Web browser. Executable is **r30cgi**. Additional executable called **r30ows** provides the interface between Reports Server and Oracle Web Application Server.

- **Report Converter** Tool allowing you to convert reports or PL/SQL libraries on one storage type for the client to another storage type for the server, and vice-versa. Can also be run stand-alone to take a built report and compile it to run in batch or interactively using Reports Runtime. Executable is **r30conv**.

- **Reports Background Engine** Tool allowing you to execute reports locally. Use is similar to Reports Runtime, but on some operating system platforms like Windows, this executable may give you better performance. Executable is **r30rbe** or **r30isv**.

This section focuses on the use of Report Builder for building new reports. There are two ways for building new reports with Developer/2000. You can build a report manually if you have an intermediate or advanced knowledge of how Report Builder works, developing the data definition for your report, the style of the report, and other features. Alternately, you can use the Report Wizard as a guide for building your report. It may be useful to start building your reports with Report Wizard, then customize later using other components of Report Builder.

Exercise

1. Identify the components of Developer/2000 and describe the uses for each component. Which component handles running existing reports from the operating system command line?

2. Spend some time exploring each Developer/2000 component for reporting.

Invoking Report Builder and Its Components

Within Report Builder, there are several components for developing new reports and modifying existing ones that you need to understand. Under the Program menu in Report Builder, you will see the same modules you found in Procedure Builder, the Object Navigator, Program Unit Editor, Stored Program Unit Editor, and Database Trigger Editor. Recall also that you cannot use Stored Program Unit Editor and Database Trigger unless you are connected to the database.

The components of Report Builder that are used in the design of reports include the Report Builder Object Navigator, Report Editor, Template Editor, and the Property Palette. Another component of Report Builder is the Parameter Form Builder, which is used for developing parameter forms for your reports. Another set of components in Report Builder include the wizards for developing reports and other items quickly. They include Report Wizard, Chart Wizard, and Web Wizard (Developer/2000 2.0 and higher). These items can all be found under the Tools menu when the Object Navigator module is in the foreground and active on Report Builder.

The Object Navigator is the master module on Report Builder. It helps you find your way through the development of a report. The Object Navigator has several drill down items available for your use, including several that should by now look familiar, including reports, templates, external SQL queries, debug actions, stack, built-in packages, and database objects. Understanding and using the Object Navigator is key to good usage of Report Builder. Figure 23-2 shows you the Object Navigator module in Report Builder. The Object Navigator module opens automatically as part of invoking Report Builder. See the next discussion for how to invoke Report Builder.

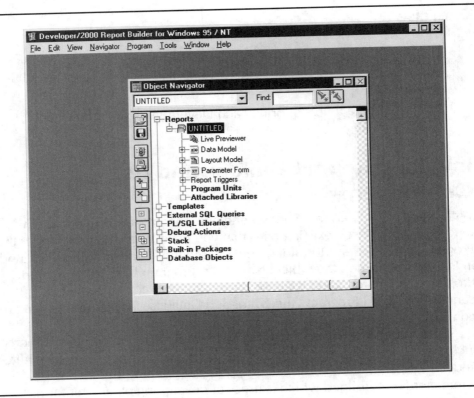

FIGURE 23-2. *Object Navigator module in Report Builder*

Another important component of Report Builder is the Report Editor module. This interface allows you to do many things in developing your reports. You can view the data definition or data model using Report Editor, you can look at the parameter form, you can view the report layout, and you can even see the report as it will look on paper. This final choice is often referred to as the Live Previewer. You toggle between these three views on your report within the Report Editor module with the use of the three buttons in the upper left-hand corner of the Report Editor module, as shown in Figure 23-3. To open the Report Editor, click on Tools | Report Editor on the Report Builder menu.

The Property Palette is another Report Builder tool allowing you to view and modify various properties and facets of your report. Overall categories

Live Previewer button
Data Model button
Layout Model button
Parameter Form button

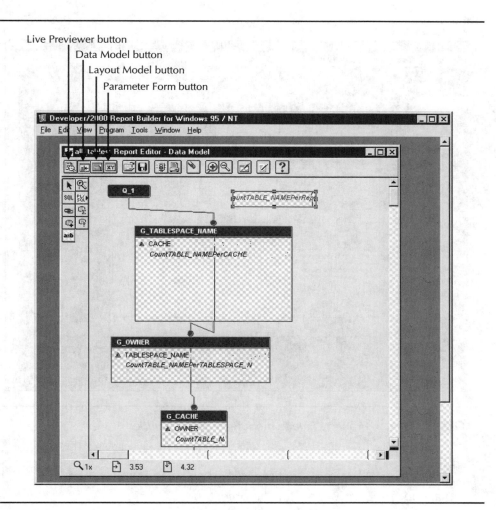

FIGURE 23-3. *Report Editor module in Report Builder*

that you can modify include general information, substitution file properties, report properties, and character mode properties. To modify an item on the Property Palette, you simply need to click on the property you want to change and its value will automatically be highlighted in such a way as to allow you to modify it easily. To open the Property Palette, click on Tools | Property Palette on the Report Builder menu. Figure 23-4 shows the Property Palette of Report Builder.

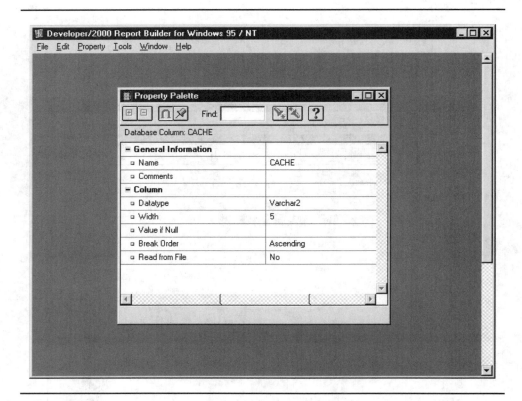

FIGURE 23-4. *Property Palette module in Report Builder*

TIP
The contents of the Property Palette are referred to as the "property sheet" for the object in question. For the rest of the unit, you will see references to invoking the Property Palette to modify object properties. Memorize that you are making modifications to the property sheet in that situation for OCP!

The Parameter Form Builder is another Report Builder tool discussed here. This module helps you build a parameter form for the current report. Figure 23-5 shows the Parameter Form Builder module running in Report Builder. Notice that several items should look familiar from your discussion of runtime parameters in Oracle Reports. Within this interface, you can enter values for these parameters that will then be used to compile your report. Clicking on Tools | Parameter Form Builder from the Report Builder menu will bring up your Parameter Form Builder. Figure 23-5 shows the Parameter Form Builder running within Report Builder. Later in this chapter, you will find out more about Report Wizard, a tool within Report Builder that helps you build new reports quickly and easily.

The final component of Report Builder is the Report Template Editor present in Developer 2.1 and higher. You can use this interface to design and modify templates used to enhance the layout and appearance of your reports. Several canned templates are included with Oracle Reports, and you may modify these report templates as you need to, or create new templates with the editor as well. Figure 23-6 shows the Report Template Editor module in Report Builder.

Invoking Report Builder

Report Builder gets run usually on a Windows-based machine. To execute it, you will usually click on an icon. Each operating system is different, so

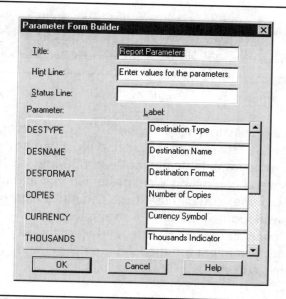

FIGURE 23-5. *Parameter Form Builder in Report Builder*

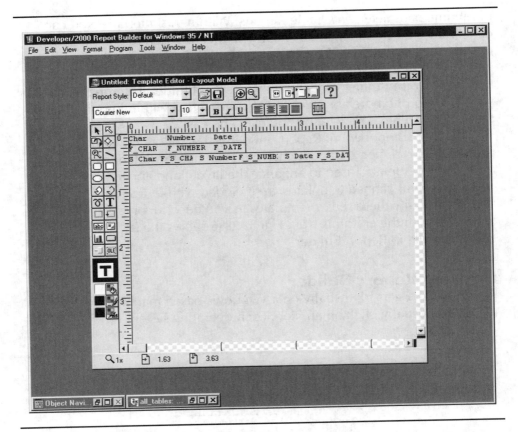

FIGURE 23-6. *Report Template Editor in Report Builder*

there is no standard way to invoke Report Builder. However, usually behind the scenes on the GUI there is an executable file. For many operating systems, that runtime executable file for Report Builder is **r30des**.

Recall that several parameters were presented in conjunction with the use of Reports Runtime. You can use these parameters for running Report Builder as well as Reports Runtime. For example, if you wanted to kick off Report Builder, connect to the database, and open the **all_tables.rdf** report in one fell swoop, you might use the following command line from your operating system to do so:

```
$> r30des userid=jason/stacy@devdb report=all_tables.rdf
```

TIP
Make sure you understand this point about
*using parameters for **r30run** and **r30des** for the*
OCP Exam 5!

Exercises

1. Identify the main use of Report Builder and name and describe its components. What are the different views of report data available as part of using the Report Editor?

2. What menu allows you to start the tools and components of Report Builder? How do you start the Object Navigator?

3. How do you invoke Report Builder? Experiment with invoking Report Builder on your operating system in conjunction with the USERID, CMDFILE, and REPORT parameters.

Main Objects in a Report

A report may have several items comprising it. To see the items comprising a report, you can open a report and view the items for that report within the Object Navigator. The following list provides insight on the main objects you will see in most reports you develop, corresponding rather directly with the nodes in the Object Navigator.

■ **Data Model**   This is the data definition for the report. The tables from which data will be drawn, along with the relationships between them, are shown in the data model for the report.

■ **Layout Model**   This is the layout definition of your report. Column headers, style definition, and other items associated with layout in the report body will be part of this mode.

■ **Parameter Form**   The report may have special items such as a comma instead of a period to indicate decimal places, or £ rather than $ for currency. The placement of these and other values is handled with the definition of parameters in the parameter form for the report.

- **Report Triggers**   A set of items that occur at various events or stages of report execution. Triggers can be defined to occur before and after the report executes, between pages, before processing the parameter form, and after processing the parameter form.

- **Program Units**   PL/SQL code blocks that can be associated with a report.

- **Attached Libraries**   Collections of PL/SQL program units associated with reports.

Exercises

1. Identify the purpose of the layout model and data model of a report. Of the two, which model is most central to determining what information from the Oracle database will be included on the report?

2. In which component of the report can you define the character used to separate the hundreds place from the thousands place in a number?

Creating Reports with Report Wizard

In this section, you will cover the following points on creating reports with Report Wizard:

- Creating simple tabular reports with Report Wizard

- Methods for building report queries

- Summarizing report values

- Modifying style and content of reports

- Other report styles available in Report Wizard

Simpler reports can be designed quickly using a feature built into the Reports tool called the Report Wizard. This utility is a graphical user interface that walks you through the steps of creating your basic report, prompting you to plug in your desired features every step of the way. This feature masks some of the challenges a beginner faces in learning Reports well enough to develop one, but there is some value for advanced Reports developers as well. This section covers the use of Report Wizard and the steps you must do every step of the way. You have a running example for this section. You are a wildlife conservator in Queensland, Australia, tracking kangaroos in the wild. Your database consists of several tables, including KGROO, KGROO_LOC, and KGROO_JOEYS. You will now generate some reports about your kangaroos using Oracle Reports.

Creating Simple Tabular Reports with Report Wizard

The most basic type of report in the Report Wizard is the tabular report. It may consist of a simple table, with headers and column values. Optionally, you can also set up a banner at the top of the report, along with other visually appealing options. The Report Wizard makes many of these options easy by providing several canned formats, which you will cover later. You encounter a welcome screen when you start Report Builder for the first time. There are several radio buttons indicating your options. They are to create a report using the Report Wizard, create a report manually, and other things. If you opt to create a report with the Report Wizard, you will then enter the Report Wizard automatically. You can also enter Report Wizard by clicking on the Tools | Report Wizard menu option. Figure 23-7 shows you the first screen you will encounter in the Report Wizard.

The first screen in Report Wizard helps you define the report style. There are several different styles available for report creation within Report Wizard. Each one is listed with a radio button next to it that allows you to select the report style. For now, you will focus on the first style in the upper left-hand corner of this interface: the tabular report. Clicking once on the radio button next to the word "Tabular" on the style window and then clicking the Next button defines the style. Later in this section, you will be introduced to the other styles available in Report Wizard, and shown how these other styles correspond to the common styles in business reports described in the beginning of the chapter.

Once you define the style, Report Wizard puts you into the next screen. Your next screen in Report Wizard helps define the data your report contains. Your options for defining data are numerous. You can write your own SQL statement, import a SQL statement from flat file, or build a SQL

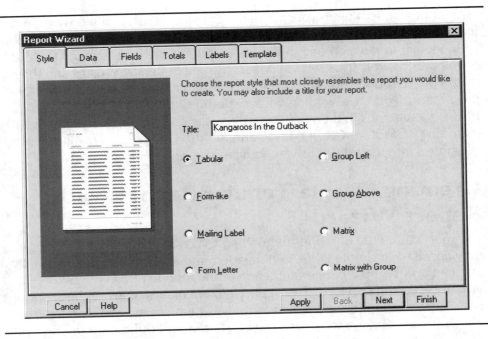

FIGURE 23-7. *Report Wizard style definition window*

statement visually using the Query Builder. The next discussion covers each of these options in more detail. For now, assume your report is really simple—merely a **select** statement to obtain all data from your KGROO and the KGROO_JOEYS table to show physical description and descendents of all kangaroos in the system. The following code block illustrates the SQL statement you will type into the text box in the center right on the Report Wizard data definition window in Figure 23-8. Once complete, click on the Next button.

```
SELECT k.kgroo_name, k.color, k.weight, k.pouch_sz, j.joey_name
FROM kgroo k, kgroo_joeys j
WHERE k.kgroo_name = j.kgroo_name;
```

The next window in Report Wizard is the field definition window. It helps you define the columns that appear in your report, based on the columns appearing in your SQL query. Figure 23-9 displays the field

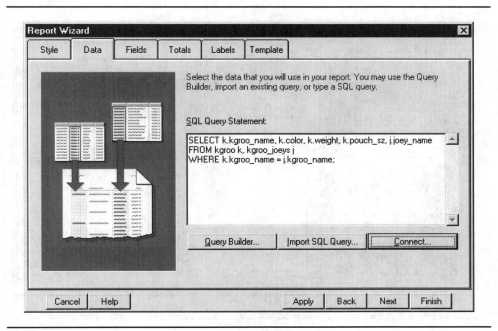

FIGURE 23-8. *Report Wizard data definition window*

definition window of Report Wizard. There are two text boxes. The one on the left contains lists of columns in your SQL query. Initially, the box on the right will be empty. You add or remove columns in your SQL query from the left to the list of columns in your report on the right with the RIGHT and LEFT ARROW buttons between the two windows. When complete, you click the Next button.

Once your field definitions are defined, you may want to perform some calculations on your data. This feature sees most of its usage in spreadsheet accounting applications that pull data from the Oracle database and perform calculations on that data. Some of these options include showing the sum of a column, a count for items in the column, average value, maximum value, or minimum value. In this example, you won't see too much of that, so for now don't worry too much about understanding the features on this screen. We will cover summarization of report values shortly. Figure 23-10 shows the Report Wizard totals definition window.

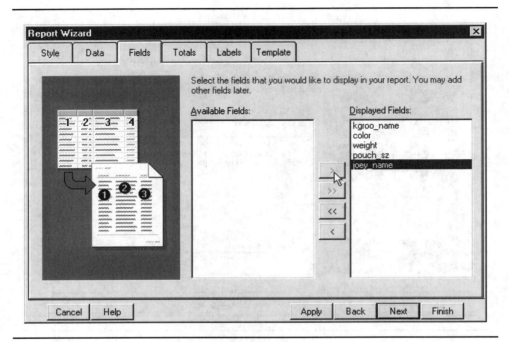

FIGURE 23-9. *Report Wizard field definition window*

After defining any totals you want to obtain on your fields, you then define the column headers you want to use to identify data in your report with the labels definition window. Report Wizard generates samples based on dropping any underscores from your column names, then displays them in text boxes next to the column names as they appeared in your SQL query. You are free to change these labels to whatever you like. In addition, you may define the column width and any format masks, such as money formats and others, to make your report more readable. Figure 23-11 displays this window.

The final touches on your report are possible with the last window of Report Wizard. This is the template definition window. Your report inherits the characteristics of the template selected, including banners, logos, and other visually appealing items. Report Wizard supplies many canned templates to work with, and the wizard allows you to preview them before making your final choice. If you do not like the canned templates, you may also provide one of your own or even none at all by selecting the appropriate

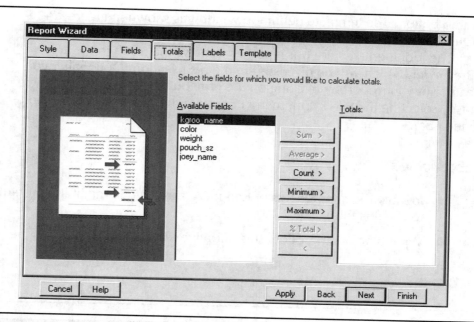

FIGURE 23-10. *Report Wizard totals definition window*

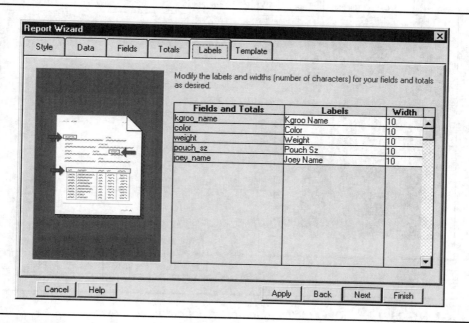

FIGURE 23-11. *Report Wizard labels definition window*

radio button. The template definition window is shown in Figure 23-12. Once you have selected your template, click the Finish button.

The tool then creates your report and shows the result in the Live Previewer, which will be discussed in the next section. Optionally, you can print your report by clicking on the Print button from the Live Previewer or by selecting the File | Print menu item from the Report Builder main menu bar.

Exercises

1. Identify the components of Report Wizard. When might it be useful to use this tool?

2. What type of report does this narrative lead you to create?

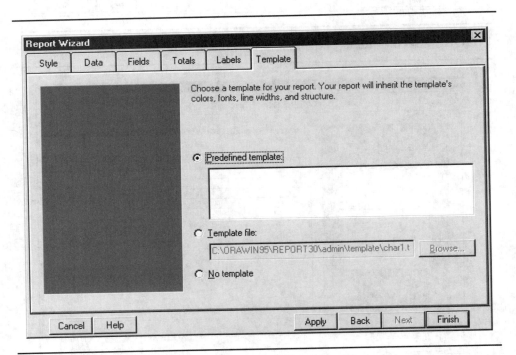

FIGURE 23-12. *Report Wizard template definition window*

Methods for Building Report Queries

As stated, several options exist for creating the query serving as the foundation for your report. Return to the data definition interface for Report Wizard in Figure 23-8 now and see if you can determine first what they might be. We have three methods for defining the SQL query. The first has already been identified: simply typing the desired SQL statement into the text box on the data definition window of Report Wizard. You can then validate that SQL statement against the database by first clicking on the Connect button and entering your username, password, and SQL*Net or Net8 connect string, and then clicking on the Check Syntax button. With this method covered, turn your attention now to the other two methods for defining your report data: importing SQL from file and using Query Builder.

TIP
You cannot check syntax on your SQL statement without first connecting to the database. If you attempt to check syntax when not logged on, Report Builder prompts you to log on.

Importing SQL from File

This option is only slightly more complex than coding the SQL statement into the text box on this interface window. You may have SQL statements stored in flat files on your computer. You can turn these into reports by importing the statements from your file in the following way. First, from the data definition window on Report Wizard, click the Import SQL Query button. A pop-up window appears to help you locate the SQL text file. Once you have identified your file, highlight it and click Open on the interface, and your SQL text will appear automatically in the text box back on the data definition window in Report Wizard.

Using Query Builder

Query Builder is a tool designed to help you define data based on visual database table representations rather than SQL statements. Some developers find Query Builder particularly useful in developing queries according to the data model for the database. Since Query Builder uses visual aids to develop

SQL, theoretically it is useful to a developer whose understanding of SQL is limited. However, your passage of OCP Exam 1 should have made you an effective user of SQL. To use Query Builder to define the data in your report, you click on the Query Builder button. If you aren't connected to the database already, Report Wizard prompts you to do so at this time. Figure 23-13 shows the data table selection interface that appears when you enter Query Builder as well. You then choose which tables to include in your report. In this case, revisit the wildlife conservator in the outback.

TIP

To add tables to your query later, click on the Select Data Tables button in the top part of the Query Builder interface shown in Figure 23-14.

You choose the schema owner of the tables you want to include in the query by clicking on the list box toward the top of the data table selection

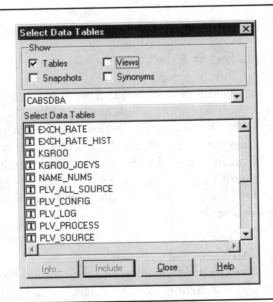

FIGURE 23-13. *Query Builder table selection interface*

interface. The default schema you will see is your own. You choose your table by clicking on its name in the list once to highlight it and then click on the Include button to include it. Once you have included all the tables you want, you then click on Close. You then click on the columns in the table box within the Query Builder interface to include those columns in your query. Query Builder will place a check mark next to the column name to show the column is included. After selecting the columns you want in the report, you then define the relationship that exists between the columns.

TIP
The only database objects you can see in the Select Data Tables interface are tables, snapshots, views, and synonyms.

In the example, the two tables selected share a common column, KGROO_NAME. To do so, you click on the Set Table Relationship button indicated by a table pointing to another table. A dialog box appears for you to key in the columns that relate. Be sure to precede the column names in both text boxes with their respective table names, especially if the column names in both tables are identical. You can choose the comparison operation, outer join condition, and whether to use the relationship in your query visually using check boxes and radio buttons. If you are happy with an ordinary table equijoin operation, simply picking the columns from both tables will establish the relationship. This is worth mentioning before you get fancy with Query Builder. Once complete, click OK and Query Builder will display the two tables again, this time with an arrow between them to display the relationship, as shown in Figure 23-14. You then click OK on the Query Builder interface to define the SQL statement. The SQL you defined will then appear in the text box back on the data definition window of Report Wizard.

TIP
Optionally, you can click on the Show SQL button next to the Set Table Relationship button to see the SQL statement before exiting Query Builder.

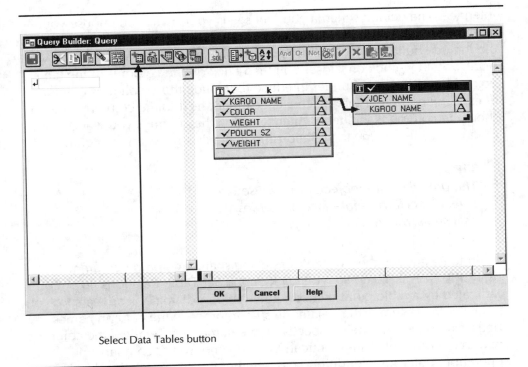

Select Data Tables button

FIGURE 23-14. *Query Builder interface with relationship defined*

Exercises

1. What are the three methods for building report queries?

2. In order to avoid Cartesian products, what activity should you perform in Query Builder when defining your SQL statement?

Summarizing Report Values

Recall in Figure 23-10 that you can define totals on your report to summarize report values. Two text boxes appear in this window, with several button between them to define the summarizations available. The button operations include Sum, Average, Count, Minimum, Maximum, and Percent Total. These buttons map to group functions of similar names, such as **sum( )**, **avg( )**, **count( )**, **min( )**, and **max( )**. If used, the report will contain a summary line at the end where the result of the corresponding group function will be displayed along with an identifier.

Exercise

Identify the summary functions available in Report Wizard.

Modifying Style and Content of Reports

Once finished, the Report Builder displays the report output in the Live Previewer interface. Your development effort needn't stop there. If you are dissatisfied with the looks of the report, you can return to the Report Wizard to alter the columns displayed, add new format templates, change the style, or just about anything else. Simply start Report Wizard again by clicking on the Tools | Report Wizard menu item on the main Report Builder, or click on the Report Wizard button in the Live Previewer button bar at the top of the interface, shown as a piece of paper with a pencil. The full Report Wizard interface is shown, with both Next and Back buttons and tabs to navigate through the wizard steps.

Any aspect of the report can be changed with Report Wizard in this mode. You can skip over to the appropriate area you wish to reconfigure by clicking on the appropriate tab at the top of the Report Wizard interface. When you have completed your changes, you click on Finish again and your changes are made to the report. Report Builder then applies the changes automatically and dynamically changes the appearance of the report in the Live Previewer according to your specifications.

You can, for example, change the style of the report from tabular to something else by clicking on the Style tab on Report Wizard and selecting a different style radio button. You can also change what columns appear in the report by changing the SQL statement generating data for the query by clicking the Data tab and modifying the data defining SQL statement. Or, you can change the columns appearing in the report by clicking the Fields tab and adding or removing columns in the data definition, or change the totals appearing in the report by clicking on the Labels tab and adding or removing items there. You can change the report template as well. In all cases, Report Wizard dynamically updates the report to contain the new features you specified as soon as you click the Finish button, and displays the new report version in the Live Previewer. Bear in mind that changing the style of your report may in some cases require a redefinition of the report's data. To redefine the data in your report, refer to the previous discussion on defining data.

Exercises

1. How do you invoke Report Wizard from the Report Builder menu bar? How does it differ from Report Wizard running automatically from the welcome screen at startup?

2. What are the different ways you can navigate through Report Wizard?

3. If you make a change to a report using Report Wizard, when will the change take effect?

Other Report Styles Available in Report Wizard

Several other report styles are available in Report Wizard. Recall from Figure 23-7 that the Report Wizard style definition window lists eight choices for report styles. They are Form-like, Mailing Label, Form Letter, Group Left, Group Above, Matrix, and Matrix with Group, in addition to the basic tabular format shown as output from queries in SQL*Plus. A description of each report, along with its appearance and ideas about usage appear here. You can alter a report style with the use of Report Wizard after you have already created the report as well, or create a report of these other types by going through Report Wizard in the same way as you went through a tabular report.

Form-Like Reports

A form-like report prints each row of output on a separate page for your report. This can be especially handy in situations where your report contains few rows with many columns, in which the column data is very wide. The labels for each field are placed to the left of the data, as opposed to the top, as in a tabular report. The following code block shows a sample of what form-like output might look like in an imaginary example:

```
NAME        Jason Scott Couchman
OCCUPATION  Consultant for Fortune 500 Companies with Oracle experience
RESIDENCE   Tennessee, has lived in North Carolina and grew up in New York
```

Mailing Label Reports

A mailing label report is straightforward—it is a list of addresses designed to be reproduced on mailing labels. The addresses can be printed several across the page, and then several down. Reports can print the labels across first, then down, or down first, then across. This is a handy feature for mailing lists maintained in an Oracle database. The following code block illustrates a simple example:

```
Flumpster           Dumpster            Bumpster
10 Oak Lane         15 Toad Street      49 Main Avenue
Mead, AL 30494      Akron, FL 403945    Sunset, CA 94049
```

Form Letter Reports

The form letter report complements the mailing label report. You can pull a key bit of text, along with names from a database, to produce form mailings efficiently. Since you have undoubtedly seen a form letter at least once, an example will be foregone in this situation.

Group Left Reports

Group-left reports are handy for producing output from SQL statements with the **group by** clause in them. The group-left report suppresses redundant printings of the same value in the leftmost column of the report. You can use the group-left report to display master-detail or parent/child relationships as well. Going back to the kangaroo example, you can see that group-left reports are handy for printing out the names of each kangaroo in such a way that those who have many joeys will not have their names repeating once for each joey in the report. The following code block shows an example of a group-left report that does all these things, literally displaying a parent/child relationship:

```
KGROO NAME     KGROO COLOR    JOEY NAME    JOEY COLOR
----------     -----------    ---------    ----------
SKIPPY         BROWN          SHELBY       RED
                              ALEXANDER    BROWN
                              THOR         BROWN
FRANCIS        RED            DINGO        RED
                              RINGO        RED
```

Group Above Reports

A group-above report is a method you can use to demonstrate a master/detail relationship in your database. You define a master group, and for every master record obtained, Oracle will obtain the related values from the detail groups. These reports can be useful for situations where you have a set of data to which other elements in another set of data belong. Consider the following example of a group-above report where the different kangaroo colors are listed across the top and the names of kangaroos are grouped according to the colors above them:

```
RED          BROWN
---------    ----------
SHELBY       SKIPPY
FRANCIS      ALEXANDER
DINGO        THOR
RINGO
```

Matrix Reports

A matrix report is a chart with two axes that display for sets of data. On the horizontal axis, the report displays one set of data, while on the vertical axis the report displays another set. Within the two axes, Oracle report displays a "matrix" or cross-product of results, where the third group of data is the locations of data within the matrix and the fourth is the actual data. The following code block shows the appearance of a matrix report of numbers whose quotient is a whole number. Key to the matrix report is the fact that the number of rows and columns are not known until the results are obtained. In the following matrix report example, imagine that your sales staff fluctuates because everyone sells on commission, and new products are added every day. Thus, there is really no way to know who sold what before the matrix report is run.

```
          YOGURT   BANANA   CHEESE   HOTDOG   LIVER
       ------------------------------------------------
CASEY  |    10       0        0        9        9
LACEY  |     0      11        7        2        3
FRED   |     1       4        0        5        5
AHMED  |   504       3        5       67       40
LARRY  |     4     105        0        3        0
```

Other Types of Reports

There are many other types of reports available in Oracle Reports. A matrix with a group report is a combination of a matrix and a group-above report. These types of reports can be good for master/detail records. You can develop multimedia reports as well, combining sound, video, and graphics to give an enticing effect along with data capture. An OLE report can be used as well to embed charts and graphs into your report along with data.

Exercises

1. Which type of report best suits the **select** statement containing a **group by** clause?

2. Which two types of reports are useful for mass mailings?

3. Explain the content of a matrix report. A group report. A matrix with group report.

Chapter Summary

This chapter gives you an introduction to Oracle Reports as a tool to design, develop, and run reports against your Oracle database. The execution of existing production reports is covered, along with design and modification of reports using Report Builder and the use of Report Wizard. This section provides a foundation for use of Oracle Reports that will serve you well in the coming chapters, on the OCP exam, and in your career with Developer/2000. All in all, the material covered in this chapter covers about 15 percent of OCP Exam 5 test content, with an additional 3 percent of content dedicated to your understanding of Developer/2000 from Chapter 11.

The first section in this chapter covers the execution of existing reports using Reports Runtime. One topic covered is the style and structure of common business reports. The most basic type of business report is the tabular report. You will see tabular reports every time you **select** information from the Oracle database, Oracle Reports will clean it up and present it to you in an elegant manner. A related type of business report is the group report. You may have several master/detail relationships in your database, such as parents to children, managers to employees, or servers to clients. There is often redundancy in showing all the individual details associated with a few masters on a simple tabular report. Thus, you can use group reports to reduce the number of times a master record is displayed. Another important type of report is the matrix report. These reports are useful when analyzing a cross-product of two different datasets. An example of a matrix report would be two lists of cities and the mileage between them.

The chapter described a common situation in the business world related to reports where the organization will have several reports already running in production that need maintenance. There is a runtime executable called Reports Runtime that allows you to run the reports from your operating system command line, or from within a script. This functionality is especially useful when running reports according to a batch schedule. You can define how your report will run with use of runtime parameters. Some parameters are required for execution, such as USERID, MODULE (formerly REPORT), DESTYPE, DESNAME, and DESFORMAT. Others are optional, and are used primarily for formatting output in the report. Some examples of these types of parameters are CURRENCY, THOUSANDS, and DECIMAL. Still other parameters are used to define how the report performs during the run and to give you status on the report's execution. These parameters include READONLY, LOGFILE, BUFFERS and ARRAYSIZE.

A report runs in one of two modes: character and bitmap. Character mode displays all US7ASCII or other text-based characters on a report page only, while bitmap reports have the capacity to display graphics like logos and that sort of thing. The mode in which a report executes is determined by the MODE parameter. This parameter can be set with the values **character**, **bitmap**, or **default**. Other parameters may have double meaning, depending on whether you run your report in character mode or bitmap. Such parameters include PAGESIZE, which can mean size of the page in inches like 8.5 × 11, or number of characters that will fit on the page like 66 × 80.

A report can find its way to many different destinations. The chapter covered several of those destinations, including the printer, email, file, the screen, the Reports Previewer, and default system output (usually also the screen). The destination for a report is defined with the DESTYPE, DESNAME, and DESFORMAT parameters. DESTYPE identifies the destination of the report, such as **file**, **printer**, or **mail**. DESNAME gives Reports Runtime the name of the printer, file, or Oracle Office email user to which the report will be sent. DESFORMAT is for use mainly with printing your reports, as it specifies what sort of print driver to use when printing the file.

If you have made an enhancement to the report or are trying to look for errors, it can sometimes be helpful to look at the report on the screen before printing it in production. To view the report in the Report Previewer, run Reports Runtime interactively (as opposed to batch mode). From the Reports Runtime GUI, you can then click on File | Run and look at the report on the screen. Alternately, you can issue the command to run Reports Runtime from the operating system command line with the BATCH parameter set to **no** and the DESTYPE parameter set to **previewer**, and Reports Runtime will execute your report and show it in the Report Previewer.

There are many executable components in Oracle Reports. Reports Runtime is one. Report Builder and Report Converter are others. Report Builder is used to develop new reports and modify existing ones, while Report Converter is designed for use when making a built report into one that can be executed using Reports Runtime. Reports Server, Reports Background Engine, and Reports Queue Manager can all be used to execute reports within a multitier architecture where an application server handles reports separate from the client machine and database server. Reports Web CGI and Oracle Web Application Server handle Web-enabling for your reports processing needs. Finally, Reports Converter can be used to change reports of one storage type on the client to another storage type for the server, or vice-versa.

Once you are used to running reports in production and know all the executable components of Oracle Reports you need to know, you will need to start thinking about using Report Builder when creating new reports. Report Builder has several components you should understand. Some of these components include the Object Navigator, Report Editor, Template Editor, and Property Palette. The Report Editor allows you to view and modify your report layout and content. The Property Palette identifies various properties of the report, such as general information, substitution, character mode, and other report properties. Another component of Report Builder is the Parameter Form Builder. This tool helps you build a runtime parameter form for the report. Several of the parameters you can set in the Parameter Form Builder are the same as parameters you can issue from the command line when using Reports Runtime to execute your report.

The chapter covers the components of a report that you should know for certification as well. Every report has a data model, or the definition of the data from your database that will appear in the report. This model includes the tables that will be used on your report and any relationships between them you define and use. In addition, the report has a layout mode, which shows how the report will look on your page. This view shows the general appearance of the report on the page, including the columns, groups, or matrices you define, along with cover or trailing pages, headers and footers, logos, graphics, or other visual enhancements. The parameter form is another component of your report. This is a set of parameters that define how Oracle Reports will display the data content to the report. Your report may contain triggers that define events occurring at various times in your report execution, such as between pages, at the beginning, or at the end. Your report may contain PL/SQL program units or libraries as well.

The final aspect of using Oracle Reports covered in this chapter is using Report Wizard to define reports of simple to medium complexity. For this section, you concentrated on building tabular reports, though Report Wizard allows you to create reports of other types as well. Report Wizard is a component of the Report Builder that helps you define different aspects of your report, such as the data definition and other report body content, a template to use with the report, layout and style, and other items. There are two ways to define your report with use of Report Wizard. The first occurs from the Oracle Reports Welcome screen, where you may opt to build a new report from scratch using Report Wizard, moving from definition of one component to another with the Back and Next buttons at the bottom of each screen. The second method of moving through the interface is to invoke it with the Tools | Report Wizard menu item after Report Builder is running.

There are tab pages available in Report Wizard. They are Style definition, Data definition, Field definition, Totals definition, Labels definition, and Template definition. Style definition is where you identify what basic format you want your report output to take, such as Tabular, Group, Mailing Label, Form Letter, Matrix, and others. Data definition is where you identify the SQL query your report will use to glean data from your Oracle database. You can define this query yourself using the SQL skills you developed for OCP Exam 1 or use the Query Builder tool to identify tables from your database and define relationships between them visually, then check off the columns you want to appear in the report. Field definition is your chance to eliminate columns that are part of the data definition from what actually appears on the page of the report. For example, to use a join statement in your SQL query, you may have included some columns to satisfy the join condition but don't want to show those columns in the report output. The field definition interface allows you to suppress those columns. The totals definition is used particularly for accounting or spreadsheet-type tabular reports where you want to show totals or other summary data on one or more columns. The labels definition gives you the chance to alter a column name in your tabular report to whatever you like. Finally, the template definition allows you to modify the overall look of your report to include graphics, logos, headers, footers, and other items to enhance the report's visual appeal. Several built-in templates exist in Oracle Reports already, and later material in this unit will cover how you can develop new templates and make them available for use within Report Wizard.

Two-Minute Drill

- Oracle Reports is the component of Developer/2000 that handles design, development, and execution of reports against the Oracle database.

- Common business reports include the following:

    - Tabular reports where the data appears in columns as in the output from SQL statements

    - Form-like reports where the column name appears on the left, the value appears on the right, and each row appears on its own page

    - Mailing labels and form letters

    - Group reports to show master/detail relationships

    - Matrix reports showing two sets of data and their cross-product

- Prebuilt or existing reports are run in Oracle Reports using Reports Runtime. This tool can be run either from the Windows-based operating system by clicking on the appropriate icon or the Start button, or from an operating system command line by passing appropriate parameters.

- The following items explain command line parameters for Oracle Reports Runtime:

  - MODULE, BATCH, and USERID identify what report to run, whether the report runs in batch, and what user to log in to the Oracle database as to run the report.

  - PARAMFORM and CMDFILE identify where Reports Runtime should pull parameters from to run the report.

  - DESNAME, DESTYPE, and DESFORMAT identify the destination name, type, and format for the report.

  - ARRAYSIZE and BUFFERS identify memory handling for array fetches and overall memory size for report execution.

  - CURRENCY, THOUSANDS, and DECIMAL identify special characters Reports Runtime should use for numeric representation in the body of the report.

  - ONSUCCESS, ONFAILURE, READONLY, AUTOCOMMIT, NONBLOCKSQL, LONGCHUNK, and ROLE define how Reports Runtime will manage transaction processing, data retrieval, and database privileges when connected to the database.

  - ORIENTATION, BACKGROUND, and PRINTJOB define how Reports Runtime aligns report data on the page, whether the report runs as a background process, and whether the Print dialog box will display to define further print options.

  - MODE, PAGESIZE, and TERM determine whether the report runs in bitmap or character mode, what the size of each page will be, and the terminal type if the report is running in character mode.

  - LOGFILE, ERRFILE, PROFILE, and RUNDEBUG identify names of runtime log, error, and performance statistics for report execution, and also determine if Reports Runtime will perform extra report debugging over and above syntactic errors (i.e., format inconsistencies).

- Reports can go to many different types of destinations, including a printer, email, screen or standard output, Report Previewer, or file.

- Sometimes it is useful to send report output to the Report Previewer. This is accomplished either by running the report in Reports Runtime interactively with the File | Run menu option or from the operating system command line by passing the parameters BATCH=**no** and DESTYPE=**previewer**.

- The runtime command for Reports Runtime is usually **r30run** for Developer/2000 2, and **r25run** for Developer/2000 1.*x*.

- Other executable components of Oracle Reports for Developer/2000 2.0 include:

  - Report Builder to create new reports using **r30des**

  - Reports Runtime to run compiled reports using **r30run**, or **r30cli** when running reports with Reports Server

  - Reports Queue Manager to manage report queuing using **r30rqv** for Unix, **r30rqm32** for Windows

  - Reports Server to run reports from a reports server, which can schedule report execution, using executable **r30mts**

  - Reports Web common gateway interface and Oracle Web Application Server to allow distribution of Oracle Reports on the Web, using executables **r30cgi** and **r30ows**

  - Report Converter to change report formats from client to server or to compile a report into something Reports Runtime can execute, using executables **r30conv** or **r30con32**

  - Report Background Engine to execute reports locally for better performance than using Reports Runtime using executable **r30bre** or **r30isv**.

- Executable components for Oracle Reports for Developer/2000 1.*x* include the ones available for Developer/2000 2.0 with appropriate downgrades on version numbers for Reports 2.5 vs. Reports 3.0.

- Report Builder is the executable used to develop new reports and modify existing ones. It has several components:

  - Object Navigator to view report components and navigate report development

- Report Editor to modify layout, template, and content of the report, and also to view what the report will look like when executed (Live Previewer)

- Property Palette to display and modify properties and aspects of the report

- Parameter Form Builder to define certain runtime parameters that affect content display in the report

- Template Editor to modify templates that may be associated with reports

- Program Unit Editor, PL/SQL Interpreter, Stored Program Unit Editor, and Database Trigger Editor.

- Main objects in a report include the following items:

  - Data model and layout model to display the data content and layout appearance of the report

  - Parameter form to define special characters such as currency indicators for report content

  - Report trigger, program units, and attached libraries to associate PL/SQL blocks with the report and define events that may execute them

  - You can see what a report will look like while developing it in Report Builder with the use of the Live Previewer.

- You can speed through development of simple reports with the use of Report Wizard. This interface helps with the development of reports by focusing your attention on six report components, corresponding to six interfaces within Report Wizard. Those six interfaces are as follows:

  - **Style definition interface**   Identify the style of the report, be it tabular, form-like, mailing label, form letter, group left, group above, matrix, or matrix with group.

  - **Data definition interface**   Identify the data from Oracle database that will be included in the report.

■ **Field definition interface**   Identify which columns from the data definition will appear on the report.

■ **Totals definition interface**   Identify summary items for columns in the report.

■ **Labels definition interface**   Identify column names for columns in the report.

■ **Template definition interface**   Identify a template for use when printing the report to enhance the report output visually.

■ Three methods exist for building report data definition queries. You can write the SQL yourself, import it from SQL file, or build a query with the use of Query Builder.

■ Query Builder is a tool that allows you to include tables and columns from the Oracle database and associate them visually by means of a graphical interface. Once you define the tables you want to include and associate them in the manner you wish, Query Builder then assembles the SQL statement for you.

■ The SQL group functions that are associated with summary options in Report Wizard include **sum( )**, **avg( )**, **max( )**, **min( )**, and **count( )**.

■ Once created, you tell Report Wizard to build your report by clicking the Finish button in the Report Wizard interface. The report you created is then displayed in the Live Previewer.

■ You can return to Report Wizard to modify your report after the fact by clicking on the Tools I Report Wizard menu item in Report Builder.

Chapter Questions

1. **Which of the following ways can be used to define the data to be included in your report? (Choose three)**

   A. SQL issued from SQL*Plus

   B. SQL statement entered manually into Report Wizard

    C. SQL statement imported from file

    D. Query generated with Query Builder

2. To compile a report or change it from one format into another, which of the following executables would you use?

    A. r30run

    B. r30des

    C. r30cli

    D. r30conv

3. Every year, the World Widgetball Association generates the regular season game schedule pairing teams in the east and the west, and assigning game dates from a set of valid game dates. What report is most likely used to obtain the result?

    A. Group left

    B. Matrix

    C. Form letter

    D. Tabular

4. The interface allowing you to design reports quickly with totals calculated on a report column is known as the

    A. Report Wizard

    B. Report Editor

    C. Command Line interface

    D. Parameter Form Builder

5. The layout model and data model are two components of reports that can be modified using what utility or component?

    A. Report Converter

    B. Reports Runtime

    C. Parameter Form Builder

    D. Report Editor

6. Command line parameters used to define special characters for report body number and money formatting work in conjunction with which of the following executables?

   A. r30run

   B. r30des

   C. r30ows

   D. r30conv

7. Which of the following parameters is used only for character mode reports?

   A. MODE

   B. TERM

   C. RUNDEBUG

   D. PAGESIZE

8. What runtime parameter can be used to specify a print driver to be associated with your report destination?

   A. DESTYPE

   B. DESNAME

   C. DESFORMAT

   D. DESDRIVER

9. The RUNDEBUG parameter allows Reports Runtime to identify what sorts of bugs in a report?

   A. Compilation bugs

   B. Server errors

   C. Report format inconsistencies

   D. All of the above

10. The output of a group-left report most closely resembles output from which of the following SQL statements?

   A. update

   B. insert as select

   C. delete

   D. select group by

Answers to Chapter Questions

1. B, C, and D.

Explanation Recall from discussion of Report Wizard there are three ways to define data incorporated into the report. They are to write your own SQL statement manually, to import a SQL statement in from file, or to define the aspects of your database data model and associate relationships between those database objects visually using Query Builder. Within Oracle Reports, it is not possible to issue SQL statements directly against the database, as in SQL*Plus. Therefore, choice A is not appropriate.

2. D. **r30conv**

Explanation Changing report format from built to executable, or PL/SQL attached library from client-side to server-side, is handled with Report Converter, the **r30conv** executable. The **r30run** executable is inappropriate because that executable is used for the Reports Runtime tool. This fact eliminates choice A. Choice B is incorrect because **r30des** is the executable that you use to launch Report Builder. Choice C is incorrect because **r30cli** is the executable you may use to execute reports using Reports Server.

3. B. Matrix

Explanation A matrix report is commonly used to generate a cross-product between one set of data on the horizontal axis and another set of data across the vertical axis. The locations within the body where a cross-product is produced become the third set, and the actual value is the fourth set. There may be more sets of data in the matrix report as well. These features of a matrix report match up well with the reporting needs identified in the question, therefore making choice B correct.

4. A. Report Wizard

Explanation The Report Wizard allows you to develop new reports with minimal effort. Report Editor helps you to refine the report, but to develop a new report from scratch with Report Editor is not as fast as development of new reports using Report Wizard, eliminating choice B. The command line interface is a little vague to be a stand-alone answer to this question, but even if it weren't, you would still know it was wrong because there is no way to develop a report from an operating system command line—only ways in Oracle Reports to execute built reports from the command line. This fact eliminates choice C. Choice D is incorrect because the Parameter Form Editor modifies parameters used when the report executes.

5. D.   Report Editor

Explanation   The layout and data model are aspects of reports that are modified from within the Report Editor interface on Report Builder. Report Converter and Reports Runtime are two tools designed to get a built report running in production. You should know to eliminate choices A and B, therefore, because the layout and data model are only of interest when building reports, not compiling or running reports. Choice C is incorrect because parameter forms are created and modified with their own interface.

6. A.   **r30run**

Explanation   Command line parameters like CURRENCY, THOUSANDS, and DECIMAL work in conjunction with the Reports Runtime to build report content. The Reports Runtime executable is **r30run**. Report Builder is used to develop new reports or modify existing ones, thereby eliminating **r30des** and choice B. The Oracle Web Application Server helps to publish your executed reports to the Web, thereby eliminating choice C, which was **r30ows**. Choice D identifies the executable used to convert built reports into executable ones, or PL/SQL program units or attached libraries from one file format to another.

7. B.   TERM

Explanation   A terminal type is only appropriate for reports running in character mode, as reports running in bitmap mode assume your terminal is a windows interface. Choice A is incorrect because the MODE parameter can be used to determine if the report runs in bitmap or character mode. Choice C is incorrect because runtime layout and format debugging can be used regardless of the report execution mode. Finally, choice D is incorrect because the page size will automatically be interpreted in two different ways depending on the mode in which the report runs.

8. C. DESFORMAT

Explanation The DESFORMAT parameter helps to identify print drivers required to print the report. Choice A, DESTYPE, is incorrect because this parameter defines the destination type from a set of options such as **printer**, **mail**, or **file**. DESNAME and choice B are incorrect because the name of the printer, Oracle Office user, or filename is defined with this parameter. Finally, choice D is incorrect because there is no parameter called DESDRIVER.

9. C. Report format inconsistencies

Explanation Any syntactic flaws in your report are ironed out when the report is built and compiled automatically by Report Builder. This eliminates the need for the RUNDEBUG parameter to force Reports Runtime to do the same, thus eliminating choice A. Choice B is incorrect as well, because server errors will cause the report execution to fail regardless of any debugging features on Reports Runtime. Finally, choice D is incorrect because choices A and B are incorrect. Recall from discussion of RUNDEBUG that the parameter is useful to find format inconsistencies such as column overlays, so that choice C is the most logical one for this question.

10. D. **select group by**

Explanation A group-left report is useful for modeling master/detail relationships in your database, such as manager to employee. Recall that in these situations you may want to eliminate redundancy in your output, so that a manager's name appears only once despite there being several employees under her. A **select group by** statement in the Oracle database will display this type of information from SQL*Plus, thus making it the logical choice for the answer to this question. Additionally, it is not usually the case that Oracle Reports will have data definition statements that modify the database, such as **update**, **insert** or **delete**, although this is not always the case. Later content in this unit will explain further the use of DML statements in Oracle Reports.

CHAPTER
24

Oracle Reports:
Introduction to
Report Builder

n this chapter, you will cover the following areas of using Report Builder to manage reports:

- Modifying reports using Live Previewer
- Managing report templates
- Report storage methods

The last chapter introduced the use of the runtime component of Oracle Reports to run existing reports and the use of Report Wizard within Report Builder to develop new reports quickly. Now, focus your attention on other topics of modifying and managing reports with Report Builder. This tool allows you to modify your report content from many perspectives such as data content and report layout. The management of report templates, which can be used to standardize the appearance of reports across an application, is covered in this chapter as well. Finally, the chapter covers storage methods for reports. Overall, the content of this chapter comprises 18 percent of OCP Exam 5 content.

Modifying Reports Using Live Previewer

In this section, you will cover the following points about the Live Previewer:

- Describing the Live Previewer
- Modifying display of report data with Live Previewer
- Modifying position of report data
- Adding page numbers and current date to reports

The design of a report needn't stop after stepping through Report Wizard. Once created, you can see what the output of your report will look like using Live Previewer. This interface shows the report in the format it will be printed in, with both the report's data and template formatting according to your specification. You can modify the report using Live Previewer and

Report Wizard, changing the position, format, and content of the report. This section shows you what Live Previewer is and how to use it.

Describing the Live Previewer

Oracle Reports provides an easy way to see your report as it looks on the page without wasting a single sheet of paper. Live Previewer gives you that functionality, along with a full set of tools to modify the report format and content. When you complete your report design with Report Wizard and click the Finish button, Oracle Reports builds your report against the database and shows the result with the Live Previewer. Figure 24-1 shows the output of your simple tabular report on kangaroos and joeys using the Live Previewer.

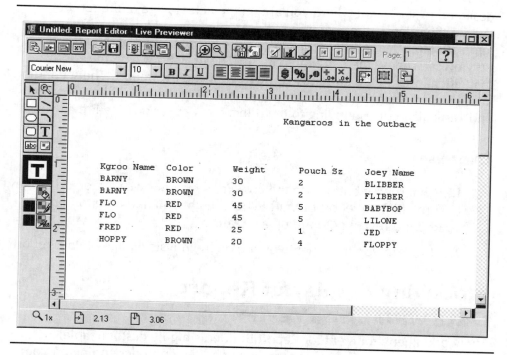

FIGURE 24-1.   *Showing your report in the Live Previewer*

Live Previewer is accessible when you run your report. There are several features about Live Previewer you should understand. On the top of the window there are two rows of control buttons you can use for switching between different viewing modes for your report. Some buttons exist on this row for opening and saving your files as well. Also possible with buttons from this row are data refreshing, printing, and sending email, activation of wizards, zooming in or out, adding certain information to the report, and other things. Below this row of buttons is another row. These buttons in the second row across the top of the interface are designed for formatting data in the report. Options available include changing font type and size, bold, italics, underline, money format, percentage, and others. Down the left side of Live Previewer is another set of buttons. These buttons handle adding other types of report formats, such as background and fill color, rectangles, lines, and other shapes to highlight the data produced by the report.

To the right and downward on Live Previewer are two sets of rulers, designed to show you where you are on the actual page of the report. Within the rulers is the actual report data, plus any added items from the template you used for the report. Along the bottom panel of the Live Previewer window there are three items. The first shows you the zoom magnification you are currently using to view the live report. The second and third tell your location on the current page of the report, horizontally and vertically, corresponding to the rulers that appear on Live Previewer.

Exercises

1. What row of buttons on the Live Previewer allows you to add money formatting to report output? Where might you find a button on the Report Previewer to fire up a wizard?

2. How can you tell where you are on the physical page of your report?

Modifying Display of Report Data with Live Previewer

The working environment for Report Builder is highly customizable, allowing you to modify the appearance of a live report depending on your needs. The View menu has many different options at the bottom of the pull-down menu that designate which features of the Live Previewer will appear. Those that will appear display a check mark next to them, while those that won't do not have a check mark. To eliminate the rulers from Live Previewer's output window, for example, click on View | Rulers to remove the check mark, and thus the ruler, from the display.

Modifying display of report data is possible with formatting options presented in the second row of buttons on the Live Previewer display as well. To modify the formatting display of report data, first click on the cell you wish to modify in the body of the report within the Live Previewer. You will be able to tell that the cell is activated by the outline appearing around the cell. You can then make changes to font type and size using the Font and Point Size list boxes in the second row. You can add bold, italics, or underline by clicking the appropriate buttons, which stand to the right of the Font type and Size list boxes in the display.

You can change the text in each cell to be left-, center-, or right-justified by clicking on the appropriate buttons, which stand to the right of the special text format buttons. You can add a dollar sign, decimal places, percentage sign, and commas every three significant digits using the special numeric format buttons to the right of the justification buttons. You can change the appearance of your report with the use of the Fill Color, Line Color, and Text Color buttons appearing vertically along the left side of the Live Previewer interface as well.

Another way to change the display of report data in Live Previewer is done with the pull-down menus on the main Report Builder module. The Format menu offers every option you have a button for in the second row of the Live Previewer. For example, if you want to make the data in a cell right-justified, you click on the cell once to activate it, then click on Format | Justify | Right menu option to set the cell to be right-justified. Your examination of the Format menu will show other formatting options that are possible as well.

TIP
You may find several questions on OCP Exam 5 that ask about the easiest way to modify layout when looking at a report in Live Previewer. Whether you think its true or not, make sure you understand that the OCP test writers think the easiest way to modify report format when looking at a report in the Live Previewer is always to make the change using Live Previewer! Be mindful of this principle when answering the OCP Exam 5 questions.

Exercises

1. What are the two methods you can use to change the display of your report data?

2. What methods are available for modifying the Live Previewer environment?

Modifying Position of Report Data with Live Previewer

You may want to change the location of data within the report in order to make it easier to understand, in addition to changing the display of data in the report as well. This functionality is possible with Live Previewer. One method available for changing the position of report data is to return to Report Wizard and reorder the column output in the Fields tab. If you want to add columns that are not currently part of the data definition for the report, you may have to modify the data definition as it appears in the Data Definition tab as well. You can also change what columns appear in the report or the order in which they are displayed by changing the SQL statement generating data for the query by clicking the Data tab and modifying the data-defining SQL statement. Or, you can change the columns appearing in the report by clicking the Fields tab and adding or removing columns in the data definition, or you can change the totals appearing in the report by clicking on the Labels tab and adding or removing items there.

Another method you may use for changing the positioning of report data is to modify the report style. For example, you may want to change a tabular report to a group-left report, or to a matrix report. These changes are made with Report Wizard, and alter the position of the data in the report. Alternately, you can modify the position of report data using the layout view of Report Builder. This activity is done by clicking on the View | Layout Model on the Report Builder main menu bar, bringing up the layout of the report in the layout model work area so that you can modify the layout of the report. You move the position of your data simply by clicking and holding an item, moving it, and releasing it with the mouse. Figure 24-2 demonstrates the appearance of your report using the layout model.

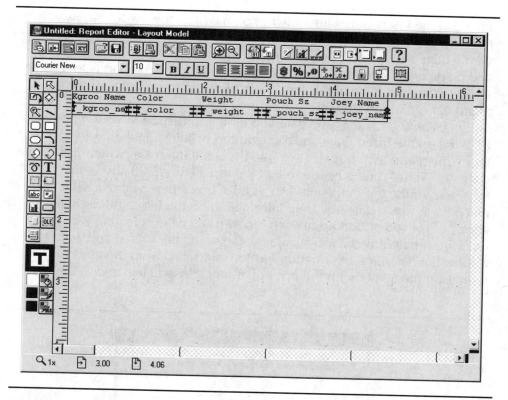

FIGURE 24-2.   *Report Builder layout model*

Exercise

Identify two different ways for modifying the position of data within a report.

Adding Page Numbers and Current Date to Reports

A simple enhancement to any report that helps identify when it ran and where you are within the report is the addition of page numbers and the current date. There are two ways to add both these items to your report. The first is with the Insert Date and Time and Insert Page Number buttons appearing in the top row of Live Previewer, toward the center of the row of buttons. The Insert Date and Time button has an arrow with a stopwatch and the number "31" on it, while the Insert Page Number button has an arrow with a page and the number "1" appearing on it. The second method for adding date/time and page number information to your report is to use the Insert | Date and Time and Insert | Page Number menu items in the main menu bar on Report Builder.

Focus now on adding the date and time information to your report. Clicking on the Insert Date and Time button or selecting the Insert | Date and Time menu item both lead you to the same interface, which has "Insert Date and Time" on the header bar at the top. Figure 24-3 shows that interface. At the top of the interface is a list box where you can select to place the inserted date and time information on the left, right, or in the center of the top or bottom of each report page. After selecting where to place your date/time information, you can select the format you want to display the date/time information in. You can select from the available formats in the text box on the center left of the Insert Date and Time

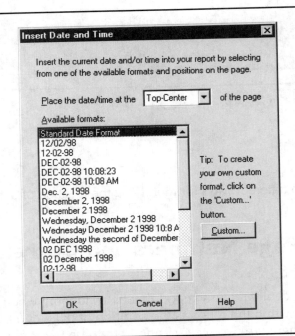

FIGURE 24-3. *Insert Date and Time interface*

interface, or click on the Custom button to create your own format. The Custom Date and Time interface will then appear, and you can enter your custom format in the text box at the top of the interface.

Below the text box is an example line where Report Builder will show you interactively what your date/time information will look like based on the formats you select from the options listed in the big display on the interface. Figure 24-4 shows one example you can type into the Custom Date and Time interface and what Report Builder will display for the date and time you configured. When finished, click the OK button to return to the Insert Date and Time Interface. The custom format you just created will then be added automatically to the available formats in the text box on the Insert Date and

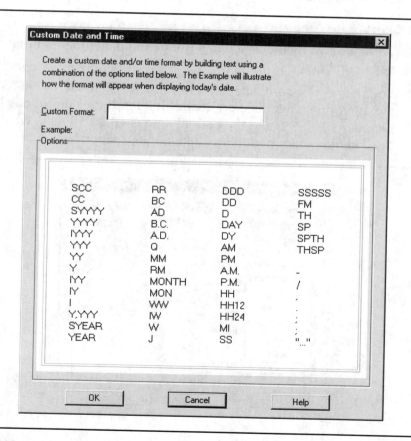

FIGURE 24-4. *Custom Date and Time interface*

Time interface. Click OK again on that interface to return to the Live Previewer to see the date/time information you added to your report.

Adding page numbers is done in roughly the same way. First, either click on the Insert Page Number button or on the Insert | Page Number menu item. This act brings up the Insert Page Number interface, shown in Figure 24-5. Defining where the page number should appear is done the same way as shown previously for adding the date and time. Once complete, you can define how you want your page numbers to appear. They can either be the page number only, or the page number with the total pages added in as well. Select the page numbering format you want to appear on your reports by clicking on the appropriate radio button and, when complete, click OK. Your selected page numbering scheme will then appear on your report.

Exercises

1. What are two methods you can use to add date/time information and page numbers?

2. You define a custom date format "YYYY RM DD, HH24-MI-SS" in the appropriate interface on Report Builder. If the current day is October 19, 1999, and the current time is 10:30:54 A.M., what will the date/time information look like on your report?

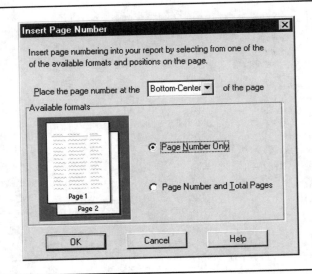

FIGURE 24-5. *Insert Page Number interface*

Managing Report Templates

In this section, you will cover the following points on managing report templates:

- Describing the template regions
- Modifying template default and override attributes
- Modifying predefined report templates
- Registering custom templates

This section covers managing report templates. The appearance of reports in your organization may be standardized easily with the use of templates. These objects can be used to encapsulate the definition of header and trailer pages for the report, corporate logos, and other visual formatting. The section will describe for you the template regions, default and override sections, modification of predefined report templates, and registering custom templates for use within Report Wizard.

Describing the Template Regions

Recall from last chapter that you can use Report Wizard to create new reports quickly and easily. Your reports can be enhanced visually with the use of templates. These templates allow you to add graphical logo displays, headings, and other items that make the data in your report more readable and understandable. They can also be used to give your reports a common appearance, based on organization, application, or any other set of criteria. You have the option of automatically applying an existing template to your report with the use of Report Wizard automatically.

A template is divided into several regions, according to the information the template supplies about the report. These regions are body region, margin region, header region, and trailer region. The body region is where you define certain aspects of the report body such as report style, text formats, font size, color, and others. The margin region includes top, bottom, and side margins. The header page and trailer page regions denote what you may want to appear on cover and trailer pages on your report. These pages may be used to distinguish it from other printed items on the printer.

Your template may predefine other aspects of reports. Aspects of the template that are applied to the report include execution parameters, report triggers, PL/SQL code, and attached libraries. These facets of a report template are all shown as drill-down items within the report template on the Object Navigator module of Report Builder.

Using Object Navigator to Create and Modify Templates

To create a new template, click once on the Templates node in the Object Navigator module, then click the Create button in the Tool Palette. Once you see the new Templates node, click on the Property icon to the left of the node to view and modify the property sheet in your Property Palette. To modify an existing template, open the template and then click the Property icon to the left of the node to view and modify the property sheet in your Property Palette.

You can drill down into the Data Model node beneath your new or existing template in the Object Navigator to view the system and user parameters predefined for the template. You can also drill down into the Layout Model node of the new or existing template to predefine template items to be included in the various regions of your report. Those regions include the body, margin, trailer, and header. Drill down into the Body node now to see there are two further nodes, called Default and Override. These nodes represent the default and override attributes of the template, an important concept that will be explained shortly. Finally, drill down into the Triggers node to see the five report triggers you can predefine for your template. Figure 24-6 displays the Object Navigator with all the Templates nodes mentioned fully expanded for your better understanding.

Modifying Templates with Template Editor

A new feature for Developer 2.1 related to modification of templates is the Template Editor. Use of this feature is accomplished by first double-clicking on the Templates drill-down item in the Object Navigator to activate that drill-down item, then clicking on the Tools | Template Editor Report Builder menu item to open the Template Editor. You should experiment with the Template Editor and an existing template that comes with the Developer/2000 release software by opening a demo template file. Template files have the extension **.tdf** and are found in the **report30/admin/template**

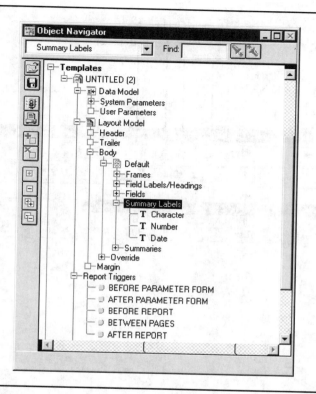

FIGURE 24-6. *Object Navigator with Template nodes displayed*

subdirectory under your Oracle software home directory on the machine where Developer/2000 is installed. This tool in Report Builder is shown in Figure 24-7 with a sample template provided with the Oracle software called **corp10.tdf**.

TIP
Be sure you understand how to modify templates using the Property Palette for OCP! Though this content is important and will complement your understanding of modifying templates with the Property Palette and Object Navigator, your understanding of the Template Editor will not be tested.

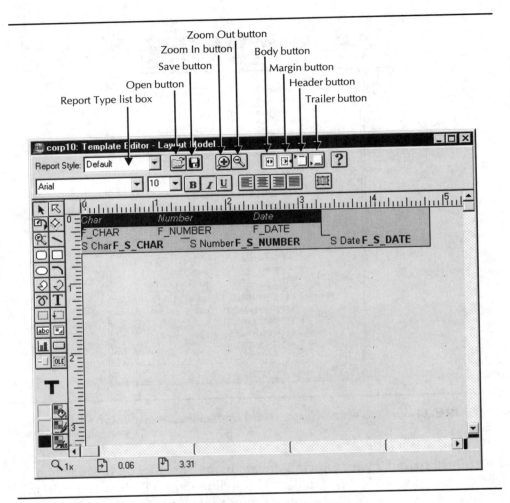

FIGURE 24-7. *Template Editor interface in Report Builder*

When you open the Template Editor, it will usually put you into the layout model of your template. Figure 24-7 shows the layout model of this sample template file provided by Oracle. Notice in that figure that there is a set of controls across the top of the interface. From left to right, they are as follows:

■ Report Type list box

■ Open and Save buttons

- Zoom In and Zoom Out buttons
- Body, Margin, Header, and Trailer buttons

The Report Type list box identifies the type of report this template enforces. The next four buttons are Open, Save, Zoom In, and Zoom Out. The functionality these buttons provide on your template should be fairly self-explanatory, so you should skip over to the last four buttons: Body, Margin, Header, and Trailer. These buttons are where the action is when you are modifying your templates. The first button navigates you to the body template region. Here, you can modify the layout of data appearing in your template body by datatype. Notice that in the **corp10.tdf** you have three datatypes defined, CHAR, NUMBER, and DATE, as part of the body region of the layout model within the Template Editor. You can see more template regions by clicking other buttons. Try clicking the Margin button now to look at that region. The change you will see is shown in Figure 24-8.

Within this perspective on the template using the Template Editor, you have several options for modifying your report template. You can easily see the header items included with this template as well, along with an item defined to display the date the report ran. Overall, however, you should notice Figure 24-8 closely resembles Figure 24-2. Hence, the explanations of different buttons available in the layout model of the Report Editor interface are also valid explanations for the layout model of the Template Editor, too.

Move on now to the header page region by clicking the Header button in the Template Editor. You will notice immediately that there is no header page developed for **corp10.tdf**. Thus, the display within Template Editor is empty. You still have the controls for changing data formats and the other options you had for your margins region view within the Template Editor interface. Finally, look at the trailer page region by clicking on the Trailer button to the right of the Header button. This view on the **corp10.tdf** template should look much the same as the header did—blank. Later in this section, we will talk about how to modify your templates using Template Editor.

Other regions where you can define items in your template include parameters. According to your view on the **corp10.tdf** template, you can define values for parameters in your template. The parameters you define fall into two categories: system and user. The system parameters include BACKGROUND, COPIES, CURRENCY, DECIMAL, DESFORMAT,

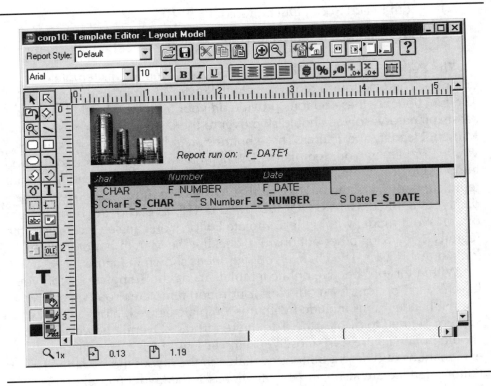

FIGURE 24-8. *Margin region shown in Template Editor*

DESNAME, DESTYPE, MODE, ORIENTATION, PRINTJOB, and THOUSANDS. You have a great deal of flexibility in defining user parameters as well.

Other template regions you may define include report triggers, which can fire at different times in the execution of the report. These times include before the parameter form is processed, after the parameter form is processed, before the report runs, between pages of the report, and after the report runs. You can define and associate PL/SQL program units and attached libraries with a template for automatic usage with your report as well. These other regions can all be found on the drill-down list under Templates in the Object Navigator.

TIP
There are a couple of questions about property value inheritance on the OCP exam. Make sure you review the topic of property value inheritance using the Report Builder online help before taking OCP.

Exercises

1. What occurs in a report when you apply a template to it? Identify some of the regions defined in a template. What tools can always be used to modify the contents of a template? What tool can only be used in Developer 2.1?

2. What extension is used to identify templates?

Modifying Template Default and Override Attributes

When you first create a report in Report Builder, the tool will define certain properties for the report automatically. These items may include runtime parameter values, physical page size, report runtime mode, margin positions, header page content, and other things. When you apply a template to a report, Report Builder changes the features for your report by imposing template components to the individual report. The items that are applied include template regions such as parameters, page size, report execution mode, margins, header and trailer page content, and other items. To apply a template to a report, you first must have the report open. Using the Object Navigator, click on the Open button and then select the Tools | Report Wizard menu item. Select the Template tab to switch to that interface, and choose either a predefined template or browse for a template of your creation. Afterward, click the Finish button to apply the template.

Modifying Template Default Attributes

A template has certain items defined within it that are consistent across all report styles available, from tabular to group to matrix. These items are called default attributes or default sections for the report template, and they will appear in the report no matter what style you select for your report, so long as you apply the template to the report. Items that can be defined as default attributes in your report include the following, corresponding to the Template | Layout Model | Body | Default node on the Object Navigator module in Report Builder: Frames, Field Labels/Headings, Fields, Summary Labels, and Summaries.

Using Object Navigator to Define Template Default Attributes

Default attributes for a template are defined in two different ways. The first way is via the use of the Object Navigator and the Property Palette. In the Object Navigator, drill down to the appropriate node listed in the bullet point above the one you wish to change. Then, click on the graphic icon next to the name. Thus, in the case of changing default attributes for summary labels of NUMBER datatype, drill down to Template | Layout Model | Body | Default | Summary Labels, and then click on the **T** icon next to the node "Number." You can look at Figure 24-6 to get a better idea.

After clicking on that icon, the Property Palette will appear to display the default attributes for summary labels of NUMBER datatype. You may then make your change. Say, for the sake of experimentation, you want to change the font of numbers displayed as summary data to blue, to contrast with the regular use of black in your report. At this point, you then click on the Text Color property. When you do so, you notice that a button with an ellipsis character appears to the right of the row. Click on that button, and a Colors interface will appear to assist you with the selection of your color. Figure 24-9 displays the Colors interface.

After making your color selection in the Colors interface, click OK. Then, close the Property Palette and return to the Template Editor module. You should notice that your summary label for NUMBER datatypes now appears in blue, corresponding to your change. Now, since this is a default attribute, it will appear in reports of different styles. In the Template Editor module, use the Report style list box in the upper left-hand corner of the interface to change from default style to tabular style. The summary label for NUMBER datatypes appears in blue as well, as it will in other report styles selected such as group left and form-like. You have now defined a default attribute for your template.

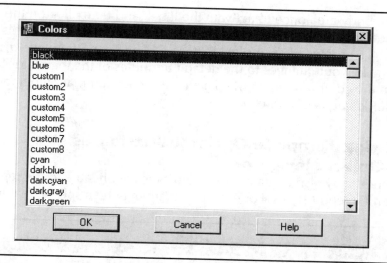

FIGURE 24-9.   *Colors interface on the Property Palette*

Using Template Editor to Define Default Template Attributes

The second method for altering template default attributes is with the Template Editor. Remember, the Template Editor is part of Developer 2.1, so be sure you understand how to do this with the Object Navigator first. Before anything else, make sure that the style displayed in the Report style list box in the upper left-hand corner of the Template Editor interface reads "Default" so that you are modifying a default attribute. Recall the similarity between the Template Editor as shown in Figure 24-7 with the Report Editor as shown in Figure 24-2. Down the left margin on this editor are several buttons, each with a different function. Notice the last three buttons on the left margin of the Template Editor interface, the ones with the four-color boxes in them. In descending order, they are the Fill Color, Line Color, and Text Color buttons.

For the sake of experimentation, modify the summary label default attribute you just changed to blue using the Object Navigator and Property Palette to red using the Template Editor. Click on the summary label in the template body area once to activate the label, and then click on the Text Color button to show the Tear Off Palette of Colors available for this label. Figure 24-10 shows the Template Editor with the Tear Off Palette displayed as you make your changes to the default attributes of the template. Then, click on the color red within the palette, and your summary label for NUMBER datatypes is now red.

Modifying Template Override Attributes with Object Navigator

Your report may also contain special attributes applicable to the report for only certain report styles. For example, there may be a special feature you

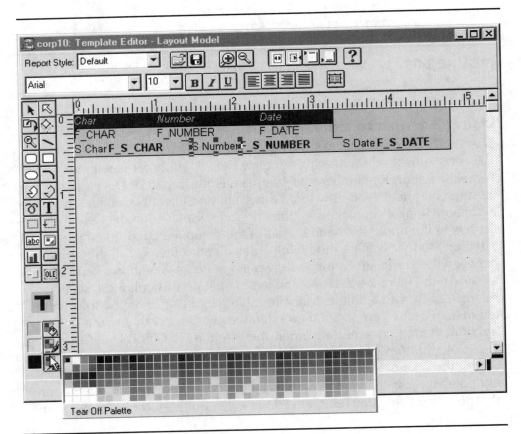

FIGURE 24-10. *Modifying default attributes with Template Editor*

want your template to contain that appears on matrix reports but not tabular reports. This component is called an override attribute. Items that can be defined as override attributes include the following sections listed under the Template | Layout Model | Body | Override drill-down item in the Object Navigator module of Report Builder: Tabular, Group left, Group Above, Form-Like, Mailing Label, Form Letter, Matrix, Matrix with Group. Under each of these items are the same sets of attributes you covered in the previous discussion on default attributes, namely frames, field labels and headings, fields, summary labels, and summaries. Override attributes for a template are defined in two ways: with the Object Navigator and Property Palette, or with the Template Editor.

Setting an override attribute on your report template with the Object Navigator and Property Palette is accomplished in the following way. In the Object Navigator, drill down to the appropriate item listed in the bullet point above the one you wish to change. For this example, assume you want to override the default attributes for summary labels on NUMBER datatypes in your group-left reports from red to green. You would first drill down to Template | Layout Model | Body | Override | Group Left | Section(1) | Summary Labels node, then click on the icon to invoke the Property Palette. Then, click on the row that reads "text color." Next to it is the word "red," for the color you defined as the default text color for summary labels in the template with the Template Editor. Click on the Ellipsis button to the right of the color definition, and the Colors interface appears. Select the color green from the interface and click OK. Repeat this operation for the second section of your group report template. When you have finished modifying override attributes for the report style, you can inspect the change you made for the override attributes by looking on the Template Editor, under the group-left style as indicated in the list box in the top left-hand corner of the Template Editor. The summary labels for NUMBER datatypes should now be green, as you have defined.

Modifying Template Override Attributes with Template Editor

The second method of defining an override attribute is to use the Template Editor module. Overall, the process is similar to defining default attributes using the Template Editor, but with the following differences. First, instead of ensuring that the style shown in the Report style list box in the upper left-hand corner of the Template Editor module shows "Default," you will want the specific report style for which you are defining an override attribute showing. In this case, it should show "Group Left." Activate the first summary label for NUMBER datatypes by clicking it. Then, click on the Text Color button appearing at the bottom left side of the Template Editor interface. The Tear Off Palette will then appear, allowing you to select the color you wish to change your text to on summary labels for numbers. Click the color, and the Template Editor will show the change.

TIP

If you use the Template Editor method to alter default or override attributes, Report Builder automatically drills down to the appropriate template item in the Object Navigator behind the scenes at the same time. After making your changes in the Template Editor, return to the Object Navigator, and you will see the change in place.

Exercises

1. Identify the meaning of a default attribute in a template. To which sections of the report may default attributes in a template be applied?

2. Identify the meaning of an override attribute in a template. In what situations do the override attributes get applied instead of the default attributes?

3. What two ways are used to modify default and override attributes in a template?

Modifying Predefined Report Templates

Oracle Developer/2000 supplies several report templates with its software release to help you get started with making your reports quickly. You may want to modify the templates that are distributed with the Oracle software for your own business purposes, however. To modify a predefined template, you must first open the template. Templates are found in the

reports30/admin/template subdirectory under the Oracle home directory, and have the extension **.tdf**. Look in this directory on your own file system to see the template files.

To open a template, click on the File I Open menu item in the Report Builder main menu bar. The Open File interface will then appear, and you can select to see the files of type template definition by using the File Type list box at the bottom of this interface. Change to the appropriate directory containing templates on your system using the Look in list box available at the top of the interface. For this exercise, you should choose the **conf2.tdf** file by clicking its name in the Open File interface and then clicking Open. Once you have opened this template definition file, you can browse the various regions of it using the appropriate drill-down nodes in the Object Navigator or the Body, Margin, Header, and Trailer buttons in the layout model of the Template Editor.

Modifying Predefined Templates with Object Navigator

You are free to modify the predefined template as you wish. For example, you may want to add content for a header page that identifies the name of the company. You can review the appropriate discussions in the previous lesson on modifying templates on what nodes to click on in the Object Navigator module. Also, review the properties you must change in your property sheet using the Property Palette.

Modifying Predefined Templates with Template Editor

To do so, you first move to the header page in the layout model of your Template Editor by clicking on the Header button. Once there, you click on the Text button in the left margin to activate your cursor to draw a text box. The Text button is shown with a "**T**" on it in the layout model of the Template Editor. Once activating the cursor, draw a text box on the header page by moving the cursor somewhere on the header page, then clicking and holding your mouse until you see a rectangle of the desired size on the header page. When you are satisfied with the size of your text box, release your mouse button and type in whatever you like. Figure 24-11 shows what the header page in your Template Editor now looks like with text defined.

Once you've mastered simple modifications like adding text to your header and trailer pages, you should practice modification of fields in your template. You can modify the default and override attributes of various items

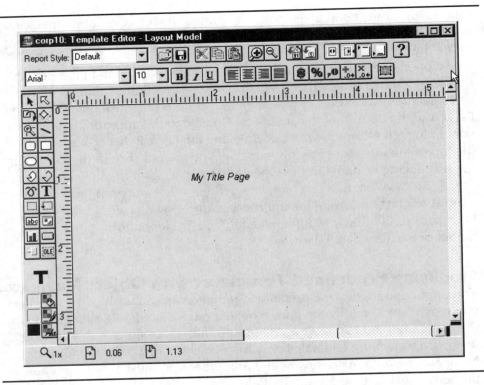

FIGURE 24-11. *Modifying templates with Template Editor: header page*

in your predefined template as described in the previous discussion. You can add date, time, and page information from the margin region of your template by clicking the appropriate button from within the layout model of the template using the Template Editor as well.

Exercises

1. Where are templates generally found in the file system containing Oracle Reports software releases?

2. Describe the process used to modify the trailer page of a template to contain a text item reading "That's all, folks!," using both the Object Navigator method and the Template Editor method?

Registering Custom Templates

In some situations, you may create new templates that you want to make available for easy inclusion and use on reports developed using Report Wizard. Recall in Chapter 22 there was some discussion about how to apply a template to a report. Within Report Wizard, there are three options for applying templates to your reports. The first is using a predefined template listed in the interface. The second is to browse for a template file in your file system. The third is to apply no template. Registering a custom template is the process of making templates of your creation available in that list interface so that you can select it easily from within Report Wizard. This task is accomplished in the following ways, depending on whether you run Developer/2000 on UNIX or Windows.

Registering your template happens in the following way. First, you open your user or global preferences file using a text editor. In Windows, the user preferences file is called **cauprefs.ora** and the global preferences file is called **cagprefs.ora**. You can find either of these files on the client machine running Developer/2000 under the Oracle software home directory on your machine (examples include c:\orawin95 or c:\orant for Windows). In UNIX, those files are both called **prefs.ora**; the only difference is that the user preferences file is located in your user home directory, while the global preferences file is located in the **tools/admin** subdirectory under the Oracle home directory.

When the user or global preferences file is opened, you then scroll through the file until you find the **Reports.***RepStyle***_Template_Desc** definition, where *RepStyle* is the report style for which your template is defined, such as **Tabular**, **BreakAbove**, **FormLetter**, and so on. You will be adding a description here for your own template to make it available for this type of report. If your template will be available for more than one type of report, then you must add your description to each appropriate area in your preferences file. The following code block shows a sample of what a preferences file contains as far as tabular template descriptions on your machine when you first install Developer/2000:

```
Reports.Tabular_Template_Desc =
  ("Corporate 1",
   "Corporate 2",
   "Confidential Heading",
   "Confidential Background",
   "Cyan Grid",
   "Bright 1",
```

```
"NCA Grey",
"NCA Yellow",
"Corporate 1 Landscape",
"Confidential Heading Landscape",
"Confidential Background Landscape",
"Cyan Grid Landscape",
Draft,
"Character Mode")
```

If you do not find a block of code like the one shown above in your user preferences file, then you should make the modification in the global preferences file. Your addition should be something descriptive, and it should be in double quotes as the others are. After adding the description for each of the report styles you want your template to be applied toward, you must also add your template's filename without the **.tdf** extension to the associated file. The following code block shows the associated **Reports.***RepStyle_***Template_File** definition for tabular reports from the preferences file:

```
Reports.Tabular_Template_File =
 (corp1,
  corp2,
  conf1,
  conf2,
  gngd1,
  brit1,
  ncagry,
  ncayel,
  corp10,
  conf10,
  conf20,
  gngd10,
  draft,
  char1)
```

TIP
Be sure to add new descriptions and files in the same order as the definition in your preferences file. For example, if you add new template descriptions at the end of the **Report.***RepStyle_***Template_Desc** *item set, make sure you add their filenames at the end of the* **Report.***RepStyle_***Template_File** *also!*

Once added to the description and filename lists, you then need to move or copy your template file in the appropriate directory. This directory is defined by your **reports30_path** environment variable defined for your machine, and should be set to the **report30/admin/template** subdirectory off your Oracle software home directory. Once these steps are complete, you should test to ensure you can apply the template to your reports using Report Wizard.

Adding a Template Image in Report Wizard (Optional)

You've probably heard the familiar pitch "for a few dollars more..." used by many salespeople. You can implement the Oracle Reports equivalent of this concept by adding an image from your template that will appear in Report Wizard. It's one nice way to make your templates a little more professional. To do so, you must accomplish the following. For each report style you want the template used for, create a report and apply the template to it. Then, use a screen capture tool to capture a portion of each sample report (2"× 3" max.), and store the screen shot in bitmap format using the naming convention *Repnamex.bmp. In this naming convention, *Repname* matches the filename specified in the **Reports.***RepStyle***_Template_File** list, while *x* identifies the report style, substituting the following characters for *x*: **a** for group above, **f** for form-like, **g** for matrix with group, **l** for group left, **m** for mailing label, **r** for form letter, **t** for tabular, **x** for matrix. After creating the bitmap file and naming it appropriately, copy it to the directory specified by the REPORTS30_PATH environment variable. Report Wizard will now display your bitmap file along with the description in the predefined template list, making it as easy for you to apply your template as it is to apply those distributed with Oracle software.

TIP
*Don't get too picky about trying to understand this for the OCP exam. As long as you know you make modifications to the **cagprefs.ora** file and some of the other high-level points made here, you should be fine.*

Exercises

1. What is the environment variable used to define the location of report template files? What is a preferences file, and how is it used?

> **2.** What are the two identifiers used in preferences files to label descriptions and filenames for predefined templates available in Reports Wizard?

Report Storage Methods

In this section, you will cover the following points on report storage methods:

■ Managing storage of report definitions

■ Report types and their portability

■ Converting reports to different storage types

■ Upgrading report and printer definition files

Understanding the use of Oracle Reports on multiple platforms in an application or system requires that you understand Oracle report storage methods. There are several methods used to store report-related files, some of which you've already seen. This section covers each of these report storage methods again in more detail. Report storage starts with report definition, so you will cover that area first. The report types and their portability between platforms and Oracle Reports executables will also be explained. A primer on what Oracle Reports executable components run which report file types will be included as well. Conversion between report storage types is a useful item to understand, and is required in some cases to use certain report types with certain files. Finally, the required tasks for upgrading report and printer definition files from Developer/2000 1.*x* to 2.0 will be covered.

Managing Storage of Report Definitions

Once created using Report Builder, reports are stored in report definition files. These file types are indicated with certain filename extensions. The following bullets explain each extension you may see used when creating and saving reports, along with the type of report the file stores and a small explanation of how the report was generated:

■ **.RDF**   The report definition file format. Binary file format containing report definition for reports runnable either in bitmap or character mode. If the report contains PL/SQL, that code is stored either as source code blocks or as compiled P-code.

- **.REP**   The report executable file format. Binary file format containing the report definition for reports runnable either in bitmap or character mode. If the report contains PL/SQL, that code is stored either as source code blocks or as compiled P-code. There are certain differences in portability between the **.rdf** and **.rep** formats that will be covered in the next discussion.

- **.REX**   The report text file format. Text file format containing one or multiple report definitions. Report Builder may use this type of file to convert to another report definition file type, depending on how Report Builder is being used.

- **.PRT**   Character mode printer definition file format. Text file format containing printer definition information for reports run in character mode. Does not actually contain a report definition, so not created by Report Builder.

- **.PLD**   PL/SQL library definition file. Text file format containing source code for PL/SQL libraries that may be used with reports. Generated using Report Builder.

- **.PLL**   PL/SQL library definition *and runnable* file. Binary file containing source code or compiled P-code for PL/SQL libraries that may be used with reports. Generated using Report Builder.

- **.PLX**   PL/SQL library executable file. Binary file format that contains PL/SQL compiled blocks that are ready to run. A PL/SQL library stored in this format cannot be modified using Report Builder, only executed.

- **.RTF**   Report output file containing contents of executed report. Generated using Report Builder or Reports Runtime.

- **.HTM or .HTML**   Report output file that is generated in the Web-enabled HTML format.

Other files used by Report Builder to support the processing of reports run in character mode include the following file types that don't necessarily have a set filename extension applicable to them:

- **Terminal definition file**   The file containing information about your terminal definition. This file is always used for Report Builder. Terminal Definition Files have the filename extension **.tdf**.

- **Keystroke file**   The file containing information about your defined keystrokes and the actions the machine should take.

- **Print screen log file**   The file created when you press the PRINT SCREEN key on your keyboard to make a screen shot of your report appearing on the screen.

There are certain files used in different versions of Developer/2000 to handle printer definitions corresponding to your reports. Later in this section, there will be a discussion of printer definition files, their use, and their upgrade from 1.*x* of Developer/2000 to 2.0. Primarily, when you store report definitions, you will be storing files with the extension **.rdf**. Later, you may want to set these reports up to be run with Reports Runtime, which means you change the format from **.rdf** to **.rep**. The discussion of file formats and their portability appears shortly.

TIP
*Make sure you know your **.rdf**, **.rep**, **.rex**, and*
***.pll** filename extensions and what they mean*
before taking the OCP exam!

Exercises

1. Identify the primary formats used to store report definitions. What are the filename extensions used to denote these formats?

2. What are the files used in conjunction with running character-based reports?

3. Identify two formats for PL/SQL libraries and their differences.

Report Types and Their Portability

Given that you will most likely be developing a lot of canned reports to include in the applications you develop, you may be concerned about portability of your report definition files. For the most part, reports developed in Developer/2000 are portable across different platforms such as Windows NT and UNIX. However, this is not always the case. Several issues exist with report definition file types and their portability across platforms.

Consider first the report definition file format, represented in your files with the **.rdf** filename extension. Files of this format are created in Report Builder whenever you create a new report. When you open your report using Report Builder for modification, this is the type of file you are modifying. This file format is stored as a binary as mentioned in the previous discussion, and is portable from one environment to another.

Now consider the report executable storage format indicated by the filename extension **.rep**. This file storage format is used for reports that are processed using Reports Runtime only. In other words, you cannot edit or modify a report in the executable format denoted by the **.rep** extension. This file format has some portability limitations as well. Although you can port these files from one environment to another for the most part without converting it, this fact is not always the case. Situations where the **.rep** file is not portable include those cases where the report contains compiled PL/SQL code. To port these files, you should first move the **.rdf** file to the other environment containing the PL/SQL code, then convert the **.rdf** file to **.rep** format. The next discussion will cover the use of Report Converter for these purposes as well.

Another type of file format you can consider is the report definition text file, denoted by the file extension **.rex**. These files are stored in plaintext, not binary format. Thus, they are highly portable between machines using the same character set, such as US7ASCII. You can use Report Converter to change the storage of a report from **.rdf** to **.rex** easily.

TIP

Both report definition binary and text files are fully portable. The report executable file is portable only if it does not contain compiled PL/SQL code.

Exercise

What restrictions are there on the portability of report definition files? What about report runtime files? What about report text files?

Converting Reports to Different Storage Types

In situations where your report does not port easily to be run from one platform or environment to another, you may have to convert the report definition file from one format to another. You perform conversion of report files from one format to another using the Report Converter, available either as a menu option in Report Builder using File | Administration | Convert, or as a stand-alone application. To run the Report Converter stand-alone, use the **r30conv** executable. This tool allows you to accomplish many things in porting your reports from one environment to another. In some cases, you can create file formats using the Report Converter tool that you would not be able to make using Report Builder. Figure 24-12 shows you the Report Converter tool in Oracle Reports.

Compiling vs. Converting

There is an area of potential confusion related to your use of Report Converter. In the list containing Oracle Developer/2000 tools you access from the Start button in Windows, you may notice a tool called Report Compiler. This tool is the same as Report Converter. The tool both compiles reports and converts them from one format to another. What's more, it is also the same tool you can access within Report Builder using the Program | Compile menu option. When you start the tool, however, notice that the window it runs in is titled Convert, and when accessed from the command line, the tool is called **r30conv**. Although this might seem confusing, it is

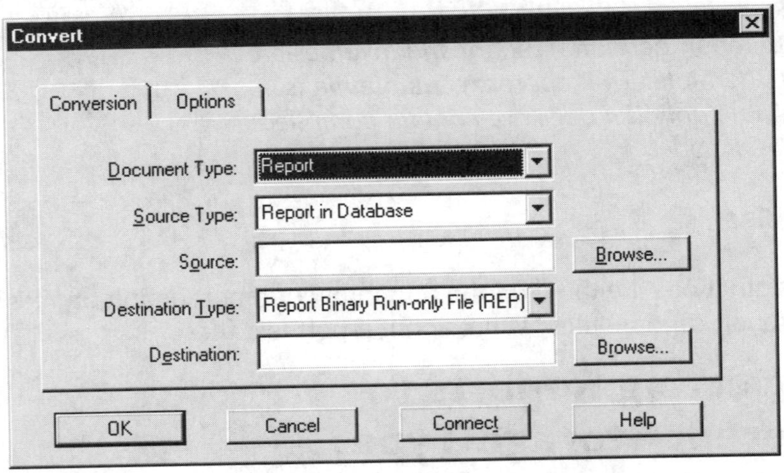

FIGURE 24-12. *Report Converter tool*

important for you to memorize that Report Converter and Report Compiler are the same tool.

Using Report Converter on Reports

Report Converter is used in the following way to convert reports from one definition type to another. First, be sure "Reports" is shown in the Document Type list box, as shown in Figure 24-12. Then, you select the report type from which you are converting using the Source Type list box. Your options in the list box for this choice are Report Binary File (**RDF**), Report ASCII File (**REX**), or Report in Database. Below that list box is a text box where you define the actual report definition file you wish to convert. You must specify the absolute path and filename for the file you wish to convert. If you do not know this information, you may click the Browse button in the Report Converter interface and the Open File interface will help you find your reports. Next, you define your destination file type and filename using the Destination Type list box. Your options as they appear in this list box include Report in Database, Report Binary Run-only File (**REP**), Report Binary File (**RDF**), Report ASCII File (**REX**), and the Report Template Binary File (**TDF**). This last option is provided to assist with creating template definitions from existing report definitions. Finally, you specify a filename for your new report storage file. When complete, click the OK button and Report Converter will convert your report file.

TIP
You can specify the filename for your destination report file without defining the file definition type extension. Oracle adds that information automatically.

It Works for PL/SQL Libraries, Too

You can use Report Converter to convert your PL/SQL library files from one type to another in the same way as you would for report definition files. To do so, you must first choose the PL/SQL Library option from the Document Type list box near the top of the Report Converter interface. Then, choose the source file definition type from the Source Type list box. Your options include Library Binary File (**PLL**), Library ASCII File (**PLD**), and Library in Database. You then identify the location of your file containing PL/SQL code in the Source text box below the Source Type list box. After this task, you define the destination type you want Report Converter to change the source file to in the Destination Type list box list box. The options as they appear in the list box include Library Binary File (**PLL**), Library ASCII File (**PLD**), Library in Database, and one other option—Library Binary Run-only File (**PLX**). This file format is similar in concept and usage to the report executable file denoted by the **.rep** filename extension. Identify your destination filename in the Destination text box, click OK, and you're there.

TIP

You can specify the filename for your destination PL/SQL Library without defining the file definition type extension. Oracle adds that information automatically.

Exercises

1. What utility handles conversion from one report type to another in Oracle Reports? What other type of file definition can this utility handle conversion for?

2. What is a PL/SQL Library executable file? What report file type is it similar to?

Upgrading Report and Printer Definition Files

Upgrading Developer/2000 from 1.*x* to 2.0 takes a bit of effort. One area where you may find yourself executing additional tasks to handle upgrades relates to report definition files and printer definition files. Some significant changes occurred in the way Oracle Reports handles printer definitions. Of course, there are changes in report definitions as well. The following discussion helps you upgrade from release 1.*x* to 2.0 of Developer/2000 with respect to Oracle Reports. Because your reports may contain and use attached PL/SQL libraries, the first topic covered is the conversion of PL/SQL code from PL/SQL 1.*x* to 2.3, the version of PL/SQL used on the Oracle Server release 7.3 and higher. It is now used in Developer/2000 2.0 and later as well. Developer/2000 1.*x* used PL/SQL 1.*x*.

TIP
You can run the Upgrade utility on reports or PL/SQL libraries only once. Even if you tell Report Converter to ignore all suggested conversions, the Upgrade utility cannot be run against the report again, preventing the utility from overwriting any manual changes made by the developer.

Upgrading PL/SQL Libraries

Your first task in upgrading your report definition files from 1.*x* to 2.0 is to upgrade any associated PL/SQL libraries. Because several keywords, features, and enhancements have been added to PL/SQL between these two versions, Report Builder has conversion utilities built in to ease the transition from one version to another. To upgrade a PL/SQL library in Report Builder interactively, simply open the library separately and then save it. The utility will process its upgrade changes automatically. If Report Builder has difficulty doing so, the PL/SQL Editor window will open, displaying both the error message and placing you in the appropriate location to make the changes.

An alternative to converting your PL/SQL programs in Report Builder is to convert them with Report Converter. Review Figure 24-12 to recognize Report Converter. Using the Report Converter GUI, opened by either clicking the appropriate icon or Start option from Windows, you first define that you want to convert a PL/SQL library with the Document Type list box, then define your source PL/SQL library filename, then define the source type as **.pll**, or PL/SQL binary containing source or P-code. If this file is not in that format, a prior conversion to that format may also be necessary. The destination file format should be **.pll** or **.plx**, whichever you prefer. The destination filename can be whatever you prefer as well. Click OK to convert, and you're on your way. Or, if you are a fan of the command line, you can issue the command shown in the following code block. Note that multiple libraries can be specified for the SOURCE parameter so long as each library is separated by a comma and all are enclosed in parentheses.

```
/home/oracle/> r30conv SOURCE=plsqllib.pll UPGRADE_PLSQL=yes
```

Upgrading Report Definitions

Once PL/SQL libraries used in your report definition are converted, you are ready to convert your report definition files as well. You will upgrade your reports in batch. The process for upgrading your report definitions can be done either with Report Converter in GUI mode or from the command line. To do so from GUI mode is done as follows. First, you open the Report Converter by double-clicking the appropriate icon or selecting the appropriate Start menu option. Next, select the Report document type from the appropriate list box in that interface. After that, choose your source type. For the destination type, make it the same as your source type. Either enter the filename for the report definition you want to upgrade using absolute pathnames or use the Browse button to find the file you want to convert. Then, enter a name for the report definition you want Report Converter to store your converted report definition in. You can browse your file system to find a destination filename as well.

TIP

*A summary of conversion activities is stored in a log file called **module.plg**.*

The alternative to running Report Converter GUI to upgrade your report definition files is to run Report Converter from the command line, passing in the appropriate command line parameters. The following code block displays the appropriate syntax. Note that multiple reports can be specified for the SOURCE parameter so long as each report is separated by a comma and all are enclosed in parentheses.

```
/home/oracle/> r30conv SOURCE=sales.rdf UPGRADE_PLSQL=yes
```

Upgrading Printer Definitions

Printer definitions allow the printer to understand how to handle special character formatting and printing. You associate these files with your reports running on character mode platforms such as UNIX command line, VMS, and the like. A printer definition file is usually a file that stores printer definition information in plaintext format. The Developer/2000 software release comes with several printer definition files already bundled in that do not require upgrade. You may, however, have printer definition files on your machine specific to your installation that require upgrade from 1.x to 2.0. You do not require printer definition files for printing reports run in bitmap mode in Oracle Reports with Developer/2000 2.0. So long as you convert the report definition, when you run the bitmap report you can print it as though it was written in 2.0 format.

Exercises

1. What needs to happen before upgrading reports that contain PL/SQL attached libraries? What utilities or Developer/2000 tools can be used to handle this activity?

2. What utility or Developer/2000 tool is used to handle upgrade of your report definitions? What is the name of the log file that contains information about the upgrade process?

3. How often can you run the Upgrade utility on your report definition files? What about upgrade for printer definitions for bitmap mode reports from 1.x to 2.0?

Chapter Summary

This chapter covers several areas of modifying and managing reports using Report Builder and other Oracle Reports executables. The topics you covered fall into modifying reports with Live Previewer, managing report templates, and report storage methods topic areas as tested on OCP Exam 5. The actual content of this chapter comprises about 18 percent of test questions you will find on OCP Exam 5.

The first area covered was modification of reports using Live Previewer. There are many fine points of your reports that cannot be modified using the Report Wizard, the tool in Report Builder that helps you assemble your reports quickly, covered last chapter. These items include display and position of data in your report and adding valuable information about when the report ran, such as date/time information.

Live Previewer consists of several components. There are buttons for switching between different report viewing modes and for modifying the format of data in the report. These controls are generally found in the horizontal toolbar of the Live Previewer interface. Additionally, there are buttons for adding rectangles, lines, and other shapes, as well as a set of buttons for altering background color, text color, and cell fill color on your report. These buttons are found on the Tool Palette of the Live Previewer interface. Additionally, there are rulers along the top and down the left side of the report viewing area, and displays to show you the current magnification of your report and your cursor's location on the physical page of the report. The View menu present when Live Previewer is in the foreground on your Report Builder GUI allows you to determine which control items are actually viewable on your display.

Modification of actual report data is performed using the button controls in the toolbar and the tool palette of Live Previewer. The generic approach to this task is a two-step process. First, you activate the field in the report you wish to modify by clicking it once to highlight it. Then, you click on whatever button, list box, or other control in the Live Previewer margins that identifies the change you wish to make to the appearance of report data. Alternately, you can select the modification to report display format you wish from the choices under the Format menu. You can, for example, add currency formatting to your report after activating the cell(s) you want the format to appear in, then clicking the Currency button or selecting the Format | Currency menu item appearing in Report Builder when Live Previewer is in the foreground. The chapter also identifies other format options available with these sets of controls.

Report data position can be modified as well. One way to do so is working with Live Previewer and Report Wizard in combination. If you wanted to change column order on your tabular report, for example, you would reenter the Report Wizard, click on the Fields tab, and add or remove columns from your report definition as you desire, then return to the Live Previewer to inspect the changes. You may also change the position or actual content of data in the report by changing the report style using that tab in the Report Wizard as well. Changes to format can be made with Live Previewer using the layout model of that tool as well. To change to the layout model of the report you created, you can either click on the Layout Model button on the left side in the horizontal toolbar of the Live Previewer interface or by choosing the View | Layout Model menu item while Live Previewer is in the foreground.

Another activity you need to understand for OCP related to Live Previewer is how to add date/time information and page numbering to your reports. Two buttons exist in Live Previewer for this purpose: the Insert Date and Time button and the Insert Page Number button. Clicking on each brings up a special interface to help you define where to place the date/time or page numbering information. The use of each interface is covered in the chapter content. Alternately, you may open the interfaces used to place date/time or page numbering information with the Insert | Date and Time or Insert | Page Number menu options in Report Builder. When adding date and time information to your report, there are some formatting conventions you need to understand, that were covered in the chapter. There will be some review of these formats in the Two-Minute Drill following this Chapter Summary as well.

Managing report templates is the next area covered in this chapter. The first area covered for this section was describing the areas or regions of a template. A template has several components, or regions. These include the template body region, margins, header pages, and trailer pages. You can define template defaults for each of these items quickly and easily. Each region has its own items for which you may define default information. The body region of the template is where you can define formatting options for each different style of report you plan to apply your template on, such as text format, font size, color, and others. You may also want to define specific items to go in your report margins such as graphics and logos to appear on your organization's reports to make for uniformity in style. These items are added or altered by defining content on your template margin region. You may want specific information to appear on the header or trailer page of your report as well, and these items are possible with the definition of template header and trailer regions. You can define default parameters for use when your report executes within your template, or special events to occur at various times during your report execution with the use of report triggers defined in your template. Template definition files in your file system are denoted with a filename extension, usually **.tdf**.

For each style of report you may apply your template to, there are attributes or sections of the template that will enforce certain formatting aspects on that report style. The attributes your template imposes can be the same across all report styles you may apply your template to, or there might be attributes your template applies to, say, tabular reports but not to form letter reports. A template attribute that gets blanket application to reports regardless of the style of report you attach the template to is called a default attribute, while a template attribute that gets applied to one report style but not another is called an override attribute.

Default attributes are defined in two ways: using the Object Navigator and Property Palette modules of Report Builder or using the Template Editor. The first method requires you to drill down to the appropriate item on your template the Object Navigator, Template | Layout Model | Body | Default. In this area of your report template, there are several attributes that can be defined. Click on the icon shown next to any of them and the Property Palette appears to help you define the default values for that attribute. Alternately, for Developer 2.1 you may want to simply open the Template Editor on your template and modify the value for the attribute using the buttons and controls in the margins on the Template Editor or with the options listed under the Format menu. If you are going to use the Template Editor to change your default attributes, however, ensure that your Report style list box in the upper left-hand corner of the Template Editor interface says "Default" so that you know you are modifying a default attribute for your template.

Modifying override attributes occurs in the same ways as the modification of default attributes, either with the Object Navigator and Property Palette or with the Template Editor. To modify an override attribute, you first drill down to the appropriate attribute you wish to change on your template in the Object Navigator, Template | Layout Model | Body | Override. Then, select the type of report you wish to define override attributes for from the set of reports appearing under this drill-down, such as Tabular, Group Above, or Matrix. After that, you drill down into the actual attribute you wish to define for this report only, click on the icon next to that attribute to invoke the Property Palette for that attribute, change your value for that attribute, and close. Alternately, for Developer 2.1 you can use the Template Editor to modify the override attribute. First, select the type of report you want to define override attributes for from the list box in the upper left-hand corner of the Template Editor. Then, define the override attributes either with the appropriate combination of format button controls or choices from the Format menu.

Rather than starting from scratch on your report, you may simply want to modify predefined report templates that come shipped with the Oracle Reports software distribution on the Developer/2000 software release. As stated, the template definition file will have the file extension **.tdf** to help you identify it. You can find the predefined templates that come with your software in the **reports30/admin/template** subdirectory under the Oracle home directory.

If you create a new template, and you want the template to be available using Report Wizard, you must do the following things. First, you must add the filename and description for your template to your user or global preferences file. This is done outside of Oracle Reports using a text editor. There are two definitions you need to look for and modify: **Reports.**_RepStyle_**_Template_Desc** and **Reports.**_RepStyle_**_Template_File**. _RepStyle_ gets replaced by the name of the report style you want your template allowed to be applied to in Report Wizard, such as **Tabular**, **FormLetter**, **BreakAbove**, and others. You must add an item to each, where the first contains short descriptions of your report template and the second contains the report filename sans the **.tdf** filename extension. Make sure you place the description and the corresponding filename in the same position on the list for each definition. For example, if you put your new template description at the end of that list, then you must place your template filename at the end of that list as well. When all descriptions and filenames are added, you may want to add a bitmap image of your report template in use on a report to be displayed in Report Wizard, but this is purely optional. Finally, you must move the template definition file (and associated bitmap images if you set any up) to the appropriate directory on your file system as defined by the REPORTS30_PATH environment variable on your machine.

The final subject area covered in this chapter is report storage methods. You covered the different report definitions and how they are stored, the different report definition types and their portability, conversion of reports from one storage type to another, and upgrade of report and printer definition files. By far the most common report storage format is the report definition file format, denoted for your files with the filename extension **.rdf**. This is a binary format file that you can both modify and run either in bitmap or character mode. PL/SQL in your report will be stored either as source or compiled code blocks. This file format type is highly portable. You may store your reports in **.rep** format as well, the report executable file format. Your **.rep** file cannot be modified in Report Builder. This is a binary file format that is ready to run using Reports Runtime. This file format is portable so long as the report doesn't contain compiled PL/SQL blocks. The final report storage format is the **.rex** format. This format is not created directly by Report Builder, but rather you convert your **.rdf** or **.rep** files to this format using Report Converter, another executable available in Oracle Reports. The **.rex** format is a text file format containing your report definitions that is as portable as any text file from one environment to another.

To convert reports or PL/SQL libraries from one form to another, you must use the Report Converter tool. You first define the document type as being report or PL/SQL library in the appropriate text box of the Report

Converter interface, then define the source filename and type using the next two text boxes in the interface. After that, you define the destination storage type and filename (without any extension) using the last two text boxes in the interface. Click OK on the interface to begin the conversion process.

The final topic in the chapter on report storage is the process you may use to upgrade report and printer definition files from 1.*x* to 2.0. You can do this for **.rdf** files by simply opening the old file and saving it, as there is an Upgrade utility built into the software release. To upgrade your **.rep** files that contain attached PL/SQL libraries, you must first upgrade the attached libraries, then the report. Report Converter is used heavily in this process. A log of conversion activities is written to a file called **module.plg** during each of these processes. An alternative to use of the Report Converter GUI is running it from the command line. Parameters appropriate in this situation include SOURCE to define the source file you would like to upgrade and UPGRADE_PLSQL, which should be set to **yes**.

Two-Minute Drill

- Live Previewer is a module allowing you to look at your report as it will appear in hard copy after developing it with Report Builder. It consists of the following items:

    - Buttons allowing you to modify the report content position and format

    - Buttons allowing you to see the report output in data or layout model

    - Buttons allowing you to send the report to printer, email, or refresh data

    - Buttons allowing you to open wizards to modify the report

    - Rulers and displays telling you the cursor's location on the report page

- To modify the controls or rulers present in Live Previewer, use the options available on the Views menu.

- To modify the display of report data execute the following tasks:

- ■ Activate the field you wish to make format changes to by clicking on it.

- ■ Apply format changes with the use of the appropriate button on the Live Previewer margin or option under Format menu.

■ To modify the position of report data using Live Previewer, you can use either of the following two options:

- ■ Report Wizard: either add, remove, or modify the order of displayed fields by clicking the Fields tab and editing; or change report style with appropriate tab.

- ■ Live Previewer: view report using layout model and move columns around.

■ Adding page numbers to a report is done with the Insert Page Number button in the Live Previewer display. This opens an interface for inserting page numbers where you can choose the location and format of your page numbers.

■ Adding date/time information to reports is done with the Insert Date and Time button in the Live Previewer display. This opens an interface for inserting date/time information where you can choose the location and format of your page numbers.

■ Displaying date/time information in Oracle Reports is done from formatting conventions that convert into actual dates on your reports. The following list shows the common format conventions and what they:

- ■ **Day, Month DD, YYYY HH12:MIAM**   Verbose date and time format converting to Saturday, December 24, 1999 3:55PM.

- ■ **DD-MON-YY**   Standard Oracle date/time format converting to 24-DEC-99.

■ Templates are generic objects that allow you to impose a set of standard features and attributes onto reports. They help enforce uniformity on reports for an organization or department easily.

■ Templates have several regions, each of which is listed, along with its contents:

- Body: report style, text formats, font size, text color, background color, cell fill color.

- Margin: banner, graphic logo, side and bottom margin captions, date/time report was run.

- Header page: cover art, report title.

- Trailer page: text appearing on a page printed at the end of the report.

- Report execution parameters: two classes of parameters, including system and user.

- Report triggers: a series of instructions written in PL/SQL that occur as prescribed events such as:

  - Before report parameters are processed

  - After parameters are processed but before the report runs

  - Between report pages

  - After report runs

- Templates contain default and override attributes. A default attribute is applied by a template to a report no matter what report style is used. An override attribute is applied by a template to only a certain style of report.

- Two methods exist for defining default and override attributes. The following list identifies each method and briefly describes its use:

  - Object Navigator working in conjunction with Property Palette: drill down to the appropriate attribute, usually found under Template I Layout Model I Body I Default or Template I Layout Model I Body I Override, click on the icon next to the attribute to open the Property Palette for that attribute, and modify the property.

  - Template Editor (Developer 2.1 only): open the layout model for that template by clicking the Layout Model button, then modify the attribute by first clicking on the cell to activate it, then clicking on the appropriate button to modify the attribute's property.

- Make sure you are modifying the attributes for the appropriate report type when using Template Editor by inspecting the contents of the Report Type list box in the upper left-hand corner of the Template Editor display.

  - For default attributes, the word "Default" should appear in the display.

  - For override attributes, the name of the appropriate report type should appear in the display.

- Several predefined report templates come packaged with the Oracle Developer/2000 software release, and they are stored in the **reports30/admin/template** subdirectory under the Oracle home directory.

- Templates have the filename extension **.tdf** to distinguish them from other files.

- You can add templates you create to the list of predefined templates available in Report Wizard by adding the filename and description for the template to the appropriate area of your user or global preferences file, **prefs.ora**.

- Your global preferences file is found in the Oracle home directory on your machine. The location of your user preferences file may either be located in the Oracle home directory or in your user home directory.

- To add a template to this file, you must add information in two places per report style you intend to apply the template to. The places where you add information are called definitions.

- Template descriptions are stored in the variable **Reports.***RepStyle*_**Template_Desc** in your preferences file. Template filenames are stored in the variable **Reports.***RepStyle*_**Template_File**. The order of descriptions stored in the first must match the order of files stored in the second.

- The identifier *RepStyle* can be replaced with the following special keywords that correspond to each of the styles of reports available in Oracle Reports: **Tabular**, **BreakAbove**, **BreakLeft**, **FormLetter**,

FormLike, **MailingLabel**, **Matrix**, and **MatrixBreak**. In these keywords, the term "break" is used to represent "group," which Oracle Reports uses in Report Builder as a report type. Note that the use of these special keywords is only appropriate in the preferences file.

- Reports Wizard also supports the use of a bitmap image of your report template to show use of your template on a report.

- After adding a template description and filename to the preferences file, move your template definition file (and associated bitmap image files, if any) to the appropriate location as defined by the **reports30_path** operating system environment variable.

- Three formats are used to store reports in Oracle Reports:

    - **.RDF**   Report definition file. Binary storage format. Modifiable and executable within Report Builder or Reports Runtime. Portable from one environment to another.

    - **.REP**   Report executable file. Binary storage format. Executable using Reports Runtime only. Not modifiable with Report Builder. Portable unless report contains attached PL/SQL libraries.

    - **.REX**   Report ASCII file. Text storage format. Can be converted into **.rdf** or **.rep** format using Report Converter. Not modifiable or executable using Report Builder or Reports Runtime. Portable from one environment to another.

- Three formats are used to store PL/SQL libraries that may be associated with Oracle Reports:

    - **.PLL**   PL/SQL library binary file. Generated and modified using Report Builder. Executed using Report Builder and Reports Runtime.

    - **.PLD**   PL/SQL library text file. Generated and modified using Report Builder. Not executable.

    - **.PLX**   PL/SQL library executable file. Generated using Report Converter. Executed using Reports Runtime.

■ Conversion of reports and PL/SQL libraries to their different storage types is handled using Report Converter. There are two ways to use the tool: GUI and command line.

■ GUI usage of the Report Converter tool requires entry of five items:

■ Document type—either a report or PL/SQL library

■ Source file type

■ Source filename

■ Destination file type

■ Destination filename

■ Use of Report Converter can happen on the command line as well.

■ Report Converter and Report Builder each have Upgrade utilities built into them for upgrading your reports automatically as well.

Chapter Questions

1. The developer is inserting date and time information into a report using the following format: DD RM YYYY BC. If today is Monday, December 25, 2013, how will the date and time information appear on the developer's report?

   A. Monday December 25 2013

   B. 25 XII 2013 AD

   C. 25 Dec 2013 AD

   D. XXV Dec 2013 AD

2. Reports with the filename extension .REX are usable with which of the following executables? (Choose two)

   A. Operating system text editor

   B. Reports Runtime

   C. Report Builder

    D. Report Converter

3. **Portability of a report with filename extension .REP depends on which of the following items?**

    A. Default attributes

    B. Override attributes

    C. PL/SQL attached libraries

    D. Parameter forms

4. **All of the following tools can be used to define an override attribute, except:**

    A. Report Wizard

    B. Object Navigator

    C. Template Editor

    D. Property Palette

5. **After upgrading your report definition files, which of the following files contains a record of conversion activities suggested by Oracle Reports but not performed?**

    A. upgrade.bad

    B. prefs.ora

    C. module.plg

    D. install.log

6. **After setting up Report Wizard to display the "IS Dept" template, the developer notices that the bitmap image for her template corresponding to use on form letters actually shows an image of this template used on tabular reports. Which of the following might have caused the error?**

    A. The filename and description items added to **prefs.ora** are in the wrong order.

    B. The **isdeptt.bmp** file was renamed **isdeptr.bmp** accidentally.

    C. None of the bitmap images for her template are in the REPORTS30_PATH directory.

    D. The predefined templates were removed from the file system.

7. **Which of the following statements must be true in order to see a report shown in Live Previewer?**

    A. The report must have been generated with Report Wizard.

    B. The report must be stored in the database.

    C. You must be connected to Oracle with a valid username and password.

    D. You must be looking at the report using the data model.

8. **Assuming standard usage of Oracle Reports filename extensions, which of the following files most likely houses a template?**

    A. depthead.rdf

    B. depthead.pld

    C. depthead.rep

    D. depthead.tdf

9. **Which of the following two definitions may be modified to make a user-defined template appear along with predefined reports in Report Wizard? (Choose two)**

    A. Reports.MatrixBreak_Template_Desc

    B. Reports.Suppress_Report_Editor_On_Open

    C. Reports.Formlike_Template_File

    D. Reports.Show_Queries

10. **The developer is producing some new reports to support a VMS system. Which of the following files are used only when running reports in character mode?**

    A. Report definition file

    B. Template definition file

    C. Report executable file

    D. Terminal definition file

Answers to Chapter Questions

1. B.   25 XII 2013 AD

Explanation   The format in the question, DD RM YYYY BC, is interpreted in the following way. DD is a two-digit day, which in this case is 25. RM stands for Roman Month, or the month of the year represented with Roman numerals, in this example it is XII for December. The YYYY represents a four-digit year. Hopefully, by 2013 the four-digit year will be standard for millenium compliance. Finally, BC indicates the "BC" or "AD" suffix should be present. Choice A would be represented symbolically as DAY MONTH DD YYYY, while Choice C would be DD Mon YYYY BC. Choice D would not be possible because there is no symbol in Oracle Reports date/time formatting that supports Roman numeral representation of days of the month.

2. A. and D.   Operating system text editor, Report Converter

Explanation   A report definition file with the **.rex** extension is a report text file. You cannot open a report text file using Report Builder nor can you execute it with Reports Runtime. You can, however, modify it as you would any other text file, using the vi text editor in UNIX. You can also convert it to another report definition file format using Report Converter.

3. C.   PL/SQL attached libraries

Explanation   Default attributes and override attributes have nothing to do with the portability of a report executable file with the extension **.rep**. Neither does the parameter form. The report executable file is not portable if there are PL/SQL attached libraries, however. Thus, the correct answer is C.

4. A.   Report Wizard

Explanation   There are two ways to define override attributes on templates. Recall that you can drill down to the appropriate override attribute using the Object Navigator and then change the properties of the attribute using the Property Palette. The second way is to modify the template using the Template Editor. The only tool left, then, is choice A, Report Wizard.

5. C. **module.plg**

Explanation The Upgrade utility built into Oracle Reports stores information about the upgrade of a report or PL/SQL library in a log file called **module.plg**. Choices A and D indicate files that are not predefined for use in Oracle, while the **prefs.ora** file has the important use of identifying user preferences.

6. B. The **isdeptt.bmp** file was renamed **isdeptr.bmp** accidentally.

Explanation This question is perhaps the most challenging in the chapter. Recall from discussion of setting up Report Wizard to use your templates that you can take bitmap image files of your template in use on a file and incorporate them into Report Wizard. This requires the peculiar naming convention *repnamex*.**bmp**, where the report name is indicated by *repname* and the report style for which the image corresponds is indicated by the last letter before the dot separating the main filename from the **.bmp** extension. For form letters, the style of report in question, that last letter before the dot needs to be **r**, but the image that shows in Report Wizard is that corresponding to the tabular report, which uses **t** as the letter before the dot. Therefore, of all these choices, choice B is most plausible.

7. C. You must be connected to Oracle with a valid username and password.

Explanation In order to see the report in Live Previewer, you must connect to the Oracle database to process the underlying data model for the report. However, you needn't have the report stored on the database, eliminating choice B. In addition, you can see your report in Live Previewer mode without it being generated using Report Wizard, eliminating choice A. Finally, you can eliminate choice D because if you were looking at the report via the data model, it is feasible you would not have even generated live data yet, and you would have little need to see the Live Previewer.

8. D. **depthead.tdf**

Explanation Your template definition file is suffixed with a **.tdf** extension if standard Oracle Reports naming conventions are followed. Report definition files are suffixed with **.rdf**, eliminating choice A. Report executable files are suffixed with **.rep**, eliminating choice C. Choice B illustrates the suffix used for PL/SQL library text files. Thus, the correct choice is choice D.

9. A. and C.   Reports.MatrixBreak_Template_Desc,
   Reports.Formlike_Template_File

Explanation   The two definitions in the preferences file that require modification if you want to add a template to the list of predefined templates available for use in Report Wizard include Reports.MatrixBreak_Template_Desc and the definition Reports.Formlike_Template_File. The other two listed as choices are used for other purposes.

10. D. Terminal definition file

Explanation   Terminal definitions are only required for character-based reports. The other files named in the example are used for both bitmap reports and for character-based reports.

CHAPTER
25

Enhancing Data Content
in Report Builder

n this chapter, you will cover the following areas of enhancing reports in Report Builder:

- Using the Data Model to create queries and groups
- Using the Data Model to create columns

The data in a report is what gives the report content. But raw data is useless unless the report developer gives the data meaning somehow. The purpose of the Data Model is to help you add meaning to your data. The Data Model displays your report queries, which extract information from the Oracle database for use in your reports. It also displays the columns of your reports in groups to organize the report columns. Both of these items are displayed pictorially in the Data Model. This chapter will cover your use of the Data Model to define and modify queries, groups, and columns in your report. Every report style has groups, but each report style may manipulate the groups differently. This chapter covers elements comprising 15 percent of OCP Exam 5 content.

Using the Data Model to Create Queries and Groups

In this section, you will cover the following points on using the Data Model to enhance reports by creating queries and groups:

- Data Model objects and their relationships
- Creating groups to modify report hierarchy
- Changing order of data in groups
- Using group filters to eliminate data from reports
- Creating data links to link data from different queries

Everyone wants reports in an organization. Analysts want to see information to make recommendations, and managers want it to make decisions. Unfortunately, everyone wants to see it in polished form, which is usually not the way it is stored in an Oracle database. When developing your reports, it is often helpful to look at data in the report in some form other than SQL statements, because, although the SQL statement assembles the data you want out of normalized databases, you may want to have a visual representation of the data you create reports from. The Data Model feature of Report Builder allows you to view the information included in your report using visual features. This section will cover the use of Data Model to show data relationships in your report. This section identifies the objects you will see in Data Model, including queries, groups, summary columns, and several others, and instructs you on how to modify each of these elements to add meaning to the overall report.

Data Model Objects and Their Relationships

Your examination of the Data Model view on your report will show you there are several items Data Model displays. These items include system parameters, user parameters, queries, groups, formula columns, summary columns, placeholder columns, and data links. Incidentally, all of these items appear under the Reports | *your_report_name* | Data Model node in the Object Navigator module within Report Builder. Note that each report may not have every item defined within the Data Model for that object. Within Report Builder, you can see a pictorial display of the Data Model objects by clicking the Data Model button in Report Editor, the second button in the top left-hand corner of that tool. Figure 25-1 shows you the items under the Data Model node in the Object Navigator, while Figure 25-2 displays the Data Model view on your report's data definition within the Report Editor.

To understand the rest of this chapter, be sure you understand the use of each object available in the Data Model. The following subsections should help you understand each component you will find in the Data Model, what each component is used for, and their relationships with one another. Bear in mind another crucial fact about objects in your Data Model appearing in your report as part of Figure 25-2. Most have had their labels altered for readability. The Property Palette is used to change labels for Data Model objects. Simply double-click on the little icon just in front of an object name and the Property Palette will appear for that object. Oracle Reports generates labels automatically for every object appearing in your reports. In each of the following lessons, pay attention to the format for the label generated automatically for each object.

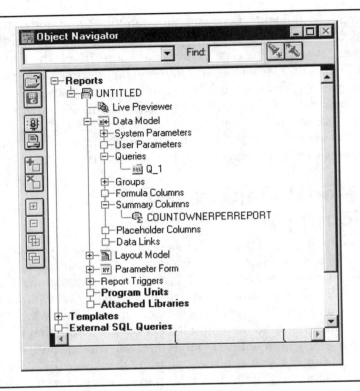

FIGURE 25-1. *Data Model node within Object Navigator*

System and User Parameters

System parameters in the Data Model are parameters created by Report Builder that accept values at the time the report is run to define how your report will run. Some system parameters include BACKGROUND, COPIES, CURRENCY, DECIMAL, DESFORMAT, DESNAME, DESTYPE, MODE, ORIENTATION, THOUSANDS, and PRINT JOB. User parameters are those parameters in the Data Model that you can create for your report. You can define an initial value and a List of Values (LOV) for your user parameters. System and user parameters do not appear in the Data Model view of your report. Instead, you examine and change their values using the Property Palette.

Queries

These items in the Data Model are the data definitions that your report will capture and present on paper. In Figure 25-2, the query is shown as the small box identified with the label ALL_TABLES Query. The automatically

Summary column

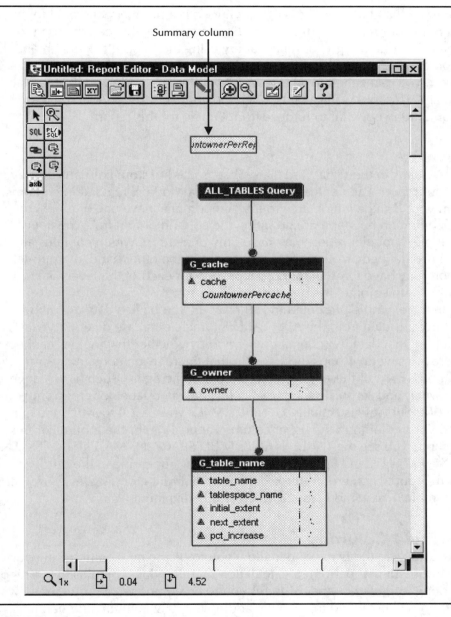

FIGURE 25-2. *Data Model view within Report Editor*

generated label for queries is Q_*n*, where *n* is a number generated for each query in your report, starting with 1. You have already been exposed to methods for defining your report query using the Report Wizard—manually, import from file, or Query Builder. With the Data Model view on your report, you can generate queries using another method as well—the Data Wizard. This tool walks you through the critical steps for defining the information you want to retrieve from Oracle for this report.

Groups

These items in the Data Model are objects used to store columns displayed in your report. Each of the boxes in the Data Model that contain columns from your data definition are groups. A report may have one or more groups, depending on how you are grouping the column output from the query. For example, a tabular report may have only one group, which contains all columns defined as output for the report. On the other hand, a group-left report may have three or more groups, one for each of the levels of grouping you want to enforce on your query.

In the example presented in Figure 25-2, you have a data definition that obtains data from the ALL_TABLES Oracle database dictionary view, grouping that data by schema owner and by whether that table is cached. There are several groups displayed in that figure, each containing some columns. Each of these groups has a label in the figure, such as G_cache, G_owner, and so on. The automatically generated label for groups in your Data Model view is actually G_*COLNAME*, where *COLNAME* is the name of the first column in the list of columns appearing for the group. For this example, you see the TABLE_NAME, TABLESPACE_NAME, INITIAL_EXTENT, NEXT_EXTENT, and PCT_INCREASE columns appearing in the third, or main, group. Each group stores data from different grouping levels in a hierarchical way, more about which will be explained later.

Formula Columns

These fields in the Data Model allow you to define new columns in your report output that perform a calculation on other data columns in the report. Creating formula columns requires you to determine what group the new column will be added to, actually adding the new column, and defining the process or formula Reports will use to calculate the new column using PL/SQL. There are no examples of a formula column in Figure 25-2, but later figures will show them with labels like *formula column group level.* The automatically generated label for these columns in Oracle Reports will have the format CF_*n*, where *n* is a number starting with 1 to uniquely identify the formula column.

Alternately, you can define formula columns at the report level that appear in separate objects from groups. The automatically generated label format for the report-level formula column is the same as that used for group-level formula columns. The steps involved in this process will be identified later in the chapter. This functionality in an Oracle report is roughly akin in concept to executing a SQL statement such as the sample code provided in the following code block:

```
SQL> SELECT empid, lastname, firstname,
  2> salary, salary*1.08 AS RAISE
  2> FROM EMPLOYEE;
```

Summary Columns

These items in the Data Model perform aggregate calculations on data in other columns, such as **sum( )** or **avg( )** operations. These columns should not be confused with formula columns, which perform a calculation on a column value for every row of data in the output or the report. The output from a SQL statement similar in concept to the one provided in the code block above illustrates a calculation on a column value for every row of data in the data **select**ed. In contrast, your summary column is a calculation performed at once for a particular column on every row of output.

Recall from the discussion of using Report Wizard in Chapter 22 that there are several different types of summaries available in Oracle Reports, similar in concept to group functions **sum( )**, **count( )**, **avg( )**, **min( )**, or **max( )**. Other options offered through manual configuration using the Data Model view in Report Builder to create a summary column and then editing that column in the Property Palette include first, last, standard deviation, and variance. For the report Data Model shown in Figure 25-2, notice the small box off to the left on the model for this report. That small box is where the summary column is defined.

Summary columns can be defined at the report level and at the group level. At the report level, they appear as separate boxes from the groups and queries of the report. One is shown in Figure 25-2 with a label generated from Report Wizard. That label is CountownerPerReport. The automatically generated label for these columns in the Data Model view is CS_n, where n is a number from 1 up. At the group level, the summary column will appear as part of the group, along with other columns in that group. The label for this object is automatically generated in the same way as those labels for the report-level summary columns.

Placeholder Columns

These columns in your Data Model view define a location where Oracle Reports will populate a report-wide or group-wide value of your choosing. Placeholder columns are similar to formula columns in that you can calculate the value in your placeholder column with a formula using PL/SQL code. Alternately, you use a special set of triggers built into Oracle Reports that fire at predefined times in the report execution to write a value to a placeholder column. There are no examples of placeholder columns in Figure 25-2, but later figures will show data models that have placeholder columns in them. Placeholder columns have the automatically generated label CP_n, where n is a number starting with 1 to uniquely identify the column.

Data Links

Finally, these items in your report are a means to draw together multiple queries designed to obtain data from the database in a master/detail format. When links are used, for each iteration of the master group, the detail query is executed. Three types of links exist in Report Builder, depending on the way they are created. The first is a query-to-query link, the next is a group-to-group link, and the last is a column-to-column link. Links are represented as a line between two queries with a special label appearing in the query Data Model object. See the discussion on linking queries that appears later in this section for more information and examples.

Exercises

1. After looking at the Data Model view of a report, what do you think are the most common elements in a report?

2. Which report elements are commonly used from Report Wizard as items that summarize other data in your report?

3. What is a link? How might a link be used in a report?

4. **(BONUS)** Find out more about summary columns and about when it may not be a good idea to mix their presence with database columns that contain equations in your data definition. Also try to find a good reason to use a data link in your report.

Creating Groups to Modify Report Hierarchy

As stated, every report contains at least one group, called either the *main* or *default* group for the report. For example, a tabular report contains a group that simply lists all columns in the report output. However, many types of reports will contain more than one group. Some of the reports that contain multiple groups include group left, group above, and matrix with group reports. Each of these types of reports uses groups to define report hierarchy. What does this mean? Take another look at the Data Model contents for your group-left report in Figure 25-2. The image clearly suggests a hierarchy of report data content.

At the top of that hierarchy is the query itself, which drives the entire data definition for the report, without which your report would be a blank sheet. Under that query is the first group, containing one column for the schema owner of tables in the ALL_TABLES dictionary view. This group is considered the level-1 group in the hierarchy of returned data in the report. The data in your report gets broken out by every unique value for every level in the hierarchy, thus giving your report a break on each schema owner with tables in the database. Below that group is another group, the level-2 group, storing the CACHE column from your dictionary view. At the bottom of the list is another group containing all other columns appearing in the report.

TIP
Combining single columns in n hierarchy group levels into one hierarchy group level containing n columns does not change the number of unique values on which your report has breaks. Only by adding unique values to a column, or adding hierarchy group levels, can you increase the total number of breaks by unique value to your report.

You can create groups to manage and alter the hierarchy of data appearing in group reports. Say, for example, that you want to add a new column to the hierarchy of your group-left report using data from the ALL_TABLES view. For this new level in the hierarchy, you want to group tables listed according to the tablespace in the Oracle database in which the table is stored.

TIP

For your information, a tablespace is a logical storage area on disk where an Oracle database can store tables, indexes, and all the other database objects you learned about in Unit I. Don't worry about understanding this concept in much detail. It is not tested on the OCP Developer track.

Adding this third level to the hierarchy is accomplished either through the use of the Data Model alone or with the use of the Report Wizard. First, you will cover the use of Report Wizard to add a third level of hierarchy on your report for breaks on TABLESPACE_NAME. From the Data Model view on your existing report in Report Editor, click on the Tools | Report Wizard menu item in the main menu of Report Builder to open that tool. From there, click on the Groups tab, appearing third over from the left whenever the report style selected for operations is a group report of some kind. If you don't see the Groups tab, then you are probably not working with a group-left, group-above, or matrix-with-group report. Since use of Report Wizard in Chapter 22 focused mainly on its use for generating tabular reports, a reprisal of Report Wizard showing the Groups tab is shown here in Figure 25-3 to help you understand the points made here.

Select the TABLESPACE_NAME column you would like to define as the third hierarchical level from the left window in the Groups tab, and add it to the right window with the Right Arrow button appearing between the two windows above the Left Arrow button. The TABLESPACE_NAME column then appears in the second window on the right side of the Groups tab under the level-3 header. Then, click the Finish button and log in to the Oracle database to allow Report Builder to generate your report, showing the output in the Live Previewer. When your report has been successfully

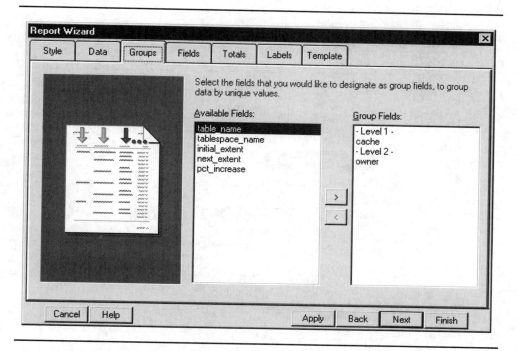

FIGURE 25-3.   *Contents of Groups tab in Report Wizard*

altered, return to the Data Model. You should now see a new level-3 group appearing between the level-2 group and the main group of columns in your report. Figure 25-4 shows what you should see in your Data Model view of the report.

TIP
You will not see a Groups tab, nor will you be able to add groups to reports that are not group reports. Group reports are those with "group" somewhere in their name.

The second way to execute this task is within the Data Model itself. Take another look at Figure 25-4 and locate the new level-3 hierarchy for grouping data you created using the TABLESPACE_NAME column. When

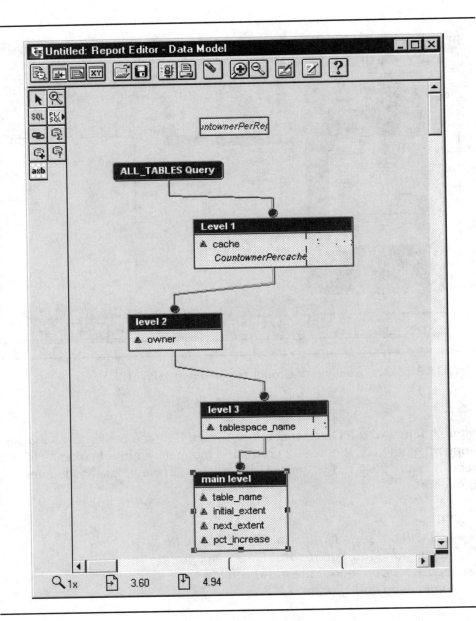

FIGURE 25-4. *Contents of Data Model after adding new group*

you locate it, point to it with your mouse and click and drag it back to the main group level of your report. When you release the mouse button, the TABLESPACE_NAME column will be returned to the bottom of the main group. Click on the now-empty level-3 group once to activate it and then press the Delete key on your keyboard. Now, point to the TABLESPACE_NAME column again and click and drag it off the main group. When you are off the main group and between the level-2 group and the main group, release your mouse button. Data Model will create a new level-3 group to store the TABLESPACE_NAME column as it looked in Figure 25-4 before you made these changes. Manually creating hierarchies has a restriction in that you can only drag one level up or down at one time.

TIP

You will encounter errors if you try to see the changes to your report Data Model by simply clicking on the Live Previewer button after making those changes. This is because the Layout Model and Data Model views are out of sync. First, click on the Layout Model button to apply the changes in the Data Model view, then click on the Live Previewer button to see the changes on your actual report.

Exercises

1. How are groups used to define data hierarchy in a report? Can you create multiple groups in tabular, form-like, form letter, or mailing label reports? Why or why not?

2. What are the two ways you can create new groups using the Data Model for your report?

3. If you have a level-1 hierarchy group containing five unique values and a level-2 hierarchy group containing two unique values, how many breaks will there be in your report? How many will there be if you combine the two groups into one? Why?

Changing Order of Data in Groups

What does changing order of data in groups mean? Actually, it can mean several things, from changing the order of data in a column, which is done with the Break Order property in the Property Palette, to changing the order of columns in your groups on the Data Model. Within any group of your report containing multiple columns, you may want to change the order of the columns in your group. This task is accomplished in one of two ways, either using the Data Model by itself or with the use of Report Wizard. First, look at the group you want to reorder columns in within the Data Model view of your report in Report Editor. For this lesson, you will modify the main group of your report developed thus far using the ALL_TABLES view. Take note of the current column order in the Data Model, which lists data columns you **select** from the ALL_TABLES view in your data definition statement for use in your report. In this case, your data definition statement appears in the following code block and corresponds directly to the fields displayed in your report.

```
select OWNER, CACHE, TABLESPACE_NAME, TABLE_NAME,
       INITIAL_EXTENT, NEXT_EXTENT, PCT_INCREASE
from ALL_TABLES;
```

Changing order of data in groups in your Data Model can be accomplished either directly in the Data Model or using Report Wizard. Note that it's really difficult to use Data Model by itself to change column order in groups if you **select** data from Oracle in your data definition columns that you don't display in the report. Although you are not required to ensure your report's data definition corresponds exactly to the fields you will display from the Oracle database (because you can limit displayed data with Report Wizard), it is advisable to do so because your Data Model groups show everything in the data definition, not just the fields displayed. For **select** * **from** *tbl_name* statements, your list of columns in the main report group won't correspond to your displayed fields, and you may have to refer back and forth between the Data Model and Report Wizard when changing the order of data in groups if you want to use Data Model.

TIP

To avoid confusion, make sure your data definition SQL statement matches your list of displayed fields in Report Wizard so that your Data Model group columns match the displayed columns.

First, attempt to change column order in your report with Report Wizard. Open Report Wizard from the Data Model now. Say that you want to put the TABLE_NAME column last in the group. From within the Data Model view of your report using the Report Editor, open the Report Wizard and click on the Fields tab. This tab shows the fields in your report. Figure 25-5 shows the contents of the Fields tab within Report Wizard containing a list of all your columns in the ALL_TABLES report.

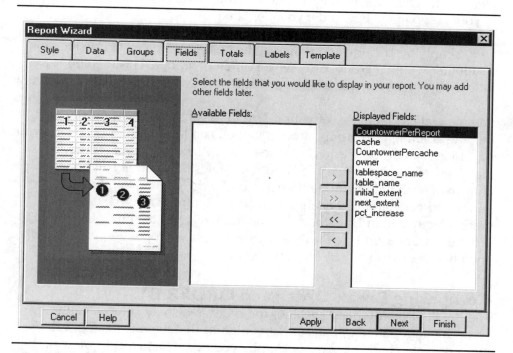

FIGURE 25-5. *Report Wizard Fields tab with columns from ALL_TABLES report*

Recall which columns are part of your main group level in the Data Model view: TABLE_NAME, INITIAL_EXTENT, NEXT_EXTENT, and PCT_INCREASE. Remove those columns from the Displayed Fields window by clicking on the column name once to highlight, and then clicking the Left Arrow button at the bottom between the Available Fields and Displayed Fields window. Or, to remove all columns and start ordering from scratch, click the Left Double Arrow button between the Available Fields and Displayed Fields windows to remove all fields from display. Then, add the fields again by highlighting each field in turn and clicking the Right Arrow button at the top between the Available Fields and Displayed Fields windows. You can drop and drag columns in the Report Wizard as well. Once complete, click the Finish button in the Report Wizard interface and Oracle Reports will generate a new version of your ALL_TABLES report, showing the output in the Live Previewer with your column order changed in the report output. If you want, you can then click on the Data Model button in Report Editor and you will see the columns in your group in the new order you identified.

You can change column order in your group within the Data Model, as well, simply by clicking and dragging the column name from one location to another within a group, or between different groups. This method is a little tricky, however, because there is a tendency for the Layout Model view

and the Data Model view of your report to get out of sync when you start moving columns and groups around in the Data Model. Your best bet if you start to get into trouble is to open the Report Wizard on your report and make whatever changes in the Groups or Fields tabs you need to, then click the Finish button and let Report Builder do its thing to fix your report. Furthermore, even if you change order on columns in your Data Model group strictly within Data Model, you won't ever see the changes in field order on your report Live Previewer view unless you open Report Wizard and click the Finish button for your report.

Comparing Break Order and ORDER BY

The Break Order property specifies the order to display column values in your Oracle report. It applies only to columns that identify distinct values of user-created break groups created by you in the Data Model view of the report. The order of column values in a default or main group is handled within the data definition by the **order by** clause of the SQL **select** statement. For column values in user-created groups, you would use Break Order to specify how Reports will order values displayed in the break column. You can specify Ascending, Descending, or None as values for the Break Order property in the property sheet for your columns. This is accomplished with the use of the Property Palette. The default value is Ascending, and it is required if the Set Break Order property is set to Yes for columns.

The mention of **order by** gives rise to some considerations you should use when specifying order in your reports. The Break Order property will take precedence over the **order by** clause in all groups except for the main or default group of the report. Consider another example, using the Australian Outback database from earlier in the text. Suppose that you created a group-left report with KGROO and JOEY. In the report query, you have the **order by** KGROO clause, where you also specify Break Order Descending for the KGROO column. Although you specified Ascending order (the default) in your **order by** clause, the listing of KGROO data is in descending order, as you specified in your Break Order property. The output of your query might appear similar to the following block:

```
KGROO    JOEY
------   ----------
FLUMPY   SKIPPY
         KANGA
DUMPY    RED
         SUPIE
         ROO
         FORD
ABE      MILLER
         CLARK
         KING
         HOPPY
         FLOPPY
```

In addition to use of Break Order being disallowed on the default or main report group, note there are some other restrictions to use of Break Order. If you use Break Order in one hierarchical group, you must use it in every group, though you needn't set it the same way (Ascending or Descending) for all groups. Break Order also cannot be used on Oracle database columns of LONG or LONG RAW datatype. Break Order also only affects the ordering of the break column, and will not change order of columns in the break group. For example, suppose that you break on KGROO and for each kangaroo you list offspring via the JOEY column. If the Break Order is Ascending, then kangaroos are printed in ascending order, but the names of offspring list in the order specified by the query. In other words, to change the order of JOEYs for each kangaroo, you need an **order by** clause in your **select** statement. Other restrictions are that a summary column cannot be a break column and cannot have Break Order set, and a formula column that depends upon a summary column cannot be a break column and cannot have Break Order set.

TIP
*Be absolutely sure you understand these points about Break Order and **order by** for use in specifying order of data in a report before taking the OCP exam!*

Exercises

1. Do your data definition columns need to match your displayed fields? Why is it a good idea to make them match?

2. How do you change column order in a group using the Data Model view only? Why isn't it necessarily a good way to do so?

3. What is Break Order? How is it set? How does its use compare to the use of **order by** in a **select** statement? Which takes precedence? What are the restrictions on using Break Order?

Using Group Filters to Eliminate Data from Reports

You may not always want to show all the data available in your database as it relates to your reporting needs. There are many ways to limit the data returned in your report. One way is to do so is at the group level using filters. A filter is a predefined operation or a PL/SQL block allowing you to limit the data returned by columns in your group. There are two predefined group filters available to eliminate data from reports. These filters can eliminate the first *n* records in a group or the last *n* records in a group.

To use the two predefined group filters to eliminate data from a group, execute the following tasks. Using the Data Model view in Report Editor on the main group in your report, double-click on the header label of the group. This action opens the Property Palette for the group. There are several items in the Property Palette that correspond to groups, one with the title Groups. Under that item there should be a property that is called Filters. Click on the value for that property, which at this time should be None. A list box will be created, where you can click on the drop-down button to see all list items. Choose either the First or Last options on this list.

TIP
Filters are an inefficient way of limiting data. A better way might be to specify the maximum number of records your report will display as part of the property sheet for the data definition query. But, understanding filters is useful for passing the OCP exam, so be sure you understand it.

A new item will appear under the Filters property called Number of Records. You can enter whatever positive integer you wish corresponding to that property. Figure 25-6 shows the Property Palette as it will appear if you want to filter out all but the first five records to show for this group. You can then switch views in the Report Editor to the Live Previewer and see the effects of your filter in action. Return to the Data Model view on your report in the Report Editor now. Notice first there is a change in the color of the dot at the end of the line leading from the next-highest group level to the main level. This change is meant to indicate that a filter exists on the group.

Creating User-Defined Filters

The third type of filter is a user-defined filter, consisting of a PL/SQL block that tests whether the record from the group will appear in the report. If the block returns TRUE, then the record will appear in the report, if the block returns FALSE, the record will not. There are three different ways to define a group filter, two of which use the Data Model, Property Palette, and PL/SQL Editor. The second uses only the Data Model and the PL/SQL Editor. The final option uses the Object Navigator and PL/SQL Editor modules.

Return now to the Group item in the Property Palette by double-clicking on the header area for the main group again. A third option exists in the drop-down list for the Filter property, called PL/SQL. After defining the

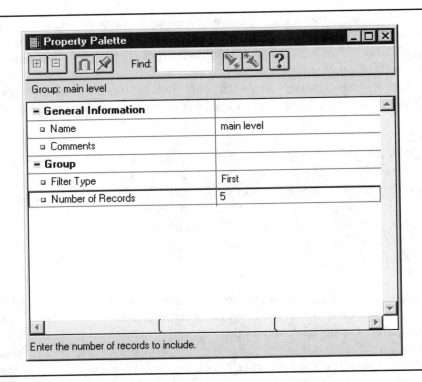

FIGURE 25-6. *Using predefined filters in the Property Palette*

PL/SQL filter value for this property, a new property appears below it called
PL/SQL Filter. A button appears immediately to the right of this property
when you click on the property name. Click the button, and the Program
Unit Editor will appear with template information to help you define your
PL/SQL code for the group filter. Figure 25-7 demonstrates the contents of
the PL/SQL Editor for a group filter that only shows records for tables where
the value in INITIAL_EXTENT is greater than 1,048,576. Once complete,
click the Compile button, and when your PL/SQL block is successfully
compiled, click the Close button.

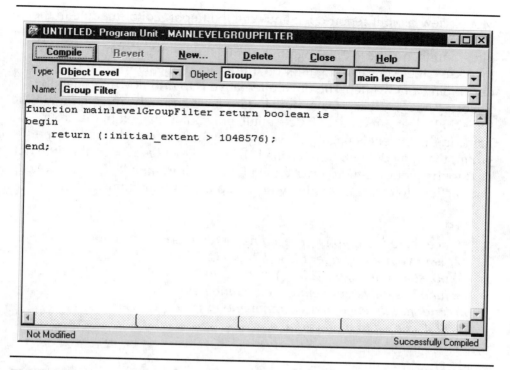

```
UNTITLED: Program Unit - MAINLEVELGROUPFILTER
```

```
function mainlevelGroupFilter return boolean is
begin
     return (:initial_extent > 1048576);
end;
```

FIGURE 25-7. *Developing group filters in PL/SQL Editor*

TIP
INITIAL_EXTENT probably won't mean much to non-DBAs. Think of it as the amount of space Oracle initially obtains in which to put the contents of a table when it is first created. Again, don't worry too much about understanding this concept, as its not covered by the OCP Developer track.

There are two other ways to open the PL/SQL Editor within Report Builder. The first is with the Report Builder main menu. With the Data

Model view of your report open and with the Report Editor module in the foreground, click once to activate the group on which you want to define a filter, and then choose the Program I PL/SQL Editor menu item. You will then see either your existing filter on this group or the template for developing a new filter. The other alternative is to drill down through the Reports I ALL_TABLES I Data Model I Groups items to the main group in the Object Navigator module. Notice a little gray dot to the left of the group name in the Object Navigator. If you already have a filter defined for the group, that gray dot will have a small "p" in it. Double-click on the little dot next to the group name to invoke the PL/SQL Editor module. Once invoked, your actions to create or modify your group filter are the same as before.

TIP
Notice there is a colon (:) preceding the column name in your group filter PL/SQL block demonstrated in Figure 25-7. You need to include this character before the column name in order to reference the column name in your PL/SQL code as a bind variable.

Exercises

1. What is a group filter? What two predefined group filters are available for group data filtering? What is the third method for defining a group filter?

2. What are the three ways to invoke the PL/SQL Editor to define a filter for a group? What special character is required before a column name to reference it in the PL/SQL block defining the group filter?

Linking Data from Different Queries

In some cases, you may want to have your report display data returned from multiple queries. For example, you may want the report to **select** certain data from one part of the database, then use that result set as master records to drive a detail query to pull data based on that master set of records. To do this task, you must create a second query for your report and then tie the two queries in the report together by means of a data link.

Recall from earlier in the discussion you learned that a data link helps you put multiple queries together in a report. You can create a data link in a report that has multiple queries that operate on intermediate forms of the data that will eventually be returned by the report. First click on the Data Link tool button in the Data Model view to activate the tool and move your pointer into the Data Model view on the report. Click and hold on one of the specific areas in the parent or master query, then move over to the appropriate area of the child or detail query and release your mouse button to draw the link from the parent to the child.

The Three Types of Data Links

There are three different types of data links between two different queries in your Data Model view on the report. The first is query to query, the second is group to group, and the third is column to column. The type of data link you want to define will influence how you actually draw the link from one query to another. An explanation of each type of data link, along with instructions on how to draw the link, is now given.

QUERY-TO-QUERY DATA LINKS   This type of data link uses data returned from the master or parent query to drive the child or detail query. The link is made at the query level by drawing the data link from the master query to the child query. Query-to-query data links can only be drawn when a foreign key in the table(s) containing columns from the child group references the primary key in table(s) of the parent group.

GROUP-TO-GROUP DATA LINKS   This type of data link uses data in the parent or master group to obtain data in the detail group. The link is made at the group level by drawing the data link from a group in the master query to a group in the detail query. Be careful not to touch the columns in the master or detail group when drawing group-to-group data links, or you will wind up drawing the next type of data link, a column-to-column data link. In order to draw a group-to-group data link, you must have common columns shared between the group.

COLUMN-TO-COLUMN DATA LINKS   This type of data link uses data in the master column to join with data obtained in the detail column. The link is made from a column in a master group to the same column in a group of the child query. In order to make this link, there must be a column shared between the two queries.

TIP
*A link is always drawn from the parent
to the child.*

Defining Data Link Properties in the Property Palette

It can be difficult to distinguish one type of link from another once the link is drawn. Sometimes the properties of the data link can help you do so. This lesson covers each of the properties of data links, describing the properties, their alternative values, and their usage on the report. The following are the properties of a data link that will appear in the Property Palette for query-to-query, group-to-group, or column-to-column data links.

SQL CLAUSE   This property defines the SQL statement clause that defines how the data from one query will relate the master group to the child query. There are three options, **where**, **having**, and **start with**. These three options relate to the original discussion of SQL statements that was covered in Unit I of this text. Of important note is the fact that your use of **start with** or **having** in the data link implies the detail query must contain a **connect by** or **group by** clause in its data definition, respectively.

CONDITION   This property defines the comparison operation between master and detail column in a data link. Valid values are =, <, >, <=, >=, <>, **like**, or **not like**. The meanings of these comparison operations were covered in Unit I. The default value for the comparison operation defined in the Condition property is =.

PARENT GROUP   This is the read-only group from the master query, that is defined as such in your data link, whose data is read as the driver for the child query. The value for this property is a label corresponding to the name of the parent group.

TIP

Beware of circular dependencies when defining parent groups, as a parent group cannot have a child query as its data source.

PARENT COLUMN   This is the read-only column from the master query that relates to the column in the detail query of the same name and data content. It can be a database, summary, or formula column.

TIP

Beware of circular dependencies when defining parent columns, as a parent summary or formula column cannot have a child query as its data source.

CHILD QUERY   This is the read-only detail query in your data link. There is a mandatory one-to-one relationship between detail queries and their master groups. In other words, no detail query can have more than one master group linked to it.

CHILD COLUMN   This is the detail column in the database link that relates to a read-only master column. These are always database columns, and should not contain lexical references. A lexical reference is a placeholder in a SQL statement that allows you to substitute a value dynamically to determine which records your query collects. An example of a lexical reference in a SQL statement is **select * from** EXCH_RATE **where** TO_CURCY = '**&TO_CURCY**'. The key indicator of a lexical reference is the ampersand. More about lexical references appears in Unit I.

Exercises

1. Identify the three types of data links. How is each one drawn?

2. What are the restrictions for defining the SQL Clause property relating to the data definition of the master or detail query?

3. What is a circular dependency? Where and why must it be avoided?

Using the Data Model to Create Columns

In this section, you will cover the following points about enhancing reports using the Data Model to create columns:

- Identifying Data Model columns
- Using database columns to display file contents
- Creating and using formula columns
- Creating and using summary columns
- Creating and populating placeholder columns

In addition to the data columns you draw from Oracle tables to populate your reports, Oracle Reports allows you to create several other columns. These reporting columns help you to add meaning to your reports in several ways. Some of these ways include column summaries like counts, totals, or other column group functions, which you have already seen in use from your mastery of Report Wizard. This section will explain the different types of columns you may have in your report, and when and how to use them.

Identifying Data Model Columns

Some mention and brief explanation of each type of column available in the Data Model view on your report has already been made. To reiterate, several types of columns can appear in your Oracle report. They include database, summary, formula, and placeholder columns. These items were already introduced earlier in the previous section. However, for reinforcement, they appear here as well. The following paragraphs explain each type of column. Figure 25-8 shows a Data Model view on a sample report that uses database, summary, placeholder, and formula columns. This figure will help you identify what these items look like within the Data Model view in Report Builder. Remember, most of the labels for these objects have been changed for readability.

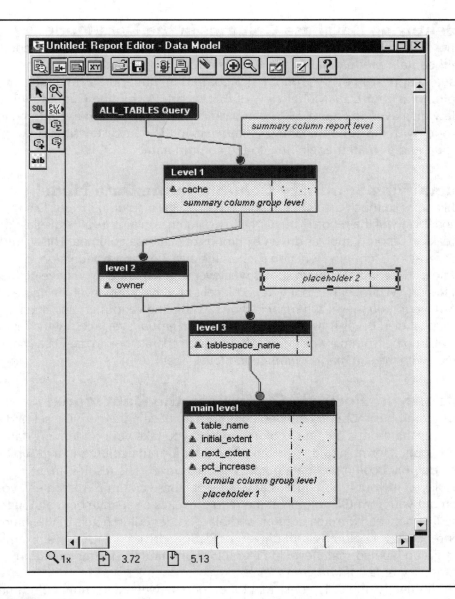

FIGURE 25-8.   *Report Data Model view with user-defined columns*

Identifying Database Columns in the Data Model

These columns store information that comes from the database. Your report will contain predominantly these types of columns. Database columns will usually appear in every group. It is a column in the report as much as it is a column in your Data Model view of that report. Within the Data Model view displayed in Figure 25-8, database columns are shown as part of each group, with the column name as it appears in the database written into the group and a small triangle next to the column name.

Identifying Summary Columns in the Data Model

This is not so much a column in your report as it is a column in your Data Model view of the report. Your summary column contains a value displayed at breaks in report output, as driven by groups of database columns. This value is the result of a grouping function such as the **avg( )** or **count( )** function in Oracle. A summary column shows whatever summarization you have defined in Report Wizard, either for the report level or for the group level. In Figure 25-8, your group-level summary is shown within the various groups, such as the group labeled Level 1, as the *summary column group level* label. At the report level, another summary column is shown as a separate box in the Data Model view, with the *summary column report level* label.

Identifying Formula Columns in the Data Model

This column is more of a derived column. You have an underlying set of data, such as that from a database column, where you take your underlying data and apply a formula to it. You can place your formula column in a group as an additional column of data output from that level. The result is then displayed in your report, just as any other database column. Alternately, you can put your formula column at the report level as a separate box, although the line between formula column and placeholder column gets a little blurry for report-level columns with trigger- or PL/SQL-driven data sources. Examine the group labeled *main level* in Figure 25-8 and find the formula column named *formula column group level*.

Ultimately, the only consistent difference between a formula column and a placeholder column comes down to the properties of each column type. In a later discussion in this chapter, you will be shown the properties of each column type. A formula column has one more property in its Property

Palette, which allows you to define the break order for the formula column within the report or at the group level. Usable break orders in the Property Palette include None, Ascending, or Descending.

Identifying Placeholder Columns in the Data Model

You can create a placeholder column at either the report level or within any group on the report to show data obtained either from report triggers or derived from formulas. In fact, there is little difference between placeholder columns and formula columns, save for the absence of the Break Order property available in formula columns that is not available in placeholder columns. Your placeholder columns at the report level appear as separate boxes such as the one in Figure 25-8 appearing with the label *placeholder2*, while placeholder columns appearing as part of groups in the Data Model will be listed within the group, such as the placeholder column labeled *placeholder1* shown in Figure 25-8 in the group labeled *main level*.

Exercises

1. What are the different data columns available for reports?

2. How are user-defined columns represented in the Data Model view for report-level data? What about those user-defined columns in groups?

3. What is the most substantial difference between a placeholder column and a formula column? Identify all the aspects of each column that are the same.

Using Columns to Display File Contents

An interesting feature columns have is the ability to read file contents—not just text files, either. You can read the contents of certain image files, Web pages, sound, video, and more. This feature allows you to develop multimedia reports. Here's how. Inside the Property Palette for database, placeholder, and formula columns is a property called Read from File. This property can be assigned Yes or No, depending on whether you want the column to draw its contents from file or not. To make any database or user-defined column read the data it displays from file, double-click on the column to invoke the Property Palette, click on the Read from File property, and select Yes from the drop-down list of valid values.

TIP
Though online help claims otherwise, this feature does not seem to be available for summary columns in Developer/2000 2.1 for Windows 95 using the Property Palette, because the necessary properties are absent.

A new property called File Format will appear when you tell Report Builder to read data from file for this column. The File Format property tells the tool what format the file takes. There are several file formats Report Builder accepts for use in your report content that allow you to display far more information in your report than text, numbers, and the like. Those types are listed in the drop-down box next to the File Format property, and they are identified and described here as well:

- **Text**   The mainstay file format. Information stored in text format, usually ASCII, or whatever text type your operating system supports.

- **Image**   Picture image stored in **.bmp**, **.cal**, **.gif**, **.jfif**, **.pic**, **.pcx**, **.ras**, **.oif**, or **.tif** format. You can create images in most of these formats with a graphics editor program such as Oracle Graphics, also part of the Developer/2000 suite, and then import or export them with Report Builder.

- **CGM**   Line drawing image file format stored with extension **.cgm**. You can generate these files using Oracle Graphics and import or export them with Report Builder.

- **Oracle Drawing Format**   Another line drawing image file format stored with extension **.odf**. You can generate these files using Oracle Graphics and import or export them using Report Builder.

- **Sound**   Listenable sound files playable in your computer. Report Builder supports the use of these only when you create buttons to display the object. More about this activity is covered in the next section. Report Builder supports the **.afc**, **.aff**, **.au**, **.snd**, and **.wav** format sound files. You create sound files using an external sound software product. This file is stored in the database in binary as a LONG RAW or BLOB datatype.

- **Video**   Viewable moving picture files. Report Builder supports the use of these only when you create buttons to display the object. More about this activity is covered in the next section. Report Builder allows the use of **.avi** or **.moo** format video files. You can create video files using external video software. This file is stored in the database in binary as a LONG RAW or BLOB datatype.

- **OLE2**   Any file format that conforms to object linking and embedding standards.

- **URL Image**   Uniform Resource Locator or link to an image on the Web, stored in any of the acceptable image formats.

Reading Data from File with Database Columns

To use the Read from File property for database columns, the way to specify a filename for the database column is to have your report obtain it from the column on the database. For example, if you choose to have your report's database column read information from file, when you try to run the report, you may receive errors stating that a particular filename corresponding to data returned from the database column was not found. It seems like a logical remedy that your database column should contain text strings corresponding to filenames and their paths. This will work, but it is not very portable. The correct thing to do is to ensure the registry REPORTS30_PATH contains the directory to search. Also, remember that the Read from File property only appears in the Property Palette when your database column datatype is CHAR or VARCHAR2.

TIP

If your Read from File property is assigned No and your column contains filenames—the filename is displayed in the report, not the contents. If Read from File is assigned Yes, then the contents of the file are displayed, not the filename.

Assigning Filenames for Columns to Read Using PL/SQL

Jump ahead a little so that we can describe what you need to do to read data from file if you are using formula columns. If you're confused, reread this lesson after covering the rest of the section. For this lesson, return to the running ALL_TABLES report example. You will change your report to include information from a small text file that explains the meaning of the CACHE column. For your information, table caching is a DBA feature in Oracle that allows you to keep the contents of small lookup tables in memory for better database performance. The file you will read from, then, is a small and simple text file explaining this fact.

You set this up to happen in your report in the following way. First, click either on the Formula Column button once or move your pointer to the level 1 group containing the CACHE column and click within the group again to put the user-defined column in place. Double-click on the column you added to open the Property Palette for it, and change the Data Type property for the new column to CHARACTER. Change the Read from File property to Yes. Ensure the File Type property is set to Text.

The final task is to explicitly define the filename to read from. Before continuing, ensure that the file already exists in the file system. The filename Report Builder uses to populate data for a column is always the contents of that column. Thus, if you want to read data from a file, your column should already contain the filename for Report Builder to use. This is accomplished for placeholder or formula columns by using the PL/SQL Formula property to assign the placeholder column a filename. Click on this property to show the Definition button, then click that button to open the PL/SQL Editor module. In the body of your PL/SQL block, identify the filename you want the report to use as the value the block returns. Figure 25-9 displays the finished block of PL/SQL where the **cachedsc.txt** file is used in your report. The existence of your file is checked at compile time, so if your file is not present when you try to compile or look at the report using Live Previewer, you will receive an error.

Remember also an important point about portability. You may want to use an environment variable such as REPORTS30_PATH to identify where your files reside. Otherwise, if your files reside outside Report Builder's

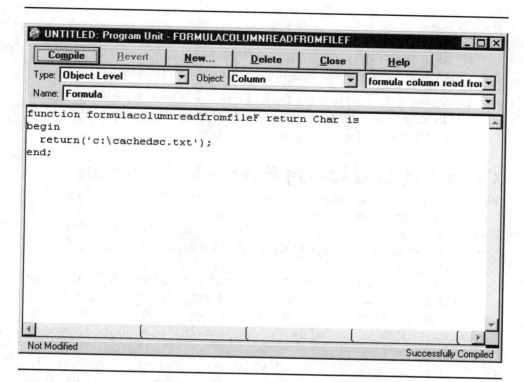

FIGURE 25-9. *Defining file read name using PL/SQL Editor*

usual search locations such as your machine's path, Report Builder will not be able to find your file unless you specify an absolute pathname, which may not be portable from machine to machine.

TIP
To assign filenames for reports to read from, formula columns are useful when you want conditionality based on the value in another database column. Placeholder columns don't seem to work well when you set them up to read from file. Database columns are used when the database stores the name of the files.

Exercises

1. What report columns support the ability to read data from files? What are the types of files these columns can read from?

2. Where is the name of the file to be read defined? If the Read from File property is set to No, what is displayed in the report? What if the Read from File property is set to Yes?

Creating and Using Formula Columns

You can create and use formula columns in two different places on your report: at the report level or at the group level. If your formula column appears at the report level, you will see it as its own object in the Data Model for the report you are writing. Formula columns at the group level appear along with other columns in the group.

Definition of a formula column for a report occurs in the following way. From within the Data Model view on your report, click on the Formula Column button on the left-hand margin of this view in Report Editor. This button has a database symbol on it with a small black "+" in the foreground. Then, move your pointer into the report Data Model definition area and click on the open area of the report, where no group or query appears. This area is sometimes referred to as the *open canvas*. After clicking once on the open area, a new object will appear with a formula column label automatically generated in it. This is your report-level formula column.

Double click on the new object to make the Property Palette appear for that object. There are several properties you can define for the formula, the number of which appearing in the Property Palette is directly related to the datatype of the column. The last property appearing in the Property Palette in Figure 25-10 is called PL/SQL formula. This property is the actual "formula" constituting your formula column.

Say for example that you want your formula column on the report level to retrieve the name of the Oracle instance this information came from and display it in the report. This information comes from the NAME column in a view in Oracle called V$DATABASE, that is owned by the SYS user. Click on the PL/SQL formula property once to make the definition button appear, and then click on that button to invoke the PL/SQL editor module to develop

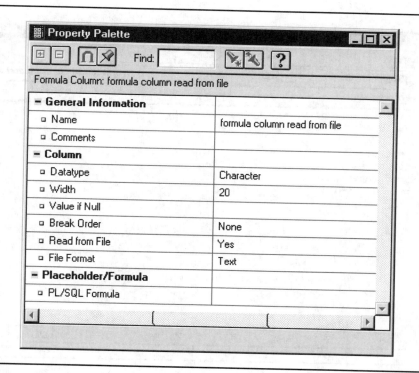

FIGURE 25-10.   *Property Palette for summary column*

your formula. In this case, your formula will be a **select** statement like the one appearing in the PL/SQL editor module in Figure 25-11. Once complete, you can press the Compile button and Oracle Reports will compile your code.

You may also want to create a formula column at the group level that generates data shown within the report. For example, your ALL_TABLES report lists the size of your tables' initial and next extents, as well as a percentage increase for each subsequent extent. There is enough information here to define another column, called THIRD_EXTENT, but you need to write a formula column to do it. In the Data Model view on your report, click on the formula column button and create a new formula column in the *main level* column group of your report by clicking once in that group. Then,

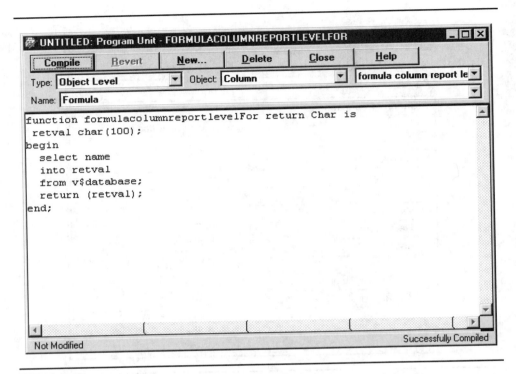

FIGURE 25-11. *Report-level formula in PL/SQL editor module*

double click on that column to invoke the Property Palette. Click on the
PL/SQL formula property and press the property definition button that
appears. In the PL/SQL editor module, define your formula using the PL/SQL
code appearing in Figure 25-12. Click the Compile button, then the Close
button, and you have defined your group-level formula. Don't forget that
you must prefix any database column in your formula PL/SQL block with a
colon (:) in order for Oracle Reports to use the column reference as
a bind variable.

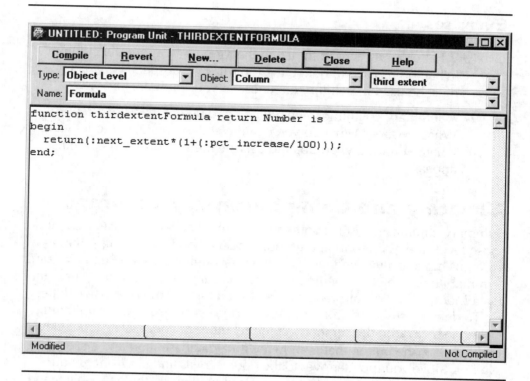

```
UNTITLED: Program Unit - THIRDEXTENTFORMULA

Compile    Revert    New...    Delete    Close    Help

Type: Object Level  ▼  Object: Column  ▼  third extent  ▼

Name: Formula  ▼

function thirdextentFormula return Number is
begin
  return(:next_extent*(1+(:pct_increase/100)));
end;

Modified                                    Not Compiled
```

FIGURE 25-12. *PL/SQL editor module with group-level formula*

TIP

*Don't try to look at your new summary column
in the Live Previewer just yet. There are some
formatting things you need to learn to do with
the Layout Model. If you really want to see
your report, open the Report Wizard Fields tab
and make sure your new formula column
appears as a displayed field.*

Exercises

1. What property is used to define the formula in a formula column? What tool is used to define the formula? What special character must be used in column references in your formula, and why?

2. A summary column can be defined at different levels of a report. What are they? What do you call the area of the Data Model view where your query, group, and user-defined report-level columns appear?

Creating and Using Summary Columns

Summary columns in your report can be defined at two levels as well, and those levels are also report and group. One method for defining summary columns has already been identified, the method that uses the Report Wizard Summary tab. The other method for defining summaries on reports uses the Data Model view on your report in Report Editor and the Property Palette.

To define a summary column at the report level, execute the following tasks. First, click on the summary column button in your Data Model view of the report, the button that is shown with a database icon and a sigma (Σ) symbol. Move your pointer over to the open canvas and click once. Your new summary column object appears. Double-click on the new object and the Property Palette appears. You can define several different types of summaries for the report, as identified in the previous section, using the list box that is accessible as soon as you click once on the Function property. You must identify a source for the summary function to use as well. This is usually going to be a database column from the report, although the source can be any user-defined column as well.

To define a summary column at the group level, execute the same tasks you would for the report-level summary column, but instead of placing the column by itself away from the groups and query object defined for your report, you will place the column inside a group. You then define the actual summarization operation and the source for your summary data as you would for a report.

TIP

If you only want to create a summary column using sum, count, minimum, maximum, average, or percent total, you can create your summary column using Report Wizard. First value, last value, standard deviation, or variance summaries can be created only by using the Data Model and Property Palette to create your summary column.

Exercises

1. Report Wizard is one way to define report summary columns. What two Report Builder tools constitute the other way? At what two levels in a report may you define a summary column?

2. Identify seven functions that you can use for summarizing your report data. Identify four summarization methods that are not available when you define summary columns using Report Wizard.

Creating and Populating Placeholder Columns

Placeholder columns and formula columns are strikingly similar in their capabilities. You can set values for both using either formulas or report triggers. Placeholder columns are designated for use when you want to display results from formulas at the report level or at the group level, or with the use of a report trigger such as the BEFORE REPORT trigger if the placeholder is for use at the report level. Recall that the placeholder column (like other user-defined columns) will appear as its own object in the Data Model view if the column is placed at the report level, but will appear in a group if created for the group level.

Populating Placeholder Columns with Report Triggers

You can populate a placeholder column with results from a report trigger if that column is placed as its own object at the report level, outside of any group. First, find the Placeholder Column button on the left margin of the Data Model for your report in the Report Editor. This button appears with a Database icon on it along with a small "**?**" in the corner. Click the button once, move your pointer onto the open canvas of your report, and click again. A new object appears to represent your placeholder column, denoted with an appropriate label. Double-click on that new object to open the Property Palette for the object. You can identify the datatype for your placeholder column as either CHARACTER, DATE, or NUMBER. Then, click on the PL/SQL Formula property, at which time the Definition button appears. Click that button now, and the PL/SQL Editor module appears in your display, in much the same way as it is shown in Figure 25-13.

Notice in Figure 25-13 there are several drop-down boxes at the top of your display, including a few with identifiers, Type, Object, and Name. The Object box is the one you are concerned with first. The following setup is required to get a report trigger feeding data into your placeholder column. If the content of the Object box do not read "Report," then you should pull down the list and make the appropriate change. After that, you may notice some changes in the Editor module. To use a report trigger to populate your placeholder column with values, you should pull down the Name list and choose the appropriate report trigger to use, such as BEFORE REPORT.

After making this choice, you will notice that some template PL/SQL code appears. The code will be used by you to define a function that returns a TRUE or FALSE value. In some situations, it may be useful to leave the report trigger definition as a function and let it return TRUE, then treat the rest of the PL/SQL block as a procedure where you execute a series of tasks on the database. For example, if your report is very complex with several different intermediate sets of data generated to produce the final result, you may want to create a temporary table to house the intermediate results with a BEFORE REPORT trigger and then remove the temporary table at the end with an AFTER REPORT trigger.

You cannot change the return datatype for this report trigger from BOOLEAN. However, you can reference the placeholder column label as a bind variable within the PL/SQL block you define for your BEFORE REPORT trigger. See Figure 25-12 for a simliar example. Be careful about the datatype of the value you assign using bind variables at this point. Oracle

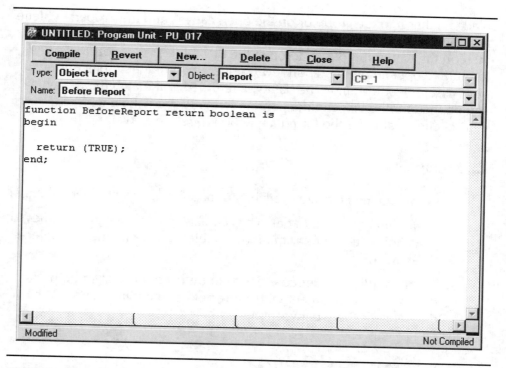

FIGURE 25-13. *PL/SQL Editor*

Reports will not check to see if the datatype for your placeholder column and the assigned value match. If there are inconsistencies, such as a CHARACTER value assigned to a placeholder that is incompatible with the DATE format, you will receive an error on your report during run time.

Populating Placeholder Columns with Formulas

The second method you can use to populate your placeholder column is with the use of a formula. This method is done for report-level and group-level placeholder columns. The method used to create your report-level placeholder column has already been covered. To create a group-level placeholder column, click on the Placeholder Column button. Move your pointer to the group in which you want the placeholder column to appear and click again. You then double-click on the placeholder column you just placed either into the group or on the open canvas and the Property Palette for that placeholder appears. Click on the PL/SQL Formula property and then on the Definition button to open the PL/SQL Editor. If you wish your formula to operate on the report level, select Report in the Object list; otherwise, select Column. The datatype returned will match the datatype you defined for the placeholder column in the Property Palette. Make sure you specify a value for the formula function to return as well.

Exercises

1. What two methods are available for populating placeholder columns?

2. What pitfalls related to datatypes can arise when assigning values to placeholder columns with bind variables? How can these problems be avoided?

3. Compare placeholder columns to formula columns from both discussions. Experiment with using both of them in a report. What difference is there between the two?

Chapter Summary

This chapter covers modification of the data definition of your report through the use of the Data Model view on your report available through the Report Editor. Using the Data Model to create queries against the database to obtain data from which to make the report is a topic covered, along with an understanding of how queries are represented within the Data Model. Understanding the concept of groups as another object in your Data Model view is also covered in this chapter. Finally, the chapter covers use of the Data Model to generate certain types of user-defined columns. This information comprises 15 percent of content in OCP Exam 5 of the Application Developer Track.

The first area of using the Data Model covers the objects in the Data Model and their relationships with one another. Several objects appear in a Data Model view on the report. The first items are system and user parameters, which impact how the report is run and certain aspects of how the output is produced. Another item in a Data Model is the query or queries that comprise the data definition. These objects are displayed as small boxes having only a query label on them. The next item in a Data Model is a group, which contains a list of columns in the data definition of the report. Groups are directly related to queries as evidenced by the line that Data Model draws between them. A query may have one or more groups as well.

Within groups there are several more objects in a Data Model view, called columns. Columns include database columns, or those columns containing data returned from the database by the query. Groups may also include user-defined columns. Examples of the user-defined columns you have in a Data Model include summary, placeholder, and formula columns. Instead of drawing data directly from the database with these columns, the user-defined column allows you to define a process that acts on the data in a database column and produce output of a different sort for the user-defined column. Finally, you can have links between multiple queries in your report that allow you to draw data together from different sources in the database. Each object in a Data Model is also represented as a drill-down item in a report's representation in the Object Navigator module of Report Builder.

Column groups in the Data Model offer a number of interesting options, such as the ability to define data hierarchy in the report. A report hierarchy can be created in group reports by placing different columns into different levels and creating breakpoints in the report output based on unique values for different columns at different levels in different groups. This activity in the Data Model is similar in concept to a regular **select** statement containing a **group by** clause, but offers the additional benefit of only one iteration of the higher-level data being printed for many lower-level records.

There are two methods used to create columns groups. One is using Report Wizard's Groups tab, the other is to draw the group using tools in the Data Model and then populate the group with database and user-defined columns. Understand, however, that you cannot create hierarchy in a report using groups for those reports that are not group reports.

Changing the order of data and data order in groups has many meanings, which were covered in the chapter. You may want to change the order of data in a column from Ascending to Descending, or vice-versa, using the Break Order property appearing in the Property Palette for that column when you double-click on the column name in the group on the Data Model view of your report. Appropriate use of Break Order is covered extensively in the text, and you should be sure you understand this concept before taking the

OCP Reports exam. You may also want to change the order of how columns appear in the report by changing them in their group. This can be handled either by clicking and dragging on column names within groups or with the Report Wizard. Note, however, that even if you change the order of columns in your group, this does not necessarily change the order of columns shown in the report.

The Data Model allows you to restrict data returned from your reports at the group level with the use of group filters. There are two predefined filters you can apply to data groups, and they allow you to filter the first n or last n number of records of output from the report. These predefined filters are defined with the use of the Filters property found in the Property Palette when you double-click on the group object for which you want to define a filter in Report Builder. Otherwise, you have the power of PL/SQL available to you to define your own filter, first selecting the PL/SQL option for the Filters property of this group and then generating a PL/SQL function for the PL/SQL Filter property appearing below Filters when you select PL/SQL. Remember that if you want to refer to a column in the data definition from within your filter or any other PL/SQL block in the report, you must precede the column name with a colon (:) in order to allow Report Builder to refer to the column as a bind variable.

Finally, you can use data links in your Data Model to create reports that combine data returned from multiple queries, where a master query's resultant data set drives the operation of a detail query. Creating data links requires you to define one query in the Data Model as the master query and another as the detail query. There are three types of data links in the Data Model, each indicating the level from master to detail. The first is query to query, where the link is drawn from the master query object to the detail query object. The second is group to group, where the data link is drawn from the group in the master query to the group in the detail. The third is column to column, where the data link is drawn from a column from a group in the master query to a column in the detail query.

In many ways, a link between queries in the Data Model for a report is similar to a join operation in a SQL statement. The properties in the Property Palette for a data link that support this concept include SQL Clause, which can be set to **where**, **having**, and **start with**. Another property fitting the bill here is Condition, which defines the comparison operation between master and detail information in the link. Be sure to review the material in the chapter that covered some important restrictions for these and other properties for data links.

The other substantial discussion of this chapter covered use of the Data Model to create user-defined columns. There are three types of user-defined columns in a report: summary columns, formula columns, and placeholder columns. The first area covered in this section was how to identify different columns in a Data Model. Database columns are identified in a Data Model by their presence in groups. Next to a database file, there will be a small triangle. User-defined columns are identified in a Data Model by their presence in groups or as stand-alone columns operating at the report level. One way to distinguish user-defined columns from one another is to look at the Report Builder–generated label for the column. For formula columns, the label will be prefixed with CF; for summary columns, the label will be prefixed with CS; and for placeholder columns, the label will be prefixed with CP. However, since you have the ability to change the name of a column by altering the appropriate property, the only foolproof way to distinguish one type of user-defined column from another is to open the Property Palette for the column and read the identification information for the column from the top of the Property Palette.

A feature of database and formula columns is their ability to read data from a flat file and incorporate that information into your report. This feature is enabled through the use of the Read from File property appearing in the Property Palette for those columns. This property is set either to Yes or No. If set to Yes, you will need to define a file format type for the File Format property, which you can choose from several options that Oracle Reports accepts. These options include text files, several formats for image files, CGM format files, Oracle drawing format files, several types of sound files, a few types of video files, OLE2 object files, or image files on the Web accessible via URL. The Two-Minute Drill and chapter content both give more detailed information about exactly which formats Oracle Reports accepts. The last item you need to address when using the Read from File feature for your database or formula column is defining the filename the column should draw its data from. For database columns, the filename is whatever the content of the column as returned from the database reads. For formula columns, the filename can be either the content of the column or it can be defined using PL/SQL functions. Either way, the filename will be a name appearing in the column, not a property defined in the Property Palette.

The chapter covered how to define and use formula columns. Formula columns can be defined either at the group level or the report level. Typically, a formula column is used when you want to modify data in a database column and show it in the report, although you have already seen that formula columns can also be used to display information from files. Defining formula columns is a two-part process in the Data Model. The two parts are defining the object and defining the formula. The first task is accomplished with the help of the Formula Column tool button in the Tool Palette on the left margin of the Data Model view. You click the tool button and click in the group in which you want the formula to appear, or draw the report-level formula column somewhere in the open canvas of the report. The second task is handled using the PL/SQL Editor module to write the program that will comprise the formula. To invoke the PL/SQL Editor module, you click on the PL/SQL Formula property in the Property Palette once to show the Definition button and then click the button to open the appropriate module.

You also covered how to create and use summary columns both in this chapter and earlier in the material covering Report Wizard. There are several different methods you can use to summarize your database and user-defined columns, corresponding to different built-in SQL functions like **sum( )**, **count( )**, and several others listed as buttons in the Totals tab of Report Wizard. There are a few summary functions in the Function property available for the summary column in the Property Palette that aren't available through Report Wizard, so be sure you understand how to define summary column behavior in that way also.

The final item covered in this chapter is the use of the Data Model to define and modify placeholder columns, and the use you may find for placeholders in your reports. As mentioned, formula columns and placeholders seem to be quite similar, though in Developer/2000 2.0, formula columns seem better supported for doing the things Oracle says they can do than placeholder columns. You can, however, populate placeholder columns with data from report triggers as well as through straight PL/SQL functions.

Two-Minute Drill

- The Data Model view on your report allows you to examine the data definition for your report in a pictorial manner.

- The objects shown in a Data Model and their usage or meaning are as follows:

  - **Query objects**   Represent the query serving as the basis for report data definition

  - **Group objects**   Object containing report database and many user-defined columns

  - **User and system parameters**   Options set at run time that affect report output

  - **Database columns**   Report columns containing data from the database

  - **Summary columns**   User-defined columns that summarize data in database or other user-defined columns.

  - **Placeholder columns**   User-defined columns that can be populated either using PL/SQL functions or report triggers

  - **Formula columns**   User-defined columns that perform activities on database columns and show the results in a separate column.

- You can see information about your Data Model objects in the Object Navigator under the Data Model node.

- Groups can be used to model report hierarchy. The columns in a level 1 group will cause breaks in your report on unique values in your level 1 group.

- Hierarchy can be created with the drawing of groups directly in the Data Model and populating those groups with columns, or with the Report Wizard Groups tab.

- Order of data in a column can be Ascending or Descending, as set with the Break Order property for the database or user-defined column on the Property Palette.

- Order of columns in a group can be changed either by clicking and dragging columns around in a group on the Data Model, or by changing the order of fields in the Fields tab on the Report Wizard. This second option is possible only if the columns in the data definition match the displayed fields in the Fields tab.

- Group filters can be used to eliminate data from reports. They are defined using the Filters property, available in the Property Palette when you double-click on a group.

- There are two types of filters: predefined and user-defined. The two predefined filters are first and last, where you can specify to see the first or last *n* records, respectively. User-defined filters are written by you using PL/SQL.

- You can reference columns in a PL/SQL function such as that which you would define for a filter by prefixing the column name with a colon, so that the PL/SQL block can refer to it like a bind variable.

- Filters are indicated in the Data Model view by changing the color of the circle at the end of the line leading to the group that has a filter defined on it.

- Two or more queries can be put together for use in a report with the use of data links. There are three types of data links:

  - Query to query

  - Group to group

  - Column to column

- There are four types of Data Model columns. They are listed and defined below:

  - **Database columns** Columns of data in the report from the database

  - **Summary columns** Columns that perform a summary operation (like **sum( )**) for all data in a column

- **Formula columns** Columns that perform an operation on another database column

- **Placeholder columns** Columns that obtain their data either from a formula or a report trigger

- The prefixes on default labels for a user-defined column can identify the column type. However, since you can alter the label, the surest way to identify a column type is to open the Property Palette for that column. The prefixes on default labels for various user-defined columns are as follows:

  - Placeholder: CP_

  - Summary: CS_

  - Formula: CF_

- Database columns are identifiable in the Data Model group by a small triangle next to the column name.

- Database and formula columns can display the contents of files. This feature is configured with specification of three details:

  - Read from File property set to Yes in the Property Palette

  - File Format property set to Text, Image, CGM, Oracle Drawing Format, Sound, Video, OLE2, or URL Image.

  - Filename determined by the content of the database or formula column, coming from the database or a PL/SQL function, respectively. Your database or formula column should specify absolute pathname so that Report Builder can find the file.

- The existence of your file is checked at report compile time, so if the file is not present, you will receive an error.

- If report portability from machine to machine is an issue, consider using the REPORTS30_PATH environment variable as an alternative to specifying absolute path for filenames to be read by database or formula columns in reports.

■ Formula, summary, and placeholder columns are created in a four-step process. The steps are as follows:

1. Click on appropriate tool buttons in the Tool Palette on the left margin of the Data Model.

2. Move pointer to open canvas in Data Model for report-level column, or to appropriate group for group-level column, and draw report-level column or click in the group to place group-level column.

3. Double-click on new user-defined column to invoke Property Palette for that column.

4. Modify properties as appropriate, such as those to define summary functions, PL/SQL formulas, or report triggers.

Chapter Questions

1. **You are defining a formula for your new formula column at the group level. The appropriate way to reference a column in your PL/SQL formula is**

   A. Using the column name, as in any PL/SQL code

   B. Prefixing the column name with a colon character, as in :COL_NM

   C. Prefixing the column name with an ampersand, as in &COL_NM

   D. You cannot reference columns in PL/SQL formulas on your reports.

2. **Your report column orders data in ascending order, but you would like to change that to descending. Which of the following tools most directly allows you to accomplish this task?**

   A. Property Palette

   B. Report Converter

   C. Report Editor

   D. Data Model

3. You are defining a database column to read what it will display in a report from file. If the READ FROM FILE property is set to NO, then what will the column display?

   A. The contents of the file and its filename

   B. The contents of the file only

   C. The name of the file only

   D. The result of a formula

4. A summary column exists in a report. Which of the following operations can a summary not perform on its summarized data?

   A. Total

   B. Maximum value

   C. Standard deviation

   D. First *n* records for the summary group

5. The circular icon containing a small "P" to indicate a PL/SQL formula has been defined for this user-defined column will appear in which of the following areas on your report?

   A. Data Model

   B. Object Navigator

   C. Property Palette

   D. Report Wizard

6. Eliminating the first or last *n* records from the output of your report is best accomplished with what Data Model feature?

   A. Summary columns

   B. Placeholder column

   C. Filters

   D. Groups

7. **A data link can be created at which of the following levels in your report? (Choose three)**

   A. Filter to filter

   B. Query to query

   C. Group to group

   D. Column to column

8. **From the Property Palette, which property determines how the information from the parent group is compared to the child column in a data link?**

   A. Child Column

   B. Parent Group

   C. Name

   D. Condition

9. **Which of the following tools is used most often with defining formulas for formula columns?**

   A. Property Palette

   B. Report Editor

   C. Data Model

   D. PL/SQL Editor

10. **Hierarchy of data within a report can be defined using which of the following Data Model objects?**

   A. Queries

   B. Groups

   C. Database columns

   D. User-defined columns

11. **Database columns can be identified in a group Data Model object by which of the following characteristics?**

A. The prefix Report Builder–generated label

B. Only by using the Property Palette

C. A small triangle appearing next to the column name in a group

D. There is no way to identify columns in the Data Model.

Answers to Chapter Questions

1. B.   Prefixing the column name with a colon character,
as in :COL_NM

Explanation   To refer to a column in a PL/SQL formula, you must prefix it as
you would a bind variable, using a colon. If you do not prefix it with a colon,
you will get an error stating that the "variable" has not been declared when you
try to compile the formula. Prefixing the column name with an ampersand, as in
&COL_NM for choice C, creates a lexical reference, which enables you to
define a value for the variable at run time in SQL*Plus. This is not permitted in
PL/SQL formulas, however. The correctness of choice B is your basic rationale
for eliminating choices A and D.

2. A.   Property Palette

Explanation   Data order in a column is set using the Break Order property
found in the Property Palette. This property can be set either to **ascending** or
descending. For choices C and D, you must return to the way the question is
asked, whereby you are trying to determine the most direct tool used to
change order of data in the column. Although Report Editor is used to open
the report for modification, and the Data Model allows you to look at the
column whose data you want to change order on, the most immediate tool
used to modify that order is the Property Palette. Choice B is inappropriate
because Report Compiler is used simply for converting reports in one format
to another.

3. C.   The name of the file only

Explanation   Answering this question correctly requires knowing that the
filename Report Builder will use in this situation is determined by the contents
of the database or formula column. In the first case, the filename comes from
the database table containing the column. In the second case, the filename
comes either from the database contents or from the PL/SQL formula
operating on the formula column. Either way, if you change the value for the
Read from File property to No, you're back to displaying the filename, not
its contents, in the report. Therefore, choice C is correct.

4. D.   First *n* records for the summary group

Explanation   Summary columns perform summarization operations on
a database or other column in the report. Choices A, B, and C describe

functions the summary column can perform. A summary column can perform most of the same grouping functions as those covered in conjunction with **group by** queries in Unit I. One operation it cannot perform, however, is the one described in choice D. That operation is handled with group filters.

5. B.   Object Navigator

Explanation   The Object Navigator module shows you all the same information the Data Model displays, only in a drill-down listing. Next to each node is usually an icon you can click on to see the Property Palette for that object. In certain cases, such as for formula columns, another circular icon appears that allows you to open the PL/SQL Editor module for a corresponding function or formula. This circular icon will contain a "P" if a PL/SQL program unit is defined for the object. The Data Model view gives no indication of this type, nor does Report Wizard. And although the Property Palette is used to define a formula, you have no indication short of opening the PL/SQL Editor as to whether one is defined for the object. Therefore, choice B is correct.

6. C.   Filters

Explanation   Filters are the best way to eliminate the first or last *n* records from the output of a report. They are expressly designed for this purpose. Summary or placeholder columns cannot accomplish this task, nor can groups by themselves eliminate records from appearing in the report. However, filters are defined on groups, so this question is a bit tricky.

7. B, C, and D.   Query to query, group to group, and column to column

Explanation   The only choice that is invalid for this question is filter to filter, which is a data link type that does not exist. You may want to take the time to review the material on data links if you got this question wrong, because the ability to identify the three types of data links is crucial for the OCP test content on data links.

8. D.   Condition

Explanation   The answer here is a little tricky, because the exam guide talks mainly about comparison operations while Oracle Reports defines this property as Condition. To refresh, the Condition property defines what comparison operation will be used between data in the parent or master set and the results of the child or detail query. Choices A and B simply identify which columns and groups partake of the comparison, while choice C simply identifies the label for the data link.

9. D.   PL/SQL Editor

Explanation   This is another one of those tricky questions whose answer may wind up being completely arbitrary. Again, you should focus on the most immediate goals the question identifies. In this case, the goal is to define formulas for formula columns. There is one main way to do this—by defining a PL/SQL function to act as the formula. This definition is handled using the PL/SQL Editor module. Again, even though you use the Report Editor to look at the Data Model, and the Data Model to look at the Property Palette, your answer is most precisely the PL/SQL Editor because that is the module that actually assists you when you define the function.

10. B.   Groups

Explanation   Hierarchy of data in a report is handled through the definition of groups
to contain the columns you want precedence to be given to on the report hierarchy. Although the query allows you to determine the overall content of the report, the report hierarchy is given through groups. Since user-defined and database columns are part of the group, it's possible for you to get tricked here, because the column data is what drives the hierarchy in the report output, but you cannot create hierarchy through manipulation of columns alone. You need to use groups, and that's why choice B is correct.

11. C.   A small triangle appearing next to the column name in a group

Explanation   Database columns are the easiest to identify in a Data Model exclusively by the way they look in the Data Model, because of the small triangle that appears next to their name in the group. You can use prefixes on labels that are generated by Report Builder, but this method backfires sometimes because you can alter the label to whatever you please using the Property Palette. You needn't open the Property Palette for database columns, however, because you can identify them with the triangle next to them in the Data Model groups. Therefore, choice C is the best.

CHAPTER
26

Enhancing Layout and
Properties in
Report Builder

n this chapter, you will cover the following areas of modifying reports using Report Builder:

■ Enhancing reports using the Layout Model

■ Modifying layout properties in reports

This chapter comprises the second big set of tasks before you when creating reports using Report Builder—the enhancement of report layout. Report Builder gives you a tool to handle the tasks related to enhancing report layout: the Layout Model. Similar to the Data Model covered in Chapter 25, the Layout Model shows you your layouts in a graphical format, where certain symbols represent either data in the report or behaviors Report Builder will assume when generating the pages of the report. There is another tool you will use quite extensively when modifying report layout, and that is the Property Palette. This is because every object in your layout has properties that can be redefined. The content of this chapter comprises about 15 percent of OCP Exam content.

Enhancing Reports Using the Layout Model

In this section, you will cover the following points on enhancing reports using the Layout Model:

■ Viewing and modifying objects in four report regions

■ Designing multipanel reports

■ Layout objects and their relationships

■ Modifying an existing report layout with Layout Model tools

■ Separating tabular data columns with lines

■ Creating buttons to display multimedia objects

■ Creating explicit anchors to alter object positions

Simply putting together the right content for your report isn't enough to complete your modification tasks. You also have to know how to perform certain tasks in the Layout Model of your report. Until now, you have let the Report Wizard handle your layout tasks for you. In this section, you will cover several key areas of defining your Layout Model view on the report. Your understanding of these areas is key both to your OCP certification and to your ability to modify report design using the Layout Model view on your report. The Layout Model view allows you to look at your report as graphical representations of its different areas—viewing and modifying objects in four report regions. You will cover designing multipanel reports. You will understand the different layout objects and their relationships with other objects in the Layout Model. You will discover processes for modifying an existing report layout with Layout Model tools. You will learn how to separate tabular data columns with lines. You will create buttons to display multimedia objects. Finally, you will also create explicit anchors to alter object positions.

Viewing and Modifying Objects in Four Report Regions

Key to your ability to handle layout issues in your report is understanding the usage of the Layout Model view on your reports available in the Report Editor. You can open the Layout Model view on your report from Report Editor in several ways. For example, you can click on the Layout Model button in the Report Editor (third from the left in that interface window), or by choosing the View | Layout Model menu option from the main menu in Report Builder. You also can click on the icon next to the Layout Model node in the Object Navigator for your report.

Your Layout Model view consists of several components. Across the top is the toolbar. Within this toolbar are controls designed to help you navigate through different views of your report, such as the Data Model, Layout Model, Parameter Form, and Live Previewer. Also, there are buttons that help you navigate through the different report regions, which will be covered shortly. The second row of buttons is called the style bar because it enables you to define text formatting and styles, fonts, and other appearance-related items. The main content of your Layout Model is the report layout, also known as the *painting region* of your report. Across the top and down the left side of the painting region are rulers. Down the left margin of the Layout Model is another set of buttons called the Tool Palette. You have already used the Tool Palette in your activities on the Data Model. Across the bottom of the window, there is a set of status controls that tell you where your pointer is located on the horizontal and vertical axes of the report, and the magnification of the report as it appears in the Editor module.

Viewing and Modifying the Layout of Report Regions

Turn your attention back to the toolbar across the top of the Layout Model. Four of the tool buttons help you to navigate through the sections or regions of your report: the Body, Margin, Header, and Trailer buttons. You have already identified these areas. To refresh the discussion, they are body, margin, header, and trailer, along with several others available as nodes in the Object Navigator module. For your purposes, however, this discussion focuses only on those four regions that are immediately accessible from within the Layout Model view on your report in Report Editor. Figure 26-1 demonstrates what you will see in the Layout Model for your ALL_TABLES report in Report Editor.

Notice in Figure 26-1 there are four buttons on the right side of the top list of command buttons. These buttons, in order of appearance, are Body, Margin, Header, and Trailer. You can navigate to each region in your report with the use of these buttons. As you navigate through your report in this way, you will notice different formatting options available, catering to the format needs of each area.

You are free to modify each item in the Layout Model view on your report, so long as you are in the appropriate region. For example, if you are looking at the margin region, you can alter the heading that appears on every page of the report by clicking on that object in the region and making an appropriate modification. However, you cannot make a change to the layout of column data appearing in the body of the report while you have

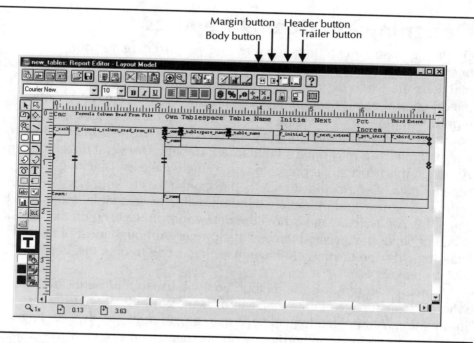

FIGURE 26-1.   *Layout Model view on your reports in Report Editor*

the margin region active in the Layout Model. Instead, you have to click on the appropriate Body button to move to that region. To modify an object in that region of a report, double-click on the object you wish to modify. The Property Palette for that object will then appear, and you can modify any of the properties you wish by clicking on that property and making the change.

Exercises

1. Identify the mechanism used to move from region to region in your report. What are the regions you can access with these methods?

2. How do you invoke the associated Property Palette for any object in a report region?

Designing Multipanel Reports

Designing multipanel reports requires that you first expand your interpretation of what a report page consists of. Recall in Oracle Reports 2.5 that there are two types of pages to consider: *physical pages* and *logical pages*. Logical pages contain data that is returned from the run of your report. In Reports 3.0, the page is referred to as a *panel*. Logical pages consist of all the data that you may logically place together in your report. For example, you may have a tabular report that has several dozen columns. Although this is usually represented on a single page by "stacking" the column data, if you could stretch the horizontal axis of your page infinitely rightward, you would ultimately wind up with a perfect table, long though it might be. A physical page is how the data winds up looking on that physical piece of paper that gets fed through the printer. Although most of the time your logical-page-to-physical-page mapping is one to one, this needn't always be the case.

A multipanel report is the method you will use to represent situations where a logical page of data maps across several physical pages of information. Although a logical page mapping to multiple physical pages cannot be represented in hard copy on one page, you can view the output of such a report using the Runtime Previewer. The scroll bars appearing in the window for this tool allow you to move across the logical page sideways or downward. In addition, you can split the screen to show a physical page (or panel) on one side of the Runtime Previewer interface while showing another on the other side.

To open the Runtime Previewer view of your report, open the report in Report Editor using the Tools I Report Editor menu bar option. Then, open the Runtime Previewer using the View I Runtime Preview menu option. If you are not connected to your database already, Reports 3.0 will prompt you to do so. Report Builder will process the report and display it in the Runtime Previewer interface. From there, you can scroll through the logical pages of the report or split the screen. Notice there is a small box appearing over the Up Arrow button in the vertical scroll bar to the right side of the Runtime Previewer interface. If you click and hold on that box, you will notice a thick dotted line appearing across the interface. To split the screen, click and hold that box, and drag it to the left or downward to split the interface vertically or horizontally, respectively. Figure 26-2 shows your activity in progress.

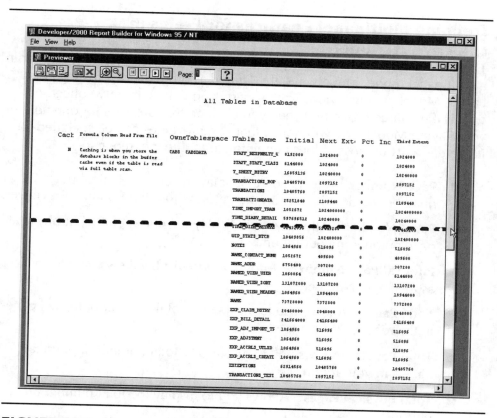

FIGURE 26-2. *Runtime Previewer interface while splitting screens*

Other Features of the Runtime Previewer

So far, primarily the Live Previewer has been covered in the chapter. However, the Runtime Previewer gives you a better representation of the running report. Some of the features Runtime Previewer allows you to use on your report include the buttons you may have embedded into your report. These buttons allow you to do things like view multimedia objects, run PL/SQL functions that call other reports or execute other operations, or use objects that are linked or embedded into your report. You will cover how to create these buttons shortly.

Defining Multipanel Features for Fields in the Layout Model

There are several ways you can specify the output for each field to appear in a multipanel report. These ways are defined as properties for fields in the Layout Model of your report. The property you will be mainly concerned with is the Source property. When you click on that property for one field in your Layout Model, you will notice that several values can be specified for it. Here is a list of those values pertaining to multipanel reports:

- **Page Number** Allows you to display the current logical page number you are viewing on the report within the Runtime Previewer.

- **Panel Number** Allows you to display the current panel or physical page number in your report.

- **Physical Page Number** Allows you to display the same information as the Panel Number.

- **Total Pages** Allows you to display the total number of logical pages in the report.

- **Total Panels** Allows you to display the total number of physical panels in your report.

- **Total Physical Pages** Allows you to display the total number of physical pages in your report.

Determining Panel Print Order

The size of the body or margin of your report in logical and physical pages can also be guided with the use of two properties: Logical Horizontal Panels and Logical Vertical Panels, which determine how many horizontal and vertical panels will map to one logical page. The maximum number of panels in either direction that a logical page may span is 50. A small note about header and trailer panels is relevant here—both can be only one logical horizontal panel or one physical page wide, while they can span multiple panels downward.

Your report will make it to print at some point or another, meaning that you have to deal with the mapping of logical pages on screen to physical pages in print. This step is accomplished with the use of the Panel Print

Order property, which can be set to Across/Down (default) in order to print your logical pages from left to right, then downward onto physical pages. This setting may be used where your logical pages are wide and you are reading them from left to right. The other setting available for the Panel Print Order property is Down/Across, which may be used to print your physical pages down the logical page first, then across. This setting is most useful when your logical panels read downward because of the report's length.

TIP

There are compelling performance reasons to beware of using of the Total Pages setting as the definition for the Source property for a field in the report. This performance problem has to do with the fact that Oracle Reports must generate and store all the pages in the report in order to calculate the total number of pages.

Exercises

1. Describe the meaning of logical pages and panels. When a report has multiple panels in a logical page, what does this mean in terms of physical pages printed to display the report?

2. What two properties set the number of panels appearing in each logical page across and downward? How wide can logical pages be in panels on the body and margin regions of your report? How wide can logical pages be in panels on the header and trailer regions?

3. What is the maximum number of panels a logical page can span in any direction?

Layout Objects and Their Relationships

Everything that appears in a report has an associated layout object that governs its appearance. Your Layout Model view shows you in miniature how your report will appear. Report Builder fills in the objects in the Layout Model with actual data when you run your report. The Layout Model will show you several types of layout objects and the relationships that exist between them. In both cases, the Layout Model uses symbols and graphical representations. The following lessons will explain those representations to you.

Types of Objects in the Layout Model

Following are descriptions of the objects displayed in the painting region of your Layout Model view on your report.

FRAMES A frame is an object that encloses other objects and prevents the contents from being written over or displaced by other objects in the layout. Your report will already have some frames in it if you used Report Wizard to create the report, and you can add more with tools in the Layout Model view.

REPEATING FRAMES A repeating frame is an object that encloses all columns in a group and appears in the report once for each record displayed in that group (i.e., once for each row of data from the database for that group). Your report will already have some frames in it if you used Report Wizard to create the report, and you can add more with tools in the Layout Model view.

FIELDS A field is a layout object used for each column in your report. Recall from the discussion of Report Wizard that you select your fields for display from the columns included in your report. Frames or repeating frames own the fields they surround.

BOILERPLATES A boilerplate is an item that appears in your report every time the report is run. Items may include column or report header text, graphical images such as logos, and that sort of thing. Like fields, boilerplates are owned by the frame or repeating frame surrounding them, or by the region they appear in.

ANCHORS An anchor handles placment of a detail layout object in relation to its master. Visually, an anchor is depicted as a line from the detail layout object to the master, with a small box delineating the termination.

TIP
There are certain situations where Report Builder creates implicit anchors between objects when those objects risk being displaced by other objects in the report. Research this topic in the Report Builder online help before taking the OCP exam.

BUTTONS   A button is designed to give interface to objects in a report by performing actions like opening and playing sound or video files, or executing PL/SQL blocks designed to launch detail reports. Some buttons are automatically created by Report Builder, such as ones supporting use of sound or video file interfaces.

OLE2 OBJECTS   An OLE2 object is one that conforms to standards for object linking and embedding. Spreadsheets are one example of an OLE2 object.

GRAPHICS OBJECTS   A graphics object is a chart or display created in Oracle Graphics, a component of the Developer/2000 suite of application development tools. You can place these objects into your reports using tools provided in the Layout Model.

Relationships Between Objects and Their Representations

In addition to displaying objects to represent each data component of your report, the Layout Model also shows several different relationships between your objects in the Layout Model. The capabilities of Report Builder's Layout Model have already been hinted at in the definition for anchors. Several different types of graphical representations are used for various Layout Model objects. For example, a frame is represented in the Layout Model as a box surrounding a field representing a database or user-defined column. Other relationships are indicated by different symbols in the Layout Model, and those symbols are indicated in Figure 26-3.

The following list identifies relationships and representations you may see in Layout Model views on your reports, as pointed out in Figure 26-3.

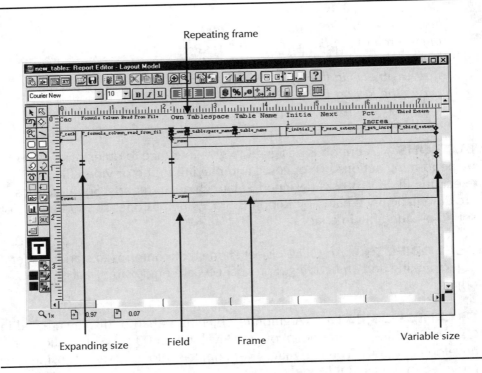

FIGURE 26-3. *Relationship symbols and their meanings*

FRAME   A frame is represented in the Layout Model as a box thinly drawn around another object. Frames surround most objects in the Layout Model of the report.

REPEATING FRAME   A repeating frame in the Layout Model is represented as a thinly drawn box. A small arrow is drawn perpendicular to one of the sides of the repeating frame to indicate the direction in which the frame will repeat. The arrow appears on the left side of the frame facing downward if the frame repeats downward. The arrow appears on the top side of the frame facing rightward if the frame repeats across. Combinations of the two are possible as well, and those combinations will be represented with arrows on two sides of the frame. If arrows appear on the left and bottom sides, the frame repeats down/across. If arrows appear on the right and top sides, the frame repeats across/down. Logically, these are the only possibilities.

MATRIX CELL   A matrix cell is represented in the Layout Model view of your report as a box with thickly drawn lines. Matrix cells appear only on matrix reports.

FIELD   A field is a label for the data that will appear in the content of the report. Fields appear within frames, repeating frames, or matrix cells.

ANCHOR   An anchor is an object that keeps one Layout Model object's location in the report rooted with respect to another object. Anchors are represented as lines with a filled-in small box attached to the end of the line.

PAGE BREAK   A page break is represented in the Layout Model as a small sheet with the edge lifting away in the corner. The lifted corner indicates whether the page break occurs before or after the object. The upper corner lifting away indicates a "before" page break; the lower corner lifting away indicates an "after" page break.

PAGE PROTECTION   Page protection is represented in the Layout Model as a box with two small ovals inside it. A line between the two ovals indicates that the page will be kept with an anchoring object.

EXPANDING SIZE   Frames may change in size depending on several factors, including the size of data in the field inside the current frame or within frames around it. Expanding-size frames are indicated by two lines drawn on the frame. If the frame expands vertically, the two lines are drawn on the upper and lower edges of the frame. If the frame expands horizontally, the two lines are drawn on the left and right edges of the frame.

CONTRACTING SIZE   Frames may change in size depending on several factors, including the size of data in the field inside the current frame or within frames around it. Contracting-size frames are indicated by a circle drawn on the frame. If the frame contracts vertically, the circle is drawn on the upper and lower edges of the frame. If the frame expands horizontally, the circle is drawn on the left and right edges of the frame.

VARIABLE SIZE   Frames may change in size depending on several factors, including the size of data in the field inside the current frame or within frames around it. Variable-size frames are indicated by a diamond drawn on the frame. If the frame contracts vertically, the diamond is drawn on the upper and lower edges of the frame. If the frame expands horizontally, the diamond is drawn on the left and right edges of the frame.

Exercises

1. Identify some of the objects you might see in the layout model for your report.

2. What symbol denotes a repeating frame layout? What symbol indicates an expanding frame, either horizontally or vertically?

Modifying Existing Report Layout with Layout Model Tools

There are at least 20 different tools available for use in the Layout Model view on your report. These tools are displayed as buttons in the left-hand margin of the display. The tools allow you to do a multitude of things. For example, you can add buttons, file links, charts, OLE2, and other objects to your report, and you can change formatting, text, background, and colors.

Layout Model Tool General Usage Procedures

Use of all the Layout Model tools falls into a general pattern. You have already seen this pattern with your use of tools in the Data Model. The next lesson will identify where and when exceptions exist to this general model for usage. The general use for these tools is given in the following list of steps:

1. Click on the appropriate tool in the Tool Palette on the Layout Model view of your report to activate the tool you wish to use.

2. Move your pointer to the appropriate area on either the open canvas or in your Layout Model view of the report.

3. Click once to create the object. In some cases, particularly with the tools that draw shapes and lines, you actually will draw the object in the Layout Model view of your report.

4. Double-click on the object you just created to invoke the Property Palette, and modify properties in your object.

Specific Layout Model Tools and Their Usage

The following paragraphs identify those tools and briefly explain their use. To identify the tools shown below, you should move your pointer over the tool button and leave it there until an identifier balloon appears with the name of the button in it. Figure 26-4 shows all the different tools in the Layout Model Tool Palette down the left margin of the Layout Model interface.

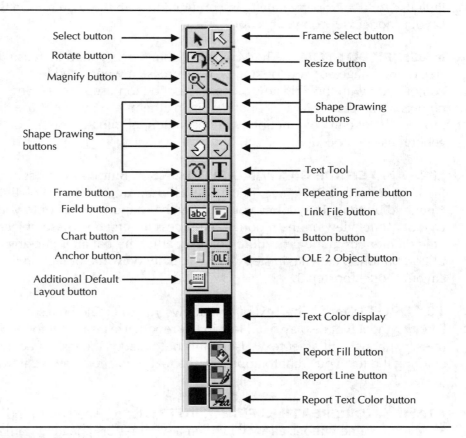

FIGURE 26-4. *Layout Model buttons and their location*

SELECT AND FRAME SELECT BUTTONS   The arrow that is activated by clicking the Select button allows you to choose an object on the Data Model view for property modification. You use this button by default when you edit reports in the Layout Model. The Frame Select button allows you to choose the frames that surround objects for property modification. These two buttons enable you to access and change properties on your objects in the Layout Model.

ROTATE AND RESIZE BUTTONS   The Rotate button allows you to rotate an object on its axis. The Resize button allows you to alter the size of the object. These buttons allow for movement of objects; therefore, there is little use for the Property Palette in conjunction with these buttons in the Layout Model view on your report.

MAGNIFY BUTTON   The Magnify button allows you to increase the size of the image you are looking at, or decrease it when used in conjunction with the Shift key. Since this is a button used for viewing objects in the Layout Model—not modifying them—you will not use the Property Palette in conjunction with this button, eliminating step 4 of the general usage procedure.

LINE AND SHAPE DRAWING BUTTONS   Buttons in this set include the Line, Rounded Rectangle, Rectangle, Ellipse, Arc, Polygon, Polyline, and Freehand buttons. They allow you to draw the shapes or lines onto your Layout Model view on the report. The process for creating these objects is a little different from the procedure defined earlier, in that after clicking on the Button button to activate in step 2, you actually draw the object on the Layout Model for step 3.

TEXT BUTTON   The Text button allows you to create boxes in your Layout Model that display fixed text in the report. This is useful for adding titles, captions, and other text. Use of this button adds the task of actually entering the text you want to appear in the text box, after drawing it as part of step 3.

FRAME AND REPEATING FRAME BUTTONS   The Frame and Repeating Frame buttons allow you to create frames or repeating frames on your report Layout Model. A frame is an object that contains a data field; a repeating frame contains every data field that is part of a group.

FIELD AND LINK FILE BUTTONS The Field and Link File buttons allow you to create fields inside of frames or objects that reference and read from files, respectively. Before creating a field, you should draw a frame to contain it using the buttons described earlier for this purpose. Also, to create your link file, you must be sure to identify the filename used in the link file Layout Model object, in step 4 when you invoke the Property Palette.

CHART AND BUTTON BUTTONS The Chart button allows you to create simple charts using the Graphics Builder button. After placing your chart into the report Layout Model, you will use the Chart Wizard to define chart layout and the data source for your chart, as well as actually creating the chart. Alternatively, you can create your chart manually using Graphics Builder and tie it into the chart object in your Layout Model using the Property Palette. The Button button allows you to create buttons that appear in your report, allowing you to access a multimedia object like a sound file from within your report.

ANCHOR AND OLE2 OBJECT BUTTON The Anchor button allows you to create an explicit anchor between a detail item and master item on your report, so that the details don't get displaced from their masters when the report is run. The OLE2 Object button allows you to embed an OLE2 object into your Data or Layout Model.

ADDITIONAL DEFAULT LAYOUT BUTTON The Additional Default Layout button allows you to create a default layout for one part of your report without overwriting any other part of your report layout. Use of this button is effectively the same as creating a report within your report, because after you draw the new object in step 3, your step 4 will be actually going through Report Wizard again to create another layout and report content—rather than the general step 4 of modifying properties in the Property Palette.

TEXT COLOR DISPLAY Though not actually a button, the Text Color display is useful as a display that allows you to see the field fill or background color, text color, and line color of these respective items in your report. It is useful for determining if the selected format using the next three buttons is visually balanced.

REPORT FILL, LINE, AND TEXT COLOR BUTTONS The Fill Color, Line Color, and Text Color buttons handle alterations to the background color, line color, and text color of your report. You can see the effects of any change in the report either in the Text Color display (defined above) or in the Layout Model for the report itself.

Exercises

1. Identify the buttons you would use to create multimedia objects in your report. What buttons would you use to embed a chart into your report?

2. What are the general steps required in creating new line and text objects in your reports? How does the creation of a text box differ from this general model?

Separating Tabular Data Columns with Lines

In some situations, you may want to create lines that separate your columns into tabular reports in order to visually distinguish the data in each of those columns. To do so, you will use the Line button to create the line in your data model according to the general steps defined in the previous discussion. Your line will be a fixed length according to how you drew it in the Data Model. The real question then becomes how to make the line extend for the depth of the column in the tabular report, however long that column becomes in your report.

To make the line extend to the length of the tabular column, you must first determine the field or column to which you want the line's extension tied, by drawing the line within the frame that contains that field. After doing so, you double-click on the line to display the Property Palette for that line. The property that defines how Report Builder should extend the line is called Line Stretch with Frame. Figure 26-5 displays the Property Palette with the options for this property.

Initially the Line Stretch with Frame property will most likely be NULL, meaning that the line length is fixed as you drew it in the Layout Model. Click on the property to make a drop-down list box appear, showing how the line can be extended. The options shown in this list are labels that identify the frames through which you drew your line, not the fields within those frames. Thus, the choices you have at this point are directly related to where you drew the line on the Layout Model. So if you don't see the frame that's associated with your line, you will have to redraw the line. Once you've identified the frame with which you want your line to stretch, click on that frame to select it and close the Property Palette. You have now defined a variable-length line that will separate your columns of data.

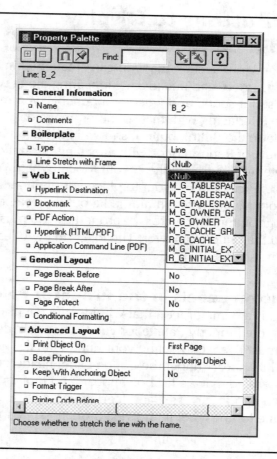

FIGURE 26-5. *Line Stretch with Frame Property in the Property Palette*

Exercises

1. How do you draw a line in the Layout Model of your report?

2. What property allows you to define a variable-length line that separates columns of data in your tabular reports?

3. Why does where you draw the line affect the ways your line will extend with the output of your report?

Creating Buttons to Display Multimedia Objects

Recall from the previous section that you can create multimedia reports containing sound, video, and image data appearing along with database columns. To do so for sound and video components, you must create a button to handle interfacing with that sound or image data. To create a button, first click on the Button button, shown in the left margin of the Layout Model view of Report Editor with a rectangular button on it. Then move your pointer to the area of the Layout Model where you want the button to appear. Click on the layout to place your button. Figure 26-6 shows your Layout Model with a multimedia button created in it. Once you have created your button, there are two properties you must define: the button label and the button behavior. The following two lessons will help you complete these tasks.

Defining Button Labels in the Property Palette

The button label is a name or icon that will identify your button to the report reader. Opening the Property Palette for your button will demonstrate the properties you must change to define your button label. The first property is Label Type, and it appears under the Button Label header. Click on the Label Type property to make a list box appear, and look in that list box to see that your two options are Text and Icon. If you choose Text, you must then enter a name for the label in the Text property appearing below Label Type.

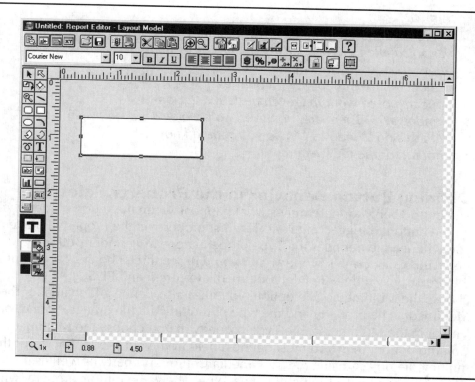

FIGURE 26-6.   *Layout Model with a multimedia button*

If you choose Icon, you must enter a filename for the icon in the Icon Name property that will substitute for Text under the Label Type property. The name for an icon will have the extension **.ico**, but you don't need to include that extension when defining the Icon Name property. Report Builder checks to see if the file is in a certain place when you define the icon. That place is the **tools/devdem20/bin/icon** subdirectory under the Oracle software home directory on Windows platforms. If you are not using an icon file that is already in this location, or if you want to use your own icon file, you must ensure the file is in this directory before associating it with a button, or else when you try to associate it with the button you will receive an error.

TIP
There is supposed to be an environment variable called TK25_ICON or TK30_ICON that allows you to specify what directory Report Builder will search for your icon files, but it appears not to work in Developer/2000 2.1 on Windows 95. There are, however, no problems with this on Windows NT, so you should know about it for the OCP exam.

Defining Button Behavior in the Property Palette

The button behavior determines what happens when the report reader clicks on the button to trigger an event. The first property in the Property Palette you will need to define is the Type property appearing under Button Behavior. Click on this property and you will see three choices appear for the property: Multimedia File, Multimedia Column, and PL/SQL. If you choose the Multimedia File option, you must also define a filename for the Multimedia File property and the type of multimedia file (Image, Sound, or Video) in the Multimedia File Type property. If you choose the Multimedia Column option, then you must define a field from your group that stores the multimedia object, using the Multimedia Column property as well as the appropriate value for Multimedia File Type. The value for this property will be NULL unless you place the button inside a field on the Layout Model view for your report. Finally, if you choose PL/SQL for your Type property, then you must only define the code for the PL/SQL Trigger property appearing in the Property Palette.

Exercises

1. What are the two general property categories that must be defined for a multimedia button? What are the two options you have for defining what appears on the face of your button?

2. Where must the icon file be located in order to use it in a button definition? What environment variable can you supposedly use for this purpose? What subdirectory of the Oracle software directory will you use for this purpose?

Creating Explicit Anchors to Alter Object Positions

Recall that anchors allow you to link two different items in your Layout Model, thereby preventing them from becoming dissociated. This feature is useful for tying master/detail records together. Since an anchor overrides the default formatting Oracle Reports will use in placing your data on the page of the report, you can use anchors to alter object positions. To create an anchor between a detail object and its master, first click on the Anchor button to activate that tool in the Layout Model of your report. An anchor has two ends, the originating end and the anchoring or terminating end. So your next task is to set the originating end for your anchor by positioning your pointer to the upper edge of the frame surrounding the detail field you want to anchor to a master. Click and hold the mouse button while you position the pointer to the lower edge of the frame surrounding the associated master field, and release the mouse button. A line will appear between the two fields. Finally, without disturbing the pointer, double-click on the anchoring or terminating end of the line you just created, and a box will appear at the terminating end of your line. Creation of your anchor object is now complete.

TIP
You might want to anchor information when you want a logo to appear in a specific area of the report with respect to the report data, or when you want certain data such as a summary field to appear near the single instance of the data it is summarizing.

Redefining Anchor Properties with the Property Palette

The next thing you can do with your anchor is redefine properties for it in the Property Palette. Double-click on the anchor again, and the Property Palette appears for your anchor. Several properties can be modified in the Property Palette for anchors, including the Child Object Name, Child Edge

Type, Child Edge Percent, Parent Object Name, Parent Edge Type, Parent Edge Percent, Collapse Horizontally, and Collapse Vertically properties. To see how an anchor looks in the Layout Model, refer to Figure 26-7.

CHILD OBJECT NAME   This is the name of the child or detail object being anchored (the anchor shown without the white box on the end in Figure 26-7). The value for this property is changed only by creating an anchor from another detail object.

CHILD EDGE TYPE   This property identifies the edge of the frame around the detail or child object field you are anchoring to a parent or master, and can have the value Top, Bottom, Left, or Right. Click on the

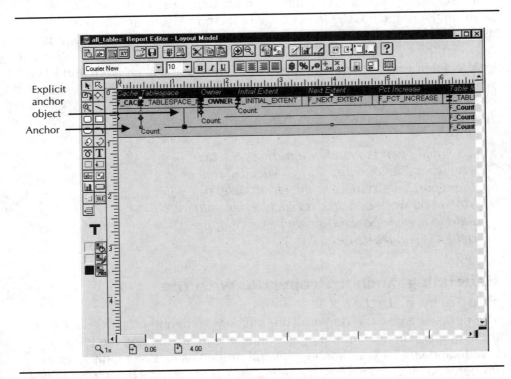

FIGURE 26-7.   *Layout Model view of an anchor*

property to make a drop-down list box appear, where you can select one of these choices. Doing so actually moves the originating end of the anchor you just created to the edge you selected. This property alters the position of the detail or child object with respect to its parent.

CHILD EDGE PERCENT   This property identifies the exact location of the originating end of the anchor on the child or detail object edge in terms of percentage from left to right for top or bottom edges, or top to bottom for left or right edges. If you alter this value, the originating end of the anchor will actually move to the place you specify. This property alters the position of the detail or child object with respect to its parent.

PARENT OBJECT NAME   This property is the name of the parent or master object. The parent object appears at the terminating end of the anchor. The terminating end is shown as a white box on the Layout Model view in Figure 26-7. Changing this value is possible only by redrawing the anchor.

PARENT EDGE TYPE   This property identifies the edge of the frame around the master or parent field to which the anchor is attached. There are four values for this property: Top, Bottom, Left, or Right. Click on the property to make a drop-down list box appear, where you can select one of these choices. Doing so actually moves the originating end of the anchor you just created to the edge you selected. This property alters the position of the detail or child object with respect to its parent.

PARENT EDGE PERCENT   This property identifies the exact location of the terminating end of the anchor on the master or parent object edge in terms of percentage from left to right for top or bottom edges, or top to bottom for left or right edges. If you alter this value, the originating end of the anchor will actually move to the place you specify. This property alters the position of the detail or child object with respect to its parent.

COLLAPSE HORIZONTALLY   Something must happen to the child or detail object if the parent does not print. This property and the next will handle that situation. Each of these properties can be defined as Yes or No. If this property is defined to be Yes, then the child or detail object will move horizontally into the parent's or master's place if the parent or master does not print.

COLLAPSE VERTICALLY   Something must happen to the child or detail object if the parent does not print. This property and the preceding one will handle that situation. Each of these properties can be defined as Yes or No. If this property is defined to be Yes, then the child or detail object will move vertically into the parent's or master's place if the parent or master does not print.

Exercises

1. What is an anchor? What is its purpose in the Layout Model?

2. How can you distinguish the originating end from the terminating end of an anchor?

3. What properties in the Property Palette can be used to move the originating or terminating end on the master or detail object once the anchor has been drawn?

4. Experiment with anchors in your report to understand how altering the edge and the anchor's position on the detail or master object will affect how the objects appear in relation to one another on the report.

Modifying Layout Properties in Reports

In this section, you will cover the following points on modifying layout properties in your reports:

■ Using link files in reports to display file contents

■ Modifying layout properties common to all object types

■ Modifying layout properties specific to one object type

From reading the last section, you should have some idea of how modifying object properties affects report layout overall. This section delves more deeply into the task of modifying layout properties. The topics include using link files to display file contents, modifying layout properties that are commonly shared by all objects in a report, and modifying layout properties specific to one object type.

Using Link Files in Reports to Display File Contents

Sometimes you may want to display the contents of a file in your report. You have already seen one way to do this by specifying a database or formula column to read its output from file and then display those contents in the column of the report. Another approach to this task is to use the Link File tool button to create an object in the Layout Model of the report and associate a file with that object.

TIP

Use link files in situations where the actual content of the file may change frequently and you always want the most current version to appear in the report. If you actually embed or import the file into the report (as an image, for example), you will only have the contents as they appeared at that moment in time.

The first set of steps in this task was covered in the preceding section. That process is to create the link file object in the Layout Model of the report by clicking on the Link File tool button, moving the pointer to the appropriate location in your report layout, and drawing the link file object to create it. These items are covered in steps 1–3 in the general model for enhancing reports with the Layout Model Tool Palette. For step 4, the General Layout and Advanced Layout properties simply identify aspects of the link file object as you created it in the Layout Model. Forget them for now. The properties you are concerned about include the Source File Format and Source Filename properties. The options available for specification in Source File Format include Text, Image, CGM, Oracle Drawing Format, and Image URL. If you have any questions, refer to the preceding chapter's explanation of these file formats and their use in the Read from File property in database or formula columns in the Data Model. A link file object is shown as part of your Layout Model for a report in Figure 26-8.

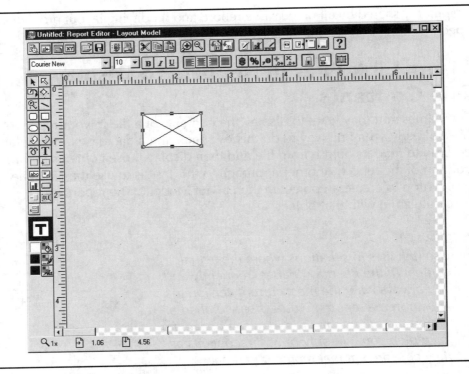

FIGURE 26-8. *Link files in your Layout Model*

The second task of defining link files is to identify to Report Builder which file you want to use as the source for this object in your Layout Model. When you click on the Source Filename property, a button will appear that you will click to select the file to be opened and read by the link file object. The file you specify must correspond to the file format you selected for that property, or the report will not behave properly at run time. Recall that this process for defining the filename is different from that used in the Data Model to obtain file contents within database or formula columns.

TIP
The existence of your link file is checked at link file-object creation time. If your link file doesn't exist, you will receive an error.

Using Web Content for Link Files in Reports

You can use pages from the Web in your data links, as well. Web pages can be either in the regular HTML format or in portable document format (PDF), which uses a special PDF reader to render your document in its original hard-copy format. There are several additional properties you will need to define within the Property Palette for Web page link files. These properties help Report Builder identify whether the document format is HTML or PDF. The following items identify the properties in the Property Palette you will need to define for link files, and the appropriate values for each. Figure 26-9 shows the Property Palette you will see for defining link files in your reports.

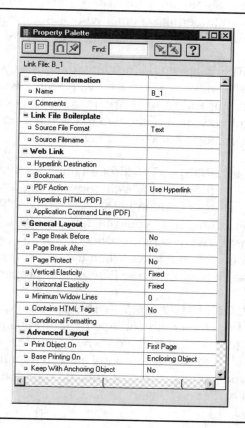

FIGURE 26-9. *Property Palette for defining link files*

HYPERLINK DESTINATION   This property accepts identifiers of 26 or fewer characters, numbers, and underscores in length. Once defined, the Hyperlink Destination property acts as a unique identifier for the link file object in the Layout Model of the report. You must specify this property if you intend to reference this object via Web link from other objects.

BOOKMARK   This property accepts an identifier that appears wherever bookmarks are displayed in your PDF document viewer or master HTML document. This identifier may or may not have ordering or indentation defined for it, using an outline number followed by the pound sign (#) that determines order but does not actually appear as part of the bookmark. If you use outline numbers, be careful about leaving gaps in the numbering of your bookmark items. Significant gaps (for example, jumping from 1.0 to 2.1.5 in your outline numbering scheme) will cause intermediate entries to be generated automatically with blank bookmark entries.

PDF ACTION   This property defines how the object will behave if clicked on from a PDF viewer. There are two possible values for this property: Use Hyperlink and Launch Application. The option you define for this property determines which of the two following properties will be activated when the object is clicked in a PDF viewer.

HYPERLINK (HTML/PDF)   This property defines a hyperlink that will be used to reach a link file via URL/Web conventions. You can specify another location in a current document with HTML anchors (**#***anchor_name*), a document on your machine (**file:///C**|/*doc_name*), or a Web-based URL (**http://www.***wherever.net/docname*), or a combination thereof. To make this property active when the report is shown as a PDF file, you must select Use Hyperlink for the PDF Action property identified earlier.

APPLICATION COMMAND LINE   This property defines a statement that can be issued from the command line of your local machine running or viewing the report that will be executed when you click on the file link object in the report. To make this property active when the report is shown as a PDF file, you must select Launch Application for the PDF Action property identified earlier.

Exercises

1. Identify the purpose and usage of a link file. How do you create one in your Layout Model?

2. What properties are set if you want to define your link file to be a text, drawing, or other type of file? How is the name of the file to be used identified in a link file?

3. What properties are set if you want to define your link file to use Web content?

Modifying Layout Properties Common to All Object Types

The main way to modify layout properties in Report Builder is to use the Property Palette. When developing Layout Model objects one at a time, as you are likely to do, you will find yourself going from one Property Palette view to another to modify the exact property you need to make the report work. This is annoying, especially if you know you have to do something tedious like add comments to every object in the Layout Model. Try to picture it yourself: opening the Property Palette for a Layout Model object, making the change, closing the Property Palette, then opening it again for another object and starting the process again. Asleep yet? It's good that there's another way to quickly modify properties across multiple objects. This method allows you to focus your efforts either on the properties that are common across different objects you selected, or on the aggregate collection of all properties for the objects you selected. To understand how to do these things, let's take a closer look at the Property Palette and its features.

The Property Palette, Revisited

One thing the Property Palette allows you to do is to open multiple Layout Model objects. You accomplish this task in the following way: First, you must select the Layout Model objects to be opened within the Property Palette, by clicking on them while simultaneously pressing the SHIFT or the

CTRL key and clicking once on the Layout Model object you wish to display in the Property Palette. After you have completed selection of all the objects in the Layout Model you wish to see, double-click on one of the objects you selected to view within the Layout Model, and the Property Palette will display all those objects' properties.

Within the Property Palette there is a set of buttons that allows you to do many different things. From left to right, the tools you will find along the top of the Property Palette include the Expand and Collapse buttons to help you drill down into the properties in your Property Palette for this object, by group. Other tools to the right include the Intersection/Union button and the Freeze/Unfreeze button. The first button is by far the most important in the Property Palette from the perspective of altering properties from multiple objects. This button toggles between views of the intersection of properties appearing in the objects you selected, and the union of those properties. In other words, you can see the common properties in the Property Palette for all the objects you selected from the Layout Model (the intersection), or you can see all the properties for every object (the union). You will see the intersection of properties when the Intersection/Union button is toggled down, and you will see the union of properties when the button is toggled up.

To make property changes to objects across all object types, you should first select every object you wish to change in the Layout Model, using the SHIFT or CTRL key and clicking on the objects. This selection of Layout Model objects can be across one particular object type or across all object types. The choice is yours. Once this step is complete, simply click on one of the objects you selected to invoke the Property Palette for all the objects, and set the Intersection/Union button toggled down to view the properties that are common to all objects you selected. Alternatively, set the Intersection/Union button toggled up to see all properties for all objects and set them all at once.

Exercises

1. How can you set up the Property Palette to view properties for multiple objects at the same time?

2. What button within the Property Palette handles toggling between views of properties shared between objects selected, and all properties for all objects selected?

Modifying Layout Properties Specific to One Object Type

Sometimes you will want to alter properties that are specific to one object, or to a subset of objects. For example, you may want to modify properties associated with only the Layout Model objects for summary columns. To do so, you would use the same methods as those outlined in the previous discussion—namely, selecting all of the summary column Layout Model objects with the SHIFT or CTRL key and clicking the mouse button, and then double-clicking on one of the objects to open the Property Palette for all of those selected. From there, you can alter properties common to all objects selected, or all the properties across all objects selected.

You may want only to change properties for one object within the multiple objects you selected, however. You already know how to accomplish this by double-clicking on the individual Layout Model object to open the Property Palette for that object and then modifying the property desired. You may be able to do it with multiple selected objects; however, one of the drawbacks to modifying properties of multiple objects in the Property Palette is that the value for the property is altered for *all* objects selected—the antithesis of what you're trying to do.

The best method in this situation is to open the Property Palette for each Layout Model object you want to change, one at a time. Though slower to accomplish, you will have more control over the values for properties at the individual object level. Finally, one other alternative you can use when altering individual properties is to open multiple Property Palettes at once, to use for comparing properties of one Layout Model object to another. This task is accomplished in the following way: First, you click on the Freeze/Unfreeze button to toggle it to Unfreeze mode, where instead of seeing a pin shown lengthwise on the button, you see only the top of its head. This step allows you to open multiple Property Palettes for different Layout Model objects, instead of having the Property Palette replace the properties it displays every time you click on a new Layout Model object. You can then place the two Property Palettes side by side for easy property comparison across Layout Model objects. Figure 26-10 displays the Property Palette with the Intersection/Union and Freeze/Unfreeze buttons identified.

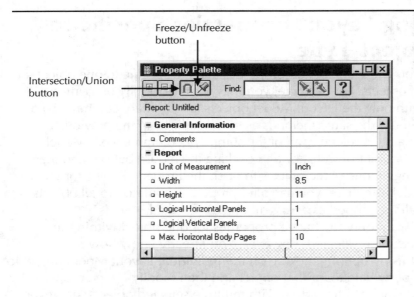

FIGURE 26-10. *Property Palette with Intersection/Union and Freeze/Unfreeze buttons*

TIP
You can view properties for multiple objects in the Data Model view just as you can in the Layout Model, by pressing SHIFT or CTRL and clicking your mouse on the object and then opening the Property Palette. You can also open multiple Property Palettes for Data Model objects using the Freeze/Unfreeze button.

Exercises

1. What tools and tasks must you accomplish to see object properties displayed in two or more Property Palettes in Report Builder at one time?

2. Why might it not be useful to show properties for multiple objects at once in the Property Palette when you want to edit values for properties in specific objects?

3. Can you accomplish tasks described in questions 1 and 2 on Layout Model objects, Data Model objects, or both? Explain.

Chapter Summary

This chapter covered several areas of enhancing layout and properties of reports in Report Builder. The key subjects in this chapter were using the Layout Model view to enhance report layout, and the intricacies of modifying the properties of a layout object using a combination of the Layout Model view and the Property Palette tool. The information in this chapter goes hand in hand with the content of Chapter 25 to form the basis of your knowledge of modifying reports. These are crucial areas of understanding in order to pass OCP Exam 5 on building reports. Toward that end, this chapter comprises 15 percent of content on that exam.

The first item covered in the chapter is using the Layout Model view to view and modify layout objects in the four regions of your report. Recall those four regions are the body, margin, header, and trailer corresponding to the body or content, top and bottom margins, header page, and trailer page on the report when it appears in hard copy or in the Live Previewer. You can view the contents of the report for that region by clicking on the appropriate region button in the Layout Model view of the Report Editor tool. Once you are in that region, you can then add objects to the layout for that region using the appropriate buttons in the Tool Palette along the left margin of the Report Editor module.

There are many different types of objects in the Layout Model view of your report. These items include frames, repeating frames, fields, boilerplates, anchors, buttons, OLE2 objects, and graphics objects. There is a tool in the Tool Palette on the left margin of the Layout Model view in Report Editor corresponding to each of these objects.

Each of the objects in the Layout Model has a representation and/or a relationship to the other objects in the model. These representations are made graphically in the Layout Model through the use of outline boxes for matrix cells, frames, and repeating frames. Other representations take the form of labels, such as those for fields. Still other objects are represented as a line connecting another object with a special box on the end, as in the case of anchors. Relationships form between these objects as well, such as those that determine whether the size of a frame is expanding, contracting, or variable. Two lines, a circle, or a diamond on the edges of a frame will identify these relationships, respectively.

The content of the chapter describes those relationships in the database and instructs you on how to create each of them. The general procedure for defining objects in the Layout Model is first clicking on the button in the

Tool Palette to allow you to create the object, then creating the object in the Layout Model view, then defining any properties that need to be associated with the object. Some of the tools that appear in the Tool Palette on the Layout Model view include Select Object and Select Frame tools, Rotate and Resize Objects tools, Magnify Report Display tool, Line and Shape Drawing tools, and tools for drawing text objects. Others include Frame and Repeating Frame creation tools; Field and Link File creation tools; Chart and Button creation tools; Anchor and OLE2 Object creation tools; additional default layout creation tools; Background, Line, Text Color tools; and Display tools.

After drawing the object onto the Layout Model view of your report, the next task is to set properties for the object. One of the tasks you may want to accomplish is to separate the tabular data output in a report with lines that extend the length of the column. This is accomplished by drawing a line on the Layout Model view inside the frame for the field with whose columnar output you want the line to extend. Then you set the Line Stretch with Frame property to the object with which the line should extend on the report.

The chapter covered the concept of logical pages in your reports, and how most of the time the logical pages showing in the Runtime Previewer will map to physical pages on a one-to-one basis. However, you can set it up so that your logical pages of the report will be multipanel, or spread across multiple physical pages. The use of the Logical Horizontal Panels and Logical Vertical Panels properties defines how logical pages will be divided into panels or physical pages printed as output. The Panel Print Order property helps you determine whether the panels are printed across or downward first. Several other aspects of report printing were covered in the chapter as well, so be sure you understand them for the exam.

Creation of buttons to support the view of multimedia objects is covered as well. First, you use the Button tool to create the button object. A button can have a label that is either an icon or a name. After creating the button, you then associate the button with the multimedia file, using the Type property and setting it to Multimedia File or Multimedia Column. If you define Type to be Multimedia File, you will also need to set a value for the filename using the Multimedia File property. When Type is defined as Multimedia Column, then you also must define a field from the Layout Model that stores the multimedia object in the report, with the Multimedia Column property along with a filename for Multimedia File.

Creating explicit anchors to set placement for an object in a report in direct relation to another object is another topic covered by the chapter. Again, the process of creating the Layout Model object comes first—in this case, the anchor. Then, you define your properties. In this case, those properties include Child Object Name, Child Edge Type, Child Edge Percent, Parent Object Name, Parent Edge Type, Parent Edge Percent, Collapse Horizontally, and Collapse Vertically. Neither the Parent Name nor the Child Name property can be altered. In those others whose values can be changed, the change will affect both the appearance of the anchor in the Layout Model view and the appearance of the two objects anchored together in the report.

Another section in the chapter concerned modification of properties for Layout Model objects in reports. Main topics of discussion were using link files to display file contents, and modifying layout properties in reports both for properties that are common across many object types and for properties that are unique to a single object. Closely related to this topic is a discussion of showing properties for multiple objects in the Property Palette, along with opening multiple Property Palettes to compare properties for several objects.

Using link files is helpful in reports when you want to display files in reports. The types of files you can display include text, images, images on the Web, and a few others. The link file is set up in the same way as other objects in the Layout Model, with the creation of the layout object followed by the definition of the properties required. In this case, the properties are Source File Format and Source Filename. Recall from the chapter that the existence of the file you set up as a file link is checked when you create the link file object. Thus, you must ensure that your file exists before creating the link to it in the report. Your file can exist on the Web, as well. There are properties you define for setting this up, including Bookmark, PDF Action, Hyperlink, and Application Command Line.

The modification of properties is done with the Property Palette, as has been explained before. You can view properties for one or several objects using this tool. To open properties for multiple objects, you first have to select multiple objects in the Layout Model by holding the SHIFT or CTRL key while pointing and clicking on the object you select. Then, when you double-click on one of the objects you selected, the Property Palette opens showing either all the properties for all the objects, or only the properties that are common across all objects you identified. You switch between these two views with the Intersection/Union button on the Property Palette. Alternatively, you can open multiple Property Palettes, each containing properties for one object, and compare them. This is accomplished with the Freeze/Unfreeze button. Use of both these tools in the Property Palette is described in the chapter.

Two-Minute Drill

- Four report regions exist in the report. They are the body, margin, header, and trailer regions.

- You access and navigate these regions using buttons shown in the Layout Model view of your report in the Report Editor module of Report Builder program.

- You can also access the Layout Model for your report using the View | Layout Model menu option in Report Builder or the Layout Model node in the Object Navigator.

- The Tool Palette appears on the left-hand side of the Layout Model interface. It has the tools you use to create new Layout Model objects.

- There are several different types of Layout Model objects: frames, repeating frames, fields, boilerplates, anchors, buttons, OLE2 objects, and graphics objects.

- Layout Model objects relate to one another. These relationships are identified pictorially in the Layout Model as well, through symbol and placement. Symbols include the following:

  - Double lines on a frame indicate expanding size

  - Circles on a frame indicate contracting size

  - Diamonds on a frame indicate variable size

- Review in the text how placement of symbols in a frame on the Layout Model indicates layout factors.

- Review for the OCP exam the mapping of logical pages to physical pages for multipanel reports.

- General usage of Layout Model tools falls in the following pattern:

  1. Click on the appropriate tool in the Tool Palette on the Layout Model view of your report to activate the tool you wish to use.

  2. Move your pointer to the appropriate area on either the open canvas or in your Layout Model view of the report.

  3. Click once to create the object. In some cases, particularly with the tools that enable you to draw shapes and lines, you actually will draw the object in the Layout Model view of your report.

  4. Double-click on the object you just created to invoke the Property Palette and modify properties in your object.

- Review the functions of the tools available in the Tool Palette focusing on the tools that handle the following:

  - Link files

  - Buttons

  - Line drawing

  - Anchors

- Step 4 in the general usage procedure given in this chapter allows you to define properties in support of various objects in the Layout Model. Some of those properties and their respective Layout Model tools or features include the following:

  - **Line button** Separating columns with lines that extend the length of a column. Extension of lines from top to bottom of a tabular column is handled with the Line Stretch with Frame property.

  - **Button button** Creating buttons to access multimedia objects from a report. Definition of button label and multimedia filename and type is handled with Label Type, Type, Multimedia File, Multimedia Column, and Multimedia File Type.

- **Anchor button** Creating anchors to hold two Layout Model objects together in the report output. Movement of origin and anchoring position on master and detail objects is handled with Child Edge Type, Child Edge Percent, Parent Edge Type, Parent Edge Percent, Collapse Horizontally, and Collapse Vertically.

- **Link File button** Create links to files to display data from a file in the report. Aspects of the file you are linking to include Source File Format and Source Filename. You can also link Web file content into your report using the Hyperlink Destination, Bookmark, PDF Action, Hyperlink, and Application Command Line properties. Certain settings may cause you to need to define values for certain properties, but not others. Review this content in the chapter for more information.

- Two features of the Property Palette allow you to modify layout properties common to many object types. Those features include the Intersection/Union button to view properties for multiple objects at once, and the Freeze/Unfreeze button to open multiple Property Palettes and compare properties.

Chapter Questions

1. **After clicking on the Text button to create that object, you should do which of the following tasks?**

   A. Draw the text box in the Layout Model view.

   B. Enter the text you want to appear in the box.

   C. Close the Layout Model view.

   D. Modify the value for the Text File property.

2. **The most efficient way to modify properties for all fields in a Layout Model view of the report is to do which of the following?**

   A. Open the Property Palettes one by one for each field in the Layout Model view.

B. Open multiple Property Palettes for each field in the Layout Model view using appropriate means.

C. Open the Property Palettes for multiple objects at once, using appropriate means, and modify the intersection of common properties shared across those objects.

D. Open the Property Palettes one by one for each nonfield object in the Layout Model view.

3. **When defining link file objects in your report, which method is used to define the filename that will be read by Report Builder to populate the report?**

   A. Database column

   B. PL/SQL formula

   C. Read from File property

   D. Source Filename property

4. **You have created a link file for a text file. When will Oracle Reports realize that the file you specified for the link file layout object does not exist?**

   A. Link file-object creation time

   B. Report compilation time

   C. Report run time

   D. When the report connects to the database

5. **Which of the following methods listed below cannot be used to reach a region of your report?**

   A. View | Layout Section menu item

   B. Reports | *Rpt_Name* | Layout Model node in the Object Navigator

    C. Arrange | Layout Region menu item

    D. Region buttons in Layout Model view

6. **The body of a multipanel report spans five physical pages across and two down for every logical page of that report. The groups shown in the report are read left to right. Which of the following value settings for properties are best with this report?**

    A. Logical Horizontal Panels 2, Logical Vertical Panels 5, Panel Print Order Down/Across

    B. Logical Horizontal Panels 5, Logical Vertical Panels 2, Panel Print Order Down/Across

    C. Logical Horizontal Panels 2, Logical Vertical Panels 5, Panel Print Order Across/Down

    D. Logical Horizontal Panels 5, Logical Vertical Panels 2, Panel Print Order Across/Down

7. **The setting for the CHILD_EDGE_TYPE property of an anchor is set to Left. If The value for CHILD_EDGE_PERCENT is increased, what happens to the anchor displayed in the Layout Model?**

    A. The placement of the anchor on the child object shifts downward along the left side.

    B. The child object is moved to the left in the Layout Model view.

    C. The placement of the anchor on the child object shifts to the right along the top.

    D. The parent object is displaced by the child if no data is selected for the parent object.

8. **Which of the following items can act as labels for your buttons in Report Builder? (Choose two)**

    A. Hypertext links

B. Sound files

C. Icons

D. Names

9. **In which of the following Reports tools can you click on the buttons you create to see how they behave in the "live" report?**

   A. Runtime Previewer

   B. Object Navigator

   C. Report Converter

   D. Report Server

10. **When using link files to read information from the Web into your reports, which of the properties determine whether the link file will behave as a hyperlink or whether it should be run as a command-line application?**

    A. Bookmark

    B. PDF Action

    C. Hyperlink

    D. Application Command Line

11. **In the Layout Model, fields are usually contained inside which of the following objects?**

    A. Anchors

    B. Buttons

    C. Boilerplates

    D. Frames

Answers to Chapter Questions

1. A. Draw the text box in the Layout Model view.

Explanation   After clicking on the Tool Palette button for any object in the Layout Model view, your next step will generally be to draw or place the object in your report's Layout Model open canvas. Text boxes are a bit of a special case after that, insofar as you will enter the text into them after drawing the object and before modifying its properties in the Property Palette. But Choice B will still happen after A, making B incorrect. Closing the Layout Model view as in choice C will prevent any further activity on the Layout Model, and therefore will be done last. There is no Text File property associated with the text object in question, making choice D incorrect.

2. C. Open the Property Palette for multiple objects at once, using appropriate means, and modify the intersection of common properties shared across those objects.

Explanation   The fastest way to modify properties for objects of the same type is to mark them for opening by clicking on them while simultaneously holding the SHIFT or CTRL key, then double-clicking on one of the elements you selected to open the Property Palette to show common properties for all objects selected. This method is much faster than altering object properties one by one, as in choice A, and comparing properties using multiple open Property Palettes as in choice B. Choice D will not change the properties for fields, and therefore is not correct.

3. D. Source Filename property

Explanation   For some columns in the Data Model view, you can set the report up to read data from file, where the filename is identified by the contents of the column. The column, in turn, can be populated by information from the database or from PL/SQL functions. The Read from File property in the column's Data Model object is used to determine whether the column will read its input from the filename specified in the column. This process, however, is not used for link files in the Layout Model, eliminating choices A, B, and C.

4. A. Link file-object creation time

Explanation The presence of the file you are creating your link to is checked when you actually create the link file object in the Layout Model, so as to avoid problems later on at run time. Thus, choice A is correct, and the rest of the choices are logically incorrect.

5. C. Arrange | Layout Region menu item

Explanation You can access the regions of a report in several ways. Those ways include the Object Navigator module using the appropriate node listed in Choice A, the main menu selection listed for choice B, and the navigation buttons in the Layout Model view shown in choice D. The only choice that isn't valid is choice C, because there is no Arrange menu in Report Builder.

6. D. Logical Horizontal Panels 5, Logical Vertical Panels 2, Panel Print Order Across/Down

Explanation To answer this question, you first need to understand the use of the three properties in the question. Recall that Logical Horizontal/Vertical Panels defines the number of physical pages or panels mapping horizontally and vertically to a logical page. In this case, you have your answer right in the question—5 across, 2 down. Thus, Logical Horizontal Panels is 5, Logical Vertical Panels is 2. The other component in the question is defining how the report will print, based on how the group data is displayed in the logical page. The answer to this question is across, then down, making the Panel Print Order appropriately defined as Across/Down. Thus, choice D is correct.

7. A. The placement of the anchor on the child object shifts downward along the left side.

Explanation Recall from the discussion of anchors that the placement of the originating and terminating ends of the anchor are displayed as properties in the Property Palette. The Child Edge Type identifies which frame edge the anchor roots to on the child. In this case, the value is Left, meaning that the anchor connects to the left side of the frame around the child field. In this situation, the Child Edge Percent property determines the exact point from top to bottom where the anchor will be placed. Lower numbers for this property put the anchor to the top, higher ones to the bottom, and 50 means dead center. Since the number for this property was said in the question to be increasing, the anchor is moving to the bottom of the left side of the frame around the child object.

8. C and D.   Icons and Names

Explanation   As explained in the chapter, a button can have an icon or a name for a label. Hypertext links or sound files may be what is activated when you press the button in the Runtime Previewer for the report, but the label on that button will always be either a name or an icon.

9. A.   Runtime Previewer

Explanation   The Runtime Previewer is the only tool described in the question that allows you to look at your report more or less as it appears on the page. The Object Navigator is a way to get around among the different elements of a report, while the Report Converter changes a report file from one format to another. The Report Server is an application that handles processing and publishing of reports separate from the client machine, and is used mainly in N-Tier architectures. These facts eliminate choices B, C, and D.

10. B.   PDF Action

Explanation   When interfacing to the Web, you can specify that a link file be treated like a URL or as an application command line, by specifying either Use Hyperlink or Launch Application for the PDF Action property in the Property Palette for the link file object. Though choices C and D are incorrect, the value you set for the PDF Action property directly affects whether the link file will use the value set for Hyperlink or Application Command Line.

11. D.   Frames

Explanation   Frames enclose fields throughout a report, to contain them and protect them from being overwritten by other objects in the report layout. Anchors keep one Layout Model object rooted with respect to the placement of another, and use frames to connect to fields but do not enclose those fields, eliminating choice A. Buttons do not enclose fields, either, but rather act as objects that allow you to interface with multimedia objects in reports or fire other reports from within a report, eliminating choice B. Boilerplates, like fields, are enclosed by frames, eliminating choice D as well.

CHAPTER 27

Developing Other Features in Reports

n this chapter, you will cover the following areas of developing other features in reports:

- Using report parameters and parameter forms
- Embedding charts in reports
- Developing and enhancing matrix reports

This chapter covers some of the final elements of basic report development in Oracle Reports, and then moves on to some advanced features and techniques. A final basic element in report development is the creation and use of report parameters, and the use of the Parameter Form tool in Report Builder. After covering that element, the chapter will move on to the creation and use of charts to enhance your reports with visually appealing contents that add value to the overall report. Finally, development of what some may argue is the most complex type of reports—matrix reports—is covered. This final section emphasizes usage of both the Layout Model and Data Model, whose features are covered extensively in the last two chapters for the purpose of creating matrix reports, and turns the knowledge of features you gained in the last two chapters into a case study of their use. The content of this chapter comprises 15 percent of material tested by OCP Exam 5.

Using Report Parameters and Parameter Forms

In this section, you will cover the following points on using report parameters and Parameter Forms:

- Controlling report output with parameters
- Creating user parameters in a report
- Creating Lists of Values for parameter input
- Incorporating user parameters into queries
- Using and modifying system parameters

- Building Parameter Form layouts for value entry
- Customizing Parameter Form layouts

The behavior and output of reports is managed with the use of parameters. Early in the section, you will cover the parameters that are used when executing reports. Some of these report parameters determine aspects about the content of the report, while others determine aspects of how the report runs on the machine. This section covers how to control the output of your report using parameters. In addition, the section covers use of Lists of Values, or LOVs, for parameter input. The use and modification of system parameters is covered as well. You will also learn how to build and customize special objects called Parameter Forms that handle input of parameter values by users of the report.

Controlling Report Output with Parameters

Two types of parameters exist in Report Builder. They are user parameters and system parameters. Recall early in the unit the discussion of parameters available for use with Report Builder running from the command line. These parameters are system-defined, and may be used to alter aspects of the report runtime behavior. The system parameters include DESFORMAT, DESNAME, and DESTYPE, used to identify the report destination device format, name, and type, respectively. Other system parameters include ORIENTATION, MODE, PRINTJOB, BACKGROUND, and COPIES, which determine various aspects of the report output, such as portrait or landscape print orientation, character or bitmap runtime mode, number of copies printed, and other features. Finally, system parameters include CURRENCY, DECIMAL, and THOUSANDS, which impact the characters Report Builder will use to represent money values, the decimal point (period in the United States, comma in Italy, etc.), and the character used to break up numbers every three digits to the left of the decimal point (such as 567,332,768,976,456,788).

The rest of the parameters are user-defined parameters. That means you can create and use them at will to alter the runtime behavior of your report. You can rename user parameters and even remove them from the report. System parameters, on the other hand, cannot be renamed or removed from the report. Reasons for incorporating user parameters into your report include wanting the ability to pass values into the report to affect its output. For example, say you are developing a master/detail report on the top 500 account executives in an organization paid expense dollars in a given year. At the master level, you may go against several tables to calculate the total expense dollars by account executive and the locations/companies they visited. In the detail level, perhaps you want to determine the total amount of revenue generated by that account executive's visit to the location mentioned. You may want to create a user parameter that passes the account executive's employee ID, date of visit, and location/companies visited by the account executive within the detail report to allow information to be passed down from the master to the detail.

Values for parameters are defined in two ways. They are either passed in as command line parameters or defined at report run time using a runtime Parameter Form. Later in the section, you will cover how this fact influences any value checks you may institute to make sure appropriate values are defined for parameters. You will also cover how to create parameter forms, values for system parameters, and the creation and use of user parameters.

Exercises

1. What is a system parameter, and how is it used in a report? Identify some of the system parameters and their uses.

2. What is a user parameter? How might a user parameter be used in the report?

Creating User Parameters in a Report

·Usually, your report won't contain any user parameters until you create some for the report. You create user parameters in the following way. First, you must drill down to the appropriate level in your report to create the user parameter. This is found in the Object Navigator module for the report using the Report | *Rpt_Name* | Data Model | User Parameters node. Once there, notice that there are no user parameters already defined. To create a new one, double-click on the User Parameters node in Object Navigator. Alternately, you can click on the Create button in the Tool Palette of the Object Navigator module along the left margin. Either of these actions causes a new item to appear as a node in the Object Navigator under User Parameters and also opens the Property Palette for you to use in defining properties on the new user parameter. The following properties can be found in the Property Palette and must be defined in support of your user parameter.

NAME   The name for your user parameter. Initially, this will be a value generated by Report Builder, but unlike system parameter names, you can invent a name for your user parameter yourself and make the change directly to the property.

COMMENTS   This one is self-explanatory. You click on the cell next to the property in the Property Palette to display the Definition button, which will appear with an ellipses displayed on it. You then click the Definition button to invoke a special interface into which you enter your comment. When finished, you click OK and the comment gets saved into the report. You can display the comment later using the Definition button again.

DATATYPE   This property defines the datatype accepted by your user parameter. Three datatypes are possible for this parameter, including CHARACTER, DATE, and NUMBER. All the following properties are relevant to all the datatypes you can choose to assign for your user parameter, except for Input Mask, for which none of these three possible datatypes requires a value. If left blank, Input Mask simply takes the old standby 'DD-MON-YY' for dates, though NLS settings may change this, and –9999 for numbers.

WIDTH   You must define a width for your different properties. The default is usually 20, but you can specify any value you like between 1 and 65535. This value specifies how wide the value accepted for the parameter will be allowed to be.

INPUT MASK   For numbers and dates, your parameter may have a special format that you want to impose on the input to make it usable, readable, or understandable. This is known as an Input Mask. Report Builder is smart enough to offer a set of masks specific to the DATE or NUMBER datatype. Some examples of date format masks use well-known terminology for date references, where YYYY represents a four-digit year, HH24 represents hours on the 24-hour clock, MM represents a two-digit month, and so on. Some examples of numeric format masks also use well-known terminology for numeric references, such as that used for money formatting, scientific notation, and other formats.

INITIAL VALUE   This is the initial or built-in value for the parameter. It can be modified using methods covered in the next lesson. The value set for the parameter in this property must correspond with the datatype you identified in that property as well.

VALIDATION TRIGGER   This is a function developed in PL/SQL that fires when Report Builder processes runtime parameter settings and again when the Parameter Form is processed. This function returns TRUE or FALSE, and has the ability to modify the value for the parameter as a bind variable.

LIST OF VALUES   This is a special object in the report that allows you to define a set or list of acceptable values to be used with your parameter (this is also abbreviated as LOV). For example, if you wanted to define a parameter that accepted a color of the rainbow as input, you might define a List of Values to go along with it that makes the only acceptable values for the parameter red, orange, yellow, green, blue, indigo, or violet. More about creating a List of Values appears in the following lesson.

Exercises

1. How is a user parameter created in the report? What are the datatypes that can be defined for a parameter?

2. What properties are definable for a user parameter? Which property is used only if the datatype acceptable for the parameter value is NUMBER or DATE?

3. What is a format mask? What are some format masks used for DATE values? What about for NUMBER values?

Creating Lists of Values for Parameter Input

As mentioned at the very end of the previous lesson, a List of Values, or LOV, is used as a validation mechanism for values defined in user parameters. To define a List of Values, you must first click on the List of Values property in the Property Palette to show the Definition button. If you then click on the Definition button, you will see an interface that facilitates the creation of the LOV. Your ability to create an LOV then depends on your ability to use the Parameter List of Values interface, which is shown in Figure 27-1. You create your LOV in one of the following two ways: either by specifying a static set of values or by **select**ing the List of Values from the database. Each method is covered in turn, over the course of this lesson.

There are several features in the interface to understand. The middle left-hand corner of the parameter List of Values interface has a pair of radio buttons, one called Static Values, the other called SELECT statement. When

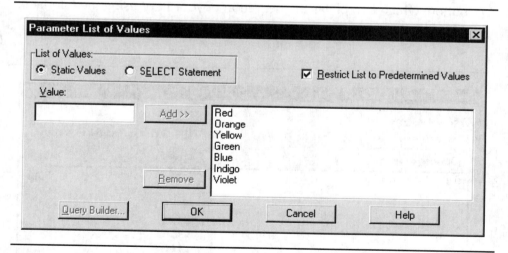

FIGURE 27-1.   *Parameter List of Values interface, Static Values display*

the Static Values button is clicked, the rest of the interface shows a text window where you key in a value for the static value list, along with two buttons used to add and remove elements from the set of static values appearing in the large text box on the right side of the interface. At the top-right side of the interface is a check box, next to which is the phrase Restrict List to Predetermined Values. The meaning of this check box is that, when checked, the value defined for the parameter must be part of the LOV you display. This interface is redrawn when you click the SELECT Statement button, as shown in Figure 27-2.

When the radio button is set to SELECT statement, the interface is drawn such that the predominant object is the text box showing the SQL query statement. A second check box appears in the right-hand side of the interface, next to which is the phrase Hide First Column. The meaning of this check box is that you can optionally hide the values in the leading column returned by your **select** statement defined in the text box in the interface. The final two items in the interface you should focus on are the Query Builder button, which allows you to use that utility as explained early in the unit to define your **select** statement for the LOV. The last item is the OK button, which completes the definition of your LOV using the interface.

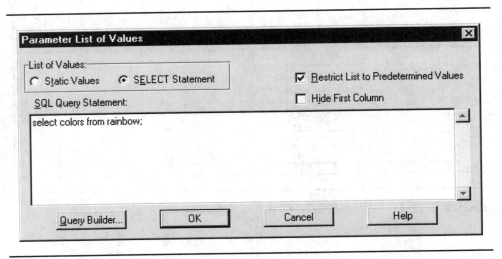

FIGURE 27-2. *Parameter List of Values interface, SELECT statement display*

Specifying a Static Set of Values in Your LOV

Your specification of a static set of values in your LOV happens in this way. First, ensure that the radio button in the upper left-hand side of the interface is set as shown in Figure 27-1 so that you can enter static values. If the interface is set to accept a **select** statement for developing your LOV, as shown in Figure 27-2, you will not be able to define a static LOV. Once this measure is taken, you are then free to enter static values in the smaller text box on the left side. Once entered, you move the new static value to the large text box on the right side by use of the Add button. If there are items in the static list you want to eliminate, you can use the Remove button to do so as well. When finished defining your static LOV, click OK.

SELECTing the Values in Your LOV from the Database

Alternately, your specification of a dynamic set of values for your LOV happens in this way. First, ensure this time that the radio button in the upper left-hand side of the interface is set as shown in Figure 27-2 so that you can enter a **select** statement or use Query Builder to develop the query. If the interface is set to accept static values for developing your LOV, as shown in Figure 27-1, you will not be able to code a **select** and the Query Builder button will be grayed out. After handling this task, you define your **select** statement to select the LOV from a table in the same way you would specify any other **select** statement in the database. Alternately, you can develop the query with Query Builder, which has already been covered earlier in this unit in relation to Report Wizard. Once complete, click the OK button.

TIP
To ensure that no other value than one in your LOV is accepted for a parameter, check the box marked Restrict List to Predetermined Values.

Exercises

1. What is an LOV? What are the two methods used to define LOVs?

2. What does it mean to hide the first column when defining an LOV? What does it mean to restrict the list to predetermined values for on LOV?

3. What property does defining an LOV correspond to in the Property Palette opened for parameters? To what parameters does defining an LOV correspond?

Incorporating User Parameters into Queries

Now that you understand how to give users the ability to specify their own parameters for a query, you need to provide a way for the report to incorporate the user parameter into how the report obtains its information. This step is accomplished through the use of lexical and bind references. Your use of user parameters in your reports depends on your ability to successfully manage the use of both these items.

Using Bind References

Values specified as your user parameter can be incorporated into SQL statements in your report data definition through the use of bind references. Bind references replace a single value in SQL or PL/SQL, such as a DATE, VARCHAR2, or NUMBER. The clauses in which bind references are used include **select**, **where**, **group by**, **order by**, **having**, **connect by**, or **start with**. You may not include a bind reference in the **from** clause or instead of some Oracle SQL reserved word, and no bind reference may ever be the same name as an Oracle reserved word. Note also that you cannot use a bind variable in an **order by** clause without also using the **decode( )** function. A bind reference is created by placing a colon (**:**) immediately before the column or parameter name. If you do not create a column or parameter before making a bind reference to it in a **select** statement, Report Builder will create a parameter for you by default. The following code blocks show some sample SQL statements containing bind variables:

```
SELECT nvl(DEPTID, :DFLTDEPT) DEPARTMENT, SUM(SALARY) TOTAL_HRCOST
FROM empl;

SELECT EMPID, SUM(REIMB_TOTAL) TOTAL_EXPENSES
FROM emp_exp_tbl
GROUP BY EMPID
HAVING SUM(REIMB_TOTAL) > :MINTOTAL;
```

Using Lexical References

Alternately, you can incorporate user parameter values through lexical references. Lexical references are placeholders for text that you include in **select** statements. You can use lexical references everywhere you can use bind references, and with one area you cannot use bind references: in a **from** clause! However, you cannot use lexical references in PL/SQL—but you can use a bind reference in PL/SQL to set a parameter value and then refer to that parameter value lexically in SQL. A lexical reference is created by placing an ampersand (**&**) in front of a column or parameter name.

Unlike bind references, a default definition is not provided for lexical references. Therefore, you must do one of the following. In the first case, you must define a column or parameter in the Data Model for each lexical reference in the query before you create your query. For columns, you must specify a value for the Value if NULL property, and for parameters you must enter a value for the Initial Value property. Report Builder then uses these values to validate a query with a lexical reference. Or, you must create your query containing lexical references. For example, you can define the following SQL query:

```
select &p_kgroo KGROO, &p_kgroo_joey OFFSPRING from JOEYS;
```

The lexical references *&p_kgroo* and *&p_kgroo_joey* can be used to change the columns selected at run time, such as through a runtime Parameter Form. If you do it this way, be sure to use column aliases; if you don't, if you change the columns selected at run time, the column names in the **select** list will not match the Report Builder columns and the report will not run. Lexical references give you many other options for dynamically altering your SQL **from** and **where** clauses, as in the following code block:

```
SELECT ITEM, VALUE FROM &MY_TABLE;
SELECT ITEM, VALUE FROM ITEMS WHERE &MY_CLAUSE
```

You can use MY_TABLE to change the table used in the query at run time, which can be helpful in developing generic reports that will be used in several different applications, client sites, or departments. For example, you could enter KGROO_JOEYS, EMPLOYEES, or just about any other table where there is a logical concept of an "item" and a "value." In some cases, you may also want to use lexical references for the **select** statement to grab the actual names of columns in the tables if there are differences.

TIP
It is important that you understand both the use of lexical and bind references in incorporating user parameters into your reports before taking OCP Exam 5.

Exercises

1. What is a bind reference? How are values specified for user parameters incorporated into reports with the use of bind references?

2. What is a lexical reference? How are values specified for user parameters incorporated into reports with the use of lexical references?

Using and Modifying System Parameters

Unlike user parameters—which you have just learned how to build from scratch, and which are fully modifiable by you, the report developer—system parameters are created by and built into Report Builder. You cannot arbitrarily remove one. You define values for system parameters in reports in the following way. Using the Object Navigator module, drill down into the Reports | *Rpt_Name* | Data Model | System Parameters node. You will notice all the system parameters mentioned above are listed, each with a small circular icon used for displaying the PL/SQL Editor module for developing PL/SQL functions to validate the value defined on the parameter. Next to that is the Properties icon, on which you can double-click in order to view the properties associated with the system parameter. The next step in the definition of a value for the system parameter is to double-click on the Properties icon and open the Property Palette for the parameter. You then can modify the value for the COMMENT, INITIAL VALUE, or VALIDATION TRIGGER properties in the Property Palette, but not the NAME, DATATYPE, or WIDTH properties.

Some notes about the properties you can modify now follow. The COMMENT property is self-explanatory. The INITIAL VALUE property is used to handle defining the value that will be used for the parameter when the report is run. The VALIDATION TRIGGER property allows you to define a PL/SQL function that validates the value against standards you define in the function. This trigger returns TRUE or FALSE based on whether or not the value was valid according to your criteria. The trigger has the ability to change the value for the parameter through the reference of the parameter as though it were a bind variable. If the validation fails, control is returned to the user within the runtime Parameter Form, where you must redefine the value for the parameter or cancel execution. Note the following restrictions on validation triggers. They must usually be small—around 32K or less. You shouldn't issue DDL statements against the database, like **create table** in a validation trigger. Finally, because of the way connection to the database is handled when a report's execution is triggered within another report, you should **commit** all outstanding changes in the parent report before kicking off the child.

TIP
Validation triggers usually fire twice during the execution of a report: once to validate the value passed for the parameter at the command line and then again in support of validating the parameter form.

Exercises

1. How are values for system parameters defined and modified?

2. What are the three properties about system parameters that can be changed by you in the Property Palette?

3. When executing detail reports from within a parent report, why is it important to **commit** changes in the parent before executing the child (HINT: Use Report Builder online help)?

Building Parameter Form Layouts for Data Entry

One of the features Report Builder extends to the developer is its ability to permit entry of parameter values by users when the report begins processing. The development of an interface to help the user with accomplishing the task of defining values for runtime parameters is greatly facilitated within Report Builder with the use of the Parameter Form Builder tool. After building all your user parameters along with their associated LOVs and determining which of the system parameters you want your report users to have access to, you can then assemble a Parameter Form for the user to enter parameters easily.

The Parameter Form is used in the following way. First, with your report open in Report Builder, click on the Tools | Parameter Form Builder menu bar option. This selection causes the Parameter Form Builder interface to be displayed. Figure 27-3 shows you the Parameter Form Builder. The other way to open the Parameter Form Builder is to move to the Parameter Form view of your report in the Report Editor, and click on the Parameter Form Builder button available in that interface, which appears second to last on the right side of the top row of buttons in the interface, with a pen and window displayed on it. Within that interface, you will see several items listed, including text boxes for you to use when defining a title, hint line, and status line. The text you define for a title will appear centered at the top of the runtime Parameter Form seen by your users when the report runs. The text you define for the hint and status lines will appear centered in the runtime Parameter Form just below the title. Below these two text boxes is a list of all system and user parameters that have been defined for this report.

You are free to include whichever parameters you want from this list by simply clicking once on the name of the parameter in the list to highlight that parameter. Also, you can change the label that will appear in the runtime Parameter Form next to the text box where users enter the value they want for the parameter by entering something into the text box next to the name of the parameter in the Parameter Form Builder interface. When you are finished defining your Parameter Form using the Parameter Form Builder interface, click on OK. You can then see the Parameter Form you defined for the report using the Report Editor interface if you click on the Parameter Form button next to the Layout Model button in the top left-hand side of the Report Editor interface. The Parameter Form view available for your report in Report Editor is shown in Figure 27-4.

Once you have created your Parameter Form for the report, you can then see how the Parameter Form behaves in action by running the report. Several ways exist for doing this step. The first is to click on the Program |

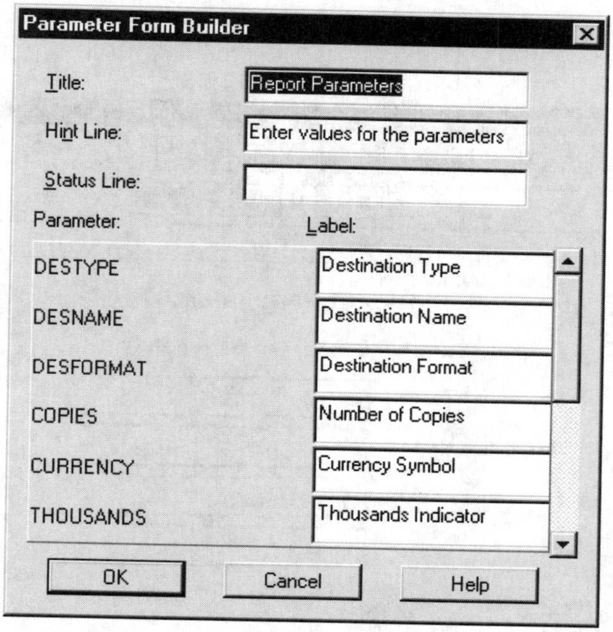

FIGURE 27-3.   *Parameter Form Builder interface*

Run Report menu item in the Report Builder interface. The second is to click on the Run button in the top middle of the Report Editor interface, which is the button displaying the Traffic Light icon in the display. You can click on View | Runtime Preview or View | Live Previewer from the menu bar to see a runtime or live preview of the report. Alternately, you can click on the Live Previewer button from within Report Editor to get to the Live Previewer view. After employing any of these methods to start running the report, the first screen you will see is the runtime Parameter Form. On it, you can enter values for any of the parameters displayed. When you are finished, click the Run button appearing in the runtime Parameter Form interface and your

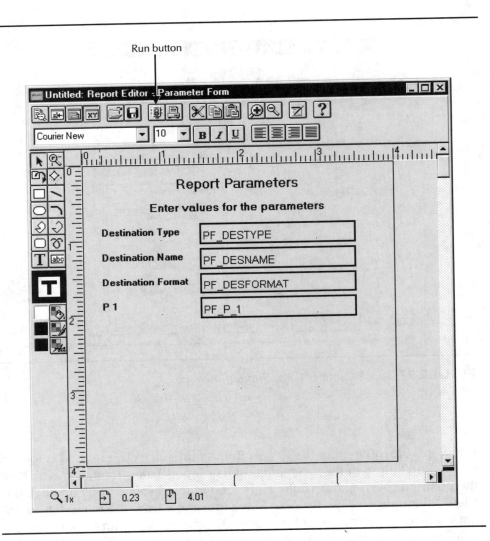

FIGURE 27-4. *Parameter Form view in Report Editor*

report will execute with the values you specified for the parameters in the Parameter Form. Figure 27-5 shows the runtime Parameter Form.

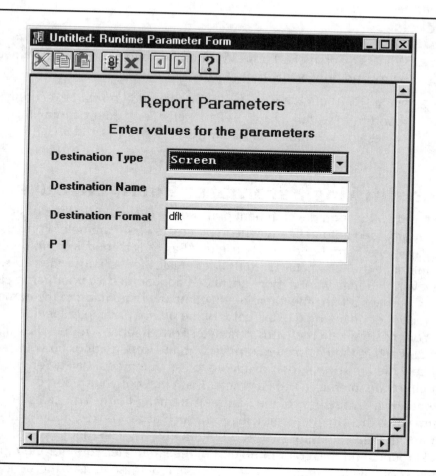

FIGURE 27-5. *The runtime Parameter Form in action*

TIP
To terminate the execution of a report from the runtime Parameter Form, simply click on the Cancel Run button shown in the runtime Parameter Form with a red "X".

Exercises

1. What is a Parameter Form? What tool is used to create a Parameter Form, and how is that tool used?

2. What is a runtime Parameter Form? How do you start executing your report from within a runtime Parameter Form after defining the values you want for your parameters?

Customizing Parameter Form Layouts

For rapid application development purposes, you should find the basic layout provided automatically when you create your Parameter Form using the Parameter Form Builder quite useful. "Basic" is a good word to describe the interface the Parameter Form Builder creates for you. In some cases, however, you may want a more advanced appearance for your Parameter Form, perhaps adding the name of the company in addition to the name of the report, or changing the text color of the title or parameter labels.

Your customization of your Parameter Form happens in the following way. Switch to the Parameter Form view in the Report Editor on your report; notice there are several tools available to use in the Tool Palette on the left margin of the interface. The Parameter Form view of your report is essentially a layout view of the runtime Parameter Form. You can add elements to the runtime Parameter Form such as text boxes, additional parameter fields, lines, or shapes. Additionally, you can modify the fill, background, and line color of objects in the Parameter Form for the report using Tool Palette buttons. The general usage of these tools is the same process as that covered for Tool Palette buttons for the Data Model and Layout Model views in previous chapters. Refer to those areas of the text for a refresher if you need it.

You can modify the settings for existing objects along with adding new ones to your report using the Parameter Form view. Simply click once on the object to activate it and double-click on it to invoke the Property Palette for the object. When active, you can alter background, line, and fill color in the Parameter Form object. Other features you can add to your runtime Parameter Form that allow it to display more parameters, text, or graphics are now described.

Adding Pages and Parameters to the Runtime Parameter Form

Sometimes if your runtime Parameter Form offers users the ability to modify several different parameters for themselves, the runtime Parameter Form tries to prevent itself from becoming cluttered. Report Builder creates the basic runtime Parameter Form with scroll bars built in. If you have seven or eight parameters to display, rather than making you scroll through a screen, the runtime Parameter Form allows you to move through pages of screens to set values for parameters. You can add pages yourself using the Property Palette. Open the Property Palette on the entire report by clicking the icon next to the name of the report in the Object Navigator module, and look for the Number of Pages property under the Parameter Form Window property node. You can alter its value to another number by keying that number in, pressing ENTER, and closing the Property Palette. If you run your report again, you will see the Next Page button that was formerly grayed out is now active and available for use.

Adding enough parameters to the Parameter Form will also cause Report Builder to automatically prompt you that more pages are needed. Return to the Parameter Form Builder interface, as shown in Figure 27-3 by clicking on the Parameter Form Builder button in the Parameter Form view of the report in Report Editor, or choose the Tools | Parameter Form Builder menu item within Report Builder. Then, click on more parameters to highlight and add them to the Parameter Form. If too many to display on one page are added to the Parameter Form, Report Builder will prompt you asking if it is all right to increase the number of pages so that your parameters can be displayed cleanly.

TIP
The Parameter Form can be hidden if the parameter values will remain constant. This is accomplished using the Parameter Form check box in Tools | Preferences, Runtime Settings tab.

Exercises

1. How are new parameters added to the Parameter Form? What are the tools that are available in the Parameter Form?

2. How are new pages added to the parameter form? Why might it be beneficial to do so?

Embedding Charts in Reports

In this section, you will cover the following points on embedding charts in reports:

- Creating graphics charts with Chart Wizard
- Displaying existing graphics charts in reports
- Using parameters for dynamic modification of chart data

Most people hate reports that just display statistics. Numbers, lists, tables, and all that are frankly boring, the stuff of endless meetings where your colleagues fall asleep and start drooling on themselves, or worse. To combat "meeting fatigue," people in business love charts—the more colorful the chart, the better. In the quest to give meaning to information, you will find yourself scoring points with everyone on the business side in your next meeting if you master the art of spicing your reports up with charts. Report Builder can help you achieve your goals with an easy-to-use tool that turns boring facts into exciting pictures. That tool is Chart Wizard, and in this section you will learn how to use it.

Creating Graphics Charts with Chart Wizard

The use of Chart Wizard is really easy. The data is already in your report—you only need to put that extra spin on it to make it easily understood. Take a simple example—a quarterly sales report from a historical perspective. It's nice to list the sales figures in tabular format, with this year's figures on one side and next year's on the other. You may even jazz it up by putting the numbers for this year in black and last year's in blue. But the icing on the cake comes when you turn it all into even a simple column chart with the same color-coding scheme.

Open the Chart Wizard in one of the following ways. You can either choose the Tools | Chart Wizard menu bar item from within Report

Builder—with or without your report being open in Report Editor—or by opening Report Editor for your report, navigating to the Layout Model, and clicking on the Chart Wizard button found near the Report Wizard and Region buttons in that view on your report. You navigate through Chart Wizard in the same way as Report Wizard, using the Next button to move forward and the Back button to return to prior screens.

Defining Chart Title and Type/Subtype

The first screen is used for defining an optional title to the chart, and it is also where you select the basic chart type and subtype. With the exception to the pie chart, each of the following charts display information in two dimensions, which in turn are represented as an axis on the chart. The horizontal (or X) axis is called the "category" axis, because on it you can separate your data shown into the categories they break down into. The vertical (or Y) axis is called the "value" axis, because on it you show the values that each category attains. For example, if you were making a chart to show unit sales by account executive, the category (X) axis would have each account executive's name, and the value (Y) axis would have numbers to represent unit sales. Another example might be to show unit sales over a period of time. In this example, the category (X) would be time, while the value (Y) would be unit sales. The exception to this paradigm is the pie chart, for which the graph represents values as an aggregate, and categories as "slices" making up that aggregate. These reports have no X or Y axes, but instead have an aggregate or "value" broken out across category. This interface used for defining chart title and type/subtype is shown in Figure 27-6, and each type and subtype is described as follows.

COLUMN CHART   This is a chart where vertical bars drawn from the horizontal (or X) axis reach values identified along the vertical (or Y) axis. Subtypes of this chart type allow for variations in the way the bars are drawn. This is often used for comparison of different items using the same criteria, such as sales figures by account executive. An example of a column chart appears in Figure 27-7.

BAR CHART   A bar chart is similar to a column chart, except that the bars are drawn horizontally from the Y axis, reaching values identified in the X axis. Subtypes of this chart type allow for variations in the way the bars

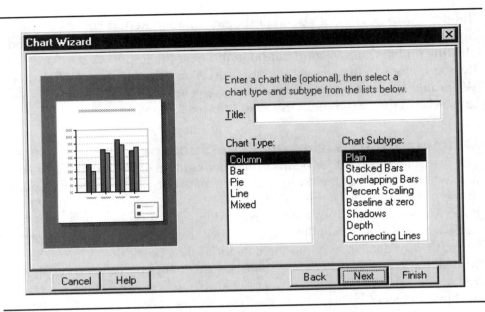

FIGURE 27-6. *Chart Wizard Title and Type/Subtype definition interface*

are drawn. Bar charts are often used for comparison of different items using the same criteria, such as sales figures by account executive. An example of a bar chart appears in Figure 27-7.

PIE CHART This is a circular chart, or "pie," that displays subsections or "slices" in different colors. Subtypes of this chart type allow for variations in the way the pie is drawn. A pie chart is often used to illustrate a market of some kind and the market share different constituents hold. An example of a pie chart appears in Figure 27-7.

LINE CHART This is a chart with an X and a Y axis, where values of one type are identified on the Y axis and values of another type are identified on the X axis. A line is drawn in the chart to show a *vector*, or points where values on X meet values on Y. Subtypes of this chart type allow for variations in the way the lines may be drawn or for the use of symbols to represent lines. A line chart is often used to illustrate trends where Y represents a set of values such as unit sales or money, while X represents time. An example of a line chart appears in Figure 27-7.

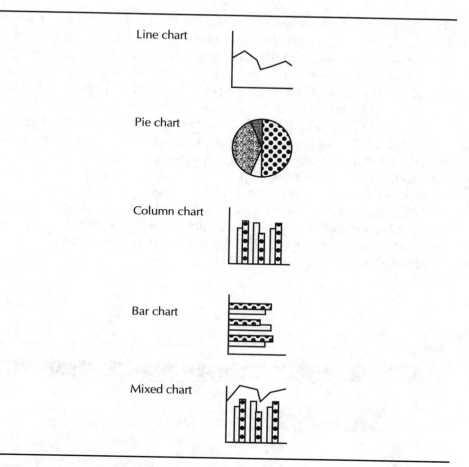

FIGURE 27-7. *Chart type examples*

MIXED CHART A combination of the line and column charts identified above and below. Subtypes for this type identify variations for the way either the lines or the columns are drawn. A mixed chart may be used to show a combination of information, such as sales figures by salesperson, along with overall sales trend. An example of a mixed chart appears in Figure 27-7.

Defining Values for Display on X and Y Axis
The next two screens in the Chart Wizard interface are used to define the values you will display on the X and Y axes of the chart. The interface shows

the columns your report will display, corresponding to the columns defined in your data model. Given the descriptions of common usage for each of the chart types, it shouldn't be difficult for you to decide which columns to use as baseline data for each axis. For example, say you were reporting on overall product sales figures per week for a six-month period. You had a table in your Oracle database called PROD_SALES, with two columns: WK_END_DATE and UNITS_SOLD. In both the interfaces used to define values for display on the X and Y axes, you would see both columns from the table. You can then use the Right Arrow button to move the WK_END_DATE column for display in the category (or X) axis. Click the Next button to move to the next interface, where you define the UNITS_SOLD column whose values will serve as the value (or Y) axis. Figure 27-8 shows the Chart Wizard interface used to identify category information, while Figure 27-9 shows the Chart Wizard interface used to identify value information.

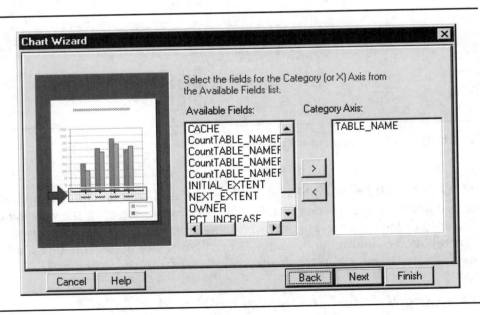

FIGURE 27-8. *Defining category (or X) axis information with Chart Wizard*

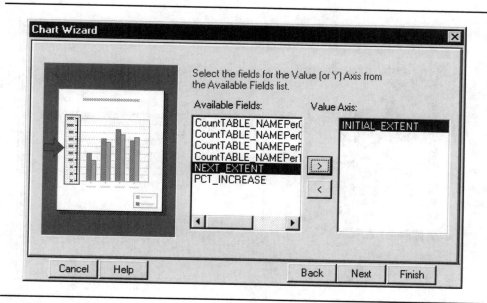

FIGURE 27-9. *Defining value (or Y) axis information with Chart Wizard*

Defining Frequency of Chart Appearance

Your new chart will have little impact on the overall value of the report if it doesn't appear appropriately within the report. Chart Wizard allows you to determine the frequency a chart is drawn into the report you just wrote by selecting the frequency from the list of frequencies in the interface. The interface where you define the frequency of chart appearance is shown in Figure 27-10. The number and names of frequencies you can choose have the following general format:

- **Beginning of report**   This frequency always appears in the list. It allows you to display the report only at the beginning of the report.

- **End of report**   This frequency always appears in the list. It allows you to display the report only at the end of the report.

- **At breakpoints in each group**   If your report is a group report, each group level you defined contains repeating frames in support of breakpoints for each of the groups. You have the option to display a chart at breakpoints for any of the groups defined in your report.

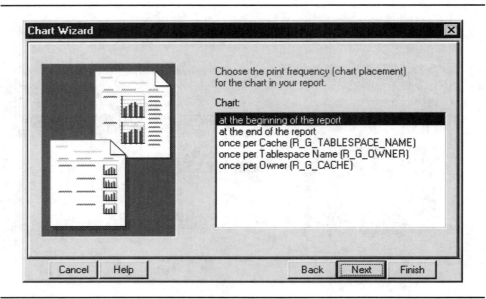

FIGURE 27-10. *Defining frequency of chart appearance in Chart Wizard*

Saving Your Chart

Once your chart definition is complete, you will be prompted within Chart Wizard to save the chart in Oracle Graphics Designer (OGD) format. The final interface of Chart Wizard prebuilds a filename for you to use to save your chart. You can use it automatically by default, or you can define your own filename by clicking on the Save As button in the window. This will cause Chart Wizard to open the Save As interface available for your operating system. Your only option to use for filename extension to use is **.ogd** because that extension indicates the type of file the chart is. Your files will be stored by default in the **bin** directory underneath your Oracle software home directory. When you are finished defining your own filename, click the Save button in that Save As interface and you will be returned to Chart Wizard, where you can click the Finish button to save the file and complete your chart definition.

Exercises

1. What are the five types of charts available in Chart Wizard? What are some situations where you might use each?

2. What is the category axis, and what sorts of information might be displayed on it in your chart? What is the value axis, and how is it used?

3. What chart type does not fit into the axis paradigm, and how does this affect the definition of category and value information for that chart type?

Displaying Existing Graphics Charts in Reports

Chart Wizard isn't the only way for you to include charts in your report, either. You may have designed more complex charts using Graphics Builder, another component in the Developer/2000 toolset. You can include existing charts in your report easily with the use of the Layout Model view in Report Editor. Covered in Chapter 26, the Layout Model offers a Tool Palette containing many buttons that allow you to draw layout objects and other objects that let you interface with objects outside your report. One of those tools is the Chart button, shown in the Tool Palette for the Layout Model view with a small column chart on it.

Recall last chapter that there are general usage guidelines for any of the tools in the Tool Palette in the Layout Model view. Those steps are first to click on the Chart button to activate the tool, then move the pointer over to your report layout and draw the chart object in the layout. After the chart object is present in the Layout Model of your report, you can double-click on that object to assign its properties. The key properties you need to define for displaying existing charts in your reports are now described.

Defining Chart Filenames

Obviously, the key element to define for your chart is the name of the file containing its definition. The Chart Filename property in the Property Palette for a chart object handles the definition of the chart filename. When you click on this property, a space appears where you can define the filename for the chart, along with a button that opens the Open File dialog interface. Key in the name of your file, or simply click the button, and then find the chart file with extension **.ogd**. When you have located your file, either in the default **bin** directory under the Oracle software home directory on your machine or elsewhere, click the Open button and you will return to the Property Palette where your filename and path appear together as the defined value for the Chart Filename property.

Defining Parameters and Columns

Since your chart may have been designed a bit more generically than the chart you would write with Chart Wizard, you must create a data source for your chart to use when drawing itself. The definition of chart parameters and columns identifies several key elements about the data source for the chart placed in your report. The properties are defined through a special interface. To invoke that interface, click on the Parameters and Columns property in your report to make the button used for invoking the interface appear in the Property Palette. Then, click on that button and the interface for defining report-to-chart column and parameter mappings will appear in the Report Builder interface. The next lesson focuses on how to use this mapping from report columns and parameters to chart columns and parameters in order to make dynamic modifications to report data.

Exercises

1. What tool and view is used to incorporate existing charts into your report? What is the property for that object that helps you to identify the chart file?

2. What property exists allowing you to map report columns and parameters to chart columns and parameters? What purpose might this serve within your report?

Using Parameters for Dynamic Modification of Chart Data

The final points made in the last lesson should indicate a few things about the use of parameters for dynamic modification of chart data. Since your chart made in Graphics Builder may be used across many reports and/or Oracle Forms applications, you will want to set it up so that the chart can accomplish these tasks easily. The best way to do this is to pass the column and/or parameter values you want the chart to use. The Parameters and Columns properties—both available in the Property Palette for chart objects in the Layout Model view of your report— together are the methods by which you can dynamically modify chart data. When you click on this property, a button appears that you can click to invoke the Chart dialog interface, where you define how chart parameters and columns match up to report columns and parameters. The next two lessons identify the methods used for both tasks.

Defining the Parameter Tab of the Chart Dialog Interface

Figure 27-11 demonstrates the Chart dialog interface used to define parameters and column matchups between chart and report. Notice there are two tabs in the dialog interface in Figure 27-11, one for defining column matchups and one for defining parameter matchups. The contents of the Parameters tab are shown in Figure 27-11. Consider the Parameters tab first. To view the contents of the Parameters tab for this interface, click on that tab in the Chart dialog interface. This interface contains two lists. The list on the left contains all report system or user parameter names, along with the names of all columns displayed in the report. Any of these report columns or parameters can function as inputs for chart parameters. On the right of the display, there is a series of text boxes. You are expected to code in the names of your chart parameters to which these report parameters will correspond.

For example, you may be writing the report that shows the weekly unit sales figures over the last six months that was described earlier in the

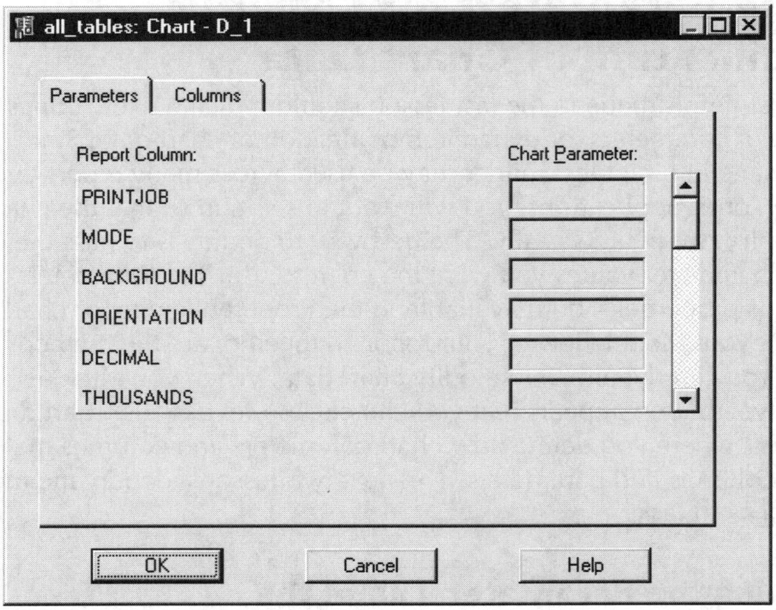

FIGURE 27-11. *Parameters tab of Chart dialog interface*

section. However, as a longtime developer of reports, you also know that there are many cases where your colleagues will want to see a line chart that displays trends over time. To speed report development, you create a generic chart that accepts a value called *chrtval* and a category called *chrtcat*. In your use of this chart on the weekly unit sales over six months report, you want to pass the product ID the user wants to see unit sales for and the end date for the six-month period, which are user-defined parameters in your report you have called PROD_PARM and END_DTTM, respectively.

You will find those two report parameters listed on the left side of the Chart dialog interface. You will first click on the name of the report parameter as you did in the interface used for defining runtime Parameter Forms described in the first section of this chapter. Then, you will enter the name of the chart parameter used to feed information from the report into the chart in the text box on the right of the line where the report parameter is listed. One final note is that defining a value in this text box is optional. If you do not specify the name of the chart parameter in the box across from the report parameter you highlight in this tab, then the Chart dialog box will assume the report and chart parameters have the same name.

TIP
A chart parameter can be fed by one and only one report parameter. However, the same report parameter can feed many different chart parameters.

Defining the Columns Tab of Chart Dialog Interface

Figure 27-12 displays the contents of the Columns tab in the Chart dialog interface. There are a few significant differences between the Columns tab and the Parameters tab. First, at the top of the Columns tab in the Chart dialog interface, there is a text box where you can define a chart query name. This feature allows you to have your chart **select** data for display in the chart out of the data in the report rather than from the database. If you have done a great deal of data filtering in the report and want to ensure your chart contains report data only, you can specify a query from the chart that should use the data extracted by Report Builder instead of data in the database. Defining a query name is optional, and should be done only when you want the chart query to use Report Builder to filter information rather than using information directly from the database.

The next significant difference between the Columns tab and Parameters tab is the presence of a report group definition item. The definition for this item consists of a drop-down box where all the report groups are listed. If you enter a value for the chart query item on the Columns tab, you must choose a report group for which the chart will summarize its data contents. Otherwise, the definition of a report group is meaningless and will be changed to NULL when you have finished defining the properties for your chart.

Identifying a report group and chart query puts a constraint on your definition of report parameters and columns appearing in the remainder of this window. If you define a chart query and associated report group, then all the columns you select from the list of columns must either be a member of the report group you defined or a member of a hierarchical group to that group in the report hierarchy. In addition, the qualifications you have in

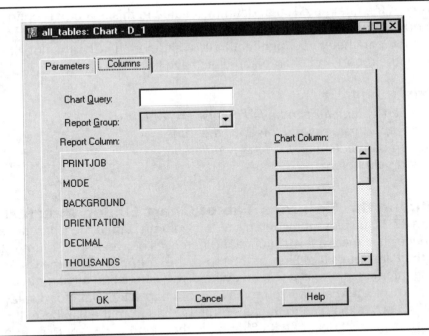

FIGURE 27-12. *Columns tab of Chart dialog interface*

defining report parameters and corresponding chart parameters for the Parameters tab also apply to those columns listed in the Columns tab.

Exercises

1. How are values defined for dynamic modification of chart data? What are the two types of values that are defined in that interface?

2. What purpose does defining a chart query serve? What about defining a report group? What is assumed about chart columns or parameters if you do not name the chart column or parameter in the text box provided to be associated with the report parameter or column?

Developing and Enhancing Matrix Reports

In this section, you will cover the following points on developing and enhancing matrix reports:

- Designing a matrix Data Model
- Designing a matrix Layout Model
- Displaying zeros in cells with no value

You have covered a tremendous amount of information about the design of reports from the data and layout perspective. You have also covered methods by which you can define parameters and use the Parameter Form built-in feature to allow your users to control the execution of their own reports with parameters. You have even added the creation of niceties such as charts and the process by which you add them to your report. So far, you have covered these items in association with simple to moderately complicated reports such as tabular and group reports. In this section, you will learn more about the most complex set of reports you can create in Report Builder: matrix reports. Creation of matrix reports from the Data Model and Layout Model perspective will be covered, along with simple replacement of zeros for NULL values in empty cells.

Designing a Matrix Data Model

Recall from early in the unit the definition of a matrix report. To refresh the discussion, a matrix report is one with at least four groups, where two of the groups contain data that will become the horizontal and vertical axes of report. A third group represents the cross-product of the elements in the groups on the horizontal and vertical axes of the report. The creation of the Data Model for a matrix report starts in the same way as it would for other reports. In this example, you will create a matrix report of information from the UNIT_SALES table, where four account executives keep track of their unit sales by product and week. The columns in this table include UNITS_SOLD, UNIT_NAME, ACCT_EXEC, and WK_END_DT. The matrix report you will design displays unit sales by account executive by product for the month of January. The rest of the lesson covers the four steps for creating a matrix Data Model.

Step 1: Creating the New Report in Object Navigator

The way you design the matrix Data Model is as follows. You create or start a new report using the Object Navigator. Click on the Reports node and then on the Create button on the Tool Palette in the left margin of the Object Navigator, or simply double-click on the Reports node. Report Builder will then prompt you to decide whether to build the report using Report Wizard or whether you will build your report manually. Although you can build a matrix report using the Report Wizard, the point of this exercise is to master the task of designing your own matrix report using the Data Model view in Report Editor, so select to build your report manually and then click OK. Your new report called *Untitled* will now appear in the Object Navigator module.

Step 2: Creating Your Data Definition

Report Builder then opens the Report Editor module and places you in the Data Model view on your new report. From there, you will need to perform the data definition for your report. For your purposes here, you will simply select all the data from the UNIT_SALES for the month of January. Follow the general usage guidelines for tools in the Tool Palette for creating the data definition. Click on the SQL Query button in the Tool Palette of the Data Model view of the report, then move your pointer to the open canvas of your report and draw a small block in that open canvas by clicking and holding while in the open canvas until a box outline appears. Then, release the button, and the SQL Query Statement dialog interface appears. You can either code the SQL query directly into the text box provided or import a SQL statement from flat file using the appropriate button, or even use Query Builder to build your SQL statement using the appropriate button. When finished, Report Builder will verify the validity of the SQL statement against the Oracle database. If you have not done so already, you will need to connect to the database so this verification can happen. The following code block displays the SQL query used in the example:

```
SELECT unit_name, acct_exec, wk_end_dt, units_sold
FROM unit_sales WHERE wk_end_dt in
('02-JAN-99','09-JAN-99','16-JAN-99','23-JAN-99','30-JAN-99');
```

Step 3: Drawing Your Additional Groups

Once finished, your newly defined query will display in the Data Model view as one group. This is the Data Model view of a query feeding into a simple tabular report. The key action in the Data Model view for this step is to create two additional groups where the cross-product will comprise the content of the report. In this case, the two groups are account executives listed in the ACCT_EXEC column of UNIT_SALES, and products listed in the UNIT_NAME column of UNIT_SALES. There are four account executives—SUE, SAMEER, DON, and TOVA—and four products sold—printers, TVs, VCRs, and stereos.

First, make enough room between the query object and the main group to draw in your matrix groups. To do so, click and hold on the header bar for the group in the Data Model view and move the entire group down to the bottom of the visible open canvas. This action stretches the line from the query object to the group object. Then, extract the account executive column from the main group in the Data Model view by clicking and holding on the ACCT_EXEC column in the main group, then dragging that column to a point toward the left between the query object and the main group on the open canvas, and then releasing the mouse button. Be sure that the column does not get placed into another group or into the query object, but rather is allowed to create its own group when you release the mouse button.

Notice now that the line from the query object no longer extends to the main group, but instead goes into the group containing the ACCT_EXEC column. You have already learned that this effectively creates a data hierarchy in your report. Extend that hierarchy to include a second group of product names by clicking and holding on the UNIT_NAME column in the main group of the query, then drag that group to a point between the query object and the main group, and to the right of the group you just created containing the ACCT_EXEC column. Now, the line that extended from the group containing the ACCT_EXEC column to the main group in the query should extend to the new group containing the UNIT_NAME column, while a new line from that new group will extend to the main group in the Data Model. Figure 27-13 shows how the new groups containing information for which you will generate a cross-product for the matrix report should appear in the Data Model view of Report Editor.

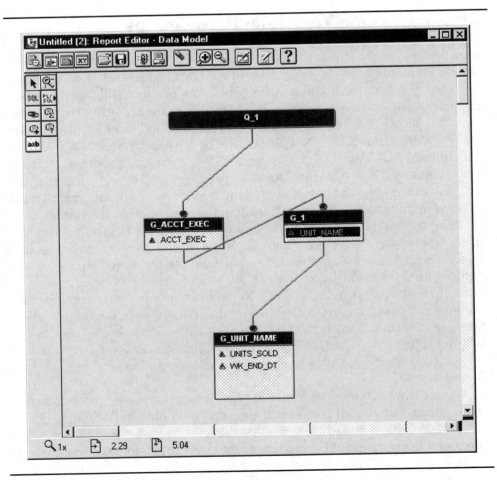

FIGURE 27-13. *Report Editor Data Model view with two groups drawn*

Step 4: Drawing the Cross-Product Group

The final step in creating the matrix Data Model is to draw the fourth group that will become the cross-product of information from the second and third group you created in the Data Model view of your report. This step is done with the use of the Cross-Product tool button in the Tool Palette. Click on that tool button to activate the tool and then move your pointer to a spot above and to the left of the second group you created. Then, click and hold on the mouse button and draw a box that encompasses the second and third group in the Data Model view of your report query. When you have completely enclosed both groups within your box, release the mouse button and Report Builder will draw your fourth group: the cross-product of data from your second and third groups. Figure 27-14 shows the full matrix Data Model as appropriately drawn.

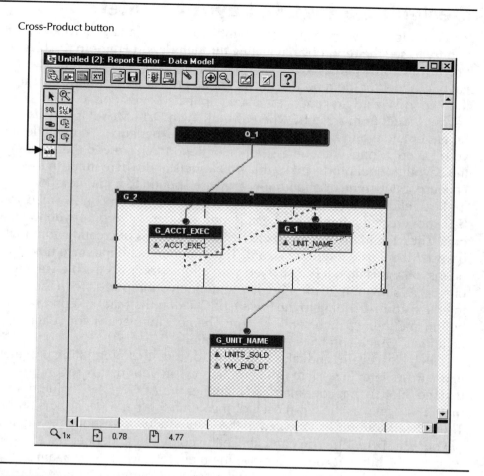

FIGURE 27-14. *Matrix Data Model for unit sales by account executive by product report*

Exercises

1. How many groups must be part of a matrix data definition? What is a cross-product group and what does it contain?

2. Describe briefly each of the steps used to build a Data Model for your matrix report.

Designing a Matrix Layout Model

You can't look at your matrix report until you design a Layout Model for it. If you try to see the report by navigating through Report Editor to the Live Previewer, you will receive an error saying that you must first create a Layout Model for the report. You can create one either manually or using the Report Wizard. In general, it is a complicated operation to build a Layout Model from scratch. Whereas building a Data Model is usually a bit easier and worth building manually for the experience. You will design your Layout Model with the assistance of Report Wizard and then review the Layout Model produced so that you understand where items in the Layout Model come from and how they are applied to a matrix report.

First, click on the Live Previewer button in the Report Editor. Since you have not created a layout for it yet, Report Builder will prompt you to create one. Click Yes in the dialog box to begin the process of creating your matrix Layout Model using Report Wizard. The Report Wizard interface now opens, only this time it is displayed with all interfaces accessible via a row of tabs, as shown in Figure 27-15. You define your report style in the interface corresponding to the Style tab. Click on the Matrix Report radio button and then click the Next button. The next interface is your data definition, which you have already identified.

Click Next again, and take a moment to study the information provided in the Rows interface. Here is where the rows in your matrix report are defined. Notice that your interface identifies the ACCT_EXEC column in the matrix row field as the top-most group column for that aspect of the report. Thus, the first group you created in the Data Model corresponds to the rows of your matrix report. You can change the column that defines the rows of your matrix, but you cannot remove them entirely. Click Next again and you can also study the information provided for the Columns interface. This is where the columns in your matrix report are defined. For your report, the

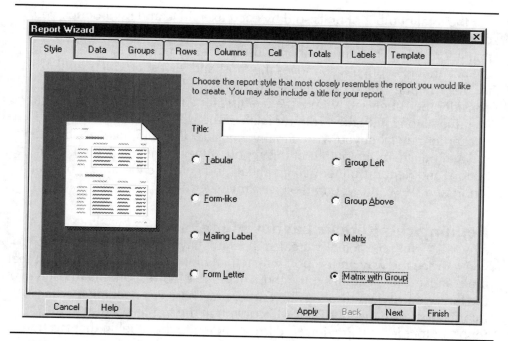

FIGURE 27-15. *Report Wizard interface with tabs shown*

columns will display the UNIT_NAME column. Finally, click Next again and you will be able to see the information defined for the Cell interface. This interface may not have anything defined for it yet, but it must have something defined for it in order for your matrix report to work right. You will want to show the information from the UNITS_SOLD column in the cells of your report, but since the data definition for the report retrieves this information for every week in January, you will want to calculate the sum of values for UNITS_SOLD for each account executive by product. To do so, click on the UNITS_SOLD column in the Available Fields text box and then click on the Sum button to display the sum of items from the UNITS_SOLD column for all weeks by account executive by product.

For the sake of simplicity, you should not consider the Totals tab, although when you see the output of your matrix report, it should be obvious the value displaying totals provides. For example, if you wanted to see the total number of units sold by each executive and by product, you could add a total for both the rows and the columns that would give you that information. This information is useful for such things as determining the account executive who moves the most and fewest products, and also for determining which products sell the most and fewest units. Next, consider the Labels tab, where the heading for each row and column are identified along with the width for each of the cells. You can change the header for any label you wish. Finally, consider the Template tab, but don't use a template for the output of this report. When done, click the Finish button, and Report Builder will go ahead and generate the output of your report and show it to you in the Live Previewer.

Refining the Report Layout Model

Now that you have actually created a default Layout Model for the report, you can see the way your report will actually look on paper. Notice first that there are several headings throughout the report, corresponding to each of the three sets of data displayed in the report. There is a heading for the information from the UNIT_NAME column in the top-left corner of the report output in Live Previewer, corresponding to the label in that tab from the Report Wizard. Another label appears below it for the information displayed from ACCT_EXEC. Still another label appears below each of the distinct values from the UNIT_NAME column, corresponding to the sum of values in the UNITS_SOLD column. Thus, it is easy for you to tell that there are three sets of data displayed in a matrix report: all the distinct values for ACCT_EXEC and UNIT_NAME, and the sum of units sold for all the weeks in January. You know this because you understand the table underlying the report and the information it stores. However, the person reading your report may not. Thus, you should modify the column and row headers to emphasize the account executives and product names, but minimize the fact that information about unit sales figures is broken out by week.

Return to the Layout Model view of your report, displayed in Figure 27-16. Since you want to eliminate the Sum Units Sold label from the report, the easiest way to do it is to find that label in the Layout Model, click on it to activate it, and then press the Delete key. You can instead display the returned values from the UNIT_NAME column directly over the UNITS_SOLD sum information by clicking on the F_UNIT_NAME field once to activate it and then dragging it down into the frame once filled with the Sum Units Sold label. Notice also at the top and left of this layout that there are repeating frames across and down, respectively. These frames are what drive the format of the matrix report. Finally, to get rid of the Acct Exec label appearing over the F_ACCT_EXEC field in the Layout Model, click once to activate it and then press the DELETE key.

Take another look at the report from within the Live Previewer again. Notice that this time the appearance of the data looks a bit less cluttered. The product names appear directly over their unit sales figures, and the names of account executives appear directly to the left for each row of sales figures. The only problem now lies with providing this report with a distinctive title so that the reader understands what he or she is looking at. Move to the margin region of this report now within the Layout Model view and click on the Text button to use that tool to assign the report a title. Follow the appropriate steps to draw the text box and then enter the title, **Sales Figures by Account Executive by Product, January**. Figure 27-17

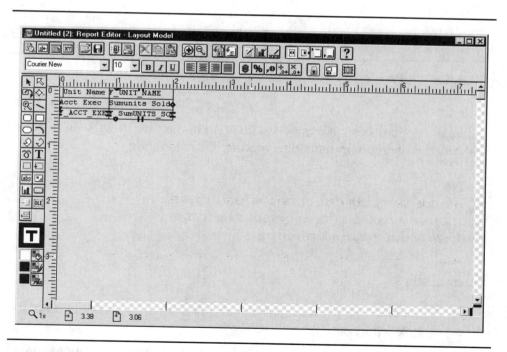

FIGURE 27-16.   *Layout Model view of unit sales by account executive by product report*

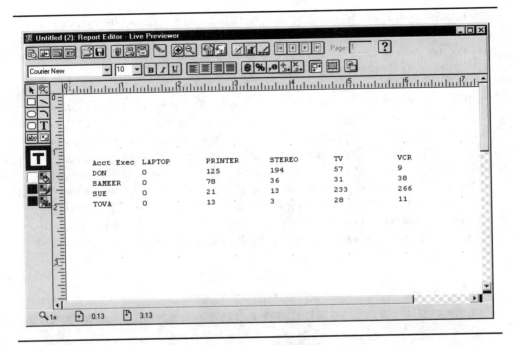

FIGURE 27-17. *Live Previewer view of matrix report output*

shows the contents of the matrix report again in the Live Previewer, this time with the data and column headers modified for readability.

TIP
The appearance of data downward and across in a matrix report is driven by repeating frames down and across, respectively.

Exercises

1. What type of Layout Model object drives the basic production of the matrix report output?

2. How do you create a title for your report within the Layout Model of the report?

Displaying Zeros in Cells with No Value

Take another look at Figure 27-17 and notice that a new product appears in the output, corresponding to a new product line added at the company where these account executives work. This new product is called LAPTOP. It's a recent addition to the product line sold at this company as of this month, and to be honest the account executives haven't figured out how to market it just yet. The report shows this—there is no data displayed for any of the executives because none of them have sold a single laptop. However, rather than simply displaying nothing for cells that have no value, it is more descriptive to show a zero instead. This is an easy task to accomplish. To do so, move to the Layout Model of your report again, and double-click on the F_sumUNITS_SOLD field to invoke the Property Palette for that field. Notice there is a property called Value if Null in the Property Palette for this item. This property has nothing defined for it if there is nothing showing in your LAPTOP column of the matrix report. You can change this by clicking on the property once to activate a cursor in it, and typing in the zero (0) character. When finished, press ENTER and then close the Property Palette. Now a zero will display in your LAPTOP column even though the database stores NULL for all account executives on sales figures for this product. Figure 27-18 demonstrates the Property Palette setting.

Exercise

What property is used to substitute zeros in a cell with NULL output from the matrix report?

Chapter Summary

This chapter covers the conclusion of the basic elements of report design along with the beginning of the advanced features of report design. The development of Parameter Forms, allowing users to specify parameter values in their reports when the report runs, is covered. The chapter then covers the design and implementation of charts in your reports, a more advanced feature of Report Builder that allows for the addition of the visual appeal that a chart can provide. Finally, a case study of matrix report creation is provided to assist in your understanding of basic elements of report design from the Data Model and Layout Model perspectives, along with an

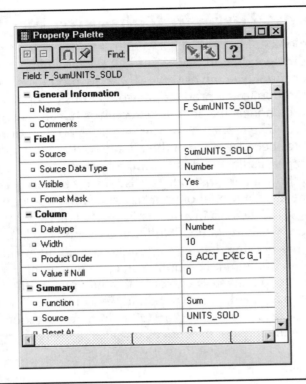

FIGURE 27-18. *Displaying zeros for NULL column values*

understanding of the development of matrix reports, an advanced type of report that allows you to assemble a cross-product of information made by several data groups. The content of this chapter comprises 15 percent of material tested by OCP Exam 5.

The chapter covered how parameters manage the behavior of reports. Two types of parameters exist in Report Builder: system parameters defined by Report Builder and assigned values by the user, and user parameters defined by the report developer and assigned values by the user. The chapter identified several system parameters as a refresher from earlier in the unit, such as those that identify the report destination (DESTYPE, DESNAME, DESFORMAT) and those that identify special character content (THOUSANDS, CURRENCY, DECIMAL). To create user parameters, double-click on the Report | *Rpt_Name* | Data Model | User Parameters node in the Object Navigator module or simply drill down to that item and click the Create button in the Object Navigator Tool Palette. You will then define values for several properties in the Property Palette for your new user parameter. The properties include NAME, COMMENTS, DATATYPE, WIDTH, INPUT MASK, INITIAL VALUE, VALIDATION TRIGGER, and List of Values. Certain constraints exist for which properties apply to user parameters of various datatypes, and you should understand these constraints for the OCP exam.

You should also make sure you understand the creation of a List of Values, or LOV, for the OCP exam. A List of Values is a set of values associated with the user parameter. If defined, it can be used to limit the value set for a parameter. The example was made in the text that if you have a parameter you define called RAINBOW_COLORS, you may want to define an LOV for the parameter that forces it to accept only the values red, orange, yellow, green, blue, indigo, and violet. Clicking on the List of Values property in the Property Palette for the user parameter causes a button to appear. Click it, and the parameter List of Values interface appears. There are two ways to define an LOV using this interface: either as a static set of values or as a **select** statement against the database. Take some time to review Figures 27-1 and 27-2 again to understand the use of the parameter List of Values interface. Remember, to ensure that no other value can be specified for the parameter than the values defined in your LOV, you must click on the check box labeled Restrict List to Predetermined Values. You can define PL/SQL functions to validate the values specified for system parameters as well. These validation triggers will usually fire twice in the report's execution—once when the report begins executing and then again when the Parameter Form is validated.

Recall that the chapter also describes a feature of Report Builder that allows you to set up an interface for your users to assign values for parameters in the report. This feature is the runtime Parameter Form. One can be assembled for your report using the Parameter Form Builder, invoked with the Tools | Parameter Form Builder menu bar item in Report Builder, or with the Parameter Form Builder button available in the Parameter Form view of Report Editor. The Parameter Form Builder interface lists out all system and user parameters available in the report. You can include any and all parameters by clicking on the name of the parameter to highlight it. You can modify the label that will appear along with the text box in the runtime

Parameter Form indicating the parameter the user is defining a value for. Three important controls are built into the runtime Parameter Form as well, including Run and Stop, and Next Page and Previous Page. The last two controls are activated automatically if you have more parameters in your Parameter Form than can fit into one page.

Your more advanced reports may make use of embedded charts, so you should understand how to assemble charts in your reports for the OCP exam. You can use an existing report created with Graphics Builder or generate one for your report on the fly with the Chart Wizard. Four aspects must be defined for your chart in order to use it, and those aspects are the chart type and subtype, values for display on both chart axes, frequency of chart appearance, and a filename and location to which to save the chart graphics file. Five types of charts exist in Chart Wizard: column charts, bar charts, pie charts, line charts, and mixed charts. For all chart types except pie charts, you must define columns for which information will be drawn to show on the category (or X) axis and the value (or Y) axis. Charts can appear at the following frequencies in a report: at the beginning, at the end, or at breakpoints in each group on the report. Finally, charts are stored as files in Oracle Graphics Designer format with the extension **.ogd** on your file system.

If you have an existing chart that you would like to use in a report, you can create a chart object in the Layout Model of your report and associate it with your existing chart file through the definition of the Chart Filename property. The chart you use may have parameters and columns already defined in it that you want to feed information into from the report. To do so, there is a special interface that allows you to map chart parameters, columns, and queries to report parameters, columns, and groups. This interface is called the Chart dialog interface, and it is invoked through a button appearing when you click on the Parameters and Columns property in the Property Palette for your chart object in the Layout Model of your report. The chapter covered the association of chart parameters to report parameters using the Parameters tab in the Chart dialog interface, as well as the association of chart queries and columns to report columns and groups using the Columns tab in the Chart dialog interface. Be sure you understand the use of this interface for the OCP exam on designing and running reports.

The final area of this chapter covers the design and modification of matrix reports using the Data Model and Layout Model views available in Report Builder. Creating the Data Model for a matrix report happens in four steps. The first of those steps is to create the report in the Object Navigator module. After that, the next step is to create the data definition through the use of the SQL Query tool button in the Data Model view of the report in the Report Editor. Your data definition can be very basic—a **select * from** *tbl_name* will suffice, if a bit slow on performance (depending on how much data is being summarized in the report). After that, you will have a query object in your Data Model with one group, which is the data definition for a simple tabular report. The third step is to create two additional groups, one for each of the datasets that will become the row and column names appearing down the left side and across the top of the matrix report. The final step is to create the fourth group, the cross-product group, whose data will appear at each juncture or cell where rows and columns intersect.

Once the Data Model has been created, you must create your Layout Model in order to view the report in the Live Previewer. To simplify things, you can use Report Wizard to create the basic layout and then modify that layout using the Layout Model. The main things that need to be addressed in the Report Wizard to create your Layout Model include defining the report style in the Style tab to be Matrix, and defining content to appear in the cells of the matrix report, where row and column values intersect. Finally, you can define a template for use in the report Live Previewer view. You can return to the Layout Model view of the report to improve the overall appearance of the report. Some things you may want to address in order to improve the appearance of the report are removing some of the labels for each of the datasets appearing in the matrix report and identifying a title for the report in the margin region of the Layout Model of the report. Note that the driving force behind the row and column layout of your matrix report is the use of repeating frames that store data from the row and column dataset into which the cross-product information lines up to in cells. The final point made in this chapter about matrix reports is the use of the Value if Null property for the fields of the report in the Layout Model, which can be used to display zeros if the cell contains a NULL value.

Two-Minute Drill

- There are two types of parameters: user parameters and system parameters.

- System parameters include DESNAME, DESTYPE, DESFORMAT, ORIENTATION, MODE, PRINTJOB, BACKGROUND, COPIES, THOUSANDS, DECIMAL, and CURRENCY.

- User parameters are defined completely by the report developer using the Report | *Rpt_Name* | Data Model | User Parameters node in the Object Navigator.

- The values you can specify for a parameter can be restricted with the use of the List of Values property in the Property Palette for the user parameter.

- Lists of Values, or LOVs, are defined with the Parameter List of Values interface. Your LOV can consist either of static values or items obtained from the database using **select** statements.

- To constrain the set of values allowable for a user parameter to those values in the LOV for that parameter, you must check the Restrict List to Predetermined Values check box.

- To constrain values for a system parameter, you must create a validation trigger.

- Validation triggers fire twice in the execution of a report: once at the beginning of report processing and then again when the Parameter Form is validated.

- A Parameter Form is a special built-in interface that you can implement in your reports that allows the user to define values for system and user parameters in the report.

- The Parameter Form Builder is the tool used to design your runtime Parameter Form. Invoke this tool either by choosing the Tools | Parameter Form Builder menu option or by clicking the Parameter Form Builder tool button in Report Editor Parameter Form view.

- The runtime Parameter Form appears whenever you run your report. To specify a value for the parameters included in the Parameter Form, you enter the value in the text box associated with the Parameter Form.

- Tools available in the runtime Parameter Form that pertain to the execution of your report include the Run and Cancel Run buttons, to control operation of your report. Click Run to continue report execution when you are finished assigning values to parameters, or Cancel Run to abort the report run.

- You can add pages to the runtime Parameter Form with the Number of Pages property associated with the Parameter Form by clicking on the icon next to the Parameter Form node in the Object Navigator module.

- Parameter Form Builder adds pages to your runtime Parameter Form automatically if you include more parameters in the Parameter Form than will fit on one page.

- Charts can be created using Chart Wizard to display visually the data in your report. Opening the Chart Wizard is handled with the Tools | Chart Wizard menu item, or with the Chart Wizard button available in the Report Editor Layout Model view of your report.

- There are four items to define for a chart in Chart Wizard, identified as follows:

  - Chart type/subtype

  - Inputs for category (X) and value (Y) axes

  - Frequency of chart appearance

  - Chart filename

- There are five types of charts definable with Chart Wizard. They are as follows:

  - **Column chart**   Vertical bars drawn from category axis to values in the value axis.

  - **Bar chart**   Horizontal bars drawn from the value axis to values in the category axis.

- **Pie chart** Circle that is cut into subsections based on percentage each section comprises of the total.

- **Line chart** Line drawn at the intersection of points on category and value axis.

- **Mixed chart** Combination of column and line chart above.

- The frequencies a chart can appear in a report include:

  - Beginning of report

  - End of report

  - At breakpoints for each group

- Charts are stored by Chart Wizard with the extension **.ogd** because they are stored in the Oracle Graphics Designer format.

- Existing chart graphics files can be incorporated into reports through the use of the chart object in the Layout Model of your report.

- Two important properties to be defined when using the chart object to include existing charts in reports are Chart Filename to define the filename for your report and Parameters and Columns to map report columns, groups, and parameters to chart parameters, columns, and queries.

- The interface used to map chart and report parameters and columns is the Chart dialog interface. This interface has two tabs, the Parameters tab for mapping the chart to report parameters and the Columns tab for mapping chart columns and queries to report columns and groups.

- Matrix reports are those reports that contain four groups of data. Three of those groups are displayed as datasets in the report. One group acts as the row name, one acts as the column name, and the third represents the cross-product of row to column dataset values.

- There are four steps to defining a matrix data model for a report:

  1. Create the new report in the Object Navigator module.

  2. Create the data definition for the matrix report.

3. Draw at least two groups to represent row and column datasets.

4. Draw a cross-product group to represent the cell dataset.

■ The easiest way to define a Layout Model is to use the Report Wizard to define the repeating frames that comprise the foundation of the Layout Model.

■ You can return to the Layout Model later to refine the report layout, such as by getting rid of the labels for the cell, column, and row content and adding a title for the report to the margin region of the Layout Model.

■ You can also substitute zeros for NULL values in cells with the use of the Value if Null property in the Property Palette.

Chapter Questions

1. **Your report has a runtime Parameter Form designed to accept a user parameter of type DATE. You want to control the format of input to this parameter. The best property to use for this purpose is which of the following?**

   A. Width

   B. Input Mask

   C. Validation Trigger

   D. List of Values

2. **Each of the following types of charts display information along an X and Y axis except for which type of chart?**

   A. Line chart

   B. Bar chart

   C. Mixed chart

   D. Pie chart

3. The mapping of parameters of a report into the parameters of a chart can be described as which of the following relationships?

   A. One to many

   B. Many to many

   C. Many to one

   D. One to one

4. You are using a predefined chart in your report. You want to restrict the data the chart uses to that data which is filtered from Report Builder. The feature you will use to enforce this requirement is which of the following?

   A. Defining a chart query by name in the Chart dialog interface

   B. Using a group filter in your Data Model

   C. Passing the data in a runtime Parameter Form

   D. Using a chart object in your Layout Model

5. Going from a group report with one hierarchical group and a main group to a matrix report with a row group, a column group, and a cross-product group requires the addition of how many groups to the report Data Model?

   A. One

   B. Two

   C. Three

   D. Four

6. You use Chart Wizard to create a pie chart in your tabular report. Which two of the following options identify frequencies that you will be able to display your chart in the report?

   A. At breakpoints in the level 1 group

   B. At the beginning of the report

    C. At the end of the report

    D. At breakpoints in the main group

7. **Charts are stored in which of the following formats?**

    A. TIFF

    B. MPEG

    C. AVI

    D. OGD

8. **A report user parameter called BEGIN_DATE is used to determine the date range for report generation. This parameter feeds a chart parameter of a different name. Which of the following statements can be made about report and chart parameters?**

    A. Report Builder assumes chart and report parameter names are the same unless told otherwise.

    B. Report Builder maps chart and report parameter names according to datatype.

    C. Report Builder does not allow the passing of data from reports to charts.

    D. The chart parameter must be called BEGIN_DATE or value passing is never allowed.

9. **Which of the following aspects of an LOV must be addressed in order to constrain values permitted for a parameter to those identified in the LOV?**

    A. LOV must use a **select** statement

    B. Restrict List to Predetermined Values check box must be checked

    C. LOV must define static values

    D. LOV must be empty

10. In the Property Palette, which of the following system parameter properties cannot be changed by the developer of the report?

    A. Comment

    B. Initial Value

    C. Validation Trigger

    D. Datatype

11. Your runtime Parameter Form contains the CURRENCY system parameters to be defined when your report is run. At which times will a validation trigger on CURRENCY fire during report execution?

    A. At the start of report execution only

    B. When the runtime Parameter Form is processed only

    C. At the start of report execution and when the runtime Parameter Form is processed only

    D. At the end of report execution only

12. Displaying zeros in any field of your report when the value returned is NULL can be accomplished using which of the following properties?

    A. Value if Null

    B. Input Mask

    C. List of Values

    D. Validation Trigger

Answers to Chapter Questions

1. B.   Input Mask

Explanation   The Input Mask property allows you to impose a predefined format onto your numeric or date inputs for a parameter. Choice A is incorrect because Width is how large (or wide) the value for the parameter can be, and cannot be changed. Choice C is incorrect because a validation trigger can return only TRUE or FALSE, and also should not be used to alter values in parameters, although it may be possible to do so. Choice D is incorrect because an LOV simply enforces the input's existence in a predefined list, but does not alter the actual value specified by the user in the way an input mask does.

2. D.   Pie chart

Explanation   Pie charts are unique in that, although you specify a value to determine "the pie" and a category to determine how the "slices are cut," these items are shown on a circle, not on a traditional graph with an X and Y axis. Choices A, B and C all are graph types that use an X and Y axis to set the stage for comparison, then draw the chart somewhere in the plane formed between the two.

3. C.   Many to one

Explanation   Each chart parameter accepts one and only one report parameter value. However, the same report parameter can feed into several different chart values. Thus, choice C is correct, while the others are incorrect.

4. A.   Defining a chart query by name in the Chart dialog interface

Explanation   Specifying a chart query by name in the Columns tab of the Chart dialog interface means that the query specified **select**s its data from the filtered data in Report Builder, not directly from the database. This feature ensures that the data comprising the chart will correspond directly to the data in the report. Although a group filter identified in choice B may be the mechanism used to restrict data in Report Builder behind the scenes, choice B is incorrect because the chart won't necessarily use that filtration unless specifically told to do so in the Chart dialog interface. The same point can be made about choice C. Choice D is incorrect because the chart object simply places the chart in the report's Layout Model, but offers no association between the data in the report and the chart unless the appropriate property is defined.

5. B.   Two

Explanation   The query in the Data Model described by this question contains two groups: a level 1 group and a main group. The level 1 group could function either as a row or column group in the matrix report, requiring only one additional group to function as the other set of row/column data, and another group to be the cross-product. Thus, choice B is correct. The only way choice C could be correct is if you removed the level 1 hierarchy group from the report and then added a new group in its place.

6. B and C.   At the beginning of the report and at the end of the report

Explanation   The general frequency of charts in reports is at the beginning and at the end, with the option to display once at every breakpoint in a group if the report is a group report. The one described in this question is a tabular report, which is not a group report, making choices B and C the only correct ones in the bunch.

7. D.   OGD

Explanation   Charts created by Chart Wizard are stored in Oracle Graphic Designer format, or OGD, making choice D correct. TIFF is a binary image format, while MPEG and AVI are video formats, making choices A, B, and C all incorrect.

8. A.   Report Builder assumes chart and report parameter names are the same unless told otherwise.

Explanation   Unless you define a chart parameter or column name in the text box next to the report parameter or column in the Chart dialog interface Parameters or Columns tab, Report Builder assumes the name of the chart and report column or parameter will be identical. You can define a different name, however, making choice D incorrect. Choice B is incorrect because no mapping between chart and report parameters and columns takes place in that interface other than that defined by name by you. Choice C is incorrect because Report Builder does permit the passing of values from reports to charts.

9. B. Restrict List to Predetermined Values check box must be checked

Explanation Even though you have defined your LOV, if you don't check the Restrict List to Predetermined Values check box in the Parameter List of Values interface, Report Builder will not enforce parameter values conforming to the contents of an LOV, making it irrelevant if the LOV is empty or how you defined it, (i.e., with a **select** or as static values).

10. D. Datatype

Explanation The other property choices given, namely Comment, Validation Trigger, and Initial Value, are all changeable by you. The only one that cannot be modified in system parameters is the Datatype parameter.

11. C. At the start of report execution and when the runtime Parameter Form is processed only

Explanation Validation triggers for parameters are fired twice during the execution of a report when a Parameter Form is defined—once when the report execution starts and then again when the runtime Parameter Form is processed. The question states that a Parameter Form is defined that contains the CURRENCY parameter, so choice C is correct. Had the Parameter Form not been defined for the report, choice A might have been acceptable, but the rest are definitely wrong.

12. A. Value if Null

Explanation The Value if Null property is used to define a default value for a field that will be displayed if the data returned from the database for the field is NULL. Input Mask is incorrect because it imposes a format on the information supplied for a parameter, not a field in the output of a report. The other two choices, C and D, also identify properties that are normally associated with the system and user parameters of a report, not the fields displayed as output.

CHAPTER
28

Advanced Topics in Report Design

n this chapter, you will cover the following advanced topics in report design:

- Coding PL/SQL triggers in reports
- Using Report Builder built-in packages
- Maximizing performance using Reports Server
- Building reports for different environments

This is the final chapter on developing reports for OCP Exam 5 in the Developer track. The chapter covers advanced topics of report design. Some of these topics include PL/SQL trigger development and the use of built-in PL/SQL packages available in Report Builder. In your report development efforts, you will encounter situations where triggers are useful, or in fact required. You have seen some of these situations already, with validation triggers for system parameters and report triggers for placeholder column value population. You will find uses for the Report Builder built-in packages as well. Another important topic covered in this final chapter is the use of Reports Server for enterprise reporting that is efficient and fast. Part of an enterprise reporting system is your recognition of the requirements for building reports for deployment in different environments and in different languages. All in all, the contents of this chapter comprise 18 percent of OCP Exam 5 content.

Coding PL/SQL Triggers in Reports

In this chapter, you will cover the following points on coding PL/SQL triggers in reports:

- Different types of triggers and their usage
- Writing and referencing common code
- Creating and referencing a PL/SQL library

PL/SQL is the programming backbone of the Oracle database and Developer/2000 suite. You can incorporate PL/SQL into many places and aspects of your reports. This section talks about some of those places and uses. In this section, you will cover the different types of triggers and their usage in the report. You will cover the development and reference of common code throughout a report. Finally, you will cover the creation and reference of PL/SQL libraries in your report. Your knowledge of OCP exam content will be rounded out by coverage provided in these crucial areas. It is important to understand these topics if you want to become certified on the Oracle Developer/2000 toolset.

Different Types of Triggers and Their Usage

You have already seen several different types of triggers and their usage in Report Builder. This lesson recaps those triggers to complete your understanding of them. There are four different types of triggers in Report Builder; action triggers, report triggers, debug triggers, and format triggers. This section covers each of these trigger types and their usage in the report. Some of this may be a review. You should take the time to understand the material to ensure your success on the OCP exam.

Action Triggers and Their Usage

Action triggers are used for the purpose of handling a set of operations associated with an event in the report. The triggering event for action triggers is the pressing of a button in the Runtime Previewer. Sometimes, in the definition of complex reports, you will want to include buttons in the output of one report that basically generate output from another report in a separate report definition (**.rdf**) file. Such reports can be thought of as "master/detail/detail" reports. The report containing the buttons that fire other reports are the master/detail reports and those reports that are fired when you press the button are the second layer of detail. The PL/SQL code contained in the action trigger needn't only fire a report, either—it can execute any PL/SQL operation permitted at that point in your report execution.

Because of the nature of buttons in Report Builder, you cannot test the functionality of an action trigger from within the Live Previewer view of your report output—you must view the report in the Runtime Previewer so that

Report Builder will both generate the button and allow you to press it. In addition, you cannot test the execution of an action trigger from within the PL/SQL interpreter module of Report Builder.

Action triggers are created in the following way. From within the Layout Model of your report, click on the Button button to activate that tool and draw the button object in the Layout Model using the general usage guidelines for Layout Model tools covered in the unit. When finished, double-click on your new button object in the Layout Model and define the Type property to be PL/SQL Trigger from the drop-down box that appears when you click on the property. Then, click on the PL/SQL Trigger property in the Property Palette and then click on the Definition button that appears next to that property. The PL/SQL Editor module then appears, where you can define the PL/SQL that will execute when the button is pressed. In this case, your action trigger fires the execution of another report with the use of a procedure called **run_report( )** that is found in the SRW built-in package. More about this package appears in the next section, while the actual PL/SQL code that might appear in such an action trigger appears in the following code block. Note that

this code is taken from the **drildone.rdf** report that comes with the Developer/2000 2.0 software release. This report is found in the **report30/demo/bitmap** subdirectory under the Oracle software home directory containing your Developer/2000 software.

```
procedure U_1ButtonAction is
begin
   srw.run_report('saledone.rdf paramform=yes
      P_custname="'||:custname||'" P_salesrep="'||:salesrep||'"');
end;
```

Report Triggers and Their Usage

Report triggers are a cornerstone of your report. Report Builder makes it possible for you to define PL/SQL for these built-in triggers that will fire at various points during the execution of your report. There are five different categories of report triggers. They are BEFORE REPORT, AFTER REPORT, BETWEEN PAGES, BEFORE PARAMETER FORM, and AFTER PARAMETER FORM. These names give an accurate indication of when the triggers fire. Your involvement with these triggers is simply to define the PL/SQL code that will run at each of the trigger firing times.

Think for a moment about validation triggers, which were mentioned last chapter in relation to the coverage of the runtime Parameter Form. Recall that validation triggers fire twice in the course of report processing. When considered in light of the report triggers, it should now be obvious both at which time the validation triggers fire, and the very fact that validation triggers are, in effect, a subset of the report triggers available for definition in Report Builder. One of the report triggers that is a validation trigger is the BEFORE PARAMETER FORM trigger, which fires before the runtime Parameter Form is displayed, and can be used to validate or even define runtime parameters for the report. The other report trigger that is a validation trigger is the AFTER PARAMETER FORM trigger, which fires after the runtime Parameter Form is displayed, and can be used to validate and change values for the parameters defined in the runtime Parameter Form. These two triggers are used to execute any PL/SQL that you might want to use to affect the data shown in the report.

The other three report triggers—BEFORE REPORT, BETWEEN PAGES, and AFTER REPORT—fire third, fourth and fifth, respectively, at the intervals described by their names. The BEFORE REPORT trigger fires after the queries used in a report are parsed and data is fetched by the Oracle RDBMS but before the report actually processes. It is a good time to perform any initialization or setup, such as creation of temporary tables to store intermediate datasets for the report. The BETWEEN PAGES trigger fires after the first page is generated but before the second page is generated, and then between each subsequent page generated by the report. This trigger is good for special formatting you want to accomplish on the second and subsequent pages of your report. This trigger only fires once within the Runtime Previewer, but fires as defined when the report is run for real. Finally, the AFTER REPORT trigger is useful for exit handling such as removal of temporary tables you created in your database as part of the BEFORE REPORT trigger or data cleanup.

Debug Triggers and Their Usage

Recall from the discussion of Procedure Builder in Unit II that there was ample coverage of debug triggers and their usage. Debug triggers in Procedure Builder give you insight on the behavior and performance of your PL/SQL block with the use of runtime debugging. Report Builder offers the same functionality for your PL/SQL blocks in reports as well. For more information about defining and using debug triggers, refer to Unit II content on debugging PL/SQL program units using Procedure Builder.

Format Triggers and Their Usage

Finally, format triggers allow for dynamic report formatting by defining a test condition to see if the object defined will appear in the report. The format trigger returns either TRUE or FALSE, depending on the criteria you define in your PL/SQL trigger block. If the trigger returns TRUE, then the object is displayed in the report output. If the trigger returns FALSE, the object is not displayed in the report output—although any data retrieved from the database or calculated in a formula will still be retrieved or calculated even though it isn't displayed. A format trigger is defined in the Layout Model view of your report through the use of the Format Trigger property in the Property Palette under the Advanced Layout node. Format triggers can either increase display prominence or eliminate the object to which they associate from report output. The methods the format trigger may use for this task include functions and procedures from the SRW package, which will be discussed in the next section.

TIP

There are several formatting and usage restrictions on format triggers, not the least of which is the inability to set values for report columns from within the PL/SQL of the format trigger. There are others, and you should consult the Report Builder online help documents to understand all of them.

Exercises

1. Identify several different types of triggers available in Report Builder. Which triggers handle validation of Parameter Form values? Which triggers handle the execution of drill-down "detail" reports fired from a master report?

2. What is the name of the package mentioned in this lesson that allows you to fire a detail report?

Writing and Referencing Common Code

It is important to know how to write and reference common PL/SQL code in Developer/2000. This understanding starts with knowing a few facts about

PL/SQL code you define for any aspect of your application, such as on your report. For every trigger you write to handle anything a trigger supports, or for any PL/SQL block you define that fires in support of an event like pressing a button, Report Builder tracks the code block and makes it available for modification in several ways. If you haven't closed it already, look at the Object Navigator contents for the **drildone.rdf** file. If you did close it, reopen the report definition file using instructions provided in the previous lesson. Figure 28-1 displays the contents of the Object Navigator module for the **drildone.rdf** report.

Open the Layout Model of this report by choosing the Tools | Report Editor menu command and then clicking on the Layout Model button in the interface. Find the button object in the report layout and double-click on it

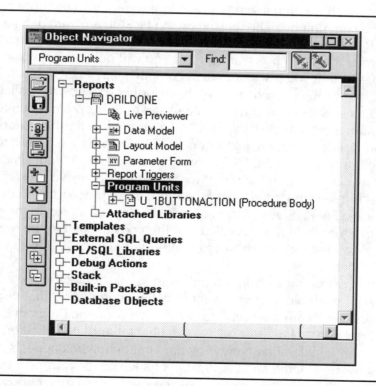

FIGURE 28-1. *Object Navigator contents for* ***drildone.rdf***

to see the Property Palette for that object. Click on the PL/SQL Trigger property in the Property Palette to make the interface button appear, and then click on the interface button to invoke the PL/SQL Editor module with the action trigger code displayed in the window. Don't make any changes—just take a second to observe the contents, and that the name of the module is **U_1ButtonAction( )**. Now click the Close button for the PL/SQL Editor module and return to the Object Navigator.

Notice that there is a drill-down node in this module called Program Units that should have a small + sign in the box next to the name of the node. Expand the node by either clicking on the + next to the node name, double-clicking on the node name, or clicking once on the node name and then clicking on the Expand button in the Tool Palette for the Object Navigator module. You should see an entry for a PL/SQL program unit of the same name as that action trigger you just looked at. Open the PL/SQL Editor for that program unit by right-clicking on the PL/SQL program unit name in the Object Navigator and choose the Program Unit Editor... option listed at the bottom of the menu box that appears. You will now be looking at the same program unit you just saw. When compiled, any PL/SQL block under this node in the Object Navigator will have further drill downs available for program unit specification and referenced and referring program units. Figure 28-2 displays the contents of the PL/SQL Editor module for this action trigger.

Report Builder, then, keeps track of all PL/SQL program units and lists them under this node in the Object Navigator module for your report. This trigger is available within the report for you to use. However, it is not available for use outside the current report. To use procedures throughout other reports, the PL/SQL program unit must either be stored in the database or in an external PL/SQL library that can then be attached to the report for use. The next lesson covers how to create external PL/SQL libraries in Report Builder.

Creation of common code is handled in Report Builder in the following way. Say, for example, that you want to define a procedure that displays a simple message, "I am a report." To do this, click on the Program Units node in the Object Navigator once to highlight it and then click on the Create button. The familiar New Program Unit dialog box appears, where you must define a name and the PL/SQL block type for your new code. Type **hello** in the text box for the name of the procedure and then choose the

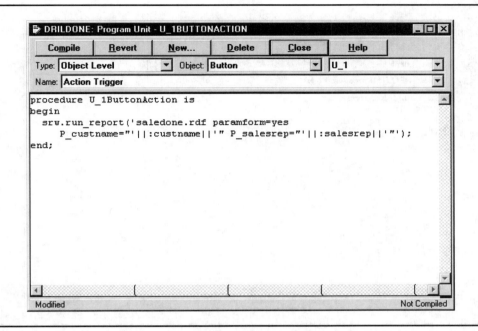

FIGURE 28-2. *PL/SQL Editor module with **U_1ButtonAction( ) displayed***

appropriate radio button, then click OK. Report Builder launches you into the PL/SQL Editor module, as shown in Figure 28-3. You can then define a simple PL/SQL block such as the one shown in the following code block:

```
procedure hello is
begin
   text_io.put_line('I am a report');
end;
```

Once written, you can reference this or any other program unit in the report from any other program unit in the report. You can reference stored procedures in the Oracle database from within your program units as well. You can also reference program units in external PL/SQL libraries that are attached to your report. You will learn how to create these libraries in the

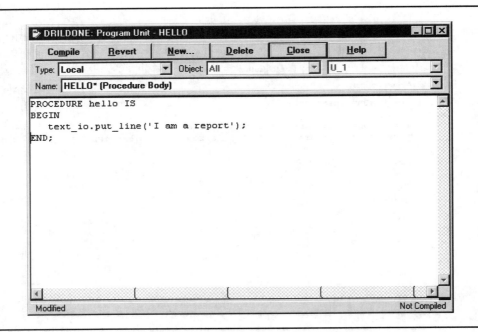

FIGURE 28-3. *PL/SQL Editor module with **HELLO( )** displayed*

next lesson. The ability to reference stored procedures in the Oracle database from your PL/SQL code in Report Builder gives rise to another interesting feature of Report Builder—the ability you have to move your program units that are local to the report into the Oracle database, and vice versa. Storing Report Builder PL/SQL blocks in the Oracle database is handled in the following way. First, you must connect to the Oracle database using any of the following ways. From within the Object Navigator with your report still open, double-click on the Database Objects node and the login prompt will appear. Enter your username, password, and database connect string to log in to the Oracle database. Or you can choose the File | Connect command and log into the database. Or you can press CTRL-J to obtain the login screen.

After logging into Oracle, you will see a + next to the Database Objects node in the Object Navigator module. Drill down into the node to see the different schema owners of objects in the database. To place your local program unit **hello( )** into the Oracle database under your username, drill down into the Database Objects node to your username. Then, drill down into your username. You will see four new nodes under your username, Stored Program Units, PL/SQL Libraries, Tables, and Views. Click and hold on the **hello( )** procedure appearing under the Program Units node in the report, and drag the program unit down to the Stored Program Units node appearing under your username until a line appears across the Object Navigator module under this node. Then release your mouse button. It may take some time for the report program unit to be copied into the database, depending on the size of the PL/SQL program, but it will get there eventually.

Exercises

1. Under what Object Navigator node will your PL/SQL trigger code appear?

2. What process is used for moving program units into the database for storage? What is the utility for doing so?

Creating and Referencing a PL/SQL Library

The final task you will cover in this section is the creation of PL/SQL libraries. Recall from Unit II that a PL/SQL library can be created on the client side to store PL/SQL code you want to make available across reports. To create a PL/SQL library, you must first have some program units to put into a library. You should write a few procedures and functions. Use some of the simple ones described in the previous lesson to get set up for building a PL/SQL library. Any of the program units stored under the Program Units node in your Object Navigator module for any of the reports can be placed in a PL/SQL library, although care should be taken to define PL/SQL blocks that are reusable across reports.

Placing Program Units in the Library

Once your code is developed, place the program units into a PL/SQL library in the following way. First, click on the PL/SQL Libraries node in the Object Navigator to highlight it. Be sure you are clicking on this node and *not* the Attached Libraries node appearing as a drill down under your report. The Attached Libraries node handles the attachment of a previously defined and working library to your report, not the development of new libraries. After clicking on the PL/SQL Library node to highlight it, click the Create button in the Tool Palette on the Object Navigator. A new set of items appears beneath this node, the most prominent of which is a new library name, which is automatically generated by Oracle in the format LIB_*nnn*. You can rename the library later, as you wish. At this point, the library is open and ready for development, but not for reference in the report you currently have open in Report Builder. Two nodes appear beneath the node for your new library, Program Units and Attached Libraries. The program units you are about to add will appear below the first node once you add them to the library. As evidenced by the second node, you can attach libraries to your libraries as well.

Add your program units to the open library in the following way. From the Program Units node appearing under the open report, click and hold on a program unit such as the **U_1ButtonAction( )** procedure appearing in **drildone.rdf**. Move the pointer down to the Program Units node underneath the node for your new library. Once you have moved to a place in the library where dropping the program unit is permitted, release the mouse button. You should now see the program unit listed under the Program Units drill-down node for the open library. Click on the Save button in the Tool Palette for Object Navigator, or choose the File | Save menu option to save the library. When using either option, be sure that the Program Units or PL/SQL Libraries node is highlighted so that you're saving the library. When finished, click on the name of the PL/SQL library you just created, and either press the Delete key or choose the File | Close menu option to close your library.

Attaching the Library to Use the Program Units

Attaching a library to use in your report is handled in the following way. First, click on the Attached Libraries node to highlight it and then click on the Create button. Actually, in this situation the name of this button is a bit of a misnomer because you are actually attaching a library that is already created. Think of it as "creating" a new attachment, if not a new library. Anyway, you click the Create button, and an interface similar to the one in Figure 28-4 appears to guide you through the attachment.

Use of the Attach Library interface is as follows. In the text box next to the word "Library," you identify your library filename using its absolute path—

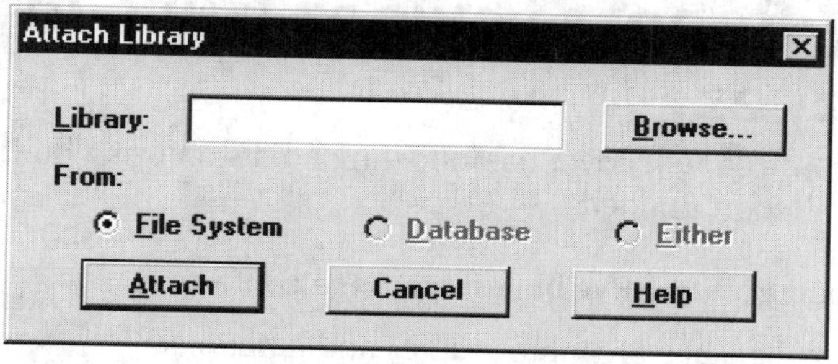

FIGURE 28-4. *Attach Library interface*

either by keying one in or by clicking on the Browse button to locate it using the Open File interface provided by the operating system. Three radio buttons appear to help you identify the source for your library. If you want to attach a library from the database, click the Database radio button. If you want to attach a library from the file system, click the File System radio button. If you don't care (though normally you will have a pretty good idea of where the library has been saved), click the Either radio button. When finished, click the Attach button, and your library will appear as a drill-down node underneath the Attached Libraries node for your report in the Object Navigator module.

With the library attached, you can now refer to PL/SQL code in the library from within your report. That PL/SQL code can be used within several different reports as well as within other libraries. Note that you cannot modify the PL/SQL code in the library, only run it. If you need to make a change to a PL/SQL program unit in an attached library, you must first open the library.

Exercises

1. Can you execute code in an open library? Why or why not? Can you modify code in an attached library? Why or why not?

2. Given several PL/SQL program units exist, how do you create a library comprised of those program units?

Using Report Builder Built-In Packages

In this section, you will cover the following points on using built-in packages in Report Builder:

- Report Builder SRW built-in package contents
- Using package SRW procedures and functions
- Output messages at run time
- Using temporary tables in reports
- Modifying visual attributes at run time

It has already been covered in these units that Developer/2000 and the Oracle database comes equipped with many built-in packages that extend the functionality of applications you develop in conjunction with them. These packages handle various tasks such as reading and writing files, embedding objects into your application, and many more. The uses of many built-in packages in Report Builder have already been described. This section covers the use of one important package that hasn't been explained but has already been mentioned. This package is called SRW, and it handles much of the key functionality provided by Report Builder. You will learn more about the use of its procedures and functions and the output messages it may give when the report executes. The use of temporary tables as intermediate storage places for report data will also be covered in this section. Finally, the processes involved in modifying visual attributes at run time is offered.

Report Builder SRW Built-In Package Contents

The SRW package offers many of the capabilities available through Report Builder's graphical interface. However, the package offers those features in procedures and functions. In fact, this package offers over 50 procedures and functions that allow you to accomplish many things with your application, including the following:

- Executing reports from within PL/SQL code
- Processing SQL statements and reference bind variables
- Tracing report activity
- Setting report format properties
- Generating temporary tables for reports
- Web-enabling reports

Without these procedures and functions, you wouldn't be able to do most of these things from within your reports. For example, you would not be able to develop "master/detail/detail" reports where next to detail records appear buttons that fire a PL/SQL block that, in turn, kicks off another report and passes it appropriate values to run. This type of depth is an enormous value-added feature for reporting on data warehouse applications. SRW makes these things possible. The following lessons give an outline of most of the functions available in the SRW package, broken out by the categories identified in the preceding list of bullets. The full list of packages available within Report Builder is displayed in Figure 28-5.

Executing Reports from PL/SQL with SRW

As identified, SRW allows you to execute another report from within PL/SQL code. The key function involved in this activity is **run_report( )**, which accepts variables to do its job—such as the name of the report to be run and parameters to feed the job—then feeds this information into Reports Runtime. Two exceptions, **run_report_batchno**, and **run_report_failure**, support the cornerstone **run_report( )** procedure by handling situations where the report was run with the BATCH parameter equaling **no** (meaning the report must be run interactively), and in general report failure situations. Another function, **geterr_run( )**, can also be used for determining exactly what error occurred when **run_report_failure** gets raised. The next lesson will cover in more detail the activity of running reports from other reports.

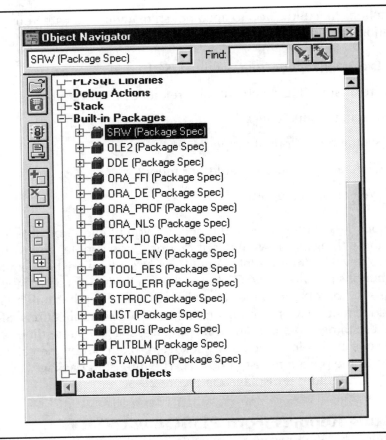

FIGURE 28-5. *Packages available in Report Builder*

Using SRW for Processing SQL

SRW offers a packaged procedure called **do_SQL( )** that handles processing of SQL statements from PL/SQL. A supporting exception called **do_SQL_failure** exists when the **do_SQL( )** procedure gets an error. Before reading any further, recall in Unit I the comment that PL/SQL integrates seamlessly with Oracle SQL and the Oracle database. Yet, here you see evidence that there is a packaged procedure that does the same thing. Is it better or worse to use a packaged procedure to execute your SQL statements? Unfortunately, the answer is yes and no. For most DML processing involving static SQL, you should simply write the SQL statement in your PL/SQL code. However, there is one situation where you can't use SQL running directly from PL/SQL, and that is the situation where you want to create tables. More on that one shortly. You can use it for **update**, **insert**, and **delete** statements, too, but **do_SQL( )** is a lot slower than regular SQL statements running in Oracle.

Tracing Report Activity with SRW

The tracing facilities offered in Report Builder are also available in the SRW package. The procedures in this category include **trace_start( )** and **trace_end( )** for starting and ending a trace, respectively. To remove and set options for the tracing run, the **trace_rem_option( )** and **trace_add_option( )** procedures are available. Special predefined types are used to pass values to these procedures, and they will be covered more in the next lesson.

SRW for Report Formatting

A blizzard of options unfolds for you in the SRW package for report formatting. There are about 25 procedures in this package, prefixed with the word "set," that handle such items as printer options, fonts, character spacing, background color, text color, borders, and more. The most important one for the OCP exam, however, is **set_attr( )**.

Using SRW to Create Temporary Tables

Picture this. You are trying to create a report that has several intermediate steps, each of which depends on the filtering activity of the previous step. Your reports work against 20 different production tables. You analyze the situation and determine that you need temporary tables that will be used as holding grounds for your report data. The question then becomes how to create them. You can, for example, create a production table that always sits out there ready for report use, but if you have several reports all needing temporary tables, this option can become hard to manage. Instead, you can use the **do_SQL( )** procedure to handle the creation and removal of temporary tables.

Web-Enabling Reports with SRW

Finally, you can deploy your reports on the Web using SRW. Several of the "set" procedures associated with formatting and output also provide Web support. The procedures available for this purpose include the following:

- **set_hyperlink( )**
- **set_pdf_action( )**
- **set_bookmark( )**
- **set_before_page_html( )**
- **set_before_form_html( )**
- **set_before_report_html( )**
- **set_after_form_html( )**
- **set_after_page_html( )**
- **set_after_report_html( )**

Exercises

1. Identify the package that contains many procedures offering functionality provided by Report Builder.

2. What are some of the capabilities this built-in package provides you? Identify at least one function or procedure from the package associated with providing that capability.

Using SRW Package Procedures and Functions

The procedures in the SRW package are used in the same way that other package procedures and functions are used. You can reference the SRW package from any PL/SQL block in Report Builder by referring to the procedure you want to use by name and prefixing the reference with the name of the package. Thus, if you wanted to use the procedure **run_report( )** in the SRW package, you might write the following block in the PL/SQL Editor for that report:

```
Procedure U_2ButtonAction is
 begin
   ...
    srw.run_report( ... );
    ...
end;
```

Using Procedures to Execute Reports

Since we've started with **run_report( )**, let's just focus on running reports from PL/SQL with the **run_report( )** procedure in SRW. This procedure accepts just one parameter: a text string. The text string you pass to this procedure should contain every item you would have included to run the same report from the command line except the **r30run** executable. Items you include in the parameter you pass to **run_report( )** include command line options, the name of the report being run, and so on. For example, say you have a report called **sfbm.rep** that outlines the sales figures by month. This report accepts a user-defined parameter called MONTH that you pass a known three-character string representing a month, such as **jan** or **nov**, along with the usual suspects for system parameters. The following code block illustrates the sample PL/SQL block again, this time with the command line parameter defined. As always, be sure you are connected to the database before you execute the Runtime Previewer to see the output for your report.

```
procedure U_2ButtonAction is
 begin
    srw.run_report('report=sfbm month=sep batch=yes');
end;
```

TIP
For the REPORT parameter, a .rep filename must be specified.

You should now understand the basic premise of using SRW procedures and functions in your PL/SQL in the report. These next few lessons will cover the use of procedures for some of the other tasks SRW allows you to do, such as creating temporary tables and formatting output.

Exercises

1. How are procedures and functions referenced in PL/SQL code if they are stored in packages?

2. What parameter is passed to **run_report( )**? What does the parameter define?

Output Messages at Run Time

An output message at run time will tell you if there are problems with the report's execution. These messages are generated when exceptions defined for the procedure or function are raised. The **run_report( )** procedure has two exceptions it raises that you should know about: the **run_report_batchno** exception and the **run_report_failure** exception. If your report does not execute properly, various errors will kick out in support of each exception. The **run_report_batchno** exception is raised when your command line string passed to **run_report( )** causes the report to run interactively. This cannot happen. In order to use **run_report( )**, you must flag the report to run in batch by specifying **yes** to the BATCH parameter. The **run_report_failure** exception is raised for general report failure.

In the course of running your reports with the SRW procedure **run_report( )**, you will generate output messages at the time of report execution that you should know how to address. You will not know if the command line you pass to **run_report( )** is valid or invalid at report compile time because all the compilation does is check to see if the text string you passed is valid text. Thus, if you want to see the output message for the error, you must get familiar with any exceptions associated with the procedure or function that you are using in SRW, and then code an explicit exception handler in the **exception** section of the PL/SQL block from which you are calling the SRW procedure.

Recall that several exceptions exist in conjunction with the procedures of SRW. The **run_report( )** procedure has **run_report_batchno** that gets raised by **run_report( )** when your report command line causes the report you attempt to run to do so in interactive (as opposed to batch) mode. This procedure has the **run_report_failure** exception that is raised when more general problems arise. If you want your report to handle these situations gracefully, you must code an exception handler in the PL/SQL block from which you call **run_report( )**. The following code block shows the code for **U_2ButtonAction( )** again, this time with exceptions defined:

```
procedure U_2ButtonAction is
   txtstr CHAR(100);
begin
    srw.run_report('report=sfbm month=sep batch=yes');
exception
   when srw.run_report_batchno then
     SRW.message(150,'Report was executed where batch did not
equal no.');
       raise SRW.program_abort;
   when srw.run_report_failure then
       txtstr := srw.geterr_run;
       SRW.message(110,txtstr);
       raise SRW.program_abort;
end;
```

Now let's talk about the actual code you have in the exception handler for this example. You identified the different exceptions raised by **run_report( )** in your **when** clauses in the exception handler by calling another SRW procedure: **message( )**. The **message( )** procedure puts a message on the screen in a dialog box that you defined in the procedure call. One of two things can happen after an exception is raised within **run_report( ).** After you review the error in the dialog box and accept it by clicking the OK button, the "master" report can either continue execution or it can abort. In the exception handler defined for **run_report_batchno**, if this exception is raised in **run_report( )** a dialog box will pop up with the message you passed to **message( )**. When you click the OK button, report execution continues. When the **run_report_failure** exception is raised by your call to **run_report( )**, the dialog box again opens with the message you passed to **message( )** for that call and you click OK to acknowledge it. But, after you click OK, the execution of your report stops because you raise the **program_abort** exception. Use of this exception is not mandatory; you should use it only when serious exceptions are raised.

TIP
*The **geterr_run( )** function returns a specific error message for failure during execution of **run_report( )**, and is used to define the text string you pass to **message( )** in this situation. The text string you define as the variable used to store the result from **geterr_run( )** should always be of type CHAR(100).*

Let's talk a little more about the **message( )** procedure in the SRW package. It accepts two parameters: a number and a text string. This procedure causes a dialog box to appear on the screen during report execution that contains the text string and number you pass to **message( )**. For example, the dialog box that will be displayed for the call to **message( )** shown in the **when run_report_failure** clause of the exception handler in the code block you just reviewed is shown in Figure 28-6.

TIP
*The **SRW.program_abort** exception kills execution of your entire report and must be raised explicitly by your PL/SQL block within the exception handler to work. There is definitely a question that pertains to this subject on the OCP exam, although it might mistakenly be referred to as a procedure or function! Don't be fooled, though, it is an exception.*

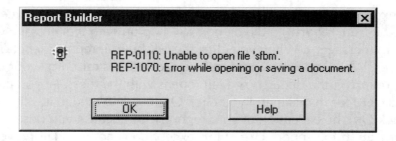

FIGURE 28-6. *Dialog box displayed by a call to **message( )***

Available Exceptions in SRW

The following is a list of exceptions that are raised within the execution of procedures and functions in SRW. Next to each exception is a basic description of when the exception is raised, and from which procedures and/or functions in SRW the exception may be raised.

- **do_SQL_failure**   Raised from **do_SQL( )**, this exception is raised when a general failure of this procedure occurs. You should *always* code exception handlers for these types of exceptions.

- **context_failure**   Raised from any procedure, this exception is raised when the call to a procedure or function in SRW is made outside of appropriate context. To determine the appropriate context for procedures in Report Builder, consult the Report Builder online help.

- **integer_error**   Raised from **message( )** or **set_maxrow( )** to indicate a noninteger value was passed where an integer was expected as a parameter to these procedures.

- **maxrow_inerr**   Raised from **set_maxrow( )** to indicate internal errors. It should never be raised, but if it is, contact Oracle. You should raise the **program_abort** exception as part of the **when** clause for handling this exception.

- **maxrow_unset**   Raised from **set_maxrow( )** due to your inability to define the maximum rows for a query once it has started execution.

- **null_arguments**   Raised from **do_SQL( )**, **set_maxrow( )**, **run_report( )**, **message( )**, or **user_exit( )** whenever NULL is passed as the value for a required parameter.

- **program_abort**   Raised by you *explicitly* within the **when** clause of an exception handler whenever you want the execution of the report to stop as the result of an occurrence of another exception. The prior code block in this lesson demonstrates its typical use.

- **run_report_batchno**   Raised from **run_report( )** indicating the report being executed is not set to run in batch mode.

- **run_report_failure**   Raised from **run_report( )** indicating the report being executed has failed. You can use the **geterr_run( )** function in conjunction with the **when** clause of your exception handler to determine the error encountered by **run_report( )**.

- **unknown_query** Raised from **set_maxrow( )** when you pass an unknown query as a parameter to the procedure.

- **unknown_user_exit** Raised from **user_exit( )** when you pass an unknown user exit as a parameter to the procedure.

- **user_exit_failure** Raised from **user_exit( )** as the result of general failure in the processing of that procedure. The **user_exit( )** procedure is designed to pass control from the report *temporarily* to another program. The program passed control by **user_exit( )** is identified as a parameter passed to the procedure. This procedure does not exit the user from report processing, as its name might imply.

TIP
*The numeric value you pass to **message( )** can be used to identify the area of PL/SQL code in the report that is the origin for the dialog box message being displayed. The number should be between 1 and 10 digits, but if the number is less than 5 (i.e., 59), leading zeros will be padded to make the number of digits shown 5 (i.e., SRW-00059). This feature can be useful for tracking down PL/SQL containing bugs.*

Exercises

1. What must you do in order to properly display messages of exceptions raised by procedures like **do_SQL( )** and **run_report( )** in the SRW package?

2. What exception kills execution of your report when it is raised? How is this exception typically raised in your PL/SQL blocks?

3. Identify the functionality of the **message( )** procedure. What parameters is it passed? Identify the functionality of the **null_arguments** exception. From where might it be raised?

4. What is the difference between **program_abort** and **user_exit( )**?

Using Temporary Tables in Reports

Temporary tables are sometimes used in reports to store data while the report runs. In some cases, your reports will obtain a set of data from the database by running the data through multiple filters. In any event, you may find it useful to store data from a report in a temporary table. However, there are some challenges for doing so. Two obvious places you will target for your creation and elimination of the temporary table include the beginning and end of the report, respectively. Report Builder answers the challenge with two built-in times in your report where a trigger fires. Those two points are the BEFORE REPORT and AFTER REPORT triggers, respectively.

TIP

Although BEFORE REPORT and AFTER REPORT may seem like obvious candidates for building temporary tables to be used in reports, you can create or remove your temporary tables anywhere in the report. Just be sure that you don't attempt to remove a temporary table before creating it, or leave a temporary table out there after the report is done.

However, as soon as you solve the obvious problem, an even bigger challenge arises. This challenge is properly executing the **create table** statement from a PL/SQL block in your report. You can explore several options for creating your table, one of which may be to create a stored procedure in the Oracle database that you call from PL/SQL code in the report. You then set up the **create table** statement through the use of the DBMS_SQL package, which allows you to open, parse, and execute SQL statements on the fly from within PL/SQL. You could even set up the calls to DBMS_SQL within the PL/SQL in your report. But a problem exists with this method in that issuing **create table** or other DDL statements via DBMS_SQL can cause hangs. Take the time now to review the comments in the package specification for DBMS_SQL to better understand the functionality it provides.

Your method for creating temporary tables in reports will be to use the **do_SQL( )** procedure available in the SRW package instead. This procedure allows you to execute any SQL statement including **create table**, **update**, and others. However, given the integration of SQL statements into PL/SQL, your best bet is to use **do_SQL( )** only in situations like creating temporary tables or other DDL operations not permitted directly in PL/SQL.

Use of the **do_SQL( )** procedure in SRW is handled as follows. You pass the procedure a text string containing any valid SQL statement, such as **create table**. The **do_SQL( )** procedure then parses and executes your statement. Unlike calls to server-side stored functions in the DBMS_SQL package, there is no need to define variables to store the address of your cursor in memory; **do_SQL( )** handles all that behind the scenes. Your BEFORE REPORT trigger for creating temporary tables used by the report may look something like the code in the following block:

```
-- Code for the BEFORE REPORT trigger
function BeforeReport return boolean is
begin
   srw.do_SQL('create table tmptbl1 (foo number(10), foo_name
varchar2(10))');
   return (TRUE);
exception
    when srw.do_SQL_failure then
        srw.message(90, 'Fatal error when creating table tmptbl1.
Abort.');
        raise srw.program_abort;
end;
```

While the code for the AFTER REPORT trigger may look something like the following code block:

```
-- Code for the AFTER REPORT trigger
function AfterReport return boolean is
begin
srw.do_SQL('drop table tmptbl1 cascade constraints');
   return (TRUE);
exception
    when srw.do_SQL_failure then
        srw.message(90, 'Fatal error when dropping table tmptbl1.
Abort.');
        raise srw.program_abort;
end;
```

TIP
*If you include reference to any objects in the
report such as columns or variables, you should
precede those references with a colon, just like
any other bind variable.*

Exercises

1. What procedure is used to execute DDL statements like **create table**
   and **drop table** from PL/SQL blocks in your report?

2. At what places in a report might you define a PL/SQL block to call
   this procedure to create and drop temporary tables in your report?

Modifying Visual Attributes at Run Time

Modifying visual attributes of your report at run time is an area of change
between Developer/2000 1.6 and 2.0. In releases of Developer/2000 prior
to 2.1, the **set_attr( )** procedure is used to modify visual attributes of your
report, and you passed both a code for the attribute you wanted to change
along with the value you wanted to change the attribute to. In 2.1 or later,
the lion's share of procedures available in the SRW package pertain to
setting and modifying visual report attributes during run time. About 25
procedures are designed for this purpose, organized around the general form
set_*attr_desc***( )**, where *attr_desc* corresponds to a short description for the
attributes that used to be passed to **set_attr( )**, while adding a few more. For
backward compatibility with Developer/2000 1.6 certification, the use of
set_attr( ) will be covered along with that for version 2.0.

Using the SRW.SET_ATTR( ) Procedure

This is a fairly complicated process where you first set an attribute mask
and then set the value for that mask in a special record called **srw.attr**.
Once the **srw.attr** record is set, you call the **set_attr( )** procedure, passing
two parameters, the first of which is almost always going to be 0. The second
is the **attr** record where your attributes are defined. The following example

presents where you set attributes for the text color to red in situations where summary values are negative numbers. Several other attributes are available—consult the Report Builder online help documents for more information. The following code block displays your use of the **attr** record and the call to **set_attr( )**:

```
function F_FormatSumValueColor return boolean is
begin
   if :colsum < 0 then
        srw.attr.mask := SRW.GCOLOR_ATTR;
        srw.attr.gcolor := 'red';
        srw.set_attr(0,srw.attr);
   end if;
   return (TRUE);
end;
```

Notice that your first step in the setup of the **set_attr( )** procedure call is to define a value for **srw.attr.mask**, an element in the **srw.attr** record. This definition sets up the next definition of the actual value for the attribute you specified for **srw.attr.mask**. Finally, you make the call to **set_attr( )**. Each attribute that is set with **set_attr( )** has a special code, like **srw.attr.gcolor** for text color. For more information about attributes and their special codes, check out the Report Builder online help documentation.

TIP
*Four situations exist where the first variable you pass to **set_attr( )** will not be 0. When you are setting attributes for **befreport_escape, aftreport_escape, befpage_escape and aftpage_escape**, you must pass the value set automatically in the SRW package corresponding to **report_id**. Even so, escape sequences are dying out with GUIs in full force.*

Using the Set of SRW.SET_ATTR_DESC( ) Procedures
With Developer/2000 2.1, the setting of visual attributes at run time is greatly simplified with the elimination of the need for defining an **srw.attr**

record. Instead, you simply call the procedure that handles defining the visual attribute you want to define, and pass it the appropriate value(s) for the attribute. The text color change example described in the previous lesson would be handled in Developer/2000 2.1 with the **set_text_color( )** procedure in the SRW package, which accepts one parameter, a text string defining color. Consider the following code block, which performs the same function as the one in the previous lesson:

```
function F_FormatSumValueColor return boolean is
begin
    if :colsum < 0 then
          srw.set_text_color('red');
    end if;
    return (TRUE);
end;
```

TIP
Several restrictions exist with setting attributes for report deployment to the Web. This topic is not covered in the OCP exam, and is therefore beyond the scope of our discussion here. If you have questions about it, consult Report Builder online help documentation.

Exercises

1. What two ways exist for defining visual report attributes with PL/SQL at run time? Which is new to Developer/2000 2.1? Which is provided for backward compatibility?

2. What is the name of the record used in conjunction with defining report attributes available in Developer/2000 prior to release 2.1? What elements exist in that record, and how are the elements in the record determined?

Maximizing Performance Using Reports Server

In this section, you will cover the following points on maximizing performance using Reports Server:

- Comparing local client and report server reporting
- The Reports Server architecture
- Viewing and scheduling reports in Queue Manager
- Invoking Oracle reporting ActiveX controls from other apps

So far, the architecture assumed for report deployment in the discussion has been the traditional client/server architecture, where reports are run and printed from either the same machine as that running the client application or the same machine as that housing the database. With the advent of N-tier applications, however, you have yet a third environment from which to run your reports—the application server. This section covers use of the Reports Server architecture in conjunction with N-tier applications. A comparison of both environments is offered, along with an overview of the architecture supporting Reports Server. The use of Queue Manager to schedule report jobs is given as well, along with an advanced topic—embedding ActiveX controls into your applications for direct interface with Reports Server.

Comparing Local Client and Report Server Reporting

Two methods exist for report processing and distribution. You can execute and print reports from the PC on your desktop, or from a server. The first method demonstrates a "fat client" setup, where the client application is packed with application logic and reporting mechanisms to handle all the needs of the distributed application. The second shows the possibility of moving toward a "thin client" setup, where most information processing is handled centrally via a server. Figure 28-7 summarizes much of the discussion that follows regarding the comparison of local client and report server reporting architectures.

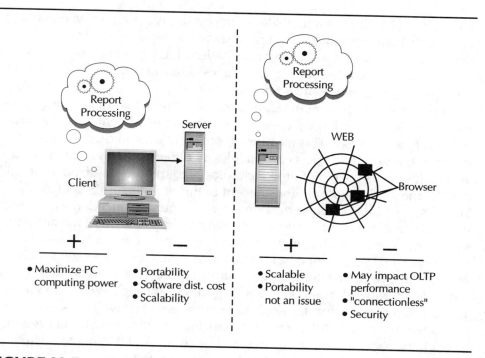

FIGURE 28-7. *Client reporting vs. server reporting comparison*

Certain benefits exist for each model. From the client perspective, the benefits are that distributed processing lessens the processing burden handled by any individual machine in the system. For example, if an OLTP application handles all transactions processed as well as all the reporting, there could be performance degradation on the application overall. The client-centric distributed processing model makes use of the explosion of processing power, memory, and disk space available on PCs today. If your report contains a lot of processing, such as heavy PL/SQL processing in conjunction with formula or summary columns, you may want to distribute the report load onto the client to improve overall performance for the system.

There are drawbacks to the client-centric processing model, however. The first problem comes when you want to distribute a new report to each client. There may arise issues with portability, such as the file systems on two PCs not being the same. Issues with portability arise also when your office uses heterogeneous operating systems on the desktop. The development cost of client/server applications has been high as well, with the cost of PC upgrades, software upgrades, and distribution. Scalability can be a challenge for these and other reasons as well.

A development has occurred in office computing that many companies including Oracle are paying attention to. That development is the explosion in Internet technology. This new development allows an organization to return to the server-centric system deployment perfected over the past 30 years with the use of mainframe technology, coupled with advances in GUI development. The most obvious benefit of this architecture is portability. Since most of your software runs on a server, you don't need to worry as much about porting applications between machines. Another advantage is scalability. The Internet is highly scalable, making it easy to add more users to the system. The overall cost for deployment may be less expensive as well, given a fixed cost for a limited number of powerful servers and inexpensive network computers working mainly through Web browsers. This architecture extends to report server processing as well, where a dedicated machine handles report processing and dissemination of reports through the organization, resolving the portability and deployment issues by using only one machine to handle all report processing.

Despite this apparent swing back in favor of centralized processing, reminiscent of mainframe processing of years gone by, there are some weaknesses in network computing that need to be addressed. The first is the very nature of connections via the Internet. You basically need to create a connection between client and server in a TCP/IP network, which is a connectionless protocol—thus, the need for an application server connected to the database synchronously, to which the thin-client browser application interacts in the connectionless paradigm. However, Oracle Reports does extend much of its current functionality to deploy reports to the Web as well. Companies like Oracle will continue to fill in other technology gaps such as security. Given the difficulties most companies have with development and maintenance of client/server applications, and as the gaps in what Internet technology can do fill, more organizations will move their systems to the Internet or an intranet.

NOTE
Since starting Reports Server varies from operating system to operating system, and because it is not a topic tested by OCP, it will not be covered here. If you want information on how to start Reports Server, refer to the Developer/2000: Guidelines for Building Applications manual that comes with your Developer/2000 software release.

Exercises

1. Describe the advantages of handling report processing from the client. What are its disadvantages?

2. Describe the advantages of handling report processing from a network-centric perspective. What are the disadvantages to network computing?

The Reports Server Architecture

With these thoughts about client/server and network computing in mind, turn your attention now toward how Oracle Reports implements a network computing paradigm with Reports Server. The server process itself runs on a machine that can be dedicated to its effort. Rather than handling report processing themselves, clients send their reports to the Reports Server for processing, where the report jobs are held in a queue. There are one or several report-processing engines running that handle the actual execution of the report. As reporting engines become free, Reports Server sends another report job from the queue to be processed. The Reports Server can also start new runtime engines if the queue gets too large, and shut down report engines if the queue is empty and the engines sit idle.

As one may imagine, Reports Server handles report job scheduling as well. The execution time and how often a report runs is tracked using features in the Queue Manager, a tool that works in conjunction with Reports Server.

A certain amount of information about job execution is tracked through the Queue Manager as well. The Report Server architecture works in the following way. You push your report to the Reports Server with the use of the **r30cli** executable. Reports Server then receives the report for processing and places the report in the report queue. Available runtime engines pick up reports to be run off the queue and process them. When finished, the output is placed in a location defined in the report definition. The report output is then printed to a destination in the report definition, sent to a user via email through Oracle Office or MAPI, or made available for Web browsers to pick up through a Web server using Reports Web cartridges or a Web server using the Common Gateway Interface (CGI) running the Reports CGI executable. This N-tier architecture is displayed in Figure 28-8.

TIP

The Queue Manager allows you to interface directly with the Reports Server to see which reports are running and those that remain to be run.

Exercises

1. What is the architecture of Reports Server? What tool is used to see the reports being executed in Reports Server?

2. What are three ways users see reports through Reports Server?

Viewing and Scheduling Reports in Queue Manager

A report is held in a queue on the Reports Server until a runtime engine becomes available for processing the report. A tool called Queue Manager handles viewing and scheduling reports for processing in the Reports Server. The use of Queue Manager is handled as follows. You first start the execution of Queue Manager by clicking the appropriate icon or by typing **r30rqv** or **r30rqv32** from the operating system command line, depending on whether you use UNIX or Windows. When you begin execution of Queue

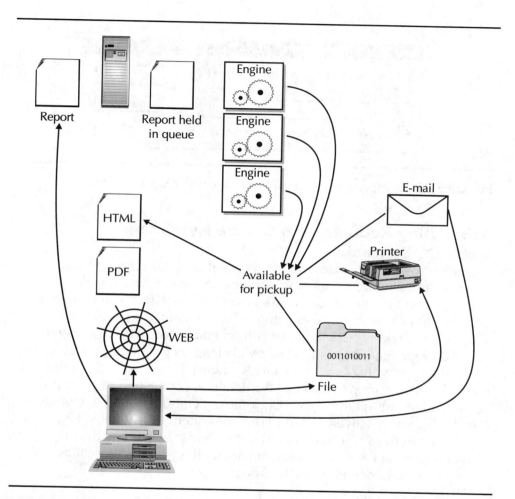

FIGURE 28-8.   *Reports Server architecture*

Manager, you will be prompted to enter the name of a queue to manage, as shown in Figure 28-9. You may choose to ignore this when opening Queue Manager by clicking the Skip button, or specify the name of a Reports Server listener on your network as it appears in the **tnsnames.ora** file or in the Oracle Names server.

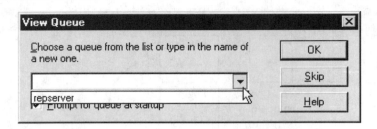

FIGURE 28-9. *Specifying a queue to manage with Queue Manager*

Scheduling Reports with Oracle Reporting ActiveX Control

Once you specify your queue to manage and click OK, Queue Manager opens to its main interface and you can begin viewing and scheduling jobs in your report queue. The Queue Manager main interface will be shown later. For now, your first task is going to be to schedule a job to run at a specific time. For this example, we will schedule execution of a new report called **db.rep**. The job is scheduled by clicking on Job | New, which opens the Run Report dialog box. Since this is a new job, you will see question marks for the report to be run and the database connection string Reports Server will use to run the report. Click the Set Options button to invoke the Oracle Reporting ActiveX Control Properties interface, shown in Figure 28-10. The ActiveX Control Properties interface has several tabs that require elements to be defined. The following discussion presents those tabs and what you need to define for each of them.

GENERAL TAB   This is where you define your report name, name of the output file, output destination, and name of the Reports Server that will handle the job. To define the report name, click the button appearing to the right of the Report Name text box to browse for your report runtime file with the **.rep** extension. Then, select the report you want to run from the file system. When finished, click OK. Your report destination may be defined from the report Destination drop-down list in this tab as well. You can define a printer, file, or Oracle InterOffice username as the output name in the text box appearing below the report Destination list. Finally, the default Reports Server shown in that drop-down list should suffice as well. Figure 28-11 shows the contents of the ActiveX Control interface General tab.

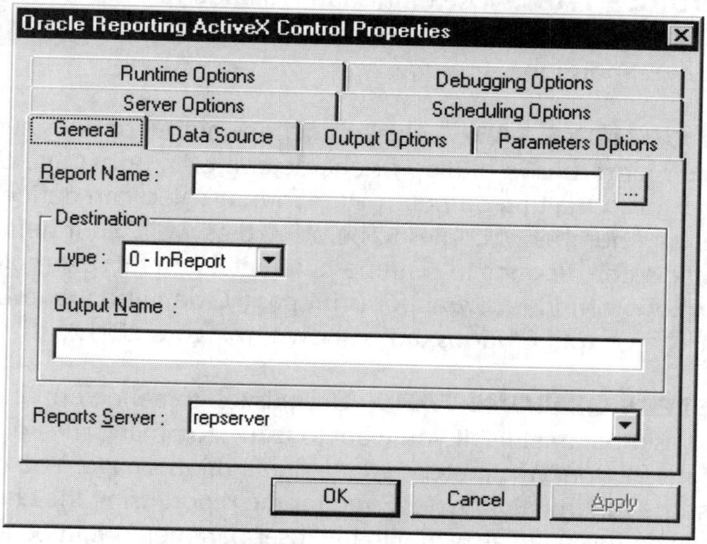

FIGURE 28-10. *Oracle Reporting ActiveX Control interface*

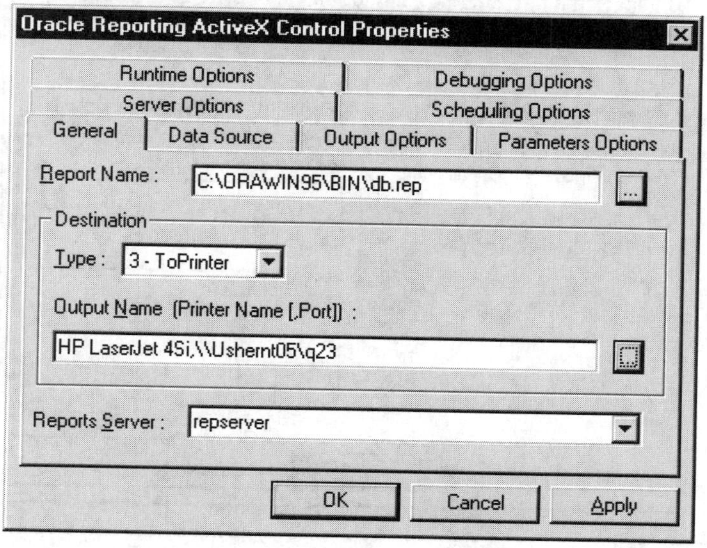

FIGURE 28-11. *General tab of Oracle Reporting ActiveX Control interface*

DATA SOURCE TAB Use of this tab is standard: simply define the username, password, and database connection string Reports Server will use to execute the report job.

OUTPUT OPTIONS TAB This tab defines output options such as whether the report runs in bitmap or character mode, print page orientation, and a driver for formatting output in Web formats. You can define the size of print pages and number of copies to be printed as well. Your definition of these elements corresponds to runtime parameters. In this example, select Bitmap for Report Mode, Portrait for print page Orientation, and Letter for Page Size. The Output Options tab is shown in Figure 28-12.

PARAMETERS OPTIONS TAB Use this tab to define options about system and user parameters. If you want to use a command file containing specifications for your parameters, you define it on this page. You can show or suppress the runtime Parameter Form for the report using the check box for that purpose on this page as well. Finally, user parameters can be identified here as well. The Parameters Options tab is shown in Figure 28-13.

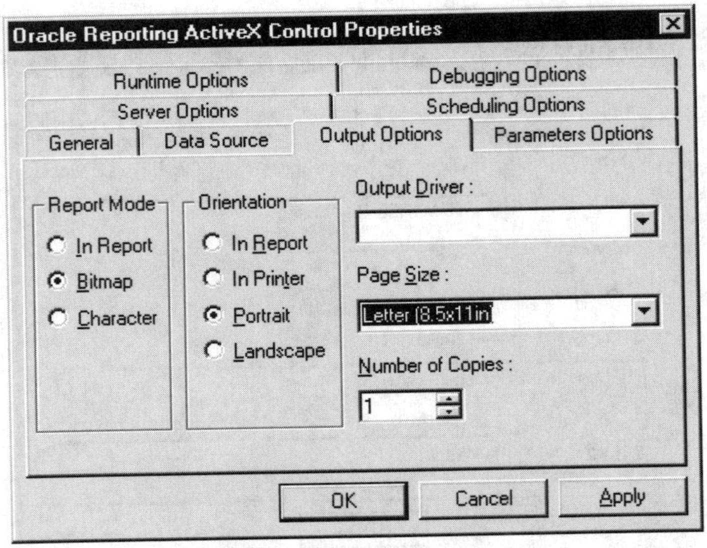

FIGURE 28-12. *Output Options tab of Oracle Reporting ActiveX Control interface*

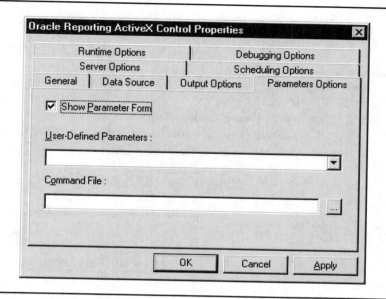

FIGURE 28-13.   *Parameters Options tab of Oracle Reporting ActiveX Control interface*

SERVER OPTIONS TAB   This tab is used to define options about how Reports Server handles the execution of this report. Items defined include how Reports Server handles the remote procedure call. Options for this item include sending the report to a local Reports Server for processing, sending to a remote Reports Server and waiting until the Reports Server comes back with report completion (synchronous execution), or sending to a remote Reports Server and polling for status until the job completes (asynchronous execution). For the most part, you will use asynchronous execution. The value specified for Report Run Progress Frequency is how long in seconds Queue Manager will wait before asking Reports Server for status again. The value specified for Report Run Timeout is how long in minutes after which if the report hasn't run, it won't be run. Specifying both to be zero means that polling and timing out features are turned off for this report. Finally, you can specify the name of the report as you want it to appear in the report queue. Figure 28-14 shows the Server Options tab in the ActiveX control. When you are finished defining your options in each tab, click OK at the bottom of the ActiveX interface.

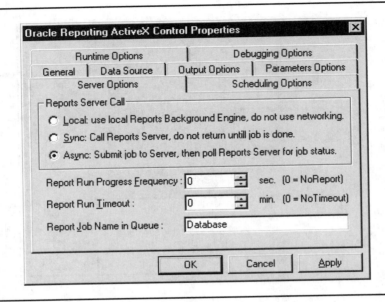

FIGURE 28-14. *Server Options tab in Reports Server ActiveX Control interface*

SCHEDULING OPTIONS TAB This tab handles the actual scheduling of your job in Reports Server. You can schedule a job to run immediately or at a specific time and date by clicking on the appropriate radio buttons in the interface. You can also specify the frequency at which the job will repeat. In this case, let's say you will schedule the job to execute at 12:30 PM on December 25, 2000, and then once a week thereafter. Figure 28-15 displays the settings you would choose for report scheduling based on this description.

RUNTIME OPTIONS TAB In this tab, you specify a few different things: how transactions behave in the report, values for CURRENCY, THOUSANDS, and DECIMAL system parameters, size of a memory array to be used for array fetching by Reports Server as it obtains your data, and the size of the buffer you will use to store chunks of data retrieved from columns of LONG datatype. You can specify transaction processing within the report to be Transactions Read-Only, Automatic Commit, or Use Non-Blocking SQL with the appropriate radio buttons. Also, you can specify what transaction-processing operation should be done if the report run succeeds or fails, such as **commit** on success or **rollback** on failure. Figure 28-16 displays this tab configured in the manner described.

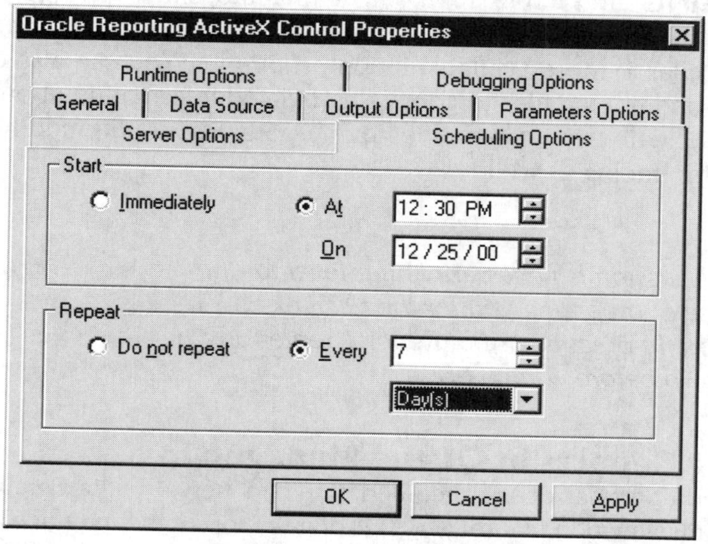

FIGURE 28-15. *Scheduling Options tab in Reports Server ActiveX Control interface*

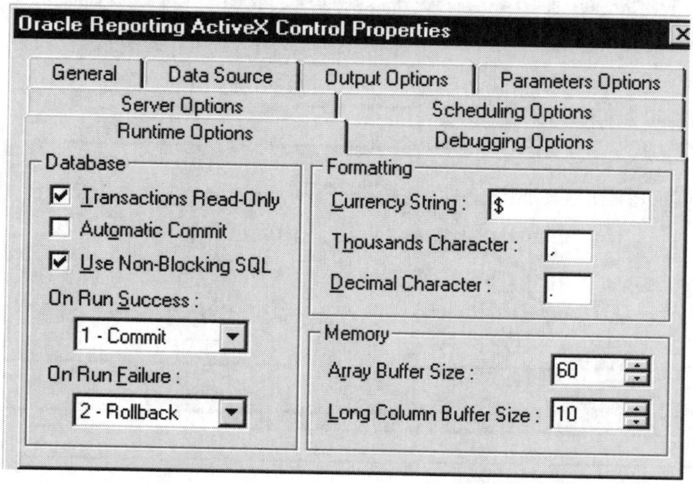

FIGURE 28-16. *Runtime Options tab in Reports Server ActiveX Control interface*

DEBUGGING OPTIONS TAB   The final tab, shown in Figure 28-17, is used for runtime debugging of your report. In it, you can define tracing options similar to those available in Report Builder. You can also define error, log, and tracing files to contain associated information about the report run. Finally, you can define how Reports Server will modify the files specified for tracing as well.

TIP
This discussion is necessarily high-level for the purpose of preparing you for the OCP exam. You should practice use of Reports Server on your own before you certify.

Viewing Reports in Queue Manager

Once your report has been scheduled, you can view it in the Queue Manager interface, displayed in Figure 28-18. Along the top of the interface are controls you can use to view different categories of reports. From left to right, the tools

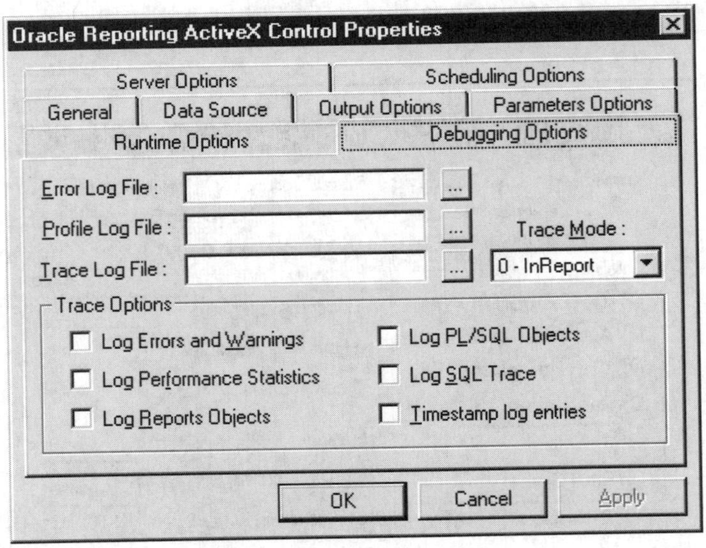

FIGURE 28-17.   *Debugging Options tab in Reports Server ActiveX Control interface*

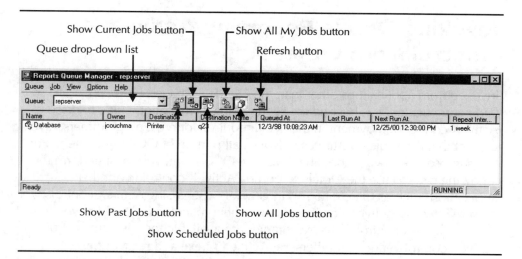

FIGURE 28-18.   *Queue Manager interface*

are the Queue drop-down list, the Show Past Jobs, Show Current Jobs, Show Scheduled Jobs, Show All My Jobs, Show All Jobs, and the Refresh buttons. These tools mirror functionality provided in the View menu in the Queue Manager interface as well. Below those tools is an open area where reports queued on the Reports Server are displayed by category depending on which button is toggled down. To see the job you just scheduled in the Queue Manager, click the Show Scheduled Jobs button in the Queue Manager interface, or the View | Scheduled Jobs menu command.

Exercises

1. Identify the interface used to schedule report jobs with the Reports Server from Queue Manager. What are some of the different features of this interface and how are they used?

2. Identify the tools in the Queue Manager interface that show different views on jobs scheduled with Reports Server. What menu contains commands that mirror these button tools?

Invoking Oracle Reporting ActiveX Control from Other Apps

The ActiveX control used to schedule reports with Reports Server can be invoked from applications other than the Queue Manager. However, to do so is fairly complicated. It is beyond the scope of this certification guide to discuss ActiveX control deployment in the detail required for most programmers, given the fact that this topic constitutes only a small portion of OCP test content. For the purpose of knowing enough to pass the OCP exam, you must perform the following tasks to use the Oracle Reporting ActiveX control in another application, such as Oracle Forms. In general, when using ActiveX controls, you must register the ActiveX control with the client machine from which you will call the ActiveX control. Two executables are available for this purpose from ActiveX control vendors or others: **regActiveX32.exe** and **regsvr32.exe**. You must also ensure that all required dynamic link library files with the extension **.dll** are placed in the **windows/system** directory on the client machine. The second task for using an ActiveX control in your application is to place the object into your application for use. The actual steps for this activity depend on the development environment into which you are deploying the ActiveX control.

TIP
Deployment of ActiveX controls in other applications is not possible on the Web or on UNIX machines.

Exercises

1. What executables are used to manually register an ActiveX control?

2. In what environments is it not possible to use ActiveX controls?

Building Reports for Different Environments

In this section, you will cover the following points on building reports for different environments:

- Character mode versus bitmap mode
- Considerations when building reports for different GUIs
- Character mode reports and their settings
- Facilities for building reports in other languages

The final area you will cover for developing reports is the requirements for building reports in different environments. The meaning of "different environments" is twofold; either a machine or another country can be a different environment. This section identifies factors for report development in both instances. The use of the MODE parameter for building character and bitmap reports in different environments and the considerations for building reports for other user interfaces are described in some detail as well. The special aspects of character-based reports will also be reiterated, along with the facilities for building reports in other human (not computer) languages.

Character Mode vs. Bitmap Mode

A report can run in one of two modes, character and bitmap. Whether the report runs in character or bitmap mode depends on the value specified for the MODE parameter. Values permitted for this parameter are character and bitmap, respectively. This parameter can be set in three ways: as a command line parameter passed in to Reports Runtime, as a runtime Parameter Form, or in the Property Palette for the MODE parameter.

As identified early in the unit, some parameters available for use on the command line when running a report can have different meanings depending on whether the report mode is bitmap or character. For example, the DESFORMAT system parameter is used to define the driver for a printer when you run a character mode report, while it means the driver that should be used for formatting output when a bitmap report is sent to a file. The PAGESIZE parameter represents the size of printed page in inches, centimeters, or picas for bitmap reports, but that same parameter defines the size of a page in characters for character-based reports. Other parameters, such as TERM, are ignored when MODE=**bitmap** because the only time Reports Runtime cares about the UNIX terminal being used is when the report is character-based. Thus, you will want to pay attention to the parameters you pass to Reports Runtime when executing reports in character or bitmap mode.

Exercises

1. Identify the parameter that determines whether the report runs in character or bitmap mode.

2. What parameters have different meanings depending on whether the report runs in bitmap or character mode?

3. Name a parameter used only when a report runs in character mode?

Considerations When Building Reports for Different GUIs

You need to take the differences between user interfaces into account when deploying reports. For example, character-based reports may look different on different terminal types. Also, your margin layout that includes a graphic for bitmap reports will not look the same on a character-based report. These are all considerations you must account for when building reports for different user interfaces.

Several factors come into play when deploying reports via the Web, as well. The appearance of a report displayed in HTML will differ from one Web browser to another, based on whether the browser window is resized on the desktop. HTML is not as precise a layout tool as other publishing formats. Several products are available that allow for precision formatting—such as what you would expect for hard copy to be deployed in the Web through the portable document format (PDF). Oracle Reports supports deployment of reports in this format to take advantage of the benefits provided.

Exercises

1. What are some factors to consider when deploying reports to different user interfaces based on character or bitmap mode?

2. What are some factors to consider when deploying reports to the Web?

Character Mode Reports and Their Settings

You should take a moment to review the list of parameters defined for Reports Runtime at the beginning of the chapter. Some of the parameters you should review have already been named. They include DESFORMAT, TERM, PAGESIZE, and MODE. For design of report Layout Model and Data Model aspects for character-based reports, you should use the appropriate settings in the Property Palette. On a new report, set the Initial Value property for the MODE parameter to Character. Set the Design in Character Units property for the report to Yes. Report page width and height properties should be set in terms of characters, 80 × 66 for letter-sized pages in portrait orientation, 132 × 41 for letter-sized pages in landscape orientation. It may be useful for you to change the font displayed in your Layout Model to Courier 12 point—the font used in character-based report output.

TIP

Remember, there are properties you can set to develop character-based reports in the property sheet for the report, opened within the Property Palette.

Exercises

1. What properties will you set for the MODE parameter to produce a character-based report? What properties will you set for the report overall for character-based reports?

2. What font is used to display output for character-based reports?

Facilities for Building Reports in Other Languages

Report Builder offers facilities for building reports that display information from languages other than English. There are procedures and functions available to test the language environment to determine if, for example, text information must be displayed from right to left, as in Hebrew and Arabic languages, or if the decimal place should be represented with a comma (,) instead of a period (.). Report Builder has a package called ORA_NLS. A partial list of functions in this package that may appear on the OCP exam and a brief description of their usage follows:

- **American( )** A function that returns TRUE or FALSE based on whether the environment character set is American English.

- **American_date( )** A function that returns TRUE or FALSE based on whether the date format for this environment is American style.

- **Right_to_left( )** A function that returns TRUE or FALSE based on whether the language defined for this environment is read right to left.

- **Single_byte( )** A function that returns TRUE or FALSE based on whether the language defined for this environment is single-byte or multibyte.

Oracle Reports displays information in a language based on the values set for language environment variables for the machine running or displaying the report. You can set variables like NLS_LANG for the purpose of determining the native language of the computer on which the report is run or displayed as well. Values for this environment variable fall into the form *language_territory.characterset*. The default value for NLS_LANG for American users is AMERICAN_AMERICA.WE8IS08859P1. In some cases, the development of the product may be done in one language while the deployment may be in another. For these situations, two other environment variables are provided. Those variables are DEVELOPER_NLS_LANG and USER_NLS_LANG, which can each be specified as different language sets.

TIP
These discussions have been necessarily brief to help you focus on the content as tested in the OCP exam. For more information about national language support, consult the Oracle Server Administrator's Guide, *Appendix C.*

Exercises

1. Identify some functions that are part of the ORA_NLS package. What are their respective purposes?

2. Identify some environment variables used to determine how language data will be displayed in a report.

Chapter Summary

This final chapter of the unit covering OCP Exam 5 instructed you on several advanced topics in Oracle Reports, including coding PL/SQL triggers, use of built-in packages in Report Builder, maximizing performance with Reports Server, and building reports for various environments. These advanced topics comprise a total of 18 percent of OCP Exam 5 test content.

The first area you covered was coding the PL/SQL triggers in reports. You learned about the differences between triggers. You covered action triggers, or those triggers that occur as the result of an event such as the clicking of a button. You also covered use of the main report triggers that fire before and after processing of the Parameter Form, before and after report processing, and between report pages. Another set of triggers you covered included debug triggers, which are helpful in ironing out problems with PL/SQL execution, and their usage in a report. The final set of triggers covered were format triggers, which are used to dynamically alter the format of a report based on certain conditions.

Tasks involved in writing common code was the next topic covered in the chapter. You identified how to reach PL/SQL blocks defined in your report through various methods using the Object Navigator module. You learned about the use of the report Runtime Previewer to get a working button to test execution of action trigger code, how to move PL/SQL program units into the database for storage, and the value of doing this. The topic of creating and referencing code in a PL/SQL library and how to attach a library to a report was covered as well.

After that, the chapter moved on to the use of Report Builder built-in packages such as the SRW package. It explained that the SRW package contains many utilities for executing reports from within other reports, processing SQL DDL statements like creating temporary tables, report tracing, formatting dynamically at run time, and Web deployment of reports. Use of the **run_report( )** was covered, along with the **geterr_run( )** function and the exceptions that can be raised by **run_report( )**. The use of **do_SQL( )** for creating temporary tables was also covered. The importance of understanding the exceptions that can be raised by SRW package procedures and functions, and coding exception handlers to make report processing go smoothly, were other topics covered. Review these topics, including the exception **srw.program_abort**, and why it may be invoked explicitly by you to cancel overall report execution, before taking the OCP exam.

The creation of temporary tables was another area covered in detail this chapter. Triggers can fire to create and remove the temporary tables, but since PL/SQL cannot execute **create_table** statements, you must use the **srw.do_SQL( )** procedure to handle these sorts of activities in your PL/SQL code. Sample PL/SQL code you may use in your BEFORE REPORT and AFTER REPORT triggers was offered, but it was also pointed out that it doesn't matter when you create or remove the temporary tables in report execution so long as the table is not removed before it is created, or left out there after the report completes.

The two methods for modifying visual attributes on your reports at run time were also covered in the chapter. The first was the use of **set_attr( )**, along with a special record called **srw.attr**, which has a **mask** element and another element depending on what attribute is being set. This is the method used in Developer/2000 versions prior to 2.1. After version 2.1, you have a large supply of procedures with names in the format **set_***attr_desc* ( ), where *attr_desc* is an attribute description. Calls to the "set" procedures in version 2.1 are generally preferred to defining the **srw.attr** record then calling **set_attr( )** in versions prior to 2.1 because of the relative ease in the former method.

Use of Reports Server was another topic of note covered in this chapter. The use of client-side reporting and its advantages and disadvantages were offered, along with a description of using Reports Server for the purpose of handling report processing. For the OCP exam, make sure you understand Figure 28-8, where the overall Reports Server architecture is explained. Queue Manager and its use for scheduling and viewing reports queued in Reports Server was another topic covered by the chapter. The scheduling of reports with the Oracle Reporting ActiveX Control interface was covered in some detail, and a brief outline for calling the ActiveX control from other applications was touched on as well.

The final topic covered was that of building reports to run in character and bitmap mode, along with the details of defining reports to run in each. Whether a report executes in character or bitmap mode depends on whether the report is run with the MODE parameter set to bitmap or character. Several parameters were identified that either mean different things or aren't used depending on which mode is used to execute the report. Other properties in a report were identified for use when you want to develop a character-based report specifically. Last, the considerations and facilities for building reports to use for other languages were offered. Use of the ORA_NLS package and environment variables like NLS_LANG, USER_NLS_LANG, and DEVELOPER_NLS_LANG were discussed. Your understanding of these elements is key to success with OCP Exam 5.

Two-Minute Drill

- There are four types of PL/SQL triggers in reports: action, report, debug, and format.

- Action triggers are used for processing as a result of an event, such as a button click.

- Report triggers are defined globally in all reports. There are five, and you should be able to name them for the OCP exam.

- Debug triggers, demonstrated in Procedure Builder, are also available in Oracle Reports.

- Format triggers are useful for conditional formatting of report content at run time, such as changing the colors of a column's total text to red when total is negative amount.

- You will need to understand and know all locations where you can find PL/SQL objects in a report from within the Object Navigator.

- You can move local program units in individual reports into the Oracle database for use from multiple reports. Make sure you know how.

- You can also move local program units into PL/SQL libraries that can then be attached to many different reports. Again, make sure you know how.

- Understand the differences between an open library and an attached library, and what can and can't be done with procedures and functions in each.

- The SRW package contains functions that allow you to do many things you need to know for OCP.

- Running reports is possible with the **run_report( )** procedure from package SRW. Problems are handled with the **run_report_batchno** and **run_report_failure** exceptions, and the **geterr_run( )** function.

- Creating temporary tables is possible with the **do_SQL( )** procedure from package SRW. The **do_SQL_failure** exception is used to alert you to problems.

- You must code exception handlers to see problems that arise when you call SRW procedures that raise exceptions.

- You can use the **message( )** function to display messages of your choosing in dialog windows.

- To stop report execution, raise the **program_abort** exception available in the SRW package.

- Review all exceptions that may be raised from the procedures and functions in the SRW package, and know which procedures and functions may raise them.

- You should know how to distinguish the two ways for modifying visual attributes at run time using procedures from the SRW package. Review this topic now.

- Reports can be run from either the client machine or from a server. Understand the architectural differences between the two and be able to list the advantages and disadvantages for each.

- Queue Manager is a tool that allows you to see the reports queued for execution by Reports Server.

- Know how to schedule report execution using the Oracle Reporting ActiveX Control interface.

- Know how to develop a bitmap and character report, and the differences between the two.

- Know the functions available in the ORA_NLS package that were covered in the text and the use of each.

- Understand the use of environment variables such as NLS_LANG, USER_NLS_LANG, and DEVELOPER_NLS_LANG.

Chapter Questions

1. When developing character-based reports, which two areas of the report will have special elements defined specifically to support the character-based report?

   A. Runtime parameters

   B. Report property sheet

   C. Data Model

   D. Report template

   E. Scheduler

2. Your report is developed to display an error message when a drill-down report executes improperly. In order to cease report execution, which of the following items may be used?

   A. program_abort( )

   B. run_report( )

   C. user_error( )

   D. user_exit( )

3. Which of the following packages contain procedures and functions designed to handle creation of temporary tables for use in your reports?

   A. ORA_FFI

   B. ORA_ENV

   C. ORA_TBL

   D. PDQ

   E. SRW

4. Which of the following procedures can be used to change the color of a summary column based on whether the value in the column is positive or negative?

   A. set_fgfill( )

   B. set_attr( )

   C. attr_set( )

   D. set_SQL( )

5. Whether your report runs as a bitmap report or character-based report is dependent on which of the following factors?

   A. Properties set in Data Model

   B. Properties set in Layout Model

   C. Value defined for MODE parameter

   D. Zero divide in data definition

6. You develop a report that calls other reports through the use of buttons. Which of the following procedures is most essential to use?

   A. run_report_batchno( )

   B. run_report( )

   C. run_report_failure( )

   D. geterr_run( )

7. Which of the following factors is not a reason to use Reports Server to process report requests?

   A. Wanting to take advantage of client-side processing power

   B. Wanting to scale report distribution via Web enablement

    C. Wanting to schedule reports with Queue Manager

    D. Wanting to reduce portability problems

8. **A format trigger is used to alter the color of text in a summary column based on whether that summary column value is positive or negative. If the procedure called to handle formatting returns TRUE, what happens?**

    A. Nothing

    B. The format change is made

    C. The report will fail

    D. The report will continue to run, but the format change will not be made

9. **When using Reports Server, how do you handle scheduling a report to execute at timed intervals?**

    A. Set the preference in Reports Server

    B. Set the preferences in Report Builder

    C. Set the scheduling in the Queue Manager Control interface

    D. Set the scheduling in the list of values static window

10. **Which two of the following triggers fire before a page of the report is laid out?**

    A. AFTER PARAMETER FORM

    B. AFTER REPORT

    C. BEFORE PARAMETER FORM

    D. BETWEEN PAGES

Answers to Chapter Questions

1. A, B. Runtime parameters and Report property sheet

Explanation   To make a report run in character mode, you can set the MODE parameter to **character** from the command line or with the use of a runtime Parameter Form. Also, in development of your report, you can set certain report properties to emphasize character-based output with the Property Palette. The other three choices are not used for either purpose.

2. A. **program_abort**

Explanation   When you raise the **program_abort** exception, the operation of your report ceases. Choice B is incorrect because **run_report( )** is the procedure you would use to handle execution of your report from within another report. The **user_exit( )** procedure temporarily passes the thread of control to another executable of your choosing, but does not quit report execution entirely. Finally, **user_error( )** is total fiction.

3. E. SRW

Explanation   The SRW package contains the **do_SQL( )** function, handling creation of temporary tables and other DDL statements from PL/SQL in your report. ORA_FFI handles interaction with non-Oracle processes and executables. ORA_ENV handles environment definition and perception from within your report. ORA_TBL and PDQ are total fiction.

4. B. **set_attr( )**

Explanation   Make sure you know that **set_attr( )** handles changing format conditions in the report at run time. The other three options in this question are made up.

5. C. Value defined for MODE parameter

Explanation   The way a report will execute can be defined with the MODE parameter, which can be set either to **bitmap** or **character**.

6. B. **run_report( )**

Explanation Since all the other choices offered require the report to be executed, they are all dependent on the call to execute the report, **run_report( )**.

7. A. Wanting to take advantage of client-side processing power

Explanation All other choices identify reasons to use network-centric processing of your report offered via the Reports Server.

8. B. The format change is made

Explanation If the procedure defined for the trigger returns TRUE, that means all went well with the trigger's execution. The format change was made, and processing of the report will continue. Based on these facts, the logical choice is B.

9. C. Set the scheduling in the Queue Manager Control interface

Explanation The only way to schedule a report job is to use the Control interface. You needn't use Queue Manager per se, because the Control interface is an ActiveX control, and thus can be embedded into other applications.

10. A, C. AFTER PARAMETER FORM and BEFORE PARAMETER FORM

Explanation These two reporting triggers both process before the report is executed, and thus before the pages of output are formatted. By the time the report triggers in choices B and D execute, data has been **select**ed and pages formatted.

APPENDIX

Preparing for Developer 2.0 New Features Upgrade Exam

ecause the book focuses so heavily on the components of Developer 2.0, the developer experienced in Developer 1.6 should find it useful especially for the purpose of preparing for the Developer 2.0 New Features Upgrade Exam. To improve your use of this book for that purpose, this appendix lists all major content areas according to the OCP Candidate Guide from Oracle, and the area of the book you can review as preparation for that topic. The topics, as well as the book content areas, are given. For practice questions, feel free to review the practice questions given at the end of each of the Forms and Reports chapters.

Be aware that this New Features Upgrade Exam focuses primarily on the new features of Developer 2.0 over 1.*x* in the areas of Forms and Reports. New features for Procedure Builder are few between these two versions of Developer/2000, so it is not important for you to review Procedure Builder or the other components of Developer/2000 for this review. For further study, check out ExamPilot.Com on the Web at **http://www.exampilot.com**.

Managing Projects with Project Builder

The information you need to learn about this topic area is contained in several areas of this book. Chapter 11 contains an explanation of how to customize Project Builder in order to develop applications. Some explanation of Project Navigator and Project Launcher is offered in Chapter 11 as well. You can further learn about Project Builder using Chapter 18. The majority of the content of Chapter 18 will help you prepare for questions in this section of the New Features Upgrade Exam.

Creating Form Documents Using Wizards

This section discusses use of Form Wizards, which are described by this book in the section in Chapter 12 on creating a basic Forms module through the use of several wizards. Chapter 12 also includes an explanation of the benefits these wizards provide. The features and types of wizards are also covered. This chapter describes use of the Data Block Wizard and the Layout Wizard. Finally, the creation of basic Forms documents using wizards is also explained. Adding charts to Form modules with a wizard is covered in Chapter 22 as well.

Representing Data Within Your Application

This section is basically a test of your knowledge of data blocks, data sources, and array DML. To prepare for questions in this section of the New Features Upgrade Exam, consult Chapters 16 and 21. Chapter 16 contains an explanation of array DML, which covers the topic bullet in this section on that topic from the Candidate Guide. Chapter 21 contains a section that explains defining data sources, a topic covered by several bullets in the corresponding section of the upgrade exam as well.

Enhancing Items

The questions in this section test knowledge of several different topics on enhancing items in your Forms application module. Several different sections in Chapters 13 and 14 will help you. The section on working with text items contains material you will find helpful. The next chapter contains two sections—one on creating input items, the other on creating noninput items—that you will find useful for questions on enhancing those items in this test.

Enhancing Interactivity

This section tests your knowledge of how to make your Forms applications more interactive and user friendly. Chapter 14 has an extensive treatment of canvases for this purpose. The sections on creating windows and content canvases and the section on working with other canvases will complement your understanding of Forms for enhancing interactivity. We suggest you read Chapter 14 with the idea in mind of making your applications more usable for people who may never have used computers before, or from the business perspective of users who will apply the software you develop.

Ensuring Consistency Across Applications

According to the *Candidate Guide*, the material in this section is similar to the content of the section on enhancing interactivity insofar as both seem to emphasize creation of canvases and tab interfaces. The main difference is that the prior one attacks the topic from the "user-friendliness" perspective while this section wants to attack the same topic from the point of the importance of uniformity in the application. We suggest you reread Chapter 14 from the perspective of making the application uniform.

Including Charts and Reports

In order to understand the information needed to answer questions correctly for this section on the New Features Upgrade Exam, look no further than Chapter 22. This chapter contains a section with the same name as this one, which describes embedding charts in Forms modules using a wizard. Embedding existing graphic displays is explained there as well. The explanation of setting up reports to run from Forms is in Chapter 22 as well, along with how to control the execution of the report with the form.

Creating Reports Using Report Wizard

To learn more about how to use the Report Wizard to create reports, you can review Chapter 23. This chapter contains a section on using Report Wizard that will explain the report styles available in Report Wizard, how to create a report in each style, using Query Builder to create the data definition for your report, and how to modify reports using Report Wizard. Complement this review by actually creating some reports with Report Wizard. The second area of this test section, applying and customizing templates, is covered in the section on managing report templates in Chapter 24. Review the appropriate section there as well.

Modifying and Enhancing Reports

The content of this section is covered amply in Chapter 26. There, you can learn about how to modify text attributes, layout, and all other items listed for this content area in the OCP Candidate Guide. These areas all relate to your use of the Layout Model in Oracle Reports, so be sure you understand thoroughly how this works by using the Layout Model extensively before the test. You can default your layout using Report Wizard as well, and you should practice how to do this.

Maximizing Performance Using Reports Server

Use of Reports Server is handled through the content of the appropriate section in Chapter 28. In that section, there is an explanation of running reports in client/server as well as in N-tier architecture applications, which is the Reports Server architecture. An explanation of how to use Queue Manager is provided there as well. For more explanation on how to enter **r30cli** and **r30mts** parameters from your operating system command line, you can review Chapter 22, where parameters and application command line names are identified and described.

Deploying Reports on the Web

For review of how to deploy reports on the Web, the following discussion will prove useful. First, understand that Oracle considers the advantages for deploying reports to the Web to be as follows:

- Low-cost deployment and maintenance through use of thin-client architecture, network computing, and Web wizards

- Platform independence and easily scalable delivery of reports using corporate intranets and Web browsers

- Dynamic reporting that supports drill-down capacity

To get your reports on the Web, certain resources are required. According to Oracle, these resources include a Web server such as Oracle Web Application Server. Another resource required is the Reports Server, a component of the Developer suite that has already been covered in some detail in Chapter 28. You may wish to review that chapter for more information. The Reports Server should be outfitted either with Web CGI or the Reports Web Cartridge so that the Reports Server and the Web server can interact. The final component of this architecture is your Web browser, present on the client machine.

The preparation of reports for Web deployment is handled with the Web Wizard in Report Builder. You should use the Web Wizard to convert existing reports into use with the Web as static HTML documents, PDF, or dynamic reports. You can add Web link properties by updating your report's property sheet through the use of the Property Palette, as you would with any other report property. These features and more allow you to view reports on the Web. For more information on Web-enabling reports, you should read *Deploying Applications on the Web*, the Oracle manual that accompanies your Oracle Developer/2000 software distribution. Additional content can be found for this test on ExamPilot.Com's Web site at **http://www.exampilot.com**.

Index

Think you're
smart?

You've built an inventory form which displays pictures of products when a user clicks on a button. Which menu item type can you create to activate and deactivate this button?

a. Magic
b. Plain
c. Check
d. Separator

Think you're ready to wear this badge?

The time is right to become an Oracle Certified Professional (OCP) and we're here to help you do it. Oracle's cutting edge Instructor-Led Training and Interactive Courseware can prepare you for certification faster than ever. OCP status is one of the top honors in your profession. Now is the time to take credit for what you know. *Call 800.441.3541 (Outside the U.S. call +1.310.335.2403)* for an OCP training solution that meets your time, budget, and learning needs. Or visit us at

http://education.oracle.com/certification for more information.

ORACLE®
E d u c a t i o n

Get Your **FREE** Subscription to Oracle Magazine

Stay informed and increase your productivity with every issue of *Oracle Magazine*. Inside each FREE, bimonthly issue you'll get:

- Up-to-date information on Oracle Data Server, Oracle Applications, Network Computing Architecture, and tools
- Third-party news and announcements
- Technical articles on Oracle products and operating environments
- Software tuning tips
- Oracle customer application stories

Three easy ways to subscribe:

1 MAIL Cut out this page, complete the questionnaire on the back, and mail it to: *Oracle Magazine*, P.O. Box 1263, Skokie, IL 60076-8263.

2 FAX Cut out this page, complete the questionnaire on the back, and fax it to **+ 847.647.9735.**

3 WEB Visit our Web site at **www.oramag.com.** You'll find a subscription form there, plus much more!

If there are other Oracle users at your location who would like to receive their own subscription to *Oracle Magazine,* please photocopy the form and pass it along.

☐ YES! Please send me a FREE subscription to Oracle Magazine. ☐ NO, I am not interested at this time.

If you wish to receive your free bimonthly subscription to *Oracle Magazine,* you must fill out the entire form, sign it, and date it (incomplete forms cannot be processed or acknowledged). You can also subscribe at our Web site at **www.oramag.com/html/subform.html** or fax your application to *Oracle Magazine* at **+847.647.9735.**

SIGNATURE (REQUIRED) ✓   **DATE**

NAME _____ TITLE _____

COMPANY _____ E-MAIL ADDRESS _____

STREET/P.O. BOX _____

CITY/STATE/ZIP _____

COUNTRY _____ TELEPHONE _____

You must answer all eight questions below.

1 What is the primary business activity of your firm at this location? *(circle only one)*
- ○ 01 Agriculture, Mining, Natural Resources
- ○ 02 Architecture, Construction
- ○ 03 Communications
- ○ 04 Consulting, Training
- ○ 05 Consumer Packaged Goods
- ○ 06 Data Processing
- ○ 07 Education
- ○ 08 Engineering
- ○ 09 Financial Services
- ○ 10 Government—Federal, Local, State, Other
- ○ 11 Government—Military
- ○ 12 Health Care
- ○ 13 Manufacturing—Aerospace, Defense
- ○ 14 Manufacturing—Computer Hardware
- ○ 15 Manufacturing—Noncomputer Products
- ○ 16 Real Estate, Insurance
- ○ 17 Research & Development
- ○ 18 Human Resources
- ○ 19 Retailing, Wholesaling, Distribution
- ○ 20 Software Development
- ○ 21 Systems Integration, VAR, VAD, OEM
- ○ 22 Transportation
- ○ 23 Utilities (Electric, Gas, Sanitation)
- ○ 24 Other Business and Services _____

2 Which of the following best describes your job function? *(circle only one)*
CORPORATE MANAGEMENT/STAFF
- ○ 01 Executive Management (President, Chair, CEO, CFO, Owner, Partner, Principal)
- ○ 02 Finance/Administrative Management (VP/Director/ Manager/Controller, Purchasing, Administration)
- ○ 03 Sales/Marketing Management (VP/Director/Manager)
- ○ 04 Computer Systems/Operations Management (CIO/VP/Director/ Manager MIS, Operations)
- ○ 05 Other Finance/Administration Staff
- ○ 06 Other Sales/Marketing Staff

IS/IT Staff
- ○ 07 Systems Development/ Programming Management
- ○ 08 Systems Development/ Programming Staff
- ○ 09 Consulting
- ○ 10 DBA/Systems Administrator
- ○ 11 Education/Training
- ○ 12 Engineering/R&D/Science Management
- ○ 13 Engineering/R&D/Science Staff
- ○ 14 Technical Support Director/ Manager
- ○ 15 Webmaster/Internet Specialist
- ○ 16 Other Technical Management/ Staff

3 What is your current primary operating platform? *(circle all that apply)*
- ○ 01 DEC UNIX
- ○ 02 DEC VAX VMS
- ○ 03 Java
- ○ 04 HP UNIX
- ○ 05 IBM AIX
- ○ 06 IBM UNIX
- ○ 07 Macintosh
- ○ 08 MPE-ix
- ○ 09 MS-DOS
- ○ 10 MVS
- ○ 11 NetWare
- ○ 12 Network Computing
- ○ 13 OpenVMS
- ○ 14 SCO UNIX
- ○ 15 Sun Solaris/ SunOS
- ○ 16 SVR4
- ○ 17 Ultrix
- ○ 18 UnixWare
- ○ 19 VM
- ○ 20 Windows
- ○ 21 Windows NT
- ○ 22 Other _____
- ○ 23 Other UNIX

4 Do you evaluate, specify, recommend, or authorize the purchase of any of the following? *(circle all that apply)*
- ○ 01 Hardware
- ○ 02 Software
- ○ 03 Application Development Tools
- ○ 04 Database Products
- ○ 05 Internet or Intranet Products

5 In your job, do you use or plan to purchase any of the following products or services? *(check all that apply)*

SOFTWARE

	Use	Plan to buy
01 Business Graphics	☐	☐
02 CAD/CAE/CAM	☐	☐
03 CASE	☐	☐
04 CIM	☐	☐
05 Communications	☐	☐
06 Database Management	☐	☐
07 File Management	☐	☐
08 Finance	☐	☐
09 Java	☐	☐
10 Materials Resource Planning	☐	☐
11 Multimedia Authoring	☐	☐
12 Networking	☐	☐
13 Office Automation	☐	☐
14 Order Entry/ Inventory Control	☐	☐
15 Programming	☐	☐
16 Project Management	☐	☐
17 Scientific and Engineering	☐	☐
18 Spreadsheets	☐	☐
19 Systems Management	☐	☐
20 Workflow	☐	☐

HARDWARE

	Use	Plan to buy
21 Macintosh	☐	☐
22 Mainframe	☐	☐
23 Massively Parallel Processing	☐	☐
24 Minicomputer	☐	☐
25 PC	☐	☐
26 Network Computer	☐	☐
27 Supercomputer	☐	☐
28 Symmetric Multiprocessing	☐	☐
29 Workstation	☐	☐

PERIPHERALS

	Use	Plan to buy
30 Bridges/Routers/Hubs/ Gateways	☐	☐
31 CD-ROM Drives	☐	☐
32 Disk Drives/Subsystems	☐	☐
33 Modems	☐	☐
34 Tape Drives/Subsystems	☐	☐
35 Video Boards/Multimedia	☐	☐

SERVICES

	Use	Plan to buy
36 Computer-Based Training	☐	☐
37 Consulting	☐	☐
38 Education/Training	☐	☐
39 Maintenance	☐	☐
40 Online Database Services	☐	☐
41 Support	☐	☐
42 **None of the above**	☐	☐

6 What Oracle products are in use at your site? *(circle all that apply)*
SERVER/SOFTWARE
- ○ 01 Oracle8
- ○ 02 Oracle7
- ○ 03 Oracle Application Server
- ○ 04 Oracle Data Mart Suites
- ○ 05 Oracle Internet Commerce Server
- ○ 06 Oracle InterOffice
- ○ 07 Oracle Lite
- ○ 08 Oracle Payment Server
- ○ 09 Oracle Rdb
- ○ 10 Oracle Security Server
- ○ 11 Oracle Video Server
- ○ 12 Oracle Workgroup Server

TOOLS
- ○ 13 Designer/2000
- ○ 14 Developer/2000 (Forms, Reports, Graphics)
- ○ 15 Oracle OLAP Tools
- ○ 16 Oracle Power Object

ORACLE APPLICATIONS
- ○ 17 Oracle Automotive
- ○ 18 Oracle Energy
- ○ 19 Oracle Consumer Packaged Goods
- ○ 20 Oracle Financials
- ○ 21 Oracle Human Resources
- ○ 22 Oracle Manufacturing
- ○ 23 Oracle Projects
- ○ 24 Oracle Sales Force Automation
- ○ 25 Oracle Supply Chain Management
- ○ 26 Other _____
- ○ 27 **None of the above**

7 What other database products are in use at your site? *(circle all that apply)*
- ○ 01 Access
- ○ 02 BAAN
- ○ 03 dbase
- ○ 04 Gupta
- ○ 05 IBM DB2
- ○ 06 Informix
- ○ 07 Ingres
- ○ 08 Microsoft Access
- ○ 09 Microsoft SQL Server
- ○ 10 Peoplesoft
- ○ 11 Progress
- ○ 12 SAP
- ○ 13 Sybase
- ○ 14 VSAM
- ○ 15 **None of the above**

8 During the next 12 months, how much do you anticipate your organization will spend on computer hardware, software, peripherals, and services for your location? *(circle only one)*
- ○ 01 Less than $10,000
- ○ 02 $10,000 to $49,999
- ○ 03 $50,000 to $99,999
- ○ 04 $100,000 to $499,999
- ○ 05 $500,000 to $999,999
- ○ 06 $1,000,000 and over

OMG